The McGraw-Hill Computer Handbook

The McGraw-Hill Computer Handbook

Editor in Chief
Harry Helms

Overview by
Adam Osborne

Foreword by
Thomas C. Bartee

McGraw-Hill Book Company

New York   St. Louis   San Francisco   Auckland
Bogotá   Hamburg   Johannesburg   London   Madrid
Mexico   Montreal   New Delhi   Panama   Paris
São Paulo   Singapore   Sydney   Tokyo   Toronto

Library of Congress Cataloging in Publication Data

Main entry under title:

The McGraw-Hill computer handbook.

Includes index.
1. Computers — Handbooks, manuals, etc.
2. Programming (Electronic computers) — Handbooks,
manuals, etc.   3. Programming languages (Electronic
computers) — Handbooks, manuals, etc.   I. Helms,
Harry L.   II. McGraw-Hill Book Company.
QA76.M37   1983   001.64   83-1044
ISBN 0-07-027972-1·

3 4 5 6 7 8 9 0   KGP/KGP   8 9 8 7 6 5 4

ISBN 0-07-027972-1

The editors for this book were Patricia Allen-Browne and Margaret Lamb,
the production supervisor was Teresa F. Leaden, and the designer was
Mark E. Safran. It was set in Times Roman by University Graphics, Inc.

Printed and bound by The Kingsport Press.

Contents

Contributors

Bartee, Thomas C.   *Harvard University*
Conroy, Thomas F.   *International Business Machines Corp.*
Erickson, Jonathan   *Radio Shack Technical Publications*
Gault, James W.   *North Carolina State University*
Gear, C. William   *University of Illinois*
Givone, Donald D.   *State University of New York at Buffalo*
Hamacher, V. Carl   *University of Toronto*
Hellerman, Herbert   *State University of New York at Binghamton*
Helms, Harry L.   *Technical Writer and Consultant*
Hohenstein, C. Louis   *Hohenstein and Associates*
House, Charles H.   *Hewlett-Packard*
Kohavi, Zvi   *University of Utah*
Koperda, Frank   *International Business Machines Corp.*
Miastkowski, Stan   *Rising Star Industries, Inc.*
Newman, William M.   *Queen Mary College, London*
Pimmel, Russell L.   *University of Missouri*
Roesser, Robert P.   *University of Detroit*
Sproull, Robert F.   *Sutherland, Sproull and Associates*
Stout, David F.   *Dataface*
Tucker, Allen, Jr.   *Georgetown University*
Vranesic, Zvonko G.   *University of Toronto*
Wiatrowski, Claude A.   *Mountain Automation Corp.*
Wiederhold, Gio M.   *Stanford University*
Zaky, Safwat G.   *University of Toronto*

Overview

TRENDS IN THE MICROCOMPUTER INDUSTRY

Without a doubt, IBM's Personal Computer strategy cast the shape of the microcomputer industry in 1982— and probably for the rest of the decade. It was not simply sales volume or market share that made IBM's Personal Computer such a formidable factor in 1982. Rather, it was the marketing strategy IBM adopted. It is a strategy all other microcomputer industry participants who wish to survive will have to adopt.

Prior to the IBM Personal Computer, industry leaders (such as Apple, Commodore, and Radio Shack) all strove to build unique hardware which, whenever possible, would run programs that could not be run on any competing machine. Furthermore, these companies vigorously fought competitors attempting to build look-alike microcomputers.

That was the old minicomputer industry philosophy, adopted by too many microcomputer manufacturers. Well in advance of IBM's entry, the ultimate fallacy of this philosophy was evident. The reason was CP/M, an operating system standard on none of the three leading personal computers (Apple, Commodore, and Radio Shack). Nevertheless, CP/M not only survived but thrived. CP/M was kept alive by more than the flock of secondary microcomputer manufacturers. A large number of Radio Shack and Apple microcomputers were also running CP/M, even though it required additional expense for unauthorized software and additional hardware for the Apple.

Was there a message in the extremes to which customers would go to thwart the intent of microcomputer manufacturers and run CP/M? Indeed there was, and it was that de facto industry standards are overwhelmingly desirable to most customers.

That message was not lost on IBM. Few messages of validity are; that is why IBM has grown to be so successful.

And so when IBM introduced its Personal Computer, it went about making its entry a new de facto standard. Any hardware manufacturer who wanted to could build a product compatible with the IBM Personal Computer. Software vendors were given every encouragement to adopt the IBM standard. The first independent microcomputer magazine dedicated to the IBM Personal Computer grew to be one of the most successful magazines in the business within six months of its first publication. People bought the magazine and advertised in it in unprecedented volumes.

There are already several microcomputers built by companies other than IBM that are compatible with the IBM Personal Computer. Already there are probably more software companies devoting themselves to the IBM standard than any other with the possible exception of CP/M.

Within a short time, I predict there will be two de facto industry standards for microcomputers: CP/M running on the Z80 for 8-bit systems and IBM (MDOS and CP/M 86) running on the 8086 or 8088 for 16-bit systems. Companies not supporting one or both of these standards have a tortuous, uphill fight ahead of them.

One can well argue that 8-bit microprocessors are generally obsolete and that the 8086 and 8088 are among the least powerful 16-bit microprocessors. But what has that to do with anything? If these microprocessors are adequate for the tasks they are being asked to perform, then any theoretical inadequacies will not be perceived by the end user. And even if the de facto standards are not the best in whatever area they have become standard, what does it matter providing their shortcomings are not apparent to the user?

The difference between the microcomputer and minicomputer industries is that microcomputers are rapidly becoming consumer products. It will be far more difficult for microcomputer industry managers to impose their will on a mass market of consumer buyers than it was for minicomputer manufacturers to manipulate a relatively small customer base (which was commonly done in the early 1970s).

This message has not been learned by many present participants in the microcomputer industry. But this message will determine more than anything else who will be the survivors when the inevitable industry shakeout occurs.

Adam Osborne
President
Osborne Computer Corporation
1983

Foreword

Since the 1950s the digital computer has progressed from a "miraculous" but expensive, rarely seen, and overheated mass of vacuum tubes, wires, and magnetic cores to a familiar, generally compact machine built from hundreds of thousands of minuscule semiconductor devices packaged in small plastic containers.

As a result, computers are everywhere. They run our cash registers, check out our groceries, ignite our spark plugs, and manage the family bank account. Moreover, because of the amazing progress in the semiconductor devices which form the basis for computers, both computers and the applications now being developed are only fragments of what will soon be in existence.

The Computer Handbook which follows presents material from the basic areas of technology for digital computers. The Handbook progresses from hardware through software to such diverse topics as artificial intelligence, robotics, and voice recognition. Microprocessors, the newest addition to computer hardware, are also discussed in some detail.

Computers are beginning to touch the lives of everyone. If you are ill, the hospital will be full of computers (there could be more computers than patients in a modern hospital; medical instrument designers make considerable use of microprocessors). Schools have been using computers for bookkeeping for years and now use computers in many courses outside computer science. Even elementary schools are beginning to use computers in basic math and science courses. Games designed around microprocessors are sold everywhere. New ovens, dishwashers, and temperature control systems all use microprocessors.

The wide range of applications brings up some basic philosophical questions about what the future will bring. System developers can now produce computers which speak simple phrases and sentences reasonably well—bank computers probably give the teller your balance over the telephone in spoken form and some of the newer cars produce spoken English phrases concerning car operation. Computers also listen well but have to work hard to unscramble what is said unless the form of communication is carefully specified. This is, however, a hot research area and some details are in this book.

The speech recognition problem previously described is a part of a larger problem called *pattern recognition*. If computers can become good at finding patterns, they can scan x-rays, check fingerprints, and perform many other useful functions (they already sort mail). The human brain is, however, very good at finding patterns even in the presence of irrelevant data (noise), and research in this area faces many challenges if computers are to become competitive. If, however, computers can become good at recognizing speech and returning answers verbally, it might be possible even to enter programs for computers and data verbally. This would make it possible literally to tell the computer what to do and have the computer respond, provided the directions were clear, contained no contradictions, etc.

While verbal communication might facilitate the programming of a computer, there would still be the problem of what language to use. There are many proponents of English, but English need not be precise and lacks the rigidity now required by the computer and its translators. Certainly much has been done in this area and the steady march from machine-like assemblers to today's high-level programming languages testifies to the need for and emphasis on this area. Much more is needed, however, and the sections of this Handbook fairly represent the state of this art and point to the direction of future work.

Robotics also presents an outstanding area for future development. Factories now use many robotic devices and research labs are beginning to fill with robots in many strange and wonderful forms. Waving aside the possibility and desirability of robots for maids, waitresses, waiters, ticket sales persons, and other functions already exploited by television and movies, there are many medical operations and precision production operations which can and will be performed by computer-guided robots (often because they are better than humans).

We often complain that others do not understand us, and at present computers do not understand us; for a while we will have to be content with computers which will simply follow our directions. Computer memories are making gains on human memories, however. Largely due to the ingenuity of memory device designers, the memory capacity of large machines now competes with our own but the different organization of the brain seems to give it substantial advantages for creative thought. Artificial intelligence delves into this area. In some areas formerly relegated to "human" thought, computers do quite well, however. For example, in such straightforward mathematical systems as Euclid's geometry, computers already perform better than might be expected; in a recent test a computer proved all the theorems in a high school test in minutes.

I think that to be really comfortable with computers it is necessary to have some knowledge of both hardware and software. In order to make computers more widely used, there is a tendency to make consumer-oriented personal computers appear to be "friendlier" than they really are. This limits their flexibility and presents users with a mystery element which needs to be and can be dissolved by a little knowledge of actual computer principles. A handbook such as this can be very helpful to users in dissolving some of the mystery. At the same time, such a handbook can open new doors in exploration and serve as a continuing reference.

Thomas C. Bartee
Harvard University
1983

The McGraw-Hill Computer Handbook

sec.1

Computer History and Concepts

Herbert Hellerman

1-1 INTRODUCTION

The modern general-purpose digital computer system, which is the subject of this book, is the most versatile and complex creation of mankind. Its versatility follows from its applicability to a very wide range of problems, limited only by human ability to give definite directions for solving a problem. A **program** gives such directions in the form of a precise, highly stylized sequence of statements detailing a problem-solution procedure. A computer system's job is to reliably and rapidly execute programs. Present speeds are indicated by the rates of arithmetic operations such as addition, subtraction, and comparison, which lie in the range of about 100,000 to 10,000,000 instructions per second, depending on the size and cost of the machine. In only a few hours, a modern large computer can do more information processing than was done by all of mankind before the electronic age, which began about 1950! It is no wonder that this tremendous amplification of human information-processing capability is precipitating a new revolution.

To most people, the words "computer" and "computer system" are probably synonymous and refer to the physical equipment, such as the central processing unit, console, tapes, disks, card reader, and printers visible to anyone visiting a computer room. Although these devices are essential, they make up only the visible "tip of the iceberg." As soon as we start to use a modern computer system, we are confronted not by the machine directly but by sets of rules called **programming languages** in which we must express whatever it is we want to do. The central importance of programming language is indicated by the fact that even the physical computer may be understood as a hardware interpreter of one particular language called the **machine language.** Machine languages are designed for machine efficiency, which is somewhat dichotomous with human convenience. Most users are shielded from the inconveniences of the machine by one or more languages designed for good man-machine communication. The versatility of the computer is illustrated by the fact that it can execute translator programs (called generically **compilers** or **interpreters**) to transform programs from user-oriented languages into machine-language form.

It should be clear from the discussion thus far that a computer system consists of a computer machine, which is a collection of physical equipment, and also programs, including those that translate user programs from any of several languages into machine language. Most of this book is devoted to examining in some detail theories and practices in the two great themes of computer systems: equipment (hardware) and programming (software). It is appropriate to begin, in the next section, by establishing a historical perspective.

1-2 HISTORICAL PERSPECTIVE

Mechanical aids to counting and calculating were known in antiquity. One of many ancient devices, the abacus, survives today as a simple practical tool in many parts of the world, especially the East, for business and even scientific calculations. (A form of the abacus was probably used by the ancient Egyptians, and it was known in China as early as the sixth century B.C.) In the hands of a skilled operator, the abacus can be a powerful adjunct to hand calculations. There are several forms of abacus; they all depend upon a positional notation for representing numbers and an arrangement of movable beads, or similar simple objects, to represent each digit. By moving beads, numbers are entered, added, and subtracted to produce an updated result. Multiplication and division are done by sequences of additions and subtractions.

Although the need to mechanize the arithmetic operations received most of the attention in early devices, storage of intermediate results was at least as important. Most devices, like the abacus, stored only the simple current result. Other storage was usually of the same type as used for any written material, e.g., clay tablets and later paper. As long as the speed of operations was modest and the use of storage also slow, there was little impetus to seek mechanization of the control of sequences of operations. Yet forerunners of such control did appear in somewhat different contexts, e.g., the Jacquard loom exhibited in 1801 used perforated (punched) cards to control patterns for weaving.

Charles Babbage (1792–1871) was probably the first to conceive of the essence of the general-purpose computer. Although he was very versatile, accomplished both as a mathematician and as an engineer, his lifework was his computing machines. It is worth noting that Babbage was first stimulated in this direction because of the unreliability of manual computation, *not* by its slow speed. In particular, he found several errors in certain astronomy tables. In determining the causes, he became convinced that error-free tables could be produced only by a machine that would accept a description of the computation by a human being but, once set up, would compute the tables and print them— all without human intervention. Babbage's culminating idea, which he proposed in great detail, was his Analytic Engine, which would have been the first general-purpose computer. It was not completed because he was unable to obtain sufficient financial support.

As Western industrial civilization developed, the need for mechanized computation grew. As the 1890 census approached in the United States, it became clear that if new processes were not developed, the reduction of the data from one census would not be complete before it was time for the next one. Dr. Herman Hollerith applied punched cards and simple machines for processing them in the 1890 census. Thereafter, punched-card machines gained wide acceptance in business and government.

The first third of the twentieth century saw the gradual development and use of many calculating devices. A highly significant contribution was made by the mathematician Alan Turing in 1937, when he published a clear and profound theory of the nature of a general-purpose computing scheme. His results were expressed in terms of a hypothetical "machine" of remarkable simplicity, which he indicated had all the necessary attributes of a general-purpose computer. Although Turing's machine was only a theoretical construct and was never seriously considered as economically feasible (it would be intolerably slow), it drew the attention of several talented people to the feasibility of a general-purpose computer.

World War II gave great stimulus to improvement and invention of computing devices and the technologies necessary to them. Howard Aiken and an IBM team completed the Harvard Mark I electric computer (using relay logic) in 1944. J. P. Eckert and J. W. Mauchly developed ENIAC, an electronic computer using vacuum tubes in 1946. Both these machines were developed with scientific calculations in mind. The first generation of computer technology began to be mass-produced with the appearance of the UNIVAC I in 1951. The term "first generation" is associated with the use of vacuum tubes as the major component of logical circuitry, but it included a large variety of memory devices such as mercury delay lines, storage tubes, drums, and magnetic cores, to name a few.

The second generation of hardware featured the transistor (invented in 1948) in place of the vacuum tube. The solid-state transistor is far more efficient than the vacuum tube partly because it requires no energy for heating a source of electrons. Just as important, the transistor, unlike the vacuum tube, has almost unlimited life and reliability and can be manufactured at much lower cost. Second-generation equipment, which appeared about 1960, saw the widespread installation and use of general-purpose computers. The third and fourth generations of computer technology (about 1964 and 1970) mark the increasing use of integrated fabrication techniques, moving to the goal of manufacturing most of a computer in one automatic continuous process without manual intervention.

Hardware developments were roughly paralleled by progress in programming, which is, however, more difficult to document. An early important development, usually credited to Grace Hopper, is the symbolic machine language which relieves the programmer from many exceedingly tedious and error-prone tasks. Another milestone was FORTRAN (about 1955), the first widely used **high-level language,** which included many elements of algebraic notation, like indexed variables and mathematical expressions of arbitrary extent. Since FORTRAN was developed by IBM, whose machines were most numerous, FORTRAN quickly became pervasive and, after several versions, remains today a very widely used language.

Other languages were invented to satisfy the needs of different classes of computer use. Among the most important are COBOL, for business-oriented data processing; ALGOL, the first widely accepted language in the international community, particularly among mathematicians and scientists; and PL/I developed by IBM and introduced in 1965 as a single language capable of satisfying the needs of scientific, commercial, and system programming.

Along with the introduction and improvements of computer languages, there was a corresponding development of programming technology, i.e., the methods of producing the compiler and interpreter translators and other aids for the programmer. A very significant idea that has undergone intensive development is the **operating system,** which is a collection of programs responsible for monitoring and allocating all systems resources in response to user requests in a way that reflects certain efficiency objectives. By 1966 or so, almost all medium to large computers ran under an operating system. Jobs were typically submitted by users as decks of punched cards, either to the computer room or by **remote-job-entry** (RJE) terminals, i.e., card reader and printer equipment connected by telephone lines to the computer. In either case, once a job was received by the computer, the operating system made almost all the scheduling decisions. A large computer could run several hundred or even thousands of jobs per 24-hour day with only one or two professional operators in the machine room.

The 1960s saw a great intensification of the symbiosis of the computer and the telephone system (**teleprocessing**). Much of this was RJE and routine non-general-purpose use, such as airline reservation systems. Considerable success was also achieved in bringing the generality and excitement of a general-purpose computer system to individual people through the use of **timesharing** systems. Here, an appropriate operating-system program interleaves the requests of several human users who may be remotely located and communicating over telephone lines using such devices as a teletype or typewriter terminal. Because of high computer speed relative to human "think" time, a single system could comfortably service 50 to 100 (or more) users, with each having the "feel" of his own private computer. The timesharing system, by bringing people closest to the computer, seems to have very great potential for amplifying human creativity.

1-3 A CLASSIFICATION OF AUTOMATIC COMPUTERS

Automatic computers may be broadly classified as analog or digital (Fig. 1-1). Analog computers make use of the analogy between the values assumed by some physical quantity, such as shaft rotation, distance, or electric voltage, and a variable in the problem of interest. Digital computers in principle manipulate numbers directly. In a sense all computers have an analog quality since a phys-

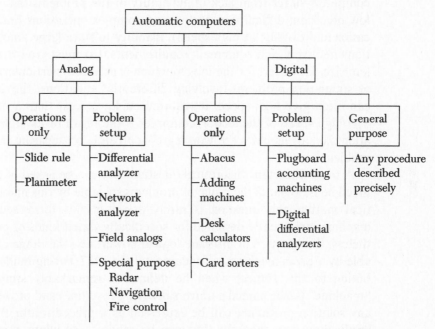

FIG. 1-1 A classification of computers

ical representation must be used for the abstraction that is a number. In the digital computer, the analogy is minimal, while the analog computer exploits it to a very great extent.

Both analog and digital computers include a subclass of rather simple machines that mechanize only specific simple operations. For example, the slide rule is an analog computer that represents numbers as distances on a logarithmic scale. Multiplication, division, finding roots of numbers, and other operations are done by adding and subtracting lengths. Examples of operation-only machines of the digital type include adding machines and desk calculators.

A second class, more sophisticated than operation-only machines, may be termed **problem-setup** machines. In addition to performing arithmetic operations they can accept a description of a procedure to link operations in sequence to solve a problem. The specification of the procedure may be built into the machine's controls, as in certain special-purpose machines, or a plugboard arrangement may be supplied for specifying the desired sequence of operations. The main idea is that the problem-solution procedure is entered in one distinct operation, and thereafter the entire execution of the work on the problem is automatic.

The electronic differential analyzer that emerged in the late 1940s is the most general form of **analog** computer. It is constructed from a few types of carefully engineered precision circuits (integrators, summing amplifiers, precision potentiometers, and capacitors) each capable of a single operation. The problem is usually set up on the machine by plugboard. Since there is usually no provision for storing results internally, the output is generally sent directly to a curve plotter. Precision, limited by drift and noise, is typically no higher than 1 part in 1000 of full scale. Compared with general-purpose digital computers, analog computers suffer from lack of generality of the problems that can be handled, low precision, difficulty in performing complex operations (including multiplication and division at high speed), inability to store large amounts of information effectively, and equipment requirements that must grow directly with problem size. However, for the jobs to which it is suited, particularly mathematical or simulation problems involving differential equations, the analog computer can often give high speed, if required, at lower cost than a digital computer. The high speed of the analog computer is the result of its highly parallel operation; i.e., all its parts are working concurrently on separate parts of the same problem.

A most important theoretical question that can be asked of a problem-setup machine is: What is the range of problems solvable by this machine? As a practical matter, this question is rarely asked in this form because plugboard machines are usually designed for specifically stated kinds of problems. Nevertheless, the question of ultimate logical power, i.e., the range of problems solvable by a given machine, is fundamental. In 1937 Turing made a direct contribution to this subject when he defined a remarkably simple hypothetical "machine" (since named a universal Turing machine) and proved, in effect, that any solution procedure can be expressed as a procedure for this machine. By implication, any machine that can be made to simulate a universal Turing machine also has its generality. The class of such machines is called **general purpose**. Most commercially available electronic digital computers are, for practical purposes, general-purpose machines. They differ in speed, cost, reliability, amount of storage, and ease of communication with other devices or people, but not in their ultimate logical capabilities.

1-4 THE NATURE OF A COMPUTER SYSTEM

A computer system is best considered as a collection of resources that are accessible to its users by programs written according to the rules of the system's programming languages. The resources are of two major classes with a wide variety of components in each:

1. **Equipment (hardware)**
   a. **Storages**   To hold both programs and data
   b. **Processing Logic**   Implementing arithmetic, logical manipulation of information

    c. **Control Logic**   Concerned with movement of information and sequencing of events

    d. **Transducers**   Devices for translating information from one physical form to another, e.g., a printer that converts electric signals to printed characters on paper

2. **Programs (software)**

    a. **Application Programs**   Programs written to satisfy some need of computer users outside the operation of the computer system itself, e.g., scientific, payroll, and inventory-control programs—in fact most of the work computers do

    b. **System Programs**   Programs concerned with the means by which the system provides certain conveniences to its users and manages its own resources, e.g., language translators and operating-system programs

1-5 PRINCIPLES OF HARDWARE ORGANIZATION

From now on we shall use the word computer to mean only the hardware part of a general-purpose computing system.

All computers have certain qualitative similarities, which will now be described. The reader will readily appreciate, however, the lack of precision in listing these common properties—our objective at present is to describe these in such a way that the essential nature of the machine, and the basis of its generality, can be intuitively understood.

From the viewpoint of the user, the machine manipulates two basic types of information: (1) operands, or data, and (2) instructions, each of which usually specifies a single airthmetic or control operation (e.g., ADD, SUBTRACT), and one or more operands which are the objects of the operation.

Within the machine, both instructions and data are represented as integers expressed in the binary number system or in some form of binary coding. This is done because the "atom" of information is then a two-state signal (called 0 or 1) which requires only the simplest and most reliable operation of electronic devices. Although the binary representation of instructions and data must appear within the machine for processing to take place, most users of computers may use the common decimal representation of numbers and alphabetic names of operations and data. Translator programs (usually supplied by the computer manufacturer) executed by the machine translate these convenient representations into the internal binary form. In other words, the binary representation of information inside the computer is important for reasons of electronic technology but is *not* an essential principle of the general-purpose computer.

The following is a list of attributes common to general-purpose digital computers:

1. The machine is capable of storing a large amount of information (both data and instructions). For economy reasons, there are usually at least three levels

of storage speed and capacity. The amount of storage is a fundamental limiting factor in the range of problems that can be handled.

2. The repertoire of instructions is typically small (from about 16 to 256 types) but is judiciously chosen to cover the requirements for any procedure.

3. Operands are referenced by name; the names of operands can be processed by instructions.

4. Instructions are accessed from storage and executed automatically. Normally, the location in storage of the next instruction is held in an instruction (or program) counter. This **pointer** is most often stepped in value (increased by 1) to specify the location of the next instruction, but certain instructions specifically modify the program counter to contain a value that depends on the outcome of comparisons between specified operands. This gives the program the ability to **branch** to alternative parts of the program, i.e., alternative instruction sequences.

The general organization of a typical computer is shown in Fig. 1-2. The heart of the system is the central processing unit (CPU), shown as comprising a main storage, which holds both program and data, an arithmetic-logic unit

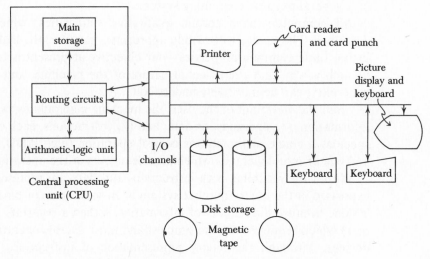

FIG. 1-2 General organization of a typical digital computer

(ALU), which contains processing circuitry such as an adder, shifter, and a few fast **registers** for holding the operands, and the instruction currently being processed. The program counter would also be included in the ALU, although in some diagrams the program control facilities are shown as a distinct function. One part of the CPU is a set of routing circuits which provide paths between storage and the ALU and input/output controllers or channels. In the type of system illustrated, many storage or input/output devices may be wired to one channel; but only one device per channel can be transmitting information from or to main storage at any one time. This is, of course, a restriction on the number of devices that can operate concurrently. It is imposed because of the economy of sharing common paths to main storage and simplicity in controlling movement of information between the devices and storage.

The major parts of a computer may be described as follows:

1. **Storage**   Means for storing a rather large volume of information and a simple economical access mechanism for routing an element of information to/from storage from/to a single point (register). Storage is usually available in several versions, even in the same system; these vary in access time, capacity, and cost.

2. **Data Flow**   The switching networks that provide paths for routing information from one part of the computer to another.

3. **Transformation**   The circuits for arithmetic and other data manipulation. This function is usually concentrated in a single arithmetic-logic unit (ALU). The centralization provides economy since a single set of fast expensive circuits is used in time sequence for all operations. Transformation circuits operate on information obtained from storage by control of the data-flow switching. As will be seen later, many of the more complex transformations such as subtraction, multiplication, and division can be obtained economically by control of sequences of very elementary operations such as addition, shifting, etc.

4. **Control**   This is a general term that includes the important function of performing time sequences of routings of information through the data flow. The control function appears on many levels in a computer. Usually the control is organized as a set of time sequences, or **cycles.** Each cycle period is commonly (but not always) divided into equally spaced time units called **clock intervals.** The term "cycle" refers to a specific type of sequence for selections on the data flow performed in a succession of clock intervals. For example, there is an **instruction fetch cycle** during which an instruction containing information about a transformation is brought from storage to an ALU register. At each clock interval within the cycle, an elementary operation is performed such as routing the storage location of the instruction to the storage-access mechanism, signaling for storage access, or routing of the instruction obtained to an ALU register.

5. **Input/Output**   Since information in the processor and storage of the computer are represented by electric signals, devices are provided to convert information from human-generated to machine-readable form on input, and in the opposite direction on output. A very common scheme for performing this transducer function uses a punched card. An operator reads the information from handwritten or typed documents and enters the information on a keyboard, much like a typewriter keyboard, of a keypunch machine. This machine translates the key strokes into holes on the card (see Fig. 1-3). The cards are then sent to the card reader, which contains the necessary equipment to READ the cards, i.e., sense the hole positions and translate them into the internal electric-signal representation. The punched card stores information in a nonvolatile form and can be read by human beings (by reading either the hole configurations or the printed characters at the top of

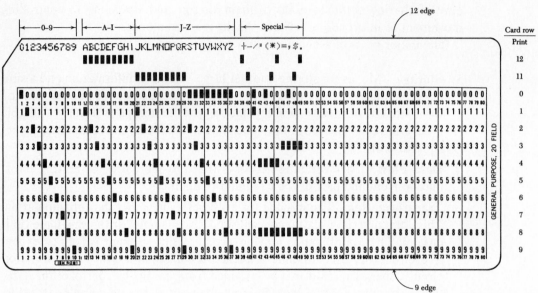

Representation of Data: Each of the 80 columns may contain one or more holes (small dark rectangles) representing an alphanumeric character. The card shown was punched to show the representations of the 10 decimal digits, 26 letters of the alphabet, and 12 special symbols (including blank) of a common symbol set.

FIG. 1-3 An 80-column IBM card showing row-column numbering and holes punched for the 48-character set used by the FORTRAN language

card). A card-punch machine may be controlled by the computer to produce punched-card output of the results of processing.

The punched card and its associated machines are examples of input/output devices. Other devices available include typewriters, punched paper tape, printers, cathode-ray-tube displays, analog-digital converters.

There is no sharp distinction between the storage function and the input/output function (the punched card was seen to contain both). However, a useful distinction can be made based on whether the output is directly machine-readable. On this basis, printers, typewriters, cathode-ray displays are input/output devices; punched cards, punched tape, magnetic tape are storage devices.

A very common terminology classifies all devices and machines not a part of the central processing unit and its directly accessible storage as input/output.

1-6 CONVENTIONS ON USE OF STORAGE

Certain conventions are almost universally assumed in using computer storage. These are independent of the physical nature of the device constituting storage—whether it uses magnetic tape, magnetic disks, semiconductors, etc. Two fundamental operations, viewed from the storage unit, are:

1. **READ** (copy)   Copies the contents of some specified portion of the storage and sends it to some standard place. Note that the copy operation is, to the user, **nondestructive;** i.e., information in storage is not modified by reading it out.

2. WRITE (replace)   Results in **replacement** of the present contents of a specified portion of storage from some standard place.

Sometimes the technology of a storage device naturally tends to violate these conventions. In such a case it is engineered with additional circuits to provide the same functional appearance to the user as described above.

1-7 ELEMENTS OF PROGRAMMING

For our present purposes, storage is assumed to consist of an array of cells which may be visualized as a long row of pigeonholes. Each cell contains information called an **operand** which may be likened to a number written on a piece of paper contained in the cell. **Each cell is given a name—the information in the cell is referenced only by the name of the cell it occupies, not by its content.** The operand referenced is then used for computation. The machine hardware usually has a wired-in name scheme whereby the cell names are the integers 0, 1, 2, etc. The user may, however, choose different names such as **X, Y, Z, I**, etc., for the cells. The translation of user names to machine names is a simple routine process since each user name is simply assigned to one machine name. This justifies our use of mnemonic symbols for names of operands.

Unless otherwise specified, numbers will denote operands, letters the *names* of operands. For example

(1)   **X←5**

is read "5 specifies **X**," which means the operand or usual number 5 replaces the contents of the cell named **X**. As another example consider the statement

(2)   **Y←1+X**

which means "the contents (operand) of the cell whose name is **X** is added to 1 and the result replaces the contents of the cell named **Y**." For brevity, we usually read this statement as "**X** plus 1 specifies **Y**." It is important to note that although the statement generally results in a change in the contents of **Y**, the contents of **X** remain unchanged. A simple program consists of a sequence of statements like the ones illustrated above. Although detailed rules of writing statements (symbols allowed, punctuation required, etc.) vary widely from program language to program language, many of the principles of programming can be illustrated adequately using a single language (APL in this case).

Since a computer normally handles large volumes of information, a key notion is designation and processing of **arrays** of information. A one-dimensional array of cells will be called a **vector.** An example of a vector is

(3)   **X≡3,29,47.4,82,⁻977.6**

An **element** or **component** of a vector will be denoted by a two-part designation. One part is the name of the entire vector; the other, written between brackets, gives the **position** of the element being referenced. In the above example

(4) $X[2] \equiv 29$

(assuming element position numbers in **X** start at 1 from the left).

Note also the meaning of a variable index. For example,

(5) $Y \leftarrow X[I]$

means "the content of cell **I** is used as a position number in **X,** and the content of the cell so designated in **X** replaces the content of **Y.**"

For example, if **X** is the vector specified in (3), the sequence

$$I \leftarrow 3$$
$$Y \leftarrow X[I]$$

results in Y being respecified by the number 47.4.

A variable such as

$$X[I] \quad \text{or} \quad X[3]$$

is said to be subscripted or indexed—the variable **I** is called an index variable. Index operations are extremely important because they allow us in effect to systematically compute cell names from other cell names or constants.

Why is it important to be able to compute names? One reason is that without this facility, it would be necessary to specify each cell explicitly by a unique name. Generating thousands of names would be tedious, and sooner or later we would probably devise a systematic naming procedure similar or identical to the indexed-variable idea. A second reason for the power of indexed variables is that the calculation of names can be included in the program for processing the data, thus greatly shortening the statement of the program but lengthening the time to execute it. For example, assume that 100 numbers have been entered into storage and called vector **X.** Two programs are shown in Fig. 1-4 to do the same job: compute **S,** the sum of the numbers.

Figure 1-4a is easy to understand immediately; it is a straight-line program consisting of all 100 executed steps written explicitly. Figure 1-4b is a much shorter program because it contains a **loop.** Note that in Fig. 1-4b, the "guts" of the program is statement 4, which adds the value in the **I** position of **X** and

∇SUM1	∇SUM2
[1] S←X[1]	[1] S←0
[2] S←S+X[2]	[2] I←1
[3] S←S+X[3]	[3] TEST:→(I>100)/0
.	[4] S←S+X[I]
.	[5] I→I+1
.	[6] →TEST
[100]S←S+X[100]	∇
∇	
(*a*) Straight line	(*b*) Loop

FIG. 1-4 Straight-line and loop programming to sum 100 numbers X

S, to produce the new **S**. This statement will be executed repetitively as we shall now see, each time with a new value of **I**. Certainly, line 5 increases **I** by 1, and line 6 directs the program to line 3 since this is where the statement labeled **TEST** is found. Line 3 says: "Compare **I** for greater than 100; if so, branch to line 0, which by convention means exit from the program. Otherwise, continue to the next statement (line 4)." With these rules, it is seen that for the case at hand, lines 4, 5, and 6 will each be executed 100 times and line 3 will be executed 101 times; in other words lines 3 to 6 constitute a program loop. Comparing the straight-line and loop programs of Fig. 1-4, we find that the number of written statements is 100 in the first case and only 6 in the second. This advantage of a short written program is somewhat offset by the fact that the loop program requires 403 **executed** statements compared to only 100 for the straight-line program. The additional executed statements in the loop program are required for index updating and testing.

1-8 PRINCIPLES OF THE SPACE-TIME RELATIONSHIP

The computer designer or user must be aware of some rather fundamental notions of how a computer and a problem can be organized to "trade" space and time. The word "space" will roughly correspond to "amount of equipment."

One simple example of this trade-off idea in the case of machine parts will now be discussed. Two ways of obtaining the same function are shown in Fig. 1-5; the function is the appearance of six signals—each of these can be either

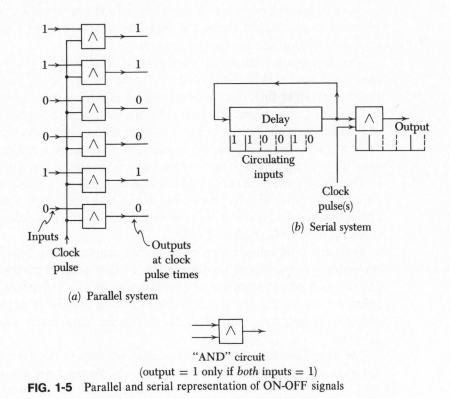

(a) Parallel system

(b) Serial system

"AND" circuit
(output = 1 only if *both* inputs = 1)

FIG. 1-5 Parallel and serial representation of ON-OFF signals

ON (=1) or OFF (=0). The circuit outputs are to appear as (, except at **timing** or **clock intervals** when the signals appear at the output point(s). To ensure that the output appears only at clock intervals, each signal and a clock pulse are fed into an AND circuit which gives a 1 output only when the signal line and clock line are both 1; at other times the output is 0.

In part (a) of Fig. 1-5 we see one representation of our set of six signals. Each signal uses its own line; the output appears on six output lines (and requires six AND circuits). In part (b) we see a second possibility—the six signals circulate as pulses in a delay-line structure—the delay is in this case six clock times. Here the signals appear in **time sequence** on a single wire.

The first circuit is extensive (and expensive) in space but concise (inexpensive-fast) in time. The second circuit has exactly dual properties. Notice also that as the number of signals grows, the parallel circuit grows proportionately but the time to receive all the signals remains the same. The serial circuit on the other hand requires no more lines (or AND circuits) to handle more signals, although the delay must increase proportionately.

Many of the desirable properties of a computer, especially its reliability, result from its use of simple components in a simple manner. Complex structures and operations are built up by using many simple components and intricate time sequences of the signals they generate or modify.

Because of the many devices for processing, control, and particularly storage, great efforts are exerted to obtain economical structures. The time-space relationship discussed above provides one method of reducing cost at the expense of time. This is an example of the idea of **time sharing,** i.e., using the same equipment (such as the adder circuit) successively in time by routing to it the numbers to be added in time sequence. The routing of information from place to place within the computer is therefore a fundamental operation. The paths provided for routing determine the **data-flow** structure of the machine—a most important characteristic of any computer.

The time-space relationship may also be illustrated by programming organization. Recall that in the procedures for summing a list of numbers, one can program **straight-line,** thereby obtaining an expensive space (storage) program but a fast-execution-time program. An alternative is to program the problem utilizing a loop; this results in great storage savings but longer execution time. In most cases, the loop program usually gains space by a much greater factor than it loses speed; it is the preferred method for all but the shortest lists.

The major point of the above discussions on time-space relationships is a fundamental property of data processing; in any task to be done, there is usually a choice of several solutions, which can be compared, to a first order, by the extent to which they trade space and time.

From the brief introduction given in this chapter, some broad properties of computer systems should be discernible. First, a general-purpose computer is one that can accept a precise stylized description of a procedure, called a **program,** for solving any problem solvable in a finite number of steps and can then execute the program automatically to process data made available to the machine.

The algorithm, or program, is important not only to the users of a computer but also, for two reasons, to its designers. (1) Product designers can perform intelligently only if they understand how the products will be used, i.e., programmed. (2) The sequences of internal switching operations necessary to implement arithmetic and other operations are also algorithms—these are the algorithms which must be specified and implemented by the logical designer.

A modern computer has been likened to a grand piano, on which the user can play Beethoven or "Chopsticks." Achieving the most value for an investment in equipment and manpower is a problem in optimizing resources that has some of the properties of combinatorial mathematics; i.e., a "slight" change in specifications or the criterion of optimization can make a very great difference in performance. The general-purpose nature of the computer rarely raises doubt that "answers" to a well-defined problem can be obtained one way or another. The central question is usually how to obtain the answers in a way that optimizes user convenience, problem-solution time, storage space, reliability, or some combination of such parameters. Needless to say, all these factors are interdependent, and some can be improved only at the expense of others. This has already been illustrated in the case of space versus time in the examples given earlier in this chapter. Some fairly general, but as yet undiscovered, "conservation" laws may relate these parameters; but at this time, the general interrelations can only be discussed qualitatively, although quantitative analysis of trade-offs is readily possible and should be done in specific cases.

sec.2

Computer Structures

V. Carl Hamacher

Zvonko G. Vranesic

Safwat G. Zaky

2-1 INTRODUCTION

The objective of this chapter is to introduce some basic concepts and associated terminology or jargon. We will give only a broad overview of the fundamental characteristics of computers, leaving the more detailed (and precise) discussion to the subsequent chapters.

Let us first define the meaning of the word "digital computer" or simply "computer," which is often misunderstood, despite the fact that most people take it for granted. In its simplest form, a contemporary computer is a fast electronic calculating machine, which accepts digitized "input" information, processes it according to a "program" stored in its "memory," and produces the resultant "output" information.

Adapted from *Computer Organization,* by V. Carl Hamacher, Zvonko G. Vranesic, and Safwat M. Zaky. Copyright © 1978. Used by permission of McGraw-Hill, Inc. All rights reserved.

2-2 FUNCTIONAL UNITS

The word **computer** encompasses a large variety of machines, widely differing in size, speed, and cost. It is fashionable to use more specific words to represent some subclasses of computers. Smaller machines are usually called **minicomputers,** which is a reflection on their relatively lower cost, size, and computing power. In the early 1970s the term **microcomputer** was coined to describe a very small computer, low in price, and consisting of only a few large-scale integrated (LSI) circuit packages.

Large computers are quite different from minicomputers and microcomputers in size, processing power, cost, and the complexity and sophistication of their design. Yet the basic concepts are essentially the same for all classes of computers, relying on a few well-defined ideas which we will attempt to explain. Thus the following discussion should be applicable to most general-purpose digital computers.

A computer consists of five functionally independent main parts: input, memory, arithmetic and logic, output, and control units, as indicated in Fig. 2-1. The input unit accepts coded information from the outside world, either from human

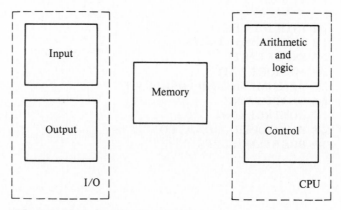

FIG. 2-1   Basic functional units of a computer

operators or from electromechanical devices. The information is either stored in the memory for later reference or immediately handled by the arithmetic and logic circuitry, which performs the desired operations. The processing steps are determined by a "program" stored in the memory. Finally, the results are sent back to the outside world through the output unit. All these actions are coordinated by the control unit. The diagram in Fig. 2-1 does not show the connections between the various functional units. Of course, such connections must exist.

It is customary to refer to the arithmetic and logic circuits in conjunction with the main control circuits as the **central processing unit** (CPU). Similarly, input and output equipment is combined under the term **input-output unit** (I/O). This is reasonable in view of the fact that some standard equipment provides both input and output functions. The simplest such example is the often encountered teletypewriter terminal. We must emphasize that input and output functions are separated within the terminal. Thus the computer sees two distinct

FIG. 2-2   A typical large computer—IBM S370/158 (IBM Corp. Ltd.)

devices, even though the human operator associates them as being part of the same unit.

In large computers the main functional units may comprise a number of separate, and often sizeable, physical parts. Fig. 2-2 is a photograph of such a computer. Minicomputers are much smaller in size. A basic minicomputer is often of desktop dimensions, as illustrated by the two machines in Fig. 2-3. Even a fairly complex minicomputer system, such as the one shown in Fig. 2-4, tends to be small in comparison with large computers.

At this point we should take a closer look at the "information" fed into the

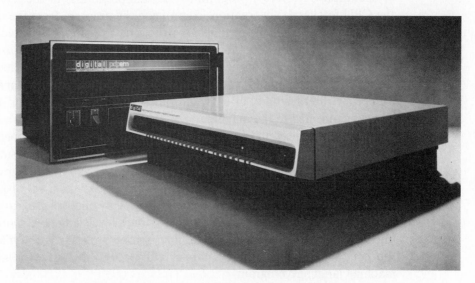

FIG. 2-3   Two minicomputers—PDP/8M and PDP11/05 (Digital Equipment Corp.)

FIG. 2-4   A minicomputer system (Digital Equipment Corp.)

computer. It is convenient to consider it as being of two types, namely, **instructions** and **data.** Instructions are explicit commands which:

• Govern the transfer of information within the machine, as well as between the machine and I/O devices
• Specify the arithmetic and logic operations to be performed

A set of instructions which perform a task is called a **program.** The usual mode of operation is to store a program (or several programs) in the memory. Then, the CPU fetches the instructions comprising the program from the memory and performs the desired operations. Instructions are normally executed in the sequential order in which they are stored, although it is possible to have deviations from this order as in the case where branching is required. Thus the actual behavior of the computer is under the complete control of the **stored program,** except for the possibility of external interruption by the operator or by digital devices connected to the machine.

Data are numbers and encoded characters which are used as operands by the instructions. This should not be interpreted as a hard definition, since the term is often used to symbolize any digital information. Even within our definition of data, it is quite feasible that an entire program (that is, a set of instructions) may be considered as data if it is to be processed by another program. An example of this is the task of **compilation** of a high-level language source program into machine instructions and data. The source program is the input data for the compiler program. The compiler translates the source program into a machine language program.

Information handled by the computer must be encoded in a suitable format.

Since most present-day hardware (that is, electronic and electromechanical equipment) employs digital circuits which have only two naturally stable states, namely, ON and OFF, binary coding is used. That is, each number, character of text, or instruction is encoded as a string of binary digits (**bits**), each having one of two possible values. Numbers are usually represented in the positional binary notation. Occasionally, the **binary-coded decimal** (BCD) format is employed, where each decimal digit is encoded by 4 bits.

Alphanumeric characters are also expressed in terms of binary codes. Several appropriate coding schemes have been developed. Two of the most widely encountered ones are ASCII (American Standard Code for Information Interchange), where each character is represented as a 7-bit code, and EBCDIC (extended binary-coded decimal interchange code), where 8 bits are used to denote a character.

2-3 INPUT UNIT

Computers accept coded information by means of input units, which consist of devices capable of "reading" such data. The simplest of these is an electric **typewriter** electronically connected to the processing part of the computer. The typewriter is wired so that whenever a key on its keyboards is depressed, the corresponding letter or digit is automatically translated into its corresponding code, which may then be sent directly to either the memory or the CPU.

A related input device is the **teletypewriter,** such as the ASR 33 (Automatic Send-Receive) terminal.[1] In addition to its typewriter function, this teletypewriter contains a paper tape reader–punch station. Its low price and sufficient versatility make the teletypewriter one of the most frequently used input (and output) devices.

While typewriters and teletypewriters are unquestionably the simplest I/O devices, they are also the slowest and most awkward to use when dealing with large volumes of data. This necessitated the development of faster equipment, such as high-speed **paper tape readers** and **card readers.** A convenient way of preparing a hard copy of a program or data is to punch the coded information on paper cards, divided into columns (usually 80), where each column corresponds to one character. A card reader may then be used to determine the location of the punched holes and thus read the input information. This is a considerably faster process, with typical readers being able to read upward of 1000 cards per minute. Fig. 2-5 shows a photograph of a card reader.

Many other kinds of input devices are available. We should particularly mention **graphic input** devices, which utilize a cathode-ray tube (CRT) display.

2-4 MEMORY UNIT

The sole function of the memory unit is to store programs and data. Again, this function can be accomplished with a variety of equipment. It is useful to distin-

---

[1]Product of Teletype Corporation.

FIG. 2-5   A punched card reader (IBM Corp. Ltd.)

guish between two classes of memory devices, which comprise the primary and secondary storage.

Primary storage, or the **main memory,** is a fast memory capable of operating at electronic speeds, where programs and data are stored during their execution. It typically consists of either magnetic cores or semiconductor circuits. The former constitute **core memories,** while the latter are referred to as **semiconductor memories.**

The main memory contains a large number of storage cells, each capable of storing 1 bit of information. These cells are seldom handled individually. Instead, it is usual to deal with them in groups of fixed size. Such groups are called **words.** The main memory is organized so that the contents of one word, containing n bits, can be stored or retrieved in one basic operation.

To provide easy access to any word in the main memory, it is useful to associate a distinct name with each word location. These names are numbers that identify successive locations, which are hence called the **addresses.** A given word is accessed by specifying its address and issuing a control command that starts the storage or retrieval process.

The number of bits in each word is often referred to as the **word length** of the given computer. Large computers usually have 32 or more bits in a word, minicomputers have between 12 and 24 (a favorite choice is 16), while some microcomputers have only 4 or 8 bits per word. The capacity of the main memory is one of the factors that characterize the size of the computer. Small machines may have only a few thousand words (4096 is a typical minimum), whereas large machines often involve a few million words. Data is usually manipulated within the machine in units of words, multiples of words, or submultiples of words. A typical access to the main memory results in one word of data being read from the memory or written into it.

FIG. 2-6 Magnetic disk storage (IBM Corp. Ltd.)

As mentioned above, programs and data must reside in the main memory during execution. Instructions and data can be written into it or read out under control of the processing unit. It is essential to be able to access any word location within the main memory as quickly as possible. Memories where any location can be reached by specifying its address are called **random access memories** (RAM). The time required to access one word is called the **memory cycle time.** This is a fixed time, usually 300 nanoseconds (ns) to 1 microsecond (μs) for most modern computers.

While primary storage is essential, it tends to be expensive. Thus additional, cheaper **secondary storage** is used when large amounts of data have to be stored, particularly if some of the data need not be accessed very frequently. Indeed, a wide selection of suitable devices are available. These include **magnetic disks, drums,** and **tapes.** Figures 2-6 and 2-7 show a bank of disk units and a tape unit, respectively.

2-5 ARITHMETIC AND LOGIC UNIT

Execution of most operations within the computer takes place in the arithmetic and logic unit (ALU). Consider a typical example. Suppose two numbers located in the main memory are to be added. They are brought into the arithmetic unit where the actual addition is carried out. The sum may then be stored in the memory.

Similarly, any other arithmetic or logic operation (for example, multiplication, division, comparison of numbers) is done by bringing the required operands into the ALU, where the necessary operation is performed. We should point out that not all operands in an ongoing computation reside in the main memory, since the CPU normally contains one or more high-speed storage cells called **registers,** which may be used for temporary storage of often used operands. Each such register can store one word of data. Access times to registers are typically 5 to 10 times faster than memory access times.

FIG. 2-7   A magnetic tape unit (IBM Corp. Ltd.)

The control and arithmetic units are usually many times faster in basic cycle time than other devices connected to the computer system. It is thus possible to design relatively complex computer systems containing a number of external devices controlled by a single CPU. These devices can be teletypes, magnetic tape and disk memories, sensors, displays, mechanical controllers, etc. Of course, this is possible only because of the vast difference in speed, enabling the fast CPU to organize and control the activity of many slower devices.

2-6 OUTPUT UNIT

The output unit is the counterpart of the input unit. Its function is to return the processed results to the outside world.

A number of devices provide both an output function and an input function. This is the case with typewriters, teletypewriters, and graphic displays. This dual role of some devices is the reason for combining input and output units under the single name of I/O unit. A photograph of a typical teletypewriter is shown in Fig. 2-8.

Of course, there exist devices used for output only, the most familiar example being the high-speed **printer.** It is possible to produce printers capable of printing as many as 10,000 lines per minute. These are tremendous speeds in the mechanical sense, but still very slow compared to the electronic speeds of the CPU.

Sometimes it is necessary to produce the output data in some form suitable for later use as input data. Punched cards may be generated with a card punch. Similarly, **paper tape punches** are available for producing a paper tape output.

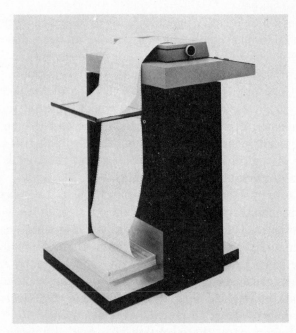

FIG. 2-8   A teletypewriter (IBM Corp. Ltd.)

Finally, we should observe that some of the bulk storage devices, used primarily for secondary storage, may also be employed for I/O purposes. As a specific case, consider the magnetic tape. Suppose that a particular job involves gathering data from a set of terminals, which is done over a relatively long period of time. It is likely that such a task can be conveniently and economically handled by a minicomputer. Using a large computer for this purpose would probably be more expensive. However, let us assume that when the data is finally collected, it must be processed in some intricate way that is beyond the capabilities of the minicomputer. A reasonable arrangement is to have the minicomputer write the collected data onto a magnetic tape as part of its output (or storage!) process. The completed tape can be transported to the large computer, which can then input the data from the tape and carry out the actual processing. In this way the large (and expensive) computer is used only where necessary, with a corresponding reduction in the overall cost of processing this particular job.

2-7 CONTROL UNIT

The previously described units provide the necessary tools for storing and processing information. Their operation must be coordinated in some organized way, which is the task of the control unit. It is effectively the nerve center of the whole machine, used to send control signals to all other units.

A line printer will print a line only if it is specifically instructed to do so. This may typically be effected by an appropriate Write instruction executed by the CPU. Processing of this instruction involves the sending of **timing signals** to and from the printer, which is the function of the control unit.

We can say, in general, that I/O transfers are controlled by software instructions which identify the devices involved and the type of transfer. However, the actual timing signals which govern the transfers during execution are generated by the control circuits. Data transfers between the CPU and memory are also controlled by the control unit in a similar fashion.

Conceptually it is reasonable to think of the control unit as a well-defined physically separable central unit which somehow interacts with the rest of the machine. In practice this is seldom the case. Much of the control circuitry is physically distributed throughout the machine. It is connected by a rather large set of control lines (wires), which carry the signals used for timing and synchronization of events in all units.

An important part of the control unit is a **display panel,** with switches and light indicators, which enables the operator to see what is happening inside the computer. The panel is particularly useful when something goes wrong in the computing process, as it often does. In such situations the operator can use the panel to discover the difficulty and hopefully remedy it. Certainly, some faults cannot be easily corrected (for example, failure of an electronic component), but many commonly occurring difficulties (minor software problems) can be diagnosed and corrected by the operator.

In summary, the operation of a typical general-purpose computer can be described as follows:

- It accepts information (programs and data) through the input unit and transfers it to the memory.
- Information stored in the memory is fetched, under program control, into the ALU to be processed.
- Processed information leaves the computer through its output unit.
- All activities inside the machine are under the control of the control unit.

2-8 BASIC OPERATIONAL CONCEPTS

In the previous section it was stated that the behavior of the computer is governed by means of instructions. To perform a given task, an appropriate program consisting of a set of instructions is stored in the main memory. Individual instructions are brought from the memory into the CPU, which executes the specified operations. In addition to the instructions, it is necessary to use some data as operands, which are also stored in the memory. A typical instruction may be

Add LOCA,R0

which adds the operand at memory location LOCA to the operand in a register in the CPU called R0, and places the sum into register R0. This instruction requires several steps to be performed. First, the instruction must be transferred from the main memory into the CPU. Then, the operand from LOCA must be fetched. This operand is added to the contents of R0. Finally, the resultant sum is stored in register R0.

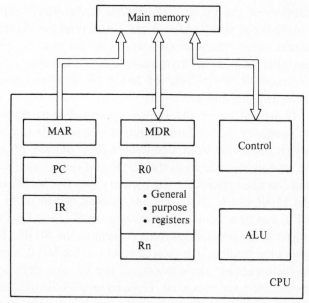

FIG. 2-9   Connections between the CPU and the main memory

Transfers between the main memory and the CPU start by sending the address of the memory location to be accessed to the memory unit and issuing the appropriate control signals. Then data is transferred from or to the memory.

Fig. 2-9 shows how the connection between the main memory and the CPU can be made. It also shows a few details of the CPU that have not been discussed yet, but which are operationally essential. The interconnection pattern for these components is not shown explicitly, since at this point we will discuss their functional characteristics only.

The CPU contains the arithmetic and logic circuitry as the main processing element. It also contains a number of registers used for temporary storage of data. Two registers are of particular interest. The **instruction register** (IR) contains the instruction that is being executed. Its output is available to the control circuits, which generate the timing signals for control of the actual processing circuits needed to execute the instruction. The **program counter** (PC) is a register which keeps track of the execution of a program. It contains the memory address of the instruction currently being executed. During the execution of the current instruction, the contents of the PC are updated to correspond to the address of the next instruction to be executed. It is customary to say that the PC points at the instruction that is to be fetched from the memory.

Besides the IR and PC there exists at least one other, and usually several other, **general-purpose registers.**

Finally, there are two registers that facilitate communication with the main memory. These are the **memory address register** (MAR) and the **memory data register** (MDR). As the name implies, the MAR is used to hold the address of the location to or from which data is to be transferred. The MDR contains the data to be written into or read out of the addressed location.

Let us now consider some typical operating steps. Programs reside in the main memory and usually get there via the input unit. Execution of a program starts by setting the PC to point at the first instruction of the program. The contents of the PC are transferred to the MAR and a Read control signal is sent to the memory. After a certain elapsed time (corresponding to the memory access time), the addressed word (in this case the first instruction of our program) is read out of the memory and loaded into the MDR. Next, the contents of the MDR are transferred to the IR, at which point the instruction is ready to be decoded and executed.

If the instruction involves an operation to be performed by the ALU, it will be necessary to obtain the required operands. If an operand resides in the memory (it could also be in a general register in the CPU), it will have to be fetched by sending its address to the MAR and initiating a Read cycle. When the operand has been read from the memory into the MDR, it may be transferred from the MDR to the ALU. Having fetched one or more operands in this way, the ALU can perform the desired operation. If the result of this operation is to be stored in the memory, it must be sent to the MDR. The address of the location where the result is to be stored is sent to the MAR and a Write cycle is initiated. In the meantime the contents of the PC are incremented to point at the next instruction to be executed. Thus, as soon as the execution of the current instruction is completed, a new instruction fetch may be started.

In addition to transferring data between the main memory and the CPU, it is necessary to have the ability to accept data from input devices and to send data to output devices. Thus some machine instructions with the capability of handling I/O transfers must be provided.

Normal execution of programs may sometimes be altered. It is often the case that some device requires urgent servicing. For example, a monitoring device in a computer-controlled industrial process may have detected a dangerous condition. To deal with such situations sufficiently quickly, the normal flow of the program that is being executed by the CPU must be interrupted. To achieve this, the device can raise an **interrupt signal.** An interrupt is a service request where the service is performed by the CPU by executing a corresponding **interrupt handling program.** Since such diversions may alter the internal state of the CPU, it is essential that its state be saved in the main memory before servicing the interrupt. This normally involves storing the contents of the PC, the general registers, and some control information. Upon termination of the interrupt handling program, the CPU's state is restored so that execution of the interrupted program may continue.

2-9 BUS STRUCTURES

So far we have discussed the functional characteristics of individual parts that constitute a computer. To form an operational system they must be connected together in some organized way. There are many ways of doing this, and we will consider the three most popular structures.

If a computer is to achieve a reasonable speed of operation, it must be organized in a **parallel** fashion. This means that all units can handle one full word of data at a given time. It also means that data transfers between units are to be done in parallel, which implies that a considerable number of wires (lines) are needed to establish the necessary connections. A collection of such wires,

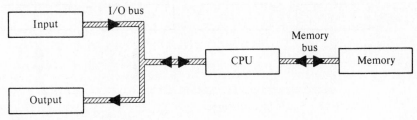

FIG. 2-10   A two-bus structure

which have some common identity, is called a **bus.** In addition to the wires which carry the data, it is essential to have some lines for control purposes. Thus a bus consists of both data and control lines.

Fig. 2-10 shows the simplest form of a **two-bus** structured computer. The CPU interacts with the memory via a **memory bus.** Input and output functions are handled by means of an **I/O bus,** so that data passes through the CPU on route to the memory. In such configurations the I/O transfers are usually under direct control of the CPU. It initiates the transfer and monitors its progress until completion. A commonly used term to describe this type of operation is programmed I/O.

A somewhat different version of a two-bus structure is given in Fig. 2-11. The relative positions of the CPU and memory are reversed. Again, a memory bus exists for communication between them. However, I/O transfers are made directly to or from the memory. Since the memory has little in the way of circuitry capable of controlling such transfers, it is necessary to establish a different control mechanism. A standard technique is to provide **I/O channels** as part of the I/O equipment, which have the necessary capability to control the transfers. In fact they resemble a small CPU and can often be thought of as computers in their own right. A typical procedure is to have the CPU initiate a transfer by passing the required information to the I/O channel, which then takes over and controls the actual transfer.

We have already mentioned that a bus consists of a collection of distinct lines, serving different purposes. While at this point it is not necessary to get into the details, it is useful to note that the memory bus in the above diagram contains a **data bus** and an **address bus.** The data bus is used for transmission of data. Hence its number of lines corresponds to the number of bits in the word. To access data in the memory it is necessary to issue an address to indicate its location. The CPU sends address bits to the memory via the address bus.

The above descriptions are representative of most computers. Fig. 2-11 usually implies a large computer. Many machines have several distinct buses, so

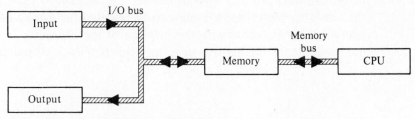

FIG. 2-11   An alternative two-bus structure

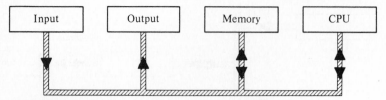

FIG. 2-12   Single-bus structure

that one could in fact treat them as **multibus** machines. However, their operation is adequately represented by the two-bus examples, since the main reason for inclusion of additional buses is to improve the operating speed through further parallelism.

A significantly different structure, which has a **single bus,** is shown in Fig. 2-12. All units are connected to this bus, so that it provides the sole means of interaction. Since the bus can be used for only one transfer at a time, it follows that only two units can be actively using the bus at any given instant. The bus is likely to consist of the data bus, the address bus, and some control lines. The main virtue of the single-bus structure is its low cost and flexibility for attaching peripheral devices. The trade-off is lower operating speed. It is not surprising that a single-bus structure is primarily found in small machines, namely, minicomputers and microcomputers.

Differences in bus structure have a pronounced effect on the performance of computers. Yet from the conceptual point of view (at least at this level of detail) they are not crucial in any functional description. Indeed, the fundamental principles of computer operation are essentially independent of the particular bus structure.

Transfer of information on the bus can seldom be done at a speed directly comparable to the operating speed of devices connected to the bus. Some electromechanical devices are relatively slow, for example, teletypewriters, card readers, printers. Others, such as disks and tapes, are considerably faster. Main memory and the CPU operate at electronic speeds, making them the fastest part of the computer. Since all these devices must communicate with each other via the bus, it is necessary to provide an efficient transfer mechanism which is not constrained by the slow devices.

A common approach is to include **buffer registers** with the devices to hold the information during transfers. To illustrate this technique, consider the transfer of an encoded character from the CPU to a teletypewriter where it is to be printed. The CPU effects the transfer by sending the character via the bus to the teletypewriter output buffer. Since the buffer is an electronic register, this transfer requires relatively little time. Once the buffer is loaded, the teletypewriter can start printing without further intervention by the CPU. At this time the bus is no longer needed and can be released for use by other devices. The teletypewriter proceeds with the printing of the character in its buffer and is not available for further transfers until this process is completed.

Number Systems and Codes

Zvi Kohavi

3-1 NUMBER SYSTEMS

Convenient as the decimal number system generally is, its usefulness in machine computation is limited because of the nature of practical electronic devices. In most present digital machines the numbers are represented, and the arithmetic operations performed, in a different number system, called the binary number system. This section is concerned with the representation of numbers in various systems and with methods of conversion from one system to another.

Number Representation

An ordinary decimal number actually represents a polynomial in powers of 10. For example, the number 123.45 represents the polynomial

$$123.45 = 1 \cdot 10^2 + 2 \cdot 10^{-1} + 3 \cdot 10^0 + 4 \cdot 10^1 + 5 \cdot 10^{-2}$$

This method of representing decimal numbers is known as the **decimal number system,** and the number 10 is referred to as the **base** (or **radix**) of the system. In a system whose base is b, a positive number N represents the polynomial

$$N = a_{q-1}b^{q-1} + \cdots + a_0b^0 + \cdots + a_{-p}b^{-p}$$
$$= \sum_{i=-p}^{q-1} a_ib^i$$

where the base b is an integer greater than 1, and the a's are integers in the range $0 \leq a_i \leq b - 1$. The sequence of digits $a_{q-1}a_{q-2} \cdots a_0$ constitutes the **integral part** of N, while the sequence $a_{-1}a_{-2} \cdots a_{-p}$ constitutes the **fractional part** of N. Thus p and q designate the number of digits in the fractional and integral parts, respectively. The integral and fractional parts are usually separated by a **radix point**. The digit a_{-p} is referred to as the **least significant digit**, while a_{q-1} is called the **most significant digit**.

When the base b equals 2, the number representation is referred to as the **binary number system**. For example, the binary number 1101.01 represents the polynomial

$$1101.01 = 1 \cdot 2^3 + 1 \cdot 2^2 + 0 \cdot 2^1 + 1 \cdot 2^0 + 0 \cdot 2^{-1} + 1 \cdot 2^{-2}$$

that is,

$$1101.01 = \sum_{i=-2}^{3} a_i 2^i$$

where $a_{-2} = a_0 = a_2 = a_3 = 1$ and $a_{-1} = a_1 = 0$.

A number N in base b is usually denoted $(N)_b$. Whenever the base is not specified, base 10 is implicit. Table 3-1 shows the representations of integers 0 through 15 in several number systems.

TABLE 3-1 Representations of Integers

2	4	Base 8	10	12
0000	0	0	0	0
0001	1	1	1	1
0010	2	2	2	2
0011	3	3	3	3
0100	10	4	4	4
0101	11	5	5	5
0110	12	6	6	6
0111	13	7	7	7
1000	20	10	8	8
1001	21	11	9	9
1010	22	12	10	α
1011	23	13	11	β
1100	30	14	12	10
1101	31	15	13	11
1110	32	16	14	12
1111	33	17	15	13

The **complement** of a digit a, denoted a', in base b is defined as

$$a' = (b - 1) - a$$

That is, the complement a' is the difference between the largest digit in base b and the digit a. In the binary number system, since $b = 2$, $0' = 1$ and $1' = 0$. In the decimal number system the largest digit is 9. Thus, for example, the complement[†] of 3 is $9 - 3 = 6$.

Conversion of Bases

Suppose that some number N, which we wish to express in base b_2, is presently expressed in base b_1. In converting a number from base b_1 to base b_2, it is convenient to distinguish two cases. In the first case, $b_1 < b_2$, and consequently base b_2 arithmetic can be used in the conversion process. The conversion technique involves expressing the number $(N)_{b_1}$ as a polynomial in powers of b_1 and evaluating the polynomial using base b_2 arithmetic.

Example We wish to express the numbers $(432.2)_8$ and $(1101.01)_2$ in base 10.

$$(432.2)_8 = 4 \cdot 8^2 + 3 \cdot 8^1 + 2 \cdot 8^0 + 2 \cdot 8^{-1} = (282.25)_{10}$$

[†]In the decimal system the complement is also referred to as the 9's complement. In the binary system it is also known as the 1's complement.

$$(1101.01)_2 = 1 \cdot 2^3 + 1 \cdot 2^2 + 0 \cdot 2^1 + 1 \cdot 2^0 + 0 \cdot 2^{-1} + 1 \cdot 2^{-2}$$

$$= (13.25)_{10}$$

In both cases the arithmetic operations are done in base 10.

When $b_1 > b_2$ it is more convenient to use base-b_1 arithmetic. The conversion procedure will be proved by considering separately the integral and fractional parts of N. Let $(N)_{b_1}$ be an integer whose value in *base b_2* is given by

$$(N)_{b_1} = a_{q-1}b_2^{q-1} + a_{q-2}b_2^{q-2} + \cdots + a_1 b_2^1 + a_0 b_2^0$$

To find the values of the a_i's, let us divide (base b_1) the above polynomial by b_2.

$$\frac{(N)_{b_1}}{b_2} = \underbrace{a_{q-1}b_2^{q-2} + a_{q-2}b_2^{q-3} + \cdots + a_1}_{Q_0} + \frac{a_0}{b_2}$$

Thus the least significant digit of $(N)_{b_2}$, i.e., a_0, is equal to the first remainder. The next significant digit, a_1, is obtained by dividing the quotient Q_0 by b_2, i.e.,

$$\left(\frac{Q_0}{b_2}\right)_{b_1} = \underbrace{a_{q-1}b_2^{q-3} + a_{q-2}b_2^{q-4} + \cdots +}_{Q_1} \frac{a_1}{b_2}$$

The remaining a's are evaluated by repeated divisions of the quotients until Q_{q-1} is equal to zero. If N is finite, the process must terminate.

If $(N)_{b_1}$ is a fraction, a dual procedure is employed. $(N)_{b_1}$ can be expressed in base b_2 as

$$(N)_{b_1} = a_{-1}b_2^{-1} + a_{-2}b_2^{-2} + \cdots + a_{-p}b_2^{-p}$$

The most significant digit, a_{-1}, can be obtained by multiplying the polynomial by b_2, i.e.,

$$b_2 \cdot (N)_{b_1} = a_{-1} + a_{-2}b_2^{-1} + \cdots + a_{-p}b_2^{-p+1}$$

If the above product is less than 1, then a_{-1} equals 0; if the product is greater than or equal to 1, then a_{-1} is equal to the integral part of the product. The next most significant digit, a_{-2}, is found by multiplying the fractional part of the above product by b_2 and determining its integral part, and so on. This process does not necessarily terminate, since it may not be possible to represent the fraction in base b_2 with a finite number of digits.

A considerably simpler conversion procedure may be employed in converting octal numbers (i.e., numbers in base 8) to binary, and vice versa. Since $8 = 2^3$, each octal digit can be expressed by three binary digits. For example, $(6)_8$ can be expressed as $(110)_2$, etc. The procedure of converting a binary number into an octal number is to partition the binary number into groups of three digits, starting from the binary point, and to determine the octal digit corresponding to each group.

Example

$$(123.4)_8 = (001\ 010\ 011.100)_2$$
$$(1010110.0101)_2 = (001\ 010\ 110.010\ 100) = (126.24)_8$$

A similar procedure may be employed in conversions from binary to hexadecimal (base 16), except that four binary digits are needed to represent a single hexadecimal digit. In fact, whenever a number is converted from base b_1 to base b_2, where $b_2 = b_1{}^k$, then k digits of that number are grouped and may be represented by a single digit from base b_2.

Binary Arithmetic

The binary number system is widely used in digital systems. Although a detailed study of digital arithmetic is beyond the scope of this book, we shall present the elementary techniques of binary arithmetic. The basic arithmetic operations are summarized in Table 3-2, where the sum and carry, difference

TABLE 3-2 Elementary Binary Operations

Bits		*Sum*	*Carry*	*Difference*	*Borrow*	*Product*
a	b	$a + b$		$a - b$		$a \cdot b$
0	0	0	0	0	0	0
0	1	1	0	1	1	0
1	0	1	0	1	0	0
1	1	0	1	0	0	1

and borrow, and product are computed for every combination of the binary digits (abbreviated **bits**) 0 and 1.

Binary addition is performed in a manner similar to that of decimal addition. Corresponding bits are added, and if a carry 1 is produced, it is added to the binary digits at the left.

Example

$$
\begin{array}{rl}
1111 & = \text{carries of } 1 \\
1111.01 & = (15.25)_{10} \\
+ \quad\quad & \\
\underline{0111.10} & = (\ 7.50)_{10} \\
10110.11 & = (22.75)_{10}
\end{array}
$$

In subtraction, if a borrow of 1 occurs and the next left digit of the minuend is 1, it is changed to 0, and the subtraction is continued in the usual manner. If, however, the next left digit of the minuend is 0, it is changed to 1, as is each successive minuend digit to the left which is equal to 0. The first minuend digit to the left which is equal to 1 is changed to 0, and the subtraction is continued.

Example

$$
\begin{array}{rl}
1 & = \text{borrows of } 1 \\
10010.11 & = (18.75)_{10} \\
- \quad\quad & \\
\underline{01100.10} & = (12.50)_{10} \\
00110.01 & = (\ 6.25)_{10}
\end{array}
$$

Just as in decimal numbers, multiplication of binary numbers is performed by successive addition, while division is done by successive subtraction.

Example   Multiply the binary numbers below.

$$11001.1 = (25.5)_{10}$$
$$\times$$
$$\underline{110.1} = (\ 6.5)_{10}$$
$$11001\ 1$$
$$000000$$
$$110011$$
$$\underline{110011}$$
$$10100101.11 = (165.75)_{10}$$

Example   Divide the binary number 1000100110 by 11001.

$$\begin{array}{r} 10110 = \text{quotient} \\ 11001\,\overline{)1000100110} \\ \underline{11001} \\ 00100101 \\ \underline{11001} \\ 0011001 \\ \underline{11001} \\ 00000 = \text{remainder} \end{array}$$

3-2 BINARY CODES

Although the binary number system has many practical advantages and is widely used in digital computers, in many cases it is convenient to work with the decimal number system, especially when the communication between human and machine is extensive, since most numerical data generated by humans are in terms of decimal numbers. To simplify the communication problem between man and machine, a number of codes have been devised so that the decimal digits are represented by sequences of binary digits.

Weighted Codes

In order to represent the 10 decimal digits 0, 1, . . . , 9 it is necessary to use at least four binary digits. Since there are 16 combinations of four binary digits, of which only 10 combinations are used, it is possible to form a very large number of distinct codes. Of particular importance is the class of **weighted codes,** whose main characteristic is that each binary digit is assigned a "weight," and for each group of four bits, the sum of the weights of those binary digits whose value is 1 is equal to the decimal digit which they represent. In other words, if w_1, w_2, w_3, and w_4 are the weights of the binary digits and x_1, x_2, x_3, x_4 are the corresponding digit values, then the decimal digit $N = w_4x_4 + w_3x_3 + w_2x_2 +$

TABLE 3-3 Examples of Weighted Binary Codes

Decimal digit	8	4	2	1	2	4	2	1	6	4	2	−3
0	0	0	0	0	0	0	0	0	0	0	0	0
1	0	0	0	1	0	0	0	1	0	1	0	1
2	0	0	1	0	0	0	1	0	0	0	1	0
3	0	0	1	1	0	0	1	1	1	0	0	1
4	0	1	0	0	0	1	0	0	0	1	0	0
5	0	1	0	1	1	0	1	1	1	0	1	1
6	0	1	1	0	1	1	0	0	0	1	1	0
7	0	1	1	1	1	1	0	1	1	1	0	1
8	1	0	0	0	1	1	1	0	1	0	1	0
9	1	0	0	1	1	1	1	1	1	1	1	1

The column group header reads $w_4 w_3 w_2 w_1$.

$w_1 x_1$ is represented by the binary sequence $x_4 x_3 x_2 x_1$. A sequence of binary digits which represents a decimal digit is called a **code word.** Thus the above sequence $x_4 x_3 x_2 x_1$ is the code word for N. A number of weighted, four-digit binary codes are shown in Table 3-3.

The binary digits in the first code in Table 3-3 are assigned the weights 8, 4, 2, 1. As a result of this weight assignment, the code word that corresponds to each decimal digit is the binary equivalence of that digit; e.g., 5 is represented by 0101, and so on. This code is known as the BCD (**Binary-Coded-Decimal**) code. For each of the codes in Table 3-3 the decimal digit that corresponds to a given code word is equal to the sum of the weights in those binary positions which are 1's. Thus, in the second code, where the weights are 2, 4, 2, 1, decimal 5 is represented by 1011, corresponding to the sum $2 \cdot 1 + 4 \cdot 0 + 2 \cdot 1 + 1 \cdot 1 = 5$. The weights assigned to the binary digits may also be negative, as is shown by the code $(6,4,2,-3)$. In this code, decimal 5 is represented by 1011, since $6 \cdot 1 + 4 \cdot 0 + 2 \cdot 1 - 3 \cdot 1 = 5$.

It is apparent that the representations of some decimal numbers in the $(2,4,2,1)$ and $(6,4,2,-3)$ codes are not unique. For example, in the $(2,4,2,1)$ code, decimal 7 may be represented by 1101 as well as by 0111. Adopting the representations shown in Table 3-3 causes the codes to become self-complementing. A code is said to be **self-complementing** if the code word of the 9's complement of N, i.e., $9 - N$, can be obtained from the code word of N by interchanging all the 1's and 0's. For example, in the $(6,4,2,-3)$ code, decimal 3 is represented by 1001, while decimal 6 is represented by 0110. In the $(2,4,2,1)$ code, decimal 2 is represented by 0010, while decimal 7 is represented by 1101. Note that the BCD code is not self-complementing. It can be shown that a necessary condition for a weighted code to be self-complementing is that the sum of the weights must equal 9. There exist only four positively weighted self-complementing codes, namely, $(2,4,2,1)$, $(3,3,2,1)$, $(4,3,1,1)$, $(5,2,1,1)$. In addition, there exist 13 self-complementing codes with positive and negative weights.

Nonweighted Codes

There are many nonweighted binary codes, two of which are shown in Table 3-4. The **Excess-3** code is formed by adding 0011 to each BCD code word. Thus,

TABLE 3-4   Nonweighted Binary Codes

Decimal digit	Excess-3				Cyclic			
0	0	0	1	1	0	0	0	0
1	0	1	0	0	0	0	0	1
2	0	1	0	1	0	0	1	1
3	0	1	1	0	0	0	1	0
4	0	1	1	1	0	1	1	0
5	1	0	0	0	1	1	1	0
6	1	0	0	1	1	0	1	0
7	1	0	1	0	1	0	0	0
8	1	0	1	1	1	1	0	0
9	1	1	0	0	0	1	0	0

for example, the representation of decimal 7 in Excess-3 is given by 0111 + 0011 = 1010. The Excess-3 code is a self-complementing code, and it possesses a number of properties that made it practical in earlier decimal computers.

In many practical applications, e.g., analog-to-digital conversion, it is desirable to use codes in which all successive code words differ in only one digit. Codes that have such a property are referred to as **cyclic codes.** The second code in Table 3-4 is an example of such a code. (Note that in this, as in all cyclic codes, the code word representing the decimal digits 0 and 9 differ in only one digit.) A particularly important cyclic code is the **Gray code.** A four-bit Gray code is shown in Table 3-5. The feature that makes this cyclic code useful is the simplicity of the procedure for converting from the binary number system into the Gray code.

Let $g_n \cdots g_2 g_1 g_0$ denote a code word in the $(n + 1)$st-bit Gray code, and let $b_n \cdots b_2 b_1 b_0$ designate the corresponding binary number, where the subscripts 0 and n denote the least significant and the most significant digits,

TABLE 3-5   The Complete Four-Bit Gray Code

Decimal number	Gray				Binary			
	g_3	g_2	g_1	g_0	b_3	b_2	b_1	b_0
0	0	0	0	0	0	0	0	0
1	0	0	0	1	0	0	0	1
2	0	0	1	1	0	0	1	0
3	0	0	1	0	0	0	1	1
4	0	1	1	0	0	1	0	0
5	0	1	1	1	0	1	0	1
6	0	1	0	1	0	1	1	0
7	0	1	0	0	0	1	1	1
8	1	1	0	0	1	0	0	0
9	1	1	0	1	1	0	0	1
10	1	1	1	1	1	0	1	0
11	1	1	1	0	1	0	1	1
12	1	0	1	0	1	1	0	0
13	1	0	1	1	1	1	0	1
14	1	0	0	1	1	1	1	0
15	1	0	0	0	1	1	1	1

respectively. Then, the ith digit g_i can be obtained from the corresponding binary number as follows:

$$g_i = b_i \oplus b_{i+1} \quad 0 \leq i \leq n - 1$$
$$g_n = b_n$$

where the symbol $\oplus$ denotes the **modulo-2 sum,** which is defined as follows:

$$0 \oplus 0 = 0 \quad 1 \oplus 1 = 0 \quad 0 \oplus 1 = 1 \quad 1 \oplus 0 = 1$$

For example, the Gray code word which corresponds to the binary number 101101 is found to be 111011 in the following manner:

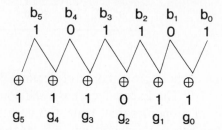

To convert from Gray code to binary, start with the leftmost digit and proceed to the least significant digit, making $b_i = g_i$ if the number of 1's preceding g_i is even, and making $b_i = g'_i$ if the number of 1's preceding g_i is odd. (Note that zero 1's is an even number of 1's.) For example, the (Gray) code word 1001011 represents the binary number 1110010. The proofs that the preceding conversion procedures indeed work are left to the reader as an exercise.

The n-bit Gray code is a member of a class called **reflected codes.** The term "reflected" is used to designate codes which have the property that the n-bit code can be generated by reflecting the $(n - 1)$st-bit code, as illustrated in Fig. 3-1. The two-bit Gray code is shown in Fig. 3-1a. The three-bit Gray code can be obtained by reflecting the two-bit code about an axis at the end of the code, and assigning a most significant bit of 0 above the axis and of 1 below the axis. The four-bit Gray code is obtained in the same manner from the three-bit code, as shown in Fig. 3-1c.

(a)	(b)	(c)
00	0 00	0 000
01	0 01	0 001
11	0 11	0 011
10	0 10	0 010
	1 10	0 110
	1 11	0 111
	1 01	0 101
	1 00	0 100
		1 100
		1 101
		1 111
		1 110
		1 010
		1 011
		1 001
		1 000

FIG. 3-1 Reflection of Gray codes

3-3 ERROR DETECTION AND CORRECTION

In the codes presented so far, each code word consists of four binary digits, which is the minimum number needed to represent the 10 decimal digits. Such codes, although adequate for the representation of the decimal digits, are very sensitive to transmission errors that may occur because of equipment failure or noise in the transmission channel. In any practical system there is always a finite probability of the occurrence of a single error. The probability that two or more errors will occur simultaneously, although nonzero, is substantially smaller. We therefore restrict our discussion mainly to the detection and correction of single errors.

Error-Detecting Codes

In a four-bit binary code, the occurrence of a single error in one of the binary digits may result in another, incorrect but valid, code word. For example, in the BCD code, if an error occurs in the least significant digit of 0110, the code word 0111 results, and since it is a valid code word, it is incorrectly interpreted by the receiver. If a code possesses the property that the occurrence of any single error transforms a valid code word into an invalid code word, it is said to be a **(single)-error-detecting code.** Two error-detecting codes are shown in Table 3-6.

The error detection in either of the codes of Table 3-6 is accomplished by a **parity check.** The basic idea in the parity check is to add an extra digit to each code word of a given code, so as to make the number of 1's in each code word either odd or even. In the codes of Table 3-6 we have used **even parity.** The even-parity BCD code is obtained directly from the BCD code of Table 3-3. The added bit, denoted p, is called **parity bit.** The **2-out-of-5 code** consists of all 10 possible combinations of two 1's in a five-bit code word. With the exception of the code word for decimal 0, the 2-out-of-5 code of Table 3-6 is a weighted code and can be derived from the (1,2,4,7) code.

In each of the codes in Table 3-6 the number of 1's in a code word is even. Now, if a single error occurs, it transforms the valid code word into an invalid one, thus making the detection of the error straightforward. Although the parity check is intended only for the detection of single errors, it in fact detects any odd number of errors and some even number of errors. For example, if the code word 10100 is received in an even-parity BCD message, it is clear that the message is erroneous, although the parity check is satisfied. We cannot determine, however, the original transmitted word.

TABLE 3-6 Error-Detecting Codes

Decimal digit	Even-parity BCD 8 4 2 1 p					2-out-of-5 0 1 2 4 7				
	8	4	2	1	p	0	1	2	4	7
0	0	0	0	0	0	0	0	0	1	1
1	0	0	0	1	1	1	1	0	0	0
2	0	0	1	0	1	1	0	1	0	0
3	0	0	1	1	0	0	1	1	0	0
4	0	1	0	0	1	1	0	0	1	0
5	0	1	0	1	0	0	1	0	1	0
6	0	1	1	0	0	0	0	1	1	0
7	0	1	1	1	1	1	0	0	0	1
8	1	0	0	0	1	0	1	0	0	1
9	1	0	0	1	0	0	0	1	0	1

In general, to obtain an n-bit error-detecting code, no more than half of the possible 2^n combinations of digits can be used. The code words are chosen in such a manner that, in order to change one valid code word into another valid code word, at least two digits must be complemented. In the case of four-bit codes, this constraint means that only 8 valid code words can be formed of the 16 possible combinations. Thus, to obtain an error-detecting code for the 10 decimal digits, at least 5 binary digits are needed. It is useful to define the **distance** between two code words as the number of digits that must change in one word so that the other word results. For example, the distance between 1010 and 0100 is three, since the two code words differ in three bit positions. The **minimum distance** of a code is the smallest number of bits in which any two code words differ. Thus the minimum distance of the BCD or the Excess-3 codes is one, while that of the codes in Table 3-6 is two. Clearly, **a code is an error-detecting code if and only if its minimum distance is two or more**.

Error-Correcting Codes

For a code to be error-correcting, its minimum distance must be further increased. For example, consider the three-bit code which consists of only two valid code words, 000 and 111. If a single error occurs in the first code word, it can be changed to 001, 010, or 100. The second code word can be changed due to a single error to 110, 101, or 011. Note that in each case the invalid code words are different. Clearly, this code is error-detecting, since its minimum distance is three. Moreover, if we assume that only a single error can occur, then this error can be located and corrected, since every error results in an invalid code word that can be associated with only one of the valid code words. Thus the two code words 000 and 111 constitute an error-correcting code whose minimum distance is three. In general, a code is said to be an **error-correcting code** if the correct code word can always be deduced from the erroneous word. In this section we shall discuss a single type of error-correcting codes, known as the **Hamming codes.**

If the minimum distance of a code is three, then any single error changes a valid code word into an invalid one, which is a distance one away from the original code word and a distance two from any other valid code word. Therefore, in a code with minimum distance of three, any single error is correctable or any double error detectable. Similarly, a code whose minimum distance is four may be used for either single-error correction **and** double-error detection **or** triple-error detection. The key to error correction is that it must be possible to **detect** and **locate** erroneous digits. If the location of an error has been determined, then by complementing the erroneous digit the message is corrected.

The basic principles in constructing a Hamming error-correcting code are as follows. To each group of **m information,** or **message, digits, k parity checking digits,** denoted $p_1, p_2, \ldots, p_k$, are added to form an $(m + k)$-digit code. The location of each of the $m + k$ digits within a code word is assigned a decimal value, starting by assigning a 1 to the most significant digit and $m + k$ to the least significant digit. k parity checks are performed on selected digits of each code word. The result of each parity check is recorded as 1 or 0, depending, respectively, on whether an error has or has not been detected. These parity checks make possible the development of a binary number, $c_1 c_2 \cdots c_k$, whose value when an error occurs is equal to the decimal value assigned to the location of the erroneous digit, and is equal to zero if no error occurs. This number is called the **position** (or **location**) **number.**

The number k of digits in the position number must be large enough to describe the location of any of the $m + k$ possible single errors, and must in addition take on the value zero to describe the "no error" condition. Consequently, k must satisfy the inequality $2^k \geq m + k + 1$. Thus, for example, if the original message is in BCD, where $m = 4$, then $k = 3$ and at least three parity checking digits must be added to the BCD code. The resultant error-correcting code thus consists of seven digits. In this case, if the position number is equal to 101, it means that an error has occurred in position 5. If, however, the position number is equal to 000, the message is correct.

In order to be able to specify the checking digits by means of only message digits and independently of each other, they are placed in positions 1, 2, 4, . . . , 2^{k-1}. Thus, if $m = 4$ and $k = 3$, the checking digits are placed in positions 1, 2, and 4, while the remaining positions contain the original (BCD) message bits. For example, in the code word **1100**110 the checking digits (in boldface) are $p_1 = 1$, $p_2 = 1$, $p_3 = 0$, while the message digits are 0, 1, 1, 0, which correspond to decimal 6.

We shall now show how the Hamming code is constructed, by constructing the code for $m = 4$ and $k = 3$. As discussed above, the parity checking digits must be so specified that, when an error occurs, the position number will take on the value assigned to the location of the erroneous digit. Table 3-7 lists the seven error positions and the corresponding values of the position number. It is evident that if an error occurs in position 1, or 3, or 5, or 7, the least significant digit, i.e., c_3, of the position number must be equal to 1. If the code is constructed so that in every code word the digits in positions 1, 3, 5, and 7 have even parity, then the occurrence of a single error in any one of these positions will cause an odd parity. In such a case the least significant digit of the position number is recorded as 1. If no error occurs among these digits, the parity check will show an even parity, and the least significant digit of the position number is recorded as 0.

TABLE 3-7   Position Numbers

Error position	Position number		
	c_1	c_2	c_3
0 (no erro.)	0	0	0
1	0	0	1
2	0	1	0
3	0	1	1
4	1	0	0
5	1	0	1
6	1	1	0
7	1	1	1

From Table 3-7 we observe that an error in position 2, or 3, or 6, or 7 should result in the recording of a 1 in the center of the position number. Hence the code must be designed so that the digits in positions 2, 3, 6, and 7 have even parity. Again, if the parity check of these digits shows an odd parity, the corresponding position number digit, i.e., c_2, is set to 1; otherwise it is set to 0. Finally, if an error occurs in position 4, or 5, or 6, or 7, the most significant digit of the position number, i.e., c_1, should be a 1. Therefore, if digits 4, 5, 6, and 7 are designed to have even parity, an error in any one of these digits will be recorded as a 1 in the most significant digit of the position number. To summarize:

p_1 is selected so as to establish even parity in positions 1, 3, 5, 7.
p_2 is selected so as to establish even parity in positions 2, 3, 6, 7.
p_3 is selected so as to establish even parity in positions 4, 5, 6, 7.

The code can now be constructed by adding the appropriate checking digits to the message digits. Consider, for example, the message 0100 (i.e., decimal 4).

Position:	1	2	3	4	5	6	7
	p_1	p_2	m_1	p_3	m_2	m_3	m_4
Original BCD message:			0		1	0	0
Parity check in positions 1,3,5,7 requires $p_1 = 1$:	**1**		**0**		**1**	**0**	**0**
Parity check in positions 2,3,6,7 requires $p_2 = 0$:	1	**0**	**0**		1	**0**	**0**
Parity check in positions 4,5,6,7 requires $p_3 = 1$:	1	0	0	**1**	**1**	**0**	**0**
Coded message:	1	0	0	1	1	0	0

p_1 is set equal to 1 so as to establish even parity in positions 1, 3, 5, and 7. Similarly, it is evident that p_2 must be a 0 and p_3 a 1, so that even parity is established in positions 2, 3, 6, and 7 and 4, 5, 6, and 7. The Hamming code for the decimal digits coded in BCD is shown in Table 3-8.

TABLE 3-8 Hamming Code for BCD

Decimal digit	Position	1 p_1	2 p_2	3 m_1	4 p_3	5 m_2	6 m_3	7 m_4
0		0	0	0	0	0	0	0
1		1	1	0	1	0	0	1
2		0	1	0	1	0	1	0
3		1	0	0	0	0	1	1
4		1	0	0	1	1	0	0
5		0	1	0	0	1	0	1
6		1	1	0	0	1	1	0
7		0	0	0	1	1	1	1
8		1	1	1	0	0	0	0
9		0	0	1	1	0	0	1

The error location and correction is performed in the following manner. Suppose, for example, that the sequence 1101001 is transmitted but, due to an error in the fifth position, the sequence 1101101 is received. The location of the error can be determined by performing three parity checks as follows:

Position:	1	2	3	4	5	6	7	
Message received:	1	1	0	1	1	0	1	
4-5-6-7 parity check:				**1**	**1**	**0**	**1**	$c_1 = 1$ since parity is odd
2-3-6-7 parity check:		**1**	**0**			**0**	**1**	$c_2 = 0$ since parity is even
1-3-5-7 parity check:	**1**		**0**		**1**		**1**	$c_3 = 1$ since parity is odd

Thus the position number formed of $c_1c_2c_3$ is 101, which means that the location of the error is in position 5. To correct the error, the digit in position 5 is complemented, and the correct message 1101001 is obtained.

It is easy to prove that the Hamming code constructed as shown above is a code whose distance is three. Consider, for example, the case where the two original four-bit code words differ in only one position, e.g., 1001 and 0001. Since each message digit appears in at least two parity checks, the parity checks that involve the digit in which the two code words differ will result in different parities, and hence different checking digits will be added to the two words, making the distance between them equal to three. For example, consider the two code words below.

Position:	1	2	3	4	5	6	7
	p_1	p_2	m_1	p_3	m_2	m_3	m_4
First word:			1		0	0	1
Second word:			0		0	0	1
First word with parity bits:	**0**	**0**	1		0	0	1
Second word with parity bits:	**1**	**1**	0		0	0	1

The two words differ in only m_1 (i.e., position 3). Parity checks 1-3-5-7 and 2-3-6-7 for these two words will give different results. Therefore the parity-checking digits p_1 and p_2 must be different for these words. Clearly, the foregoing argument is valid in the case where the original code words differ in two of the four positions. Thus the Hamming code has a distance of three.

If the distance is increased to four, by adding a parity bit to the code in Table 3-8, so that all eight digits will have even parity, the code may be used for single-error correction and double-error detection in the following manner. Suppose that two errors occur; then the overall parity check is satisfied but the position number (determined as before from the first seven digits) will indicate an error. Clearly, such a situation indicates the existence of a double error. The error positions, however, cannot be located. If only a single error occurs, the overall parity check will detect it. Now, if the position number is 0, then the error is in the last parity bit; otherwise it is in the position given by the position number. If all four parity checks indicate even parities, then the message is correct.

sec. 4

Boolean Algebra and Logic Networks

Donald D. Givone
Robert P. Roesser

4-1 INTRODUCTION

A simple algebra, called **Boolean algebra,** can be used to describe the behavior and structure of logic networks. Such a formal mathematical tool is convenient in discussing the internal workings of a computer and as an aid in the design of logic systems. Furthermore, since one of the main applications of microprocessors is as a software replacement for hard-wired logic, the operations of Boolean algebra occur frequently in a microcomputer program.

This chapter will introduce a Boolean algebra for two-valued logic. The various mathematical operations will be defined and several types of Boolean algebraic expressions will be introduced. Manipulations of algebraic expressions will be illustrated. Finally, the association between the Boolean algebra expressions and logic diagrams will be established.

4-2 BOOLEAN ALGEBRA

In general, a formal mathematical system consists of a set of elements, a set of operations, and a set of postulates. Boolean algebra, being a mathematical system, is also defined in terms of these three sets.

Some of the circuits in a computer provide for manipulating binary symbols comprising numbers or other information. Other circuits are used for communication purposes by providing appropriate paths through a logic network for information to travel. Finally, still other circuits are intended for control purposes, such as the activation of particular functions and the indication of various conditions. In all three cases, the signals at the various points within a circuit are two-valued. That is, the signals can represent the binary symbols, or they can correspond to true-false conditions depending upon whether or not certain events are to be caused or have occurred. Thus, the Boolean algebra that we will use needs two elements to correspond to the two values of the signals. In all our future discussions, this two-valued Boolean algebra will be assumed. This algebra is also known as the **switching algebra.**

The two elements of the Boolean algebra are called its **constants,** and we will use the convention of denoting them by 0 and 1. To avoid confusion with the binary digits, these symbols frequently are called **logic-0** and **logic-1.** At times a correspondence will be established between logic-0 and logic-1 and the binary digits 0 and 1. At other times logic-1 will correspond to a certain affirmative condition and logic-0 to its negative counterpart. The power of an abstract algebra is that its results are valid regardless of the nature of its elements as long as they satisfy the postulates.

For the purpose of having an algebra that describes the behavior and structure of logic networks, the terminals and internal points of a network are associated with **Boolean variables** that are restricted to the two values logic-0 and logic-1. Formally, a variable x in a two-valued Boolean algebra is a symbol such that

$$x = 0 \quad \text{if } x \neq 1$$
and
$$x = 1 \quad \text{if } x \neq 0$$

The letters of the alphabet will be used to denote Boolean variables.

Now that the elements of the Boolean algebra have been defined, it is necessary to introduce a set of operations and a set of postulates that indicate the behavior of the operations. There are several Boolean operations. The most important are AND, OR, and NOT.

The AND operation is denoted by the dot product sign ($\cdot$) or simply by the juxtaposition of Boolean variables. Thus, the AND operation between two variables x and y is written as

$$x \cdot y \quad \text{or} \quad xy$$

This operation is often referred to as **logical multiplication.**

The postulates for the AND operation are given in Table 4-1. From this table it can be seen that the value of $x \cdot y$ is logic-1 if and only if both x and y are logic-1; otherwise, $x \cdot y$ has the value of logic-0. Although Table 4-1 defines logical multiplication between only two variables, the concept of the AND oper-

TABLE 4-1
Definition of the AND Operation

x	y	$x \cdot y$	x	y	$x \cdot y$
$0 \cdot 0 = 0$			$1 \cdot 0 = 0$		
$0 \cdot 1 = 0$			$1 \cdot 1 = 1$		

TABLE 4-2
Definition of the OR Operation

x	y	$x + y$	x	y	$x + y$
$0 + 0 = 0$			$1 + 0 = 1$		
$0 + 1 = 1$			$1 + 1 = 1$		

ation can be generalized to any number of variables. Thus, $x_1 \cdot x_2 \cdots x_n$ is logic-1 if and only if $x_1, x_2, \ldots, x_n$ are each logic-1; otherwise, $x_1 \cdot x_2 \cdots x_n$ is logic-0.

As indicated above, the dot product symbol or juxtaposition will be used to denote the AND operation. Frequently in literature, however, the AND operation is denoted by the symbol $\wedge$. The AND operation between the two variables x and y is then written as $x \wedge y$.

The next Boolean operation to be introduced is the OR operation. This operation is denoted by a plus sign ($+$). Thus, the OR operation between two variables x and y is written as

$$x + y$$

This operation is often referred to as **logical addition**.

The postulates for the OR operation are given in Table 4-2. From this table it can be seen that the value of $x + y$ is logic-0 if and only if both x and y are logic-0; otherwise, $x + y$ has the value of logic-1. This operation can also be generalized for the case of n variables. Thus, $x_1 + x_2 + \cdots + x_n$ is logic-1 if and only if at least one of the variables is logic-1; otherwise, $x_1 + x_2 + \cdots + x_n$ is logic-0.

Although the plus sign will always be used to indicate the OR operation in this book, the symbol $\vee$ frequently appears in computer literature. In this case the OR operation between the two variables x and y is written as $x \vee y$.

The final operation to be introduced at this time is the NOT operation. This operation is also known as **complementation, negation,** and **inversion.** An overbar ($^{-}$) will be used to denote the NOT operation. Thus, the negation of the single variable x is written $\bar{x}$.

As indicated in Table 4-3, the postulates of the NOT operation are

$$\bar{x} = 1 \quad \text{if } x = 0$$

and
$$\bar{x} = 0 \quad \text{if } x = 1$$

or, equivalently,
$$\bar{0} = 1 \quad \text{and} \quad \bar{1} = 0$$

The prime symbol ($'$) is also used to indicate the NOT operation in computer literature. In this case the complementation of x is written as x'.

TABLE 4-3
Definition of the NOT Operation

x	$\bar{x}$	x	$\bar{x}$
0	1	1	0

A two-valued Boolean algebra can now be defined as a mathematical system with the elements logic-0 and logic-1 and the three operations AND, OR, and NOT, whose postulates are given by Tables 4-1 to 4-3.

4-3 TRUTH TABLES AND BOOLEAN EXPRESSIONS

Now that the constituents of a Boolean algebra have been defined, it is next necessary to show how they are used. The object of a Boolean algebra is to describe the behavior and structure of a logic network. Fig. 4-1 shows a logic network as a black box. The inputs are the Boolean variables $x_1, x_2, \ldots, x_n$, and the output is f. To describe the terminal behavior of the black box, it is necessary to express the output f as a function of the input variables $x_1, x_2, \ldots, x_n$. This can be done by using a truth table (or table of combinations) or by using Boolean expressions.

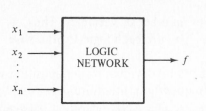

FIG. 4-1 The logic network as a black box

Logic networks that are readily described by truth tables or Boolean expressions are said to be **combinational networks.** A combinational network is one in which the values of the input variables at any instant determine the values of the output variables. A second class of logic networks is that in which there is an internal memory. Such networks are said to be **sequential** and have the property that the past as well as the present input values determine the output values from the network. This chapter will concentrate on combinational networks.

As indicated earlier, each of the Boolean variables $x_1, x_2, \ldots, x_n$ is restricted to the two values logic-0 and logic-1. Furthermore, all points within the black box, including the output line, are also restricted to these values. A tabulation of all the possible input combinations of values and their corresponding output values, i.e., functional values, is known as a **truth table** (or **table of combinations**). If there are n input variables and one functional output, this table will consist of 2^n rows and $n + 1$ columns. The general form of a truth table is shown in Table 4-4. It should be noted that a simple way of including all possible input values in a truth table is to count in the binary number system from 0 to $2^n - 1$. The value of f will, of course, be 0 or 1 in each row, depending upon the specific function.

The second method of describing the terminal behavior of a combinational logic network uses a **Boolean expression.** This is a formula consisting of Boolean constants and variables connected by the Boolean operators AND, OR, and NOT. Parentheses may also be used as in regular algebra to indicate a hierar-

TABLE 4-4 The Truth Table

x_1	x_2	$\cdots$	x_{n-1}	x_n	f
0	0	$\cdots$	0	0	$f(0, 0, \ldots, 0, 0)$
0	0	$\cdots$	0	1	$f(0, 0, \ldots, 0, 1)$
0	0	$\cdots$	1	0	$f(0, 0, \ldots, 1, 0)$
0	0	$\cdots$	1	1	$f(0, 0, \ldots, 1, 1)$
$\cdots$	$\cdots$	$\cdots$	$\cdots$	$\cdots$	$\ldots\ldots\ldots\ldots$
1	1	$\cdots$	1	1	$f(1, 1, \ldots, 1, 1)$

chical ordering of the operations. For example, a three-variable Boolean expression might be

$$f(x_1, x_2, x_3) = [(x_1 + \bar{x}_2)(\bar{x}_1 + x_3)] + (x_2 x_3)$$

In order to reduce the number of parentheses, however, it is usually assumed that the AND operation (i.e., logical multiplication) takes precedence over the OR operation (i.e., logical addition). Thus, the above expression is normally written as

$$f(x_1, x_2, x_3) = (x_1 + \bar{x}_2)(\bar{x}_1 + x_3) + x_2 x_3$$

Obtaining a Truth Table from a Boolean Expression

Both truth tables and Boolean expressions are useful tools for describing the terminal behavior of a logic network. Since they both can describe the same network, it is desirable at times to be able to convert each of these descriptions into the other. Clearly, by replacing each of the variables in a Boolean expression with its corresponding logic value and by evaluating the expressions with the use of the definitions of the AND, OR, and NOT operations, a value for the expression can be obtained. This evaluation corresponds precisely to one row of the truth table. If this procedure is carried out for each input combination, the corresponding truth table can be readily obtained.

To illustrate the manner in which the truth table is obtained from a Boolean expression, again consider the formula

$$f(x_1, x_2, x_3) = (x_1 + \bar{x}_2)(\bar{x}_1 + x_3) + x_2 x_3 \qquad (4.1)$$

Since this expression is a function of three variables, the truth must consist of $2^3 = 8$ rows. In Table 4-5 the eight combinations of values for the three variables x_1, x_2, and x_3 are listed in the first three columns.

To complete the construction of the truth table, we can evaluate Eq. (4.1) for each of the eight combinations of values. For example, when $x_1 = 0$, $x_2 = 1$, and $x_3 = 1$, we have

$$
\begin{aligned}
f(0, 1, 1) &= (0 + \bar{1})(\bar{0} + 1) + 1 \cdot 1 \\
&= (0 + 0)(1 + 1) + 1 \\
&= 0 \cdot 1 + 1 \\
&= 0 + 1 \\
&= 1
\end{aligned}
$$

The last column of Table 4-5, showing the functional values of the expression, is the result of the eight evaluations.

There is an alternate procedure for obtaining a truth table from a Boolean expression. This procedure involves carrying out the Boolean operations on the columns of the table in accordance with the expression to be evaluated. To illustrate this approach, again consider Eq. (4.1). Since both $\bar{x}_1$ and $\bar{x}_2$ appear in the expression, two columns are added to Table 4-5 such that the logic values in these columns are the complements of those in the first two columns. Next,

TABLE 4-5 Truth Table for the Boolean Expression
$f(x_1, x_2, x_3) = (x_1 + \bar{x}_2)(\bar{x}_1 + x_3) + x_2 x_3$

x_1	x_2	x_3	$\bar{x}_1$	$\bar{x}_2$	$x_1 + \bar{x}_2$	$\bar{x}_1 + x_3$	$(x_1 + \bar{x}_2)(\bar{x}_1 + x_3)$	$x_2 x_3$	f
0	0	0	1	1	1	1	1	0	1
0	0	1	1	1	1	1	1	0	1
0	1	0	1	0	0	1	0	0	0
0	1	1	1	0	0	1	0	1	1
1	0	0	0	1	1	0	0	0	0
1	0	1	0	1	1	1	1	0	1
1	1	0	0	0	1	0	0	0	0
1	1	1	0	0	1	1	1	1	1

the values of x_1 given in the first column are ORed with the values of $\bar{x}_2$ given in the fifth column. This operation results in the sixth column of Table 4-5, which shows the evaluation of $x_1 + \bar{x}_2$. In a similar manner the values of $\bar{x}_1$ and x_3 are used to obtain the evaluation of $\bar{x}_1 + x_3$ given in the seventh column. The results in the sixth and seventh columns are then ANDed to obtain the evaluation of $(x_1 + \bar{x}_2)(\bar{x}_1 + x_3)$ indicated in the eighth column. The evaluation of $x_2 x_3$, in the ninth column, is also easily obtained by the use of the second and third columns. Finally, the entries in the eighth and ninth columns are ORed. This operation produces the final column, giving the value of Eq. (4.1) for each possible combination of values for the variables x_1, x_2, and x_3.

The Minterm Canonical Form

It is also possible to write Boolean expressions from a truth table. One such expression is known as the minterm canonical form or standard sum-of-products.

To see how the minterm canonical form is obtained, consider Table 4-6. The first row of the table in which the functional value is logic-1 has the combination $x_1 = 0$, $x_2 = 0$, and $x_3 = 1$. Now consider the product term $\bar{x}_1\bar{x}_2 x_3$. Substituting the logic values 0, 0, and 1 for x_1, x_2, and x_3 in the term $\bar{x}_1\bar{x}_2 x_3$, we can see that the value of the term is logic-1. Furthermore, for any of the other seven combinations of logic values of x_1, x_2, and x_3, this term will have the value logic-0. In a sense, then, the product term $\bar{x}_1\bar{x}_2 x_3$ can be used to describe the condition given by the second row of Table 4-6.

Proceeding further along these lines, we find that the next row in which Table 4-6 has a functional value of logic-1 is the third row, which corresponds to the combination $x_1 = 0$, $x_2 = 1$, and $x_3 = 0$. If this set of values is substituted into the product term $\bar{x}_1 x_2 \bar{x}_3$, the resulting value will be logic-1. Again the property holds that for only a single combination of values does this product term have the value logic-1. Thus, we can conclude that the third row of Table 4-6 can be described by the product term $\bar{x}_1 x_2 \bar{x}_3$. Finally, by similar reasoning, we find that the sixth

TABLE 4-6 A Truth Table

x_1	x_2	x_3	f
0	0	0	0
0	0	1	1
0	1	0	1
0	1	1	0
1	0	0	0
1	0	1	1
1	1	0	0
1	1	1	0

row of Table 4-6, in which $x_1 = 1$, $x_2 = 0$, and $x_3 = 1$, can be described by the product term $x_1\bar{x}_2x_3$.

Combining the above results, we can see that the Boolean expression

$$f(x_1, x_2, x_3) = \bar{x}_1\bar{x}_2x_3 + \bar{x}_1x_2\bar{x}_3 + x_1\bar{x}_2x_3$$

precisely describes Table 4-6, since each product term in the expression corresponds to exactly one row in which the functional value is logic-1 and the sum corresponds to the collection of the three rows. For the remaining five combinations of values, the expression has the value logic-0. An expression of this type is called the **minterm canonical form** or **standard sum-of-products.** Such an expression is characterized as a sum of product terms in which every variable appears exactly once, either complemented or uncomplemented, in each product term. The product terms that comprise the expression are called **minterms.**

In general, each row of a truth table that has a functional value of logic-1 can be described by a minterm. The minterm, which is a product term, has a complemented variable if the value of that variable is logic-0 in the row in question and contains an uncomplemented variable if the value of the variable is logic-1. Connecting all the product terms constructed for rows that have a functional value of logic-1 by the Boolean OR operation results in the minterm canonical form for the given truth table.

4-4 BOOLEAN ALGEBRA THEOREMS

Several theorems can be developed that show the basic relationships in a Boolean algebra. The most important of these are listed in Table 4-7.

TABLE 4-7   Boolean Algebra Theorems

1a	$\bar{0} = 1$	1b	$\bar{1} = 0$	
2a	$x + 0 = x$	2b	$x \cdot 1 = x$	
3a	$x + 1 = 1$	3b	$x \cdot 0 = 0$	
4a	$x + x = x$	4b	$xx = x$	Idempotent law
5a	$x + \bar{x} = 1$	5b	$x\bar{x} = 0$	
6	$(\bar{x}) = x$			Involution law
7a	$x + y = y + x$	7b	$xy = yx$	Commutative law
8a	$x + xy = x$	8b	$x(x + y) = x$	Absorption law
9a	$x + \bar{x}y = x + y$	9b	$x(\bar{x} + y) = xy$	
10a	$\overline{(x + y)} = \bar{x}\bar{y}$	10b	$\overline{(xy)} = \bar{x} + \bar{y}$	DeMorgan's law
11a	$(x + y) + z = x + (y + z)$	11b	$(xy)z = x(yz)$	
	$= x + y + z$		$= xyz$	Associative law
12a	$x + yz = (x + y)(x + z)$	12b	$x(y + z) = xy + xz$	Distributive law

The first three theorems essentially reiterate the properties of the Boolean operations AND, OR, and NOT. Since the variables in these theorems are generic,† each variable can denote an entire Boolean expression. Thus, Theorem 3a states that ORing logic-1 with anything will always result in a logic-1. The fourth theorem, which is also known as the **idempotent law,** states that repeti-

---

†A generic variable is one that can denote a single variable, the complement of a single variable, a Boolean expression, or the complement of a Boolean expression.

tions of variables in an expression are redundant and may be deleted. Thus, the concepts of raising a variable to a power and having coefficients other than logic-0 and logic-1 do not exist in this algebra. The fifth and sixth theorems emphasize the complementary nature of the Boolean variables. The **involution law** states that double complementation has a cancellation effect.

The next four theorems involve two generic variables. The first of these, the **commutative law,** states that the order in which an operation is performed on a pair of variables does not affect the result of the operation. Theorems 8 and 9 provide for the simplification of Boolean expressions. Theorem 10, **DeMorgan's law,** shows the effect of complementation on generic variables when connected by the AND and OR operations.

The final two theorems pertain to three generic variables. The **associative law** states that when ANDing variables or when ORing variables, they may be grouped in any order. The **distributive law** states that factoring is permissible in a Boolean algebra. Special attention should be given to the type of factoring possible by Theorem 12a.

It should be noted that a symmetrical property exists in the Boolean algebra theorems. In particular, each theorem in Table 4-7, except Theorem 6, appears in pairs. These pairs are related by interchanging each occurrence of the AND operation with an OR operation, each occurrence of the OR operation with an AND operation, each occurrence of a logic-0 with a logic-1, and each occurrence of a logic-1 with a logic-0. This symmetrical property is known as the **principle of duality.**

Many of the theorems given in Table 4-7 can be generalized for a larger number of variables. For example, the generalized form of DeMorgan's law can be written as

$$\overline{(x + y + \cdots + z)} = \overline{x}\,\overline{y} \cdots \overline{z}$$

and
$$\overline{(xy \cdots z)} = \overline{x} + \overline{y} + \cdots + \overline{z}$$

while the generalized form of the distributive law is

$$w + xy \cdots z = (w + x)(w + y) \cdots (w + z)$$

and
$$w(x + y + \cdots + z) = wx + wy + \cdots + wz$$

The theorems listed in Table 4-7 can readily be proved by the method of **perfect induction.** Perfect induction is proof by exhaustion. That is, the validity of the theorem can be established by substituting all possible combinations of values of the variables in both sides of the expression and verifying that the equality holds for every combination. Since the variables are limted to two values in our Boolean algebra, such a procedure is not prohibitive.

To illustrate a proof by perfect induction, consider the distributive law

$$x + yz = (x + y)(x + z)$$

A truth table can be constructed for $x + yz$ and $(x + y)(x + z)$ as explained in the preceding section. This has been done in Table 4-8. In the fifth column, the expression $x + yz$ is evaluated for the eight combinations of values of the three variables, and the expression $(x + y)(x + z)$ is evaluated in the eighth column. Since these two columns are identical, it can be concluded that the

TABLE 4-8   Proof of the Distributive Law $x + yz = (x + y)(x + z)$ by Perfect Induction

x	y	z	yz	$x + yz$	$x + y$	$x + z$	$(x + y)(x + z)$
0	0	0	0	0	0	0	0
0	0	1	0	0	0	1	0
0	1	0	0	0	1	0	0
0	1	1	1	1	1	1	1
1	0	0	0	1	1	1	1
1	0	1	0	1	1	1	1
1	1	0	0	1	1	1	1
1	1	1	1	1	1	1	1

equality $x + yz = (x + y)(x + z)$ holds under all possible conditions. Thus, the validity of the theorem is established.

4-5   USING THE BOOLEAN ALGEBRA THEOREMS

There are many ways in which the Boolean algebra theorems can be used. In general, they provide rules for the manipulation of Boolean expressions. Thus, equivalent expressions can be derived. These derived expressions can be simpler or more complex than the original expressions, depending upon the objective of the manipulation. For example, the simplest expression, as measured by the number of symbols within the expression, may be desired; or the objective may be to obtain the minterm canonical form without having to construct the truth table first.

Equation Simplification

To illustrate the process of equation simplification, consider the following three examples.

Example 4.1   To simplify the expression

$$(x_1 + x_3)(x_1 + \bar{x}_3)(\bar{x}_2 + x_3)$$

we can proceed as follows:

$$
\begin{aligned}
(x_1 + x_3)(x_1 + \bar{x}_3)(\bar{x}_2 + x_3) &= (x_1 + x_3\bar{x}_3)(\bar{x}_2 + x_3) & \text{by Theorem } 12a \\
&= (x_1 + 0)(\bar{x}_2 + x_3) & \text{by Theorem } 5b \\
&= x_1(\bar{x}_2 + x_3) & \text{by Theorem } 2a
\end{aligned}
$$

Example 4.2   To simplify the expression

$$\bar{x}_1\bar{x}_2 + x_1\bar{x}_2 + x_1x_2 + x_2x_3$$

we can proceed as follows:

$$
\begin{aligned}
\bar{x}_1\bar{x}_2 + x_1\bar{x}_2 &+ x_1x_2 + x_2x_3 \\
&= \bar{x}_1\bar{x}_2 + x_1\bar{x}_2 + x_1\bar{x}_2 + x_1x_2 + x_2x_3 & \text{by Theorem } 4a
\end{aligned}
$$

$$= \bar{x}_2\bar{x}_1 + \bar{x}_2x_1 + x_1\bar{x}_2 + x_1x_2 + x_2x_3 \qquad \text{by Theorem } 7b$$
$$= \bar{x}_2(\bar{x}_1 + x_1) + x_1(\bar{x}_2 + x_2) + x_2x_3 \qquad \text{by Theorem } 12b$$
$$= \bar{x}_2(x_1 + \bar{x}_1) + x_1(x_2 + \bar{x}_2) + x_2x_3 \qquad \text{by Theorem } 7a$$
$$= \bar{x}_2 \cdot 1 + x_1 \cdot 1 + x_2x_3 \qquad \text{by Theorem } 5a$$
$$= \bar{x}_2 + x_1 + x_2x_3 \qquad \text{by Theorem } 2b$$
$$= x_1 + \bar{x}_2 + x_2x_3 \qquad \text{by Theorem } 7a$$
$$= x_1 + \bar{x}_2 + x_3 \qquad \text{by Theorem } 9a$$

Example 4.3 To simplify the expression

$$x_1x_2 + x_2x_3 + \bar{x}_1x_3$$

we can proceed as follows:

$$x_1x_2 + x_2x_3 + \bar{x}_1x_3$$
$$= x_1x_2 + x_2x_3 \cdot 1 + \bar{x}_1x_3 \qquad \text{by Theorem } 2b$$
$$= x_1x_2 + x_2x_3(x_1 + \bar{x}_1) + \bar{x}_1x_3 \qquad \text{by Theorem } 5a$$
$$= x_1x_2 + x_2x_3x_1 + x_2x_3\bar{x}_1 + \bar{x}_1x_3 \qquad \text{by Theorem } 12b$$
$$= x_1x_2 + x_1x_2x_3 + \bar{x}_1x_3x_2 + \bar{x}_1x_3 \qquad \text{by Theorem } 7b$$
$$= x_1x_2 + x_1x_2x_3 + \bar{x}_1x_3 + \bar{x}_1x_3x_2 \qquad \text{by Theorem } 7a$$
$$= x_1x_2 + \bar{x}_1x_3 \qquad \text{by Theorem } 8a$$

As can be seen from the above examples, the simplification of Boolean expressions is not algorithmic. Hence, it is not always obvious which theorem to apply at each step. Proficiency in this process comes from experience. For this reason, algorithmic techniques have been developed for the simplification of Boolean expressions.

Equation Complementation

Frequently a Boolean expression must be complemented. This complementation is achieved by using DeMorgan's law. The following example illustrates how complementation of an expression is performed:

Example 4.4 To complement the expression

$$(\bar{x}_1\bar{x}_2 + x_3)\bar{x}_1x_4$$

we proceed as follows:

$$\overline{[(\bar{x}_1\bar{x}_2 + x_3)\bar{x}_1x_4]} = \overline{(\bar{x}_1\bar{x}_2 + x_3)} + \overline{(\bar{x}_1)} + \bar{x}_4$$
$$= \overline{(\bar{x}_1\bar{x}_2 + x_3)} + x_1 + \bar{x}_4$$
$$= \overline{(\bar{x}_1\bar{x}_2)}\bar{x}_3 + x_1 + \bar{x}_4$$
$$= [\overline{(\bar{x}_1)} + \overline{(\bar{x}_2)}]\bar{x}_3 + x_1 + \bar{x}_4$$
$$= (x_1 + x_2)\bar{x}_3 + x_1 + \bar{x}_4$$

The Minterm Canonical Form

Another use of the Boolean algebra theorems is to obtain the minterm canoncial form of a given expression. Clearly, given a Boolean expression, we can first construct its truth table and then write the minterm canonical form. However, by use of the theorem $x + \bar{x} = 1$ and the distributive law $x(y + z) = xy + xz$, it is possible for us to expand an equation directly into its minterm canonical form.

To illustrate the procedure, consider the expression

$$x + \bar{x}(z + y\bar{z})$$

To start the process, we apply the distributive law so that the expression consists of only a sum of product terms. In this case, we have

$$x + \bar{x}z + \bar{x}y\bar{z}$$

Next, the product terms that are not minterms must be modified to include the missing variables. The first term x is not a minterm, since it does not contain the y and z variables. These variables can be introduced by ANDing x with $(y + \bar{y})(z + \bar{z})$, which is equivalent to ANDing x with logic-1. By similar reasoning, the variable y can be introduced into the second term $\bar{x}z$ by ANDing it with $y + \bar{y}$. Finally, the last term is a minterm since all three variables appear. Combining our results, we can rewrite the given expression as

$$x(y + \bar{y})(z + \bar{z}) + \bar{x}(y + \bar{y})z + \bar{x}y\bar{z}$$

If the distributive law is now applied to this expression and duplicate terms are dropped when they appear, the minterm canonical form will result. In this case we have

$$xyz + xy\bar{z} + x\bar{y}z + x\bar{y}\bar{z} + \bar{x}\bar{y}z + \bar{x}y\bar{z}$$

The Maxterm Canonical Form

A canonical expression for a function is one that is unique and has a standard form. It can therefore be of value in determining the equivalence of functions. That is, two functions are equivalent if their canonical expressions are the same. The minterm canonical form consists of a sum of product terms in which every variable appears within each product term. Another standard formula in Boolean algebra is known as the maxterm canonical form or standard product-of-sums. As in the case of the minterm canonical form, the maxterm canonical form can be obtained from the truth table or by expanding a given Boolean expression.

Again consider Table 4-6. This truth table denotes a Boolean function f. The truth table for the complement of this function, i.e., f, is constructed by complementing each of the values in the last column, i.e., the functional values. The resulting truth table is shown in Table 4-9. Using the procedure of Sec. 4.3, we can now write the minterm canonical form for the complementary function $\bar{f}$ as

$$\bar{f}(x_1, x_2, x_3) = \bar{x}_1\bar{x}_2\bar{x}_3 + \bar{x}_1x_2x_3 + x_1\bar{x}_2\bar{x}_3 + x_1\bar{x}_2x_3 + x_1x_2x_3$$

If both sides of the above equation are complemented with the use of DeMorgan's law, an equation for the function f will result:

$$\overline{[f(x_1, x_2, x_3)]} = f(x_1, x_2, x_3) = \overline{(\overline{x}_1\overline{x}_2\overline{x}_3 + \overline{x}_1x_2x_3 + x_1\overline{x}_2\overline{x}_3 + x_1x_2\overline{x}_3 + x_1x_2x_3)}$$

$$= (\overline{\overline{x}_1\overline{x}_2\overline{x}_3})(\overline{\overline{x}_1x_2x_3})(\overline{x_1\overline{x}_2\overline{x}_3})(\overline{x_1x_2\overline{x}_3})(\overline{x_1x_2x_3})$$

$$= (x_1 + x_2 + x_3)(x_1 + \overline{x}_2 + \overline{x}_3)(\overline{x}_1 + x_2 + x_3)(\overline{x}_1 + \overline{x}_2 + x_3)$$
$$(\overline{x}_1 + \overline{x}_2 + \overline{x}_3)$$

This last expression is the maxterm canonical form for the function f.

The **maxterm canonical form** or **standard product-of-sums** is characterized as a product of sum terms in which every variable of the function appears exactly once, either complemented or uncomplemented, in each sum term. The sum terms that comprise the expression are called **maxterms**.

TABLE 4-9 The Truth Table for the Complement of the Function Given in Table 4-6

x_1	x_2	x_3	f	$\overline{f}$
0	0	0	0	1
0	0	1	1	0
0	1	0	1	0
0	1	1	0	1
1	0	0	0	1
1	0	1	1	0
1	1	0	0	1
1	1	1	0	1

In general, to obtain the maxterm canonical form from a truth table, the truth table of the complementary function is first written by changing each logic-1 functional value to logic-0 and vice versa. The minterm canonical form is then written for the complementary function. Finally, the resulting expression is complemented by DeMorgan's law to obtain the maxterm canonical form.

The maxterm canonical form can also be arrived at algebraically if a Boolean expression is given. In this process, use is made of the theorem $x\overline{x} = 0$ and the distributive law $x + yz = (x + y)(x + z)$.

To illustrate the procedure, consider the expression

$$\overline{x}y + \overline{y}z$$

Since the maxterm canonical form consists of a product of sum terms, it is first necessary to rewrite the expression in this general form. This rewriting can be done by use of the distributive law. In this case,

$$\overline{x}y + \overline{y}z = (\overline{x}y + \overline{y})(\overline{x}y + z)$$
$$= (\overline{x} + \overline{y})(y + \overline{y})(\overline{x} + z)(y + z)$$
$$= (\overline{x} + \overline{y}) \cdot 1 \cdot (\overline{x} + z)(y + z)$$
$$= (\overline{x} + \overline{y})(\overline{x} + z)(y + z)$$

Once an expression is obtained that consists of only a product of sum terms, it is next necessary to determine whether each sum term is a maxterm. If not, we can introduce the appropriate variables by using the theorem $x\overline{x} = 0$. Thus, for the above example, we get

$$(\overline{x} + \overline{y})(\overline{x} + z)(y + z) = (\overline{x} + \overline{y} + 0)(\overline{x} + 0 + z)(0 + y + z)$$
$$= (\overline{x} + \overline{y} + z\overline{z})(\overline{x} + y\overline{y} + z)(x\overline{x} + y + z)$$

Finally, the distributive law is applied and duplicate terms are removed by the idempotent law. Thus, we have

$(\bar{x} + \bar{y})(\bar{x} + z)(y + z)$
$$= (\bar{x} + \bar{y} + z)\,(\bar{x} + \bar{y} + \bar{z})(\bar{x} + y + z)$$
$$(\bar{x} + \bar{y} + z)(x + y + z)(\bar{x} + y + z)$$
$$= (\bar{x} + \bar{y} + z)(\bar{x} + \bar{y} + \bar{z})(\bar{x} + y + z)(x + y + z)$$

4-6 THE KARNAUGH MAP METHOD OF BOOLEAN SIMPLIFICATION

In the previous section it was stated that the Boolean algebra theorems provide a means for the manipulation of Boolean expressions. Since the expressions resulting from such manipulation are equivalent, the combinational logic networks that they describe will be equivalent. It is therefore of interest to determine what is, in some sense, the "simplest" expression. Unfortunately, such an expression may be difficult to determine by algebraic manipulations. Several methods have been developed for deriving simple expressions. One such method, utilizing Karnaugh maps, will be presented in this section.

Karnaugh Maps

A **Karnaugh map** is a graphic representation of a truth table. The structure of the Karnaugh maps for two-, three-, and four-variable functions is shown in Fig. 4-2 to 4-4 along with the general form of the corresponding truth tables. It can be seen that for each row of a truth table, there is one cell in a Karnaugh map, and vice versa. Each cell in a map is located by a coordinate system according to its axis labelings, and the entry in the cell is the value of the function for the corresponding assignment of values associated with the cell. Fig. 4-5 gives the truth table and Karnaugh map for the particular Boolean function

x	y	$f(x, y)$
0	0	$f(0, 0)$
0	1	$f(0, 1)$
1	0	$f(1, 0)$
1	1	$f(1, 1)$

(a)

FIG. 4-2 A two-variable Boolean function (a) Truth table (b) Karnaugh map

$$f(x, y, z) = \bar{x}(\bar{y} + \bar{z}) + xz$$

The truth table is arrived at by evaluating the expression for the eight combinations of values as described in Sec. 4.3, and the Karnaugh map is then constructed as indicated by the general form shown in Fig. 4-3.

When Karnaugh maps are used for simplifying Boolean expressions, rectangular groupings of cells are formed. In general, every $2^a \times 2^b$ rectangular grouping of cells corresponds to a product term with $n - a - b$ variables, where n is the total number of variables associated with the map and a and b are nonnegative integers. Since the dimensions of these groupings are $2^a \times 2^b$, it

x	y	z	$f(x, y, z)$
0	0	0	$f(0, 0, 0)$
0	0	1	$f(0, 0, 1)$
0	1	0	$f(0, 1, 0)$
0	1	1	$f(0, 1, 1)$
1	0	0	$f(1, 0, 0)$
1	0	1	$f(1, 0, 1)$
1	1	0	$f(1, 1, 0)$
1	1	1	$f(1, 1, 1)$

(a)

yz

x	00	01	11	10
0	$f(0,0,0)$	$f(0,0,1)$	$f(0,1,1)$	$f(0,1,0)$
1	$f(1,0,0)$	$f(1,0,1)$	$f(1,1,1)$	$f(1,1,0)$

(b)

FIG. 4-3 A three-variable Boolean function (a) Truth table (b) Karnaugh map

w	x	y	z	$f(w, x, y, z)$
0	0	0	0	$f(0, 0, 0, 0)$
0	0	0	1	$f(0, 0, 0, 1)$
0	0	1	0	$f(0, 0, 1, 0)$
0	0	1	1	$f(0, 0, 1, 1)$
0	1	0	0	$f(0, 1, 0, 0)$
0	1	0	1	$f(0, 1, 0, 1)$
0	1	1	0	$f(0, 1, 1, 0)$
0	1	1	1	$f(0, 1, 1, 1)$
1	0	0	0	$f(1, 0, 0, 0)$
1	0	0	1	$f(1, 0, 0, 1)$
1	0	1	0	$f(1, 0, 1, 0)$
1	0	1	1	$f(1, 0, 1, 1)$
1	1	0	0	$f(1, 1, 0, 0)$
1	1	0	1	$f(1, 1, 0, 1)$
1	1	1	0	$f(1, 1, 1, 0)$
1	1	1	1	$f(1, 1, 1, 1)$

(a)

yz

wx	00	01	11	10
00	$f(0,0,0,0)$	$f(0,0,0,1)$	$f(0,0,1,1)$	$f(0,0,1,0)$
01	$f(0,1,0,0)$	$f(0,1,0,1)$	$f(0,1,1,1)$	$f(0,1,1,0)$
11	$f(1,1,0,0)$	$f(1,1,0,1)$	$f(1,1,1,1)$	$f(1,1,1,0)$
10	$f(1,0,0,0)$	$f(1,0,0,1)$	$f(1,0,1,1)$	$f(1,0,1,0)$

(b)

FIG. 4-4 A four-variable Boolean function (a) Truth table (b) Karnaugh map

x	y	z	f
0	0	0	1
0	0	1	1
0	1	0	1
0	1	1	0
1	0	0	0
1	0	1	1
1	1	0	0
1	1	1	1

(a)

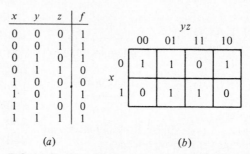

(b)

FIG. 4-5 The Boolean function $f(x,y,z) = \bar{x}(\bar{y} + \bar{z} + xz$ (a) Truth table (b) Karnaugh map

follows that the total number of cells in a grouping must always be a power of 2. All future references to groupings will pertain only to those whose dimensions are $2^a \times 2^b$.

Minimal Sums

One method of obtaining a Boolean expression from a Karnaugh map is to consider only those cells that have a logic-1 entry. These are called **1-cells.** They correspond to the minterms of the canonical expression. Every $2^a \times 2^b$ grouping of 1-cells will correspond to a product term that can be used in describing part of the truth table. If a sufficient number of groupings are selected such that every 1-cell appears in at least one grouping, the ORing of these product terms will completely describe the function. By a judicious selection of groupings, simple Boolean expressions can be obtained. One measure of the degree of simplicity of a Boolean expression is a count of the number of occurrences of letters, i.e., variables and their complements, called **literals,** in the expression. Expressions consisting of a sum of product terms and having a minimum number of literals are called **minimal sums.**

There are two guidelines for a judicious selection of groupings that will enable a minimal sum to be written. First, the groupings should be as large as possible. This guideline follows from the fact that the larger the grouping, the fewer will be the number of literals in its corresponding product term. Second, a minimum number of groupings should be used. This guideline stems from the fact that each grouping corresponds to a product term. By using a minimum number of groupings the number of product terms, and consequently the number of literals in the expression, can be kept to a minimum.

In Fig. 4-6 a four-variable Karnaugh map and the optimal groupings of 1-cells are shown. No larger groupings are possible on this map. Also, no fewer than three groupings will encompass all the 1-cells. The columnar grouping corresponds to the rectangle with dimensions $2^2 \times 2^0 = 4 \times 1$, the square grouping has dimensions $2^1 \times 2^1 = 2 \times 2$, and the small grouping of two cells has dimensions $2^1 \times 2^0 = 2 \times 1$. It should be noted that the rectangular groupings may overlap.

In order to write the Boolean expression from a Karnaugh map, reference must be made to the labels along the map's axes. It is necessary to determine which axis variables do not change value within each grouping.

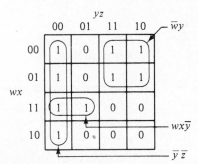

FIG. 4-6 Groupings on a four-variable Karnaugh map

Those variables whose values are the same for each cell in the grouping will appear in the product term. A variable will be complemented if its value is always logic-0 in the grouping and will be uncomplemented if its value is always logic-1.

To illustrate the writing of a Boolean expression, again consider Fig. 4-6. Referring to the square grouping, we can see that the grouping appears in the first and second rows of the map. In these rows the variable w has the value of logic-0. Thus, the product term for this grouping must contain $\overline{w}$. Furthermore, since the x variable changes value in these two rows, this variable will not appear in the product term. When we now consider the two columns that contain the grouping, the y variable has the same value in these two columns, i.e., logic-1, and hence, the literal y must appear in the product term. Finally, we can see that the z variable changes value in these two columns and, hence, will not appear in the product term. Combining the results, we find that the square grouping corresponds to the product term $\overline{w}y$.

If this procedure is applied to the remaining two groupings in Fig. 4-6, their corresponding product terms can be determined. The columnar grouping corresponds to the term $\overline{y}\,\overline{z}$, since the variables y and z both have the value logic-

0 associated with every cell in this grouping. Furthermore, since no row variables have the same logic value for every cell of the grouping, neither the w nor x variables appear in the product term. In a similar manner, the two-cell grouping corresponds to the product term $wx\bar{y}$. Thus, the minimal sum for this Karnaugh map is given by the expression

$$f(w, x, y, z) = \overline{w}y + \overline{y}\overline{z} + wx\bar{y}$$

Although the three- and four-variable Karnaugh maps are normally drawn as the two-dimensional configurations shown in Figs. 4-3 to 4-4, from the point of view of the permissible rectangular groupings that can be formed, it is necessary to regard them as three-dimensional configurations.

For the three-variable map of Fig. 4-3, it is necessary to regard the left and right edges of the map as being connected, thus forming a cylinder. It is on the surface of this cylinder that the rectangular groupings are formed. Hence, rectangular groupings may appear split when drawn. Figure 4-7 shows a split rectangular grouping. The corresponding product term is obtained as explained previously and is $\overline{x}\overline{z}$ for the case shown in Fig. 4.7.

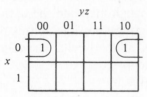

FIG. 4-7 Split grouping on a three-variable Karnaugh map

Split rectangular groupings can also appear on four-variable maps. In general, the left and right edges of a four-variable map are connected as well as the top and bottom edges. Thus, the four-variable map of Fig. 4-4 should be regarded as appearing on the surface of a toroid. Fig. 4-8 shows some examples of split rectangular groupings on a four-variable map. In Fig. 4-8a the grouping of the four cells corresponds to the term $x\overline{z}$ and the grouping of the two cells corresponds to $\overline{x}yz$. Special attention should be paid to the grouping illustrated in Fig. 4-8b. The four corners form a $2^1 \times 2^1$ rectangular grouping if the map is visualized as being a toroid. The corresponding product term is $\overline{x}\overline{z}$.

In summary, the basic approach to determining the optimal groupings on a Karnaugh map leading to a minimal sum is as follows. First a 1-cell is selected that can be placed in only one grouping that is not a subgrouping of some larger grouping. The largest grouping containing this 1-cell is then formed. Next, another 1-cell with the above property, not already grouped, is selected and its

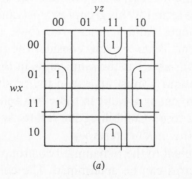
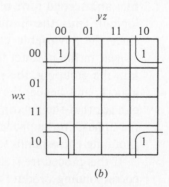

FIG. 4-8 Examples of split groupings on a four-variable Karnaugh map

grouping formed. This process is repeated until all the 1-cells are in some grouping or there remain ungrouped 1-cells that can be grouped in more than one way. At this point, a minimum number of additional groupings are formed to account for the remaining 1-cells. The following examples illustrate this procedure for obtaining minimal sums from Karnaugh maps.

Example 4.5 Consider the Karnaugh map shown in Fig. 4-9. The 1-cell in the upper right-hand corner can be grouped with the 1-cells in the other three corners. Furthermore, this 1-cell can appear in no other groupings that are not subgroupings of these four cells. Thus, the term $\overline{x}\overline{z}$ must appear in the minimal sum. Next, it is noted that the 1-cell in the first row, second column, still is not in a grouping. It can be placed in a grouping of four cells to yield the term $\overline{x}\overline{y}$. Finally, the remaining ungrouped 1-cell can be grouped with the cell just below it to produce the term $wy\overline{z}$. The minimal sum is

$$f(w, x, y, z) = \overline{x}\overline{z} + \overline{x}\overline{y} + wy\overline{z}$$

which consists of seven literals.

Example 4.6 Consider the Karnaugh map shown in Fig. 4-10. The 1-cell in the upper left-hand corner can be grouped only with the 1-cell next to it.

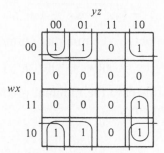

FIG. 4-9 Example 4.5

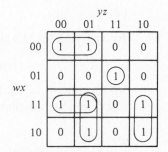

FIG. 4-10 Example 4.6

Similarly, the 1-cell in the lower right-hand corner can be grouped only with the 1-cell above it. The 1-cell in the second row, third column, can be grouped only by itself. At this point there still remain three 1-cells that have not been placed in some grouping. It should be noticed that these 1-cells, unlike the other cases, can be placed into more than one grouping. To complete the process, a minimum number of groupings must be selected to account for these remaining 1-cells. The groupings shown on the map correspond to the minimal sum

$$f(w, x, y, z) = \overline{w}\overline{x}\overline{y} + wy\overline{z} + \overline{w}xyz + wx\overline{y} + w\overline{y}\overline{z}$$

which consists of 16 literals. There are two other equally good minimal sums that could have been formed:

$$f(w, x, y, z) = \overline{w}\overline{x}\overline{y} + wy\overline{z} + \overline{w}xyz + w\overline{y}\overline{z} + wx\overline{z}$$

and $$f(w, x, y, z) = \overline{w}\overline{x}\overline{y} + wy\overline{z} + \overline{w}xyz + wx\overline{y} + \overline{x}yz$$

It can be seen from this example that more than one minimal sum can exist for a given function.

Minimal Products

Thus far it has been shown how a minimal sum can be obtained from a Karnaugh map. Karnaugh maps can also be used to construct minimal expressions, as measured by a literal count, consisting of a product of sum terms. These expressions are called **minimal products.**

To obtain a minimal product, attention is given to those cells in the Karnaugh map that contain a logic-0. These are called **0-cells.** In this case a minimal sum is written for the complement of a given function by including every 0-cell, and only 0-cells, in at least one grouping while satisfying the requirements of using the largest and the fewest groupings possible. Again, the three-dimensional nature of the maps must be kept in mind. Then, DeMorgan's law is applied to the complement of the expression. This results in an expression for the Karnaugh map (and, hence, the truth table). Furthermore, it consists of a product of sum terms and a minimum number of literals.

Example 4.7 Consider the function in Example 4.5, whose Karnaugh map is given in Fig. 4-9. The map is redrawn in Fig. 4-11, where the 0-cells are grouped to form a minimal sum for the complement of the function:

$$\bar{f}(w, x, y, z) = yz + \bar{w}x + x\bar{y}$$

or

$$f(w, x, y, z) = \overline{(yz + \bar{w}x + x\bar{y})}$$

By applying DeMorgan's law, we obtain the minimal product

$$f(w, x, y, z) = (\bar{y} + \bar{z})(w + \bar{x})(\bar{x} + y)$$

which consists of six literals. In this case the minimal product of the function has fewer literals than its minimal sum.

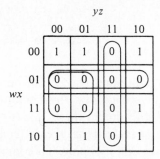   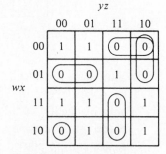

FIG. 4-11 Example 4.7   **FIG. 4-12** Example 4.8

Example 4.8 Consider the function in Example 4.6, whose Karnaugh map is shown in Fig. 4-10 and is redrawn in Fig. 4-12. By grouping the 0-cells, there are three minimal products that can be formed. The minimal product corresponding to the groupings in Fig. 4-12 is

$$f(w, x, y, z)$$
$$= (w + \bar{x} + y)(\bar{w} + \bar{y} + \bar{z})(\bar{w} + x + y + z)(w + \bar{y} + z)(w + x + \bar{y})$$

The two other minimal products are

$$f(w, x, y, z)$$
$$= (w + \bar{x} + y)(\bar{w} + \bar{y} + \bar{z})(\bar{w} + x + y + z)(w + \bar{y} + z)(x + \bar{y} + \bar{z})$$

and

$$f(w, x, y, z)$$
$$= (w + \bar{x} + y)(\bar{w} + \bar{y} + \bar{z})(\bar{w} + x + y + z)(w + x + \bar{y})(w + \bar{x} + z)$$

In each of these expressions, 16 literals appear. Hence, the same number of literals appear in the minimal product descriptions of this function as in its minimal sum descriptions.

Don't-Care Conditions

Before we close this discussion on Karnaugh maps, one more situation must be considered. It should be recalled that Boolean expressions are used to describe the behavior and structure of logic networks. Each row of a truth table (or cell of a Karnaugh map) corresponds to the response (i.e., output) of the network as a result of a combination of logic values on its input terminals (i.e., the values of the input variables). Occasionally, a certain input combination is known never to occur, or if it does occur, the network response is not pertinent. In such cases, it is not necessary to specify the response of the network (i.e., the functional value in the truth table). These situations are known as **don't-care conditions.** When don't-care conditions exist, minimal sums and products can still be obtained with Karnaugh maps.

Don't-care conditions are indicated on the Karnaugh maps by dash entries. To obtain a minimal sum or product, the cells with dash entries, called **don't-care cells,** may be used optionally in order to form the best possible groupings. Any of the don't-care cells can be used when grouping the 1-cells or the 0-cells. Furthermore, it is not necessary that they be used at all or that they be used only for one particular type of grouping.

Figure 4-13 shows a Karnaugh map with don't-care conditions. The map of Fig. 4-13a can be used to obtain a minimal sum

$$f(w, x, y, z) = y\bar{z} + \bar{w}x\bar{y}$$

while the map of Fig. 4-13b can be used to obtain a minimal product

$$f(w, x, y, z) = (y + z)(\bar{y} + \bar{z})(\bar{w} + y)$$

It should be noted that the cell corresponding to the values $w = 0$, $x = 1$, $y = 0$, and $z = 0$ is used for both a minimal sum and a minimal product; while the

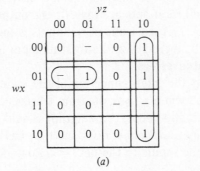

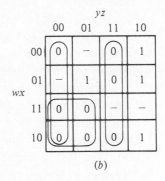

(a)   (b)

FIG. 4-13 Karnaugh maps involving don't-care conditions

cell corresponding to the values $w = 0$, $x = 0$, $y = 0$, and $z = 1$ is not used at all.

Although the Karnaugh map method can be extended to more than four variables, the maps get increasingly difficult to analyze. To handle these larger problems, computer techniques have been developed.

4-7 LOGIC NETWORKS

Boolean algebra serves to describe the logical aspects of the behavior and structure of logic networks. Thus far we have considered only its behavioral descriptive properties. That is, the algebraic expression or the truth table provides a mechanism for describing the output logic value of a network in terms of the logic values on its input lines. However, Boolean algebra expressions can also provide an indication of the structure of a logic network.

The Boolean algebra, as described in the preceding sections, includes the three logic operators: AND, OR, and NOT. If there are circuits whose terminal logic properties in some sense correspond to these three operators, then the interconnection of such circuits, as indicated by a Boolean expression, will provide a logic network. Furthermore, the terminal logic behavior of this network will be described by the expression. In the next chapter it will be seen that such circuits exist and are called **gates.** Of course, electrical signals really appear at the terminals of the gates. However, if these signals are classified as two-valued, then logic-0 can be associated with one of the signal values and logic-1 with the other. In this way, the actual signal values can be disregarded at the terminals of the gate circuits, and the logic values themselves can be assumed to appear.

The gate symbols for the three Boolean operations introduced thus far are shown in Fig. 4-14. Inasmuch as these symbols denote the Boolean operators,

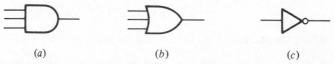

(a)   (b)   (c)

FIG. 4-14   Gate symbols (a) AND gate (b) OR gate (c) NOT gate (or inverter)

the terminal characteristics for these gates are described by the definitions previously stated in Tables 4-1 to 4-3. That is, the output from the AND gate will be logic-1 if and only if all its inputs are logic-1; the output from the OR gate will be logic-1 if and only if at least one of its inputs is logic-1; and the output from the NOT gate will be logic-1 if and only if its input is logic-0. NOT gates are also commonly called **inverters.**

A drawing that depicts the interconnection of the logic elements is called a **logic diagram.** In general, when a logic diagram consists only of gate elements with no feedback lines around them, the diagram is said to be of a **combinational network.** A combinational network is one that has no memory property and, thus, one in which the inputs to the network alone determine the outputs from the network.

There is a correspondence between the logic diagram of a combinational net-

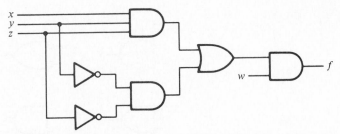

FIG. 4-15   Logic diagram whose terminal behavior is described by
the Boolean expression $f(w,x,y,z) = w(xyz + \overline{y}\overline{z})$

work and a Boolean expression. Hence, Boolean expressions serve as descriptions of combinational networks. As an example, consider the logic diagram shown in Fig. 4-15. The two NOT gates are used to generate $\overline{y}$ and $\overline{z}$. The output from the upper-left-hand AND gate is described by xyz, and the output from the lower-left-hand AND gate is given by $\overline{y}\overline{z}$. These two outputs serve as inputs to the OR gate. Thus, the output from the OR gate is described by $xyz + \overline{y}\overline{z}$. Finally, the output from the OR gate enters the remaining AND gate along with a w input. Hence, the logic diagram of Fig. 4-15 is described by the equation

$$f(w, x, y, z) = w(xyz + \overline{y}\overline{z})$$

Clearly, it is just as easy to reverse the above process. That is, from a given Boolean expression, it is a simple matter to construct a corresponding logic diagram.

In order that the gate symbols can all be kept the same size in a logic diagram and in order to prevent the crowding of several inputs to AND gates or OR gates, the generalized symbols shown in Fig. 4-16 are frequently used when a single gate has a large number of input lines.

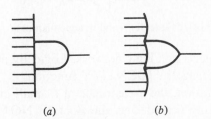

(a) (b)

FIG. 4-16   Gate symbols to accommodate a large number of inputs (a) AND gate (b) OR gate

4-8 ADDITIONAL LOGIC GATES

Three logic gates were introduced in the previous section. However, several additional ones frequently appear in logic diagrams. Fig. 4-17 summarizes the commonly encountered gate symbols. First, it should be noted that several additional logic functions are symbolized. Second, two gate symbols are shown for each function. These symbols utilize the **inversion bubble notation.**

The Inversion Bubble Notation

As indicated in Fig. 4-17, a simple triangle denotes a **buffer amplifier.** These circuits are needed to provide isolation, amplification, signal restoration, and

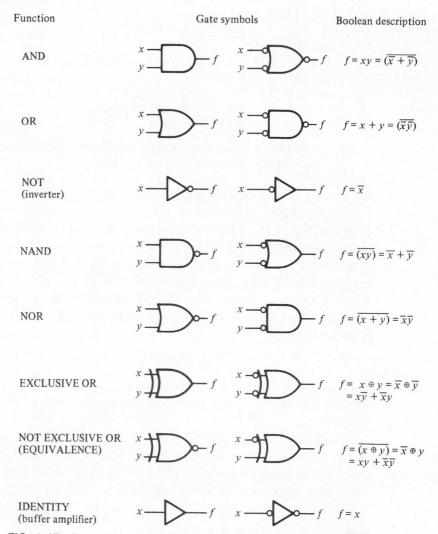

Function	Gate symbols	Boolean description

FIG. 4-17 Summary of gate symbols frequently found in logic diagrams

impedance matching in various parts of a logic network. Logically, its output is the same as its input; i.e., it performs the IDENTITY function.

With the inversion bubble notation, the appearance of a small circle on the input or output of a gate is simply regarded as the Boolean NOT operation. Thus, a triangle with a small circle on its input or output, but not both, becomes the NOT-gate symbol introduced previously; and an inversion bubble on both the input and output of a buffer amplifier is simply another symbol for a buffer amplifier, since $f = x = (\overline{\overline{x}})$.

Inversion bubbles can also be applied to the basic AND-gate and OR-gate symbols. For example, the Boolean expression $f = xy$ can be written as $f = (\overline{\overline{x} + \overline{y}})$. This expression serves as the basis for the second AND-gate symbol shown in Fig. 4-17. Similarly, $f = x + y$ can be written as $f = (\overline{\overline{x}\overline{y}})$. This expression implies a second OR-gate symbol.

The NAND Function

Fig. 4-17 also introduces four new logic functions: NAND, NOR, EXCLUSIVE OR, and NOT EXCLUSIVE OR. Consider first the NAND operation.

Table 4-10 gives the definition of this operation as performed on two variables x and y. Algebraically this operation can be written as $\overline{(xy)}$, and symbolically it can be regarded as an AND gate, with inputs x and y, followed by a NOT gate. Furthermore, since $\overline{(xy)} = \bar{x} + \bar{y}$, the NAND operation can also be regarded as an OR gate preceded by NOT gates at its inputs. These two interpretations suggest the gate symbols shown in Fig. 4-17.

In general, the output of a NAND gate is defined as $\overline{(x_1 x_2 \cdots x_n)} = \bar{x}_1 + \bar{x}_2 + \cdots + \bar{x}_n$. Thus, the output is a logic-1 if and only if at least one of its inputs has the value of logic-0; otherwise, the output is logic-0.

One reason for the popularity of the NAND gate in logic networks stems from the fact that the NAND operation is a **universal operation.** A universal operation is one that can be used to implement the three basic Boolean operations AND, OR, and NOT. Fig. 4-18 illustrates this universal property. As a consequence of the universal property, it follows that any combinational logic network can be realized by using only NAND gates.

One procedure for obtaining a logic diagram consisting of only NAND gates from a Boolean expression involves applying the algebraic definition of the NAND gate, i.e., $f(x_1, x_2, \ldots, x_n) = \overline{(x_1 x_2 \cdots x_n)}$. To illustrate this, consider the Boolean expression

$$f(w, x, y, z) = w + \bar{y}z + \bar{w}(x + y)$$

By applying DeMorgan's law, this expression can be written as

$$f(w, x, y, z) = \overline{\{\overline{w(\overline{yz})}[\overline{w(x + y)}]\}}$$

Since this is the general algebraic descriptive form for a NAND gate with inputs $\bar{w}$, $(\bar{y}z)$, and $[\overline{w(x + y)}]$, the logic network shown in Fig. 4-19a can be constructed. Furthermore, the term $(\bar{y}z)$ is the algebraic form for a NAND

TABLE 4-10 Definition of the NAND Operation

x	y	$f = \overline{(xy)}$
0	0	1
0	1	1
1	0	1
1	1	0

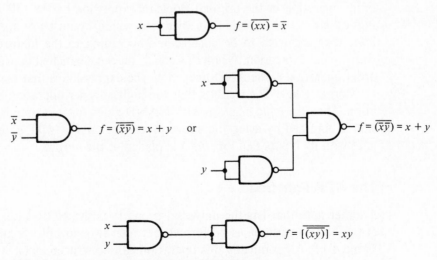

FIG. 4-18 The universal property of NAND gates

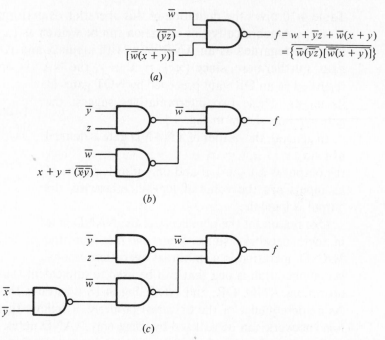

FIG. 4-19 Procedure to obtain the logic diagram consisting only of NAND gates for the Boolean expression $f(w,x,y,z) = w + y\bar{z} + \bar{w}(x + y)$

gate with inputs $\bar{y}$ and z, and the term $[\overline{\bar{w}(x + y)}]$ is the algebraic form for a NAND gate with inputs $\bar{w}$ and $(x + y)$. The resulting network is shown in Fig. 4-19b. Finally, the term $x + y$ can be written as $(\overline{\bar{x}\bar{y}})$, which implies the network of Fig. 4-19c. Assuming that the complemented form of the input variables is available, the logic network of Fig. 4-19c is a NAND-gate realization of the Boolean function

$$f(w, x, y, z) = w + \bar{y}z + \bar{w}(x + y)$$

Clearly, if the complemented form of the input variables is not available, NOT gates can always be used.

In order to carry out the above procedure, it is necessary that the highest-order operation in the original Boolean expression be the OR operation. The highest-order operation is that operation which would be performed last if the logic diagram were to be constructed according to the hierarchical order of the original expression. When this condition is not satisfied because the highest-order operation is the AND operation, the expression is first complemented by DeMorgan's law. The result is that the highest-order operation is the OR operation. Then the logic diagram with NAND gates for the complemented expression is obtained by using the above procedure, and a NOT gate (or a NAND gate with its inputs tied together) is placed at the output.

The NOR Function

Another gate that has the universal property is the NOR gate. The definition of the NOR operation as performed between two variables x and y is given in Table 4-11. Algebraically this operation can be written as $\overline{(x + y)}$, and symbolically it can be regarded as an OR gate, with inputs x and y, followed by a NOT gate. Since $\overline{(x + y)} = \overline{x}\overline{y}$, the NOR operation can also be regarded as an AND gate preceded by NOT gates at its inputs. These two interpretations suggest the gate symbols shown in Fig. 4-17.

In general, the output of a NOR gate is defined as $\overline{(x_1 + x_2 + \cdots + x_n)} = \overline{x}_1 \overline{x}_2 \cdots \overline{x}_n$. Thus, the output is logic-1 if and only if all its inputs have the value of logic-0; otherwise, the output is logic-0. The universal nature of NOR gates is illustrated in Fig. 4-20, where it is shown that by the use of these gates alone, the three basic Boolean operations can be realized.

As a consequence of the universal property of NOR gates, any combinational logic network can be realized by the use of just this one type of gate. One procedure for obtaining a logic diagram with NOR gates from a Boolean expression involves applying the algebraic definition of the NOR gate, i.e., $f(x_1, x_2, \ldots, x_n) = \overline{(x_1 + x_2 + \cdots + x_n)}$. The only restriction placed on the initial Boolean expression is that the highest-order operation must be the AND operation. When this condition is not satisfied because the highest-order operation is the OR operation, the logic diagram with NOR gates for the complement of the expression is first obtained. Then a NOT gate (or a NOR gate with its inputs tied together) is placed at the output.

To illustrate the construction of a logic diagram, again consider the expression

$$f(w, x, y, z) = w + \overline{y}z + \overline{w}(x + y)$$

Since the highest-order operation in this expression is the OR operation, the expression is complemented:

$$\overline{f}(w, x, y, z) = \overline{[w + \overline{y}z + \overline{w}(x + y)]}$$

TABLE 4-11
Definition of the NOR Operation

x	y	$f = \overline{(x + y)}$
0	0	1
0	1	0
1	0	0
1	1	0

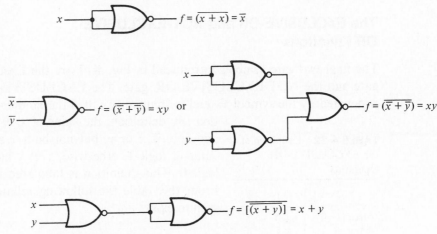

FIG. 4-20 The universal property of NOR gates

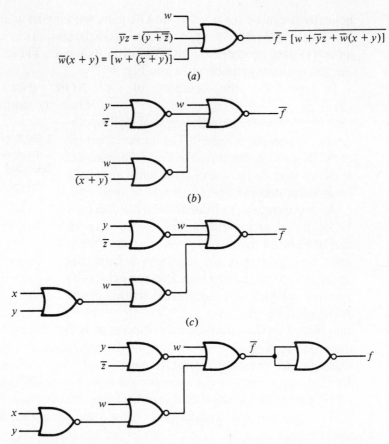

FIG. 4-21 Procedure to obtain the logic diagram consisting only of NOR gates for the Boolean expression $f(w,x,y,z) = w + \bar{y}z + \bar{w}(x + y)$

The logic diagram for the complemented expression is then constructed as indicated in Fig. 4-21a–c. The logic diagram is completed by placing a NOR gate with its inputs tied together at the output of the network, as shown in Fig. 4-21d.

The EXCLUSIVE-OR and NOT-EXCLUSIVE-OR Functions

The final two gate symbols introduced in Fig. 4-17 are the EXCLUSIVE-OR gate and the NOT-EXCLUSIVE-OR gate. The EXCLUSIVE-OR operation is denoted by the symbol $\oplus$ and is frequently called the **modulo-2-sum** operation. By definition, the value of $x \oplus y$ is logic-1 if and only if x or y, but not both x and y, has the value of logic-1; otherwise, $x \oplus y$ has the value of logic-0. This definition is tabulated in Table 4-12. From this table the following relationship can be seen to exist:

$$x \oplus y = \bar{x}y + x\bar{y}$$

TABLE 4-12 Definition of the EXCLUSIVE-OR Operation

x	y	$x \oplus y$	x	y	$x \oplus y$
$0 \oplus 0$		$= 0$	$1 \oplus 0$		$= 1$
$0 \oplus 1$		$= 1$	$1 \oplus 1$		$= 0$

The complement of the EXCLUSIVE-OR operation is the NOT-EXCLU-SIVE-OR operation. Algebraically,

$$\overline{(x \oplus y)} = \overline{(\overline{x}y + x\overline{y})} = (x + \overline{y})(\overline{x} + y) = xy + \overline{xy}$$

From this equation it can be seen that $\overline{(x \oplus y)}$ has the value of logic-1 if and only if the logic value of both x and y are the same; otherwise, $\overline{(x \oplus y)}$ has the value of logic-0. For this reason, the NOT-EXCLUSIVE-OR gate is also called the EQUIVALENCE gate.

Although NAND and NOR gates are available with several input lines, the EXCLUSIVE-OR and NOT-EXCLUSIVE-OR gates are typically available with only two input lines.

As with all the other functions described, two gate symbols are given in Fig. 4-17 for both the EXCLUSIVE-OR and the NOT-EXCLUSIVE-OR operations. It can easily be shown that by regarding the bubble symbol as a NOT gate, the alternate gate symbols shown each correspond to the indicated function.

sec. 5

Sequential Networks

James W. Gault
Russell L. Pimmel

5-1 INTRODUCTION

A **sequential digital** network is one whose outputs depend not only on the current inputs but also on the sequence of previous inputs. We therefore say that sequential networks have memory.

5-2 THE FLIP-FLOP ELEMENT

The flip-flop is the basic sequential element. The name may be used to refer both to the electronic circuit, whose inputs and outputs are voltage levels L and H, and to the logic element, whose inputs and outputs are logic values 0 and 1.

Flip-Flop Circuit

The flip-flop circuit is a special electronic circuit with two output signals Q and $\overline{Q}$, as shown in Fig. 5-1. The Q output is referred to as the **true output;** $\overline{Q}$ is the

complementary or **false output.** These signals assume one of two voltage levels and are complementary; i.e., if Q is at the high voltage level H, $\overline{Q}$ must be at the low voltage level L, and vice versa. Since the flip-flop maintains its outputs until changed by the input signals, it has two stable conditions: Q = H and $\overline{Q}$ = L or Q = L and $\overline{Q}$ = H. These two conditions are referred to as **states.** The

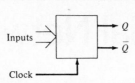

Inputs

Clock

FIG. 5-1 Flip-flop symbol

first, Q = H, is called the **set state,** and the second, Q = L, is the **reset** state. We say that a flip-flop is **set** when it is driven into the set state, and we say that it is **reset** or **cleared** when driven into the reset state. In general, the positive-logic assumption is used with flip-flops. Thus, the set and reset states often are referred to as the **1 state** and the **0 state,** respectively.

We shall describe four common flip-flop circuits, the *D*, *T*, *SR*, and *JK*. Each type has a unique relationship between its input signals and the associated state transitions. This relationship is represented by a **state voltage table,** which indicates the voltage on the Q output after the clock transition for all input conditions for both the set and reset states. Figure 5-2 shows the symbol and the state voltage tables for the *D*, *T*, *SR*, and *JK* flip-flop circuits. In these tables **present state** and **next state** are used to define the condition before and after the transition.

The *D* flip-flop circuit has only one input signal, and the circuit assumes the state defined by this signal; i.e., the circuit is driven to the reset state when the input is low and to the set state when the input is high. The *T* flip-flop circuit changes states if its single input signal is high; otherwise it remains in the same state. The *SR* flip-flop circuit can be selectively set or reset by activating the appropriate input; i.e., the circuit is set if the *S* input is high and reset if the *R*

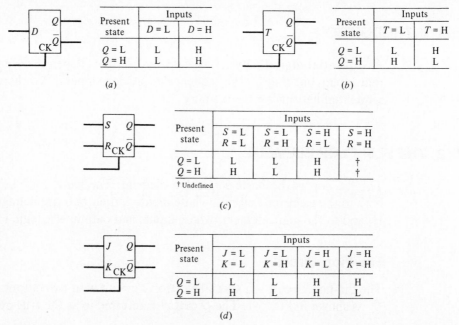

FIG. 5-2 Symbol and voltage state table for (a) D flip-flop circuit, (b) T flip-flop circuit, (c) SR flip-flop circuit, and (d) JK flip-flop circuit

input is high. If both inputs are low, there is no change in the state, but if both are high, the next state is undefined. The *JK* flip-flop circuit is similar to the *SR* flip-flop circuit except that the condition when both inputs are high is defined as a toggle signal; i.e., the flip-flop changes states regardless of the present state.

A flip-flop circuit is asynchronous or synchronous depending on whether a clock signal is used or not. **Asynchronous flip-flop** circuits operate without clock signals, and state transitions are initiated as soon as the input signals are altered. **Synchronous flip-flop** circuits operate with a clock signal, so that the input signals are valid and the corresponding state transitions are initiated only during a specific portion of the clock signal. As a consequence, the input signals must be stable during this portion of the clock cycle. We shall consider the clock signal as a periodic pulse; the **rising** and **falling edges** provide two distinct time events which can be defined as **active phases.** Flip-flop circuits may be **edge-triggered** devices, which use the same active phase both to recognize input signals and to initiate state transitions, or **master-slave devices,** which use the rising edge of the clock pulse to recognize input signals and the falling edge of the clock pulse to initiate state transitions. The second type derives its name from the fact that it consists of two internal flip-flop circuit stages: the first stage, the master, recognizes the inputs signals and initiates its state transitions on the rising edge of the clock pulse; the second stage, the slave, accepts the outputs of the master as its input signals and initiates its state transitions on the falling edge of the clock pulse.

Figure 5-3 shows timing diagrams for a rising-edge-triggered *T* flip-flop circuit, for a falling-edge-triggered *SR* flip-flop circuit, and for a master-slave *JK* flip-flop circuit. In these timing diagrams we assume that the flip-flop circuits are reset initially. In Fig. 5-3a, the *T* input signal is low on the rising edge of the first and last clock pulses, so that the flip-flop circuit remains in the same state. With the middle two clock pulses the *T* input is high, so that the flip-flop circuit changes states. Just as with combinational digital circuits, there is a time delay, referred to as the **propagation delay** t_p, before the output signal has stabilized when a transition occurs. Again, this is a characteristic of the device, and the length of delay depends on the technology used in its manufacture. With flip-flop circuits, a second important timing constraint, the flip-flop **setup time,** is an interval just before the active phase of the clock pulse during which the input signals must be stable. It also is a characteristic of the device depending on the manufacturing technology.

For the *D* flip-flop circuit in Fig. 5-3b, the active phase of the clock pulse is the trailing edge, as indicated by the small circle on the *C* input in the flip-flop symbol. On the first clock pulse, the *D* input is low, but since the flip-flop circuit is already reset, there is no change in state. On the second clock pulse the *D* input is high, and so the flip-flop circuit is set. There is no state change on the third clock pulse when the *D* input is high since the flip-flop circuit is already set. The flip-flop circuit is reset on the fourth clock pulse.

In Fig. 5-3c, the output change is initiated on the falling edge of the clock pulse, as indicated by the circle on the *C* input. However, the inputs are valid on the rising edge of the clock pulse because the device is a master-slave flip-flop circuit. On the first clock pulse the *J* input is high and *K* input is low, and

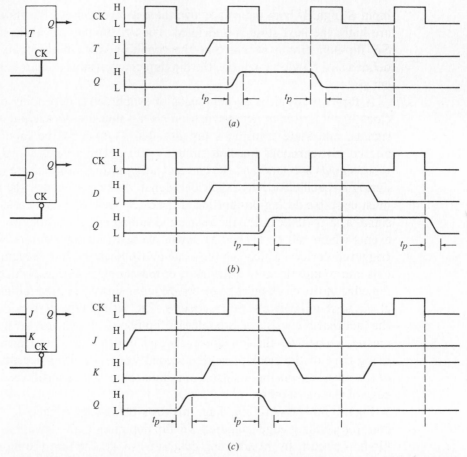

FIG. 5-3 Timing diagrams: (a) rising-edge-triggered T flip-flop circuit; (b) falling-edge triggered D flip-flop circuit, and (c) master-slave JK flip-flop circuit

so the flip-flop circuit is set. Both input signals are high during the second clock pulse, and so the flip-flop circuit toggles. Nothing happens on the third clock pulse since both inputs are low. On the fourth, the inputs are defined to reset the flip-flop circuit, but since it is already reset, there is no change in its state.

Flip-Flop Logic Element

In associating the voltages on the flip-flop circuit inputs and outputs with binary values, we shall use the positive-logic assumption. The logic behavior of the flip-flop is described by the logic state tables or simply state tables, as shown in Table 5-1. The flip-flop state tables are analogous to the voltage state tables in Fig. 5-2 and indicate the binary value of Q after the clock pulse for all inputs conditions for both initial states ($Q = 0$ and $Q = 1$). These state tables are obtained by substituting 0 for L and 1 for H in the corresponding voltage table in Fig. 5-2.

In designing sequential networks, we use the transition table, an alternative description of the flip-flop's behavior. The **transition table,** which can be derived from the state table, defines the input condition necessary for each possible state transition. Transition tables for all four flip-flop types also are shown in Table 5-1.

TABLE 5-1 State Tables and Transition Tables for Four Flip-Flop Logic Elements (d = Don't Care Condition)

D flip-flop

State table			Transition table		

Present state	Input		Present state	Next state	D
	D = 0	D = 1			
Q = 0	0	1	0	0	0
Q = 1	0	1	0	1	1
			1	0	0
			1	1	1

T flip-flop

State table			Transition table		

Present state	Input		Present state	Next state	T
	T = 0	T = 1			
Q = 0	0	1	0	0	0
Q = 1	1	0	0	1	1
			1	0	1
			1	1	0

SR flip-flop

State table					Transition table			

Present state	Inputs SR				Present state	Next state	S	R
	0 0	0 1	1 0	1 1				
Q = 0	0	0	1	†	0	0	0	d
Q = 1	1	0	1	†	0	1	1	0
					1	0	0	1
					1	1	d	0

JK flip-flop

State table					Transition table			

Present state	Inputs JK				Present state	Next state	J	K
	0 0	0 1	1 0	1 1				
Q = 0	0	0	1	1	0	0	0	d
Q = 1	1	0	1	0	0	1	1	d
					1	0	d	1
					1	1	d	0

†Undefined.

We shall use the *JK* flip-flop to illustrate the procedure for converting a state table into a transition table. The first state transition in the table, the 0-to-0 transition, results if $J = 0$ and $K = 0$, the input condition specifying no change, or if $J = 0$ and $K = 1$, the input condition to reset the flip-flop. Thus, since K can be either 0 or 1, it can be considered a don't-care condition. Thus, the 0-to-0 transition requires that $J = 0$ and $K = $ d. For the 0-to-1 transition, the inputs must be $J = 1$ and $K = 0$, the input condition to set the flip-flop, or $J = 1$ and $K = 1$, the input condition to toggle the flip-flop. Thus, for this transition the required inputs are $J = 1$ and $K = $ d. Input requirements for the other two transitions are similarly defined.

5-3 STATE TABLES AND STATE DIAGRAMS

In describing the behavior of sequential networks containing several flip-flops we shall use the concept of states. Earlier in this chapter we defined a state as a recognizable condition and pointed out that a flip-flop has two stable states, the reset state, with $Q = 0$, and the set state, with $Q = 1$. In a network with N flip-flops the states are characterized by an N-bit binary word, where each bit is associated with one of the flip-flops. Since there are 2^N distinct patterns in an N-bit word. there are 2^N stable states.

Symbolic Notation

Instead of using binary code words to define the input conditions, output conditions, and states, it is sometimes convenient to define a symbolic code representing each valid input condition, output condition, and state. We shall use the symbols $I_0, I_1, I_2, \ldots$, $R_0, R_1, R_2, \ldots$, and $S_0, S_1, S_2, \ldots$ to represent the valid input conditions, output or response conditions, and states, respectively. Just as a flip-flop is characterized by its state table defining the next state for all combinations of inputs and present states, a sequential network, which is constructed from flip-flops, is characterized by a **network state table,** or **state table,** defining the current output condition and next state for all combinations of input conditions and present states. Alternatively, the information in the network state table can be represented by a **network state diagram,** or **state diagram,** pictorially defining the current output and next state for all combinations of input conditions and present states. Figure 5-4 shows the state table and state diagram for a sequential network. The network has two valid input conditions (I_0 and I_1), three valid output conditions (R_0, R_1, and R_2), and four valid states (S_0, S_1, S_2, and S_3).

Present state	Inputs	
	I_0	I_1
S_0	S_1/R_1	S_3/R_2
S_1	S_2/R_2	S_2/R_1
S_2	S_0/R_2	S_2/R_1
S_3	S_0/R_0	S_0/R_0

(a)

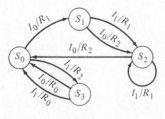

(b)

FIG. 5-4 (a) Network state table and (b) state diagram

In the state table in Fig. 5-4 the current inputs are listed across the top, and the present states are listed in the leftmost column. Entries in the internal squares define the next state and the current output for each combination of input condition and present state. For example, when the network is in state S_0 and the input is I_0, the current output is R_1 and the next state is S_1. Similarly if the input is I_1 and the present state is S_0, the current output is R_2 and the next state is S_3. As another example, for state S_3 the current output is R_0 and the next state is S_0, regardless of the input. Finally, for present state S_2 and input I_1 there is no change in state, and the current output is R_1.

In the state diagram in Fig. 5-4b, a circle represents each state, and for each input condition a directed line points to the next state. Input conditions and current output conditions are defined above each directed line. In this example, there are two lines leaving state S_0, one for each valid input. If the input is I_0, the current output is R_1 and the next state is S_1; whereas if the input is I_1, the current output is R_2 and the next state is S_3. For state S_3 the next state is S_0 and the current output is R_0, regardless of the input. Also, for state S_2 with an input of I_1, there is no change in state and the current output is R_1.

Since the state table and state diagram provide the same information, it is possible to convert one into the other. In converting a state table into a state diagram a circle is drawn for each state in the leftmost column of the state table. Each internal square is translated into a directed line segment between circles. For example, for the present state S_0 in Fig. 5-4a, there are two internal squares, one for each input condition, and so there are two directed lines leaving the S_0 circle in the state diagram. For the input condition I_0, the directed line terminates on the circle for S_1 and the input and output conditions are defined by I_0/R_1. For the input condition I_1, the line is terminated on the circle for state S_3, and the input and output conditions are I_1/R_2. This same procedure would be followed for the other three present states.

The procedure for converting a state diagram into a state table is analogous. First the structure of the table is defined, a row for each state in the state diagram and a column for each unique input condition. Next each directed line is translated into an internal square. For example, for S_0 in Fig. 5-4b, the directed line for I_0 has an output of R_1 and a next state of S_1; this information is entered into the upper left internal square as S_1/R_1. The directed line for I_1 has an output of R_2 and a next state of S_3; this information is entered into the upper right square as S_3/R_2. The other three states are handled in the same way.

State Sequences

To illustrate that both the network state table and the network state diagram characterize the behavior of a sequential network, let us consider how the network defined in Fig. 5-4 responds to the input sequence $I_1, I_1, I_0, I_1,$ and I_0 if the initial state is S_1. At the time of the first clock pulse, the input is I_1, and the present state is S_1. From the state table or diagram in Fig. 5-4 we see that for the combination of S_1 and I_1 the output at this clock pulse is R_1 and the next state after the clock pulse is S_2. as shown in Fig. 5-5a. For the second clock pulse, the input is specified as I_1 and the new present state defined by the transition on the previous clock pulse is S_2. From the state table or diagram we see that with the combination of I_1 and S_2 the output is R_1 and the next state is S_2. For the third clock pulse, the specified input is I_0 and the present state is S_2.

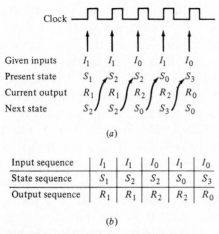

(a)

Input sequence	I_1	I_1	I_0	I_1	I_0
State sequence	S_1	S_2	S_2	S_0	S_3
Output sequence	R_1	R_1	R_2	R_2	R_0

(b)

FIG. 5-5 Sequence of inputs, outputs, and states for the network defined in Fig. 5-4

This combination produces an output of R_2 and results in the new state S_0. Outputs and transition for the fourth and fifth clock pulse can be analyzed similarly.

The table in Fig. 5-5b more concisely defines the sequence of states and outputs produced by the given sequence of inputs. We may consider each vertical line to be a clock pulse, and the entries in the previous column indicate the condition at the clock pulse. For example, at the first clock pulse the valid conditions are I_1, S_1, and R_1; at the second clock pulse they are I_1, S_2, and R_1.

Example A sequential network is defined by the state table below. Define the sequence of outputs and states for the input sequence I_0, I_2, I_2, I_3, and I_1. The initial state is S_2.

Present state	Input			
	I_0	I_1	I_2	I_3
S_0	S_0/R_0	S_1/R_1	S_2/R_0	S_1/R_0
S_1	S_0/R_0	S_1/R_0	S_1/R_0	S_0/R_0
S_2	S_1/R_2	S_1/R_0	S_2/R_0	S_1/R_0

SOLUTION

Input sequence	I_0	I_2	I_2	I_3	I_1
State sequence	S_2	S_1	S_1	S_1	S_0
Output sequence	R_2	R_0	R_0	R_0	R_1

Binary-Coded State Tables and Diagrams

State tables and state diagrams can be constructed using binary codes to represent the input conditions, output conditions, and states. Figure 5-6a describes one set of code words for the sequential network defined by the state table† and state diagram in Fig. 5-4.

Coding the two input conditions requires only one binary variable, X_0. There are two choices for defining the code: letting $X_0 = 0$ for I_0 and $X_0 = 1$ for I_1 or letting $X_0 = 0$ for I_1 and $X_0 = 1$ for I_0. In Fig. 5-6a we have chosen the former.

†In all encoded state tables the next state and output variable entries are ordered with decreasing subscripts from left to right.

Input code		Output code			State code		
Symbol	X_0	Symbol	Z_1	Z_0	Symbol	Q_1	Q_0
I_0	0	R_0	1	1	S_0	0	0
I_1	1	R_1	0	1	S_1	1	0
		R_2	1	0	S_2	1	1
					S_3	0	1

(a)

Present state	X_0	
$Q_1 Q_0$	0	1
0 0	10/01	01/10
1 0	11/10	11/01
1 1	00/10	11/01
0 1	00/11	00/11

$$Q_1 Q_0 / Z_1 Z_0$$

(b)

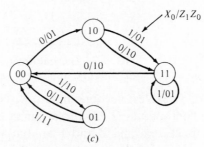

(c)

FIG. 5-6 (a) One set of code words for network described by Fig. 5-4, (b) resulting encoded state table, and (c) diagram

Two variables (Z_1 and Z_0) are required for coding the three output conditions. In defining the code, there are several choices, and the only constraint is the requirement of uniqueness of the code word for each condition. The code defined in Fig. 5-6a assigns the code word 11 to the condition R_0, the code word 01 to the condition R_1, and the code word 10 to the condition R_2, the code word 00 being unassigned. These code words specify the value of the binary variables Z_1 and Z_0, Z_1 being the more significant bit. In coding the four states, we must use two binary variables, which implies that the network contains two flip-flops represented by Q_1 and Q_0. Again, there are several choices for defining the code; that used in Fig. 5-6a assigns the code word 00 to S_0, the code word 10 to S_1, the code word 11 to S_2, and the code word 01 to S_3. These code words specify the values of Q_1 and Q_0 with Q_1 the more significant.

The codes defined in Fig. 5-6a represent arbitrary choices. There are techniques for defining codes which by some criterion or other minimize the complexity of the network. We shall not be concerned with this aspect of sequential network design and shall limit ourselves to defining unique but arbitrary codes for each condition and state.

Figure 5-6b and c shows the encoded state table and state diagram derived from the symbolic versions in Fig. 5-4. These encoded versions are obtained by replacing each symbol by its assigned code word. For example, I_0 is replaced by 0. R_0 by 11, and S_0 by 00.

5-4 CONVERTING A STATE TABLE INTO A LOGIC DIAGRAM

In this section we describe a method for converting an encoded state table for a sequential network into an efficient logic diagram using the general structural model in Fig. 5-7. This model separates the sequential network into a combinational subnetwork and a flip-flop subnetwork. It also identifies four distinct

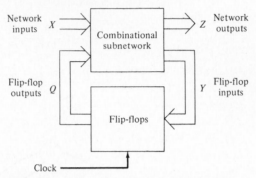

FIG. 5-7 General structural model of a sequential network

groups of variables: network inputs X, network outputs Z, flip-flop inputs Y, and flip-flop outputs Q. Of these signals, X and Q are inputs to the combinational subnetwork, and Z and Y are outputs of this subnetwork.

Let us consider the encoded state table shown in Fig. 5-8a and develop an

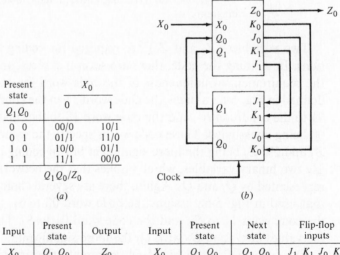

Present state	X_0	
$Q_1 Q_0$	0	1
0 0	00/0	10/1
0 1	01/1	11/0
1 0	10/0	01/1
1 1	11/1	00/0

$Q_1 Q_0 / Z_0$

(a)

(b)

Input	Present state	Output
X_0	Q_1 Q_0	Z_0
0	0 0	0
0	0 1	1
0	1 0	0
0	1 1	1
1	0 0	1
1	0 1	0
1	1 0	1
1	1 1	0

(c)

Input	Present state	Next state	Flip-flop inputs			
X_0	Q_1 Q_0	Q_1 Q_0	J_1	K_1	J_0	K_0
0	0 0	0 0	0	d	0	d
0	0 1	0 1	0	d	d	0
0	1 0	1 0	d	0	0	d
0	1 1	1 1	d	0	d	0
1	0 0	1 0	1	d	0	d
1	0 1	1 1	1	d	d	0
1	1 0	0 1	d	1	1	d
1	1 1	0 0	d	1	d	1

(d)

FIG. 5-8 (a) State table, (b) structural model, (c) output truth table, and (d) extended truth table for a sequential network

efficient logic diagram for it using JK flip-flops. From the state table we note that there is one input variable X_0, one output variable Z_0, and two flip-flop outputs Q_1 and Q_0. Since JK flip-flops are specified, Y contains four variables (J_1, K_1, J_0, and K_0). Figure 5-8b shows the general structural model with these variables identified explicitly. This figure points out that defining the logic diagram for this sequential network basically reduces to defining an efficient logic diagram for the combinational subnetwork. The first step in this procedure then is defining a truth table for this combinational subnetwork from the information in the state table.

The state table explicitly defines the value of Z_0 for all combinations of values for X_0, Q_1, and Q_0. Thus the truth table for Z_0 is obtained simply by rewriting the information in a more standard form. Figure 5-8c shows the resulting **output truth table.** All combinations of values for X_0, Q_1, and Q_0 were enumerated using a binary count. Each row corresponds to an internal square in the state table. For example, the first row corresponds to the upper left internal square, where the input is 0 and the present state is 00. In the state table the output for this combination is 0, which is entered under Z_0 in the first row of the truth table. The second row corresponds to the internal square where the input is 0 and the present state is 01. In the state table the output for this combination is 1, which is entered in the truth table. This procedure is repeated until all entries in the output truth table are defined.

Although the state table does not define the values for J_1, K_1, J_0, and K_0 explicitly, it does define the next state of Q_1 and Q_0, thereby indirectly defining the flip-flop inputs. Since this information is not directly available and must be derived, we use an extended truth table to transform it into the desired format.

The **extended truth table** for this problem (Fig. 5-8d) lists combinations of values for the input and present states, and for each combination it defines values for the associated next states and flip-flop inputs to produce the specified transition. In this table all combinations of values for X_0, Q_1, and Q_0 were enumerated by a binary count. Entries in the next-state columns were found in the corresponding internal square of the network state table, just as we found the values of Z_0 for the output truth table above. For example, the last row in the extended truth table corresponds to the internal square in the state table where the input is 1 and the present state is 11. For this combination the next state is 00, which is entered in the last row of the extended truth table. The next-to-last row in the extended truth table corresponds to the internal square in the state table where the input is 1 and the present state is 10. For this combination the next state is 01, which is entered in the extended truth table. This procedure is repeated until all next states are defined in the extended truth table.

The extended truth table now defines the present and next state for all input combinations. The next step is to define values for the flip-flop inputs to produce each transition for each flip-flop. To help complete this table we shall use the flip-flop transition table (Table 5-1), which defines the values on J and K for all possible transitions. In the first row, Q_1 undergoes a 0-to-0 transition; from the flip-flop transition table we see that $J_1 = 0$ and $K_1 = $ d produces this transition. These values are therefore entered in the first row of the extended truth table. In the last row, Q_1 undergoes a 1-to-0 transition, and so the inputs are $J_1 = $ d and $K_1 = 1$. These values are entered in the extended truth table. This

	$\bar{Q}_1\bar{Q}_0$	$\bar{Q}_1Q_0$	Q_1Q_0	$Q_1\bar{Q}_0$
$\bar{X}_0$	0	1	1	0
X_0	1	0	0	1

$Z_0 = \bar{X}_0 \cdot Q_0 + X_0 \cdot \bar{Q}_0$

(a)

	$\bar{Q}_1\bar{Q}_0$	$\bar{Q}_1Q_0$	Q_1Q_0	$Q_1\bar{Q}_0$
$\bar{X}_0$	0	0	d	d
X_0	1	1	d	d

$J_1 = X_0$

(b)

	$\bar{Q}_1\bar{Q}_0$	$\bar{Q}_1Q_0$	Q_1Q_0	$Q_1\bar{Q}_0$
$\bar{X}_0$	d	d	0	0
X_0	d	d	1	1

$K_1 = X_0$

(c)

	$\bar{Q}_1\bar{Q}_0$	$\bar{Q}_1Q_0$	Q_1Q_0	$Q_1\bar{Q}_0$
$\bar{X}_0$	0	d	d	0
X_0	0	d	d	1

$J_0 = X_0 \cdot Q_1$

(d)

	$\bar{Q}_1\bar{Q}_0$	$\bar{Q}_1Q_0$	Q_1Q_0	$Q_1\bar{Q}_0$
$\bar{X}_0$	d	0	0	d
X_0	d	0	1	d

$K_0 = X_0 \cdot Q_1$

(e)

FIG. 5-9 K maps for the sequential network defined in Fig. 5-8

procedure is repeated until J_1 and K_1 are completely defined. This procedure is then applied to define J_0 and K_0 from the specified transitions of Q_0.

The output truth table (Fig. 5-8c) and the extended truth table (Fig. 5-8d) combine to define the behavior of the combinational subnetwork. To obtain an efficient logic diagram we construct maps for Z_0, J_1, K_1, J_0, and K_0 and obtain a minimum sum-of-products form for each variable. These maps and the minimization are shown in Fig. 5-9. Figure 5-10 shows the AND, OR, and NOT logic

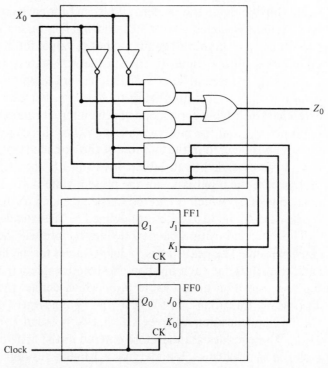

FIG. 5-10 An efficient logic diagram for the sequential network defined in Fig. 5-8

diagram implementing these equations and the interconnections between logic elements in the two subnetworks. This figure emphasizes that X_0 and Z_0 are the only external signals; the flip-flop inputs and outputs are internal signals.

Example For the state table below derive all minimum sum-of-products equations needed to construct a logic diagram using *JK* flip-flops.

Present state Q_1Q_0	X_1X_0			
	00	01	10	11
00	01/01	10/01	11/10	00/00
01	10/01	11/10	00/00	01/01
10	11/10	00/00	01/01	10/01
11	00/00	01/01	10/01	11/10

SOLUTION First we construct the standard and extended truth tables. In the latter we use the *JK* flip-flop transition table.

X_1	X_0	Present state Q_1	Q_0	Z_1	Z_0	X_1	X_0	Present state Q_1	Q_0	Next state Q_1	Q_0	J_1	K_1	J_0	K_0
0	0	0	0	0	1	0	0	0	0	0	1	0	d	1	d
		0	1	0	1			0	1	1	0	1	d	d	1
		1	0	1	0			1	0	1	1	d	0	1	d
		1	1	0	0			1	1	0	0	d	1	d	1
0	1	0	0	0	1	0	1	0	0	1	0	1	d	0	d
		0	1	1	0			0	1	1	1	1	d	d	0
		1	0	0	0			1	0	0	0	d	1	0	d
		1	1	0	1			1	1	0	1	d	1	d	0
1	0	0	0	1	0	1	0	0	0	1	1	1	d	1	d
		0	1	0	0			0	1	0	0	0	d	d	1
		1	0	0	1			1	0	0	1	d	1	1	d
		1	1	0	1			1	1	1	0	d	0	d	1
1	1	0	0	0	0	1	1	0	0	0	0	0	d	0	d
		0	1	0	1			0	1	0	1	0	d	d	0
		1	0	0	1			1	0	1	0	d	0	0	d
		1	1	1	0			1	1	1	1	d	0	d	0

K maps are drawn and used to define minimum sum-of-products equations (Fig. 5-11).

$$Z_1 = \overline{X}_1 \cdot \overline{X}_0 \cdot Q_1 \cdot \overline{Q}_0 + \overline{X}_1 \cdot X_0 \cdot \overline{Q}_1 \cdot Q_0 + X_1 \cdot X_0 \cdot Q_1 \cdot Q_0$$
$$+ X_1 \cdot \overline{X}_0 \cdot \overline{Q}_1 \cdot \overline{Q}_0$$
$$Z_0 = \overline{X}_1 \cdot \overline{X}_0 \cdot \overline{Q}_1 + \overline{X}_1 \cdot \overline{Q}_1 \cdot \overline{Q}_0 + X_1 \cdot \overline{X}_0 \cdot Q_1 + X_1 \cdot Q_1 \cdot \overline{Q}_0$$
$$+ \overline{X}_1 \cdot X_0 \cdot Q_1 \cdot Q_0 + X_1 \cdot X_0 \cdot \overline{Q}_1 \cdot Q_0$$
$$J_1 = \overline{X}_1 \cdot X_0 + \overline{X}_1 \cdot Q_0 + X_1 \cdot \overline{X}_0 \cdot \overline{Q}_0$$
$$K_1 = \overline{X}_1 \cdot X_0 + \overline{X}_1 \cdot Q_0 + X_1 \cdot \overline{X}_0 \cdot \overline{Q}_0$$
$$J_0 = \overline{X}_0$$
$$K_0 = \overline{X}_0$$

A logic diagram can be drawn directly from these equations.

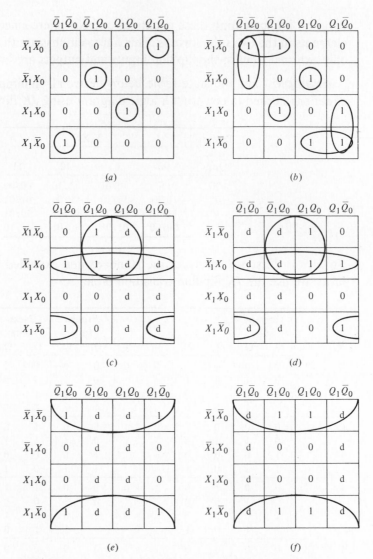

FIG. 5-11 K maps: (a) Z_1, (b) Z_0, (c) J_1, (d) K_1, (e) J_0, (f) K_0

5-5 CONVERTING A LOGIC DIAGRAM INTO A STATE TABLE

This section describes a method for converting a logic diagram for a sequential network into a state table. This conversion, the counterpart of that described in the previous section, is an essential step in the analysis of sequential networks.

Figure 5-12 shows the logic diagram for a sequential network. There are one input variable X_0, one output variable Z_0, and two T flip-flops FF0 and FF1. The combinational network is described with AND, OR, and NOT gates. Z_0 and the two flip-flop inputs T_0 and T_1 can be described in terms of the combinational subnetwork inputs X_0, Q_1, and Q_0

$$Z_0 = \overline{X}_0 \cdot Q_1 \cdot Q_0 + X_0 \cdot \overline{Q}_1 \cdot \overline{Q}_0 \qquad (5\text{-}1)$$

$$T_1 = X_0 \cdot \overline{Q}_0 + \overline{X}_0 \cdot Q_0 \qquad (5\text{-}2)$$

$$T_0 = 1 \qquad (5\text{-}3)$$

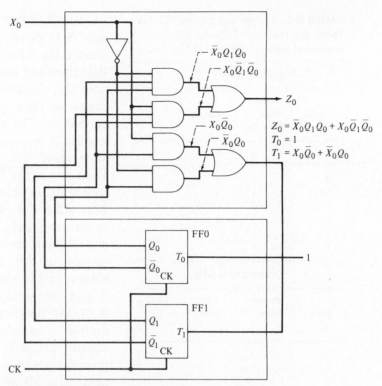

FIG. 5-12   Logic diagram for a sequential network

Table 5-2 shows the output truth table for the output Z_0 constructed from Eq. (5-1). The first three columns, X_0, Q_1, and Q_0, represent inputs to the combinational subnetwork, and the entries in these columns represent an enumeration of all possible combinations. As before, this enumeration is done using a binary count. Entries under Z_0 were obtained by rewriting Eq. (5-1) as $Z_0 = m_3 + m_4$ and then placing a 1 in the rows corresponding to minterms m_3 and m_4 and a 0 in all other rows.

Table 5-2 also shows the extended truth table for the flip-flop inputs. Entries in the input and present-state columns were enumerated just as before. Entries in the flip-flop input columns were obtained from Eqs. (5-2) and (5-3). The equation for T_1 can be rewritten as $T_1 = m_1 + m_3 + m_4 + m_6$ to define explicitly the rows where T_1 has a value of 1. Equation (5-3) indicates that T_0 is always 1, and these values are entered in the extended truth table.

This table now defines the present state and the flip-flop inputs for all combinations. Next we define the next state of each flip-flop defined by each transition. This is done in the two next state columns in the extended truth table. Entries in these columns are obtained by applying the T flip-flop state table (Table 5-1) to each specified transition for each flip-flop in each row of the extended truth table. To illustrate this technique consider FF1. In the first row $Q_1 = 0$ and $T_1 = 0$; so, from the flip-flop state table, the next state is $Q_1 = 0$; in the second row $Q_1 = 0$ and $T_1 = 1$, so the next state is $Q_1 = 1$; in the third, $Q_1 = 1$ and $T_1 = 0$, so the next state is $Q_1 = 1$; in the fourth, $Q_1 = 1$ and $T_1 = 1$, so the next is $Q_1 = 0$; and so on for the remaining four rows. Entries for FF0 are processed in the same way.

Table 5-2 also shows the state table corresponding to the two truth tables just

TABLE 5-2 Output and Extended Truth Tables and the State Table for the Sequential Network Defined in Fig. 5-12

Output truth table

Input X_0	Present state Q_1	Q_0	Output Z_0
0	0	0	0
0	0	1	0
0	1	0	0
0	1	1	1
1	0	0	1
1	0	1	0
1	1	0	0
1	1	1	0

Extended truth table

Input X_0	Present state Q_1	Q_0	Next state Q_1	Q_0	Flip-flop input T_1	T_0
0	0	0	0	1	0	1
0	0	1	1	0	1	1
0	1	0	1	1	0	1
0	1	1	0	0	1	1
1	0	0	1	1	1	1
1	0	1	0	0	0	1
1	1	0	0	1	1	1
1	1	1	1	0	0	1

State table

Q_1	Q_0	X_0 0	1
0	0	01/0	11/1
0	1	10/0	00/0
1	0	11/0	01/0
1	1	00/1	10/0

derived. The first step in this conversion is to define the structure of the state table. The truth tables indicate that there are two state variables (Q_1 and Q_0), implying $2^2 = 4$ present states, so there are four rows in the state table. The one input variable X_0 implies $2^1 = 2$ input conditions, so the state table will have two columns. Each row in the truth tables is transferred to an internal square in the state table. For example, the first row in the truth tables represents a present state 00 and an input 0, which corresponds to the upper left internal square in the state table. From the truth tables we see that the next state is 01 and the output is 0. This information is entered as 01/0 in that square. The next row represents the present state 01 with an input of 0. Its next state 10 and the output 0 are entered into the appropriate square in the state table. This process is repeated until each row in the truth tables is transferred to the appropriate square in the state table.

Example For the network shown in Fig. 5-13 derive the output sequence which results if the initial state is $Q_1 = 0$ and $Q_0 = 1$ and the input sequence is $X = 1, 0, 1, 1, 0$.

SOLUTION To derive the sequence of output we need to obtain the state table. First, we define equation for the output Z and the flip-flop inputs J_0, K_0, J_1, and K_1

$$Z = (\overline{\overline{\overline{X} \cdot \overline{Q}_1}}) + \overline{Q}_0 = \overline{X} \cdot \overline{Q}_1 + \overline{Q}_0$$
$$J_0 = \overline{\overline{Q}_1 + \overline{Q}_0} = Q_1 + \overline{Q}_0$$
$$K_0 = (\overline{\overline{X} \cdot \overline{Q}_1}) + \overline{\overline{Q}_0} = \overline{X} \cdot \overline{Q}_1 + Q_0$$
$$J_1 = Q_0$$
$$K_1 = (\overline{\overline{X} \cdot \overline{Q}_0}) + (\overline{\overline{X} \cdot \overline{Q}_1}) = X \cdot Q_0 + \overline{X} \cdot \overline{Q}_1$$

The output and extended truth table are now developed from these equations and the transition table for the *JK* flip-flop.

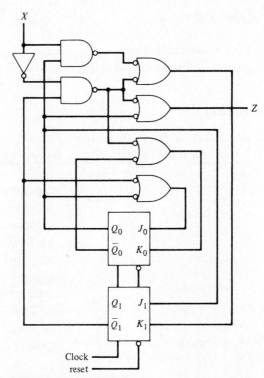

FIG. 5-13   Logic diagram

X	Present state Q_1	Q_0	Z
0	0	0	1
0	0	1	1
0	1	0	1
0	1	1	0
1	0	0	1
1	0	1	0
1	1	0	1
1	1	1	0

X	Present state Q_1	Q_0	Next state Q_1	Q_0	J_1	K_1	J_0	K_0
0	0	0	0	1	0	1	1	1
0	0	1	1	0	1	1	0	1
0	1	0	1	1	0	0	1	0
0	1	1	1	0	1	0	1	1
1	0	0	0	1	0	0	1	0
1	0	1	1	0	1	1	0	1
1	1	0	1	1	0	0	1	0
1	1	1	0	0	1	1	1	1

From these tables we define the state table

Present state Q_1	Q_0	X = 0	X = 1
0	0	01/1	01/1
0	1	10/1	10/0
1	0	11/1	11/1
1	1	10/0	00/0

The sequence for the given conditions is

Input X	1	0	1	1	0
Present state Q_1Q_0	0 1	1 0	1 1	0 0	0 1
Output Z	0	1	0	1	1

5-6 DESIGN EXAMPLES

In this section we shall illustrate the process of designing simple sequential networks from a precise verbal specification.

Decade Counter

In the first example we shall design a decade counter using T flip-flops. This network contains four flip-flops whose outputs form a code word interpreted as a BCD-coded decimal value. On each clock pulse the coded value is incremented, and when 9 is reached, it returns to 0 on the next clock pulse. On the 9-to-0 transition the network activates an output line to indicate the counter overflowed; this signal frequently is referred to as a carry.

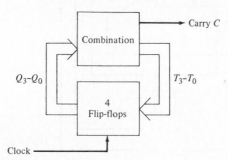

FIG. 5-14 Structural model for a decade counter

The first step in the design process is defining a structural model and using it to identify the input and output variables. Figure 5-14 shows such a model for the decade counter. Aside from the clock signal there are no other inputs to this network. The only output from the combinational subnetwork is the carry signal C.

The next step is to define either the state table or state diagram describing the behavior of the network. Figure 5-15a shows the state diagram for this counter. It indicates that the network has 10 acceptable states and that the sequence of states is 0000, 0001, 0010, . . . , 1000, 1001, and then repeats with 0000, 0001, and so on. Since there are no inputs to the network, the values on the directed lines show only the current output associated with each state. These have a value of 0 for all valid states except 1001. Figure 5-15b shows the cor-

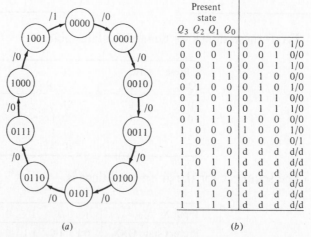

	Present state $Q_3 \ Q_2 \ Q_1 \ Q_0$								
0	0	0	0	0	0	0	1/0
0	0	0	1	0	0	1	0/0
0	0	1	0	0	0	1	1/0
0	0	1	1	0	1	0	0/0
0	1	0	0	0	1	0	1/0
0	1	0	1	0	1	1	0/0
0	1	1	0	0	1	1	1/0
0	1	1	1	1	0	0	0/0
1	0	0	0	1	0	0	1/0
1	0	0	1	0	0	0	0/1
1	0	1	0	d	d	d	d/d
1	0	1	1	d	d	d	d/d
1	1	0	0	d	d	d	d/d
1	1	0	1	d	d	d	d/d
1	1	1	0	d	d	d	d/d
1	1	1	1	d	d	d	d/d

(a)   (b)

FIG. 5-15 (a) State diagram and (b) table for a decade counter

TABLE 5-3 Output Truth Table and Extended Truth Table for
Decade Counter Defined in Figs. 5-14 and 5-15

Present state				Output	Present state				Next state				Flip-flop input			
Q_3	Q_2	Q_1	Q_0	C	Q_3	Q_2	Q_1	Q_0	Q_3	Q_2	Q_1	Q_0	T_3	T_2	T_1	T_0
0	0	0	0	0	0	0	0	0	0	0	0	1	0	0	0	1
0	0	0	1	0	0	0	0	1	0	0	1	0	0	0	1	1
0	0	1	0	0	0	0	1	0	0	0	1	1	0	0	0	1
0	0	1	1	0	0	0	1	1	0	1	0	0	0	1	1	1
0	1	0	0	0	0	1	0	0	0	1	0	1	0	0	0	1
0	1	0	1	0	0	1	0	1	0	1	1	0	0	0	1	1
0	1	1	0	0	0	1	1	0	0	1	1	1	0	0	0	1
0	1	1	1	0	0	1	1	1	1	0	0	0	1	1	1	1
1	0	0	0	0	1	0	0	0	1	0	0	1	0	0	0	1
1	0	0	1	1	1	0	0	1	0	0	0	0	1	0	0	1
1	0	1	0	d	1	0	1	0	d	d	d	d	d	d	d	d
1	0	1	1	d	1	0	1	1	d	d	d	d	d	d	d	d
1	1	0	0	d	1	1	0	0	d	d	d	d	d	d	d	d
1	1	0	1	d	1	1	0	1	d	d	d	d	d	d	d	d
1	1	1	0	d	1	1	1	0	d	d	d	d	d	d	d	d
1	1	1	1	d	1	1	1	1	d	d	d	d	d	d	d	d

responding state table. Since the network has no inputs, there is only one internal column in the table. Note that since the next state for the six unused states 1010 to 1111 is undefined, they are designated as don't-care conditions.

Table 5-3 shows the truth table for the network output C and the extended truth table for the flip-flop inputs T_3, T_2, T_1, and T_0. Briefly, the present states were enumerated. Values for the output in the truth table and the next states in the extended truth table were transferred row by row from the corresponding squares in the state table or the corresponding directed line in the state diagram. Values for the flip-flop inputs were defined in order to produce each specified state transition. In defining these values we used the T flip-flop transition table (Table 5-1).

The next step is to obtain efficient equations for the output C and for the flip-flop inputs T_3, T_2, T_1, and T_0. Figure 5-16 shows the maps used in obtaining these minimum sum-of-products expressions. The logic diagram showing an AND, OR, NOT implementation corresponding to these equations is given in Fig. 5-17.

A 3-Bit Up-Down Binary Counter

The second example is a 3-bit up-down binary counter with one input signal, to control the direction of the count, and two output signals, one indicating the counter overflow and one indicating counter underflow. This network contains three flip-flops whose outputs form a code word interpreted as a binary value. On each clock pulse the counter increments the coded value if the input signal is active and decrements the coded value if the input signal is inactive. The output signal indicating counter overflow, sometimes called the carry signal, is active on the 111-to-000 transition. The second output signal indicating that the counter underflowed, sometimes called the borrow signal, is active on the 000-

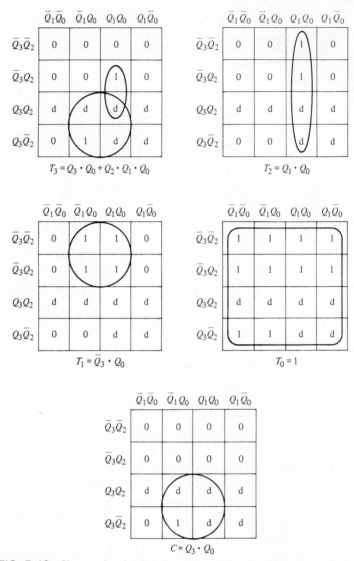

FIG. 5-16 K maps for the decade counter defined in Figs. 5-14 and 5-15

to-111 transition. We do not specify a flip-flop type since we shall stop our development after we have defined the state table.

Figure 5-18 shows the structural model for the 3-bit up-down binary counter. The input signal controlling the count is symbolized by U, the carry signal by C, and the borrow signal by B.

Figure 5-19 shows the state diagram and table for this network with the positive-logic assumption. When the input U has the value 0, the next state is obtained by decrementing the binary value defined by the present state. This is true even for the state 000, which when decremented produces 111. On this transition the borrow signal is active and B is set to 1. When the input U has the value of 1, the next state is obtained by incrementing the binary value defined by the present state. This is also true for the state 111, which when incremented produces 000. On this transition the carry signal is active and C is set to 1.

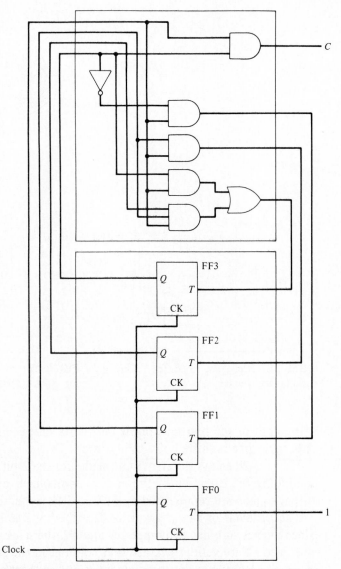

FIG. 5-17 Logic diagram for the decade counter defined in Figs. 5-14 and 5-15

The truth table for C and B and the extended truth table for the flip-flop inputs can be developed from either the state table or diagram using the transition table for the selected flip-flop type. From these truth tables, minimum sum-of-products equations can be obtained and used in drawing a logic diagram.

A 2-Bit Shift Register

As a third example let us consider a 2-bit shift register, a sequential network that transfers the contents of each flip-flop to an adjacent one. In this example, the direction of the transfer is controlled by an input signal; the contents are shifted to the right if this signal is active and to the left if it is inactive. Data

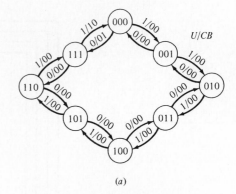

(a)

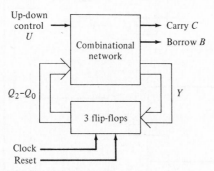

FIG. 5-18 Structural model for a 3-bit up-down binary counter

Present state $Q_2\,Q_1\,Q_0$			Input							
			0				1			
0 0 0			1	1	1/0	1	0	0	1/0	0
0 0 1			0	0	0/0	0	0	1	0/0	0
0 1 0			0	0	1/0	0	0	1	1/0	0
0 1 1			0	1	0/0	0	1	0	0/0	0
1 0 0			0	1	1/0	0	1	0	1/0	0
1 0 1			1	0	0/0	0	1	1	0/0	0
1 1 0			1	0	1/0	0	1	1	1/0	0
1 1 1			1	1	0/0	0	0	0	0/1	0

(b)

FIG. 5-19 (a) State diagram and (b) table for a 3-bit up-down binary counter

shifted out of the register appear on a data output line, and the value on the data input line is shifted into the register.

Figure 5-20 shows the structural model for the 2-bit shift register. The signal controlling the direction of the shift is symbolized by R; the data input and output signals are represented by DI and DO, respectively.

The behavior of this network is described by the state table in Table 5-4. Since the network has two inputs, R and DI, there are four input combinations; and since all are valid, there are four columns in the state table. There are two flip-flops, resulting in four present states, and so there are four rows in the table.

Internal entries are found by first recognizing the direction of the shift defined by R and then evaluating the output data and the effect of the shift on the contents of the register with the given input data. As an example, consider

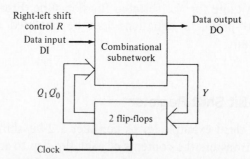

FIG. 5-20 Structural model for a 2-bit shift register

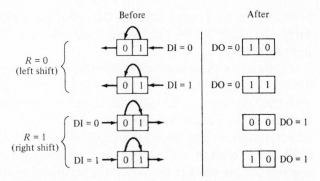

FIG. 5-21   Operation of a 2-bit shift register for present state of 01

each entry in the second row where the present state is 01. We shall use Fig. 5-21 to help define the corresponding next state and output.

In the upper two examples in Fig. 5-21 where $R = 0$, a shift toward the left results. Thus, the 0 in the left position is shifted to the data output; the 1 in the right position is shifted to the left position; and the input datum, regardless of whether it is 0 or 1, is shifted to the right position. In the lower two examples in this figure, where $R = 1$, a shift toward the right results. Thus, the 1 in the right position is shifted to the data output; the 0 in the left position is shifted to the right position; and the input datum is shifted to the left position. The first example indicates that for the input condition 00 and the present state 01, the next state is 10 and the output is 0. This is entered as 10/0 in the first internal column of the second row of Table 5-4. Similarly, the second example indicates that for input condition 01 and present state 01, the next state is 11 and the output is 0. The third example indicates that for input condition 10 and present state 01, the next state is 00 and the output is 1. The fourth example indicates that for input condition 11 and present state 01, the next state is 10 and the output is 1.

Entries in the other three rows are obtained in a similar manner. This state table can be transformed into truth tables and then into a logic diagram representing a minimum sum-of-products implementation.

An 8-Bit Shift Register

Although the approach based on the state table works with simple networks, it becomes too cumbersome as the number of flip-flops increases. Frequently the

TABLE 5-4   State Table for a 2-Bit Shift Register

Present State Q_1Q_0	Inputs R DI			
	0 0	0 1	1 0	1 1
00	00/0	01/0	00/0	10/0
01	10/0	11/0	00/1	10/1
10	00/1	01/1	01/0	11/0
11	10/1	11/1	01/1	11/1

network can be divided into smaller, identical units. These can be designed using the state table; the overall network is designed by specifying their interconnection.

To illustrate the use of subdivision we shall design a register which accepts 8 bits of parallel data and then shifts them out serially, i.e., bit by bit, starting with the least significant bit. This circuit is referred to as a **parallel-to-serial converter.** The circuit will have two control inputs: a data strobe signal (DS), which is active when the input parallel data is valid, and a shift-enable signal (SE), which must be active when the serial data are transferred. The first signal is active for one clock pulse to load the parallel data into the register; the second signal must be active for eight clock pulses to shift out all 8 bits. Figure 5-22a shows an input-output model for this network. The input-output model for a 1-bit unit is shown in Fig. 5-22b, and the interconnection of eight 1-bit units is shown in Fig. 5-22c.

Let us now define the state table for the identical unit. Since it contains only one flip-flop, it has just two present states. Also, it has four distinct input signals

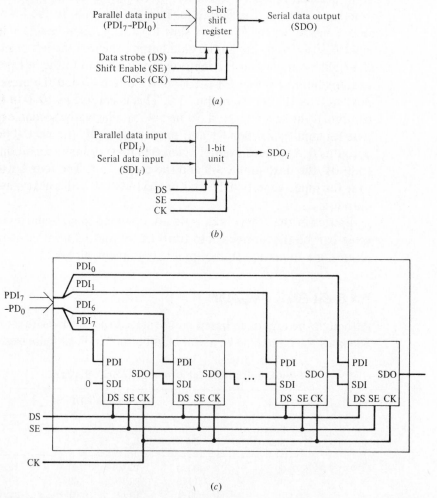

FIG. 5-22 An 8-bit shift register: (a) input-output model, (b) input-output model for a 1-bit unit, and (c) diagram showing interconnections

TABLE 5-5   State Table for Single Stage of 8-Bit Shift Register

Present state Q	Inputs DS SE PDI SDI			
	0000	0001	0010	0011
0	0/d	0/d	0/d	0/d
1	1/d	1/d	1/d	1/d
	0100	0101	0110	0111
	0/0	1/0	0/0	1/0
	0/1	1/1	0/1	1/1
	1000	1001	1010	1011
	0/d	0/d	1/d	1/d
	0/d	0/d	1/d	1/d
	1100	1101	1110	1111
	d/d	d/d	d/d	d/d
	d/d	d/d	d/d	d/d

so there are sixteen input combinations. Table 5-5 shows the state table for the 1-bit unit. In the first four columns since both control inputs are 0, there is no change in state and the output is a don't-care condition. In the second four columns, DS = 0 and SE = 1, and so the data on SDI will be shifted into the flip-flop and the present state will be shifted out of the flip-flop. Thus, the next state is defined by the value of SDI and the output is defined by the present state. In the next four columns, DS = 1 and SE = 0, and so data on PDI will be loaded into the flip-flop and the condition of the output is unimportant. Thus, the next state is defined by the value of PDI and the output is a don't-care condition. In the last four columns, DS = 1 and SE = 1. Because this represents an invalid input, both the next state and the output are don't-care conditions.

The state table in Table 5-5 can be transformed into a logic diagram using the techniques described in previous examples. The fact that there are four input variables and one state variable presents a small complication since we have not discussed the five-variable map. Instead we present a more intuitive approach for designing this identical unit. Note that its flip-flop must be set if both the data strobe signal DS and the parallel data input PDI are active or if both the shift-enable signal SE and the serial data input SDI are active. These conditions are summarized as

$$\text{SET} = \text{DS} \cdot \text{PDI}_i + \text{SE} \cdot \text{SDI}_i \qquad (5\text{-}4)$$

where SET is the signal to set the flip-flop. A similar relationship can be developed for the RESET signal:

$$\text{RESET} = \text{DS} \cdot \overline{\text{PDI}_i} + \text{SE} \cdot \overline{\text{SDI}_i} \qquad (5\text{-}5)$$

We also note that SDO$_i$ simply represents the true output of the flip-flop. From

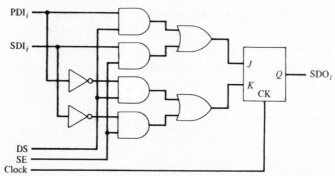

FIG. 5-23 Logic diagram for the 1-bit unit of the 8-bit shift register

this development we can construct a logic diagram for the single stage. Figure 5-23 shows this diagram using a *JK* flip-flop, where the logic gates implementing Eq. (5-4) are connected to the *J* input and those implementing Eq. (5-5) are connected to the *K* input.

5-7 IMPORTANT SEQUENTIAL NETWORKS

In this section we present examples of several important sequential networks available as single integrated circuits. They generally fit into three classes: counters, shift registers, and memory elements. Instead of the detailed models presented earlier in the chapter, we shall use abbreviated voltage tables to describe the behavior of these networks.

Counters

Counters are sequential networks that proceed through a sequence of states following a counting scheme. There are two general types, decade counters and binary counters. **Decade counters** contain four flip-flops and generate the sequence corresponding to $0, 1, \ldots, 8, 9, 0, 1$, and so on. **Binary counters** may contain three, four, or more flip-flops. An *N*-bit binary counter generates the sequence corresponding to $0, 1, \ldots, (2^N - 1), 0, 1$, and so on.

In addition to the clock, counters have other types of inputs which are useful in various applications. One example is an input to control the direction of the counting sequence. This input is referred to as the **up-down control line.** Many counters have a clear input which when active resets all flip-flops in the counter. A related group of inputs allows selective setting and resetting of all flip-flops in the counter. This group contains a control input, called the **load line** or **preset control line,** which when active transfers the data on a group of **preset input lines** to the flip-flops. Thus the counter can be preset to any value by placing the appropriate pattern on the preset inputs and activating the load line.

It is common to use the negative-logic assumption on the clear and load inputs so that these signals are active when at the low voltage level. Even in synchronous counters, these inputs may be asynchronous, so that the resulting transitions occur as soon as the input becomes active. Frequently these inputs are assigned a priority to define the dominant input if both are active at the same time.

In addition to the flip-flop outputs, there may be a **carry output,** indicating counter overflow, and a **borrow output,** indicating counter underflow.

As an example of a counter, we shall consider a presettable decade counter with asynchronous clear and preset inputs. Fig. 5-24 shows an input-output model of this network and an abbreviated voltage table describing its behavior. The outputs Q_3 to Q_0 represent the true outputs of the four flip-flops. The small circle on the CLEAR input indicates the negative-logic assumption, so that this input is active when at the low voltage level. The LOAD input uses the positive-logic assumption and is active at the high voltage level. The preset inputs X_3 to X_0 are connected to corresponding flip-flops. The CLOCK signal is active on the falling edge, as indicated by the small circle on this input in the model. The active phase of the clock pulse produces state transitions which correspond to incrementing the value stored in the flip-flops. Because the network is a decade counter, the sequence will correspond to 0, 1, 2, . . . , 8, 9, 0, 1, and so on.

The first row in the abbreviated voltage table indicates that the counter will be cleared if the CLEAR input is at the low voltage level regardless of the condition of the other inputs. Thus, the CLEAR signal has the highest priority. The second row indicates that if the CLEAR signal is inactive, i.e., at the high voltage level, and the LOAD signal is at the high voltage level, the flip-flops will be loaded or preset as defined by the preset inputs X_3 to X_0, regardless of the condition of the CLOCK signal. Thus, the LOAD signal has the second highest priority. The third row indicates that if the CLEAR and LOAD signals are inactive and the clock is stable, there will be no change in the flip-flops. The fourth row indicates that if the CLEAR and LOAD signals are inactive, the counter will increment its contents on the falling edge of the CLOCK pulse.

This network (or integrated-circuit device) can be used in many ways. Figure 5-25, a circuit containing two of these devices divides the input clock rate by 100; that is, it generates one clock pulse at the output for every 100 applied to the input. The INITIALIZE signal, generally applied at the start of operation,

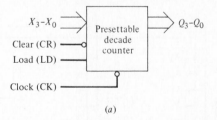

(*a*)

Inputs			Next	
Clear	Load	Clock	state	Comments
L	d	d	L L L L	All flip-flops cleared asynchronously
H	H	d	$X_3 X_2 X_1 X_0$	All flip-flops preset asynchronously
H	L	L or H	$(Q_3 Q_2 Q_1 Q_0)$	No change
H	L	↓	$(Q_3 Q_2 Q_1 Q_0) + 1$	Incremented with active phase

(*b*)

FIG. 5-24 Presettable decade counter: L = low voltage level, H = high voltage level, d = don't care condition, ↑ = falling-edge-triggered

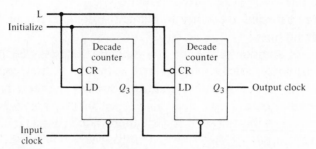

FIG. 5-25 Divide-by-100 network using the presettable decade counter in Fig. 5-24

ensures that the flip-flops are all reset. The first 10 input clock pulses will overflow the decade counter on the left, referred to as the less significant decade counter. On the tenth pulse, its Q_3 output will fall from the high to the low voltage level, and this transition will increment the decade counter on the right, referred to as the more significant decade counter. Since the more significant decade counter will increment once for each 10 input clock pulses, it will overflow after 100 input clock pulses and generate a high- to low-voltage-level transition on its Q_3 output. When this occurs, all flip-flops in the two-decade counter are reset and ready to repeat the process. Thus, the output clock rate will be one-hundredth the input rate.

Figure 5-26 shows a second application of the counter described in Fig. 5-24. This network, which divides the input clock rate by 360, makes use of the preset capability of the device. Without any presetting, a three-stage decade counter will divide by 1000; that is, there will be a high-to-low transition on Q_3 of the most significant decade counter after each 1000 input clock pulses. If the count is preset to 640, only 360 pulses will be required to produce this high-to-low transition. The preset inputs for the least significant decade counter, the one on the left, are all connected to the low voltage level; those for the middle one are arranged to preset with the value 4; while those for the most significant, the one

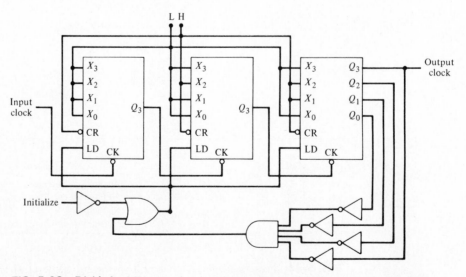

FIG. 5-26 Divide-by-360 network using the presettable decade counter in Fig. 5-24

on the right, are arranged to preset with the value 6. The preset enable signal LOAD can be activated by the INITIALIZE signal, assumed to be active when at the low level, or by an AND gate that detects when the contents of the most significant decade counter have a value zero. The last connection is necessary so that the overall network will repeatedly generate an output for every 360 input pulses.

Shift Registers

The **shift register** is a sequential network in which the contents of each flip-flop are transferred to the adjacent flip-flop in the register. The value in the last flip-flop in the register is shifted out of the register, and the value on the input line is shifted into the first flip-flop in the register. Frequently, shift registers have an additional input that controls whether the shift is to the left or to the right. In many shift registers a control line is provided to enable the loading of all flip-flops in parallel from their individual inputs. It is rare to find all these inputs, outputs, and controls on a single packaged shift register, but various combinations are available.

Two important shift-register configurations represent parallel-to-serial converters and serial-to-parallel converters. When each bit in a binary word is transferred simultaneously during a single time interval using a line for each bit, a **parallel transfer** is performed. When a multibit binary word is transferred bit by bit during successive time intervals using a single line, a **serial transfer** is performed. The terms parallel and serial also are used to describe binary words and information transferred in the corresponding way. With the **parallel-to-serial converter**, the shift register has a control line that loads each flip-flop simultaneously with the input parallel word and a second control line that shifts the data out as a serial word. With the **serial-to-parallel converter**, the serial data are shifted into the shift register and then transferred out as a parallel word. Figure 5-27 shows an input-output model and abbreviated voltage table for the 8-bit serial-to-parallel converter. The network has three input signals. The CLEAR signal, which is active when low and has the highest priority, resets all eight flip-flops. The other two inputs, the CLOCK signal and the DATA INPUT

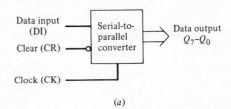

(a)

Inputs		Next state								Comments
Clear	Clock	Q_7	Q_6	Q_5	Q_4	Q_3	Q_2	Q_1	Q_0	
L	d	L	L	L	L	L	L	L	L	Clear
H	H or L	Q_7	Q_6	Q_5	Q_4	Q_3	Q_2	Q_1	Q_0	No change
H	↑	DI	Q_7	Q_6	Q_5	Q_4	Q_3	Q_2	Q_1	Shift

(b)

FIG. 5-27 An 8-bit serial-to-parallel converter

(DI) signal, control the serial loading of the network. During the active phase of the CLOCK cycle, which in this case is defined by the low to high transition, the contents of all flip-flops are transferred to the right position, and the level on DI is loaded into Q_7. After eight clock cycles, an 8-bit serial word will be loaded into the register and available in parallel form at the outputs Q_7 to Q_0.

Memory Elements

The simplest memory element is a single register, frequently referred to as a **latch** or **data buffer.** It serves as temporary storage for a parallel word which may be valid only during a specific time interval. This type of circuit is used in interfacing digital systems. Figure 5-28 shows the input-output model and an abbreviated voltage table for a synchronous 4-bit latch. The circuit has four data inputs D_3 to D_0, each connected to a flip-flop. The voltage levels on these lines are transferred to the flip-flops during the active phase of the CLOCK signal when the STROBE input is at the high level. The data, which are then stored in the register, are available at the outputs Q_3 to Q_0.

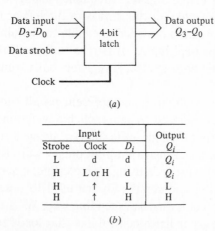

Input			Output
Strobe	Clock	D_i	Q_i
L	d	d	Q_i
H	L or H	d	Q_i
H	↑	L	L
H	↑	H	H

(b)

FIG. 5-28 A 4-bit latch

Integrated circuits with more than one register on the chip are available. Figure 5-29 shows the input-output model for a 4×8 **register file,** which has 32 flip-flops organized as four 8-bit words. There are eight data input lines DI_7 to DI_0, and the values on these lines can be loaded or written into any of the four 8-bit registers. There are also eight data output lines DO_7 to DO_0, and the contents of any of the four registers can be placed on these lines. The direction of data flow, i.e., whether it is written into a register or read from a register, is controlled by the read-write (R/W) line. When this line is at the low voltage level, data will be transferred or written into the network; when it is high level, data will be transferred or read from the network. The specific register involved in the transfer is defined by the two address lines. These two lines can assume four conditions, LL, LH, HL, and HH. Each condition is used to designate one of the four registers. As an example of the operation of this network, the condition where R/W = L, A_1 = H, and A_0 = L stores or writes the value on the data input lines DI_7 to DI_0 into register 2 and holds the output lines DO_7 to DO_0 at the high voltage level. Similarly, when R/W = H, A_1 = L, A_0 = H, the contents of register 1 appear on the output lines and the data on DI_7 to DI_0 are ignored.

As semiconductor technology advanced, the size of the register files grew. This increasing complexity required more and more input and output connections. Since the number of input and output connections is a complicating factor in both the manufacture and use of the devices, methods for reducing the number of connections were introduced. An important development was the intro-

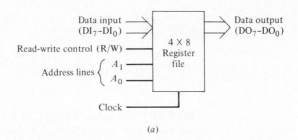

(a)

Inputs			Register contents				Output
R/W	A_1	A_2	Reg 0	Reg 1	Reg 2	Reg 3	D_o
L	L	L	DI	—	—	—	H
L	L	H	—	DI	—	—	H
L	H	L	—	—	DI	—	H
L	H	H	—	—	—	DI	H
H	L	L	—	—	—	—	Reg 0
H	L	H	—	—	—	—	Reg 1
H	H	L	—	—	—	—	Reg 2
H	H	H	—	—	—	—	Reg 3

Dash indicates no change

(b)

FIG. 5-29 A 4 X 8 register file

duction of the bidirectional data line. Figure 5-30 shows the input-output model for the 4 × 8 register file using bidirectional data lines.

The connection of a bidirectional line to a flip-flop cell is shown in Fig. 5-31. In addition to the bidirectional data line and the read-write control line, there is another input enabling this specific cell. This signal is generated elsewhere on the integrated circuit from the input address lines. A new symbol representing a **three-state buffer** is shown in the figure. The behavior of this element is described in Fig. 5-32. Note that the output of this element has three states, the

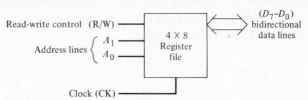

FIG. 5-30 A 4 X 8 register file with bidirectional data lines

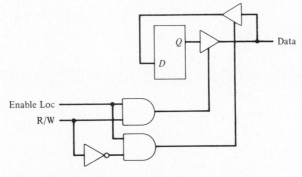

FIG. 5-31 Flip-flop cell with bidirectional data lines

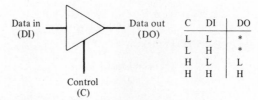

C	DI	DO
L	L	*
L	H	*
H	L	L
H	H	H

FIG. 5-32 Three-state buffer; L = low voltage level, H = high voltage level, * = high-impedance state

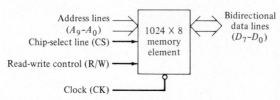

FIG. 5-33 Input-output model for memory element

standard low and high voltage states and a third state referred to as the high-impedance state. When the circuit is in this state, its output essentially is an open circuit. If the control input is at the high level, the output is at the same level as the input. However, if the control input is at the low level, the output is in the high-impedance state. This arrangement is necessary for two reasons: (1) it coordinates the use of a single data line with the flip-flop input and output, and (2), more important, it eliminates electrical problems that could result from connecting the same data line to a large number of flip-flop cells.

Currently register files containing hundreds and even thousands of registers are available on a single integrated circuit. Because of the large storage capacity, they are called **memory elements.** Fig. 5-33 shows the input-output model for a 1024 × 8 memory element requiring 10 address lines to specify uniquely the 1024 8-bit registers. In addition, there is a chip-select line that also must be activated for any data transfers.

sec.6

The Arithmetic-Logic Unit

Thomas C. Bartee

6-1 INTRODUCTION

The arithmetic-logic unit (ALU) is the section of the computer that performs arithmetic and logical operations on the data processed by the computer. This section of the machine can be relatively small, consisting of perhaps one or more large-scale integration (LSI) chips, or, for large "number crunchers" (scientific-oriented computers), it can consist of a considerable array of high-speed logic components. Despite the variations in size and complexity, the small machines generally perform their arithmetic and logical operations using the same principles as the large machines. What changes is the speed of the logic gates and flip-flops used; also, special techniques are used for speeding up operations and performing several operations in parallel.

Although many functions can be performed by the ALUs of present-day machines, the basic arithmetic operations—addition, subtraction, multiplication, and division—continue to be "bread-and-butter" operations. Even the literature gives evidence of the fundamental nature of these operations, for when a new machine is described, the times required for addition and multiplication are always included as significant features. Accordingly, this chapter first describes the means by which a computer adds, subtracts, multiplies, and divides. Other basic operations, such as shifting, logical multiplication, and logical addition, are then described.

It should be remembered that the control unit directs the operation of the ALU. What the ALU does is to add, subtract, shift, etc., when it is provided with the correct sequence of input signals. It is up to the control element to provide these signals, as it is the function of the memory units to provide the arithmetic element with the information that is to be used. It will therefore be assumed that the control and memory sections of the machine are capable of delivering the correct control signals, and that the data on which the operations are to be performed are available. The function of the ALU is therefore to add, subtract, or perform whatever operation the control element directs.

6-2 CONSTRUCTION OF THE ALU

The information handled in a computer is generally divided into "words," each consisting of a fixed number of bits. For instance, the words handled by a given binary machine may be 32 bits in length. In this case, the ALU would have to be capable of adding, subtracting, etc., words of 32 bits in length. The operands used are then supplied from computer storage, and the control element directs the operations that are performed. If addition is to be performed, the addend and augend will be supplied to the ALU which must add the numbers and then, at least temporarily, store the results (sum).

To introduce several concepts, let us consider the construction of a typical computer ALU. The storage devices will consist of a set of flip-flop **registers,** each of which consists of one or more flip-flops. The **length** of each register is defined as the maximum amount of information the register can store. In a binary register, the register length is equal to the maximum number of binary digits that can be stored; and in a binary-coded-decimal (BCD) register, the register length will be the number of decimal digits the register can store.

For convenience, the various registers of the ALU are generally given names such as X register, B register, MQ register, etc., and the flip-flops are then given the same names, so that the X register would contain flip-flops X_1, X_2, X_3, etc.

Most computers (especially microprocessors) have a register called an **accu-**

mulator which is the principal register for arithmetic and logical operations. This register stores the result of each arithmetic or logical operation, and gating circuitry is attached to this register so that the necessary operations can be performed on its contents and any other registers involved.

An accumulator is therefore a basic storage register of the arithmetic element. If the machine is instructed to **load** the accumulator, the control element will first clear the accumulator of whatever may have been stored in it and then put the operand selected in storage into the accumulator register. If the computer is instructed to add, the number stored in the accumulator will represent the augend. The addend will then be located in memory, and the computer's circuitry will add this number (the addend) to the number previously stored in the accumulator (the augend) and store the sum in the accumulator. Notice that the original augend will no longer be stored in the accumulator after the addition. Furthermore, the sum may then either remain in the accumulator or be transferred to memory, depending on the type of computer. This chapter will deal only with the processes of adding, subtracting, etc., and not the process of locating the number to be added in memory or the transferring of numbers to memory.

Some computers, instead of having a single accumulator, will have two or more accumulators, and these are called, for instance, accumulator A and accumulator B (as in the 6800 Microprocessor) or ACC1, ACC2, etc. (as in the Data General Corporation computers). When the number of registers provided to hold operands becomes larger than four, however, the registers are often called **general registers,** and individual registers are given names, such as general register 4, general register 8, etc.

6-3 INTEGER REPRESENTATION

The numbers used in digital machines must be represented using such storage devices as flip-flops. The most direct number representation system for binary-valued storage devices is an **integer representation system.** Figure 6-1(a) shows

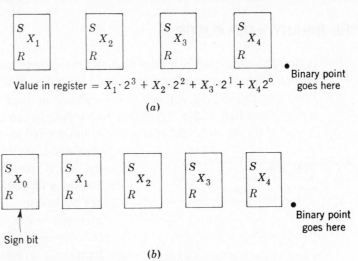

FIG. 6-1 Representation systems (a) Integer representation (b) Sign-plus-magnitude system

a register of four flip-flops, X_1, X_2, X_3, and X_4, used to store numbers. Simply writing the values or states of the flip-flops gives the number in integer form, so that $X_1 = 1$, $X_2 = 1$, $X_3 = 0$, $X_4 = 0$ gives 1100, or decimal 12, while $X_1 = 0$, $X_2 = 1$, $X_3 = 0$, $X_4 = 1$ gives 0101, or decimal 5.

It is generally necessary to represent both positive and negative numbers; so an additional bit is required, called the **sign bit.** This is generally placed to the left of the magnitude bits. In Fig. 6-1(b) we choose X_0 as the sign bit, and X_1, X_2, X_3, and X_4 will give the magnitude. A 0 in X_0 means that the number is positive, and a 1 in X_0 means that the number is negative (this is the usual convention); so $X_0 = 0$, $X_1 = 1$, $X_2 = 1$, $X_3 = 0$, and $X_4 = 1$ gives positive 1101, or $+13$ in decimal, and $X_0 = 1$, $X_1 = 1$, $X_2 = 1$, $X_3 = 0$, and $X_4 = 1$ gives negative 1101, or -13 in decimal.

This system is called the **signed-integer binary system,** or **signed magnitude binary integer system.**

If a register contains eight flip-flops, a signed binary number in the system would have 7 magnitude, or integer, bits and a single sign bit. So 00001111 would be $+15$ and 10001111 would be -15, since the leading 0 and 1 give the $+$ and $-$ only.

The magnitudes of numbers which can be stored in the two representative systems in Fig. 6-1 are as follows:

1. For binary integer representation, an n-flip-flop register can store from (decimal) 0 to $2^n - 1$. Thus for a 6-bit register, we can store from 000000 to 111111, where 111111 is 63, which is $2^6 - 1$, or $64 - 1$.

2. The signed binary integer representation system has a range of from $-(2^{n-1} - 1)$ to $+(2^{n-1} - 1)$ for a binary register. For instance, a 7-flip-flop register can store from -111111 to $+111111$, which is -63 to $+63[-(2^6 - 1)$ to $+(2^6 - 1)]$.

In the following sections we shall learn how to perform various arithmetic and logical operations on registers.

6-4   THE BINARY HALF ADDER

A basic module used in binary arithmetic elements is the **half adder.** The function of the half adder is to add two binary digits, producing a sum and a carry according to the binary addition rules shown in Table 6-1. Figure 6-2 shows a design for a half adder. There are two inputs to the half adder, designated as X and Y in Fig. 6-2, and two outputs, designated as S and C. The half adder performs the binary addition operation for two binary inputs shown in Table 6-1. This is **arithmetic addition,** not logical or Boolean algebra addition.

As shown in Fig. 6-2, there are two inputs to the half adder and two outputs. If either of the inputs is a 1, but not both, the output on the S line will be a 1. If both of the inputs are

TABLE 6-1

INPUTS	SUM BIT
0 + 0	0
0 + 1	1
1 + 0	1
1 + 1	0 with a carry of 1

1s, the output on the C (for carry) line will be a 1. For all other states there will be a 0 output on the CARRY line. These relationships may be written in Boolean form as follows:

$$S = X\overline{Y} + \overline{X}Y$$
$$C = XY$$

A **quarter adder** consists of the two inputs to the half adder and the S output only. The logical expression for this circuit is therefore $S = X\overline{Y} + \overline{X}Y$. This is also the **exclusive OR** relationship for Boolean algebra.

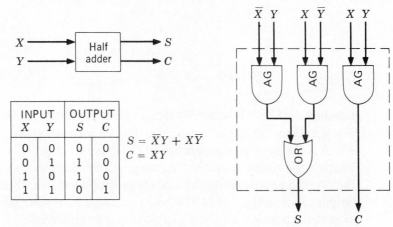

FIG. 6-2 Half adder

6-5 THE FULL ADDER

When more than two binary digits are to be added, several half adders will not be adequate, for the half adder has no input to handle carries from other digits. Consider the addition of the following two binary numbers:

$$
\begin{array}{ll}
\quad 1011 & \quad 1011 \\
+\ 1110 & +\ 1110 \\
\hline
11001 = \text{sum} & \quad 0101 = \text{partial sum} \\
& \quad \underline{1\ 1} \quad = \text{carry bits} \\
& \ 11001 = \text{complete sum}
\end{array}
$$

As shown, the carries generated in each column must be considered during the addition process. Therefore adder circuitry capable of adding the contents of two registers together must include provision for handling carries as well as addend and augend bits. There must therefore be three inputs to each stage of a multidigit adder—except the stage for the least significant bits—one for each input from the numbers being added and one for any carry that might have been generated or propagated by the previous stage.

The block diagram symbol for a **full binary adder,** which will handle these carries, is illustrated in Fig. 6-3, as is the complete table of input-output rela-

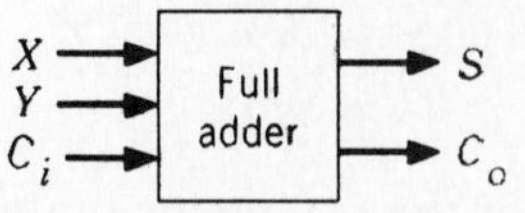

INPUT			OUTPUT	
X	Y	C_i	S	C_o
0	0	0	0	0
0	0	1	1	0
0	1	0	1	0
0	1	1	0	1
1	0	0	1	0
1	0	1	0	1
1	1	0	0	1
1	1	1	1	1

$$S = \overline{X}\,\overline{Y}C_i + \overline{X}Y\overline{C}_i + X\overline{Y}\,\overline{C}_i + XYC_i$$
$$C_o = \overline{X}YC_i + X\overline{Y}C_i + XY\overline{C}_i + XYC_i$$
$$\text{or}$$
$$C_o = XC_i + XY + YC_i$$

FIG. 6-3   Full adder

tionships for the full adder. There are three inputs to the full adder: the X and Y inputs from the respective digits of the registers to be added, and the C_i input, which is for any carry generated by the previous stage. The two outputs are S, which is the output value for that stage of the addition, and C_o, which produces the carry to be added into the next stage. The Boolean expressions for the input-output relationships for each of the two outputs are also presented in Fig. 6-3, as is the expression for the C_o output in simplified form.

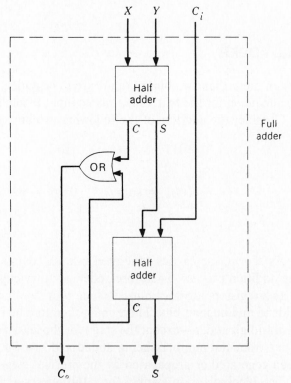

FIG. 6-4   Half-adder and full-adder relationship

A full adder may be constructed of two half adders, as illustrated in Fig. 6-4. Constructing a full adder from two half adders may not necessarily be the most economical technique, however, and generally full adders are designed directly from the input-output relations illustrated in Fig. 6-3.

6-6 A PARALLEL BINARY ADDER

A 4-bit parallel binary adder is illustrated in Fig. 6-5. The purpose of this adder is to add together two 4-bit binary integers. The addend inputs are named X_1 through X_4, and the augend bits are represented by Y_1 through Y_4. The adder shown does not possess the ability to handle sign bits for the binary words to be added, but only adds together the magnitudes of the numbers stored. The additional circuitry needed to handle sign bits is dependent on whether negative numbers are represented in true magnitude or in the 1s or 2s complement systems, and this problem will be described later.

Consider the addition of the following two 4-bit binary numbers:

$$0111 \text{ where } X_1 = 0, X_2 = 1, X_3 = 1, \text{ and } X_4 = 1$$
$$\underline{0011} \text{ where } Y_1 = 0, Y_2 = 0, Y_3 = 1, \text{ and } Y_4 = 1$$
$$\text{sum} = 1010$$

The sum should therefore be $S_1 = 1, S_2 = 0, S_3 = 1,$ and $S_4 = 0$.

The operation of the adder may be checked as follows. Since X_4 and Y_4 are the least significant digits, they cannot receive a carry from a previous stage. In the problem above, X_4 and Y_4 are both 1s, their sum is therefore 0, and a carry is generated and added into the full adder for bits X_3 and Y_3. Bits X_3 and Y_3 are also both 1s, as is the carry input to this stage. Therefore the sum output line S_3 carries a 1 and the CARRY line to the next stage also carries a 1. Since X_2 is a 1, Y_2 a zero, and the carry input is 1, the sum output line S_2 will carry a 0, and the carry to the next stage will be a 1. Both inputs X_1 and Y_1 are equal

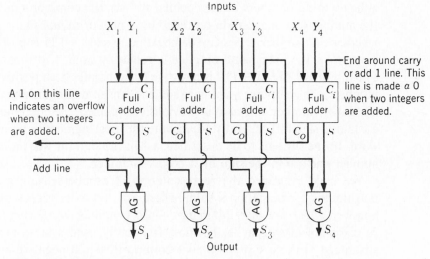

FIG. 6-5 Parallel adder

to 0, and the CARRY input line to this adder stage is equal to 1. Therefore the sum output line S_l will represent a 1 and the CARRY output line, designated as "overflow" in Fig. 6-5, will have a zero output.

The same basic configuration illustrated in Fig. 6-5 may be extended to any number of bits. A 7-bit adder may be constructed using 7 full adders, and a 20-bit adder using 20 full adders.

It should be noted that the OVERFLOW line could be used to enable the 4-bit adder in Fig. 6-5 to have a 5-bit output. This is not generally done, however, because the addend and augend both come from storage, and so their length is the length of the basic computer word, and a longer word cannot be readily stored by the machine. It was explained earlier that a machine with a word length of n bits [consisting of sign bit and $(n - 1)$ bits to designate the magnitude] could express binary numbers from $(-2^{n-1} + 1)$ to $(2^{n-1} - 1)$. A number within these limits is called **representable.** Since the simple 4-bit adder in Fig. 6-5 has no sign bit, it can only represent binary integers from 0 to 15. If 1100 and 1100 are added in the adder illustrated in Fig. 6-5, there will be a 1 output on the OVERFLOW line because the sum of these two numbers is 11000. This number is 24 decimal and cannot be represented in this system. Such a number is referred to as **nonrepresentable** for this particular very small register, and when two integers are added such that their sum is nonrepresentable (that is, contains too many bits), then we say the sum **overflows,** or an **overflow** occurs. A 1 on the CARRY line for the full adder connected to the most significant digits indicates this. The overflow generated in this case is often connected to circuitry which alerts the computer, generating an indication that an overflow operation has occurred. It is one of the functions of the arithmetic element to detect such overflows.

The AND gates connected to the S output lines from the four adders are used to gate the sum into the correct register.

6-7 POSITIVE AND NEGATIVE NUMBERS

When writing numbers in the decimal system, the common practice is to write the number as a magnitude preceded by a plus or minus sign, which indicates whether the number is positive or negative. Hence $+125$ is positive and -125 is negative 125. The same practice is generally used with binary numbers: $+111$ is positive 7, and -110 is negative 6. To handle both positive and negative numbers, the computer must have some means of distinguishing a positive from a negative number, and as was previously explained, the computer word usually contains a sign bit, generally adjacent to the most significant bit in the computer word. In the systems to be described, a 1 in the sign bit will indicate a negative number and a 0 in the sign bit a positive number.

We have examined the representation of numbers using a signed-integer magnitude representation system. There are two other representation systems, however, which are more often used—the 1s and 2s complement systems. (The 2s complement system is the most frequently used system at present.) The advantage of these systems is that both positive and negative numbers can be added or subtracted using only an adder of the type already explained.

Here are the three basic systems.

1. Negative numbers may be stored in their **true magnitude form.** The binary number − 0011 will therefore be stored as 1.0011, where the 1 indicates that the number stored is negative and the 0011 indicates the magnitude of the number.

2. The **1s complement** of the magnitude may be used to represent a negative number. The binary number −0111 will therefore be represented as 1.1000, where the 1 indicates that the number is negative and 1000 is the 1s complement of the magnitude. (The 1s complement is formed by simply complementing each bit of the positive magnitude.)

3. The **2s complement** may be used to represent a negative binary number. For instance, −0111 would be stored as 1.1001, where the 1 in the sign bit indicates that the number is negative and the 1001 is the 2s complement of the magnitude of the number. (The 2s complement is formed by 1s complementing the magnitude part 0111, giving 1000, and then adding 1 to the least significant digit, giving 1001.)

6-8 ADDITION IN THE 1S COMPLEMENT SYSTEM

The 1s complement system for representing negative numbers is often used in parallel binary machines. The main reason for this is the ease with which the 1s complement of a binary number may be formed, since only complementing each bit of a binary number stored in a flip-flop register is required. Before discussing the implementations of an adder for the 1s complement system, the four possible basic situations which may arise in adding combinations of positive and negative numbers in the 1s complement system will be noted:

1. When a positive number is added to another positive number, the addition of all bits, including the sign bit, is straightforward. Since both sign bits will be 0s, no sum or carry will be generated in the sign-bit adder and the output will remain 0. Here is an example of the addition of two 4-bit positive numbers.

NORMAL NOTATION	COMPUTER WORD
+0011	0.0011
+0100	0.0100
+0111	0.0111

2. When a positive and a negative number are added together, the sum may be either positive or negative. If the positive number has a greater magnitude, the sum will be positive; and if the negative number is greater in magnitude, the sum will be negative. In the 1s complement system, the answer will be correct as is if the sum of the two numbers is negative in value. In this case no overflow will be generated when the numbers are added. For instance:

+0011	0.0011
−1100	1.0011
−1001	1.0110

In this case the output of the adder will be 10110, the last 4 bits which are the 1s complement of 1001, the correct magnitude of the sum. The 1 in the sign bit is also correct, indicating a negative number.

3. If the positive number is larger than the negative number, the sum before the end-around carry is added will be incorrect. The addition of the end-around carry will correct this sum. There will be a 0 in the sign bit, indicating that the sum is positive.

$$
\begin{array}{rcl}
+1001 &=& 0.1001 \\
-0100 &=& 1.1011 \\
\hline
+0101 & & 0.0100 \\
& & \qquad\longrightarrow 1 \\
\hline
& & 0.0101
\end{array}
\qquad
\begin{array}{rcl}
+0011 &=& 0.0011 \\
-0010 &=& 1.1101 \\
\hline
+0001 & & 0.0000 \\
& & \qquad\longrightarrow 1 \\
\hline
& & 0.0001
\end{array}
$$

Notice what happens when two numbers of equal magnitude but opposite signs are added:

$$
\begin{array}{rcl}
+1011 &=& 0.1011 \\
-1011 &=& 1.0100 \\
\hline
0000 & & 1.1111
\end{array}
\qquad
\begin{array}{rcl}
+0000 &=& 0.0000 \\
-0000 &=& 1.1111 \\
\hline
0000 & & 1.1111
\end{array}
$$

The result in these cases will be a negative zero (1.1111), which is correct.

4. When two negative numbers are added together, an end-around carry will always be generated, as will a carry from the adder for the first bits of the magnitudes of the numbers. This will place a 1 in the sign bit.

$$
\begin{array}{rcl}
-0011 &=& 1.1100 \\
-1011 &=& 1.0100 \\
\hline
-1110 & & 1.0000 \\
& & \qquad\longrightarrow 1 \\
\hline
& & 1.0001
\end{array}
\qquad
\begin{array}{rcl}
-0100 &=& 1.1011 \\
-0111 &=& 1.1000 \\
\hline
-1011 & & 1.0011 \\
& & \qquad\longrightarrow 1 \\
\hline
& & 1.0100
\end{array}
$$

The output of the adder will be in 1s complement form in each case, with a 1 in the sign-bit position.

From the above we see that in order to implement an adder which will handle 4-bit magnitude signed 1s complement numbers, we can simply add another full adder to the configuration in Fig. 6-5. The sign inputs will be labeled X_0 and Y_0, and the C_o output from the adder connected to X_1 and Y_1 will be connected to the C_i input of the new full adder for X_0 and Y_0. The C_o output from the adder for X_0 and Y_0 will be connected to the C_i input for the adder for X_4 and Y_4. The S_0 output from the new adder will give the sign digit for the sum. (Overflow will not be detected in this adder; additional gates are required.)

6-9 ADDITION IN THE 2S COMPLEMENT SYSTEM

When negative numbers are represented in the 2s complement system, the operation of addition is very similar to that in the 1s complement system. In parallel machines, the 2s complement of a number stored in a register may be formed by first complementing the register and then adding 1 to the least significant bit of the register. This process requires two steps and is therefore more time-consuming than the 1s complement system. However, the 2s complement system has the advantage of not requiring an end-around carry during addition.

The four situations which may occur in adding two numbers when the 2s complement system is used are as follows:

1. When both numbers are positive, the situation is completely identical with that in case 1 in the 1s complement system which has been discussed.

2. When one number is positive and the other negative, and the larger number is the positive number, a carry will be generated through the sign bit. This carry may be discarded, since the outputs of the adder are correct, as shown below:

$$
\begin{array}{rr}
+0111 = & 0.0111 \\
-0011 = & +1.1101 \\
\hline
+0100 & 0.0100 \\
& \llcorner\!\!\rightarrow \text{carry is discarded}
\end{array}
\qquad
\begin{array}{rr}
+1000 = & 0.1000 \\
-0111 = & +1.1001 \\
\hline
+0001 & 0.0001 \\
& \llcorner\!\!\rightarrow \text{carry is discarded}
\end{array}
$$

3. When a positive and negative number are added and the negative number is the larger, no carry will result in the sign bit, and the answer will again be correct as it stands:

$$
\begin{array}{rl}
+0011 = & 0.0011 \\
-0100 = & 1.1100 \\
\hline
-0001 & 1.1111
\end{array}
\qquad
\begin{array}{rl}
+0100 = & 0.0100 \\
-1000 = & 1.1000 \\
\hline
-0100 & 1.1100
\end{array}
$$

Note: A 1 must be added to the least significant bit of a 2s complement negative number when converting it to a magnitude. For example:

$$
\begin{array}{rl}
1.0011 = & 1100 \text{ form the 1s complement} \\
& \underline{0001} \text{ add 1} \\
\hline
& -1101
\end{array}
$$

When both numbers are the same magnitude, the result is as follows:

$$
\begin{array}{rl}
+0011 = & 0.0011 \\
-0011 = & 1.1101 \\
\hline
0000 & 0.0000
\end{array}
$$

When a positive and a negative number of the same magnitude are added, the result will be a positive zero.

4. When the two negative numbers are added together, a carry will be generated in the sign bit and also in the bit to the right of the sign bit. This will cause a 1 to be placed in the sign bit, which is correct, and the carry from the sign bit may be discarded.

$$
\begin{array}{rr}
-0011 = & 1.1101 \\
-0100 = & 1.1100 \\
\hline
-0111 & 1.1001 \\
& \llcorner\!\!\rightarrow \text{carry is discarded}
\end{array}
\qquad
\begin{array}{rl}
-0011 = & 1.1101 \\
-1011 = & 1.0101 \\
\hline
1110 & 1.0010
\end{array}
$$

For parallel machines, addition of positive and negative numbers is quite simple, since any overflow from the sign bit is simply discarded. Thus for the parallel adder in Fig. 6-5 we simply add another full adder, with X_0 and Y_0 as inputs and with the CARRY line C_o from the full adder, which adds X_1 and Y_1, connected to the carry input C_i to the full adder for X_0 and Y_0. A 0 is placed on the C_i input to the adder connected to X_4 and Y_4.

This simplicity in adding and subtracting has made the 2s complement system the most popular for parallel machines. In fact, when signed-magnitude systems are used, the numbers generally are converted to 2s complement before addition of negative numbers or subtraction is performed. Then the numbers are changed back to signed magnitude.

6-10 ADDITION AND SUBTRACTION IN A PARALLEL ARITHMETIC ELEMENT

We now examine the design of a gating network which will either add or subtract two numbers. The network is to have an ADD input line and a SUBTRACT input line as well as the lines that carry the representation of the numbers to be added or subtracted. When the ADD line is a 1, the sum of the numbers is to be on the output lines, and when the SUBTRACT line is a 1, the difference is to be on the output lines. If both ADD and SUBTRACT are 0s, the output is to be 0.

First we note that if the machine is capable of adding both positive and negative numbers, subtraction may be performed by complementing the subtrahend and then adding. For instance, $8 - 4$ yields the same result as $8 + (-4)$, and $6 - (-2)$ yields the same result as $6 + 2$. Subtraction therefore may be performed by an arithmetic element capable of adding, by forming the complement of the subtrahend and then adding. For instance, in the 1s complement system, four cases may arise:

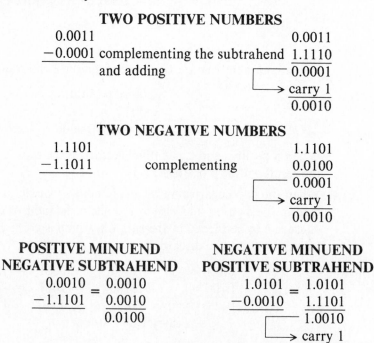

TWO POSITIVE NUMBERS

0.0011	0.0011
-0.0001 complementing the subtrahend	1.1110
and adding	0.0001
	carry 1
	0.0010

TWO NEGATIVE NUMBERS

1.1101	1.1101
-1.1011 complementing	0.0100
	0.0001
	carry 1
	0.0010

POSITIVE MINUEND NEGATIVE SUBTRAHEND

$$\begin{array}{c} 0.0010 \\ -1.1101 \end{array} = \begin{array}{c} 0.0010 \\ 0.0010 \\ \hline 0.0100 \end{array}$$

NEGATIVE MINUEND POSITIVE SUBTRAHEND

$$\begin{array}{c} 1.0101 \\ -0.0010 \end{array} = \begin{array}{c} 1.0101 \\ 1.1101 \\ \hline 1.0010 \end{array}$$
carry 1
1.0011

The same basic rules apply to subtraction in the 2s complement system, except that any carry generated in the sign-bit adders is simply dropped. In this case the 2s complement of the subtrahend is formed, and the complemented number is then added to the minuend with no end-around carry.

We now examine the implementation of a combined adder and subtracter network. The primary problem is to form the complement of the number to be subtracted. This complementation of the subtrahend may be performed in several ways. For the 1s complement system, if the storage register is composed of flip-flops, the 1s complement can be formed by simply connecting the complement of each input to the adder. The 1 which must be added to the least significant position to form a 2s complement may be added when the two numbers are added by connecting a 1 at the CARRY input of the adder for the least significant bits.

A complete logical circuit capable of adding or subtracting two signed 2s complement numbers is shown in Fig. 6-6. One number is represented by X_0, X_1, X_2, X_3, and X_4, and the other number by Y/Y_1, Y_2, Y_3, and Y_4. There are two control signals, ADD and SUBTRACT. If neither control signal is a 1 (that is, both are 0s), then the outputs from the five full adders, which are S_0, S_1, S_2, S_3, and S_4 will all be 0s. If the ADD control line is made a 1, the sum of the number X and the number Y will appear as S_0, S_1, S_2, S_3, and S_4. If the SUBTRACT line is made a 1, the difference between X and Y (that is, $X - Y$) will appear on S_0, S_1, S_2, S_3, and S_4.

Notice that the AND-to-OR gate network connected to each Y input selects either Y or $\overline{Y}$, so that, for instance, an ADD causes Y_1 to enter the appropriate full adder, while a SUBTRACT causes $\overline{Y}_1$ to enter the full adder.

To either add or subtract, each X input is connected to the appropriate full adder. When a subtraction is called for, the complement of each Y flip-flop is gated into the full adder, and a 1 is added by connecting the SUBTRACT signal to the C_i input of the full adder for the lowest order bits X_4 and Y_4. Since the SUBTRACT line will be a 0 when we add, a 0 carry will be on this line when addition is performed.

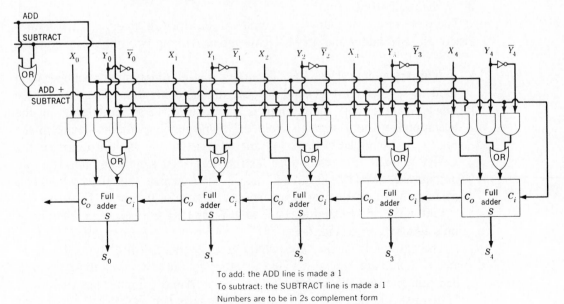

To add: the ADD line is made a 1
To subtract: the SUBTRACT line is made a 1
Numbers are to be in 2s complement form

FIG. 6-6 Parallel addition and subtraction

The simplicity of the operation of Fig. 6-6 makes 2s complement addition and subtraction very attractive for computer use, and it is the most frequently used system.

The configuration in Fig. 6-6 is the most frequently used for addition and subtraction because it provides a simple direct means for either adding or subtracting positive or negative numbers. Quite often the $S_0, S_1, \ldots, S_4$ lines are gated back into the X flip-flops, so that the sum or difference or the numbers X and Y replaces the original value of X.

An important consideration is overflow. In digital computers an **overflow** is said to occur when the performance of an operation results in a quantity beyond the capacity of the register (or storage register) which is to receive the result. Since the registers in Fig. 6-6 have a sign bit plus 4 magnitude bits, they can store from $+15$ to -16 in 2s complement form. Therefore, if the result of an addition or subtraction were greater than $+15$ or less than -16, we would say that an overflow had occurred. Suppose we add $+8$ to $+12$; the result should be $+20$, and this cannot be represented (fairly) in 2s complement on the lines $S_0, S_1, S_2, S_3,$ and S_4. The same thing happens if we add -13 and -7 or if we subtract -8 from $+12$. In each case logical circuitry is used to detect the overflow condition and signal the computer control element. Various options are then available, and what is done can depend on the type of instruction being executed. (Deliberate overflows are sometimes used in double-precision routines. Multiplication and division use the results as are.)

6-11 FULL ADDER DESIGNS

The full adder is a basic component of an arithmetic element. Figure 6-3 illustrated the block diagram symbol for the full adder, along with a table of combinations for the input-output values and the expressions describing the sum and carry lines. Succeeding figures and text described the operation of the full adder. Notice that a parallel addition system requires one full adder for each bit in the basic word.

There are of course many gate configurations for full binary adders. Examples of an IBM adder and an MSI package containing two full adders follow.

1. **Full binary adder**   Figure 6-7 illustrates the full binary adder configuration used in several IBM general-purpose digital computers. There are three inputs to the circuit: the X input is from one of the storage devices in the accumulator, the Y input is from the corresponding storage device in the register to be added to the accumulator register, and the third input is the CARRY input from the adder for the next least significant bit. The two outputs are the SUM output and the CARRY output. The SUM output will contain the sum value for this particular digit of the output. The CARRY output will be connected to the CARRY input of the next most significant bit's adder (refer to Fig. 6-5).

   The outputs from the three AND gates connected directly to the X, Y, and C inputs are logically added together by the OR gate circuit directly beneath. If either the X and Y, X and C, or Y and C input lines contains a 1, there should be a CARRY output. The output of this circuit, written in

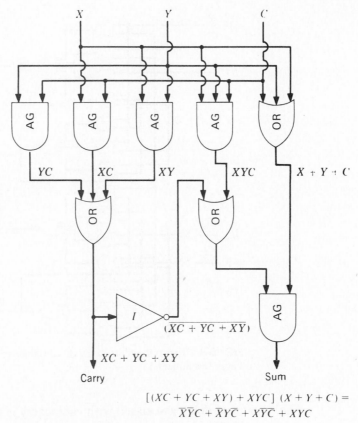

$$[(XC + YC + XY) + XYC](X + Y + C) =$$
$$\overline{X}\overline{Y}C + \overline{X}Y\overline{C} + X\overline{Y}\overline{C} + XYC$$

FIG. 6-7   Full adder used in IBM machines

logical equation form, is shown on the figure. This may be compared with the expression derived in Fig. 6-3.

The derivation of the SUM output is not so straightforward. The CARRY output expression $XY + XC + YC$ is first inverted (complemented), yielding $(\overline{XY + XC + YC})$. The logical product of X, Y, and C is formed by an AND gate and is logically added to this, forming $(\overline{XY + XC + YC})$ + XYC. The logical sum of X, Y, and C is then multiplied times this, forming the expression

$$[(\overline{XY + XC + YC}) + XYC](X + Y + C)$$

When multiplied out and simplified, this expression will be $\overline{X}\overline{Y}C + \overline{X}Y\overline{C}$ + $X\overline{Y}\overline{C} + XYC$, the expression derived in Fig. 6-3. Tracing through the logical operation of the circuit for various values will indicate that the SUM output will be 1 when only one of the input values is equal to 1, or when all three input values are equal to 1. For all other combinations of inputs the output value will be a 0.

2. **Two full adders in an integrated circuit (IC) container**   Figure 6-8 shows two full adders. This package was developed for integrated circuits using transistor-transistor logic (TTL). The entire circuitry is packaged in one IC container. The maximum delay from an input change to an output change for an S output is on the order of 8 nanoseconds (ns). The maximum delay from input to the $C2$ output is about 6 ns.

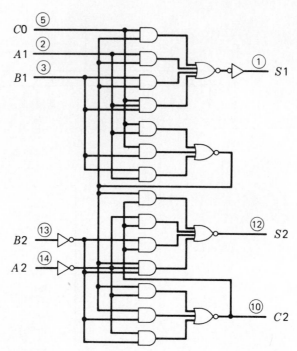

FIG. 6-8 Two full adders in an IC container (courtesy Texas Instruments)

The amount of delay associated with each carry is an important figure in evaluating a full adder for a parallel system, because the amount of time required to add two numbers is determined by the maximum time it takes for a carry to propagate through the adders. For instance, if we add 01111 to 10001 in the 2s complement system, the carry generated by the 1s in the least significant digit of each number must propagate through four carry stages and a sum stage before we can safely gate the sum into the accumulator. A study of the addition of these two numbers using the configuration in Fig. 6-5 will make this clear. The problem is called the **carry-ripple problem.**

There are a number of techniques which are used in high-speed machines to alleviate this problem. The most used is a bridging or carry-look-ahead circuit which calculates the carry-out of a number of stages simultaneously and then delivers this carry to the succeeding stages.

6-12 THE BINARY-CODED-DECIMAL (BCD) ADDER

Arithmetic units which perform operations on numbers stored in BCD form must have the ability to add 4-bit representations of decimal digits. To do this a BCD adder is used. A block diagram symbol for an adder is shown in Fig. 6-9. The adder has an augend digit input consisting of four lines, an addend digit input of four lines, a carry-in and a carry-out, and a sum digit with four output lines. The augend digit, addend digit, and sum digit are each represented in 8, 4, 2, 1 BCD code.

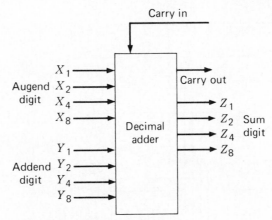

FIG. 6-9 Serial-parallel addition

The purpose of the BCD adder in Fig. 6-9 is to add the augend and addend digits and the carry-in and produce a sum digit and carry-out. It is possible to make a BCD adder using full adders and AND or OR gates. An adder made in this way is shown in Fig. 6-10.

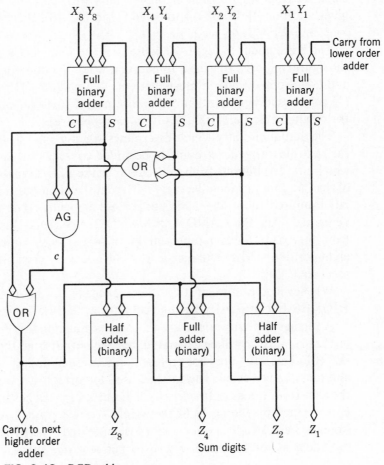

FIG. 6-10 BCD adder

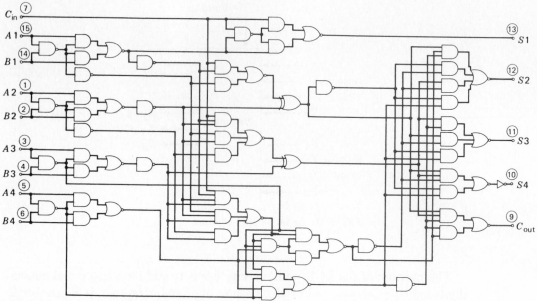

FIG. 6-11 Complete BCD adder in an IC package

There are eight inputs to the BCD adder, four X_i, or augend, inputs and four Y_i, or addend, digits. Each of these inputs will represent a 0 or a 1 during a given addition. If 3(0011) is to be added to 2(0010), then $X_8 = 0$, $X_4 = 0$, $X_2 = 1$, and $X_1 = 1$; $Y_8 = 0$, $Y_4 = 0$, $Y_2 = 1$, and $Y_1 = 0$.

The basic adder in Fig. 6-10 consists of the four binary adders at the top of the figure and performs base 16 addition when the intent is to perform base 10 addition. Some provision must therefore be made to (1) generate carries and (2) correct sums greater than 9. For instance, if $3_{10}(0011)$ is added to $8_{10}(1000)$, the result should be $1_{10}(0001)$ with a carry generated.

The actual circuitry which determines when a carry is to be transmitted to the next most significant digits to be added consists of the full binary adder to which sum (S) outputs from the adders for the 8, 4, 2 inputs are connected and of the OR gate to which the carry (C) from the eight-position bits is connected. An examination of the addition process indicates that a carry should be generated when the 8 AND 4, or 8 AND 2, or 8 AND 4 AND 2 sum outputs from the base 16 adder represent 1s, or when the CARRY output from the eight-position adder contains a 1. (This occurs when 8s or 9s are added together.)

Whenever the sum of two digits exceeds 9, the CARRY TO NEXT HIGHER ORDER ADDER line contains a 1 for the adder in Fig. 6-10.

A further difficulty arises when a carry is generated. If $7_{10}(0111)$ is added to $6_{10}(0110)$, a carry will be generated, but the output from the base 16 adder will be 1101. This 1101 does not represent any decimal digit in the 8, 4, 2, 1 system and must be corrected. The method used to correct this is to add $6_{10}(0110)$ to the sum from the base 16 adders whenever a carry is generated. This addition is performed by adding 1s to the weight 4 and weight 2 position output lines from the base 16 adder when a carry is generated. The two half adders and the full adder at the bottom of Fig. 6-10 perform this function. Essentially then, the adder performs base 16 addition and corrects the sum, if it is greater than 9, by adding 6. Several examples of this are shown below.

$$
\begin{array}{cccc}
 & (8) & (4) & (2) & (1) \\
\end{array}
$$

$$
8 + 7 = 15 \quad 1000 + 0111 =
\begin{array}{cccc}
1 & 1 & 1 & 1 \\
+0 & 1 & 1 & 0 \\
\hline
1 \quad 0 & 1 & 0 & 1 & = 5 \\
\end{array}
$$

└ with a carry generated

$$
\begin{array}{cccc}
 & (8) & (4) & (2) & (1) \\
\end{array}
$$

$$
9 + 5 = 14 \quad
\begin{array}{cccc}
1 & 0 & 0 & 1 \\
0 & 1 & 0 & 1 \\
\hline
1 & 1 & 1 & 0 \\
+0 & 1 & 1 & 0 \\
\hline
1 \quad 0 & 1 & 0 & 0 & \text{or } 4 \\
\end{array}
$$

└ with a carry generated

Figure 6-11 shows a complete BCD adder in an IC package. The inputs are digits A and digits B, and the outputs are S. A carry-in and a carry-out are included. The circuit line used is CMOS.

6-13 POSITIVE AND NEGATIVE BCD NUMBERS

The techniques for handling BCD numbers greatly resemble those for handling binary numbers. A sign bit is used to indicate whether the number is positive or negative, and there are three methods of representing negative numbers which must be considered. The first and most obvious method is, of course, to represent a negative number in true magnitude form with a sign bit, so that -645 is represented as 1.645. The other two possibilities are to represent negative numbers in a 9s or a 10s complement form, which resembles the binary 1s and 2s complement forms.

6-14 ADDITION AND SUBTRACTION IN THE 9S COMPLEMENT SYSTEM

When decimal numbers are represented in a binary code in which the 9s complement is formed when the number is complemented, the situation is roughly the same as when the 1s complement is used to represent a binary number. Four cases may arise: two positive numbers may be added; a positive and negative number may be added, yielding a positive result; a positive and a negative number may be added, yielding a negative result; and two negative numbers may be added. Since there is no problem when two positive numbers are added, the three latter situations will be illustrated.

Negative and positive number—positive sum:

$$+692 = 0.692$$
$$\underline{-342} = \underline{1.657}$$
$$+350 \ulcorner 0.349$$
$$ \llcorner\!\!\rightarrow 1$$
$$ 0.350$$

Positive and negative number—negative sum:

$$-631 = 1.368$$
$$\underline{+342} = \underline{0.342}$$
$$-289 1.710 = -289$$

Two negative numbers:

$$-248 = 1.751$$
$$\underline{-329} = \underline{1.670}$$
$$-577 \ulcorner 1.421$$
$$ \llcorner\!\!\rightarrow 1$$
$$ 1.422 = -577$$

The rules for handling negative numbers in the 10s complement system are the same as those for the binary 2s complement system in that no carry must be ended-around. A parallel BCD adder may therefore be constructed using only the full BCD adder as the basic component, and all combinations of positive and negative numbers may thus be handled.

There is an additional complexity in BCD addition, however, because the 9s complement of a BCD digit cannot be formed by simply complementing each bit in the representation. As a result, a gating block called a **complementer** must be used.

To illustrate the type of circuit which may be used to form complements of the code groups for BCD numbers, a block diagram of a logical circuit which will form the 9s complement of a code group representing a decimal number in

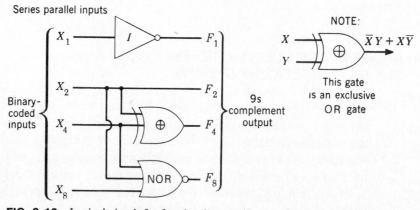

FIG. 6-12 Logical circuit for forming 9s complement of 8, 4, 2, 1 BCD digits

8, 4, 2, 1 BCD form is shown in Fig. 6-12. There are four inputs in the circuit, X_1, X_2, X_4, and X_8. Each of these inputs carries a different weight: X_1 has weight 1, X_2 has weight 2, X_4 has weight 4, and X_8 has weight 8. If the inputs represent a decimal digit of the number to be complemented, the outputs will represent the 9s complement of the input digit. For instance, if the input is 0010 (decimal 2), the output will be 0111 (decimal 7), the 9s complement of the input.

Figure 6-13 shows a complete 9s complementer in an IC package. The circuits used are CMOS, and so transmission gates appear in the block diagram as well as conventional gates. (This does not bother the circuit's user because the user is primarily interested in the circuit's function.) When the COMP input is a 1, the outputs $F1$-$F4$ represent the complement of the digit on $A1$-$A4$; while if COMP is a 0, the $A1$-$A4$ inputs are simply placed on $F1$-$F4$ without change.

By connecting the IC packages in Figs. 6-11 and 6-13 together, a BCD adder-subtracter can be formed as shown in Fig. 6-14. This shows that a two-digit adder-subtracter IC package would be required for more digits. In order to add the digits in the inputs, the ADD-SUBTRACT input is made a 1; to subtract, this signal is made a 0. (Making the ZERO input a 1 will cause the value of B to pass through unchanged.) BCD numbers may also be represented in parallel form, as we have shown, but a mode of operation called **series-parallel** is often used. If a decimal number is written in binary-coded form, the resulting number consists of a set of code groups, each of which represents a single decimal digit. For instance, decimal 463 in a BCD 8, 4, 2, 1 code is 0100 0110 0011. Each group of 4 bits represents one decimal digit. It is convenient to handle each code group which represents a decimal digit as a unit, that is, in parallel. At the same time, as the word lengths for decimal computers are apt to be rather long, it is desirable to economize in the amount of equipment used.

The **series-parallel** system provides a compromise in which each code group is handled in parallel, but the decimal digits are handled sequentially. This requires four lines for each 8, 4, 2, 1 BCD character, each input line of which carries a different weight. The block diagram for an adder operating in this system is shown in Fig. 6-15. There are two sets of inputs to the adder; one consists of the four input lines which carry the coded digit for the addend, and the other four input lines carry a coded augend digit. The sets of inputs arrive sequentially from the A and B registers, each of which consists of four shift registers; the least significant addend and augend BCD digits arrive first, followed by the more significant decimal digits.

If the 8, 4, 2, 1 code is used, let 324 represent the augend and 238 the addend. The ADD signal will be a 0. The adder will first receive 0100 on the augend lines, and at the same time it will receive 1000 on the addend lines. After the first clock pulse, these inputs will be replaced by 0010 on the augend lines and 0011 on the addend lines. Before the first clock signal, the sum lines should contain 0010, and before the second, 0110. A carry will be generated during the addition of the first two digits; this will be delayed and added in using the D flip-flop. The process will continue until each of the three digits has been added. To subtract B from A, we have only to make the ADD-SUBTRACT input a 1 and then apply the clocks.

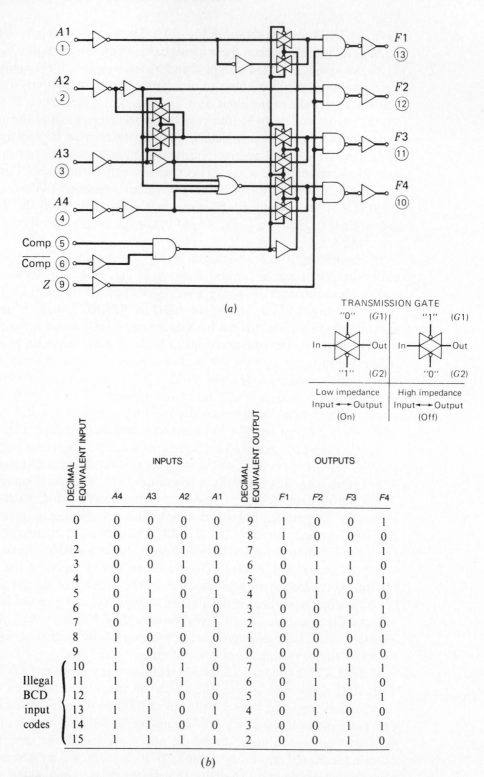

(a)

TRANSMISSION GATE

Low impedance		High impedance
Input ←→ Output		Input ←→ Output
(On)		(Off)

DECIMAL EQUIVALENT INPUT	INPUTS				DECIMAL EQUIVALENT OUTPUT	OUTPUTS			
	A4	A3	A2	A1		F1	F2	F3	F4
0	0	0	0	0	9	1	0	0	1
1	0	0	0	1	8	1	0	0	0
2	0	0	1	0	7	0	1	1	1
3	0	0	1	1	6	0	1	1	0
4	0	1	0	0	5	0	1	0	1
5	0	1	0	1	4	0	1	0	0
6	0	1	1	0	3	0	0	1	1
7	0	1	1	1	2	0	0	1	0
8	1	0	0	0	1	0	0	0	1
9	1	0	0	1	0	0	0	0	0
10	1	0	1	0	7	0	1	1	1
11	1	0	1	1	6	0	1	1	0
12	1	1	0	0	5	0	1	0	1
13	1	1	0	1	4	0	1	0	0
14	1	1	0	0	3	0	0	1	1
15	1	1	1	1	2	0	0	1	0

Illegal BCD input codes { 10–15

(b)

FIG. 6-13 9s complements in IC package (a) Logic diagram (b) Truth table

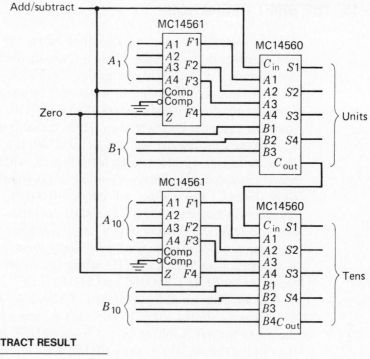

ZERO ADD/SUBTRACT RESULT

0	0	$B + A$
0	1	$B - A$
1	d	B

d = don't care

FIG. 6-14   Parallel add-subtract circuit (10s complement)

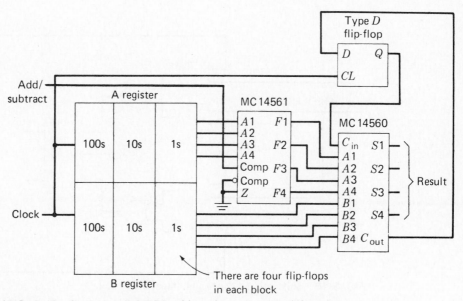

FIG. 6-15   Series-parallel BCD adder-subtractor using shift register

6-15 THE SHIFT OPERATION

A **shift operation** is an operation which moves the digits **stored** in a register to new positions in the register. There are two distinct shift operations, a shift-left operation and a shift-right operation. A shift-left operation moves each bit of information stored in a register to the left by some specified number of digits. Consider the following six binary digits, 000110, which we will assume to be stored in a parallel binary register. If the contents of the register are shifted left 1, after the shift register will contain 001100. If a shift right of 1 is performed on the word 000110, after the shift the register will contain 000011. The shifting process in a decimal register is similar: if the register contains 0.01234, after a right shift of 1 the register will contain 0.00123, or after a left shift of 1 the register will contain 0.12340. The shift operation is used in the MULTIPLY and the DIVIDE instructions of most machines and also is provided as an instruction which may be used by programmers. For instance, a machine may have instructions SHR and SHL, where the letters represent in mnemonic form the order for SHIFT-RIGHT and SHIFT-LEFT instructions.

A block diagram of logic circuitry for a single stage (flip-flop) in a register which can be shifted either left or right is shown in Fig. 6-16. As can be seen, the bit to the left is shifted into X when SHIFT RIGHT is a 1 and the bit to the right is shifted into X when SHIFT LEFT is a 1.

Figure 6-17 shows an MIS package which contains four flip-flops and gating circuitry so that the register can be shifted right or left, and also so that the four flip-flops can be parallel loaded from four input lines W, X, Y, and Z. The circuits are TTL circuits and are clocked in parallel. By combining modules such as this one, a register of a chosen length can be formed which can be shifted left or right or parallel loaded.

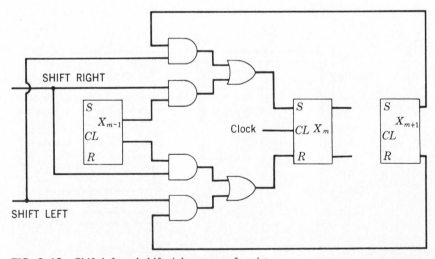

FIG. 6-16 Shift-left and shift-right stages of register

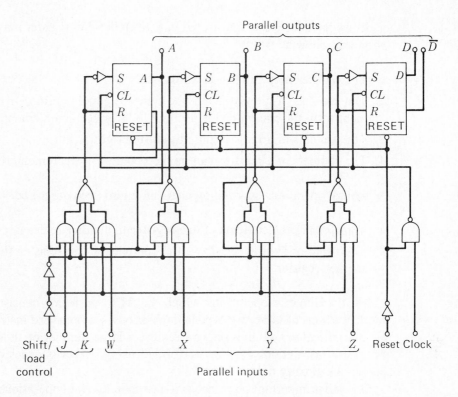

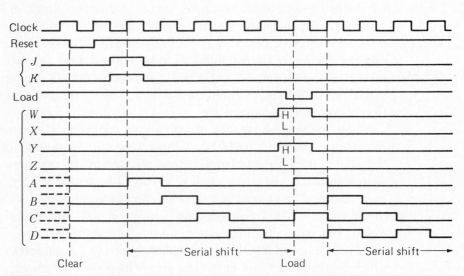

FIG. 6-17 Shift register (model SN74195) with a parallel load ability (courtesy Texas Instruments)

6-16 BASIC OPERATIONS

The arithmetic-logic unit of a digital computer consists of a number of registers in which information can be stored and a set of logic circuits which make it possible to perform certain operations on the information stored in the registers and to perform certain operations between registers.

As we have seen, the data stored in a given flip-flop register may be operated on in the following ways:

1. The register may be reset to all 0s.
2. The contents of a register may be complemented to either 1s or 2s complement form for binary, or for decimal to 9s or 10s complement form.
3. The contents of a register may be shifted right or left.
4. The contents of a register can be incremented or decremented.

Several operations between registers have also been described. These include:

1. Transferring the contents of one register to another register.
2. Adding to or subtracting from the contents of one register the contents of another register.

Most arithmetic operations which an ALU performs consist of these or sequenced sets of these two types of operations. Complicated instructions, such as multiplication and division, can require a large number of these operations, but these instructions may be performed using only sequences of the simple operations already described.

One other important point needs to be made. Certain operations which occur within instructions are **conditional;** that is, a given operation may or may not take place, depending on the value of certain bits of the numbers stored. For instance, it may be desirable to multiply using only positive numbers. In this case the sign bits of the two numbers to be multiplied together will be examined by control circuitry, and if either is a 1, the corresponding number will be complemented before the multiplication begins. This operation, complementing of the register, is a conditional one.

Many different sequences of operations can yield the same result. For instance, two numbers could be multiplied together by simply adding the multiplicand to itself the number of times indicated by the multiplier. If this were done with pencil and paper, 369 $\times$ 12 would be performed by adding 369 to itself 12 times. This would be a laborious process compared with the easier algorithm which we have developed for multiplying, but we would get the same result. The same principle applies to machine multiplication. Two numbers could be multiplied together by transferring one of the numbers into a counter which counted downward each time an addition was performed, and then adding the other number to itself until the counter reached zero. This technique has been used, but much faster techniques are also used and will be explained.

Many algorithms have been used to multiply and divide numbers in digital machines. Division, especially, is a complicated process, and in decimal machines in particular, many different techniques are used. The particular technique used by a machine is generally based on the cost of the machine and the premium on speed for the machine. As in almost all operations, speed is expensive, and a faster division process generally means a more expensive machine.

To explain the operations of binary multiplication and division, we will use a block diagram of a generalized binary machine. Figure 6-18 illustrates, in block

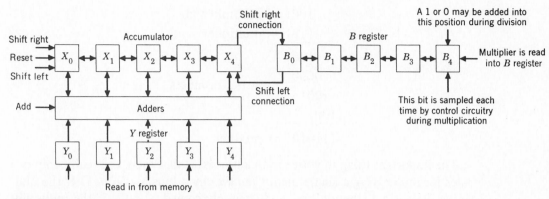

FIG. 6-18   Generalized parallel arithmetic element

diagram form, the registers of an ALU. The machine has three basic registers, an accumulator, a Y register, and a B register. The operations which can be performed have been described:

1. The accumulator can be cleared.

2. The contents of the accumulator can be shifted right or left. Further, the accumulator and the B register may be formed into one long shift register. If we then shift this register right two digits, the two least significant digits of the accumulator will be shifted into the first two places of the B register. Several left shifts will shift the most significant digits of the B register into the accumulator. Since there are 5 bits in the basic machine word, there are five binary storage devices in each register. A right shift of five places will transfer the contents of the accumulator into the B register, and a left shift of five places will shift the contents of the B register into the accumulator.

3. The contents of the Y register can be either added to or subtracted from the accumulator. The sum or difference will then be stored in the accumulator register.

4. Words from memory may be read into the Y register. To read a word into the accumulator, it is necessary first to clear the accumulator, then to read the word from memory into the Y register, and then to add the Y register to the accumulator.

An arithmetic element which can perform these operations on its registers can be sequenced to perform all arithmetic operations. It is, in fact, possible to construct a machine using fewer operations than these, but most general-purpose computers will usually have an arithmetic element with at least these capabilities.

6-17 BINARY MULTIPLICATION

The process of multiplying binary numbers together may be best examined by writing out the multiplication of two binary numbers:

$$
\begin{array}{r}
1001 = \text{multiplicand} \\
\underline{1101} = \text{multiplier}
\end{array}
$$

$$
\left.\begin{array}{r}
1001 \\
0000 \\
1001 \\
\underline{1001}
\end{array}\right\} \text{partial products}
$$

$$
1110101 = \text{product}
$$

The important thing to notice in this process is that there are really only two rules for mulitplying a single binary *number* by a binary *digit*: (1) If the multiplier digit is a 1, the multiplicand is simply copied, and (2) if the multiplier digit is a 0, the product is 0. The above example illustrates these rules as follows: The first digit to the right of the multiplier is a 1; therefore the multiplicand is copied as the first partial product. The next digit of the multiplier to the left is a 0; therefore the partial product is 0. Notice that each time a partial product is formed, it is shifted one place to the left of the previous partial product. Even if the partial product is a 0, the next partial product is shifted one place to the left of the previous partial product. This process is continued until all the multiplier digits have been used, and then the partial products are summed.

The three operations which the computer must be able to perform to multiply in this manner are therefore: (1) the ability to sense whether a multiplier bit is either a 1 or a 0, (2) the ability to shift partial products, and (3) the ability to add the partial products.

It is not necessary to wait until all the partial products have been formed before summing them. They may be summed two at a time. For instance, starting with the first two parital products in the above example,

$$
\begin{array}{r}
1001 \\
\underline{0000} \\
01001
\end{array}
$$

The next partial product may then be added to this sum, displacing it one position to the left:

$$
\begin{array}{r}
01001 \\
\underline{1001} \\
101101
\end{array}
$$

and finally,

$$
\begin{array}{r}
101101 \\
\underline{1001} \\
1110101
\end{array}
$$

A multiplier can be constructed in just this fashion. By sampling each bit of the multiplier in turn, adding the multiplicand into some register, and then shifting the multiplicand left each time a new multiplier bit was sampled, a product would be formed of the sum of the partial products. In fact, the process of multiplying in most binary machines is performed in a manner very similar to this.

To examine the typical technique for multiplying, the generalized arithmetic elements in Fig. 6-18 will be used. Referring to Fig. 6-18, let the multiplier be stored in the *B* register, and the multiplicand in the *Y* register; the accumulator contains all 0s as shown below:

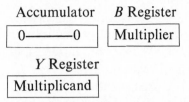

Let us also assume that both multiplier and multiplicand are positive. If either is negative, it must be converted to positive form before the multiplication begins. Assume *n* bits in each operand. For Fig. 6-18, $n = 4$.

The desired result format is shown below with the product being the combined accumulator and *B* register.

Accumulator	*B* Register
Product	Product

Y Register   Product, with most significant

Multiplicand part in accumulator

A multiplication requires *n* basic steps, where *n* is the number of bits in the magnitude of the numbers to be multiplied, and a final right shift to position the product. Each basic step is initiated by the control circuitry examining the rightmost bit in the *B* register. The basic step is as follows.

Basic step If the rightmost bit in the *B* register is a 0, the combined accumulator and *B* register is shifted right one place. If the rightmost bit in the *B* register is a 1, the number in the *Y* register is added to the contents of the accumulator, and the combined accumulator and *B* register is then shifted right one place.

After each basic step the new rightmost bit of the *B* register is again examined, and the next of the *n* steps is initiated.

Let us consider the same multiplication that was used in the previous example, that is, 1101×1001, where 1101 is the multiplier. In this case, in the beginning the accumulator contains 0.0000, the *B* register 0.1101, and the *Y* register 0.1001. Four steps will be required and a final shift.

Step 1. Since the rightmost bit of the *B* register contains a 1 (the least significant bit of the multiplier), during the first step the contents of the *Y* register are added to the accumulator, and the combined accumulator and *B* register are then shifted to the right. The second least significant bit of the multiplier will now occupy the rightmost bit of the *B* register and will control the next operation. The *Y* register will still contain the multiplicand 0.1001, the contents of the accumulator will be 0.0100, and the contents of the *B* register will be 1.0110.

Step 2. The rightmost bit of the B register is a 0, and since it controls the next operation, a SHIFT-RIGHT signal will be initiated, and the accumulator and B register will be shifted right, giving 0.0010 in the accumulator and 0.1011 in the B register.

Step 3. A 1 is now in the rightmost bit of the B register. The Y register will therefore again be added to the accumulator, and the combined accumulator and B register will again be shifted right, giving 0.0101 in the accumulator and 1.0101 in the B register.

Step 4. The least significant bit of the B register will be another 1; so the Y register will again be added to the accumulator and the accumulator shifted right. After the above shift right, the combined accumulator and B register will contain 0.011101010. A final right shift gives 0.001110101, the correct product for our integer number system. The most significant digits will be stored in the accumulator, and the least significant digits in the B register.

Accumulator	B register	
0.0000	0.1101	At beginning
0.0100	1.0110	After Step 1
0.0010	0.1011	After Step 2
0.0101	1.0101	After Step 3
0.0111	0.1010	After Step 4
0.0011	1.0101	After shift right

The reason for the combined accumulator and B register can now be seen. The product of two 5-bit signed numbers can contain up to nine significant digits (including the sign bit), and so two 5-bit registers, not one, are required to hold the product. The final product is treated like a 10-bit number extending through the two registers with the leftmost bits (most significant bits) in the left register, and the rightmost bits (least significant bits) in the right register, and the least significant binary digit in the product. Thus our result in the two combined registers was 0.001110101, which is $+117$ in decimal.

The control circuitry is designed to perform the examination of the multiplier bits, then either shift or add and shift the correct number of times, and then stop. In this case the length of the multiplier, or Y register, is 4 bits plus a sign bit; so four such steps are performed. The general practice is to examine each bit of the machine word except the sign bit, in turn. For instance, if the basic machine word is 25 bits, that is, 24 bits in which the magnitude of a number is stored plus a sign bit, each time a multiplication is performed, the machine will examine 24 bits, each in turn, performing the add-and-shift or just the shift operation 24 times. As may be seen, this makes the multiplication operation longer than such operations as add or subtract. Some parallel machines double their normal rate of operation during multiplication: if the machine performs such operations as addition, complement, transfers, etc., at a rate of 4 MHz/s for ordinary instructions, the rate will be increased to 8 MHz for the add-and-shift combinations performed while multiplying. Some machines are able to shift right while adding; that is, the sum of the accumulator and Y register appears shifted one place to the right each time, and the shift-right operation after each addition may be omitted.

The sign bits of the multiplier and multiplicand may be handled in a number of ways. For instance, the sign of the product can be determined by means of control circuitry before the multiplication procedure is initiated. This sign bit is stored during the multiplication process, after which it is placed into the sign bit of the accumulator, and the accumulator is then complemented, if necessary. Therefore the sign bits of the multiplier and multiplicand are first examined; if they are both 0s, the sign of the product should be 0; if both are 1s, the sign of the product should be 0; and if either but not both is a 1, the sign of the product should be 1. This information, retained in a flip-flop while the multiplication is taking place, may be transferred into the sign bit afterward. If the machine handles numbers in the 1s or 2s complement system, both multiplier and multiplicand may be handled as positive magnitudes during the multiplication, and if the sign of either number is negative, the number is complemented to a positive magnitude before the multiplication begins. Sometimes the multiplication is performed on complemented numbers using more complicated algorithms.

6-18 DECIMAL MULTIPLICATION

Decimal multiplication is a more involved process than binary multiplication. Whereas the product of a binary digit and a binary number is either the number or 0, the product of a decimal digit and decimal number involves the use of a multiplication table plus carrying and adding. For instance,

$$7 \times 24 = (7 \times 4) + (7 \times 20) = 28 + 140 = 168$$

Even the multiplying of two decimal digits may involve two output digits; for instance, 7×8 equal 56. In the following discussion we call the two digits which may result when a decimal digit is multiplied times a decimal digit the **left-hand** and the **right-hand digits.** Thus for 3×6 we have 1 for the left-hand digit and 8 for the right-hand digit. For 2×3 we have 0 for the left-hand digit and 6 for the right-hand digit.

Except for simply adding the multiplicand to itself the number of times indicated by the multiplier, a simple but time-consuming process, the simplest method for decimal multiplication involves loading the rightmost digit of the multiplier into a counter that counts downward and then adding the multiplicand to itself and simultaneously indexing the counter until the counter reaches 0. The partial product thus formed may be shifted right one decimal digit, the next multiplier digit loaded into the counter, and the process repeated until all the multiplier digits have been used. This is a relatively slow but straightforward technique.

The process may be speeded up by forming products using the multiplicand and the rightmost digit of the multiplier as in the previous scheme, except by actually forming the left-hand and right-hand partial products obtained when multiplying a digit by a number and then summing them. For instance, 6×7164 would yield 2664 for the right-hand product digits and 4032 for the left-hand product digits. The sum would then be

$$
\begin{array}{r}
2664 \\
+\ \ 4032 \\
\hline
42984
\end{array}
$$

Decimal-machine multiplication is in general a complicated process if speed is desired, and there are almost as many techniques for multiplying BCD numbers as there are types of machines. IC packages are produced containing a gate network that has two BCD characters as inputs which produce the two-digit output required.

6-19 DIVISION

The operation of division is the most difficult and time-consuming that the ALU of most general-purpose machines performs. Although division may appear no more difficult than multiplication, there are several problems in connection with the division process which introduce time-consuming extra steps.

Division, using pencil and paper, is a trial-and-error process. For instance, if we are to divide 77 into 4610, we first notice that 77 will not "go" into 46; so we attempt to divide 77 into 461. We may guess that it will go six times; however,

$$
\begin{array}{r}
6\ \ \ \ \ \\
77\,\overline{)4610} \\
462\ \ \\
\hline
-1\ \
\end{array}
$$

Therefore we have guessed too high and must reduce the first digit of the quotient, which we will develop, to 5.

The same problem confronts the computer when it attempts to divide in this manner. It must "try" a subtraction each step of the process and then see if the remainder is negative. Consider the division of 1111 by 11:

$$
\begin{array}{r}
101\ \ \\
11\,\overline{)1111} \\
11\ \ \ \ \\
\hline
0011\ \\
11\ \\
\hline
00\
\end{array}
$$

It is easy to determine visually at any step of the process whether the quotient is to be a 1 or a 0, but the computer cannot determine this without making a trial subtraction each time. After a trial quotient has been tried and the divisor subtracted, if the result is negative, either the current dividend must be "restored" or some other technique for dividing used.

There are several points to be noted concerning binary fixed-point integer-value division. The division is generally performed with two signed binary integers of the same fixed length. The result, or quotient, is stored as a number, with as many digits as the divisor or dividend, and the remainder is also stored as a number of the same length.

Using the registers shown in Fig. 6-18, we will show how to divide a number stored in the accumulator by a number in the Y register. The quotient is then stored in the B register and the remainder in the accumulator. This is the most common division format.

Assume the B and Y registers in Fig. 6-18 to be 5 bits in length (4 bits + sign bit) and the accumulator also 5 bits in length. Before starting the procedure, the dividend is read into the accumulator, and the divisor into the Y register. After the division, the quotient will be stored in the B register, and the remainder will be in the accumulator. Both divisor and dividend are to be positive.

The following shows an example. The accumulator (dividend) originally contains 11 (decimal) and the Y register (divisor) contains 4. The desired result then gives the quotient 2 in the B register and the remainder 3 in the accumulator.

Accumulator B Register

| 01011 |

| 00000 |

At beginning of division

Y Register

| 00100 |

Accumulator B Register

| 00011 |

| 00010 |

After division

Y Register

| 00100 |

There are two general techniques for division for binary machines: the **restoring** and the **nonrestoring** techniques. Our first example will use the restoring technique.

Just as in multiplication, the restoring technique for division requires that a **basic step** be performed repeatedly (in this case as many times as there are significant bits in the subtrahend).

Basic step In the restoring technique the basic step consists of a "trial division" which is made by first subtracting the Y register from the accumulator. After the subtraction, one of the following is executed.

1. If the result is negative, the divisor will not "go"; a 0 is therefore placed in the rightmost bit of the B register, and the dividend (accumulator) is restored by adding the divisor to the result of the subtraction. The combined B register and accumulator will then be shifted left.

2. If the result of a subtraction is positive or zero, there is no need to restore the partial dividend in the accumulator for the trial division has succeeded. The accumulator and B register are both shifted left and then a 1 is placed in the rightmost bit of the B register.

The computer determines whether or not the result of a trial division is positive or negative by examining the sign bit of the accumulator after each subtraction.

In order to demonstrate the entire procedure, it is first necessary to explain how to initiate the division and how to start and stop performing the basic steps. Unfortunately these are complicated procedures, just as determining the start, stop, and position of the decimal point is complicated for "ordinary" division.

1. As described above, if the divisor is larger than the dividend, then the quotient should be 0, and the remainder is the value of the dividend. (For instance, if we attempt to divide 7 by 17, the quotient is 0, and the remainder is 7.) To test this, the dividend in Y can be subtracted from the accumulator, and if the result is negative, all that remains is to restore the accumulator by adding the Y register to the accumulator. The B register now has value 0 which is right for the quotient, and the accumulator has the original value which is the remainder.

2. After the above test is made, it is necessary to align the leftmost 1 bit in the divisor with the leftmost 1 bit in the dividend by shifting the divisor left, and to record the number of shifts required to make this alignment. If the number of shifts is M, then the basic step must be performed $M + 1$ times.

3. Now, the basic step is performed the necessary $M + 1$ times.

4. Finally, to adjust the remainder, the accumulator must be shifted right $M + 1$ times after the last basic step is performed. Examples are shown in Tables 6-2 and 6-3. Step 1 above, testing for a zero quotient, is not shown in the two examples.

Figure 6-19 shows a flowchart of the algorithm. Flowcharts are often used to represent algorithms. A more detailed flowchart would separate some of the steps, such as "shift the accumulator right $M + 1$ times," into single shifts performed in a loop which is controlled by a counter. Often, when algorithms are reasonably complicated, as this algorithm is, it is convenient to draw a flowchart of the algorithm before attempting to implement the control circuitry.

During division, the sign bits are handled in much the same way as during multiplication. The first step is to convert both the divisor and the dividend to positive magnitude form. The value of the sign bit for the quotient must be stored while the division is taking place. The rule is that if the signs of the dividend and divisor are both either 0s or 1s, the quotient will be positive. If either but not both of their signs is a 1, the quotient will be negative. The relationship of the sign bit of the quotient to the sign bit of the divisor and dividend is therefore the quarter adder, or exclusive OR, relationship, that is, $S = X\overline{Y} + \overline{X}Y$. The value for the correct sign of the quotient may be read into a flip-flop while the division is taking place, and this value may then be placed in the sign bit of the register containing the quotient after the division of magnitudes has been completed.

There are several techniques for nonrestoring division. One widely used algorithm employs a procedure in which the divisor is alternately subtracted and added. Another uses a technique where the divisor is compared to the dividend at each trial division.

TABLE 6-2

B REGISTER	ACCUMULATOR	Y REGISTER	REMARKS
0.0000	0.0110	0.0011	We divide 6 by 3.
0.0000	0.0110	0.0110	Y register is shifted left once, aligning 1s in accumulator and Y register. The basic step must be performed two times.
0.0000	0.0000	0.0110	Y register has been subtracted from accumulator. The result is 0, so B register and accumulator are shifted left, and a 1 is placed in the rightmost bit of B register.
0.0001	0.0000	0.0110	
0.0001	1.1010	0.0110	Y register is subtracted from accumulator.
0.0010	0.0000	0.0110	Y register is added to accumulator, and B register and accumulator are shifted left 1. A 0 is placed in B register's last bit.
0.0010	0.0000	0.0110	Accumulator must now be shifted right two times, but it is 0 so no change results. The quotient in B register is 2, and the remainder in accumulator is 0.

TABLE 6-3

B REGISTER	ACCUMULATOR	Y REGISTER	REMARKS
0.0000	0.1101	0.0011	We divide 13 by 3.
0.0000	0.1101	0.0110	Shift Y register left.
0.0000	0.1101	0.1100	Shift Y register left. Leftmost 1 bits in accumulator and Y register are aligned. Basic step will be performed three times.
0.0000	0.0001	0.1100	Y register has been subtracted from accumulator. Result is positive.
0.0001	0.0010	0.1100	B register and accumulator are shifted left, and 1 is placed in B register.
0.0001	1.0110	0.1100	Y register is subtracted from accumulator. Result is negative.
0.0010	0.0100	0.1100	Y register is added to accumulator. Both are then shifted left, and a 0 is placed in B register.
0.0010	1.1000	0.1100	Y register is subtracted from accumulator. Result is negative.
0.0100	0.1000	0.1100	Y register is added to accumulator. Accumulator and B register are shifted left. A 0 is placed in B register's bit.
0.0100	0.0001	0.1100	Accumulator has been shifted right three times. The quotient is 4, and the remainder is 1.

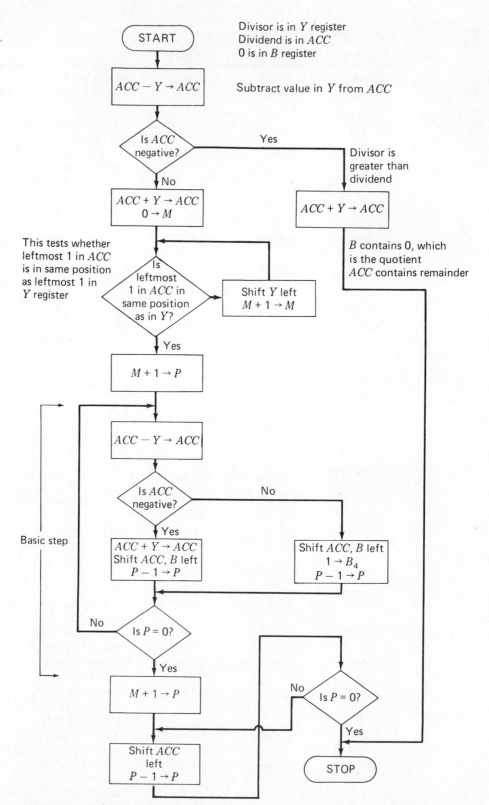

FIG. 6-19 Flowchart of division algorithm

6-20 LOGICAL OPERATIONS

In addition to the arithmetic operations, many logical operations are performed by ALUs. Three logical operations will be described here: logical multiplication, logical addition, and **sum modulo 2** addition (the exclusive OR operation). Each of these will be operations between registers, where the operation specified will be performed on each of the corresponding digits in the two registers. The result will be stored in one of the registers.

The first operation, logical multiplication, is often referred to as an **extract, masking,** or **AND operation.** The rules for logical multiplication have been defined as $0 \cdot 0 = 0; 0 \cdot 1 = 0; 1 \cdot 0 = 0;$ and $1 \cdot 1 = 1.$ Suppose that the contents of the accumulator register are "logically multiplied" by another register. Let each register be five binary digits in length. If the accumulator contains 01101 and the other register 00111, the contents of the accumulator after the operation will be 00101.

The masking, or extracting, operation is useful in "packaging" computer words. To save space in memory and keep associated data together, several pieces of information may be stored in the same word. For instance, a word may contain an item number, wholesale price, and retail price, packaged as follows:

S	1 → 6	7 → 15	16 → 24
	item number	wholesale price	retail price

To extract the retail price, the programmer will simply logically multiply the word above by a word containing 0s in the sign digit through digit 15, and with 1s in positions 16 through 24. After the operation, only the retail price will remain in the word.

The logical addition operation, or the sum modulo 2 operation, is also provided in most computers. The rules for these operations are:

LOGICAL ADDITION	MODULO 2 ADDITION
$0 + 0 = 0$	$0 \oplus 0 = 0$
$0 + 1 = 1$	$0 \oplus 1 = 1$
$1 + 0 = 1$	$1 \oplus 0 = 1$
$1 + 1 = 1$	$1 \oplus 1 = 0$

Figure 6-20 shows how a single accumulator flip-flop and B flip-flop can be gated together so that all three of these logical operations can be performed. The circuit in Fig. 6-20 would be repeated for each stage of the accumulator register.

There are three control signals, LOGICAL MULTIPLY, LOGICAL ADD, and MOD 2 ADD. If one of these is up, or 1, when a clock pulse arrives, this operation is performed and the result placed in the ACC (accumulator) flip-flop. If none of the control signals is a 1, nothing happens, and the ACC remains as it is.

The actual values desired are found by three sets of gates; that is, ACC $\cdot$ B, and ACC $+$ B, and ACC $\oplus$ B are all formed first. Each of these is then AND-

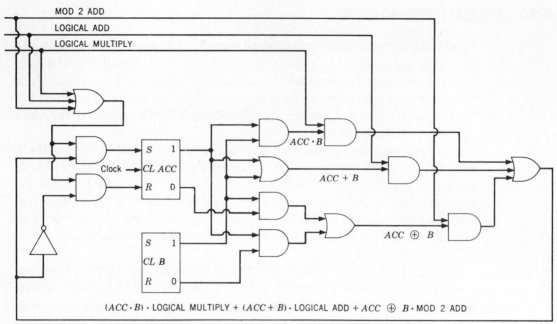

FIG. 6-20 Circuit for gating logical operations into accumulator flip-flop

gated with the appropriate control signal. Finally the three control signals are ORed together, and this signal is used to gate the appropriate value into the ACC flip-flop when one of the control signals is a 1.

Figure 6-20 shows how a choice of several different function values can be gated into a single flip-flop using control signals. We could include an ADD signal and a SHIFT RIGHT and a SHIFT LEFT by simply adding more gates.

Figure 6-21 shows an example of the logic circuitry used in modern computers to form sections of an ALU. All the gates shown in this block diagram are contained in a single IC chip (package) with 24 pins. The chip is widely used (in the DEC PDP-11 series and Data General NOVAs, for example). With TTL (Schottky) circuits the maximum delay from input to output is 11 ns. (There is an ECL version with a 7 ns maximum delay.)

This chip is called a **4-bit arithmetic-logic unit** and can add, subtract, AND, OR, etc., two 4-bit register sections. Two chips could be used for the logic in an 8-bit accumulator, four chips would form a 16-bit accumulator, etc.

The function performed by this chip is controlled by the mode input M and four function select inputs S_0, S_1, S_2, and S_3. When the mode input M is low (a 0), the 74S181 performs such arithmetic operations as ADD or SUB-TRACT. When the mode input M is high (a 1), the ALU does logic operations on the A and B inputs "a bit-at-a-time." (Notice in Fig. 6-21 that the carry generating gates are disabled by $M = 1$.) For instance, if M is a 0, S_1 and S_2 are also 0s, and S_0 and S_3 are 1s, the 74S181 performs arithmetic addition. If M is a 1, S_0 and S_3 are 1s, and S_1 and S_2 are 0s, the 74S181 chip exclusive ORs (mod 2 adds) A and B. (It forms $A_0 \oplus B_0$, $A_1 \oplus B_1$, $A_2 \oplus B_2$ and $A_3 \oplus B_3$.)

The table in Fig. 6-21 further describes the operation of this chip.

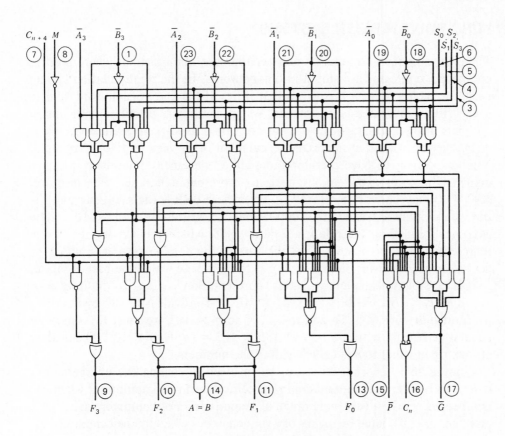

MODE SELECT INPUTS*				ACTIVE LOW INPUTS AND OUTPUTS	
				LOGIC	ARITHMETIC
S_3	S_2	S_1	S_0	$(M = H)$	$(M = L)\ (C_n = L)$
L	L	L	L	$\overline{A}$	$A - 1$
L	L	L	H	$\overline{AB}$	$AB - 1$
L	L	H	L	$\overline{A} + B$	$A\overline{B} - 1$
L	L	H	H	Logical 1	-1
L	H	L	L	$\overline{A + B}$	$A \mp (A + \overline{B})$
L	H	L	H	$\overline{B}$	$AB \mp (A + \overline{B})$
L	H	H	L	$\overline{A \oplus B}$	$A - B - 1$
L	H	H	H	$A + \overline{B}$	$A + \overline{B}$
H	L	L	L	$\overline{A} B$	$A \mp (A + B)$
H	L	L	H	$A \oplus B$	$A \mp B$
H	L	H	L	B	$A\overline{B} \mp (A + B)$
H	L	H	H	$A + B$	$A + B$
H	H	L	L	Logical 0	$A \mp A$*
H	H	L	H	$A\overline{B}$	$AB \mp A$
H	H	H	L	AB	$A\overline{B} \mp A$
H	H	H	H	A	A

*$L = 0;\ H = 1$.

Note:

$$x \oplus y$$

is the symbol for a mod 2 adder (exclusive OR gate)
$z = x \oplus y$

$\mp$ is the sign for arithmetic addition

FIG. 6-21   4-bit arithmetic-logic unit

6-21 FLOATING-POINT NUMBER SYSTEMS

The preceding sections describe number representation systems where positive and negative integers are stored in binary words. In the representation system used, the binary point is "fixed" in that it lies at the end of each word, and so each value represented is an integer. When computers calculate with binary numbers in this format, the operations are called **fixed-point arithmetic.**

In science it is often necessary to calculate with very large or very small numbers. Scientists have therefore adopted a convenient notation in which a **mantissa** plus an **exponent** are used to represent a number. For instance, 4,900,000 may be written as 0.49×10^7, where 0.49 is the mantissa and 7 is the value of the exponent, or 0.00023 may be written as 0.23×10^{-3}. The notation is based on the relation $y = a \times r^p$, where y is the number to be represented, a is the mantissa, r is the base of the number system ($r = 10$ for decimal, and $r = 2$ for binary), and p is the power to which the base is raised.

It is possible to calculate with this representation system. To multiply $a \times 10^n$ times $b \times 10^m$, we form $(a \times b) \times 10^{m+n}$. To divide $a \times 10^m$ by $b \times 10^n$, we form $a/b \times 10^{m-n}$. To add $a \times 10^m$ to $b \times 10^n$, we must first make m equal to n. If $m = n$, then $a \times 10^m + b \times 10^n = (a + b) \times 10^m$. The process of making m equal to n is called **scaling** the numbers.

Considerable "bookkeeping" can be involved in scaling the numbers, and there can be difficulty in maintaining precision during computations when the numbers vary over a very wide range of magnitudes. For computer usage these problems are alleviated by means of two techniques whereby the computer (not the programmer) keeps track of the radix (decimal) point, automatically scaling the numbers. In the first, programmed **floating-point routines** automatically scale the numbers used during the computations while maintaining the precision of the results and keeping track of the scale factors. These routines are used with small computers having only fixed-point operations. A second technique lies in building what are called **floating-point operations** into the computer's hardware. The logical circuitry of the computer is then used to perform the scaling automatically and to keep track of the exponents when calculations are performed. To effect this, a number representation system called the **floating-point system,** is used.

A floating-point number in a computer uses the exponential notation system described above, and during calculations the computer keeps track of the exponent as well as the mantissa. A computer number word in a floating-point system may be divided into three pieces: the first is the sign bit, indicating whether the number is negative or positive; the second part contains the exponent for the number to be represented; and the third part is the mantissa.

As an example, let us consider a 12-bit word length computer with a floating-point word. Figure 6-22 shows this. It is common practice to call the exponent

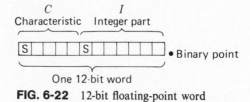

FIG. 6-22   12-bit floating-point word

part of the word the **characteristic** and the mantissa section the **integer part;** we shall adhere to this practice.

The integer part of the floating-point word shown represents its value in signed-magnitude form (rather than 2s complement, although this has been used). The characteristic is also in signed-magnitude form. The value of the number expressed is $I \times 2^c$, where I is the value of the integer part, and C is the value of the characteristic.

Figure 6-23 shows several values of floating-point numbers both in binary form and after being converted to decimal. Since the characteristic has 5 bits

$$\underbrace{}_{C} \quad \underbrace{}_{I}$$

| 0 | 0 | 1 | 1 | 1 | 0 | 0 | 0 | 1 | 0 | 1 | 1 | Value is $2^7 \times 11 = 1408$

$C = +7 \qquad I = +11$

| 0 | 0 | 0 | 1 | 1 | 1 | 0 | 0 | 0 | 1 | 1 | 1 | Value is $2^3 \times (-7) = -56$

$C = +3 \qquad I = -7$

| 1 | 0 | 1 | 0 | 1 | 0 | 0 | 0 | 0 | 1 | 0 | 1 | Value is $2^{-5} \times 5 = \frac{5}{32}$

$C = -5 \qquad I = +5$

| 1 | 0 | 1 | 1 | 0 | 1 | 0 | 0 | 1 | 0 | 0 | 1 | Value is $2^{-6} \times -9 = -\frac{9}{64}$

$C = -6 \qquad I = -9$

FIG. 6-23 Values of floating-point numbers in 12-bit all-integer systems

and is in signed-magnitude form, the C in $I \times 2^c$ can have values from -15 to $+15$. The value of I is a sign-plus-magnitude binary integer of 7 bits, and so I can have values from -63 to $+63$. The largest number represented by this system would have a maximum I and would be 63×2^{15}. The least number would be -63×2^{15}.

This example shows the use of a floating-point number representation system to store "real" numbers of considerable range in a binary word.

One other widely followed practice is to express the mantissa of the word as a fraction instead of as an integer. This is in accord with common scientific usage since we commonly say that 0.93×10^4 is in "normal" form for exponential notation (and not 93×10^2). In this usage a mantissa in decimal normally has a value from 0.1 to 0.999. . . . Similarly, a binary mantissa in normal form would have a value from 0.5 (decimal) to less than 1. Most computers maintain their mantissa sections in normal form, continually adjusting words so that a significant (1) bit is always in the leftmost mantissa position (next to the sign bit).

When the mantissa is in fraction form, this section is called the **fraction.** For our 12-bit example we can express floating-point numbers with characteristic and fraction by simply supposing the binary point to be to the left of the magnitude (and not to the right as in integer representation). In this system a number to be represented has value $F \times 2^c$, where F is the binary fraction and C is the characteristic.

For the 12-bit word considered before, fractions would have values from $1 - 2^{-6}$, which is 0.111111, to $-(1 - 2^{-6})$, which is 1.111111. Thus numbers from $(1 - 2^{-6}) \times 2^{15}$ to $-(1 - 2^{-6}) \times 2^{15}$ can be represented, or about $+32,000$ to $-32,000$. The smallest value the fraction part could have is now the fraction 0.1000000, which is 2^{-1}, and the smallest characteristic, which is 2^{-15}, so the smallest positive number representable is $2^{-1} \times 2^{-15}$ or 2^{-16}. Most computers use this fractional system for the mantissa, although computers of Burroughs Corporation and the National Cash Register Company use the integer system previously described.

The Univac 1108 represents single-precision floating-point numbers in this format:

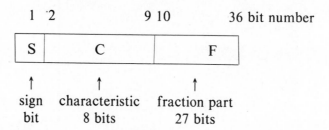

For positive numbers, the characteristic C is treated as a binary integer, the sign bit is a 0, and the fraction part is a binary fraction with value $0.5 \le F < 1$. The value of the number represented is $2^{C-128} \times F$. This is called an **offset system** because the value of the characteristic is simply the integer value in that portion of the word minus an offset which in this case is 128. The exponent can therefore range from -128 to $+127$, since the integer in the characteristic section is 8 bits in length.

As an example, the binary word

$$0.10000001 \quad 1100\ldots\ldots0$$

characteristic   fraction

has value $2^{129-128} \times \tfrac{3}{4} = 2 \times \tfrac{3}{4} = 1.5$. The representation for a negative number can be derived by forming the representation for the positive number with the same magnitude and then forming the 1s complement of this representation (considering all 36 bits as a single binary number).

In computers using 16-bit words (including some made by DEC, Hewlett-Packard, Data General, and IBM), floating-point words are represented by two adjacent words and thus have 32 bits per word. The actual format for floating-point words for several of these computers is shown in Fig. 6-24. In these computers the fraction part F consists of 24 bits representing a 23-bit fraction and

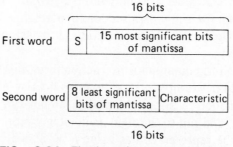

FIG. 6-24 Floating-point representation using two words

a sign bit. The exponent or characteristic consists of 8 bits. (In Hewlett-Packard computers the fraction part and the characteristic part are represented in 2s complement form, as programmed for FORTRAN.) Each of these computers can represent magnitudes of up to 2^{127} (or about 10^{38}) and fractions of about as small as 2^{-138} (about 10^{-38}).

Another example of a computer with internal circuitry which performs floating-point operations and uses a single computer word representation of floating-point numbers is the IBM 360/370 series.

IBM calls the exponent part of the **characteristic** and the mantissa part the **fraction.** In the 360/370 series floating-point data words can be either 32 or 64 bits in length. The basic formats are as follows:

short or single-word floating-point number:

S characteristic fraction

0	1 → 7	8 → 31

long or double-word floating-point number:

S characteristic fraction

0	1 → 7	8 → 63

In both cases the sign bit S is in the leftmost position and gives the sign of the number. The characteristic part of the word then comprises bits 1–7 and is simply a binary integer, which we shall call C, ranging from 0 to 127. The actual value of the scale factor is formed by subtracting 64 from this integer C and raising 16 to this power. Thus the value 64 in bits 1–7 gives a scale factor of $16^{C-64} = 16^{64-64} = 16^0$; a 93 (decimal) in bits 1–7 gives a scale factor of $16^{C-64} = 16^{93-64}$, which is 16^{29}; and a 24 in bits 1–7 gives a 16^{-40}.

The magnitude of the actual number represented in a given floating-point word is equal to this scale factor times the fraction contained in bits 8–31 for the short number, or 8–63 for a long number. The radix point is assumed to be to the left of bit 8 in either case. So if bits 8–31 contain 10000 . . . 00, the fraction has value ½ (decimal); that is, the fraction .1000 . . . 000 in binary. Similarly, if bits 8–31 contain 11000 . . . 000, the fraction value is ¾ decimal, or .11000 . . . 000 binary.

The actual number represented then has magnitude equal to the value of the fraction times the value determined by the characteristic. Consider a short number:

	sign	characteristic	fraction
floating-point number:	0	1 0 0 0 0 0 1	1 1 1 0 0 . . . 0
bit position:	0	1 2 3 4 5 6 7	8 9 10 11 12 . . . 31

The sign bit is a 0, and so the number represented is positive. The characteristic has binary value 1000001, which is 65 decimal, and so the scale factor is 16^1. The fraction part has value .111 binary, or ⅞ decimal, and so the number represented is ⅞ × 16, or 14 decimal.

Again, consider the following number:

	sign	characteristic	fraction
floating-point number:	1	1 0 0 0 0 0 1	1 1 1 0 0 . . . 0
bit position:	0	1 2 3 4 5 6 7	8 9 10 11 12 . . . 31

This has value -14 since every bit is the same as before, except for the sign bit. (The number representation system is signed magnitude.)

As further examples:

sign	characteristic	fraction	
0	1 0 0 0 0 1 1	1 1 0 . . . 0	$16^3 \times \frac{3}{4} = 3072$
0	0 1 1 1 1 1 1	1 1 0 . . . 0	$16^{-1} \times \frac{3}{4} = \frac{3}{64}$

6-22 PERFORMING ARITHMETIC OPERATIONS WITH FLOATING-POINT NUMBERS

A computer obviously requires additional circuitry to handle floating-point numbers automatically. Some machines come equipped with floating-point instructions. (For computers such as DEC PDP-11/45 and others, floating-point circuitry can be purchased and added to enable them to perform floating-point operations.)

To handle the floating-point numbers, the machine must be capable of extensive shifting and comparing operations. The rules for multiplying and dividing are

$$(a \times r^p) \times (b \times r^q) = ab \times r^{p+q}$$

$$(a \times r^p) \div (b \times r^q) = \frac{a}{b} \times r^{p-q}$$

The computer must be able to add or subtract the exponent sections of the floating-point numbers, and also to perform the multiplication or division operations on the mantissa sections of the numbers. In addition, precision is generally maintained by shifting the numbers stored until significant digits are in the leftmost sections of the word. With each shift the exponent must be changed. If the machine is shifting the mantissa section left, for each left shift the exponent must be decreased.

For instance, in a BCD computer, consider the word

0	10	0064
sign	exponent	mantissa

To attain precision, the computer shifts the mantissa section left until the 6 is in the most significant position. Since two shifts are required, the exponent must be decreased by 2, and the resulting word is 0.08 6400. If all numbers to be used are scaled in this manner, the maximum precision may be maintained throughout the calculations.

For addition and subtraction the exponent values must agree. For instance, to add 0.24×10^5 to 0.25×10^6, we must scale the numbers so that the exponents agree. Thus

$$(0.024 \times 10^6) + (0.25 \times 10^6) = 0.274 \times 10^6$$

The machine must also follow this procedure. The numbers are scaled as was described, so that the most significant digit of the computer mantissa section of each word contains the most significant digit of the number stored. Then the larger of the two exponents for the operands is selected, and the other number's mantissa is shifted and its exponent adjusted until the exponents for both numbers agree. The numbers may then be added or subtracted according to these rules:

$$(a \times r^p) + (b \times r^p) = (a + b) \times r^p$$
$$(a \times r^p) - (b \times r^p) = (a - b) \times r^p$$

sec. 7

The Memory Element

Thomas C. Bartee

7-1 INTRODUCTION

The memory of a computer is not actually concentrated in one place; storage devices are scattered throughout the machine. For instance, the **operation registers** are flip-flop registers which are used in the arithmetic and control units of the computer and arithmetic operations including additions, multiplications, shifts, etc., are all performed in these registers of the machine. The actual processing of information is performed in and at the direction of these registers.

Looking outward, the next category of storage device which is encountered is called the **high-speed memory, inner memory,** or **main memory.** This section of the computer's memory consists of a set of storage registers, each of which is identified with an address that enables the control unit either to write into or read from a particular register.

It is desirable that the operating speed of this section of the computer's memory be as fast as possible, for most of the transfers of data to and from the information processing section of the machine will be via the main memory. For this reason, storage devices with very fast access times are generally chosen for the main memory; unfortunately the presently available devices which are fast enough to perform this function satisfactorily do not possess the storage capacity that is sometimes required. As a result, additional memory, which is called the **auxiliary memory** or **secondary memory,** is added to most computers. This section of the computer's memory is characterized by low cost per digit stored, but it generally has an operating speed far slower than that of either the operation registers or the main memory. This section of the memory is sometimes designated the **backup store,** for its function is to handle quantities of data in excess of those that may be stored in the inner memory.

The final and outermost storage devices are those that are used to introduce information into the computer from the "outside world" and to store results from the computer to the computer user. The storage media in this case generally consist of such input media as punched cards or perforated paper tape, and the outputs from the machine generally consist of printed characters. Again, the cost per bit is low, but the operating speeds of the tape and card readers, printers, etc., are liable to be on the order of 1000 times slower than the speeds of the operation registers. This chapter will be limited to the **internal storage** of the machine, which is defined as those storage devices that form an integral part of the machine and are directly controlled by the machine.

Each of the divisions of memory has certain characteristics. For instance, the premium on speed is very high for the operation registers. These registers must generally perform operations at several times the speed of the main memory. The main memory also requires high operating speeds, but because it is desirable to store larger quantities of data (perhaps 10^4 to 10^9 bits) in this section of the memory, a compromise between cost and speed must generally be made. The same sort of compromise must often be made in the case of the auxiliary memory. In a large machine the auxiliary memory may have to store from 10^8 to 10^{12} binary digits, and in these instances it might prove too expensive to use devices such as those used in the main memory.

An important point to notice when considering operating speed is that, before a word can be read, it is necessary to locate it. The time required to locate and read a word from memory is called the **access time.** The procedures for locating information may be divided into two classes, random access and sequential access. A **random-access** storage device is one in which any location in the device may be selected at random, access to the information stored is direct, and approximately equal access time is required for each location. A flip-flop register is an example of a random-access storage device, as are the IC and magnetic core memories, which will be described. A **sequential-access** device is one in which the arrival at the location desired may be preceded by sequencing through other locations, so that access time varies according to location. For instance, if we try to read a word stored on a reel of magnetic tape and the piece of tape on which the word is stored is near the center of the reel, it will be necessary to sequence through all the intervening tape before the word can be read.

Another way to subdivide storage devices is according to whether they are static or dynamic storage devices. A **static** storage device is one in which the information does not change position; flip-flop registers, magnetic core registers, and even punched cards or tape are examples of static storage devices. **Dynamic** storage devices, on the other hand, are devices in which the information stored is continually changing position. Circulating registers utilizing charge coupled device (CCD) delay lines are examples of dynamic storage devices.

This chapter will concentrate on the four most frequently used devices for storing digital information in the internal memory sections of computers. These are (1) IC memories, which are high speed and of moderate cost; (2) magnetic core memories, which are random-access devices used principally in the inner memory because of their high operating speeds and moderate cost per bit; (3) magnetic drum and disk memories, which are direct-access storage devices generally used for auxiliary storage; and (4) magnetic tape memories, which are used exclusively as an auxiliary, or backup, storage but which are capable of storing large quantities of information at low cost. Following the sections on drum, disk, and magnetic tape devices, the techniques used to record digital information on a magnetic surface will be described.

7-2 RANDOM-ACCESS MEMORIES

The main memory of a computer is organized in a way which is particularly desirable. Figure 7-1 shows that a high-speed main memory in a computer is organized into words of fixed lengths. As the figure indicates, a given memory is divided into N words, where N generally is some power of 2, and each word is assigned an **address** or **location** in the memory. Each word has the same number of bits, called the **word length,** and if we read, for instance, the word at location 72, we shall receive a word from the memory with this word length.

The addresses or address numbers in the memory run consecutively, starting with the address 0 and running up the largest address. Thus at address 0 we find a word, at address 1 a second word, at address 2 a third word, and so on up to the final word at the largest address.

Generally, the computer can read a word from or write a word into each location in the memory. For a memory with an 8-bit word, if we write the word

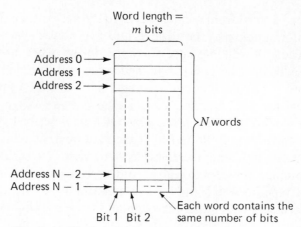

FIG. 7-1 Words in high-speed memory

01001011 into memory address 17 and later read from this same address, we shall read the word 01001011. If we again read from this address at a later time (and have not written another word in), the word 01001011 will again be read. This means the memory is **nondestructive read** in that reading does not destroy or change a stored word.

It is important to understand the difference between the **contents** of a memory address and the address itself. A memory is like a large cabinet containing as many drawers as there are addresses in memory. In each drawer is a word, and the address of each word is written on the outside of the drawer. If we write or store a word at address 17, it is like placing the word in the drawer labeled 17. Later, reading from address 17 is like looking in that drawer to see its contents. We do not remove the word at an address when we read, but change the contents at an address only when we store or write a new word.

From an exterior viewpoint, a high-speed main memory looks very much like a "black box" with a number of locations or addresses into which data can be stored or from which data can be read. Each address or location contains a fixed number of binary bits, the number being called the **word length** for the memory. A memory with 4096 locations, each with a different address, and with each location storing 16 bits, is called a **4096-word 16-bit memory,** or, in the vernacular of the computer trade, a **4K 16-bit memory.** (Since memories generally come with a number of words equal to 2^n for some n, if a memory has $2^{14} =$ 16,384 words, computer literature and jargon would refer to it as a 16K memory, because it is always understood that the full 2^n words actually occur in the memory. Thus, 2^{15}-word 16-bit memory is called a 32K 16-bit memory.)

Memories can be read from (that is, data can be taken out) or written into (that is, data can be entered into the memory). Memories which can be both read from and written into are called **read-write memories.** Some memories have programs or data permanently stored and are called **read-only memories.**

A block diagram of a read-write memory is shown in Fig. 7-2. The computer places the address of the location into which the data are to be read into the **memory address register.** This register consists of n binary devices (generally flip-flops), where 2^n is the number of words that can be stored in the memory. The data to be written into the memory are placed in the **memory buffer reg-**

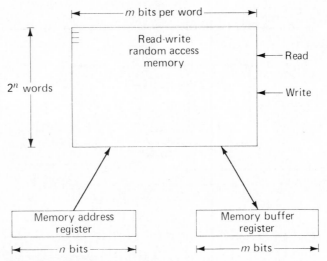

FIG. 7-2 Read-write random-access memory

ister, which has as many binary storage devices as there are bits in each memory word. The memory is told to write by means of a 1 signal on the WRITE line. The memory will then store the contents of the memory buffer register in the location specified by the memory address register.

Words are read by placing the address of the location to be read from into the memory address register. A 1 signal is then placed on the READ line, and the contents of that location are placed by the memory in the memory buffer register.

As can be seen, the computer communicates with the memory by means of the memory address register, the memory buffer register, and the READ and WRITE inputs. Memories are generally packaged in separate modules or packages. It is possible to buy a memory module of a specified size from a number of different manufacturers, and, for instance, an 8K 16-bit memory module can be purchased on a circuit board ready for use. Similarly, if a computer is purchased with a certain amount of main memory, more memory can generally later be added by purchasing additional modules and "plugging them in."

If it is possible to read from or write into any location "at once," that is, if there is no more delay in reaching one location as opposed to another location, the memory is called a **random-access memory** (RAM). Computers almost invariably use random-access read-write memories for their high-speed main memory and then use backup or slower speed memories to hold auxiliary data.

7-3 LINEAR-SELECT MEMORY ORGANIZATION

The most used random-access memories are IC memories and magnetic core memories. Both are organized in a similar manner, as will be shown.

In order to present the basic principles, an idealized IC memory will be shown, followed by details of several actual commercial memories.

In any memory there must be a basic memory cell. Figure 7-3 shows a basic memory cell consisting of an RS flip-flop with associated control circuitry. In

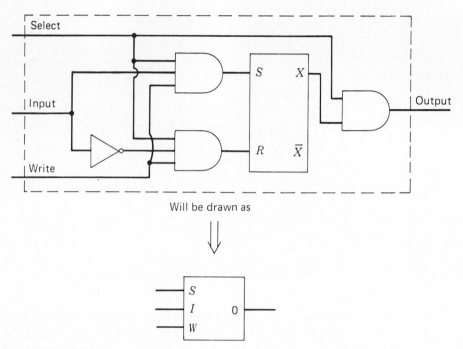

Will be drawn as

FIG. 7-3 Basic memory cell

order to use this cell in a memory, however, a technique for selecting those cells addressed by the memory address register must be used, as must a method to control whether the selected cells are written into or read from.

Figure 7-4 shows the basic memory organization for a **linear-select** IC memory. This is a four-address memory with 3 bits per word. The memory address register (MAR) selects the memory cells (flip-flops) to be read from or written into through a **decoder** which selects three flip-flops for each address that can be in the memory address register.

Figure 7-5(a) shows the decoder in expanded form. It has an input from each flip-flop (bit) to be decoded. If there are two input bits as in Fig. 7-5(a), then there will be four output lines, one for each state (value) the input register can take. For instance, if the MAR contains 0 in both flip-flops, then the upper line of the decoder will be a 1 and the remaining three lines a 0. Similarly, if both memory cells contain a 1, the lowest output line will be a 1 and the remaining three lines a 0. Similar reasoning will show that there will be a single output line with a 1 output for each possible input state, and the remaining lines will always be a 0.

Figure 7-5(b) shows a decoder for three inputs. The decoder has eight output lines. In general, for n input bits a decoder will have 2^n output lines.

The decoder in Fig. 7-5(b) operates in the same manner as that in Fig. 7-5(a). For each input state the decoder will select a particular output line, placing a 1 on the selected line and a 0 on the remaining lines.

Returning to Fig. 7-4, we now see that corresponding to each value that can be placed in the MAR, a particular output line from the decoder will be selected and carry a 1 value. The remaining output lines from the decoder will contain

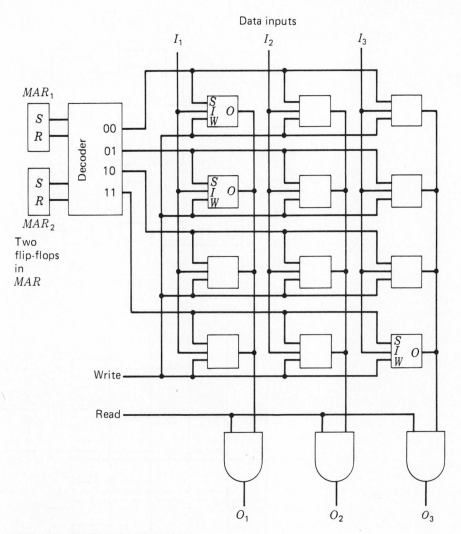

FIG. 7-4 Linear-select IC memory

0s, not selecting the AND gates at the inputs and outputs of the flip-flops for these rows. (Refer also to Fig. 7-3.)

The memory in Fig. 7-4 is organized as follows: There are four words, and each row of three memory cells comprises a word. At any given time the MAR selects a word in memory. If the READ line is a 1, the contents of the three cells in the selected word are read out on the O_1, O_2, and O_3 lines. If the WRITE line is a 1, the values on I_1, I_2, and I_3 will be read into the memory.

The AND gates connected to the OUT lines on the memory cells in Fig. 7-3 must have the property that when a number of AND gate output lines are connected together, the output goes to the highest level. (If any OUT is a 1, the line goes to 1, otherwise it is a 0.) This is called a **wired** OR. In Fig. 7-4 all four memory cells in the first column are wire-ORed together, so if any output line is a 1, the entire line will be a 1. (Memory cells in IC memories are constructed in this manner.)

Now if the READ line is a 1 in Fig. 7-4, the output values for the flip-flops

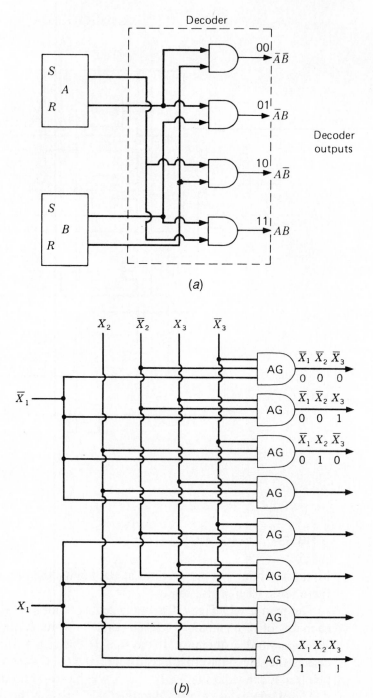

FIG. 7-5 (a) Four-output decoder (b) Parallel decoder

in the selected row will all be gated onto the output line for each bit in the memory.

For example, if the second row in the memory contains 110 in the three memory cells, and if the MAR contains 01, then the second output line from the decoder (marked 01) will be a 1, and the input gates and output gates to these three memory cells will be selected. If the READ line is a 1, then the outputs from the three memory cells in the second row will be 110 to the AND gates at the bottom of the figure, which will transmit the value 110 as an output from the memory.

If the WRITE line is a 1 and the MAR again contains 01, the second row of flip-flops will have selected inputs. The input values on I_1, I_2, and I_3 will then be read into the flip-flops in the second row.

As may be seen, this is a complete memory, fully capable of reading and writing. The memory will store data for an indefinite period and will operate as fast as the gates and flip-flops will permit. There is only one problem with the memory—its complexity. The basic memory cell (the flip-flop with its associated circuitry) is complicated, and for large memories the decoder will be large in size.

In order to further explore memory organization, we will first examine decoder construction in more detail, the selection schemes that are commonly used, and finally some examples of IC memories now in production.

7-4 DECODERS

An important part of the system which selects the cells to be read from and written into is the decoder. This particular circuit is called a **many-to-one decoder,** a **decoder matrix,** or simply a **decoder,** and has the characteristic that for each of the possible 2^n binary input numbers which can be taken by the n input cells, the matrix will have a unique one of its 2^n output lines selected.

Figure 7-5(b) shows a decoder which is completely parallel in construction and designed to decode three flip-flops. There are then $2^3 = 8$ output lines, and for each of the eight states which the three inputs (flip-flops) may take, a unique output line will be selected. This type of decoder is often constructed using diodes (or transistors) in the AND gates. The rule is: the number of diodes (or transistors) used in each AND gate is equal to the number of inputs to each AND gate. For Fig. 7-5(b) this is equal to the number of input lines (flip-flops which are being decoded). Further, the number of AND gates is equal to the number of output lines, which is equal to 2^n (n is the number of input flip-flops being decoded). The total number of diodes is therefore equal to $n \times 2^n$, and for the binary decoding matrix in Fig. 7-5(b) 24 diodes are required to construct the network. As may be seen, the number of diodes required increases sharply with the number of inputs to the network. For instance, to decode an eight-flip-flop register, we would require $8 \times 2^8 = 2048$ diodes if the decoder were constructed in this manner.

As a result there are several other types of structures which are often used in building decoder networks. One such structure, called a **tree-type** decoding network, is shown in Fig. 7-6. This tree network decodes four flip-flops and therefore has $2^4 = 16$ output lines, a unique one of which is selected for each state of the flip-flops. An examination will show that 56 diodes are required to build this particular network, while $2^4 \times 4 = 64$ diodes would be required to build the parallel decoder type shown in Fig. 7-5.

Still another type of decoder network is shown in Fig. 7-7. It is called a **balanced multiplicative decoder network.** Notice that this network requires only

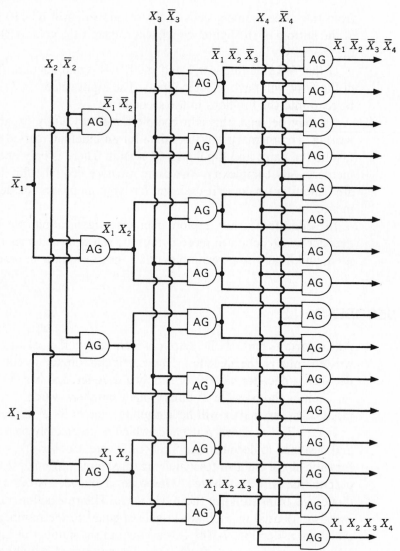

FIG. 7-6 Tree decoder

48 diodes. It can be shown that the type of decoder network illustrated in Fig. 7-7 requires the minimum number of diodes for a complete decoder network. The difference in the number of diodes, or decoding elements, to construct a network such as shown in Fig. 7-7, compared with those in Figs. 7-5 and 7-6, becomes more significant as the number of flip-flops to be decoded increases. The network shown in Fig. 7-5, however, has the advantage of being the fastest and most regular in construction of the three types of networks.

Having studied the three types of decoding matrices which are now used in digital machines, we will henceforth simply draw the decoder networks as a box with n inputs and 2^n outputs, with the understanding that one of the three types of circuits shown in Figs. 7-5–7-7 will be used in the box. Often only the uncomplemented inputs are connected to decoders, and inverters are included in the decoder package. Then a three-input (or three-flip-flop) decoder will have only three input lines and eight outputs.

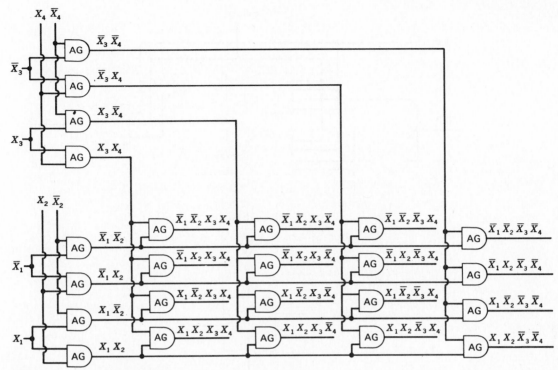

FIG. 7-7 Balanced decoder

7-5 DIMENSIONS OF MEMORY ACCESS

The memory organization in Fig. 7-4 has a basic linear-select (one-dimensional) selection system. This is the simplest organization. However, the decoder in the selection system becomes quite large as the memory size increases.

As an example we assume a parallel decoder as shown in Fig. 7-5b. These are widely used in IC packages because of their speed and regular (symmetric) construction.

Consider now a decoder for a 4096-word memory, a common size for an IC package. There will be 12 inputs per AND gate, and 4096 AND gates are required. If a diode (or transistor) is required at each AND gate's input, then $12 \times 4096 = 49,152$ diodes (or transistors) will be required. This large number of components is the primary objection to this memory organization.

Let us now consider a **two-dimensional selection system.** First we will need to add another SELECT input to our basic memory cell. This is shown in Fig. 7-8. Now both the SELECT 1 and the SELECT 2 must be 1s for a flip-flop to be selected.

Figure 7-9 shows a two-dimensional memory selection system using this cell. Two decoders are required for this memory, which has 16 words of only 1 bit per word (for clarity of explanation). The MAR has 4 bits and thus 16 states. Two of the MAR inputs go to one decoder and two to the other.

To illustrate the memory's operation, if the MAR contains 0111, then the value 01 goes to the left decoder and 11 goes to the upper decoder. This will select the second row (line) from the left decoder and the rightmost column from the top decoder. The result is that only the cell (flip-flop) at this intersec-

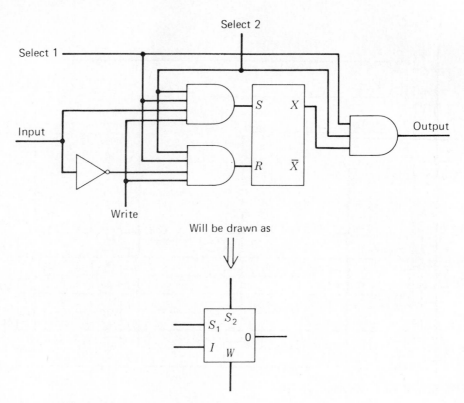

FIG. 7-8 Two-dimensional memory cell

tion of the second row and the rightmost column will have both its SELECT lines (and as a result its AND gates) enabled. As a result, only this particular single cell will be selected, and only this flip-flop can be read from or written into.

As another example, if the MAR contains 1001, the line for the third row of the left decoder will be a 1 as will be the second column line. The memory cell at the intersection of this row and column will be enabled, but no other cell will be enabled. If the READ line is a 1, the enabled cell will be read from; if the WRITE line is a 1, the enabled cell will be written into.

Now let us examine the number of components used. If a 16-word 1-bit memory was designed using the linear-select or one-dimensional system, then a decoder with 16 × 4 inputs and therefore 64 diodes (or transistors) would be required.

For the two-dimensional system two 2-input 4-output decoders are required, each requiring 8 diodes (transistors); so 16 diodes are required for both decoders.

For a 4096-word 1-bit-per-word memory the numbers are more striking. A 4096-word linear-select (one-dimensional) memory requires a 12-bit MAR. This decoder therefore requires 4096 × 12 = 49,152 diodes or transistors. The two-dimensional selection system would have two decoders, each with six inputs. Thus each would require $2^6 \times 6 = 384$ diodes or transistors, that is, a total of 768 diodes or transistors for the decoders. This is a remarkable saving, and extends to even larger memories.

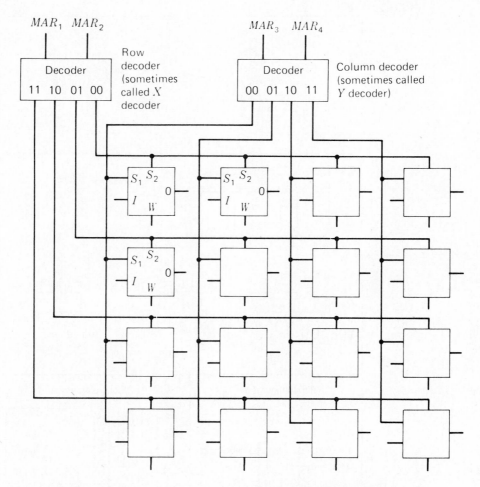

WRITE— (All W inputs on cells are connected to this input)

INPUT— (All I inputs on cells are connected to this input line)

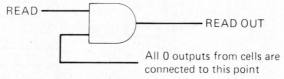

FIG. 7-9   Two-dimensional IC memory organization

In order to make a memory with more bits per word, we simply make a memory like that shown in Fig. 7-9 for each bit in the word (except that only one MAR and the original two decoders are required).

The above memory employs a classic two-dimensional selection system. This is the organization used in most core memories and in some IC memories. Figure 7-10 shows an IC memory with 256 bits on a single chip. As can be seen, this is a two-dimensional select memory.

In a two-dimensional memory, however, simplification in decoder complexity is paid for with cell complexity. In some cases this extra cell complexity is inexpensive, but it is often a problem, and so a variation of this scheme is used.

A variation on the basic two-dimensional selection system is illustrated in

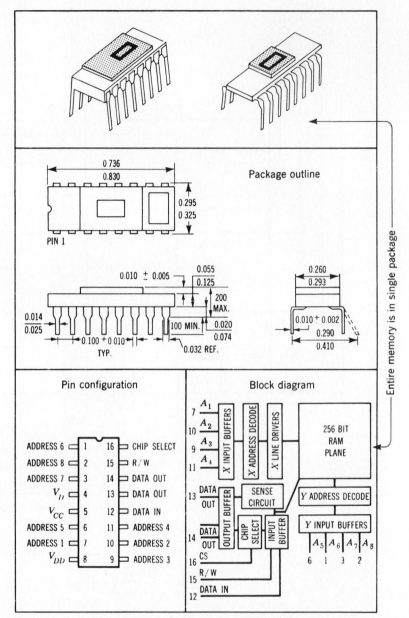

FIG. 7-10 Single-chip 256-bit memory (courtesy of Intel Corp.)

Fig. 7-11. This memory uses two decoders, as in the previous scheme; however, the memory cells are basic memory cells, as shown in Fig. 7-3.

The selection scheme uses gating on the READ and WRITE inputs to achieve the desired two-dimensionality.

Let us consider a WRITE operation. First assume that the MAR contains 0010. This will cause the 00 output from the upper decoder to be a 1, selecting the top row of memory cells. In the lower decoder the 10 output will become a 1, and this is gated with an AND gate near the bottom of the diagram, turning the W inputs on in the third column. As a result, for the memory cell in the top row and third column the S input and the W input will be a 1. For no other

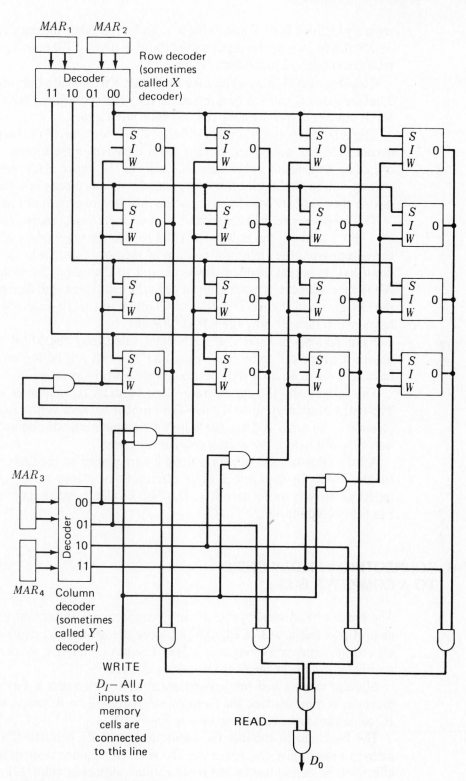

FIG. 7-11 IC memory chip layout

memory cell will both S and W be a 1, and so no other memory cell will have its RS flip-flop set to the input value. (Notice that all I inputs on the memory cells are connected to the input value D_l.)

Consideration of other values for the MAR will indicate that for each value a unique memory cell will be selected for the write operation. Therefore for each MAR state only one memory cell will be written into.

The read operation is similar. If the MAR contains 0111, then the upper decoder's 01 line will be a 1, turning the S inputs on in the second row of memory cells. As a result only these four cells in the entire array are capable of writing a 1 on the output lines. (Again, the memory cells are wire-ORed by having their outputs connected together, this time in groups of four.)

The lower decoder will have input 11, and so its lowest output line will carry a 1. This 1 turns on the rightmost AND gate in the lowest row, which enables the output from the rightmost column of memory cells. Only the second cell down has its output enabled, however, and so the output from the rightmost AND gate will have as output the value in the cell. This value then goes through the OR gate and the AND gate at the bottom of the diagram, the AND gate having been turned on by the READ signal.

Examination will show that each input value from the MAR will select a unique memory cell to be read from, and that cell will be the same as would have been written into if the operation were a write operation.

This is basically the organization used by most IC memories at this time. The chips contain up to 64K bits. The number of rows versus the number of columns in an array is determined by the designers who decide upon the numbers that will reduce the overall component count.

All the circuits necessary for a memory are placed on the same chip, except for the MAR flip-flops which quite often are not placed on the chip, but the inputs go directly to the decoders. This will be clearer when interfacing with a bus has been discussed.

7-6 CONNECTING MEMORY CHIPS TO A COMPUTER BUS

The present trend in computer memory connection is to connect the computer central processing unit (CPU), which does the arithmetic, generates control, etc., to the memory by means of a **bus.** The bus is simply a set of wires which are shared by all the memory elements to be used.

Microprocessors and minicomputers almost always use a bus to interface memory, and in this case the memory elements will be IC chips, which are in IC containers just like those shown in Fig. 7-10.

The bus used to connect the memories generally consists of (1) a set of **address lines** to give the address of the word in memory to be used (these are effectively an output from a MAR on the microprocessor chip); (2) a set of **data wires** to input data from the memory and output data to the memory; and (3) a set of **control wires** to control the read and write operations.

Figure 7-12 shows a bus for a microcomputer. In order to simplify drawings and clarify explanations, we will use a memory bus with only three address

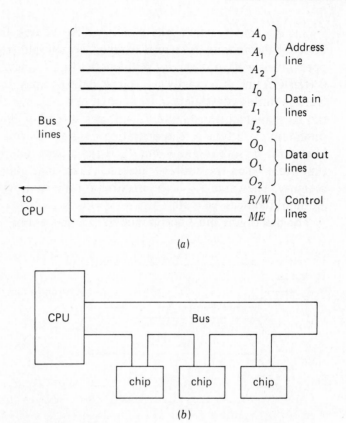

(a)

(b)

FIG. 7-12 Bus for computer system (a) Bus lines (b) Bus/ CPU/memory organization

lines, three output data lines, two control signals, and three input data lines. The memory to be used is therefore an 8-word 3-bit-per-word memory.

The two control signals work as follows. When the R/W line is a 1, the memory is to be read from; when the R/W line is a 0, the memory is to be written into. The MEMORY ENABLE signal ME is a 1 when the memory is either to be read from or to be written into; otherwise it is a 0.

The IC memory package to be used is shown in Fig. 7-13. Each IC package has three address inputs A_0, A_1, and A_2, an R/W input, an output bit D_O, an input bit D_I, and a CHIP SELECT $\overline{CS}$. Each package contains an 8-word 1-bit memory.

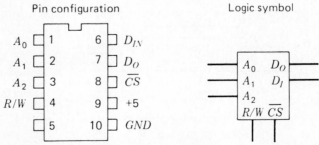

FIG. 7-13 IC package and block diagram symbol for RAM chip (a) Pin configuration (b) Logic symbol

The IC memory chip works as follows. The address lines A_0, A_1, and A_2 must be set to the address to be read from or written into (refer to Fig. 7-13). If the operation is a READ, the R/W line is set to a 1, and the $\overline{CS}$ line is brought to 0 (the $\overline{CS}$ line is normally a 1). The data bit may then be read on line D_O. Certain timing constraints must be met, however, and these will be supplied by the IC manufacturer. Figure 7-14 shows several of these. The value T_R is the minimum cycle time a read operation requires. During this period the address lines must be stable. The value T_A is the access time, which is the maximum time from when the address lines are stable until data can be read from the memory. The value T_{C0} is the maximum time from when the $\overline{CS}$ line is made a 0 until data can be read.

The bus timing must accommodate the above time. It is important that the

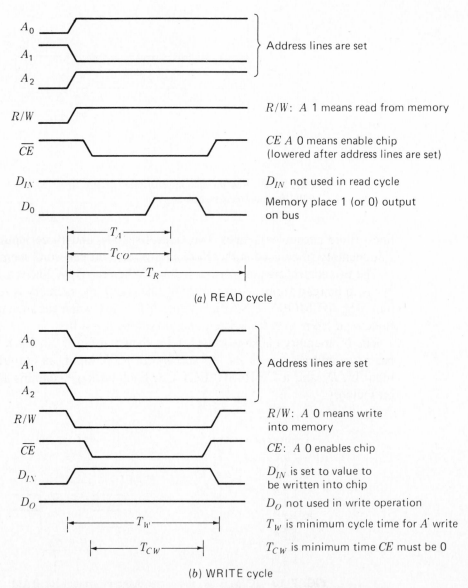

(a) READ cycle

(b) WRITE cycle

FIG. 7-14   Timing for bus IC memory (a) READ cycle (b) WRITE cycle

bus not operate too fast for the chip and that the bus wait for at least the time T_A after setting its address lines before reading and wait at least T_{C0} after lowering the $\overline{CS}$ line before reading. Also, the address line must be held stable for at least the period T_R.

For a WRITE operation the address to be written into is set up on the address lines, the R/W line is made a 0, $\overline{CS}$ is brought down, and the data to be read are placed on the D_I line.

The time interval T_W is the minimum time for a WRITE cycle; the time T_H is the time the data to be written into the chip must be held stable. Different types of memories have different timing constraints which the bus must accommodate. We will assume that our bus meets these constraints.

In order to form an 8-word 3-bit memory from these IC packages (chips), the interconnection scheme in Fig. 7-15 is used. Here the address line to each chip is connected to a corresponding address output on the microcomputer bus. The CHIP ENABLE input of $\overline{CS}$ of each chip is connected to the MEMORY ENABLE output ME from the microprocessor via an inverter, and the R/W bus line is connected to the R/W input on each chip.

If the microprocessor CPU wishes to read from the memory, it simply places the address to be read from on the address lines, puts a 1 on the R/W line, and then raises the ME line. Each chip then reads the selected bit onto its output line, and the CPU can read these values on its I_1, I_2, and I_3 lines. (Notice that a chip's output is a bus input.)

Similarly, to write a word into the memory, the CPU places the address to

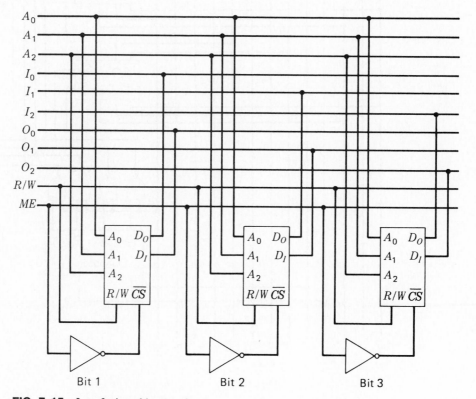

FIG. 7-15   Interfacing chips to a bus

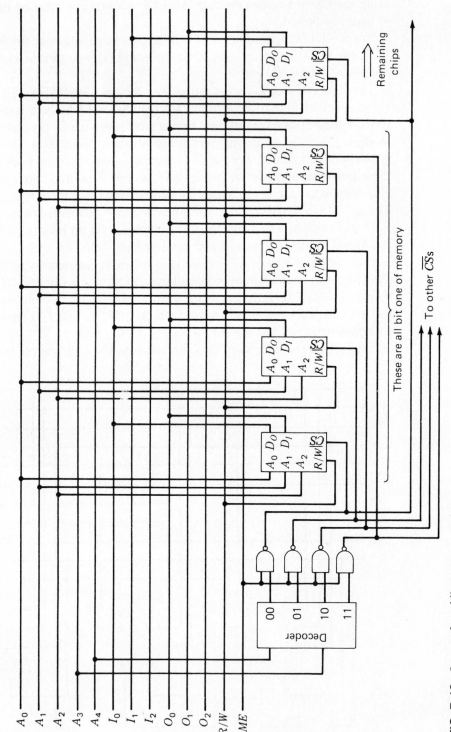

FIG. 7-16 Layout for adding memory to bus

be written into on the address lines, the bits to be written on the O_1, O_2, O_3 lines, lowers R/W, and then raises ME.

In practice, for microprocessors the memory words now generally contain 8 bits each. (Some new large microprocessors have 16-bit words.) There are generally 16 address lines, and so 2^{16} words can be used in the memory. On the other hand, memory chips tend to have from 8 to 14 (at most) memory address lines. Fortunately there is a simple way to expand memories, and this is shown for our small system in Fig. 7-16.

In this example the chips again have three address lines, but the microprocessor bus has five lines. In order to enable connection, a two-input decoder is connected to the two most significant bits of the address section of the bus, while the three least significant bits are connected to the chip address buses as before.

Now the decoder outputs are each gated with the ME control signal using a NAND gate, so when ME is raised, a single CHIP SELECT line is lowered (the outputs from the NAND gates are normally high). The decoder therefore picks the chip that is enabled, and the address lines on the enabled chip select the memory cell to be written into or read from. The decoding on the chip then selects the particular memory cell to be read from or written into.

The principle shown in Fig. 7-16 is widely used in computers. Memory chips almost invariably have fewer address inputs than buses, and so this expansion technique is necessary to memory usage. Notice that only 1 bit of the memory word is completely drawn in Fig. 7-16. (One chip from the second bit is also shown.) An entire 32-word 3-bit memory would require 12 chips of the type shown here.

As may be seen, a micro- or minicomputer can be purchased with a minimal memory, and the memory can then be expanded by adding more chips, up to the size that the bus address lines can accommodate.

7-7 RANDOM-ACCESS SEMICONDUCTOR MEMORIES

The ability to fabricate large arrays of electronic components using straightforward processing techniques and to make these arrays in small containers at reasonable prices has made semiconductor memories the most popular at this time.

Although there are a number of different schemes and devices available, there are at present six main categories of IC memories.

1. **Bipolar memories** These are essentially flip-flop memories with the flip-flops fabricated using standard *pn* junction transistors. These memories are fast but tend to be expensive.

2. **Static MOS memories** These are fabricated using MOS field effect devices to make flip-flop circuits. These memories are lower in speed than the bipolar memories but cost less, consume less power, and have high packing densities.

3. **Dynamic MOS memories** These are fabricated using MOS devices, but instead of using a flip-flop for the basic memory cell, a charge is deposited

on a capacitor (or capacitors) fabricated on the IC chip, and the presence or absence of this charge determines the state of the cell. The MOS devices are used to sense and to deposit the charge on the capacitors used. Since the charge used will slowly dissipate in time, it is necessary to periodically refresh this charge, and the memories are therefore called **dynamic memories.** (MOS or bipolar flip-flop memories are called **static memories.**) These memories tend to be slower than the other types, but they are also less expensive, consume less power, and have a high packing density.

4. **CMOS memories** CMOS utilizes both p- and n-channel devices on the same substrate. As a result it involves more complex processing. CMOS has improved speed power output over n- and p-channel MOS, but is higher in cost.

5. **Silicon on sapphire (SOS) memories** SOS is similar to CMOS. Devices are formed on an insulating substrate of sapphire. This reduces the device capacitance and improves speed. However, SOS is the highest in cost.

6. **Integrated injection logic (IIL) memories** The IIL circuits eliminate the load resistors and current sources of TTL circuits. This reduces power consumption over bipolar memories, giving greater packing density than bipolar. As a result, IIL mixes speed of bipolar memories with packing density of MOS. It is medium-cost.

The selection techniques, sensing techniques, and other basic ideas used in core memories also apply to semiconductor memories. Since the storage devices are fabricated on a chip, the sense amplifiers, decoders, etc., can be placed on the same chip, and quite often individual chips contain essentially complete small memories. The following sections cover some of the important features and details of semiconductor memories. Table 7-1 lists some key memory characteristics.

TABLE 7-1 Semiconductor Memory Characteristics

CHARACTERISTIC	MOS n-CHANNEL HIGH SPEED	MOS n-CHANNEL HIGH DENSITY	BIPOLAR
Number of bits per chip	4096	65,536	16,364
Access time, ns	10	100	40
Power dissipation, mW/bit	0.05	0.01	0.1
Average large-quantity cost, cents/bit	0.1	0.05	0.1

7-8 BIPOLAR IC MEMORIES

Bipolar memories are fabricated using high-density versions of the bipolar transistor flip-flop. One problem in increasing the density is isolating individual transistors from one another, but manufacturers have developed processes for reducing the space needed for transistor isolation. An advantage of bipolar devices is the simplicity of the interface circuitry required because of compatibility with bipolar logic. Another is the speed attainable.

Figure 7-17 shows a basic bipolar memory cell. The circuit consists of two

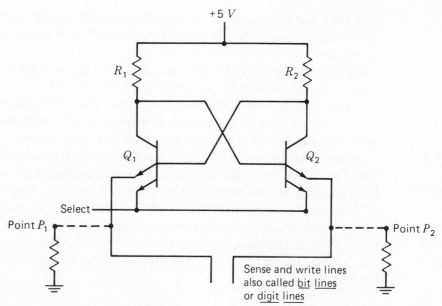

FIG. 7-17 Basic bipolar memory cell

transistors which are cross-coupled to form a conventional flip-flop. Each transistor has two emitters, however, and one of these is used to select the cell in an array. The other emitter is used to sense the state of the flip-flop and to write into the flip-flop.

The connections to the top emitters in $Q1$ and $Q2$ form what is called a **digit line.** It is used to both sense the state of the flip-flop and write into it.

The circuit operates as follows. If the SELECT line is low (at about 0 V), the flip-flop will be stable with current from the on transistor being conducted to ground by the emitter connected to the SELECT line. The transmitter will be off. As long as the digit lines are at 0 V or positive, which they normally are, they will not disturb the flip-flop's state.

If the SELECT line is raised positive (to +5 V, for instance), the emitters connected to the digit lines now control current flow. Figure 7-17 shows dashed lines to indicate resistors connected to ground from the digit lines.

Now suppose SELECT is high and we wish to read the flip-flop's state. If $Q1$ is on, then current will flow through the left resistor connected to ground. At the same time $Q2$ will be off and so no current will flow through the rightmost resistor. This means that point $P1$ will be positive with regard to $P2$. (The amount that $P1$ will be positive is determined by the value of the resistor in that part of the circuit.)

If $Q2$ is on and $Q1$ is off, current will flow through the rightmost resistor to ground and will not flow through the leftmost resistor, and $P2$ will be positive relative to $P1$.

The above shows that with the SELECT line positive, we can determine the state of the flip-flop by measuring the voltage at $P1$ and $P2$. This is normally done by an amplifier circuit called a **sense amplifier** which measures this difference and outputs a 1 or a 0, depending on whether $P1$ or $P2$ is more positive.

It is also possible to write into the cell using the digit lines. Suppose the

SELECT line is high, and if we force $P1$ high with regard to $P2$, then $Q2$ will go on and will force $Q1$ off. Similarly, raising $P2$ with regard to $P1$ will force $Q1$ on and $Q2$ off.

As may now be seen, the same two digit lines can be used to both sense the state of the flip-flop and force a given value into the cell.

Figure 7-18 shows an arrangement with two SELECT lines and two memory cells in order to show how these cells can be combined in memory. As indicated, more cells can be added in either the vertical or the horizontal direction.

Assume that the upper SELECT line is high and the lower SELECT line is low. This selects the upper cell. Now if we wish to read from the memory, the sense amplifier will tell the state of the selected flip-flop because the other cell(s) in that column will have low SELECT lines conducting current to ground for the on transistors, and only the selected cell will have the current flow to ground for its on transistor pass through the sense amplifier. This means that a single cell in each column can be selected and read from by connecting a decoder to the SELECT inputs.

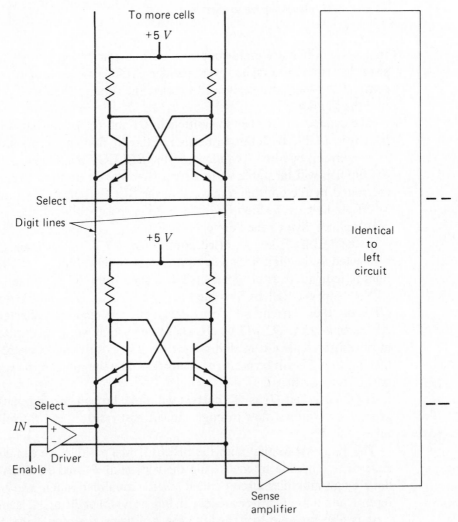

FIG. 7-18 Bipolar memory cells in array

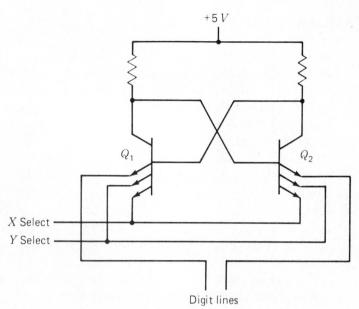

FIG. 7-19   Two-dimensional select bipolar cell

Similarly, we can write a 1 or a 0 into the selected cell in a column using the driver circuit, which will force either one of the digit lines positive with respect to the other.

This memory is organized like that in Fig. 7-11, except that the two digit lines are used to both read from and write into a cell instead of having separate READ and WRITE lines. Also, a sense amplifier is used to read column output values and a column driver (which can be disabled) to write into a cell.

Figure 7-19 shows a bipolar memory cell for a two-dimensional selection system. Both SELECT lines must be high to select the cell. Otherwise the circuit operates like that in Figs. 7-17 and 7-18, using digit lines to both sense the state of the cell and write into a selected cell.

The memory cell in Fig. 7-19 would be used in a memory organized like that in Figs. 7-9 and 7-10.

Table 7-2 lists some characteristics of commercially available bipolar memory chips.

TABLE 7-2   IC Bipolar Memories

ORGANIZATION	PART NUMBER	MAXIMUM ACCESS TIME *ns*	MAXIMUM CURRENT REQUIRED mA
1024 $\times$ 4	6250/6251-1	50	175
1024 $\times$ 8	6282/6283-2	35	170
	6280/6281-1		
4096 $\times$ 1	93L471	45	165
4096 $\times$ 1	93F471	30	195

7-9 STATIC MOS MEMORIES

It was realized very early in semiconductor memory development that MOS devices offer simplicity of manufacture and economy of layout. (MOS is made with only one diffusion and perhaps two-thirds the number of masks of bipolar devices.) MOS cells take up only one-half to one-fourth the area of bipolar cells, and hence they offer a considerable cost advantage. Figure 7-20 illustrates a MOS flip-flop analogous to the bipolar device of Fig. 7-17.

A cell is selected by simply raising the SELECT line. $Q1$ and $Q3$ serve as gates, connecting to the digit lines. $Q2$ and $Q4$ form a conventional flip-flop. The state of the storage cell can be read by raising the SELECT line which will turn on either $Q1$ or $Q3$, depending on the state of the flip-flop. The write operation is carried out by raising the SELECT line and then setting the desired value in by placing a high and a low voltage on the correct digit lines, just as in Fig. 7-17.

The predominant type of MOS device in early memories was the p-channel enhancement mode (PMOS) unit, where holes are the vehicle of current flow. Although easy to produce, inexpensive, and reliable, PMOS is relatively slow and limited in LSI packing density. n-channel devices have now become the most popular, offering important performance advantages over their p-channel counterparts, such as low operating voltage and higher speed. Because electron mobility is greater than hole mobility, n-channel transistors are two to three times faster than p-channel transistors, which is equivalent to saying that n-channel devices have greater gain than p-channel devices of the same size. For equal speeds, n-channel units are smaller, permitting greater packing density, and higher substrate doping levels may be employed, increasing density even further. Further, there are many variations in NMOS technology, including VMOS, HMOS, etc.

If we compare bipolar and MOS technologies, bipolar offers a speed advantage, although, until recently, limitations imposed by the need for isolation between transistors have limited packing density and hence per-chip storage capacity. Bipolar components can provide access times of under 10 ns, in con-

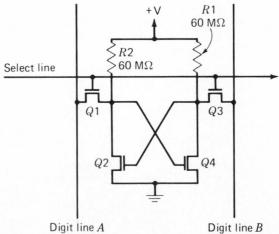

FIG. 7-20 MOS static memory cell (courtesy of GTE Microcircuits Division, GTE Products Corporation)

trast with 300 ns or more for PMOS and 20 ns for NMOS. MOS devices have relatively high internal capacitance and impedance, leading to longer time constants and access times. Our schematic symbols will not show the channel connections on the FETs, as is conventional for memory devices. All devices are NMOS.

The operation of a typical 4096-bit static NMOS memory chip is detailed in Figs. 7-21–7-23. The 4096 bits of memory are organized in an array of 64 rows by 64 columns. The memory bits are accessed by simultaneously decoding the X address A_0–A_5 for the rows and the Y address A_6–A_{11} for the columns. (Each column contains a **presence amplifier,** the outputs of which are ORed and connected to the output stage.) Each bit or memory cell is a standard flip-flop as shown in Fig. 7-21, consisting of R_1, R_2 (which are actually MOS devices), $Q2$, $Q4$, $Q1$, and $Q3$. $Q1$ and $Q3$ are used to connect the cell to the digit lines whenever the X SELECT is high. To read from this cell, the SELECT line is raised; then the cell will pull one of the digit lines low from its normally high state. The sense circuit selected by the Y column decoder will detect the differential voltage on the digit line selected and amplify it. To write into the cell, an X line is selected and forced low by the circuit, and the selected cell assumes the state forced by the selected digit line.

The CHIP SELECT (CS) input controls the operation of the memory. When CS is low, the input address buffers, decoders, sensing circuits, and output stages are held in the off state, and power is supplied only to the memory elements. When the CS goes high, the memory is enabled. The CS pulse clocks the TTL logic level addresses, READ-WRITE, and DATA input into D flip-

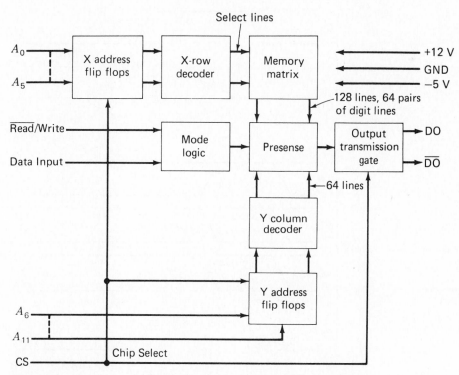

FIG. 7-21 Block diagram of MOS static memory (courtesy of GTE Microcircuits Division, GTE Products Corporation)

Top view

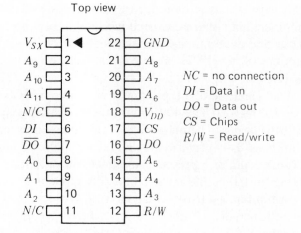

Pin assignment

FIG. 7-22 MOS static memory pin assignment (courtesy of GTE Microcircuits Division, GTE Products Corporation)

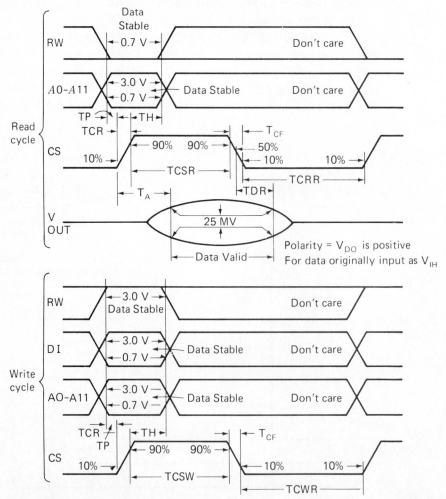

FIG. 7-23 Timing diagrams (courtesy of GTE Microcircuits Division, GTE Products Corporation)

flops and enables the output stage. When a cell is read from, one of the two outputs will be a 1 (DO for data originally input as a 1, $\overline{DO}$ for data originally input as a 0).

As shown in Fig. 7-22, this memory chip is packaged in a 22-pin dual in-line package. By assembling a number of these chips, a large, moderately fast memory can be constructed. Memory cycle times for this chip are on the order of 50 ns. Figure 7-23 shows the timing for the memory cycles.

Notice that the basic memory cell in this memory is a device as shown in Fig. 7-3. A two-dimensional selection is obtained by breaking the memory into rows and columns and using many (64) sense amplifiers and INHIBIT, or digit, drivers on these columns. When a read or write operation is performed, the appropriate digit driver or "presence" amplifier is selected by the Y decoder. Thus a row of memory cells is enabled by the ROW SELECT line, but only the cell at the intersection of the enabled row and the selected sense amplifier or digit line driver will be actually used, as was shown in Fig. 7-11. This scheme requires more digit drivers and sense amplifiers, but simplifies construction of the individual flip-flop memory cells. (Two more MOS transistors per cell are required to make a conventional two-dimensional selection as in the bipolar cell previously shown.) In general, two-dimensional selection of semiconductor cells requires more circuitry (generally two transistors per cell) but simplifies the decoders used. A pure one-dimensional (linear) selection makes for larger decoders but simpler individual cells. As a result, compromise strategies such as that shown are often used.

The characteristics of several NMOS memories are shown in Table 7-3.

TABLE 7-3 NMOS Static Memories

PART NUMBER, MANUFACTURER, ORGANIZATION	POWER DISSIPATION mW	MAXIMUM ACCESS TIME ns	MAXIMUM CYCLE TIME ns	PACKAGE
91L30/AMD (1K × 4)	350	500	840	22-pin
9135/AMD (4K × 1)	675	80	130	18-pin
SEMI 4402 (4K × 1)	500	100	100	22-pin
5256/National (1K × 4)	400	250	400	22-pin
2147H/Intel (4K × 1)	500	45	60	18-pin
TMS4045/TI (1K × 4)	400	150	150	18-pin

7-10 DYNAMIC MEMORIES

MOS cells are generally used as the basis for a dynamic memory system. In a given memory cell, a 1 is written in by placing a charge on a capacitor; not charging or discharging the capacitor stores a 0. Reading then entails sensing the presence or absence of a charge on the capacitor. However, because there is always some leakage of the charge to ground, periodic refreshing is necessary.

Figure 7-24 depicts the simplest and most used type of data storage cell, using a single MOS switching transistor and a storage capacitor (also a MOS device). Although the single-transistor memory cell requires sophisticated sense and write circuits, its small size makes it suitable for high-density storage, such as in memories with 64,000 cells per IC chip.

In Fig. 7-24 the ROW SELECT line operates as in other memories: making this line high selects a cell. The DATA line is used to read from the cell. Cells are arranged in a two-dimensional array with sense amplifiers connected to each DATA line and in turn to all the cells in that column. When a row is enabled by the ROW SELECT line, all the transistors in that row conduct (the transistors in other rows are off). These on transistors transfer any charge on the capacitors to the DATA line, destructively reading the data. Each column in the array has its own sense amplifier which detects the charge, amplifying the detected level to a logic 1 (outputting a 0 for no charge). (These sense amplifiers must be carefully designed because the charge is attenuated by the capacitance formed by the entire column's DATA line.)

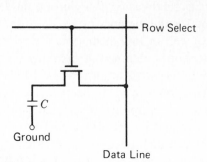

FIG. 7-24
Single-transistor memory cell

A cell is written into by forcing the DATA line to a high or low voltage (for 1 or 0) and then raising the ROW SELECT, forcing or not forcing a charge into the capacitor.

Figure 7-25 shows the address timing and pin layout for a 16K-bit dynamic RAM. There are not enough address lines into these chips, and so the addresses are **time multiplexed** (that is, put on in two sections, one right after the other). First the (first half) row address is placed on A_0-A_6 and RAS is lowered, then the column address is placed on A_0-A_6 and $\overline{\text{CAS}}$ is lowered. In order to use RAMs of this kind, extra circuitry for multiplexing address lines and to generate the REFRESH signal must be used. Nevertheless, because of the high packing density and low cost, the extra complexity of these specialized circuits is compensated for, and these memories are widely used.

The primary advantages of dynamic MOS memories lie in the simplicity of the individual cells. There is a secondary advantage in the fact that power need not be applied to the cells when they are not being read from or written into. This makes for higher packing densities per chip. The obvious disadvantage lies in the need to refresh these cells every few milliseconds since charge continually leaks from the capacitors (generally less than every 2 ms). External circuitry to control refresh rewrite is generally required, or sometimes the memories may include special circuits to refresh when commanded. As a result, extra refresh memory cycles are required, but these occupy only a small percentage of the overall operating time. Table 7-4 lists some of the characteristics of dynamic memories.

The selection systems and sense and write operations for dynamic memories are similar to those for static memories, except that more complicated timing

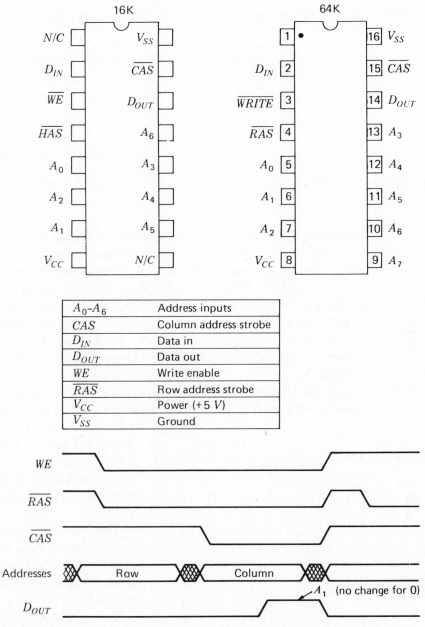

FIG. 7-25 16K and 64K dynamic memory pin layout and address timing

is required. Dynamic memories are generally slower than static memories but also tend to cost less per bit.

7-11 READ-ONLY MEMORIES

A type of storage device called a **read-only memory** (ROM) is widely used. ROMs have the unique characteristic that they can be read from, but not written into. The information stored in these memories is therefore introduced into the memory in some manner such that the information is semipermanent or

TABLE 7-4 Several Commercially Available 16K NMOS Dynamic Memories

MANUFACTURER	PART NUMBER	ACCESS TIME ns	READ CYCLE TIME ns	WRITE CYCLE TIME ns	OPERATING POWER mW	NUMBER OF PINS	OUTPUTS
Intel	2116	150	375	375	720	16	Latched, 3-state, TTL compatible
TI	TMS4070	150	550	550	550	16	Unlatched, 3-state, TTL compatible
Mostek	MK4116	120	375	375	600	16	Unlatched, 3-state, TTL compatible
Motorola	MCM6616	250	375	375	500	16	Latched, 3-state, TTL compatible

permanent. Sometimes the information stored in a ROM is placed in the memory at the time of construction, and sometimes devices are used where the information can be changed. In this section we shall study several types of ROMs. These are characteristic of this particular class of memory devices, and most devices are variations on the principles that will be presented.

Basically a ROM is a device with several input and output lines such that for each input value there is a unique output value. Thus a ROM physically realizes a truth table, or table of combinations. A typical (small) one is shown in Table 7-5.

This list of input-output values is actually a list of binary-to-Gray code values. It is important to see that the list can be looked at in two ways: first as a table for a gating network with four inputs and four outputs, and second as a list of addresses from 0 to 15, as given by the X values, and the contents of each address, as given by the values of Z.

TABLE 7-5 Binary-to-Gray Code Values

INPUT				OUTPUT			
X_1	X_2	X_3	X_4	Z_1	Z_2	Z_3	Z_4
0	0	0	0	0	0	0	0
0	0	0	1	0	0	0	1
0	0	1	0	0	0	1	1
0	0	1	1	0	0	1	0
0	1	0	0	0	1	1	0
0	1	0	1	0	1	1	1
0	1	1	0	0	1	0	1
0	1	1	1	0	1	0	0
1	0	0	0	1	1	0	0
1	0	0	1	1	1	0	1
1	0	1	0	1	1	1	1
1	0	1	1	1	1	1	0
1	1	0	0	1	0	1	0
1	1	0	1	1	0	1	1
1	1	1	0	1	0	0	1
1	1	1	1	1	0	0	0

Thus we might construct a gating network as in Fig. 7-26 which would give the correct Z output for each X input. (The boxes with + are mod 2 adders.)

Table 7-5 could also be realized by a 16-word 4-bit-per-word core memory into which we had read 0000 at the address 0; 0001 at the address 1; 0011 in the next address; and so on until 1000 in the last address. If we did not ever thereafter write into this memory, it would be a ROM memory and would serve the same purpose as the gating network in Fig. 7-26.

Figure 7-27(a) shows a scheme for implementing Table 7-5 using a decoder network with four inputs X_1, X_2, X_3, and X_4 and a number of diodes. With a given input combination (or address), a single output line from the decoder will be high. Let us assume that the input value is $X_1 = 0$, $X_2 = 1$, $X_3 = 1$, $X_4 =$

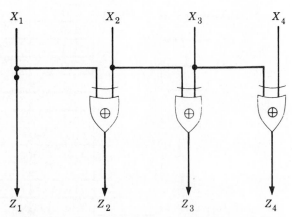

$$X \oplus Y = \overline{X}Y + X\overline{Y}$$

FIG. 7-26 Combinational network for binary-to-Gray code

1. This corresponds to 0111 on the decoder output in Fig. 7-27(a). Diodes are connected at the junction of this line, and the output lines which are 1s, and no diodes are placed where 0s are to appear. Thus for the input 0111 we have a single diode connected to output line Z_2, since the desired output is to be 0100. Similarly, for the input 0110 we connect diodes to Z_2 and Z_4, since the output is to be 0101. The operation of the network is as follows. Only one decoder line output will be high at a time. Current flows from this line to only those output lines to which a diode is connected. Thus for the input 0101, current flows into lines Z_2, Z_3, and Z_4 but not Z_1; so Z_2, Z_3, Z_4 will be 1s and Z_1 a 0.

The entire scheme outlined above realizes the ROM with electronic gates (the diodes form OR gates). By using LSI techniques, arrays of this sort can be inexpensively fabricated in small containers at low prices. 512-word 8-bit memories are of about average size for the LSI ROMs; these memories effectively store 4096 bits in all.

The diodes in Fig. 7-27(a) are often transistors, and the manufacturing processes are of various types. Figure 7-27(b) shows typical memory cells for semiconductor ROMs using MOS and bipolar transistors. These cells are from a one-dimensional selection system; notice the word-selection lines and the bit line. Both one- and two-dimensional selection is used in ROMs. MOS ROMS generally have 40-ns to 200-ns access times; access times of bipolar memories range from 10 ns to 100 ns.

When a ROM is constructed so that the user can electrically (or using other techniques) write in the contents of the memory, the memory is called a **programmable ROM,** or **PROM.** Often a scheme is used where a memory chip is delivered with 1s in every position, but 0s can be introduced at given positions by placing an address on the input lines and then raising each output line which is to be a 0 to a specified voltage, thus destroying a connection to the selected cell. (Sometimes the memories contain all 0s, and 1s are written in by the user.)

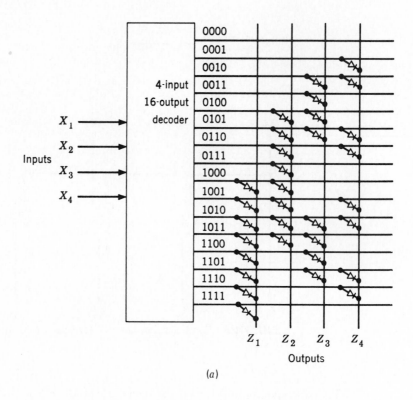

(a)

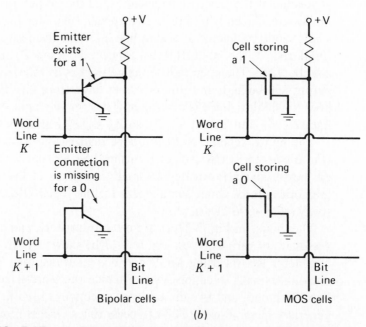

(b)

FIG. 7-27 (a) Diode ROM (b) ROM cells using MOS and bipolar transistors

Devices are also manufactured which program PROMs by reading paper tapes, magnetic tapes, punched cards, etc., and placing their contents into the PROM.

Custom ROM manufacturers provide forms whereby a user can fill 1s and 0s on a form that is provided, and the manufacturer will produce a custom-made mask and will then produce LSI chips which will realize the memory contents specified by the user. A single chip may cost more for such a memory, but large production runs generally cost less per chip. These devices come with up to 64K bits per IC package.

Figure 7-28 shows a block diagram of a 64K-bit MOS memory which is organized as a 4096-word 8-bit-per-word memory. The user places the address on the thirteen input lines A_0–A_{12} and then raises CS_1 and CS_2 ($\overline{CE}$ must be low). This will enable the output, and the desired word will appear on lines O_0–O_7. This is a custom-made memory where the desired memory contents are supplied to the manufacturer by the user on a form. The manufacturer then makes

PIN CONFIGURATION

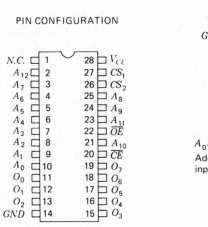

BLOCK DIAGRAM

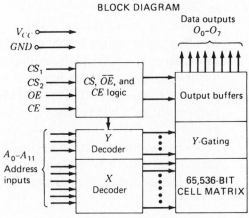

PIN NAMES

A_0–A_{12}	Addresses
$\overline{OE}$	Output enable
$\overline{CE}$	Chip enable
CS	Chip select
$N.C.$	No connection

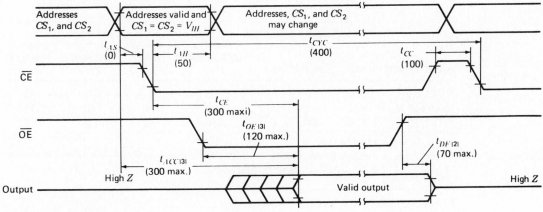

Notes
1. All times shown in parentheses are minimum times and are nanoseconds unless otherwise specified.
2. t_{DF} is specified from $\overline{OE}$ or $\overline{CE}$, whichever occurs first.
3. t_{ACC} may be delayed up to 180 ns after the falling edge of $\overline{CE}$ without impact on t_{ACC}.

FIG. 7-28 64K ROM (courtesy of Intel Corp.)

a mask to create the desired bit patterns on an IC chip and manufactures ROMs with this pattern to order. Delay time for the memory is on the order of 75 ns.

When a ROM is manufactured so that the memory's contents can be set as desired by the user and the memory can later have the contents erased and new values written in, the ROM is said to be **erasable and reprogrammable,** and is often called an **EPROM.**

For example, some memory chips are made with a transparent lid. Exposing the chip (through the lid) to ultraviolet light will erase the pattern on the chip, and a new pattern can be written in electrically. This can be repeated as often as desired.

Table 7-6 shows characteristics of some bipolar ROMs and of several electrically programmable ROMs (EPROMs) which can have their contents erased by exposure to ultraviolet light and can be programmed (written into) by placing designated voltages on inputs. Also shown in Table 7-6 are some characteristics for electrically alterable ROMs (EAROMs) which can have their contents rewritten while in place in a circuit by means of properly applied input voltages.

Several companies make devices for programming PROMs and EPROMs. Some of these devices are operated from a keyboard, some from tape, and some from external inputs such as microprocessors.

TABLE 7-6 ROM Characteristics

BIPOLAR ROMS

ORGANIZATION	PART NUMBER†	ACCESS TIME ns	CURRENT REQUIRED mA
512 × 8	6240/6241-1	90	170
1014 × 4	6252/6253-1	60	175
1024 × 8	6282/6283-1	55	170
1024 × 10	6255/6256-1	100	165/175
2048 × 8	6275/6276-1	110	190

MOS EPROMS

MODEL NUMBER	SIZE	ORGANIZATION	MAXIMUM ACCESS TIME (ns)	POWER SUPPLY (V)	MAXIMUM ACTIVE CURRENT (mA)	STANDBY CURRENT (mA)
TI 2716	16K	2048 × 8	450	12, ±5	45	45
Intel 2732	32K	4096 × 8	300	5	40	15
Ti 2532	32K	4096 × 8	450	5	168	10

MOS EAROMS

MODEL NUMBER	SIZE	ACCESS TIME μs
Nitron NC7050	256 × 4	2–5
Nitron NC7051	1024 × 1	2–5
GI ER3402	1024 × 4	0.95
GI ER3800	2048 × 4	2.6

†Courtesy of Monolithic Memories.

When an EPROM or a PROM chip is to be programmed, there is generally a write enable to be raised, which makes output lines able to accept data. Address lines are then set to the location to be written into. Then, for some chips, the output lines to have 1s on them are raised to high voltages (or a sequence of large-amplitude pulses are applied to them) or, for some chips, the normal logic levels are placed on the output lines and a special program input is placed with a sequence of high-voltage (25 V) pulses. In either case each memory location must be written into by setting the address lines and then writing the desired contents into the output lines. Applying an erase (by means of raising the lid to the IC container and applying an ultraviolet light for some specified time) generally erases all the contents of the memory.

7-12 MAGNETIC CORE STORAGE

For about 20 years magnetic core memories dominated computer main memory usage. In the past few years, however, IC memories have passed cores in terms of total sales. Total core memory sales increase every year, however, and many existing computers still use them. The invention of the core memory was the technological breakthrough that brought the computer industry to life in the early 1950s.

The basic storage device in a magnetic core memory consists of a small toroidal (ring-shaped) piece of magnetic material, called a **magnetic core.** The magnetic core is generally a solid piece of ferromagnetic ceramic material.

Figure 7-29 illustrates a magnetic core, many times actual size. An input winding (wire) is shown threaded through this core. If current is passed through this winding, magnetic flux will be produced, with a direction dependent on the direction of the current through the winding. The core is ring-shaped and formed of material with high permeability, so that it will present a low-reluctance path for the magnetic flux. Depending on the direction of the current through the input winding, the core will become magnetized in either a clockwise or a counterclockwise direction. The retentivity of the material used in the core is such that when the magnetizing force is removed, the core remains magnetized, retaining a large part of its flux.

The characteristics of a given type of magnetic core are generally studied by means of a graph, with the magnetizing force H produced by the winding current plotted along the abscissa, and the resulting flux density B through the core plotted along the ordinate (Fig. 7-30). If a cyclical current which is alternately

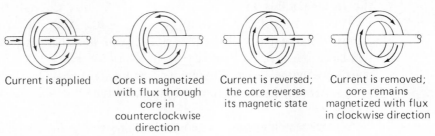

Current is applied   Core is magnetized with flux through core in counterclockwise direction   Current is reversed; the core reverses its magnetic state   Current is removed; core remains magnetized with flux in clockwise direction

FIG. 7-29 The magnetic core

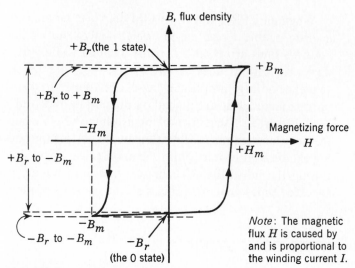

FIG. 7-30 Hysteresis loop for a magnetic material

positive and negative is applied to the input winding in Fig. 7-29, for each value of the input current there will be a magnetizing force H applied to the core. If the flux density B in the core is then plotted against this magnetizing force, the resulting curve is called a **hysteresis loop.** In Fig. 7-30, the force H applied is sufficient to saturate the core material at both the positive and the negative extremities of the input current. The maximum flux density through the core when the core is saturated with a positive value of H is designated $+B_m$, and the corresponding negative value of H is denoted by $-B_m$.

Notice that for each value of magnetizing force there are two values of flux density. One occurs when the magnetizing force is increasing, and the other when the magnetizing force is decreasing. If the magnetizing force is varied from $-H_m$ to $+H_m$, the flux density will move along the lower part of the curve, and if the magnetizing force is moved from $+H_m$ to $-H_m$, the flux density will move along the upper part of the curve, again following the arrows, to point $-B_m$.

If a current sufficient to cause the core to be saturated is applied at the input winding and then removed, the flux density through the core will revert to either point $+B_r$ or point $-B_r$, depending on the polarity of the current. These two operating points are called the **remanent points,** and when the flux through the core is at either of these points, the core resembles a small permanent magnet. If a core is at the $+B_r$ point of the graph and a current of sufficient amplitude to cause a force of $-H_m$ is applied, the flux produced will be in opposition to the remanent flux in the core $+B_r$, and the flux through the core will be reversed, moving the operating point to $-B_m$. After the current has been removed, the majority of the flux will remain, and the flux density in the core will be at the $-B_r$ point of the curve. The fact that the core can be in either one of two unique states of magnetization makes it possible to consider one state as representing a 0 ($-B_r$ in the figure) and the other state as a 1 ($+B_r$ in the figure).

Another winding, called a **sense winding** [see Fig. 7-31(b)], is used to determine whether a core contains a 0 or a 1. To sense the state of the core, a current

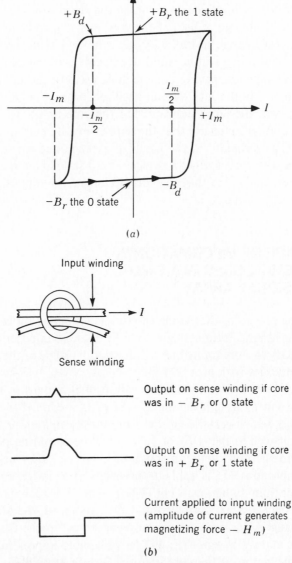

FIG. 7-31 (a) Current versus flux density hysteresis loop for a magnetic core (b) Sense winding

sufficient to produce a magnetizing force $-H_m$ is applied to the input winding. If the core was at $+B_r$, the operating point will be moved downward along the arrows in Fig. 7-30 to the $-B_m$ point. If the core was at the $-B_r$ point, the operating point will be moved horizontally to $-B_m$. The amount of change in flux in the core will be quite different for each of these cases. If the core was initially in the 1 state (at point $+B_r$ on the hysteresis curve), the direction of magnetization of the core will be changed, and the flux through the core will change from $+B_r$ to $-B_m$. The magnitude of this change in the magnetization of the core is indicated as $+B_r$ to $-B_m$ on the figure. If, however, the core was originally in the 0 state at $-B_r$ on the curve, the change in magnetization will be small, only from $-B_r$ to $-B_m$, and the magnitude of this change in flux is indicated as $-B_r$ to $-B_m$ on the figure. A change in the flux density through the core will induce a voltage in the sense winding, which is proportional to the rate of change of flux. If the core was originally in the 0 state, the change and rate of change in flux will be small, and therefore the voltage induced in the sense winding will be small. If the core was originally in the 1 state, the amount of change and rate of change in flux will be large, and consequently the voltage induced in the sense winding will be large. A small output from the sense winding will therefore indicate that the core originally contained a 0, and a large output will indicate that the core originally contained a 1.

The difficulty in the use of this technique for sensing the state of a core is that the core is always reset to the 0 state. This readout technique is therefore "destructive" in that the core no longer contains the information that was previously stored in it.

7-13 STORAGE OF INFORMATION IN MAGNETIC CORES IN A TWO-DIMENSIONAL ARRAY

The preceding discussion showed how a single bit of information may be stored in and read from a single core. In digital computer systems, however, it is necessary to store many bits of information; some of the larger computers have core memories with over 10 million cores.

Figure 7-31(a) plots the values of flux density for a magnetic core versus current I through the input winding of a core. If the current reaches a value of $+I_m$, which is sufficient to saturate the core, and is then removed, the core will be placed in the $+B_r$, or 1, state. If the operating point on the curve is at $+B_r$ with no input current through the winding, and a negative pulse of current with amplitude $-I_m$ is applied, the core will be switched to the 0 state. The important thing to notice in Fig. 7-31 is that, if the core is in the 1 state and a current of only $-I_m/2$ is applied and then removed, the state of the core will not be changed. Instead, the operating point will move from $+B_r$ to $+B_d$ and, when the current is removed, will move back to approximately $+B_r$. The same principle applies if the core is in the 0 state at point $-B_r$ on the curve. A current of $+I_m$ will switch the core to the 1 state, but a current of $+I_m/2$ will only move the operating point to $-B_d$, and when the current is removed, the core will return to point $-B_r$.

Figure 7-32(a) shows 16 cores arranged in a square array. Each core has two input windings, one from a set of X input lines and one from a set of Y input lines. Assume that all the cores are in the 0 state and a 1 is to be written into core X_2Y_2. If a current with an amplitude of $+I_m$ is applied on the X_2 line, core X_2Y_2 will be switched to the 1 state. However, all the cores connected to the X_2 input line will also be switched to the 1 state. The same holds true if a current of $+I_m$ is applied to input line Y_2, in which case all the cores connected to this Y input line would be switched to the 1 state.

If, however, currents of $+I_m/2$ are applied to both the X_2 line and the Y_2 line at the same time, only core X_2Y_2 will receive a total current of $+I_m$ [Fig. 7-32(b)]. Each of the other cores along the Y_2 input line will receive a current of

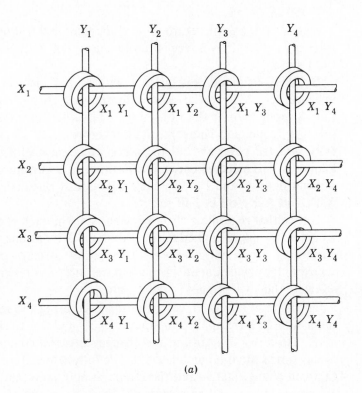

(a)

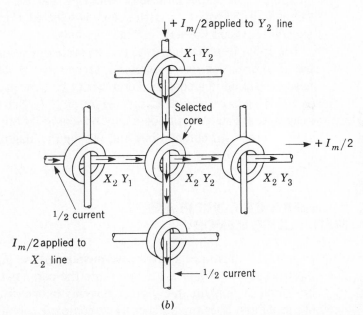

(b)

FIG. 7-32 Two-dimensional core plane (a) Wiring (b) Selection of X_2Y_2

$+I_m/2$, as will each of the cores along the X_2 input line. Since these cores will have started at point $-B_r$ on the graph and will receive a current of $+I_m/2$, their operating point will be moved as far as $-B_d$ on the curve. However, the operating point will not be moved as far as the steep incline which leads to the $+B_r$ section of the graph. When the current is removed, these cores, with the exception of X_2Y_2, will return to the $-B_r$ point and will be in the 0 state. Therefore only core X_2Y_2 will receive a total current of $+I_m$ and will be switched into the 1 state.

By this technique, any given core can be selected from the array. For instance, core X_1Y_3 can be selected by applying currents of $+I_m/2$ to the X_1 and the Y_3 input lines at the same time. This is known as the coincident-current selection technique. The core which receives a full $+I_m$ current is known as a **fully selected core,** and all the cores which receive a current of $+I_m/2$ are known as **half selected cores.** For instance, if a current of $+I_m/2$ is connected to input lines X_1 and Y_3, core X_1Y_3 will be fully selected, and cores X_1Y_1, X_1Y_2, X_2Y_3, and X_3Y_3 will be half selected.

Notice that regardless of the previous state of each of the cores in the array, a current of $+I_m/2$ applied to one X and one Y input line will result in sufficient current to switch only one core of the array. If cores in the 0 state are half selected, they will remain in the 0 state; and if cores in the 1 state are half selected, they will remain in the 1 state.

The state of any given core can be sensed using the same technique. If currents of $-I_m/2$ are applied to input lines X_2 and Y_2, a full $-I_m$ current will be applied to core X_2Y_2, causing it to change states if it contained a 1 and to remain in the same state if it contained a 0. The fully selected core will be the only core that can change states, and therefore the only core that is capable of causing an appreciable output on a sense winding. A sense winding would be threaded through all the cores; if a certain core is selected, the output at the sense winding will represent the state of that core only.

It may be seen that there are two separate operations involved: first, the writing of information into a core and, second, the reading of information which has been stored in a core. A 0 or a 1 may be written into any core in the array by applying a current of either $-I_m/2$ or $+I_m/2$ to the correct pair of input lines, and the state of any core may be sensed by applying a current of $-I_m/2$ to the correct pair of input lines and sensing the magnitude of the output voltage on the sense winding.

7-14 ASSEMBLY OF CORE PLANES INTO A CORE MEMORY

Figure 7-33 illustrates a small **core-memory plane.** Any core in this plane may be selected, and a 0 or a 1 written into the core, or the state of any core may be sensed by applying the correct currents to one of the X input lines and one of the Y input lines simultaneously. A complete core memory consists of a number of such planes, stacked in a rectangular array. The X windings of each plane are connected in series, so that current applied to the X_1 winding of the first plane must travel through the X_1 winding of the second plane, and so on, until it passes through the X_1 winding for the last plane in the array. If the plane illustrated in Fig. 7-33 were connected in an array, the X_1 winding at the top left of the drawing would be connected to one end of the X_1 winding from the preceding core plane, and the X_1 winding at the bottom left would be connected to the X_1 winding of the following core plane. If 10 core planes of the size shown in Fig. 7-33 were stacked in this manner, a pulse on the X_1 input line would

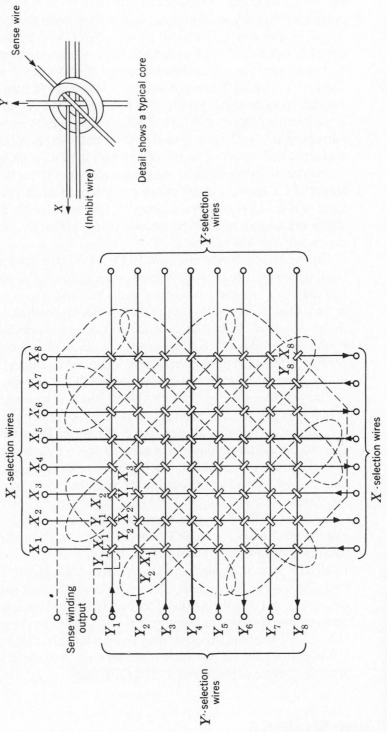

Sense wire

Y

X

(Inhibit wire)

Detail shows a typical core

Y-selection wires

X-selection wires

X-selection wires

Y-selection wires

Sense winding output

X_1 X_2 X_3 X_4 X_5 X_6 X_7 X_8

Y_1 X_1 X_2

Y_2 X_2 Y_1 X_3

Y_2 X_1

Y_8 X_8

Y_1 Y_2 Y_3 Y_4 Y_5 Y_6 Y_7 Y_8

FIG. 7-33   Core-memory plane

have to travel through 80 cores. The Y windings are connected in the same manner. Each plane has its own sense winding, however, and the sense windings for the planes are not connected together in any way; instead, a **sense amplifier** is connected to the sense-winding output from each plane.

Let us call a $+I_m/2$ current pulse a WRITE 1 pulse, for such a current applied to an X or Y winding tends to write a 1 into the cores along the winding. It may be seen that simultaneously applying a WRITE 1 pulse on a selected Y line and a selected X line will write a 1 into a single core in the same relative position in each of the planes. For instance, if the X_3 and Y_4 input lines are pulsed with a current of $+I_m/2$, the X_3Y_4 core in each plane will receive a $+I_m$ current. If a $-I_m/2$ pulse is then applied to the same X- and Y-selection lines, an output will be sensed on the sense winding of each plane.

In general there will be as many core planes in the array as bits in the word length of the memory in which the array is used. If the word length is 15 bits, there will be 15 planes in the array; if the word length is 35 bits, 35 planes. There will be a sense winding for each plane, so that the output from each core that is selected will be sensed.

One problem still remains. A WRITE 1 ($+I_m/2$) pulse on a pair of X and Y input lines will write a 1 into the core in the same relative position of each plane, and therefore into every position of the word, and it may be necessary to write 0s into some cores and 1s into others. A fourth winding through each core is therefore added. This winding is called the **inhibit winding,** and it is used to inhibit the writing of a 1 into a given selected core in a plane. A single inhibit winding is threaded through each core in a plane in a direction so that a current of $-I_m/2$ on the winding will oppose the WRITE 1 current. There are therefore as many inhibit windings as core planes. There is also a single driver for each inhibit winding, which can be gated on or off, depending on whether a 1 or a 0 is to be written into the selected core of the plane. The amplitude of the current through the inhibit winding is the same as the $-I_m/2$ current used in the X and Y selection lines. The inhibit winding is threaded through the cores so that the magnetizing force from the current through the inhibit winding always opposes the magnetizing force of the WRITE 1 currents.

Since the WRITE 1 pulse from the X and Y drivers is of $+I_m/2$ amplitude and the pulse from the INHIBIT driver is of $-I_m/2$ amplitude, if a WRITE 1 pulse is applied from a given pair of X and Y drivers at the same time as an INHIBIT pulse is applied, the total current through the selected core will be $(+I_m/2) + (+I_m/2) + (-I_m/2) = +I_m/2$, which is not sufficient to switch the core to a 1. A 1 or a 0 may therefore be written into the selected core of a given plane by first clearing the cores with a $-I_m/2$ pulse on the correct pair of X and Y SELECT lines, and then turning the inhibit driver on for each plane where a 0 is desired and off for each plane where a 1 is desired, while applying a WRITE 1 pulse to the X and Y SELECT lines.

7-15 TIMING SEQUENCE

The same timing sequence is generally used whether the computer is to write information in the core memory or to read information from the core memory. The total time taken by the entire timing sequence is called a **memory cycle,** and is one of the principal speed-determining factors for a core memory. Figure 7-34 shows a complete memory cycle. The operation of writing a word into the memory will be examined first, then the read operation. Assume that there are five core planes in the total array and that each core plane contains 64 cores, as in Fig. 7-33.

1. **Writing into a core memory** Assume that the binary number 10100 is to be written into core location X_3Y_4 of the memory. Zeros are therefore to be written into the selected cores of planes 2, 4, and 5.

   First the correct drivers are selected. Since core X_3Y_4 in each plane is to be written into, the drivers connected to the X_3 line are enabled, as are the drivers connected to the Y_4 line of the array. When the READ TIME pulses are applied, 0s are written into the X_3Y_4 core in each of the five planes. After 0.4 μs each of the selected cores will contain a 0. At 0.5 μs after the sequence is initiated, the INHIBIT drivers connected to planes 2, 4, and 5 are turned on; in addition, the write time begins. A 1 will then be written into the selected core in planes 1 and 3, and the subtraction of the inhibit current from the coincident current through the selected cores in planes 2, 4, and 5 will result in the selected cores in these planes remaining in the 0 state. After the sequence of pulses, the selected cores in planes 1 and 3 will contain 1s, the selected cores in planes 2, 4, and 5 will contain 0s, and the computer word 10100 will have been stored in the memory in location X_3Y_4.

2. **Reading from a core memory** Assume that at a later time the location X_3Y_4, which was written into in the write operation above, is to be read from. The timing sequence illustrated in Fig. 7-34 still applies, although there are several differences in operation. First the read currents are applied to the selected cores (from 0 time to 0.5 μs in Fig. 7-34). If a large signal is received at the sense amplifier connected to a given plane during this period, the selected core in that plane contained a 1; if a small signal is received, the selected core in the plane contained a 0. The sense windings connected to planes 1 and 3 will therefore produce signals indicating 1s, and the sense windings connected to planes 2, 4, and 5 will produce small signals, indicating 0s. The word stored was therefore 10100. This word must now be written back into the memory array. The output of each sense winding is amplified and used to set a storage device to the 0 or 1 state during the read time, and

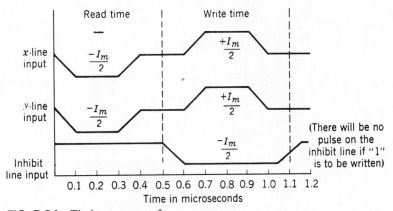

FIG. 7-34 Timing sequence for core memory

the contents of each of these storage devices are then used to control the INHIBIT drivers during the write time. Only the inhibit drivers connected to planes 2, 4, and 5 will therefore be enabled by signals from the respective storage devices and conduct during the write time, and the selected cores in these planes will remain in the 0 state. After the write time, the selected cores will again contain 10100, just as before the read operation.

7-16 DRIVING THE *X*- AND *Y*-SELECTION LINES

Let us examine the sequencing of current through a core memory using a simple idealized model. Flip-flops are generally used as the storage devices for both the memory address register and the memory buffer register. Figure 7-35 illustrates, in block diagram form, the operation of a selection system for a core memory, with each plane the size of the plane illustrated in Fig. 7-33. Since there are eight *X*- selection lines and eight *Y*-selection lines, three flip-flops will be required to select an *X* line and three more to select a *Y* line. There are therefore six flip-flops in the memory address register, so that any one of the 64

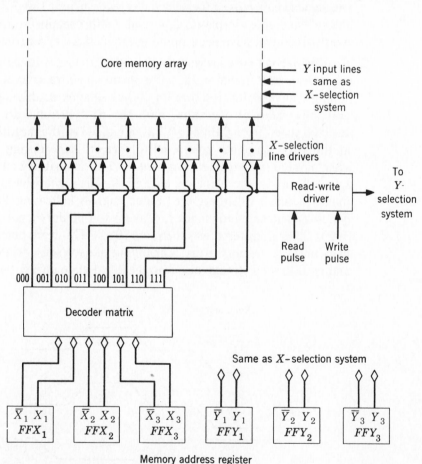

FIG. 7-35 *X*- and *Y*-selection system

(2^6) locations in each plane may be selected. The flip-flops in the register illustrated have been designated X_1, X_2, X_3, and Y_1, Y_2, Y_3 to indicate that the first three are used to select the X winding and the second three to select the Y winding.

1. **X-selection line drivers** There are eight X- selection line drivers in Fig. 7-35, each of which has two inputs, one from the decoder and one from the READ-WRITE driver. The output currents from the READ-WRITE driver may be either negative or positive; the X-selection line drivers are therefore capable of passing current in either direction. The X-selection line drivers also function as AND gates, for they will pass current only when the input signal from the decoder matrix represents a 1. Only one of the X-selection line drivers will be enabled by the decoder at any given time. For instance, if the X flip-flops in the memory address register contain 000, only the leftmost driver in the illustration will be enabled. All the X-selection line drivers will receive a READ and then a WRITE current pulse (of opposite polarity) from the READ-WRITE driver. Since only one X-selection line driver is enabled by a 1 signal from the decoder, only one of the X windings in the array will receive the drive currents. The same holds true for the Y-selection line system, which is identical with the X system. Since only one X line and only one Y line are pulsed during each memory cycle, only one core in each plane will receive a full-select READ-WRITE pulse.

2. **READ-WRITE driver** The READ-WRITE driver receives two clock pulses each memory cycle. The first is the READ pulse, which causes the READ-WRITE driver to deliver a positive HALF-SELECT pulse of current to both the X- and Y-selection line drivers. The second input pulse to the READ-WRITE driver is the WRITE pulse, which initiates a negative pulse of current to the X- and Y-selection line drivers. The current supplied by the READ-WRITE drivers is generally on the order of 0.1 to 1 A.

The operation of the memory address register and its associated circuitry causes a single core in each plane of the memory to receive a FULL-READ and then a FULL-WRITE current pulse. The memory address register is generally loaded directly from the instruction which is being interpreted by the machine; that is, the address section of the word is read directly into the memory address register.

7-17 MEMORY BUFFER REGISTER AND ASSOCIATED CIRCUITRY

The memory buffer register consists of a flip-flop register which contains one flip-flop for each plane in the array. The number of planes in the array, and hence the length of the memory buffer register, is equal to the number of bits in the basic computer word. The arithmetic element and control element of the machine generally communicate directly with the memory buffer, either loading the word to be written in storage into it or reading from it.

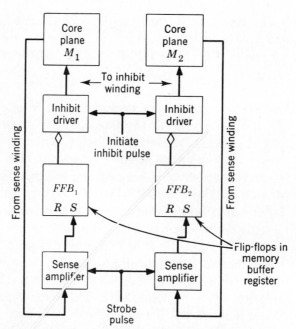

FIG. 7-36 Operation of memory buffer register

Figure 7-36 illustrates two flip-flops of a memory buffer register along with their associated circuitry. Each bit in the memory buffer register has identical circuitry. Two distinct sequences may occur, the first involves the reading of a word from memory and the second the writing of a word into the memory.

1. **Reading from memory** The location of the word to be read from the memory is first loaded into the memory address register (Fig. 7-35). The memory buffer register is then cleared. During the read time (Fig. 7-34) the selected core in each plane receives a full-current pulse and is set to 0. If the selected core in a given plane contains a 1, a signal is received on the sense winding. This is amplified by the sense amplifier and then used to set a 1 into the memory buffer flip-flop used to control the INHIBIT driver for the core plane. If the selected core in the plane contains a 0, the signal received by the sense amplifier will be small, and no pulse will appear at the output of the sense amplifier, and the flip-flop will remain in the 0 state.

   The sense amplifier is "strobed" (Fig. 7-36) with a narrow pulse because, despite the fact that a core containing a 0 will produce a small signal when "sensed," many of the cores in each plane will receive HALF-SELECT pulses, and each will generate a small amount of noise on the sense winding. If this noise is additive, it may approach the level of the signal from a core whose polarity is reversed. It has been found that the noise generated by the half-selected cores dies out shortly after the HALF-SELECT pulses are started. Therefore the sense amplifier is strobed during the latter part of the read time, when the output from a selected core reversing states is highest in proportion to the noise from half-selected cores. Only the output signal during the strobe pulse is gated into the SET line of the flip-flop.

   During write time (Fig. 7-34) each of the selected cores receives a full-select current from the X- and Y-selection system. As a result of the read operation, all these cores have previously been set in the 0 state. However, the memory buffer flip-flops now contain 1s for each plane in which a 1 was stored in the full-selected core. The outputs from these flip-flops are used to enable the INHIBIT drivers for each plane in which a 0 is to remain. All other full-selected cores will be set to the 1 state. The 0 output from each flip-flop is therefore used to enable the INHIBIT driver for the plane associated with the flip-flop. After the write time, the selected core in each plane will be in its original state.

2. **Writing into core memory** The X- and Y-selection system goes through the same timing sequence when a word is to be written into memory as when a word is read from memory. The operation of the memory buffer register differs, however. The word to be written into the selected location is loaded into the memory buffer register, and the address in memory to be written into is loaded into the memory address register. During the read time the sense amplifier is not strobed; so the memory buffer register is not disturbed.

After the read time, all the selected cores will have been set to 0. During the write time, the same cores all receive full-current WRITE pulses from the X- and Y-selection systems. However, the planes in which 0s are to remain have their INHIBIT drivers enabled by the memory buffer flip-flops (Figs. 7-35 and 7-36), and the half-current pulses from these drivers cancel the selection current, leaving the full-selected cores in the 0 state. All other full-selected cores are set to 1.

After the write time, the word in the memory buffer register will have been written into the cores.

7-18 CORE-MEMORY ORGANIZATION AND WIRING SCHEMES

The core-memory organization which has been described is the classic **coincident-current four-wire random-access core memory.** Several variations on this basic scheme will be outlined in this section.

First notice that the SENSE-line and the INHIBIT-line windings can be combined into a single winding. The sense amplifier is used only during the read section of the memory timing cycle, while the INHIBIT driver is on only during the write portion of the memory timing cycle. By simply connecting the sense amplifier to the inhibit winding and removing the sense winding, an array with only three wires per core can be formed. To visualize this, picture Fig. 7-33 with the sense winding removed. The sense amplifier is then connected to the inhibit winding, and this winding is called the **digit winding** or **bit winding.** The sense amplifier must, of course, be capable of withstanding the large input from the inhibit driver. A three-wire coincident-current memory of this type is shown in Fig. 7-37, which is a 16-word 4-bit memory.

Aside from simplifying memory construction, reducing the number of windings through the cores has the desirable effect of making it possible to reduce the size of the cores. Smaller cores can be switched faster than larger cores, and the limiting factor on core size is often the number of wires through the cores;

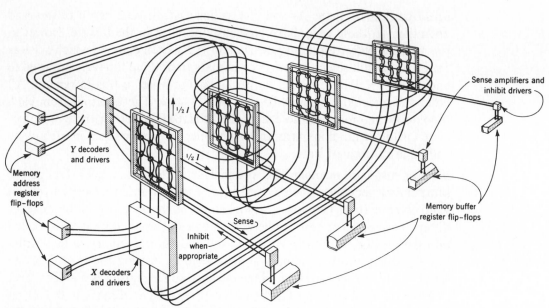

FIG. 7-37 Three-wire coincident-current memory

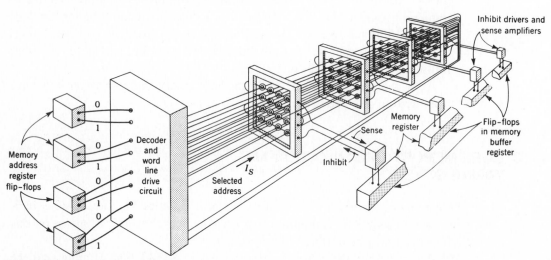

FIG. 7-38 Linear-select memory

so the fastest memories are made with fewer wires. The price that is paid is in additional circuit complexity.

A 16-word 4-bit linear-select memory is shown in Fig. 7-38.

There is another core-memory arrangement called a 2½D memory. One variation of the 2½D memory is used for large inexpensive memories, and another for small fast memories. We shall not study this type of memory in detail except to note that the basic principle consists in making a stack, which is basically a coincident-current selection stack, but where the X windings are continuous from plane to plane. However, each plane has a separate Y winding. During the READ cycle, current is then gated through the selected X winding, which goes through all planes, and also through all Y windings; so each selected Y driver is turned on. During the WRITE cycle only those Y drivers for planes in which a 1 is to be written are turned on, while the X drivers are used in the customary way. CDC has a core memory with 12-mil cores which has a 275-ns memory cycle and a 2½D organization. The organization is basically that illustrated in Fig. 7-11.

The 2½D memory can be three wires with a separate sense winding, or there are some two-wire memories where the output of the selected core is sensed on the Y drive line by a circuit technique. (This is used in a very large IBM memory.) The 2½D memory is a strategy that uses the coincident-current selection technique of half currents, but uses a divident Y winding to facilitate writing, using more complicated gating of the Y windings rather than inhibit windings.

7-19 MAGNETIC DRUM STORAGE

The storage devices which have been described utilize the principle of setting a device that is essentially bistable into one of its two states. Access to the devices was essentially random—once addressed, a core is immediately available and a flip-flop or dynamic cell continuously produces an indication of its state. The limitations on this type of storage are based on the complexity, and therefore the cost and reliability, of storing a large number of bits. While IC memories have been constructed which can store tens of millions of bits, some large machines require the storage of as many as 10^{13} bits. This would require 1 million IC memories. The high speed of IC storage is therefore paid for with the complexity and the cost of the storage.

Magnetic drums were among the first devices to provide a relatively inexpensive means of storing information and have reasonably short access times. A magnetic drum consists basically of a rotating cylinder coated with a thin layer of magnetic material which possesses a hysteresis loop similar to that of the material used in magnetic cores (Fig. 7-30). A number of recording heads [Fig. 7-39(a)] are mounted along the surface of the drum. These are used to write and read information from the surface of the drum by magnetizing small areas, or sensing the magnetization of the areas on which information has been recorded. While Fig. 7-39(a) shows only a few heads, some magnetic drums have several hundred recording heads scattered about their periphery.

As the drum rotates, a small area continually passes under each of the heads. This area is known as a **track** [Fig. 7-39(a)]. Each track is subdivided into cells, each of which can store 1 binary bit.

Generally one of the tracks is used to provide the timing for the drum. A series of timing signals is permanently recorded around this timing track, and each signal defines a **time unit** for the drum system. The timing track is then used to determine the location of each set of storage cells around the tracks. For instance, if the timing track is 60 in. in length and timing pulses are recorded at a density of 100 per inch, there will be 6,000 locations for bits (cells) around each of the tracks. If the drum has 30 tracks plus the timing track, the drum will have the capacity to store a total of 180,000 bits.

Information is written onto the drum by passing current through a winding on the write heads. This current causes flux to be created through the core mate-

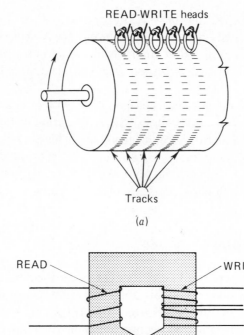

READ-WRITE heads

Tracks

(a)

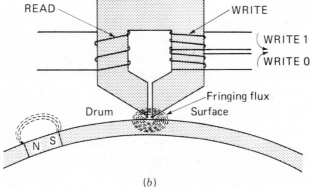

(b)

FIG. 7-39 Magnetic drum memory (a) Magnetic drum tracks (b) Read-write head

rial of the head. Figure 7-39(b) illustrates a head for writing or reading information from a drum. Some drum systems use separate heads for reading and writing, and others use combined read-write heads. The head in Fig. 7-39(b) consists of a ring formed of high-permeability material around which wire is wound. When information is to be written on the surface of the drum, pulses of current are driven through the write 0 or write 1 winding. The direction of flux through the head and, in turn, the polarization of the magnetic field recorded on the surface of the drum depend upon whether write 1 or write 0 is on.

The gap in the core presents a relatively high-reluctance path to the flux generated by the current through the coil. Since the magnetic material on the surface of the drum is passing near the gap, most of the flux passes through this material. This causes a small area of the drum surface to be magnetized, and since the material used to coat the surface of the drum has a relatively high retentivity, the magnetic field remains after the area has passed from under the head, or the current through the coil is discontinued. It should be noted that the head does not actually touch the surface of the drum. Instead, to prevent wear, the heads are located very close to the drum surface but not touching it. The drum must therefore be of very constant diameter in order to keep the heads at a constant distance. If the head moves farther from the surface of the drum, the signals recorded will become weaker. In practice the heads are able to move slightly into or away from the surface and are pushed toward the surface by a spring-loading mechanism. A cushion of air between the head and the rotating surface then maintains the required relatively constant distance from the magnetic surface.

The signals recorded on the surface of the drum are read in a similar manner. When the areas which have been magnetized pass under the head, some of the magnetic flux is coupled into the head, and changes in this flux induce signals in the winding. These signals are then amplified and interpreted. A description of the recording techniques used will be found in the final section of this chapter.

The sizes and storage capacities of magnetic drums vary greatly. Small drums with capacities of less than 200,000 bits have been constructed. Drums of this size generally have from 15 to 25 tracks and from 15 to 50 heads. To decrease access time, heads are sometimes located in sets around the periphery of the drum, so that a drum with 15 tracks may have 30 heads divided into two sets of 15 heads, each set located 180° from the other. For very fast access time there may be even more than two sets of heads.

Much larger drums can store up to 10^9 bits and may have from 500 to 1000 tracks. The larger drums are generally rotated much more slowly than small drums, and speeds vary from 120 rpm up to 75,000 rpm. The access times obviously decrease as the drum speeds increase. However, there is another important factor, the packing density along a track. Most present-day drums have a packing density of from 600 to 2000 bits/in. (By maintaining the heads very close to the drum surface and rotating the drum slowly, packing densities in excess of 1000 bits/in. may be achieved.) One drum system, the IBM 2303, has 800 tracks and 4892 bytes per track (and so about a 3.9 million-byte capacity), and the drum makes a complete rotation in 17.5 ms. Table 7-7 gives some characteristics of present-day drum systems.

TABLE 7-7 Magnetic Drum Characteristics

CHARACTERISTICS	FH 432 UNIVAC 1108	2301 IBM 360	2303 IBM 360	1964 ICL 1900 SERIES	FASTRAND II UNIVAC 1108
Tracks per drum	144	220	800	512	6,144
Characters per track	12,288	20,483	4,892	4,048	10,752
Characters per unit	1,572,864	4,096,600	3,910,000	2,072,576	132,120,756
Transfer rate, kbits	1,440	1,200	312	100	153
Head arrangement (fixed or movable)	Fixed	Fixed	Fixed	Fixed	Movable
Heads per drum	128	200	800	512	32 × 192 positions
Drum diameter, in.	10.5	10.7		18.5	32.8
Drum speed, rpm	7,100	3,490	3,428	1,500	870
Packing density, bits/in.	627	1,250	1,105	1,000	1,000
Average access time, ms	4.25	8.6	8.75	20.5	93
Approximate cost per 6-bit character stored, cents	8	5	4	3	0.2

7-20 PARALLEL AND SERIAL OPERATION OF A MAGNETIC DRUM

It is possible to operate a drum in either a serial or a parallel mode. For parallel operation all the bits of a word may be written simultaneously and read in the same manner. If the basic computer word contains 40 bits, the drum might read from 41 tracks (one for timing) simultaneously, thus reading an entire computer word in 1-bit time. When the drum is read from and written into in parallel, a separate read and write amplifier is required for each track that is used simultaneously, so that to read a 40-bit word in 1-bit time, 40 read amplifiers are required. The correct set of heads is then selected, and the drum system locates the selected set of cells.

Notice that words in a parallel system may be located by means of a timing track. If each track contains 8192 bits, a 13-bit counter may be set to zero at the same position each time the drum revolves, and stepped by one each time a timing pulse appears. In this way location 1096 will be the 1096th slot around the track from the 0 location. If the address of the word to be read is loaded into a register, the signals from the drum can be gated into the computer when the counter agrees with the register's contents. In this way words may be located on the drum.

A magnetic drum may also be operated in a serial mode. In this case only one track will be read from or written into at a given time. Since there are a number of tracks for each drum, the correct track as well as the location of the desired bits around the track must be selected.

Each track is therefore assigned a number. In addition, each track is divided into sectors, each sector containing one or more full computer words.

To specify the address of a word on a magnetic drum operated serially, both the track number and the sector number must first be given. If only one word is in a sector, this will suffice; if more than one word is in each sector, this word must be specified also. Consider a drum with 32 tracks plus a timing track and 32 words (sectors) around each track. The address of a word on the drum in a binary machine will consist of 10 bits, 5 bits to specify the track and 5 bits the sector.

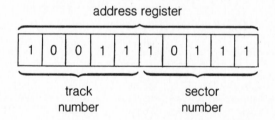

The five flip-flops containing the track number may be connected to a decoder, which will then select the correct read-write head.

Several techniques involving the timing tracks may be used to locate the selected sector. One technique involves the use of several timing tracks instead of one. Figure 7-40 shows a technique utilizing three timing tracks. One of the tracks contains a set of signals indicating the location of each bit around the tracks. The second track contains a set of pulses with a pulse at the beginning of each word time. (The word-time signals illustrated are 12 bits apart; so the basic word would be 11 or 12 bits in length.) In addition, the sector number of the next word around the drum is recorded around a third timing track. The computer reads sector numbers from this track, and when the number read agrees with the sector number in the address, the computer can then read the selected word from the next sector, beginning with the next word-time pulse.

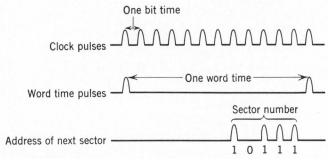

FIG. 7-40   Timing signals for a magnetic drum

7-21 MAGNETIC DISK MEMORIES

Another type of memory, called a **magnetic disk memory,** greatly resembles the magnetic drum memory in operation. The magnetic disk memory provides very large storage capabilities with moderate operating speeds. There are quite a large number of different types of magnetic disk memories now on the market. Although differing in specific details, all of them are based on the same principles of operation.

A magnetic disk memory resembles the coin-operated automatic record player, or "juke box." Rotating disks coated with a magnetic material are stacked with space between each disk (refer to Fig. 7-41). Information is recorded on the surface of the rotating disks by magnetic heads which are positioned against the disks. (Information is recorded in bands rather than on a spiral.) Each band of information around a given disk is called a **track.** On one side of a typical disk there may be from one hundred to several thousand of these data tracks. Bits are recorded along a track at a density of from perhaps 500 to 9000 bits/in. In some systems the outer tracks contain more bits than the inner tracks, because the circumference of an outer track is greater than that of an inner track, but many disks have the same number of bits around each track. The speed at which the disks rotate varies, of course, with the manufacturer, but typical speeds are on the order of 3600 rpm.

Since each disk contains a number of tracks of information and there may be several disks in a given memory, several techniques have evolved for placing the magnetic read-write head in the correct position on a selected track. Since the same head is generally used for reading and for writing, the problem becomes that of placing this head accurately and quickly on the track that has been selected.

There are two basic types of disk head placement systems. The first type of system has its heads fixed in position on each track. These are called **fixed-head systems.** The second kind of system has one or more pairs of read-write heads for each pair of adjacent disk surfaces (because information is generally written on both the top and the bottom of each disk). These read-write heads are mounted on arms which can be moved in and out. These are called **movable-head systems.**

The positioning of the heads by means of the mechanical movement of arms is a difficult and tricky business, particularly since the tracks are often recorded less than hundredths of an inch apart on the disk. It should be apparent that

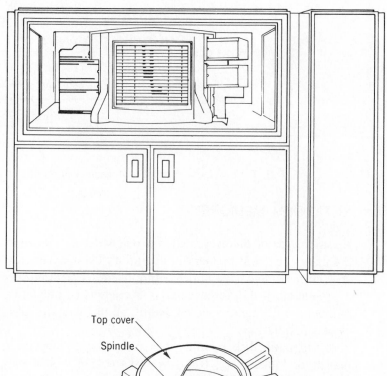

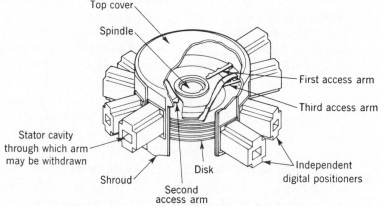

FIG. 7-41 Magnetic disk memory system

disk-file memories with many heads can locate and record or read from a selected track faster than the ones with only a few heads, since the amount of mechanical movement before the track is reached will be less for the multihead system.

The total time it takes to begin reading selected data or to begin writing one selected track in a particular place is called the **access time.**

The time it takes to position a head on the selected track is called the **seek time,** and it is generally somewhere between an average of several milliseconds to fractions of a second. The other delay in locating selected data is the **latency,** or **rotational, delay,** which is the time required for the desired data to reach the magnetic head once the head is positioned. Thus the total access time for a disk is the seek time plus the latency.

For a rotational speed of 2400 rpm, for example, latency is a maximum of 25 ms and averages 12.5 ms. Latency represents a lower limit to access time in systems using fixed heads. As a result, for minimum access time fixed heads are used. Typically heads are arranged in groups of eight or nine, perhaps including a spare, and are carefully aligned in fixed positions with respect to the disk. Although head spacing in each group is typically 8–16/in., track densities of 30–60/in. can be achieved by interlacing groups.

Although they are faster, fixed-head systems provide less storage capacity than moving-head systems having comparable disk recording areas because the moving-head systems have more tracks per inch. Further, the large number of heads required can increase cost for a given capacity.

An important advantage of moving magnetic heads concerns their alignment with very closely spaced data tracks. Although track spacing is limited by "crosstalk" between adjacent tracks and mechanical tolerances, spacing of 10 mils between adjacent tracks is common. Further, track widths of approximately 2.5–5 mils are consistent with head positioning accuracies of 0.5–1.5 mils.

The read-write heads used on magnetic disk memories are almost invariably of the type called **flying heads.** A simplified diagram of a flying head is shown in Fig. 7-42. When a disk rotates at a high speed, a thin but resilient boundary layer of air rotates with the disk. The head is so shaped that it rides on this layer of rotating air, which causes the disk to maintain separation from the head, thus preventing wear on the surface of the disk. In effect, the layer of air rotating with the disk acts like a spring with a stiffness exceeding several thousand pounds per inch, thus forcing the head away from the surface of the disk. To force the head into the correct proximity with the disk, a number of mechanisms have been used. Often compressed air is simply blown into a mechanism which forces the head toward the surface of the disk, using a pistonlike arrangement, as shown in Fig. 7-42.

There are many sizes and speeds for disk memories. Some disks are quite large, running up to 4 ft in diameter. Others are smaller, rotate faster, are changeable, etc. Because of the large market for these memories and the seemingly infinite variety of configurations in which they can be manufactured, the system user is afforded considerable freedom in selection.

Disk memories which have changeable disk packs (or **modules**) are very pop-

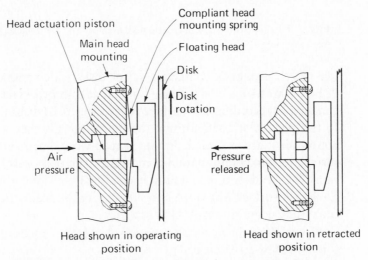

FIG. 7-42 Flying head for magnetic drum or magnetic disk memory

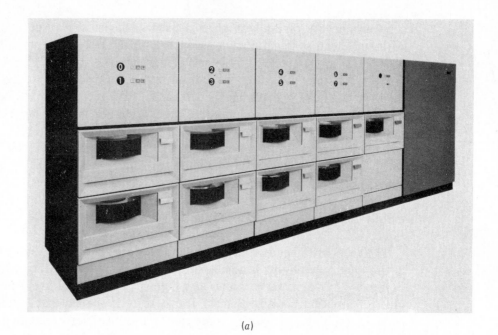

(a)

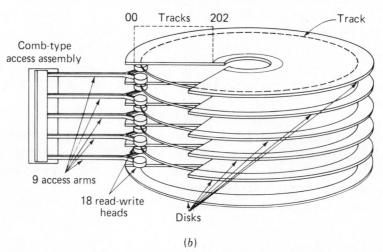

(b)

FIG. 7-43 (a) IBM 2314 magnetic disk memory (b) Disk pack for IBM 2314 (only five disks are shown)

ular. Each disk pack contains a set of disks which rotate together. The IBM 2314 shown in Fig. 7-43(a) uses a changeable disk pack, for instance, which contains 20 recording disk surfaces consisting of 10 disks [refer to Fig. 7-43(b)]. In this particular configuration the top of the top disk and the bottom of the bottom disk are not used. Eighteen read-write heads are used, two for each surface on which information is recorded. The disks revolve at a speed of 2400 rpm. The heads are mounted in a comblike positioning mechanism as shown. Each disk surface is divided into 200 concentric magnetic tracks per inch, and each track contains about 4400 bits/in.

Figure 7-44 shows characteristics of a lower priced disk system manufactured by Hewlett-Packard.

Table 7-8 lists the characteristics of several of the larger disk pack systems.

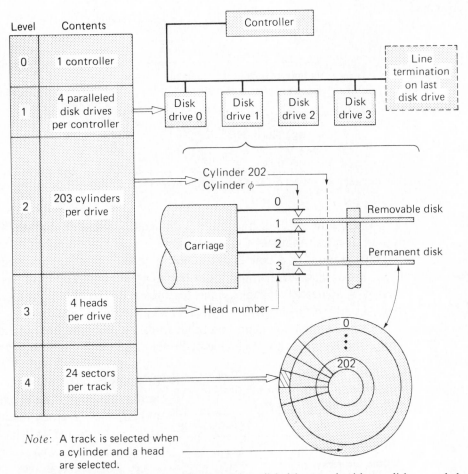

FIG. 7-44 Storage system containing up to four disk drives, each with two disks recorded on both sides (courtesy Hewlett-Packard Co.)

TABLE 7-8 Disk Drive/Disk Pack Technology

DISK DRIVE TECHNOLOGY	IBM 2314	CDC 215	UNIVAC 8440	IBM 3330	IBM 3330-11	IBM 3340
Pack design	IBM 2316	IBM 2316	2316†	IBM 3336	IBM 3336-11	IBM 3348
Number of surfaces	20	20	20	19	19	24
Storage capacity, Mbytes	29	54	108	100	200	35 to 70
Tracks per inch	200	200	200	192	384	300
Transitions per inch	4,400	4,400	4,400	4,040	4,040	5,072
Data rate, million bits/s	2.5	2.5	5.0	6.5	6.5	7.1
Average access time, ms	60	30	30	30	30	25
Rpm	2,400	2,400	2,400	3,600	3,600	3,000
Detent	Mechanical‡	Optical	Optical	Servo	Servo	Servo
Actuator	Hydraulic‡	Voice coil	Voice coil	Voice coil	Voice coil	Voice coil
Disk coating, minimum, μin.	90	90	50	50	40	40
Head fly height, minimum, μin.	80	80	70	50	30	30

†Special pack made with 2,316-pack hardware and 3,336 disks.
‡Non-IBM hybrids exist with voice coil and optical mask.

TABLE 7-9   Large Fixed Disk Drive Characteristics (For CDC 9776†)

CHARACTERISTIC	SPECIFICATION
Number of spindles per cabinet	2
Capacity per spindle	400 Mbytes (movable head)
	1.72 Mbytes (fixed head)
Data rate	9.6 MHz
Average access time	25 ms
Rotational speed	3600 rpm
Latency time	8.4 ms

†Courtesy CDC Corp.

In the mid 1970s disk units with changeable packs or modules were the most used devices. At about that time, however, an IBM unit with fixed disks, the 3350, brought in a new disk technology with greater recording density, more tracks per data surface, and faster transfer rate. This disk technology is referred to as **Winchester** technology and features a low head loading force (10 grams versus 300 grams on earlier devices) and a low mass head. Also, since disks are not changeable, alignment and other tracking problems are reduced. Disks are also lubricated so the lightweight heads can "crash" without damage. (They bounce.) The original Winchester disk drives were used for large storage systems; however, the technology was quickly picked up by manufacturers of smaller drives and so Winchester drives are now made by many companies, and fixed disk systems are popular with mini- and microcomputer systems as well as with large systems.

Some specifications for a large CDC drive are shown in Table 7-9, while specifications for typical small Winchester drives are shown in Table 7-10.

TABLE 7-10   Typical Fixed Disk Winchester Drive Characteristics (For Small to Medium Systems)

CHARACTERISTIC	SPECIFICATION
Number of disks	1 to 4
Data surfaces	1 to 7
Bit density	6400 bits/in.
Track density	500 tracks/in.
Tracks per surface	690
Surface capacity	7.6 Mbytes
Rotational speed	3600 rpm
4-disk capacity	53.2 Mbytes

Because of the relative inexpensiveness per bit of information stored in disk memories and because of the relatively low access times and the high transfer rates attainable when reading or writing data from or into a disk file, magnetic disk memories have become one of the most important storage devices in modern digital computers.

7-22 FLEXIBLE DISK STORAGE SYSTEMS— THE FLOPPY DISK

An innovation in disk storage, originally developed at IBM, uses a flexible, "floppy" disk with a plastic base in place of the more conventional rigid, metal-based disk. This storage medium is approximately the size and shape of a 45-rpm record and can be "plugged in" about as easily as a tape cartridge. Each floppy disk costs only a few dollars.

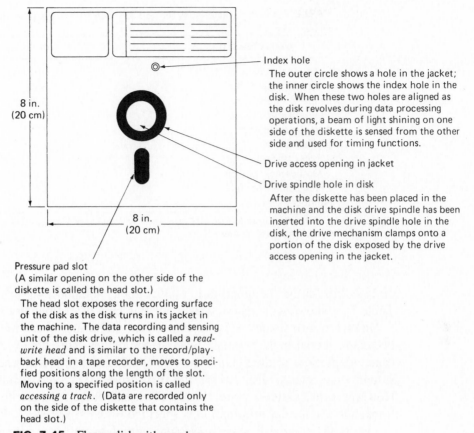

Index hole

The outer circle shows a hole in the jacket; the inner circle shows the index hole in the disk. When these two holes are aligned as the disk revolves during data processing operations, a beam of light shining on one side of the diskette is sensed from the other side and used for timing functions.

Drive access opening in jacket

Drive spindle hole in disk

After the diskette has been placed in the machine and the disk drive spindle has been inserted into the drive spindle hole in the disk, the drive mechanism clamps onto a portion of the disk exposed by the drive access opening in the jacket.

8 in. (20 cm)

8 in. (20 cm)

Pressure pad slot
(A similar opening on the other side of the diskette is called the head slot.)

The head slot exposes the recording surface of the disk as the disk turns in its jacket in the machine. The data recording and sensing unit of the disk drive, which is called a *read-write head* and is similar to the record/play-back head in a tape recorder, moves to specified positions along the length of the slot. Moving to a specified position is called *accessing a track*. (Data are recorded only on the side of the diskette that contains the head slot.)

FIG. 7-45 Floppy disk with envelope

The floppy disks are changeable, and each disk comes in an envelope as shown in Fig. 7-45. The disks are mounted on the disk drive with the envelope in place, and information is written and read through an aperture in the envelope. (Some systems require removing the envelope.) Several manufacturers now provide complete systems for under $500 for use with these disks. Convenience in use and low prices have broadened the use of floppy disk memories in many applications.

On most floppy disk drives the read-write head assembly is in actual physical contact with the recording material. (For increased life, head contact is generally maintained only when reading or writing.) Track life on a diskette is generally on the order of 3 to 5 million contact revolutions. The standard flexible disk is enclosed in an 8-in. square jacket, and the disk has a diameter of 7.88 in. The recording surface is a 100-μin.-thick layer of magnetic oxide on a 0.003-in.-thick polyester substrate. The jacket gives handling protection, and, in addition, it has a special liner that provides a wiping action to remove wear products and other dirt which would be abrasive to the media and head if left on the surface.

In the original IBM version there is a single 0.100-in.-diameter index hole 1.5 in. from the center of the disk to indicate the start of a track. A written track is 0.012-in. wide, and standard track spacing is 48/in. The number of tracks is 77. The capacity of a surface using a standard code and a bit density

TABLE 7-11 Characteristics for an IBM Compatible Flexible Disk Drive

CHARACTERISTIC	SPECIFICATION
Capacity, bytes†	400,000
Rotational speed, rpm	360
Transfer rate, bits/s	250,000
Track-to-track access time, ms	16–20
Average access time, ms	176
Bit density	
Inner track, bits/in.	3,268
Outer track, bits/in.	1,836
Track density per inch	48
Number of tracks	77

†This is a maximum; using IBM's formatted recording system, only 250,000 bytes of data are recorded per disk.

of 3268 bits/in. on the innermost track is about 400,000 bytes of 8 bits each. Table 7-11 shows some characteristics of this kind of flexible disk system.

Disks are also made in 5¼-in. and 3½-in. sizes, and these mini disks are becoming increasingly popular. Several companies offer floppy disk systems using adaptations of the flying-head concept. Some floppy disks use an address system (like regular disk) where the disk drive, track, and sector are given. However, other systems write "headers" on each block of recorded data on a track, and the header information is specified for each access.

The "IBM standard" system uses one complete track for formatting information. Sync bits and headers as well as check bits are interlaced with data on the remaining tracks.

In order to increase disk capacity, manufacturers now supply two-sided double-track-density (100 tracks/in.) and double-density (5–6 kbits/in.) drives. Less expensive drives normally have fewer tracks.

Table 7-12 shows some characteristics for small system disks.

TABLE 7-12 Disk Characteristics

	8-in. DISK DRIVE		5.25 in. DISK DRIVE	
	SINGLE SIDED	DOUBLE SIDED	SINGLE SIDED	DOUBLE SIDED
Capacity (unformatted)				
Single density, kbytes	400	800	110	220
Double density, kbytes	800	1600	220	440
Average access time, ms	225	100	450	300
Transfer rates				
Single density, kbits/s	250	250	125	125
Double density, kbits/s	500	500	250	250
Number of tracks	77	154	35	70
Rotational speed, rpm	360	360	300	300
Track density per inch	48	48	48	48

7-23 MAGNETIC TAPE

At present the most popular medium for storing very large quantities of information is magnetic tape. Although because of its long access time, magnetic tape is not a desirable medium for the main high-speed storage of a computer, modern mass-production techniques have made the cost of tape very low, so that vast quantities of information may be stored inexpensively. Furthermore, since it is possible to erase and rewrite information on tape, the same tape may be used again and again. Another advantage of magnetic tape is that the information stored does not "fade away," and therefore data or programs stored one month may be used again the next.

Another advantage of using magnetic tape for storing large quantities of data derives from the fact that the reels of tape on a tape mechanism may be changed. In this way the same magnetic tape handling mechanism and its associated circuitry may be used with many different reels of tape, each reel containing different data.

There are four basic parts of a digital magnetic tape system:

1. **Magnetic tape** This is generally a flexible plastic tape with a thin coating of some ferromagnetic material along the surface.

2. **The tape transport** This consists of a mechanism designed to move the tape past the recording heads at the command of the computer. Included are the heads themselves and the storage facilities for the tape being used, such as the reels on which the tape is wound.

3. **The reading and writing system** This part of the system includes the reading and writing amplifiers and the "translators" which convert the signals from the tape to digital signals which may be used in the central computing system.

4. **The switching and buffering equipment** This section consists of the equipment necessary to select the correct tape mechanism if there are several, to store information from the tape and also information to be read onto the tape (provide buffering), and to provide such facilities as manually directed rewinding of the tape.

The tape transports used in digital systems have two unique characteristics: (1) the ability to start and stop very quickly, and (2) a high tape speed. The ability to start and stop the tape very quickly is important for two reasons. First, since the writing or reading process cannot begin until the tape is moving at a sufficient speed, a delay is introduced until the tape gains speed, slowing down operation. Second, information is generally recorded on magnetic tape in "blocks" or "records." Since the tape may be stopped between blocks of information, the tape which passes under the heads during the stopping and starting processes is wasted. This is called the **interblock** or **interrecord gap.** Fast starting and stopping conserves tape.

Figure 7-46(a) shows a typical tape system. To accelerate and decelerate the tape very quickly, an effort is made to isolate the tape reels, which have a high inertia, from the mechanism that moves the tape past the recording heads. Fig-

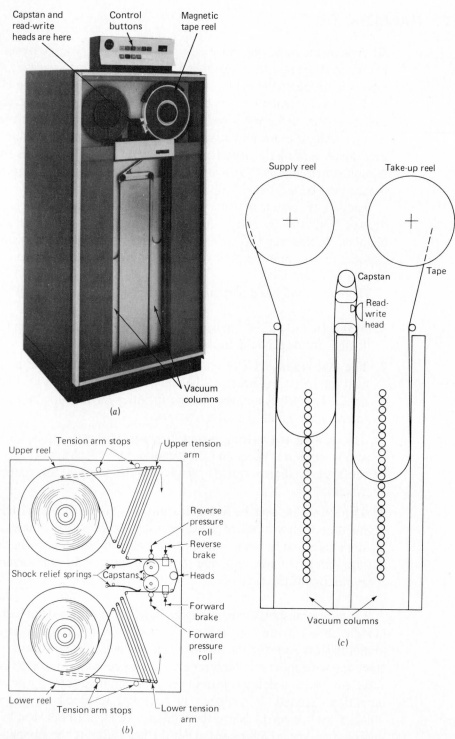

Capstan and read-write heads are here

Control buttons

Magnetic tape reel

Vacuum columns

(a)

Supply reel

Take-up reel

Capstan

Tape

Read-write head

Vacuum columns

(c)

Upper reel

Tension arm stops

Upper tension arm

Reverse pressure roll

Reverse brake

Shock relief springs

Capstans

Heads

Forward brake

Forward pressure roll

Lower reel

Tension arm stops

Lower tension arm

(b)

FIG. 7-46 (a) IBM 3420 tape system (b) Magnetic tape mechanism using vacuum columns

TABLE 7-13 Typical Tension Arm Tape Drive Characteristics

REEL SIZE in.	bits/in.	DATA RATE kbits	START-STOP TIMES ms	CAPACITY Mbytes	COST OF A TYPICAL REEL OF TAPE $
7	1600	40	15	11.5	7.50
8.5	1600	60	10	23	8.50
10.5	1600	72 kbits/s at 45 in./s; 120 kbits/s at 75 in./s	8.33 (5 ms at 75 in./s)	46	11.00

ure 7-46(b) shows a high-speed start-stop tape mechanism which uses a set of tension arms around which the tape is laced. The upper and lower tension arms in Fig. 7-46(b) are movable, and when the tape is suddenly driven past the heads by the capstan, the mechanism provides a buffering supply of tape. A servomechanism is used to drive the upper and lower reels, maintaining enough tape between the capstan and the tape reels to keep the supply of tape around the tension arms constant. Table 7-13 shows some characteristics of this kind of system.

Another arrangement for isolating the high-inertia tape reels from the basis tape drive is shown in Fig. 7-46(c). This system isolates the tape from the capstan drive by means of two columns of tape held in place by a vacuum. A servosystem then maintains the correct length of tape between reel and capstan drive. Both this and the previous systems use continuously rotating capstans to actually drive the tape, and "pressure rolls" to press the tape against the capstan when the transport is activated. Brakes are also provided for fast stopping. Table 7-14 shows some typical figures on this kind of system.

Using systems of this sort, the start and stop times can be less than 5 ms. These are the times required to accelerate a tape to a speed suitable for reading or writing and the time required to fully stop a moving tape. The speeds at which the tapes are moved past the heads vary greatly, most tape transports having speeds in the range from 12.5 to 250 in./s. Lincoln Laboratory has constructed a very fast (900 in./s) mechanism in which the tape is driven directly by the reels of the tape transport. A tape system of this sort is designed to transfer only large quantities of data to and from the machine's main fast-access storage in a single operation. The slower tape speeds, combined with fast starting and stopping, are probably more adaptable to systems in which smaller amounts of data must be transferred. Some systems have changeable cartridges

TABLE 7-14 Typical Vacuum Column Tape Drive Characteristics for 10.5-in. Tape Reel Systems

SPEED in./s	bits/in.	MAXIMUM DATA RATE kbytes/s	START-STOP TIMES ms	CAPACITY Mbytes
50	1600	80	7.5	46
75	1600	120	5	46
200	1600	320	3	62
200	6250	1250	1.2	350

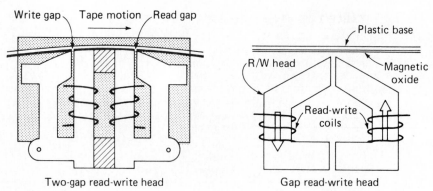

Write gap   Tape motion   Read gap

Plastic base

R/W head

Magnetic oxide

Read-write coils

Two-gap read-write head   Gap read-write head

FIG. 7-47   One- and two-gap tape heads

with a reel of tape in each cartridge. The manufacturers of these systems feel that this protects the tape and facilitates changing the reels. These will be discussed in a following section.

Most tape systems have two-gap read-write heads. The two gaps (refer to Fig. 7-47) are useful because, during writing, the read gap is positioned after the write gap and is used to check what has been written by reading and comparing.

Tapes vary from ¼ to 3 in. in width; however, most tape is ½-in.-wide 1.5-mil-thick Mylar tape. A 10.5-in. reel typically has 2400 or 3600 ft of tape. Generally about nine channels or tracks are used for ½ in. of width. The surface of the tape is usually in contact with the read-write head. Output signals from the read heads are generally in the 0.1- to 0.5-V range. The recording density varies; however, 200, 556, 800, 1600, 6250, and even 12,500 bits/in. per channel are fairly standard.

Data are recorded on magnetic tape using some coding system. Generally one character is stored per row (refer to Fig. 7-48) along the tape. The tape in Fig. 7-48 has seven tracks, or channels, one of which is a parity bit, which is added to make the number of 1s in every row odd (this will be studied in the next chapter, as will the codes used for magnetic tape). Data are recorded on magnetic tape in blocks, with gaps between the blocks and usually with unique start and stop characters to signal the beginning and the end of a block.

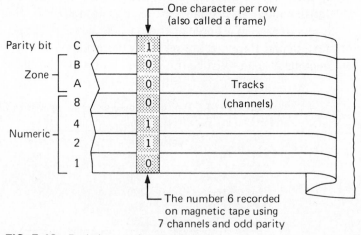

One character per row (also called a frame)

Parity bit   C   1
Zone   B   0
        A   0   Tracks
        8   0   (channels)
Numeric 4   1
        2   1
        1   0

The number 6 recorded on magnetic tape using 7 channels and odd parity

FIG. 7-48   Basic layout of magnetic tape

A small piece of metallic reflective material is fastened to the tape at the beginning and end of the reel, and photoelectric cells are used to sense these markers and prevent overrunning of the tape [refer to Fig. 7-49(a)].

The codes used to record on tape vary, but two commonly used IBM codes are shown in Fig. 7-49(b) and (c). IBM standard tape is ½ in. wide and 1.5 milliinch thick, with either seven or nine tracks. The seven-track code is shown in Fig. 7-49(b), where the 0s are simply blank and 1s are indicated by a vertical line. Figure 7-49(c) shows the nine-track code. Recording densities are 200, 556, 800, 1600, or 6250 bits (or rows) per inch [which means 200, 556, 800, 1600, or 6250 characters (or bytes) per inch, since a character is recorded in each row].

Some characteristics of a medium-priced vacuum column tape system are shown in Table 7-15, and Table 7-16 gives the characteristics for an inexpensive tension arm Hewlett-Packard system.

TABLE 7-15 Vacuum Column Digital Tape Transport Characteristics

KENNEDY MODEL 9300†	
CHARACTERISTIC	SPECIFICATION
Data density	9 tracks, 800 characters/in., 1600 characters/in.
Tape velocity	125 in./s
Start-stop time	3 ms at 125 in./s
Start-stop displacement	0.6825 in.
Reel size diameter	10.5 in.
Tape	
Length	2,400 ft
Width	0.5 in.
Thickness	1.5 mil
Rewind speed	300 in./s nominal

†(Courtesy Kennedy Company, an Allegheny International Company)

TABLE 7-16 Hewlett-Packard 7090E Tape Systems

CHARACTERISTIC	SPECIFICATION
Number of tracks	9
Read-write speed	
2100-based systems	25, 37.5, 45 in./s
3000 system	45 in./s
Density	1600 characters/in. (8 bits/character)
Data transfer rate	72,000 characters/s max
Reel diameter	10.5 in. maximum
Tape (computer grade)	
Width	0.5 in.
Thickness	1.5 mils
Rewind speed	160 in./s
Start-stop times	8.33 ms (read-after-write) at 45 in./s
End of tape and beginning of tape reflective strip detection	IBM compatible

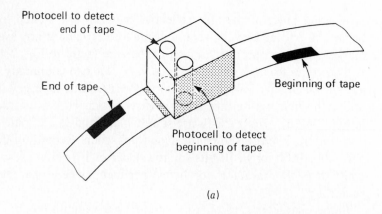

(a)

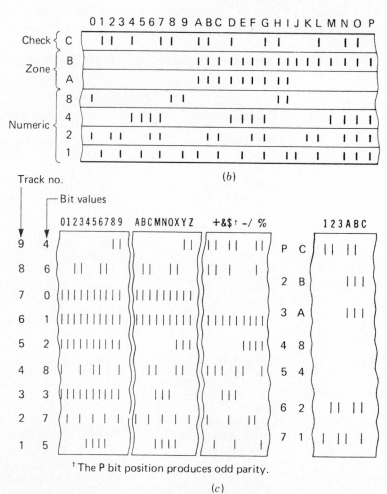

† The P bit position produces odd parity.

(c)

FIG. 7-49 Magnetic tape coding (a) Beginning and end of tape marking (b) Magnetic recording of seven-track BCD code on tape (c) Nine-track (EBCDIC) and seven-track tape data format comparison

7-24 TAPE CASSETTES AND CARTRIDGES

The changeable tape cassette used in the familiar home recorder is an attractive means for recording digital data. The cassettes are small, changeable, and inexpensive; they are frequently used in small and "home" computers. The tape moving mechanism in the conventional home tape cassette often used for small systems is not of sufficient quality for larger business and scientific computer usage. However, a number of high-quality digital cassettes with prices in the dollar region ($2 to $15 in general) have been developed. These are of small size—on the order of the familiar cassette—and have a similar appearance.

There are also larger **tape cartridges** which contain long strips of magnetic tape and which resemble large cassettes. These cartridges provide a more convenient way to package tape, and greatly simplify the mounting of tape reels (which can be a problem with conventional reels of tape where the tape must be manually positioned on the mechanism). The tape cartridges also provide protection against dirt and contamination, since the tape is sealed in the cartridge.

Figure 7-50 shows a typical cassette. A number of different digital cassettes and cassette drives are now in production, and each has different characteristics. As an example, Data General Corporation offers a cassette drive with an average tape speed of 31 in./s, a 282-ft. 0.15-in. magnetic tape per cassette, storage per tape of 800,000 bits, and transfer (reading) rate of 12,800 bits/s. The cassette can rewind in 85 s. A 22-in. reflective leader and trailer are used to mark the beginning and the end of the tape (a photodiode senses this strip).

Cartridges are a high-performance magnetic tape storage medium. There are several cartridge designs available. These vary not only in performance capabilities, but also in the division of hardware between cartridge and transport. The 3M cartridge and drive shown in Fig. 7-51 is representative. The cartridge contains 300 ft of ¼-in. tape capable of recording up to four tracks at 1600 bits/ in. for a maximum storage capacity of more than 2×10^7 bits. The 3M transport operates at 30 in./s when reading or writing, and at 90 in./s in search mode. A novel elastic band drive moves the tape and also supplies tape tension. Tape drive, hub, and guide components are referenced to the base of the cartridge and require no external guidance. There are several new cartridge systems designed to "back up" Winchester disk drives.

tape cassette.

FIG. 7-50   Magnetic tape cassette

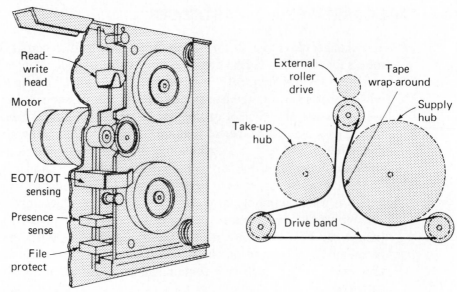

FIG. 7-51   Digital cartridge and interface (courtesy 3M)

Table 7-17 gives some specifications of the 3M cartridge and the 3M cartridge drive. Table 7-18 compares some of the standard memory devices which have been described. Notice that these are standard systems, and some newer devices exceed these characteristics. Table 7-19 gives some data on the newer low-cost devices suitable for minicomputers and microcomputers as opposed to more expensive devices. These are again representative figures for the latest systems.

TABLE 7-17   Specifications of 3M Cartridge and DCD-3 Cartridge Drive

CHARACTERISTIC	SPECIFICATION
Operating speed	
Read-write	30 in./s forward and reverse
Fast forward, rewind, gap search	90 in./s forward and reverse
Packing density	1600 bits/in.
Transfer rate	48 kbits/s maximum
Interrecord gap	1.33 in. typical; 1.2 in. minimum per ANSI standard
Maximum recommended start-stop rate	Three operations per second without forced air cooling
Total speed variation	±4% max
Tape head	1-, 2-, 4-channel read-while-write heads available
Interface logic	TTL compatible
Power	5 V dc ± 5%, ± 18 V dc ± 5%

†For instance, the heads may or may not be included in each cartridge.

TABLE 7-18 Storage Media Comparisons

	5-in. REEL	PHILLIPS CASSETTE	3M-TYPE CARTRIDGE	FLOPPY DISK	LARGE HARD DISK FIXED MEDIA
Capacity, kbytes	18,500	550	2500	250	571,000
Transfer rate, kbits/s	180	9.6	48	250	14,000
Number of tracks	9	2	4	77	600
Density, bits/in.	880	880	1600	3200	1600
Interrecord gap, in.	0.6	0.8	1.3	Not applicable	Not applicable
Mechanism cost	2000	400	500	400	30,000
Media cost, cents/byte	0.06×10^{-3}	1.2×10^{-3}	0.6×10^{-3}	2.6×10^{-3}	0.185×10^{-3}

TABLE 7-19 Low-Cost Storage System Characteristics

CHARACTERISTIC	CAPACITY	COST cents/byte
Floppy disk	2.4 Mbits	2.6×10^{-3}
High-performance cassette	1 Mbytes	5×10^{-4}
Phillips cassette	1.44 Mbytes	1.2×10^{-3}
Low-performance cassette	200 kbits	20×10^{-4}
3M cartridge	11.5 Mbytes	0.6×10^{-3}
7-in. tape reels	40 Mbits	0.5×10^{-4}

7-25 MAGNETIC BUBBLE AND CCD MEMORIES

The secondary or backup memory devices that have so far been really successful have all been electromechanical devices (drums, disks, tape, etc.) which store bits as magnetic fields on a surface and rely on mechanical motion to locate the data. However, two devices for secondary storage having no moving parts are now being developed and have started to appear in some commercial applications. These are magnetic bubble and CCD memories.

Magnetic bubble memories are primarily competing with floppy disks, small disks, cartridges, and small tape devices. Bubble memories are more reliable (having no moving parts), consume less power, are smaller, and cost less per unit. However, disks have higher transfer rates, and the cost per bit is lower except for very small systems.

Bubble memories trace their history to research at the Bell Laboratories, which showed that bits can be stored as "bubbles" in a thin magnetic film formed on a crystalline substrate. A bubble device operates as a set of shift registers. The storage mechanism consists of cylindrically shaped magnetic domains, called **bubbles.** These bubbles are formed in a thin film layer of single-crystal synthetic ferrite (or garnet) when a magnetic field is applied perpendicular to the film's surface. A separate rotating field moves the bubbles through the film in shift-register fashion. The presence of a bubble is a 1, no bubble is a 0. The bubbles move along a path determined by patterns of soft magnetic material deposited on the magnetic expitaxial film.

To the user, the physics of the bubble memory's operation are less important than its operating characteristics. The memories appear as long shift registers which can be shifted under external control. Storage is permanent since if shifting is stopped, the bits in the memory will remain indefinitely.

To utilize the shift register characteristics better and reduce access time, the shift registers are generally made of only modest lengths of perhaps 50–100 kbits. A memory package is liable to contain from a few hundred kilobits to several megabits.

The shift rate is relatively slow, perhaps 200 kHz, so access times are on the order of a few milliseconds. (Reading and writing are only performed at the ends of the shift register.)

Bubble memories require relatively complex interface circuitry, but IC manufacturers have produced reasonable IC packages for this purpose.

Charged coupled devices (CCDs) are constructed using IC technology. The bits are stored on capacitors as charges similar to the dynamic IC memories, except that the storage is arranged in a shift register configuration with the charge "packets" being shifted from cell to cell under clock control.

Since the storage mechanism is a charge on a capacitor, if shifting stops for very long (a few milliseconds), the charges will leak from the capacitors and the memory's contents will be lost.

CCD memories generally have from 500 kbits to several megabits of storage. The shift registers are read from and written into from the ends, so access time is dependent on shift-register lengths. The shift rate is generally 200–500 kHz, and so for reasonable-length shift registers access times are in the milliseconds.

Since CCD memories use IC technology, they require less interface circuitry than bubble memories. The strategy involved in determining how long the shift registers should be for both bubbles and CCDs is based on a cost/performance analysis. A greater number of shorter loops results in faster access times, but more interface circuits and more complicated system usage strategies. Long loops give economy but long access times.

Both bubble and CCD technologies are in the early stages, but they are already considered competitive with the smaller more conventional disk memories.

7-26 DIGITAL RECORDING TECHNIQUES

Although the characteristics and construction of such storage devices as magnetic drums, tape recorders, and magnetic disk storage devices may vary greatly, the fundamental storage process in each consists of storing a binary 0 or 1 on a small area of magnetic material. Storage in each case is dynamic, for the medium on which the information is recorded is moved past the reading or writing device.

Although the process of recording a 0 or a 1 on a surface may appear straightforward, considerable research has gone into both the development of the recorded patterns used to represent 0s and 1s and the means for determining the value recorded. There are two necessities here: (1) the packing density should be made as great as is possible, that is, each cell or bit should occupy as little space as possible, thus economizing, for instance, on the amount of tape used to store a given amount of information; and (2) the reading and writing procedure should be made as reliable as is possible. These two interests are conflicting because, when the recorded bits are packed more and more closely together, the distortion of the playback signal is greatly increased.

In writing information on a magnetic surface, the digital information is supplied to the recording circuitry, which then codes this information into a pattern which is recorded by the write head. The techniques used to write information on a magnetic medium can be divided into several categories, the **return-to-zero** (RZ) technique, the **return-to-bias** (RB) technique, and the **non-return-to zero** (NRZ) technique. The methods for reading information written using these techniques also vary. The basic techniques will be described below, along with the recorded waveshapes and the waveshapes later read by the read heads and translated by the reading system.

7-27 RETURN-TO-ZERO AND RETURN-TO-BIAS RECORDING TECHNIQUES

Figure 7-52 illustrates the return-to-zero recording technique. In Fig. 7-52(a) no current goes through the winding of the write head, except when a 1 or a 0 is to be recorded. If a 1 is to be recorded, a pulse of positive polarity is applied to the winding on the write head, and if a 0 is to be written, a negative pulse is applied to the winding. In either case the current through the write-head winding is returned to zero after the pulse, and remains there until the next bit is recorded. The second set of waveforms on this drawing illustrates the remanent flux pattern on the magnetic surface after the write head has passed. There is some distortion in this pattern due to the fringing of flux around the head.

If this pattern of magnetization is passed under a read head, some of the magnetic flux will be coupled into the core of the head. The flux takes the lower reluctance path through the core material of the head instead of bridging the gap in the head (Fig. 7-39), and when the amount of flux through the core material changes, a voltage will be induced in the coil wound around the core. Thus a change in the amplitude of the recorded magnetic field will result in a voltage being induced in the coil on the read head. The waveforms in Fig. 7-52(a) and (b) illustrate typical output signals on the read-head windings for each of the techniques. Notice that the waveform at the read head is not a reproduction of the input current during the write process, nor of the pattern actually magnetized on the magnetic material.

The problem is, therefore, to distinguish a 1 or a 0 output at the sense winding. Several techniques have been used for this. One consists in first amplifying the output waveform from the output waveform from the read winding in a linear amplifier. The output of this amplifier is then strobed in the same manner

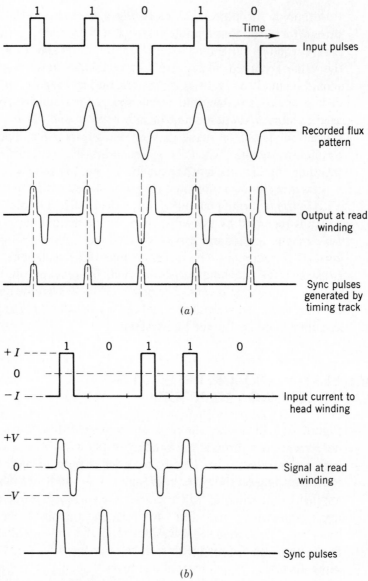

FIG. 7-52 Recording techniques (a) Return-to-zero (RZ) recording (b) Return-to-bias (RB) technique

that the output from the sense winding of a core plane is strobed. For drum systems the correct timing for the strobe, which must be very accurate, may be determined by the timing signals recorded on the timing track. If the output from the read amplifier is connected to an AND gate, and the strobe pulse is also connected as an input to the same AND gate, the output will be a positive pulse when the recorded signal represents a 1.

It is important that the timing pulse be very sharp and occur at the right time relative to the reading and writing of the bits.

A fundamental characteristic of return-to-zero recording [(Fig. 7-52(a)] is that, for a 1, the output signal during the first half of each bit time will be positive with regard to the second half; and that for a 0, the first half of the output signal during each bit time will be negative in regard to the second half of the signal. This is sometimes exploited in translating the signal read back.

In the return-to-zero system in Fig. 7-52(a) the magnetic field returns to zero flux when a 1 or a 0 pulse is not present. This makes it impossible to write over information which has previously been written, unless the position of each cell is very accurately located. If a 0 pulse is written directly over a previously recorded 1, the flux generated will reverse the polarity of the recorded field only if the write head is in exactly the right position when the 0 is recorded. The timing of the writing of information is therefore very critical for this system, and it is rarely used except with magnetic drums, where the timing may be accurately established by timing tracks. An alternative technique involves erasing all flux before writing new information, but this involves an additional erase head and is seldom used.

The second method for recording information is the return-to-bias system, illustrated in Fig. 7-52(b). In this case the current through the winding maintains the head saturated in the negative direction unless a 1 is to be written. When a 1 is written, a pulse of current in the opposite direction is applied to the winding at the center of the bit time. The outputs at the sense winding are also illustrated in the figure. In this case there will be an output at the sense winding only when a 1 is written. This output may be amplified and strobed just as in the previous case. The timing here is not so critical when information is being "written over," because the negative flux from the head will magnetize the surface in the correct direction, regardless of what was previously recorded. The current through the winding in this case, and in all those which follow, is assumed to be sufficient to saturate the material on which the signals are being recorded. A primary problem here concerns sequences of 0s. For magnetic tape, either a clock track must be used or the code used must be such that at least one 1 occurs in each line of the tape. Notice that this is because only 1s generate magnetic flux changes, and therefore output signals at the read head.

7-28 NON-RETURN-TO-ZERO RECORDING TECHNIQUES

Figure 7-53 illustrates three recording techniques, each of which is classified as a non-return-to-zero system. In the first, the current through the winding is negative through the entire bit time when a 0 is recorded, and is positive through the entire bit time when a 1 is recorded. The current through the winding will therefore remain constant when a sequence of 0s or 1s is being written, and will change only when a 0 is followed by a 1 or when a 1 followed by a 0 is written. In this case a signal will be induced in the sense winding only when the information recorded changes from a 1 to a 0, or vice versa.

The second technique illustrated is sometimes referred to as a **modified non-return-to-zero,** or **non-return-to-zero mark** (NRZI), technique. In this system the polarity of the current through the write winding is reversed each time a 1 is recorded and remains constant when a 0 is recorded. If a series of 1s is recorded, the polarity of the recorded flux will therefore change for each 1. If a series of 0s is recorded, no changes will occur. Notice that the polarity has no

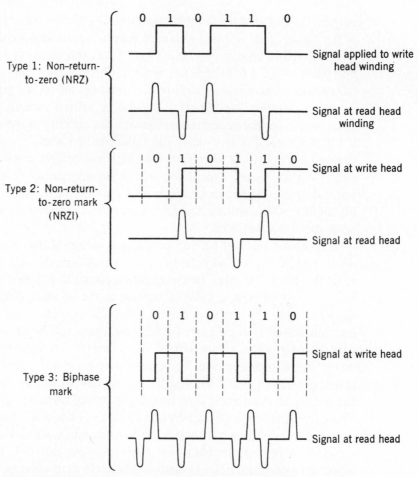

FIG. 7-53 Three types of non-return-to-zero recording

meaning in this system; only changes in polarity. Therefore a signal will be read back only when a 1 has been recorded. This system is often used for tape recording when, in order to generate a clock or strobe, a 1 must be recorded somewhere in each cell along the tape width. That is, if 10 tracks are recorded along the tape, one of these must be a timing track which records a sequence of 1s, each of which defines a different set of cells to be read, or the information must be coded so that a 1 occurs in each set of 10 cells which are read. Alphanumeric coded information is often recorded on tape, and the code may be arranged so that a 1 occurs in each code group.

The third non-return-to-zero technique in Fig. 7-53 is sometimes called a **phase-encoded, biphase-mark, Harvard, Manchester,** or **split-frequency system.** In this case a 0 is recorded as a ½-bit-time negative pulse followed by a ½-bit-time positive pulse, and a 1 is recorded as a ½-bit-time positive pulse followed by a ½-bit-time negative pulse. This technique is often used in high-speed systems.

The reading of information which has been recorded consists of two steps. First the output from the read head is amplified, and then the amplified signals are translated by logic circuitry. Figure 7-54 shows a translation technique for

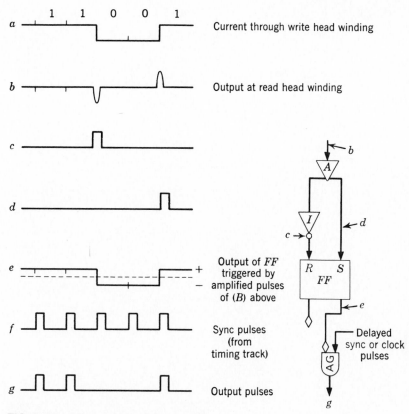

a   1   1   0   0   1   Current through write head winding

b   Output at read head winding

e   Output of *FF*
triggered by
amplified pulses
of (*B*) above

f   Sync pulses
(from
timing track)

g   Output pulses

FIG. 7-54   Non-return-to-zero recording

the first non-return-to-zero system illustrated in Fig. 7-53. The output signals may be either from the output flip-flop or from serial pulses. The sync pulses occur each time a cell passes under the read heads in the system.

The flip-flop (Fig. 7-54) responds to positive pulses only. Positive-pulse signals at the recording head will therefore "set" the flip-flop to 1. The inverter at the C input will cause negative pulses to be made positive. These positive pulses then will clear the flip-flop. The output of the flip-flop may be used directly by the computer, or pulse outputs can be generated by connecting an AND gate to the 1 output, delaying the sync pulses, and connecting them to the AND gate. Also, a serial representation of the number stored along the surface may be formed.

sec. 8

Software

V. Carl Hamacher
Zvonko G. Vranesic
Safwat G. Zaky

8-1 INTRODUCTION
8-2 LANGUAGES AND TRANSLATORS
8-3 LOADERS
8-4 LINKERS
8-5 OPERATING SYSTEMS

8-1 INTRODUCTION

The name software refers to all programs that are written to be executed on a computer. These programs may be written in any of a number of different languages. The size of programs has a wide range. Student programs for small numerical problems may consist of only 20 to 50 statements in a high-level, problem-oriented language such as FORTRAN. At the other end of the scale, the accounting and management information programs that are used by large corporations or governments have many thousands of statements. These examples are from the area that is usually called application or user programs. They are programs written by people who use computers to solve scientific and business operation problems.

The suppliers of computer systems and services are responsible for the provision of another class of programs, collectively called computer system programs, or system software, to distinguish them from user programs. System software includes the programs that translate user programs into machine language programs. Other system programs are used to load these translated programs into the main memory prior to execution. The translators are sometimes called language processors. An important component of system software is the set of routines that are used to manage the operation of the physical resources [CPU, main memory (MM), mass storage, I/O devices, etc.] in a complete computing system. These routines comprise the operating system programs.

To reduce the cost of individual user computations, the resources in large computer systems are almost always shared among a number of independent user programs. The purpose of operating system software is to control this resource sharing so that the system is utilized as efficiently as possible, while at the same time it is made easy to use from the customer standpoint. This is an elusive goal, and a large amount of research and development effort has gone into the design and production of operating systems.

8-2 LANGUAGES AND TRANSLATORS

The most basic language is machine language, in which programs are represented by a listing of the binary patterns for the machine instructions and data elements (bytes or words). Fig. 8-1 shows a machine language. The binary patterns of the machine language program are represented in both the octal and hexadecimal notations. The hexadecimal system is very convenient for representing bytes and words in both 16-bit and 32-bit word-length machines, since patterns of 8, 16, and 32 bits can be encoded by two, four, and eight hexadecimal digits, respectively.

A machine language program for a specific computer can be executed on that computer without the aid of any other program. However, since programming in machine language is a cumbersome process, programs are usually written in a language that has a more symbolic and stylized form. The simplest of these are the assembly languages. The problem-oriented languages such as FORTRAN, PL/I, COBOL, ALGOL, etc., are often called high-level languages to denote the fact that they have a powerful set of operational and control state-

Main memory location		Memory word contents (16 bits)				
Octal byte address	Hexadecimal byte address	Machine language version		Assembly language version		
		Octal	Hexadecimal			
212	8A	005000	0A00		CLR	RO
214	8C	012703	15C3		MOV	#-16.,R3
216	8E	177760	FFF0			
220	90	006300	0CC0	MLOOP:	ASL	R0
222	92	006101	0C41		ROL	R1
224	94	103002	8602		BCC	NOADD
226	96	060200	6080		ADD	R2,R0
230	98	005501	0B41		ADC	R1
232	9A	005203	0A83	NOADD:	INC	R3
234	9C	001371	02F9		BNE	MLOOP
236	9E	000000	0000		HALT	

FIG. 8-1 Program for multiplication in machine and assembly language

ments which are substantially above the basic statement types provided in assembly languages.

A program written in any language above machine language is called a **source program.** Source programs are translated into machine language by system programs called **translators.** In the case of assembly languages, these translators are called assemblers. When the source program is in a high-level language, the translator is called a **compiler.** The output of the language translation process is called an **object program.** In the simplest situation, the object program is in machine language and can be loaded into the MM and executed directly. Sometimes, parts of large source programs are translated in separate operations into separate object programs. Further processing is required on these object programs to link them together into a single machine language program that can be executed directly.

A few remarks are in order regarding assembly and high-level languages. Basically, an assembly language is just an orderly and structured set of mnemonics for a corresponding machine language. There are exceptions to this simple viewpoint that merit comment. In some of the more extensive assembly languages, single statements (with parameters) can correspond to short sequences of machine instructions. These types of statements are often called **macroinstructions** or **macros.** The assembler that generates the machine language version of these types of statements automatically expands them into the appropriate sequence of machine instructions. Such an assembler is sometimes called a **macroassembler.** Assembly languages, even with macro facilities, are closely related to machine languages. On the other hand, high-level languages have many statements that must be translated into separate but interconnected sequences of machine instructions. This is a more complicated process than the expansion of macroinstructions. The high-level languages make it easier for programmers to express what they want the computer to do, without having to directly specify how the machine instructions should be assembled to do it. Control structures such as DO loops, IF . . . THEN . . . ELSE . . . statements, PROCEDURES with parameters, as well as data structures such as ARRAYS, with various data types, characterize these languages.

It is not essential to translate high-level language programs into machine language in order to execute the programs. It is sometimes desirable to perform a translation into an intermediate language form that is then executed by another program called an **interpreter.** The interpreter is a program that reads the program to be interpreted and executes it statement by statement. This is a much slower execution process, but there are situations where the interpretive method is the best choice from the overall system standpoint. For example, interpretive execution of short student jobs that are run only once after being debugged may be the most efficient method. The controlled execution implied by the interpretive technique allows much more extensive and meaningful error diagnostics to be returned to the user at execution time. Interactive computing, in which the user enters a few statements, requests that they be executed and the answers returned to the terminal before proceeding to more computations, is naturally handled by interpretive methods. On the other hand, it is usually best to compile programs into machine language if they are to be run a large number of times using different data. Examples of this would be the frequently used mathematical subroutine packages for numerical integration, linear equation solution, or the large business data processing programs.

8-3 LOADERS

Let us assume that a program has been translated into machine language form. To execute this program, it must be loaded into the MM of the computer. Since this is not a trivial process, we will discuss some of the steps required.

The principles involved in loading the program into the MM for execution can be described through an example. Consider a machine language program that has been punched onto paper tape in the format shown in Fig. 8-2. The paper tape characters are 8 bits wide (a byte), so that two characters are required to specify the contents of a word in a 16-bit word-length computer. Blank tape is read as all zeros by the paper tape reader mechanism, so that the beginning of the information is signified by a start byte of value 1. The next two bytes specify a 16-bit number that states the total number of bytes in the program segment to follow. The starting address of the program is defined by the next two bytes. The program segment then lists each word, low-order byte first, of the program to be loaded. At the end of the program segment, an 8-bit check sum, which is the sum of the program bytes modulo 256, is included. The check sum provides a limited form of error detection on the correctness of the electro-

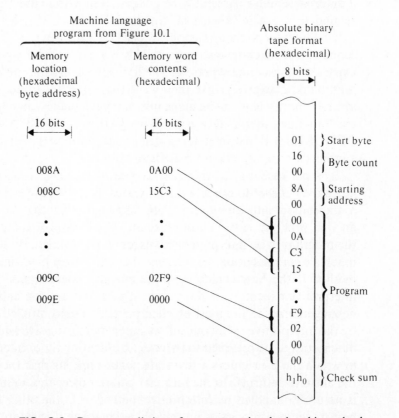

FIG. 8-2 Paper tape listing of a program in absolute-binary-loader format

mechanical conversion of hole sensing to byte patterns in the paper tape reader mechanism. Any single error in reading the program segment will be detectable by comparing the check sum read with an internal count.

To load such a program into the MM, it is necessary to use another program already residing in the memory. The latter program is called the **absolute binary loader.** It is not a long program and can be placed into the memory manually via the front panel switches that exist on all computers. We have discussed program-controlled I/O earlier. Therefore, it should not be very difficult for the reader to construct an absolute-binary-loader program that reads in bytes from a paper tape prepared in the format of Fig. 8-2. The loader places the program words in the proper area in memory, accumulating the internal check-sum count as it proceeds. A flowchart for such a program is shown in Fig. 8-3. A program corresponding to this flowchart might take about 50 instructions to encode in a typical minicomputer. This is quite a few bits to manually toggle into the MM from console switches.

A simpler loader program can be written to load programs such as this absolute binary loader into the memory. The name **bootstrap loader** is usually given to this simpler loader. It does not accumulate a check sum for error detection and can be constructed so that it does not need to keep an explicit count of the number of bytes to be loaded. To have the latter feature, the format of programs that are to be loaded by the bootstrap loader is more complicated than that of Fig. 8-2. We will not give the details of how bootstrap loaders operate because they tend to be machine-dependent, and, to make them as short as possible, clever coding tricks are usually employed.

The above discussion has sketched the ideas involved in the simplest form of loaders for machine language programs. In many computer systems, particularly larger ones, there is a requirement for a more complex loader, called a **relocating loader.** First, let us motivate the need for such a loader. In the case of the absolute binary loader, the starting point of the program to be loaded is fixed at the time the program is written. In general, the program will run correctly only if it is loaded starting at that particular MM location. A normal operating environment for many computers is that a number of different programs are in the MM at any one time. These programs are usually of different sizes so that we would like some flexibility in determining where a particular program is placed at load time. Therefore, the function of a relocating loader is to take a machine language program which was generated on the assumption that it would be loaded starting at some location x, usually chosen as 0 for convenience, and load it starting at location y. In general, such a loader will need to make some changes to the program so that it will run correctly at the new location.

Let us look at the format that an object program must have if it is to be relocatable. When all addresses in a program are specified relative to the program counter, the program will execute correctly no matter where it is placed in the memory. On the other hand, suppose an absolute memory address mode is used somewhere in a program. Such address values are called **address constants.** The relocating loader must adjust these address constants according to where the program is to be loaded. If the object program is generated so that it will run correctly if loaded at location 0, the adjustment simply consists of add-

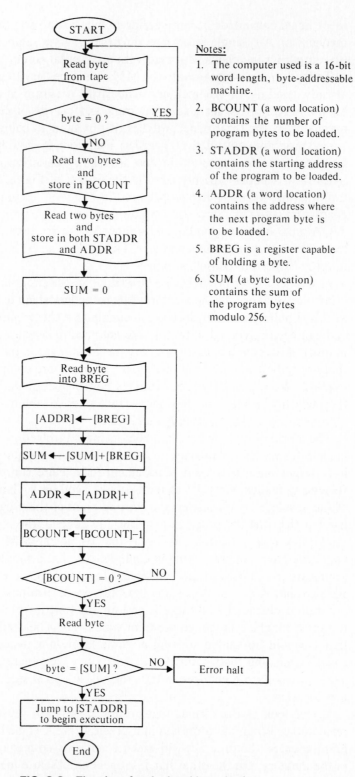

Notes:

1. The computer used is a 16-bit word length, byte-addressable machine.

2. BCOUNT (a word location) contains the number of program bytes to be loaded.

3. STADDR (a word location) contains the starting address of the program to be loaded.

4. ADDR (a word location) contains the address where the next program byte is to be loaded.

5. BREG is a register capable of holding a byte.

6. SUM (a byte location) contains the sum of the program bytes modulo 256.

FIG. 8-3 Flowchart for absolute binary loader

ing the address of the actual starting location as an offset to all address constants in the program. Obviously, the position of the address constants in the object program must be indicated by the translator. We will see an example of how this can be done in the next section.

Some computers have features that facilitate program relocatability. Suppose all addresses are generated relative to a base register. At execution time, the value in the base register is taken as an offset to addresses generated by the remainder of the addressing mode information. In this case, program relocation can be achieved by simply loading the starting address into the base register. Thus the complexity of address handling by the translator and loader can be greatly reduced by a particular machine organization feature. This interaction of machine hardware features with basic system software is an important aspect of the design of complete computing systems.

8-4 LINKERS

Until now we have considered the simple case of loading complete programs that have been translated into machine language as a single unit. In more practical situations, a large program consists of a number of routines that have been written separately, possibly by different people. It is often useful to be able to translate these routines independently into machine language. We will use the term **object module** to denote the output from each of these independent translations. Object modules must be in a format that allows them to be collected together and linked into a single program that can be passed to a loader. This means that the programmer must identify certain symbols as being **external** in the source programs. External symbols are simply those variables or line labels that are referenced by more than one of the separately translated programs or subprograms. The program that links the object modules into a single machine language program that can be passed to a loader is called a **linker.** Let us denote its output as a **load module.** We should note that it is quite common to consolidate the functions of the linker and loader into one system program called a linking loader. The generation of the load module would then be an intermediate step in the execution of the linking loader.

There are some trade-offs involved here. Instead of trying to link and load separately translated programs, it is sometimes feasible, and perfectly reasonable, to collect all source programs and subprograms required for some composite task and present them as a single entity to the translator which directly generates the load module. The complexity of cross-referencing is then moved back into the translator. In this section, however, we assume that separate translations have been justified.

The easiest starting point is the same as the one taken in the case of the absolute-binary-loader program. We will specify a format for the object modules generated by the separate translations. The major new idea in this format is the specification of external symbols as defined earlier. Fig. 8-4 shows a possible format for object modules. This general format starts with a table of external symbols, called the external symbol dictionary (ESD), followed by the machine language listing of the program. A listing of the location of address constants that must be relocated by the loader is placed after the program in a section called the relocation dictionary (RD). Address constants must be flagged. We are now making this more specific by assuming that these items are identified by a listing of their locations.

Let us take the specific example of two programs A and B that have been translated separately. Program A defines two memory locations DATAWORD1 and DATAWORD2 that are to be accessed by both programs. Program A also calls program B as a subroutine, so it needs to reference the entry point SUBRB of program B. A possible format in which these programs may be presented to the linker is shown in Fig. 8-5. An identification tag is included in each line of the ESD. The first line gives the length of the program along with its name, identified by the tag P. The second and third lines in the ESD for program A declare (D) DATAWORD1 and DATAWORD2 as being external. They are the addresses of locations 120 and 121 of this program. The fourth line, SUBRB, is a reference (R) to an address in program B. This reference appears in location 180 of program A. The address SUBRB must be defined in the ESD of program B. When the location of the word labeled SUBRB is determined during the linking process, its value must be entered at word 180 of program A. The fact that this value must be relocated when the final load module is loaded into the MM is also indicated by entering the location 180 in the RD. Similar comments apply to the object module for program B. An additional example, comprising a local reference represented by the internal address constant LOCALBR, is included in this module. The reference is made in word 74, and this fact is indicated in the RD. The figure shows this address constant to be 7. The other two entries in the RD refer to the locations of the address constants DATAWORD1 and DATAWORD2.

External symbol dictionary (ESD)

Program

Relocation dictionary (RD)

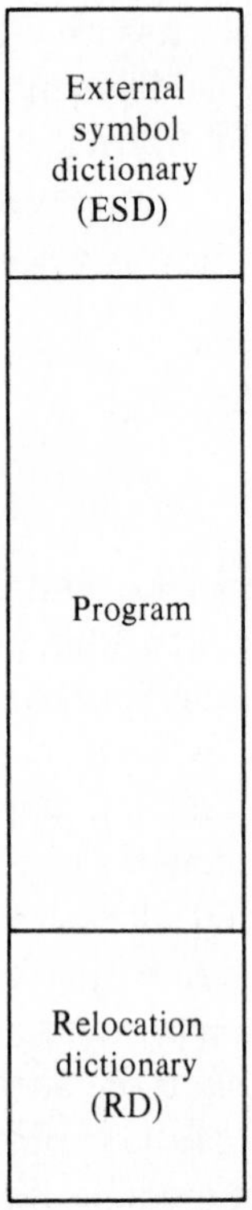

FIG. 8-4 An object module

Suppose now that these two object modules are presented to the linker in the order A followed by B. The linking process must create a load module consisting of the 375 words of the program bodies of A and B, preceded by a length declaration and followed by a composite RD. It should be easy to convince oneself that there is enough information in the individual ESDs and RDs to create the load module shown in Fig. 8-6. For example, the linking process determines that SUBRB is the 251st location of the composite load module. Therefore, the address constant 251 is entered in word 180 of the program body of the load module. Similarly, the address constant 7 in line 74 of the program B module gets changed to address constant 257 (= 250 + 7) when it is entered in line 324 (= 250 + 74) of the final load module. This load module can now be passed to the loader program. When a starting address S is specified to the

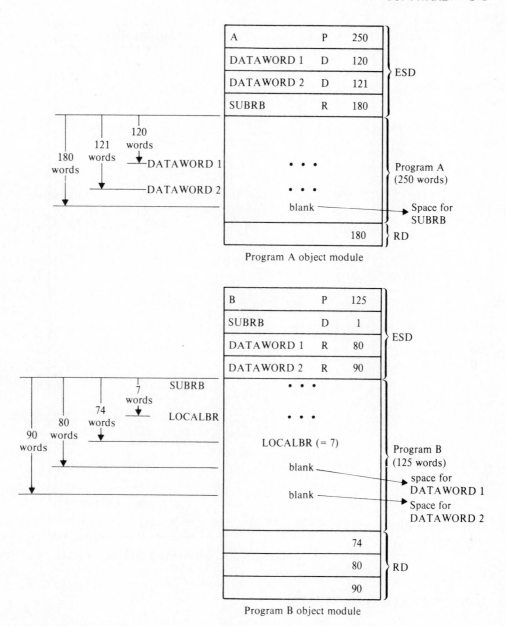

FIG. 8-5 Object modules for programs A and B

loader, it loads the 375-word program in the MM beginning at that location. Then it adds the value S − 1 to the constants 251, 257, 120, and 121 in load module locations 180, 324, 330, and 340. The final appearance of the 375-word program in the MM is shown in Fig. 8-7, where a starting address of 3401 has been assumed.

The model of linking and loading that has been presented here is a simplified version of the main ideas involved in the specification of ESDs and RDs. A practical implementation will normally require a number of different classes of external symbols. This provides greater user flexibility in writing programs that must communicate with each other but which are to be translated separately.

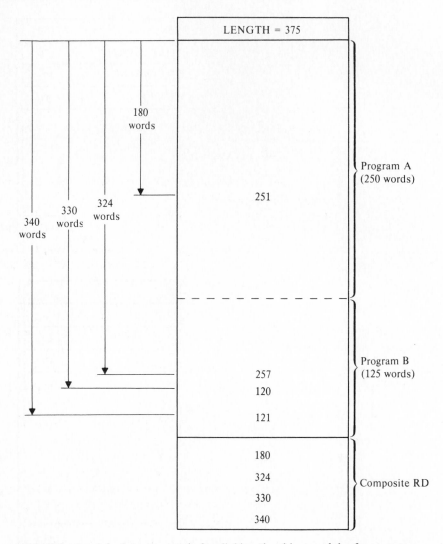

FIG. 8-6 Load module generated after linking the object modules for programs A and B

8-5 OPERATING SYSTEMS

In the introduction to this chapter we stated that the resources in a computer system are usually shared among a number of user programs to reduce the cost of computation for the individual user. Resource sharing will reduce costs only if it leads to an increase in system throughput, that is, if more user programs can be run per unit time. The purpose of this section is to discuss the ways that user jobs share the resources and to describe how the operating system (OS) programs try to make this sharing efficient, thus resulting in high throughput.

Let us assume that the computer system consists of a CPU, MM, card reader, line printer, and magnetic-disk auxiliary storage. The reader, printer, and disk communicate with the MM through three logically independent channels. The channels permit data transfers between the MM and these three peripheral devices to proceed concurrently with the execution of programs by the CPU. It is this possibility for concurrency that must be exploited to achieve a high rate of processing of user programs. A main function of the OS programs is the scheduling, initiation, and monitoring of both channel and CPU activity.

We will use the term **job** to refer to all the I/O and computation associated with a given user program. Furthermore, it is convenient to use the name **step** to identify phases of input, computation, or output as called for by a job. For now, we will assume that the user presents a complete job request to the system in the form of a deck of punched cards defining the program and data, and then waits for printed output when the job has been completely processed. The user is not involved in the processing in any way.

Consider the processing of a number of jobs whose card decks have the form shown in Fig. 8-8. The job header, data header, and end-of-job cards perform obvious separator functions. The job header has another function, that of job description. A sequence of actions that may occur in a computer system during the processing of a typical job is indicated in Table 8-1. During the first job step, the program is read into the MM from the card reader. The form of the program is not specified in Fig. 8-8. If it is in high-level source form, the operating system will direct the program text to the appropriate compiler for translation to machine language.

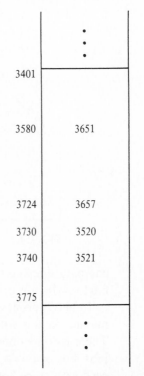

FIG. 8-7 Load module of Fig. 8-6 placed in the main memory starting at location 3401

For our purposes here, we can assume that any processing required to transform the program into executable form is included in computation step C1. This step will also include the initial phase of execution of the program. Execution continues until data input is required at step R2. This data input step requires the card reader to transfer the information from some of the data cards into the MM for subsequent processing during

TABLE 8-1 Example of Job Sequencing

Job step no.	Operation	System component involved
1	Program input step R1	Card reader
2	Computation step C1	CPU
3	Data input step R2	Card reader
4	Computation step C2	CPU
5	Data input step R3	Card reader
6	Computation step C3	CPU
7	Data output step W1	Line printer

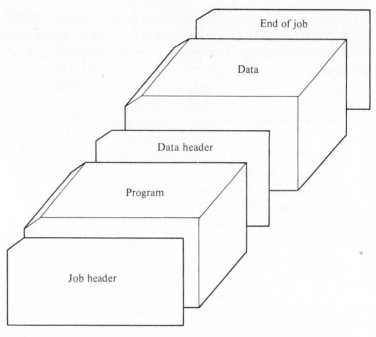

FIG. 8-8 A job deck

computation step C2. The remainder of the data is read during step R3, and final results are printed in step W1.

In **batch processing,** jobs are processed one at a time in a strictly sequential manner in the order in which the batch of jobs is placed in the card reader. There is some opportunity for overlapping I/O with computation in individual jobs. For example, in the job outlined in Table 8-1, the card reader could proceed with steps 3 and 5 as soon as step 1 is completed. The data is read into a buffer area in the MM by the card reader channel while computation step C1 is in progress. Output printing in this particular job is the last step. If we assume that it cannot begin until computation step C3 is completed, then there is no chance to overlap output with either input or computation. In other jobs, it might be possible to overlap some output steps with computation steps. What we can now conclude is that some overlapping of I/O and computation is possible within individual jobs. However, the extent of this overlapping is highly variable from job to job.

There are more opportunities for overlapping the activity of the physical resources in the system if we consider the requests of a number of jobs instead of just one job at a time. Therefore, an obvious extension of the simple batch-processing system described above is to read the job deck for jobs N + 1, N + 2, . . . into a MM buffer area, while computation is proceeding on job N. The card deck for job N is assumed to have been read earlier. As computation proceeds on job N, output from jobs . . . , N − 2, N − 1 can be transferred from another MM buffer to the line printer. The jobs are still processed in the order in which they are placed in the batch, but there is a potential gain in efficiency in overlapping processing of adjacent jobs as well as within jobs.

Let us consider some of the details of how overlapping may occur in a specific example. It is convenient to introduce a time line diagram that shows the time required to execute each step of a user job. Fig. 8-9a gives the diagrams for the user job of Table 8-1, which we will refer to as job X, and two other jobs, Y and Z. As mentioned above, it is possible to overlap job steps of individual jobs as well as those of different jobs. However, there are limits to the amount of overlapping that can be achieved, since some steps on a given facility cannot be started until associated steps on other facilities are finished. For example, step C2 of job X cannot begin until step R2 is completed for that job. Taking such limitations into account, Fig. 8-9b shows the amount of overlapping achievable among the various steps of the three jobs X, Y, and Z. We have assumed that they follow each other in the batch in the order stated and that the system begins operation at t_0. Maximum overlapping occurs during time period t_3 to t_4. The CPU idle time from t_1 to t_2 occurs because of the above restriction that

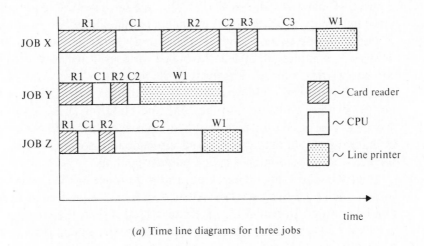

(a) Time line diagrams for three jobs

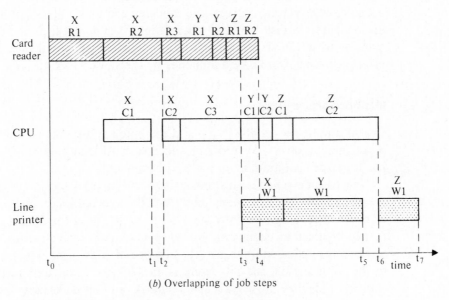

(b) Overlapping of job steps

FIG. 8-9 I/O—compute overlap in a batch system

step C2 of job X cannot be started until step R2 is completed. Similarly, the printer idle time from t_5 to t_6 results from the fact that step W1 for job Z must follow step C2 for job Z.

A few other comments are in order about Fig. 8-9b. If the time from t_0 to t_7 is considered as a period of time that occurs after the system has been operating for a while, then output from jobs processed before job X could be printed during the period t_0 to t_3. Also, job decks following the deck for job Z could be read after t_4.

Spooling

In the above discussion, we have assumed that there is sufficient MM capacity for the input and output buffers required to achieve a reasonable level of overlapping. If this is not the case, the extra storage capacity required can be provided by a magnetic disk. We now should consider whether the added overhead of buffering information from the MM onto the disk, and then back into the MM as it is requested, offsets the hoped for overall increase in efficiency. We will not attempt a detailed analysis of the problem. However, it has been found that such systems do achieve increased overall efficiency. The process of continuously reading job decks into the MM and buffering them onto the disk until the CPU is assigned to them is called **input spooling.** The companion process of buffering output onto the disk and subsequently moving it back into the MM for transfer to the printer is called **output spooling.**

In general, spooling smooths out the wide range of demands by individual jobs on the I/O devices so that a steady work load is created at the card reader and line printer. In the batch system discussed earlier, there can be times when the card reader is idle, and other times where the remainder of the system is idle while the card reader reads in the next job. Similar statements apply to the line printer. Because both these electromechanical devices have relatively much slower data transfer rates than disks, the spooling system can be made to operate efficiently. When programs are executed and they call for input, card images are read from a disk file, and when output is generated, print line images are transferred to a disk file. Computation rates on individual programs are then effectively freed from direct influence by the slower I/O devices.

Multiprogramming

In both the simple batch system and the batch system with spooling, the CPU is assigned to jobs X, Y, and Z in succession. All computation is completed on job X before computation on job Y is begun, etc.

Now consider a generalization of this situation in which an OS routine selects a few (maybe three or four) jobs from the spooled-input queue on disk and transfers their programs into the MM in preparation for execution. The CPU is then assigned to begin computation (which may include translation, linking to system-supplied subroutines, etc.) on one of these jobs. Then, at some point in the computation, the job requests an I/O operation that results in a disk transfer. This may involve the spooling disk or other disks assigned to that user for the user's own files. The operating system initiates this transfer and then assigns the CPU to one of the other jobs in the MM.

This situation of having a few jobs in the MM at any time tends to free the CPU from having to wait for disk transfers (or any other type of independently processed I/O activity). The chances are increased that the CPU can be more highly utilized on user program computations if this is done. The technique is called **multiprogramming.** It clearly involves reasonably complex OS procedures to achieve the desired efficiency. There is a danger that the required OS programs themselves may take too much CPU time. However, multiprogramming systems have been successfully employed in practice and are being continually improved.

To give a simple example of activity in a multiprogrammed system, let us again consider the steps of jobs X, Y, and Z in Fig. 8-9a. Here, we will assume that all R1 steps correspond to loading the program from the input-spooling disk to the MM. The relative times would actually be different, but that won't affect our discussion. Further, assume that the remaining read steps R2 and R3 of job X refer to input data on the spooling disk but that steps R2 of jobs Y and Z refer to input from two other auxiliary storage devices that can operate through other channels concurrently with the spooling disk. As before, the logical sequence of events for each job must proceed as shown in Fig. 8-9a. Suppose that all R1 steps have been performed. Then, any of the C1 steps can be initiated in the CPU by the operating system. Fig. 8-10 shows one possible sequence of events that begins by assigning the CPU to step C1 of job X. When step C1 of X is completed, step R2 of X is begun, and at the same time step C1 of Y is started. The rest of the steps can be easily followed from the diagram. In this example, the CPU is kept busy all the time.

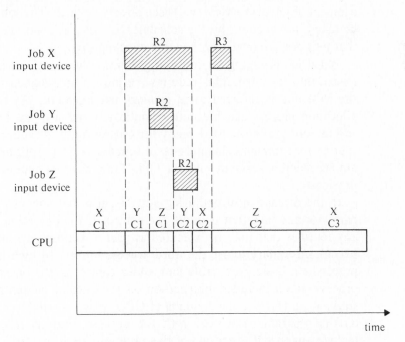

FIG. 8-10 Possible sequence of activities in a multiprogramming system

Operating System Control of Multiprogramming

The previous sections have suggested how spooling and multiprogramming can be used to achieve high system throughput of jobs. We gave examples to show how input, computation, and output steps from different jobs could be overlapped. This increases the utilization of the computer system components (I/O devices, channels, CPU) by increasing the amount of parallel activity.

The purpose of this section is to discuss some rudimentary aspects of the OS routines that are required to schedule, initiate, and monitor the parallel activity. It is common to have a few jobs at various stages of processing in a multiprogramming system. The grouping of jobs for multiprogramming is done by an OS scheduling routine. This is called **long-term scheduling,** and it is done on the basis of the job control information that the user supplies at the front of the job. Such information is usually collected into a **job list** during input spooling. The user declares the resources the job will require in job control statements, which typically include estimates for MM space, CPU time, as well as peripheral device requirements. Jobs that operate on data files that exist on magnetic tapes or disks also need to specify the particular storage volume (tape or disk) required.

By examining the resource requirements of jobs on the job list, the OS scheduler routine can group jobs for multiprogramming in an attempt to use the system resources in the most efficient manner. Jobs that require a lot of I/O operations can be grouped with jobs that require a lot of CPU activity so that a balanced demand on all system components is created. There is an aspect of scheduling that is not directly related to system efficiency. Users can often request high-priority service by paying a premium rate. This leads to the establishment of job-priority classes based on service rates. The job priority must also be taken into account by the scheduler, if it is not done manually at the time that jobs are submitted to the input-spooling process.

When job grouping for multiprogramming has been done, the jobs must be loaded into the MM. This requires the jobs to be assigned to specific parts of the MM and is referred to as **memory management.** OS procedures for this allocation process can be quite complicated and will not be discussed. Once several jobs are in the MM ready for processing, it is necessary to have an OS routine that implements **short-term scheduling.** The routine resolves conflicts among memory-resident jobs for CPU time, channel access, etc., as discussed previously.

In the discussion of operating systems, it is convenient to have a common name for any task that is under the control of the operating system, including any routines that may be executed as part of running a scheduled job. It has become customary to use the word **process** to refer to such tasks. Generally, a process is a basic executable unit under control of the operating system. The process notion includes information on the current contents of the processor status word (PSW), the contents of CPU registers, etc., as execution proceeds on the program associated with the process. Enough information must be included so that if execution of this program is interrupted, it can be resumed at some later time and proceed correctly. With this informal idea of process in mind, let us give some examples. Consider a user job that contains the program PROG. During the execution of PROG, it requests an input operation from a disk via I/O channel A. While the input operation is being performed, execution of PROG is temporarily suspended, and the CPU is assigned to some other job. Upon completion of the input transfer, PROG is ready to resume execution and the CPU is reassigned to it. When computation is completed, a request is made to print some output data. I/O channel B transfers the data to a disk file that accumulates all printing associated with the job. Output spooling will later print this file in a separate operation. There are three processes associated with this job:

P_1 The program PROG
P_2 The input routine executed by channel A
P_3 The output routine executed by channel B

Individual input and output processes such as P_2 and P_3 are relatively simple from the standpoint of their management by the operating system. Once initiated, they usually run continuously to completion because of the nature of channel operation. On the other hand, processes such as P_1 can have a complicated activity pattern. They may be blocked a number of times by I/O calls or preempted by other higher-priority processes. The result is that a process may go through a number of state transitions between states such as "runnable," "running," "blocked."

A useful mechanism for graphically showing the possible state transitions that can occur for a process is the **state** diagram. Fig. 8-11 shows a general state diagram. The arrows between states indicate the cause of the transition. One of the responsibilities of the operating system is **process management,** that is, the control of the activities implied by the state diagram model. For example, consider a situation where program X is running while a higher-priority program Y is blocked waiting for an external interrupt. When this interrupt is received, control will be passed to the operating system, and program Y will be

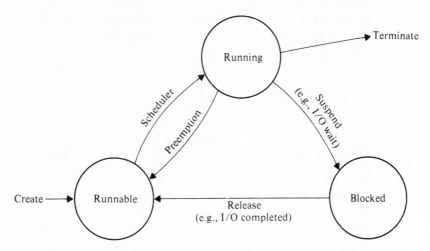

FIG. 8-11   Process state diagram

released into the runnable state. Since program Y has higher priority than X, the OS scheduler will suspend execution of program X and resume execution of program Y.

By now, the reader is probably aware that users in multiprogramming systems do not provide the actual I/O machine instructions and/or channel commands as part of their programs. Also, the user does not service the interrupts that result from completion of his I/O requests. The user simply requests the operating system to perform an I/O operation and to return control when I/O is completed. The I/O routines of the operating system execute the actual transfer. There are a number of reasons why the individual user does not write the actual I/O routines. First of all, most users only want to specify their logical input and output in simple statements in a high-level language. This type of user cares only about reading in information from cards and printing out results on a line printer. These users are completely isolated from the mechanics of I/O spooling and multiprogramming. Even in the case of users who could program some of these machine-dependent functions, there is still a need for central control by an operating system to ensure that (1) users do not interfere with each others' data or programs, and (2) no single user unfairly monopolizes the resources and lowers system efficiency. In summary, OS routines must perform all I/O operations and control the use of shared resources to protect individual jobs and to keep the system throughput high.

We should mention that the CPUs of some computers have both a supervisor mode and a user mode. One difference between supervisor mode and user mode is that certain instructions, such as those that modify the PSW, can only be executed when the CPU is in the supervisor mode. This helps in providing the protection among users mentioned above. In general, when the CPU is in the user mode, it can be interrupted by any peripheral device, causing a transfer to an OS interrupt-servicing routine that executes in the supervisory mode. When the CPU is in the supervisory mode, usually only the most time-critical I/O devices can interrupt it.

At this point, we should be more explicit about the role of I/O device interrupt priorities as opposed to the more general concept of user job-process priorities. Priority in scheduling user job processes for the use of shared resources is usually determined by the requirements stated on the job control cards, including the user-determined choice of paying more for faster service. Suppose the operating system determines the job-request priorities based on the other job characteristics. A possible strategy is as follows: The requests for CPU processing from jobs that require a lot of I/O are given high priority; correspondingly, the I/O requests of jobs that require a lot of CPU processing are given a high priority. The objective of this strategy is to allow jobs to proceed in such a way that they tend toward always being ready to use the resource that they depend on most. In this way, a steady demand on all system resources may be achieved, resulting in maximum component utilization and job throughput. In some cases, as we will see in the next section on interactive systems, scheduling priorities are determined by the urgency of individual process requests, and the system does not have as much freedom in scheduling processes as it does when job throughput is the only performance criterion.

Let us now turn to a discussion of the I/O device interrupt priorities associated with the hardware interrupt requests generated by peripheral devices. These priorities are usually independent of any of the scheduling priorities among user job processes. The device interrupt priorities are determined by the urgency of response of the servicing routines that are a part of the operating system. These response demands of the devices are a function of their own operating characteristics, and they are independent of the user process demands.

Operating System Control of Interactive Computing

Interactive computing has become a very common method of using a computer. The general idea is that users prepare their programs at a teletypewriter or CRT terminal in an **on-line** mode. That is, the user I/O device is under control of the CPU, and as characters are entered at the device keyboard, they are sent directly into the computer system. In some cases, simple computations are executed, line by line, as they are entered. In other situations, the user can name and type in a routine, or a function, and then request that it be executed. A number of different languages have been developed for this purpose. Two of the more popular ones are APL and BASIC. Because of the relatively slow rates at which users require character and line processing, a typical large computer can handle a number of the order of 25 to 50 user terminals doing small-scale computations.

In batch processing, the major objective is to achieve high-throughput rates. Little importance is attached to the time required to complete an individual job. On the other hand, the main objective in an interactive computing system is to achieve fast response to individual users. This requirement is a more severe constraint on scheduling the use of the CPU than is the case in the general multiprogramming situation. When a user enters a command at a terminal requesting the computer to perform some computation and print back an answer, it is important that the computer respond within a few seconds. For purposes of later discussion, let T denote this response delay.

Consider a large computer system with a single CPU that performs interactive computation for up to 50 terminals. A scheduling technique called **time-slicing** or **round-robin** servicing can be used to provide the required response times to all users. In this technique, the CPU is assigned to service each terminal in turn for a short interval of time. To meet the response-time requirements, an upper limit must be imposed on these intervals. This upper limit is called a **quantum,** t. An interval timer is used to interrupt a user process that tries to execute beyond t s. In such a case, control is returned to the operating system. It then assigns a quantum to the next terminal. If there are n active terminals, the value of t can be chosen as $t = T/n$, ignoring OS overhead for the moment. Consider a specific example where the allowable delay T is at most 2 s and all 50 terminals are active. Then, each user gets 40 ms of computation time every 2 s. On a machine that fetches and executes an instruction every 4 μs on the average, 40 ms of computation time corresponds to the execution of 10,000 instructions. This should be adequate for complete execution of most routines used in interactive computing.

The above numerical example is only an estimate of the computation time assignable to each user every T s. A number of details have been overlooked. The parameter T was defined to be the time between a user request for a computation and the response by the computer. We have implied that all the CPU time is assignable to user computations. This is not actually the case. Among other things, CPU time may be required to transfer individual characters from terminals to memory buffers. An alternative is to use a separate processor to collect input characters and assemble them in its memory. Whenever a complete line has been assembled for a terminal, it is transferred to the memory of the main computer. However, we shall first consider the case where the main CPU performs all tasks related to character collection and buffering. The characters from a specific terminal are collected into an input buffer assigned to that terminal. The computer may also echo back each character to be printed at the terminal immediately after it is received. The echoback must appear to the user to be instantaneous, which in practice should be a fraction of a second.

The buffering of input strings and the associated echoback of individual characters for all the interactive terminals should then be viewed as an independent ongoing OS process. The same applies to the buffering of output strings that constitute computer responses (answers) and their subsequent printing. Interrupts can be used to call the OS processes associated with reading and printing characters. Alternatively, the CPU can poll the terminals for individual character transfers. Obviously, this must be done at a much higher rate than the assignment of quanta by the round-robin scheduler.

The tasks of reading and printing individual characters constitute overhead that decreases the amount of CPU time available for computation. Thus the effective quantum time is less than the previously defined t. However, not all the terminals are likely to request a computation every T s. This means that, on the average, each terminal can expect more than one quantum of computation time during every T s.

It is instructive to obtain a rough estimate of the time overhead due to individual character handling. A convenient way to proceed is to postulate a "typical" session at a terminal by an "average" user. Consider an engineering student who wishes to perform a calculation associated with determining the voltages in an electric network. Assume that the major calculation involves solving four simultaneous linear equations. A system subroutine is available for such a problem. The student has to type in the parameters and a subroutine call command to get the solution. Each parameter is represented in decimal floating-point format by at most 10 characters. Since a maximum of 16 parameters is required, the student will type at most 160 characters to enter the data for the problem. Assuming that another 40 characters are used in initiating the session and calling the subroutine, the student will type about 200 characters in this simple session. The computer responses will consist of four answer values of about 10 characters each, and various replies during initiation and termination of the session that might amount to a total of 50 to 60 characters. The computer will then type about 100 characters during the session. Thus a total of 300 characters will be printed. Let the total elapsed time for the session be 5 min. Hence each terminal represents a character-processing load of 60 characters per minute. If there are 50 active terminals, the total estimated character-processing rate is 3000 characters per minute.

Let us now determine the time required to process a single character. Assume that the system we are considering has interrupt facilities. Upon receiving an interrupt request from a terminal, the current state of the CPU must be saved. Let this procedure take 10 instructions. Servicing of the interrupt consists of identifying the terminal, transferring the character to the appropriate input buffer, adjusting the buffer pointer, and echoing the character back to the terminal printer. This may take another 20 instructions. Finally, about 10 instructions are needed to restore the state of the CPU and branch back to the interrupted program. Therefore, as a rough estimate, 40 instructions are required to process a single character. Assuming that each instruction needs 4 μs for execution, the time required for character handling is $3000 \times 40 \times 4 = 480,000$ μs/min. This represents an overhead of only 0.8 percent.

In the above discussion, we have assumed that a single CPU supports all the processes required to accomplish interactive computing, including the handling of individual characters. Since the latter is an independent task, it may be, and often is, delegated to a separate "front-end" processor. This processor gathers characters from all terminals and transfers them in larger blocks to the main processor. Then the main CPU has to deal with only one interrupt, that of the block transfer, instead of individual interrupts from the terminals. Although our example calculations showed that this amounted to only about 1 percent of the main CPU time, the situation we chose to examine was very much simplified. All the terminals were assumed to be slow-speed teletypewriter devices and no character translations were performed. Front-end processors are used to perform a number of other tasks related to buffering character input and output. There may be different types of terminals, each having different communication protocols. The identification of individual terminals and character transfers inbound and outbound may be much more complicated than we assumed above. Also, character set codes may differ from terminal to terminal. The front-end processor can then be used to translate all codes into some standard format before transferring them to the main computer.

Another practical aspect involves the utilization of computers that provide interactive services. If the interactive computing load does not use all the CPU time available, it is quite feasible to occupy the computer with noninteractive batch processing during the spare time intervals. In such cases, interactive processing should be given higher priority. The batch processing is done at a lower-priority level and is often referred to as background computation.

sec. 9

Input, Output, and Secondary Storage Devices

C. William Gear

9-1 INTRODUCTION

The function of a computer system is to process information. We have seen how this is done using the memory and processor units. The computer system must also be able to transmit information between itself and its environment. The information to be processed must be input to the system, and the results must be output back to the external world. The computer may be in one of various different environments which affect the type of input-output communication required. In the most familiar systems, the computer primarily communicates with humans who prepare the problem for solution, provide the initial data, and wish to interpret the answers. In other applications, the input can be directly from a physical device. Complex experiments in the physical sciences can be measured automatically by computer. In such a case, the principal inputs to the computer are digital readings taken directly from the various instruments used to monitor the experiment. In other applications, both input and output may connect directly to mechanical or electrical equipment. For example, an airborne computer may be used to calculate the position of the plane at any instant (by use of inputs from gyroscopes and other inertial devices), to compare this position with the desired flight path derived by computation, and then to output correction signals to the control mechanisms of the aircraft. Computers for online instrumentation and process control applications are usually smaller and more specialized than the general-purpose computers that we have been discussing. In this chapter, we shall discuss the input and output that are common to the general-purpose systems. However, the principles involved do not differ from those in online computers.

The general-purpose computer may need to communicate either directly with the user or with a computer-readable medium. The former is referred to as **input-output,** whereas the latter is called **secondary storage,** since the information is not yet "out" of its computer representation. Secondary storage is also called **backup storage.** Secondary storage can be used to transmit data to another computer either immediately or at a later time. Immediate transfer can only be accomplished by a direct data connection between two computers. With a direct data connection, each computer looks like a secondary storage device to the other. This sort of connection is frequently used between small special-purpose control computers and large general-purpose computers. Delayed transfers are achieved by first storing the information on a machine-readable medium, such as magnetic tape (discussed below), and then transferring the storage medium to the other machine. An important application of this storage is for transferring the information back to the machine that originally wrote it. This provides a mechanism for storing a large amount of data for a long period of time without using the expensive main memory. We shall see that some devices have the ability to store information on a medium that can be physically moved from one computer to another, while others do not. This could form one basis for classifying secondary storage. Input-output would always fall into the former category. Devices also differ in their speeds and capacities, and this forms another basis for classification which we use below. We refer to long-term storage devices, which are frequently used to save information over long periods of time, and to medium-term storage devices, which are frequently used either to save information from one short computer run to another, for additional storage during a single execution of a program, or to provide rapid access to frequently used system programs. Generally speaking, higher-speed devices have less capacity and are less likely to have removable storage media.

9-2 INPUT-OUTPUT DEVICES

Input-output devices are of two basic types: **hard-copy** devices and non-hard-copy devices. The latter present the output directly to the user in a nonpermanent form, or read the input directly as the result of some action by the user, such as the pressing of a key on a typewriter keyboard.

Online Terminals

One of the most common I/O devices today is the online terminal. It consists of a keyboard by which the user can enter alphabetic and numeric data and an output device. The output device may be either a printing device such as a type-writerlike mechanism, or a cathode-ray-tube (CRT) alphanumeric display. The latter can display a number of lines of characters, typically 20 to 24 lines of 60 to 80 characters per line. When a CRT is used, it normally displays the last 20 or 24 lines output by the computer and operates in the **scroll** mode; that is, as each new line is output, it is placed at the bottom of the screen and the other lines on the screen are moved up one position. In this process, the top line on the screen disappears.

Input to the keyboard is limited to typing speed (perhaps a peak of 10 to 15 characters a second in very short bursts with an average closer to 8 for a very good typist). Output speed is determined by the capacity of the line connecting the terminal to the computer. For typewriters, this is normally about 15 to 30 characters per second, although some printing mechanisms will operate more rapidly. For CRT terminals, much higher rates are possible, and one frequently transmits at 120 to 960 characters per second. Users of these terminals may find a switch that indicates "baud rate." This is the speed in bits per second. Since most transmission systems transmit 10 bits to send one ASCII 8-bit char-acter, the baud rate is normally 10 times the character rate. Many terminals are connected to the computer via telephone lines. In that case, the baud rate is limited to about 1200.

Most terminals are connected to the computer by two independent circuits: one connecting the keyboard to the computer for input and the other connecting the computer to the output device for output. (Even when one phone circuit is used, the two independent circuits are present. They are **multiplexed** over the one phone line.) The use of two independent circuits is called **full duplex;** it allows simultaneous transmission in both directions. Although in many cases it appears to the user that each character typed on the keyboard is immediately printed or displayed on the output, in fact the character is being sent to the computer and retransmitted from the computer back to the terminal. This is called **echoing.** In some systems it is possible to type faster than the computer can generate the response so that the echo is noticeable. A few systems use **half duplex** in which there is only one transmission line. In such systems the user has to be careful not to type while the computer is transmitting information back to the terminal because if both occur at the same time the two signals on the transmission line will conflict with each other and information will be lost. A third system is called **simplex.** It uses one line which can only be used in one direction at a time. Some sort of **protocol** is needed for communications between the terminal and the computer so that each knows when it has per-mission to transmit and so that each can be guaranteed to get a turn. Simplex systems are seldom used for terminals.

The Line Printer

The typewriterlike output device in terminals is a character-at-a-time printer. This limits its speed because it is difficult to print a single character in much less than 4 milliseconds. The **line printer** is a device which prints a line at a time. The computer transmits a complete line of information to the printer unit, and then it is printed. A printing mechanism exists at every print position across the line, which can vary in width from 80 characters to 150 characters in common printers. Because of the parallelism preset in such a printer, it can achieve speeds of 1000 to 2000 lines per minute by mechanical means. Nonmechanical printing techniques (photographic, for example) can achieve even higher speeds (up to 30,000 lines per minute).

Plotters and Display Devices Although printer output is very convenient for many purposes, frequently the user needs to present the information graphically in order to be able to understand its significance. This may be in the form of a single graph plotting one variable against another, or it may be a complex pictorial display representing a multidimensional item. For example, three-dimensional pictures are frequently represented by two-dimensional contour maps, where lines represent the paths of constancy in the third dimension (weather maps, for example, in which the contours of constant pressure are drawn to indicate the high-pressure and low-pressure regions).

If graphs have to be prepared by hand from numerical output by the computer, a large amount of output is typically needed and time-consuming drawing must be undertaken by the human. Therefore, direct graphical output devices have been developed for computer use. There are two basic types of output device: one which allows the user to put a point at any location on the output **page,** and one which allows the user to move a **pen** in any direction a given distance, with the pen either on the paper making a mark or off the paper not making a mark. The words **pen** and **paper** are not meant literally, in that the output could be on any medium which can be marked. In many devices, the two basic techniques are both available, but it is convenient to examine them separately.

The **incremental plotter** is an example of the second form of output. It is a device with a pen and a large sheet of paper. The pen can be moved a small increment in any one of several directions. In a typical plotter, it can move in any one of the eight directions separated by 45 degrees a distance of $\frac{5}{1000}$ inch vertically or horizontally, or $\frac{7}{1000}$ inch in any of the four 45-degree directions. All lines must be made up of these short, straight-line segments. The computer commands the plotter with a series of characters to make each basic plot step.

The use of a plotter to draw a 45-degree triangle lying on its hypotenuse is shown in Fig. 9-1. The computer subroutine library will usually contain subroutines to simplify the use of the plotter. A common package of subroutines for a plotter allows the user to move the pen from where it is currently to any given position on the page, with the pen either writing or not, to draw many of the common curves such as ellipses and to print letters and numbers. The subroutines convert the demands of the user into sequences of the basic steps for the plotter. The time

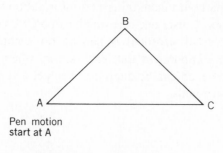

Pen motion
start at A

Pen down
Move up, right (100 steps)
Move down, right (100 steps)
Move left (200 steps)
Pen up

FIG. 9-1 Plotting a triangle

to plot a figure is dependent on the linear distance that the pen moves. The speed is of the order of 1 to 10 inches per second.

The cathode-ray-tube output device basically allows the user to illuminate spots on the face of the CRT by specifying X and Y coordinates to the output device. With such a device, a line must be built up from many small points. Typically about 500 to 4000 points can be displayed in each direction, and adjacent points are sufficiently close that they are joined together as far as the eye can see. Other CRT displays have built-in **vector** and **character** facilities which allow them to generate straight lines and standard characters directly. This serves to decrease the computer time needed to generate a display, but not to increase the flexibility of the display from the user's point of view. The basic operations are used by subroutines to provide the same facilities as are available for the plotter. An important additional facility available with a cathode-ray tube is the **light pen.** This is a photoelectric device, shaped like an ordinary pen, which can be placed on any point on the face of the CRT. When the spot touched is illuminated by the program in control, a signal is generated by the photocell. This signal is sent to the computer, usually in the form of an interrupt. Thus the programmer can tell where the pen is positioned. By suitable programs, it is possible to follow the light pen around the screen and store inside the computer the coordinates of the various points indicated by the user. Thus the user can **draw** on the face of the CRT, and the light pen can be used as an input device. Its most common use is for pointing at sections of the total display on the tube.

Other devices can be used for indicating a point on the screen. One is a special tablet that is sensitive to an electronic pen held by the user. Another is a small hand-held box that the user moves over the surface of the table. Pickup devices measure the position of the hand and transmit it to the computer, which then displays a circle or a cross on the screen corresponding to the hand's position.

Another form of CRT output is coupled with a camera so that microfilm or microfiche can be produced directly from computer output. In addition to the commands to plot lines and display text on the CRT screen, there are commands to advance the film or position the microfiche negative. These devices are capable of very high speed output. They have a second advantage: the physical size of the output is quite small compared to a large listing. (Some very high speed computers used in large numerical calculations have used line printers as fast as 30,000 lines per minute. Such printers require forklift trucks to move the volume of paper produced in a modest time, since it represents about an 8-inch stack of 11- by 14-inch paper every minute. Output on a microfiche can be carried away by hand. It is doubtful that either can be read.)

The next two types of input-output are almost obsolete. Punched cards are still used in some business applications in which a small amount of information is to be received by mail from a large number of sources (for example, identifying information returned with bill payment), and punched paper tape is occasionally used for low-speed recording of data from experiments and on extremely low cost microcomputers. We discuss them here because they have an important historical contribution, and understanding paper tape makes the understanding of the use of magnetic tape much simpler.

Punched Cards

The most common form of punched card is a rectangle of heavy card stock (usually about 7½ inches by 3¼ inches) that can be punched with a hole in any one of 960 positions on a 12 by 80 rectangular array of positions. Other sizes of cards—with 51 or 90 columns instead of the 80 columns mentioned above—are in use, but the 80-column card is the most common. Punched cards were used for machine control in the weaving industry long before they were used in data processing. The first major application of punched cards to data handling occurred during the late 1800's, when Herman Hollerith adapted them for use in the 1890 census. Because of his work, the cards are called **Hollerith cards,** and one way in which they were punched is called the **Hollerith card code.** This code is a means of representing alphanumeric data (that is, the alphabetic letters and the 10 decimal digits) and a few special characters such as period, comma, etc. One column is used to represent each character, so that up to 80 characters can be punched on one card. As shown in Fig. 9-2, the card rows are labeled 12, 11, 0, 1, 2, 3, 4, 5, 6, 7, 8, and 9. A blank character or space is represented as no holes punched, the numerical digits 0 through 9 by a punch in the corresponding row, and the letters by double punches. A through I are represented by a 12-row punch together with a digit punch from 1 to 9, respectively, J through R by an 11-row punch with the digit 1 through 9, respectively, and S through Z by a 0-row punch with the digit 2 through 9, respectively. Other characters are represented by other combinations of punched holes.

When a card written in this format is read into the machine, it is converted into a string of characters in memory in a suitable code. If the standard 48-character set is used, then only 6 bits are needed to represent 48 characters. Therefore one of the 6-bit codes, such as the BCD code, can be used. This conversion is usually done by hardware, so that the programmer does not have to concern himself with the Hollerith code. In many recent machines an 8-bit code is used, allowing up to 256 different characters. The two most common 8-bit codes are ASCII (American Standard Code for Information Interchange) and EBCDIC (Extended Binary Coded Decimal Interchange Code). The latter is an IBM internal standard.

Each column of a punched card can contain up to 12 punches for a total of $2^{12} = 4096$ different combinations. However, if 6-bit or 8-bit codes are used, far fewer combinations are used. In some systems the **binary card** is introduced to combat this inefficiency. The binary card can be punched in any position, so that each column contains 12 bits of information. If a binary card is read into the computer, each column is mapped in a direct manner into 12 bits of memory, and vice versa on output punching. Since cards so punched are not readable by most printing equipment, this use of cards is solely for storage of information to be read back in at a later stage. It is very common, for example, to store programs on binary cards after they have been translated by the machine (to avoid having to retranslate them). If an 8-bit code is used in the computer, there exists a mapping from 8-bit bytes to combination of punches in a single column. Since 8 of the 12 bits of information are being used, the inefficiency is not too bad. The IBM 370, for example, uses EBCDIC code for storing binary information on cards rather than provide a special set of instructions to handle

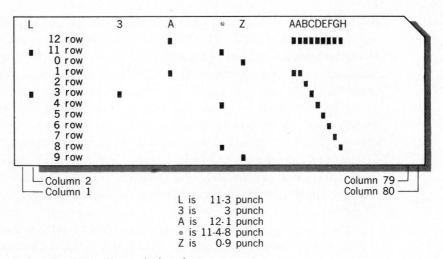

FIG. 9-2   Hollerith punched card

binary cards. If a 6-bit code is used, binary cards can allocate two 6-bit characters to each card column. However, binary information is seldom kept on punched cards these days; so the inefficiency is not critical.

Cards can be read at speeds in the range of 1000 to 2000 per minute and punched at speeds of 200 to 400 per minute. Because card reading is prone to error, the card reader usually reads each card twice to check for reading errors, and card punches usually also read the punched result to perform similar checking.

Punched Paper Tape

Punched paper tape is very similar to punched cards in that it consists of a heavy paper stock in which information is represented by the presence or absence of punched holes. It differs from cards in that paper tape is in continuous strips of arbitrary lengths, whereas cards are a fixed size. Tape is commonly used in three different widths containing five, seven, or eight possible information-hole positions across the tape. Each of these positions is called a **channel.** A 1-inch eight-channel tape is shown in Fig. 9-3. Notice that, in addition to the eight information positions or channels, there is a ninth position that

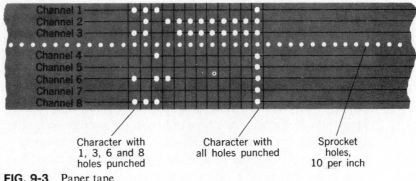

FIG. 9-3   Paper tape

is always punched with a sprocket hole. This is to locate the position where the information should appear along the tape. Without this sprocket hole, a series of characters consisting of no punched holes would lead to a strip of completely blank tape. It would then be impossible to tell how many characters there were in such a string except by measuring the length of the tape, a procedure which would be very prone to error. The sprocket hole is also used to mesh with a sprocket gear on the slower mechanical readers. Since paper tape is prone to error, it is very common to use one of the information channels as a parity bit for the other information channels. Paper tape can be read at speeds of 1000 to 2000 characters per second, and punched at 300 characters per second, although the lowest-cost devices handle only about 10 characters per second in either direction.

Many other forms of input and output devices have been developed for special purposes. Optical scanners can **read** sets of typed characters, and some devices have achieved a limited ability to read handwritten characters. Three-dimensional pens that enable the computer to track the user's hand in three-dimensional space have been designed; and analog input and output converters not only read information directly from experimental measuring equipment but also control experiments directly. Voice output is possible either by controlling sets of audio recorders similar to tape recorders, or by passing signals to an audio generator that produces basic sounds of speech directly. Experimentally, limited acoustic input has been performed using the computer to analyze the signals from microphones.

9-3 LONG-TERM STORAGE AND INTERMEDIATE INPUT-OUTPUT

Problems that involve the use of very large amounts of data and that are run on many different occasions have a requirement for long-term storage devices. Problems in this class include commercial jobs such as the record keeping associated with the maintenance of customer accounts and scientific jobs such as the comparison of data gathered from a particular physics experiment with the data gathered from many previous experiments. Both of these jobs have the characteristic that very large amounts of data are involved (100 million characters should be considered typical in designing systems for this type of problem) and the characteristic that the data is to be changed in a small way (some customer accounts are changed, or some additional experimental data is added to the history file). These characteristics dictate the need for a storage device that has virtually unlimited total capacity, although it only need be accessed in a serial fashion (that is, in sequential order, one unit of information at a time). Since the electronics associated with storage devices is the expensive part of the device, a desirable form of storage is one in which the storage is on a simple medium which can be removed, kept on a shelf, and replaced. To a limited extent, punched cards are a type of long-term storage, since the card reader and punch are, in principle, capable of handling an arbitrarily large number of cards. However, cards cannot be changed (holes cannot be filled in any practical way), and cards have a nonnegligible cost (a couple of cents per card). Also, card equipment is comparatively slow. However, there are a number of other devices which do not have these drawbacks, specifically, magnetic tapes, disk files, and variations on both. These are all forms of the familiar tape recorder used for audio storage. This section will discuss the principles of a number of such devices. It is not intended to be exhaustive, since new versions are marketed almost every day. Although the manufacturer may claim a "breakthrough," the operating principles remain very similar; the speed and capacity may increase and the cost decrease.

Magnetic Tape

Magnetic-tape storage was derived directly from audio-tape principles. The storage medium is a long strip of tape with a fixed width. Common tape systems are available with ½-inch and 1-inch tape widths. The length of the tape is typically about 2400 feet, and it is wound on a reel for easy handling. Microcomputer systems often use smaller cassette tapes and other cartridges. Functionally, these are identical. The tape itself is about ⅟₅₀₀ to ⅟₁₀₀₀ of an inch thick, and it consists of a backing of flexible material, such as Mylar, with a coating of a magnetic material (an iron oxide). Information is stored on the tape by magnetizing the oxide coating in one direction or another. A **track** on the tape is a section of the width of the tape in which the magnetically coded information is stored. See Fig. 9-4. Since a track is less than ⅟₁₆ of an inch wide, several tracks

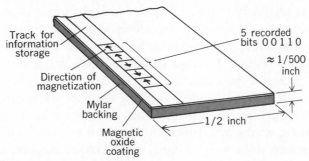

FIG. 9-4   Magnetic tape

can be placed across the tape. Half-inch tape commonly has either 7 or 9 tracks across the width; hence 7 or 9 bits can be stored in **parallel.** These are used to store one 6- or 8-bit character plus a parity bit. To read or write on tape, the reel of tape is mounted on a **tape drive,** which is a mechanism with two drive reels, **read heads, write heads,** and a **capstan** (a rotating wheel against which the tape is pressed by a **pinch roller**) which pulls the tape across the heads at an approximately constant speed (see Fig. 9-5). When the tape is written, it is pulled across the heads by the capstan, and amplifiers drive current through the write heads in order to magnetize the tape. It is read by pulling the tape across the read heads with the capstan and sensing the voltages induced in the read heads.

   In practice, the bits of information are packed very closely together along the tape; for example, 200, 556, 800, and 1600 bits per inch (bpi) in each track are standard **densities.** Since the tape is moved at speeds around 120 inches per

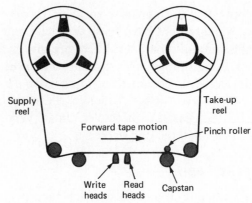

Supply reel

Take-up reel

Forward tape motion

Pinch roller

Write heads

Read heads

Capstan

FIG. 9-5 A tape drive

second, it is out of the question to start or stop the tape between characters. Therefore, the information is usually written on the tape in continuous **records** or **blocks** with gaps between for starting and stopping the tape motion. These gaps are called **interrecord gaps** and are about 3/4-inch long. The length of the blocks is either fixed by the computer or is allowed to vary according to the use by the programmer. It is important to understand the difference between these two possibilities, so we shall first examine the reason for their use.

We recall that paper tape had a sprocket hole in order to allow the tape reader to know where a character was punched on the tape. In a similar manner, it is necessary for the computer to know where a set of bits (a character) is written on the magnetic tape. This is not done by a sprocket hole (it is difficult to punch 1600 holes to the inch), but in some systems the equivalent—a **timing track**—is used. A timing track is a tape track that contains a magnetic signal in every bit position. The tape reader can use this track to indicate when a character position across the tape has been encountered, and then it can read the actual information bits. The alternative is to demand that every character written on the tape contain at least one magnetic signal, so that the **OR** of all channels will contain a signal when a character is read. This is not too difficult, since it is normal to use a parity bit in every character. By using appropriate parity, at least one signal is assured. Other recording techniques can be used to guarantee that a signal can be sensed in every character position, even if each track is considered separately. The important difference is that if timing tracks are used, the tape must be **formatted** before use by writing a timing track all the way along the tape and leaving it there permanently. It is always possible to return to the same point on the tape by counting the timing bits. If, however, a timing track is not used, the tape drive must provide its own timing information during the writing of new information via an electronic clock. Since it is impossible to guarantee that the tape moves at exactly the same speed on two successive operations, a written block of a given number of characters may vary in length from one WRITE operation to another. The effect of this is shown in Fig. 9-6. In the top diagram, the tape has been written with two blocks of information of 10,000 characters each at 800 bpi (about 12½ inches each). In the second diagram, the first block has been rewritten when the tape moved 10 percent faster. Consequently, 1¼ inches of the next block have been overwritten.

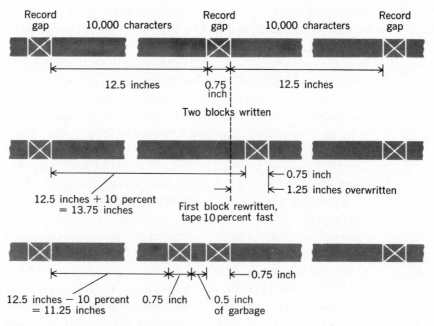

FIG. 9-6 Effect of nonconstant tape speeds

The bottom diagram shows the effect of rewriting the first block with the tape moving 10 percent slower. This time, about ½ inch of the previous block remains. If the user attempted to read the second block, errors would occur in both cases.

Tape that uses timing tracks can be rewritten at any point. In general, tape without timing tracks cannot be used in this manner, but must be used sequentially. That is, before a block can be written, all blocks earlier than it on the tape must first be written. However, some manufacturers are claiming to be able to produce tape units which are sufficiently accurate that blocks can be written at arbitrary points.

A comparison of formatted and unformatted tape is difficult. On the one hand, formatted tape can be changed at any point. On the other, part of the space on the tape is used for timing information that could be used for storage. (The problem of writing precisely where the bit appears in the timing track is also more difficult than writing whenever the tape-unit clock indicates.) If tape is to be rewritten at any point, then it is easier for the programmer to use **fixed-length blocks,** and, indeed, tape is often formatted in this way. However, the tendency has been to use fixed-length blocks even on unformatted tape, for system reasons. The largest computer manufacturer, IBM, uses unformatted tape, and such tape is therefore the most common.

Basic tape operations include writing and reading blocks of information. In addition, tape-handling operations are necessary to enable the program to reach the particular block needed. After a tape block has been written, it is necessary to backspace the tape to the beginning of the block in order to reread it. (Some systems allow tape to be read or written in either direction, but the majority only allow reading and writing in the forward direction.) Sometimes it is necessary to space forward over one or more blocks in order to reach something further down the tape; therefore a forward space operation is desirable.

Magnetic tape is only sequentially accessible. That is, it is more like a scroll than a book. A scroll is read by unwinding it from one end; in order to reach a paragraph in the middle, it is necessary to roll through all previous paragraphs. In general, there are no operations to access an arbitrary block on a tape. Instead, it is necessary to skip through all the preceding blocks, one at a time.

Many of the terms introduced below are derived from business data processing. The basic unit of information in business data is the **character,** which may be part of a name, address, or numeric record. Characters are grouped together into **fields** representing the names, etc. Groups of fields are combined into one **record,** which may be the basic block written onto the tape. Historically, the word **record** was used to mean a recorded block of information. We shall reserve the word to signify a logical group of information typically handled as a unit by the user, and we shall use the word **block** to mean the physically recorded group of information. A record might, for example, contain all of the employment information relating to one employee. Finally, all of the employee records are grouped into one **file,** or **data set.** In a large organization, one file may occupy many reels of tape; whereas in a small company, it may occupy only a small part of one reel. (A reel of tape may contain 30 million characters.) The file concept is used in magnetic tape recording by providing a special **end-of-file** mark which can be written by the computer instead of a regular block. When it is read, an indicator is set which can be sensed by the program to indicate that the end of the file has been reached. A common analogy to draw for files, records, and characters on tape is with a book. The paragraphs are similar to records, and the file is the whole book. This does not take into account divisions into sections and chapters. These the programmer must handle by careful use of multiple end-of-file marks or other techniques. Following this analogy, fixed-length blocks are similar to the pages of a book. Blocks do not usually correspond to the natural division of the information into sections, paragraphs, etc., but they **do** provide an easy way of locating a piece of information if an index is provided. On tape, fixed blocks may not correspond to the requirements of the information, but they can be used to advantage if the information is indexed.

To make use of file marks, two operations are usually provided, a backspace file and a skip-to-end-of-file operation. These make it easier to move over multiple files with minimum program effort. The operations allowed on typical unformatted and formatted systems are shown in tabular form below. Many tape units, those with separate read and write heads, check the information as it is being written by reading it back. If a parity bit is used (almost all magnetic recording devices use parity), and if the tape passes over the read head after it has passed over the write head, the information can be checked for parity. This will allow any single error to be detected. If an error is detected, the operation can be repeated, which requires that the tape be backspaced to the start of the block and the write repeated.

When a file of information on magnetic tape is to be updated (that is, some of the information is to be changed), it is necessary to read the original from one tape and make updated copy on another tape on a second tape drive. The

TABLE 9-1 Unformatted and Formatted Tape

Operation	Unformatted tape	Formatted tape
Write	Program specifies the number of words.	A multiple of a fixed number of words (the block length).
Read	Option. Either the whole block written or a number of words specified by the program. Restriction: cannot read downstream of a write operation.	Fixed block as written or a given number of words.
Backspace	Block or file possible.	Block only†
Forward space (skip)	Block or file possible.	Block only†
Rewind	O.K.	O.K.
Write end of file	O.K.	Not available†
Sense end of file on read	O.K.	Not available†

†It is possible to allow an extra character at the start of each block to represent a file mark, in which case all file operations are possible.

only time that this is not necessary is when fixed-length-block formatted tapes are used and the updated material is not longer than the original. The minimum number of unformatted tape drives for any useful operation is two, while four is a more practical minimum for most data manipulation tasks. Two tapes are needed so that one can be updated onto the other. An unlimited number of reels of tape can be stored on shelves and, given enough time, processed by the computer. Therefore the upper limit of storage is unbounded. The speed of operation varies between different drives and manufacturers, and the range of character rates is from a few thousand per second to 20,000 per second. Moving the tape over records and files takes about the same length of time as reading or writing, while rewinding takes from 1 to 2 minutes maximum. The time to start and stop the tape in the record gap varies from 1 to 20 milliseconds. Formatted and unformatted tape are compared in Table 9-1.

Disk Units

A **disk,** also called a **disk file,** is a device which resembles a phonograph record and its playback mechanism. Physically, a single disk platter is a circular sheet of metal about 10 to 20 inches in diameter and $\frac{1}{16}$ to $\frac{1}{4}$ inch thick. It is coated on both surfaces with a magnetic material, so that the thickness of the disk is for mechanical strength only. Information is recorded on the disk surface magnetically, just as information is recorded on magnetic tape. The difference between the recording on a phonograph record and a disk platter (in addition to the means of storing information) is that whereas a record contains one continuous groove or track in a spiral, a disk surface contains many tracks arranged in concentric circles. The read-write heads (the same head is used for both) are mounted on movable arms which can be positioned over any one of the tracks: there may be from 100 to 1000 tracks on a surface. A diagram of a single disk surface is shown in Fig. 9-7.

A disk unit may be able to access a single surface at a time, or it may contain several platters, each with a read-write head on an arm, such that any surface

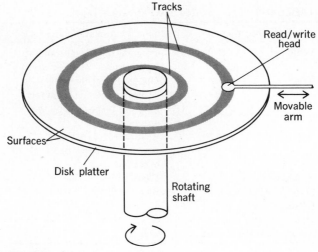

FIG. 9-7 Disk

can be accessed. As long as the set of disk platters can be removed, the disk file satisfies our definition of long-term, essentially unlimited storage. It has characteristics similar to magnetic tapes in that it can take a relatively long time to move from the track currently under the head to another track, just as it can take a tape reader a long time to move from one position on the tape to another relative to the transmission time for one character. However, both figures are much faster for disk files, in that a typical maximum head-movement time for a disk file is about $\frac{1}{10}$ second, whereas for a tape it is up to 4 minutes. The data rate for characters from disk is typically between 100 KC (KC = 1000 characters) and 400 KC per second compared to 30 KC to 180 KC for tape. A large disk file will contain the same amount of information as a tape to within an order of magnitude. (Tapes contain about 1000 characters per inch over 2400 feet, for about 30×10^6 characters; disks typically contain from 10 to 400×10^6 characters.)

The method of recording on disks is almost always a fixed-block mode, since each track is of a fixed length. The disk pack contains **sector marks** which are physical marks that can be read by the disk drive to determine the current position of the disk. Typically, a disk pack contains between 20 and 40 sector marks. One of these is special (often a double mark is used), and it is called an **index mark.** It indicates the beginning of a track. Blocks may be recorded starting at any of the sector marks. During writing, the disk unit uses a clock to determine timing. During reading, the data from the disk itself contains enough information to give the timing. The speed of a disk file is sufficiently precise that it is possible to write in any block without changing the others.

Many disk drives use a fairly elaborate procedure to ensure that the correct track and sector are under the head before a read or write is permitted. Most disks use a **header,** consisting of about 50 bits of information that contain the track, sector, and length of the block in front of each block. This information is written on the disk pack when it is first placed in operation in what is called a **formatting** operation. The system programmers choose blocks sizes once and for all for the system, and cause these headers to be written in front of every

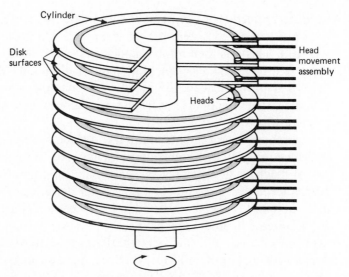

FIG. 9-8   Multiple-surface disk file (cutaway view)

block. When the disk is used subsequently, the program must first move the head to the right track (this is called a **seek** operation), then specify the header information before the read or write can be performed. The disk drive compares the information and does not permit the operation until a match occurs. Most users are not aware of this process, as it is done by system programs when a disk operation is requested.

While the heads are fixed in any one position, the computer has access to one track on each surface. If we visualize this set of tracks on the disk surfaces shown in Fig. 9-8, we see that they lie on the surface of a cylinder. For this reason, disks are often addressed by the **cylinder address** and the **surface address.** The former refers to the position of the heads, the latter to the surface being used. Taken together, these components form the **track address.** When several blocks of information are to be transmitted between the disk unit and the computer, it is faster if they are on the same cylinder, so that no head movement is involved.

A recent form of disk is called a **floppy disk** because the disk is a circular sheet of flexible Mylar coated with a magnetic oxide. The device is very low cost—about one tenth the cost of a modest size standard disk unit, and is often used in microcomputer systems.

Variations of Tapes and Disks

Many devices have been marketed which are in the same class as tapes and disks: that is, they have the characteristics of removability (so that storage is virtually unlimited) and a reasonable speed and capacity for a single load. They take the form of packages of disklike or tapelike storage media which can be accessed so that an individual piece of the medium can be placed under the read-write mechanism. With devices of this form, capacities in excess of 10^9 characters **online** (that is, in the machine at one time) are achievable.

One such device was the **data-cell,** a unit that contained cartridges, each of which contained strips of flexible base coated with a magnetic material. The read mechanism consisted of a drum around which one of the strips could be wrapped. This was then rotated under read-write heads to record or play back data. A mechanical access system could load or unload any one of the strips. Once a strip was loaded, the speed was about the same as disk speeds, but it took a considerable time to access a strip if it was some distance from the access mechanism.

The major improvements in the last decade have been decreases in the cost of devices coupled with some increases in speed. Without reducing the physical size of mechanical mechanisms, it is difficult to move them reliably at a much higher speed than present, although higher densities have led to some improvement in speed. However, the reduction of costs of integrated circuits and the great increase in production have served to lower cost considerably. Small, slow tape units based on ⅛-inch wide audio tape cassettes are under $100, while floppy disk units are $500 to $1000. Large disk drives with one-third billion characters are up to 20 times that price.

9-4 MEDIUM-TERM STORAGE DEVICES

By **medium-term** storage we mean the retention of information for times of a few seconds to a few days, where it is not practical to **unload** the storage medium for physical storage in a cabinet. Devices in this category are characterized by speeds ranging from those available with the long-term devices to speeds of the order of several million characters per second. The capacities of these devices range from those of long-term devices down to the order of a million characters. Applications of these devices are as extensions of the directly addressable main memory in problems in which there is inadequate main memory, and for the retention of information from one problem run to another when it is not convenient to physically reload a storage medium onto a reader. Typical situations that call for these applications are, in the former case, the sorting of large amounts of input information (probably contained on a magnetic tape) which requires many passes over the data, copying them from one storage area to another, and, in the latter case, the saving of user programs and data in a timesharing, remote-console system, where it is necessary for each user to have almost immediate access to private information each time a console is used.

The needs of the examples given above can be satisfied by the use of the long-term devices mentioned above, but some problems exist for which the maximum data rate or the average access time (to move the heads or the tape) are inadequate; so improvements must be sought. However, in a typical installation, some of the disk units available will be used mainly as **scratch** storage; that is, for the temporary storage of information during the execution of a program only. In addition, a number of other devices can be used.

The Disk

The disk was discussed above as a unit with removable disk platters for long-term storage. If the platters do not have to be removable, then it is possible to put more platters in a single unit. In fact, this was the first form of disk developed. It is physically similar to the removable-platter disk and is used in the same manner. However, its storage capability can be increased and, by using more than one head to read or write bits on several tracks at once, its speed can be increased considerably. The extreme form of such a disk file is one in which there is one head for every track. This is often called a **drum,** although we usually distinguish between **fixed-head disks** and drums. Since a large disk file can have 8000 tracks, the one-head-for-one-track arranagement is only possible for the smaller disk units. This type of arrangement does, however, eliminate the positioning of the arms carrying the heads—the slowest part of a disk-file operation. The average access time then drops down to half the rotation time (about half of 35 milliseconds), since the user will have to wait—on the average—a half revolution before the desired information rotates to a position underneath the reading head so that it can be transmitted to the computer. The average delay caused by rotation is called **latency.**

The Drum

Historically, the drum was developed before the disk file, but it is convenient to think of it as a variant of the disk file with fixed heads. Instead of information being stored on a set of disk surfaces, it is stored on the surface of the drum, which may be about 10 inches in diameter and perhaps 20 inches long (although much larger drums have been developed). Because drums are more compact, they can achieve much higher revolution speeds than can disk-file mechanisms. Hence, the average access time can be reduced. Typically, revolution times are in the range of 8 to 35 milliseconds. Information is usually stored in fixed-length blocks on a drum. A drum is shown pictorially in Fig. 9-9. It is like a single

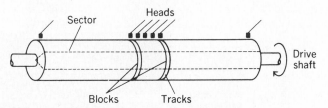

FIG. 9-9   Drum

cylinder of a disk file but, for engineering reasons, it is possible to get a higher bit density on a drum than on a disk. To achieve high data rates, several tracks may be read in parallel, so that a large number of words can be read in a single revolution. To keep the blocks to a manageable size, the tracks are divided into **sectors.** Each sector contains a block for reading and writing purposes. The computer accesses the drum by specifying a track and a sector address. After one sector has been read or written, the next-higher-numbered sector can be accessed immediately because it is possible to switch from one set of heads to another almost instantaneously.

Bulk Storage Devices

The primary memory of the computer is constructed from many identical elements, each of which can store 1 bit, and each of which can be accessed in about the same amount of time. The elements may be cores, or magnetic thin films, or integrated circuit elements. Speeds are typically from 0.1 to 1 microsecond for reading and writing one word composed of from 16 to 64 bits. A bulk store is a similar device in which the number of words has been greatly increased from the typical main memory sizes of 10^4 to 10^6 words. A bulk store may hold about 10 million characters. As a consequence of the increase in size, the speed is worse, typically 2 microseconds or more for an access. One organization, adopted by CDC in their extended core storage (ECS), is to make the "word" in the bulk memory very wide. Whereas the regular memory contains 60-bit words, the bulk memory contains 480-bit words. Thus eight words can be read in parallel from each of four banks of bulk store simultaneously to achieve a maximum rate of 100 nanoseconds per word, which is the peak speed of the main memory, achieved by overlapping four banks of 400-nanosecond memory. Because these speeds can only be achieved if many consecutive words are moved (the first word takes 3.2 microseconds), it can only be used as a block transfer device between the main memory and the bulk store. Thus it looks rather like a drum or disk file, but it is much faster and has no delays waiting for the

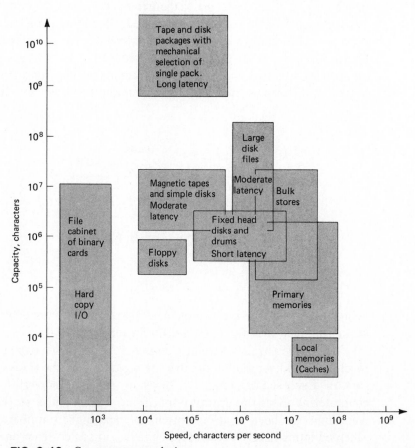

FIG. 9-10 Current memory devices

rotation to the start of a block. It cannot be used to provide instructions and data directly to the CPU. However, the program can fetch data (or instructions) from ECS by executing a block copy instruction which copies a block of words sequentially from ECS memory to primary memory. Then the data or instructions can be used in the next section of code.

9-5 SPEED AND CAPACITY COMPARISONS

The speeds and capacities of various types of storage media are shown and compared with the speed and capacity of main memories in Fig. 9-10.

sec. 10

Timesharing Systems

Herbert Hellerman
Thomas F. Conroy

10-1 INTRODUCTION

The timesharing type of computer system first appeared in its present form in the early 1960s. Although related in some ways to earlier military "command and control" and airline reservation systems, the term **timesharing** now usually denotes a multiuser system in which each user has the ability to define and run his own programs on what he perceives as his own private general-purpose computer, with the added proviso that the system must respond to certain of his requests quickly enough to be comfortable for man-machine interaction. Compared to the more common "batch system," timesharing is then a different way for people to interact with a computer. Since it is a much more intimate way, activities such as problem solving, engineering design, and all types of program construction and debugging are very convenient. This major enhancement of the creative environment not only results in economies arising from more productive uses of human resources, but also presents us with an open-ended challenge to enhance human creativity.

In addition to user-oriented justifications, resource efficiencies (at least potential ones) tend to favor timesharing. One of these is the hope that the high demand rate of the many users connected to the system together with a batch workload will improve CPU utilization, which typically runs as low as 30 to 40 percent in many batch systems. However, this potential may be offset at least in part by swapping "overhead" (see below).

The "timesharing" of the central processor from which the system derives its generic name is only one of several increased opportunities for sharing. Others include the sharing of main storage and other devices, as well as the sharing of programs, especially translator programs (interpreters and compilers), libraries of subroutines, and users' programs. This accessibility, available at human reaction times, means that a timesharing system becomes a vast communication medium whereby people can quickly access the experience of others.

Having introduced the key motivations for timesharing, we now turn to some characteristic features of the implementation of such systems. One issue, which has been resolved in a surprisingly simple manner, is that the equipment of a modern medium-large computer system requires relatively little in the way of additional types of devices or features to run many timesharing systems. Three essential CPU features: an **interrupt scheme, real-time clock,** and a **storage protection mechanism** were already common in most computers emerging in the 1960s, since they are also needed to run modern multiprogrammed-batch operating systems efficiently. The one type of device essential and somewhat unique to the timesharing environment is the **terminal,** which today typically consists of a typewriter-like device such as a teletype or IBM "golf-ball" typewriter with appropriate electronics to connect the device to a telephone line. Terminals of this kind are relatively cheap, and users can then connect to any timesharing system that expects the given type of terminal (provided, of course, that prior billing arrangements are made). It is thus quite feasible for a single terminal to connect (**dial up**) through the usual telephone facilities to several different remotely located central-processing facilities at various times to accommodate different needs for computer languages and other conveniences and facilities. The common very extensive telephone system is then often a part of a timesharing system. At the computer site, the signals on each of the incoming lines are changed electrically by a modem (modulator-demodulator), then usually multiplexed into a single register, and thence distributed to the buffer areas of main storage where system programs process their messages. This multiplexing function requires a device that is typically called a **transmission control unit.**

A timesharing system must recover its costs by servicing a fairly large number of users concurrently. A typical medium-sized computer services on the order of 50 users. A large number is essential for economic viability and is also technically feasible, since each individual user is likely to be a light load on the system. This is because even during long sessions at the terminal, much time is usually spent in thinking and keying. Of course one major objective of timesharing is fast response to certain critical human demands like editing a program; these usually require relatively little processing from a reasonably fast computer.

The many connected users (in aggregate) require considerable storage to hold their current programs and data. This storage is usually well beyond the economical sizes of high-speed main storage. Only a few (sometimes only one) users' required storage space can be held in main storage at a time and the rest must be kept on a cheaper, slower, but higher capacity auxiliary store like a drum or disk. When the system decides to work on a particular job, if it is not in main storage (as will often be the case), it must first move a current resident job out of main storage to the (say) drum (so that its state is thereby saved for later resumption of processing). The desired job is then sent from the drum to the just-vacated part of main storage. This process is called **swapping** and is characteristic of most timeshared systems. Swapping is done automatically by the operating system program. Many other rules have been developed also; we shall examine some of them. All such rules must satisfy one key requirement: fast response to those requests that are essential to man-machine interaction.

A word is in order about terminology. In discussing communication-computer systems, the work required for one interaction between the user and the system will be called a **tract,** which is an abbreviated form of **transaction.** A tract is somewhat similar to what we have previously called a **job,** but to the individual user, a "job" (like getting some program to work) usually takes many interactions and hence many tracts.

Some timesharing systems provide their terminal users with only a single programming language, in which case the system is sometimes said to be **dedicated.** Examples of dedicated systems include IBM's QUIKTRAN and some APL and BASIC systems. Some analysts use the term dedicated to mean that timesharing users may be given more than one language, but a background (batch) workload cannot run concurrently. Since programs in a batch mode can often require greater machine resources, a desirable feature is that the languages and compilers used at the terminals be **compatible** with those used in the batch system. If compatibility is not available, this can cause much frustration, especially if a job evolves from the small-scale algorithm-development stage to handling large volumes of data. The trend is definitely towards multilanguage (i.e., nondedicated) timesharing systems with batch-compatible languages.

To summarize some essential points made above, the timesharing system's primary objective is effective, economical, and comfortable man-machine interaction. The sharing of common resources, including hardware, programs, and data on the time scale of human reaction times, requires certain fairly unique equipment at each user location (terminals and communication devices). It can make good use of existing telephone equipment for communications and requires a major reorientation of the system's internal management of its own resources, i.e., a different operating system from the usual batch type.

10-2 THE USER VIEWPOINT AND SOME CONSEQUENCES

In our introduction, some major user benefits of timesharing were stated. We now turn to one study that gives at least some organized evidence that supports such claims. Evidence of this type is quite difficult to obtain and analyze, since it involves the work habits of people, which is a most difficult subject from which to draw any general conclusions. One study done at MIT involved 66 students in a management class that used a simulation model of the construction industry implemented by DYNAMO, a simulation language. Each student was given certain information about the industry and market conditions and was to use the model (on a computer) to optimize his return. The class was divided into two groups. Both used the same model, but to one group the computer was available as a timeshared system, while to the other as a batch system. Data on the student's performance and attitudes was obtained by questionnaires, by instructor's analysis of problem solutions, and by the usual computer accounting of the use of its resources. The major outcomes of this experiment may be summarized as follows:

1. Total cost (system plus user's worktime) for both groups did not differ appreciably. The costs were, however, distributed quite differently. The timeshared group had a lower man-effort cost, but a higher computer cost.
2. The timesharing users achieved a significantly better solution to the assigned problem.
3. More than twice as many people in the batch processing group did not obtain a useful answer to the assigned problem.
4. More people liked the timesharing system.

The experiment indicates the importance of including the benefit of a better solution to the problem and user attitudes, as well as the easy-to-measure direct costs. Other similar studies point to another important conclusion: **there was more variability of user performance within each group than between groups.** This suggests that differences between people's skills are probably more significant than the type of system used.

One important aspect of the individual user's viewpoint must include the costs for the equipment and services he directly uses. Figure 10-1 gives a listing which is primarily of interest because of the categories of costs rather than the specific values (which will undoubtedly change with time). Terminal rental, telephone data-set, and telephone line costs need no further elaboration. The **CPU rate** is applied only to the time the system works for the individual user.

Category	Typical Rate	Assumed Usage	Cost/month	
Terminal rental (IBM2741)	$100/month	1	$100	
Telephone data-set	28	1	28	
Telephone leased line*	3/mile/month	50 mile		150
CPU charge*	5/minute	20		100
Connect charge*	12/hour	40	480	
File charge	1/7k byte/month	70k byte	10	

*Connect charge typically includes:
    1 minute CPU time/hour of connect time
    Prorated share of leased telephone line

FIG. 10-1 Typical rates (year 1971)

The connected rate is applied to each hour the user is "signed on" to the system, whether he uses it or not, and is justified by the need to tie up some central computer resources, such as main-storage areas for terminal buffering, and a subchannel for communication line control. Figure 10-1 gives rates for the various categories of charge; costs will depend on times also. For typical times, most of the cost may well be for the communications part of the system rather than CPU use. This is often the justification for using a device, called a **telephone-line concentrator,** that can combine the signals of several terminals in the same locality in order that they can more economically share an expensive leased line to the central system. This becomes more important as distances (hence costs) between clusters of terminals and the computer become longer.

In order to understand the performance issues in timesharing systems, we now consider how the user would like the system to appear to him. It is relatively easy to make a long "laundry list" of desirable features, most of which are also common to any other kind of general-purpose computing system, but this will shed little light on the special concerns of the timesharing user. We rather ask the question: What system properties are unique or at least most important to the user of a timesharing system? We may begin an answer by concisely restating some of the considerations discussed in the introduction to this chapter: The primary objective of a timesharing system is to provide fast, convenient, and economical man-machine interaction. To make this statement as clear as possible and to illustrate it by several examples is the major objective of this section.

We first examine the context of only one person interacting with his "private" computer through his terminal; we shall momentarily set aside those performance issues that are due to the many users who share resources (see later sections).

Most timesharing systems are often said to be **conversational** because the user-machine interaction may be considered to take the form of a "polite" conversation whereby each transmits messages to the other in strict alternation. This is usually imposed by the system locking the keyboard after receipt of a user's typed line of transmission until it finally responds either with results, a message of its own, or sometimes simply a keyboard unlock.

The major types of functions needed by the user are listed in Fig. 10-2. They are provided by system-supplied programs that interpret the commands by which the user may make various kinds of requests for service. To help sharpen our understanding of these facilities, we shall be comparing them to the needs of a user of a batch system. Likewise, we shall initially assume that the language translator that converts the user's programs to machine-executable form is of the compiler type commonly found in batch systems.

Most of the items of Fig. 10-2 imply the requirement that user programs and data must be stored within the system from session to session. Items 1 and 4 are usually supplied to the named objects by a naming scheme implemented by a collection of directories. To prevent confusion between identically named objects of different users, most systems keep a hierarchy of directories. In effect, each user's objects automatically and implicitly have his name (or identifier) included as part of their names.

Program and data editing are usually supplied in the form of a program that

1. *Program and Data Objects*
   - (*a*) List current names & descriptions
   - (*b*) Assign & delete names
   - (*c*) Reference objects by name
2. *Program Editing (statements and entire programs) By Line Number and Context*
   - (*a*) *Display*
   - (*b*) *Modify*
   - (*c*) *Delete*
   - (*d*) *Insert*
   - (*Note:* Modify can be done by: *Delete,* then *Insert.*)
3. *Data Editing on*
   - (*a*) Input to program
   - (*b*) Computed data
4. *Composition*
   - Combine named objects (programs, files) into new named objects
5. *Sequence Control*
   - (*a*) Sign on & off (Log-on & off)
   - (*b*) Start a program
   - (*c*) Interrupt a program
   - (*d*) Resume an interrupted program
6. *Detection of User Errors*
   - (*a*) Line by line at entry
   - (*b*) After program entry
   - (*c*) During execution

FIG. 10-2 Checklist of desirable user facilities

appears to the user as a set of "edit commands" corresponding to the operations mentioned in item 2. The editing of source data intended for entry under control of the user's program can be handled by much the same facilities as for program editing.

The major difficulties in satisfying the listed requirements center on item 5—the interruptibility of programs. (Remember, we are here talking only about the interruptibility required by one user, not by the system for its swapping functions.) We may begin by asking whether this is really essential. If so, what is the minimal facility to satisfy the fundamental need? The ability to interrupt a program is indeed essential because the theory of computation tells us that there is no way to tell in advance whether programs will end. Thus, a long-running program may be executing properly or be in an endless loop. For this reason, batch systems always provide some means to abort a program in order to prevent it from unduly monopolizing system resources. Usually, this is done by the machine operator, who receives a message from the operating system if a program runs longer than some user-estimated time specified on a job card. The same type of scheme could be used in a timesharing system. However, having only this would not be appropriate. The reason is the immediate physical presence of the user, who can often (but not always) recognize that a program is running too long and is probably in error. Also, he may well come to this conclusion by observing the printout of intermediate results (which no one sees during running of a batch system).

Although the user must be permitted to interrupt a program, say by using an "attention" button on his terminal, the facilities he then requires to respond are not so clear. The simplest requires him to restart the translation and run of the program (usually after he has modified the source statements or input data).

This needs no special capabilities of the compiler. With this convention, a time-sharing system may use a compiler taken from an existing batch system with little change (at least to respond to the interrupt requirement), since after every interruption, there is a new complete compilation. To reduce compile time (often at the expense of object speed), a fast-compile compiler like the highly successful WATFOR for FORTRAN IV, developed at the University of Waterloo, is desirable. If the system must permit the user to resume an inter-rupted program at a later time without a recompile, then additional facilities must be provided. To see what is needed and how these may be provided, let us consider what a user might want to do following his requested interrupt. First, he probably will want to "see" some data values (like a loop-control variable). Of course, he should only need to refer to this by its name used in his program. To translate this name to the address (location) in memory of the data value requires the symbol table (and possibly other tables, like a relocation table) that has usually been discarded after compilation. Thus, to satisfy this requirement, the system must retain the symbol table produced by the compiler. Also, the requested data must be displayed to the user in source-language form, which requires at least some of the usual compiler's facilities. To summarize, the abil-ity to display and modify computed values in response to on-demand user requests requires features not necessary, and hence not usually available, in compilers written for the batch environment.

The problem of responding to the user's syntactical errors (item 6 of Fig. 10-2) is essential to any programming system, timesharing or batch. Whether the timesharing system has unique requirements here is somewhat controversial. Some people believe (strongly) that every line of program should be syntacti-cally checked upon entry and any errors sent to the user as fast as possible. Others feel (strongly) that a concise report listing all errors after the entire program has been entered is sufficient, and even preferable. It is possible that this issue can never be resolved once and for all, since it may depend on the work habits of individual people. At this writing (1975) some of the most suc-cessful timesharing systems, like IBM's APL and CMS systems, do not syn-tactically check line-by-line, while others do. To provide the line-by-line syntax-check feature is not too difficult if the compiler is being written from the begin-ning; it requires nontrivial changes to modify a compiler to have this feature.

We may summarize the above discussion by saying that it is possible to sup-ply adequate interaction facilities for many purposes by using a fast-compile compiler, even one designed for a batch system, together with a good human-engineered file-edit and handling subsystem. However, such a system will not supply certain facilities desirable (if not essential) for debugging, especially the ability to modify computed data (referenced in source form) and to resume the interrupted program.

All of the above desirable functions (and some others) may be supplied most conveniently to both the user and the translator programmer if the translator program is an **interpreter** rather than a **compiler.** An interpreter translates each statement of the source program each time the statement is executed, while a compiler translates the entire user program once to a machine (object) program in a distinct translation phase, and only then executes the resulting object code. Interpreters usually spend most of their time on the repetitive translation of

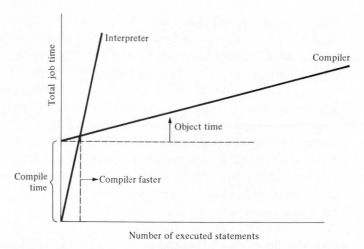

FIG. 10-3 Sketch of compiler vs. interpreter performance considerations

statements rather than on productive execution. The relative performance properties of compilers vs. interpreters is sketched in Fig. 10-3. It is seen that the interpreter may be faster for very short-running programs (especially one with no loops, due to the initialization of the compiler), but that the compiler is better for almost any looping program. However, the interpreter, since it translates each statement as it executes the statement, can easily permit changes in the program without the need to recompile. It can also permit the language to be somewhat more convenient, since it depends on "last-moment" information about storage allocation and resource use, while the compiler must know by user declaration or rules about these things **before** the program is run (when it is translated). To put it another way, an interpreter requires the latest possible binding time of user-oriented names and parameters to machine resources. Actually, the distinction between compiler and interpreter need not be as strict as it might seem from the above discussion, which for exposition purposes emphasizes the differences. Nevertheless, the more a compiler uses interpreter techniques, the better the convenience for the user, but the poorer the running time.

It cannot be too strongly emphasized that the essential man-machine interaction facilities, which include editing of program and data operations, are usually very frequent, but usually require very little computation time. For this reason, they will be called **trivial tracts.** In a sense, this is an unfortunate term, since they rank highest in the importance of being serviced quickly. In other words, fast responses to trivial requests are not only possible, but essential.

The requirement of fast response to trivial tracts may be viewed as a special case of a more general principle of man-machine psychology:

A Response Design Principle

The system should be designed to give fastest response to those requests that the human user expects to be quickly processed, provided that each such request, when run alone, can be processed in a short time.

This principle may seem at first glance to be rather obvious, but if accepted, it can give a very useful guide to the design of resource schedules. Thus, beyond giving highest priority to the trivial tracts of program editing and display, other short-time tracts should also be given higher priority than longer runs. Since run times are often not known in advance, a scheduler like round robin can complete short tracts quickly, even when it cannot identify them. It is also worth noting that the user may well expect the time required to service a tract to be much less than the system's processing time for the tract. In this case, the response will necessarily be unsatisfactory. The above principle insists however that where this conflict is not present, the system should respond so as to meet human expectations.

Knowledge of expected "length of run" (and storage required in some systems) can be a very valuable aid to the scheduler. Although the round-robin scheduler does not make use of such knowledge, this scheduler in its simple form can require appreciable swapping delays, which tends to undo some of its scheduling advantages. The question of prior knowledge of tract processing times is a profound one. In dedicated systems with only one (or a very few) specific language and file-edit processors, the designers and the scheduler can easily get information about the resource needs of important classes of tracts. For example, the IBM RAX system, which used one compiler of the FORTRAN language, reduced swap overhead by being designed to do a complete compilation without swapping, since most compile times were judged to be short enough so as not unduly to affect trivial responses. RAX did however "time slice" (and swap) object program executions, since their run times were unpredictable.

The more general the system in terms of variety of language translators, file-edit facilities, etc., the more difficult it will be to make use of prior knowledge of use of resources. Thus, general systems must depend increasingly on their own observations and measurements of resource use for resource scheduling.

10-3 CHOICE OF TIME SLICE

The fundamental purpose of time slicing is to force the operating system to reconsider its resource-scheduling decisions. This is essential to most measures of good response performance because the scheduling variables and hence priorities, often change their values as time progresses. Since computation of these variables and their relative ranks requires use of the same central computer that services users, it is essential to interrupt the CPU from time to time (time-slice intervals) to do these computations and make resource allocation decisions based on them.

From the most simplistic view, which neglects overhead in scheduling variable updating and job switching, the time slice should be very short in order to ensure very fast response to changes in state of the scheduling variables. More realistically, however, a switch of the CPU from one tract to another really involves two switches: (1) current user program to operating system (scheduler), and (2) operating system to user program. In most systems, the first step is fairly fast. The second step can also be fast if the return is to the program mentioned in step 1. However, if a new program is involved in step 2, and if this program must be swapped into main storage from slow storage, and if this must be preceded by swap out of a program already in main storage, the process of job switching can be quite time consuming. The job switching overhead then should influence the lower limit of feasible time-slice values. However, in many systems there are two sets of jobs to which the system can switch—those currently resident in main storage and those currently not resident. Since switching overhead is much lower for the first class than for the second, this suggests using **two time slices.** Some systems have variable time slices, but in such cases, if the maximum time slice is long (say several seconds), the CPU is interruptible to new tracts, since they may well be in the critical trivial-response category.

To summarize, too large a time-slice value tends to make a system sluggish in response, and too small a value tends to increase CPU task-switching overhead. To reduce swapping, another major source of inefficiency, and yet seek to retain as much response sensitivity as possible, separate time-slice intervals are often chosen for (1) the time a tract is to remain in main storage before swap out, and (2) the time the CPU is allocated to one tract before being switched to another tract in main storage. The length of the time slice(s) may be fixed at system-design time, it may be specified as a parameter to be supplied by system programmers/operators, or it may be automatically computed by the operating system based on its own observations of job and system activity.

10-4 THE MIT CTSS SYSTEM

The Compatible Time-Sharing System (CTSS) developed at MIT in the early 1960s is among the first reported in detail in the literature. As its name suggests, the system was designed so that **any** program that ran on a conventional IBM 7090 computer would run without change (compatibly) on the timeshared system. This requirement (which is desirable but not essential to timesharing systems per se) has the advantage that users may construct, debug, and modify programs on the timesharing system and be sure that these will run as production jobs in the more machine-efficient batch system. This also means that all of the resources, especially all of main storage, that are available to the batch user are also available under timesharing.

A sketch of the CTSS equipment configuration is shown in Fig. 10-4. It is seen to consist of a single IBM 7094 central processing unit with two 32k-word, 2-microsecond core-storage boxes. One of these was used only for one problem program at a time, and hence satisfied the compatibility requirement, since the standard 7094 system had only 32k words of storage. The other 32k-word core box was used for CTSS's system programs. Like most other IBM 7090/7094 systems, this one also used the special-purpose IBM 7750 computer for line multiplexing and control. A high-speed channel controlled transmission between the main core boxes and a drum and disk. The drum was the major "swap" device.

The compatibility feature, which ensures the greatest possible storage space available to the user, eliminated many of the scheduling and control problems that occur in systems that manage resources in a more flexible manner. Thus, since CTSS kept only one user program at a time in core storage, there was no

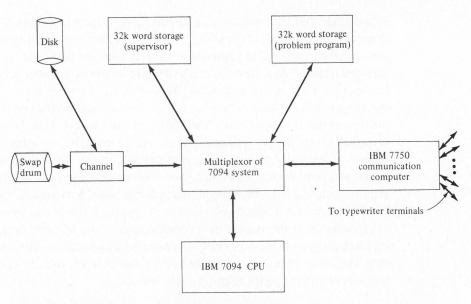

FIG. 10-4 MIT CTSS system configuration (partial)

space sharing or need for dynamic program relocation. The IBM 7090 computer originally used by CTSS had these as specially designed features; they were not used. Another consequence of keeping only one program in main storage at a time is the impossibility of "overlap swap" of one user's job with CPU work on another. As is true of most systems, to reduce swap time, CTSS only swapped the used portion of the maximum space of 32k words.

Although many scheduling problems common to later timesharing systems were not present in CTSS, the system did its one major scheduling function, i.e., deciding which tract should next receive service and for how long, in an elegant and interesting manner. Figure 10-5 summarizes CTSS's "exponential"

1. *9 priority levels; several jobs can be in each level*

Highest	0	
priority	1	
	2	New jobs: space < 4095 words
	3	New jobs: space ≥ 4095 words
	4	
	5	
	6	
	7	
Lowest	8	
priority		

2. *Job scheduling algorithm*

    (*a*) Tract for next CPU service from highest priority nonempty level.

    (*b*) A tract not selected for 60 seconds is moved to next higher priority level.

    (*c*) A tract in level q, once selected for service, is run until first occurrence of an I/O request, job completion or 0.5×2^q seconds. Longest possible burst time = 128 seconds.

    (*d*) If a tract does not complete by end of the burst, it is moved down one priority level.

    (*e*) A tract currently in execution (burst) is preempted (swapped out) in favor of a new arrival to level q if the current job has run at least 0.5×2^q seconds. A preempted job is returned to the queue level just before its current burst started.

FIG. 10-5 CTSS exponential scheduler

scheduling algorithm, which may be briefly described as follows. The scheduler gives a **new** incoming request high priority, since it may well be a short interactive one for which fast response is most critical. In that case the tract will be serviced quickly. As a tract proves to require longer and longer processing time, its priority is set lower and lower. However, as the priority of a tract drops, meaning it is less likely to be selected for service, its service period (time slice) once selected is longer than for high-priority tracts. This latter feature is intended to reduce swapping (during which the CPU is idle) for jobs that require long CPU times, thus improving thruput. To summarize, CTSS assumed a new job was short and gave it good service at first. As a job lingered, thus proving itself to be long, it slipped into the "background" where it was treated more like a batch job. One refinement of the above principles was a crude attempt at estimating the probable rank of job lengths for incoming jobs by presuming a correlation between space required and the (unknown) time to run. Thus jobs requiring more than 4095 words were initially set one priority level lower than the jobs requiring less space.

10-5 THE APL SYSTEM

The APL system is named for K. E. Iverson's book (**A P**rogramming **L**anguage) in which a powerful and elegant programming language was described and applied to a wide variety of algorithms. The language was intensively used "on paper" by a small but dedicated collection of people for at least six years before the first machine translation appeared. Thus, unlike most other programming languages, this one enjoyed a long period of careful conceptual development before being frozen by an implementation and its inevitable pressures for expediency and compatibility.

Although not designed explicitly for timesharing, the Iverson language is ideally suited to the man-machine environment, due to its philosophy, which permits and even encourages the user to specify much processing with a minimum of symbols and hence keystrokes. The following language features will help make this clear:

1. A name can denote an array, i.e., a vector, matrix, or multidimensional structure that is permitted to shrink or expand in size without specific attention by the user.

2. A wide variety of operators, each denoted by its own special symbol (or simple symbol combination), are applicable to entire arrays, as well as to the usual single values or indexed variables. These include profound generalizations of the operators of matrix algebra, as well as many others.

3. Three data types (number, bit, and character) are provided with automatic translation between bit and number types (and also between integer and floating-point numbers) without any explicit act from the user.

The value of many of these properties to man-machine interaction was demonstrated in 1964 by a "pilot" system that used many of APL's language ideas.

The language evolved through the preimplementation years and was improved even further during the implementation, where for example, the strict right-to-left rule for scanning statements was finally refined, and the extension to multidimensional arrays was completed. The implementation of APL was done under the overall supervision of K. E. Iverson and A. D. Falkoff at IBM's Watson Research Center in Yorktown, N.Y.

The translator for the IBM System/360 is an interpreter (as opposed to a compiler) and is mainly the work of two people, L. Breed and R. Lathwell, over a period of less than a year. This pair of young wizards, with the help of R. Moore of I. M. Sharp Associates (Toronto, Canada), also built the software for terminal handling and swapping, as well as a simple command language to permit the user to access a limited amount of disk space. The early APL system ran under DOS, the major IBM operating system used on small and intermediate-sized System/360s in the mid 1960s. Later (about 1968), APL was available under the more comprehensive OS/360 operating system. Although many Mod 40 and Mod 50 systems with as little as 250k bytes of main storage serviced about 50 connected APL users, the system more typically included a Mod 50 (or faster CPU) with at least 500k bytes. These were able to run an OS batch workload, as well as say 50 or more APL terminals with response times to APL trivial requests usually well within the comfortable range of 3 seconds.

From a performance viewpoint, APL may be considered from two aspects. First there is the language and its translator. These can be analyzed neglecting the timesharing environment. The second aspect is concerned with the multiuser resource-allocation problems such as swapping.

It was decided to use an interpreter translator to help ensure that the elegance and user convenience of the language would be compromised as little as possible. It is almost certain that any compiler implementation of the language would require declarations and possibly other user annoyances. However, the price of the interpreter in execution time is considerable, since it must translate every statement every time it is executed (instead of only once per program, as for a compiler). This great inefficiency of the interpreter is, however, somewhat softened (compared to other languages) because the APL language tends to result in much execution per statement, owing to the powerful array operators. Yet performance tends to be poor in programs that loop appreciably. The **space efficiency** of the interpreter method of translation for APL would seem to be better than that of a compiler. APL uses a single resident copy of the interpreter shared by all users. This requires space comparable to the storage that would be taken for a resident compiler designed for fast response. The real saving in space is, however, due to the fact that the language permits concise programs of what in other languages are extensive programs. The interpreter only requires intermediate scratch storage for one statement at a time; a compiler requires storage of the larger object program.

There is an interesting interplay between APL's time and space use. Many of the operations that make best use of arrays and result in very compact statements, which themselves require little storage and are fast to translate, unfortunately require quite a bit of storage space. As an extremely simple example, to sum the first N integers in the simplest and fastest APL fashion, the statement is

$$+ /\iota N$$

However, this statement requires APL to store N numbers, far more (for large N) than would be required if the same calculation was programmed with a loop. However, the loop is more inconvenient to program and would run much slower (in APL).

These considerations can easily be used to "prove" all sorts of things (both favorable and otherwise) about APL's translator performance. A fair statement would appear to be that with the interpreter translator, the user pays a considerable time price for the conveniences of the language, and this price can be lessened by the often lavish use of space that results from many of the array operators. Of course, space efficiency is only really important when one's space is exhausted. Until then, and this applies to small problems, the most concise program (with as little looping as possible) is most convenient and reasonably fast.

One interesting and important performance feature of APL is the set of "I-beam" operators (so called because the operator invoking them is a composite of two symbols that give the appearance of the cross section of a steel beam). A partial listing of these operators that can be used at any terminal and can be included in any program is given in Fig. 10-6. Certain of the I-beams can be of

X	Definition of IX:
19	Accumulated keying time (total time of keyboard-unlock) during this session[1]
20	The time of day
21	The CPU time used in this session
22	The no. of bytes remaining in the workspace
23	The no. of terminals currently signed on
24	Time at the start of the session
25	The date[2]
26	The first element of $I27$
27	Vector of statement numbers in the state vector

Notes: 1. All times are in $1 \div 60$ of second.

2. The date is represented by a 6-digit integer; the pairs give month, day, and year.

FIG. 10-6 Some APL I beams

great value to the individual programmer in assessing and improving the performance of his programs. These include I22, which gives the amount of storage remaining in his workspace, and I21, which gives the reading on his particular CPU clock. Using the latter, the CPU time to execute any portion of a program can be obtained as an APL variable. Note that CPU time for a program depends only on the performance of the timed program, and not on the sharing of the system by many users. Other I-beams (numbered 14 and lower) refer to vectors of frequency distributions of various types of system activity. These I-beams may be restricted to only "privileged" terminals in order to conserve valuable core-memory space. In all, the I-beams give any user access to valuable aspects of individual user and system performance.

We now turn to the second aspect of APL performance, that is, the handling of multiple users. Figure 10-7 shows a sketch of main storage. A small storage area (about 600 bytes) is reserved in main storage for **each** signed-on user to

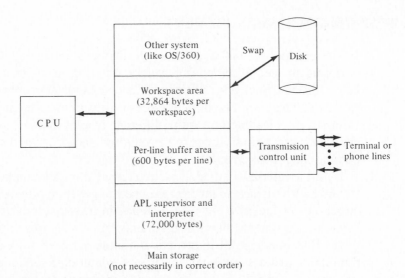

Main storage
(not necessarily in correct order)

FIG. 10-7 Typical APL resources

buffer terminal messages. Since transmission between this space and the terminal is controlled by the machine's multiplexor channel, which can operate independently of the CPU, many such transmissions can occur concurrently with each other and with CPU processing. This means that the user can be entering a program or data or receiving output, at least for a limited time, even when his workspace has been swapped out. The system is also designed so that the overlap between CPU time and terminal transmission is possible even for the same program (as well as between programs). Thus, a program that repeats the sequence: compute-a-line/type-a-line appears at the terminal to run at printout speed, provided the computation part is not excessive and the number of demands for CPU service is not too high.

A single copy of the APL translator in main memory is shared by all users. The Installation may specify that two or more workspaces (each 32k bytes) be held in main storage concurrently. Swapping is between these areas and a disk (IBM 2311 or 2314/3330). Because more than one workspace may be held in main storage concurrently, overlap is possible between input and output swapping and computation (on different APL jobs). One limitation of IBM-supplied APL systems (as of 1972) is the restriction of the user to fixed-size workspaces (usually 32k bytes). Only one can be "active," i.e., accessible to his program at one time. A manually executed command is required to access a nonactive workspace. This serious practical restriction was removed by at least one APL system (provided by the Scientific Time-sharing Co.). The SV (shared variable) version of APL announced in 1973 for System/370 machines can also provide file accessibility. It is worth noting that APL runs on any standard IBM S/360 or S/370 with the requisite configuration. No special (nonstandard) equipment of any kind is necessary.

Unusually high reliability was evident even in the first days of APL operation. In part this is due to the use of the system by the designers and implementers during development and debug. An APL system typically runs "unattended" (no machine-room operator) for several days over holidays.

10-6 PERFORMANCE MEASUREMENT

In this section we confine attention to methods applicable to the timesharing environment, i.e., a computing system servicing many terminals manned by human beings. Such a system may of course (and often does) also run a batch workload. There are two basic classes of measurement technique, internal and external, each leading to a quite different type of measuring experiment with greatly different implications to the required knowledge and skills of those conducting the measurements.

With the **internal** method, those interested in measurement must have access to, and may even have to modify, the operating system program (although many measurement facilities are now included in most modern operating systems). Timesharing systems, like batch systems, often have interrupt-interpreter programs that intercept all interrupts and store a record for each, thus giving a time stamp and description of the event for later data reduction. A timesharing system will, in addition, need to capture in some way the activities of each of its terminal users. Since this data is usually much more voluminous than for a batch system, greater care must be taken to prevent the mechanics of measurement from significantly degrading performance. Many, if not most timesharing systems reported in the literature describe some internal measurement scheme. Note, however, that **any** internal software measurement instrument is almost sure to be particular to a **single** operating system. Although it is a valuable, if not indispensable, tool in the development phase and can also be of great value to those installing a system, users of internal measurements must usually be quite knowledgeable about internal system structure. This need not be inherent in internal methods; with care, performance data obtained this way could be displayed in a form not requiring knowledge of the internals of a system. But at present at least, this is a statement more of hope than fact.

The **external** method of measurement treats the system as a kind of "black box" with only the usual user terminals available for conducting all measurements. Unlike internal methods, the external scheme depends critically on control of the workload and how the system appears to the user, but needs no knowledge of the details of internal system behavior and no access to the internals of the operating system.

The performance of any system, including a timesharing system, depends on three kinds of factors:

1. The workload
2. The system structure (hardware and software)
3. The performance measures

Since we are now considering **measurement** of performance, an actual system must of course be presented to us. The system structure is then completely determined; there remains the task of including a careful description of it in the report. Item 3, performance measures, also need not be a formidable problem. In particular, the following criteria are representative:

1. Response times:

(a) Mean, median, standard deviation

(b) Frequency distribution (in execution-time ranges)

2. Central system utilizations:
A vector of percent busy time of each component, such as CPU, channel
swap devices, etc., while running the workload

The remaining item, the **workload,** is the most difficult one to fix for measurements; this is the reason that most of this section centers on this problem. The reason is easy enough to understand. Since the workload on a timesharing system is applied by people personally interacting with the system, their behavior at the terminal must be part of the workload specification. One immediate consequence is a disturbing one for a physical scientist, although not unfamiliar to behavioral scientists; it will be most difficult to obtain reproducible results if one insists on using live user activity. However, with care, the results may be statistically reproducible. For example, if measurements are made on the same system at the same time of day for successive workdays, although the details of each user's activity will almost certainly be different, the frequency distributions of their collective activity may well be similar. Needless to say, this is not a statement of fact, but rather of plausibility, and should itself be checked by measurement. The monitoring of actual system activity is readily possible with an internal-measurement instrument. It is much more difficult using the external-measurement technique, although some performance information can be obtained externally by the use of a **snooper terminal.** A snooper terminal (or terminals) consists of an ordinary user terminal at which the measurement user requests a known and measurable quantity of work, like a sequence of interactive requests for service or selected compile-and-run jobs. During this time, other users are behaving in their usual manner. The snooper measures the system's responsiveness to his requests and records how this varies with (say) time of day and the nature of the snooper request. He may also wish to compare these times to those of another system on which he snoops (preferably with the same snooper workload).

The most basic concept of workload characterization for a timesharing system is the **script.** A script consists of a collection of records of the interactions of real or imagined users with the system, with the time stamps for each item on each record. To visualize a script for a single user, imagine a session at the terminal with the terminal printout annotated so that each line is stamped with the time at which the line appeared as output or input. The script for a measurement experiment consists of a collection of such individual user scripts. After such a collection is obtained and concurrence is achieved on its suitability, it is then possible to reproduce the response of the system to that script. The same script may be used as a workload description to investigate changes in configuration or the operating system. The script is then the input data to a simulator of the system.

Selecting a script is a similar problem to choosing any benchmark. We shall not discuss this problem now, but simply assume a script is available. Although the script data is simple enough in principle, even when an acceptable script exists, the mechanics of representing and applying it can be formidable. Since the information volume of a script can be large and the time sequencing crucial, manual input of any but the simplest script is not feasible. We shall presently consider machine representations of scripts. However, it is worth digressing briefly to suggest that it is possible, economical, and feasible to apply very simple scripts manually to a system as follows:

1. **Pretest preparation:**
   (a) Choose and debug some test programs and store them in several test users' files. A script will typically be one of j people calling for a test program (see below).
   (b) Arrange for time to "take over" the system for testing.
   (c) Arrange for a team of people who will physically enter the scripts at test time. They should have some familiarity (as users) with the system under test.

2. **Measurement tests (some typical ones):**
   (a) Trivial-response test: Have j users concurrently make trivial requests as fast as they can and measure the response times by stop watch. First make $j = 1$, then 2, 3, etc.
   (b) Run-response tests: Have j users synchronously call the same program and record response times. Repeat the test for $j = 1, 2, 3$, etc.
   (c) A mixture of trivial-response and run-response tests.

Although the above kind of test is simple in principle, actual execution of it requires considerable human coordination. However, it requires no special equipment or tampering with the system itself. By judicious choice of the test programs, this method can quickly uncover many performance properties and difficulties.

It is necessary and feasible to represent complex scripts in machine-readable form so that a computer can supply them to the system under test. The procedure for translating script information into requests for service and recording the system responses may be implemented as a program to which the script is input data. It is even possible for the system under test to run this program, in which case, the system resources are not only shared by the tested scripts, but also by the mechanics of the test itself! There are some obvious problems here, such as

1. The system under test has its resources (especially main storage) diminished by the test.
2. The test procedures require tested-system time.
3. The terminals to which the script outputs should be applied may not be available.
4. Some software interface will be necessary so that the computer is shared between the test generator-recorder program and the tested system.

The first two and the last points are obvious. The third point is worth some comment. In the actual system, the user's requests typically arrive over tele-

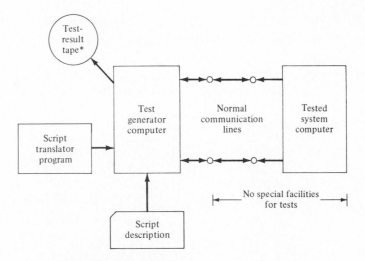

*Test-result tape processed later (so test generator computer can respond as quickly as possible during script)

FIG. 10-8 Using one computer to test another

phone lines to the transmission-control multiplexor device connected to the computer. In most systems, it is **not** possible for the same computer to generate inputs to these terminals! Such a feature is, incidentally, valuable in system tests as well as performance measurements, but many systems do not as yet have it. Of course, the measurements can still be made using self-generated tests, but now the generated requests must be supplied to some internal system region, like the terminal buffer areas of main storage, in a form suitable for these areas.

A much purer scheme that surmounts the self-test difficulties at the expense of more hardware is to use a separate computer to supply the tests and to receive and record the results. A sketch of such a system is shown in Fig. 10-8. The test-generator computer is first loaded with its program to translate scripts to machine form and receive and record the tested service response. The scripts themselves (say in card or tape form) are then sent to the test-generator computer. The tested system is started up in the usual manner, and care should be taken that no human users are permitted to "sign on." Since the scripts all start with sign on, as soon as the test-generator system sends out its first messages, the tested system will start to respond. Note that a hypothetical observer at the tested system would have no way of knowing that there are not real people at the other end of the telephone lines (rather than the test-generator computer)!

10-7 A TIMESHARING SYSTEM SIMULATOR

A simple simulation model of the swapped-workspace kind of timesharing system will now be described and used to provide a concrete mechanism for investigating certain performance issues. The model is essentially a variant of a general job-processing model, with the addition of certain characteristic features of computer timesharing systems like swapping.

Figure 10-9 shows a sketch of the resources modelled by the simulator and

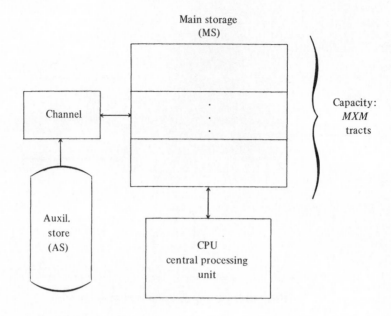

Resource Parameters

MXM = Max. no. of tracts resident in MS concurrently
ST = One-way swap time
H = Time slice
PSV = Per swap CPU overhead time
V = 0 − No overlap of swap with compute
           1 − overlap
STS = 0 − No time slicing
           1 − Time slicing
SC = Scheduler code
RB = Bias value for jobs not in MS

Workload Parameters

For each tract (I)
$A[I]$ = Time-of-tract request
$X[I]$ = Execution time

FIG. 10-9   Simulation model

lists the parameters that the user must supply to the model. It is seen that up to MXM tracts may be resident in main storage (MS) concurrently. A one-way swap of a workspace between MS and AS requires ST seconds, and a CPU overhead time of PSV seconds is required to initiate a swap. Overlapped swapping is (or is not) specified ($V = 1$ or 0), and any of six schedulers is specified by SC, which may or may not be time sliced, as specified by the variable STS ($= 1$ or 0). The time slice is specified by H.

A Type I workload of the direct class describes each tract with its time of arrival and execution time. Figure 10-10 shows a state diagram with the definitions of states and state transitions. Figure 10-11 gives some idea of the data structures used inside the simulator which, together with the state diagram of Fig. 10-10, can help us begin to visualize how the simulator logic is organized.

The scheduling decision selecting the tract to next receive a time slice or to be swapped into or out of MS is done at the end of each time slice or at the end of a tract. Scheduling is considered in two parts with a simple, interesting dual-

Tract states:

1. Not arrived
2. Arrived: in AS
3. In channel: AS to MS (swap in)
4. Arrived: in MS (CPU not executing)
5. CPU executing (in MS)
6. In channel: MS to AS (swap out)
7. Tract complete: in MS
8. Tract complete: in AS

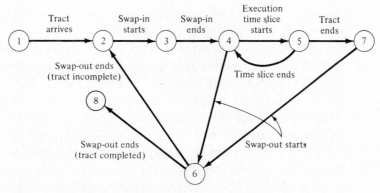

FIG. 10-10 State definitions and transition diagram for a tract

ity relationship between them. The first part, called **admission rule,** decides which tract should receive the next time slice. This is done by finding among the tracts eligible for service the one that has the smallest value of the scheduling variable (we assume also some suitable tie-breaking rule). When the tract has been identified, there are two major cases: (1) the tract is in MS, and (2)

		1	2	3	4	etc.
		Tract →				
Arrival times	A					
Execution times	X					
State vector	S					
Execution times complete	P					
Times of last slice	L					
Completion times	Q					

(*a*) Tract variables.

		Alu. 1	Chan. 2
Times of completion	CV		
Tracts in service	ID		
Utilization times	U		
Required execution times	XT		

(*b*) Resource variables.

FIG. 10-11 Some internal simulator variables

the tract is not in MS (being therefore in AS). In the first case, the tract is given the next time slice. In the second case, if there is an empty workspace in MS, "swap in" of the selected tract starts to that space. During swap in, if the overlapped swapping option is specified, the scheduler will apply the admission rule to those tracts in MS and select the best one for a time slice during swap in.

In the event that there is no empty space in MS, the scheduler first seeks a completed tract in MS as the tract to be swapped out. If such a tract is found, it is swapped out, and again a tract in MS may be given a time slice during this period. If there is no completed tract in MS, then the system invokes the **complementary replacement rule** to select the tract that should be swapped out from MS to AS to make room for the selected tract. This rule works as follows: The admission rule is applied to those tracts already in MS and the **poorest** ranking tract is the one selected to be swapped out (replaced). During swap out, another tract in MS may be given a time slice. Once swap out is completed, there is in effect an empty workspace in MS, and the admission rule described above is then applicable. The complementary replacement rule is not simply a single scheduling algorithm, but rather a statement about scheduling replacement rules. More specifically, it tells how to derive a replacement rule from a given admission rule.

Figure 10-12 is a flow chart of the logic of the simulator. The simulator as described thus far is a useful educational device for learning about the interrelationship of various system parameters. The workload description can be a stream of number pairs, each pair being an arrival time and execution time for each tract. By synthesizing a few such streams with very few tracts in each (say ten), a user can get a good feel for the effects of different scheduling algorithms, more than one workspace in MS at a time, swap times, etc.

We have now completed our description of the logic of a simulator which, through parameter selection, can simulate a class of timesharing systems. How can this simulator be used? We turn now to this important question by identifying two classes of activity that must be addressed by the designers of any simulation model:

1. Obtaining data about the workload to drive the simulator
2. Establishing confidence that the simulator gives correct and useful results

Since the simulator described earlier can, by parameter selection, be made to approximate the logic of APL's management of resources, this system will be used as the example in what follows.

Any practical evaluation tool, including a simulator, must be driven by some realistic representation of the workload the system actually encounters. An ideal source of such data is a software monitor. Our simulator requires arrival and execution times. The APL system includes a software monitor that supplies histograms, i.e., frequency distributions of the occurrences of various events. One of these is the cumulative frequency distribution of think times, i.e., interarrival times between user requests (tracts). One measured distribution is plotted in Fig. 10-13 together with the exponential distribution, which has the same mean value. The two functions are seen to agree quite closely.

Figure 10-14 shows a similar plot of the measured histogram of **execution**

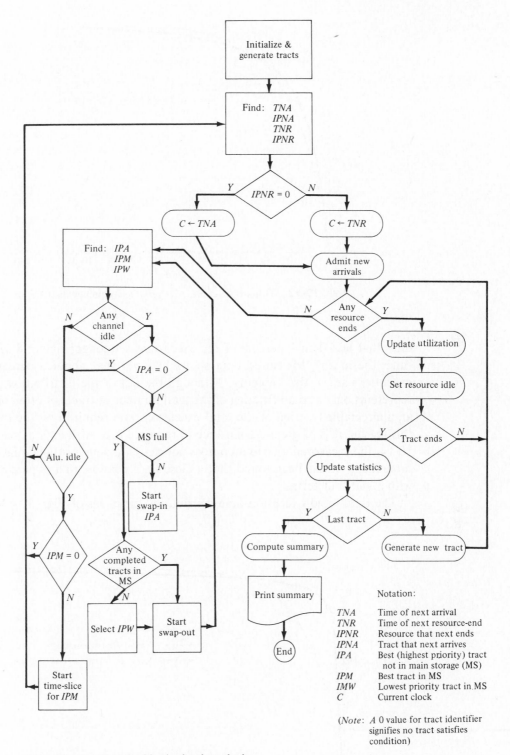

FIG. 10-12 Sketch of basic simulator logic

times, again with an exponential plot, but which is seen to be in poor agreement with the measured distribution. This is due to the "long tail" of the measured execution-time distribution, which indicates that execution times that are several multiples of the mean are much more common in the measured data than is predicted by the exponential law. Thus, for example, the exponential law pre-

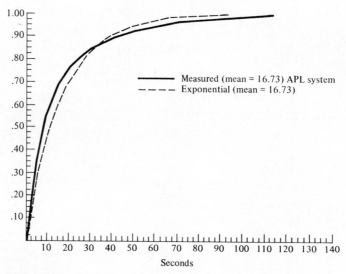

FIG. 10-13 Think-time cumulative relative-frequency distribution

dicts that less than 1 percent of the executions are longer than 1.8 seconds (6 times the mean). Measured data shows however that about 3 percent of the executions are in this category. Although the tail of the distribution of course represents only a small fraction of the total number of tracts, it often represents an appreciable fraction of the total execution time required by the tracts. For this reason, it is of great significance in resource use. Although as seen in Fig. 10-14, the measured distribution does not match a single exponential with the same mean, it has been found that a close fit is possible to a hyperexponential with about four terms.

The think- and execution-time distribution functions of Figs. 10-13 and 10-

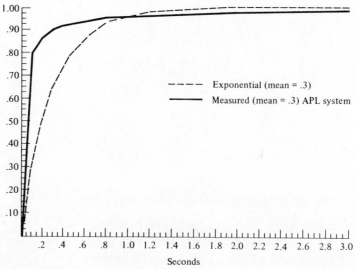

FIG. 10-14 Execution-time cumulative relative-frequency distribution

14 can be used with a programmed random-number generator to supply the arrival and execution times for each simulated tract.

Having at hand the data to drive the simulator, we now turn to the second point made earlier, i.e., establishing confidence in the logic of the simulator. One way to do this is to verify that it gives the same results as obtained by mathematical analysis. This kind of test is, of course, a necessary but not a sufficient test of the simulator logic, since it usually involves model degeneration, that is, using a highly simplified case of the model for which an analytic solution exists. Figure 10-15 shows the results of use of the simulator in this way. Two schedulers, RR and FIFO, were used with exponential arrival- and execution-time distributions. The analytic and simulated results are seen to be very close.

Another and more important way to establish confidence in a simulator is to compare its results with measured results. One of the first choices to be made here is the set of variable values to be compared. For example, it is possible to select a variable that is rather **insensitive** (or as the statisticians say, **robust**) to many of the system parameters that determine performance. It is then relatively easy to obtain good agreement between measurement and simulation. Conversely, it is possible to choose variables for comparison that are quite sensitive to many system parameters. Excellent agreement will now be difficult because small differences between the model and the system will produce large differences in the selected variable values. In what follows, we have chosen variables

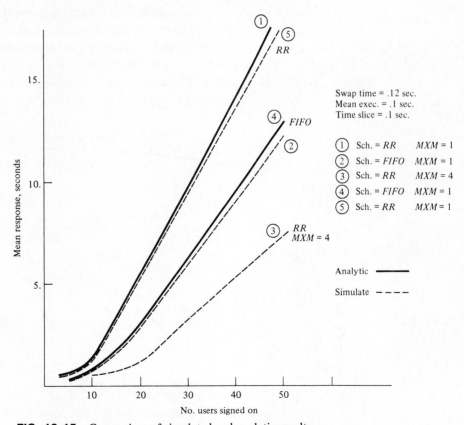

FIG. 10-15 Comparison of simulated and analytic results

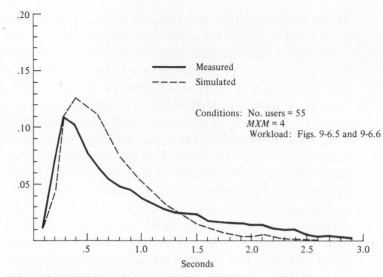

FIG. 10-16 Reaction-time relative frequency distribution

that are (1) most-significant indicators of performance (given the objectives of a timesharing system), and (2) available as measured values from the APL system. These variables are quite sensitive to system parameters, so that appreciable differences between measured and simulated results are to be expected and are observed. Perhaps more important than actual agreement between values are closeness of function shape and tracking of trends, all of which are quite good, as will now be seen. The measurements were taken on an IBM S/360 Mod 50 running only APL with 55 signed-on users.

Figure 10-16 shows measured and simulated reaction-time distributions.

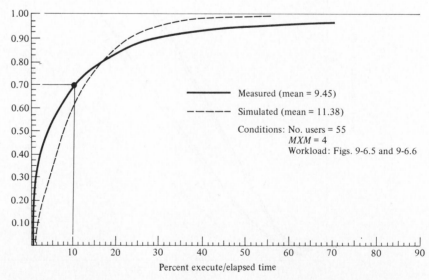

FIG. 10-17 Percent execute/elapsed times cumulative relative-frequency distribution

Reaction time is defined as the time between tract arrival and first time slice. Figure 10-17 shows the cumulative relative distributions of execute/elapsed times, i.e., the reciprocal of the "stretch factors." Thus, for example, the point on solid curve (10%, .7) means that "70 percent of the (measured) tracts had execute/elapsed time ratios of .1 or less." In other words, 70 percent of the tracts had stretch factors of 10 or more times.

Both Figs. 10-16 and 10-17 give performance measures for all tracts together. It is recalled from our earlier discussions that the success of a time-sharing system depends most critically on its ability to service trivial tracts (and other short ones) quickly. How well does APL do this? We can begin to get some idea by noticing from Fig. 10-14 that about 80 percent of the tracts are in the trivial category that requires one time slice (.1 second in this system) or less of execution time. Figure 10-16 indicates that most requests receive their first time slice (the only one the trivial tracts require) in less than 1 second. These facts strongly indicate that APL is very responsive to trivial requests. It can be shown that this characteristic degrades only very slowly with the number of signed-on users (unlike the response to long nontrivial tracts). All these observations are qualitatively confirmed by the experience of APL users.

Figure 10-18 shows the results of a simulator study to determine the effects of keeping more workspaces in main storage concurrently (but with only two

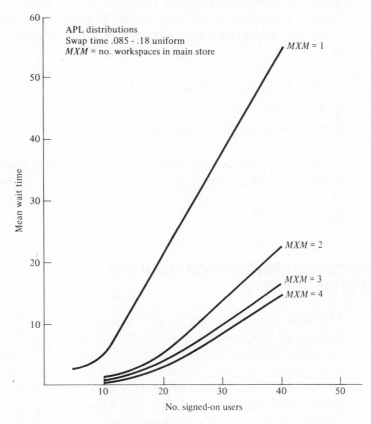

FIG. 10-18 Simulated APL performance with various numbers of workspaces

No. Signed-on users	30	30	50	50	30	30	50	50
CPU *Speed factor*	4	4	4	4	1	1	1	1
MXM (Max. no. in MS)	2	3	2	3	2	3	2	3
Mean think time	16.75	16.75	16.75	16.75	16.75	16.75	16.75	16.75
Mean execute time	0.08	0.08	0.07	0.08	0.28	0.29	0.21	0.25
Mean wait time	0.44	0.34	1.30	0.73	1.37	0.80	5.69	2.44
Mean queue length	0.85	0.66	0.82	2.2	2.86	1.82	15.35	7.48
Mean new queue length	0.5	0.5	2.0	1.9	0.7	0.6	1.3	1.7
Fig. of merit	0.41	0.43	0.18	0.21	0.37	0.42	0.17	0.20
Thruput	2.99	3.28	2.96	3.40	1.95	2.28	2.05	2.58
% CPU utilization	17	17	27	28	52	55	58	79
% channel utilization	50	46	84	77	63	54	88	89
% overlap	9	9	17	20	33	34	45	69

Conditions for all runs in this table:

No. tracts/run = 2000
Workload = APL distributions (see Figs. 9-6.5 and 9-6.6)
Time slice = 0.1 second
Swap times = 0.025 to 0.25 second
Per-swap CPU overhead = 0.01 second
Channel interference = 0.15

FIG. 10-19 Representative simulation results

swapping channels). It is seen that for the same number of signed-on users, performance improves greatly from one to two resident workspaces, but the improvements beyond that (say for *MXM* from 3 to 4) are marginal.

Figure 10-19 gives a summary table showing the effects of selected variations in

1. Number of signed-on users
2. CPU speed factors
3. Number of resident workspaces

on mean wait time, queue length, new queue length (new arrivals), figure-of-merit (short job), thruput, resource utilization, and overlap. It shows the type of summary display that is useful in making judgments about major system-design parameters.

10-8 IBM TIMESHARING OPTION (TSO) FOR SYSTEM/360/370

The main idea of this system, first released in 1971, is to provide the extensive facilities of IBM's general-purpose Operating System (OS/360) in a timesharing mode. TSO also gives its interactive users access to certain language facilities designed especially for the timesharing environment and not provided in the batch system. However, the user may choose to develop programs completely compatible with OS batch. Batch runs may be initiated from a terminal, and the system can run a batch workload concurrently with servicing the timesharing (foreground) jobs.

We shall now briefly describe TSO in two contexts. The first considers facilities available to each individual user, and the second covers the resource-management and sharing-scheduling aspects.

Single-User Facilities

Each user sees TSO first via a **command language** that performs the same functions as the job control language in the batch system, but which is extended and "humanized" for the timesharing environment. The command language includes:

1. EDIT commands for conveniently entering, storing, displaying, and modifying stored information called data-sets. Edit facilities include both context-search and line-number referencing.
2. Commands to associate data-set names and names used in programs (file names) to achieve late binding of stored objects and devices to program names.
3. Execution of programs.

A significant feature is the ability to **store sequences of commands as command procedures** (i.e., subroutines in the command language). These are the counterparts of OS JCL-cataloged procedures. Each such sequence is given a name and may be supplied parameters that are much the same as in the usual subroutine-linking or macro-call manner. In fact, the syntax of the TSO command language closely resembles the OS Assembler Macro Language. A command procedure may process both positional and key-word (self-identifying) parameters. The latter may be assigned "standard" (i.e., default) values. For example, consider the following **header** of a stored command procedure called (say) PLICLGO (this name is not included in the procedure itself)

$$\text{PROC 1,\&X, SYS1 (*), SYS2 (*)}$$

The writer of this procedure has specified by the "1" that there is one positional parameter; its name is X (the first name following the number). The SYS1 and SYS2 are key-word parameter names, their default values are *, which is the symbol for the terminal as a device. Thus, a user may call this procedure (named PLICLGO) by statements like

$$\text{PLICLGO STAT SYS1 (DATA)}$$
or
$$\text{PLICLGO STAT}$$

In the first case, the procedure is invoked, the name STAT will replace X everywhere it appears in the procedure, and the name DATA will be used wherever SYS1 appears in the procedure. Note that since no mention of SYS2 was made in the call, each time it appears in the procedure, its default value * (meaning the terminal) will be used. To summarize, the first above version calls the command procedure named PLICLGO which, with the above PROC header, can result in (say) compilation then execution of the program stored in the data-set named STAT. This program expects input data from the data-set named DATA and gives its output at the terminal. The second above version of the call is similar, but because SYS1 is also omitted, input data as well as output data devices are both defaulted to the terminal.

The idea of stored command procedures is very important. It not only relieves tedium in repeating commonly used sequences, but it also permits language subsystems to be built and supplied to application-oreinted users who have little interest and knowledge of internal system operations. Such subsystems may be programmed by IBM or, more commonly, by installation system programmers. Even ordinary users may, if they desire, construct their own command procedures.

At this writing (1975), experience with TSO's command language indicates its great potential, which is presently somewhat marred by certain oversights in its architecture. TSO provides, at optional charge, three language versions intended for interactive use: ITF/BASIC, ITF/PL/I, and code-and-go FORTRAN. All feature line-by-line syntax checking at entry time and other debugging facilities.

The standard OS/360 compilers for FORTRAN, COBOL, PL/I, ALGOL, and Assembler are also available. OS sequential-access methods (BSAM and QSAM) may be directed to the terminal. Some of the processors are offered in somewhat modified versions for the timesharing environment. A TEST command permits START/STOP and trace of running programs from the terminal. Unfortunately, this tool does **not** offer source-language debugging. Since outputs are in machine language, the user must eventually translate TEST outputs to symbolic outputs using a symbol table.

Resource Management in TSO

To begin to understand resource management in TSO, consider Fig. 10-20, which shows the major objects as they appear in a logical hierarchy. The central resource scheduler is called the **driver.** It communicates with all other major control functions through its **timesharing interface program.** The driver receives reports about both task and resource states and, together with certain parameters specified by the installation, decides on which job should be swapped into and out of storage and how much CPU time each should receive (more on this later). The driver also is a major control over the batch (background) component of the workload.

The flow of system control may be roughly traced using Fig. 10-20. Consider the system just after the system operator has started MVT, but before he has started TSO. He starts TSO by giving a command that intitiates a system program called the time sharing control task (TSC), which can further communicate with him (to accept parameters) and can also initiate a region control task (RCT) for each foreground region. Each RCT in turn can call a copy of the LOGON scheduler in response to a LOGON command entered from a terminal. The LOGON scheduler accepts the information in the user's LOGON message and also has access to a data-set called the **user attribute data set** (UADS) that contains prestored information about each authorized user (account number, LOGON passwords, etc.). Included in the UADS is the name

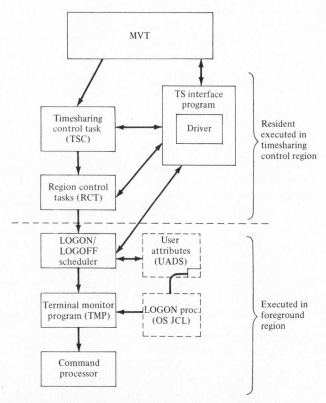

FIG. 10-20   Logical hierarchy of control in TSO

of an OS JCL (job control language) cataloged procedure called the LOGON procedure. A LOGON procedure specifies a single OS job step, and for this reason each TSO session from LOGON to LOGOFF at any single terminal is considered as a single-step OS job. The EXEC statement specifies a program to be executed. In the case of a LOGON procedure (Fig. 10-21), the program thus called is one for interpreting all terminal commands that the user will enter during the session. Although this interpreter program may be written by the

```
//NFSPROC    EXEC    PGM=IKJEFTO1,ROLL=(NO,NO)
//SYSUDUMP   DD      SYSOUT=R
//SYSHELP    DD      DSN=SYS1.HELP,DISP=SHR
//SYSEDIT    DD      DSN=&EDIT,UNIT=SYSDA,SPACE=(1688,(50,20))
//SYSPROC    DD      DSN=SYS1.CMDPROC,DISP=SHR
//DD1        DD      DYNAM
//DD2        DD      DYNAM
//DD3        DD      DYNAM
//DD4        DD      DYNAM
//DD5        DD      DYNAM
//DD6        DD      DYNAM
//DD7        DD      DYNAM
//DD8        DD      DYNAM
//DD9        DD      DYNAM
//DD10       DD      DYNAM
```

FIG. 10-21   A typical LOGON procedure

Object	Abbr.	Type	Number	Active residence	Major functions
Driver	–	System program	One per system	T.S. control region	Master resource allocator for TSO and batch
Timesharing control task	TSC	System program	One per system	T.S. control region	1. Starts RCT's 2. Communicates with TSO system operator 3. Controls swapping
Region control task	RCT	System program	One per foreground region	T.S. control region	1. Quiescing control 2. Starts LOGON/LOGOFF procedures
Terminal monitor program	TMP	System or user program	One per signed-on user	Foreground region	Interprets commands directly from terminal, calls command processor
User attribute data-set	UADS	Partition of data-set	One per authorized user	Disk	1. Names of LOGON procedures 2. Account number, LOGON passwords 3. User profile
LOGON procedure	–	OS JCL cataloged procedure	One or more per user	Disk	Starts TMP, specifies data-sets needed in terminal session (including procedures)
Command procedure	–	Partition of data-set	Any	Disk	Stored subroutine of commands that: 1. Calls system and user programs to execution 2. Reserves space 3. Binds data-sets (names of physical space) to files (program names)

FIG. 10-22   Important system objects in TSO

user for his specific purposes, we shall assume (as is often the case) that the program called is the one supplied by IBM, called the terminal monitor program (TMP). The TMP may be thought of as a "local supervisor," since it interprets user commands (it may call a command interpreter for syntax analysis) and starts the process of calling whatever programs are needed to satisfy the commands. In addition to the EXEC statement, the LOGON-cataloged procedure specifies several DD statements (for reserving disk space and binding data-sets to names) that will be needed during the user session. Each user may have several LOGON procedures in his catalog; their names are stored in his UADS and he specifies which one he wishes in his LOGON message (or one is supplied by default). All of these events connected with LOGON may be thought of as a way to get each user's "private" logical machine specified and started.

Figure 10-22 gives a summary of each of the logical objects. Figure 10-23 shows the layout of main storage in a typical TSO system with one foreground and one background region. Note that most of the areas are those required by OS MVT. The new ones include the timesharing control region holding most of the permanently resident TSO system programs and, of course, the foreground region. Note that the latter is divided into two parts; one is assigned from the top down and the other from the bottom up. The second of these is called the **local system queue area** and is reserved for storing control-block information connected with the current activity in the region; this will be swapped out (and later swapped back in) along with the other valid information in the region. (Only that part of the region that contains valid information is swapped.)

One major performance issue can be discussed using Fig. 10-23. The **extended link-pack area** in the timesharing control region holds copies of commonly used system programs needed by TSO users. As in any conventional (nonvirtual storage) OS system, each installation must specify how much space is to be used for this purpose and which routines and data are to be made resident there. Since any routines not resident here will have to be fetched from disk (or drum) for each use, the selection of high-activity modules is essential for good performance. The manufacturer supplies some suggestions to help an installation get started. However, good performance requires use of a software monitor to identify the best collection of modules to make resident. This is perhaps the primary performance issue in an OS-like system that features highly modularized and complex data and program structures. Unless residences are chosen very judiciously, I/O activity for OS data management (still very much a part of TSO) may play a greater role in device contention than swapping.

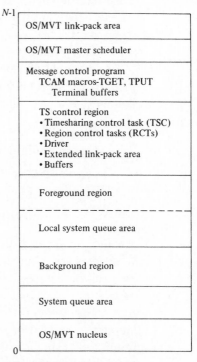

FIG. 10-23 Main-storage layout for typical TSO system

We now turn to another important performance issue, i.e., the scheduling of terminal jobs into main storage (called **major time slicing** or servicing) and the scheduling of the CPU among the jobs already in main storage (including background jobs). TSO's control programs (driver and TSC) schedule movement of information between the foreground region(s) and a swap device. Only the actually used part of a region, called the **swap load,** is actually swapped, and **swap out is started only after any ongoing nonterminal I/O involving the region is completed,** a process called **quiescing.** Buffer space for each terminal is kept permanently resident in main storage (as is done in APL) so that terminal messages may proceed even when a user's region is swapped out. Thus, there is no need for quiescing terminal I/O.

Scheduling of the vital resources of CPU and a main-storage region center on two scheduling time intervals. The first is called a job's **major time slice,** which is defined as the time the job gets to remain in main storage between its swap in and its next swap out. The second, called its **minor time slice** is the maximum contiguous time the CPU is allocated to a currently resident job. Both types of time slice depend on several parameters, some of which are supplied by the Installation (system programmers) and others of which are measured by the system itself. A collection of specific parameter values will be called a **logical queue.** A collection of user jobs with a common logical queue constitute a queue of jobs to be serviced. In TSO, "servicing a job" refers only to swapping it into a main-storage region. A logical queue is, therefore, a collection of scheduling parameters that determine the major time slice of every job that belongs to the queue. Note that there may be several queues on a single main-storage region. The jobs awaiting service on any single queue are serviced in round-robin order. However, TSO may maintain several queues so that jobs may be assigned different classes of service. We shall shortly discuss in some detail the scheduling parameters that determine a logical queue, how a job gets assigned to a queue, and how it may be moved among queues. Before doing so, we must mention that the scheduling of minor slices (i.e., CPU time slices) to those jobs currently in main storage (and ready to run) also depends on certain scheduling parameters, as will be described later.

As indicated above, each main-storage region may have several queues of jobs. Any given queue is managed by reference to fixed values assigned by the Installation to the following parameters that can only be changed manually:

$A_{R,Q}$ = average service time for jobs in the queue

$M_{R,Q}$ = minimum major time slice

$SL_{R,Q}$ = swap-load limit

$IL_{R,Q}$ = interaction time limit

$SC_{R,Q}$ = number of service cycles before advance to the next queue

An additional parameter $(N_{R,Q})$ is determined by the system from time to time. It denotes the number of ready jobs in the queue. $A_{R,Q}$ is the time interval between two successive swap ins of any given job in the queue. The purpose of $M_{R,Q}$ is to ensure that jobs on the queue remain in main storage long enough so that some productive work is done on each. $SL_{R,Q}$ measures the maximum amount of main storage that jobs on this queue may require. $IL_{R,Q}$ is the maximum total time in main storage permitted since the user's last request for service. Any specific set of these four values describes the nature of a class of jobs' scheduling properties. From the above parameters for a queue, the scheduler computes the major time slice for each job on the queue as follows:

$$T_{R,Q} = \text{Max}\left(M_{R,Q}\, \frac{A_{R,Q}}{N_{R,Q}}\right)$$

Each job is then kept in main storage for the time $T_{R,Q}$; all jobs in the queue are serviced in this way in round-robin order. After $SC_{R,Q}$ cycles on the current queue, the next queue is serviced.

The limit parameters SL_R and $IL_{R,Q}$, if exceeded by a job, cause the system to seek a new queue for the job that can contain that job's parameters. The new queue must be on the same region, since the lack of dynamic relocation in System/360 does not permit a program to be moved to a new region once its execution starts. Such a new queue will, however, in general specify different values for the parameters. For example, consider two queues as follows:

	Q1	Q2
A	1	10
M	.2	1
SL	100k	100k
IL	.1	5

Here, $Q1$ with its small IL and A values is clearly intended for rapid swapping to service highly interactive requests, while $Q2$ is intended for jobs already found to be fairly long. Note that the large A value will tend to retain $Q2$ jobs in main storage longer, thus giving them a better chance for productive CPU work between swap ins.

Of the jobs occupying the TSO regions of main storage at a given time that are ready to execute (i.e., not waiting on I/O) one is selected (**dispatched**) for a CPU interval called a **minor time slice**. TSO permits the systems people running the system to specify some guaranteed percentage of total CPU time for the batch workload. The remaining CPU time is called **foreground time,** and it is the subdivision of this time into minor time slices that will now be described.

The time available for foreground CPU time may be allocated into minor time slices according to any one of three schemes (selected by system programmers):

1. Simple dispatching: The minor time slice is set equal to the foreground time; this time is given to the highest priority job (i.e., the job swapped in the longest time ago). Simple dispatching is always used whenever only one foreground region is used in the system.

2. Even dispatching: The minor time slice is the foreground time divided by the number of ready foreground jobs in main storage.

3. Weighted dispatching: The system computes an estimated wait-time percentage for each job based on its past behavior with respect to I/O wait (not counting terminal I/O, which does not require swap in). The longer the estimated I/O wait time, the longer the minor slice that is computed. This compensates for the parts of a time slice that I/O-bound jobs will lose to CPU-bound jobs due to I/O wait.

10-9 THE G.E. INFORMATION SERVICE NETWORK

Until now we have discussed timesharing of a single CPU system to which several users may be connected via telephone lines. Such systems are in common use to service a single organization's needs, where the same equipment is often shared with a batch workload. A somewhat different type of marketing scheme is the case where a company offers timesharing services on a subscription basis to anyone having access to a terminal.

The General Electric Company's information services network is a subscription service composed of an equipment and software configuration designed to service many remote users; subsets of these may or may not belong to the same organization and may or may not share common information (like user files). Furthermore, the system resources (as well as the users) may be widely dispersed geographically and may change in time with minimum disruption to subscribers. Such a system is sometimes called an information utility because in many ways it resembles other utilities like those that supply electric power, telephone communications, etc. Each user, considered as a subscriber, only pays for the facilities he uses (including his share of space time of central facilities), but

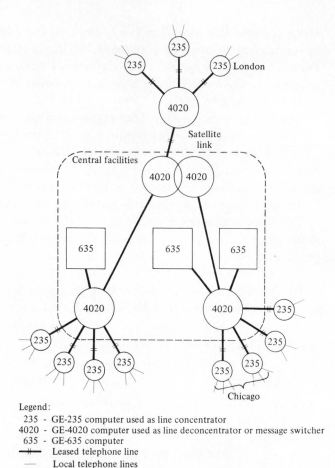

Legend:
235 - GE-235 computer used as line concentrator
4020 - GE-4020 computer used as line deconcentrator or message switcher
635 - GE-635 computer
━━╫━━ Leased telephone line
─── Local telephone lines

FIG. 10-24 Sketch of a fragment of G.E. information services network (© 1972)

he is shielded from the burden and responsibility of heavy investment, development, and management of system resources. The organization supplying these earns its revenue by providing acceptable user services.

Figure 10-24 shows a fragment of the network to illustrate some principles of the communication configuration. Starting at the user end, terminals (not shown) connect to a small computer (GE 235) in the locality by dialing an appropriate telephone number. Once connected, all communication (from a hardware viewpoint) is directly with the GE 235, which can service several terminals in the locality (like Chicago, Illinois). The local computer serves as a concentrator of messages. It accumulates (buffers) incoming (and outgoing) messages from several local lines and eventually transmits the messages to a single long-distance leased telephone line that reaches the site of the central computer (say in Cleveland, Ohio). At the central-computer location, another computer (4020) deconcentrates the messages, performs error checking (and requests retransmit if errors are found), and forwards the messages to a G.E. 635 central-computer system. This description has been in terms of messages inbound from terminals to the computer; a similar process is done in the outbound direction. As mentioned in the introduction to this chapter, the line concentrator can substantially reduce telephone charges by efficiently sharing a single leased line. Each user directly pays only local telephone charges (a share of the leased line is included in his subscription rate).

Some other features of the network evident from Fig. 10-24 are worth noting. Subscribers in the same city may reach any of several concentrator computers, each with direct access to a specific central facility; this is seen on the diagram in the case of two concentrators in Chicago. Each central concentrator computer (4020) is connected to others in such a way that each computer-processing facility can communicate with every other one, and each user's terminal can in principle reach any of the several central computers.

One of the potentially great advantages of a network is the ability to pool resources so that they may be partitioned in different ways as the actual demands develop. There are several possible ways that this may conceivably be done; we now mention some of these for the G.E. network. As of this writing (mid 1972), each subscriber's account number is associated with file storage at a particular G.E. 635 system location. This association is done automatically by the system so that services for a given subscriber number are not moved between systems automatically. However, in making the assignments, an attempt is made to load balance the system by assigning the subscriber number to a 635 whose load is relatively light. Another useful load-balance factor is the time difference between various geographic locations (i.e., New York is 3 hours later than Los Angeles) so that business days, and hence activities, are staggered.

Thus far we have discussed only the communications aspects of the G.E. network. A brief description will now be given of the facilities available to individual users, with emphasis on those features not found in the APL or TSO systems discussed previously.

The system presently supplies three languages: BASIC, FORTRAN, and REMAPT (a previous version also provided ALGOL). BASIC is a FORTRAN-like language originally designed at Dartmouth College and since greatly expanded to include file handling and character-string manipulation operators (among other types). Both BASIC and FORTRAN use compiler translators. REMAPT is a language for conveniently describing parts; the descriptions are translated into programs for numerically controlled machine tools. A central program library is available to all users and includes statistical programs, scientific computation programs, management games, etc. A convenient text editor facility is available for easily creating, displaying, and modifying source programs and data. Rather extensive files may be kept on disk (the user pays for what he uses by the kilobyte per month). The file system, holding both programs and data, is notable for its careful attention to security and privacy features. For example, when a file is deleted by a user, its contents are overwritten to prevent the new user assigned this space from inadvertently reading the file. It is relatively easy to design a secure file system as long as shared access is not also required. The G.E. system provides both sharing and security. First, some security is provided by the usual password scheme. A password may be assigned by the user to a file; access requires the password as well as the file name. Second, user X may give permission to selected other users (or exclude them) to access X's files. Four types of access may be specified by a PERMIT command

EXECUTE
READ (implies EXECUTE)
WRITE (implies APPEND)
APPEND

The PERMIT status may be changed only by the X user.

There has been no published description of the G.E. network. Informally at this writing, it is said to contain twelve G.E. 635 computers. Each of these has a memory-cycle time of 1 microsecond (36 bits) and a fixed-point ADD/SUB-TRACT/COMPARE time of 1.9 microseconds. A 635 machine has an interrupt system, privileged mode, and a single address register for relocation (and protection). Drums are among the devices that can be attached; each drum has 4.7 million bytes, an average access of 18 microseconds, and a 370 kbyte/second transmission rate. Fixed-head and removable disks may also be attached. Some of these devices are undoubtedly included in the system.

No system configuration or performance information has been published. Informally, it has been learned that the network presently serves about 1000 users concurrently with "comfortable" response times.

Assembly and System Level Programming

C. William Gear

11-1 INTRODUCTION

A job that is normally done on an elaborate system can be done on a very simple computer with a minimal system, provided only that there is sufficient memory space and computer time available. However, the amount of time involved in the preparation of programs for minimum systems, as well as the difficulty of checking them, makes the task prohibitively expensive. The objective of a system is not only to make it possible to execute programs rapidly, but also to make it possible to prepare programs rapidly. It is often pointed out that the computer can do nothing that cannot be done by hand; that it cannot, therefore, provide the human with powers not previously had. It has also been pointed out that the car does not enable a person to go anywhere not possible by foot, but it does enable a person to go many more places a lot more quickly. The car is only about 10 times faster than the person; the computer is about 10^9 times faster than the hand calculator. The development of automatic programming and operating systems over the last 25 years has increased the speed with which programs can be written by a factor of 10 to 100. This not only enables the user to complete some tasks more quickly and less expensively, but makes the computer solution of other tasks possible in a reasonable time.

The purpose of system software is twofold: to make it easier for the user to get a job onto the computer, and to make it easier for that user to run it and test it when it is on the computer. At the machine level the computer executes instructions represented as patterns of digits. At the assembly level, not only is it easier for humans to read and write the programs; we can also provide additional language features that improve the ease of use of the computer. Additional power is provided by the operating system, so that the user sees a language enhanced with additional commands. Whether the additional commands are part of the hardware or provided by software is of no concern to the ordinary user; the effect is to provide a more powerful system at the higher level. In this chapter we are going to look at the additional facilities necessary to get a program into the computer and to run it.

11-2 THE RAW MACHINE: INITIAL PROGRAM LOAD

The basic hardware is capable of executing sequences of instructions drawn from the computer memory. It is the job of the user and the system to get a user program into the memory and begin execution at the correct point. The input-output section of the computer is capable of reading data into memory; so this is the hardware that must be used to load the program. Internally, program, numbers, and other data are represented by "words" (or groups of words) of binary digits. The input instructions on a machine are capable of reading an external representation of these bits into memory. Therefore, if the program to be executed is specified in its binary form exactly as it should appear inside the memory of the computer, input instructions can be used to load it. Unfortunately, this begs the question, since these input instructions must themselves be loaded into memory before they can be executed. To get around this difficulty, an **initial load sequence,** also known as an **initial program load** (IPL), or a **bootstrap sequence,** is usually employed.

An initial load sequence is brought into action by pressing a button on the main computer console. This button initiates a single short segment of code that is prewired into the computer and contains a program to start the loading process. Very few programmers need be concerned with this process since it is built in by the manufacturer and is not usually changed. (Some mini- and microcomputers are an exception, as the initial load program is not wired in, but must be loaded by the programmer using console switches to deposit the appropriate bit patterns in specified memory cells.) The intitial load sequence is the start of a complex loading process that is used to bring system programs into the computer which will, in turn, load the user programs and assist in their execution. Most of the time, these additional system programs are resident in the computer; the initial program load only has to be used after some catastrophic stoppage of the computer such as power off, or major hardware or system software error. We will briefly follow the sequence of events that take place after the initial program load button is pressed because each process illustrates an important aspect of the operating system and its historical development.

Because the IPL sequence must be permanently stored in memory (or worse still, entered by hand), it is kept very short. On some computers it is a single word, but generally it is several. Let us suppose that the computer has an input instruction that reads a single **record,** such as the contents of a single 80-column care image, into a set of consecutive cells in memory. On such a computer, the IPL button could force the computer into the state in which it would be if such an instruction had just been fetched from memory and was about to be executed. Suppose that the instruction supplied by the IPL button indicates that the contents of a record should be read into locations 0 through 19 (assuming that four characters can provide enough information to fill one word). If the IPL button also forces the control counter to 0, the computer will execute the input instruction, filling locations 0 through 19, and then execute the contents of location 0 for the next instruction. Since this has just been filled by the input instruction, control of the computer is now in the hands of the program just read. This program, although limited to 20 words, is long enough to read in additional program. (For example, if it contained 20 input instructions, it could

Program 11-1   Absolute Loader

```
do forever
    INPUT next card to A to A+19
    X1 ← C(A+1)
    X2 ← C(A)
    if X1 = 0 then go to Address in X2 endif
    do for J = 0 to X1−1
        C(X2+J) ← C(A+J)
    enddo
enddo
```

fill another 400 locations with code. This process is called **bootstrapping** because the program is pulling itself in "by its bootstraps.") If the initial record is read from disk or tape, it need not be restricted to 20 words; so the complete program could be read by the single read instruction provided in the IPL sequence.

As additional records are input, additional program can be read into memory. Some early computers, and some very simple current microcomputers, use this process to load user programs directly, but this assumes that the program has already been converted into a final binary form. Even if that is true, the process of having to provide the input instructions to input the program is messy; so it is convenient to have, even at this primitive level, a standard format for input of **absolute binary code.** Usually, each record of the program in its absolute binary form contains a number of consecutive words, the address of the first word, and the number of words. If the records are in card images, the format could be as shown in Fig. 11-1. Since the length of the program is not known in advance, the final record must contain an indicator. This can be a zero word count N in the second group of four characters. The location L in the

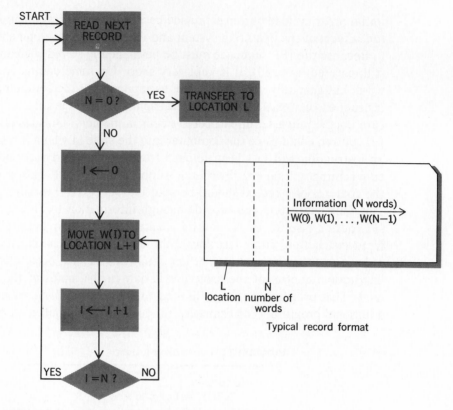

FIG. 11-1 Absolute loader format

first group of four characters can then contain the initial execution address of the program loaded.

A program which reads in information in this format is called an **absolute loader.** Usually, this is the program read by the IPL sequence. If this program is short (as it certainly is for simple computers), it probably can be read by a single input instruction in the IPL sequence. An absolute loader for a computer with an input instruction which loads 20 words is given in Program 11-1. The format of the input is assumed to be that shown in Figure 11-1, with the first two sets of four characters containing the location address and word count, respectively, and up to 18 words in the next 18 groups of four characters. **X1** and **X2** are assumed to be two index registers. **C(A)** means the content of cell **A,** while **C(X1 + J)** means the content of cell whose address is the content of **X1** plus the value of **J.** Since **J** would undoubtedly be held in another index register, it is likely that a specific implementation of this code would require **X1** to be incremented along with **J** to avoid the double indexing suggested by **C(X1 + J).**

11-3 THE ASSEMBLER

The absolute loader requires that the user prepare a program completely, specifying the addresses of all instructions and data, and giving the binary form of all instructions and data to be input. This detail is not only tedious, but unnecessary for the specification of a program. It does not matter to a user if a given variable, which may be called **X,** is in location **1026** or **10260.** Neither is the execution of the program affected by the value of a particular address as long as all references to a particular variable use the same address. For this reason we want to allow the user to talk about a variable by its name, **X,** instead of requiring an absolute address; that is, we want to work with symbolic addresses. Similarly, we want to be able to talk about instructions by using their mnemonics, such as **ADD.**

The hardware is only capable of understanding binary. It can accept neither symbols as addresses nor mnemonics as instructions. (That is not to say that hardware could not be constructed to accept such forms, but practical machines do not.) To get around this difficulty, we must advance from the simple absolute loader discussed in the previous section to a program that translates the source language of mnemonics and symbols (assembly language) to an object language of binary instructions and addresses. Such a translation program is called an **assembler.** Note that the loading process is becoming more complex, but as it does, the job for the user is becoming simpler. To get an assembly language program into the computer it is necessary, first, to obey the IPL sequence to bring in an absolute loader. This, in turn, can be used to bring in an assembler, which can then be used to translate a user program.

The Two-Pass Assembler

To translate the source assembly language, the assembler must replace each mnemonic operation with its equivalent binary code and replace each symbolic address with its numerical equivalent. For example, if the assembler reads the code segment

```
              LOAD      A
    LOOP      STORE     B
              ADD       C
              BMI       LOOP
              STOP
    A         ................
    B         ................
    C         ................
```

it must replace the operation mnemonics **LOAD, STORE, ADD, BMI,** and **STOP** with whatever binary equivalent they have on the computer for which the code is being assembled, and it must replace the symbols **A, B, C,** and **LOOP** with their equivalent addresses. If this code is to start at location 100, and the operation codes for **LOAD, STORE, ADD, BMI,** and **STOP** are **52, 53, 48, 32,** and **03,** respectively, then the assembler should translate the program to the following numerical form. (We give the numeric form in decimal to aid the reader.)

Location	Content		Input form	
100	52 105		LOAD	A
101	53 106	LOOP	STORE	B
102	48 107		ADD	C
103	32 101		BMI	LOOP
104	03 000		STOP	
105	......			
106	......			
107	......			

Converting the operation mnemonics can be done easily if the assembler keeps a table of all mnemonic instruction names. When a mnemonic is read, the table can be consulted and the equivalent binary code found. To do the same for symbolic addresses, it is necessary to construct an equivalent table. The operation codes are known ahead of time, but the relation between the symbols that a programmer uses and addresses in memory cannot be known until the program has been coded and read by the machine. In this example, the assembler cannot know that the symbol **LOOP** is associated with location **101** until the program is read. Thus, there are two distinct actions to be taken for all programmer-defined symbols. The first is to set up a table of all symbols and assign them numeric values; the second is to take those values and substitute them for the symbols. These two phases are usually associated with two scans, or **passes,** over the source code. On the first pass, a **symbol table** is constructed in memory, giving the equivalent address for each symbol. For the example above, the symbol table is as shown after the first pass. On the second pass, the substitution is made to translate the code into binary. Note that these two passes of the assembler take place before the user program is ready to load into memory and execute. That is, the translation is done at **assembly time,** which is the time when the assembler is in control. After the translation process has been completed, the user program can be put into execution. This is called **run time.**

Symbol	Value
LOOP	101
A	105
B	106
C	107

The first pass has to use rules for determining which location is to be assigned to each distinct symbol. The basic principle used is to count the instructions as they are read. If each instruction is to be assembled into the location following the preceding instruction, this count indicates its address. The count is kept by the assembler, and is called the **location counter.**

We will first discuss a common form of assembler, then take a brief look at some of the special features of the assemblers for each of the four systems we have studied. The reader should be aware that there are as many different assemblers as there are different systems, in fact more because some computer systems offer more than one assembler. An assembler has to recognize and handle the idiosyncrasies of the particular machine. However, within these constraints, many of the features of different assemblers are very similar; so the student should concentrate on learning the basic principles, not the details particular to any one system.

External Representation of Instructions

The programmer has to be able to specify the name of an instruction and its operand address or addresses and to indicate if a symbolic address is associated with the location containing the instruction. **Fields** of the input record are associated with each of these items. (We assume that the input record is a line or a card image. It could just as well come from a disk file or tape unit.) Many of the early assemblers used **fixed-format** input in which each field occupied a fixed position in the input line. This was convenient when punched cards were used, as was the case on many early computers, but it is less convenient for terminal input and does prevent the use of identation to display structure. Consequently, most current assemblers use variable-format input. In variable-format input, each field is separated from the next by one or more separator characters. Virtually all assemblers use a format in which the four items

Location symbol
Operation
Address(es)
Comment

are specified in the order listed. One or more of the fields may be empty. A typical format requires the location symbol to start by an early column (1 in the IBM 370, 2 in the Cyber 170). It is terminated by one or more blanks. Thus, the absence of a location symbol is indicated by an appropriate number of blanks at the start of the line. The operation mnemonic comes next, also terminated by one or more blanks. Next appears the address field. If the instruction contains several addresses, these are usually separated by commas, although this is an area in which assemblers differ quite a bit. The address is also terminated by one or more blank columns. Everything thereafter is comment, and should be so used. Assemblers for smaller machines frequently use special characters to separate fields. For example, the PDP-11 and Intel 8080 assemblers terminate the location symbol with a colon, the mnemonic with a blank, and the address field with a semicolon. (End-of-line also terminates any of the fields.) These formats have the advantage that blanks can appear anywhere, and that a line with nothing but a comment is allowed; the first nonblank character must be a semicolon. Lines with nothing but comments are normally allowed in other types of assembler by interpreting a line with a particular character, usually *, in column 1 as a comment line.

If card images are used, it is not uncommon to use the last eight columns as line identification by punching a four-character code word for the program section in columns 73 to 76 and a 4-digit sequence number in columns 77 to 80. This forms part of the comment field, and is a good idea for programs kept on cards. It is not usually a good idea for programs kept on disk file because many systems do not store the complete card image, only the contents of columns up to the last nonblank character. (This frequently results in a 50 percent saving in disk space.)

Since only one column or separator character is needed to separate fields, it is possible to write a program "squeezed to the left." For example,

```
            GCD LOAD FF1
               SUB X2
               BZ XT
               BPL Y
               SMI
               STORE X2
               BR YNOT
            Y STORE F1
            YNOT BR GCD
            XT LOAD F1
               RET
```

This is a terrible piece of code for several reasons, not the least of which is that nothing is lined up, and so it is almost impossible to tell where the various fields begin and end. The assembler does not care how many blanks are in the input, or what variable names are used; so these degrees of freedom should be used by the programmer to make the program as clear as possible to the human reader. What is not clear should be told in comment (which is noticeably missing from the code above). Names of variables and instruction location should be chosen for their informative value, not at random, or for their "cuteness." Thus, we could and should rewrite the fragment of code above as follows:

```
***********************************************************************
*       THIS SECTION OF CODE COMPUTES THE GREATEST COMMON             *

*       DIVISOR OF FACT1 AND FACT2.   IT IS CALLED AS A               *

*       SUBROUTINE.   THE RESULT IS LEFT IN THE ACCUMULATOR.          *

*       FACT1 AND FACT2 ARE CHANGED.                                  *

*       EULER'S ALGORITHM IS USED.                                    *

*       REFER TO . . . FOR A DESCRIPTION OF THIS METHOD.              *
***********************************************************************

GCD       LOAD    FACT1           Start of loop
          SUB     FACT2           Compute difference
          BZ      DONE            Terminate if FACT1 = FACT2
          BPL     F1LARGE         If FACT1 < FACT2 then . . .
*                                 FACT2 is the larger
          SMI                     Change sign to get FACT2 − FACT1
          STORE   FACT2           Set FACT2 = FACT2 − FACT1
          BR      IFEND

*                                 else (FACT1 is the larger)
F1LARGE   STORE   FACT1           Set FACT1 = FACT1 − FACT2
IFEND     BR      GCD             Repeat loop
DONE      LOAD    FACT1           Result to accumulator
          RET                     Return to calling program
```

Note that probably nobody but the author could make this change as it is doubtful that anybody else could have understood the original code! (This is still not a good piece of code, as the algorithm functions only for strictly positive integers. The code should really check to see that the initial data satisfies this requirement. As it stands, the code could easily get stuck in an infinite loop for invalid data.)

Assemblers place restrictions on the form of symbolic names used. These are similar to the restrictions on identifiers in higher-level languages. Usually, names must start with a letter and contain nothing but alphanumeric characters (the letters and decimal digits, although some systems define additional characters as alphanumeric). The length is usually restricted, typically to somewhere between five and eight characters maximum. Most assemblers allow expressions to be used in any place where an address can appear. For example, if the symbol **BLK1** represents memory address **105, BLK1 + 2** would represent address **107.** Expressions may involve the usual arithmetic operators and possibly some additional ones, but the form allowed is very dependent on the assembler.

Definition of Data and Storage by Pseudo-Instructions

When a symbol is placed in the location field, a symbolic address used to reference instructions is defined. In addition to these symbolic addresses which are typically used in branch instructions, it is necessary to provide a mechanism for defining the addresses of locations, containing constants and variables. In some assemblers, the symbolic addresses of locations holding single variables, such as **X,** need not be defined; in those assemblers the omission of a definition causes the assembler to allocate a single cell at the end of the program for the variable. This is analogous to the action of a Fortran compiler which allocates space for all variables otherwise undefined. In current program practice this is not viewed with favor as it can hide serious program errors. Consequently, most assemblers require that all symbolic addresses be defined at some point in the program so that an omission can be detected as an error. **Pseudo-instructions** are used for this purpose. A pseudo-instruction (pseudo for short) is an instruction, or direction, to the assembler to tell the assembler what to do, rather than an instruction that has to be assembled for the computer to execute. Thus, a pseudo is "executed" at assembly time. There are two basic types of pseudos, those that cause data to be loaded as constants or initial values of variables, and those that just tell the assembler some facts about the program, such as the need for space for variables. We will call the latter type **directives.**

Data Loading Psuedos   Typical of pseudos that load data into memory are the pseudos that allow for the definition or declaration of numerical values and character strings. Two approaches to this group of pseudos exist. One provides a different psuedo for each data type (decimal data, octal data, character strings, etc.), while the other uses a single pseudo and determines the data type from the format of the data. The IBM 370 assembler uses the latter method, while the PDP-11, Cyber 170, and Intel 8080 assemblers use a combination of the two. General forms of these pseudos are illustrated in the following examples:

```
NUMB      WORD      10B,27.3,FFFH
PIECE     BYTE      101B,23,A1H,−1
NAMES     CHAR      'ABCDEFGHIJK'
```

The first, **WORD,** loads a sequence of words of data into consecutive cells. The symbolic address in the location field, **NUMB,** is assigned the address of the first word loaded. In this example, three words are loaded; each word is specified by an item in the address field. Items are separated with commas. The conversion used for the data is determined by the format of the data. Here we show the use of a trailing **B** to indicate Binary, a trailing **H** to indicate Hexadecimal, and nothing to indicate decimal. Most but not all assemblers expect decimal numeric values unless specified otherwise. Some allow the base of numbers to be set by the user. The first example above also illustrates the specification of floating-point constants. The second item in **WORD** is a floating-point value because there is a decimal point present. Usually the conversion rules for integers and floating point are similar to those in many higher-level languages such as FORTRAN and Pascal. The second example above, **BYTE,** appears in some computers that have byte addressing. It allows individual bytes to be loaded with 8-bit data quantities. Otherwise, it is similar to **WORD.** The address, **PIECE** in the example, is assigned the address of the first byte loaded. **CHAR** loads character strings into consecutive bytes. In the example above, 11 characters are loaded into consecutive bytes of memory (or into whatever unit of memory is used to hold 11 characters). The symbol **NAMES** is assinged the address of the first character. The address field in **CHAR** is a string surrounded by single quotes. Just those characters inside the quotes are loaded. If the string is to contain a note as a character, it must be input as a two quotes. Thus,

```
QUOTE      CHAR      ''''
```

is a string consisting of a single quote. In addition to allowing the user to specify constants via pseudos, many assemblers allow the use of **literals.** These are constants that are written in the address field of the instruction that refers to them. In most assemblers, they are preceded by the character =. The assembler places the constant following the literal character (=) in a storage cell at the end of the program and generates a symbolic address to refer to it. For example

```
LOAD      =6
```

might be translated to

```
          LOAD      D$001
          ...................
D$001     WORD      6
```

Note that the assembler generates a symbol for the literal of a form that is unlikely to be used by the programmer. In fact, in many assemblers, the generated symbol will have a form that cannot be used by the programmer. The assembler keeps a list of all literals specified and generates a table of them in cells following the program. Whenever constants are used, it is preferable to use literals; the code is easier to read, and many assemblers check to see if the same literal is used twice, so that only one copy need be kept. Needless to say, one should not write an instruction such as **STORE = 6,** even if the assembler allows it! The reason for this can be seen in the code segment

```
LOAD      =3
STORE     =6
LOAD      =6
STORE     RESULT
```

Execution of this will store the value 3 in **RESULT,** a fact not apparent if one reads only the last two lines!

Assembler Directives   These pseudos are used to place code into memory locations out of normal sequence, to reserve blocks for multiword items, and to define symbolic addresses and other names. Typical of these pseudos are **BSS, EQU, SET,** and **ORG,** which are pseudos found in almost all assemblers. For example,

```
QARRAY    BSS       100
```

reserves the next 100 words of memory for a block of data. The address, **QARRAY** in this example, is identified with the first of these words. (**BSS** stands for Block Started by Symbol.) The address field of a **BSS** instruction can usually be an expression depending on other, previously defined, symbols.

Whereas **BSS** is used to allocate space, and thereby advances the location counter, the **ORG** (origin) psuedo sets the location counter to a specified value. For example,

```
ORG       200+A
```

sets the location counter to the value of the expression **200 + A.**

EQU (EQUivalent to) is used to assign the value of a symbol directly. For example,

```
N         EQU       100
```

states that the value of the symbol N is 100 so that **N** is a symbolic name for 100. The principal use of **EQU** is in defining the values of "parameters" of programs that are known prior to assembly. For example, if one is writing a program to sort blocks of data, it will need arrays of space in which to manipulate that data. If the program needs, say, two arrays, one twice the size of the other, it should be written with a parameter, say **N,** which gives the size of one array. It might start with the statements

```
N         EQU       100
REG1      BSS       N
REG2      BSS       2*N
```

which allocate the two blocks. If it is necessary to change the size of the arrays, it is only necessary to change the **EQU** statement.

The **SET** pseudo is related to **EQU** in that it assigns a value to a symbol. However, it is done in the sense of assignment, and a symbol may be assigned a value in one **SET** statement and then have this value changed by a later **SET** statement. For example,

```
MEMSZ   SET   300
MEMSZ   SET   MEMSZ/3
REG1    BSS   MEMSZ
MEMSZ   SET   MEMSZ*2
REG2    BSS   MEMSZ
```

achieves the same effect as the previous example. It first sets the symbol **MEMSZ** to a value of 300. Then that value is changed to 100 and a block of 100 locations is allocated to **REG1**. Finally, **MEMSZ** is changed to 200 and 200 locations are allocated to **REG2**. It is important to understand that **SET** is a pseudo and is handled by the assembler at assembly time when the statement is processed. It does not generate any code and has no effect at execution time. For example, in code of the form

```
XX      SET   20
        code to execute the following loop 20 times
           (part of the body of a program loop)
XX      SET   XX+1
        (rest of body of program loop)
        end of loop
YY      SET   XX
```

the value of the symbol **YY** is 21 because the assembler reads the code from top to bottom, even if it assembles code to repeat the body of the loop at execution time.

The assembler produces object code to be loaded into locations sequentially, usually starting at location 0. Initially, the location counter is set to 0. It is modified by each instruction or pseudo that allocates space or changes the place at which subsequent code and data are to be loaded. Many assemblers have several location counters. Pseudos allow the programmer to switch from one location counter to another. The programmer can think of these as representing different pads of coding paper; each pad has its own location counter. When a switch is made to another location counter, it is as if the code were being written on the associated pad of paper. The assembler assembles the code from each pad (called a **control section** in some assemblers, a **block** in others) in such a way that the code from one pad occupies consecutive locations in memory, followed by code from the next pad.

The last line in an assembly language program has to be indicated. The usual way is with the pseudo **END,** which tells the assembler to start the next pass or to finish.

The Second Pass

On the second scan through the input, the assembler produces the binary object code consisting of the machine-language equivalent of the input and the binary form of the data specified. Where does the assembler place this output? One possibility is to place it directly into memory in the locations requested by the user. This way, execution of the program can begin immediately after translation is finished. Such a scheme is called a **load-and-go** scheme. It suffers from many drawbacks, although it has a very definite advantage of speed over most other schemes to be discussed. Among the disadvantages are the facts that

1 A program cannot be loaded into locations occupied by the assembler program. Fancy assemblers on small computers frequently occupy most of the primary memory, ruling out the possibility of direct loading.

2 Each time that the program is to be executed, it has to be reassembled. (This is only serious if the assembler is slow.)

The first problem can be overcome by placing the object code onto a secondary storage device during the second pass of the assembler. This is not strictly a load-and-go system, but can still retain some of the speed advantages if the secondary storage is reasonably fast. If a copy can also be retained for later use, either on a disk storage unit or on hard copy such as punched cards, the next execution does not require reassembly, just a reloading. Hence, the output of the assembler should be in a form acceptable to a loader such as the absolute loader described earlier.

An example of an assembly language program for a typical one-address machine is given below.

```
START       LOAD        A
            ADD         B
            STORE       C
            BRANCH      D
A           WORD        13,15
B           EQU         A+1
C           BSS         2
D           ADD         =10
            STORE       C+1
            HALT
            END         START
```

The address field of the **END** statement on the last line tells the assembler that execution is to commence at the line labeled **START**. When this program is assembled, the assembler produces the binary equivalent of the code below. For human ease, the operations are left in mnemonic form.

Note that the assembler has placed the literal value 10 at the end of the code in location **11**. The program stops on the **HALT** instruction at location **10**. In many computer systems, the operating system takes over at this point. If we had omitted the **HALT**, the computer would have tried to execute the data in

Location	Instruction	Address or decimal content of cell
0	LOAD	4
1	ADD	5
2	STORE	6
3	BRANCH	8
4	WORD	13
5	WORD	15
8	ADD	11
9	STORE	7
10	HALT	
11	WORD	10

the location following the last store as an instruction. This would have caused an immediate error indication if the data did not look like a valid instruction. If it did look like a valid instruction, the problem is more serious, because the error would not be noticed immediately, but only when the first location containing a data pattern equivalent to an illegal instruction or an instruction that violates protection is encountered. Programmers must be very careful to be certain that their code and data remain distinct so that this type of error not occur. For this reason, the example above does not represent a good program style; it is better to separate instructions and data completely.

The IBM 370 Assembler

The assembler for the IBM 370 machines differs in a number of ways from the design just discussed. Some of these differences are due to additional burdens imposed on the assembler by the complexity of the machine; others stem from an attempt to provide a more uniform approach to many of the pseudos concerned with data loading. This section will discuss the assembler briefly in order to point out some of its features.

Input is in the form of card images with variable-format fields separated by blanks. Columns 73 to 80 are ignored. Symbolic names can contain up to eight characters. Conventionally, many people start the mnemonic in column 10 and the address field in column 16. However, if indentation is used to present program structure, it is better to start the address field at column 20 or later. Operation mnemonics for the IBM 370 are built around the idea that certain letters indicate basic functions, and these can be qualified with other letters. Thus, **A, S, M,** and **D** indicate the four arithmetic operations, while **L** and **ST** indicate Load and STore. Addition of **E** indicates floating point; **D,** double-precision floating point; etc. An **RR** instruction is indicated by appending an **R;** an immediate address instruction, by appending an **I;** etc. Thus, **ADR** means **add double-precision from a register.** The simplicity of the scheme can trap the unwary. For example, after seeing the instruction **LTR** (Load and Test Register) one might be tempted to use **LT.** It does not exist.

The addresses in multiple-address instructions are separated with commas, while indexing is represented with parentheses. For example,

A   R3,B(R7)

is an addition to **R3** of address **B** indexed by register **7.** In fact, the **R** in **R7** is unnecessary, but many assemblers predefine the symbols **R0** through **R15** to be equivalent to **0** through **15,** respectively, so that this more mnemonic form can be used. It is as if every program were preceded with

R0	EQU	0
R1	EQU	1
. . . .		
R15	EQU	15

Except for a few cases, IBM 370 instructions have no more than two addresses. (**LM** and **STM,** Load and STore Multiple, are among the exceptions. They move the contents of several general registers to and from memory with one instruction.) The lengths of character and decimal operands are also specified in parentheses. For example,

AP   B(6),C(4)

adds the 4-byte packed decimal string starting at address **C** to the 6-byte packed decimal string starting at **B.**

Naturally, the programmer prefers not to have to specify the length. If so, the assembler will provide it. How can the assembler do this, since it has to know the length? It examines the operand definition. When the symbolic addresses **B** and **C** are defined, an amount of memory space is specified. This is the length used by the assembler. For example, is space is allocated for data with the **DS** (Define Storage) pseudo, the programmer can indicate the length in a variety of ways.

B	DS	PL6
C	DS	PL4

indicates that **B** and **C** are storage areas for packed decimal strings of length 6 and 4 bytes, respectively. (The **P** stands for Packed, and the **L** for Length.) The general format of the DS pseudo is

symbol   DS   item1,item2, . . ., item−n

Each of the items is a specification of a set of storage areas which are described by letters and numbers. For example, "F" describes a Fixed-point, single-precision quantity, that is, a 32-bit word, while "D" describes a Double-precision, floating-point word, that is, a 64-bit quantity. Each can be preceded by an integer indicating repetition. For example

```
        XVAR    DS        3F,2D
```

describes a set of three 32-bit words followed by a set of two 64-bit words. Because quantities of each specific length had to lie on corresponding boundaries in memory in the IBM 360 and early versions of the IBM 370, descriptors of halfword, word, and doubleword items align space on boundaries of the same size. For example,

```
        MSG     DS        CL7
        YVAR    DS        F,2D
```

first allocates a character string space of length 7 bytes such that the address of the first byte is **MSG.** Next it allocates a single-precision word followed by two double-precision words for **YVAR.** Let us suppose that **MSG** is in byte address 64. Since it occupies 7 bytes, the next available space is address 71. Because **F** is a 32-bit, word aligned descriptor, **YVAR** will be allocated to the next word after byte 71, that is, bytes 72 to 75. Note that **YVAR** is given the address 72, the address of the first item allocated by the **DS.** Finally, two double-precision words of 64 bits each are allocated. Since double-precision words must start on double boundaries (addresses divisible by 8), these are allocated byte addresses 80 to 87 and 88 to 95, respectively.

The principal difference between **DS** and the general pseudo **BSS** we discussed earlier is due to the need to specify the length of the various data fields for the IBM 370 instructions. When a symbol is defined in the IBM 370 assembler, its length as well as its address is being defined; its length is defined by the descriptor (**F, D,** etc.), while its address is defined by the position in which it appears.

The IBM 370 assembler uses one constant-defining pseudo-instruction for all classes of data; the type of data is specified in the address field. The descriptors are similar to those in the **DS** pseudo, but in the **DC** (Define Constant) pseudo they must be followed by the data value in quotes. For example,

```
        XARRAY    DC        F'12',F'−24',F'36'
```

defines a set of three fixed-point words with values 12, −24, and 36. These are word aligned exactly as in the **DS** pseudo. These can be abbreviated to the form

```
        XARRAY    DC        F'12,−24,36'
```

Other examples are illustrated in the following section of data definitions:

```
        D1        DC        2PL3'45'
        XSTR      DC        C'1234 A'
        SHORT     DC        H'34'
        YDEC      DC        P'13',C'AB,CD'
        HEX       DC        X'5555FFFF'
                  DS        0F
        HEX1      DC        X'5555FFFF'
        FPDATA    DC        E'43.5',D'−56.2'
```

The first defines two strings of length 3 bytes, each containing the packed decimal value **45**. The next specifies a string of the six characters **1234ƀA,** where **ƀ** is the blank character. Note that it is not necessary to give a length if one is prepared to accept the length implied by the data item itself. The next defines a halfword (16 bits) containing the integer **34**. **YDEC** is a packed decimal string of length 2 bytes with value **13** followed by a five-character string including a comma. **HEX** is a group of 32 bits whose HEXadecimal value is **5555FFFF.** Note that it may not lie on a word boundary. If it is necessary to force word alignment, the **DS** following can be used. It forces alignment to an **F** boundary (word boundary) but allocates no space. Consequently, **HEX1** will be word aligned. The final entry defines single- and double-precision floating-point numbers with values **43.5** and **−56.2,** respectively.

There are many other data descriptors that can be found in the IBM assembler manual. One very important one is the **A** descriptor which describes an address.

```
YADDR     DC      A(Y)
```

specifies a 32-bit quantity, word aligned, whose value is the address of **Y**.

Literals Literals follow naturally from the above discussion. A literal is generated by writing an = sign followed by any valid address field item of a DC pseudo. Some examples are

```
A       R4,=F'23'         Add fixed-point 23
AE      FPR2,='E13.5'     Add floating-point 13.5
AH      R1,=H'−9'         Add halfword −9
AP      A,=P'−235'        Add packed 2-byte value −235
N       R6,=X'0000FFFF'   AND the hex value 0000FFFF
```

These have the effect of putting the constants at the end of the program, and replacing the literal with the address of the constant.

Base Register Assignment Recall that an IBM 370 address has to be represented by a 12-bit displacement and a base register address. This means that when a programmer writes an instruction such as **A R4,X** the assembler must convert the address **X** into such a form. Therefore, it must know which registers can be used as base registers and what their contents will be at execution time. The programmer must give the assembler this information, and it is done with the **USING** pseudo. For example, suppose the programmer decides to use register 15 as a base register. The sequence

```
        L       R15,=A(NEXT)
        USING   NEXT,R15
NEXT    ......  next instruction
```

first loads register 15 with the address of location **NEXT** at execution time. Then it tells the assembler (at assembly time) that register 15 is being used to hold the address **NEXT**. This sequence can be written several ways. The Load instruction can be replaced with **BAL R15,NEXT. BAL** stands for Branch and

Link. It branches to the specified address (**NEXT**), and places the address of the byte following the **BAL** into register 15. This happens to be the same as **NEXT.** Even better is the **BALR** instruction. The sequence

```
BALR    R15,0
USING   *,R15
```

first executes the Branch and Link Register instruction which stores the address of the byte following the instruction in register 15, and then branches to the address in the second register specified. In this case, the second register is **R0,** which cannot be used for indexing; so the instruction would appear to branch to location 0. However, the IBM 370 interprets this special case to mean no branch so the only effect of the instruction is to set **R15** to the address of the following instruction. The **USING** pseudo tells the assembler that **R15** is being used to hold '*', which is the name of the current value of the location counter.

After a **USING** instruction, the assembler knows that certain registers contain values it can use to construct an address. For example, if the sequence

```
        BALR    R15,0
        USING   *,R15
T       SR      R5,R6
U       BP      T
        AR      R5,R7
        BM      U
```

is assembled, the assembler must assemble the address **T** in the **BP** instruction. At assembly time it knows that **R15** contains the address corresponding to **T,** and so it assembles an address of the form **0(15);** that is, the **BP T** is the same as **BP 0(15).** The **BM** instruction will assemble as **BM 2(15)** because the address **U** is a displacement of 2 bytes beyond the contents of base register **15.**

Obviously, the programmer must not change the contents of base registers without informing the assembler. To inform the assembler we use the **DROP** pseudo. **DROP R15,R12** tells the assembler that registers **15** and **12** can no longer be used as base registers. Equally, the programmer must also ensure that the assembler has base registers available so that it can construct any addresses given. It is usually necessary to use at least two, one for program addresses and one for data. The only assembler limit is 15, the number of registers that can be used for indexing in the machine, but the objective of the programmer is to keep the number reasonable so that registers are available for other arithmetic and indexing.

The PDP-11 Assembler MACRO-11

The PDP-11 assembler uses the standard four fields for input lines. They are separated with special characters and optional blanks. The symbolic address is followed by a colon if present. Absence of a colon after the first nonblank character string generally indicates that the string is an operation mnemonic. The operation field is followed by at least one blank, and the address field is separated from comment by a semicolon. Multiple addresses can be separated by blanks or commas. These constructs are illustrated in the code segment

```
START:  MOV     A,R0        ;Load index
        MOV     ZERO R1     ;Initialize R1
        ADD     D(R0) R1
```

Symbolic addresses in MACRO-11 are strings of alphanumeric characters starting with an alphabetic character. Alphabetic characters include period and dollar characters, but these are normally reserved for system and macro use. Any number of characters can be used, but only the first six are checked; so it is wise to restrict oneself to six.

A series of special characters are used to indicate the type of address structure required. A complete set is shown in Table 11-1.

TABLE 11-1 Address Construction Indicators in MACRO-11

#	Immediate address
@	Deferred (indirect) address
( )	Deferred (from register only) or indexing
−	Auto-decrement
+	Auto-increment
%	Register address

From this table we see that **%3** means register **3**, so that **MOV %3,3** means move the content of register **3** to memory address **3**. Earlier we were using **R3** to mean register **3**. Many versions of MACRO-11 have defined **R0** through **R7** to be equivalent to **%0** through **%7**. If not, the user can precede a program with the lines

```
R0 = %0
R1 = %1
.........
R6 = %6
R7 = %7
PC = %7
```

The character = acts like the pseudo **SET;** for example, **R3 = %3** sets the value of the name **R3** to the value **%3**. Symbolic names have an address value and other qualifiers associated with them. In this case, the fact that **R3** represents a register is one of the qualifying pieces of information recorded for **R3;** this fact is given to the assembler when it reads "**R3 = %3**."

Other examples of MACRO-11 addressing are

```
MOV     #10,%2      ;Move the integer 10 to register 2
ADD     A(2),(4)    ;Move A indexed by R2 to address
                    ;held in R4
```

```
SUB       (R0)+,−(R2)   ;Move (R0) to −2(R2)
                        ;R0 and R2 are incremented and
                        ;decremented by 2, respectively
```

The data loading pseudos include

```
.WORD
.BYTE
.ASCII
```

The address field of the **.WORD** and **.BYTE** pseudo is a series of items separated with commas. These items can be arbitrary expressions, including symbolic addresses. They are evaluated and stored in 16 or 8 bits, respectively. In the case of **.WORD,** the information starts on a word boundary. Any symbol in the location field is assigned the address of the first byte loaded.

Expression evaluation in MACRO-11 is ready to trap the unwary. For starters, all numeric information is in octal. Secondly, evaluation proceeds from left to right unless parenthesization is used. Thirdly, angle brackets ⟨ and ⟩ are used to parenthesize. Thus, **13 + 3*2** is **28** decimal to MACRO-11 because **13** is octal, or **11** decimal, and addition is performed before the multiplication. If the "conventional" result is needed, it must be written as **13. + ⟨3*2⟩** in which we have indicated that **13** is decimal by following it with a period and have parenthesized the multiplicative term.

The **.ASCII** pseudo allows a string of characters to be assembled in the ASCII code. Thus

```
STR:      .ASCII   /ABCDEFGHIJKL/
```

loads 12 bytes containing the string shown. The address of the first is **STR.** Assembly directives include

```
.ODD
.EVEN
.BLKW
.BLKB
.RADIX
```

.ODD and **.EVEN** set the location counter to the address of the next odd or even byte, respectively. This is done by advancing it one byte if necessary. **.BLKB** and **.BLKW** allocate bytes and words of storage, respectively. For example,

```
X:        .BLKW    40
```

allocates 40 octal words of storage, starting on a word boundary. **X** is the address of the first word. The **.RADIX** pseudo allows the user to specify the radix used. The default value is 8 (octal), but the user may change it to 2, 4, 8, or 10 by writing, for example,

.RADIX   10

Once a radix has been declared, it will be in effect until another declaration has been made. The radix in effect can be overruled temporarily by one of the constructions shown in the example below:

.WORD   54,↑D231,↑B1101,↑F3.6,↑O7777

The first word is assembled in the current radix. Subsequent words are converted as a decimal integer (**D**), a binary integer (**B**), a floating-point number in 16-bit format (**F**), and an octal integer (**O**).

The assembler name for the location counter is the period character. For example, the location counter can be incremented by 7 by writing

. = . + 7

The Cyber 170 Assembler COMPASS

The format of instructions accepted by the COMPASS assembler differs somewhat from most other assemblers, but the principles are similar, and the pseudo orders use a conventional format. The input lines have the usual four fields. The first, the location field, may start in columns 1 or 2. If columns 1 and 2 are both blank, there is no symbolic address associated with the instruction or pseudo. Otherwise, the name, which consists of one to seven alphanumeric characters starting with an alphabetic character, is terminated by one or more blanks. The operation field may start anywhere from columns 3 to 29 inclusive. The address field, called the **variable field** in COMPASS documentation, follows the operation field, separated from it by one or more blanks. It must also start by column 29. Finally the comments field appears, starting anywhere on or after column 30. The requirement that comments cannot start until column 30 has several effects. One is that blanks can appear in the address field before column 30 (this is not recommended). However, note that any characters following the first blank on or after column 29 are comment. Thus, a line with blanks in columns 1 to 29 is solely a comment line. A comment line may also be indicated by an * in column 1 (a feature common to many assemblers). Ths user should also be careful that the address field starts before column 30, otherwise it is taken as a comment field.

Conventionally in COMPASS assembler programs, column 1 is reserved for the comment asterisk or a comma which indicates the line is a continuation of the previous line, columns 2 to 9 are used for the location field, columns 11 to 16 for the operation field, and columns 18 to 29 for the address. Some programmers like to vary this to allow indentation for documentation of the program structure. (The column at which the comments start can be changed by the assembler directive COL.)

Instructions in the Cyber 170 can be loosely classified into two types, those that do arithmetic and logic, and the remaining (which are mainly test instructions). The former use a format in which part of the instruction is indicated in the address field and part of the address is in the operation field. For example, in

$$RX3 \qquad X4+X5$$

one of the three addresses is in the operation field and the + sign in the address field tells us that this is an addition instruction. Immediate instructions indicate some of the instruction in the address field. For example, in

$$SB3 \qquad A5-B4$$

the minus sign is part of the op code. In other instructions, such as

$$SB3 \qquad A5-L$$

the minus sign simply tells the assembler to form the negative of the address L (in ones complement) and to use the instruction

$$SB3 \qquad A5+(-L)$$

The other instructions are written in a more conventional form. For example,

$$NE \qquad B3,B6,T$$

causes a branch if the contents of registers **B3** and **B6** are not equal. COMPASS allows considerable flexibility in the way many of the instructions are written. For example, the two instructions

$$GT \qquad B5,B6,T$$
$$LT \qquad B6,B5,T$$

are identical, branching to **T** if **B5** is greater than **B6** (or **B6** is less than **B5**).

The register names **X0** to **X7**, **B0** to **B7**, and **A0** to **A7** are fixed in the assembler; so the user cannot redefine them. If a symbolic name is to be used for a register, it must be written in the form **A.name, X.name,** or **B.name.** For example, if the name **REGSUM** has been defined to be **5** (perhaps by use of the **EQU** pseudo), the name **X.REGSUM** can be used in place of **X5.**

Pseudo Orders Two pseudo orders must appear in every COMPASS program. The first is **IDENT.** This must be the first line of a program. It assigns a name to the program. For example

$$IDENT \qquad TEST1$$

says that the program name is **TEST1.** The last line of a program must be an **END,** written in the form

$$symbol \quad END \qquad start$$

where the symbol in the location field, if present, is set equal to the total length of the program, and the address field "start," if present, is the location at which execution should begin.

There are a vast number of other pseudos in COMPASS. For full documentation, the reader should refer to the COMPASS manual. Symbols may be defined and memory space allocated with the **EQU, SET,** and **BSS** pseudos. Symbols, and expressions involving symbols, may appear in the address field of these pseudos, but they must in general be predefined; that is, it must be possible to calculate the address value during the first pass of the assembler.

The principal data generation pseudos are **BSSZ** (which generates words of zero data but is otherwise like **BSS**), **DATA** (which generates words of data in a large number of formats), **DIS** (which generates character string data), **VFD** (which converts a series of expressions into a set of fields of specified length), and **CON** (which generates word-size constants whose value is given by an expression). For example,

```
A       BSSZ       10
B       DATA       -56,1.5E3,B7700,O777,D4.5,3HABC,A.WXYZ.
C       DIS        2,ABCDE
D       DIS        ,*0123456789ABCDEF*
X       VFD        10/D-C,40/Z,25/-1
Y       CON        D-A,B,2*B-A
```

generates 26 words of data. The first line generates 10 words of zero data. The second generates seven words of data consisting of the integer **−56,** the floating-point number **1500.,** the octal integer **7700,** the octal integer **777,** the decimal floating-point value **4.5** (values are usually decimal, but the user has the option of changing the base), followed by two words containing character strings. The first contains **ABC** padded with seven blanks on the right and the second contains **WXYZ** padded with six blanks on the left. The initial character determines the type of conversion used; in this example we have used **B** or **O** for octal, **D** for decimal, **H** for left-justified character strings, and **A** for right-justified character string. Others can be referenced in the COMPASS manual cited above.

The **DIS** pseudo has two forms, both used in the example above. The number of words to be generated can be specified in front of the comma, in which case 10 times that number of characters are read from the columns following the comma. (Recall that the Cyber 170 has 60-bit words, and characters occupy 6 bits.) Alternatively, zero (or null) can be specified as the number of words, in which case the first character following the comma is used as a string delimiter. In the second example above, the * is the string delimiter. The string consists of all characters following the first * up to the next one.

The address field in the **VFD** in the example above consists of a series of subfields separated by commas. Each subfield consists of a length specification in bits, followed by an expression which is converted to an integer and placed in the number of bits specified. Thus **10/D−A** causes the 10-bit value equal to **19 (= D−A)** to be assembled. **25/−1** causes the bit string **11 · · · 110** to be assembled (note that the arithmetic is ones complement). Thus, the **VFD** above generates 75 bits, or one and one-quarter words. If the next instruction or pseudo is one which causes assembly to start on a word boundary (**forces upper** in COMPASS terminology), the remaining three-quarters of a word is filled with 0s.

CON is similar to **VFD** except that it generates 60-bit words of data. Its address field is a series of expressions which are evaluated by the assembler and placed in consecutive words.

The Location and Origin Counters COMPASS uses the name origin counter for the location in which code is to be loaded. During assembly, an origin counter is maintained and incremented by one for each word assembled. It can be set by means of the **ORG** pseudo. For example,

$$X \qquad DATA \qquad 1$$
$$ORG \qquad X+10$$

sets the origin counter so as to leave a gap of nine words after word **X.** In addition to the origin counter, COMPASS has a **location counter** which normally has the same value as the origin counter. When a symbolic address is defined by appearing in the location field of an instruction, the value in the location counter is used to assign a value to the symbol. The location counter can be set by the **LOC** pseudo to a value different than the origin counter. If it is set to a value 100 larger than the origin counter, it will retain that difference until changed again. One case in which the user may want this flexibility is when code is to be assembled in one location but must be moved to another location by the user program before that code is to be executed. **LOC** can be used to set the location counter to the ultimate destination of the code. This use is not recommended as it leads to confusing programs, but the structure of the Cyber 170 I/O can make this option useful.

The Intel 8080 Assembler

This is an example of an assembler for a very small computer. Consequently, it has fewer features than the assemblers discussed in the previous three sections. It is similar to the PDP-11 assembler in that it is oriented to paper-tape or keyboard input. The four fields of an assembler statement are standard:

Label (symbolic address)—terminated by a semicolon if present

Operation—terminated by a blank

Address—terminated by a semicolon or end of line

Comment—terminated by end of line

Additional blanks may appear with the terminators. Symbolic addresses (names) are limited to five characters and may not be the names of the registers (**A, B, C, D, E, F, H, L, or SP**) or of operation codes. Otherwise, the assembler is very standard, allowing general expressions in any address field as long as these expressions evaluate to a number whose length can be represented in the number of bits permitted. For example,

MVI   B,X*(Y+Z)

is valid if **X, Y,** and **Z** have numeric values such that **X*(Y + Z)** is between 0 and 255 inclusive, because the **MVI** (Mo Ve Immediate) requires 1 byte (8 bits) of immediate address. Expressions may also use the operators

AND	
OR	
NOT	
XOR	Exclusive or
MOD	Remainder of left operand divided by right
SHR	First operand shifted right N places, where N is second operand
SHL	As SHR, but left shift

In the shift operators, the 0 bits are shifted into the appropriate end. For example, to move a byte equal to the top 8 bits of address **X** into the accumulator, we can write

MVI   A,X SHR 8

The eight 0 bits shifted in ensure that the address fits into 8 bits. On the other hand, to move the bottom 8 bits of the address **X** into the **C** register, we must execute

MVI   C,X AND 0FF

The constant **0FF** is obviously hexadecimal and consists of eight binary 1s. The **AND** operation extracts the 8 least significant bits of **X** so that the address is valid. Address calculation is done in 16-bit twos complement arithmetic. The location counter is represented by the charater **$.** Thus,

JMP $+10

causes a transfer to 10 bytes beyond the location of the **JMP** instruction. An instruction can be used as an operand in an address by surrounding it with parentheses. For example, to load the register pair **B,C** with the binary representation of the instruction **MVI E,′X′,** we can execute

LXI   B,(MVI E,′X′)

The data locating pseudos are

DB	;define bytes
DW	;define words

DW can be used to specify a sequence of 16-bit words. It takes the form

DW   item1,item2, . . . , itemn

If this is preceded by a symbol, that symbol will be equated with the address of the first byte loaded. Each item is translated into a 16-bit quantity and loaded into two consecutive bytes; the least significant byte of the item is stored in the location with the lower address. Each item can be one of

A decimal constant, for example, 373, −27, or 31D

An octal constant, for example, +2770, 1350, or −11110

A binary constant, for example, 101B or −111B

A hexadecimal constant, for example, 375H or OFFF

A symbolic address that is defined somewhere

A character surrounded by quotes

An expression involving any of the above provided it evaluates to a 16-bit quantity

Note that the base of numeric quantities is decimal unless it is followed by one of the characters **O, B,** or **H,** or it uses a hexadecimal digit. Hexadecimal numbers must start with a digit (which can be a zero). Otherwise, they would be confused with names. The pseudo instruction **DB** is similar except that 8-bit quantities are loaded and therefore the items must evaluate to 8 bits. The address field of a **DB** pseudo may also be a string of characters surrounded by single quotes, for example,

```
MSG:    DB        'END OF INPUT'
```

This generates the ASCII encoding of the character string in a set of consecutive bytes. **MSG** is the address of the first byte. (A single quote in the string is represented by two quotes in the usual way.)

Space is allocated with the **DS** (Define Storage) pseudo. For example,

```
W:      DS        4*KW
```

allocates a block of **4*KW** bytes. All symbols in the address field must have been defined earlier so that the assembler knows how many bytes to allocate.

The Intel 8080 assembler includes a minimum set of other pseudos, including **ORG, EQU, SET,** and **END.** One slight peculiarity is that the label (which must appear in an **EQU** and **SET,** but must not appear in **ORG** and **END**) is not followed by a colon in **EQU** and **SET.**

11-4 RELOCATING LOADERS AND LINKAGE EDITORS

It was stated that the assembler prepares code as though the first instruction is to be loaded into location 0. There are many circumstances in which it is necessary to be able to control the point at which loading starts. If several sections of program are to be placed in memory simultaneously, it is obviously necessary that they not overlap. This situation can occur when one user combines several sections of code to form one larger program, or when several programs from different coders are placed in memory simultaneously. It is desirable to be able to load any segment of code into any place in memory and to be able to make the decision concerning the point at which to start loading after assembly. In this way, code can be assembled once and not reassembled unless its function has to be changed or errors have to be removed. This flexibility is a necessary condition for the availability of libraries of precompiled or preassembled programs.

It is also desirable to leave the determination of the load point until the last minute so that the system can take account of the current environment when loading another program. (In fact, programming encourages lazy habits in many ways. As a general rule, it is better to leave as many decisions until the last minute as possible to retain as much flexibility as possible.)

Now we are at a seeming impasse. The assembler prepares code as if it is to be loaded starting at location 0, but we want to be able to load it anywhere. The solution is to require the assembler to tell the loader what must be changed if the program is moved. Consider the assembly language code

```
        LOAD     A
        ADD      B
        BRANCH   C
A       BSS      1
B       EQU      9900
C       STORE    A
```

for a one-address machine that places one instruction per word. If this is loaded starting at location 0, the values of the symbols used are

```
A = 3
B = 9900
C = 4
```

On the other hand, if this is loaded starting at location 2300, the values of the symbols used are

```
A = 2303
B = 9900
C = 2304
```

Thus, some of the operand addresses in the code must be changed by addition of the starting address 2300. The assembler can tell which addresses are to be changed if it knows which symbols change. It can tell which symbols change by the way they are defined. Those that are defined absolutely in pseudos such as **EQU** do not change. The ones that do change are those defined in such a way that their value depends on the counting mechanism used to assign successive instructions, blocks of storage, or data; that is, those whose value depends on the location counter. Symbols and addresses that change when the program moves are called **relocatable symbols and addresses.** The assembler keeps track of all symbols used by the programmer. As each new one is defined, it must record not only the value of the symbol, but also whether or not it is relocatable.

The absolute loader described in Section 11-2 makes no changes to the code as it is loaded. When we want to relocate code in memory we must use a **relocating loader.** This type of loader modifies the operand addresses as it loads the program. So that the relocating loader knows which operand addresses to change, the assembler must indicate whether or not each operand address in each instruction is relocatable. This can be done by allocating an additional bit position in the input to the loader for each operand address position in each word to be loaded. If, for example, we have a machine with one-address instructions and one instruction per word, 1 bit is passed from the assembler to the loader for each word generated. This bit tells the loader whether or not to add the starting address to the word. The code given in the example above would assemble to the equivalent of

0	LOAD	3R
1	ADD	9900
2	BRANCH	4R
4	STORE	3R

where we have indicated relocatable addresses by a trailing **R.** If this program is loaded starting at location **4108** we get

4108	LOAD	4111
4109	ADD	9900
4110	BRANCH	4112
4112	STORE	4111

The programmer should realize that the use of relocatable addresses may restrict the use of arithmetic expressions in address fields. The scheme just described permits single positive relocation only; that is, the relocation amount can be added once or not at all. Therefore, it would not be possible to write an address such as $100 - XVAR$, where **XVAR** is relocatable, since it requires negative relocation. Similarly, an address such as $A + B$ is not allowed if both **A** and **B** are relocatable, because $A + B$ requires double relocation. Addresses such as $A - B$, where **A** and **B** are both relocatable, are valid because they indicate no relocation.

The assembler can put the **relocatable object code** in secondary storage as the translation proceeds. When assembly is over, the object can be left on secondary storage devices semipermanently for later use and/or loaded immediately. In the latter case the user frequently wishes to load the object code from several assemblies or from assemblies and compilations. For that reason, the format acceptable to the relocatable loader is normally generated by all of the translators in the system.

With this technique, a number of programs can be loaded in primary memory without interference. The loader loads each one in turn, noting where it starts and how long it is. Usually, the loader loads each program into consecutive areas in memory, starting at location 0 and working up. One of the code sections must be the main program that is to be executed initially, since execution must start at one specific place. Others must be subprograms called into play by the main program or by programs previously called by the main program. Frequently, the loader assumes that the first program loaded is the main program unless a specific indication otherwise is given.

When one of the programs is written, say the main program, the programmer will have no knowledge of the location in memory of other subroutines that may be used. For example, the program may need to call a square root subroutine from the library, but its location will not be known until the main program has been assembled and loaded. Therefore, there must be a mechanism for branching to other subprograms that does not rely on a knowledge of their addresses at assembly time. There are a number of mechanisms for this purpose. Some of the common ones will be discussed below.

When the user writes the assembly language code for one section and wishes to branch to another (which has been, or will be, assembled separately), it is desirable to use a symbolic name for the other section. One very common way of doing this is to use a pseudo such as **CALL** which is similar to the **CALL** statement in a number of high-level languages. We would like to be able to write

CALL   SQRT

to indicate that we want to branch to the program named **SQRT** which will be loaded with our program. The assembler does not know what address to place in the branch instruction because it does not know where **SQRT** will be loaded.

One of the earliest methods used to get around this problem is called the **transfer-vector** technique. It would be better called a **branch-vector** technique today because the word **transfer** is used here in the sense of branch. In the transfer-vector technique, the assembler generates a table of all different subrouting names used and assigns a unique integer to each, starting at 0 and working up. This is done in the first pass. During the second pass the object code is generated starting at location N, where N is the number of different subroutines names found in pass I. Each **CALL** pseudo is replaced by a branch instruction to the relocatable location corresponding to the name in the **CALL,** that is, to a location between O and $N - 1$. If, for example, **SQRT** is equated with the integer **3**, a **CALL SQRT** assembles as a branch to location **3** in the program. This means that when a **CALL** is executed, it will branch to one of the first N locations in this program section. It is up to the loader to fill these locations with branch instructions to the place where the desired program is actually loaded. This collection of branch instructions is called the **transfer vector.** To allow the loader to construct the transfer vector, the assembler tells the loader the names of the desired programs. It does this by passing a list of the N different names of programs needed. This is illustrated in the center column of Fig. 11-2. It is also necessary for the loader to find out which sections of code have which names so that it can fill in the branch instructions in the transfer vector. This information must be provided by the programmer. Most assemblers provide a pseudo such as **ENTRY** for this purpose. The statement

ENTRY   A,B

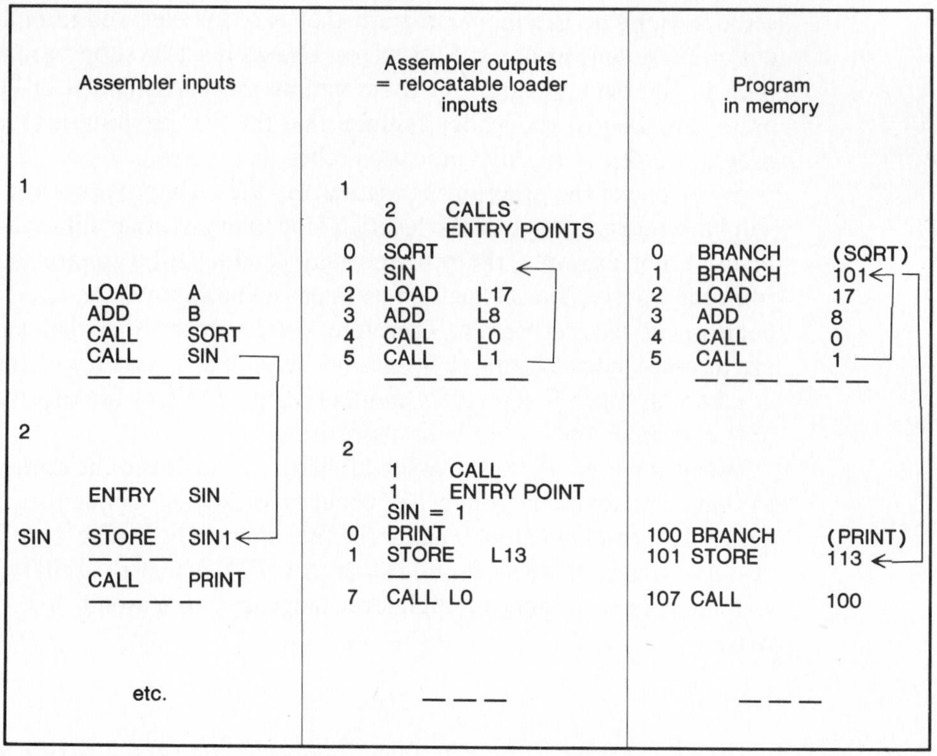

```
        Assembler inputs          Assembler outputs              Program
                                  = relocatable loader           in memory
                                         inputs

1                            1
                                   2    CALLS
                                   0    ENTRY POINTS
                                 0 SQRT                      0  BRANCH   (SQRT)
                                 1 SIN          ←            1  BRANCH   101←
     LOAD    A                   2 LOAD   L17                2  LOAD     17
     ADD     B                   3 ADD    L8                 3  ADD      8
     CALL    SORT                4 CALL   L0                 4  CALL     0
     CALL    SIN                 5 CALL   L1                 5  CALL     1
     — — — — —                   — — — — —

2                            2
                                   1    CALL
                                   1    ENTRY POINT
                                 SIN = 1
     ENTRY   SIN                 0 PRINT                   100 BRANCH   (PRINT)
 SIN STORE   SIN1←               1 STORE   L13             101 STORE    113 ←
     — — —                       — — —
     CALL    PRINT               7 CALL L0                 107 CALL     100
     — — — —


        etc.                     — — —                          — — —
```

FIG. 11-2 Relocatable binary with transfer vectors

tells the assembler that the symbols **A** and **B** are to be passed to the loader as the names of **entry points** in the current program. The symbols **A** and **B** must be defined somewhere in the current program as addresses. For example, a piece of the **SQRT** program might have the form

```
            ENTRY    SQRT
    SQRT    LOAD     . . .
```

The **ENTRY** pseudo can usually be placed anywhere in the section of code containing the definitions of any symbols it uses. It is best to place it very near the front because it is valuable documentary information. When the assembler processes an **ENTRY** pseudo, it simply records the names (in pass I) and the corresponding addresses (in pass II). At the end of assembly, it can generate a list of all entry points and corresponding addresses for the loader. This technique is illustrated in Fig. 11-2.

A second method used to tie several subprograms together employs a **linking** technique. A linker, also called a **linkage editor,** is essentially another assembler that accepts partially assembled programs and completes the assembly. As with the transfer-vector technique, during assembly some of the symbolic addresses are undefined because they are in other sections being assembled separately. A pseudo, such as **CALL,** causes a table of such symbols to be generated. These symbols are left undefined in the segment being assembled, just as in the transfer-vector technique. However, in the linking method, the number of the entry in the table is not put in the address field, rather the address of the instruction containing the undefined symbol is saved together with the symbol. This table is passed to the linker so that it can place the address of the symbol in the instructions that used it.

One of the advantages of the linking method is that there is one less branch instruction executed. A more significant advantage is that it is not limited to branching to other programs; it can also be used to reference data in other sections. All that is necessary is for the programmer to tell the assembler that a symbol will be defined in a different program, and the assembler can place that symbol in its table of **external symbols.** The declaration can be made with a pseudo such as **EXTERNAL.** For example,

EXTERNAL SQRT,TRPDAT,XYZ

says that the three symbols given are to be passed on to the loader for linking. A program that contains such a segment can refer to addresses using these symbols in code such as

LOAD   XYZ+6
BRANCH   SQRT

etc. The assembler will assemble the addresses by substituting **O** for the external symbols, but it will pass the names of the external symbols to the loader along with a list of each place in which each external symbol is used. The symbols must be defined in some section of the program and be declared to be **ENTRY** points in that section. (Some assemblers use the declaration **EXTERNAL** for both purposes. Any name declared external but also defined in the program is clearly an entry point.) Many assemblers allow expressions involving external symbols, but the result must not require more than single relocation by any given external symbol. As a general rule in any assembly language program, not more than one relocatable or external address should appear in any expression, except when the difference of two addresses defined in the current program segment is used. An example of the use of external variables is shown in Fig. 11-3.

The output of a linker can remain in relocatable binary form for later loading. Indeed, it can continue to contain **unsatisfied external references,** that is, references to external symbols not yet defined, so that it can be linked to additional code later. At some point it must be converted to absolute binary ready to execute. If the linking and loading are done in one step by a single program, we call that program a linking loader.

When the programmer uses external declarations to reference data in other program sections, all the symbols are normally defined in the input somewhere. On the other hand, when subroutine names are specified, such as **SQRT,** the programmer may mean that the program is to be obtained from the library. Therefore, the linker first checks the input to see if all external symbols are defined somewhere. Any that are still missing are then searched for in the library. (Large systems frequently have many separate libraries and the user may have the flexibility of requesting searches through several libraries in a particular order.)

ASSEMBLER INPUTS			ASSEMBLER OUTPUTS			PROGRAM IN MEMORY		
Main program								
	ENTRY	X, Y		ENTRY POINTS:				
	EXTERNAL	DSUB		X = 21				
				Y = 25				
				EXTERNAL REFS				
				DSUB IN 17				
. . .				. . .			. . .	
	LOAD	X	11	LOAD	L21	511	LOAD	521
	STORE	B	12	STORE	L22	512	STORE	522
	ADD	X	13	ADD	L21	513	ADD	523
	STORE	B+1	14	STORE	L23	514	STORE	524
	STORE	B+2	15	STORE	L24	515	STORE	525
	LOAD	Y	16	LOAD	L25	516	LOAD	723
	CALL	DSUB	17	CALL	0	517	CALL	525
	STORE	Y	18	STORE	L25	518	STORE	
	. . .			. . .			. . .	
X	DEC	5	21	5		521	5	
B	BSS	3		—				
Y	DEC	4	25	4		525	4	
Subroutine				ENTRY POINTS				
				DSUB = 0				
				EXTERNAL REFS				
	EXTERNAL	X,B		X IN	2, . . .			
	ENTRY	DSUB		B IN	1, . . .			
DSUB	STORE	Z	0	STORE	L13	723	STORE	736
D1	ADD	B+2	1	ADD	2	724	ADD	524
	MPY	X	2	MPY	0	725	MPY	521
	. . .			. . .				
	BRANCH	D1	12	BRANCH	L1	735	BRANCH	724
	BSS	1		—				

FIG. 11-3 External referencing for data and subroutines

The IBM 370 Linkage Editor and Loader

In assembly language, the IBM 370 programmer uses the pseudos **ENTRY** and **EXTRN** to pass information to the linkage editor. The loader has very little to do because the base register hardware addressing system removes the need for much of the relocation work that would otherwise be needed. At assembly time the address field of an instruction is put into a base-plus-displacement form, where the displacement is an absolute integer no more than 4095. Since base registers are loaded dynamically at execution time, they contain an address determined by the loaded position of the program. The assembler input that gives rise to relocatable addresses is the **A** field in the **DC** pseudo. If **LOOP** is a program address, then

$$DC \qquad A(LOOP)$$

is a 32-bit word whose value is the address **LOOP,** and which is therefore relocatable. This construction is frequently used for external addresses. If the address **X** is external, the instruction **L R4,X** is invalid because it is not possible to assemble the address **X** in base-plus-displacement form. Instead, the code

```
        EXTRN   X
        L       R4,AX
        L       R4,0(R4)
        ................
AX      DC      A(X)
```

must be used. (The first line can be written as **L R4, = A(X)** using a literal address. Then the last line can be omitted.) With this form, the loader has 32 bits to which it can add the address of **X** at load time. This group can also be written in the form

```
        L       R4,=V(X)
        L       R4,0(R4)
```

It uses the literal **= V(X)**. The construction **V(X)** is similar to **A(X)** but it also declares **X** to be external.

Address expressions may be used in **A** fields but not **V** fields. An expression in an **A** field may not be relocated more than once by any address in a program segment or once by each external address.

The PDP-11 Loader LINK-11

The assembly programmer defines external variables and entry points using the single pseudo **.GLOBL.** Thus, the declaration

```
        .GLOBL   X1,AAA,DEF
```

declares the three symbols **X1, AAA,** and **DEF** to be external if they are not defined in the same program segment, but entry points if they are defined. The program may use expressions involving global variables, but the result must not require more than single relocation by an external variable or the current program origin. Thus, the code

```
            .GLOBL  A,B
C = 4
D:          MOV     R1,R2
E:          ADD     R1,R3
            MOV     #A,D-E(R2)
            MOV     D+C,A+C
```

is valid because each address is either absolute or singly relocatable. With the above definitions of symbolic addresses, the instruction **MOV D + E,A∗B** contains two errors. The address **D+E** is doubly relocatable by the origin of the current program section, and the expression **A∗B** contains a product of relocations.

Loading in the Cyber 170

External symbols and entry points are declared in **EXT** and **ENTRY** pseudos. Address expressions can use external or internal relocatable symbols provided that after evaluation the expression reduces to either an absolute value, an address relocated positively by a single external symbol, or an address relocated positively or negatively by the address of a single internal block. For example, expressions of the form

$$3*ALPHA-2*BETA$$

are valid if **ALPHA** and **BETA** are either both absolute or both relocatable by the same amount (in which case these are a single positive relocation).

Loading in the Intel 8080

The Intel 8080 assembler is of the load-and-go form; so there is no separate loader on the simplest systems.

11-5 THE LIBRARY

To avoid loading many programs from external input, installations usually make the commonly used programs available in a program library. This, as the name suggests, is nothing more than a collection of programs which can be used with other programs. To make the collection useful and accessible, it is put on a high-speed secondary storage device such as a disk, and the user can obtain a copy of any member for the loading process. The loader first combines the sections of code provided by the user, linking them by one of the above methods. If some of the external names are not defined in the user supplied programs, the loader attempts to find a library program of the same name. It does this by consulting an index, or directory, of the names of all programs in a library file. When a program is located, it is read by the loader and linked to the other user code. This means that the library can be kept in assembled form and does not have to be retranslated each time it is used. Many systems allow the user to specify a collection of libraries. For example, a group of users in, say, chemistry may have its own library of chemical analysis programs which is to be used, followed by the public library, on the computer. The chemists would instruct the computer to search the chemistry library first. Some users may also have their personal library which they wish to be consulted before a group library. Programs common to everybody, such as **SQRT,** are kept in the public library. If programs with the same name are in more than one library, the loader selects the one from the first library in which it is found. This points out a very important principle: the user does not have to know the name of every program in the libraries consulted. If the job submitted contains an external symbol which is defined in another part of the same job, the loader does not look for it in a library at all. If the job refers to a program in the user's personal library, the loader will find it there and not check further. Thus, the programmer need not avoid using the names of library programs in a section of code if those library programs are not wanted. The definition in the user code will be taken first. This also allows the user to define substitute copies of library programs to be loaded in place of the system versions.

11-6 OTHER TRANSLATORS

The repetoire of the computer usually includes a number of higher-level translators. They are all faced with the same basic task—converting the input source program into a binary output object program which has meaning to the machine. Some translators will translate into assembly language code and then leave the assembler to translate to binary; others produce binary directly.

It is highly desirable that all translators that are part of a system produce compatible object code. Then a single loader can be used in all cases and programs written in one language can call on programs written in another. In some instances, load-and-go compilers are written. In compilers, the designers are faced with a choice between fast translation and fast execution (in some cases it seems that neither goal is achieved). The load-and-go compiler is normally used as a very fast compile method. If there is adequate memory space, the compiler can be kept in memory and used to process a number of source programs. Then, the compiler does not have to be read into primary memory before each compilation. The loading of a compiler from secondary storage is a significant part of the compilation time for short programs, so that a load-and-go system can be very efficient for short jobs such as those that occur during program testing.

11-7 RUNNING THE PROGRAM, MONITORING

The most carefully written code will contain errors of various sorts. The programmer may have stated a program improperly so that, say, $A - B$ is formed instead of $B - A$. Errors of this sort can only be found by comparing answers with the results of alternate calculations or by checking **invariants** of the problem. An invariant is an expression or fact that does not change. For example, in a physical problem, the total energy of a system plus the incoming energy minus the energy lost is an invariant. In a sorting problem, the number of items is an invariant. It is possible to check that such quantities do not change (although, in numerical problems, roundoff errors may cause small changes). Errors of a numerical type cannot be detected by a programming system, although some help can be provided; for example, overflow can be detected and reported.

Other errors are due to mistakes in transcribing the desired algorithm into source language, or to mistakes in the use of library programs. Frequently, these will lead the program to behave wildly. The program may, for example, try to execute the content of a memory location that was never loaded with instructions or was incorrectly written over by data. It may also get into an infinite loop. Whenever any of these situations arise, the programmer can use help.

Immediately a program tries to execute an illegal instruction, the user must be notified. If too much time has elapsed, the program must be stopped, and the user told what was being executed at the time of termination.

To take care of these things, a program is monitored in execution by another program and the trap and interrupt features of the hardware. We shall call this other program a **monitor** because of its function. It is frequently referred to as a **supervisor** or an **executive** program. The trap and interrupt mechanisms cause control to be transferred to specific locations in the memory when any of various unusual conditions arise. When the monitor program—which occupies the locations around the area to which the trap or interrupt branches—senses an illegal instruction, it uses programs to identify the location of the illegal instruction and report it to the user, together with a printout of sections of primary memory likely to be of interest to the user. Before a new program is put into execution, the monitor sets a timer to the amount of time requested by the user for execution. If the monitor receives a timer interrupt indicating that too much time has been used, the monitor prints a message to the user and terminates the program, again providing a dump for the user if requested.

Memory protection allows sections of memory to be declared off limits to the user program. Any attempt to reference this area of memory will result in a trap to the monitor. In this way, a user program can be restrained from changing or reading areas of memory that are of no concern to it. Prior to starting execution of a program, the monitor sets the memory limits for that program. Some systems allow separate read and write protection. This allows some areas of memory to contain system data or program that is accessible to anybody but can be changed by authorized programs only. The most common use of this is for shared programs in a timesharing environment.

The chief purposes of memory protection are twofold:

1. To help detect potential errors within the user program
2. To facilitate the assignment of memory to user programs only when needed

Both read and write protection are used to detect errors. It is obvious that an attempt to store into memory not within the range of addresses allocated to a program is an error; so write protection can be used to detect any out-of-range address on storing. Read protection need not be as restrictive because there are valid reasons for allowing a user program to read some system locations such as those containing time of day or date. However, an attempt to read other users' data should be prevented because there is always a need to provide security of data to some users of a system. Read and write protection can also be used to prevent programs from accessing areas of memory currently in use for input and output. Since input and output may be in progress between primary memory and other devices, it is clear that errors could occur if the user read or changed the contents of memory involved in I/O transfers.

Secondly, there is the problem of assignment of memory space. In an advanced operating system, it is likely that many user programs are in primary memory at the same time. Although each user is unaware of the others, at any particular time less memory space may be available in primary memory to a user program than it needs. However, each user program refers to memory as required. If primary memory space is not available, an interrupt occurs because the unavailable addresses are protected. The monitor uses this as an indication that it must provide more memory to the interrupting program as soon as it is available.

The monitor is stored in a protected area of memory. So that it may reference memory anywhere, various levels of protection are defined. These are called **modes** in some systems, **ring levels** in others. In the **supervisor mode** a program may reference any part of memory. Consequently, the monitor executes in supervisor mode. In user mode, protection applies; so user programs execute in user mode. Interrupts and traps cause a change of mode, usually to supervisor mode. (There may be other levels of protection between these two. These may be used to execute some of the system programs that do not need access to the whole of memory. By providing protection for them, there is a check against errors in the system programs, which, surprisingly enough, do happen occasionally.)

Because data and programs for many users are stored on secondary devices and I/O units at any given time, hardware I/O operations must also be protected from unauthorized use. In most systems, all I/O operations are **privileged instructions** which can be executed in supervisor mode only.

Many features of the monitor and associated protection are negative—they are designed to prevent the user from doing certain things such as using too much time. However, the monitor also provides the user with a number of positive benefits. The main facilities usually provided are for control of I/O equipment. There we will see that they are complicated to use, and thus the monitor normally provides sets of subroutines that simplify their use. Other programs are provided in the monitor to take special actions on unusual conditions that the user may wish to control. For example, a user may wish to regain control after a numerical overflow so that corrective action can be taken in the program.

The monitor often calls in additional aids for the user after a trap on an error. These include programs which will give dumps of the user region of primary memory after certain types of program termination. Other debugging aids are usually provided by system programs that function as subroutines in the user area. Among these are trace programs that print the results of selected variables each time specified instructions are executed. Trace programs usually operate by requiring that the program be assembled (or compiled) in the "trace mode," meaning that the list of information wanted at execution time is assembled in with the program. However, some trace systems execute at a lower level by allowing the user to plant "traps" in the loaded copy of the program. These trace systems use a copy of the symbol table generated by a translator, and a copy of the **memory map,** which is the table of memory allocation generated by the linking loader. With this information, the trace program can translate a symbol into a memory address as used at execution time so that the user can request traps at various points in a program. This symbolic information can also be used to provide symbolic dumps of memory showing the value of each variable used alongside its name. Sometimes it is convenient to take a series of short dumps of selected areas of memory periodically. These are called **snapshots. A comparison postmortem** is also useful. This compares the state of the memory at the end of execution to the initial state, and tells the user which locations have been changed.

Interpretation

Interpretation can be used to enhance the capabilities of the computer. One way in which it is used is in conjunction with the trap mechanism to provide what appears to the user to be additional machine instructions. For example, input and output are handled by the monitor in most systems. The user activates this code by "executing" certain "instructions" that are actually invalid. These cause a trap to the monitor so that it can perform the I/O. When the trap occurs, the monitor examines data in the user area of memory to determine the meaning of the trap. For example, the assembler may provide an "instruction" such as

READ   A,10,IN3

meaning that 10 words are to be read into locations **A** to **A+9** from input **IN3**. The assembler could translate this into a particular illegal instruction with an operand address giving the location of a block of three words containing the information **A, 10,** and **IN3**. At execution time, this illegal instruction can be trapped and examined by the monitor. It will realize that the illegal instruction indicates a read operation and execute that operation using the information **A, 10,** and **IN3**. From the machine point of view, the **READ** is being interpreted. From the user point of view, the system executes the **READ** instruction. Thus, the user sees a higher-level machine, called a **virtual machine.**

Interpretation is also very useful in tracking down programming errors. In this case, an interpreter interprets every machine instruction in the program. An interpreter of machine language is basically the same as an interpreter of a high-level language. The interpreter program behaves just like a computer, fetching successive instructions of the interpreted program from memory, examining them, and performing the action indicated. If, for example, the instruction is a **STORE,** the interpreter places a copy of a cell being used to hold the contents of the accumulator for the interpreted program into the cell with the memory address indicated. However, it can do several other things. If the cell is not part of the data area of the program it can print an error. (If the interpreter is provided with a table of all data areas defined by the program it has the information needed for this checking.) This is more error detection than is normally available with simple memory protection. The interpreter can also keep a list of cells which the programmer would like monitored. Any stores or reads on these cells can also be reported to the user.

11-8 TASK AND JOB SCHEDULING, COMMANDS

We have seen that system programs are provided for translating, loading, and monitoring of user programs. In some of the very early systems it was necessary for the user or operator to sequence the separate tasks which made up a single job through the computer. For example, if a job consisted of a section of FOR-TRAN code and a section of assembler code, and it required three library subroutines, the operator of an early machine performed the following steps:

1. Load the FORTRAN compiler. This was done with an absolute loader which was either kept in memory or was loaded by an initial load sequence.

2. Compile the FORTRAN section of code. The output was saved for later loading.

3. Load the assembler in the same manner as the compiler was loaded.

4. Assemble the next section of code. Save the output for the loading process.

5. Load the relocatable loader via the absolute loader.

6. Feed the output from the compiler and assembler into the loader. Since three subroutines were still required, the loader typed out their names to the operator. Copies of these programs had to be obtained and fed into the relocatable loader.

7. Commence execution. When it stopped, actions requested by the user had to be taken. For example, if a dump was wanted, it was necessary to load a dump program.

This process was slow on early systems for two reasons. First, the intermediate storage was on very slow hard-copy media such as punched cards or paper tape. Second, the operator had to initiate each step. When secondary storage devices are available, as they are on almost all systems today, use of the hard copy is not necessary for system programs or intermediate storage and the computer can sequence automatically through the steps. Instead of the user giving (written) commands to the operator indicating the steps to be followed, they must be given to the computer. Therefore, we need another system program whose job is to process these commands. Not surprisingly, this is called a **command interpreter,** and the statements made by the user are written in a language called a **command language.** [Operating system 370 calls the language **job control language** (JCL) and the statements are **job control statements.** Unfortunately, JCL is one of the worst languages ever designed for computer use or control; so we will not discuss it here.] When the user prepares a job, the programs and data must be surrounded by suitable commands that tell the system exactly what is to be done. Computer installations normally provide descriptions of simple sets of commands needed to perform standard operations, and the user is recommended to get those. They are often installation dependent anyway. We will discuss a simple example of a command language which is similar to the language available on some Cyber installations. However, it is illustrative of the features found in all modern command languages.

A command language is similar to any other language; it uses operators and operands to tell the computer system what to do. In this case, the operators are requests to compile, assemble, load, etc., and the operands are programs and data. The programs and data are stored on secondary storage as named files, and their names are used in the commands. For example, the command

FORTRAN,PROG1,OBJECTA

says that the **FORTRAN** compiler is to be executed using a set of data named **PROG1** as its input. The output (relocatable binary) is to be placed into a file called **OBJECTA.** (We have ignored what happens to the listing generated by most compilers; that might require an additional file name in the command.) If the command

ASSEMBLE,PROG3,OBJECTA

is next, it tells the computer to assemble the file name **PROG3,** placing the relocatable binary also into file **OBJECTA.** If this is placed on the end of the earlier information, file **OBJECTA** now contains the relocatable binary for **PROG1** and **PROG3.** Next we might issue the command

LOAD,OBJECTA,MYJOB

which would load the information in **OBJECTA,** producing an absolute binary file named **MYJOB** ready to execute. Finally, executing the command

MYJOB,INPUT,OUTPUT

would cause the program just prepared to be executed, using file **INPUT** for input, and file **OUTPUT** for output. If we wanted to save the compiled form for later, we could also execute a command such as

SAVE,MYJOB

which would keep a permanent copy of **MYJOB** on the disk files for later use.

The format of the commands we have used above is

Operator   input file, output file

It would be nice if we could keep everything that simple. In practice, other file names and additional information must be provided, but we will not complicate the picture here. Because a lot of information is needed, systems include a number of default options. For example, the Cyber system assumes that if an input or output file name is omitted, the input file comes from the standard input device, and the output file goes to the standard output device. If the programmer is using a terminal, these refer to the keyboard and CRT screen or typed output. If the programmer runs the job through batch, these refer to the input reader and the output printer, respectively.

The user at an interactive terminal can issue these commands by entering them as they are to be executed. However, it is also convenient to be able to create a file of commands and have them executed without further human intervention. This is useful not only for batch jobs in which the whole job is left for later processing, but also in interactive work when the user would like to apply the same set of commands repeatedly to different sets of programs and data.

We will describe the input for a batch job first. The first lines in a batch job are usually concerned with identification and charging. Subsequent lines contain the commands, and finally we will have the programs and data. In the example above, we want to FORTRAN compile the first part of the job, assemble the next part, load the two objects together with the library programs, and finally execute the result using the data following the program. Some systems start each command statement with a special character (JCL uses the two characters //), but other systems simply group all commands together in front of any program or data cards. We will describe the latter organization as it is more flexible, but the former is very similar. A typical job makeup for the example above would be

```
ID information (User name, account number, password, etc.)
FORTRAN,,OBJECTA
ASSEMBLE,,OBJECTA
LOAD,OBJECTA,MYJOB
MYJOB,,
end-of-record mark
FORTRAN source program
end-of-record mark
Assembly source program
end-of-record mark
Data for run
end-of-file mark
```

The first two commands after the identification have a missing input file name; so the input is assumed to be from the standard input device which is the one reading this stream of data. Hence, the FORTRAN program is the first record following the record containing the commands. (We are using Cyber terminology here. A **record** is a group of information terminated by an end-of-record indicator. It may consist of many line images.) The program to be assembled is the record following the FORTRAN program. Finally, the data, which is used in the execution step, is the last record. The output from the execution step goes to the standard output device because a file is not specified. The whole thing is followed by an end-of-file mark.

We see that a set of commands is simply another type of program, one that is executed by the command interpreter. Its statements are executed sequentially just as the instructions in a machine language program are executed sequentially. There is no reason why one cannot have control statements in these **control programs,** and many systems have such statements. Typical of these are the selection group

```
IF,expression
. . . . . . . . . . . .
ELSE
. . . . . . . . . . . .
ENDIF
```

which tests the value of a logical expression and decides which group of commands to execute, and the looping group

```
WHILE,expression
. . . . . . . . . . . . . . . .
ENDWHILE
```

which repeats a group of commands as long as the logical expression is true. The use of these is shown in the following example. It processes a file **STUDJOBS** which consists of a series of records, each record being a FORTRAN program written by a student in a class. The task is to compile each of these, and, for each job that compiles, execute it using the data file **TEST,** and then check the output with the program **GRADE** which places the grading information in the file named **CLASSGRADE.** If the program does not compile, the program **DIAGNOSE** is to be used to record the failure. The command **REWIND** positions a file at the first item. The logical expression **FILE(name,NO__EOF)** tests the file name for no end-of-file condition. The expression **ERRORFLAG** is true if there was an error in the previous (FORTRAN) step.

```
REWIND,STUDJOBS
WHILE,FILE(STUDJOBS,NO__EOF)
  FORTRAN,STUDJOBS,OBJECT
  IF,ERRORFLAG
    DIAGNOSE,OBJECT,CLASSGRADE
  ELSE
    REWIND,TEST
    REWIND,OUT
    LOAD,OBJECT,RUNFILE
    RUNFILE,TEST,OUT
    REWIND,OUT
    GRADE,OUT,CLASSGRADE
  ENDIF
ENDWHILE
```

(Many command interpreters do not allow identation as used above; we have used it to make the structure clear to the reader.)

A command program, such as the one above, could be entered with the job, or it could be stored in a file. In the latter case, it can be given parameters, just as a subprogram in any language can be given parameters. For example, the names of the files **STUDJOBS, TEST,** and **CLASSGRADE** could be set as parameters. Then the command file could be used for several classes. Command languages also allow the programmer to send messages to the operator requesting that tapes and other storage media be mounted on tape drives and other units.

The system processes sequences of jobs. As each job terminates, the system decides which job to execute next. In the simplest batch processing system, the next job waiting in a card reader or on disk is selected. In complex multiprogramming systems, a scheduling program examines the jobs waiting and selects one according to some combination of priority information, length of job, and the ease with which it can be placed in operation in the current environment.

sec.12

Survey of High-Level Programming Languages

Harry L. Helms

12-1 INTRODUCTION

A **high-level language** is one in which numerous instructions must be executed at the machine language level to perform a function or task specified. Instructions written in a high-level language must be translated into the machine language used by the computer system the program will be executed on. The "translator" in such a case is the **compiler.** The high-level language program is known as the **source program** and the resulting machine language program is the **object program.** The compiler is itself a program. On some computer systems (particularly microcomputers), an **interpreter** is used instead of a compiler. Interpreters translate the instructions of a source program in a one-by-one manner. As a result, interpreters produce object programs more slowly than compilers. However, interpreters require less memory than compilers.

High-level languages are sometimes described as being **machine independent.** This means that a program written in a high-level language such as COBOL should run on any computer system with a COBOL compiler. In actual practice, however, several variations have crept into high-level languages so that no high-level language is totally "portable" to all computer systems with a compiler for the language in question. Efforts to standardize high-level languages and compilers have received much attention in recent years.

High-level languages greatly simplify programming tasks when compared to assembly or machine level languages. Fewer errors are likely to result. Programs written in one language may be used on other machines with little or no revisions. High-level languages execute slower and occupy more space in memory than machine or assembly languages, however.

12-2 DEVELOPMENT OF HIGH-LEVEL LANGUAGES

The first high-level language of lasting significance was FORTRAN (an acronym for FORmula TRANslator). The first specification of the language was published in 1954; the first use was on an IBM computer in 1956. The leader of the project that developed FORTRAN was John Backus, who was employed at that time by IBM. He later participated in the development of a formal method for defining the syntax of programming languages which became known as the Backus-Naur Form (BNF).

In 1958, representatives of the Association for Computing Machinery met with representatives of European computing societies. The result was ALGOL (ALGOrithmic Language). Like FORTRAN, ALGOL was effective in solving a wide variety of mathematical problems. Unlike FORTRAN, ALGOL was not actively supported by hardware manufacturers in the United States. Thus, ALGOL was much more popular in Europe than the United States.

The U.S. Department of Defense undertook the development in 1959 of a common language for businesses working under contract to the Department and other government agencies. The result was COBOL (COmmon Business Oriented Language). Unlike FORTRAN and ALGOL, COBOL emphasized readability of programs; a COBOL program can often be read and interpreted by a non-programmer. COBOL programs also are largely self-documenting, making them easy to revise and update.

1965 saw the introduction of two significant new languages. At Dartmouth College, Professors Thomas Kurtz and John Kemeny developed a teaching language loosely based on FORTRAN which became known as BASIC (Beginner's All-purpose Symbolic Instruction Code). BASIC has strong interactive facilities: it is possible for a user to "converse" with a BASIC program as the program is executed. This makes it possible for the program to "ask" the user to supply data, verify data, make choices, etc., as the program is executed. BASIC's popularity exploded with the introduction of microcomputers beginning in 1975. Today, BASIC may well be the most widely known and used high-level language in the world.

The second language introduced in 1965 was PL/I (Programming Language I). PL/I was developed under the auspices of IBM, and was an attempt to produce a language combining the best features of ALGOL, COBOL, and FORTRAN. PL/I is indeed suited for a wide variety of purposes and is more versatile than ALGOL, COBOL, or FORTRAN. At the time of its introduction, it was predicted by some that PL/I would emerge as the dominant high-level language and eventually replace COBOL and FORTRAN. This obviously did not take place. One reason apparently was that existing COBOL and FORTRAN users did not feel the additional features of PL/I justified converting to PL/I. Another problem may have been PL/I's "size"; its facilities and statements are quite numerous compared to COBOL and FORTRAN and consequently PL/I takes longer to learn.

Professor Niklaus Wirth of the Technical University in Zurich, Switzerland developed a significant new language in 1971 known as Pascal (after Blaise Pascal, the well-known seventeenth century mathematician). Pascal was based upon ALGOL but incorporated several refinements. Pascal's facilities for manipulating non-numeric data is far superior to ALGOL. Pascal also has superior input and output features. Data structures (such as lists and tables) can be easily manipulated in Pascal, and it is possible for the users to define and use their own data types. Like ALGOL, Pascal is a **block structured** language. This means that programs are divided into sections, or blocks, to accomplish specific functions and that alterations can be made to one block without affecting the others.

A recent language which promises to have a great impact is Ada. It was developed in 1979 under the direction of the U.S. Department of Defense as a replacement for the numerous languages used by the American armed forces and their suppliers. Ada is based upon Pascal, but includes several extensions and new features. It is especially suited for real-time applications.

12-3 HIGH-LEVEL LANGUAGE DESCRIPTIONS

There are numerous high-level languages in existence today and new ones are introduced each year (although few are actually implemented or used to any extent). As such, it is impossible to mention all high-level languages here. The following will be brief descriptions of the most significant high-level languages.

Ada. Ada is a relatively new language based on Pascal. Like Pascal, it is a highly structured language. A major advantage over Pascal is improved real-time capabilities. Ada programs are built from modules; modules are constructed from smaller units known as packages and procedures. Ada is a rather "large" language and of moderate difficulty to learn.

ALGOL. ALGOL (ALGOrithmic Language) was the first block structured language. An ALGOL program is actually a single statement, known as a block, describing the steps to be taken to accomplish a desired action. The beginning and end of each block is clearly indicated. Blocks may be nested within each other. ALGOL has poor input and output facilities, however.

APL. APL (A Programming Language) is strong in its interactive capabilities and is relatively easy to learn. It also has a simple syntax, numerous operators, and refined data structure features. APL has been widely used in education, but not extensively in commercial applications.

BASIC. BASIC (Beginner's All-purpose Symbolic Instruction Code) is widely used today in microcomputer systems. BASIC was originally designed as a teaching language loosely based on FORTRAN and is simple to learn. Its capabilities are limited compared to most other high-level languages, however, and many different, incompatible implementations of the language are in use.

C. C is a language originally developed for minicomputers using the UNIX operating system. It is a comparatively small language; there are no operations for character strings or lists, for example. It is widely used for writing numerical and operating system programs; it is a highly efficient language in terms of its operating speed and memory requirements.

CBASIC. CBASIC is a variation of BASIC designed to encourage a more structured approach to programming. The most immediately noticeable difference is that statements in CBASIC do not need line numbers unless referenced by another statement. CBASIC is mainly used for business applications programs.

COBOL. COBOL (COmmon Business Oriented Language) features strong record, file, and field description and manipulation capabilities. A COBOL program is divided into different divisions (such as environment division and data division) according to the functions performed.

FORTH. FORTH is a language that allows users to define and use their own commands, functions, and procedures. FORTH has been implemented successfully on microprocessor systems for such diverse tasks as control of motorized drives and video games.

FORTRAN. FORTRAN (FORmula TRANslator) is a popular language for mathematical and scientific computation. Its numerical abilities are strong (particularly its ability to handle complex numbers) although it is weak in handling character strings. It is of moderate difficulty to learn and use.

LISP. LISP (LISt Processing) is a language designed for the manipulation of strings and recursive data. It also has facilities for mathematical and logical operations. It has been used extensively in research on artificial intelligence.

Pascal. Pascal is an ALGOL-based language that has achieved wide popularity. It is block structured and encourages a systematic, disciplined approach to programming. It features a large set of control statements and allows users to define their own data types.

PL/I. PL/I combines many of the features of ALGOL, COBOL, and FORTRAN. The result is a language with applicability to a large number of situations. However, PL/I has a large number of features, making it somewhat difficult to learn and use.

RPG. RPG (Report Program Generator) incorporates many of the concepts and terms of punched-card accounting machine methods. It is a limited-scope language primarily useful for producing written reports on the data contained in one or more input files. As such, many systems on which RPG is available have another high-level language available to handle tasks for which RPG is not suited.

SNOBOL. SNOBOL was developed in 1962 by Bell Laboratories. It has strong string manipulation and pattern matching facilities. The prime use of SNOBOL has been in text processing.

12-4 SUMMARY

As is readily apparent, there is no high-level language ideal for all applications. The task to be performed is perhaps the most important factor in determining which language is "best" for a given situation.

The following sections will describe some popular high-level languages in greater detail.

sec.13

BASIC

Harry L. Helms

13-1 INTRODUCTION

BASIC is an acronym for Beginners' All-purpose Symbolic Instruction Code. BASIC was developed in the early 1960's at Dartmouth College by John Kemeny and Thomas Kurtz as a teaching language. It largely remained a teaching language until the introduction of microcomputer systems in the mid-1970s. BASIC was selected as the high-level language for such systems due to its simplicity and "compactness" in memory compared to other high-level languages. The rapid growth of microcomputer systems since the late 1970s has now resulted in BASIC being very likely the most widely used computer language in the world.

Such popularity has been at the expense of uniformity. ANSI developed a standard BASIC; however, most microcomputer systems use their own particular implementation of BASIC. This is largely because microcomputer technology has advanced at a very rapid rate and the language has been changed to take advantage of the capabilities of the hardware. The result is that someone able to program in the BASIC used by one computer system (such as Apple) may be unable to program in the BASIC used by another computer system (such as IBM).

The wide variation in different implementations of BASIC makes it impossible to cover every possible variation in this chapter. For our purposes, we will restrict our discussion to the following popular implementations:

- Apple II Applesoft
- Atari 400/800
- Commodore PET
- IBM Personal Computer Advanced
- Radio Shack Level II
- Radio Shack Color Computer Extended
- Texas Instruments 99/4(A)

Most other implementations of BASIC will be similar to these implementations. Consult the system or programming manual for the system you are using for variations not covered here.

13-2 SYSTEM COMMANDS

Commands are instructions to the computer system. They are independent of the program in the system memory and are executed immediately. The following is a list of commands and the implementations in which they are found. If no system(s) are given in parentheses following the command, the command is found in all seven implementations mentioned in the previous section.

AUDIO Connects or disconnects cassette output to a television speaker (Radio Shack Extended Color).

AUTO Automatically numbers program lines as they are entered from the keyboard (Atari, IBM Advanced, and Radio Shack Level II).

BLOAD Loads binary data or machine language programs into memory (IBM Advanced).

BREAK Sets up a breakpoint to halt program execution at a specified line number (Texas Instruments 99/4).

BSAVE Saves binary data onto a diskette (IBM Advanced).

BYE Goes to calculator mode of operation from BASIC (Atari and Texas Instruments 99/4).

CALL-151 Puts system into monitor mode for machine language program execution (Apple II).

CALL CLEAR Clears the video monitor screen (Texas Instruments 99/4).

CLEAR Sets all numeric variables to 0 and all string variables to null (Apple II and Atari).

Sets aside a specified number of bytes of memory for string storage; also sets numeric variables to 0 and string variables to null (Radio Shack Level II and Extended Color).

Clears all program variables and optionally sets memory area (IBM Advanced).

CLOAD Loads a BASIC program from a cassette tape (Atari, Radio Shack Level II and Extended Color).

CLOADM Loads a machine language program from cassette tape (Radio Shack Extended Color).

CLOAD? Compares a program in memory to one on cassette tape. If there are differences, BAD will be displayed on the video terminal (Radio Shack Level II).

CLR Same function as **CLEAR** (Apple II and Commodore PET).

CONT Continues execution of a program after it has been halted (not available on Texas Instruments 99/4).

CONTINUE Same function as **CONT** (Texas Instruments 99/4).

CSAVE Saves a program in memory onto a cassette tape (Atari, Radio Shack Level II and Extended Color).

CSAVEM Writes out a machine language file (Radio Shack Extended Color).

DEL Deletes indicated program lines from a program. The form for is

DEL program line(s)

(Apple II and Radio Shack Extended Color).

DELETE Same function as **DEL** (IBM Advanced and Radio Shack Level II).

Deletes programs or data files from filing system (Texas Instruments 99/4).

DLOADM Loads machine language programs at baud rate specified; 0 for 300 baud or 1 for 1200 baud (Radio Shack Extended Color).

EDIT Allows editing of line numbers specified (IBM Advanced, Radio Shack Level II and Extended Color).

FILES Lists files in diskette directory that match file name specified (IBM Advanced).

HIMEN Sets addresses of highest memory address available during program execution (Apple II).

HOME Moves cursor to top left of video display (Apple II).

KILL Erases a diskette file (IBM Advanced).

LIST Displays a list of all program lines specified. If no lines are specified, the entire program is displayed. The form is

LIST first line number—last line number

LOAD Same function as **CLOAD** (Apple II, Commodore PET and IBM Advanced).

LOMEN   Sets lowest address available in a program (Apple II).

MERGE   Merges saved program with one in memory (IBM Advanced).

MOTOR   Turns cassette recorder on or off (Radio Shack Extended Color).

NAME . . . AS   Renames a diskette file. The form is

NAME old diskette name **AS** new diskette name

(IBM Advanced).

NEW   Deletes entire program from memory and clears all variables.

NOTRACE   Turns off **TRACE** mode feature (Apple II).

NUM   Similar to **AUTO,** but begins line numbering at 100 and advances in increments of 10 (Texas Instruments 99/4).

OLD   Similar function to **CLOAD** (Texas Instruments 99/4).

RENUM   Renumbers program lines in specified increments. The form is

RENUM new, start, inc

where new is the first new line number, start is the line number in the original program where renumbering is to start and inc is the increment by which the renumbering increases. If inc is omitted, line numbers increase by 10 (IBM Advanced and Radio Shack Extended Color).

RESEQUENCE   Renumbers program lines in a specified increment beginning at indicated line number. The form is

RESEQUENCE beginning line, increment

(Texas Instruments 99/4).

RESET   Reinitializes all diskette information (IBM Advanced).

RUN   Begins program execution. If a line number follows, program execution begins at that line.

SAVE   Same function as **CSAVE** (Apple II, Commodore PET, IBM Advanced and Texas Instruments 99/4).

SKIPF   Skips to next program on a cassette tape or to end of specified program (Radio Shack Extended Color).

SYS   Same function as **CALL-151** (Commodore PET).

SYSTEM   Same function as **CALL-151** (IBM Advanced and Radio Shack Level II).

TRACE   Indicates which line number in a program is being executed (Apple II and Texas Instruments 99/4).

TROFF   Same function as **NOTRACE** (IBM Advanced, Radio Shack Level II and Extended Color).

TRON   Same function as **TRACE** (IBM Advanced, Radio Shack Level II and Extended Color).

UNBREAK   Ends breakpoint established by **BREAK** (Texas Instruments 99/4).

UNTRACE   Same function as **NOTRACE** (Texas Instruments 99/4).

VERIFY   Same function as **CLOAD?** (Commodore PET).

13-3 PROGRAM STRUCTURE

Each line in a BASIC Program must have a line number. Program execution begins with the lowest line number and proceeds with other line numbers in order of their ascending values. Common programming practice calls for using line numbers from 0 to 999, increasing in increments of 10. Using increments of 10 allows inserting additional statements later as needed. It is also normal practice to use line numbers from 0 to 999 for the main body of the program and line numbers over 1000 for subroutines.

More than one statement may be placed on a program line if the statements are separated by colons (:). (This is not available in the Texas Instruments 99/4(A) implementation of BASIC.)

It is normal programming practice to conclude programs with an **END** statement, although this is not mandatory. However, if a program uses subroutines, **END** must be the last statement in the main program. This prevents all subroutines from being executed following the conclusion of the main program.

Explanatory remarks may be placed in a program by using **REM** statements. **REM** statements do not affect program operation in any manner, although they occupy space in memory. The form is

100 REM THIS IS A REMARK

REM statements should be added as necessary for clarity if the program listing is to be reviewed as others. They are also useful for documentation in program development as well.

BASIC does not have any specified divisions or sections within the main body of the program to accomplish designated functions such as input/output, arithmetic operations, etc. However, good programming practice calls for statements accomplishing certain functions to be grouped together.

13-4 VARIABLES AND CONSTANTS

The names of all variables and constants must begin with a letter of the alphabet (A through Z). The remaining characters of the name may be either letters or numbers; no other characters (!, %, etc.) are all allowed.

Most implementations of BASIC allow variable names to contain up to 255 letters or digits. However, only the first two letters or digits will be significant to the computer in distinguishing between variable names. For example, to the computer the names **DOLLARS** and **DOWNTIME** would represent the same variable. The major exceptions to this rule are Texas Instruments 99/4(A) BASIC, in which variable names are significant to the first 15 characters, and IBM Advanced, in which variable names are significant to the first 40 characters.

Variable names may represent either integer or real values. Specific types of variables may be represented by adding an appropriate character following a variable name, as follows:

Character	Type	Definition
$	String	Variable containing up to 255 characters
%	Integer	Variable storing a whole number from -32767 to 32767
! or **E**	Single Precision	Variable storing value using six significant figures
#	Double Precision	Variable storing value using sixteen significant figures
D	Double Precision with Scientific Notation	Used for constants or for output for very large/very small numbers

Variables without declaration characters are assumed to be single precision.

Values may be assigned to variable names using the **LET** statement:

LET X = 10

However, values may be assigned to variables without **LET:**

X = 10

Values may be assigned to variables as the results of operations:

X = A/B

Arrays are items of data arranged and stored using a single variable name. The individual parts of an array are known as **elements.** Elements may be numbers or strings. Each element is identified by the array name followed by an integer (known as a subscript). Array names follow the same rules as variable names.

The number of elements in an array is set by the **DIM** statement. The statement

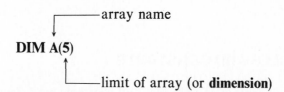

would set up a **one-dimensional** array containing the elements **A(0), A(1), A(2), A(3), A(4)** and **A(5).** The **0** subscripted variable name is usually not used but is available.

Arrays may have more than one dimension. The statement

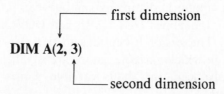

sets up a **two-dimensional** array with elements such as **A(0, 0), A(1, 1), A(1, 2), A(2, 1),** etc.

The dimensions of an array may be either numbers or expressions. **DIM** statements may be placed anywhere in a BASIC program.

IBM Advanced BASIC and Texas Instruments 99/4A BASIC include the **OPTION BASE** statement. This allows specifying the lowest subscript limit of an array. For example, the statements

100 OPTION BASE = 5

200 DIM X(10)

would define an array having the element **X(5)** through **X(10)**.

IBM Advanced also includes the **ERASE** and **SWAP** statements. The **ERASE** statement allows elimination of specified variables from the program. The form is

ERASE list of variables

The **SWAP** statement permits the values of two variables to be exchanged. The form is

SWAP first variable, second variable

IBM Advanced BASIC and Radio Shack Level II BASIC both contain statements which allow declaration of a list of variables as a certain type without having to add type declaration characters to each variable name. They are as follows:

DEFDBL   Causes variables beginning with any letter in a specified range to be stored and treated as double precision variables. The form is

DEFDBL letters

DEFINT   Similar to **DEFDBL,** but causes variable beginning with any letter in a specified range to be stored and treated as integer variables.

DEFSNG   Similar to **DEFDBL,** but causes variables beginning with any letter in a specified range to be stored and treated as single precision variables.

DEFSTR   Similar to **DEFDBL,** but causes variables beginning with any letter in a specified range to be stored and treated as string variables.

13-5 ARITHMETIC OPERATORS

Arithmetic operators are indicated in BASIC by the following symbols:

+	Addition
−	Subtraction
*	Multiplication
/	Division
\	Integer division (IBM Advanced)
∧ or ↑	Exponentiation
MOD	Gives integer remainder of integer division (Apple and IBM Advanced)

13-6 RELATIONAL OPERATORS

BASIC includes the following relational symbols, although not all are available in every implementation of BASIC:

$<$	Less than
$>$	Greater than
$=$	Equal to
$<>$	Not equal to
$<=$	Less than or equal to
$>=$	Greater than or equal to

13-7 LOGICAL OPERATORS

BASIC includes the following logical operators:

AND   Expression is true if both parts are true; otherwise expression is false.

OR   Expression is true if either part is true; otherwise expression is false.

NOT   Makes an expression not true.

XOR   Expression is false if both parts are false or if both parts are true; expression is true if one part is true and other part is false (IBM Advanced).

IMP   Expression is false if first part is true and second part is false; otherwise expression is true (IBM Advanced).

EQV   Expression is true if both parts are true or both parts are false; otherwise expression is false (IBM Advanced).

An expression may be made negative by placing the symbol $-$ before it.

13-8 ORDER OF OPERATIONS

Arithmetic, relational and logical operations are performed in the following order of precedence:

1. Exponentiation
2. Negation
3. Multiplication and division from left to right
4. Addition and subtraction from left to right
5. Relational operators from left to right
6. NOT
7. AND
8. OR

9. XOR
10. IMP
11. EQV

The order of operations may be altered by placing expressions and operations in parentheses. When parentheses are nested, operations in the innermost set of parentheses are performed first. Evaluation is performed on the next level of parentheses outward, etc.

13-9 PROGRAM LOGIC AND CONTROL

BASIC normally executes programs beginning with the lowest line number, continuing with the next highest line number, and so forth in ascending order. It is possible to alter this execution using control and transfer statements. Transfer statements may be classified as **unconditional,** meaning they always alter the flow of program execution, and **conditional,** in which program execution is altered only if certain conditions are met.

BASIC includes the following control statements:

END   Terminates execution of a program.

RETURN   Ends a subroutine and returns control to the statement immediately following the last executed GOSUB statement.

STOP   Interrupts execution of a program.

WAIT   Suspends program execution until conditions specified following **WAIT** are met (Apple II, Commodore PET and IBM Advanced).

There are two unconditional transfer statements:

GOSUB   Transfers program control to subroutine beginning at line number indicated by expression following GOSUB.

GOTO   Transfers program control to line number indicated by expression following **GOTO.**

Conditional transfer statements are far more numerous:

ELSE   Used in conjunction with the **IF** statement to specify an alternative action when the **IF** test is false.

alternative action
↑
⌐IF A = B PRINT "A = B" ELSE PRINT "A DOES NOT EQUAL B"⌐
↓
IF test

(Available in IBM Advanced, Radio Shack Level II and Extended Color.)

ERROR   Used in conjunction with **IF . . . THEN** to cause printing of an error message when a specified condition is found (Radio Shack Level II).

Simulates the occurence of an error or allows definition of error codes (IBM Advanced).

FOR . . . TO Sets up a loop of statements to be repeated for a specified number of times. The **FOR . . . TO** loop is terminated by **NEXT**:

10 FOR I = 1 TO 10
20 PRINT I;
30 NEXT

I is known as the **index variable.** Each time the loop is executed, 1 is added to the value of the index variable. When the value of the index variable exceeds the upper limit of its range (10 in the example above), execution of the loop ends and program execution continues normally. STEP may be used to specify the increment by which I increases. In the program line

10 FOR I = 1 TO 50 STEP 5

I will increase from 1 to 50 in jumps of 5 and the loop will terminate when the value of **I** exceeds 50. If **STEP** is omitted, **I** will increase in increments of 1. The increment, starting value and ending value of **I** may be negative numbers.

IF . . . GOSUB Tests the expression following **IF** to see if it is true or false. If the expression is true, the subroutine beginning at the line number following **GOSUB** is executed. If the expression is false, the next line in the program is executed. (Not available in Atari, IBM Advanced, or Texas Instruments 99/4.)

IF . . . GOTO Tests the expression following **IF** to see if it is true or false. If the expression is true, program control is transferred to the line number following **GOTO**. If the expression is false, the next line in the program is executed. (Not available in Atari or Texas Instruments 99/4.)

IF . . . THEN Tests the expression following **IF** to see if it is true or false. If the expression is true, the statement following **THEN** is executed. If the expression is false, the next line in the program is then executed. An alternative action to the one following **THEN** may be specified by using **ELSE**:

IF A = B THEN PRINT "A = B" ELSE STOP

(Texas Instruments 99/4 allows only line numbers following **THEN** and **ELSE**.)

ON COM(n) GOSUB Branches to subroutine beginning at line number following **GOSUB** when information enters the communications buffer through the communications adapter (1 or 2) indicated by **n** (available in IBM Advanced).

ON ERROR . . . GOTO Transfers program control to line number following **GOTO** when error is found during program execution. The **ON ERROR . . . GOTO** statement must be executed before an error occurs to have effect (available in IBM Advanced and Radio Shack Level II).

ONERR . . . GOTO Same function as **ON ERROR . . . GOTO** (Apple II).

ON . . . GOTO Transfers program control to a line number depending upon an integer obtained by evaluating the expression following **ON:**

$$\text{100 ON I GOTO 300, 400, 500}$$

when **I** = 1   2   3

I is an expression evaluating to an integer. If the value of **I** is greater than the number of elements following **GOTO,** the next line in the program is executed.

ON . . . GOSUB Similar to **ON . . . GOTO,** but transfers control to subroutines instead of line numbers.

ON KEY(n) GOSUB Enables trap routine for a key specified by **n,** where **n** is an expression between 1 and 14 (IBM Advanced).

ON PEN GOSUB Transfers control to subroutines beginning at line number following **GOSUB** when light pen is activated (IBM Advanced).

ON STRIG(n) GOSUB Enables trap routine when one of the joysticks is pressed. If **n** = 0, the first joystick controls; if **n** = 2, the second joystick controls (IBM Advanced).

WHILE . . . WEND Sets up a loop of statements which is executed as long as a given condition is true. The usual form is

WHILE expression

Loop of statements

WEND

The expression is true as long as it is not equal to zero. After each loop execution, the expression following **WHILE** is checked. If the expression is not true, program execution resumes at the first statement following **WEND** (IBM Advanced).

13-10 SUBROUTINES

A **subroutine** is a grouped sequence of statements accomplishing a certain action. A subroutine may be used as often as needed in a program.

Program control shifts to a subroutine through a **GOSUB** statement or a variant of **GOSUB.** When the subroutine is executed, program control shifts back (through a **RETURN** statement) to the main program at the first statement following **GOSUB.**

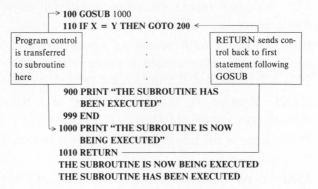

Subroutines are placed at the end of the main program. Good programming practice calls for using 0 through 999 for line numbers in the main program and 1000 through 9999 for line numbers in subroutines.

END should be added as the last statement in the main program when subroutines are used. This prevents program control from flowing directly to subroutines when execution of the main program is finished.

13-11 NUMERIC FUNCTIONS

The various implementations of BASIC include several numeric functions. The general form of a numeric function is

numeric function (number or expression)

ABS   Returns the absolute value of an expression.

ATN   Returns the arctangent of an expression.

CDBL   Returns a double-precision representation of the number or expression (IBM Advanced and Radio Shack Level II).

CINT   Returns the largest integer not greater than the number or expression (IBM Advanced and Radio Shack Level II).

CLOG   Returns the common logarithm of an expression (Apple II and Atari).

COS   Returns the cosine of an expression.

CSNG   Returns a single-precision representation of a number or expression (IBM Advanced and Radio Shack Level II).

DEF   Allows defining of new numeric functions (Texas Instruments 99/4).

DEF FN   Same function as **DEF** (Apple II, Commodore PET, IBM Advanced, and Radio Shack Extended Color).

ERL   Returns the line number where an error has occurred (IBM Advanced and Radio Shack Level II).

ERR   Returns a value related to the code of an error (IBM Advanced and Radio Shack Level II).

EXP   Returns the value of the natural number (e) raised to the power specified by a following expression.

FIX   Returns a truncated representation of an argument (IBM Advanced and Radio Shack Level II).

FRE   Gives the total number of unused bytes in memory. If followed by a string variable, gives amount of unused string space (Atari, Commodore PET, IBM Advanced, and Radio Shack Level II).

HEX$ Returns the hexadecimal value of a number (IBM Advanced and Radio Shack Extended Color).

INT   Returns the integer portion of an expression that is less than or equal to the expression.

LOG   Returns the natural logarithm of an argument.

MEM   Returns the amount of free memory available (Radio Shack Level II and Extended Color).

MKD$ Converts a single precision number to a 8-byte string (IBM Advanced).

MKI$ Converts an integer to a 2-byte string (IBM Advanced).

MKS$ Converts a single precision number to a 4-byte string (IBM Advanced).

NULL   Prints the number of spaces specified (Atari).

OCT$ Returns the octal value of a number (IBM Advanced).

POS   Returns a number from 0 to 63 indicating the cursor position on the video terminal (Apple II, Commodore PET, IBM Advanced, Radio Shack Level II and Extended Color).

PPOINT   Returns color code of a specified graphics cell (Radio Shack Extended Color).

RANDOM   Reseeds the random number generator (Commodore PET and Radio Shack Level II).

RANDOMIZE   Same function as **RANDOM** (IBM Advanced and Texas Instruments 99/4).

RND   Generates a pseudo-random number (not available in Radio Shack Extended Color).

SGN   Returns a -1 if an expression is negative, a 0 if it is 0, and a 1 if it is positive.

SIN   Returns the sine value of an expression in radians.

SPC   Returns the number of skips specified (Commodore PET and IBM Advanced).

SQR   Returns the square root of an expression (not available on Atari).

TAN   Returns the tangent of an expression (not available on Atari).

TI   Sets real-time clock to specified value (Commodore PET).

TIMER   Returns contents of or allows setting of timer (Radio Shack Extended Color).

TIME$ Sets or displays current time (IBM Advanced).

13-12 STRING FUNCTIONS

BASIC also includes several different string functions. The general form of a string function is

string function (string variable or argument)

ADR   Returns the address where the name, value, and pointer of the variable are located in memory (Atari).

ASC   Returns the ASCII value of the first character of a string.

CALL KEY   Checks keyboard and returns key being pressed or null string if no key is pressed (Texas Instruments 99/4).

CHR$ Returns a one-character string whose character has an ASCII graphics or control code specified by a number or expression evaluating to 0 through 255.

CVD   Converts an 8-byte string to a double precision number (IBM Advanced).

CVI   Converts a 2-byte string to an integer (IBM Advanced).

CVS   Converts a 4-byte string to a single precision number (IBM Advanced).

FRE   Returns amount of free memory available for string variable storage (Atari, Commodore PET, IBM Advanced, and Radio Shack Level II).

GET   Same function as **CALL KEY** (Apple II and Commodore PET).

Reads a record from a random file into a random buffer (IBM Advanced).

INKEY$ Same function as **CALL KEY** (IBM Advanced, Radio Shack Level II and Extended Color).

INSTR   Searches a designated string beginning at an indicated position for another designated string and returns position at which target string is found (IBM Advanced and Radio Shack Extended Color).

LEFT$ Returns specified number of characters, n, from a string starting at the left. The form is

LEFT$ (string, n)

(Not available in Atari or Texas Instruments 99/4.)

LEN   Returns the length of a specified string or 0 if the string is null.

MID$ Returns specified number of characters, n, from a string starting at position p. The form is

MID$ (string position, n, p)

(Not available in Atari or Texas Instruments 99/4.)

POS   Returns a substring from a string beginning at position n in the string. The form is

POS (string, substring, n)

(Available in IBM Advanced, Radio Shack Level II and Extended Color, and Texas Instruments 99/4.)

RIGHT$**   Similar to **LEFT$, but returns specified number of characters from a string starting at the right (not available in Atari or Texas Instruments 99/4).

SEG$ Returns a specified number of characters, n, from a string beginning at position p, where p is a number representing a character numbered from left to right in the string. The form is

SEG$ (string, p, n)

(Texas Instruments 99/4.)

STR$ Converts a numeric expression into a string.

STRING$ Returns a string of length n composed of a character c. The form is

STRING$ (n, c)

(Available in IBM Advanced, Radio Shack Level II and Extended Color.)

VAL   Converts a string to a number.

VARPTR   Same function as **ADR** (IBM Advanced, Radio Shack Level II and Extended Color).

13-13 ASSEMBLY LANGUAGE STATEMENTS AND ROUTINES

The widespread use of BASIC with microprocessor-based computer systems has resulted in most implementations of BASIC having statements and routines to directly access the microprocessor and associated semiconductor memories.

To properly use assembly language statements and routines, one must have the memory maps for the system and must be familiar with the instruction set for the microprocessor used in the system. Assembly language routines offer the advantages of faster execution speed and more efficient use of available memory space; however, assembly language programming is often difficult and time consuming.

The following statements allow direct access to the computer system's memory:

PEEK   Returns the value stored at the address specified (Atari restricts use to video locations only; not available in Texas Instruments 99/4).

GO GCHAR   Same function as **PEEK** (Texas Instruments 99/4).

POKE   Places a specified value at a designated memory location. The form is

POKE addr, val

where addr is the memory address and val is the value (not available in Texas Instruments 99/4).

The following statements are used to add routines written in the instruction code of the system's microprocessor:

CALL   Causes program control to shift from the main program to the assembly language subroutine located at the specified memory address. The form is

CALL memory address

Instructions to return to the main program are contained within the assembly language subroutine (Apple II and IBM Advanced).

DEFUSR   Defines the starting address of a machine language subroutine (IBM Advanced and Radio Shack Extended Color).

EXEC   Transfers control to assembly language programs located at specified address (Radio Shack Extended Color).

POP   Removes the most recent addition from the memory register stack (Apple II and Atari).

USR Similar function to **CALL** (not available in Atari or Texas Instruments 99/4).

13-14 GRAPHICS STATEMENTS

The greatest differences between various implementations of BASIC involve graphics statements. Computer systems vary greatly in their graphics capabilities and the implementations of BASIC they use reflect these differences. Graphics statements are also the most "volatile" area of BASIC; new graphics statements are being introduced regularly as microcomputer manufacturers constantly seek to improve the graphics capabilities of their systems.

CALL CHAR Defines a new character for the video display (Texas Instruments 99/4).

CALL CLEAR Erases video display but does not affect program in memory (Texas Instruments 99/4).

CALL COLOR Defines the background color used by individual characters (Texas Instruments 99/4).

CALL HCAR Draws a horizontal line at a specified line number (Texas Instruments 99/4).

CALL SCREEN Defines background color of the video display (Texas Instruments 99/4).

CALL VCHAR Draws a vertical line at a specified column (Texas Instruments 99/4).

CIRCLE Draws a circle on the video display (IBM Advanced and Radio Shack Extended Color).

CLS Same function as **CALL CLEAR** (Apple II, IBM Advanced, Radio Shack Level II and Extended Color).

COLOR Sets the color of the point for the next plot (Apple II).

Defines the background color used for individual characters (Atari).

Sets foreground and background colors (Radio Shack Extended Color).

Sets the foreground, background, and border colors (IBM Advanced).

DRAW Draws a line beginning at a specified starting point for a specified length and of an indicated color (Radio Shack Extended Color).

Draws an object as specified by characters in the string following **DRAW** (IBM Advanced).

DRAWTO Draws a line from the last plotted point to new position specified (Atari).

GET Reads graphics contents of a rectangle into memory (Radio Shack Extended Color).

In text mode, reads record from random file into random buffer; in graphics mode, reads points from an area of the screen (IBM Advanced).

GR Turns on low resolution graphics (Apple II).

GRAPHICS Similar function to **CALL HCAR** (Atari).

HCOLOR Selects the background color of the video display screen (Apple II).

HLIN ... AT Similar function to **CALL HCAR** (Apple II).

HPLOT Similar function to **DRAWTO** (Apple II).

LINE Draws a line from one specified point to another (IBM Advanced and Radio Shack Extended Color).

PAINT "Paints" video display starting at a specified point and continuing until a designated point is reached (IBM Advanced and Radio Shack Extended Color).

PCLEAR Reserves specified amount of graphics memory (Radio Shack Extended Color).

PCLS Clears video display using specified background color (Radio Shack Extended Color).

PCOPY Copies graphics from source page to destination page (Radio Shack Extended Color).

PLOT Turns on specified graphics block (Apple II and Atari).

PMODE Selects graphics resolution and first memory page (Radio Shack Extended Color).

POINT Checks specified video location and returns a 1 if it is on, a 0 if off (Radio Shack Level II).

Returns a color of specified point on the screen (IBM Advanced).

PRESET Resets a point to specified background color (IBM Advanced and Radio Shack Extended Color).

PSET Sets a specified point to a designated color (IBM Advanced and Radio Shack Extended Color).

PUT Stores graphics from source onto start/end rectangle (Radio Shack Extended Color).

In text mode, writes record from a random buffer to a random file. In graphics mode, writes colors onto specified area of screen (IBM Advanced).

RESET Resets a graphics point (Radio Shack Level II and Extended Color).

SCREEN Selects graphics or text screen and color (Radio Shack Extended Color).

Returns the ASCII code for the character on the screen at a specified line and column (IBM Advanced).

SET Similar function to **PLOT** (Radio Shack Level II and Extended Color).

SETCOLOR Similar function to **CALL SCREEN** (Atari).

TEXT Switches from graphics to text mode (Apple II).

VLIN ... AT Similar function to **CALL VCHAR** (Apple II).

VTAB Moves cursor down a specified number of lines (Apple II).

13-15 INPUT AND OUTPUT STATEMENTS

Most implementations of BASIC share a common group of input and output statements such as **PRINT, INPUT,** and **READ.** However, many implementations include certain variations on these statements as well.

Output Statements

PRINT   Outputs string variables, numbers, variables, or material enclosed in quotes:

100 X = 10
200 PRINT X
10

100 A$ = "OUTPUT"
200 PRINT A$
OUTPUT

100 PRINT "OUTPUT"
OUTPUT

More than one item can follow a **PRINT** statement. If the items are separated by commas, each item is printed in a separate printing zone on the microcomputer system's video display.

100 PRINT "OUTPUT", "OUTPUT"
OUTPUT   OUTPUT

If the items are separated by semicolons, no space is inserted between items on the display:

100 PRINT "OUTPUT"; "OUTPUT"
OUTPUTOUTPUT

PRINT can also be used to perform calculations:

100 PRINT 5 + 2
7

PRINT @   Specifies the exact position where printing is to begin. The usual form is

PRINT @ n, output

where n is an integer from 0 to 1023 and output is the data to be printed (Radio Shack Level II and Extended Color).

POSITION   Similar function to **PRINT @** (Atari).

PRINT USING   Prints string and numeric values according to format specified. The form is

PRINT USING format specifier; value

PRINT USING uses the following symbols in format specifiers:

Specifies position of a digit

.   Specifies the decimal point in a value

,	Specifies that a comma is to be inserted after every third digit
**	Specifies that all unused spaces to the left of the decimal will be filled with asterisks
$$	Specifies a dollar sign will occupy the first position preceding the number
**$	Specifies a dollar sign in the first position preceding the number and all unused spaces to the left will be filled with asterisks
∧ **or** ↑	Specifies that the value is to be printed in exponential form
+	Specifies a + for positive numbers and a − for negative numbers when placed at the beginning of the format specifier
/n/	Specifies that n plus two additional characters from a string are to be printed (IBM Advanced)
%n%	Specifies a string field of more than one character; the length of the field will be the number of spaces equal to n plus 2 (Radio Shack Level II and Extended Color)
!	Specifies that the first string character of the current value will be returned

(**PRINT USING** statement is available in IBM Advanced, Radio Shack Level II and Extended Color.)

TAB   Used with **PRINT** to specify printing begins in a specified column position. The form is

$$\text{PRINT TAB (exp)}$$

where exp is an integer or expression that evaluates to an integer (not available in Atari).

PRINT #   Prints the values of specified data onto a file or cassette tape (not available in Atari).

DISPLAY   Similar in function to **PRINT** (Texas Instruments 99/4).

WRITE   Similar to **PRINT,** but commas are inserted between items as they are output (IBM Advanced).

WIDTH   Sets output line width in number of characters (IBM Advanced).

Input Statements

INPUT   Halts program execution and waits for input from the keyboard. A prompting message may be added in quotes; it will appear on the display. The form is

$$\text{INPUT ``prompt''; variables}$$

INPUT#   Inputs data from a cassette and assigns it to variables (not available in Apple II or Atari).

RECALL   Similar function to **INPUT#** (Apple II).

READ   Reads values accompanying a **DATA** statement and assigns them to specified variables. The form is

READ list of variables

DATA   Shows data in a list in a program. It can be accessed by a **READ** statement. The form is

DATA list of items

READ and **DATA** statements are used together in the following manner:

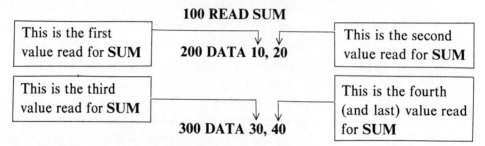

RESTORE   Causes the next **READ** statement to begin inputting data beginning with the first data item in the first **DATA** input.

13-16 SPECIALIZED INPUT AND OUTPUT STATEMENTS

The rapidly developing capabilities of microcomputer hardware has resulted in such systems being able to input and output data from more peripherals than the usual keyboard and video terminal. New statements have been added to the implementations of BASIC used on such systems to make use of such capabilities.

Output Statements

BEEP   Procedures a "beep" sound from the speaker (IBM Advanced).

CALL SOUND   Selects sound output from the system (Texas Instruments 99/4).

CLOSE   Closes peripheral data file (Commodore PET, IBM Advanced, Radio Shack Extended Color and Texas Instruments 99/4).

LLIST   Lists program or specified line on a printing peripheral (IBM Advanced, Radio Shack Level II and Extended Color).

LPRINT   Similar to **PRINT,** but sends output to a printing peripheral (Atari, IBM Advanced, and Radio Shack Level II).

LPRINT USING   Similar to **PRINT USING,** but with a printing peripheral (IBM Advanced).

OPEN   Opens a peripheral to input or output a data file (Commodore PET, IBM Advanced, and Texas Instruments 99/4).

DSP   Displays line number where value of variables is changed (Apple II).

OPEN COM . . . AS   Opens data file for communications (IBM Advanced).

OUT Sends specified value to a designated port (IBM Advanced and Radio Shack Level II).

PLAY Plays music of a specified note, octave, volume and length (IBM Advanced and Radio Shack Extended Color).

PR# Similar to **OUT** (Apple II).

SOUND Produces specified tone for selected duration (Atari, IBM Advanced, and Radio Shack Extended Color).

SPEED Selects speed at which characters are sent to an output device (Apple II).

STORE Sends contents of a numeric array to a cassette (Apple II).

UPDATE Reads and writes an opened file stored on a cassette (Texas Instruments 99/4).

Input Statements

APPEND Allows additional data to be added to the end of a data file (Texas Instruments 99/4).

CALL JOYSTK Checks for and accepts input from a joystick (Texas Instruments 99/4).

IN Goes to input port and receives value there (Radio Shack Level II).

IN# Similar function to **IN** (Apple II).

JOYSTK Returns the horizontal or vertical coordinate of a joystick (Radio Shack Extended Color).

LINE INPUT Inputs line from keyboard to a string variable (IBM Advanced and Radio Shack Extended Color).

PADDLE Accepts value from a control paddle (Atari).

PDL Similar function to **PADDLE** (Apple II).

PTRIG Returns a 0 if the game paddle button is presented or a 1 if it is not pressed (Atari).

STICK Similar function to **JOYSTK** (IBM Advanced).

STRIG Similar function to **PTRIG**, but is used with joysticks (Atari and IBM Advanced).

13-17 RESERVED WORDS

Reserved words vary between the different implementations of BASIC. As a general rule, no word used as a command, function, or statement in an implementation of BASIC should be used as a variable name in that implementation of BASIC.

sec.14

COBOL

Allen B. Tucker, Jr.

14-1 INTRODUCTION

COBOL (Common Business Oriented Language) is currently the most widely used language for data processing applications. It was designed and refined as a common language that would enable programs and programming techniques to be easily shared and transferred from one machine to another. Furthermore, COBOL is an Englishlike language; its syntax was designed so that the casual observer as well as the programmer could intelligently read a program and understand it. In this section, we will study COBOL and assess how well it has achieved these goals.

Brief History of COBOL

In the late 1950s, data processing installations began to realize the need for a common data processing language. In May 1959, representative computer manufacturers and users from industry and government met in Washington, D.C., to discuss the feasibility and desirability of such a development.

The CODASYL (Conference on Data Systems Languages) committee was thus formed; soon thereafter it had developed a draft description for such a language. A revised version of that draft was published in April of 1960 by the Government Printing Office, and became known as "COBOL-60."

The second version, called "COBOL-61," was published the following year, and became widely implemented. In 1963 an extended version of COBOL, called "COBOL-61 Extended," was published. Further extensions and refinements to the language were made in a 1965 version, called "COBOL, Edition 1965." This version was finally approved as an American National Standard in 1968. Meanwhile, COBOL development continued and new versions were published in 1968, 1969, 1970, and 1973 in the COBOL Journal of Development. A revised American National Standard for COBOL was approved in 1974. This standard reflects all COBOL modifications which had been published since the acceptance of the 1968 COBOL standard.

Implementations and Variations of COBOL

The version of COBOL which we will discuss in this section is the 1974 American National Standard COBOL. Since those features which differ from the 1968 standard version are not universally implemented at this writing, we will identify such features as they occur throughout this section.

COBOL is implemented on most medium and large computers, including the following.

Manufacturer	Implementation
Burroughs	B1700, B6700
CDC	3000, 6000, Cyber Series
DEC	PDP-10
Honeywell	Multics, 600, 6000 Series
IBM	360, 370 Series
Univac	1100 Series

Some manufacturers provide a number of implementations of COBOL, each having slightly different programming features. All of the above COBOL implementations, however, conform in their features with those of the 1968 American National Standard COBOL. In addition, most of the above implementations contain (implementation dependent) language extensions.

In addition to the manufacturer-supplied implementations of COBOL, other implementations have been developed by software houses and university groups. Perhaps the best known among these is WATBOL, a fast-compiling implementation of COBOL developed at the University of Waterloo.

Major Applications of COBOL

The application area for which COBOL was designed is the data processing area. Although COBOL may be used in scientific or text processing applications, the result is usually less satisfactory than what would be achieved by using a language which was designed for that application area.

The recent versions of COBOL are well suited to data processing applications, since these versions contain such powerful built-in functional elements as a report writer feature, a table search function, and a sort facility. Essentially, these features of COBOL are designed to aid the programmer in organizing, accessing, updating, reordering, and reporting data in files.

Writing COBOL programs, however, is a somewhat more arduous task than writing in another language. This stems from COBOL's basic philosophy of having English phrases (rather than more succinct formulas), sentences, paragraphs, and sections as its basic syntactic building blocks. The programmer's freedom to structure a program's text is restricted by COBOL's column-specific orientation for statements and statement labels.

In response to these problems, recent versions of COBOL have provided certain abbreviation and formatting options. Also, the ability to automatically insert source program text from a library helps alleviate the programmer's writing burden.

14-2 WRITING COBOL PROGRAMS

As suggested in the foregoing section, a COBOL program is organized along the lines of an English text. The highest level of program organization is the "division," and every COBOL program consists of four divisions. The four divisions and their purposes in the program are as follows.

Division name	Purpose
IDENTIFICATION DIVISION	Identifies the program, its author, its purpose, and other general operational characteristics.
ENVIRONMENT DIVISION	Specifies certain characteristics of the physical computer environment on which the program is run, especially those of the input-output devices used by the program.
DATA DIVISION	Describes the nature and organization of data used by the program. Generally, this includes the record layouts of external files as well as the nature of internal variables and tables that are local to the program.
PROCEDURE DIVISION	Describes the algorithm to be performed when the program is executed.

These four divisions must occur in this order within a COBOL program. Each one is delineated by the occurrence of its respective division name at its beginning. That division name must be written exactly as shown above, and with its terminating period (.).

The next level of organization within a COBOL program is the "section." Each division, with the exception of the Identification Division, may have more than one section. Within each section there may be more than one "paragraph." Paragraphs, in turn, are composed of "sentences," which are composed of "words." These terms all have fairly precise meanings in COBOL, as we shall see.

Our presentation of COBOL will not include all features of the language. Rather, it will include what we consider to be the most useful features in a programming environment. In doing this, we have attempted specifically not to present an oversimplified view of the language. Rather, we have stripped off marginally useful features, in order that attention may be properly focused on the essential elements of COBOL.

Data Types and Constants

A COBOL data item may be represented as a "literal," which is composed of two classes, "numeric literal" and "nonnumeric literal." Numeric literals are written as ordinary decimal numbers. They are composed of from 1 to 18 decimal digits, possibly preceded by a sign (+ or −), and possibly containing a decimal point (.). The following are examples of COBOL numeric literals.

$$1.73 \quad 0 \quad -17 \quad 250$$

A nonnumeric literal is any string, enclosed in quotes ("), of one or more characters from the implementation-defined character set. That set must contain at least the following fifty-one characters that compose the COBOL character set.

$$\text{ʋ(blank)} \ . < (+ \$ *) ; - /, > = \text{"} A B \ldots Z 0 1 \ldots 9$$

Furthermore, if the literal itself is to contain a quote ("), then that quote must be written twice in succession so that it may be distinguished from an enclosing quote. The value of a nonnumeric literal is exactly that sequence of characters that occur between its enclosing quotes, except that an embedded quote (") is represented as two successive quotes (" "). The following are examples of COBOL nonnumeric literals.

"ABC"

"AʋBʋC"

"WHAT""SʋTHIS?"

The reader should note that blanks (ʋ) are significant within a literal, so that the first two literals are **not** equivalent in any sense.

Certain COBOL constants may be represented alternatively as "figurative constants." A figurative constant is a COBOL word which denotes a particular (class of) literal value(s).

Figurative constant	Class of literals represented
ZERO ZEROS ZEROES	A numeric literal 0 or a nonnumeric literal composed entirely of zeros, such as "0" and "00" and "000".
SPACE SPACES	A nonnumeric literal composed entirely of blanks (ʋ), such as "ʋ" and "ʋʋ" and "ʋʋʋ".
HIGH-VALUE HIGH-VALUES	A nonnumeric literal composed entirely of the highest value in the collating sequence for the implementation's character set, such as "9" and "99" and "999".
LOW-VALUE LOW-VALUES	A nonnumeric literal composed entirely of the lowest value in the collating sequence for the implementation's character set, such as "ʋ" and "ʋʋ" and "ʋʋʋ".
ALL literal	A nonnumeric literal composed of a sequence of occurrences of 'literal'; e.g., 'ALL "14"' means "14" or "1414" or "141414", etc.

As shown, each figurative constant except the last may be written in more than one way. The particular value represented by an occurrence of a figurative constant in the program depends upon the context in which it is used.

Names, Variables, and Data Structures

A COBOL variable is called an "elementary data item." It is a "data name" associated with one or more values that may change while the program is executing. A data name must be either a valid COBOL "user-defined word" or filler and must be both unique from all other data names and "procedure names" in the program and not among the COBOL "reserved words."

A COBOL **user-defined word** is a sequence of at most 30 alphabetic (A–Z), numeric (0–9), and dash (-) characters, except that dash (-) may not be the first or last character.

Additionally, a COBOL data name must contain at least one alphabetic (A–Z) character. The following are valid COBOL data names.

GROSS-PAY   X   N19   19N

"Procedure names" are used to label sections and paragraphs in the program. Unlike data names, they are not required to contain an alphabetic character.

The COBOL "reserved words" may not be used as data names or procedure names. They have specific preassigned uses in a COBOL program. A complete list of the COBOL reserved words is given below. Here, an underlined part of a reserved word indicates an allowable abbreviation for the word. For example, the word **CORRESPONDING** may be written more briefly as **CORR** without any change in its meaning.

ACCEPT	BEFORE	74 COLLATING	74 DAY
ACCESS	68 BEGINNING	COLUMN	74 DEBUG-CONTENTS
68 ACTUAL	BLANK	COMMA	74 DEBUG-ITEM
ADD	BLOCK	74 COMMUNICATION	74 DEBUG-LINE
68 ADDRESS	74 BOTTOM	COMPUTATIONAL	74 DEBUG-NAME
ADVANCING	BY	COMPUTE	74 DEBUG-SUB-1
AFTER		CONFIGURATION	74 DEBUG-SUB-2
ALL	74 CALL	CONTAINS	74 DEBUG-SUB-3
ALPHABETIC	74 CANCEL	CONTROL	74 DEBUGGING
74 ALSO	74 CD	CONTROLS	DECIMAL-POINT
ALTER	CF	COPY	DECLARATIVES
ALTERNATE	CH	CORRESPONDING	74 DELETE
AND	74 CHARACTER	74 COUNT	74 DELIMITED
ARE	CHARACTERS	CURRENCY	74 DELIMITER
AREAS	CLOCK-UNITS		DEPENDING
ASCENDING	CLOSE	DATA	DESCENDING
ASSIGN	COBOL	74 DATE	74 DESTINATION
AT	CODE	DATE-COMPILED	DETAIL
AUTHOR	74 CODE-SET	DATE-WRITTEN	74 DISABLE

DISPLAY	INDEX	OBJECT-COMPUTER	REPORTING
DIVIDE	INDEXED	OCCURS	REPORTS
DIVISION	INDICATE	OF	RERUN
DOWN	74 INITIAL	OFF	RESERVE
74 DUPLICATES	INITIATE	OMITTED	RESET
74 DYNAMIC	INPUT	ON	RETURN
	INPUT-OUTPUT	OPEN	REVERSED
74 EGI	74 INSPECT	OPTIONAL	REWIND
ELSE	INSTALLATION	OR	74 REWRITE
74 EMI	INTO	74 ORGANIZATION	RF
74 ENABLE	INVALID	OUTPUT	RH
END	IS	74 OVERFLOW	RIGHT
END-OF-PAGE			ROUNDED
ENTER	JUSTIFIED	PAGE	RUN
ENVIRONMENT		PAGE-COUNTER	
74 EOP	KEY	PERFORM	SAME
EQUAL		PF	SD
ERROR	LABEL	PH	SEARCH
74 ESI	LAST	PICTURE	SECTION
EVERY	LEADING	PLUS	SECURITY
68 EXAMINE	LEFT	74 POINTER	68 SEEK
74 EXCEPTION	74 LENGTH	POSITION	74 SEGMENT
EXIT	LESS	POSITIVE	SEGMENT-LIMIT
74 EXTEND	LIMIT	74 PRINTING	SELECT
	LIMITS	PROCEDURE	74 SEND
FD	74 LINAGE	74 PROCEDURES	SENTENCE
FILE	74 LINAGE-COUNTER	PROCEED	74 SEPARATE
FILE-CONTROL	LINE	68 PROCESSING	74 SEQUENCE
68 FILE-LIMIT	LINE-COUNTER	74 PROGRAM	SEQUENTIAL
68 FILE-LIMITS	LINES	PROGRAM-ID	SET
FILLER	74 LINKAGE		SIGN
FINAL	LOCK	74 QUEUE	SIZE
FIRST	LOW-VALUES	QUOTES	SORT
FOOTING			74 SORT-MERGE
FOR	MEMORY	RANDOM	SOURCE
FROM	74 MERGE	RD	SOURCE-COMPUTER
	74 MESSAGE	READ	SPACES
GENERATE	MODE	74 RECEIVE	SPECIAL-NAMES
GIVING	MODULES	RECORD	STANDARD
GO	MOVE	RECORDS	74 STANDARD-1
GREATER	MULTIPLE	REDEFINES	74 START
GROUP	MULTIPLY	REEL	STATUS
		74 REFERENCES	STOP
HEADING	74 NATIVE	74 RELATIVE	74 STRING
HIGH-VALUES	NEGATIVE	RELEASE	74 SUB-QUEUE-1
	NEXT	REMAINDER	74 SUB-QUEUE-2
I-O	NO	68 REMARKS	74 SUB-QUEUE-3
I-O-CONTROL	NOT	74 REMOVAL	SUBTRACT
IDENTIFICATION	68 NOTE	RENAMES	SUM
IF	NUMBER	REPLACING	74 SUPPRESS
IN	NUMERIC	REPORT	

74 SYMBOLIC	74 TIME	USAGE	WRITE
SYNCHRONIZED	TIMES	USE	ZERO
	TO	USING	ZEROES
74 TABLE	74 TOP		
68 TALLY	74 TRAILING	VALUE	+
TALLYING	TYPE	VALUES	−
TAPE		VARYING	*
74 TERMINAL	UNIT		/
TERMINATE	74 UNSTRING	WHEN	**
74 TEXT	UNTIL	WITH	>
THAN	UP	WORDS	<
THROUGH	UPON	WORKING-STORAGE	=

Most COBOL implementations have additional reserved words, to suit the needs of their extensions to the language. The reader is encouraged to become aware of them, since the names chosen for variables must not be identical with any reserved word. This is somewhat of a nuisance, since some of the reserved words (e.g., **PAGE**) are natural candidates for variable names.

All variables used in a COBOL program must be declared within the program's Data Division. A variable may occur by itself, as an entry within a table (i.e., array), or as an element within a data structure (i.e., a field within a record). Accordingly, a variable is declared in one of the following ways.

1. 77 data-name description

2. level data-name description

Form 1 is used when a variable occurs as an independent item, while form 2 is used when it occurs either as an entry within a table or as an element within a data structure. Here, "data-name" identifies the variable. "Description" denotes a series of so-called "clauses" which describe the range and kind of values the variable can contain. "Level" denotes a two-digit number which identifies the hierarchical level of the variable within the table or data structure.

There are a number of different clauses which can occur in a variable's description. Among them, the most important ones are the following.

Clause	Purpose
REDEFINES clause	Causes a variable to share the same storage as another variable. (See section 14.7.)
JUSTIFIED clause	Causes a nonnumeric variable's value to be right-justified (with blank-fill on the left) rather than left-justified. (See section 14.7.)
PICTURE clause	Identifies whether the variable will have numeric or nonnumeric values, as well as the range of values it can accommodate. It also may describe any editing characteristics (e.g., "$") that might be inserted when its value is printed.
USAGE clause	Identifies whether a numeric-valued variable will be used in calculations, and thus dictates how its value is stored internally.
VALUE clause	Causes an initial value to be assigned to the variable at the beginning of program execution.

Of these, the PICTURE clause is the most important, since it describes the nature of the variable. The PICTURE clause has the following general form.

PICTURE   **[IS]**   string

Here, "string" describes the variable's class (alphabetic, numeric, or alphanumeric), range of values, and other editing characteristics. It is written as a sequence of characters from the following list.

PICTURE character	Meaning
A	A single alphabetic (A–Z) or blank (Ƀ) character position.
B	A single blank character position.
S	A numeric sign (+ or −) position, which will not appear when the value is printed.
V	The position of a decimal point within a numeric value, which will not appear when the value is printed.
X	A single alphanumeric character position.
Z	A leading zero position in a numeric value which, if the digit is zero, will suppress its appearance when the value is printed.
9	A single decimal digit (0–9) position in a numeric value.
	The position of a decimal point within a numeric value, which will appear when the value is printed.
$	The position of a leading dollar sign to be printed with a numeric value.
—	A numeric sign position, which will appear as "−" when the value printed is negative, and as "Ƀ" otherwise.

A variable is said to be Alphabetic, Alphanumeric, Numeric, Alphanumeric Edited, or Numeric Edited according to the appearance of its **PICTURE** clause. These five classes are defined and illustrated in the following paragraphs.

Alphabetic variable: PICTURE string contains a sequence of A's, denoting that the variable can contain any nonnumeric value which has only alphabetic (A–Z) and/or blank (Ƀ) characters. The number of A's defines the length of any value that the variable may have. For example, that the variable named **TITLE** shall contain some fifteen-character alphabetic value is declared in either of the following two equivalent ways (assuming **TITLE** is not part of a table or other structure).

77 TITLE PIC AAAAAAAAAAAAAAA.

77 TITLE PIC A(15).

The value of **TITLE** may thus be any fifteen-character value, as long as it is composed of only blanks (Ƀ) and letters (A-Z). For example, **TITLE**'s value may be **"ANNUALƀREPORTƀƀ"**. The "*A(15)*" in the second version is simply a convenient way to abbreviate a sequence of 15 consecutive A's.

Alphanumeric variable: PICTURE string contains a sequence of X's, denoting that the variable can contain any nonnumeric value which has any alphabetic (A-Z), numeric (0-9), or special (Ƀ. +, *, etc.) characters. The number of X's defines the length of any value that the variable may have. For example, that the variable named **TITLE** shall contain instead *any* fifteen-character value is declared in either of the following two ways.

77 TITLE PIC XXXXXXXXXXXXXXX.
77 TITLE PIC X(15).

For example, **TITLE**'s value may be either "**ANNUALℓℓREPORTℓℓ**" or "**1975ℓℓREPORTℓℓℓℓ**" or any other fifteen-character value.

Numeric variable: PICTURE string contains a sequence of 9s, optionally headed by S and optionally containing V. The number of 9s denotes the number of decimal digits in the variable's value. The presence of S denotes that negative, as well as positive, values may be assigned to the variable. The position of V among the 9s denotes the (fixed) position of a decimal point in the variable's value. For example, that the variable named **GROSS-PAY** shall contain a numeric value in the range 0 to 99999.99, the variable I shall contain a numeric value in the range 0 to 999, and the variable **NET-INCOME** shall contain a value in the range −99999.99 to 99999.99 are declared in the following way (assuming that these variables are not part of a table or other structure).

77 GROSS-PAY	**PIC 99999V99.**
77 I	**PIC 999.**
77 NET-INCOME	**PIC S99999V99.**

Alphanumeric Edited variable: PICTURE string contains a sequence of the characters A, X, 9, and B. The variable's value is dictated by the particular sequence of A's, X's, and 9s in its PICTURE string, and additionally each occurrence of B indicates the presence of an embedded blank in the variable's value. For example, suppose the variable **TITLE** were declared as follows.

77 TITLE PIC 9999BA(10).

This says that **TITLE** may contain any fifteen-character string whose first four characters are numeric (0–9), whose fifth character is blank (ℓ), and whose remaining characters are alphabetic (A–Z) or blank (ℓ). Thus, **TITLE** may again have the value "**1975ℓREPORTℓℓℓℓ**".

Numeric Edited variable: PICTURE string contains a sequence of the following characters.

B V Z 9 . − $

The meanings of **B**, **V**, and **9** are the same as above. Additionally, one or more leading 9s in the PICTURE string may be written as Z's, to indicate suppression of leading zeros when the value is printed. Similarly, the occurrence of V in the PICTURE string may be replaced by . to indicate the position of the decimal point which additionally will appear when the value is printed. The $ may be written at the left of the leftmost 9 or Z to indicate printing of a dollar sign. Additional dollar signs may be written in place of leading 9s or Z's to indicate a dollar sign which will "float" immediately to the left of the leftmost nonzero (significant) digit when the value is printed. Finally, − may be written at the extreme left of the PICTURE string to denote insertion of ℓ or − on the left of the printed value as it is nonnegative or negative, respectively. Too, − is similar to S in the numeric variable's picture, in the sense that it permits the variable to have negative, as well as nonnegative, values. For example, suppose that **GROSS-PAY** and **NET-INCOME** were to contain the same range of values as described above, but were to be displayed with decimal points. Additionally, suppose that leading zeros were to be suppressed (replaced by ƀ) in the display of **NET-INCOME,** and that a "floating" dollar sign were to be displayed immediately before the leftmost significant digit of **GROSS-PAY.** Then they would be declared as follows.

77 GROSS-PAY   PIC $$$$$$.99
77 NET-INCOME PIC −ZZZZZ.99.

If the value of **GROSS-PAY** were, for example, 03571.52 then it would be displayed as ƀ$3571.52. If the value of **NET-INCOME** were −00025.53 then it would be printed as −ƀƀƀ25.53. We should note that the sign − may also be designated to float by using the same convention used for $.

There are many variations available for describing a variable's range of values and editing characteristics. We have illustrated here only the most common ones.

The **USAGE** clause may be written for a variable to specify the manner in which its value is represented in storage. It has the following form.

$$[\text{USAGE} \quad [\text{IS}]] \begin{Bmatrix} \textbf{DISPLAY} \\ \textbf{COMPUTATIONAL} \\ \textbf{INDEX} \end{Bmatrix}$$

If the **DISPLAY** alternative is chosen, then the variable's value will be stored in exactly the form that it will be printed. If the **COMPUTATIONAL** alternative is chosen, then the variable must be Numeric (as indicated by its **PICTURE** clause). In that case, its value will be stored in binary form. If the **INDEX** alternative is chosen, then the variable must be Numeric and can be used only in a restricted way. If, on the other hand, the **USAGE** clause is omitted, then it is assumed to be **DISPLAY.**

The **VALUE** clause is used when a variable is to be initialized to a constant value at the beginning of the program's execution. This does not, of course, prevent the variable's value from being altered later on. It has the following general form.

VALUE [IS] literal

Here, "literal" denotes either a numeric literal (if the variable's **PICTURE** is Numeric or Numeric Edited), a nonnumeric literal (if the variable's **PICTURE** is otherwise), or a figurative constant.

For example, suppose the above variables named **TITLE, I,** and **GROSS-PAY** were to be initialized with the values "ANNUALƀREPORTƀƀ", 0, and 3571.52, respectively, at the beginning of execution. Suppose additionally that the variable I were to be used heavily in arithmetic calculations. Then they would be declared as follows.

77 TITLE   PIC X(15) VALUE "ANNUAL₿REPORT₿₿".
77 I   PIC 999   VALUE 0 COMP.
77 GROSS-PAY PIC $$$$$$.99 VALUE "₿$3571.52".

The reader should note here that the **PICTURE** and **VALUE** clauses have been written in their abbreviated form in all three declarations, while the **USAGE** clause has also been abbreviated in the second declaration.

COBOL provides two ways in which a single data name may be associated with more than one value. One is the so-called "table," and the other is the so-called "record description entry."

A table is a one-, two-, or three-dimensional collection of values, all of which have the same characteristics. Consider, for example, Fig. 14-1, in which table A is a one-dimensional table (or, simply, a list) of five entries, each a three-digit nonnegative integer, and table B is a two-dimensional table with five rows and four entries in each row, each entry a two-digit integer. The particular values stored in A and B are illustrative, and of no consequence to the following discussion.

A			B			
006			17	42	00	−10
035			18	03	00	−11
217			19	47	19	−12
001			20	48	49	22
023			00	00	−2	−3

FIG. 14-1

A one-dimensional table is declared in the following way.

>   01 table-name.
>   02 entry-name description **OCCURS** clause.

A two-dimensional table is declared in the following way.

>   01 table-name.
>   02 row-name **OCCURS** clause.
>   03 entry-name description **OCCURS** clause.

A three-dimensional table is declared in the following way.

>   01 table-name.
>   02 row-name **OCCURS** clause.
>   03 column-name **OCCURS** clause.
>   04 entry-name description **OCCURS** clause.

In each of these cases, "table-name" denotes any unique user-defined word which names the table, while "description" denotes the particular clauses (e.g., **PICTURE** clause) which describe the nature of a typical entry in the table. These are written exactly as they would be for an ordinary 77-level (single-valued) variable. "Row-name," "column-name," and "entry-name" denote user-defined words which name a table's typical row, column, and single entry.

"**OCCURS** clause" is used to define the number of elements in each dimension of the table. It has the following two forms.

1. **OCCURS** integer **[TIMES]** **[INDEXED [BY]** indices]
2. **OCCURS** integer-1 **TO** integer-2 **[TIMES]**
   [DEPENDING [ON] data-name]
   [INDEXED [BY] indices]

Here, "integer" denotes the number of entries in the dimension where the **OCCURS** clause appears. "Integer-1" and "integer-2" denote lower and upper bounds for the number of entries in a given dimension, in the event that that number varies during program execution. When the **"DEPENDING ON"** option of form 2 is used, then the value of "data-name" defines the dimension's current number of entries throughout program execution. "Data name" itself must be separately defined as a Numeric variable. The **"INDEXED BY"** option is used when an entry in the table is referenced by one or more variables whose usage is **INDEX**. These variables' names are then listed as "indices" within that option.

Returning to our example tables, we can declare **A** and **B** (but not their indicated values) as follows.

> **01 TABLE-A.**
> **02 A PIC 999 OCCURS 5.**
> **01 TABLE-B.**
> **02 ROW-B OCCURS 5.**
> **03 B OCCURS 4 PIC S99.**

The declaration of **B** illustrates also that the **OCCURS** clause may precede, as well as follow, the **PICTURE** clause.

The values shown in the diagrams for **A** and **B** cannot be initialized from within **A**'s or **B**'s declaration. The **VALUE** clause can be used to initialize an array, but only if all entries are to have the same value and, in addition, all entries have **USAGE DISPLAY** (as opposed to **COMP** or **INDEX**). Thus, initialization of arrays is usually deferred to the Procedure Division.

An ordinary variable's value is referenced from within the Procedure Division by simply giving that variable's name. However, an entry in a table is referenced from within the Procedure Division in one of two ways, depending on whether or not the table is indexed (i.e., contains an **"INDEXED BY"** option in its declaration).

If the table is not indexed, then an individual entry is referenced using "subscripts" as follows.

> entry-name ƀ (subscript [,ƀ subscript][,ƀ subscript])

Here, "entry-name" denotes the name of an individual entry in the table's declaration (e.g., **A** and **B** are the entry-names in our declarations). The number of "subscripts" given must agree with the number (1, 2, or 3) of dimensions in the table's declaration. The symbol "ƀ" indicates the requirement for exactly one blank in the locations indicated. Each subscript must be either a numeric literal or the name of a Numeric variable. The subscript's value must be within the range permitted by the **OCCURS** clause for that dimension.

For example, when referring to the third element in the table **A**, we would write the following.

$$A \, \not{b} \, (3)$$

When referring to the Ith entry in **A**, we would write the following.

$$A \, \not{b} \, (I)$$

Here **I** must be a Numeric variable whose value is 1, 2, 3, 4, or 5 (since **A** has 5 elements).

Similarly, when referring to the item in the third row and second column of **B**, we would write the following.

$$B \, \not{b} \, (3, \not{b} \, 2)$$

The item in the Ith row and Jth column of **B** is referenced by

$$B \, \not{b} \, (I, \not{b} \, J)$$

where **I** and **J** must be Numeric variables whose values are in the ranges 1, 2, 3, 4, or 5 and 1, 2, 3, or 4, respectively.

If, on the other hand, the table is indexed, then an individual element in the table may additionally be referenced by a similar expression, having the following form.

$$\text{entry-name} \, \not{b} \, (\text{index-name} \, [\not{b} \, \{\pm\} \, \not{b} \, \text{integer}]$$
$$[, \not{b} \, \text{index-name} \, [\not{b} \, \{\pm\} \, \not{b} \, \text{integer}]]$$
$$[, \not{b} \, \text{index-name} \, [\not{b} \, \{\pm\} \, \not{b} \, \text{integer}]]$$

Here, "entry-name" again denotes the name of an individual entry in the table's declaration, and the number of occurrences of "index-name" is the same as the number of dimensions (1, 2, or 3) in the table.

Suppose, for example, that table **B** were redeclared as follows.

01 TABLE-B.
    02 ROW-B OCCURS 5 INDEXED BY I.
        03 B OCCURS 4 PIC S99 INDEXED BY J.

Here, **B** represents the same configuration (5 $\times$ 4) of the same kinds of values as in its previous declaration. However, the variables **I** and **J** are identified as "indices" for referencing a row and column, respectively, in **B**. Now, **I** and **J** must have values in the range 1 to 5 and 1 to 4, respectively, when they are used as indices to reference a single element in **B**. Again the expression

$$B \, \not{b} \, (I, \not{b} \, J)$$

references the item in the Ith row and Jth column of **B**.

A bit more flexibility is available when indices are used instead of subscripts to reference an item in a table. For instance, the expression

$$B\not{b}(I\not{b}+\not{b}1, \not{b}J\not{b}-\not{b}2)$$

references the entry in the **I** + 1st row and **J** — 2d column of **B**. Again, this is valid only if **I** + 1 is in the range 1 to 5 and **J** — 2 is in the range 1 to 4.

A record description entry is the description of a structured collection of individual variables which generally are not all of the same type. For example, we may describe a record named **PERSON** as a collection of four variables; a twenty-five-character alphanumeric **NAME,** a nine-digit numeric social security number (**SS-NO**), a numeric **GROSS-PAY** in the range 0 to 99999.99, and a forty-character alphanumeric **PADDRESS.** (Recall that the preferred name, **ADDRESS,** is a reserved word, and thus cannot be used for this purpose.) A set of sample data for one **PERSON** appears in Fig. 14-2. This particular exam-

ALLEN ♭ B. ♭ TUCKER ♭♭♭♭♭♭♭♭♭♭

275407437

25400.00

1800 ♭ BULL ♭ RUN, ♭ ALEXANDRIA, ♭ VA. ♭ 22200 ♭♭♭♭

FIG. 14-2

ple shows two levels of structure; at the elementary level are four variables, and at a higher level is the variable **PERSON,** which includes all four as subordinates. Another way to picture a record description entry is in the form of a tree. There, the name (e.g., **PERSON**) of the record description entry is the "root" of the tree, and the individual elements are its "leaves." This is illustrated in Fig. 14-3 for the example.

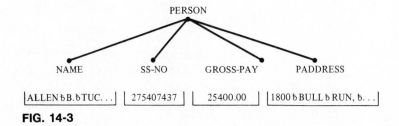

FIG. 14-3

To define a record description entry in COBOL, one writes "level numbers" prefixed to the various names in the structure. The name of the entire structure (e.g., **PERSON**) is prefixed by level number 01, the names of all items at the next level are prefixed by level number 02, and so on. Within an individual level, names are listed from left to right. Thus, the above structure could be defined in the following way.

```
01 PERSON.
    02 NAME          PIC X(25).
    02 SS-NO         PIC 9(9).
    02 GROSS-PAY     PIC 9(5)V99.
    02 PADDRESS      PIC X(40).
```

Note also that each individual item of a record description entry must be terminated by a period (.), and that the elementary items are the only ones which have a **PICTURE** clause.

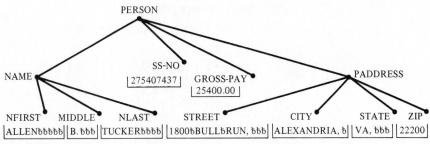

FIG. 14-4

Some of the variables at level 02 in this example can themselves be structured. The tree in Fig. 14-4 shows how **NAME** can be subdivided into three items and **PADDRESS** into four. If this were done, then we would have the following corresponding record description entry.

```
01 PERSON.
    02 NAME.
        03 NFIRST      PIC X(10).
        03 MIDDLE      PIC X(5).
        03 NLAST       PIC X(10).
    02 SS-NO           PIC 9(9).
    02 GROSS-PAY       PIC 9(5)V99.
    02 PADDRESS.
        03 STREET      PIC X(17).
        03 CITY        PIC X(12).
        03 STATE       PIC X(6).
        03 ZIP         PIC 9(5).
```

The reader should notice again that only those variables which are not themselves subdivided have **PICTURE** clauses. These are known as the "elementary items," and correspond to the leaves in the tree description. The other items in a record description entry are known as "group items." In this example, **PERSON, NAME,** and **PADDRESS** are group items.

To reference an entire record description entry from within the Procedure Division of a COBOL program, one simply gives that entry's name, which appears at the 01 level. For instance, to reference the entire collection of values defined in the above example, one uses the name **PERSON.** Thus, all record description entries within a single COBOL program must have mutually unique names (i.e., unique at the 01 level).

However, names at subordinate levels (e.g., 02, 03, etc.), within a record description entry may be identical with subordinate names of another record description entry. Suppose, for example, that we wanted to simultaneously store the **NAME, SS-NO, GROSS-PAY,** and **PADDRESS** of two different persons, say **PERSON-A** and **PERSON-B.** Then we would write the following record description entries.

```
01 PERSON-A.
   02 NAME        PIC X(25).
   02 SS-NO       PIC 9(9).
   02 GROSS-PAY   PIC 9(5)V99.
   02 PADDRESS    PIC X(40).
01 PERSON-B.
   02 NAME        PIC X(25).
   02 SS-NO       PIC 9(9).
   02 GROSS-PAY   PIC 9(5)V99.
   02 PADDRESS    PIC X(40).
```

To reference, for example, the **SS-NO** of **PERSON-A,** one writes a "qualified reference" as follows.

SS-NO OF PERSON-A

If, on the other hand, we wanted to reference **PERSON-B's SS-NO,** we would write the following.

SS-NO OF PERSON-B

It should be evident that such qualification is necessary only when the indicated name (**SS-NO,** in this case) is not unique. If it were unique, then the name itself would be adequate to unambiguously reference the item.

We note also that a table can occur within a record description entry, as well as by itself. For example, suppose that we wanted to store the last five addresses for each **PERSON,** rather than just the current one. Then we could rewrite the record description entry for a person as follows.

```
01 PERSON.
   02 NAME      PIC X(25).
   02 SS-NO     PIC 9(9).
   02 GROSS-PAYPIC 9(5)V99.
   02 PADDRESS PIC X(40) OCCURS 5.
```

The use of subscripts, indices, and qualification for tables occurring in this way is exactly the same as described in the foregoing paragraphs. Finally, a reference to any unique data item, whether it occurs alone, within a table, or at the elementary level of a record description entry, is known in COBOL as an "identifier."

14-3 COBOL STATEMENTS

We will not discuss all of the COBOL statements in this chapter, because of the importance of focusing attention on the most widely used ones. The ones we will cover are listed in the following table, together with a brief description of their purpose in a COBOL program.

Statement	Purpose
ADD statement SUBTRACT statement MULTIPLY statement DIVIDE statement COMPUTE statement	To perform one or more arithmetic (add, subtract, . . .) operations and then assign the result as the new value of a variable or table entry.
CALL statement EXIT PROGRAM statement	To initiate execution of a subprogram, and to return control from the subprogram to the calling program, respectively. These are discussed in section 14.5.
CLOSE statement DELETE statement OPEN statement READ statement REWRITE statement WRITE statement	To perform the various input-output operations. These are discussed in section 14.4.
COPY statement	To cause insertion of source text from a library into a COBOL program at compile time. This is discussed in section 14.7.
GENERATE statement INITIATE statement TERMINATE statement	To aid in the generation of reports. These are discussed in section 14.7.
GO TO statement IF statement	To alter the sequence of program statement execution.
INSPECT statement SEARCH statement SET statement	To search a character string or table.
MERGE statement RELEASE statement RETURN statement SORT statement	To sort a file or merge two files. These are discussed in section 14.7.
MOVE statement STRING statement UNSTRING statement	To move, concatenate, or separate data values, respectively.
PERFORM statement	To control repeated execution of a group of statements.
STOP statement	To terminate program execution.

In the remainder of this section we will discuss all statements listed above which are not designated for discussion in another section. To begin our discussion, consider the simple COBOL program in Fig. 14-5. In spite of its practical uselessness, this program does illustrate many of the basic COBOL statement types.

Every COBOL program contains four divisions, whose purposes were described above. The four divisions must appear in the order indicated in this sample program. Each division begins with its "division header" (such as **IDENTIFICATION DIVISION.**), which identifies its beginning.

The reader should recognize the declarations of variables (**H, I,** and **J**), record description entry (**PERSON**), and tables (**A** and **B**) within the Data Division. The statements which actually control program execution occur within the Procedure Division. The reader should note also a fairly rigid syntactic structure in this program.

Let us focus attention for a moment on this program's Procedure Division. In general, it may consist of one or more "sections." Each section consists of one or more "paragraphs," and each paragraph consists of one or more "statements."

```
         IDENTIFICATION DIVISION.
           PROGRAM-ID. SIMPLE.
         ENVIRONMENT DIVISION.
           CONFIGURATION SECTION.
             SOURCE-COMPUTER. IBM-370-145.
             OBJECT-COMPUTER. IBM-370-145.
         DATA DIVISION.
           WORKING-STORAGE SECTION.
           77 H PIC 9(5) COMP.
           77 I PIC 9(5) COMP.
           77 J PIC 9(5) COMP.
           01 ARRAY-A.
             02 A PIC 999 OCCURS 5.
           01 ARRAY-B.
             02 ROW-B OCCURS 5.
               03 B PIC S99 OCCURS 4.
           01 PERSON.
             02 NAME PIC X(25).
             02 SS-NO PIC 9(9).
             02 GROSS-PAY PIC 9(5)V99.
         PROCEDURE DIVISION.
         *  THIS PROGRAM DOES LITTLE MORE THAN ILLUSTRATE SOME OF
         *  COBOL'S BASIC STATEMENTS.
             PERFORM S1 VARYING I FROM 1 BY 1 UNTIL I = 5.
         S1. COMPUTE A (I) = 6 - I.
         S2. MOVE 1 TO H.
         LOOP. IF H < 6 THEN
                 MOVE 1 TO B (H, 1)
                 COMPUTE B (H, 2) = 5 + 3 * (4 - A (H))
                 ADD 1 TO H
                 GO TO LOOP.
             PERFORM S3 VARYING I FROM 1 BY 1 UNTIL I = 5.
         S3. MOVE A (I) TO B (I, 3).
             COMPUTE B (I, 4) = B (I, 1) + B (I, 2) + B (I, 3).
         S4. MOVE 'ALLEN B. TUCKER' TO NAME.
             MOVE 25400.00 TO GROSS-PAY.
             STOP RUN.
```

FIG. 14-5

A section is always begun by a "section header," which has the following form.

section-name **SECTION.**

Here, "section-name" names the section and may be any unique, nonreserved, user-defined word. In the special case that the Procedure Division has only one section, its section header may be omitted. This is the case for our sample program.

A "paragraph" always has the following form.

paragraph-name. sentence-sequence

Here, "paragraph-name" names the paragraph and may be any unique, non-reserved, user-defined word. "Sentence-sequence" denotes a sequence of sentences which comprise the paragraph. The end of a paragraph is delimited by the beginning of the next paragraph (or by the end of the program if there are no more paragraphs). The example program's Procedure Division contains five paragraphs, named **S1, S2, LOOP, S3,** and **S4.**

A sentence is a sequence of one or more statements, and is always terminated by a period (.) and a space (ƀ). Each of the example program's first two paragraphs contains one sentence, which contains one statement. Its third paragraph contains two sentences; the first contains five statements (**IF, MOVE, COMPUTE, ADD,** and **GO TO**) and the second contains one statement. The fourth paragraph contains two sentences and the fifth contains three.

Section and paragraph names, as well as the Procedure Division header itself, must begin in a tab position (called "Area A") to the left of that (called "Area B") for sentences which are not prefixed by a paragraph name. Furthermore, section headers and the Procedure Division header must appear on a line by themselves.

The GO TO Statement

The statements in a COBOL program are generally executed in the order in which they are written, unless a statement which can alter that order is encountered. One such statement is the **GO TO** statement, which has either of the following general forms.

    1. GO TO procedure-name
    2. GO TO procedure-name-list **DEPENDING [ON]** identifier

Here, "procedure-name" denotes any paragraph-name or section-name appearing in the Procedure Division. "Procedure-name-list" denotes a list of one or more (say **n**) procedure-names, which are mutually separated by comma-space (,ʙ). "Identifier" denotes the name of an elementary Numeric variable which can have integer values only.

When executed, form 1 of the **GO TO** statement causes control to pass directly to the first statement within the first sentence of the paragraph or section having the indicated procedure-name. In the example program, execution of the **GO TO** statement

GO TO LOOP

causes control to pass to the statement beginning "**IF H < 6 THEN . . .**" since it is the first one in the paragraph named **LOOP.**

Form 2 of the **GO TO** statement causes control to pass directly to the beginning of the first, second, . . . , or **n**th named paragraph (or section) in the procedure-name-list depending on whether the current value of identifier is 1, 2, . . . , or **n**, espectively. If, on the other hand, the current value of identifier is not within this range, the next statement following the **GO TO** statement is executed. Form 2 is not illustrated in the example program.

The STOP Statement

The **STOP** statement causes program execution to cease. It has the following form.

STOP RUN

The **STOP** statement is not necessarily the last statement in the program. Its position(s) in the Procedure Division is (are) dictated by the logical point(s) where program execution could cease. The only **STOP** statement in the example program is its last statement.

Arithmetic Expressions

Arithmetic expressions are used in a COBOL program to designate that a certain series of arithmetic computations (e.g., add, subtract, . . .) take place. They occur in the **COMPUTE** statement and in the **IF** statement.

An arithmetic expression may be any one of the following.

1. A Numeric elementary variable name
2. A numeric literal
3. Two arithmetic expressions separated by an "arithmetic operator"
4. An arithmetic expression enclosed in parentheses.

The "arithmetic operators" and their meanings appear in the following list.

Arithmetic operator	Meaning
+	Addition
−	Subtraction
*	Multiplication
/	Division
**	Exponentiation

Each of these operators always operates on two values, the one at its left and the one at its right. For instance, the arithmetic expression

$$H + 2$$

denotes addition of the value of the variable named **H** and (the numeric literal) 2.

When two or more arithmetic operations are specified, they are executed sequentially. For instance, if we wanted to add the value of **I** to the sum **H** + 2, then we would write the following (omitting the numbered arrows).

$$H + 2 + I$$
$$\uparrow \quad \uparrow$$
$$① \quad ②$$

Here, the addition **H** + 2 takes place first, and the addition of that sum and the value of **I** takes place second, as shown by the numbered arrows.

A series of two or more operations within an arithmetic expression is generally carried out from left to right, with the following two exceptions. First, there is a hierarchy among the operators, as follows. All exponentiations (**) are performed first (from left to right), all multiplications (*) and divisions (/) are performed second (from left to right), and finally all additions (+) and subtractions (−) are performed (from left to right). This means that

$$H + 2 * I$$
$$\uparrow \quad \uparrow$$
$$② \quad ①$$

denotes the sum of **H** and 2 * **I**, rather than the product of **H** + 2 and **I**.

Second, whenever the ordering thus defined is not desired, the programmer may override it by enclosing in parentheses the operations he wants performed first. For instance, to specify the product of **H** + 2 and **I**, the programmer writes the following.

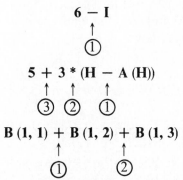

The following three arithmetic expressions appear in the example program's Procedure Division.

The reader should notice the very careful spacing that has been used in writing these arithmetic expressions. That is not accidental. COBOL requires that at least one blank space (ƀ) both precede and follow every arithmetic operator within an arithmetic expression. Thus, for instance,

$$6-I \text{ and } 6 - I$$

are not equivalent, and only the latter is legal.

Arithmetic Statements

The five COBOL arithmetic statements are the **ADD, SUBTRACT, MUL-TIPLY, DIVIDE,** and **COMPUTE** statements. These statements have the following options in common.

ROUNDED option
SIZE ERROR option

These options will be discussed and illustrated at the end of this section.

The **ADD** statement may be written in either of the following forms.

1. **ADD** value-list **TO** identifier-list **[ROUNDED]**
   [SIZE ERROR option]
2. **ADD** value, value-list **GIVING** identifier-list **[ROUNDED]**
   [SIZE ERROR option]

Here, "value-list" denotes a list of one or more Numeric identifiers and/or numeric literals, mutually separated by comma-blank (,ƀ). "Identifier-list" denotes a list of one or more Numeric identifiers, mutually separated by comma-blank (,ƀ). "Value" denotes a single Numeric identifier or literal.

Execution of form 1 leaves in each identifier of "identifier-list" the result of adding to its current value the sum of all the values in "value-list." The example program contains an illustration of form 1 as follows.

ADD 1 TO H

Here, "value-list" has only one value, which is added to the current value of the variable named **H** (the only member of "variable-list").

Execution of form 2 leaves in each identifier of "identifier-list" the result of adding the identifier or literal "value" and the sum of the identifiers and literals in "value-list." The previous value of each identifier in "identifier-list" need not, therefore, play a role in this calculation. Although form 2 is not illustrated in the example program, the following statement is equivalent to the example of form 1 shown above.

ADD 1, H GIVING H

The **SUBTRACT** statement may be written in either of the following forms.

1. **SUBTRACT** value-list **FROM** identifier-list **[ROUNDED]**
    [**SIZE ERROR** option]
2. **SUBTRACT** value-list **FROM** identifier **[ROUNDED]**
    GIVING identifier-list
    [**SIZE ERROR** option]

Here, "value-list" and "identifier-list" have the same denotations as they did in the **ADD** statement.

Execution of form 1 leaves in each identifier of "identifier-list" the result of subtracting from its current value the sum of all the values in "value-list." For example,

SUBTRACT 1 FROM I

leaves as the new value of I the result of subtracting 1 from its current value.

Execution of form 2 leaves in each identifier of "identifier-list" the result of subtracting from the current value of "identifier" the sum of all the values in "value-list." The current value of "identifier," however, is not affected by this execution unless it appears also in "identifier-list." For example, to leave in the variable **H** the result of subtracting 1 from the variable **I**, one could write the following.

SUBTRACT 1 FROM I GIVING H

The current value of **I** here is not affected.

The **MULTIPLY** and **DIVIDE** statements have the following general forms, respectively.

MULTIPLY value-1 **BY** value-2 **[GIVING** identifier-3**]** **[ROUNDED]**
    [**SIZE ERROR** option]
DIVIDE value-1 **BY** value-2 **GIVING** identifier-3 **[ROUNDED]**
    [**REMAINDER** identifier-4]
    [**SIZE ERROR** option]

Here, "value-1" and "value-2" each denotes a Numeric identifier or numeric literal, while "identifier-3" and "identifier-4" denote Numeric identifiers.

Execution of the **MULTIPLY** statement leaves in identifier-3 the product of value-1 and value-2. If the optional "**GIVING** identifier-3" is omitted, then value-2 must be an identifier, and the product becomes that identifier's new value. For example,

MULTIPLY 3 BY H GIVING I

leaves in **I** the product of 3 and the current value of **H.** However,

MULTIPLY 3 BY H

leaves that product as the new value of **H**.

Execution of the **DIVIDE** statement leaves in identifier-3 the quotient of value-1 and value-2. Additionally, if the optional "**REMAINDER** identifier-4" is included, then the result of subtracting from value-1 the product of value-2 and the quotient is defined as the "remainder," and it is stored in identifier-4. For example,

DIVIDE 5 BY 2 GIVING I REMAINDER J

leaves in **I** the value 2 and in **J** the value 1.

The **COMPUTE** statement permits several arithmetic operations to be designated, with the result assigned to an identifier. It has the following general form.

COMPUTE identifier **[ROUNDED]** = arithmetic expression
[SIZE ERROR option]

Here, "identifier" denotes any Numeric identifier. Execution of the **COMPUTE** statement causes the numeric result of evaluating the arithmetic expression to become the new value of the identifier. For instance, the following **COMPUTE** statement appears in the example program.

COMPUTE A (I) = 6 − I

Execution of this statement leaves in the Ith entry of the table **A** the difference of 6 and **I**. It is equivalent, therefore, to the following **SUBTRACT** statement.

SUBTRACT I FROM 6 GIVING A (I)

The **ROUNDED** option allows rounding of the final result of an arithmetic operation before it is assigned to the identifier which is the "target" of the result. It may be used for any of the five arithmetic statements described above. It is specified by placing the reserved word **ROUNDED** immediately after those target identifiers for which the result should be rounded. We will illustrate this using the **MULTIPLY** statement, assuming that the following declarations have been made.

77 HOURS PIC 9(2)V9.
77 RATE PIC 9V99.
77 GROSS-PAY PIC 9(5)V99.

Suppose that we want to compute a person's **GROSS-PAY** as the product of the **HOURS** worked (say 37.5) and the **RATE** per hour (say $5.25), rounding to the nearest penny. Then we would write the following.

MULTIPLY HOURS BY RATE GIVING GROSS-PAY ROUNDED

This would leave **GROSS-PAY** at 196.88, the result of rounding the product 196.875 to two decimal places. Omission of the **ROUNDED** option would have left **GROSS-PAY** at 196.87. The decimal place to which rounding takes place is always the rightmost decimal digit of the target identifier.

A "size error condition" arises whenever the result of performing an arithmetic operation has more significant nondecimal digits than the number allowed by the target variable (as defined in its **PICTURE** clause). Furthermore, the size error condition arises whenever division by zero is attempted. For example, if **GROSS-PAY** had been declared with **PICTURE 9(2)V99** rather than **9(5)V99** and the above **MULTIPLY** statement had been executed, a size error condition would have been raised.

If the arithmetic statement in which a size error condition occurs does not contain a **SIZE ERROR** option, then the resulting value of the target identifier becomes undefined. On the other hand, the arithmetic statement may contain a **SIZE ERROR** option, which has the following general form.

[ON] SIZE ERROR statement

Here, "statement" denotes any imperative statement, such as a **GO TO** statement that would transfer control to an error-handling paragraph whenever the size error condition arises. If the arithmetic statement contains the **SIZE ERROR** option, then both the current value of the target identifier is not changed and "statement" is executed, whenever execution of that arithmetic statement causes the size error condition to arise. If that condition does not arise, execution of the statement proceeds normally. Continuing the example where **GROSS-PAY** is declared with **PICTURE 9(2)V99,** consider the following statement.

**MULTIPLY RATE BY HOURS GIVING GROSS-PAY
ON SIZE ERROR GO TO BAD-GROSS**

Execution of this statement will leave in **GROSS-PAY** the correct product of **RATE** and **HOURS,** provided it does not exceed 99.99. If that product does, however, exceed 99.99 then the size error condition will be raised and control will pass to the paragraph named **BAD-GROSS.**

Conditions and IF Statements

An **IF** statement is used to test whether a so-called "condition" is true or false, and then select the subsequent sequence of statement execution accordingly.

Conditions serve to specify relations that exist among variables and values. COBOL allows specification of conditions in a variety of ways. Conditions fall into the following categories.

Relations
Class conditions
Condition-name conditions
Sign conditions

A relation consists of any two arithmetic expressions (a and b) separated by a relational operator that must be preceded and followed by blank (Ƅ). The relational operators (op) and the meanings of "a op b" are as follows.

Relational operator (op)	Meaning of "a op b"
=	The values of a and b are equal
<	The value of a is less than the value of b
>	The value of a is greater than the value of b
NOT =	Either a < b or a > b (i.e., a ≠ b)
NOT <	Either a = b or a > b (i.e., a ≧ b)
NOT >	Either a < b or a = b (i.e., a ≦ b)

Evaluation of the relation "a op b" yields the value "true" or "false," respectively, as the meaning of "a op b" is or is not true. That is, the arithmetic expressions a and b are first evaluated, and the stated relation between these two values is tested (in the usual arithmetic sense). An illustration of a relation occurs in the example program as follows.

$$H < 6$$

Evaluation of this yields the value "true" exactly when the current value of **H** is less than 6.

A relation can also be written using nonnumeric literals and/or nonnumeric variables instead of arithmetic expressions. For example, to specify a test of whether or not the current value of **NAME** (as defined in the example program) is **"ALLEN B. TUCKER"** the following relation would suffice:

NAME = "ALLENƀB.ƀTUCKERƀƀƀƀƀƀƀƀƀ"

Evaluation of this delivers the value "true" or "false" as the current value of **NAME** is or is not identical (character by character) with the literal **"ALLENƀB.ƀTUCKERƀƀƀƀƀƀƀƀƀ"**.

The relations < and > are defined for nonnumeric values on the basis of an implementation dependent collating sequence among the characters in the COBOL character set. For example, **"A"** < **"B"** is true, **"B"** < **"C"** is true, and so forth. Now, for two nonnumeric literals, say **a** and **b**, the relation **"a"** < **"b"** is true if one of the following is true.

1. **a** and **b** have the same number of characters, the first **k** (for some **k** ≧ 0) characters in **a** are respectively identical with the first **k** characters in **b**, and the **k** + 1st character in **a** is less than the **k** + 1st character in **b**.

2. **a** and **b** do not have the same number of characters, but the result of extending the shorter of the two with enough blanks at its right to make their lengths identical leaves 1 true.

The relation **"a = b"** is similarly defined when the lengths of **a** and **b** are not identical. Thus, the following relation is equivalent to the one written above.

NAME = "ALLENƀB.ƀTUCKER"

The relation **"a > b"** for nonnumeric values is true whenever neither **"a < b"** nor **"a = b"** is true. The relations **"a NOT < b,"** **"a NOT = b,"** and **"a NOT > b"** are defined for nonnumeric values as they were for arithmetic expressions.

A class condition is used to test whether a value is numeric (composed entirely of digits and, possibly, signed) or whether a value is alphabetic (composed entirely of letters A–Z and/or spaces). It may be written as follows.

$$\text{identifier } \textbf{IS [NOT]} \begin{Bmatrix} \textbf{NUMERIC} \\ \textbf{ALPHABETIC} \end{Bmatrix}$$

Here, "identifier" denotes any identifier whose **USAGE** is **DISPLAY** (rather than **INDEX** or **COMPUTATIONAL**). Evaluation of a class condition yields the value "true" or "false" as identifier's current value does or does not satisfy the indicated test, respectively. For example, reconsider the variable **NAME** used above, and assume that it has the value **"ALLENƁB.ƁTUCKER"**. Then the conditions

NAME IS NUMERIC

NAME IS ALPHABETIC

both yield the value "false," since (1) the value of **NAME** is not a number, and (2) the value of **NAME** contains a character (specifically, ".") which is not alphabetic or blank.

A condition-name condition is used to test whether an elementary variable's current value satisfies a particular condition, as defined by a "condition-name" in the variable's declaration. This is done by following the variable's declaration immediately by an "88-level" condition-name declaration as follows.

88 condition-name **VALUE**-clause-list.

Here, "condition-name" denotes any unique nonreserved, user-defined word, while **"VALUE-clause-list"** denotes a sequence of one or more **"VALUE clauses"** which are mutually separated by comma-blank (,Ɓ). A **VALUE** clause has either of the following forms.

1. **VALUE [IS]** literal-1
2. **VALUES [ARE]** literal-1 **THROUGH** literal-2

Here, "literal-1" and "literal-2" denote any numeric or nonnumeric literal which is consistent with the variable's **PICTURE**.

For instance, suppose we redeclared **GROSS-PAY** in the example program as follows.

02 GROSS-PAY PIC 9(5)V99.
   88 LOW-PAY VALUES 0 THRU 6000.
   88 AVERAGE-PAY VALUE 10000.
   88 HIGH-PAY VALUES 20000 THRU 99999.

Here, we have defined three condition-names to be associated with the variable **GROSS-PAY**: **LOW-PAY**, **AVERAGE-PAY**, and **HIGH-PAY**. Each identifies a value, or range of values, for **GROSS-PAY** by an explicit name.

Now, the condition-name condition is written simply by stating any condition-name which has been defined for some variable. Its evaluation yields the value "true" or "false," respectively, as the current value of that condition-name's associated variable falls within the range of values identified by that condition name. For example, if the condition-name

LOW-PAY

is written, and the value of **GROSS-PAY** is currently 25400.00, then the value "false" will be returned. The condition-names **AVERAGE-PAY** and **HIGH-PAY** will yield the values "false" and "true," respectively, since only the range defined for **HIGH-PAY** is satisfied by the value 25400.

A sign condition is used to test whether the current value of an arithmetic expression is positive, negative, or zero. It has the following form.

$$\text{arithmetic expression } \textbf{IS [NOT]} \begin{cases} \textbf{POSITIVE} \\ \textbf{NEGATIVE} \\ \textbf{ZERO} \end{cases}$$

Evaluation of this condition yields the value "true" or "false," accordingly as the expression's value does or does not satisfy the indicated condition.

Finally, several of these conditions may be combined, using the logical operators **"AND"** and **"OR"**. Evaluation of

$$C_1 \textbf{ AND } C_2$$

where C_1 and C_2 denote any of the four kinds of conditions described above, yields the value "true" or "false" accordingly as both C_1 and C_2 are true or not. Similarly, "C_1 **OR** C_2" is "true" or "false" accordingly as either one or both of C_1 and C_2 are "false." **AND** has higher priority than **OR**, so that "C_1 **OR** C_2 **AND** C_3" means "C_1 **OR** (C_2 **AND** C_3)" rather than "(C_1 **OR** C_2) **AND** C_3". As suggested here, priority may be overridden by appropriate use of parentheses.

An **IF** statement may be written in one of the following ways.

1. **IF** condition statement-1
2. **IF** condition statement-1 **ELSE** statement-2

Here, "condition" denotes any of the conditions discussed above, while "statement-1" and "statement-2" each denotes any (sequence of) statement(s), containing at most one conditional statement.

Execution of form 1 proceeds in two major steps. First, the designated "condition" is evaluated. Second, if that result is "true" then control passes to the (first statement in the sequence of) statement(s) designated by "statement-1." Otherwise, control passes to the first statement of the next sentence textually following the IF statement.

Execution of form 2 proceeds also in two steps. First, the designated "condition" is evaluated. Second, control passes either to (the beginning of) "statement-1" or to (the beginning of) "statement-2," depending respectively on whether that result is "true" or "false."

An illustration of form 1 occurs in the example program, as follows.

Condition

LOOP. IF H < 6

Statement-1
$\left\{\begin{array}{l}\text{MOVE 1 to B (H, 1)}\\\text{COMPUTE B (H, 2) = 5 + 3 * (H − A (H))}\\\text{ADD 1 TO H}\\\text{GO TO LOOP.}\end{array}\right.$

Here, note that several statements make up "statement-1," and thus that control will pass to the first of them (**MOVE . . .**) if "**H < 6**" is true. Otherwise, control will bypass them all by going to the beginning of the next sentence.

The PERFORM Statement

Much of programming is concerned with the proper specification of controlled loops. COBOL provides the **PERFORM** statement as an aid to writing such loops.

A controlled loop is the repeated specification of statements until a certain condition becomes true. Many such loops are "counter-controlled," which means that a counting variable is initialized and then incremented and tested each time a sequence of statements is executed. This is pictured in two different forms in Fig. 14-6. Here, **i** denotes the control variable, while m_1, m_2, and m_3 denote Numeric variables or Numeric literals which are, respectively, the initial value, the limit value, and the increment value for the control variable. An illus-

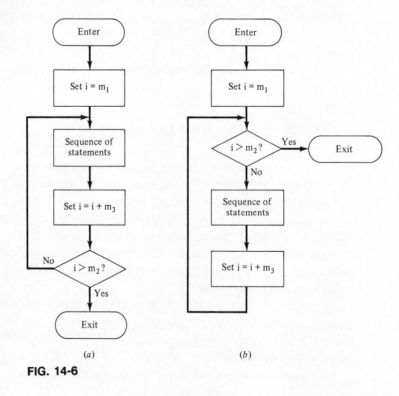

(a)   (b)

FIG. 14-6

tration of flowchart (b) is given in the example program. There, the control variable is **H,** its initial value is 1, its limit is 5, and its increment is 1.

Flowchart (b) can be written using the **PERFORM** statement as follows.

PERFORM procedure-name

VARYING i FROM m$_1$ BY m$_3$ UNTIL i $>$ m$_2$

procedure-name . . . | Sequence of statements |

For instance, the paragraphs named **S2** and **LOOP** in the example program can be equivalently rewritten using the **PERFORM** statement as follows.

S2.   **PERFORM LOOP VARYING H FROM 1 BY 1 UNTIL H $>$ 5.**
         GO TO LOOP-EXIT.
LOOP.   **MOVE 1 TO B (H, 1)**
         COMPUTE B (H, 2) = 5 + 3 * (H − A (H)).
LOOP-EXIT.   **EXIT.**

More generally, the **PERFORM** statement has several different forms. Some of them are as follows.

1. PERFORM pn-1 [**THROUGH** pn-2] [number **TIMES**]

2. PERFORM pn-1 [**THROUGH** pn-2] **UNTIL** condition-1

3. PERFORM pn-1 [**THROUGH** pn-2]
      VARYING i FROM m$_1$ BY m$_3$ UNTIL condition-1
      [**AFTER j FROM n$_1$ BY n$_3$ UNTIL** condition-2
      [**AFTER k FROM p$_1$ BY p$_3$ UNTIL** condition-3]]

Here, "pn-1" and "pn-2" denote procedure names, and "number" denotes an integer-valued variable or integer constant. "Condition-1," "condition-2," and "condition-3" denote arbitrary conditions, i, j, and k denote Numeric variables, while m$_1$, m$_3$, n$_1$, n$_3$, p$_1$, and p$_3$ each denotes a Numeric variable or Numeric literal.

Execution of form 1, without either of the two indicated options, causes execution of all statements in the paragraph or section named "pn-1," after which control passes to the next statement following the **PERFORM** statement.

In fact, execution of all forms of the **PERFORM** statement finally return control to the next statement following it. If the "**THROUGH** pn-2" option is used in any of these forms, then all sections or paragraphs from the one named "pn-1" to the one named "pn-2," inclusive, are executed. If the "number **TIMES**" option is used in form 1, the designated pn's are executed the number of times dictated by "number."

Execution of form 2 causes repeated execution of the designated pn's until "condition" becomes true. The condition is reevaluated before each execution of the pn's, so that the pn's may be executed zero times.

Execution of form 3 without any of the options shown is as depicted by flowchart (b), with the test in Fig. 14-7 replaced by the one in Fig. 14-8. If one or both of the options are included in form 3, then two or three "nested" loops

FIG. 14-7   **FIG. 14-8**

would be described. Here, the variable i would vary least frequently and k would vary most frequently. For example,

PERFORM LOOP VARYING H FROM 1 BY 1 UNTIL H > 5
AFTER I FROM 1 BY 1 UNTIL I > 2
AFTER J FROM 1 BY 1 UNTIL J > 3

would cause the paragraph named **LOOP** to be executed $5 \times 2 \times 3 = 30$ times. The sequence of values of **H, I,** and **J,** as execution of **LOOP** repeats, are as follows.

Step	1	2	3	4	5	6	7	...	30
H	1	1	1	1	1	1	2	...	5
I	1	1	1	2	2	2	1	...	2
J	1	2	3	1	2	3	1	...	3

Immediately before the 31st execution of **LOOP, J, I,** and **H** would be incremented beyond their limit values, in that order, and control would thus pass to the next statement following the **PERFORM** statement.

Note that if the statement itself marks the beginning of the paragraph that had been **PERFORM**ed, then it will be executed once more than the number of times designated by the **PERFORM** statement. For that reason, we inserted the statement **"GO TO LOOP-EXIT"** and the paragraph name **"LOOP-EXIT"** in the previous example. Equivalently, we could have eliminated that **GO TO** statement by a slight change in the condition for exit, as follows.

S2.   PERFORM LOOP VARYING H FROM 1 BY 1 UNTIL H = 5.
LOOP. MOVE ...
COMPUTE ...
LOOP-EXIT. EXIT.

The need for **LOOP-EXIT** still exists, however, in order to delimit the end of the paragraph.

The MOVE Statement

The **MOVE** statement, when executed, causes one or more values to become the new value(s) of one or more variables. It has the following basic form.

MOVE value **TO** identifier-list

Here, "value" denotes either an identifier or a literal, while "identifier-list" denotes a list of one or more identifiers which are mutually separated by comma-space (‚ƀ). "Identifier-1" and "identifier-2" denote identifiers.

Execution of the **MOVE** statement causes "value" to become the new value of each identifier in "identifier-list." For instance, the **MOVE** statement

MOVE 1 TO H

in the example program causes the variable **H** to have the value 1.

On the other hand, "value" and "identifier-list" may designate group items, rather than elementary items. In this case, each one should be identically structured, so that the result of the **MOVE** is identical with that which would occur if it were replaced by a sequence of **MOVE** statements, one for each pair of corresponding elementary items in the two groups.

When "value" and "identifier-list" designate elementary items, then they should belong to the same category. That is, they should either be both numeric or both nonnumeric (i.e., alphabetic, alphanumeric, or alphanumeric edited). For instance, in **"MOVE 1 TO H"** both 1 and **H** are numeric.

Furthermore, whenever an identifier in "identifier-list" has a **PICTURE** which is not the same as that of "value," then conversion of "value" takes place before it is **MOVE**d to the identifier. Conversion from one numeric value to another is accomplished by decimal point alignment, adding leading zeros to or truncating leading digits from "value," and adding decimal zeros or truncating decimal digits from "value," as required by identifier's **PICTURE**. Conversion from one nonnumeric value to another requires only that the length of the value being moved be made equal to the length of the identifier where it will be stored. This is accomplished by either truncating right-hand characters or adding right-hand blanks (ƀ) to "value." The following examples illustrate the results of some common **MOVE** operations.

Value to be MOVEd	PICTURE of result	Value after MOVE
3.19	9V9	3.1
	V99	.19
	99V999	03.190
'TEXT'	X(3)	'TEX'
	X(4)	'TEXT'
	X(5)	'TEXTƀ'

We must emphasize here that conversion occurs only when both "value" and "identifier" are elementary items. When they are not the **MOVE** operation thus takes place without regard for either the value's type or the result's **PICTURE**. It is executed as if an elementary nonnumeric value were **MOVE**d to an elementary nonnumeric item, with padding or truncation on the right as required. For example, execution of

MOVE 'TEXT' TO C, D

where **C** and **D** are defined as follows

```
              01 C.
                  02 C1 PIC X.
                  02 C2 PIC X.
              01 D.
                  02 D1 PIC X(3).
                  02 D2 PIC X(3).
```

will leave the following results in the elements of **C** and **D**.

C1	T	D1	TEX
C2	E	D2	TЬЬ

This rule suggests some strong advice. Namely, when **MOVE**ing data from one group to another, be sure that the two groups are identically structured and that corresponding elements have identical **PICTURE**s.

STRING and UNSTRING Statements

The **STRING** and **UNSTRING** statements provide COBOL with a primitive character-manipulation facility. The **STRING** statement allows concatenation (joining) of several nonnumeric values (strings) into one, while the **UNSTRING** statement allows decomposing a single string into several. Their formats are as follows.

$$\text{STRING value-list-1} \begin{bmatrix} \textbf{DELIMITED} \begin{bmatrix} \textbf{BY} \end{bmatrix} \begin{Bmatrix} \text{value-1} \\ \textbf{SIZE} \end{Bmatrix} \end{bmatrix}$$

$$\begin{bmatrix} , & \text{value-list-2} \begin{bmatrix} \textbf{DELIMITED} \begin{bmatrix} \textbf{BY} \end{bmatrix} \begin{Bmatrix} \text{value-2} \\ \textbf{SIZE} \end{Bmatrix} \end{bmatrix} \end{bmatrix}$$

$$\vdots$$

> **INTO** identifier [[**WITH**] **POINTER** ptr]
> [; [**ON**] **OVERFLOW** statement]
> **UNSTRING** identifier [**DELIMITED BY** delimiter-list]
> **INTO** identifier-list
> [; [**ON**] **OVERFLOW** statement]

Here, "value-list-1" and "value-list-2" denote lists of elementary nonnumeric items or literals that are mutually separated by comma-space (,Ь). "Value-1" and "value-2" each denotes an individual nonnumeric elementary item or literal. "Identifier" denotes a nonnumeric identifier, "identifier-list" denotes a list of the same that are mutually separated by comma-space (,Ь), and "ptr" denotes a numeric identifier. "Statement" denotes any unconditional statement. "Delimiter-list" denotes a list of one or more nonnumeric identifiers and/or literals, mutually separated by the reserved word **OR**.

Execution of the **STRING** statement causes "identifier" to be filled from left to right with the result of concatenating the values in value-list-1, value-list-2, . . . , in the order in which they are written. If that result has more characters than allowed by identifier's **PICTURE**, then the **OVERFLOW** condition is raised and "statement" is executed (if the **"ON OVERFLOW"** clause is present). Otherwise (i.e., either the **OVERFLOW** condition is not raised or the **"ON OVERFLOW"** clause is not present), control passes to the next statement following the **STRING** statement. If, on the other hand, that result is not as long as that allowed by identifier's **PICTURE,** then the remaining (rightmost) characters in "identifier" are left unchanged. (The reader should note that the **MOVE** statement is different in this respect.)

When the **"DELIMITED BY SIZE"** alternative is used, each of the values in the corresponding value-list is taken in its entirety. When, on the other hand, the **"DELIMITED BY** value-1" alternative is used, the first (leftmost) occurrence of "value-1" within each of the values in the corresponding value-list delimits the end of that value. (If "value-1" does not occur within one or more of the values in value-list, then the entire value is used—as in the **SIZE** alternative.)

When the **"WITH POINTER** ptr" option is specified, the current integer value of ptr dictates the position in "Identifier" where the leftmost character of "value-list-1" will be stored.

For example, suppose we had the following values and identifiers.

Identifier	PICTURE	Current value
STREET	X(17)	"1800ƀBULLƀRUN,ƀƀƀ"
CITY	X(12)	"ALEXANDRIA,ƀ"
STATE	X(6)	"VA.ƀƀƀ"
ZIP	9(5)	22200
ADDR	X(40)	SPACES

Then execution of the statement

STRING STREET, CITY, STATE, ZIP DELIMITED BY SIZE
            INTO ADDR

will leave **ADDR** as shown below.

        "1800ƀBULLƀRUN,ƀƀƀALEXANDRIA,ƀVA.ƀƀƀ22200"

However, if we wanted to pack out extra trailing blanks, as well as trailing commas and periods, we would instead rewrite the statement as follows.

STRING	**STREET**	**DELIMITED BY ",",**
	"ƀ"	**DELIMITED BY SIZE,**
	CITY	**DELIMITED BY ",",**
	"ƀ"	**DELIMITED BY SIZE,**
	STATE	**DELIMITED BY ".",**
	"ƀ"	**DELIMITED BY SIZE,**
	ZIP	**DELIMITED BY SIZE,**
INTO	**ADDR**	

This would leave **ADDR** instead as shown below.

        "1800ƀBULLƀRUNƀALEXANDRIAƀVAƀ22200ƀƀƀƀƀƀ"

Note that the trailing blanks here were already present before the **STRING** statement was executed; they were not added during the process.

Execution of the **UNSTRING** statement causes the value of "identifier" to be split up and moved to the identifiers in "identifier-list" in the order that they are listed. If the "**DELIMITED BY** delimiter-list" option is used, then if any of the values in "delimiter-list" occurs within the value being split up, then it (prematurely) terminates movement of that value. For example, reconsider the identifiers declared above, where **STREET, CITY, STATE,** and **ZIP** are all blank-filled, and **ADDR** has the following value.

"1800ƀBULLƀRUN,ƀALEXANDRIA,ƀVA.ƀ22200ƀƀƀƀ"

Execution of the following statement will cause **STREET, CITY, STATE,** and **ZIP** to regain their original values, except that commas and periods will not be transmitted.

**UNSTRING ADDR DELIMITED BY ",ƀ" OR ".ƀ"
INTO STREET, CITY, STATE, ZIP**

Here, the delimiters are ",ƀ" and ".ƀ". Scanning of **ADDR** begins at its left, and characters are moved from it into **STREET** until either ",ƀ" occurs, ".ƀ" occurs, or **STREET** is filled (whichever comes first). Since they are delimiters, ",ƀ" and ".ƀ" will not be moved. Then **CITY** is filled, beginning with the next character in **ADDR** after the leftmost delimiter ",ƀ". Similarly, **STATE** and **ZIP** are filled.

The INSPECT Statement

COBOL character manipulation is enhanced greatly by the **INSPECT** statement. (See next page.) It permits the program to search a character string (i.e., **DISPLAY** item) for occurrences of some other character string, possibly replacing such occurrences by yet another string. The form of the **INSPECT** statement is as follows.

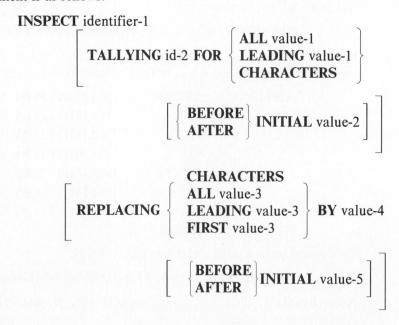

Here, "identifier-1" denotes any data item whose usage is **DISPLAY.** "Id-2" denotes any elementary numeric data item, which serves to contain the integer count of the number of occurrences of the designated string "value-1" in "identifier-1." "Value-1," "value-2," "value-3," "value-4," and "value-5" each denotes a nonnumeric elementary identifier or literal.

When the **BEFORE** (or **AFTER**) option is included, the ending point (or starting point, respectively) of the search is identified as the position in "identifier-1" immediately before (after) the leftmost occurrence of "value-2" or "value-5." When it is omitted, the ending point and starting point are identified as the right and left ends of "identifier-1," respectively.

Execution of the **INSPECT** statement thus occurs as follows. If the **TALLYING** option is included, then "id-2" will be left with the total number of characters counted. Counting is governed by the choice given after the word **"FOR."** **"ALL** value-1" dictates that the total number of occurrences of "value-1" from the starting point to the ending point of the search be counted. **"LEADING** value-1" dictates that only those occurrences of "value-1" that occur before any non-"value-1" be counted. **"CHARACTERS"** dictates that the total number of characters from the starting point to the ending point be counted. In all of these cases, "id-2" is not initialized by the **INSPECT** statement, and thus must be done elsewhere in the program.

If the **REPLACING** option is included, then the starting and ending points for replacement of characters within "identifier-1" are similarly defined, depending on the presence or absence of "value-5." Here, "value-3" identifies the characters to be replaced (or else **"CHARACTERS"** designates that all characters be replaced), while "value-4" designates the value which will replace the characters.

Either the **TALLYING** option or the **REPLACING** option must be present in an **INSPECT** statement. Consider the following examples, using the seventeen-character variable named **STREET** as "identifier-1" with the following value in each case.

$$\text{"bb1800bBULLbRUN,b"}$$

Also we assume the presence of the counting variable **I,** with **PICTURE 99** and current value 0, in each case.

Example	Resulting value of STREET	Resulting value of I
1 INSPECT STREET TALLYING I FOR ALL "b"	Unchanged	5

2 INSPECT STREET
   TALLYING I FOR ALL "b"
     AFTER INITIAL "b"
	Unchanged	4

3 INSPECT STREET REPLACING LEADING "b" BY "*"	"**1800bBULLbRUN,b"	0 (unchanged)

4 INSPECT STREET
   REPLACING ALL "b" BY "*"
     AFTER INITIAL ","
	"bb1800bBULLbRUN,*"	0 (unchanged)

The SEARCH and SET Statements

While **INSPECT** allows searching a character string for a particular value, the **SEARCH** statement allows searching a table for a particular value. The **SET** statement is used to assign a value to an **INDEX** variable that is associated with the table being **SEARCH**ed. These statements have the following forms.

1. SEARCH   identifier-1   [**VARYING** index]
          [**AT END** statement-1]
             WHEN condition statement-2

2. SET index-list $\begin{Bmatrix} \textbf{TO} \\ \textbf{UP BY} \\ \textbf{DOWN BY} \end{Bmatrix}$ value

Here, "identifier-1" identifies the table to be searched. It must be a group-level name which contains both an "**OCCURS** clause" and an "**INDEXED BY** clause." "Index" denotes an index variable, which is defined in an "**INDEXED BY** var" part of the table's **OCCURS** clause. "Index-list" denotes a list of such items, mutually separated by comma-space (,ƀ). "Statement-1" and "statement-2" both denote imperative statements. "Value" denotes either an index variable or an integer constant.

When executed, the **SEARCH** statement performs a serial search of the indicated table, varying the table's own index (and, concurrently, the "index" if the **VARYING** clause is present) until either the designated "condition" is true or the end of the table is reached. Accordingly, either "statement-2" or "statement-1" is executed (and the other one is skipped). When "statement-1" is not specified and the search reaches the end of the table before "condition" becomes true, control passes to the next sentence.

A

43
19
−5
0
−19

FIG. 14-9

Execution of the **SET** statement causes each variable in "index-list" to be initialized at (**TO**), incremented by (**UP BY**), or decremented by (**DOWN BY**) the integer "value."

Consider the following example, where the table named **TABLE-A** is searched for the first occurrence of zero. Here, **TABLE-A** and index **I** are declared as follows.

> **01 TABLE-A.**
> **02 A PIC S99 OCCURS 5 INDEXED BY I.**

Note that our mention of **I** as an index in the declaration of **TABLE-A** implicitly declares **I.** Now assume that **A** has the values given in Fig. 14-9. Then the search is designated as follows.

> **SET I TO 1.**
> **SEARCH TABLE-A**
>   **AT END GO TO ZERO-NOT-FOUND**
>   **WHEN A (I) = 0 GO TO ZERO-FOUND.**

Execution of the search will pass control to **ZERO-FOUND,** leaving **I** with value 4.

14-4 INPUT-OUTPUT CONVENTIONS

COBOL provides extensive facilities for reading and writing data values during program execution. A COBOL "file" is a collection of records, each one formatted into fields in the same way as the next. A file may be accessed by a program sequentially for either input or output, or randomly for either input, output, or input-output (i.e., records may be both read and written).

Sequential accessing takes a file's records in the order in which they are stored, one at a time beginning with the first. Random accessing takes a file's records in no particular order, as dictated by the program. Thus any record in a randomly accessed file may be read (written) zero, one, or more times in a single program run.

For each file accessed by a COBOL program, the following must be included in the program.

1. In the Environment Division, identify the physical device (e.g., card reader, magnetic tape) class where the file resides.

2. In the File Section of the Data Division, define the file's attributes and provide an area (by way of a record description entry) into (from) which records will be read (written) from (to) the file.

3. In the Procedure Division, provide statements which will read (write) records from (to) the file, as well as statements which will "open" and "close" the file.

Device Assignment in the Environment Division

Whenever a program uses one or more files, its Environment Division must contain a so-called "Input-Output Section" and "File-Control Paragraph." The file-control paragraph contains for each file one "file-control-entry," which principally assigns the file to a particular (implementation dependent) physical input-output device. The Input-Output Section is thus headed as follows.

INPUT-OUTPUT SECTION.

FILE-CONTROL.   file-control-entry . . .

Each file-control-entry has the following form.

SELECT file-name **ASSIGN TO** device-name

[**RESERVE** integer **AREAS**]

$$\left[\textbf{ORGANIZATION IS} \begin{Bmatrix} \textbf{SEQUENTIAL} \\ \textbf{INDEXED} \end{Bmatrix} \right]$$

$$\left[\textbf{ACCESS MODE IS} \begin{Bmatrix} \textbf{SEQUENTIAL} \\ \textbf{RANDOM} \end{Bmatrix} \right]$$

[**RECORD KEY IS** data-name].

The reader should note first that this entry always terminates with a period (.). Here, "file-name" denotes any nonreserved, user-defined word containing at least one alphabetic (A–Z) character. "Device-name" is implementation dependent. The following are valid device-names for IBM OS ANS COBOL implementations.

Device-name	Meaning
DA-S-ddname	Some direct-access (DA) device and a sequentially organized (S) file.
DA-I-ddname	Same, except that the file has indexed (I) organization.
UT-S-ddname	Some magnetic tape (UT) device and a sequentially organized file.
UR-S-ddname	Some unit record (UR) device—card reader, punch, or line printer—and a sequentially organized file.

Here, a file whose organization is indexed may be accessed either sequentially or randomly, but must reside on a direct-access device. Also, "ddname" denotes a one- to eight-character name which appears on the data-definition job control card ("dd card") for that file at execution time.

The **RESERVE** clause is optional, and is used to specify the number of input-output buffers (**AREAS**) to be assigned to the file. If omitted, the number of buffers is implementation dependent.

The **ORGANIZATION** and **ACCESS** clauses are also optional. If omitted, then **SEQUENTIAL** is assumed for each. If a file has **INDEXED** organization, then its **ACCESS MODE** may be either **SEQUENTIAL** or **RANDOM.**

When organization is **INDEXED** and **ACCESS MODE** is **RANDOM** for a file, then an individual record is retrieved by its "key." The key of a record is a value which uniquely distinguishes that record from all others in the file. For example, the key for an employee master file can be an employee's social security number, so that no two employees will have the same key. Thus, for random access to an **INDEXED** file, the **RECORD KEY** clause identifies the "data-name" (or field) within the file's record description entry which serves as the key for the file. This clause is, of course, not used for **SEQUENTIAL** access.

For example, suppose we have an input punched-card file named **CARDS,** an output print file named **PAPER,** and an output magnetic tape file named **MAG-TAPE.** Then a program with these three files would have the following Input-Output Section in its Environment Division.

```
        INPUT-OUTPUT SECTION.
        FILE-CONTROL.
            SELECT-CARDS        ASSIGN TO UR-S-SYSIN.
            SELECT PAPER         ASSIGN TO UR-S-SYSPRINT.
            SELECT MAG-TAPE     ASSIGN TO UT-S-TAPEDD.
```

File and Record Definition in the Data Division

For each file used by a program, there must be one file description which is immediately followed by one or more record descriptions, in the File Section of the Data Division. Basic organization of the Data Division is as follows.

        DATA DIVISION.
          FILE SECTION.
          {file-description
          record-description ... } ...
          WORKING-STORAGE SECTION.
          {declarations of variables, tables, and record-descriptions}

A file's "file-description" has the following form.

        FD file-name
            [BLOCK [CONTAINS] integer-1 [CHARACTERS]]
            [RECORD [CONTAINS] integer-2 [CHARACTERS]]
            LABEL RECORDS ARE $\begin{Bmatrix} \text{STANDARD} \\ \text{OMITTED} \end{Bmatrix}$
            [LINAGE IS value LINES].

The reader should note first that each file description must end with a period (.). "File-name" must be the same as the file's file-name given in its **SELECT** clause in the Environment Division. The **BLOCK CONTAINS** clause is used when each physical record in the file contains more than one logical record (i.e., the records are "blocked"). In this case, "integer-1" denotes the total number of characters in a physical record. When the file's records are unblocked (as in the case of unit record files), the **BLOCK CONTAINS** clause is not required.

The **RECORD CONTAINS** clause identifies the number of characters in a logical record, denoted by "integer-2." This clause may be omitted when the logical record length is fixed by the file's device class, which is implementation dependent.

The **LABEL RECORDS** clause is always present, and identifies whether (**STANDARD**) or not (**OMITTED**) the file has standard labels. The format of file labels is implementation dependent.

The **LINAGE** clause may be used only for print files. It defines the number of lines on a logical page as "value." "Value" itself denotes any integer-valued variable or constant. If the **LINAGE** clause is present, a system-generated **LINAGE-COUNTER** is available to the program. It contains an integer value which defines the next line to be written on the current page. Its value is maintained by the system and it may be referenced by the program.

Following the file's "file-description" is one or more of the "record descriptions," which define the structure and layout of a logical record in the file. Sometimes a file will have records of two, three, or more different structures, and thus will require two, three, or more different record-descriptions. Additionally, the number of character positions defined in the combined **PICTURE** clauses of the elementary items of a record description must be the same as the file's logical record size.

For example, reconsider the three files named **CARDS, PAPER,** and **MAG-TAPE** presented in the foregoing paragraph. Let us assume additionally that the **CARDS** file is an input deck of standard 80-character punched cards, the **PAPER** file is an output sheet of 132-character-per-line paper, and the **MAG-TAPE** file is a sequence of 80-character logical records, combined into 800-

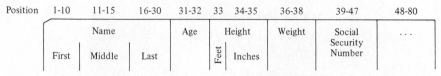

FIG. 14-10

character blocks (physical records). Furthermore, the tape file has standard labels (but the others do not) and a tape record has the layout shown in Fig. 14-10. Then we could write file and record descriptions in the Data Division for these files as follows.

```
FD CARDS
    RECORD CONTAINS 80 CHARACTERS
    LABEL RECORDS ARE OMITTED.
01 CARDS-RECORD.
    02 CARD PIC X(80).
FD PAPER
    RECORD CONTAINS 133 CHARACTERS
    LABEL RECORDS ARE OMITTED
    LINAGE IS 60 LINES.
01 PAPER-RECORD.
    02 FILLER      PIC X.
    02 DATA-LINE PIC X(132).
FD MAG-TAPE
    BLOCK CONTAINS 800 CHARACTERS
    RECORD CONTAINS 80 CHARACTERS
    LABEL RECORDS ARE STANDARD.
01 MAG-TAPE-RECORD.
    02 NAME.
        03 NFIRST       PIC X(10).
        03 MIDDLE       PIC X(5).
        03 NLAST        PIC X(15).
    02 AGE              PIC 99.
    02 HEIGHT.
        03 FEET         PIC 9.
        03 INCHES       PIC 99.
    02 WEIGHT           PIC 999.
    02 SS-NO            PIC 9(9).
    02 FILLER           PIC X(33).
```

We should point out that the reserved word **FILLER** is used to name any portion of a record which will not be referenced in the Procedure Division. This is true for positions 48–80 of our **MAG-TAPE-RECORD**.

Note also that the **PAPER** file's record is 133 (not 132) characters long, with provision for one leading position at the beginning of its record description. This is an implementation dependent characteristic. The extra position is used by the system for controlling vertical printer spacing, as dictated by **WRITE** statements for that file.

File Accessing in the Procedure Division

A file is accessed during execution of a COBOL program whenever an **OPEN, CLOSE, READ, WRITE, REWRITE,** or **DELETE** statement is executed.

The **OPEN** statement initiates access to a file. No records may be read (written) from (to) a file before the file is opened. The **OPEN** statement has the following form.

$$\text{\textbf{OPEN}} \left\{ \begin{array}{l} \textbf{INPUT} \\ \textbf{OUTPUT} \\ \textbf{I-O} \end{array} \right\} \text{file-name-list}$$

Here, "file-name-list" denotes a list of names of the files to be opened, mutually separated by comma-space (,ɓ). The choice of **INPUT, OUTPUT,** or **I-O** depends on how the file is to be accessed. When the file is opened for **INPUT,** records may only be read from the file (sequentially or randomly) using the **READ** statement. When the file is opened for **OUTPUT,** records may be written to the file (sequentially or randomly) using the **WRITE** statement. When the file is opened for **I-O,** records may be read from the file (sequentially or randomly) using the **READ** statement, (re)written to the file randomly using the **WRITE** or **REWRITE** statement, rewritten to the file sequentially using the **REWRITE** statement, or deleted from the file (sequentially or randomly) using the **DELETE** statement. However, the **DELETE** statement may be used only when the file's organization is **INDEXED.**

The **CLOSE** statement terminates access to the file. It should occur only after all other accesses (**READ, WRITE,** etc.) to the file have been executed. Its form is as follows.

CLOSE file-name-list

Execution of a **CLOSE** statement effectively disconnects the listed files from use by the program. However, any of these files may be subsequently accessed after another **OPEN** statement for that file has been executed.

The **READ** statement is used to transfer a single logical record from a file to the program. It has the following form.

READ file-name **[RECORD]**
[AT END statement-1**]**
[INVALID KEY statement-2**]**

Here, "file-name" denotes the file from which a record is to be read. The record itself is stored in the area described by the record-description entry (or entries) for that file's description. No conversion is performed. "Statement-1" denotes an imperative statement to be executed when end-of-file occurs. "End-of-file" is an attempt to read a record from a sequentially accessed file when the last record has already been read. "Statement-2" denotes an imperative statement to be executed when an attempt to read a record from a randomly accessed file has been unsuccessfully made. That is, there was no record on the file whose key matched the current value of the variable whose data-name appears in the **RECORD-KEY** clause of the file's **SELECT** statement in the Input-Output Section of the Environment Division. Responsibility for setting that variable's value is, of course, in the hands of the program.

The **WRITE** statement is used to transfer a single record from the program to a file. It has the following form.

WRITE record-name
$$\left[\text{AFTER} \left[\text{ADVANCING} \right] \left\{ \begin{matrix} \text{value } \underline{\textbf{LINES}} \\ \underline{\textbf{PAGE}} \end{matrix} \right\} \right]$$
[**AT END-OF-PAGE** statement-1]
[**INVALID KEY** statement-2]

"Record-name" denotes the group-level name of some record-description entry for the file (note that "file-name" is not used here). The **AFTER** clause is used only for print files, and "value" denotes an integer variable or constant which denotes the number of lines to advance before the line is printed. The **PAGE** alternative denotes a skip to the top of the next page. The **AT END-OF-PAGE** clause is also used only for print files, and "statement-1" denotes an imperative statement to be executed whenever the writing causes an advance beyond the last line of the current page.

The **INVALID KEY** clause is used only when the file has **INDEXED** organization. If it is accessed sequentially the **INVALID KEY** condition occurs whenever an attempt is made to write a record whose key is less than or equal to the most recently written record. If the file is accessed randomly, the **INVALID KEY** condition occurs whenever an attempt is made to write a record whose key is identical with that of some other record in the file. In either case, "statement-2" denotes an imperative statement to be executed whenever the **INVALID KEY** condition occurs during execution of the **WRITE** statement.

The **REWRITE** statement causes a record to be replaced in a file that resides on a direct access (DA) device. The file may be either a sequential or an indexed file. It has the following form.

DELETE file-name [**RECORD**]
[**INVALID KEY** statement-2]

The file must be opened in the input-output mode for a **DELETE** statement to be valid for it, but it may be accessed either sequentially or randomly. If it is accessed sequentially, then the most recently read record is deleted. If it is accessed randomly, then the record whose key matches the current value of the variable containing the file's key is deleted from the file. Raising of the **INVALID KEY** condition on a **DELETE** statement is the same as that for the **REWRITE** statement.

To illustrate some of these statements, let us reconsider the files **CARDS**, **PAPER**, and **MAG-TAPE** defined above. The following Procedure Division statements will read the **CARDS** file, print it (double-spaced), and copy it on magnetic tape.

```
                OPEN INPUT CARDS, OUTPUT PAPER, OUTPUT
                MAG-TAPE.
L1.             MOVE SPACES TO DATA-LINE.
                WRITE PAPER-RECORD AFTER PAGE.
LOOP.           READ CARDS AT END GO TO ALL-DONE.
                MOVE CARD TO DATA-LINE, MAG-TAPE-RECORD.
                WRITE MAG-TAPE-RECORD.
                WRITE PAPER-RECORD AFTER ADVANCING 2 LINES
                    AT END-OF-PAGE GO TO L1.
                GO TO LOOP.
ALL-DONE.       CLOSE CARDS, PAPER, MAG-TAPE.
                STOP RUN.
```

14-5 SUBPROGRAMS

In most practical programming situations, the task is large enough to warrant subdividing the program into a number of functional blocks. These may be linked together by a main program which controls the sequence in which the functional blocks will be executed. Another advantage of subprograms is that they permit the reuse of code without rewriting and debugging it each time it is needed.

COBOL provides facilities that permit subprogramming. A COBOL subprogram is a complete program that has certain additional features which allow it to be invoked during the execution of another COBOL program or subprogram. In fact, a subprogram may be executed only by invocation from another program. In this section, we shall describe and illustrate both writing and invoking COBOL subprograms.

Here, we will consider the task of computing the "factorial," say f, of an integer n, which is defined as follows.

If $n < 2$ then its factorial $f = 1$.
Otherwise, its factorial $f = 2 \times 3 \times \ldots \times n$.

For example, the factorial of 5 is $2 \times 3 \times 4 \times 5 = 120$.

Writing Subprograms

The subprogram itself is actually a definition of a task, such as computing a factorial, to be performed. In COBOL, the following special provisions must be made when writing a subprogram.

1. The Data Division must contain a Linkage Section, which defines the nature and structure of all variables that will be "passed" to the subprogram from the invoking program.
2. The Procedure Division header must be expanded to identify those variables and the order in which they should be listed at the time the invoking program calls the subprogram.

3. The Procedure Division should contain an **EXIT** statement at location(s) where control should logically return to the invoking program.

The Linkage Section immediately follows the Working-Storage Section in the Data Division. It contains a declaration of each parameter that will be passed to the subprogram, according to the same conventions used for defining ordinary variables and record-description entries in the Working-Storage Section. It begins with the following section header.

LINKAGE SECTION.

For example, for the factorial subprogram, two parameters are required, *n* and *f*. We will assume that both must have **PICTURE S9(9)** and **USAGE COMPUTATIONAL** when they are passed by the invoking program. Thus, the Linkage Section would be written as follows.

LINKAGE SECTION.
77 N PIC S9(9) COMP.
77 F PIC S9(9) COMP.

The Procedure Division header for subprograms has the following general form.

PROCEDURE DIVISION USING parameter-list.

Here "parameter-list" denotes a list of the parameters defined in the Linkage Section, mutually separated by comma-space (,ɓ). In our example, the Procedure Division header would be written as follows.

PROCEDURE DIVISION USING N, F.

The Procedure Division itself is written just as though it were an ordinary program performing its designated task. However, when it has completed the task, it must return control to the invoking program, using the following statement.

p-name.   **EXIT PROGRAM.**

As indicated, the **EXIT PROGRAM** statement must appear in a paragraph (named "p-name") by itself.

Thus, we may write the entire factorial subprogram, which we will name **FACT,** as follows.

IDENTIFICATION DIVISION.
  PROGRAM-ID.   FACT.
ENVIRONMENT DIVISION.
  CONFIGURATION SECTION.
    SOURCE-COMPUTER.   IBM-370-145.
    OBJECT-COMPUTER.   IBM-370-145.
DATA DIVISION.
  WORKING-STORAGE SECTION.
    77 I PIC S9(9) COMP.

```
LINKAGE SECTION.
   77 N PIC S9(9) COMP.
   77 F PIC S9(9) COMP.
PROCEDURE DIVISION USING N, F.
   MOVE 1 TO F.
   PERFORM S1 VARYING I FROM 1 BY 1 UNTIL I = N OR I > N.
      S1. COMPUTE F = F * I.
      S2. EXIT PROGRAM.
```

We emphasize here that **N** and **F** are not variables, as is **I**. They are parameters which "hold the place" of variables that will be provided by the invoking program at the time **FACT** begins execution.

Invoking Subprograms

Once written, a subprogram is invoked from another subprogram or ordinary program via the **CALL** statement. The **CALL** statement also lists the particular variable(s) that will be identified with the subprogram's parameter(s) throughout execution of the subprogram's Procedure Division for that invocation. The **CALL** statement has the following form.

CALL "name" USING variable-list

Here "name" denotes the subprogram's name as defined in the **PROGRAM-ID** paragraph of its Identification Division. "Variable-list" denotes a list of those variables in the calling program's Data Division which are to be accessed by the subprogram during this particular invocation.

There is a one-to-one left-right correspondence between the variables in "variable-list" and the parameters in the subprogram's "parameter-list." To illustrate, suppose we want to write a program which, using the **FACT** subroutine, computes and prints binomial coefficients,

$$a_i = \frac{n!}{i! \, (n - i)!} \qquad \text{for each } i = 0, 1, \ldots, n$$

given any two-digit positive integer n as input. Then the program could be written as follows.

```
IDENTIFICATION DIVISION.
   PROGRAM-ID.  BINOMIAL.
ENVIRONMENT DIVISION.
   CONFIGURATION SECTION.
      SOURCE-COMPUTER.  IBM-370-145.
      OBJECT-COMPUTER.  IBM-370-145.
   INPUT-OUTPUT SECTION.
      SELECT CARDS ASSIGN TO UR-S-SYSIN.
      SELECT PAPER ASSIGN TO UR-S-SYSPRINT.
DATA DIVISION.
FILE SECTION.
```

```
FD CARDS RECORD CONTAINS 80, LABEL RECORDS ARE
OMITTED.
    01 CARD.
        02 N PIC 99.
        02 FILLER PIC X (78).
FD PAPER RECORD CONTAINS 133 LABEL RECORDS ARE
OMITTED.
    01 PRINT-LINE.
        02 FILLER PIC X.
        02 I        PIC 99.
        02 FILLER PIC X(2).
        02 AI       PIC 9(9).
        02 FILLER PIC X(119).
WORKING-STORAGE SECTION.
    77 NC PIC 9(9) COMP.
    77 IC PIC 9(9) COMP.
    77 NMIC PIC 9(9) COMP.
    77 NFACT PIC 9(9) COMP.
    77 IFACT PIC 9(9) COMP.
    77 NMIFACT PIC 9(9) COMP.
PROCEDURE DIVISION.
    OPEN INPUT CARDS, OUTPUT PAPER.
    MOVE SPACES TO PRINT-LINE.
    READ CARDS AT END GO TO P2.
    MOVE N TO NC.
    CALL FACT USING NC, NFACT.
    PERFORM P1 VARYING IC FROM 0 BY 1 UNTIL IC = NC.
P1. CALL FACT USING IC, IFACT.
    SUBTRACT IC FROM NC GIVING NMIC.
    CALL FACT USING NMIC, NMIFACT.
    COMPUTE AI = NFACT/(IFACT * NMIFACT).
    MOVE IC TO I.
    WRITE PRINT-LINE AFTER ADVANCING 1.
P2. CLOSE CARDS, PAPER.
    STOP RUN.
```

Now let's look at the first **CALL** statement in this program, which is underlined. The correspondence between the variables listed here and the parameters listed in the **FACT** subprogram is as follows.

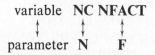

When the called program is executed, every occurrence of a parameter in its Procedure Division is, in effect, replaced by its corresponding variable from the **CALL.** Thus, execution of this particular **CALL** statement results in a computation of the factorial of the current value of the variable named **NC** and the storing of that factorial in the variable named **NFACT.**

If the input value of N is 05, the following results will be printed.

0	**1**
1	**5**
2	**10**
3	**10**
4	**5**
5	**1**

In this case, the reader should see that the value of **NFACT** will be 120, **NC** will vary from 0 to 5, and paragraph **P1** will be executed six times.

14-6 COMPLETE PROGRAMS

Throughout the foregoing sections, the reader may have noticed a certain rigidity in the syntax of statement forms and examples. Here we describe more exactly the syntactic requirements that COBOL programs must satisfy.

The Identification Division in a COBOL program serves mainly as documentation. Although only its division header and the **PROGRAM-ID** paragraph are required there, additional paragraphs can optionally be written to further document the program. The general Identification Division syntax is as follows.

> **IDENTIFICATION DIVISION.**
> **PROGRAM-ID.** program-name.
> [**AUTHOR.** comment.]
> [**INSTALLATION.** comment.]
> [**DATE-WRITTEN.** comment.]
> [**DATE-COMPILED.** comment.]
> [**SECURITY.** comment.]

Here, "program-name" denotes the name of the program and may be any unique nonreserved word (perhaps subject to other implementation dependent restrictions). "Comment" denotes any appropriate documentary information that identifies the author, the installation, and so forth.

The order of the four Divisions, as well as the order of the various Sections within the Environment and Data Divisions, must not vary. Additionally all 77-level items in the Working-Storage and Linkage Sections of a program must physically precede all record description entries in that Section. The ordering of individual 77-level items or record-description entries among themselves, however, is immaterial.

The layout of an individual line within a COBOL program is somewhat restricted. **"Area A"** of a line is defined as positions 8–11, while **"Area B"** is defined as positions 12 through the end of the line. (The length of a line is implementation dependent.)

Positions 1–6 of a line are normally left blank. Position 7 serves one of two purposes, as follows. If it contains an asterisk (∗), then the remainder of the line is taken as commentary documentation for the program. If it contains a dash (-) then the remainder of the line has the continuation of a literal constant which would not entirely fit on the previous line. Otherwise, position 7 should be left blank.

Area A of the line is reserved for Division headers, Section headers, paragraph names, 01-level items in record-description entries, 77-level items, and file-description (FD) entries. Each of these must begin somewhere within Area A, although not necessarily in position 8. All other elements of a program—principally words, statements, sentences, and non-01-level items of record-description entries—must be entirely within Area B, but need not begin exactly in position 12. Moreover, any element may continue from one line of the program to the next, provided that its continuation is in Area B.

Generally, a sentence may occupy one or more lines and a line may contain one or more sentences. When a sentence continues from one line to the next, it may be broken between any two adjacent words, where a space would naturally occur. Furthermore, wherever a single space occurs, two or more spaces may also be written. Finally, the comma-space (,б) given for various lists in several types of statements may equivalently be replaced by one or more spaces.

With this freedom, the programmer has the responsibility of laying out the program so that logic can be easily seen.

14-7 ADDITIONAL FEATURES

We cannot cover with justice all the additional features of COBOL. In this section we focus attention on the following features.

> The **VALUE, REDEFINES,** and **JUSTIFIED** clauses
> The Debug and Library facilities
> The Sort-Merge facility
> The Report Writer facility

Only the essential aspects of these features will be presented here. For more detailed information, the reader should consult a COBOL reference manual.

The VALUE, REDEFINES, and JUSTIFIED Clauses

One way to initialize the value of either a variable or elementary item in a record-description entry at the beginning of program execution is to specify that initial value in a **VALUE** clause, which has the following form.

VALUE [IS] literal

Here, "literal" denotes any numeric or nonnumeric constant which is consistent with the variable's **PICTURE**. For example, if we want to initialize the numeric variable named **I** with value 0 we could write either of the following declarations.

77 I PIC S9(5) VALUE 0.
77 I PIC S9(5) VALUE ZERO.

The reader should note that this has rather restricted use, since a variable having the **OCCURS** clause or the **REDEFINES** clause cannot be initialized in this way. Furthermore, this convention can be used only in the Working-Storage Section of the Data Division.

The **REDEFINES** clause allows the program to rename a storage area in two or more different ways. This is useful, for instance, when a single eighty-character value is to be treated occasionally as eighty contiguous single-character values. It has the following form.

REDEFINES data-name

Here "data-name" denotes the name of the area being redefined. The item which redefines that area must be declared immediately after it. For our example, consider the following declarations.

> **01 CARD-AREA.**
>   **02 CARD PIC X(80).**
>   **02 CARD-POS REDEFINES CARD PIC X OCCURS 80.**

Now, if we want to reference the entire **CARD-AREA** as a single entity, we write **"CARD."** If, on the other hand, we want to reference the Ith position (where I is an integer-valued variable) of that same **CARD-AREA,** we write **"CARD-POS (I)."**

The **JUSTIFIED** clause allows nonnumeric data being moved to a receiving area to be right-justified, rather than left-justified (which occurs if the **JUSTIFIED** clause is omitted). It has the following form.

JUSTIFIED [RIGHT]

This clause can be used only at the elementary level. For example, suppose we redeclare the **CARD** area as follows.

> **01 CARD-AREA.**
>   **02 CARD PIC X(80) JUSTIFIED RIGHT.**

Then execution of the following **MOVE** statement

MOVE "ALLEN" TO CARD

leaves **CARD** with the value **"ALLEN"** in its rightmost five (rather than leftmost five) positions and blank-filled on the left (rather than on the right).

The Debug and Library Facilities

To serve the programmer's needs for (1) tracing execution and dumping intermediate results during program testing, and (2) continually changing and extending existing programs, COBOL has facilities intended to ease the tedium of program modification and testing.

The Debug facility allows the programmer to add a "debugging algorithm" to a program while it is being tested. That algorithm may specify conditions under which to dump certain variables' values, initiate program trace, and so forth. Unfortunately, most current COBOL implementations do not contain the Debug facility described in the 1974 standard. Rather, they support either different debugging features or none at all; the 1968 COBOL standard failed to provide such features.

The Library facility permits the programmer to save certain often-used segments of COBOL source programs on a library, and then have one or more of them dynamically inserted into a program at compile time. A natural use for this facility occurs when a large record description (e.g., and employee master file's record description) is shared among several programs that process that file. This permits writing and editing that record description only once, and then obtaining an automatic copy of it as it is needed, eliminating duplication of effort and the errors that would occur therein.

The Sort-Merge Facility

File sorting and merging occurs so frequently in data processing applications that COBOL provides a very powerful facility to directly specify these actions within a program. To specify a file sort or merge, the program must make the following provisions.

1. Identify the file to be sorted (merged) in the File-Control paragraph of the Environment Division.

2. Describe the file to be sorted (merged) and its record layout in Sort Description (SD) entries of the File Section in the Data Division.

3. Specify that the sort or merge function be executed by writing a **SORT** or **MERGE** statement within the Procedure Division. Additional processing of records, as they either enter into or exit from the **SORT** or **MERGE** operation, is provided by the **RELEASE** and **RETURN** statements, respectively.

The file to be sorted (merged) is defined and identified with a physical input-output medium by using the **SELECT** and **ASSIGN** clauses (in the Environment Division's File-Control paragraph) exactly as if the files were ordinary files used by the program. For the sort or merge to take place, however, the files must have sequential, rather than indexed, organization.

A Sort Description (**SD**) entry in the File Section of the Data Division must be written for the file to be sorted (merged). It has the following form.

> SD file-name
>> **RECORD CONTAINS** integer [**CHARACTERS**].

Here, "integer" denotes the file's logical record length. Following this must be one or more record description entries for the file.

The **SORT** statement has the following form.

SORT file-name-1
    [ON] $\begin{Bmatrix} \textbf{ASCENDING} \\ \textbf{DESCENDING} \end{Bmatrix}$ **KEY** data-name-list
  $\begin{Bmatrix} \textbf{INPUT PROCEDURE} \text{ [IS] section-name-1 [\underline{\textbf{THROUGH}} section-name-2]} \\ \textbf{USING} \text{ file-name-2} \end{Bmatrix}$
  $\begin{Bmatrix} \textbf{OUTPUT PROCEDURE} \text{ [IS] section-name-3 [\underline{\textbf{THROUGH}} section-name-4]} \\ \textbf{GIVING} \text{ file-name-3} \end{Bmatrix}$

Here, "file-name-1" is the so-called "sort file," and is the same as "file-name" that was defined in the **SD** entry. "File-name-2" and "file-name-3" denote the input file to the sort and the output file from the sort, respectively. They must be defined in ordinary **FD** entries of the Data Division's File Section. "Data-name-list" denotes a list of one or more data-names that are defined within the sort file's record description. These together constitute the controlling key to the sort. Section-name-1, -2, -3, and -4 denote the names of Procedure Division sections.

Either the **"INPUT PROCEDURE"** clause or the **"USING"** clause, but not both, must be specified in the **SORT** statement. If the **"INPUT PROCE-DURE"** clause is specified, then "section-name-1" (through "section-name-2") is executed to create the sort file, "file-name-1." Each time a record is to be transferred to the sort file, the following statement within the input procedure must be executed.

RELEASE record-name

Here, "record-name" denotes a record-description entry defined under the sort-description (**SD**) entry for the sort file. Further, the input procedure must be self-contained, so that control may not transfer either out of it from within or into it from elsewhere in the program. If, on the other hand, the **"USING"** clause is specified, then records are automatically passed to the sort file directly from "file-name-2." However, "file-name-2" must be **OPEN**ed by the program before the **SORT** statement is executed.

Similarly, if the **"OUTPUT PROCEDURE"** clause is specified, then the resulting sort file at the end of the sort operation is accessed by the program's "section-name-3" (through "section-name-4"). To retrieve an individual record from the sort file, the **OUTPUT PROCEDURE** must have a **"RETURN** statement," whose form is as follows.

RETURN file-name **[RECORD]**
AT END statement

Here, "file-name" identifies the sort file from which a record will be retrieved and placed into the sort file's record-description entry. "Statement" denotes an imperative statement to be executed when end-of-life occurs on the sorted file. If, on the other hand, the **"GIVING"** clause is specified, then the sorted file will be written directly onto the file named "file-name-4," which also must be **OPEN**ed by the program in advance of the **SORT** statement's execution.

The Report Writer Facility

COBOL applications usually require one or more carefully formatted reports to be produced by the program. The Report Writer facility attempts to ease this burden by allowing the programmer to specify the physical layout of a report, rather than the program logic that would be required to produce that report. In this section we describe the essential characteristics of this facility, leaving much detail to be obtained by the interested reader from other references.

To use the Report Writer facility, a COBOL program must have the following elements.

Data Division

1. A file-description (**FD**) entry in the File Section that identifies the output file upon which each report is to be written.

2. A Report Section, containing a description of each report to be generated.

Procedure Division

1. Initialize the generation of a report, using the **"INITIATE"** statement.

2. Perform the generation of a report, using the **"GENERATE"** statement.

3. Complete the generation of a report, using the **"TERMINATE"** statement.

The program must also establish access to a sequential input file, whose individual records supply the basic data for the report.

That file must be sorted according to some known set of fields, known as "controls." For example, extracted records from the order file of Case Study 3 are sorted to ascending sequence by **STATE-DIST** and **SALESPSN-ID.** Whenever a record is read whose controls differ from those of the previous record, a "control break" is said to occur.

Now, any report is said to be divided into a sequence of groups, each having three different kinds of information:

Heading lines; identify the report and control values for the current group.

Detail lines; report individual records' data.

Footing lines; summarize (total) detail lines for the current group.

For instance, the Sales Summary report is divided into a sequence of groups, one for each different **STATE** and **DISTRICT** represented on the file. Each group's heading lines identify its **STATE** and **DISTRICT,** as well as other literal information. Its detail lines contain totals for individual salespersons, and its footing line contains totals for all salespersons in that **STATE** and **DISTRICT.**

An ordinary **FD** entry must be provided in the File Section of the Data Division for the file(s) upon which the report(s) are to be generated. It must contain the following special clause.

REPORT IS report-name

Here, "report-name" denotes any unique nonreserved user-defined word which identifies the report.

The Report Section contains one "Report Description (**RD**) entry" and a set of "report group description entries" for each report to be generated. It must always be the last section in the Data Division, and its header is written as follows, beginning in Area A.

REPORT SECTION.

A Report Description entry defines the report's overall characteristics; mainly its control fields, its name, and the number of lines on a page. It has the following form, beginning in Area A.

> **RD** report-name **CONTROLS ARE** name-list
> **PAGE LIMIT IS** integer **LINES.**

Here, "report-name" again denotes the name of the report, while "name-list" denotes a list of names of the fields which constitute the report's controls (e.g., **STATE-DIST** and **SALESPSN-ID**), mutually separated by comma-space (,ᗐ). The order in which these names are listed denotes the hierarchy of controls; the first name listed denotes the major control, and so forth.

Following the **RD** entry for a report, a set of report group description entries defines the layout and content of a typical group's heading lines, detail lines, and footing lines. Here the control break(s) are also defined. Each of these three types of "report groups" is described using a hierarchical structure similar in form to a record-description entry.

A report group describing the heading lines of a report has the following form.

> **01 TYPE CONTROL HEADING** name **LINE NEXT PAGE.**
> {heading-description}

Here, "name" identifies the control break upon which the heading for a new group will be generated. "Heading-description" denotes the actual values which compose the heading. It is a hierarchy of record-description entries having the following form.

$$
\begin{aligned}
&\text{level-number [name]} \\
&\left[\textbf{LINE} \left\{ \begin{array}{l} \text{integer-1} \\ \textbf{NEXT PAGE} \end{array} \right\} \right] \\
&[\textbf{COLUMN} \text{ integer-2}] \\
&[\textbf{PICTURE} \text{ picture}] \\
&\left[\left\{ \begin{array}{l} \textbf{SOURCE} \text{ identifier} \\ \textbf{VALUE} \text{ literal} \end{array} \right\} \right]
\end{aligned}
$$

Here, "level-number" denotes a two-digit integer from 02 to 49 which defines the hierarchical level of the entry named "name."

The **LINE** clause denotes vertical spacing either to the line given as "integer-1" or the first line on the **NEXT PAGE.** Its omission signifies remaining on the current line. The **COLUMN** clause denotes horizontal spacing to the position given as "integer-2" on the line.

The **PICTURE** and **SOURCE(VALUE)** clauses either both appear or both do not appear. The **PICTURE** clause describes, in its usual way, the format of the heading item to be printed, while the **SOURCE** or **VALUE** clause is used to designate the actual value that will appear. The **VALUE** clause is used when a literal constant is to be printed, while the **SOURCE** clause is used when a value stored in "identifier" is to be printed.

The **CONTROL HEADING** description items consist of four different lines, which are presented in ascending order from the top of the page. On line 1 there are two items, one a literal constant title such as **"SALES SUMMARY REPORT"** and the other a variable taken from the **SOURCE "THIS-MONTH."**

Detail lines are similarly defined, except that they have **TYPE DETAIL** rather than **TYPE CONTROL HEADING.** Also a detail line's vertical positioning may be described by

LINE PLUS integer

which says that it occurs "integer" lines below the previous line. On the other hand, a report may be defined so that individual detail lines are not printed. This is accomplished by omitting both the **LINE** and **COLUMN** clauses from the line's description.

Control footing lines are similarly defined, but with the following additional considerations. First, its 01-level entry has the following form.

01 TYPE CONTROL FOOTING name.

Here, "name" identifies the control break upon which a control footing will be generated. Second, the value printed on a control footing line may be designated by the **SOURCE, VALUE,** or **SUM** clause. The latter is selected when the value is to be computed as the sum of all values of all occurrences of an "identifier" before the control break occurred. The **SUM** clause has the following form.

SUM identifier

This brief discussion and illustration should enable the reader to assimilate the basic facilities of the Report Writer feature. The interested reader should consult a COBOL reference manual for more extensive information.

14-8 COMPARISON OF 1968 AND 1974 STANDARDS

The following list summarizes the main differences between the 1968 and 1974 COBOL standards.

1. The 1968 standard's **REMARKS** paragraph and **NOTE** statement have been replaced by the asterisk (∗) in position 7 for inserting documentary comments anywhere within a program.

2. The 1968 standard's **EXAMINE** statement has been replaced and generalized in the form of the new **INSPECT** statement.

3. Certain syntax rules in the 1968 standard have been relaxed: 77-level items need not precede all 01-level items; commas, periods, and semi-colons may be preceded by a space; a space need not intervene between a variable and its subscript.

4. String manipulation facilities have been enhanced by addition of the **STRING** and **UNSTRING** statements. Also the programmer can dynamically redefine the collating sequence which is used as a basis for string comparisons.

5. The 1968 standard's Random Access Input-Output facility has been augmented with a new Indexed Input-Output facility. An Indexed file can be

accessed either randomly or sequentially, while a Random Access (renamed "Relative") file can be accessed only randomly.

6. The 1968 standard's sort facility has been renamed Sort-Merge, and extended to include the capability to merge two files using a single (**MERGE**) statement.

7. The Report-Writer facility has been extended and defined more clearly in the 1974 standard.

8. The 1974 standard's Debugging facilities are completely new.

9. The 1974 standard's subroutine linkage facilities (**CALL** and **EXIT PRO-GRAM** statements, Linkage Section) are completely new.

10. The 1974 standard includes new facilities for writing programs which support communications applications.

FORTRAN

Harry L. Helms

15-1 INTRODUCTION

FORTRAN is an acronym for FORmula TRANSlator. It is one of the oldest high-level languages and is still one of the most widely used.

The first implementation of FORTRAN, FORTRAN I, was developed in 1954 and was first used in 1956 on an IBM 704 computer. In 1958 an enhanced version known as FORTRAN II was introduced. FORTRAN II was followed a few years later by FORTRAN III. However, FORTRAN III was never put into any widespread use.

A major advance was the development of FORTRAN IV in 1962. Thanks to its implementation on IBM systems, it soon achieved wide use. Also in 1962, the American Standards Association organized a committee to develop a uniform version of FORTRAN. In 1966 the committee completed its work, and the result became known as ANSI FORTRAN or FORTRAN-66.

Following 1966 there were several teaching versions of FORTRAN developed. Particularly noteworthy were WATFOR and WATFIV, designed at the University of Waterloo (Ontario). Several other variations of FORTRAN were also developed. These culminated in a revision of FORTRAN in 1977 which became known as FORTRAN-77. It replaced FORTRAN-66 as the ANSI version of FORTRAN. FORTRAN-77 incorporates several of the most useful features of WATFOR and WATFIV. FORTRAN-77 is also the implementation that will be discussed in this section.

FORTRAN is an especially useful language for problems which can be expressed in mathematical or algebraic form. Its ability to handle complex numbers has made it popular for scientific engineering applications. However, it is not limited to those applications.

15-2 PROGRAM FORMAT

FORTRAN programs consist of lines known as statements. Program execution normally begins with the first statement in the program and continues sequentially until the last statement in the program has been executed. However, the order of execution may be altered through the use of control and transfer statements. Normally, FORTRAN programs will be terminated with the **STOP** and **END** statements. The **STOP** statement finishes the execution of the program, while **END** is a message to the compiler that the end of the FORTRAN source program has been reached. The **END** statement must be the last statement in every FORTRAN program.

Comments may be added to a FORTRAN program as needed by placing an asterisk (*) or the letter **C** in the first column position on a program line. Comments do not affect program execution in any way.

FORTRAN statements may be assigned line numbers if desired. These are not mandatory unless a statement is referenced by another statement in the program (such as a control or transfer statement). Line numbers can be any number of five digits or less. Line numbers are placed in the first five column positions on a program. They do not have to be in any order; larger value line numbers may precede smaller value line numbers in a program. However, good programming practice dictates that line number assignment be done in a logical rather than haphazard fashion.

If a FORTRAN statement is too long for a single line, it may be continued on succeeding lines by placing any character other than zero in the sixth column position from the left. The first line of the statement to be continued does not require a character in the sixth column position.

15-3 KEY PUNCH AND TERMINAL ENTRY

For many years, FORTRAN programs were entered into a computer by means of a deck of punched cards. Recently, there has been the introduction of video terminals for the entry of FORTRAN programs. There are some differences in the way a FORTRAN program is prepared for entry depending upon whether punched cards or a video terminal is used.

Punched cards are divided into 80 column positions running from left to right across the card. The first column position is used for indicating whether the line is a comment. The first five column positions can be used for line numbers. The sixth column position is reserved for a character indicating the statement is continued from a previous line. Column positions 7 through 72 are used for the FORTRAN statement. The remaining column positions, 73 through 80, are not read by the computer system. They may be left blank; however, they are commonly used to sequentially number the punched cards so as to insure the statements of the FORTRAN program are in proper order.

The major difference to the above format when a video terminal is used is that each line of the program must be assigned a line sequencing number. Line sequencing numbers are normally five-digit numbers in the range of 00001 to 99999. The statements will be executed in the order of the values of the line numbers.

Continued statements are indicated by a plus sign (+) in the column position immediately following the lines sequencing number. If there is any other character in the column position immediately following the line sequencing number, the line is treated as a comment.

Line sequencing numbers do not replace optional statement numbers. Statement numbers may come between the line sequencing number and the statement itself, as in this example:

$$00010* \text{ THIS IS A COMMENT LINE}$$
$$00020 \text{ } 100 \text{ A } = \text{ B } + \text{ C}$$

15-4 CONSTANTS AND VARIABLES

The same rules apply to constant and variable names in FORTRAN. The first character must be a letter of the alphabet. The remaining characters may be letters of the alphabet or digits (0–9). The maximum length of a constant or variable name is six letters.

FORTRAN differentiates between real and integer names for constants and variables by the first letter of the name. Name for integer constants and variables begin with the letters I, J, K, L, M, or N. Names for real constants and variables begin with the remaining letters of the alphabet (A through H and O through Z). There are FORTRAN statements which allow this convention to be overturned, however, and they will be discussed later in this chapter.

FORTRAN permits six types of constants and variables: integer, real, double-precision, complex, logical, and character. They are as follows:

Integer   a value without a decimal point, the letter E, or the letter D. It may contain a sign; if one is not given, the value is treated as positive.

Real   a value with a decimal point or expressed in exponential form using the letter E. This type of value has seven significant digits.

Double Precision   a real value with sixteen significant digits instead of seven. It is written in exponential form using the letter D instead of E.

Complex   a value comprised of a real number component and an imaginary number component. A complex value is represented by two real values. For example, the expression

$$(1.7, 7.98)$$

represents the complex value

$$1.7 + 7.98i$$

Logical   a constant or variable that can assume one of two values, .TRUE. or .FALSE.

Character   a value that is a string of characters enclosed in single quotes, as in

$$\text{‘CHARACTER’}$$

If a single quote is desired within a string, two consecutive single quotes should be used. Thus, the string VARIABLE'S NAME could be represented as **‘VARIABLE''S NAME’**.

15-5   TYPE DECLARATIONS

As mentioned before, FORTRAN has the intrinsic ability to specify whether a constant or variable name is integer or real by the first letter of the name. However, there may be situations where one wishes to have an integer variable name beginning with A or a real constant name such as **IXT**. Also, the programmer needs a way to specify names which represent complex constants, logical variables, etc. FORTRAN handles such situations through the **TYPE** and **IMPLICIT** declarations.

The **TYPE** declaration specifies the data type to be represented by a variable name. The form is

$$\text{\textbf{type} variable name(s)}$$

where type is **INTEGER, REAL, CHARACTER, DOUBLE PRECISION, COMPLEX,** or **LOGICAL.** Suppose one wished to declare the variable name **VECTOR** as a complex type. The form would be

$$\text{\textbf{COMPLEX VECTOR}}$$

In a similar situation, suppose one wished to declare **TEST1** and **TEST2** as logical constants. The form would be

$$\text{\textbf{LOGICAL TEST1, TEST2}}$$

The **IMPLICIT** declaration allows the specification of all variable and constant names beginning with a given first letter as being of a certain type. The form is

IMPLICIT type (letters)

where type is **REAL, COMPLEX,** etc., and the letters are the first letters of the variable names to be of the type specified. The letters in parentheses may be separated by commas (A, B, D, F) or by a dash if a range of letters is to be declared. For example, (A,B,C,D,E,F) is equivalent to (A–F).

It is possible to overturn the effect of an **IMPLICIT** declaration for specific constant or variable names by a following **TYPE** declaration. For example, the program lines

IMPLICIT DOUBLE PRECISION (A–Z)
COMPLEX VECTOR, FUNC

would declare all constant and variable names to be double-precision, with the exception of **FUNC** and **VECTOR,** which are declared to be complex.

15-6 ARRAYS

An array in FORTRAN is a group of data referred to by a single variable name. Individual items of the group are referred to by the variable name followed by one or more numbers in parentheses. The numbers in parentheses are known as subscripts. An array may have up to seven subscripts. Each subscript is separated from the other by commas.

Arrays are established by the **DIMENSION** statement. The general form is

DIMENSION variable name (first subscript, second subscript, etc.)

For example, the statement **DIMENSION ABLE (2, 3)** would establish an array with the elements **ABLE (1, 1), ABLE (1, 2), ABLE (1, 3), ABLE (2, 1), ABLE (2, 2),** and **ABLE (2, 3).**

All subscripts must be integers, integer expressions, or integer non-subscripted variables.

DIMENSION statements must appear at the beginning of a program, before all executable statements.

It is also possible to express the subscripts of a **DIMENSION** statement in terms of lower and upper boundaries. For example, the statement **DIMENSION YEAR (1952:1982)** would set up an array having the elements **YEAR (1952), YEAR (1953), YEAR (1954),** etc., up through **YEAR (1982).**

15-7 ASSIGNMENT OF VALUES

Often it is necessary to assign an initial value to a variable name. This is done by the **DATA** statement. It has two forms:

DATA variable names/values
DATA variable names/values, variable names/values, etc.

If several variable names are to be assigned the same value, the repeator symbol may be used to save space. The repeator symbol is an integer specifying the number of repetitions plus an asterisk before the value to be repeated. For example, the statement

DATA A, B, C, D, E /5 * 1.5/

would assign the value of 1.5 to the variable names **A, B, C, D,** and **E.**

Variable names must agree with the type of data being assigned to them by a **DATA** statement. For example, if a real value is assigned to a variable name beginning with I, an error will result.

DATA statements must be placed after specification statements such as **DIMENSION** but before any executable statements.

15-8 ARITHMETIC OPERATORS

FORTRAN uses the following symbols for arithmetic operations:

+	Addition
−	Subtraction
/	Division
*	Multiplication
**	Exponentiation

Arithmetic operations are performed from left to right on a program line in the following order of priority:

1. Exponentiation

2. Multiplication and division

3. Addition, subtraction, and negation

However, the above order may be overruled by placing operations in parentheses. Operations in parentheses are always performed first.

FORTRAN allows arithmetic operations involving both integer and real values. (This is known as mixed-mode arithmetic.) However, the result will be a real value.

If a fractional part is obtained from integer division, it is truncated. For example, 5/2 will give a result of 2, not 2.5.

15-9 RELATIONAL OPERATORS

Two arithmetic expressions or variables may be compared by using the following arithmetic expressions:

.LT.	Less than
.LE.	Less than or equal to

.EQ.	Equal to
.NE.	Not equal to
.GT.	Greater than
.GE.	Greater than or equal to

15-10 THE EQUALS SYMBOL

The = symbol can be used in arithmetic expressions to indicate the outcome of an operation and to assign the outcome to a variable name. For example, the expression $5/2 = A$ would result in the value of 2.5 being assigned to **A**. Initial values may be assigned to variables by using = instead of a **DATA** statement, as in $A = 2.5$.

15-11 CONTROL AND TRANSFER STATEMENTS

As mentioned earlier, a FORTRAN program is normally executed beginning with the first statement in the program and continuing with each succeeding statement until the last statement in the program is reached. However, FORTRAN has several statements which alter this pattern. The following is a brief description of each:

GO TO   The **GO TO** statement has three variations: unconditional, conditional, and assigned.

Unconditional. The unconditional **GO TO** statement causes program control to shift to the statement whose line number follows **GO TO.** The statement

GO TO 100

will cause the program to immediately shift to line number 100 and execute the statement. The program would next execute the statement immediately following the one on line number 100 and continue executing succeeding statements in a normal manner.

Conditional. The unconditional **GO TO** is executed when found in a program regardless of other conditions. In contrast, the conditional **GO TO** shifts program control to various line numbers depending upon the value of an index variable. Its form is

GO TO (line numbers), index variable

where the line numbers within parentheses are separated from each other by commas and the index variable is an integer variable.

In a conditional **GO TO** statement, program control shifts to the first line number within parentheses if the value of the index variable is 1. If the value of the index variable is 2, program control shifts to the second line number in the parentheses. If the index variable value is 3, control shifts to the third line number, and so forth. If the value of the index variable is greater than the number of line numbers in parentheses, the next statement immediately following the conditional **GO TO** is executed. The following is an example of a conditional **GO TO** statement:

GO TO (50, 20, 75) N

IF N = 1   2   3   4

The statement immediately following is executed

Assigned. The assigned **GO TO** statement requires the use of two statements; **GO TO** and **ASSIGN.** The general form of an assigned **GO TO** statement is

ASSIGN first variable **TO** second variable

GO TO second variable (line numbers)

where the first and second variables are both integer variables. The first variable can be an integer constant as well. The **ASSIGN** statement must be executed before the assigned **GO TO** statement is executed.

The **ASSIGN** statement transfers the value of the first variable to the second variable, which is then used in the assigned **GO TO** statement. The assigned **GO TO** statement then shifts program control to one of the line numbers within parentheses depending upon the value of the second variable in a similar fashion to the computed **GO TO** statement. However, the value of the second variable must be one of the line numbers within parentheses. Further, the name for the second variable must not be used for another purpose within the program.

IF ... THEN ... ELSE   The **IF ... THEN ... ELSE** statement construct allows selection of alternative actions depending upon a given condition. The general form of this is

IF (condition) **THEN** first consequence

ELSE second consequence

END IF

where condition is a relational or logical expression and the first and second consequences are one or more statements. The condition in parentheses is evaluated. If it is true, the first consequence following **THEN** is executed. If it is false, the second consequence following **ELSE** is executed. It is also possible to use **IF** with an **ELSE IF** statement as follows:

IF (first condition) **THEN** first consequence

ELSE IF (second condition) **THEN** second consequence

END IF

END IF

In the above example, the first condition is evaluated. If it is true, the first consequence is executed. If it is false, the second condition is evaluated. If the second condition is true, the second consequence is executed. If the second condition is false, the third consequence is executed.

Computer IF   This statement transfers program to different line numbers depending upon the value of an arithmetic expression. Its form is

IF (expression) num1, num2, num3

where the arithmetic expression is in parentheses and num1, num2, and num3 represent three statement line numbers. If the expression in parentheses evaluates to a value less than zero, program control shifts to num1. If the expression equals zero, program control shifts to num2. If the expression is greater than zero, program control shifts to num3.

Logical IF   This statement evaluates a logical expression in parentheses. If the logical expression is true, the consequence statement on the same line is executed. If the logical expression is false, the statement immediately following the **IF** statement is executed. For example

IF (A .LT. B) STOP

while stop program execution is **A** is less than **B**; otherwise, the statement will be ignored. The consequence statement can be any FORTRAN statement with the exception of another logical **IF** or a **DO** statement (to be described later).

In addition to the relational operators described previously, logical expressions may use the **.NOT.**, **.AND.**, and **.OR.** logical operators. Their effects are as follows:

.NOT.   Returns a value of **.TRUE.** if the value of an expression is **.FALSE.** Returns value of **.FALSE.** if the value of the expression is **.TRUE.**

.AND.   Used to join two expressions; returns a value of **.TRUE.** if both expressions are **.TRUE.** Otherwise, returns a value of **.FALSE.**

.OR.   Used to join two expressions; returns a value of **.TRUE.** if either or both expressions are **.TRUE.** Returns a value of **.FALSE.** if both expressions are **.FALSE.**

When logical, relational, and arithmetic operators are contained in the same expression, the expression is evaluated from left to right in the following order:

1. Exponentiation
2. Multiplication and division
3. Addition and subtraction
4. Relational operators
5. .NOT.
6. .AND.
7. .OR.

DO   The **DO** statement allows a statement or series of statements to be repetitively executed for as many times as desired. The usual form of the **DO** statement is

DO label **I** = int, ter, incr

. . . . .

statements to be executed

. . . . .

label **CONTINUE**

where label is a statement line number, **I** is an integer variable (known as the index or control variable), int is the initial value of the index variable, ter is the terminal or final value of the index variable, and incr is the increment by which the index variable increases with each repetition. The values of int, ter, and incr may be negative. FORTRAN does not require that the repetitive loops established by the **DO** statement end with **CONTINUE.** However, it is considered good programming practice to do so.

A typical **DO** statement might look like this:

$$\text{DO } 100 \text{ I} = 5, 1000, 10$$
$$\text{N} = \text{N} + 1$$
$$\text{100 CONTINUE}$$

This **DO** statement will cause 1 to be added to the value of **N** repetitively. The initial value of the index variable is 5. The first time the loop is executed, 10 is added to the index variable, giving a value of 15. This process repeats as long as the index value is less than or equal to 1000. When the value of the index variable exceeds 1000, the first statement following **CONTINUE** is executed.

PAUSE   This statement temporarily stops execution of a program and causes the word **PAUSE** to be displayed on the output device of the computer system. The form of this statement is

PAUSE integer constant

where the integer constant has five or fewer digits. **PAUSE** is used to allow the computer operator to change storage tapes or disks, check on program results at a desired point, etc.

STOP   This statement terminates execution of the program. As mentioned previously, it comes at the end of a program, before the **END** statement. It is also used as a consequence of **IF** and **IF . . . THEN . . . ELSE** statements.

END   This statement alerts the compiler that the end of the program has been reached. It must be the last statement in the program and should have no line number.

15-12 SUBPROGRAMS

FORTRAN allows routines to be written separately from the main program and for these routines to be used by the main program. This allows a desired function to be obtained as needed without writing the same group of statements each time.

FORTRAN allows two types of subprograms: functions and subroutines. Functions return only one result while subroutines can return more than one result.

Functions are created using the **FUNCTION** statement. The form is

FUNCTION name (dummy arguments)

. . . . .

valid FORTRAN statements (except **FUNCTION,**
    SUBROUTINE, and **BLOCK DATA** statements)

. . . . .

RETURN

. . . . .

END

in which name follows the same rules as those for constant and variable names. The dummy arguments are variable names used within the function to represent values "transferred" to the function from the main program. The type of result (real, complex, etc.) must agree with the name following **FUNCTION.** If not, the appropriate type declaration (**REAL, COMPLEX,** etc.) must precede **FUNCTION.** Also, there must be one statement within the function that assigns the function name to a value.

In the main program, the function is referred to by its name. Suppose we have defined a function named **RATIO** as follows:

> **FUNCTION RATIO (A, B)**
> **RATIO = A/B**
> **RETURN**
> **END**

Suppose in the main program we wish to use the function **RATIO** with the values 15 and 2 and assign the result to the variable name **RESULT.** The statement to do so would be

> **RESULT = RATIO (15, 2)**

In the function **RATIO, A** would have a value of 15 and **B** would have a value of 2. After the function is executed, the name **RATIO** would have a value of 7.5 in the main program. The value of **RATIO** would then be assigned to **RESULT.**

Subroutines are similar to functions, but can return more than one result. The usual form is

> **SUBROUTINE** name (dummy arguments)
>
> . . . . .
>
> Valid FORTRAN statements (except **FUNCTION,**
>   **SUBROUTINE,** and **BLOCK DATA** statements)
>
> . . . . .
>
> **RETURN**
>
> . . . . .
>
> **END**

The subroutine name must be a valid variable or constant name, as was the case with functions.

Subroutines are referred to by the main program using **CALL** statements. Their form is

> **CALL** name (actual arguments)

where name is the name of the subroutine. The actual and dummy arguments must correspond in order, number, type, and mode. Values are transferred from the actual arguments to the dummy arguments when **CALL** is executed. When the subroutine execution is finished, values are transferred back from the dummy arguments to the actual arguments. Dummy arguments may be non-subscripted variables or an array name. The actual arguments may be constants, non-subscripted variables, array elements, expressions, an array name, or a reference to another subprogram.

It is possible to have main programs and subprograms share the same storage locations for data through the **COMMON** statement. The form is

COMMON names

where names represent the list of data to be shared by both the main program and subprogram(s). Suppose the statement

COMMON X, Y, Z

appears in the main program. To refer to the same data storage locations in a subprogram, the statement

COMMON X, Y, Z

or

COMMON A, B, C

may be used, although normal practice is to use the same variable names for both main program and subroutine **COMMON** statement. Corresponding variable names must agree in type.

It is also possible to reserve "blocks" of **COMMON** storage by labeling such blocks. The form is

COMMON/label/names/label/names

where both the labels and names follow the rules for naming constant and variable names. The labeled **COMMON** is useful when subprograms need to share only a portion of the data common to the main program and subprograms. In such a case, the subprogram **COMMON** statement will have the label(s) of only the data storage locations common to that subprogram and the main program.

Data may be entered into a labeled **COMMON** statement through a **BLOCK DATA** subprogram. The form is

BLOCK DATA

. . . . .

DATA, DIMENSION, IMPLICIT, TYPE, SAVE,
     EQUIVALENT, COMMON, PARAMETER statements

. . . . .

END

The **BLOCK DATA** statement will define initial values for the main program and subprograms.

The **EQUIVALENCE** statement can also be used to indicate that two variable names share the same memory location. The statement

EQUIVALENCE (A, B, C)

would reserve the same memory locations for the variable names **A, B,** and **C.**

Variables in a subprogram that are not in an unlabeled **COMMON** statement or in the argument list are "lost" when control returns to the main program. These can be retained by the **SAVE** statement. Its form is

SAVE subprogram name

or

SAVE variable name(s)

If the subprogram name follows **SAVE**, all variables in the subroutine are saved. Otherwise, only the variable(s) specified will be retained.

FORTRAN contains many "built-in" functions, which are known as intrinsic functions. These will be discussed later. However, there may be occasions when it is necessary to use the name of an intrinsic function, a user-defined function, or subroutine in the argument list of a subprogram call. Since subprogram names and variable names follow the same rules, the compiler cannot distinguish between the two unless an **INTRINSIC** or **EXTERNAL** statement is used. The form for both is either **INTRINSIC** or **EXTERNAL** followed by the name to be declared. **INTRINSIC** is used with the FORTRAN-supplied intrinsic while **EXTERNAL** is used with user-defined subprograms.

It is possible to enter a subprogram through a point other than the normal entry point using the **ENTRY** statement. The **ENTRY** statement is placed within the subroutine at the desired alternate entry point(s). The form is

ENTRY name (dummy arguments)

and it may be accessed by a **CALL** statement in the same manner as an ordinary subroutine.

15-13 INTRINSIC FUNCTIONS

FORTRAN includes numerous functions that are intrinsic (pre-defined and declared) to the language. Many of these functions are to be used only with certain types of expressions, such as real, complex, etc. The usual form of function is

function (expression)

The following is a listing of functions by type:

Complex

CABS Returns the absolute value of an expression.

CCOS Returns the cosine of an angle in radians.

CEXP Exponential (e) raised to power of the expression.

CLOG Returns the natural logarithm e of the expression.

CMPLX Converts expression to complex number.

CONJ Returns the conjugate of a complex function.

CSQRT Returns the square root of the expression.

CSIN Returns the sine of an angle in radians.

Integer

IABS Returns the absolute value of an expression.

IDIM Returns the positive differences between two values.

IDINT Converts a double-precision value to integer.

IFIX Converts a real value to integer.

INT Truncates the decimal part of a value.

ISIGN Transfers the sign from one integer value to another.

MAXO Selects the largest of several values.

MINO Selects the smallest of several values.

MIN1 Selects the smallest of several values but converts any real result to integer.

Double Precision

DABS Returns the absolute value of an expression.

DACOS Returns the arccosine of an expression.

DASIN Returns the arcsine of an expression.

DATAN Returns the arctangent of one argument.

DANTAN2 Returns the arctangent of two arguments.

DBLE Converts an expression to double-precision.

DCOS Returns the cosine of an argument in radians.

DCOSH Returns the hyperbolic cosine of an argument.

DDIM Returns the positive difference between two arguments.

DEXP Returns the exponential (e) raised to the power of the expression.

DINT Truncates the decimal part of an expression.

DLOG Returns the natural logarithm e of an expression.

DLOG10 Returns the common logarithm of an expression.

DMAX1 Selects the largest of several values.

DMIN1 Selects the smallest of several values.

DMOD Returns the remainder from division by two values.

DNINT Returns the whole number closest in value to the expression.

DPROD Converts a real value to double-precision.

DSIGN Transfers the sign from one value to another.

DSIN Returns the sine of an expression in radians.

DSINH Returns the hyperbolic sine of an argument.

DSQRT Returns the square root of an expression.

DTAN Returns the tangent of an argument in radians.

DTANH Returns the hyperbolic tangent of an expression.

IDINT Converts the expression to the nearest integer value.

Real

ABS Returns the absolute value of an expression.

ACOS Returns the arccosine of an an expression.

AIMAG Returns the imaginary part of a complex number.

AINT Truncates the decimal part of an expression.

ALOG   Returns the natural logarithm of an expression.

ALOG10   Returns the common logarithm of an expression.

AMAX1   Selects the largest value of several arguments.

AMIN1   Selects the smallest value of several arguments.

AMOD   Returns the remainder from division of two values.

ANINT   Returns the nearest whole number in value to the argument.

ASIN   Returns the arcsine of an argument.

ATAN   Returns the arctangent of an expression in radians.

ATAN2   Returns the arctangent of two arguments in radians.

COS   Returns the cosine of an argument in radians.

COSH   Returns the hyperbolic cosine of an argument.

DIM   Returns the positive difference between two arguments.

EXP   Returns the exponential (e) raised to the power of the expression.

FLOAT   Converts an expression to a real number.

NINT   Returns the nearest integer value.

REAL   Converts a complex value to a real value.

SIGN   Transfers the sign from one value to another.

SIN   Returns the sine of an argument in radians.

SINH   Returns the hyperbolic sine of an argument.

SORT   Returns the square root of an argument.

SNGL   Converts a double-precision value to a single-precision value.

TAN   Returns the tangent of an argument in radians.

TANH   Returns the hyperbolic tangent of an argument.

15-14 PARAMETERS

A constant can be given a name by the **PARAMETER** statement. The form is

PARAMETER name

where name follows the same rules as variable names. Once a constant has been named by a **PARAMETER** statement, its value cannot be altered in the program.

15-15 NAMING PROGRAMS

FORTRAN permits the naming of a program if desired. This is done by a **PROGRAM** statement. The form is

PROGRAM name

If used, **PROGRAM** should be the first statement in a program.

15-16 CHARACTER MANIPULATION

Earlier, the data type **CHARACTER** was defined as a value that is a string of characters enclosed in single quotes. Difficulties in handling character data had long been a weakness of FORTRAN; however, FORTRAN-77 includes several new features for manipulating character (or string) data.

Two-character strings may be concatenated by the concatenation operator //. Suppose that

$$A = \text{'ABC' } B = \text{'CBA'}$$

thus

$$C = A//B$$

would result in

$$C = \text{'ABCCBA'}$$

It is also possible to obtain a substring of a character string. The form is

substring name = string name (int1 : int2)

where substring name is the name to identify the substring, string name identifies the string the substring is to be taken from, int1 identifies the position of the beginning of the substring, and int2 identifies the position of the end of the substring. Suppose there is a character string **DIGITS = '1 2 3 4 5 6 7 8'**. Thus

$$\textbf{INTS} = \textbf{DIGITS (2:7)}$$

would produce the substring **INTS = '2 3 4 5 6 7'**.

There are four intrinsic functions for comparing two character strings. Their form is

function (string1, string 2)

and each function returns a value of **.TRUE.** if the condition described is met. They are as follows:

LGE   The first string is equal to the second string or follows it in collating sequence.

LGT   The first string follows the second in collating sequence.

LLE   The first string is equal to the second or precedes it in collating sequence.

LLT   The first string precedes the second in the collating sequence.

There are also four intrinsic functions for manipulating character data, as follows:

CHAR   Converts a single digit to a character.

ICAR   Converts a single character to a string.

INDEX   Returns an integer indicating the starting position of a substring in a longer string. The form is

INDEX (string, substring)

where string and substring are represented by variable names.

LEN   Returns the length of a character string.

15-17 EQUIVALENCE OPERATORS

FORTRAN also includes two operators to test whether two expressions are equivalent to each other. They are:

.EQV.   Statement is **.TRUE.** if the expressions are equivalent.

.NEQV.   Statement is **.TRUE.** if the expressions are not equivalent.

   .EQV. and **.NEQV.** have the lowest priority of all operational symbols, with **.NEQV.** lower than **.EQV.**

15-18 FILE ORGANIZATION

FORTRAN includes facilities to mainpulate sequential, random, and stream files, although its capabilities in this regard are not as extensive as COBOL.

   Individual compilers and computer systems have varying techniques for the creation and handling of files on disk and tape. Because of these differences file statements will be discussed only in general terms. For a more precise description of a computer system's file handling capabilities, consult the operating manual for the system in question.

OPEN   This statement connects an existing file to an input/output device or generates a new file. It is followed by a list of specifiers in parentheses which describe the file. The specifiers are as follows:

   UNIT=   the file unit number
   IOSTAT   integer variable for input/output status
   FILE   name of the file
   ERR   statement label to transfer to in case of error
   STATUS   describes the status of the file using the following descriptors:
      OLD, NEW, SCRATCH, or **UNKNOWN**
   ACCESS   **SEQUENTIAL** or **DIRECT**
   FORM   **FORMATTED** or **UNFORMATTED**
   RECL   length of record if file is direct access type
   BLANK   specifies handling of blanks, either **NULL** or **ZERO**

CLOSE   This statement disconnects a peripheral from a file. It is followed by a list of specifiers in parentheses as follows:
   UNIT=   the file unit number
   IOSTAT   integer variable for input/output status
   ERR   statement label to transfer to in case of error
   STATUS   **KEEP** or **DELETE**

INQUIRE   This statement returns information about the attributes of a file. Information about a file is returned as **"YES," "NO,"** or **"UNKNOWN"**; for other specifiers, the information is **.TRUE.** or **.FALSE.** Besides the **UNIT=**, **IOSTAT,** and **ERR** specifiers, the **INQUIRE** statement also uses the following:
   EXIST   **.TRUE.** if file exists
   OPENED   **.TRUE.** if is open
   NUMBER   number of peripheral connected to file

NAMED .TRUE. if file has a name
NAME returns name of the file
ACCESS returns "SEQUENTIAL" or "DIRECT"
FORM returns whether a file is formatted or unformatted
FORMATTED returns a "yes" or "no"
UNFORMATTED returns a "yes" or "no"
RECL returns length of records in file
NEXTREC returns number of next record in a direct access file
BLANK returns whether blanks or zeroes are being used

REWIND Causes a file on tape to be rewound to its beginning.

BACKSPACE Causes a tape file to backspace one record.

ENDFILE Places an end of file mark on a tape.

15-19 LIST-DIRECTED (STREAM) INPUT/ OUTPUT

Data can be entered and output in FORTRAN using a preset format. This is known as list-directed or stream input and output. This can be done with the **READ, PRINT,** and **WRITE** statements using an asterisk (*) in place of a format identifier. The general definitions of **READ, PRINT** and **WRITE** are:

READ Inputs data and assigns it to variable names.

PRINT prints out the values associated with a list of variables.

WRITE Similar to **PRINT,** but can also output data to memory and peripheral devices

In list-directed operations, these statements would be used as follows:

READ* variable 1, variable 2, . . .
PRINT* variable 1, variable 2, . . .
WRITE* variable 1, variable 2, . . .

Each compiler will have its own rules for spacing between data items, maximum number of digits, etc. The system operating manual should be consulted for such information.

15-20 FORMATTED INPUT/OUTPUT

It is possible to specify the form in which data is read into or written from a computer system by the **FORMAT** statement. The **FORMAT** statement must be used with a **READ, WRITE,** or **PRINT** statement. The forms for formatted input/output are:

READ (d, fsn) list of variables
WRITE (d, fsn) list of variables
PRINT fsn list of variables

where d represents the unit number of the input/output device to be used, fsn is the **FORMAT** statement line number, and the list of variables are those to be input or output in the desired format. Some computer systems allow the use of **READ** without indicating the unit number of the input/output device. For example, the statement

WRITE (1, 700) A, B, C

would cause variables **A, B,** and **C** to be output to the device identified by 1 using the format specified by the **FORMAT** statement at line number 700. The form of the format statement is:

line number **FORMAT** (specifications)

where the line number follows the usual rules of FORTRAN and the specifications within parentheses are separated from each other by commas. The following codes are used to create specifications:

A   character values

B   double-precision values

E   exponential form real values

F   real values

G   general form

H   character constants

I   integer values

L   logical values

P   scale factors, used with B, E, F, and G specifications to shift the decimal point and size of the exponent when a value is output

S   restores the optional + convention to the compiler

SP   prints + with all subsequent positive data

SS   suppresses + for all subsequent positive data

TL   next character is input or output the number of spaces indicated to the left of the current position

TR   next character is input or output the number of spaces indicated to the right of the current position

X   allows editing to the left or right the number of spaces specified

:   ends format control if there are no more items in list

/   skips a record

(The following are used for input only)

BN   specifies blank characters are to be ignored

BZ   specifies all blank spaces are to be treated as zeroes

Specifications for the four most common types of data—integer, real, character, and exponential—follow the forms below:

Integer Iw

Real Fw.d

Character Aw

Exponential Ew.d

where w represents the spaces allocated for the value during input or output, . represents the decimal point, and d represents the number of places to the right of the decimal point. Format specifications for other value types can be created by using format codes in a manner similar to those for the specifications for integer, real, character, and exponential values.

As previously mentioned, **FORMAT** statements must be used with a **READ, WRITE,** or **PRINT** statement. Suppose one wished to reserve five spaces for integer data and ten spaces for real data with seven places to the right of the decimal point on input. This could be done with a pair of statements such as

> **READ (1, 750) INT, REALVR**
> **750 FORMAT (I5, F3.7)**

In the **READ** statement, **1** could refer to the input device (such as terminal or card reader). **750** is the line number of the **FORMAT** statement, and **INT** and **REALVR** are the variable names data will be assigned to. In the **FORMAT** statement specification, **I5** will allocate five spaces (known as a *field*) for the integer variable **INT** and ten places, seven of them to the right of the decimal point, for the real variable **REALVR**.

In this example, the decimal point seems to occupy no space; that is there could be three digits to the left of the decimal point and seven to the right of the decimal point. This applies only to input of data. If this **FORMAT** statement had been used with a **WRITE** or **PRINT** statement, **REALVR** could have only two spaces to the left of the decimal point and seven to the right of the decimal point.

On output, if the integer portion of a field does not occupy all the space allocated to it, all unused spaces to the left are filled with blanks. If the portion to the right of the decimal point does not allocate all the space allocated to it, all unused spaces to the right are filled with zeroes. If the integer portion occupies more spaces than allocated, an error results and a string of asterisks is output. If the portion to the right of the decimal exceeds the spaces allocated to it, the decimal part is truncated and rounded to fit the space allocated to it.

On input, there is no need to insert spaces between data on a line. The **FORMAT** statement will "divide" the line according to the specifications following **FORMAT**. In the previous example, the first five spaces of the line would be read as integer data and the next ten as real data. A line of input data such as **1 2 3 4 5 6 7 8 9 0 1 2 3 4 5** would have assigned the value of **1 2 3 4 5** to **INT** and **6 7 8 9 0 1 2 3 4 5** to **REALVR**. However, if the field specification does not agree with the type of data to be input or output, an error will result.

A field specification may be repeated by placing an integer before it representing the number of times it is to be repeated. For example, **3I5** would set up three fields of five spaces each for integer data.

Descriptive headings and labels can be added by placing characters in single quotes as part of the **FORMAT** statement specification. If one wished to allocate five spaces for integer data on output and to add a descriptive label, it could be done as follows:

WRITE (1, 725) INT
725 FORMAT ('THE ANSWER IS', I5)

FORTRAN includes specification characters to control the printer carriage and other output peripherals, although these vary from system to system.

15-21 RESERVED WORDS

No word used as a statement, function name, or command should be used as a variable or constant name in FORTRAN.

sec.16

Pascal

Harry L. Helms

16-1 INTRODUCTION

Pascal is named for the seventeenth century mathematician Blaise Pascal. It was developed by Niklaus Wirth of the Technical University in Zurich, Switzerland. Prof. Wirth published the first definition of Pascal in 1971.

Pascal was based upon ALGOL. As a teacher, Prof. Wirth was keenly aware that the first programming language a student learns has a great influence on a person's programming style. Thus, one important consideration in Pascal's development was that it should be conducive to teaching good programming style. As a result, Pascal encourages the writing of disciplined, organized programs and fosters increased programmer productivity.

Like ALGOL, Pascal is a block structured language. The various "blocks" compose programs that have clear beginnings and endings with program functions clearly spelled out in separate blocks. This makes modification of a program easier, since changes made to one block need not affect any of the other blocks.

Besides the "standard" Pascal defined by Wirth, there are two other major implementations used. One has become known as "UCSD Pascal," developed by Kenneth Bowles of the University of California at San Diego. UCSD Pascal is a subset of standard Pascal intended primarily for use on minicomputers and microcomputers. Another popular implementation is "Apple Pascal," developed by the Apple Computer Company for its popular line of Apple microcomputers. Apple Pascal is essentially a variant of UCSD Pascal but with extensions for graphics and other hardware capabilities of the Apple microcomputers. We will restrict our discussion here to standard Pascal.

16-2 PROGRAM STRUCTURE

The format of a Pascal program is as follows:

> **PROGRAM** name (**INPUT,OUTPUT**);
> **BEGIN**
> . . . . .
> Statements, each of which must end
> with a semicolon (;)
> . . . . .
> **END.**

The **PROGRAM** declaration establishes the name or identifier of the program. (**INPUT, OUTPUT**) are program parameters. Program parameters will be discussed later; at this point it is sufficient to note that any program accepting input or giving output needs program parameters. At the end of the **PROGRAM** declaration line is a semicolon.

Following the **PROGRAM** declaration come declarations of the constants and variables used in the program (these declarations will be detailed later). The main body of the program is contained between **BEGIN** and **END.** There is no punctuation following **BEGIN.** A period (.) follows **END** rather than a semicolon.

Program statements, each ending with a semicolon, come between **BEGIN** and **END.** They are executed in the order they appear.

Non-executable comments may be included in a program by placing the comment between the symbols (* and *). An example is

(*This is how a comment is made*)

Such comments have no effect on the program and are ignored by the compiler. They should be inserted to identify major sections of the program and to document why certain actions were taken. This is especially useful if there is a possibility that others will examine the program or that the program will need to be revised or updated.

Spacing on program lines has no effect on program execution. It is good programming practice to use spacing and indentation for clarity in reading the program.

16-3 IDENTIFIERS

The name following the **PROGRAM** declaration is an example of an identifier. Identifiers are also used to name constants, variables, and various parts of a program (such as procedures). Identifiers must start with a letter and the characters that follow must be letters or numbers. Spaces or other symbols are not allowed. Identifiers may contain Pascal reserved words but cannot be reserved words. Identifiers may be as long as desired.

16-4 DATA TYPES

One of Pascal's great strengths is its data typing ability. In addition to the data types provided by Pascal, it is also possible to define and use other data types as needed.

The following are data types provided by Pascal:

BOOLEAN: Data types having the logical values of **TRUE** or **FALSE.**

CHAR: Data types whose values are characters.

INTEGER: Data types having values in a range of integer numbers. On minicomputer and microcomputer systems, the range is commonly -32767 to $+32767$. On large computers, it may be as large as -2147483647 to $+2147483647$.

REAL: Data types having values in a range of real numbers. There are limits to the magnitude and precision of real numbers which can be handled by a computer; this varies from system to system.

Definition of other data types will be discussed later.

16-5 DEFINITIONS AND DECLARATIONS

Constants and variables are named using identifiers. However, constants and variables and their associated identifiers must be defined or declared before they can be used in a Pascal program.

Constant definitions and variable declarations may come immediately after the **PROGRAM** declaration and before any executable statements. When they are located in this manner, they are said to be **global.** Global constants and variables may be used anywhere in the program. In addition, constant definitions and variable declarations may be located within the various blocks of a Pascal program and such definitions and declarations are used within that block; they are known as **local** definitions and declarations. It is possible to use the same identifiers for local definitions and declarations in other blocks, although this is usually poor programming practice.

Constant definitions must always precede any variable declarations. Each constant to be defined must be separated from each other by a semicolon. The constant definitions must be preceded by **CONST**, as in the following:

> **CONST**
> > **MILE = 5280;**
> > **FOOT = 12;**
> > **METER = 39.36;**

This definition establishes two integer constants, **MILE** and **FOOT,** and one real constant, **METER.** Once defined, neither the value nor type of a constant may change.

Pascal includes a predefined constant identifier in **MAXINT,** which represents the largest integer value the computer system can handle. The largest negative integer is represented by −**MAXINT** and the largest positive integer by +**MAXINT.**

Each variable that is used in a Pascal program must be declared by a **VAR** statement. The **VAR** statement associates an identifier with each variable and defines its type. An example is as follows:

> **VAR**
> > **COUNT, TOTAL: INTEGER:**
> > **TEMPERATURE: REAL;**
> > **RESULTS: BOOLEAN;**

This statement declares **COUNT** and **TOTAL** to be identifiers associated with integer variables, **TEMPERATURE** to be an identifier associated with a real variable, and **RESULT** to be a variable associated with a Boolean value. Once declared, the type of a variable may not change.

Pascal allows the definition and use of data types other than **BOOLEAN, CHAR, INTEGER,** and **REAL** (in fact, **BOOLEAN, CHAR, INTEGER,** and **REAL** can be considered pre-defined data types). To define new data types, the **TYPE** statement is used. The form is

> **TYPE**
> > **COLORS = (RED, WHITE, YELLOW, BLUE)**

TYPE declarations come between **CONST** and **VAR** declarations. All variables of a defined type must be declared in a **VAR** statement.

Each program block should have only one **CONST, TYPE,** and **VAR** declaration in the block.

16-6 ARRAYS

An array in Pascal is defined as a fixed number of data elements of the same type sharing a common identifier. An array is declared using an ARRAY statement. Its form is

> identifier: **ARRAY** [index] **OF** type

where identifier is an identifier following the rules discussed, index represents the limits of the array, and type is the type of the array elements. The index includes the lowest and highest ranges of the array separated by two dots. The declaration

SUMTOTAL: ARRAY [1..10] OF INTEGER

would set up an array with the elements **SUMTOTAL [1], SUMTOTAL [2],** etc., up to **SUMTOTAL [10].** The number in brackets is known as a **subscript.** If the program tries to reference or use an element outside the range determined by the index, the program will fail.

Arrays may have more than one subscript, or **dimensions.** The form is

identifier: **ARRAY** [index] **OF ARRAY** [index] **OF** type

16-7 ASSIGNMENT OPERATORS

Assignment statements compute a value and assign it to a variable. Values are assigned to variables by inputting data in corresponding order to declaration of the variables. Assignment statements assign new values to variables and are written using the following operators:

:=	A generalized equivalency statement similar to = in algebra
+	Addition
−	Subtraction and negation
*	Multiplication
/	Division with real number result; operands may be real or integer
DIV	Division with integer number result; both operands must be integers
MOD	Gives remainder from integer division

Assignment statements are executed as they appear from left to right. With multiple operators in one line, operations are performed in the following order:

1. Operations in parentheses
2. Negation
3. Multiplication and division
4. Addition and subtraction

16-8 RELATIONAL OPERATORS

Relationships between Pascal expressions are expressed using the following relational operators:

=	Is equal to

<>	Is not equal to
>	Is greater than
>=	Is greater than or equal to
<	Is less than
<=	Is less than or equal to

Pascal also includes three relational operators used only with **BOOLEAN** operands. They are:

AND	Statement is true if both expressions are true
OR	Statement is true if either expression is true
NOT	Statement is true if the operand is false.

16-9 CONTROL STATEMENTS

Pascal includes several statements to control the execution of a program. These statements can be divided into two broad categories. The first category consists of statements controlling how many times a certain action is repeated, while the second group is composed of statements which control whether an action is to be performed or which action is to be performed.

One method of repetitively performing a desired action is the **WHILE** statement, which is used in conjunction with **DO**. The form is as follows:

> **WHILE** Boolean expression **DO**
>> statement

Each time the action is repeated, the Boolean expression is evaluated. As long as the value is **TRUE,** the statement following **DO** is performed. When the value is **FALSE,** the statement is not executed; instead, the next following statement is executed.

Often the "statement" to be repetitively performed actually consists of several different program lines. In such cases, the **WHILE** statement has the following form:

> **WHILE** Boolean expression **DO**
>> **BEGIN**
>>> statements (separated by semicolons)
>> **END**

In this case, note that no punctuation appears after **BEGIN** or **END.** In addition, no punctuation appears after the program line immediately preceding **END.**

Another method of repetitively performing an action is the **REPEAT** statement, used in conjunction with **UNTIL.** The form of this is

> **REPEAT**
>> statement
> **UNTIL** Boolean expression

In this case, the statement is performed and the Boolean expression following **UNTIL** is evaluated. If the value is **FALSE,** the statement is again executed. The statement will be executed continuously until the value is **TRUE.**

As with the **WHILE** statement, the "statement" between **REPEAT** and **UNTIL** may consist of several program lines separated by semicolons. However, unlike the **WHILE** statement, it is not necessary to bracket the program lines between **BEGIN** and **END.** However, the last program line before **UNTIL** should not have a semicolon.

Pascal also contains a version of the **IF . . . THEN . . . ELSE** statement construct. The first form is

> **IF** Boolean expression
> **THEN** statement

In this example, the Boolean expression is evaluated. If it is **TRUE,** the statement following **THEN** is executed. If it is **FALSE,** the statement following **THEN** is not executed and program control shifts to the next line.

The second form is

> **IF** Boolean expression
> **THEN** first statement
> **ELSE** second statement

The Boolean expression is evaluated. If it is **TRUE,** the statement following **THEN** is executed. If it is **FALSE,** the statement following **ELSE** is executed.

Several different alternative actions may be selected through the **CASE** statement. Its form is

> **CASE** selector expression **OF**
>   label: statement;
>   label: statement:
>   label: statement:
>   . . . . .
>   label: statement
> **END**

When the **CASE** statement is executed, the selector expression is evaluated and produces an integer or ordinal value. The labels preceding each statement following **CASE . . .OF** represent integer or ordinal values. When the selector expression value matches a label value, the statement following the label is executed.

Pascal also has a **GOTO** statement. It is the only statement in Pascal that makes use of a line number. The form is

> **GOTO** line number
> line number statement

When the **GOTO** statement is executed, program control shifts immediately to the statement beginning with the line number following **GOTO.** (Frequently, **GOTO** is used in conjunction with an **IF . . .THEN** statement.)

All line numbers used with **GOTO** must be declared with a **LABEL** declaration. The form is

LABEL line number

LABEL declarations follow the **PROGRAM** heading and preceed the **CONST** and **VAR** declarations.

Programming practice in Pascal calls for avoiding the **GOTO** statement. It should be used only when no alternative method of structuring the problem exists.

16-10 FUNCTIONS AND PROCEDURES

A **function** is a set of actions which may be invoked as needed during program execution; it takes one or more given values and returns a single result. A **procedure** is similar to a function, but can return several results or no results at all. A procedure can "stand alone" as a statement; a function can be used in almost any situation where a constant or variable could be used. In short, procedures can be considered as replacements for statements while functions can be considered replacements for expressions. Both functions and procedures must be declared.

The **FUNCTION** declaration has the following form:

> **FUNCTION** identifier (parameter list): type;
> > **BEGIN**
> > > statements
> > **END;**

where identifier is a standard Pascal identifier, parameter list represents the parameters used in the funciton, and type defines the type of the value associated with the function.

Parameters are variables whose values are not assigned to them by an assignment statement. Instead, values are passed to the parameters from the statement that calls the function or procedure. There is usually another type declaration within the same parentheses as the parameter list which declares the types of the parameters.

Each function or procedure is, in effect, an independent Pascal program. Variables and constants can be declared and defined within a function or procedure just as in the main program. Since each function or procedure is independent of the rest of the program and other functions and procedures, identifiers are used in one function or procedure (although this is not considered good programming practice).

Procedures are declared in a manner similar to functions, with **PROCEDURE** substituted for **FUNCTION**. Since a procedure does not itself return a value, there is no type declaration in a **PROCEDURE** declaration.

16-11 PREDEFINED FUNCTIONS

Pascal includes the following predefined functions:

ABS: Result is the absolute value of an expression.

ARCTAN: Result is a real value representing the arctangent in radians of an expression.

CHR: Result is a character (**CHAR** type) in the position in the collating sequence given by the argument.

COS: Result is the cosine of an expression in radians.

EOF: Result is **TRUE** if the end of a file has been reached; otherwise, it is **FALSE.**

EXP: Result is e raised to indicated power, where e is the logarithmic natural number.

LN: Result is the natural logarithm of an expression.

ODD: Result is **TRUE** if an integer value is odd; otherwise, it is false.

ORD: Result is the ordinal number of an argument in a set of values of which the argument is a member.

PRED: Result is the predecessor value relative to the argument value.

RESET: Initializes an input file to accept values.

REWRITE: Initializes an output file to output values.

ROUND: Gives integer result of rounding from a real value.

SIN: Result is sine of an expression expressed in radians.

SQR: Result is the square of an expression.

SQRT: Result is square root of an expression.

SUCC: Result is successor value relative to the argument value.

TRUNC: Result is an integer value obtaining by truncating the fractional part of a real value.

16-12 INPUT AND OUTPUT

In Pascal, the **READ** statement reads an item of data and stores it in a location associated with a variable. The form of this is

READ (variable list);

The data items to be read come after the program; each data item is separated from the others by at least one space. Data items are assigned to variables in the order in which they are input. For example, if the first data item is 1, and the first identifier in the variable list is **A,** then **A** would be associated with the value of 1. The types of the data items to be input should agree with the types of the variables in the list. If variables of the **CHAR** type read numeric data, the data items will be input as characters and treated as such by the program.

However, if characters are read for a variable list of numeric variables, an error will result.

There may be situations in which it is preferable to have the data items read one line at a time. For this purpose, **READLN** is used. **READLN** causes input control to shift to the next line of input when the end of the variable list or line of input is reached.

Data may be output using the **WRITE** statement. The general form is

WRITE (variable list)

Characters may be output by **WRITE** by placing the character string, enclosed by single quotes, inside the parentheses following **WRITE**. If an apostrophe is desired in the output, a pair of single quotes should be included in the character string.

It is possible to allocate a desired number of spaces, known as a **field**, for data items on output. This is done by indicating the number of spaces desired in the field with an integer and separating the integer from the appropriate data item identifier with a colon. For example, **SUM:5** would allocate a total of five spaces to the data item represented by **SUM**.

Greater control over output is provided by the **WRITELN** statement. It is identical to **WRITE,** except that output control shifts to the next line whenever the output list following **WRITELN** has been output.

16-13 PACKED ARRAYS

A more efficient use of memory for data storage is possible with packed arrays. The declaration to set up a packed array is

identifier: **PACKED ARRAY** [index] **OF** type

Packed arrays have no effect upon the results produced by a program. However, program execution is slowed down because of the greater time necessary to access individual items in a packed array.

16-14 SETS

Pascal allows the mathematical concept of a set to be used in programming. A set may be defined by the definition

SET OF type

where the type must be ordinal. Thus, sets of real numbers or strings are not allowed. Moreover, sets must be processed as a whole since Pascal provides no operations to break a set down into its individual elements.

Pascal includes the following set operators:

*	Intersection
+	Union
−	Difference

Pascal also provides the comparison operator **IN.** It has the following typical form:

IF variable **IN**[set] **THEN** statement

IN can be used in conjunction with other conditional statements and relational operators.

16-15 FILES AND RECORDS

A file is a data structure composed of elements of the same type. Pascal files are sequential; elements may be added, deleted, or examined only by going through the entire file in order. Files may be declared by

identifier: **FILE OF** type

To generate a file, components are written to it one at a time. The file is readied for writing by the predeclared procedure

REWRITE (file)

which clears the file of all components. To add elements, **WRITE** is used along with the file identifier and desired component in parentheses. The file identifier and component should be separated by a comma.

A file may be read by using the predeclared procedure **RESET** followed by the file name in parentheses. This prepares the file reading. The file can then read by using **READ** followed by the file name and a variable name in parentheses.

The **(INPUT, OUTPUT)** declaration following the **PROGRAM** heading establishes files for input and output. They are known as external files. Additional external files may be added following the **PROGRAM** heading but they must be declared as a variable in the program. Files used for purposes other than input and output are known as internal files.

In Pascal, a record is a data structure whose elements may be of different types and may be accessed at random. The general form of a record declaration is

RECORD
Identifier(s): types
END

The identifiers and types are known as fields of the record.

The individual components of a variable may be accessed as if they are simple variables by the **WITH** statement. The form is

WITH record variable **DO** statement

WITH does away with the requirement that the identifiers of a record variable's fields be qualified. This saves programming time, since the elements of a record are usually processed by a series of statements.

16-16 RESERVED WORDS

AND	NIL
ARRAY	NOT
BEGIN	OF
CASE	OR
CONST	PACKED
DIV	PROCEDURE
DO	PROGRAM
DOWNTO	RECORD
ELSE	REPEAT
END	SET
FILE	THEN
FOR	TO
FUNCTION	TYPE
GOTO	UNTIL
IF	VAR
IN	WHILE
LABEL	WITH
MOD	

sec. 17

PL/I

Allen B. Tucker, Jr.

17-1 INTRODUCTION

PL/I has received much interest and increased usage in the past few years. There are several reasons for this. First, it is a more modern language than most others, and thus its features relate more directly to those of current computers and applications. Second, PL/I is a general-purpose language, supporting scientific, data processing, text processing, and systems programming applications. Third, implementations of PL/I have become widespread, efficient, and reliable. In this chapter, we will study PL/I and evaluate its effectiveness in the scientific, data processing, and text processing application areas.

Brief History of PL/I

The first version of PL/I was presented to SHARE by the Advanced Language Development Committee of the SHARE FORTRAN project. This version was called NPL (New Programming Language). It was first implemented in 1965 by IBM, under the name PL/I.

PL/I was slow to gain acceptance in the 1960s. Its first compilers were inefficient and unreliable. Although its programming features were many and varied, it was not considered an acceptable alternative in any one particular application area. However, for the reasons listed above, PL/I has begun to experience substantial usage.

In February 1975 a Draft Proposed Standard for PL/I was published jointly by Technical Committee X3J1-PL/I of the American National Standards Committee X3 and Technical Committee TC10-PL/I of the European Computer Manufacturers Association. We therefore use the draft standard version of PL/I as our basis for presentation and evaluation in this chapter.

As we discuss the features of PL/I, it will be important to keep a good historical perspective. The main features of PL/I are drawn directly from its predecessors ALGOL, FORTRAN, and COBOL. Indeed, if we combined the syntactic structure and dynamic storage allocation features of ALGOL, record structures and input-output of COBOL, and arithmetic capabilities of FORTRAN, and then added some string processing, list processing, and interrupt-trapping features, we would have a language remarkably similar to PL/I.

Implementations and Variations of PL/I

Since the language was first implemented in 1965, PL/I compilers have been developed for a number of computers and operating systems, including the following.

Burroughs	B6700 System
CDC	Cyber Series
Honeywell	Multics System
IBM	360, 370 Series

For the following reasons, implementations of PL/I are not as widespread as those of FORTRAN or COBOL.

1. PL/I has not yet been standardized.
2. The cost of developing and maintaining a PL/I compiler is much greater than that for a special purpose language.

In addition to manufacturer-supplied implementations, a number of independently developed PL/I compilers are available. These vary in the completeness with which they implement PL/I's programming features. Perhaps the best known among these is PL/C, which was developed at Cornell University.

Major Applications of PL/I

Unlike the other languages covered in this text, PL/I is a general-purpose language. It was intentionally designed to be used equally well in scientific, data processing, text processing, and systems programming applications. It has, in fact, become widely known in all these areas. In none of these areas, however, has the dominant language (FORTRAN, COBOL, SNOBOL, and assembly languages, respectively) been overtaken by PL/I.

17-2 WRITING PL/I PROGRAMS

A PL/I program is a sequence of statements which describes an algorithm. Because of its generality, PL/I provides a wide variety of statement types and functional capabilities. We will present only those which seem to have the widest usage in scientific, data processing, and text processing applications. Specifically, we will not discuss PL/I's compile-time or multitasking features. Also, a number of built-in functions, interrupt conditions, and statement-writing options will not be included. What remains to be covered is what we might view as "essential PL/I," but certainly not "simplified PL/I."

Data Types and Constants

Strictly speaking, PL/I data types fall into two classes; "problem data" and "program control data." PL/I's problem data includes items which a programmer normally identifies as data: character strings, numbers, and other codes that occur as input, output, and working values in the program. PL/I's program control data includes such items as statement labels and pointers (which connect the nodes of a linked list).

PL/I's problem data consists of two classes; **arithmetic** and **string**. An arithmetic data item is a number, and as such has all the following attributes.

Attribute	Options
base	DECIMAL or BINARY
mode	REAL or COMPLEX
scale	FIXED or FLOAT
precision	(p,q) or (p)

The "options" listed here are written in upper-case letters to identify that they are part of the PL/I language. In addition, many of these PL/I "keywords" can be abbreviated. A keyword's proper abbreviation is indicated by underlining those letters which compose it. For example, **COMPLEX** can be equivalently written as **CPLX, DECIMAL** as **DEC,** and so forth.

A **REAL FIXED DECIMAL** arithmetic data value is nothing more than an ordinary decimal number, with or without a fractional part, such as the following.

$$1.73 \qquad 0 \qquad -17 \qquad 250$$

A **REAL FIXED BINARY** data value is a binary number, with or without a fractional part, and written with a "B" at its right end, such as the following.

$$1.01B \qquad 0B \qquad -11B \qquad 111110B$$

The precision of a **REAL FIXED (DECIMAL** or **BINARY)** arithmetic data value is always of the form (p,q); p and q are positive integers defining that value's total number of digits and total number of fractional digits, respectively. For instance, the **REAL FIXED DECIMAL** constant 1.73 has precision (3,2), as does the **REAL FIXED BINARY** constant 1.01B. The maximum precision for a **FIXED** arithmetic data value is implementation dependent.

A **REAL FLOAT DECIMAL** arithmetic data value is an ordinary decimal number followed by an exponent part which indicates multiplication by a power of 10. For example, the decimal number 105000 may be written as a **REAL FLOAT DECIMAL** value as 1.05E5. This is an encoding convention which describes the number 1.05×10^5 or 105000. A **REAL FLOAT BINARY** value, similarly, is written as a binary number followed by an exponent part, which indicates multiplication by a power of 2. For example, the binary number 101000 may be written as a **REAL FLOAT BINARY** number as 1.01E5B, which denotes 1.01×2^5 (the point here is a binary point, not a decimal point). Again the symbol "B" distinguishes the value as **BINARY** rather than **DECIMAL.**

The precision for a **REAL FLOAT (DECIMAL** or **BINARY)** arithmetic data value is always of the form (p); p is a positive integer which defines that value's total number of significant (decimal or binary) digits. For instance, the **REAL FLOAT DECIMAL** constant 1.05E5 has precision (3), since it has 3 significant digits (preceding the exponent). Similarly, 1.01E5B has precision (3). The precision with which a **FLOAT** value is actually stored is implementation dependent.

A **COMPLEX** arithmetic data value is written in two parts; a real part followed by an imaginary part. An imaginary part is identified by writing the letter "I" at its right end. Although PL/I fully supports **COMPLEX** arithmetic, we will not discuss it further in this section.

Generally, **FLOAT** data are used in scientific computations, since they can represent a wide range of values. **FIXED DECIMAL** data are generally preferred in data processing applications, since they can represent decimal fractions exactly. For instance, the number 10.53 will be converted to binary if it is stored in **FLOAT,** and thus accuracy will be lost (that is, it might be represented as something like 10.5299). If it is stored in **FIXED DECIMAL,** however, the number is not converted to binary and no accuracy is lost. This is important when it denotes the dollars-and-cents value $10.53. Finally, **FIXED BINARY** data are usually preferred for performing integer arithmetic, as in integer counters, loop-control variables, and so forth.

We now turn to the other class of PL/I problem data, string data. A PL/I string may be either a character string (denoted by the attribute **CHARACTER**) or a bit string (denoted by the attribute **BIT**).

A character string is a sequence of zero or more characters taken from an (implementation-defined) alphabet. For the purposes of this section, we will assume that that alphabet contains the following characters.

ƀ . (+ & $ *) ; - / , % ? : # @ ' = "
A B C D E F G H I J K L M N O P Q R S T U V W X Y Z
0 1 2 3 4 5 6 7 8 9

Furthermore, we will assume that they are ordered exactly as they are written here. That is, "ƀ" is less than ".", which is less than "(", and so forth. This means that the alphabetic characters (A–Z) are ordered in the usual way, that the numeric characters (0–9) are also ordered in the usual way, and that the special characters precede the alphabetics, which in turn precede the numerics.

When written within a PL/I program a character string must be enclosed at either end by a single quote ('). Here are five examples of character strings.

'ABC'
'AƂBƂC'
"
'WHAT "SƂTHIS?'
(5) 'ABC'

The first two strings are not equivalent in any sense; remember that the blank (Ƃ) is significant within a character string. The third string is empty—i.e., it contains no characters. The fourth string illustrates what to do if, indeed, the string itself contains a single quote ('). That quote must be written twice in succession, in order that it be syntactically distinguishable from the enclosing quotes. The enclosing quotes are not part of the string; they merely define its beginning and its end. The fifth string illustrates how a string which is simply a repetition of a shorter string can be abbreviated. This one is merely another way of writing the string **'ABCABCABCABCABC'**.

In addition to its value, a character string always has a length attribute: the integer number of characters contained within it (excluding the enclosing quotes). The lengths of the five character strings shown are, respectively, 3, 5, 0, 12, and 15. Note that the occurrence of a quote (') within a string contributes only 1 to the length, even though it is written twice ("). The maximum length of a PL/I character string varies among implementations.

A bit string is a sequence of zero or more binary digits (0s and 1s), which are often referred to as "bits." When written within a PL/I program, a bit string is enclosed in single quotes and followed immediately by **"B."** Here are five examples of bit strings.

'0'B
'1'B
"B
'01001'B
(3) '01'B

Like character strings, bit strings have the length attribute. The lengths of the above bit strings are 1, 1, 0, 5 and 6, respectively. Note here that the convention for abbreviating is available for bit strings as well as for character strings.

An important use for bit strings in PL/I programming is for representing logical (truth) values. Specifically, the bit strings '0'B and '1'B are interpreted as "false" and "true," respectively, when they are used in this way.

Names, Variables, and Data Structures

A PL/I variable is a name which is associated with one or more values that may change during program execution. A variable's name may be any sequence of alphabetic (A–Z, @, #, $), numeric (0–9) and/or break (_) characters, the first of which much be alphabetic. The following are valid variable names.

> X
>
> GROSS_PAY
>
> #19

Some implementations impose a maximum length on variable names.

When the variable is associated with exactly one value, then it is said to be an "element variable." When it is associated with more than one value, then the variable is either an "array variable" or a "structure variable."

Every element variable in a PL/I program has a set of attributes associated with it. Those attributes describe the kind of data values which may be assigned to that variable during program execution. Suppose **X** and **GROSS_PAY** and **TITLE** are variables in a program. Let **X** have attributes **REAL FLOAT DECIMAL** and precision (6). Let **GROSS_PAY** have the attributes **REAL FIXED DECIMAL** and precision (7,2). Finally, let **TITLE** have the attributes **CHARACTER** and length (25). This means the following.

1. **X** may contain any arithmetic data value which is **REAL FLOAT DECIMAL** and has 6 or fewer significant decimal digits. For example, the value of **X** may be 3.59847E-5.

2. **GROSS_PAY** may contain any arithmetic data value which is **REAL FIXED DECIMAL** and whose value lies within the range −99999.99 to 99999.99. For example, the value of **GROSS_PAY** may be 23400.00.

3. **TITLE** may contain any character string data value which has a length of 25 characters. For example, the value of **TITLE** may be '1975ƀANNUALƀBUDGETƀREPORT', or perhaps '1975ƀANNUAL ƀBUDGETƀƀƀƀƀƀ'.

The attributes associated with an element variable are established either by explicit declaration or by default. That is, when a variable's attributes are not explicitly declared, the system assigns attributes to it according to a well-defined set of rules.

To declare a variable's attributes explicitly, the programmer writes a "declaration statement" which may take the following form.

> <u>DEC</u>LARE name attributes;

Here, "name" identifies the variable's name and "attributes" denotes a sequence of attributes which are to be associated with that name. Continuing the examples presented above, we could declare attributes for the variables named **X, GROSS_PAY,** and **TITLE** as follows.

> **DECLARE X FLOAT DECIMAL (6);**
>
> **DECLARE GROSS_PAY FIXED DECIMAL (7,2);**
>
> **DECLARE TITLE CHARACTER (25);**

Note that at least one space separates the various parts of the declaration statement. This series of declarations, if they all appeared in the same program, could have been written more briefly by (1) using allowable abbreviations for keywords and (2) combining the declaration of several variables into one declaration, as shown here.

DCL X FLOAT DEC (6),

GROSS_PAY FIXED DEC (7,2),

TITLE CHAR (25);

Another kind of abbreviation is useful when several variables all have the same attributes. For example, if **I, J,** and **K** have attributes **FIXED BINARY** and precision (31,0) then they can be declared as follows.

DCL (I,J,K) FIXED BIN (31, 0);

That is, the attributes **FIXED BIN (31,0)** can be "factored" outside the parentheses which enclose the variables that have those attributes in common. Finally, any **FIXED** precision (p,q) in which q = 0 can be abbreviated simply as (p). Thus, (31,0) in the above declaration could have been written as (31).

As implied in an example above, a character string variable must be declared with the attributes **CHARACTER** and length **I**. Similarly, a bit string variable must be declared with the attributes **BIT** and length **I**. In either case, the length **I** denotes the number of characters (bits) comprising all character (bit) string values that will become associated with that variable's name. For example, once we declare that **TITLE** is a **CHARACTER (25)** variable, every value stored in **TITLE** must be a twenty-five character string.

There is another attribute, called **VARYING**, which allows the length, as well as the value, of a character or bit string variable to change during program execution. For example, if we redeclare **TITLE** as follows

DCL TITLE CHAR (25) VARYING;

then we permit any character strings, of length 0 to 25 inclusive, to become the value of **TITLE**. Thus, the following two strings may become the value of **TITLE** at different times during execution of the program.

'1975ƀANNUALƀBUDGETƀREPORT'

'1975ƀANNUALƀBUDGET'

It is not always necessary to explicitly declare a variable in a program. A variable exists in a program as soon as its name is used in an executable statement, whether or not it has been declared. Furthermore, not all attributes for a declared variable need to be explicitly written. When one or more attributes for a declared variable are omitted, or when the variable is totally undeclared, its attributes are assigned (by "default") by the system as follows.

1. When the variable is either undeclared or none of its attributes appear in its declaration. If its name begins with I,J,K,L,M, or N then it assumes the arithmetic attributes

REAL FIXED BIN (15,0).

Otherwise, it assumes the arithmetic attributes

REAL FLOAT DEC (6).

2. When the variable is declared and at least one, but not all, of its arithmetic mode, scale, and base attributes is missing in the declaration, then the missing one(s) are assigned from the following list.

Attribute missing	Assign
mode	REAL
scale	FLOAT
base	DECIMAL

3. When an arithmetic variable is declared without a precision attribute, then the latter is assigned as follows. For reasons which will be seen later, no variable may be declared with only a precision attribute. (At least one additional attribute must textually precede the variable's precision in the declaration.)

Scale and base	Precision assigned
FIXED DEC	(5,0)
FIXED BIN	(15,0)
FLOAT DEC	(6)
FLOAT BIN	(21)

4. When a string variable is declared without a length attribute, its length is assigned as 1.

Thus, for example, we need not have declared the variable named **X** in the foregoing example, although we did have to declare **GROSS_PAY** and **TITLE**. If we did not, then they would both have defaulted to **REAL FLOAT DEC (6)**. A degree of abbreviation for our declaration of **GROSS_PAY**, however, is possible as follows.

DCL GROSS_PAY FIXED (7,2);

Our omission of **REAL** or **COMPLEX** (mode) here defaults to **REAL,** and our omission of **DEC** or **BIN** (base) here defaults to **DEC**. This is exactly what we required.

The decision whether to explicitly declare a variable in a program depends upon both the programmer's own style and the program's logical structure, as well as the default rules themselves.

PL/I provides an alternate method of declaring certain arithmetic and string variables: the **PICTURE** specification. This kind of declaration has the following form.

DCL name **PICTURE** 'specification';

Here, the specification may take a variety of forms. We present only two forms below.

To declare a character variable like **TITLE** in the foregoing example, we could have equivalently said one of the following.

DCL TITLE PIC 'XXXXXXXXXXXXXXXXXXXXXXXXX';
DCL TITLE PIC '(25)X';

Specifically, "**X**" is the character specification, and the number of X's defines the length of the string. The second declaration shows how a long sequence of X's can be abbreviated.

To declare a **REAL FIXED DECIMAL** variable, such as **GROSS_PAY** in the foregoing example, we could have equivalently said the following.

DCL GROSS_PAY PIC '99999V99';

Specifically, "9" is the decimal digit specification, and the number of 9s defines the number of digits accommodated by the variable. Also, the position of "V" locates the decimal point. If **V** is omitted, the decimal point is assumed to be at the right of the rightmost 9. Thus, we have here the equivalent of declaring **GROSS_PAY** to be **REAL FIXED DECIMAL (7,2).**

This so-called "numeric character" **PICTURE** specification offers, however, a bit more flexibility than its alternative **REAL FIXED DECIMAL (7,2).** That is, one can include editing characters, such as "$" and ".", to control printing of the value of the variable. For example, if **GROSS_PAY** were redeclared as follows,

DCL GROSS_PAY PIC '$99999V.99';

had the value 23400.00, and then were printed, the value would be $23400.00. The interested reader should consult his PL/I reference manual for more information on editing numeric character variables.

PL/I provides two ways in which a variable may represent a number of values, rather than just one. One is called the **array** and the other is called the **structure.** An array is an *n*-dimensional collection of elements, all of which have the same attributes. For instance, an array named **A** may be a one-dimensional list of five elements, each one having the attributes **REAL FLOAT DEC (6).** Similarly, **B** may name a two-dimensional array, with five rows and four columns of elements, each one having the attributes **REAL FIXED**

A
1.50000 E0
2.70000 E-3
1.49999 E1
0.00000 E0
1.11001 E17

B			
17	42	00	-10
18	03	00	-11
19	47	19	-12
20	48	49	22
00	00	-2	-3

FIG. 17-1

DEC (2,0). **A** and **B** are illustrated in Fig. 17-1. As shown, although all elements in either **A** or **B** must possess the same attributes, the values of the elements themselves will typically differ from each other and change as program execution progresses. The maximum number of dimensions allowed for an array is implementation dependent.

To define an array, its dimensionality *n,* and number of elements in each dimension, the program must declare the array in the following way.

DCL name (size) attributes;

Here, "name" identifies the array's name, "size" defines its dimensionality and number of elements in each dimension, and "attributes" identifies the attributes possessed by each element in the array. If one or more attributes are omitted, they will be assigned (by default) according to the rules for element variables.

"Size" may appear as a sequence of one or more positive integer constants, separated by commas. The number of constants identifies the number of dimensions in the array, while the value of each constant identifies the number of elements in the dimension. For example,

DCL A(5) FLOAT DEC (6);

defines an array **A** with one dimension and five elements (i.e., a simple list of five elements). Note that the attributes **FLOAT DEC (6)** could have been omitted here without changing the meaning of the declaration. Similarly,

DCL B(5,4) FIXED DEC (2,0);

defines an array **B** with two dimensions, five elements in the first dimension (rows), and four elements in the second dimension (columns). Thus, these declarations define the arrays **A** and **B** as pictured above (but they do not assign values to the individual elements).

The size of a PL/I array need not be constant, even though that is the case for these two arrays. In general, an array may be declared with a variable number of elements in each dimension, as suggested by the following valid declaration.

DCL A(N) FLOAT DEC (6);

However, we defer discussion of this valuable alternative until after we have gained a firmer understanding of PL/I program structure.

The PL/I structure is the second way by which a variable name may refer to a number of elements. Unlike an array, the individual elements of a structure may have different attributes from each other. For example, a structure named **PERSON** may have four different elements; a **NAME** which is a twenty-five-character string, a social security number (**SS#**) which is a nine-digit numeric character value, a **GROSS_PAY** which is a **REAL FIXED DECIMAL (7,2)** value, and an **ADDRESS** which is a forty-character string. Figure 17-2 is a set of example data for one **PERSON.**

| ALLENbB.bTUCKERbbbbbbbbbb |

| 275407437 |

| 25400.00 |

| 1800bBULLbRUN, bALEXANDRIA, bVA. b22200bbbb |

FIG. 17-2

This particular example shows two levels of variables. At the elementary level are four variables, and at a higher level is the variable **PERSON,** which includes all four as subordinates. Another way to visualize the structure is in its tree form, where the structure name (**PERSON,** in this case) is the "root" and the individual elements are the "leaves." This is shown in Fig. 17-3 for the foregoing example.

To define a structure in PL/I, one uses a **DECLARE** statement. The individual levels of the variables within the structure are defined by prefixing the integer 1 to the structure name (**PERSON,** in this case), 2 to all variables at the next level, and so on. Within an individual level, variables are listed from left to right. Thus, the above structure would be declared as follows.

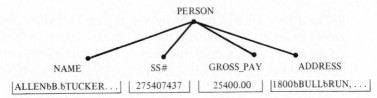

FIG. 17-3

> **DCL 1 PERSON,**
> > **2 NAME**   **CHAR (25),**
> > **2 SS#**   **PIC '(9)9',**
> > **2 GROSS_PAY**   **FIXED DEC (7,2),**
> > **2 ADDRESS**   **CHAR (40);**

Note also that the individual elements in the structure are separated by commas, while the entire declaration is terminated by semicolon (;).

Some of the variables at level 2 in this example can themselves be structures. For example, **NAME** can subdivide into **FIRST, MIDDLE,** and **LAST,** and **ADDRESS** can subdivide into **STREET, CITY, STATE,** and **ZIP,** as illustrated in the tree in Fig. 17-4. If this were done, then we would have the following corresponding structure declaration.

> **DCL 1 PERSON,**
> > **2 NAME,**
> > > **3 FIRST CHAR (10),**
> > > **3 MIDDLE CHAR (5),**
> > > **3 LAST CHAR (10),**
> > **2 SS# PIC '(9)9',**
> > **2 GROSS_PAY FIXED DEC (7,2),**
> > **2 ADDRESS,**
> > > **3 STREET CHAR (17),**
> > > **3 CITY CHAR (12),**
> > > **3 STATE CHAR (6),**
> > > **3 ZIP PIC '99999';**

The reader should notice that only those variables within a structure which are not themselves subdivided have attributes associated with them. These are the elementary variables in a structure; they are the ones which are the "leaves"

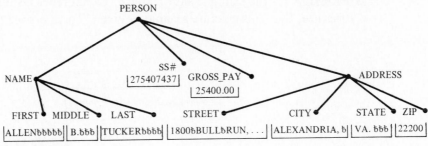

FIG. 17-4

in the structure's tree representation. It should also be clear that the particular values assigned to this structure are shown only for illustrative purposes, and would not be assigned by anything stated or implied by any of these declarations. We will discuss later the various ways in which values can be assigned to elementary variables, arrays, and structures.

The value of an elementary variable, the elements of an array, and the elements of a structure may be changed (assigned) by execution of any one of a variety of statements. To reference the value of an elementary variable within a statement, one simply provides the variable's name.

To reference the entire collection of elements within an array, one provides the array's name. However, to reference a single element within an array, one provides the array's name followed by a list of subscripts which is enclosed in parentheses. The number of subscripts given must be identical with the number of dimensions in the array as declared. Let's recall the two arrays **A** and **B** declared above. To reference the fourth element within **A**, we would write **A(4)**. Similarly, if we want to reference that element in the third row and second column of **B**, we would write **B(3,2)**. Although the subscripts in these two examples are integer constants, that is not a general requirement. For example, if **I** is an integer-valued variable [e.g., **REAL FIXED BIN (15,0)**], whose value is 1, 2, 3, 4, or 5, then the expression **A(I)** identifies the first, second, third, fourth, or fifth element of **A** accordingly. That is, each time **I** changes value, the expression **A(I)** references a different element of **A**. Similarly, if **I** and **J** are both integer-valued variables, then the expression **B(I,J)** references the element in the *I*th row and *J*th column of **B**.

Another way to reference selected elements of an array is by using the so-called "cross-section." Consider once again the 5 × 4 array of **B** defined above. If we want to reference all elements in a single row of **B**, say the second row, then we would write **B(2,*)**. Similarly, we could reference the entire fourth column of **B** by saying **B(*,4)**. These two cross sections of **B** are pictured in Fig. 17-5.

Thus, a cross section serves to reduce the dimensionality of an array; the result is an array of fewer dimensions. In this example, we took one-dimensional cross sections **B(2,*)** and **B(*,4)** from the two-dimensional array **B**. As with single elements, cross sections may be defined by the use of variables instead of constants. For instance, **B(I,*)** denotes the *I*th row of **B** and **B(*,J)** denotes the *J*th column. The use of cross sections is especially convenient in applications using matrix algebra, as we shall see later.

To reference an entire structure, one simply gives the structure's name, such as **PERSON** for the example shown above. To reference a substructure, within a structure, that substructure's name is given. To reference a single element

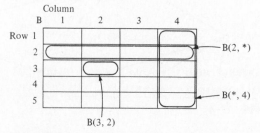

FIG. 17-5

within a structure, only that element's name needs to be given. In addition, it is possible to have two different elements (or substructures) with the same name, as shown in the following example.

```
DCL 1 PERSON_A,
        2 NAME CHAR (25),
        2 SS# PIC '(9)9',
        2 GROSS_PAY FIXED DEC (7,2),
        2 ADDRESS CHAR (40),
     1 PERSON_B,
        2 NAME CHAR (25),
        2 SS# PIC '(9)9',
        2 GROSS_PAY FIXED DEC (7,2),
        2 ADDRESS CHAR (40);
```

These two structures, **PERSON_A** and **PERSON_B,** have identically named elements. (The structures themselves must have mutually unique names.) In order to distinguish the **SS#,** for example, of **PERSON_A** from that of **PERSON_B,** a "qualified name" must be given. If **PERSON_B's SS#** is to be referenced, then the qualified name **PERSON_B.SS#** must be written, while **PERSON_A's SS#** is referenced by **PERSON_A.SS#.** Such qualification must be used whenever the name by itself would be ambiguous.

Finally, we should mention that PL/I permits arrays to occur within structures and structures to occur within arrays. In most practical situations, however, the occurrence of an array within a structure involves only a one-dimensional array.

Initialization of Variables, Arrays, and Structures

It is often convenient to have the initial values of variables, arrays, or structures assigned initially (at the time the program segment in which they are declared begins execution). This is accomplished in PL/I by writing the "INITIAL attribute" within the declaration of the variable, array, or structure. It has the following form.

<u>INITIAL</u> (value-list)

Here, "value-list" denotes a list of one or more values to be assigned to the declared variable, array, or structure. Each value may be a constant or a repetitive specification, which abbreviates a list of constants.

For example, reconsider the variables **X** and **TITLE** and the array **B** that were discussed in the previous section. The values that were shown there may be initialized in the following way.

```
DCL X FLOAT DEC (6) INIT(3.59847E-5),
    TITLE CHAR (25) INIT('1975ʙANNUALʙBUDGET'),
    B(5,4) FIXED DEC (2,0) INIT (17,42,0,−10,18,3,0,
        −11,19,47,19,−12,20,48,49,22,0,0,−2,−3);
```

The elementary items in a structure are initialized similarly.

Two points should be noted about the use of the **INITIAL** attribute. First, when an array is initialized, the list of values are assigned in **row-major** order. Second, if several adjacent (or all) entries in an array are to be initialized to the same value, then the number of repetitions for that value may be indicated by placing that number before it, enclosed in parentheses. For example, if we want to initialize all the entries of **B** to the value zero, we can write the following.

DCL B(5,4) FIXED DEC (2,0) INIT ((20)0);

Note carefully that the specification, "INIT (0)", here would have initialized only **B(1,1)** to zero, leaving undefined the values of the remaining entries in **B**.

Finally, we note that if the initial value differs in any of its attributes from those of its associated variable, then that value is "converted" to an equivalent value whose attributes agree.

17-3 BASIC STATEMENTS

We will not discuss all the PL/I statements in this chapter because of the importance of focusing our attention on the most widely used ones. The ones we will cover are listed below, together with a brief discussion of their purpose in a PL/I program.

Statement	Purpose
ALLOCATE statement **FREE** statement	To accomplish dynamic storage allocation
Assignment statement	To perform a series of arithmetic (add, subtract, . . .) or string (concatenate) operations, and then assign the result as the new value of a variable, array (element), or structure (element)
BEGIN statement	To delimit the logical beginning of a program section
CALL statement **RETURN** statement	To cause the invocation of a subprogram, and the return of control from a subprogram
CLOSE statement **OPEN** statement	To perform the various input-output operations
GET statement **PUT** statement **FORMAT** statement **READ** statement **WRITE** statement	To perform the various input-output operations
DECLARE statement	To define variables and their attributes
DO statement	To delimit the beginning of a group of statements which is to be either repeated a number of times or executed conditionally
END statement	To delimit either (1) the end of a program or subprogram, (2) the end of a program section headed by a **BEGIN** statement, or (3) the end of a group of statements headed by a **DO** statement
GO TO statement **IF** statement	To alter the sequence of program statement execution
ON statement	To describe an action to be taken in the event that an exceptional condition, such as end-of-file or division by zero, occurs during program execution
PROCEDURE statement	To delimit the beginning of a PL/I program or subprogram
STOP statement	Causes program execution to terminate, and return control to the system

In the remainder of this section, we will discuss the assignment, **DECLARE, DO, END, GO TO, IF, PROCEDURE,** and **STOP** statements. Discussion of the remaining statements in this list will be presented in subsequent sections, as indicated above. To start our discussion of these statements, consider the following simple PL/I program.

```
SIMPLE: PROCEDURE OPTIONS (MAIN);
    DCL A(5) FLOAT, (H,I,J) FIXED BIN (15,0),
        B(5,4) FIXED DEC (2,0);
    DCL 1 PERSON,
        2 NAME CHAR (25),
        2 GROSS_PAY FIXED DEC (7,2);
/* THIS PROGRAM DOES LITTLE MORE THAN ILLUSTRATE SOME
OF PL/I's BASIC STATEMENTS */
    DO I = 1 TO 5;
    A(I) = 6 − I;
    END;
    H = 1;
LOOP: IF H < = 5
    THEN DO;
        B(H,1) = 1;
        B(H,2) = 5 + 3 * (H − A(H));
        H = H + 1;
        GO TO LOOP;
        END;
    B(*,3) = A;        /* FILL 3RD COLUMN OF B */
    B(*,4) = B(*,1) + B(*,2) + B(*,3);        /* SUM ROWS OF B */
    NAME = 'ALLEN B. TUCKER';
    GROSS_PAY = 25400;
    STOP;
END SIMPLE;
```

This program has little practical value, but it does illustrate each of the statement types discussed in this section.

A PL/I program begins with a statement of the form

name: <u>**PROCEDURE OPTIONS (MAIN)**</u>;

and ends with a statement of the following form.

END name;

The "**OPTIONS(MAIN)**" part designates that the program is not a subprogram, and thereby is immediately executable. In both of the statements above, "name" identifies the program, and must be the same in both places. In our example, the program name is **SIMPLE**. The name may be any sequence of letters (A–Z), digits (0–9), or the characters @, #, $, or ⌣, provided that it begins with either a letter or one of the characters @, #, or $.

In all statements, including these, adjacent keywords and names must be separated by at least one space (ɓ). For instance, there must be a space between **PROCEDURE** and **OPTIONS** in the first statement. But spaces are not required if there is an intervening delimiter, such as a colon (:), a semicolon (;), parentheses, a plus sign (+), and so forth.

The seventh and eighth lines of the example program illustrate a PL/I "comment." A comment can be any sequence of characters which begins with /* and ends with */. Comments may appear anywhere within a PL/I program, and they have no other effect than to provide program documentation.

The GO TO Statement

The statements in a PL/I program are generally executed in the order in which they are written, unless a statement is encountered which can alter that order. One such statement is the **GO TO** statement, which has the following general form.

GO TO label;

Here, "label" denotes the label of some other statement between the program's first (**PROCEDURE**) statement and its **END** statement (including the **END** statement itself). Any statement in the list given above can thus be the "target" of a **GO TO** except for the **PROCEDURE** statement, the **DECLARE** statement, the **FORMAT** statement, and the **ON** statement. Certain other restrictions exist and will be noted later.

A statement is labeled by prefixing it with a "label" and a colon (:) as shown.

label : statement

Here, "label" may be any sequence of characters, the first of which is alphabetic (A–Z, $, @, #), and the rest of which are alphabetic, numeric (0–9), or the break character (_). A statement may, in fact, be so prefixed any number of times. (This writer sees little use for that "flexibility.") For instance, the example program contains a statement labeled **LOOP** and a **GO TO** statement, which causes control to return to that statement labeled **LOOP**.

The STOP Statement

The **STOP** statement simply causes program execution to cease. It may be included or not if program execution would normally cease upon reaching the program's **END** (last) statement. Otherwise, it must be placed at whatever place in the program where execution could cease. Its form is always the following.

STOP;

Expressions

The remaining statements to be discussed in the section are the assignment, **DO,** and **IF** statements. They all require an understanding of an extremely important concept: the PL/I expression.

The expression is the central vehicle in PL/I for specifying that a computation takes place. The computation may involve numbers or strings. It may deliver as a result a single-value or a number of values (by way of an array or structure). Although it is not strictly part of the PL/I language, we will for pedagogical purposes partition expressions into the following classes.

Elementary expressions
   Arithmetic expressions
   String expressions
   Logical expressions
Array expressions
Structure expressions

The "elementary expressions" have the common characteristic that their execution yields a single value as a result. For an arithmetic expression, the result is always a numeric value. For a string expression, the result is always a character or bit string value. For a logical expression, the result is always a one-bit string value. In this context, the values **'1'B** and **'0'B** are interpreted "true" and "false," respectively.

An arithmetic expression is either a single term or a series of such terms separated by arithmetic operators, and perhaps by parentheses (as described below). A single term may be either a numeric constant, a numeric-valued variable name, a numeric-valued function reference, or a numeric-valued array reference as illustrated by the following examples.

10   I   GROSS_PAY   SQRT(X)   A(H)

Each of these terms denotes a single value; the first is a constant, the next two are variable names, the fourth is a function reference, and the last is an array reference.

The arithmetic operators and their meanings are as follows.

Operator	Meaning
+	addition
−	subtraction
*	multiplication
/	division
**	exponentiation

Each of these operators always operates on two values, the one at its left and the one at its right within the arithmetic expression. For instance,

H + 2

denotes addition of the current value of the variable **H** and the constant 2.

When two or more operations are required, they are executed from left to right. For instance, if we wanted to add the value of **I** to the sum of **H + 2**, we would write the following (omitting the numbered arrows).

H + 2 + I
  ↑   ↑
  ①   ②

Here, the addition **H + 2** takes place first, and then the addition of that sum and **I** takes place second, as shown by the numbered arrows.

A series of two or more operations are generally carried out from left to right, with the following two exceptions. First, there is a hierarchy among the operators. All exponentiations (******) are performed first (from right to left), all multiplications (*****) and divisions (**/**) are performed next (from left to right), and finally all additions (**+**) and subtractions (**−**) are performed (from left to right). This means that

$$H + 2 * I$$
$$\uparrow \quad \uparrow$$
$$② \quad ①$$

denotes the sum of **H** and **2 * I** rather than the product of **H + 2** and **I**.

Second, whenever this ordering is not what is desired, the programmer may override it by enclosing in parentheses the operations to be performed first. For instance, to specify the product of **H + 2** and **I**, the programmer writes the following.

$$(H + 2) * I$$
$$\uparrow \quad \uparrow$$
$$① \quad ②$$

Here, the addition will take place first, as the numbered arrows indicate.

A string expression is either a single term or a series of such terms separated by the string operator ‖.

A single term in a string expression may be a string constant or a string-valued variable name, array reference, or function reference, as illustrated below.

'ABABABƁƁ'   **NAME**   **S(I)**   **SUBSTR (NAME, 1, 5)**

The string operator ‖ denotes concatenation of two strings, forming one string as a result. For instance, if we want to concatenate **'ABA'** and **'BABƁƁ'** to form the one string, **'ABABABƁƁ'**, then we write the following.

'ABA' ‖ 'BABƁƁ'

Although concatenation is the only PL/I string operator, PL/I's capability for supporting string-processing applications is largely derived from its string built-in functions.

A logical expression is either a one-bit string constant (**'0'B** or **'1'B**), a one-bit string variable, a function reference which returns a one-bit string constant as a result, a relation between two arithmetic expressions or two string expressions, or a series of such logical expressions connected by the logical operators "**&**" or "**|**" and/or prefixed by the logical operator "**¬**". A relation is formed by separating the two arithmetic expressions or string expressions by one of the following "relational operators:" **<, <=, =, >=, >**.

Several examples are given in the following table to illustrate these various kinds of logical expression. In the examples, it is assumed that **P** is a variable declared as **BIT(1)**, **H** is **FIXED BIN**, **GROSS_PAY** is **FIXED DEC (7,2)**, **NUMERIC** is a function which returns a value of **'0'B** or **'1'B**, and **S** and **NAME** are string variables.

Kind of logical expression	Example	Meaning
One-bit constant	'0'B	"False"
One-bit string variable	P	"True" or "False," as the value of P is '1'B or '0'B, respectively
Function reference	NUMERIC(S)	"True" or "false," as the value returned is '1'B or '0'B, respectively
Relation between two arithmetic expressions	H < = 5	"True" or "false," as the value of H is less than or equal to 5 or not respectively
Relation between two string expressions	NAME = 'ALLEN'	"True" or "false," as the value of NAME is or is not equal to 'ALLEN', respectively
Series of these connected by logical operators	H < = 5 | NAME = 'ALLEN'	"True" or "false" as either the value of H is less than or equal to 5 or the value of NAME is 'ALLEN' or not, respectively
	0 < H & H < 5	"True" or "false" as both 0 is less than the value of H and the value of H is less than 5 or not, respectively
	¬NUMERIC(S)	True or false as the complement of the value returned is '1'B or '0'B, respectively

The relational operators $<$, $< =$, $=$, $\neg =$, $> =$, and $>$ are the logical operators and & and | are all binary operators. They represent the conditions listed in the following table.

Operator	Condition represented by "A operator B"
$<$	A is less than B
$< =$	A is less than or equal to B
$=$	A is equal to B
$\neg =$	A is not equal to B
$> =$	A is greater than or equal to B
$>$	A is greater than B
|	Either A or B (or both) is true.
&	Both A and B are true.

The expression "**A** operator **B**" yields the value "true" or "false" depending respectively on whether or not the condition represented is true. Finally, the logical operator "¬" is a unary prefix operator. The expression ¬**A** represents a condition whose value is true exactly when the value of the logical expression **A** is false. Otherwise, the value of ¬**A** is false.

The relational operators all share the same precedence, have higher precedence than the logical operators, and have lower precedence than the arithmetic operators. Furthermore, "&" has precedence over "|", and "¬" has precedence over both "&" and "|". Parentheses are used in logical expressions to override that precedence, just as for arithmetic expressions. Thus, for example,

0 < H & H < 5

has the interpretation given above. On the other hand, the expression

$$P \mid Q \text{ \& } (H <= 5 \mid NAME = \text{‘ALLEN’})$$

$$\underset{⑤}{\uparrow} \quad \underset{④}{\uparrow} \quad \underset{①}{\uparrow} \quad \underset{③}{\uparrow} \quad \underset{②}{\uparrow}$$

is evaluated in the order indicated by the numbered arrows, since the parentheses override the precedence that "&" would otherwise have over the second "|".

The relations $<$, $<=$, $\neg =$, $>=$, and $>$, when applied to arithmetic expressions, reflect the usual ordering that exists among the numbers. That is, the condition

$$H <= 5$$

is a test of whether the value of **H** is less than or equal to 5 in the numerical sense. Thus any of the following values of **H** would give an answer of "true" (**‘1’B**).

$$5 \quad 4.9999 \quad 0 \quad -3 \quad -100$$

When applied to string expressions, the relations reflect the so-called "collating sequence," or predefined ordering that exists among the characters in the character set. This may be an implementation dependent definition. However, the following useful fact is always true of such an ordering.

$$ᵬ < \{\text{all special characters}\} < A < B \ldots < Z < 0 < 1 < \ldots < 9$$

By "special characters" we mean all those which are neither letters nor digits, such as "+", ";", and so forth.

For two **single-character** strings, say **S** and **T**, **S** is less than **T** if and only if **S** precedes **T** in the collating sequence given above. Thus, for example, **‘A’** < **‘B’** is true, **ᵬ** < **‘A’** is true, and so forth. If **S** and **T** have lengths which are equal but greater than 1, then **S** is less than **T** if one of the following is true.

1. The leftmost character in **S** is less than the leftmost character in **T**.

2. The first k characters in **S** and **T** are identical ($1 \leq k <$ length of **S** or **T**), but the $k + 1$st character in **S** is less than the $k + 1$st character in **T**.

This means, for instance, that **‘ALLEN’** < **‘BROWN’** is true since **‘A’** < **‘B’**. It also means that **‘ALLAN’** < **‘ALLEN’** is true, since (for $k = 3$) the first three characters in the two strings are identical, but the fourth character (**A**) in **‘ALLAN’** is less than the fourth character (**E**) in **‘ALLEN’**.

Finally, if **S** and **T** are of unequal lengths, the shorter of the two is extended on its *right* with enough blanks (**ᵬ**) to equalize their lengths and the test described above is then applied. Thus, **‘ALL’** < **‘ALLEN’** is true, since **‘ALLᵬᵬ’** < **‘ALLEN’** is true by rule (2) above.

A relation between two bit strings is identically defined, with the initial fact that **‘0’B** < **‘1’B** is true. If the two bit strings being compared are of *unequal* length, then the shorter one is padded on the right with zeros (rather than blanks) before the conditions (1) and (2) above are tested.

Two character strings, **S** and **T**, are *equal* (i.e., **S** = **T** is true) only if one of the following conditions is satisfied.

1. S and T are of equal length, and they are composed of the same characters in the same order (i.e., they are identical).

2. S and T are of unequal length, but the result of adding enough blanks on the right of the shorter one to equalize their lengths renders them identical.

Thus, **'ABC'** is equal to only **'ABC'**, **'ABCƀƀ'**, **'ABCƀƀƀƀ'**, and so on. It is not equal to **'ƀƀABC'**, or **'AƀƀBC'**, or **'BAC'**.

Equality between two bit strings is similarly defined, except that the shorter one is again padded on the right with zeros (instead of blanks).

The other relations ($<=$, $\neg=$, $>=$, and $>$) are defined for strings in terms of $<$ and $=$ in the following table.

Relation	Meaning of "A relation B"
$<=$	Either A $<$ B or A $=$ B is true
$\neg=$	A $=$ B is not true
$>=$	Either B $=$ A or B $<$ A is true
$>$	B $<$ A is true.

This concludes our discussion of elementary expressions.

PL/I expressions can contain arrays or structures, in addition to elementary values, as operands. An expression which contains array names is called an "array expression," and its execution yields an array, rather than a single value, as the result. An expression which contains structure names is called a "structure expression," and its execution yields a structure as a result. We will not further discuss structure expressions here.

Let A and B be two 4 $\times$ 3 arrays of **REAL FIXED DEC (5,0)** values, as shown.

$$A \begin{bmatrix} 5 & 2 & 0 \\ -1 & 0 & 0 \\ 3 & 7 & 0 \\ 9 & 4 & 0 \end{bmatrix} \qquad B \begin{bmatrix} 1 & 2 & 4 \\ 3 & 2 & 3 \\ 2 & 1 & 1 \\ 0 & 5 & 3 \end{bmatrix}$$

If we write the expression 3 * A, we are describing that 4 $\times$ 3 array which is formed by multiplying each element of A by 3, as shown.

$$\begin{bmatrix} 15 & 6 & 0 \\ -3 & 0 & 0 \\ 9 & 21 & 0 \\ 27 & 12 & 0 \end{bmatrix}$$

If we write A + B, we are describing that 4 $\times$ 3 array which is formed by adding corresponding elements of A and B, as shown.

$$\begin{bmatrix} 6 & 4 & 4 \\ 2 & 2 & 3 \\ 5 & 8 & 1 \\ 9 & 9 & 3 \end{bmatrix}$$

Similarly, the expression A *op* B, where "op" is any one of $-$, *, /, or **, denotes the 4 $\times$ 3 array which is formed by subtracting, multiplying, dividing, or exponentiating corresponding elements of A and B, respectively.

Although there is a natural analogy between the PL/I array and the algebraic notion of matrix, the mathematically oriented programmer should be careful to note that the analogy breaks down in the case of multiplication; array multiplication, e.g., A ∗ B, does not represent the matrix product. The latter is not achievable in a single PL/I statement.

There are some general restrictions which should be kept in mind when writing array expressions. First, the number of dimensions and number of elements in each dimension should be the same for all arrays referenced in a single expression. For instance, the only array that we can add to a 4 × 3 array is another 4 × 3 array. Second, array cross sections can be used in arithmetic expressions. For instance, if we wanted to compute the one-dimensional, three-element array which is formed by taking the product of corresponding elements from the third row of A and the second row of B (as shown above), we would write the following expression.

$$A(3,*) * B(2,*)$$

The following array would result from its execution.

$$\begin{bmatrix} 9 \\ 14 \\ 0 \end{bmatrix}$$

Attributes of the Result of Expression Evaluation

When an elementary expression is executed, the result is always a single number, character string, or bit string. Although an arithmetic expression's operands are all numbers, they typically do not all have the same attributes. For instance, even the simple expression

$$I + 1$$

has two operands which most likely will have different attributes; those of the variable I may be **REAL FIXED BIN (15,0),** while those of the constant 1 are **REAL FIXED DEC (1,0).**

The mode, base, and scale attributes of the result of executing an arithmetic operation are defined in the following table, when one operand does not totally agree in these attributes with the other.

One operand's attributes	Other operand's attributes	Result's attributes
REAL	COMPLEX	COMPLEX
FIXED	FLOAT	FLOAT
DECIMAL	BINARY	BINARY

If the two operands agree in all these attributes, then the result carries their common attributes. The precision of the result depends both upon the nature of the arithmetic operation and the implementation. The rules constituting its definition are so obtuse that any sensible presentation of them here would be extremely cumbersome. Suffice it to say that the precision defined for the result of an operation of the form

$$A \; op \; B$$

where "op" denotes $+$, $-$, $*$, $/$, or $**$, is adequate to accommodate the largest (smallest) value that would reasonably be achieved by executing that operation. For instance, $I + 1$ will yield a result with attributes **FIXED BIN (15,0)** if those of **I** are **FIXED BIN (15,0).**

The precision of the result of an arithmetic operation is also bound by implementation dependent maximum values. For PL/I(F), those values are listed in the following table.

Base and scale or result	Maximum precision of result
FIXED DECIMAL	(15,q) where $0 \leq q \leq 15$
FIXED BINARY	(31,q) where $0 \leq q \leq 31$
FLOAT DECIMAL	(16)
FLOAT BINARY	(53)

When the result of a **FIXED (DEC** or **BIN)** arithmetic operation is a value so large that its leftmost significant digit exceeds the maximum allowable precision, then the so-called **FIXEDOVERFLOW** condition is raised. For example, if we perform the following **FIXED DEC** addition,

$$999999999999999 + 1$$

the result will have 16 significant digits. Raising of that condition causes the program's execution to be interrupted. Whether execution resumes, and from what place, is up to the programmer.

The Assignment Statement

The main vehicle for computing and assigning a new value to a variable, array, or structure is the assignment statement. Its form is as follows.

$$\text{variable} = \text{expression};$$

Here, "variable" denotes either an elementary variable, an array variable, or a structure variable, and "expression" denotes an elementary expression, array expression, or structure expression. Not all variations implied by a strict interpretation of this definition are permissible, as we will discuss further below.

When an assignment statement is executed, the expression on its right is first evaluated. Then the result of that evaluation becomes the new value of (is "assigned to") the variable. For example, suppose I is a **FIXED BIN (15,0)** variable with current value 43 at the time the following assignment statement is executed.

$$I = I + 1;$$

First the value of the expression **I + 1**, or 44, is computed, and then that becomes the new value of the variable I.

The variable on the left of the assignment's "=" sign may also be an array reference. For instance, let **KA** be a one-dimensional array of **10 FIXED BIN (15,0)** values. Then **KA(3) = I + 1**; would assign the value of **I + 1** to the 3rd element in **KA**.

More than one variable may be listed on the left of the assignment's "=" sign, forming a so-called multiple assignment statement. This is a convenient device to initialize a number of variables to the same value. For instance, we could write

I, J, K = 0;

to initialize the variables **I, J,** and **K** to zero. This is slightly more convenient to write than the following equivalent sequence of statements.

I = 0;   J = 0;   K = 0;

If the result designated by the expression on the right of the assignment's "=" sign has attributes different from those of the variable on the left, then "conversion" occurs. Conversion is the transformation of a value with one set of attributes to an equivalent, or nearly equivalent, value with a different set of attributes. For example, the value 15 has attributes **REAL FIXED DEC (2,0).** If we converted it to **REAL FIXED BIN (15,0),** we would obtain the following equivalent value.

000000000001111B

Conversion is a difficult issue to master completely. Perhaps the main reason for this difficulty is that some of the rules for conversion are implementation dependent, and vary from one implementation to another. Nevertheless, the programmer must be aware that conversion will take place on any assignment statement where the left-hand variable's attributes disagree with those of the value being assigned. Conversion takes place not only with the execution of assignment statements, but also with the execution of the so-called "stream input" statements.

In most PL/I implementations, all "reasonable" conversions are well defined. Even the conversion of a character string containing a valid number, like '1.23', to its "equivalent" arithmetic value, 1.23, is performed by most implementations. Some conversions are impossible, however. For instance, if we were asked to convert the character string **'ALLEN'** to an "equivalent" arithmetic value, we would throw up our hands. Situations like this one, in which there is no reasonable conversion possible, will cause the so-called "CONVERSION condition" to be raised. This is an exceptional condition which causes program execution to be interrupted. Whether execution is resumed, and from what point in the program, is up to the programmer.

Conversion between **FIXED** and **FLOAT,** and between **DECIMAL** and **BINARY,** is fairly straightforward. The result is what one would expect in the numerical sense. Conversion of the precision of an arithmetic value, however, is not always suitable. Specifically, conversion of a **FIXED** value from one precision to another precision results either in the padding of leading or trailing zeros, or the truncation of leading or trailing digits, in the original value. The following table illustrates exactly what happens when an initial value is converted to a value with the given target attributes.

Initial value	Target attributes	Result of conversion
3.19	FIXED DEC (2,1)	3.1
3.19	FIXED DEC (2,2)	.19
3.19	FIXED DEC (4,3)	3.190
3.19	FIXED DEC (4,2)	03.19

As the reader can see, both trailing and leading significant digits can be truncated as a result of conversion. The truncation of trailing digits results in a loss of significance, but causes no error condition to be raised. However, the truncation of leading significant digits, like the "3" in the second example in the table, raises the so-called "SIZE condition." This event causes program execution to be interrupted. Whether execution resumes, and at what point in the program, is decided by the programmer.

Another common kind of conversion, so-called "length conversion," occurs when a fixed-length **CHAR** (or **BIT**) string variable is assigned a character (or bit) string value whose length is different from that of the variable. For instance, let **S** and **T** be string variables declared as follows.

DCL S CHAR (5), T CHAR (1);

If the length of the variable is greater than that of the value being assigned to it, then the value is padded on the right with enough blanks to make its length equal that of the target variable. For instance,

S = 'ALL';

leaves **S** with the value **'ALLƀƀ'.** If the length of the variable is less than that of the value being assigned to it, then the value is truncated on the right accordingly. For instance,

T = 'ALL';

leaves **T** with the value **'A'.**

This particular conversion can often be advantageous to the programmer. For instance, if it is desired to clear a long, say 132-character, variable **V** to blanks, the programmer can simply say

V = 'ƀ';

with the knowledge that blanks will be padded throughout **V.**

Assignment to a varying-length string variable, however, changes the length of that variable as well as its value. For instance, if **S** is **CHAR (5) VARYING,** then the assignment **S = 'ALL';** will leave the value of **S** as **'ALL'** and the length of **S** as 3.

So far, we have discussed only the assignment of elementary values to elementary variables. That is indeed the most common use of the assignment statement. Sometimes, however, we would like to assign an entire array or structure a new set of values. For this, we may be able to use the array assignment or structure assignment statement.

One situation which often occurs is that of initialization. If we want to set all elements of an array named **A** to some elementary value, say 0, then we may simply write

A = 0;

Note that the array name, **A**, is written without subscripts. Similarly, we may assign such a value to a cross section of an array by designating that cross section on the left of the assignment. Finally, we may initialize all elements of a structure to a single value in a similar fashion, by giving that structure's name on the left.

The other situation which occurs is that in which an array of values, computed by an array expression, is to be assigned to an entire array or cross section. For example, suppose **B**, **C**, and **D** are arrays declared as follows.

$$\text{DCL (B(5,3), C(3), D(5,3))   FIXED BIN (15,0)};$$

Then we could directly assign to **B** the values of corresponding elements in **D** by simply writing the following:

$$\text{B} = \text{D};$$

On the other hand, we could assign to the second row of **B** the three values computed by taking the sum of **C** and twice the fourth row of **D**, as follows.

$$\text{B(2,*)} = \text{C} + 2 * \text{D(4,*)};$$

One absolute rule to remember when assigning an array the values resulting from an array expression is the following. The array being assigned new values must agree, in dimensionality and number of elements in each dimension, with that array which is the result of the array expression being evaluated.

The IF Statement

When a statement or sequence of statements, **S**, is to be executed only in the event that the condition designated by some logical expression, **e**, is true (i.e., has the value '1'B), the **IF** statement is used. It has either one of the following two forms.

1. IF e THEN S

2. IF e THEN S_1 ELSE S_2

Here, **e** designates the logical expression, while **S**, S_1, and S_2 designate any single statement, "**DO** group," or "**BEGIN** block." **DO** groups and **BEGIN** blocks are extremely useful aids to writing well-structured programs; we shall discuss them later. Note also that no semicolon explicitly appears to terminate the **IF** statement. However, **S**, S_1, and S_2 each terminates with a semicolon, so that the end of the **IF** statement is always uniquely identified.

Execution of form 1 of the **IF** statement involves two steps. First, the expression of **e** is evaluated, obtaining a result of '1'B (true) or '0'B (false). If the result is true, then **S** is executed. Otherwise, **S** is bypassed.

Execution of form 2 also involves two steps. First, the expression **e** is evaluated, again obtaining a true or false result. Either S_1 or S_2 is then executed, and the other is bypassed, depending on whether the result is true or false, respectively.

Let's look at some examples of the **IF** statement. Suppose we want to compute **FED_TAX** as 22 percent of **GROSS_PAY** provided **GROSS_PAY** is under $18,000.00. We assume here that **GROSS_PAY** and **FED_TAX** are either numeric character variables with **PICTURE '(5)9V99'** or **FIXED DEC (7,2)** variables. Then we could write the following **IF** statement (form 1).

> **IF GROSS_PAY < 1800**
> **THEN FED_TAX = .22 ∗ GROSS_PAY;**

Here, we note that an assignment statement occurs as **S**, while the expression **e** is simply **"GROSS_PAY < 18000"**.

Suppose, in addition, we want to compute **FED_TAX** as 25 percent of **GROSS_PAY** whenever **GROSS_PAY** is not under 18,000.00. Then we would expand the **IF** statement to form 2 as follows.

> **IF GROSS_PAY < 18000**
> **THEN FED_TAX = .22 ∗ GROSS_PAY;**
> **ELSE FED_TAX = .25 ∗ GROSS_PAY;**

Now **FED_TAX** will be computed one way or the other depending on the value of **GROSS_PAY**. In the former example, **FED_TAX** would have been computed only if **GROSS PAY** were under $18,000.00.

A **DO** group has several forms, most of which will be discussed in a later paragraph. We introduce its simplest form here, however, because of its natural association with the **IF** statement. The simplest form of the **DO** group is composed of a sequence of executable statements headed by **"DO;"** and ended by **"END;"**. The example program given above contains this kind of **DO** group, which is rewritten and outlined below.

> **LOOP: IF H < = 5**
>
> **THEN**
> ```
> DO;
> B(H,1) = 1;
> B(H,2) = 5 + 3 ∗ (H − A(H));
> H = H + 1;
> GO TO LOOP;
> END;
> ```

As shown, this **DO** group appears within an **IF** statement, and thus is executed only if the condition **H < = 5** is true. Otherwise, it is completely bypassed.

For a more practical example, consider solving, for real roots **x**, the quadratic equation

$$ax^2 + bx + c = 0 \qquad (a \neq 0)$$

where **a**, **b**, and **c** are real and given.

The number of roots and their values can be determined by first computing the discriminant **d** from **a**, **b**, and **c** as follows.

$$d = b^2 − 4ac$$

If **d < 0**, then there are no real roots. If **d = 0**, then there is one real root **x1**, given by

$$x1 = −b/(2a)$$

If $d > 0$, then there are two real roots, $x1$ and $x2$, given by

$$x1 = (-b + \sqrt{d})/(2a)$$
$$x2 = (-b - \sqrt{d})/(2a)$$

The program segment to compute the number of roots, say **NROOTS,** and their values, say **X1** and **X2,** given coefficients **A, B,** and **C,** can be written as follows.

```
D = B ** 2 − 4 * A * C;
IF D < 0 THEN NROOTS = 0;
ELSE IF D = 0
    THEN DO;
      NROOTS = 1;
      X1 = −B/(2 * A);
    END;
  ELSE DO;
    NROOTS = 2;
    X1 = (−B + D ** .5)/(2 * A);
    X2 = (−B − D ** .5)/(2 * A);
    END;
```

As shown, the **ELSE** of the first **IF** statement is followed by another **IF** statement of form 2. Each part of that **IF** statement contains a separate **DO** group. As the reader can see, this structuring renders a very clear and straightforward encoding of the problem solution.

The DO Statement and Loops

Much of programming is concerned with the proper specification of controlled (as opposed to infinite) loops. PL/I provides several forms of the **DO** statement as an aid to writing such loops.

A controlled loop is the repeated execution of a sequence of statements until a certain specific condition becomes true. Many such loops are "counter-controlled" loops, in which a counting variable is initialized and then incremented and tested each time the sequence of statements is executed. When the variable is incremented beyond a specific limit, the loop's execution terminates. This is pictured in two different forms in Fig. 17-6. Here, i denotes the loop-control variable, while m_1, m_2, and m_3 denote expressions which are, respectively, the initial value, the limit value, and the increment value for the control variable. An illustration of flowchart (b) is given in the example program. There the control variable is **H,** the initial value m_1 is 1, the limit m_2 is 5 and the increment m_3 is 1. Flowchart (b) can be encoded as a "**DO** loop" as follows.

DO i = m_1 **TO** m_2 **BY** m_3;

> Sequence of
> statements

END;

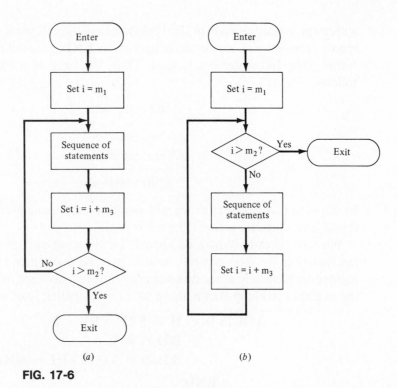

FIG. 17-6

For instance, the loop in the example program can be rewritten equivalently as follows.

$$\textbf{LOOP: DO} \quad \textbf{H} = \textbf{1 TO 5 BY 1;}$$
$$\textbf{B(H,1)} = \textbf{1;}$$
$$\textbf{B(H,2)} = \textbf{5} + \textbf{3} * (\textbf{H} - \textbf{A(H))};$$
$$\textbf{END;}$$

As indicated, the single **DO** statement incorporates the initialization, test, and increment steps of the loop depicted in flowchart (b).

The reader should note that flowchart (a) is not equivalent to flowchart (b), since it does not permit the case where the sequence of statements is executed zero times. The PL/I **DO** loop, therefore, does include provision for that event.

There are many forms in which the **DO** statement may be written, in order to permit a variety of commonly used loops to be conveniently described. We will discuss what we consider to be the most useful among these forms, as follows.

1. **DO** $i = m_1$ **TO** m_2 **BY** m_3;
2. **DO** $i = m_1$ **TO** m_2;
3. **DO** $i = m_1$ **BY** m_3;
4. **DO** $i = v_1, v_2, \ldots, v_n$;
5. **DO WHILE** (e);
6. **DO** $i = m_1$ [**TO** m_2][**BY** m_3] **WHILE** (e);

Here, i denotes a variable; $m_1, m_2, m_3, v_1, v_2 \ldots, v_n$ denote arithmetic expressions; and e denotes a logical expression. In each of these six forms, the **DO** statement is used to control the repeated execution of some sequence of statements. The latter is always delimited by an **END** statement, no matter which form of the **DO** statement is used. Thus, the form of a PL/I **DO** loop is as follows.

DO statement

Sequence of statements

END statement

In the next few paragraphs we will describe the meaning of each of these six forms, and illustrate a case where it is useful.

We have already illustrated form 1, for the most part. We did not mention the fact that the loop control variable may be decremented instead of incremented by providing a negative value for m_3. For instance, we could redescribe the example **DO** loop shown above as a decrementing loop, as follows.

LOOP: DO   H = 5 TO 1 BY −1;

B(H,1) = 1;

B(H,2) = 5 + 3 ∗ (H − A(H));

END;

If m_3 is negative, then the sense of the test performed before execution of the sequence of statements in flowchart (b) is reversed, as shown in Fig. 17-7.

Form 2 is an abbreviation for form 1 when the increment value m_3 is 1. For instance, the following **DO** statements are equivalent.

DO H = 1 TO 5 BY 1;

DO H = 1 TO 5;

Form 3 is used when exit from the loop is not naturally specifiable by either an upper limit or a **WHILE** clause. Its meaning is the same as that of form 1, except that no test for exit is performed. The programmer must ensure that such a loop remains controlled by providing some other means by which the loop will eventually be exited. Perhaps the most common use for this form is the loop which controls the sequential reading of records in a file. Exit occurs when the end of the file is reached; the loop-control variable in this case plays the role of a record counter.

Form 4 is used when the succession of values taken on by the loop control variable does not form a sequence describable by a constant increment or decrement. For example, suppose we want to perform a sequence of statements once for each of the following values of **H**: 1, 3, and 4. Then we would use form 4 as follows.

DO H = 1, 3, 4;

Sequence of statements

END;

This is equivalent to the repeated writing of "Sequence of statements" shown in Fig. 17-8.

Form 5 is used when exit from the loop is taken only when a certain condition, specified by e, becomes false. This test is performed before each execution of the sequence of statements, so that the possibility for those statements to be executed zero times is not excluded. One common use for this form occurs in numerical analysis, where a sequence of approximations is computed until a specified convergence condition is satisfied. For example, suppose we are developing an approximation to $\sqrt{A}$ by Newton's method. Then the next approximation Y is computed from the previous one X by the formula

$$Y = \tfrac{1}{2}(X + A/X)$$

and this is repeated until the absolute value of the difference between two successive approximations is sufficiently small, say less than 0.0001. Then the following loop will exist when that condition occurs.

DO WHILE (ABS (Y − X) > = 0.0001);
      X = Y;
      Y = 0.5 ∗ (X + A/X);
END;

Form 6 is used when either the attainment of an upper limit or the falsity of an exit condition, whichever occurs first, is reached. The semantics of this case are defined in Fig. 17-9 (for $m_2 > 0$). We see here that both tests are performed before the sequence of statements is executed.

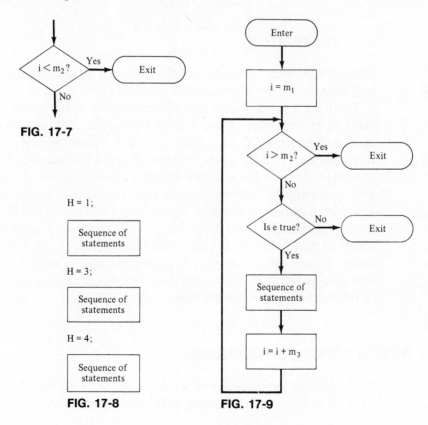

FIG. 17-7

H = 1;

Sequence of statements

H = 3;

Sequence of statements

H = 4;

Sequence of statements

FIG. 17-8   **FIG. 17-9**

One use for this "combined" form of the loop is to prevent the program from going into an infinite loop. For instance, the previous example tacitly assumes that the condition.

$$\text{ABS} (Y - X) > = 0.0001$$

will eventually become false. There are, however, certain conditions under which that will never happen. Thus, it behooves the programmer to ensure exit from the loop (one way or the other) by forcing an upper limit of, say, 50 on the number of times the code is executed. Thus, he replaces the above **DO** statement as follows.

$$\text{DO I} = 1 \text{ TO } 50 \text{ WHILE (ABS } (Y - X) > = 0.0001);$$

Now when this loop exits, the program can test which of the conditions actually caused the exit to occur.

Another case where form 6 is useful is that of sequential table search. Suppose, for instance, that **NAMES** is an array of 50 fifteen-character strings, and **NAME** is a simple fifteen-character string variable. The following code searches **NAMES** to see whether or not the value of **NAME** is there.

> **DO I = 1 TO 50 WHILE (NAMES (I) ¬ = NAME);**
> **END;**
> **IF I > 50 THEN GO TO NOT_FOUND;**

FOUND: _____

_____

_____

NOT_FOUND: _____

This example illustrates also that the value of a loop control variable is indeed well defined, and sometimes useful, upon exit from the loop that it controls.

There are a number of reasonable restrictions on the use of **DO** loops which ought to be mentioned. First, it is illegal to cause control to transfer into any statement within a **DO** loop from outside it, unless the transfer is to the **DO** statement itself (which causes initiation of the loop). Second, it is of course legal to transfer from within the loop to any statement within or without the loop. The reader should distinguish, however, that transfer to the **END** statement from within causes **continuation** of the loop, while transfer to the **DO** statement causes **reinitiation** of the loop. Third, a **DO** loop may be completely nested within another **DO** loop, provided that the rules for transfer of control are followed. Fourth, the value of a loop control variable should not explicitly be **altered** from within the loop. However, that variable's value can be, and usually is, **referenced** from within the loop.

17-4 INPUT-OUTPUT CONVENTIONS

PL/I facilities for reading and writing data are extensive. They fall into two different classes, called "stream I/O" and "record I/O." It is important to understand the fundamental nature of these two classes, since each one is essential to a significantly wide application area.

When data are read or written by a program using stream I/O, the data are considered to form a continuous sequence, or stream, of individual values. Indeed, the individual (card) records are taken as if they were attached, end to end, to form one very long card accommodating all data values in the file. For example, consider the input data deck in Fig. 17-10. When read as input under stream I/O, this data appears to the program in a left-to-right order, as if the cards were attached as in Fig.

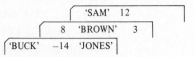

FIG. 17-10

17-11. Under stream I/O, it is the individual data value, rather than the individual record, which is the fundamental unit of input (or output).

Stream input operations are always specified by a **GET** statement, while stream output operations are specified by a **PUT** statement. When the **GET** statement is executed, a specified number of individual data values are read from the current position of the data stream. When the **PUT** statement is executed, a specified number of data values are placed into the current position of the data stream. After completion of either of these statements, the current position of the data stream is advanced. We can visualize this by picturing an imaginary pointer initially placed at the first value in the data stream, as shown in Fig. 17-12. When the first **GET** statement is executed, assume that two values are read as input: **'BUCK'** and −14. Now the "current position" of the pointer is moved past these two, as shown in Fig. 17-13. The next execution of a **GET** statement will cause data to be read beginning with **'JONES'**.

Finally, stream I/O always takes place sequentially. Data values are read from a file in the order that they appear; data values are written to a file in the order that **PUT** statements are executed. The file cannot be "backed up" so that a value may be reread, or spaced forward so that values may be skipped.

When data is read or written using **record I/O,** the file is considered to be a collection of records. Any individual input or output operation causes the reading or writing of an entire record. Record I/O usually takes place sequentially. Record I/O also permits records to be read (written) randomly provided the

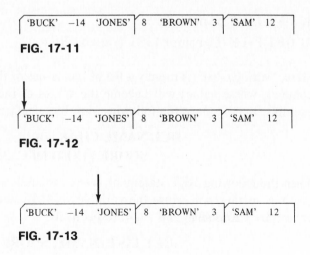

FIG. 17-11

FIG. 17-12

FIG. 17-13

file in question is located on a random access input-output device. This is an important alternative for many applications; we will discuss random processing of files in this section.

Record input operations are always specified by a **READ** statement, while record output operations are specified by a **WRITE** or a **REWRITE** statement. When a **READ** statement is executed (for a file that is being processed sequentially) the next **record** in the file is read. Similarly, when a **WRITE** statement is executed the next record is written out into the file.

Whether stream or record I/O is used, the concept and physical aspects of a file are the same. A "file" is any collection of data which resides on a computer-readable medium (e.g., a deck of cards, a reel of magnetic tape, an area of a disk, a continuous sheet of paper). An "input file" is one which is used to supply data to the program. An "output file" is one which is used to store results computed by the program. An "update file" is one which is used both to supply data and to store results. In most applications a file is either an input file or an output file.

Stream I/O

When stream I/O is used, the data in a file may appear either as a sequence of data values separated from each other by blanks or as a sequence of records which are identically laid out (formatted), as illustrated in Fig. 17-14. In the former case the program uses so-called "list-directed" techniques, while in the latter case the program uses "edit-directed" techniques to access the data.

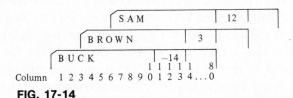

FIG. 17-14

List-directed input is specified by a **GET** statement in one of the following forms.

1. GET LIST (variable-list);

2. GET FILE (filename) **LIST** (variable-list);

Here, "variable-list" is merely a list of the names of the variables, separated by commas, whose values will become the values of the data read. Suppose, for example, that we have the following variables declared in a program.

DCL NAME CHAR (10),
SCORE FIXED DEC (3,0);

Then the following **GET** statement, when executed with the data shown in the previous section, will cause the variables **NAME** and **SCORE** to take on the values **'BUCKƀƀƀƀƀƀ'** and −14, respectively.

GET LIST (NAME, SCORE);

The order in which the variables are listed in the **GET** statement defines the order in which input values are assigned. Note also that character string data is represented with its enclosing single quotes; this is required for any string read under list-directed input. Note finally that individual data values must be separated from each other by at least one blank space when read under list-directed input.

The difference between form 1 and form 2 of the list-directed input statement is that form 1 implies that input data will be taken from the "standard input file," while form 2 allows data to be taken from any particular file, as designated by "filename."

Every file used by a PL/I program, whether for input or for output, has a unique file name. That is a character sequence which begins with an alphabetic (A–Z, @, #, $) character and contains only alphabetic, numeric (0–9), and/or break (_) characters. Because they are used so commonly, two particular files are singled out and designated as the "standard input file" and the "standard output file." The former is merely the system's standard input medium, usually punched cards. The latter is the system's standard output medium, usually printed paper. These files' names vary among implementations; for IBM's PL/I(F) compiler, they are named **SYSIN** and **SYSPRINT,** respectively.

The important point is that, if form 1 of the **GET LIST** statement is used, the system assumes (by default) that the program wants data read from the standard input file (**SYSIN**). If any other file is required, then form 2 must be used to specify it.

Similarly, list-directed output is specified by a **PUT** statement in one of the following forms.

1. **PUT LIST** (expression-list);
2. **PUT SKIP LIST** (expression-list);
3. **PUT FILE** (filename) **LIST** (expression-list);

Here, "expression-list" designates a number of expressions, separated by commas. Form 1 or 2 may be used when the standard output file is desired; otherwise, form 3 may be used in order to indicate a different "filename." When executed, the **PUT** statement causes the resulting values of the listed expressions to be transferred to the output file, and in the order they are listed.

For example, reconsider the variables **NAME** and **SCORE** declared above, and with values 'BUCKℓℓℓℓℓℓ' and −14, respectively. Suppose we want to print these values. Then we could say the following.

PUT LIST (NAME, SCORE);

The values printed would be BUCKℓℓℓℓℓℓ and −14. Where they are printed depends upon both the current position of the output file and the (system-defined) tab settings for that file.

For printed, list-directed output each line on the page is segmented into a fixed number of horizontal tab positions. For this chapter, we will assume that they are positions 1, 21, 41, 61, 81, and 101 on a 120-character line size. Readers are encouraged to learn the tab positions for their implementations.

Suppose the current position of the print file is as shown in Fig. 17-15 when

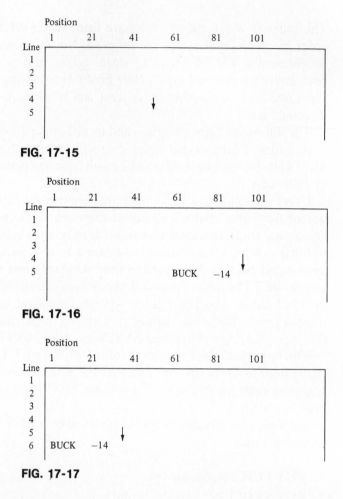

FIG. 17-15

FIG. 17-16

FIG. 17-17

the above **PUT** statement is executed. Then execution will leave the values of **NAME** and **SCORE** as shown in Fig. 17-16. Note that the current position has also changed in preparation for the next **PUT** statement to be executed. Note also that character strings are printed without their enclosing quotes.

Form 2 of the **PUT** statement will cause a skip to the beginning of the next line before printing begins. For instance, **"PUT SKIP LIST (NAME, SCORE);"** would leave the results printed instead as shown in Fig. 17-17. Form 3 of the **PUT** statement is used when the output is destined for a file different from the standard output file. In this case the file may not be printed, and individual data values may instead be separated by a single blank space rather than a number of spaces to the next tab position. Tab positions are defined only for printed output files.

Edit-directed input is specified by a **GET** statement in one of the following forms.

1. GET EDIT (variable-list) (format-list);

2. GET FILE (filename) **EDIT** (variable-list) (format-list);

The choice between form 1 and form 2 is again governed by whether input is to be read from the standard input file or not. The "variable list" serves the same purpose as it did for the list-directed **GET** statement. The "format-list" describes the layout and form of the individual data values on the medium (e.g., cards) where they reside. It is composed of a sequence of format items separated by commas. A format item serves one of the following two purposes:

1. It controls the forward positioning of the pointer which indicates the location from which the next data value is to be read. This kind is called a "control format item."

2. It describes the physical layout in which a data item is stored on the input medium (e.g., punched card). This kind is called a "data format item."

Some commonly used control format items, data format items, and their meanings are described in the following tables.

Control format item	Meaning (input)
COLUMN(n)	Skip forward to column (position) n on the current record (e.g., card) before reading the next value. Here, n denotes any integer-valued expression. If column n has already been passed in the current record, skip forward to column n of the next record.
X(n)	Skip forward n positions past the present position in the input stream; "n" denotes any integer-valued expression greater than 0.
SKIP(n)	Skip to the beginning of the nth record beyond the current one in the input stream; "n" denotes any integer-valued expression greater than 0. A skip to the beginning of the next record can be written simply as SKIP instead of SKIP (1).

Data format item	Meaning (input)
F(w,d)	A FIXED DECIMAL arithmetic data value, stored in the next w positions in the input stream. The "field width" w can be any integer-valued expression, as can d; "d" denotes the number of digits, beginning with the right position in the field, to be taken as the value's fractional part. If the value in the field has a decimal point already, then its position overrides d (see examples below). If d = 0, then F(w,0) can be equivalently written as F(w), indicating an integer input value.
E(w,d)	A FLOAT DECIMAL arithmetic data value, stored in the next w positions in the input stream; "d" denotes the number of digits in the mantissa which follow the decimal point, and is overridden if the point appears explicitly in the number. (See examples below.)
A(w)	A character string data value, stored in the next w positions (without its enclosing quotes) in the input stream; "w" may be any positive interger-valued expression.
B(w)	A BIT string data value, stored in the next positions (without its enclosing quotes or "B"), in the input stream; "w" may be any positive integer-valued expression.

To illustrate how these work, let us first apply edit-directed input to read the first two data values, from the formatted data shown in Fig. 17-14, into **NAME** and **SCORE**.

GET EDIT (NAME, SCORE) (COL(1), A(10), F(3,0));

First, there is a left-to-right matching of the variables listed with the data format items in the format-list (the control format items—**COL (1)** in this case—are ignored in this matching process). To each variable there corresponds a format item which is used to control the input of the datum that will become its new value. Second, the individual format items are obeyed from left to right (as they appear), when the statement is executed.

For example, this statement says literally the following.

"Proceed to column 1 of the next card if you are not already there. The next ten columns (1–10) contain a character string which should be stored in **NAME**. The next three columns contain a three-digit integer, which should be stored in **SCORE**."

This is precisely what's desired if we want to use this **GET** statement to read a sequence of cards, one by one, which are formatted as illustrated in Fig. 17-14. Note, specifically, that the **COL (1)** specification is required. If it were omitted, then the second execution of the **GET** statement would begin at position 14 of the first card, rather than position 1 of the second.

There are a number of "what if" situations that can arise using edit-directed input. We illustrate a large majority of them with the following examples. Study them carefully, so that the definitions of the various data format items become more meaningful. Let's look first at some **FIXED DECIMAL VALUES** and corresponding **F** format items. Any value which is not either a valid fixed decimal constant or entirely blank will raise the **CONVERSION** condition. Furthermore, the attributes of the variable where the "value as interpreted" will be stored should accommodate those of the value itself.

Value in input stream	Format item	Value as interpreted
1234	F(4,3)	1.234
ƀƀ34	F(4,3)	0.034
ƀ34ƀ	F(4,3)	0.034
1.23	F(4,3)	1.230
ƀƀƀƀ	F(4,3)	0.000
1234	F(4)	1234
ƀƀ34	F(4)	34
ƀ34ƀ	F(4)	34
1.23	F(4)	1.230

For example, it would be unusual to read the value of 1.234 using an **F** format item into a variable which did not have arithmetic (rather than string) attributes. Furthermore, if the variable were **FIXED DECIMAL**, it would be unusual if the variable's precision were not sufficient to accommodate the significant digits in the value; for example, (3,3) precision would not accommodate the value of 1.234. If this occurs, then the **SIZE** condition will be raised.

Yet, a variable may well accommodate the "value as interpreted," and also require that the value be converted to fit the attributes of the variable as declared. Suppose, for example, that we have the value 1.236. The following list shows the different ways that this value can be converted if it is to be stored in a variable, say **X**, with the following different attributes.

Attributes of X	Result of conversion
REAL FIXED DEC (6,3)	001.236
REAL FIXED DEC (6,2)	0001.23
REAL FIXED DEC (5,0)	00001
REAL FLOAT DEC (6)	0.123600E1

That is, the value is stored in one of its representations as dictated by the attributes of the variable where it is to reside. Note that trailing (right-hand) digits are truncated without rounding, and that this does not raise an error condition.

Let's now look at some examples to illustrate the **E** format item.

Value in input stream	Format item	Value as interpreted
1234ƀƀƀƀ	E(8,3)	1.234E0
12.34ƀƀƀ	E(8,3)	12.34E0
−1234E1ƀ	E(8,3)	−1.234E1
1234ƀƀƀƀ	E(8,0)	1234E0
12.34ƀƀƀ	E(8,0)	12.34E0
−1234E1ƀ	E(8,0)	−1234E1

Any value which is not either a valid fixed decimal constant or a valid float decimal constant will raise the **CONVERSION** condition. Specifically, a totally blank value will raise the **CONVERSION** condition when read under **E** format. Furthermore, the attributes of the variable where the "value as interpreted" will be stored should accommodate those of the value itself, in the same sense as that described above for values read under **F** format.

Finally, let's look at some examples to illustrate the **A** and **B** format items.

Value in input stream	Format item	Value as interpreted
TITLEƀ17	A(8)	'TITLEƀ17'
TITLEƀ17	A(7)	'TITLEƀ1'
ƀTITLEƀ17	A(7)	'ƀTITLEƀ'
1011	B(4)	'1011'B
1011	B(3)	'101'B

Two points are worth mentioning here. First, the input values are not enclosed in quotes. Second, the value is taken from left to right, and as many characters are taken as dictated by w in the **A** or **B** format item. Note also that leading and embedded blanks are retained in the "value as interpreted."

The variable where the "value as interpreted" is to be stored should accommodate the value. That is, it should be a character or bit string variable, as the format item is **A** or **B** respectively. If that variable's length is less than that of the value as interpreted, then the value is truncated on the right as required to fit the variable. If the variable's length is greater than that of the value as interpreted, then trailing blanks or zeros are added at the right end as required to fit the variable, as it is a character or bit string variable, respectively. For example, let **S** and **T** be declared as follows.

DCL S CHAR(4), T CHAR(10);

If the value as interpreted were 'TITLEƀ17', then it would be stored as 'TITL' in **S** and 'TITLEƀ17ƀƀ' in **T**. Finally, we should note that any value in the input stream to be read under **B** format control must be composed entirely of 0s and 1s. Otherwise, an error condition will be raised.

Edit-directed output is specified by a **PUT** statement in one of the following forms.

1. PUT EDIT (variable-list) (format-list);

2. PUT FILE (filename) **EDIT** (variable-list) (format-list);

Again, the choice between form 1 and form 2 is governed by whether or not output is to be directed to the standard output file, **SYSPRINT.** The "variable-list" serves the same purpose as it did for the list-directed **PUT** statement. The format list is identical in purpose to the format list accompanying edit-directed input; it describes the layout and form of the individual data values on the medium (e.g., printed paper) where they will be placed when the **PUT** statement is executed.

The various kinds of control and data format items for output are similar with those used for edit-directed input. Their meanings for edit-directed output are described here.

Control format item	Meaning (output)
PAGE	Skip forward to the first position (column) on the first line of the next page before printing the next value.
LINE(n)	Skip forward to the first position of the nth line on the current page before printing the next value. If the nth line has already been reached, skip forward to the first line on the next page.*
COLUMN(n)	Skip forward on the current line to the nth column for printing the next data value. If the nth column has already been passed, the nth column on the next line will be accessed.*
X(n)	Skip forward n positions in the stream; line or page boundaries may be crossed by the X format item.
	Skip forward to the beginning of the nth line following the present one. SKIP(1) may be abbreviated as simply SKIP.

*These exceptional actions are implementation dependent. Our presentation reflects the IBM PL/I(F) implementation.

Data format item	Meaning (output)
F(w,d)	A FIXED DECIMAL arithmetic value will be stored in the next w positions of the output stream, rounded to d digits on the right of the decimal point. For an integer, F(w,0) can be abbreviated as F(w).
E(w,d)	A FLOAT DECIMAL arithmetic value is stored in the next w positions of the output stream, rounded to d digits on the right of the decimal point, as shown below. $$\underbrace{x.xxx \ldots x \text{ E} \pm yy}_{d}$$
A(w)	The interpretation of this value is the same as that for FLOAT data values. A CHARACTER string value is written in the next w positions of the output stream, without its enclosing quotes; "(w)" may be omitted here, in which case the remaining "A" specification implies a value of w identical with the length of the character string being written.

Data format item	Meaning (output)
B(w)	A BIT string value is written in the next w positions of the output stream, without its enclosing quotes or "B". Again, "(w)" may be omitted, in which case it is assumed to be identical with the length of the bit string being written.
P'picture-spec'	A numeric character data value is stored in the output stream, as specified by the "picture-spec."

The **PAGE** and **LINE** control format items described above apply only to files which are destined for the printer; so-called "print files." The others apply equally as well to any stream output file.

There are a variety of exceptional situations that can occur during edit-directed output. We point out the most common among these situations via the examples below. First, let's apply edit-directed output to print the values of **NAME** and **SCORE,** which are declared and initialized as follows.

> **DCL NAME CHAR(10) INIT ('BUCK'),**
> **SCORE FIXED DEC(3) INIT (−14);**

Suppose the current position of the output data stream is the first position of the first line on the page. Then the following statement

> **PUT EDIT (NAME, SCORE) (A(10), X(10), F(3,0));**

will leave the values printed as shown in Fig. 17-18. The same result would have been obtained if the "A(10)" format item had been replaced by "A" (since the length of **NAME** is 10), the "F(3,0)" format item had been replaced by "F(3)", or the "X(10)" format item had been replaced by "COL(21)".

```
      Position
                 1 1 1      2 2 2 2
        1 2 3 4 5 6 7 8 9 0 1 2 . . . . . 0 1 2 3 . . .
Line
  1   | BUCK ƀ ƀ ƀ ƀ ƀ ƀ            − 1 4
  2   |
  3   |
```

FIG. 17-18

The examples in the following table illustrate some more situations that can occur during edit-directed output. Study them carefully, so that you obtain a firm understanding of these special situations.

Value as stored	Format item	Value as printed
1.236	F(6,3)	ƀ1.236
1.236E2	F(7,3)	123.600
1236	F(8,3)	1236.000
1236	F(6)	ƀƀ1236
1.236	F(6,2)	ƀƀ1.24
1.236	F(6,1)	ƀƀƀ1.2
1.236	E(12,6)	0.123600E+ƀ1
1.236E2	E(12,3)	ƀƀƀ0.124E+ƀ3
'BUCK'	A(6)	BUCKƀƀ
'BUCK'	A(3)	BUC
'101'B	B(6)	101ƀƀƀ
'101'B	B(2)	10

Any value which is improper for the format item provided, such as **'BUCK'** or 1000.5 for the format item **F(6,3)**, will cause an error condition to be raised.

We conclude this discussion of edit-directed input-output with some additional important points. First, if the number of data format items exceeds the number of values to be read (written), then they and the intervening control format items will be ignored. For example, consider the following statement.

PUT EDIT (NAME, SCORE) (A,F(3), **COL(50), A** **);**

The boxed items in the format list will be ignored upon execution of this statement. Similarly, any control format item which follows the data format item for the last value to be printed (**SCORE** in this case) will be ignored, whether or not a data format item follows it. **"COL(50)"** would be ignored in the above example even if **",A"** were omitted immediately after it.

Second, if the number of data format items is insufficient to accommodate the number of data value to be read (written), then the format list is repeated from its beginning. For example,

PUT EDIT (NAME, SCORE, NAME, SCORE) (A, F(3));

and

PUT EDIT (NAME, SCORE, NAME, SCORE) (A, F(3), A, F(3));

are effectively equivalent.

Third, the repetition of any part of a format list may be specified by (enclosing that part in parentheses and) preceding that part by an integer expression to indicate the number of repetitions desired. For example,

PUT EDIT (NAME, SCORE, SCORE, NAME) (A, F(3), F(3), A);

and

PUT EDIT (NAME, SCORE, SCORE, NAME) (A,2ƀF(3), A);

are effectively equivalent. Enclosure in parentheses must be done if the part to be repeated consists of more than one format item. Note that a blank (ƀ) is required before the part being repeated.

Finally, a general comment about stream I/O should be made before we conclude its discussion. That is, an array or structure may be read (written) under stream I/O in any one of a variety of ways. To illustrate, let's declare the following array **B** and structure **S**.

> **DCL B(5,4) FIXED DEC (2,0),**
> **1   S,**
> **2 T FIXED DEC (3,2),**
> **2 U CHAR (5),**
> **2 V FLOAT DEC (6);**

To read the next twenty values into **B**, and then the next three values into **S**, we could say any of the following, equivalently.

1. GET LIST (B1,1), B(1,2), B(1,3), B(1,4), B(2,1), . . . , B(5,4), T, U, V);

2. GET LIST (((B(I,J) DO J = 1 TO 4) DO I = 1 TO 5), T, U, V);

3. GET LIST ((B(I,*) DO I = 1 TO 5); S);

4. GET LIST (B,S);

Choice 2 illustrates that a **DO** specification can be placed within an input-output list to help abbreviate the length of the list. Choice 3 illustrates that the cross section and/or the structure name can be used to further abbreviate the explicit specification of all variable names in question. Choice 4 illustrates the ultimate degree of abbreviation possible, as well as the implied (row-major) order when explicit **DO** specifications for array input-output are omitted. No matter which of these alternatives is used, the twenty-three individual data values in the input stream are stored in **B** and **S** in precisely the same way. If **EDIT**-directed, rather than **LIST**-directed, input had been used the format list would be written to accommodate all twenty-three values to be read, no matter which of the four alternatives for specifying **B** and **S** in the data list were used.

Record I/O

In this section, we will discuss two different modes of accessing files using record I/O; "sequential" input and output, and "direct" input, output, and update. Sequential accessing takes a file's records in the order in which they are stored, one at a time and beginning with the first. Direct accessing takes a file's records in no particular order, as dictated by the program. Thus any record in a directly accessed file may be read or written zero, one, or many times in a single program run.

To define a file's attributes, the file declaration is used. Its form is as follows.

$$\text{DCL filename \textbf{FILE RECORD} } \begin{Bmatrix} \textbf{SEQUENTIAL} \\ \textbf{DIRECT} \end{Bmatrix} \begin{Bmatrix} \textbf{INPUT} \\ \textbf{OUTPUT} \\ \textbf{UPDATE} \end{Bmatrix} ;$$

Here, "filename" is the name of the file, and the keywords **FILE** and **RECORD** (as opposed to **STREAM**) identify that a file using record I/O, as opposed to stream I/O, has been declared. One of the alternatives in braces is given to indicate **SEQUENTIAL** or **DIRECT** access, and one is given to indicate whether the file is to be used for **INPUT, OUTPUT,** or **UPDATE.** "**UPDATE**" means that records may be both read and written on the file in a single run of the program.

To process an **INPUT RECORD** file sequentially, the following statement may be used.

READ FILE (filename) INTO (variable);

Here, "filename" identifies the file itself, and "variable" identifies the location where the record's contents will be stored. For example, suppose that we have the file named **CARDS** and a variable named **CARD,** declared as follows.

DCL CARDS FILE RECORD INPUT SEQUENTIAL,
CARD CHAR (80);

Then the following statement,

READ FILE (CARDS) INTO (CARD);

when executed, causes the next record in the file **CARDS** to be read and stored in **CARD.**

We assume here that the length of a record (e.g., a single punched card) is eighty characters; the variable into which an input record is read must always be the same length as that of a record in the file. Yet the variable need not be declared with the **CHARACTER** attribute. Alternatively, it is often useful to define a structure to accommodate a single input record.

Column	1-10	11-15	16-30	31-32	33	34-35	36-38	39-47	48-80
		Name		Age		Height	Weight	Social Security Number	ƀƀ...ƀ
	First	Middle	Last		Feet	Inches			

FIG. 17-19

For example, assume that a card contains information for a person, as shown in Fig. 17-19. The following structure would then accommodate a single such record.

```
DCL 1 PERSON,
      2 NAME,
         3 FIRST CHAR (10),
         3 MIDDLE CHAR (5),
         3 LAST CHAR (15),
      2 AGE PIC '99'
      2 HEIGHT,
         3 FEET PIC '9',
         3 INCHES PIC '99',
      2 WEIGHT PIC '999',
      2 SS# PIC '(9)9',
      2 REST CHAR (33);
```

The following **READ** statement would cause a record to be read into this structure filling all its elementary fields with values.

READ FILE (CARDS) INTO (PERSON);

It is important to emphasize that record I/O operations, when executed, cause no conversions of data. Thus, it is the responsibility of the program to be sure that the data items as stored on a record will be accommodated by the attributes of the variables where the data items will be stored upon execution of an input-output operation like **READ.** In the IBM 360/370 implementations, the *internal* representations of **FIXED (FLOAT) DECIMAL (BINARY)** values are *not* identical with their *external* representations; conversion is required to get from one to the other. Thus, record I/O is appropriate for such values only if their *internal* representations are recorded in the file! In most applications, this will mean that the variables be declared as character strings (**CHAR**) or as numeric character (**PICTURE**) items.

To process an **OUTPUT RECORD** file **SEQUENTIAL**ly the following statement may be used.

WRITE FILE (filename) **FROM** (variable);

Here, "filename" and "variable" identify the file and the location from which the record will be written, respectively. For example, if we are outputting card images (e.g., tape or punched cards), we might declare the output file as follows.

DCL IMAGES FILE RECORD OUTPUT SEQUENTIAL;

We then would use the following **WRITE** statement to output a single card image from **CARD** (as declared above).

WRITE FILE (IMAGES) FROM (CARD);

To process a **RECORD** file **DIRECT**ly, whether for **INPUT, OUTPUT,** or **UPDATE,** each record must have associated with it a "key," which serves to uniquely identify the record and thus distinguish it from the other records in the file. To illustrate, suppose that our file of **PERSON**s described above is to be processed **DIRECT**ly, and that the **SS#** (positions 39–47) serves as each record's key.

To process a **DIRECT RECORD** file for **INPUT,** the **READ** statement must not only identify the particular file and location where the input record is to be stored; it must also identify the desired record by its key. Thus, the **READ** statement takes the following form.

READ FILE (filename) **INTO** (variable) **KEY** (expression);

The "expression" is evaluated to determine the desired record's key. For example, if we wanted to read directly from our file of **PERSON**s that record with **SS# = '025308235',** then we would say the following.

READ FILE (CARDS) INTO (PERSON) KEY ('025308235');

If a record exists in that file with that key, then it will be retrieved and stored in the structure **PERSON.** If not, then the **KEY** condition will be raised.

To process a **DIRECT RECORD** file for **OUTPUT,** the **WRITE** statement must also identify the particular key which will be stored in the record. Thus, the **WRITE** statement takes the following form.

WRITE FILE (filename) **FROM** (variable) **KEYFROM** (expression);

The value of the "expression" is interpreted as a character string and inserted into the position of the record where the key is stored. For example, if we want to add to our file (now declared as **OUTPUT** rather than **INPUT**) a record which is stored in **PERSON,** with **KEY = '025308235',** we would say the following.

WRITE FILE (CARDS) FROM (PERSON) KEYFROM ('025308235');

If a record already exists in that file with the identical key, then the KEY condition would be raised.

To process a **DIRECT RECORD** file for **UPDATE,** three possible elementary operations can take place;

1. Change an existing record on the file.
2. Add a new record to the file.
3. Delete an existing record from the file.

The first operation is achieved by the following pair of statements.

> **READ FILE** (filename) **INTO** (variable) **KEY** (expression);
> **REWRITE FILE** (filename) **FROM** (variable) **KEY** (expression);

The two statements may be separated by other statements which perform individual changes to the record stored in the "variable." In any event, the record which is finally rewritten from the "variable" physically replaces the record that was just read.

The second operation, adding a record, is achieved by an ordinary **WRITE** statement as follows.

> **WRITE FILE** (filename) **FROM** (variable) **KEYFROM** (expression);

The program must assure that the "expression" designating the new record's key is unique from the other keys on the file. Otherwise the **KEY** condition will be raised.

The third operation, deleting a record, is achieved by the following statement.

> **DELETE FILE** (filename) **KEY** (expression);

The result of executing this statement is that that record on the file whose key matches the "expression" is deleted from the file. If there is no such record, then the **KEY** condition is raised.

Input-Output Conditions

The foregoing discussion noted that certain extraordinary conditions may be raised upon the occurrence of particular events during execution of a PL/I program's input-output operations. We discuss the most common input-output conditions, specifically the **ENDFILE** condition, the **ENDPAGE** condition, the **KEY** condition, and the **TRANSMIT** condition, in the following paragraphs.

The **ENDFILE** condition is raised when a sequential input operation (**READ** or **GET** statement) is to be executed but there is no more data remaining in the file to read.

The **ENDPAGE** condition is raised when a sequential stream output operation (**PUT** statement) is being executed for a print file and causes the last line of the current page to be exceeded.

The **KEY** condition may be raised when a direct record input or output operation is to be executed. The various situations which can cause the **KEY** condition to be raised are defined in the preceding section.

The **TRANSMIT** condition may be raised during any input or output operation, whether it be record or stream. It means that an uncorrectable transmission error has occurred during an attempt to read (write) the current record in the file, and thus the record was not properly transferred from (to) the physical device to (from) memory.

When any one of these conditions is raised for a given file, the action that takes place depends upon whether or not the program contains a so-called "on-unit" for that condition and that file. If such an on-unit is absent from the program, the following action takes place for these conditions.

Condition	Action in the absence of an on-unit
ENDFILE KEY TRANSMIT	Print a message which indicates that the condition has occurred, and then raise the ERROR condition.
ENDPAGE	Skip to the top of the next page and then resume executing the PUT statement at the point where the ENDPAGE condition was raised.

If the programmer prefers that some other action take place when one of these conditions takes place, then he may write a so-called "ON statement" for that condition, which has the following form.

ON condition (filename) on-unit;

Here, "condition" is one of the conditions **ENDFILE, ENDPAGE, KEY,** or **TRANSMIT,** while "filename" identifies the particular file on which the indicated condition's occurrence is being trapped. For example, if two different sequential input files are being processed by a program, then two different **ON** statements may be provided for the condition **ENDFILE.** The "on-unit" designates what action should take place when the designated condition occurs with the designated file. The on-unit may be either a single statement or a sequence of statements headed by "**BEGIN;**" and terminated by "**END;**". Such a sequence is called a "**BEGIN** block."

For example, suppose that whenever the **ENDPAGE** condition is raised on the **SYSPRINT** file we want to skip to the top of the next page and print the following title before proceeding.

position 1   position 91
↘ LISTING OF INPUT DATA   ↘PAGE xxx

Here, the pages will be numbered in the upper righthand corner. Suppose that the program's purpose is to list a deck of input cards. Then it might be written as follows.

```
LISTER: PROC OPTIONS (MAIN);
    DCL CARD CHAR (80), PNO FIXED BIN (31) INIT (0);
    ON ENDFILE (SYSIN) STOP;
    ON ENDPAGE (SYSPRINT) BEGIN;
        PNO = PNO + 1;
        PUT PAGE EDIT ('LISTING OF INPUT DATA',
        'PAGE', PNO) (A, COL (91), A, F(4));
        PUT SKIP;
        END;
    SIGNAL ENDPAGE (SYSPRINT);
    DO I = 1 BY 1;
        GET EDIT (CARD) (A(80)):
        PUT SKIP EDIT (CARD) (A(80));
        END;
    END LISTER;
```

The **ENDPAGE** condition will be raised whenever the **PUT** statement is about to be executed and its **SKIP** part would cause a skip beyond the last line on the page. The **ON** statement specified the action that will occur in that event, which is simply to increment the page number (**PNO**) and print the title at the top of the next page.

If the on-unit contains neither a **STOP** statement nor a **GO TO** statement that would cause control to transfer into another part of the program, then execution of the on-unit is immediately followed by a "normal return" of control to a point in the program near where the condition originally was raised. The exact point of normal return depends upon the particular condition, as shown in the following list.

Condition	Point of normal return
ENDFILE	The statement immediately following the particular GET or READ statement where ENDFILE was raised is the next to be executed.
ENDPAGE	The PUT statement that was being executed when ENDPAGE was raised is resumed as if ENDPAGE had never been raised.
KEY	The statement immediately following the (READ, WRITE, REWRITE, or DELETE) statement where KEY was raised is the next to be executed. The actual input-output operation, however, will not have taken place.
TRANSMIT	The statement immediately following the input-output statement where TRANSMIT was raised is the next to be executed. The actual input-output operation, however, will not have taken place.

Thus, for our example, normal return from the **ENDPAGE** on-unit will pass control back to the **PUT** statement within the **DO** loop where **ENDPAGE** was raised; the line that was about to be printed will appear immediately after the heading on the new page.

Finally, note in this program the "**SIGNAL** statement." Its execution causes the designated condition [in this case, **ENDPAGE (SYSPRINT)**] to be raised, even though it hasn't actually occurred. Thus, this particular **SIGNAL** statement forces a heading to be printed at the top of the first page output.

17-5 SUBPROGRAMS

In most practical programming situations, the task is large enough to warrant segmenting the program into a number of functional blocks. These are linked together by a "main" program that controls the sequence in which these functional blocks will be executed. Another advantage of program segmentation is that it permits the reuse of code without rewriting and debugging it each time it is needed.

PL/I has facilities which support such segmentation. A PL/I subprogram is a procedure which may be invoked during execution of the main program [designated by "**PROCEDURE OPTIONS (MAIN)**"] or another subprogram. A PL/I subprogram is classified as either a "function procedure" or a "subroutine procedure." In either case, there are two aspects to the use of subprograms: writing the subprogram itself, and invoking it to perform its function.

Certain functions have such widespread utility that they are provided as part of the PL/I language. They are known as the "built-in functions," and have already been written as function procedures. Thus, when one of these functions—such as finding the square root of a number—is required, the programmer need only invoke it. A complete description of the PL/I built-in functions may be found in any appropriate reference manual. We describe in Tables 17-1, 17-2, and 17-3 the ones which seem to be most useful in the various application areas.

For each of the given arithmetic built-in functions (Table 17-1), the arguments may be any expression x having a numeric (rather than string) value.

TABLE 17-1 Some of PL/I's Arithmetic Built-In Functions

	Function	Name	Arguments	Result
1	Absolute value	ABS	x	The absolute value of the argument x, where x is any arithmetic value.
2	Ceiling	CEIL	x	The smallest integer i which is greater than or equal to x.
3	Cosine	COS	x	The cosine of x, where x represents an angle in radians.
4	Exponential	EXP	x	The result of raising e to the power x.
5	Natural logarithm	LOG	x	The logarithm (to the base e) of x, where $x > 0$.
6	Common logarithm	LOG10	x	The logarithm (to the base 10) of x, where $x > 0$.
7	Maximum value	MAX	$x_1, x_2, \ldots, x_n$	The largest value from among the n values ($n \geq 2$) given.
8	Minimum value	MIN	$x_1, x_2, \ldots, x_n$	The smallest value from among the n values given.
9	Remainder (Modulus)	MOD	x_1, x_2	The remainder when x_1 is divided by x_2.
10	Sine	SIN	x	The sine of x, where x represents an angle in radians.
11	Square root	SQRT	x	The square root of x, where $x \geq 0$.

TABLE 17-2 Some of PL/I's Array Built-In Functions

	Function	Name	Arguments	Result
1	High bound	HBOUND	a, i	For the ith dimension of the array a, the highest valid subscript value.
2	Product	PROD	a	The product of all elements in the array a.
3	Sum	SUM	a	The sum of all elements in the array a.

TABLE 17-3 Some of PL/I's String Built-In Functions

	Function	Name	Arguments	Result
1	Index	INDEX	s, t	If the string t occurs in the string s, then the result is an integer i > 0 defining the position of the leftmost character of the leftmost occurrence of t in s. Otherwise, the result is 0.
2	Length	LENGTH	s	The length (number of characters) of the string s.
3	Substring	SUBSTR	s, i, l	That substring within the string s which begins in position i and has length l. If l is omitted, then the substring extends to the end of s.
4	Verify	VERIFY	s, t	If all characters of the string s are also in the string t, then the result is 0. Otherwise, the result is an integer i > 0 defining the position of the leftmost character in s which is not in t.

Thus, the various functions are generic, in the sense that any one of them can be applied to a numeric argument with attributes **FIXED** or **FLOAT, DEC** or **BIN,** and so forth. The result returned by any of these functions generally has attributes which are consistent with the attributes of the arguments and the nature of the function.

Similarly, the array built-in functions are generic, in the sense that each may be applied to an array of values having any numeric attributes. In addition, **HBOUND** may be applied to any array, including an array of strings. The result returned by it is an integer. The result returned by either of the last two has attributes identical with those of the array itself.

Note that all of these built-in functions share the common characteristic of delivering a *single* value, rather than a number of values, as a result. This is required by the way in which functions are invoked.

A function must be invoked by using a "function reference" in place of a variable or constant in an expression. A function reference always takes the following form.

$$\textbf{name} \text{ (arguments)}$$

Here, "name" denotes the name of the function and "arguments" denotes a list of expressions (separated by commas) which describe the values to which the function is to be applied. When so invoked, the function returns a single elementary result (whether it be a number or a string), which subsequently becomes the operand in the remaining evaluation of the expression in which the function reference appears. For example, suppose we have **FLOAT** variables **A, B,** and **C;** the values of **A** and **B** are 2 and 3, respectively; and we want to compute **C** as follows.

$$C = \frac{A + B}{\sqrt{A^2 + B^2}}$$

Then we would use the built-in function named **SQRT** as follows.

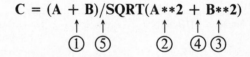

Variable	Attributes	Value (s)				
X	FLOAT (6)	−3.5				
Y	"	+2.9				
I	FIXED BIN (31)	17				
A	(5) FLOAT (6)	8	3	0	−1	5
B	(5, 4) FLOAT (6)	1	−1	2	0	
		7	2	−1	2	
		9	2	4	−1	
		6	7	8	−7	
		3	1	0	2	
S	CHAR (25)	ƀ THESE ƀ ARE ƀ THE ƀ TIMES. ƀƀƀƀ				

FIG. 17-20

As the reader can see, the function reference calls for evaluation of $A**2 + B**2$, yielding 13, which is passed to the **SQRT** function. The result returned is the **FLOAT** value which is (a close approximation to) the square root of 13, say 3.60555. This value then becomes the divisor in the subsequent evaluation of the expression.

To illustrate how various other built-in functions may be used, let's assume the variables and values shown in Fig. 17-20. Then the following function references, when executed, would deliver results as indicated.

Function reference	Result delivered
COS(Y)	$-0.970958E0$ (2.9 radians $\approx$ 166 degrees)
SUM(A)	15
SUM(A * B(*,3))	The "inner product" of A and the 3rd column of B, i.e., $A_1 * B_{13} + A_2 * B_{23} + A_3 * B_{33} + A_4 * B_{43} + A_5 * B_{53} = 5$
SUBSTR (S, I, 6)	'IMES.ʙ'
SUBSTR (S, I)	'IMES.ʙʙʙʙ'
INDEX (S, 'THE')	2
INDEX (S, 'THEʙ')	12
INDEX (S, '?')	0
VERIFY (S, 'ʙ')	2 (the position in S of the leftmost nonblank character)
INDEX (SUBSTR (S,VERIFY(S, 'ʙ')), 'ʙ')	6 (the position of the leftmost blank within that substring which begins 'THESEʙARE . . .')

Note that these last two examples illustrate how the **INDEX** and **VERIFY** built-in functions can be used to easily isolate a word (i.e., a sequence of characters followed by a blank) within a text. Specifically, **VERIFY** locates the word's leftmost character and **INDEX** locates its rightmost.

Writing Function Definitions

When the program requires the performance of a function which is not among the built-in functions, the programmer can define a "function procedure" and then invoke it in the same way that a built-in function is invoked. Because a programmer-written function is invoked in generally the same way as a built-in function, it must always deliver a single value as a result. Procedures which expressly deliver a number of different results must be written as "subroutine procedures." These will be discussed in a later section.

To define a function procedure, the programmer must (1) identify the particular parameters which will be required for the function to deliver a result; (2) determine the attributes of these parameters, together with the attributes of the delivered result; (3) determine the algorithm to be used for the function's definition; (4) set this all down as a PL/I function procedure.

The first three of these tasks must be done regardless of the particular programming language used. Let us consider the following problem as an illustration.

Write a function subprogram which will deliver as a result the factorial of any integer *n*.

Here, we see that only one parameter, an integer n, is required. The factorial is defined as follows.

$$\text{fact } (n) = n \cdot (n - 1) \cdots 3 \cdot 2 \text{ if } n > 1$$
$$= 1 \qquad\qquad\qquad \text{if } n \leq 1$$

The result to be returned is thus an integer, which is either 1 (if $n \leq 1$) or the product of the first n positive integers (if $n > 1$).

To define a PL/I function, one always begins with a **PROCEDURE** statement of the following form.

entry-name: **PROCEDURE** [(parameter-list)] [**RETURNS** (attributes)];

Here, "entry-name" denotes the procedure's name and the optional "parameter-list" denotes a list of parameters which are separated from each other by commas. The attributes of the result returned are determined either by default or from the "attributes" part of the optional **RETURNS** clause shown here, depending respectively on whether or not that clause is omitted. The rules for assigning attributes by default to the returned value are the same as those for assigning attributes by default to ordinary variables.

Following the procedure statement is the body of the procedure, which defines the computations that will take place when the function is invoked. The function is written much like an ordinary program segment designed for the same purpose, except that parameters are written where variable names would otherwise occur in the program segment. The procedure's body is always terminated by an **END** statement.

END entry-name;

Here, "entry-name" again denotes the name of the function, and is thus identical with that given in the function's **PROCEDURE** statement.

To illustrate these ideas let us write a function procedure named **FACT** to compute the factorial of an integer n. Here, we identify one parameter, N, to denote the number whose factorial will be computed.

```
FACT: PROC (N) RETURNS (FIXED BIN);
    DCL (F, I, N) FIXED BIN;
    F = 1;
    DO I = 2 TO N;
        F = F * I;
    END;
    RETURN (F);
END FACT;
```

Note first that the procedure's body designates the factorial computations as if N were an ordinary variable. As a parameter, it takes the place of a value which will be supplied at the time the function is invoked. We will further describe this process in the next section.

At the place(s) where it is logically appropriate to return the computed result to the calling program, the function must contain a **RETURN** statement, of the following form.

RETURN (expression);

The result of evaluating the "expression" is returned to the calling program. Since that result must be a single value, the expression must be one which delivers one value, be it arithmetic or string.

In our example, the reader will notice that the computed value of the variable **F** is returned to the calling program. Both **F** and **I** are merely local variables used by the function to compute the desired result.

Invoking Functions

Functions which are written by the programmer are invoked in exactly the same way as the built-in functions; by using the function reference. However, there are some additional considerations which apply to programmer-defined functions; we discuss them in this section.

Suppose we want to compute the binomial coefficients

$$a_i = \frac{n!}{i!(n-i)!} \qquad i = 0, 1, \ldots, n$$

for the familiar polynomial shown below.

$$(x + y)^n = a_n x^n + a_{n-1} x^{n-1} y + \ldots + a_i x^i y^{n-i} + \ldots + a_0 y^n$$

Then we could write the following program, which prints the desired sequence of coefficients, **A**.

```
P: PROC OPTIONS (MAIN);
    DCL (A, I, N) FIXED BIN;
        FACT ENTRY RETURNS (FIXED BIN);
    GET LIST (N);
    DO I = 0 TO N;
        A = FACT (N)/(FACT (I) * FACT (N − I));
        PUT SKIP LIST (I,A);
    END;
END P;
```

We focus attention on the two underlined parts of this program. The first serves to identify the attributes of the result returned by the **FACT** function. It is required when both the following conditions hold.

The function definition is external to the procedure calling it.

The result returned by the function, as defined, has attributes different from those that would be assigned by default.

When the function definition is "internal" (i.e., not external) to the procedure which invokes it, then the attributes of the result returned are immediately known to the system. Thus the **ENTRY** declaration shown here would not be required in that case.

The second underlined statement shows three different invocations of the function **FACT.** Each argument of a function reference may be any expression, as shown by the expression "N − I" in the third invocation. Such expressions are evaluated before the function is invoked. In any event, a function reference must always contain exactly as many arguments as there are parameters in the function's definition. A left-right one-to-one correspondence is established between the arguments and the parameters.

When the function is invoked, the following steps take place:

1. Each argument, or its value, replaces each occurrence of its corresponding parameter in the function procedure's body.
2. The resulting procedure body is executed as if it were an ordinary section of the calling program.
3. The result returned by that execution is the value of the expression in the **RETURN** statement of the body. That returned result then is used for subsequent evaluation of the expression where the function reference occurs.

A number of details should be added to this rather terse description. Before they are discussed, let us trace execution of the above example program. Suppose that the **GET** statement for this program leaves **N** = 5. Then the program will list the following outputs.

0	1
1	5
2	10
3	10
4	5
5	1

Let us consider the last execution of the assignment statement (where **I** = 5) that contains our three function references. In the course of evaluating the arithmetic expression, **FACT (I)** is the first invocation of **FACT** to be executed. Since the value of the argument (**I**) is 5, the function is executed to compute the factorial of 5, or 120. This returned value then takes place in the original arithmetic expression as if the assignment statement had been written as follows.

$$A = FACT (N)/(120 * FACT (N − I));$$

Next, the **FACT** function is again invoked; this time by the function reference, **FACT (N − I).** The argument value 0 is passed to the function (since it is the current value of **N − I**), replacing the parameter **N**. The result returned, 1, then replaced **FACT (N − I)** for subsequent evaluation of the expression. After the product 120 * 1 is computed, the remaining **FACT(N)** causes the third invocation to be executed, returning the value 120. Evaluation of the arithmetic expression is then completed, and the quotient, 1, is assigned to **A.**

An important additional detail to remember when writing and invoking programmer-defined functions is the requirement that one of the following two conditions be met by the calling program.

1. Each argument agrees in all its attributes with its corresponding parameter.

2. If one or more arguments disagrees in any of its attributes with its corresponding parameter, an entry declaration must be provided in the calling program to indicate such disagreement. This provision allows proper conversion to take place at the time of the invocation.

The form of an entry declaration is slightly more general than the one underlined in the example above.

DCL entry-name **ENTRY** [(attributes-list)] [**RETURNS** (attributes)];

Here, "attributes-list" denotes a list of sets of attributes, each set separated from the next by a comma. The number of sets of attributes in the list is identical with the number of parameters in the function as defined. Each such set must agree with the attributes of its corresponding parameter in the function's definition.

Now, since each of the three function references in our example program has an argument with attributes **FIXED BINARY,** the first condition is met. An entry declaration of the kind described above is therefore not required. Suppose, on the other hand, that we wanted to invoke the **FACT** function to compute the factorial of, say, 5. Then we could write

FACT (5)

to designate that computation. However, the argument **(5)** in this invocation has attributes **FIXED DECIMAL (1, 0).** To indicate that such disagreement should be resolved by an appropriate conversion, the following revision of the entry declaration for **FACT** is required.

DCL FACT ENTRY (FIXED BIN) RETURNS (FIXED BIN);

A second important detail to remember when writing and invoking programmer-defined functions is the requirement that conversion must be **possible** in the event that an argument's attributes disagree with those of its corresponding parameter. Specifically, this means that an array or structure argument cannot be supplied when the corresponding parameter designates an elementary variable, and an array or structure must be supplied when the corresponding parameter designates one.

Additional details regarding argument-parameter correspondence are also important; these will be discussed when we illustrate subroutine definition and invocation. Others will become apparent as the reader becomes familiar with PL/I. The best approach to take when defining and invoking subprograms is probably the conservative one. Provide a full entry declaration whenever the defined function is external to the calling program. In addition, ensure that arguments are supplied in the proper order. Finally, for any substantial function procedure definition, provide within it an adequate documentation for each parameter, as well as the result.

Writing Subroutine Definitions

A subroutine does not return a value to the calling program in the sense that a function does. The result of invoking a subroutine may be one or more elementary values, arrays, or structures. Additional parameters are provided in the subroutine's definition to designate each of the results. These parameters are usually listed last in the **PROCEDURE** statement that begins the subroutine's definition.

Other than this, there is little additional distinction between a subroutine definition and a function definition. In a subroutine definition, the **RETURN** statement must not contain an expression (since one result may not be returned). Instead, those parameters which designate results returned by the subroutine are written in an appropriate context within the subroutine's body, in order to allow values to be assigned to their corresponding arguments at the time of invocation.

Let us illustrate these conventions by rewriting the function **FACT** as a subroutine. In this rewriting, the additional parameter **F** is used to designate the resulting factorial. Recall that **F** was an ordinary variable in the original function definition.

```
FACT: PROC (N, F);
      DCL (N, F, I) FIXED BIN;
      F = 1;
      DO I = 2 TO N;
        F = F * I;
      END;
      RETURN;
END FACT;
```

Comparing this with the original function definition, we see that the **RETURN** statement has been shortened. This indicates the point at which control will return to the calling program. Note also that the **RETURNS** clause has been omitted, since it is meaningless for subroutines.

At this point, we give another example to illustrate two additional conventions; a subroutine which computes a number of results (rather than just one), and the handling of arrays in subroutine definitions. The problem is this:

Write a subroutine which, for any one-dimensional array of **FLOAT DEC** values, computes their mean, maximum value, and minimum value.

When an array is a parameter of a subroutine (or a function), its number of dimensions must be fixed in the subroutine's (function's) definition. However, its number of elements (subscript range) in each dimension need not either be fixed in the definition or be passed as an additional parameter.

For this problem, we identify four parameters: **A** designates the array of values supplied by the calling program, while **MEAN, MAX,** and **MIN** designate the results to be computed by the subroutine. We will name the subroutine **MMM.**

```
MMM: PROC (A, MEAN, MAX, MIN);
     DCL A(*) FLOAT DEC,
```

```
        (MEAN, MAX, MIN) FLOAT DEC;
    N = HBOUND (A, 1);
    MEAN, MAX, MIN = A(1);/* INITIALIZE RESULTS*/
    DO I = 2 TO N;
        MEAN = MEAN + A(I);
        IF A (I) > MAX THEN MAX = A(I);
        ELSE IF A (I) < MIN THEN MIN = A(I);
    END;
    MEAN = MEAN/N;
END MMM;
```

This is a fairly straightforward subprogram, once familiarity is established with the handling of subscripts. As written, this subprogram can adapt itself to any one-dimensional array of numbers, regardless of its size.

Invoking a Subroutine

A subroutine must be invoked by execution of a **CALL** statement. The general form of the **CALL** statement is as follows.

CALL entry-name   [(argument-list)];

Here, "entry-name" identifies the name of the subroutine being invoked, and the optional "(argument-list)" part designates the actual arguments to be used for this particular invocation.

For example, let us rewrite the main program above which computed the binomial coefficients. This rewriting, however, will use the factorial subroutine named **FACT** rather than the factorial function named **FACT.**

```
P: PROC OPTIONS (MAIN);
    DCL (A, I, N, F1, F2, F3) FIXED BIN,
        FACT ENTRY (FIXED BIN, FIXED BIN);

    GET LIST (N);
    DO I = 0 to N;
        CALL FACT (N, F1);
        CALL FACT (I, F2);
        CALL FACT (N - I, F3);
        A = F1/(F2 * F3);
        PUT SKIP LIST (I, A);
    END;
END P;
```

The most noticeable difference between this and the original version is the addition of three new variables, **F1, F2,** and **F3**. These hold the results computed by the three different calls to the **FACT** subroutine. Note also that the **ENTRY** declaration for **FACT** does not have a **RETURNS** clause. That clause is meaningful only for functions. Note finally that we have described the attributes of the two parameters in the **ENTRY** declaration. That was not necessary for this program, since the actual arguments in the three **CALL** statements already possess those attributes. (Yet that extra declaration helps to document the program.)

The argument-parameter correspondence for subroutines is exactly like that for functions. Here we provide some additional details on that correspondence. Some common pitfalls can be easily avoided by a good understanding of these additional details.

In executing a subroutine call or function reference, any argument having one of the following characteristics will have a "dummy argument" created for it.

1. The argument is an arithmetic expression with operators (e.g., "N − I" in the third **CALL** statement above).
2. The argument is a constant [e.g., "7" in **CALL FACT (7, F1);**].
3. The argument is a variable, array, or structure name whose attributes are not identical with those of its corresponding parameter [e.g., **"P"** in **CALL FACT (P, F1);** where **P** is **FLOAT DEC,** rather than **FIXED BIN**].
4. The argument is enclosed in parentheses.
5. The argument is itself a function reference.

The creation of a dummy argument means that the name of a temporary location containing the argument's current value, rather than the argument's name itself, replaces all occurrences of the corresponding parameter in the subroutine's or function's body, and the resulting code is then executed.

When an argument is used strictly as input to the invoked subprogram, the creation of a dummy argument does not disrupt the proper functioning of the subprogram. For instance, in the above program **P** it matters not in the first **CALL** statement whether the variable N's attributes are **FIXED BIN (31)** or **FIXED BIN (15)** or **FIXED DEC (5)** or **FLOAT DEC (6)** or any other set of numeric attributes. If **N** disagrees in its attributes with those of its corresponding parameter (**N**, coincidentally) in the subroutine's definition, a dummy argument will be created with the required attributes, and the value of **N** will be stored there. The dummy argument is then treated just as **N** would have been had **N** possessed the right attributes. Thus, the factorial of **N** will be correctly returned to **F1** in any event.

However, when an argument is used to hold output from the invoked subprogram, it **must not** be one for which a dummy argument will be created. If it is, then the result delivered will become the value of the dummy argument, and thus becomes inaccessible to the calling program. Specifically, this means that an output argument must always be a simple variable (or array or structure, as appropriate) which agrees in all its attributes with its corresponding parameter in the subprogram's definition. For instance, **F1 must** have the attributes **FIXED BIN** in order that the factorial of **N** be properly stored in it as a result of the first **CALL** statement in the above program.

Internal Subprograms, EXTERNAL
Variables, and Side Effects

So far, we have discussed PL/I subprogramming facilities as if the calling program and the called subprogram were mutually external to each other, and the only way that information can be passed between the two is through the use of parameters and corresponding arguments. Other options, however, are available. A subprogram's definition may be embedded totally within the (sub)program that invokes it. Information may be passed between the invoking program and the subprogram in essentially two other ways than by the use of parameters. In this section, we present these alternatives, their advantages, and their pitfalls.

Let us reconsider the **FACT** function and the program **P** which invoked it. The definition of **FACT** could have been placed entirely within **P**, as shown below.

```
P: PROC OPTIONS (MAIN);
    DCL (A, I, N) FIXED BIN;
    FACT: PROC (N) RETURNS (FIXED BIN);
        DCL (F, I, N) FIXED BIN;
        F = 1;
        DO I = 2 TO N;
            F = F * I;
        END;
        RETURN (F);
        END FACT;
    GET LIST (N);
    DO I = 0 TO N;
        A = FACT (N)/(FACT (I) * FACT (N − I));
        PUT SKIP LIST (I, A);
    END;
END P;
```

When this is done, the need for an **ENTRY** declaration for **FACT** is eliminated. Otherwise, the program **P** is identically the same as it was before.

Another point to notice here is the occurrence of **I** as a working variable in both the main program **P** and the subprogram **FACT**. The declaration of **I** in **P** identifies one variable, and the declaration of **I** in **FACT** identifies another (distinct) variable, even though their names are coincidentally identical. When a reference to **I** occurs in the main program **P**, as in the statement "**DO I = 0 TO N;**", the program is referring to the variable **I** which was declared in **P**. But when a reference to **I** occurs in the subprogram **FACT,** as in the statement "**DO I = 2 TO N;**", the subprogram is talking about the variable named **I** which was declared in **FACT.** Thus, no confusion will result.

Technically, the range of statements which can legally reference a variable is known as that variable's "scope." The scope of a variable is defined in such a way that no two variables with the same name can be referenced by the same statement. The scope of a variable is defined differently depending on whether that variable is explicitly declared. If it is explicitly declared, that variable has as its scope only that procedure (or **BEGIN** block) where it is declared, together with all procedures which are internal to that procedure and do not themselves contain a declaration of a variable with the same name. Otherwise, its scope includes all procedures which contain the procedure which uses it.

These two situations are depicted graphically below. In the first case, the variable **I** is not declared, and thus its scope transcends both procedures **P** and **Q**.

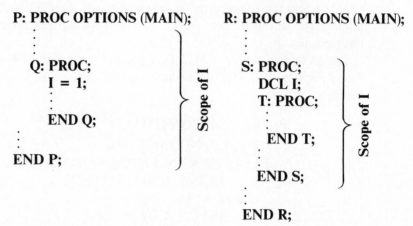

In the second case, assuming that **I** is declared **only** in **S**, its scope includes both procedures **S** and **T**, but not **R**. Thus, any reference to **I** from **R** will be talking about another (undeclared) variable with the same name.

There is much practical advantage in having a firm understanding of a variable's scope. For instance, had we not delimited the scope of **I** by declaring it in the function **FACT** when **FACT** was internal to **P**, that reference to **I** within **FACT** would have altered the value of the same variable named **I** which was controlling the loop out in **P**. The effects would have been disastrous.

By the same token, one can intentionally not delimit the scope of a variable so that it may be referenced both from within and from without an internally embedded subprogram. This device can sometimes be used to avoid the use of a parameter.

Finally, one can achieve the same effect when two (sub)programs are mutually external to each other, as indicated below.

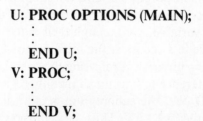

In this case, if we want **U** and **V** to share access to a common variable, say **I**, then we can declare that that variable is **EXTERNAL** to each procedure, as follows.

```
U: PROC OPTIONS (MAIN);
   DCL I EXTERNAL;
   . . .
   END U;
V: PROC;
   DCL I EXTERNAL;
   . . .
   END V;
```

Now there is one variable named **I** which can be referenced either from **U** or from **V**. Whenever such a variable is so shared among two or more mutually external procedures, it must be declared to have the **same attributes** in each place where it is declared. The use of **EXTERNAL** variables is thus a viable alternative to the use of parameters and arguments for sharing information between a calling program and a called program.

The final issue to be considered when defining subprograms is that of so-called "side-effects." A side effect is an alteration by a subprogram to the value of a variable which is not among the arguments supplied in the invocation, and is not local to the subprogram. Most side effects in actual programming situations are undesirable and unnecessary. For example, the failure of the internally embedded function **FACT** to delimit the scope of its local variable **I** would have caused the undesirable kind of side effect. Some side effects are intentional and unavoidable. When they are included, the programmer should give fair warning that they exist by including proper documentation within the subprogram's definition.

Recursion

Some applications require the use of functions that are defined recursively. That is, the function uses itself in its own definition. Examples of recursive function definitions are found in elementary calculus, number theory, and applications of formal languages.

PL/I permits the declaration of procedures that call themselves, and thus can directly realize recursively defined functions. Such procedures are called "recursive procedures." To illustrate, let us reconsider the factorial function, which may be redefined recursively as follows.

$$\text{factorial }(n) = 1 \qquad\qquad \text{if } n < 2$$
$$= n \times \text{factorial }(n - 1) \qquad \text{if } n \geq 2$$

This definition can be directly encoded in PL/I as a recursive procedure in the following way.

```
FACT: PROC (N) RETURNS (FIXED BIN);
      DCL N FIXED BIN;
      IF N < 2 THEN RETURN (1);
      ELSE RETURN (N * FACT(N − 1));
END FACT;
```

IBM's PL/I compilers have the additional requirement that a recursively defined procedure be explicitly identified by the appearance of the keyword **RECURSIVE** before the **RETURNS** portion of its **PROCEDURE** statement. Others allow that keyword to be included or excluded at the programmer's option.

In either case, the reader should see that **FACT** invokes itself each time the expression **N** * **FACT(N − 1)** is evaluated. This leads to the following sequence of invocations for an evaluation of **FACT(4).**

Invocation	Result returned by it
1	4 * FACT(3)
2	3 * FACT(2)
3	2 * FACT(1)
4	1

The fourth invocation then returns **1** to the third, which computes **2 * 1** and returns that result to the second, and so forth.

The reader should also be aware that the use of recursive procedures in actual computing must be accompanied by an understanding of the process actually being represented. Recursion is not efficiently implemented on most current computers; iteration (the use of **DO** loops) is usually preferred for that reason.

17-6 COMPLETE PROGRAMS

When preparing a PL/I program for execution, the programmer must follow certain mild restrictions. These restrictions vary from one implementation to another. We will discuss the common restrictions here, and advise readers to become familiar with those others which are unique to their installations.

When recorded on punched cards, a PL/I program may be laid out in a fairly free-form manner. IBM implementations generally require that the program not use column 1 or columns 73–80 of any card. Beyond that, however, there is no required starting position for statements or statement labels. A statement may be continued from one card to another without addition of an explicit symbol to indicate it. Similarly, two or more statements may be recorded on a single card. The statement delimiter is, in every case, the semicolon (;) rather than the card boundary.

With such syntactic freedom at hand, the programmer has an added responsibility to lay out the program so that its logic can be easily seen. Usually, this means at least the following.

1. Statement labels begin in a tab position to the left of that for statements.

2. Statements begin at a common tab position.

3. When a new logical level occurs for a group of statements, such as a DO group or BEGIN block, that group of statements begins at a tab position which would indent it from its surrounding text.

When a PL/I program consists of a single main program followed by one or more external subprograms, some implementations require that the subprograms be separated from each other and from the main program by an additional card. For IBM's PL/I(F) implementation, this separator card has the basic form shown in Fig. 17-21. For more information on this, the reader should consult the installation's PL/I reference manual.

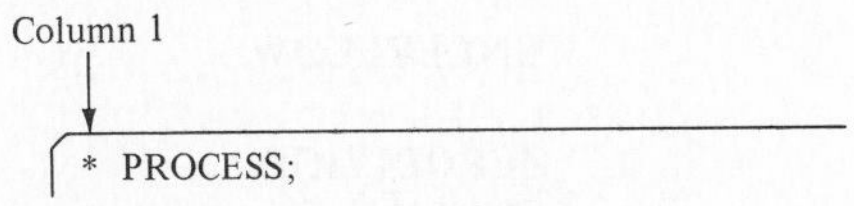

Column 1

* PROCESS;

FIG. 17-21

Any number of blank spaces may be inserted anywhere within a statement except within a variable name, statement label, procedure name, or PL/I keyword. For example, **DECLARE** must not contain any embedded blanks.

On the other hand, no two adjacent PL/I keywords or names may be written **without** at least one blank space between them. For instance, the following are **not** equivalent.

$$DCL \quad X \quad FLOAT \quad DEC;$$
$$DCL \quad X \quad FLOATDEC;$$
$$DCL \quad XFLOAT \quad DEC;$$
$$DCLX \quad FLOAT \quad DEC;$$

The second and fourth of these are invalid statements, the first declares a variable named **X**, and the third declares a variable named **XFLOAT**.

17-7   ADDITIONAL FEATURES

It would be impossible to treat with justice all the many additional features of PL/I. In this section, we focus attention on the following two features.

Conditions, Interrupts, and on-units.
Storage classes and program control of storage allocation.

Only the essential aspects of these features will be discussed here. For more detailed information, the reader should consult a PL/I reference manual.

Conditions, Interrupts, and On-Units

In previous sections, we mentioned a number of so-called "conditions" that could be raised in the event that one or another unusual occurrence happened during execution of a program. In addition to those we mentioned, PL/I has a number of other conditions. We will not discuss them all here, but the following table describes the most important ones.

Condition	Meaning
CONVERSION	A character string value, such as 'ABC', cannot be converted to an equivalent arithmetic value.
FIXEDOVERFLOW	An arithmetic operation has a FIXED result which exceeds the maximum precision allowed by the implementation.
OVERFLOW	A FLOAT value exceeds the maximum allowed by the implementation.
SIZE	A high order significant digit is dropped when a value is assigned to a FIXED variable.
UNDERFLOW	A FLOAT value is smaller than the minimum allowed by the implementation.
ZERODIVIDE	The denominator in a division (/) operation has value zero.
ENDFILE	An attempt was made to read from a sequential input file after the last record had already been read.
ENDPAGE	An attempt was made to execute a PUT statement for a print file whose output would exceed the last line of the page. (The number of lines on a page varies among implementations, but is usually 60.)
KEY	(1) An attempt was made to read a record from a DIRECT file, and no record exists on the file with the specified key, or (2) an attempt was made to write a record to a DIRECT file and there was already a record on the file with the same key.
TRANSMIT	A physical input-output error has occurred during the transmission of a record to or from an input-output medium.
SUBSCRIPTRANGE	A subscript is outside the range for that dimension of the array in question.
STRINGRANGE	A SUBSTR function reference improperly describes a substring which is partly or fully outside the string in question.
CHECK	One of the variables in the so-called "check list" has been assigned a new value, or one of the statements whose label appears in the check list has been executed.

The uses of these conditions will be illustrated below. Here, it is important first to understand what happens when one of these conditions occurs during program execution.

First, each condition is said to be in one of two states at any time during program execution: "enabled" and "disabled." Program execution is, in fact, **interrupted** upon the occurrence of one of these conditions only if that condition is **enabled** at the time the condition occurs. If the condition is disabled, program execution continues as if it never occurred.

Certain of these conditions are permanently enabled by the system throughout program execution. Those are **ENDFILE, ENDPAGE, KEY,** and **TRANSMIT.** Certain other of these conditions are initially enabled by the system, but may be explicitly disabled within the program. Those are **CONVERSION, FIXEDOVERFLOW, OVERFLOW, UNDERFLOW,** and **ZERODIVIDE.** The rest of these are initially disabled by the system, but may be explicitly enabled within the program.

To enable one or more otherwise-disabled conditions for the duration of the program, the program is preceded by a "condition prefix," which has the following form.

(condition-list):

Here, "condition-list" denotes a list of those conditions, separated by commas. For example, if we wanted to enable the **SIZE** and **SUBSCRIPTRANGE** conditions through execution of program **P**, we would write the following.

(SIZE, SUBRG):
P: PROC OPTIONS (MAIN);
      .
      .
      .
END P;

Similarly, to disable one or more otherwise-enabled conditions throughout execution of a program, we would write a condition prefix in which each of the disabled conditions is written with **NO** affixed to its left end. For example, if we also wanted to disable the **CONVERSION** condition in the above program, we would rewrite the condition prefix as follows.

(SIZE, SUBRG, NOCONV):

Now suppose that an enabled condition actually arises and program execution is interrupted. What happens next depends upon whether the program wants to take its own action when the condition arises, or is willing to accept the "Standard System Action" for that condition. This choice is indicated by the presence or absence in the program of an **ON** statement for that condition, respectively.

Suppose for the moment that no **ON** statement is present in the program for any condition, and that all conditions are enabled. The following table tells what will occur as the Standard System Action when one of these conditions arises.

Condition(s)	Standard system action
CONVERSION FIXEDOVERFLOW OVERFLOW SIZE UNDERFLOW ZERODIVIDE ENDFILE KEY TRANSMIT SUBSCRIPTRANGE	An error message is printed and execution terminates.
ENDPAGE	The print file is advanced to the top of the next page; execution of the output statement then resumes as if ENDPAGE had not occurred.
STRINGRANGE	Execution continues with some string different from the ill-specified substring.
CHECK	This is a special condition used for program tracing, and will be treated separately.

The reader has already seen the use of **ON** statements to direct program execution when an input-output condition arises. The general form of an **ON** statement is the following.

ON condition on-unit

Here, "condition" denotes any of the conditions listed above, and "on-unit" denotes either a single unlabeled statement or an unlabeled **BEGIN** block.

A **BEGIN** block, like a **DO** group, is used to delimit an entire sequence of statements. It has the following form.

BEGIN:

> Sequence of
> statements

END;

When used as an on-unit, the **BEGIN** block may contain any statement except a **RETURN** statement.

To illustrate the use of **ON** statements, let us consider the following program.

```
P: PROC OPTIONS (MAIN);
   DCL NZ FIXED BIN INIT (0);
   ON ENDFILE (SYSIN) BEGIN;
        PUT SKIP LIST (NZ, 'DIVISIONS BY ZERO.');
        STOP;
        END;
   ON ZDIV NZ = NZ + 1;
LOOP:  DO I = 1 BY 1;
        GET LIST (A, B);
        C = A/B;
        END;
   END P;
```

The purpose of this program is simply to read pairs of numbers, **A** and **B**, divide the first by the second, and keep track of the number of times division by zero occurs.

Execution begins with the statement labeled **LOOP**. This **DO** loop continues normally until one of the two conditions, **ENDFILE (SYSIN)** and **ZDIV**, occurs. **ZDIV** can occur only during execution of the statement "**C = A/B;**". When that condition arises, program execution is interrupted and the **ON** statement for **ZDIV** is executed. This causes incrementing of the counter **NZ**.

Now, when execution of an **ON** statement terminates without either a transfer of control back to the program (via a **GO TO** statement in the on-unit) or a termination of the program (via a **STOP** statement in the on-unit), this causes so-called "normal return" to the program. The particular point in the program where control returns in this fashion depends on the particular condition that arose. The table below describes the point of normal return for each of the conditions discussed here.

Condition	Normal return from an on-unit
CONVERSION	Conversion is retried with the string which caused the condition to arise, and within the statement where it arose.
FIXEDOVERFLOW OVERFLOW SIZE UNDERFLOW ZERODIVIDE	Control returns to a point immediately following that place in the statement where the condition arose. The numerical result of the operation causing the condition is undefined.
ENDFILE KEY TRANSMIT	Control returns to the statement immediately following that statement which caused the condition to arise.
ENDPAGE	Control returns to that point in the PUT statement which caused the condition to arise.
SUBSCRIPTRANGE STRINGRANGE CHECK	Control returns to a point immediately following that place in the statement where the condition arose.

Returning to our example program, we see from this table that control will return from the **ON** statement to assign the undefined result of $A/0$ to **C**, in the statement "**C = A/B;**". The loop thus continues, exercising the statement "**NZ = NZ + 1;**" whenever the condition **ZDIV** arises, until the condition **END-FILE (SYSIN)** arises. At that point, the other **ON** statement is executed, causing the counter **NZ** to be printed and program execution to stop. "Normal return" is not at issue in this case, since the **STOP** statement precludes it.

Before concluding this section, we give some practical situations in which these interrupt-trapping facilities are useful.

Recall that the **CONVERSION** condition occurs when a character string cannot be successfully converted to a number, as in the case of '**ABC**'. Thus, it may occur either during execution of an assignment statement or during execution of a stream input (**GET**) statement. When **CONVERSION** does occur, the programmer (i.e., the **ON** statement) may wish to examine, or at least display, the string which caused the condition to occur, or the "source string." That string is saved in a special PL/I system variable named **ONSOURCE.** Any reference to **ONSOURCE** within the **CONVERSION** on-unit will deliver as a result the value of that source string.

The arithmetic conditions, **FIXEDOVERFLOW, OVERFLOW, SIZE, UNDERFLOW,** and **ZERODIVIDE,** should generally be enabled for all applications. It is unfortunate that IBM's PL/I(F) implementation does not initially enable the **SIZE** condition, requiring the programmer to list it explicitly in a condition prefix.

The conditions **SUBSCRIPTRANGE** and **STRINGRANGE** should generally be employed to protect the program's integrity during its development. After the program has been fully checked out and prepared for productive use, however, it is usually unnecessary to continue with these conditions enabled. First, the program should at this point have steps built into it which prevent these conditions from occurring. Second, performance of a program (in speed and storage requirements) which has a large number of array references or character string references may be significantly degraded by the enabling of these conditions.

Finally, let us turn to the **CHECK** condition. This is PL/I's main vehicle for program tracing and checking of intermediate results during program development. Although it is a debugging tool, the **CHECK** condition is nevertheless an intrinsic part of the PL/I language.

To obtain a printed value of a variable, say **I**, each time it gets reassigned (by execution of either an assignment or an input statement), the program appends a **CHECK** prefix to the program as follows.

(CHECK (I)):

When a programmer wants a statement label, say **L**, printed each time that statement is executed, he appends a **CHECK** prefix to the program as follows.

(CHECK (L)):

The sample program and output in Fig. 17-22 illustrate the use of the **CHECK** condition. Recall that the variable **I** will be assigned four times, even though the statement labeled **L** will be executed three times, because of the definition of the PL/I **DO** statement.

```
            Program                    Output

(CHECK (I, L)):                    I = 1;
  P:  PROC OPTIONS (MAIN);         L
      X = 53;                      I = 2;
      DO I = 1 TO 3;               L
  L:  X = SQRT(X);                 I = 3;
      END;                         L
  END P;                           I = 4;
```

FIG. 17-22

Like the **STRINGRANGE** and **SUBSCRIPTRANGE** conditions, the **CHECK** condition comes not without its price in execution speed and storage requirements. Thus its use outside the program development environment is ill advised.

Storage Classes and Program Control of Storage Allocation

From time to time an application program will not be able to predict its storage requirement for certain data until after it has begun executing. This usually occurs in systems programming applications. It occurs often enough in the other application areas that PL/I facilities for "dynamic storage allocation" are widely useful.

Every PL/I variable (including arrays and structures) has a "storage class" attribute, which defines when, how, and by whom storage is allocated for that variable. A variable's storage class must be one of those listed in the following table.

Storage class	Meaning
STATIC	Storage is allocated once for the variable, and its initial value (if any) is assigned by the system when the entire program is loaded for execution.
AUTOMATIC	Storage is allocated for the variable and its initial value (if any) is reassigned by the system each time the procedure, or BEGIN block, that declares it begins execution.
CONTROLLED	Storage is allocated for the variable by the program upon execution of an "ALLOCATE statement." Until that time, the variable may not be referenced in the program, since it does not yet exist in storage. However, several "copies" of the variable may thus exist simultaneously. In this case, only the most recently allocated copy may be referenced.
BASED	As in the CONTROLLED case, storage is allocated by the program. Unlike CONTROLLED, a BASED variable may exist in several "copies," all of which may be referenced during program execution.

If the program does not explicitly declare a variable's storage class, then **AUTOMATIC** is assigned by default.

The **STATIC** storage class is the most efficient in time, since storage is allocated and initial values are assigned when the program is first loaded for execution. It is usually preferred for arrays which represent tables of constants, such as the following.

DCL MONTHS (12) CHAR (3) STATIC
INIT ('JAN', 'FEB', 'MAR', · · · , 'DEC');

However, when using the **STATIC** storage class, the programmer must remember that the **INITIAL** attribute applies only once, when the program begins execution.

Because **AUTOMATIC** is generally the most widely used storage class, it occurs by default. The system allocates storage for an **AUTOMATIC** variable, but not until the **PROCEDURE** or **BEGIN** block in which it is declared actually begins execution. This accommodates an important practical situation: the one in which the program cannot predict the size N of an array A before execution begins. Consider the following example.

P: PROC OPTIONS (MAIN);

. . .

GET LIST (N);
BEGIN;
DCL A(N) FLOAT;

. . .

END;

. . .

END P;

Here, we have localized the declaration of **A** so that its scope includes only the statements within the **BEGIN** block. Each time that block is entered, N will have an integer value, and that will determine the size of the array **A**. When control exits the **BEGIN** block, storage allocated for **A** will be released and **A** will thus become undefined again. (This quality of **AUTOMATIC** variables applies to **PROCEDURE**s as well as **BEGIN** blocks, even though a **PROCEDURE** may be entered only via a **CALL** statement or a function reference. It does not apply to **DO** groups since the **DO** statement does not delimit the scope of a declared variable.)

The **CONTROLLED** storage class passes responsibility for allocating and freeing a variable's storage to the program. Storage allocation occurs upon execution of an **ALLOCATE** statement; freeing occurs upon execution of a **FREE** statement. They have the following basic forms.

> **ALLOCATE**   variable-list;
>
> **FREE**   variable-list;

Here, "variable-list" denotes a list of one or more variable (including array or structure) names, each of which has the **CONTROLLED** attribute, separated by commas.

A **CONTROLLED** variable, say **X**, cannot be referenced until after an "**ALLOCATE X;**" statement has been executed. However, several instances of **X** may simultaneously exist, since a new instance is defined each time an "**ALLOCATE X;**" statement is executed. A reference to **X**, as in "**Y = X + 1;**", refers to the instance of **X** which was most recently allocated. The next most recently allocated instance of **X** is accessible only after a "**FREE X;**" statement is executed, which deallocates the most recently allocated instance of **X**. Thus, a series of allocations for the same variable tends to create a pushdown stack, whose top is identified as the most recently allocated instance of the variable. **ALLOCATE** and **FREE,** in this setting, tend to simulate the stack's elementary "push" and "pop" operations. Since there is little application of this concept outside the systems programming area, we will discuss it no longer. The interested reader should consult a PL/I reference manual for more information.

However, when the **CONTROLLED** variable is an array whose size is unpredictable, its allocation can be done explicitly in the program as follows. First, the array's unknown size is indicated by "*" as a dimension in its declaration. For example.

> **DCL A(∗) FLOAT CONTROLLED;**

This declares **A** to be a one-dimensional array of an unknown number of **FLOAT** values, for which storage will be allocated and freed by the program. The program must then keep that promise. For example, the following program has the same effect as did the previous example program, but uses the **CONTROLLED** array **A** in place of the **BEGIN** block.

> **P: PROC OPTIONS(MAIN);**
>
> **DCL A(∗) CONTROLLED FLOAT;**
>
> . . .
>
> **GET LIST (N);**

ALLOCATE A(N);

. . .

FREE A;

. . .

END P;

Note here that the number of elements, **N**, in **A** is specified in the **ALLOCATE** statement, but not in the **FREE** statement.

The **BASED** storage class is similar to the **CONTROLLED** storage class, with the additional capability that all existing (rather than just the most recently allocated) copies of **BASED** variable may be referenced at any time during program execution. We will discuss **BASED** variables in only a cursory manner, since their applications lie primarily in the systems programming areas which heavily employ stacking, queuing, and other linked-list manipulation disciplines.

The mechanism for referencing a **BASED** variable is the so-called **POINTER** variable. This is a different kind of variable from the ones we have discussed so far. A **POINTER** variable's sole purpose is to point to a BASED variable, rather than contain a value itself. This is depicted in Fig. 17-23. If we want to refer to that version of **B** whose value is 15, we would write the following "qualified reference" to **B**.

$$P \rightarrow B$$

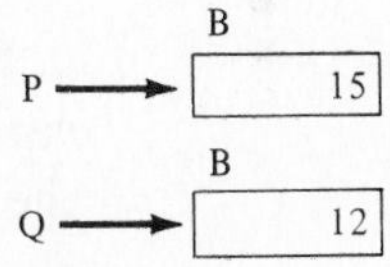

B

P ⟶ [15]

B

Q ⟶ [12]

FIG. 17-23

The other version may be referenced by "**Q → B.**"

Although any number of variables may be used within a program, one must be identified uniquely as the **BASED** variable's "home pointer." This is done at the time of declaration as follows.

DCL variable **BASED** (pointer-variable);

For example, we may write

DCL B FIXED BASED (P);

to declare that **B** is **BASED** and its home pointer is **P**.

When storage is to be allocated for a **BASED** variable, one of the following forms of the **ALLOCATE** statement must be used.

1. **ALLOCATE** variable;
2. **ALLOCATE** variable **SET** (pointer-variable);

Form 1 causes a new version of the "variable" to be created, and sets that variable's home pointer to point to it. Form 2 is equivalent to form 1, except that the particular choice of pointer variation is given explicitly. Thus either of the following

ALLOCATE B;
ALLOCATE B SET (P);

causes storage to be allocated for **B** and **P** to point to that version, as shown in Fig. 17-24. The following statements cause (1) another version of **B** to be allocated and pointed to by **Q**, and (2) the values 15 and 12 to be assigned the two versions, respectively, as depicted in Fig. 17-24.

ALLOCATE B SET (Q);
P → B = 15;
Q → B = 12;

As shown here, the particular version of a **BASED** variable in question may be explicitly specified by a "qualified reference," such as **P → B** or **Q → B.** In the event that the version desired is the one pointed to by the based variable's home pointer, the qualification (**P → **) may be dropped. Thus, for instance, the second statement above may be equivalently rewritten as "**B = 15;**".

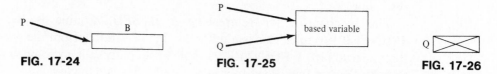

FIG. 17-24   **FIG. 17-25**   **FIG. 17-26**

Pointer variables may be declared either by their identification as a **BASED** variable's home pointer or explicitly, with the **POINTER** attribute. For instance the pointer **Q** used above should be declared as follows.

DCL Q PTR;

A pointer variable may be assigned a value either by execution of an **ALLOCATE** statement or by execution of an assignment statement. For instance,

Q = P;

assigns to **Q** the value of **P**. Effectively, this makes **Q** point to the same version of a based variable as **P** currently does (Fig. 17-25). There is a special value **NULL** which, when assigned to a pointer variable, means that that variable "points nowhere." It is depicted in Fig. 17-26 (for the pointer **Q**). It can be assigned explicitly, as shown.

Q = NULL;

For an illustration of the rudiments of based and pointer variable use in list processing, consider the problem of creating a list of names from a deck of input cards, such as that shown in Fig. 17-27. Specifically, assume that the program does not know how many names there are, but wants in any case to create an internal linked list of the form shown in Fig. 17-28 (for the data given above).

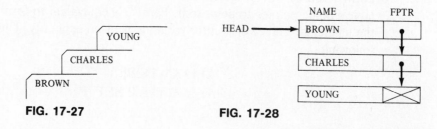

FIG. 17-27   **FIG. 17-28**

Each version of the **BASED** variable has two parts, a **NAME** and a "forward" pointer (**FPTR**) to the next version. The end of the list is depicted by a **NULL** forward pointer, while the beginning, or head, of the list is indicated by the pointer **HEAD.** This is an example of the most basic list structure, a so-called "single-linked list."

Thus, the **BASED** variable is logically declared as a structure. We present the program which creates this list and then discuss its execution on the given data.

```
LISTER:PROC OPTIONS (MAIN);
      DCL 1 NODE BASED (P),
            2 NAME CHAR (15);
            2 FPTR POINTER,
        (Q, HEAD) PTR;
      ON ENDFILE (SYSIN) BEGIN;
            FREE NODE;
            IF Q ¬ = NULL THEN Q → FPTR = NULL;
                        ELSE HEAD = NULL;
            STOP;
            END;
      ALLOCATE NODE SET (P);
      HEAD = P; Q = NULL;
      DO I = 1 BY 1;
            GET EDIT (P → NAME) (COL(1), A(15));
            Q = P;
            ALLOCATE NODE SET (P);
            Q → FPTR = P;
      END;
   END LISTER;
```

The first executable statement is the first **ALLOCATE** statement, which causes a copy of the **BASED** variable **NODE** to exist, as shown in Fig. 17-29. Note that, as yet, neither **NAME** nor **FPTR** has values. The next two statements set the **HEAD** pointer to point to this first node, and initialize an auxiliary pointer, **Q**, to **NULL**.

The first execution of the **DO** loop leaves the configuration shown in Fig. 17-30 (for the example data). Specifically, the first **NAME** is read, **Q** is set, and then a new **NODE** is allocated and pointed to by **P**. Finally, the previous node's **FPTR** is set to point to this new node, thus linking the two together.

This process continues as long as there are cards to be read. The reader should recognize that **Q** always keeps track of the next-to-last **NODE** allocated,

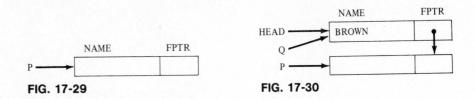

FIG. 17-29   **FIG. 17-30**

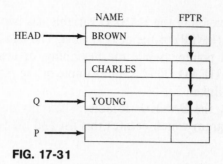

FIG. 17-31

while **P** points to the next node to contain a name in the event that there is yet another **NAME** to be read. When **ENDFILE** occurs for this data, the situation is as shown in Fig. 17-31. Thus, the on-unit frees the most recently allocated **NODE** and sets **Q**'s **NODE**'s **FPTR** to **NULL**, marking the end of the list. Note that the **IF** statement in the on-unit applies to the case where there are no cards, in which case the **HEAD** pointer would be set to **NULL** to identify an empty list.

Hardware and Software Documentation

Jonathan Erickson

18-1 INTRODUCTION

Documentation may be defined as the printed material accompanying computer hardware and software. It has been the center of increasing controversy and importance in recent years as computer technology has come into wide use by those who are not data processing or computer science professionals. Often documentation is the last part of a computer system to be developed, the first part the user sees, and the part most widely criticized.

There are two major reasons why documentation is so vulnerable to criticism:

1. The quality of the documentation is limited by the quality of the information provided to the documentation writer ("garbage in, garbage out").
2. Writer specialization is difficult because of the wide range of documentation needed to support various computer products.

Consequently, it has become increasingly important for anyone concerned with computer-related publications (either as a user or writer) to be able to exactly define the characteristics of good documentation.

18-2 CHARACTERISTICS OF GOOD DOCUMENTATION

The "bottom line" for any documentation is that it be complete and accurate. Most complaints about documentation concern inaccurate information. This is understandable. A person who has just spent several hundred dollars on a software package or several thousands of dollars for a computer system expects information that is correct and sufficient to allow the software or hardware to be used.

"Accuracy" means more than sample programs should work or that hardware is properly described. The documentation should also accurately reflect the environment in which the software or hardware is to be used. For example, a business applications package should be technically correct regarding standard business practices and normal office procedures.

Another common complaint about documentation is that it does not provide enough information (although it may seem there can never be enough information about some software or hardware). If the documentation has sufficient information—even if poorly presented or organized—the documentation user should be able to eventually root it out. Such a situation is bad, but it is preferable to a case where necessary information has been left out of the documentation. If sufficient information is not included, the user has every right (indeed, almost an obligation) to complain to the software or hardware vendor responsible.

18-3 TYPES OF DOCUMENTATION

Computer documentation falls into one of the following broad categories:

Systems manuals
Applications manuals
Tutorial manuals
Reference manuals

A systems manual describes the operation of a piece of hardware or a collection of programs. Applications manuals describe how particular hardware items or programs solve specific problems, achieve certain results, or perform desired functions. A tutorial manual instructs the user in the operation and use of software or hardware, while a reference manual is a compilation of information about software or hardware arranged for easy and rapid reference. Sometimes these types may be combined. For example, a tutorial may include a separate reference section.

Before the quality of documentation can be judged, the intent of the documentation must be considered. A good tutorial manual does not always make a good reference manual, nor does a good reference manual make a good tutorial manual.

Thus, some of the complaints about documentation arise because users expect the manual to supply information it was never intended to furnish. By its very nature, a tutorial manual will seldom offer the ease and rapidity of access found in a reference manual. And a reference manual will not be as helpful to a first-time user as a tutorial manual would be.

From the preceeding, it is obvious that a documentation writer must keep both the intended audience and purpose of the documentation in mind as the material is prepared.

18-4 REFERENCE DOCUMENTATION

In most cases, it is assumed that the user of reference documentation is already familiar with the subject(s) under discussion. Just as one must have a knowledge of the English language to use a dictionary, some knowledge of COBOL would be essential to use a COBOL reference manual.

One of the most crucial decisions in preparing reference documentation is how the material should be organized. For example, suppose the task is to prepare a reference manual of the various statements and commands used by a high-level language. How should the information be organized? One approach would be to organize the statements and commands in alphabetical order. An alternative would be to group the material by categories, with separate sections devoted to input and output statements, control and transfer statements, functions, etc.

If the documentation writer cannot be certain of the level of sophistication of the user, presenting information in alphabetical or numeric sequence is the best choice. If the user sophistication will be high, more elaborate methods may be used to present the information. The important point is to maintain the criteria of ease and rapidity of access to the information for the intended users.

It should be noted that, in many cases, some information will be needed more frequently than other information. Such frequently-needed information could be extracted and placed in a separate section. Another approach would be to use special design techniques such as boldface or italic type to indicate frequently-needed information.

Efforts should be made to keep each entry in reference documentation self-contained. Entries that refer to previous entries or examples are often frustrating and confusing to users.

18-5 TUTORIAL DOCUMENTATION

Tutorial documentation is designed to teach such concepts as programming or the proper use of a computer system. The basic assumption in tutorial documentation is that the reader is a novice to the techniques discussed and wants to learn about such techniques.

Tutorial documentation should be structured according to how users should learn the material. A tutorial on programming in the BASIC language might begin with a discussion of the CLS statement. This would be because it is one of the first statements used in BASIC programming, not because it comes early in an alphabetical listing of BASIC statements.

A good tutorial manual should have numerous practical examples. These examples should be relevant and meaningful to the user. Many tutorial manuals for microcomputer systems have made use of interaction between the user and the microcomputer, requiring the user to enter data into the microcomputer and become an active participant in the learning process.

One common failing of many tutorial manuals is the assumption of too much knowledge on the part of the user. Documentation writers use the concepts of computing on a regular basis and it is easy to forget that the user of a tutorial manual will likely be unaware of many basic concepts and terms. It is also useful to break information down to small chunks in a tutorial manual.

It is misleading to think of a tutorial manual as being a simpler project than a reference manual. A tutorial manual will contain about the same amount of information as a reference manual on the same topic.

18-6 DEVELOPING DOCUMENTATION

Documentation cannot be created by the writer alone. It must be a joint product of the writer, appropriate marketing personnel, and programming or engineering specialists.

Marketing personnel will be able to contribute information on who the customers for the product will be and how it will be sold. If the product is a $500.00 software package intended for scientific users, the documentation can be written on a level as sophisticated as the user. However, a video game software package priced at $15.00 would require documentation simple enough for a child to understand and use. In many cases, the documentation writer's "customer" is actually marketing personnel, and documentation is actually written for their approval.

Programming or engineering specialists supply information on the technical aspects of a software package or item of hardware. Programming and engineering specialists have much the same relationship to marketing personnel that the documentation writer has. Both must provide a final product that meets the requirements of marketing personnel in addition to furnishing input to the documentation writer.

As a consequence, documentation development usually proceeds in parallel with software or hardware development. Scheduling is essential, or a company could find itself unable to sell a software package or hardware item because the documentation is not finished.

However, this can have consequences that documentation writers and users must be aware of. Often, a documentation writer will be unable to actually verify the documentation against a final version of the hardware or software prior to publication of the documentation. In such cases, some minor (or even major) errors in the documentation are almost inevitable. Further, there is a possibility that the coordination between the documentation writer, marketing personnel, and technical specialists could break down.

An effective method of insuring that documentation is appropriate for the intended users is to let a sampling of typical users actually use the hardware or software with the documentation. At a minimum, the documentation should be reviewed by marketing personnel and the engineering or programming specialists prior to preparation of the final version by the documentation writer.

Considering the many constraints imposed upon the documentation writer, the quality of documentation is on the average quite good. Where some major book publishers may take a year or more to develop a 200 page book, a 200 page manual may be written or produced in a matter of weeks.

Databases and File-System Organization

Gio Wiederhold

19-1 INTRODUCTION

When we talk informally about a **database,** we refer to a collection of mutually related data, to the computer hardware that is used to store it, and to the programs used to manipulate it.

By mutually related we mean that the data represents knowledge about a specific enterprise, say a company, a university, or a governmental institution. The data may also be related because it deals with a certain problem area, perhaps about a disease which is of concern to the staff of a number of hospitals. The data should be organized so that it can be processed to yield information.

The organization of the data in a database has to represent the underlying meaning or semantics of the data correctly and efficiently. In conventional programs the structure of data is arranged for the convenience of the program. A database contains data to be used by many and diverse programs. The organization of a database can hence not be solely determined by decisions made while programming specific functions.

19-2 FILES

A database is a collection of related data. The data storage for a database is accomplished by the use of one or more files. A **file** is defined to be a collection of similar records kept on secondary computer-storage devices. Typical of **secondary storage** devices are disk drives with magnetic disks. A **record** is defined at this point to be a collection of related **fields** containing elemental data items. A data item typically represents a value which is part of a description of an object or an event. Computational processes can manipulate such values.

Size

To warrant the attention and the approaches discussed in this section, the database should be reasonably **large.** We will be discussing only processes that are applicable to large external files. Collections of data that can be processed in their entirety in the directly addressable memory of a computer, its primary storage, allow techniques that will not be covered here. The use of the term database also implies that a number of people are involved. Not only may data entry be done by people far removed from the users, but the data may contain information suitable for a variety of purposes. The quantity of data to be handled may range from moderately large to very large. These measures of size depend on the hardware and on operational constraints which may apply in a given environment.

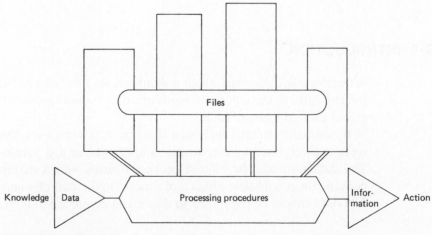

FIG. 19-1 A database

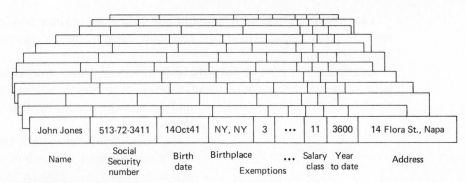

John Jones	513-72-3411	14Oct41	NY, NY	3	...	11	3600	14 Flora St., Napa
Name	Social Security number	Birth date	Birthplace	Exemptions ...		Salary class	Year to date	Address

FIG. 19-2 A payroll file

Large implies a quantity of data which is greater than a single person can handle wholly by himself, even when he or she has access to a computer system. The actual quantity will vary depending on the complexity of the data and applications. An example of a large database is the integrated personnel and product data system in a manufacturing company of about 6000 employees, with more than 300,000 records of 21 types.

A **very large** database is an essential part of an enterprise and will be in continuous use by many people. At the same time it will extend over many storage units. An example of a very large database is found at a telephone company with 5 million subscribers. Much larger yet are databases at the social security administration and other national systems.

To have a copy of the contents of a file frozen at a certain instant in time is important for many purposes, including periodic analysis of data, backup for reliability purposes, and auditing. To avoid problems, it is best not to permit a file to be used and modified while it is being copied. In a very large database these two considerations conflict. This is a useful functional definition which imposes certain design constraints on the systems which we will be discussing.

File Organization

Files not only are characterized by their size but are further distinguished by their organization. Differences in the organizations of files lead to differences in performance when storing and retrieving records.

Six basic file-organization types will be analyzed in detail later. A database often requires more than one type of file.

Input-Output

When reading or writing files, data is transferred between storage units of the computer system. When reading input or writing output, data enters or leaves the computer system. A database is concerned with the data which remains within the scope of the system. Data which is written on tape, stored, and later mounted and read again can be part of the database. Data which is taken out, modified externally, and reentered has to be considered new input.

Examples of devices used for input and output are keypunched cards, printed reports, tapes shipped to other computer systems, and computer-generated microfilm output.

Examples of devices for files are fixed disks and drums, master tapes or disks kept at the computer site, archival tapes kept in remote vaults for protection, and card decks containing lists of customer or personnel.

In many computer system the categories of file versus input and output are not well delineated. We will assume that adequate **input** and output capabilities are available, including on-line terminals where appropriate, when we talk about database systems.

We will not discuss file organizations that are based on input and output facilities. These tend to regard data as a continuous stream of characters. *Stream files*, as defined by PL/1, and their equivalents in other systems, are based on the reading and writing of continuous lines of text. Continuous text streams are important for communication but are not suitable for data manipulation. The word "file" will also not be used to refer to the hardware employed to store the data comprising the files.

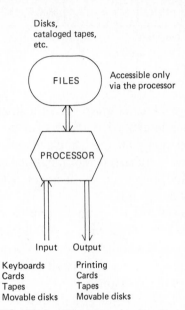

Disks, cataloged tapes, etc.

FILES — Accessible only via the processor

PROCESSOR

Input Output

Keyboards Printing
Cards Cards
Tapes Tapes
Movable disks Movable disks

FIG. 19-3 Files versus input-output

19-3 COMPUTATIONS ON A DATABASE

In the first section we considered some of the static aspects of a database, namely, the storage of data as files, records, and fields. We now will look at a database from a dynamic point of view. The dynamic behavior of programming structures has been studied whenever operating systems have been analyzed. The term *computation* is used to denote a section of an application which manipulates the database. Most of the computations which are used to manipulate data collections are conceptually simple. We recognize four types of computations related to databases:

1. Building of the data collection
2. Updating of data elements in the data collection
3. Retrieval of data from the data collection
4. Reduction of large quantities of data to usable form

They are sketched in Fig. 19-4; it is obvious that calculations are only a part of the computations to be performed. A database application will use all four types of computations, but certain applications will stress one type more than others.

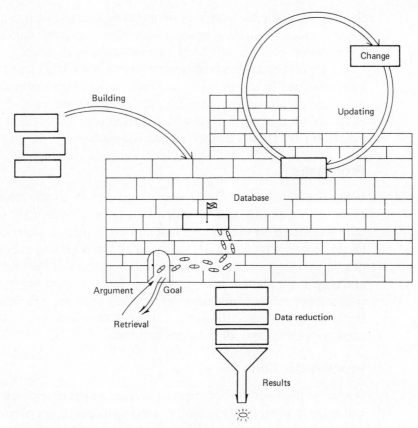

FIG. 19-4 Computations with a database system

The building of a database includes data collection, data organization, and data storage. This aspect is often the most costly part of a database operation.

The updating of a database includes the addition of new data, the changing of data values when necessary, and the deletion of invalidated or obsoleted elements. The relative activity in this area varies much between applications. A static database may be used in a retrospective study where all the data is collected prior to analysis. A dynamic or volatile database is encountered in applications such as reservations systems.

Data retrieval can consist of the fetching of a specific element in order to obtain a stored value or fact, or the collection of a series of related elements to obtain data regarding some relationship which manifests itself when data are joined. To fetch a specific data record, the database will be entered using a search **argument,** which will be matched with a **key** in the database records. The usage of the word key in computing is unfortunately the opposite of the key concept in common household usage: a person who desires something from a house uses a key which will open the lock of the proper house; here a person uses the argument to match the key of the proper record. The argument of a search is also often called the **search key.** Context in general clarifies the distinction.

When the desired information is diffused throughout the database, it may be necessary to access most of its contents and summarize or abstract the data, so that the volume presented is of manageable and usable form. Statistical summaries, annual business operating statements, or graphical data presentations are examples of frequently used data-reduction techniques.

Conceptual descriptions of computations for a particular problem frequently can be written in a few lines; the procedures to implement them may be diagrammed on a one-page flowchart and programmed in a short time. Yet the effort required to bring a database system into operation frequently involves expenditure of large amounts of time and money.

Processes

While a user views an update or retrieval request as the basic unit of computation, the operating system which schedules the execution of a computation may decompose computations into a number of distinct **processes.** Processes are the basic computational units managed by the operating system. The processes of a single computation may require different units of the computer's hardware and may be executed in parallel. Various types of operating systems will require different properties from the processes they manage. The scheduling and performance of processes, and hence of the computations that were specified, determine the performance of database systems.

Process Sections

A process itself can be decomposed into a number of sections. A **section** is the collection of program steps during which the operating system does not have to worry about the process. When a process stops, requests data from a file, requires a new allocation of storage space, and so on, the operating system has to step in and take action. When, for instance, a record from a file is requested, the operating system has to assure that the record is not currently being modified by another process. A section of a process which presents such interaction potential is known as a **critical section**. Figure 19-5 sketches a process with its sections.

19-4 A HIERARCHICAL VIEW OF DATA

Two aspects of the environment within which a database operates are important. There is the overall view, in which the database is a component of an overall system involving people, organizations, and communication; in contrast there is the microscopic view, in which the elements comprising the database are the hardware bits and bytes provided by the technology. When the content of a database is viewed as a structured representation of information regarding a subtest of the real world, we are concerned with the meaning of the information represented by the data and the relevance of the results that may be obtained. When the database is viewed from the specifics of its operation, we note the structure of the electronic devices which make possible the mechanization of the data-processing tasks. Figure 19-6 presents the structure in the form of a pyramid to symbolize the breadth of the base required to obtain information.

Since the subjects of this section are the storage and the manipulation of data, little can or will be said here regarding the information content of the

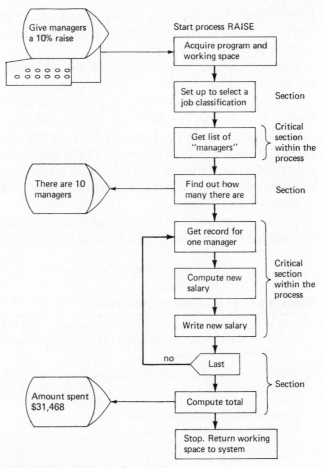

FIG. 19-5 Sections of a process

data. The technical aspects of database implementations can be discussed independently of the informational significance of the data value stored. The fact that this section will only casually touch on the value of data is not intended to imply that people who actually implement information-processing systems should ignore these considerations in their particular applications. It is clearly irresponsible if computer professionals ignore the ramifications of the task at

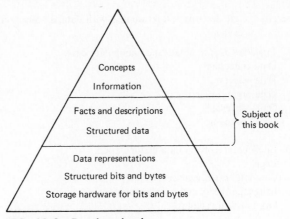

FIG. 19-6 Database levels

hand or their contribution to the social and human environment. A number of textbooks deal with the proper use of information for business and governmental operations and decision making.

This section also avoids subjects on the other side of the database domain, the design and construction of data-storage devices. Although the design and performance of computer hardware is central to the evaluation of database systems, little discussion of hardware-design alternatives will take place. Obviously, familiarity with the hardware that provides the building blocks of computer systems can only be beneficial to the system developer. Again textbooks are available for the computer engineer at many levels of sophistication. A sufficiently large body of material is available between these two extremes to keep us busy for some time.

Table 19-1 attempts to present and place the various areas of discussion in relationship to each other. The table also lists some of the fields of study which

TABLE 19-1 Levels of Database Structure

Level 1 At the conceptual level we deal with information data with sufficient significance to make us act. Information has the essence of newness and nonredundancy, so that its acquisition increases our knowledge.

A: Some processes used to obtain information:
Cross tabulation
Exception reporting
Mathematical and statistical analysis
Linear and dynamic programming
Decision analysis
Deductive inference

B: Intellectual tools for managing information:
Intuitive or formal models of the area of concern
Information theory
Heuristic processes
Formalized conceptual relationships

C: Requirements for the production of information:
Named and described data
Means to select and collect data according to description and content
Means to analyze such data intellectually or automatically

Level 2 At the descriptive level we deal with data, a collection of text or numbers describing items or events.

A: Processes used to obtain and manipulate data:
Data collection
Data selection
Data organization
Data retrieval
Data reduction

B: Intellectual tools for data manipulation:
Logic
Computer-science concepts
Language theory and metalanguage
Propositional calculus

C: Required for large-scale data mainpulation:
Named files
Named or addressable records
Addressable data elements
Catalogs and descriptions of available facilities
Facilities to obtain resources from the system
Procedure libraries

Level 3 At the organizational level we deal with data representation, data removed from context but named and processable.

A: Processes used to represent data and manipulate the results which carry out functions:
Encoding and decoding
Storage definition
File management
Space management and cataloging
Moving and comparing of fields containing coded data
Control of errors

B: Intellectual tools for the design of data representation and manipulation:
Information theory
Arithmetic processes
Programming languages
Knowledge of computer architecture and component performance

C: Required for the representation of data:
Storage devices for encoded data
Hardware to move addressed fields in storage
Elementary capability for code comparison

Level 4 At the material level finally we find hardware, the equipment used to provide largely unformatted addressable storage.

A: Processes used to obtain hardware:
Engineering design
Production

B: Tools required for the engineer who is designing hardware:
Knowledge of electronics, physics, and logic
Experience in production practice

C: What the engineer in turn has to rely on:
Availability of components, devices, and measurement tools
Availability of production facilities

provide background or further material appropriate to the levels presented. The reader is not expected to be knowledgeable in these areas; they are listed merely as navigational aids.

The term **naming** in the table is used to mean the creation of symbolic references to data with minimal concern as to location and form. The term **addressing** is used to denote the exact specification of position and representation. We see in Table 19-1 that as we descend to more primitive levels, naming is replaced more and more by addressing.

A Comparison A comparison can be made here between the levels discussed in Table 19-1 and the operation of a railroad.

1. The *conceptual level* concerns itself with the idea of value added because of the transportation of the goods and their relevance to the economic structure.
2. The *descriptive level* concerns itself with scheduling, train sizes, and equipment combinations required to move goods at a reasonable cost and with adequate flexibility.
3. The *organizational level* concerns itself with the building of trackage, the operation of marshaling yards, and the operational efficiency of the complex.
4. The *material level* concerns itself with design of locomotives, freight cars, signaling mechanisms, rails, and ties, and all the myriad pieces of equipment required to actually run a railroad.

Description and Organization This text considers the two central levels shown in the diagram: the descriptive level and the organizational level.

On the **descriptive level**, we present the processes carried out to satisfy demands for data according to its meaning or utility relative to some problem. We have to specify the data in terms which aid its selection by such processes. The content of data elements is quite important. Database systems provide tools to relate data according to their meaning.

On the **organizational level**, we present the processes which locate and move data according to demands of efficiency. Descriptions of data may be manipulated at this level as well as the data itself. Here it is not the content but the size and the position of the data element which is of concern. File systems provide tools to fetch records containing data according to relative position or name.

The two levels are highly dependent on each other. The descriptive level can easily specify requirements that the organizational level cannot reasonably supply using any given set of hardware. On the other hand, a file organization that expands the basic hardware capabilities only minimally may impose restrictions that prevent the descriptive level from being effective.

The two levels are required to separate database support systems and application systems. The structures at the file level are designed using general support requirements as a basis. These requirements can be satisfied by programs which will remain similar from application to application.

The applications of database will be a reflection of the decision maker's concept of the information problems and will vary over time as the needs, the analysis tools, and the insight of the users of the database mature.

In order to ensure that the separation of levels is not evaded, systems which attempt to support the concept of distinct levels may hide the structural detail of lower levels from users at the higher levels. This idea of **information hiding** can remain valid only when lower-level functions are reliable, complete, and reasonably efficient.

19-5 CURRENT PRACTICE

The previous section developed concepts in an abstract fashion. Past experience has to be placed into the framework which has been developed. This will be done with the aid of some examples.

A File Program

To illustrate the use of the file, we will use a simple program to carry out the actions that were presented in Fig. 19-5. The program is intended not to be especially good or bad, but rather typical.

Example 19-1

```
/*Program to process "raise" transactions*/
  raise:PROCEDURE(message);
        DECLARE message CHAR(200);
     s1:DECLARE emp_list(5000) INITIAL((5000)0);
     s2:DECLARE workspace(20), title CHAR(8), pct CHAR(2);
        title = SUBSTR(message,6,8);pct = SUBSTR(message,17,2);
     s3:OPEN FILE(job_classification)DIRECT;
     s4:READ FILE(job_classification) KEY(title) INTO(emp_list);
        CLOSE FILE(job_classification);
        DO i = 1 TO 5000 WHILE emp_list(i)¬ = 0;END;
        no_employees = i − 1;
        PUT SKIP EDIT (no_employees,title) ('There are',I5,' ',A8);
        OPEN FILE(payroll)SEQUENTIAL UPDATE;
        total_increase = 0;
        DO j = 1 TO no_employees;
        s5:READ FILE(payroll) KEY(emp_list (j)) INTO(workspace);
           /* Increase salary field of record */
           increase = workspace(18)*pct/100;
           total_increase = total_increase + increase;
           workspace(18) = workspace(18) + increase;
           REWRITE FILE(payroll) FROM(workspace); END;
        CLOSE FILE(payroll);
        PUT SKIP EDIT(total_increase) ('Amount spent $', F(8,2));
        RETURN;
  END raise;
```

The **DECLARE** statements **s1** and **s2** define working areas for a copy of the record within the program. All items of one record are related by being kept in adjoining cells on the file and in the declared arrays. The **OPEN** statements name the files and their usage and assign the file to the process. The name of the requested file will have to be looked up in a directory of file names. The programmer who wrote the programs expects that the file from this point on is under exclusive control of the program until the file is released with a **CLOSE** statement. The execution of the **OPEN** statements can involve a number of sections and may take a relatively long time.

The **READ** statement **s4** fetches the particular record named **'Managers'** to obtain a list of employee numbers. The **READ** statement **s5** names a particular record of the file identified with the employee and moves a copy of this record into the **workspace.** The system will have to look up and compute the proper record address in the files corresponding to the identification. It will use primary or core storage for the **workspace.** The address for the **workspace** is determined during program compilation and loading.

The program now can extract information, such as the salary, by addressing fields in the copy of the record. The copy of the record is modified to reflect the employee's raise. The comment provides some help in understanding the content of the addressed fields. The final **REWRITE** completes the update of a record in the file. For its proper operation, it depends on the record address that was generated by the file system during the execution of the **READ** statement. The file system must have saved this address at the time of the **READ** for use in the **REWRITE.**

Naming versus Addressing In this example the records on the file have been specified using a **name,** namely, the title or the **employee_number.** The file system performs some computational procedure to determine an actual address for the corresponding record and then fetches the record. It remembers this address on files which are to be updated in order to perform a **REWRITE** properly. Within the record fetched, we have located data by providing **addresses;** the salary field was addressed as field 18. When an address is used, the programmer controls position and size of the data unit.

Operating-System Control

System facilities were used to handle the larger units of data, the files. This has provided independence in the task description from specification of the hardware used. The writer of the file program expects that there is somewhere an expert who controls, directly or through programs, where the records actually are located. This expert controls the file system, which is generally a part of a computer **operating system.**

Statements outside the programming language are used to provide information to the operating system regarding the program. These statements form the **control language** for the operating system. The lack of communication between the programming language and the control language is often a barrier to effective utilization of computer systems.

A control-language statement for the above example may read as shown in Example 19-2.

Example 19-2

```
FILE(data):(NAME("payroll"), DEVICE(diskdrive),
    LOCATION(disk5), ORGANIZATION(fixed records
    (80 bytes), indexed, sequential, buffered),
    SIZE(60 tracks), etc.)
```

The statement has been made prettier than most control languages permit in order to aid comprehension. Once this statement is processed, the payroll file is allocated to the program throughout the entire computation.

It is not clear if the payroll file belongs exclusively to the entire program, to the program during the period between **OPEN** and **CLOSE** statements, or to the program only during the interval between **READ** and **REWRITE** statements. The answer depends on the operating system in use. Another transaction, to add up all the salaries in order to prepare a budget, should wait until the entire **raise** computation is completed if inconsistent results are to be avoided.

The knowledge required for applications programming may be separate from the knowledge to write control language statements; but in order to write effective database systems, both aspects have to be understood. In order to design the database application, considerably broader knowledge is required. The analysis of retrieved data can also require a different type of expertise from that required for the design, organization, or the collection and updating of the data. In order to manage an entire database, a specialist in database administration may be needed.

Modularity

As database applications become more complex, a further separation of functions can be expected to take place. The programs which operate on the database will be **modules;** they will use other program modules, and they will themselves be used by higher-level modules. The raise program implements one transaction type of a transaction-processing system and is called upon when the **message** entered says **raise.** The **OPEN, READ, REWRITE,** etc., statements are calls on modules of the file system. A high degree of modularity is needed because:

1. Projects are undertaken that are of a size where many people have to work together, and individuals take on more specialized functions.
2. Many projects may make use of a single database or of some part of it, and the specification of the database becomes the sum of many requirements.
3. The information in a database has a value that makes unlimited access by everyone involved unreasonable. In order to provide protection of access to private data, the access processes are controlled by the operating system.

In the example above, all the lines programmed must have been written by someone who was aware of the application. The control-language statement may have been generated with the assistance of a specialist. The processes carried out by the system (invoked by the **OPEN, READ,** and **REWRITE** statements) were probably written by someone not aware of the application, and at an earlier time and a different place.

The separation of function and facilities in the development of a system is primarily based on convenience, size of computations, and knowledge of the particular programmer. More formal criteria of modularity are being developed and are becoming an important aspect of computing management.

The example is not intended as an indictment of PL/1 as a programming language. No computer language exists that forces structuring of programming elements according to the levels we discussed, although there are a number of languages which make structuring truly difficult.

19-6 DESCRIPTIONS

In order to permit implementation and use of a system by a number of people, some documentation will have to exist to describe both the static aspects, the **file structure,** and the dynamic aspects, the **computations,** which carry out the data transformations.

A picture of the data in terms of files, records, fields, and the relation between items of data contained in these elements is appropriate for the static aspect. Such a data-structure definition may be available in the form of a document containing guidelines to the people who program the file operations on this database. An alternative is to materialize the structure definitions in the form of a collection of computer-readable codes, a **schema** which guides file processes automatically. Much of the content of this book will be concerned with the design and use of such schemas.

The computational description may be given as a formula, a description of a number of sections to be executed, or a flowchart. In many commercial programming groups much effort is put into **systems analysis** which prepares process descriptions in minute detail for subsequent implementation by coders. It is easy for errors to develop because of communication problems between systems analysts and coders. The analyst may assume the coders are aware of conditions which are not recognized by the coders. Coders may program for cases which cannot occur. The determination of critical sections is often a source of difficulty. No formal methods are yet adequate to verify completeness of descriptions for interacting processes. Sometimes flowcharts of the programs written are generated automatically to allow a posteriori verification of the design or to satisfy documentation aesthetics.

Static versus Dynamic Descriptions   The static and dynamic aspects are not always distinguishable when we describe files. For simple data-processing problems the process description may be dispensed with entirely. The computation is described indirectly by providing two pictures of a file, specifying the form and contents before and after the computation. This method could also apply to the movement of data between two separate files. Dispensing with process coding entirely is the intent of **report generators,** which accept the description of the source files and a layout of the output report which is desired. All processing steps are implied. The same intent is found in the use of high-level query systems where an information-retrieval request is stated as a formula and its resolution is the task of an information-retrieval system.

At other times one may find that the data organization is implicitly defined by a listing of the steps of the process which puts the data into the database.

Complex interlinked structures are often described in this manner, since the static picture could be incomprehensible. The two choices available are implied in the existence of two terms for the description of storage structures: **file organization** versus **access methods.**

If multiple processes are operating on the file, a static description, together with the specification of conditions when this description is valid, may be essential. These conditions have to be recognized by these processes, or by critical sections invoked, before they can process the file properly.

Such a condition could state simply that the file has been completely updated. More detailed conditions may specify that certain records have not been updated yet, maybe because of lack of information such as hours worked by some employees. Some computations could be programmed to decide not to proceed at all; other processes would not be impeded unless they require one of the records which have not yet been brought up to date.

We see that there is a relationship between the quality or completeness of our description of the data and our ability to refine and classify the sections which combine to form data-processing computations.

Flowcharts   In order to describe complex processes and data flow, we will sometimes in this section have to resort to a graphic description of the dynamics of an algorithm, a **flowchart** as shown in Fig. 19-7. In these we will distinguish three types of activity:

Control flow, the sequence of instruction executed by the processing unit under various conditions. This sequence is described when flowcharts are used to document a programming algorithm.

Control-data flow, the flow of data elements whose effect is on the control flow of the computations. Typical examples are counts, control switches that indicate whether an operation is permitted, whether an area is full or empty, and so forth. These may be set by one program and used by another program.

Data flow, the flow of the bulk of the coded data to generate information for the benefit of the users of the process rather than for the control of the process itself. This flow is typically between files and input or output devices.

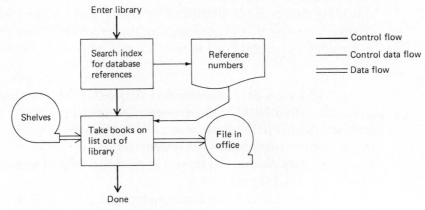

FIG. 19-7 Flowchart notation

The last two activities are sometimes difficult to distinguish, since often some control data are extracted during data processing. In many cases, however, the distinction is very useful to the understanding of processes. Figure 19-7 indicates the three types of flow in a process.

With modern techniques of programming, including the use of higher-level languages, well-defined modules, well-structured processes, and documented standard algorithms, the need for descriptions of the program dynamics has lessened. A detailed description of file and program state is much preferable unless process interactions are unusually complex.

19-7 BINDING

It still is accepted by many people in data processing that the contents and the structure of the database have to be fully determined before procedures that operate on it can be written. This assumption defeats one of the major advantages that can be accomplished when we consign our processes to computer technology. When designing and implementing a database system, it is desirable that methods be employed that allow development and change, so that we are not wholly dependent on perfect foresight. The fact that all our data and procedures are themselves computer manipulatable should make it possible to add data and relationships to the database at a later time. The operations involved in such a change may not be trivial, but a system that takes advantage of such growth possibilities can avoid obsolescence.

Whenever a decision is implemented which defines a fixed relationship between data elements, the number of choices available from that point on is reduced. The process of fixing data or processing relationships is referred to as **binding.** At the final stage of data processing all relationships needed to generate information have to be bound.

Binding Time   The concept of binding is in common use to distinguish compiling, **early binding,** versus interpretive, **late binding,** processes. The range of binding choices in the database area is considerably greater than in the area of programming. Binding frequently takes place years before a new database system produces its first results.

Binding choices can be illustrated by expanding Example 19-1. Given that a manager's identification is not found within the job-classification list but has to be obtained by scanning a file with records describing the departments, we write:

```
        s3:OPEN FILE(department) SEQUENTIAL; no_employees = 0;
           ON ENDFILE(department) GO TO tell;
read_next:READ FILE(department) INTO(workspace);
        s6:no_employees = no_employees + 1;
           emp_list(no_employees) = workspace(8); /*manager number*/
           GO TO read_next;
        tell:PUT SKIP EDIT(no_employees, . . .
```

This program is bound to the assumption that there is a one-to-one correspondence between departments and managers. If one manager becomes responsible for two departments, **raise** will give him a 21 percent raise instead of a 10 percent raise. Inserting between **read_next** and **s6** the statement,

DO i = 1 TO /* check for duplicate managers */

   IF emp_list(i) = workspace(8) THEN GO TO read_next;

END;

would defer the binding to the time that **raise** is executed. If binding is deferred until each individual element is accessed, much computational effort is spent during the actual processing. Late binding can be especially costly both because it is done at a critical time when the answer is needed and because it has to be done on an element-by-element basis, rather than once and for all when the structure is defined.

Early binding may be chosen because it can provide considerable initial efficiencies. In a database a significant amount of binding occurs as soon as the designer has specified the position of data elements within the files. Later modifications of bound structures will be extremely awkward and often also cause inefficient processing. When new data types or relationships are to be added, a complete reorganization of the file structure and modification of the associated programs are required.

To avoid the cost of change, the decision may be to put additional data elements into positions originally intended for other purposes. This situation is analogous to the making of machine-language changes in the output of compilers. Such situations are no longer acceptable in programming because of the low cost of recompilation; in the area of file management, the patching of data structures is still common. An example of such a patch is given in Example 19-3.

Example 19-3   Given that records of a personnel-file have fields as follows:

name,address, sex, salary,military_service,date_employed;

and a field for maternity_leave is required. The records are used by many programs, even though only a few of them deal with the military_service field. The solution adopted may be to use this field for maternity_leave whenever the sex field indicates a female employee.

In this example the decisions made at an earlier binding time determine the implementation of later system features. The patch will cause further problems as progress in sexual equality invalidates the assumptions made.

The lack of proper programming methodology and the pressures to patch rather than to do changes properly are a cause of frustration in many computer shops. The consequences are often cynicism and low productivity of professional personnel. Much of the design process presented in this section can be reduced to the making of decisions in regard to binding in a knowledgeable manner. The designer's choice of binding time represents his decision on the optimal compromise between efficiency and flexibility.

19-8 CLASSIFICATION OF OPERATING SYSTEMS

Databases can be established under any of the large variety of operating systems that are available. Operating systems provide a variety of services, of which the major ones can be classified as:

Process management
File-system support
Input and output support
Usage measurement

This section will be concerned with file systems. Process management is performed by a system process which allocates the resources available to user processes or to jobs containing a sequence of processes that are submitted for execution on a computer. The **resources** consist of the computing capability provided by the Central Processing Unit (CPU), the core memory which contains the process, the file storage, and the input and output capability including the control of user terminals. The scheduling system will of necessity consume computing resources themselves in direct proportion to its complexity.

Batch Processing

Sequential scheduling of computations or **batch processing** makes all or most of the resources of the computer available to one process during the required time period. Figure 19-8 provides diagrams of this method and of those methods discussed in the remainder of this section. It is obvious that only few jobs will be able to use all the available resources effectively when we use the single job-stream batch method.

The sketches present the allocation of one resource. In reality all the resources mentioned above participate in the execution of a computation. It is generally the limit of capability of one resource which prevents the full utilization by a computation of the other resources.

A typical example is found when reading data which is to be processed. The reading may proceed at the maximum speed of the input device, but the central processor can do the required computation on the data which has been read using only a few percent of its capacity. Subsequently a large calculation may take place, and the reading device has to wait for instructions on what to read next.

Multiprogramming

Multiprogramming attempts to utilize resources more effectively by allowing sharing of the resources among a number of computations according to their current requirements. If a computation cannot use a resource, it will give up its claim so that the operating system can start a process which has been waiting to use the resource. Individual computations will take longer, but if the

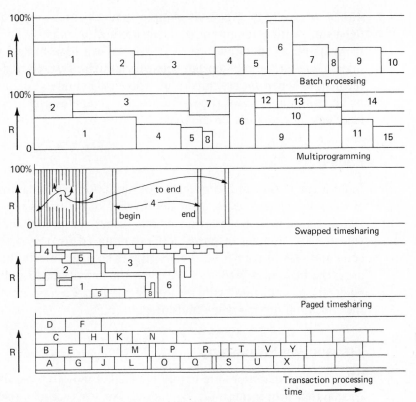

FIG. 19-8 Resource allocation for five modes of system operation

resources can be distributed better among the computations, the total productivity will be larger. Some amount of processor capability will be taken from the total available in order to effect the switching between computations.

Timesharing

Timesharing provides a mechanism to split computations into slices and allocate only the critical resources to the active computations according to rules which attempt to strike a balance between the productivity of users and the system. The user at the terminal can now be considered also as a critical resource. Unfortunately, users are very slow in execution, but demanding when they require computation. Fast response for such users is provided by limiting the competing computational slices to a fraction of a second by means of a timer-driven interrupt. When users signal that they are ready to use the computer, their process will be put in the queue and executed after a very short delay. The hardware resources which are most critical in most timesharing systems are the CPU and core memory. During inactive periods the users' processes may be "swapped out" of the primary resources. The inactive processes will be occupying disk or drum space, and this space may not be organized according to the criteria we use for data files.

Timeshared use of CPU and core provides an effective resource utilization when the computations are of a type that cannot make use of these resources during relatively long periods of time. These pauses are frequently related to delays in waiting for responses from users at terminals. The requirements of many database operations are such that we will have to deal with users at terminals, so that the relationship between database systems and resource-sharing techniques becomes very important. This mode of operation, because of the frequent switching costs of slices of a process, promotes user efficiency at a significant cost in computer productivity.

Paging

Since a single slice of a timeshared computation rarely can make use of much of the available resources, a further division of the user's processing space into pages can allow better sharing of this resource and a reduction of swapping volume. The number of pages actually required for the allocated quantity of computation will vary from slice to slice. The pages are brought in on demand or on the basis of a prediction based on the activity history. Pages which show recent usage are kept in core memory if possible. **Paging** capability also can aid the allocation process when multiprogramming.

Transaction Processing

When the computations are naturally small, a mode of operation referred to as **transaction processing** may be chosen. An instance of a small computation could be the processing of a retrieval request for a single item of stored data. Here the processes are started as soon as possible after the request for a computation and are permitted to use the CPU as long as possible. When they come to a point where they have to wait for a response from terminals or for data from files, they will yield to the system and enable another transaction process to be started or resumed. A process may even avoid yielding, if it is within a critical section, to prevent release of a file which is not in a well-defined state. When a transaction is finished, it will inform the system, which then can free all allocated resources. Example 19-1 was written to show a typical transaction program.

Here more control is required over the computations to be executed to avoid the possibility that one computation monopolizes the entire system. This control is applied when the computation is specified or bound. At execution time little checking is performed, and hence the operating system can be considerably less complex. A computation which grossly exceeds reasonable limits of resource consumption can be abruptly terminated. Many database actions can be handled effectively in a transaction-processing environment.

Cost of Sharing

Any form of resource sharing is associated with considerable operational and management overhead costs. If there is no significant benefit to the use of shared resources, a dedicated system that is of just adequate size is preferable. Such a system will, of course, not be able to cope well with irregular high-intensity demands. Mixed systems which have local capability as well as access to central shared resources are of great interest to system designers. Because they are in the early stage of their development, such systems are not analyzed in this section.

19-9 APPLICATIONS

Application areas that employ database systems currently include:

Manufacturing with inventory management, *Bills-of-Materials* processing, and production-equipment scheduling

Service industries with lists of service capabilities and allocation schedules

Economic models with production and consumption data for allocation and planning

Financial institutions with lists of individual accounts, assets, and convertibility of funds

Scientific research with collections of previously gathered data used to determine future research directions

Medical services with patient records, disease histories, problem classification, treatment-effectiveness data

Descriptive data on individuals and property

Libraries cataloging abstracts and indexes of their holdings

The management of inventories in manufacturing, particularly where assemblies consist of many parts and subassemblies, was one of the earliest and is one of the most productive areas of database systems. A particular objective of these *Bills-of-Materials* systems is the proper accounting and order scheduling of parts that are components of diverse end products and hence particularly critical. We will draw many examples from personnel files, since their contents and function are frequently self-evident. More interesting and potentially more significant applications are in food and energy-resource planning.

Definition of an Application of a Database   In any application of computers, the purpose of the effort should be spelled out in detail. Only then can one identify and judge the relevance of the data elements contained in the files, the processes required to manipulate the data, and the file structures which will enable the processes to be effective. Knowledge of the environment is needed to determine the value of the produced information. We also have to know the response time intervals required to ensure timely delivery of the system outputs. All these items provide the data for system analysis and the subsequent selection of the hardware. The dynamics of the application environment will provide useful information to decide the degree of formalization of the data organization and the corresponding binding times.

A statement of objectives and constraints, which specifies the goal and environment of the application, is an essential part of any project carried out in practice. Such a statement should also be presented with any project carried out as an exercise within the scope of this book. A frequent error in the formulation of objectives is the inclusion of the method or technology to be used as part of the objective. A proper place for such an account is the section which describes the results of the system analysis.

Objective statements which imply that the desire to **computerize** was the reason for development of a database should send a shiver down the spine of any computing professional. If the choice of methods or technology has been intentionally limited, a separate section of the objective statement should clarify such conditions.

19-10 FILE-SYSTEM ORGANIZATION

The basic features desired of systems that store large amounts of data are fast access for retrieval, convenient update, and economy of storage. Important secondary criteria are the capability to represent real-world structures, reliability, protection of privacy, and the maintenance of integrity. For analysis the design should be easy to abstract. These criteria tend to conflict with each other. The choice of the method of file organization will determine the relative performance of a system in these areas. We will initially evaluate files according to the basic criteria. A good match of the capabilities provided by the file system to the priorities determined by the database system, is vital to the success of the resulting system.

In order to simplify the choice, we will describe and measure six basic file-design alternatives. Most structures used in practice either fall into one of these categories or can be reduced to combinations of these methods.

The six types covered in this section are the pile, the sequential file, the indexed-sequential file, the indexed file, the direct file, and the multiring file. The choice of these six has been influenced by the fact that all these basic models are closely related to systems in actual use. In other words, the collection of these six is not intended to represent a mathematically minimal set of independent file-organization methods.

The previous definition of a file can now be expanded to state that a file not only consists of similar records but also has a consistent organization.

File Directories

Associated with a file may be a header or a directory record. This record contains information describing the position and the format of the records comprising the file. Different types of file organization put different requirements on the contents of the file directory. Much of the information that is kept in the directory is associated with storage allocation and with database concepts, and for that reason directory records are not discussed as part of the subsequent file analyses. Typical data elements kept in a directory include the name, the owner, the begin point, the end point, the amount of space allowed, and the amount of space actually used. It is worth noting here that the collection of the directory records for a number of files may in turn form a file. The owner of such a directory file is typically the operating system for the computer.

A practical procedure to deal with directory records is to read these records once, when a computation begins to use the file, and to retain the information for further reference. This process is referred to as the **opening** of a file. A corresponding process at termination of the use of a file, the **closing** of the file, will update the file directory if changes in the file have occurred that should be reflected in the directory.

File Descriptions

With each description of a file organization, new definitions will be encountered that are relevant for the subsequent file-organization methods. This implies that it is best to follow the material of this section in the sequence in which it is presented.

Each file-organization method is described and analyzed in conjunction with one specific record organization. While the combination presented may be typical in practice, it should be realized that many other combinations are valid. Such alternative combinations will produce different formulas for the performance parameters. The derivations of these measures are sufficiently simple to allow readers to evaluate other alternatives on their own.

Measures of Performance

Quantitative measures are necessary to evaluate file-system performance. Seven measures are provided for each of the six file-organization methods. The seven measures used are:

Storage required for a record

Time to fetch an arbitrary record from the file

Time to get the next record within the file

Time to update by insertion of a record into the file

Time to update by changing a record of the file

Time for exhaustive reading of the entire file

Time for reorganization of the file

The six operations on files are executed by combining seeks, reads, and writes of blocks, so that the measures to be derived are based on the hardware parameters obtained in the preceding chapter. The use of generalized parameters provides a certain amount of independence from the physical specifics of the hardware, so that the analysis of file methods can proceed without considering details of the possible hardware implementation. The critical decisions in the evaluation of file performance in specific cases are reduced to the four questions below:

Is a seek required, or are we positioned appropriately; i.e., is s to be used?

Are we passing directly to the next record, or not; i.e., is the latency 0, r, or $2r$?

TABLE 19-2 A Dense, a Sparse, and a Redundant File

(a) A dense file: database course attendees

	Student no.	Class	Credits	Incompletes	Current work	Age	Grade
1	721	S	43	5	12	20	PF
2	843	S	51	0	15	21	Reg
3	1019	F	25	2	12	19	Reg
4	1021	F	26	0	12	19	Reg
5	1027	F	28	0	13	18	Reg
6	1028	F	24	3	12	19	PF
7	1029	F	25	0	15	19	Reg
8	1031	F	15	8	12	20	Aud
9	1033	E	23	0	14	19	PF
10	1034	F	20	3	10	19	Reg

(b) A sparse file: database course attendees

	Student no.	Courses taken					Exp. years
		CS101	CS102	Bus3	EE5	IE103	
1	721	F72	F73		W73		
2	843	F72	W73				
3	1019		S72	S73			1
4	1021		S72			F73	
5	1027	F73		S73			
6	1028				W73		1
7	1029	F73	W73				
8	1031	F73					
9	1033						3
10	1034					F73	

(c) A redundant file: database course attendees

	Prerequisite	Student no.	When taken	Years exp.	Acc. credits	. . .	Grade
1	CS102	721	F73		43	. . .	PF
2	CS102	843	W73		51	. . .	Reg
3	CS102	1019	S72		25	. . .	Reg
4	CS102	1021	S72		26	. . .	Reg
5	CS102	1029	W73		25	. . .	Reg
6	Bus3	1019	S73		25	. . .	Reg
7	Bus3	1027	S73		28	. . .	Reg
8	EE5	721	W73		43	. . .	PF
9	EE5	1027	W73		28	. . .	Reg
10	IE103	1021	F72		26	. . .	Reg
11	IE103	1034	F73		20	. . .	Reg
12	Exp.	1019		3	25	. . .	Reg
13	Exp.	1028		1	24	. . .	PF
14	Exp.	1033		1	23	. . .	PF
15	None	1031			20	. . .	Aud

Are we reading significant data only, or are we spacing through a file; i.e., do we use t or t' for the transfer rate?

Are we measuring the net quantity of data or the space required; i.e., do we use R or $(R + W)$ as a measure?

In this section we will measure the cost of these operations in terms of time required.

Record Size   In order to gain economy of **storage,** we wish to store the data with a minimum of **redundancy.** Redundancy of data elements also increases the effort required when values of data elements have to be changed. Redundancy exists when data fields are duplicated (for instance, in records 1 and 8 of Table 19-2c) or when the description of the contents of the data fields is repeated with every entry. Reduction of the latter form of redundancy can be aided by imposing structure, so that the position of a data element serves as a component of the description. If the data is highly heterogeneous, such a tabular organization may actually be wasteful because of the need to maintain many empty spaces. Table 19-2 shows a dense file, a sparse file, and a redundant file. Each of these files presents information in a form useful for a particular purpose.

Fetch Record   In order to be able to use data from a file, a record combining the data has to be read into a processor. Fetching a record consists of two steps: locating the position of the record followed by the actual reading. We use the term **fetch** when the retrieval of the record is **out of the blue;** that is, no operations to prepare for a simpler locate and read sequence have preceded this fetch. To read data efficiently, we have to locate the element to be read fast. A simple address computation, similar to the determination of the location for an array element in core memory, seems most desirable but leads to inflexibility in terms of data storage whenever the data is not tabular in nature, or the entries in the table are not dense, so that entries cannot be directly located on the basis of a subscript value. The use of look-up tables or indexes helps in data retrieval when the position cannot be directly computed, but their existence increases redundancy. A look-up table, helpful in obtaining access to the other files, is shown in Table 19-3.

TABLE 19-3   A Look-up Table

Name	Student no.		Prerequisite entries	
Allmeyer, John	1031	15		
Bushman, Wilde	1028	13		
Conte, Mary	843	2		
Erickson, Sylvia	1034	11		
Gee, Otto	1021	4	10	
Heston, Charles	721	1	8	
Hotten, Donna	1029	5		
Jason, Pete	1027	7	9	
Makale, Verna	1019	3	6	12
Punouth, Remington	1033	14		

Get-Next Record   Isolated data rarely provides information. Information is mainly generated by relating one fact with another; this implies getting the next record according to some criterion. While **Fetch** can be characterized as an **associative** retrieval of a data element based on a key value, **Get-Next** can be characterized through a **structural** dependency. A successor record can be obtained most efficiently when related data are kept together, that is, when the **locality** of these data is strong. Since there may be multiple dimensions to data relationships, but only a few efficient access sequences through the physical devices in which the data resides, a highly redundant storage design can help; or a liberal use of pointers to provide linkages to successor records can provide assistance. The reading, or writing, of records in a particular order is referred to as **serial** reading. If serial reading is simplified by a physical ordering of the records, we can read the file containing these records **sequentially.** Table 19-2c shows the use of redundancy to simplify grouping of records that identify the prerequisite courses.

Insert   Many files require the regular insertion or addition of new data records in order to remain up to date. Writing into a file is a task which is frequently more complex than reading the file. Adding records is easiest if they can be placed at the end of a file, extending the file. The address of the end, the end point, is often kept in the directory to make the end easy to locate. When a record has to be put in a specific place to simplify serial access, other records may have to be shifted or modified to accommodate the insertion. When data is stored redundantly, multiple write operations will have to be carried out to perform a complete file-update operation.

If an "incomplete" has to be removed in the files shown in Table 19-2, only one record is changed. If, however, the removal implies that a new prerequisite is fulfilled, many operations are required.

Each write into a blocked file will require the reading of the block in order to be able to merge the data from the surrounding records before rewriting the entire block. If we produce information, rather than operate an archive, the read frequencies should exceed the number of updates of files and records by a considerable margin. Hence we are often willing to use data organizations which provide fast retrieval, even when this makes update operations more complex.

Update Record   When data within an existing record have to be changed the new, updated record is created using some information from the previous instance of the record. The file is updated with the new record. It may not be possible to use the old space if the record has grown in size. The old record will then have to be invalidated. The look-up table shown in Table 19-3 presents such a problem if a prerequisite is to be added.

Read Entire File   Some application functions require the reading of the entire file. Here again we prefer a dense, nonredundant file to avoid excessive time and errors due to the multiple occurrence of the same data item. If this cannot be achieved, the process of exhaustive reading has to maintain additional information either within the file or in separate tables. There is, for instance, no simple way to use the file shown in Table 19-2c to count the number of students or to compute the average credits accumulated by them.

Reorganization   Finally, it may be necessary to clean up files periodically, especially those that have undergone regular dynamic change. The frequency of this operation is not directly dependent on application requirements but varies greatly with the type of file organization used. This operation, called file reorganization, has many similarities with the process of garbage collection encountered in some computer-language systems which provide dynamic storage allocation.

In a more informal manner we will use the term **retrieve** for both fetch and get-next, and use the term **access** to denote any reference to a file. The word **search** is used sometimes to describe file activity for access prior to the read or write of a block.

19-11 THE PILE

The initial method presented is a minimal method. Data in a **pile** (Fig. 19-9) is collected in the order that it arrives. It is not analyzed, categorized, or normalized. At best the order may be chronological. The records may be of variable length and need not have similar sets of data elements.

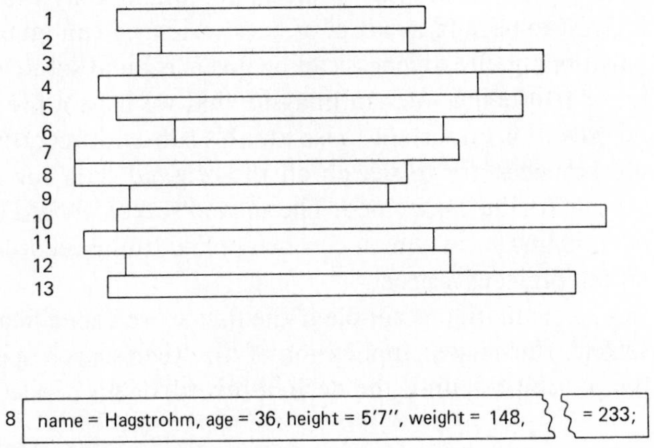
1
2
3
4
5
6
7
8
9
10
11
12
13
8
name = Hagstrohm, age = 36, height = 5'7", weight = 148,
= 233;

FIG. 19-9 A pile file with representative record

Structure and Manipulation

Some restrictions, though, will have to be observed to allow processing of data in order to extract information. A record has to consist of related data elements, and each data value needs to have an identification of its meaning. This identification may be an explicit name, a code, or a position which indicates its *attribute* type, such as **height;** and if multiple identical domains exist in a record, the attribute type also specifies the relationship to the object or event described by the record: **height of doorway, height of tower.** We will use in pile files an explicit name for the attribute description, since this matches best the unstructured form of the file.

Example 19-4 Data Element

height = 95

In this example, the value of the data element is **95** and the description is **height.**

The pair in Example 19-4 is referred to as an *attribute name-value pair*.

Just one such pair does not make a significant record. We need a number of such pairs to define an object adequately, and then, if we want to associate factual data regarding this object, we will want to define additional attribute pairs that contain further data. Different sets of attributes in a record may be used for various searches, so that we do not wish to preassign attributes to the key or goal data function.

Example 19-5 Data Record

name = Hoover, type = Tower, street = Serra Road, height = 95;

The key attributes of a record are to be matched to the search argument of the fetch request. The terms **key** and **goal** define two parts of the record. The key identifies the record wanted in the file, and the goal is defined to be the remainder of the record. The number of attributes required for a search is a function of the **partitioning effectiveness** of the key attributes. Partitioning takes place whenever we check the set of data for some specified attribute, and then separate the set of data into a subset containing only those records that are still of interest to us, and a subset of data which we can ignore from this point on. The partitioning effectiveness can be given as an absolute count or a ratio. After the first partitioning, we can imagine that we have a file with a smaller number of records. It is important to isolate this subset of records in such a way that it will not be necessary to search all the original data for a match according to the second attribute specified. The second search should be measured in terms of a partitioning ratio, which can be applied to the records selected to be of interest by the previous search.

The evaluation is simple if the first search specification is independent of the second. Successive application of all other search specifications narrows down the possibilities until the desired record, or set of records, is obtained.

Using the above example, the specification **Tower** applied to a file containing all objects in this world, or at least all towers, would restrict our search to the 10^7 towers in this world [assumption: one tower per 300 people and $3(10^9)$ people in this world]. The name **Hoover** may have a partitioning ratio of $4(10^{-6})$ (fraction of Hoovers in the world, extrapolated from the San Francisco telephone book, combined with the assumption that half the towers are named after people), so that the second search attribute would yield 25 possible records. (Assumption: as many towers are named after Hoovers as after other family names.) A third specification (the street name) should be sufficient to determine which tower is desired, or the nonexistence of a tower answering the given request.

If no attribute pairs are left in our record beyond those required for the search, the only information retrievable is the fact that this object exists in our file; many attribute types may exist which defy a priori compartmentalization; tower still is available as a goal-data element.

Example 19-6 Complex Attribute

**place = (street = Serra Road, town = Stanford,
county = Santa Clara, state = Cal);**

An attribute value may in itself be divided into a number of attribute name-value pairs to simplify the conceptual organization of the record, as shown in Example 19-6.

Throughout the remainder of this section, we will assign to the symbol a the total number of attribute types in the file under consideration, and to the symbol a' the average number of attributes occurring in a record. If the record in Example 19-5 is representative for the file, then a' for that file would be 4. In Example 19-6 we would choose a' to be 4 greater. We do not need to know the value of the total attribute count a of an entire file in the pile organization.

Use of Piles

Pile files are found where data is collected prior to processing, where data is not easy to organize, and in some research on file structures. They also provide a basis for performance comparison within this text.

Data banks that have been established for military intelligence sometimes have this form, since the potential usage of a record is difficult to assess. In this file many attribute types may exist which defy a priori compartmentalization. Many manual data collections, such as medical records, also have the form of a pile. In pile files, data analysis can become very costly because of the time required for retrieval of a statistically adequate number of sample records.

Performance of Piles

The following performance-parameter values can be associated with a pile organization.

Record Size in a Pile   File density in a pile is affected by two factors: negatively, by the need to store the attribute names with the data, and positively, by the fact that nonexistent data need not be indicated at all. The effect is a relatively high density when the material collected is heterogeneous or sparse, and a relatively low density when the data is dense and the same attribute names occur in successive records. Since name and data are of variable length, some separation characters (=, and ;, in the examples above) are stored to mark the data. We will denote the average length of the name portion of an attribute name-value pair in terms of bytes as A, and the average length of the value portion as V. For the last two examples above A is 5 and V is 6.

Using these definitions, we can state that the expected average record length will be

$$R = a'(A + V + 2)$$

Appropriate values for a', A, and V will have to be based on an adequately sized sample.

Fetch Record in a Pile   The time required to locate a record in a pile is high, since all the records may have to be searched to locate a data item that has a single instance in the file. If it has an equal probability of appearance anywhere in the file, we consider that at least one, and maybe all (b) blocks will have to be read. The expected average then is the sum of all the times to reach and read any of the blocks, divided by the number of choices, or

$$\text{Average blocks read} = \sum_{i=1}^{b} \frac{i}{b} = \frac{1}{2}(1 + b)$$

$$\approx \frac{1}{2}b \qquad \text{if } b \gg 1$$

The time to read this number of blocks sequentially is then

$$T_F = \frac{1}{2}b\,\frac{B}{t'}$$

Figure 19-10 illustrates the process. We use the assumptions about buffers made previously, so that blocks are read into one buffer while the previous

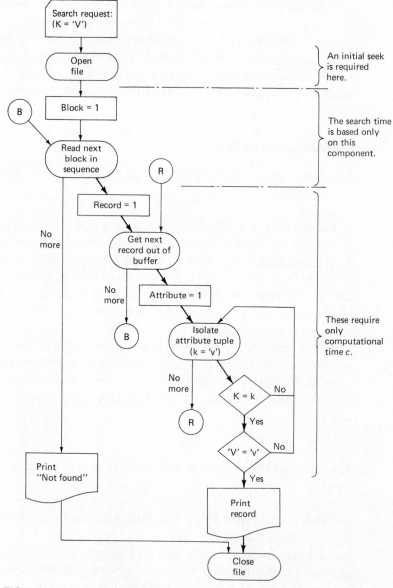

FIG. 19-10 Search through a pile

buffer contents are being processed. Due to the relationship between blocks and records, we now can restate the sequential fetch time in a more useful form:

$$T_F = \frac{1}{2} n \frac{R}{t'}$$

The use of the sequential transfer rate t' is appropriate here, since we read the file from its begin point, passing over gaps and cylinder boundaries, until we find the block containing the desired record.

Batching of Requests   Partial solutions to the problem of long search times include the collection of search requests into batches, since a batch of many requests can be processed in one pass through the entire file. The average search-time factor will increase from the value ½ above to ¾ or ⅚ for two or three requests. For more requests, this factor will approach 1, so that we simply state for the expected cost of executing a batch of L fetch requests

$$T_F(L) = 2 T_F \; L \gg 1$$

While this lowers the cost per item searched to $2/L(T_F)$, the responsiveness to an individual request doubles the original value of T_F. In addition, there is delay due to the amount of time required to collect an adequate batch (L) of requests. Such batch operations frequently are carried out only on a daily cycle to make them profitable. In a medical data file which, from the point of view of this type of search, had a pile format, the search time in fact exceeded 24 hours. If requests arrive at a very high rate, a single search program, handling multiple requests, may cycle continuously through the file taking requests as they arrive and immediately processing each request through the n records of the file. Here the search costs are reduced as indicated above, and the expected delay is T_F as before for an individual request. If we process many requests in one batch, an efficient record data-processing algorithm is required to ensure that our condition $c < R/t$ still holds.

Get-Next Record of a Pile   Since no ordering of records is provided here, the potential successor record may be anywhere in the file. Since the position is not known, the time required to find an arbitrary successor record is also

$$T_N = T_F$$

We have to assume that information from the previous record is required to search for the successor record. If the specification of required attributes for the successor record were known initially, the test for this record could be made during the one combined search, similar to the method for batched requests described above.

Insert into a Pile   The time required for inserting a new record into a pile file will be fast because of its lack of structure. The address of the end of the file is known and data is simply added to the end, and the end pointer is updated. To obtain dense packing of records, the last block is read into core memory, the new record is appended, and the block is rewritten. The time required will be then

$$T_I = s + r + btt + T_{RW}$$

We can simplify:

$$T_I = s + 3r + btt$$

New records will not always fit into the last block of a file. For a simple, unspanned, variable-length record organization the current block does not have to be read when the value of the end point of the file, as kept in the directory, indicates that this block is already too full to take the new record. Then only a new block will be allocated to the file and written. For a variable spanned organization the previous block will have to be read, updated, rewritten, and an additional block written since the record did not fit.

The relative frequency of encountering a block boundary which will require the use of either of the two procedures is R/B. This factor can be used to correct the above value of the insertion time.

We will ignore this variation in the discussions following and assume that two accesses provide read and rewriting capability for file extension. When a batch of file extensions is being processed, the time per record will be less, since the block at the end can remain available in core.

Update Record in a Pile Updating of a record consists of locating and invalidating the old record, and writing a new, probably larger, record at the end of the file, so that

$$T_U = T_F + T_{RW} + T_I$$

If only a deletion is to be made, the T_I term drops out. Deletion is actually effected by rewriting the old record space with **NULL** characters or a message as "Deleted xxx . . . x;".

Read Entire Pile An exhaustive search in this file organization only is twice as costly as a specific search:

$$T_X = 2T_F$$

If, however, we wish to read this file serially according to some attribute, the repetitive use of n individual fetches would cost

$$T_X \text{ (serial)} = nT_F = \frac{1}{2} n^2 \frac{R}{t'}$$

This is avoided by putting the records into a sequential order to match the seriality of the attribute values. It is now well known that sorts can be performed using order $n \log_2 n$ steps. A typical sort step may involve a sequential read and a sequential write of one record. Hence a rough estimate is that using sorting of the file,

$$T_X \text{ (serial)} = T_X + T_{\text{sort}} + T_X = (2n + 2n \log_2 n) \frac{R}{t'}$$

which will be considerably less than nT_F on any nontrivial file.

Reorganization of a Pile   If the pile file is updated as described above, then periodically a removal of the invalidated areas is desired. This is accomplished by copying the file, excluding records marked deleted, and reblocking the remaining records. If the number of records added during a period is o and the number flagged for deletion is d, the file will have grown from n to $n + o$ so that the time to copy the file will be

$$T_Y = (n + o)\,\frac{R}{t'} + (n + o - d)\,\frac{R}{t'}$$

The number of overflow records o is not identical in the various file-organization methods evaluated but depends on the algorithms used. Here

$$o = \#\,(\text{new records}) + \#\,(\text{updated records})$$

and d, the number of records to be deleted during reorganization is

$$d = \#\,(\text{removed records}) + \#\,(\text{updated records})$$

It also is assumed here and in the other evaluations of the term T_Y that the reading and the writing during the reorganization do not interfere with each other. This means specifically that if moving-head disks are used, separate devices must be used for the old and the new file. It also requires that sufficient buffers are available to utilize the disks fully. Since reorganization generally can be scheduled at times of low utilization, this condition frequently can be met.

19-12 THE SEQUENTIAL FILE

This method provides two distinct structural changes relative to the pile organization. The first improvement is that the data records are ordered into a specific sequence, and the second improvement is that the data attributes are categorized so that the individual records contain all the data-attribute values in the same order and possibly in the same position. The data-attribute names then need to appear only once in the description of the file. Instead of storing attribute name-value pairs, an entire set of values (a column) is associated with each name. This organization looks similar to the familiar tabular output that is generally associated with computers, and as shown in Fig. 19-11 here uses fixed-length records.

Structure and Manipulation of Sequential Files

One or more attribute-value sets will become the key attribute(s) for the records in the file. It is generally necessary to be able to identify records uniquely on the basis of their keys. The records in the file are then ordered according to the key attributes. One key attribute will provide the primary, high-order sort key, and if this attribute does not uniquely determine the order, then secondary and further key attributes can be specified until the order is completely determined. Serial reading of the file in this order now can be performed sequentially. In

Table 19-1*a* and *b* the student number provides such an attribute, but in Table 19-1*c* there is no single field usable as a key. Two attributes, prerequisite and student number, can be combined to form a key.

Sometimes artificial fields containing sequence or identification numbers are added to obtain unique key attributes. The partitioning of the file, discussed with the pile-file description, now is performed explicitly: the identification number is chosen to be unique for each record and hence partitions the file into *n* individual records. Unfortunately, a separate computation may be needed to determine the identification number pertaining to a desired data record.

With this increase in structure, and the attendant increased efficiency in tabular-oriented processing, a great deal of flexibility is lost. Updates or extensions to a sequential file are not easily accommodated. The fact that only the key attribute determines the sequence of the records introduces an asymmetry which makes sequential files unsuitable for general information retrieval. The common procedure to handle insertions to a sequential file is to collect them in a pile, the **transaction log file,** until the pile becomes large and then to perform a **batch update.** This is done by reorganizing the file. The transaction log file is sorted according to the same keys used for the main file, and the changes are merged into a new copy of the sequential file.

	Name	Age	Height	IQ
1	Antwerp	55	5'8''	95
2	Berringer	39	5'6''	75
3	Bigley	36	5'7''	70
4	Breslow	25	5'6''	49
5	Calhoun	27	5'11''	80
6	Finnerty	42	5'9''	178
7	Garson	61	5'6''	169
8	Hagstrohm	36	5'7''	83
9	Halgard	31	5'6''	95
10	Kroner	59	5'5''	145
11	McCloud	26	5'8''	47
12	Miasma	27	5'2''	75
13	Mirro	38	5'8''	52
14	Moskowitz	23	5'7''	50
15	Pop	38	5'3''	53
16	Proteus	41	5'8''	152
17	Purdy	37	5'9''	48
18	Roseberry	38	5'7''	70
19	Wheeler	23	5'8''	67
20	Young	18	5'8''	89

FIG. 19-11 A sequential file

A sequential file is restricted to a limited and predetermined set of attributes. A single description applies to all records, and all records are structurally identical. If a new attribute has to be added to a record, the entire file has to be reorganized. Every record of the file will be rewritten to provide space for the new data item. To avoid this problem, one finds that sequential files are sometimes initially allocated with space to spare; a few columns are left empty.

The fixed record layout is easy to construct by processing programs, since programs are easier to write when information of the same type is found in identical positions of successive records. The written record is often simply a copy of the information in processor storage. Even where data is transformed by the processing languages, strong support is given to such record-oriented data through PICTURE specifications in COBOL and FORMAT statements in FORTRAN and PL/1.

Example 19-7 A Record Declaration

> **DECLARE 1 payroll_record,**
>
> **2 name,**

        3 initials CHAR(2),

        3 last_name CHAR(28),

     2 date_born CHAR(6),

     2 date_hired CHAR(6),

     2 salary FIXED BINARY,

     2 exemptions FIXED BINARY,

     2 sex CHAR(1),

     2 maternity_leave FIXED BINARY;

     etc.

   . . .

   . . .

       WRITE (payroll_file) FROM (payroll_record);

The record layout which will appear on the file for Example 19-7 is a direct representation of the **DECLARE** statement in the program.

Use of Sequential Files

Sequential files are the most frequently used type of file in batch-oriented commercial processing. In order to combine data from multiple sequential files, sorts are performed to make the records of the files **consequential** (Fig. 19-12). Then

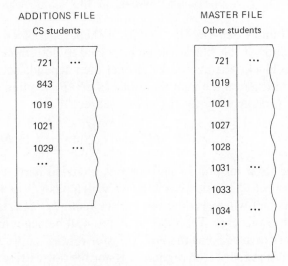

FIG. 19-12 Cosequential files

all required data can be found by spacing only forward over the files involved. A disadvantage is that files can be in sequence only according to one primary key, so that frequently such a file has to be sorted again according to another key in order to match other sets of files. Where data is processed only cyclically, as in monthly billings, sequential files show cost advantages that are hard to achieve by other methods.

Performance of Sequential Files

The performance of sequential files ranges from excellent to next to impossible, depending on the operations desired.

Record Size in a Sequential File   The file-storage requirement when using a fixed record format is a factor which depends on all the possible attributes a. The description of the attributes which frequently is outside the file itself appears only once per file, and thus the space required for the attribute names can be neglected. However, space will be used when attributes have an undefined value or are unimportant in combination with other attributes. The last two entries shown in Example 19-7 illustrate such an attribute dependency where for the category **sex = 'Male'** the last maternity_leave will frequently be **NULL.** The fixed record size is the product of the number of fields and their average size.

$$R = aV$$

If many values are undefined, the file density will be low. If the value a' is close to the value for a, the file density will be high. If insertions are expected, space for o new records of length R must also be allocated in an associated area.

Fetch Record in a Sequential File   The common approach to fetch a record from a sequential file consists of a serial search through the file. The time required to fetch an arbitrary record can be significantly reduced if we use a direct-access device and a binary search technique. This search is possible only for the attribute type for which the file has been put in sequence.

Binary Search (Fig. 19-13)   Whenever a block is fetched, the first and last records in this block will be inspected to determine if the goal record is within this block. The number of fetches then depends not on the number of records n but rather on the number of blocks nR/B. We find, using the expected number of block accesses for the binary search, that

$$T_F = \log_2\left(n\frac{R}{B}\right)(s + r + btt + c)$$

The term for processing time c is included here, since, until the record range has been checked, it is not known which block is to be read next. The efficiencies obtained when reading the file sequentially using alternate buffers have been lost in this case. The value of c may well be negligible compared with the other times involved, but the bulk transfer rate t' is always inappropriate.

When the search argument is not the key attribute used to sequence the file, the search is similar to the search through a pile file. Since the total size of the file will be different from the size of a pile file because of the difference in record organization, the relative performance will depend on the attribute density a'/a as well as on the relative length of attribute descriptors A and data values V. Half the file will be searched on the average to fetch a record, so that

$$T_F = \frac{1}{2}n\frac{R}{t'}$$

For small files this may be comparable with the binary search time.

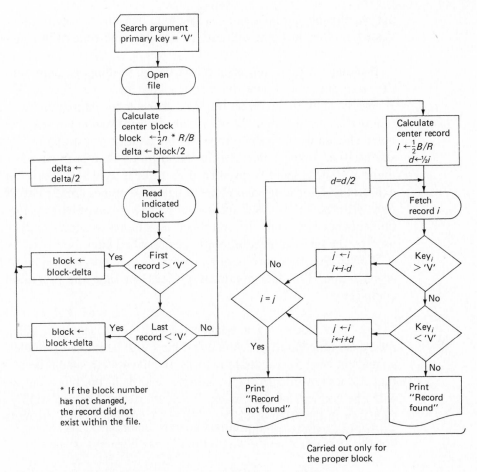

FIG. 19-13 Nested binary search in a blocked sequential file

If the file has received o' new records into a transaction log or overflow file, this file should be searched also. This file will be in chronological order, so that the additional term is always

$$T_{FO} = \frac{1}{2} o' \frac{R}{t'}$$

to allow for a sequential search. The total fetch time, if both parts of the file are searched sequentially, is

$$T_F = \frac{1}{2}(n + o') \frac{R}{t'}$$

or with the assumption that the transaction log file is on the average half full,

$$T_F = \frac{1}{2}\left(n + \frac{1}{2} o\right) \frac{R}{t'}$$

where o is the capacity of the transaction log file.

If fetching of individual records is frequent, the sequential search through a transaction log file could be excessively expensive. It may pay off to use some technique to keep the transaction log file in a sequence permitting faster searching. Applicable methods such as chaining and direct access, which will be discussed in other sections, will add to the effort and time of insertions.

Probing   A third approach to searching, **probing,** is more difficult to quantify. It applies only where the search argument is the sequence key for the file. It consists of an initial direct fetch, or probe, to an estimated position in the file, followed by a sequential search. If only forward sequential searches can be executed efficiently, the initial probe will be made at an estimated lowest matching key position. Likely values for an initial probe have been based on the leading digits of a social security number, if its value is used as a key; or on a percentile expectation for leading characters of names, if names are the key. Names beginning with the letters "Sc," for instance, may be found after $0.79n$ records in a file sequenced by name. More refined techniques to access records directly are used by the file-organization methods described later.

We see that there are here three access methods applicable to a single file organization. The data organization does not bind the programming choices completely.

Get-Next Record of a Sequential File   In a sequential file, a successor record is immediately accessible and may well be in the same block. If there is a frequent need for successor records, the file system should be programmed so that it does not discard the remaining records in the block but keeps a buffer with the contents of the current block available. The probability of finding a successor in the same block is $(B/R - 1)/(B/R)$, so that the expected time to get the next record is only

$$T_N = \left(1 - \frac{B/R - 1}{B/R}\right)\frac{B}{t'} = \frac{R}{t'}$$

If the file-system design does not take into consideration the need to get successor records and does not keep the current block available, then

$$T_N = r + btt$$

will be incurred since the buffer has to be refilled.

Insert into a Sequential File   Adding a record to the main file is normally impossible, since the sequence would not be maintained if new records were to be added to the end. For small data collections, records beyond the point of insertion can be moved up to make space for the new record. This effort involves the reading and rewriting of half of the blocks of the file on the average, so that

$$T_I = \frac{1}{2}\,n\,\frac{R}{B}\left(\frac{B}{t'} + T_{RW}\right)$$

In practice, this is rarely feasible. The usual procedure is to collect new records into a transaction log file and at a later time execute a batch update. We will use o to indicate the number of records collected for deferred insertion.

The actual cost of extending the file is hence a function of the time required to write the records to the transaction log file and the cost of the reorganization run. The cost of the reorganization T_Y is allocated below to the o records that had been saved on the transaction log file between reorganization periods. For a simple unblocked transaction log file the update and allocated reorganization time give

$$T_I = s + r + \frac{R}{t} + \frac{T_Y}{o}$$

The response time that users sense when they enter a record for update includes only the initial three terms. The reorganization time T_Y and the transaction record count o are defined below. A blocked transaction log file will involve reading and rewriting the last block, so that

$$T_I = s + r + btt + T_{RW} + \frac{T_Y}{o}$$

If the file is blocked and updates are frequent, the last block of the transaction log file can be kept available in an update buffer so that seeks and writes occur less frequently.

$$T_I = \frac{R}{B}(s + r + btt) + \frac{T_Y}{o}$$

If searches have to be carried out on such incomplete files, both the sequential file and the transaction log file will have to be searched.

Update Record in a Sequential File   The definition of this file does not allow insertion of larger records than the original record stored. If the key value does not change, the record could be rewritten into the main file. If the key value is different, the update is similar to the process of adding a record but also involves the deletion of a record at another position in the sequential file. Instead of modifying the record in the main sequential file, a flag record indicating this action can be added onto the transaction log file and used for fetches and in the reorganization process. This type of change causes two entries in the transaction log file. If there are d record deletions and v record updates, $d + 2v$ records have to be added into the count o, the size of the transaction log file. Then $T_U \approx T_I$. Since complex updating is rarely done using this file organization, we will skip further evaluation of updating performance.

Read Entire Sequential File   An exhaustive processing of the file consists of sequentially reading the main and the transaction log file. This means that data will be processed serially for the key used to establish the physical sequence of the file. The transaction log file should be sorted first to establish this sequence. Then

$$T_X = \text{sort}(o) + n\frac{R}{t'} + o\left(s + r + \frac{R}{t}\right)$$

for unblocked overflows, or

$$T_X = \text{sort}(o) + (n + o)\frac{R}{t'}$$

for a blocked transaction log file with double buffers, so that both files can be processed in bulk.

If serial processing is not important, the transaction sort can be omitted. It is obvious that the time to process records in sequential order is much less than the time to process records in any other serial order, namely,

$$T_X \text{ (seq)} \approx 2T_s$$

while

$$T_X \text{ (not seq)} = nT_s$$

If the transaction log file is relatively large ($o \rceil \ll n$), it may be best to reorganize the file first. The records can be analyzed during the reorganization, so that

$$T_X = T_Y$$

We find from the comments in the preceding paragraphs that

$$o = (n_{\text{new}} - n_{\text{old}}) + 2v + d$$

or in words, the value of the transaction count o is here the sum of the number of new records, plus twice the number of records to be changed, plus the number of records to be deleted.

Reorganization of a Sequential File Reorganization consists of taking the old file and the transaction log file and combining them into a new file. In order to carry out the merge effectively, the transaction log file will first be sorted according to the same key field used for the old file. During the merge the sorted data from the transaction log file and the records from the old sequential file are copied into the new file, omitting any records which are marked for deletion in the transaction log file. The time required for the reorganization run consists of the sort time for the transaction log file plus the merge time. The time required to reorganize the file is the sum of the times to read both files and write a new one, plus the time required to sort the transaction log file.

$$T_Y = n_{\text{old}} \left(\frac{R}{t'} \right) + \text{sort} (o) + o \left(\frac{R}{t'} \right) + n_{\text{new}} \left(\frac{R}{t'} \right)$$

or if the number of records being deleted $d + v$ can be neglected,

$$T_Y = 2(n + o) \frac{R}{t'} + \text{sort} (o)$$

Estimates for the time required to sort files were provided with the discussion of exhaustive reading of a pile file.

19-13 THE INDEXED-SEQUENTIAL FILE

The indexed-sequential-file design attempts to overcome the access problem inherent in the sequential-file organization without losing all the benefits and

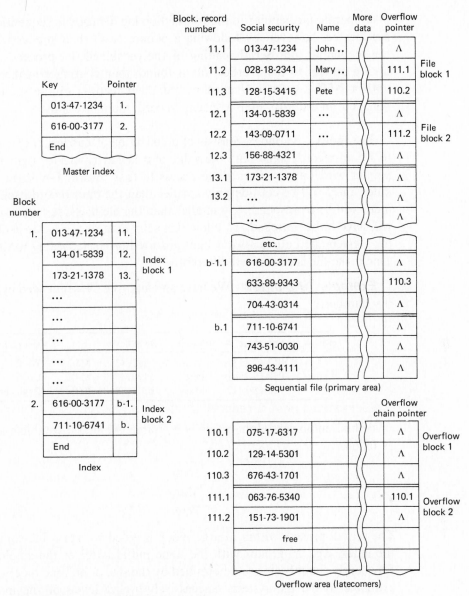

FIG. 19-14 An indexed-sequential file

tradition associated with sequential files. One additional feature is an index to the file to provide better random access; another provides a means to handle additions to the file. Figure 19-14 shows a particular example of an indexed-sequential file. We find in this figure the three important components: the sequential file, the index, and an overflow area. The sketch also has a number of details which we will discuss below.

Structure and Manipulation of Indexed-Sequential Files

This file organization allows, when reading data serially, sequential access to the original record areas of the file. Records which have been inserted are found in a separate file, similar to the transaction log file used in sequential files. They are located, however, by following a pointer from their predecessor record in the sequential file. Serial reading of the combined file proceeds sequentially until a pointer to the overflow file is found, then continues in the overflow file until a **NULL** pointer is encountered; then reading of the sequential file is resumed. In order to fetch a specific record, the index is used.

The Index An index consists of a collection of **entries,** each corresponding to a data record, containing the value of a key attribute for that record, and a pointer which allows immediate access to that record. For large records, the index entry will be considerably smaller than the data record itself. The entire index will be correspondingly smaller than the file itself, so that a smaller space will have to be searched. To allow fast searching of the index itself, the index for a given attribute is always kept in sorted order according to this attribute, even if the file is sequenced differently.

Example 19-8 Index We have an employee file sequenced by social security number:

Rec #	Social sec #	Name	Birth date	Sex	Occupation
1	013-47-1234	John	1/1/43	Male	Welder
2	028-18-2341	Pete	11/5/45	Male	Creep
3	128-15-3412	Mary	6/31/39	Fem	Engineer

To find employees alphabetically by name, we might establish an index file as follows:

John	1
Mary	3
Pete	2

The search process within a large index is aided by again indexing subsets of the index, e.g., 26 groups with the same initial letter of the employee names. Frequently the subsets are determined by the size of buffers, blocks, and tracks available to the file system. Successively higher levels of the index become smaller and smaller until there remains only a small, highest-level index that can be kept in core memory. It will be shown later that there is rarely a need for many levels of indexing. An alternative to multilevel indexing is to provide for a binary search on the index file. Binary searching was discussed when sequential files were evaluated in the preceding section. In Fig. 19-14 the subsetting of the index is based on the number of index entries (8) which fit into a block.

A Primary Index The index for an indexed-sequential file is usually based on the same key attribute which has been used to determine the sequence of the file itself. For such a primary index a number of refinements can be applied.

Block Anchors Individual records in a block can be found by a sequential search within the block, so that it is not necessary to keep in the index an entry for every record but only to reference one record per block. Such a reference record is called an **anchor point,** and only the anchor's key value and the block pointer are kept in the index. Natural anchor points are based on blocks, tracks, or cylinders. In Fig. 19-14 the choice of anchor point has been the first record of a block; at times other choices may be better. The cost of searching within a block for a record is minimal, since the entire block is brought into memory whenever required and can be kept available in a buffer. A block will contain a number of records equal to B/R. The number of entries in the index is hence $n(R/B)$, and the size of an index entry is $V + P$.

When only block anchors are kept in the index, it cannot be determined by checking the index alone if there exists a record corresponding to a specific argument. The appropriate data block has to be read also. To determine if the value of a search argument is beyond the last entry in the file, the last data block will have to be fetched, since the anchor point refers to the first record in this block. If records are to be inserted often at the end of the file, it can be more convenient to keep the key value of the last record of each block in the index instead of the key for the first record. The appropriate block for a given argument is then found in the index through a sequential less-than-or-equal match.

Cylinder Indexes   Since much of the overhead of fetching a block is due to the time required to reach a particular cylinder, a reduction of seek effort can be made by placing subsets of the index according to hardware boundaries. There will then be a master index which contains only key attribute values and addresses of cylinder anchors. Then on the initial track of each cylinder there will be a cylinder index using tracks, blocks, or records for that particular cylinder as anchors. No seek delay will be incurred between cylinder index and data records.

Fanout Ratio of an Index   To evaluate the number of **levels** of indexing that might be required, we will take an example of a fairly large file (one million records) and a block-anchored index. In order to estimate the access time to fetch a record, we wish to know how many levels of index are needed for a file of this size.

Example 19-9 Index Design   Given is a block size B of 2000 bytes, a value size V of 14 bytes, a pointer size P of 6 bytes, and data records having a total length R of 200 bytes. With this blocking factor (B/R) of 10, the 10^6 records require 10^5 blocks and hence as many index pointer entries. The quotient of block size B and index-entry size provides the referencing capability per block of index storage or the **fanout ratio y** of each index level. Each index block provides

$$y = \frac{B}{V + P}$$

index entries. The size of the index entry is here $(14 + 6) = 20$ bytes and the block size B is still 2000. Now $y = 100$, so that the 10^5 lowest-index-level entries occupy 10^3 blocks which can be pointed at by 10^3 second-level index entries. This second-level index will occupy a total of 20(1000) = 20,000 bytes. The latter number is excessive for core storage, so that a third index level to the second index level will be created. Only (20,000/2000) = 10 entries occupying 200 bytes would be required at the top level. The terms **master index** indicates the topmost level, and the index levels are numbered from 1, for the level closest to the data, to x (here 3) for the master level.

It can be seen that index blocks hold many entries, that is, have a large fanout ratio, so that the number of levels remains small. In the case above, during processing two levels of the index will be used from disk while the master index remains available in core memory, and we can expect a total of three accesses which read blocks in order to fetch a data record.

A record-oriented index for the same file would be B/R, or 10, times as large but would use the same number of levels, as can be seen by recomputing Example 19-9 for 10^6 index entries. The case of a block-anchored index kept on the same cylinder as the data referenced can be evaluated for the same file as follows:

Example 19-10 Hardware-Oriented Index Design Using a disk with cylinders capable of holding 266,000 bytes, we find on each cylinder (266,000/2000) = 133 blocks. Index entries which match sequential hardware units do not need a pointer field, since entry 1 simply corresponds to block 1, etc. The index will require 133(14) = 1862 bytes or one block on each cylinder, leaving 132 blocks for data. There also will be the next higher level index to the indexes to the data. The file occupies $10^6(200)/(132(2000))$ = 758 cylinders. The cylinder index does not require a pointer field either, since it simply has one entry per sequential cylinder. The total cylinder index requires 758(14) = 10,612 bytes, or 6 blocks with 142 entries each. In practice, when using cylinder-resident first-level indexes, the cylinder index will also reside within the diskpack. Given diskpacks of 200 cylinders, each cylinder index will use 2800 bytes (two blocks), and a master index will have one entry per diskpack, or four entries for this file. If block sizes cannot be increased for the index, the access to the cylinder index here requires two block reads. With two buffers the loss of one revolution can yet be avoided.

We find in this example that the hardware-oriented indexing structure has a higher fanout (132,142) and hence a smaller master index. The actual values will depend on blocking size and file size. The software index structure is more flexible to adapt to specific file requirements. It can be seen that the trees describing these index organizations are very broad, rather than high.

The measure of the breadth of a tree is the fanout ratio. In Fig. 19-15 there are symbolic examples of a small and a large fanout ratio. The trees are not presented in the traditional computer-science upside-down fashion, so that the process to fetch a leaf on the tree starts in the figure from the bottom, at the root. The fanout ratio is a very important parameter in the analysis of indexed file organizations and will be encountered frequently.

The Overflow In order to insert records into the file, some free space has to be reserved. We can place insertions to the file in a separate file, or reserve space

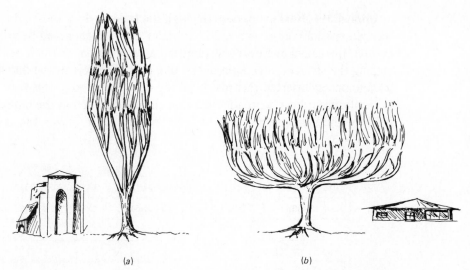

FIG. 19-15   Italian and Monterey cypress (a) Low fanout (b) High fanout

in every block for insertions, or reserve space in every cylinder for inserted records. A separate insertion file requires a separate access with seek and latency overhead at any point where an insertion had been made. Allocating space in every block is feasible only if blocks are large and insertions are well distributed; otherwise it is too easy to run out of space.

Keeping spare space in every cylinder provides a reasonable compromise: to locate an overflow record will require rotational latency but not a seek. The cylinder address is obtained from the index using the attribute key value of the record being inserted by matching the entry for the nearest predecessor. The new record is placed in the next sequential free position in the cylinder-overflow area.

Cylinder-overflow areas have to be carefully dimensioned. If insertions cluster in certain areas, the corresponding cylinders will need large overflow areas. If the system provides a space allocation so that all cylinder-overflow areas are of equal size, as most do, much space can be wasted in cylinders that are not receiving many insertions. An escape hatch can be the provision of a single and separate secondary overflow area that is used when any cylinder-overflow area itself overflows. Now the objective of avoiding seek time is lost for the records placed in the secondary overflow area; specifically, serial access will be quite slow. There are two alternatives to gain access to the primary overflow.

Indirect Overflow Access through the Sequential File   The pointers to inserted records are commonly placed with the predecessor records in the primary data blocks (see Fig. 19-14). The key of the inserted record is not kept there; only the pointer is put into the sequential file, so that a search for any intervening record is directed to the overflow area. This procedure avoids modification of the index to reflect the insertion but adds one block reading time to every fetch for an inserted record. A request for a nonexistent record will require going to the overflow file if the search argument follows the key of a primary record with an overflow indication.

Immediate Overflow Access through the Index   To indicate that an inserted record exists, a pointer is used. If an index entry is anchored to every record of the file, the associated overflow pointer can also be put in the index. When processing the sequential portion of the file, these pointers in the index entries are used to access inserted records. Now the decision to go to the overflow area for a specific record can be made based on the information in the index, so that the fetch of the primary block is avoided. Figure 19-16 shows the corresponding

		Primary entries		Overflow entries	
		013-04-1234	11	075-17-6317	110.3
	1	134-01-5839	12	156-88-4321	111.2
		173-21-1378	13	—	Λ
		...	...	...	...
	2	...	...	...	...
		...	...	...	...
		...	...	...	...
		...	...	....	...
	3	616-00-3177	b-1	704-43-0314	111.1
		711-10-6714	b	—	Λ
		End			

Master index / Index to data records

013-47-1234	1
307-10-4837	2
616-00-3177	3
End	

FIG. 19-16   Index for immediate access to overflow area

index; the primary file does not have fields pointing to the overflow area. The maintenance of an expanding index requires a processing effort when the file is being updated. Maintenance is simplified in the design shown above by allocating an overflow pointer space with every record entry, doubling the size of the index. The large index will, however, increase index processing time. For block-anchored indexes the increase in index size would be very great. This method is mainly of interest when the overflow area is not on the same cylinders as the corresponding primary records, so that the saving in fetch time becomes important.

Chaining of Overflow Records   In order to locate multiple overflows from one primary record, pointers are also placed in the records in the overflow areas. All such records are linked into a **chain,** possibly through many blocks of the overflow area. A new record can be linked into the chain, so that sequential order is maintained.

When the fetch has to proceed via many inserted records, in a large number of blocks, following the chain to a specific record may actually be less efficient than simply searching the overflow area exhaustively. On the other hand, serial processing is greatly simplified when we can follow the chain. In order not to lose the records from the sequential file buffer when processing, a separate overflow buffer should be available. To avoid this cost, IBM ISAM uses blocks based on the record size in the overflow area.

Push-through   An alternate method of placing overflow records maintains the key sequence in the blocks of the primary file. New records are inserted after their proper predecessor; successor records are pushed toward the end of the block. Records from the end of the primary block are pushed out into the overflow area. Figure 19-17 illustrates the **push-through** process using the same

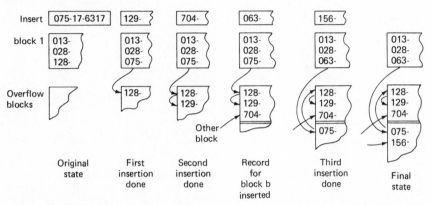

FIG. 19-17   Successive insertions into a block of an indexed-sequential file with push-through

insertion sequence which led to Fig. 19-14. The final state of the file is shown in Fig. 19-18. The index is identical, does not change, and is depicted symbolically. Now only one overflow pointer is required per primary block and only one jump is made to the overflow file per block. The overflow file still is processed as indicated earlier. The chains, however, will be longer. A fetch of a record placed in the overflow area will take longer on the average. If the access time between the sequential-file area and the overflow file area is greater than the access time between overflow blocks (i.e., the two areas are not on the same cylinder), then serial processing will be faster when using push-through.

Reorganization   At or before the time when the overflow areas themselves overflow, a file reorganization is required. Reorganization can also be needed when, owing to the creation of long chains, the fetch or serial processing time becomes excessive. Such a reorganization consists of reading the file in the manner that would be used when doing serial processing and writing it anew, leaving out all records that are marked deleted, and writing all new and old remaining records sequentially into the main areas of the new file. During this processing, the reorganization programs will create new indexes based on new anchor-point values.

The frequency of such reorganization is dependent on the insertion activity within the file. In practice one finds time intervals ranging from a day to a year between reorganization runs. Since a reorganization run can take a long time, the reorganization is generally performed before the file is actually full to avoid unpleasant surprises at busy times. It may simply be scheduled on a periodic

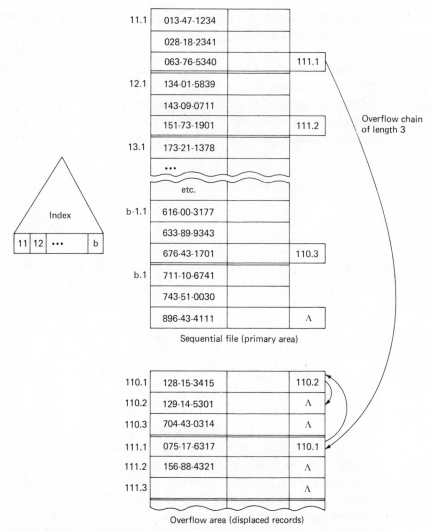

FIG. 19-18 Indexed-sequential file overflow with push-through of records

basis or be done in the next convenient period after the overflow area exceeds a certain limit of entries.

Use of Indexed-Sequential Files

Indexed-sequential files of the limited type discussed above are in common use in modern commercial processing. They are used especially where there is a need to keep files up to date within time frames that are less than the processing intervals which are possible with cyclical reorganization of sequential files. An indexed-sequential file can, for instance, be used to produce an inventory listing on a daily basis but be reorganized on a weekly basis in concert with a process which generates orders for goods for which the stock is low.

Indexed-sequential files are also in common use to handle inquiries, with the restriction that the query must specify the key attribute. Sometimes copies of the same data are found sequenced according to different keys in separate indexed-sequential files to overcome this restriction. Updating cost and space requirements are multiplied in that case.

The effects of the alternate design choices frequently are not understood by the users, so that many systems which are indexed-sequential files take longer to process data than seems warranted. In situations where files receive updates in clusters, the generated chains can be long and costly to follow. Often clustered updates are actually additions to the end of a file. By treating these separately or by preallocating space and index values in the indexed-sequential file during the prior reorganization, the liabilities of appended records can be reduced. Within one indexed-sequential-file method the options are often limited, but a number of alternative indexed-sequential-file designs are available from computer manufacturers and from independent software producers. The restriction that only one attribute key determines the major order of the file and hence that all other attribute values are less suitable as search arguments is common to all sequential files.

Performance of Indexed-Sequential Files

The performance evaluation of indexed-sequential files is more complex than the evaluation of the two preceding file-organization methods because of the many options possible in the detailed design. We will base the evaluation on a simple form similar to the most common commercial designs.

The index is parallel in sequence to the data file itself. The first-level index is anchored to blocks of data, and a second-level index has one entry per first-level index block. The first-level index, the data areas, and the overflow area are all kept on the same cylinder. The total file occupies multiple cylinders.

After a reorganization the data areas and the index areas are full and the overflow areas are empty. When a record is added, it is placed into the overflow area and linked between the data records in order to maintain a functional sequence. To make this possible, a pointer position is allocated in every record. Records to be deleted are not actually removed but only marked as invalid. An additional field or a null indicator in the record is required for such a deletion flag. The pointer has to be maintained for references to the overflow area. No change of the index takes place between reorganizations, which simplifies the insertion procedure. All areas are blocked to an equal size B.

Record Size in an Indexed-Sequential File   In the sequential part of the file, a record requires space for a data values and for the pointer to a possible overflow area.

$$R = aV + P$$

Additional space is allocated for o overflow records. These records also have a pointer to take care of chaining; each overflow record also requires

$$R_o = aV + P$$

In addition, there exists an index with key values and pointers. The size of an index entry is $V + P$. The first-level index contains one entry per data block, so that

$$i1 = \left\lceil n \left/ \left\lfloor \frac{B}{R} \right\rfloor \right. \right\rceil$$

entries are required. For the second-level index there will be one entry per first-level index block. The fanout ratio for the index itself is

$$y = \left\lfloor \frac{B}{V + P} \right\rfloor$$

so that the number of entries for the second and higher levels of the index is

$$i_{\text{level}} = \left\lceil \frac{i_{\text{level}-1}}{y} \right\rceil$$

The number of blocks required for the first-level index is equal to i_2 and the number of blocks at successive levels is equal to the number of entries at the level below, until one block can contain the entire root of the index tree. The total space for a three-level index will be

$$SI = (i_2 + i_3 + i_4)B = (i_2 + i_3 + 1)B$$

When blocks of the first-level index reside on the same cylinder as the indexed data, an amount of space adequate for one index entry per data block should be reserved.

A sample calculation for the total space required for a file as shown in Fig. 19-19, using record-anchored indexes, is given in Example 19-11. The calculation evaluates the capacity of one cylinder.

Example 19-11 Calculation of Cylinder Capacity For an Indexed-Sequential File

Parameters:
  $R = 200$ (including the linkage pointer of 6 bytes length)
  $B = 2000$
  $V = 14, P = 6$
  Blocks per track = 7, surfaces per cylinder = 19, overflow allocation = 20 percent
Allocation:
  Primary-index size per record = $(14 + 6)/[2000/200] = 2$ bytes
  Overflow space per record = $0.20(200) = 40$ bytes
  Maximum number of primary data records per cylinder
= $[(19(7)(2000))/(200 + 2 + 40)] = 1099$
  Net number of data records, truncated to a multiple of $B/R = 10$, per cylinder = 1090
  Space for overflow records in whole blocks/cylinder = $1090(0.20) = 220$
  Number of primary index entries/cylinder = $1090(200/2000) = 109$
  Number of primary index blocks/cylinder = $\lceil(109(20))/2000\rceil = 2$
  Verification: blocks used versus blocks available = $(1090 + 220)/\lceil(2000/200) + 2\rceil$ versus $19(7)$ or $133 \leq 133$ is just adequate.
  Note: If this verification indicates that a larger number of blocks was required because of the rounding-up procedures, then the number of data blocks has to be reduced. The total space per record (excluding the relatively very small higher-level indexes) is now $133(2000)/1090 = 245$ bytes.

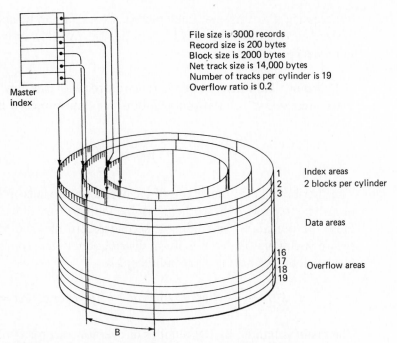

File size is 3000 records
Record size is 200 bytes
Block size is 2000 bytes
Net track size is 14,000 bytes
Number of tracks per cylinder is 19
Overflow ratio is 0.2

Master
index

Index areas
2 blocks per cylinder

Data areas

Overflow areas

FIG. 19-19 Illustration of indexed-sequential-file layout

The file in Fig. 19-19 now requires $\lceil 3000/1090 \rceil = 3$ cylinders with a master index of 6 entries. The total space per record after reorganization is then

$$R_{\text{total}} = R + \frac{o}{n} R_o + \frac{SI}{n}$$

In general, the record sizes R and R_o will be equal.

Fetch Record in an Indexed-Sequential File   To locate a specific record, the index will be used. Given a file which has a size similar to the file used in Example 19-11, the master index will not require a disk access, since it will have been placed into a table in core storage when the file was opened. The fetch process will consist of a look-up in the master table, a seek to the cylinder, a read of the index, and a read of the data block, requiring

$$T_{FO} = c + s + r + btt + r + btt \qquad \text{if } o = 0$$

However, if insertions have occurred, the procedure will fail to find an inserted record and will have to continue to the overflow-file area. The probability that the desired record is in the overflow area Pov depends on the number of insertions o' that the file has received. For a fetch where any record is equally probable,

$$Pov = \frac{o'}{n + o'}$$

The number of records in the sequential file which will have overflow pointers rop will be equal to or less than o', since multiple overflows may be chained from one primary record. The expected length of the chains determines the cost of accessing the overflows. Each record of the chain to be accessed will, in general, require the reading of a block, since the overflow area is not maintained in sequence.

Overflow Chain Length   Given *rop* records with overflow pointers in the Primary area, $rop \le o'$, the probability of a primary record having an overflow pointer is

$$P1f = \frac{rop}{n}$$

The distribution over the chains of the overflows depends on the pattern of keys of arriving records. We will here assume the best case, a **uniform distribution.** Here the probability of finding a second record chained to a given overflow record, assuming the same uniform distribution, is also rop/n, so that the overall probability of having a second record is

$$P2f = \frac{rop}{n} P1f = P1f^2 \text{ or } \quad \text{in general, } Pif = P1f^i.$$

The chain is limited by the number of overflow records o'. The total expected sum of records *Ptf* chained to a primary record is hence

$$Ptf = P1f + P2f + \cdots + Po'f$$

and this accounts for all overflow records, so that also

$$Pov = Ptf$$

The expression for *Ptf* in terms of *Pif* is a geometric series (without the initial term of 1 for $i = 0$), so that

$$Pov = Ptf = \sum_{i=1}^{o'} P1f^i = \frac{1 - P1f^{o'+1}}{1 - P1f} - 1$$

which, as o' gets large (>20) while $P1f \ll 1$ (<0.5) becomes

$$Pov = Ptf = \frac{P1f}{1 - P1f} \quad \text{so that} \quad P1f = \frac{Pov}{1 + Pov}$$

Then the expected length of the chains *Lc* is

$$Lc = \frac{Pov}{P1f} = 1 + Pov$$

An insertion requires traversal of the entire chain to link the record at the end.

$$Lc_I = Lc = 1 + Pov$$

A fetch requires the average length to be traversed.

$$Lc_F = \frac{1 + Lc}{2} = 1 + \frac{1}{2} Pov$$

Now, if s_{ov} is the seek time to the overflow area,

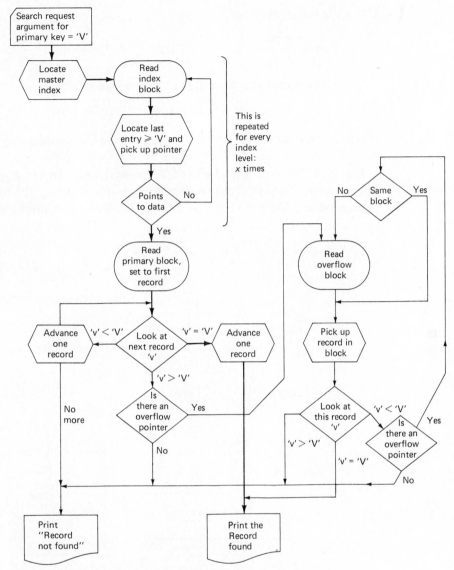

FIG. 19-20 Fetch a specific record in an indexed-sequential file

$$T_F = T_{FO} + Pov(s_{ov} + Lc_F(r + btt))$$

The process is illustrated in Fig. 19-20. Using cylinder-based overflow areas $s_{ov} = 0$, and

$$T_F = T_{FO} + PovLc_F(r + btt)$$

$$= c + s + \left(2 + Pov\left(1 + \frac{1}{2}Pov\right)\right)(r + btt)$$

Estimation of Fetch Time   If reorganizations are made when the overflow area is 80 percent full, the average value of o' will be $0.4o$. If in this case an overflow area equal to 20 percent of the prime file has been allocated, then

$$o' = (0.20)(0.4)n = 0.08n$$

Using the relations above,

$$Pov = \frac{0.08}{1.08} = 0.0741 \quad \text{and} \quad Lc_F = 1 + \frac{0.0741}{2} = 1.037$$

With these assumptions we arrive at an average fetch time of

$$T_F = c + s + 2.077(r + btt)$$

Nonuniform insertion distributions can increase T_F considerably.

Get-Next Record of an Indexed-Sequential File In order to locate a successor record, we start from the last data record, ignoring the index. We have to determine whether serial reading can be done sequentially or whether we

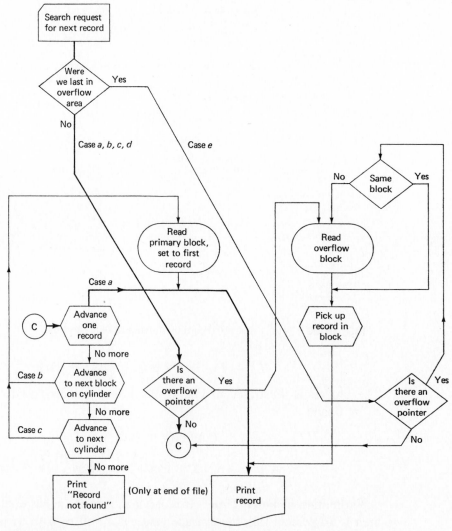

FIG. 19-21 Get the successor record in an indexed-sequential file. Note that the flow in this figure overlaps Fig. 19-20 to a great extent

have to go to another area. A number of possibilities exist depending on the locations of the predecessor and the successor record. The five cases distinguished are illustrated using the record numbers of Fig. 19-14. The process is flowcharted in Fig. 19-21.

Path Choices for Next Record

- There has been no insertion following the last record, and the successor record is in the same primary data block already available in core (last record is 12.1).
- There has been no intervening insertion, but the record is in a following block on the same cylinder (last record is 12.3).
- There has been no insertion, but the record is in a new block on another cylinder [given that there are β blocks per cylinder, and the file begins at a new cylinder, this would happen between records $\beta.3$ and $(\beta + 1).1$, $2\beta.3$ and $(2\beta + 1).1$, etc.].
- There has been an insertion, and the successor record will be in an overflow block (last record is 12.2).
- The last record is an inserted record, so that for the successor, a new block, data or overflow, on the same cylinder has to be read (last record is 110.1 or 111.1).

We will summarize the conditions using Fig. 19-21 to illustrate the probabilities of these cases with the following notation:

Pd Current record is in a primary data block $= 1 - Pov$.

Pm There has been no intervening insertion $= 1 - Plf$ (see definition above).

Pb The record is in the same block $= 1 - R/B$.

Pc The block is in the same cylinder $= 1 - 1/\beta$.

Figure 19-22 indicates the conditions based on the previous figure. We can state then that, by applying the appropriate combination of probabilities to their costs,

$$
\begin{aligned}
T_N = & (Pd)(Pm)(Pb)(c) + & &/* \text{ case } a */\\
& (Pd)(Pm)(1 - Pb)(Pc)(r + btt) + & &/* \text{ case } b */\\
& (Pd)(Pm)(1 - Pb)(1 - Pc)(s + r + btt) + & &/* \text{ case } c */\\
& (Pd)(1 - Pm)(r + btt) + & &/* \text{ case } d */\\
& (1 - Pd)(r + btt) & &/* \text{ case } e */
\end{aligned}
$$

Both Pd and Pm can be rewritten in terms of Pov using the chain-length results as derived above.

The result found above can be simplified if cylinder seeks can be ignored (i.e., β is large, so that the value of $Pc \approx 1$), if we neglect the core-search time c for

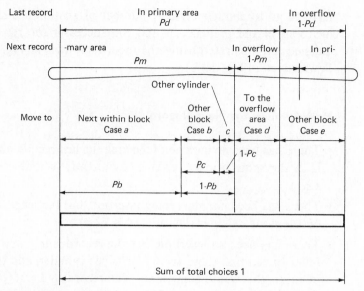

FIG. 19-22 Conditions in the search for a successor record

records within the block and if we consider Pov to be sufficiently small so that terms containing Pov^2 can be neglected.

$$T_N = \left(\frac{R}{B} + 2Pov \left(1 - \frac{R}{B} \right) \right) (r + btt)$$

Insert into an Indexed-Sequential File Adding records to the file will always require the reading and rewriting of the predecessor record, since a pointer will have to be inserted or changed. The new record also requires a read and rewrite of the current overflow block. The fetch time for the predecessor is equal to T_F, the overflow block is on the same cylinder and requires $r + btt$ to be reached, and each rewrite will take one revolution $T_{RW} = 2r$, so that

$$T_I = T_F + 2r + r + btt + 2r = T_F + 5r + btt$$

Update Record in an Indexed-Sequential File An update of equal size and identical key could be put into the original spot, so that the process is similar to the fetch strategy but incorporates an extra write of time T_{RW}

$$T_{Uid} = T_F + 2r \qquad \text{for nonkey field changes}$$

In the general case, the previous version of the record is deleted and the new record inserted appropriately. A deletion rewrites the old record with an **invalid** indicator but keeps the key and pointer fields intact so that the structure of the file is not violated. Then

$$T_U = T_{Uid} + T_I = 2T_F + 7r + btt$$

The special case of T_{Uid} is not recognized by many systems except for explicit deletions, so that all updates require T_U.

Read Entire Indexed-Sequential File An exhaustive search of the file has to be made when the search argument is not the indexed attribute. A choice exists whether the file still is to be read serially or whether the entire data area on a cylinder is to be read sequentially, followed by sequential reading of the entire overflow area. Most systems provide only the ability to read serially, so that for **serial reading,**

$$T_X = T_F + (n + o' - 1)T_N \approx (n + o')T_N$$

If the primary data block can be kept available, the primary area can be read, using the bulk transfer rate, while overflows are still processed serially. Then for **serial buffered reading,**

$$T_X = n\frac{R}{t'} + o'(r + btt)$$

While an overflow block is being read, the main block can be retained and processed further.

In the alternative case, **sequential reading,** the evaluation would consider the effective transfer rate, neglecting the delay when skipping from data blocks to overflow blocks, since this occurs at most once per cylinder. For sequential reading,

$$T_X = (n + o')\frac{R}{t'}$$

Reorganization of an Indexed-Sequential File   To reorganize the old file, the entire file is read serially and rewritten without the use of overflow areas. As a by-product a new index is constructed. The prior index can be ignored, since the file is read serially. We now assume that o' new records are in the overflow areas. We also assume that the reorganization program can handle multiple blocks simultaneously as in the serial buffered case above. Two additional buffers in core are needed to collect the new data and index information. These can be written out sequentially whenever they are filled. Then

$$T_Y = n\frac{R}{t'} + o'(r + btt) + (n + o' - d)\left(\frac{R}{t'} + \frac{SI}{t'}\right)$$

The value of o' will be less than o, the number of records for which overflow space has been allocated. We assumed earlier $o' = 0.8\,o$. Such a value would be justified if the reorganization policy were as follows:

Reorganization of a file is to be done the first night the overflow area exceeds 75 percent utilization and the average daily increase of the overflow area is 10 percent.

A simpler assumption that $o' = o$ will provide a conservative approximation for the number of overflow records to be processed.

19-14 THE INDEXED FILE

When there is no requirement for sequentiality to provide efficient serial access, an **indexed file** can be used. In an indexed file (Fig. 19-23) the records are

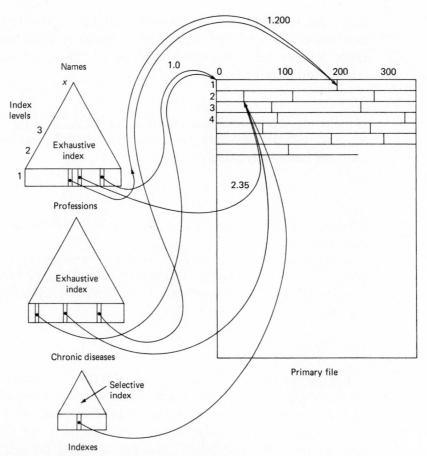

FIG. 19-23 Record linkage in an indexed file

accessed only through one or more indexes. Now there is no restriction on the placement of a data record, as long as a pointer exists in some index that allows the record to be fetched when the goal data from the record is wanted. One index will be associated with one key attribute, and indexes can exist for all attributes for which a search argument can be expected. With the loss of sequentiality relative to a primary key attribute, a gain in flexibility is obtained which may make this organization preferable to the indexed-sequential file organization.

Inverted Files A file for which indexes have been created is sometimes referred to as an **inverted file.** This term has its origin in bibliographic indexing and will be used carefully in this section. An exhaustive index to a file that contains only English text may have as entries all the unique words (types) in the file, and is essentially a vocabulary, with pointers to all the instances (tokens) in the text where the words appear. If the pointers are augmented by a sample of the text, the result assumes the form of a **concordance.** The language used for the text is, of course, not restricted to English. An excerpt from a concordance is shown in Fig. 19-24. In a text file there is only one attribute domain, **words,** and the index has multiple entries per record, one for each word. Partial inversions may exclude high-frequency words or other words not of

Sample of text

Key—attribute value   Pointer

, quant vit pasmer Rollant, / dunc out tel	doel unkes mais n'out si grant. / Tendit sa mai	2223
la sele en remeint guaste. / Mult ad grant	doel Carlemagnes li reis, / quant Naimun veit	3451
c. / Co dist li reis: "Seignurs, vengez voz	doels, / si esclargiez voz talenz e voz coers,	3627
chevaler." / Respont li quens: " Deus le me	doinst venger!" / Sun cheval brochet des esperu	1548
ad mort France ad mis en exill. / Si grant	dol ai que ne voldreie vivre, / de ma maisnee,	2936
d sanc. / Franceis murrunt, Carles en ert	dolent. / Tere Majur vos metrum en present.	951
ent, / e cil d' Espaigne s'en cleiment tuit	dolent. / Dient Franceis: "Ben fiert nostre gu	1651
alchet ireement, / e li Franceis curucus e	dolent; / n'i ad celoi n'i plurt e se dement,	1835
ma gent." / E cil respunt "Tant sy jo plus	dolent. / Ne pois a vos tenir lung parlement:	2835
sil duluset; / jamais en tere n'orrez plus	dolent hume! / Or veit Rollant gue mort est su	2023
devers les porz d' Espairne: / veeir poez,	dolente est la rereguarde; / ki ceste fait, jan	1104
e vient curant cuntre lui; / si li ad dit:	"Dolente, si mare fui! / A itel hunte, sire, mon	2823
pereres cevalchet par irur / e li Franceis	dolenz e curucus; / n'i ad celoi ki durement ne	1813
aienur, / plurent e crient, demeinent grant	dolor, / pleignent lur deus, Tervagan e Mahum	2695
perere,' co dist Gefrei d' Anjou, / "ceste	dolor ne demenez tant fort! / Par tut le camp f	2946
ance ad en baillie, / que me remembre de la	dolur e l'ire, / co est de Basan e de sun frer	489
amimunde, / pluret e criet, mult forment se	doluset; / ensembl'od li plus de xx. mil humes,	2577
out mais en avant. / Par tuz les prez or se	dorment li Franc. / N'i ad cheval ki puisset e	2521
ad apris ki bien conuist ahan. / Karles se	dort cum hume traveillet. / Seint Gabriel li a	2525
poeent plus faire. / Ki mult est las, il se	dort cuntre tere. / Icele noit n'unt unkes esca	2494
it le jur, la noit se aserie. / Carles se	dort, li empereres riches. / Sunjat qu'il eret	718
ent liquels d'els la veintrat. / Carles se	dort, mie ne s'esveillat. AOI. / Tresvait la no	736
le cel en volent les escicles. / Carles se	dort, qu'il ne s'esveillet mie. / Apres iceste,	724
s Deu co ad mustret al barun. / Carles se	dort tresqu'al demain, al cler jur. / Li reis	2569
et les os, / tute l'eschine li desevret del	dos, / od sun espiet l'anme li getet fors,	1201
gemmet ad or, / e al cheval parfundement el	dos; / ambure ocit, ki quel blasme ne quil lot.	1588
eruns a or, / fiert Oliver derere en mi le	dos. / Le blanc osberc li ad descust el cors,	1945
ros: / sur les eschines qu'il unt en mi les	dos / cil sunt seiet ensement cume porc. AOI.	3222
re joe en ad tute sanglente; / l'osberc del	dos josque par sum le ventre. / Deus le guarit	3922
ele les dous alves d'argent / e al ceval le	dos parfundement; / ambure ocist seinz nul reco	1649
t li ber. / De cels d' Espaigne unt lur les	dos turnez, / tenent l'enchalz, tuit en sunt cu	2445
a fuls: / de cent millers n'en poent guarir	dous. / Rollant dist: "Nostre jume sunt mult p	1440
s e l'osberc jazerenc, / de l'oree sele les	dous alves d'argent / e al ceval le dos parfund	1648
tet en ad, ne poet muer n'en plurt. / Desuz	dous arbres parvenuz est . . . . li reis. / Les c	2874
Dedesuz Ais est la pree mult large: / des	dous baruns justee est la bataille. / Cil suṇt	3874
agne, ki est canuz e vielz! / Men escientre	dous cenz anz ad e mielz. / Par tantes teres ad	539
t vielz, si ad sun tens uset: / men escient	dous cenz anz ad passet. / Par tantes teres at	524

FIG. 19-24 Sample of a concordance of the Chanson de Roland. (From Joseph J. Duggan, "A Concordance of the Chanson de Roland," Ohio State University Press, Columbus, 1969)

interest, such as initials of authors. The terms inverted index, inverted list, inverted file, and partially inverted file are used very inconsistently in the literature, and frequently imply indexing as described below. Indexing in a bibliographic context is the selection or creation of significant attribute values for subsequent retrieval. Sometimes a copy of a sequential file, when sorted according to another key attribute, has been called an inverted file.

Structure and Manipulation of Indexed Files

There may be as many indexes as there are attribute types in the file. An index for an attribute of an indexed file consists of an entry for every record placed in the sequence determined by the attribute values. Each entry consists of the attribute value and a pointer to the record. In indexed files successor records are reached using the next index entry rather than sequentiality or pointers from the predecessor record. Each index may require multiple levels as shown with the index for an indexed-sequential file.

The data-record format may be similar to any of the previous organizations. Records containing attribute name-value pairs, as seen in the pile file, will be preferred if the attribute density a'/a is low; otherwise structured records may be employed. Since the pointers in the index specify the block address and record position for every record, there is essentially no restriction on record size or on the placement of records within a specific block. Records can be inserted wherever the file system determines that sufficient free space is available.

Exhaustive and Selective Indexes   Indexes may be **exhaustive,** that is, have pointers to every record in the file, or **selective,** that is, have only pointers to records where the attribute value is significant. Significance can be defined by the fact that a value exists (is not undefined or zero) or can be limited to instances where attribute values fall within a range which makes them likely keys for retrieval.

An example of such a selective index could occur in a personnel health file where only indexes of current or chronic diseases are maintained, although a more complete record is kept for statistical or individual purposes in the data file itself. Such an instance is shown symbolically in Fig. 19-23 as a "chronic disease" index. Another selected index for a health file could point to all individuals with a cholesterol level greater than 250, if frequent reference to this fact is made, for instance, in regular meal preparation.

If there is not even one exhaustive index, a space-allocation table is required to allow the file to be properly maintained. Such a table gives an accounting of all the space allocated to the file. If the file is read serially according to this table, a record ordering similar to the pile file may be perceived.

Maintenance of Indexes   The major problem in the use of indexed files is caused by the need to update all the indexes that refer to a record whenever a record has been added, deleted, or moved; and the need to change single indexes when a field value has been changed. In indexed-sequential files updating of the index was avoided through the use of pointer chains to insertions. The use of multiple overflow chains would not be consistent with the design of the indexed file, so that index maintenance is essential. It can be impractical to attempt to change all indexes immediately. High-priority fetch requests using the file may want to be processed before all indexes are brought up to date.

The continuous maintenance of indexes can be quite time-consuming. Sometimes indexes are created from a file for a particular analysis but are not kept up to date when the file changes. Sometimes indexes are updated only periodically, which causes recent information to be inaccessible.

The updating of the indexes may then be done at times when the computer is relatively idle. If such updating can be performed incrementally, a periodic wholesale reorganization can be avoided so that the file is kept available. Such index updating will be done by a process which is active at a low priority until it is completed. It is necessary to keep the old record in place until assurance exists that all referring indexes have been updated. Updating while the file is otherwise active requires careful sequencing of update operations and the maintenance of status information on incomplete updates. In some applications, use of recently obsoleted data may not matter. If it does, however, the old record is best marked as invalid: **deleted** or **moved.** In the latter case, the marker can provide an indication of the new location. For new attribute values, the new record will not be retrievable according to the corresponding attribute key until the relevant index has been updated. A relatively higher priority may be assigned to a process which updates important attribute indexes than to other index-update processes.

Anchor Points   The important technique of only assigning blocks or anchor points to reduce index size, which was used in the indexed-sequential file organization, is not available here, since index and data are not cosequential. This makes it necessary for the lowest-level index to have an entry for every significant record.

Use of Indexed Files

Indexed files are used mainly in areas where timeliness of information is highly critical. Examples are found in airline-reservation systems, job banks, military data systems, and other inventory-type areas. Here data is rarely processed serially, other than for occasional, maybe only yearly, stocktaking.

When an item of information is obtained, e.g., a free seat on a certain flight, the data should be correct at that time, and if the item is updated, i.e., a seat is sold on that flight, that fact should be immediately known throughout the system.

Another aspect of multi-indexing of such information is that one now can find the information of flight number, by passenger name, by interline transfer record, and so forth, without file reorganization or data redundancy. There is, of course, redundancy between the contents of the index and the data.

Other instances where indexed files are desirable occur when data is highly variable and dynamic. The flexibility of the record format and placement available with indexed files does not exist in other file systems. If only one key attribute is required, such flexibility can also be provided by tree-structured files. When the data is all indexed, all information is also contained in the index, and one could conceivably eliminate the data file itself. This possibility is referred to as a **phantom** file. A transposed file presents an alternative to an indexed file when serial access is important.

Performance of Indexed Files

The performance of indexed files is easier to evaluate than the performance of the preceding indexed-sequential file designs. The critical decisions are made when the number of attributes that are to be indexed is determined. Exhaustive indexes for all attributes will easily exceed the size of the original file. In practice, there are always some attributes for which indexing is not justified. This will reduce the size of the index but will not affect the other performance factors as long as no searches try to use this index. Attributes that have low partitioning effectiveness are poor candidates for indexing.

The evaluation considers a completely indexed file, only one level of indexing per attribute, with sparse occurrence of data attribute values so that variable-length data records and selective indexes are used.

Record Size in an Indexed File The space requirement for the data portion of such a file is identical to the pile-file requirement. In addition, there will be a indexes to provide an index for every attribute. Since the data attributes are sparse, there are only a' attributes per record; the average index contains $n\, a'/a$ index entries referring to data records, and each entry is of size $V' + P$. The space requirement per record is equal to the sum of index and data space. Since all attribute values which exist in a given record are indexed, the space allocated to a record is

$$R_{\text{total}} = a'(V' + P) + a'(A + V + 2)$$

for index and data.

The value field in an index may be required to be of fixed length to allow fast searches through the index, so that V' may be larger than the average value field V in a data record. On the other hand, if there frequently are multiple records related to a certain attribute value (for example, the attribute category is "profession," so that we have many entries in this index for an attribute value like "welder"), then one value entry may serve many pointers. Techniques can reduce key-value sizes of indexes further, so that $V' < V$. If V' is assumed to be equal to V, then

$$R\text{total} = a'\,(A + 2V + P + 2)$$

based on the above relation.

Additional index blocks will be used if multilevel indexing is required. In most designs, that additional number amounts to only a small percentage of storage space, as will be shown in Example 19-12.

Index Loading and Growth When there are frequent insertions, it can be desirable to leave extra space in the index blocks. If the index is initially 80 percent loaded, we have allowed for up to 20 percent additions, or for $o = n/4$. This can be expressed as an initial **loading density** of 0.8. The index will be larger, inversely proportional to the initial loading density, so that

$$R_{\text{total}} = a'\,\frac{n + o}{n}\,(V' + P) + a'(A + V + 2)$$

but the data area will expand only in proportion to the actual number of records. An algorithm to handle index-block growth, **B-trees,** creates two half-full index blocks whenever one index block overflows, which replace the overflowing block. With every split one more entry is put into the next level up. When the top level splits, a new master level is created beginning with just two entries. Except for the initial loading density, the number of entries per index block will range from $\frac{1}{2}(y + 1)$ (just after a split) to y (just before a split), so that the average loading density will be

$$\text{Density} = \frac{1}{2}\,\frac{\frac{1}{2}\,(y + 1),\, + y}{y} = 75 \text{ percent}$$

This determines the ongoing space requirement for the index: as the index grows, new blocks will be required, since on the average this loading ratio will be maintained. Distribution of entries over adjoining blocks before splitting a block has been suggested to increase the density of a B–tree.

A directory of attributes is also needed to locate the index corresponding to an attribute name.

Fetch Record in an Indexed File   The expected fetch time for an indexed file is similar to the time used for an indexed-sequential file. However, no overflow areas exist, and hence the term that accounts for the chasing after overflow records is eliminated. Since there will be, in general, several index subfiles, we cannot assume any more that these indexes and data will both occupy the same cylinder. The indexes will be of the larger record-anchored variety and also contain entries for recently inserted records, so that the value n here includes the o' insertions considered in indexed-sequential files. We add the accesses for index and data and find

$$T_F = s + r + btt + s + r + btt$$
$$\text{or } T_F = 2(s + r + btt)$$

for files with a single-level index.

If the assumption of a small index does not hold, additional delays are incurred. We will first consider a single index. There are two access methods. The index can be searched using a binary search, or additional levels of index can be added.

A Multilevel Index   The number of levels of indexing required is a function of the number of index elements that can be put into one index block. In order to evaluate the access, we will assume here that all indexes partition their data evenly. One index then will refer to $n(a'/a)$ records, where a' is again the expected number of attributes existing in a record. The number of data records accessible per index block is equal to the fanout ratio $y = B/(V + P)$, so that the number of first-level index blocks required is

$$N1IB = n\frac{a'/a}{B/(V + P)}$$

Higher-level indexes require one entry per lower-level index block, so that the number of second-level index blocks is

$$N2IB = \frac{N1IB}{B/(V + P)}$$

and similarly, for levels (3,4, . . . , x), until $NxIB$ is 1 or less. The number of levels required is therefore

$$x = \left\lceil \log_y\left(n\frac{a'}{a}\right) \right\rceil$$

where $y = \left\lfloor \frac{B}{V + P} \right\rfloor$

The search process is flowcharted in Fig. 19-25.

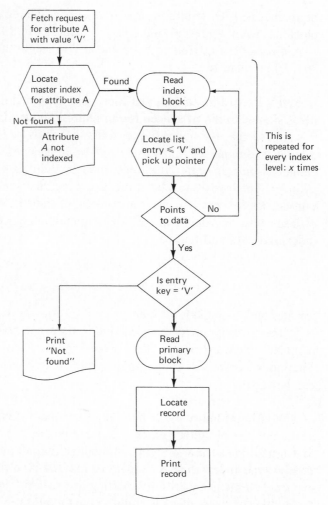

FIG. 19-25   Fetch using one index of a multi-indexed file

The value of x was evaluated iteratively in the previous section; with indexed-sequential files, the first level may be based on block-anchor points, so that there this formula was applied not to n but rather to $n R/B$.

Master Indexes in Core   The effective value of x can be reduced by 1 if either all or the currently used index blocks at level x can be kept available in core memory. To keep all master indexes available might require up to aB characters of primary storage. Since the master-level index blocks tend not to be full, about half as much space may be required in practice. Even this will generally be excessive. This possibility will not be further considered, since it requires significant scarce resources and complex core-storage management.

Example 19-12   Consider a personnel file of $n = 20{,}000$ employees, containing an inventory of their skills. Each employee has an average of 2.5 skills, so that here a'/a is actually greater than 1.

The skills are given a code of 6 characters. To find an employee record, an 8-digit pointer is used which occupies 4 character positions, giving 10 bytes per index entry. The blocks in the file system are 1000 characters long, so that 100 index elements can appear per block.

$$N1IB = 20{,}000(2.5)/100 \rightarrow 500$$
$$N2IB = 500/100 \rightarrow 5$$
$$N3IB = 5/100 \rightarrow \; < 1 \text{ block, or a table of five entries in primary memory}$$

Computing x directly,

$$x = \log_{100}(20{,}000(2.5)) = 2.69897 < 3$$

For a multilevel indexed file the fetch time is now

$$T_F = (1 + x)(s + r + btt)$$

If a single index can be kept within a cylinder, then

$$T_F = 2s + (1 + x)(r + btt)$$

Get-Next Record of an Indexed File   The search for a successor record is based on the asusmption that the last index block is still available, so that only a new record has to be fetched.

$$T_N = s + r + btt$$

This holds as long as the fanout ratio $y \gg 1$, since the probability that the current index block contains also the pointer to the next record is $(y - 1)/y$.

Insert into an Indexed File   To add a record to an indexed file, the record is placed in any free area, and then all a' indexes referring to existing attributes for this record have to be updated. If there is enough space within the index blocks (the index loading density < 1), the insertion process will only have to find, read, and rewrite updated index blocks.

Summing the times for data-block fetch and rewrite, for following the a' indexes down x levels, and for first-level index rewrites, we find

$$T_I' = s + r + btt + 2r + xa'(s + r + btt) + a'2r$$
$$\text{or } T_I' = (1 + xa')s + (3 + xa' + 2a')r + (1 + xa')btt$$

Keeping indexes within a cylinder can reduce these times also. If all indexes are small so that $x = 1$,

$$T_I' = (1 + a')(s + 3r + btt)$$

Index Overflows   In the worst case the insertion causes all index blocks to overflow so that they have to be extended or split. Then $a'x$ index blocks have to be written in addition.

The creation of one index block requires the movement of data from the one which is overflowing into a new buffer, the rewriting of the old one, the writing of the new one, and an update of the next higher-level index block. We have accounted in T_I' above for the rewriting of the old lower-level block and the reading of the higher-level block. If the higher-level block is still available in the buffer, the additional work for a single overflow is the sum of the time to write a new block and the time to rewrite the second-level block.

$$T_{Iov} = c + s + r + btt + r + btt$$

Since the rewriting of the second-level block here has been interrupted by the writing of a level 1 block, a new seek may have to occur, replacing the $r + btt$ term with $s + r + btt$ above for indexes not residing within a cylinder.

Considering all a indexes, there will be na' index entries in use. If a B-tree algorithm is used, the index blocks will vary from half full to full. There will be $N1IB$ level 1 index blocks. At a hypothetical point when all index blocks have just overflowed and been split, there will be $n\,a'$ empty entries. Each insertion requires a' new index entries. Given an optimum, uniform distribution of index updates, there will be $a\,N1IB$ index splits after n insertions, so that

$$Pov = \frac{a}{n}\,N1IB = \frac{a'}{B/(V + P)}$$

Including the above terms for lower-level index updating makes

$$T_I = T'_I + Po_v\,T_{Iov}$$

$$= (1 + a')(s + 3r + btt) + a'\,\frac{V + P}{B}\,(c + s + 2r + 2btt)$$

Index splitting at levels two or above can safely be discounted owing to the typically high value of $y = B/(V + P)$ which makes terms containing $1/y^2$ etc., insignificant. Master indexes tend to be even less full, and a master index can be dimensioned not to overflow at maximum file size using the above relationship.

Update Record in an Indexed File   An update of a record in an indexed file consists of a search followed by a change of those indexes for which the new record contains changed values. A minimal update, one field only, changes only one data record and changes only one index. When the new field value is so far removed from the old one that the old index entry is in a different block from the new one, the update requires the fetching and rewriting of the two index blocks, the old one and the new one.

$$T_U = T_F + 2r + 2(s + 3r + btt)$$

If both old and new values fall into the same index block, one fetch and rewrite may be saved, so that

$$T_U = T_F + s + 5r + btt$$

The ratio between these two types of occurrences is difficult to predict and depends on the behavior of the attribute change. For instance, if the attribute type is a person's weight, we can expect the simpler case to be predominant. Furthermore, if the update changes a value from undefined to a defined value, only a new index entry has to be created. Conservatively, we have to assume the index changes to be randomly distributed among the blocks of an index. Given an average loading density of 75 percent, there will be

$$bi = \frac{n}{y} \frac{a'}{a} \frac{1.0}{0.75}$$

primary index blocks for one attribute; then the probability, given random data changes, of requiring another index block is $Pi = (bi - 1)/bi$, so that

$$T_U = T_F + s + 5r + btt + Pi(s + 3r + btt)$$

For large files and frequent attributes Pi will be close to 1, so that

$$T_U = T_F + 2s + 8r + 2btt$$

The index seek time can again be avoided.

If multiple (a_U) attribute values change, then that many index blocks will have to be found and changed. This will make

$$T_U = T_F + 2r + 2a_U(s + 3r + btt)$$

Index blocks also may overflow here. The considerations used in insertions may be applied here also.

The uniform behavior assumed for insertion and update patterns represents the best behavior over the long term. Updating tends to be periodically heavy in one area, and then concentrate again on other attributes. These irregularities can specifically affect system response time. The additional term for these requires statistics of update behavior which we do not have available here, and we will not evaluate their effect. If a good understanding of the frequency of attribute changes and of the value-change ranges exists, a more precise estimate of update cost can be made, using the concepts discussed above.

Read Entire Indexed File The fully indexed organization effectively precludes exhaustive searches. When necessary, such searches may be accomplished by using the space-allocation information, or by serial reading of the file using some exhaustive index. An exhaustive index is created when the referred data element is required to exist in every record. A brute-force approach using such an index will cost

$$T_X = nT_F$$

If one follows the space-allocation pointers, seeks need to be done only once per block, so that here the read time for a consecutively allocated file would be equal to the time needed to read a sequential file. If the blocks are distributed randomly or found from the space allocation in a random fashion, then

$$T_X = n \frac{R}{B}\left(s + r + \frac{B}{t'}\right)$$

The records here will appear in an unpredictable order. A reduction in actual search efficiency may be caused by the processing of empty spaces created by previous deletions.

Reorganization of an Indexed File Indexed files are not as dependent on periodic reorganization as are the previous file organizations. Some implementations of indexed files in fact never need to reorganize the files. Reorganization need never affect the database itself, only a specific index, and as such it can be done incrementally, one index at a time. An average index will consist of

$$b_i = (n + o') \frac{a'}{a} \frac{V + P}{B} + bhi$$

blocks, where bhi is the number of blocks due to higher-level indexes. The time requirement then is

$$T_Y = 2ab_i(s + r + btt)$$

to reorganize all a indexes. The new index blocks are, in general, put into new disk areas so that the T_{RW} based relations are not valid. The average seek time can be reduced by using separate devices for the old and the new index.

19-15 THE DIRECT FILE

The direct file relates most closely the search argument used in the fetch of a record to the physical capabilities of direct-access mechanisms. Direct access to a file means simply that data are placed in a known position on the device (Fig. 19-26). The earliest direct-access disk files were used by electromechanical accounting machines which would use a number, punched on a card, to determine where the remainder of the card contents was to be filed. The direct-access

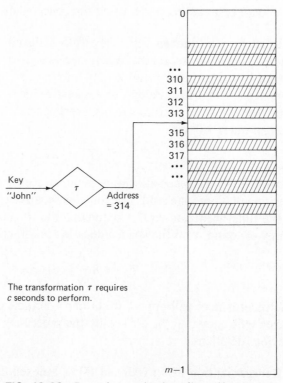

FIG. 19-26 Record accessing in a direct file

method is relatively fast, since it avoids intermediate file operations, but the method forces the data to be located according to a single key attribute, similar to the case of sequential and indexed-sequential files but not necessarily related to any predecessor records. The searches through index tables that aid in the location of a record in the indexed file organization are replaced by a computation τ whose objective it is to provide the record address.

Structure and Manipulation of Direct Files

In the simplest realization of a direct-access method, identification numbers are assigned to the data records that are equal to the disk, track, and record addresses of the file. Thus employee Joe is designated as 25-4-7, and that sequence tells us directly that his payroll record is to be found on disk number 25, track 4, as record 7. We will list a number of problems associated with the use of file addresses to identify data records, and then skip intermediate solutions to arrive at the more common current methodology.

File Addresses   The addresses in a random-access device tend not to be contiguous; i.e., they may go from 0 to 200, and then from 1000 to 1200, and so on. Apart from the fact that nobody wants to be called a zero, this causes confusion on the clerical side, since hardware knowledge has to be imparted to staff remote from the computer departments.

When the device becomes obsolete and is replaced, everything and everybody may have to be renumbered.

Identification numbers may be needed in more than one file; in fact, different subsets may be required, causing one individual or item to carry a variety of numbers.

To reuse space, the identification number has to be reassigned when a record has been deleted, causing confusion when processing past and present data together.

One may not wish to be restricted to a dense set of numbers to identify records. Natural keys are names, social security numbers, or inventory numbers where groups of successive digits have meaning. In general, the number of people or items which may be referred to or addressed by these keys is much larger than the number of records to be kept on file. In other words, the key space is much larger than the file-address space.

Key-to-Address Transformations   The solution to the problems associated with the use of file addresses involves the use of a computational procedure that translates existing identification data, i.e., key attribute values, into the address space of a disk. The procedure can be adjusted to cope with changes and multiple uses of the key. Such methods are referred to as **key-to-address transformations.** Two categories of these methods may be employed here, **deterministic procedures** which translate identification fields into unique addresses and **probabilistic techniques** which translate the keys into addresses which are as unique as possible. Figure 19-26 shows the access to a direct file for a new record with key "John." The key-to-address transformation algorithm τ applied to the string "John" has generated the relative record address "314." The same key-to-address transformation is applied to a search argument when a record is to be fetched.

A **deterministic procedure** takes the set of all key values and computes a unique corresponding disk address. Algorithms for such transformations become difficult to construct if the number of file entries is larger than a few dozen. Adding a new entry will require a new algorithm, since the algorithm is dependent on the distribution of the source keys; hence only static files can be handled conveniently. The replacement of a computational algorithm with a table makes the problem of transformation more tractable: we have invented again the indexed file! We will not discuss deterministic direct access further.

The **probabilistic transformations** translate the identification value into numeric addresses that are within the file-address space available for the file—using an algorithmic procedure. A uniform distribution of addresses is desired, since this will place an equal fraction of the keys into each and every slot.

Duplicate addresses may be generated from different source keys and this causes collisions, and we will discuss later in this section what is to be done in that case. The probabilistic transformation may try to preserve the order of the records, or it may be designed to maximize the degree of uniqueness of the resulting address. Most transformations take the latter as their only goal. The first class of transformations are called **sequence maintaining;** the other algorithms are referred to as **random key-to-address transformations** or **hashing techniques.** A family tree of key-to-address transformations is displayed in Fig. 19-27. A simple technique is illustrated in Example 19-13.

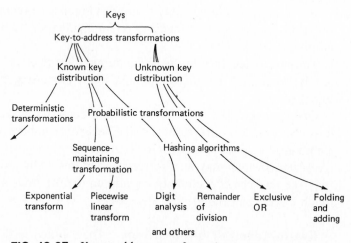

FIG. 19-27 Key-to-address transformation types

Example 19-13 Key-to-Address Transformation A randomizing transformation for a personnel file uses the social security number as the key. We assume that the value of the low-order digits of these numbers is evenly distributed and hence there is a high probability of deriving out of these digits a unique number for every employee. If one wants to allow space for 500 employees, the value of the key may be divided by 500, leaving a remainder with values between 0 and 499. Obviously identical addresses can occur:

Al	**or**	**322-45-6678**	**giving**	**178**
Joe	**or**	**123-45-6392**		**392**
Mary	**or**	**036-23-0373**		**373**
Pete	**or**	**901-23-4892**		**392**

Here Joe and Pete will both be assigned to a record number 392; the records for Joe and Pete will collide if both are placed directly into a file. Collisions are a topic presented below.

Key and Address Space A key value may range over a large number of possible values, limited only by the maximum size of the key field V. The number of legal keys may be 10^V for a numeric key, 26^V for a simple alphabetic key. For a social security number the key space size is 999,999,999. The space on the file will be much less for most users outside of the Social Security Administration. The available address space can be defined in terms of its record capacity m. The number of actual records put in the file cannot exceed the available space; hence

$$base^V \gg m \geq n$$

Since many of the key-to-address algorithms depend on a numeric key value, it may be desirable to convert alphabetic keys into numeric representations. If a value from 0 to 25 (**lettervalue**) can be assigned to the 26 letters used, a dense numeric representation can be obtained without any loss of information, using a polynomial conversion as

```
/* Letters to integers */
numeric_value = 0;
DO i = 1 TO number_of_letters;
  numeric_value = numeric_value * 26 + lettervalue (letter(i));
END;
```

Numbers and blanks require appropriate expansion of this routine, and computer-word overflow has to be considered.

To simplify the process, we assume the existence of relative-addressing capability. This provides an algorithm which translates sequential record numbers in the range from 0 to $m - 1$ into the physical address space of the disk units or whatever device is being used for the storage of the data. Now we only need to generate integers in the range 0 to $m - 1$ from the source key. It is often desirable to compute block addresses instead of addresses of specific record spaces. Multiple records can be placed into a block or bucket. The use of buckets is evaluated later.

Distribution-dependent methods depend on at least approximate knowledge of the keys to be expected. The benefits that can be gained by distribution-dependent methods depend on **open addressing,** bucket size, file density, and appropriateness of the transformation. For small buckets and a good algorithm the improvement over randomizing transforms can be significant; on the other hand, the liabilities of distribution-dependent transformations are major, since a change in key distribution can cause these methods to generate many more collisions than a randomization would generate in that case. A benefit of some distribution-dependent key-to-address transformations is that they can allow maintenance of sequentiality. Such a **sequence-maintaining key-to-address transformation** achieves this goal by letting the addresses produced increase with increasing keys. Serial access is made possible in this case. Otherwise basic direct files do not have the capability for serial access.

Survey of Methods   Only two distribution-dependent methods (digit analysis and sequence-maintaining transformations) are discussed. The hashing methods presented (remainder of division, exclusive-OR, and folding and adding) try to make use of the random properties in the digits of the key. Operations such as arithmetic multiplication and addition, which tend to produce normally distributed random values, are undesirable when hashing.

The **digit-analysis method** attempts to capitalize on the existing distributions of key digits. An estimate or a tabulation is made for each of the successive digit positions of the keys using a sample of the records to be stored. In Example 19-13 the three low order digits of a social security number were estimated to have a uniform distribution.

A tabulation lists the frequency of distribution of zeros, ones, twos, and so on. The digit positions that show a reasonably uniform, even distribution are candidates for use as digits in the file address. A sufficient number of such digit positions has to be found to make up the full address; otherwise combinations of other digit positions (taken modulo 10 or as appropriate) can be tested.

Similar tests can be made on character-oriented keys. Here the set of 26 possible letters may be divided into 10 groups to yield digits, or into groups of different sizes to yield factors other than 10 which can be used to produce an access record number.

A **sequence-maintaining transformation function** can be obtained by taking a simplified inverse of the distribution of keys found. The addresses are generated to maintain sequentiality with respect to the source key. In a **piece-wise linear transformation** the observed distribution is approximated, automatically or manually, by simple line segments. This approximation then is used to distribute the addresses in a complementary manner.

The **remainder of the division** of the key by a divisor equal to the number of record spaces allocated, m, can be used to obtain the desired address. Division is in some sense similar to taking the low-order digits, but when the divisor is not a multiple of the base (10 in Example 19-13) of the number system of the key (or the number system used by the computer), information from the high-order portions of the key will be included; and this additional information has a positive effect on the number of choices and hence on the uniformity of the generated address. Large prime numbers are generally used as divisors, since their quotients exhibit a well-distributed behavior, even when parts of the key do not. In general, divisors that do not contain small primes (≤ 19) are adequate. Tests have shown that division tends to preserve better than other methods preexisting uniform distributions, especially uniformity due to sequences of low-order digits in assigned identification numbers. The remainder does not preserve sequentiality. The problem with division is in the capability of the available division operation itself. Frequently the key field to be transformed is larger than the largest dividend the divide operation can accept, and some computers do not have divide instructions which provide a remainder. The remainder has then to be computed using the expression

$$\text{address} = \text{key} - \text{FLOOR}(\text{key}/\text{m}) * \text{m}$$

The explicit **FLOOR** operation is included to prevent a smart optimizer from generating address $= 0$ for every **key,** which would lead to an extreme number of collisions ($n - 1$). These operations can be avoided by replacing division with a multiplication by the reciprocal of m. This means that the operation uses binary fractions and the result has to be adjusted by shifting. When key lengths are excessive, this transformation can be preceded by the **exclusive-OR** operation.

An **exclusive-OR** operation is available on most binary computers or can be obtained by such statements as

```
DECLARE (address,keypart1,keypart2) BIT(19);
. . .
x_or: PROCEDURE(arg1,arg2); DECLARE(arg1,arg2) BIT (*);
      RETURN ( (arg1,arg2)(⌐(arg1,arg2)) );
      END x_or;

. . .
address = x_or (keypart1,keypart2);
```

As the example shows, the key is segmented into parts which match the required address size. Using this operation results in random patterns for random binary inputs. If the segments contain characters, then **x_or('MA', 'RA')** will be equal to **x_or ('RA', 'MA'),** so that "MARA" will collide with "RAMA." Care has to be taken where the binary representation of decimal digits or characters is such that certain bit positions always will be zero or one. These problems can be controlled by making the segment sizes such that they have no common divisor relative to character or word sizes. This operation is generally among the fastest computational alternatives provided by the hardware.

Folding and adding of the key digit string to give a shorter string for the address has been often used. Alternate segments are bit-reversed. This method is available in the hardware of some recent large HONEYWELL computers.

Several other techniques have been used and can be found in the literature; more have been proposed and evaluated; for files none seem promising.

Summary   It is obvious from the above that many choices exist here. It is necessary to remember that random direct files can be accessed only via one precise attribute value and not by range or serially. Serial access can be achieved only by stepping through every possible key value. Unless the keys are very dense, the great majority of fetches would result in a **record-not-found** condition. In practice this choice is excluded from consideration. Another inherent restriction in a computation of record addresses is that data records are expected to be of fixed length.

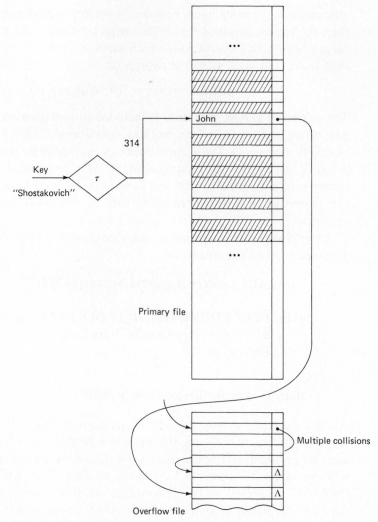

FIG. 19-28 Direct file with collision

Collisions (Fig. 19-28) Any probabilistic procedure may produce some identical addresses from different keys, and the resolution of the resulting collisions will occupy us in this section.

The larger the record-address space is relative to the number of records to be stored into this space, the lower is the probability of collisions. While we will evaluate such probabilities in detail subsequently, we will note that given about 50 percent excess space ($m/n = 1.5$), we incur costs due to collisions that become quite bearable; depending on the detailed design, we expect collisions less than 34 percent of the times we access the file.

To determine whether such a collision has occurred, we have to compare the key value found at the computed address with the key value given. Assume that we are reading a file constructed from Example 19-13. The fact that the algorithm computed for Pete, with social security number 901-23-4785, a record number of 392 does not necessarily provide a space for Pete's record. The content of the record space itself has to be tested. The space can be empty, it can contain an older record for Pete, or it can already contain a colliding record for

Joe. The choice is determined by matching the key fields. If the key field in the file is not **NULL** and the new and old key fields do not match then there is a collision. A similar process is followed for the search argument when a record is to be fetched. The corresponding outcomes are: no record found, record found, or look further at the results of the collisions. We will discuss methods of handling collisions from the point of view of adding a new record to a direct file. Three strategies are in use to resolve collisions, sometimes in combination. Two methods, linear search and rerandomization, which use the main file for storage of the overflow, are referred to as **open-addressing** techniques. The third method uses a separate overflow file.

Linear Search   A search through successive record positions may be used to locate unused space for the new record.

Search in the Bucket   An important approach to collision handling is the grouping of all records in one block as one bucket, as shown in Fig. 19-29. Only

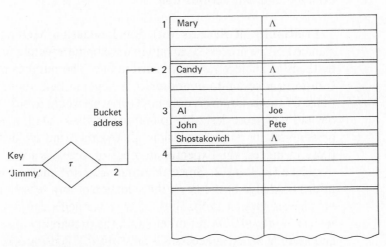

FIG. 19-29   Buckets

computational time is required to access the records within a bucket. Only when the bucket itself is filled will disk access time be required. If the bucket is of block size, there will be space for *ovpb* collisions in the bucket, where

$$ovpb = \left(1 - \frac{n}{m} \right) \left\lfloor \frac{B}{R} \right\rfloor$$

namely, the fraction of free space times the number of records per block.

Search in the File   When an overflow does occur, the search can proceed to the next sequential block. This avoids the costs of seek times to new areas but tends to cluster overflows together. This method is used frequently in practice both for files and for primary storage. As long as the number of entries is less than the number of spaces available ($n < m$), a record space will eventually be found. Since this can be determined a priori, no alternate termination method is required. The problem with clustering is that, when an area of the storage space is densely used, fetches need many search steps. Additional insertions tend to increase the size of the dense area. An example of this effect is shown in Fig. 19-34. Clustering has been shown to become detrimental even for moderately loaded storage.

Rerandomization Techniques other than searching the next bucket for free space have been used to avoid or to distribute the clusters. A new address computation taking other identifying data or an alternate algorithm can be used to compute a new record address in the same space. This technique, when applied to devices such as disk files, will cause a high overhead since generally a new seek is required. Further collisions can occur, and the procedure may have to be repeated a number of times. We cannot guarantee in fact that the process will ever locate an empty space. These techniques are used in primary storage, although they probably should be used with care on systems using paging for memory management. Applications of this approach are found when associative memories are implemented by software. The method used has to provide for an eventual alternate termination.

Probability of Success with Randomization Methods A graphic understanding of the processes can aid in developing a feeling for the effects of various methods to achieve random distributions. The number of possible methods to transform n keys into m addresses is huge; in fact, there are m^n possible functions. Of these, however, only $m!/(m - n)!$ would avoid any collisions. It would obviously be most desirable to find one of these. On the other hand, we have m possibilities for a total collision; all records wind up in the same slot, and in those instances, the expected number of accesses for a fetch, using a chain, would be $(n + 1)/2$. Since the randomization method is chosen without any prior knowledge of the keys, the selection of any reasonable method out of the m^n choices gives a probability of that method's causing no overflows of only $m!/(m - n)!/m^n$. On the other hand, the probability of selecting the worst case and needing $\frac{1}{2}n$ extra accesses is only m/m^n. Choosing a key-to-address randomization itself at random, we can see from Fig. 19-30 that we may expect $p = 0.30$ additional accesses for $m = 5$ and $n = 4$.

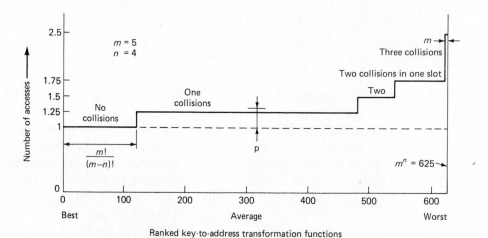

FIG. 19-30 Fetch-length distribution

The curve shows a similar shape for other values of m and n. Estimates for the number of collisions in the general case can be derived, but the intent of this subsection is to show the relative unimportance of the specific choice of randomization method, as long as it is chosen to be outside the obviously worst areas. It might be mentioned here that a change of keys, that is, a new set of data to be randomized, will completely reorder the position of the m^n methods in the figure, but the form of the distribution remains the same.

Overflow Area   It also is possible to put all records which cause collisions or bucket overflows into a separate file with a linkage from the primary record, similar to the overflow chains used in indexed-sequential files. If such a separate overflow area is established, no clustering will take place. An overflow causes a new seek but avoids the recursive search problem of the first method. A difficulty lies in the allocation of sufficient overflow space, since the number of collisions is not absolutely predictable. The use of an initial linear search within a bucket can drastically reduce the overflow load.

The cost of overflows can be lowered again by allocating overflow areas on each cylinder. This requires modification of the key-to-address transformation to account for the gaps in the primary addressing space. If buckets are already used, it may be better to use this space to reduce the density per bucket.

Bucket Addresses   We have discussed earlier the use of buckets to reduce the effort of collision processing. Where multiple records are kept in one block, and the entire block is fetched when a record is required, a shorter address can be used. If there are B/R records in a block, the address space reduces from m to mR/B.

Use of Direct Files

Direct files find frequent use for directories, pricing tables, schedules, name lists, and so forth. In such applications where the record sizes are small and fixed, where fast access is essential, and where the data is always simply accessed, the direct-file organization is uniquely suitable. Direct files also play an important role as a subsidiary part of more complex file organizations.

Performance of Direct Files

The performance of direct files has been more thoroughly analyzed than the performance of any of the preceding methods. The initial parameter in these evaluations is the number of record spaces or buckets m that are available for the storage of the n records. In general, n is smaller than m. The number of records that still cause collisions is denoted here as o. We will analyze a simple direct-access structure with buckets that hold a single fixed-length record and a separate area to contain up to o records that caused collisions. We will, when appropriate, also make comments which pertain to direct files using open addressing and to the use of buckets holding multiple records, since these methods are used frequently.

Record Size in a Direct File   The space required for a file SF as described above is

$$SF = m(aV + P) + o(nV + P)$$

or per record,

$$R_{\text{effective}} = \frac{m + o}{n}(aV + P) = \frac{m + o}{n} R$$

Fetch Record in a Direct File   In order to predict an average for time to locate a record in a direct file, we must determine the probability of collision p, since the predicted fetch time is simply the time required for randomization, the time for the single direct access, plus the average cost of a collision.

$$T_F = c + s + r + btt + p(s + r + btt)$$

An analysis which estimates the collision probability for this design has been done. The result of the analysis shows that for direct files, buckets of size R with overflow areas for collisions, the expected value of p is

$$p = \frac{1}{2}\frac{n}{m}$$

Measurements have produced results which are in close agreement with these figures.

Effect of Open Addressing   The tests also show the detrimental effect of clustering in open addressing with a linear search. The problem of clusters increases rapidly with the loading density n/m (Fig. 19-31). Knuth has derived,

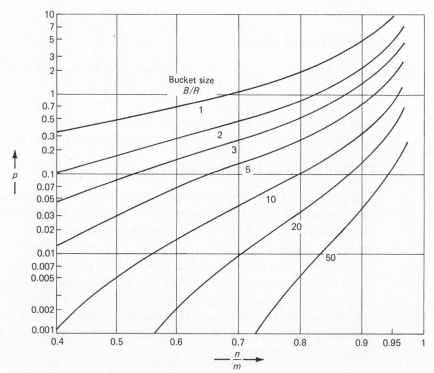

FIG. 19-31 Overflow probability for open addressing and linear search

using the arguments of a randomly selected randomization discussed above, that the appropriate value for the number of additional accesses becomes

$$p = \frac{1}{2} \frac{n}{m - n}$$

The result for bucket sizes $B/R > 1$ is complex and hence is presented here in graphical form. These values have been compared and match experimental results using the remainder of division quite well. For poorly distributed keys, the results are validated when bucket sizes $B/R \geq 5$. It should be noted that no overflow area is required when open addressing is used, so that the equivalent value of m may be appropriately larger. This will not compensate fully for the increased number of collisions.

Example 19-14 The assumption stated previously was that only one record space is provided per bucket and that there is a separate overflow area. It may be adequate to provide 50 percent more primary space than the amount required for the file itself, giving as a result a collision probability of

$$p = \frac{1}{2} \frac{n}{1.5n} = 0.3333 \qquad \text{or about 33 percent}$$

extra accesses due to collisions when the file is fully loaded.

With open addressing, using the same primary space m and bucket sizes equal to R, the value of p becomes

$$p = \frac{1}{2} \frac{1}{1.5 - 1} = 1.0$$

indicating 100 percent extra accesses. If the record size $R = 200$ and the block size $B = 2000$, the bucket size can be made 10, increasing only the computational overhead. The value of p obtained from Fig. 19-31 is now

$$p = 0.03$$

so that only 3 percent of the fetches will have to access another block.

In linear searching, if the decision to read the next block can be made immediately, no revolution needs to be wasted. In general, however, one revolution is required to read the next block if the read decision is based on the contents of the predecessor block, so that the access time for an overflow is $2r + btt$. Alternate-block accessing, as shown in Fig. 19-32 can reduce this delay to $2btt$, leaving a time $c < btt$ for the comparisons within a bucket. This technique does not require any general block renumbering, since the decision where to place overflows is arbitrary. In summary

$$T_F = c + s + r + btt + p\, t_{\text{overflow}}$$

where the choices for p are given above for separate overflow areas or linear searching and various bucket sizes; the values for t_{overflow} are:

$s + r + btt$ for a separate overflow area

$r + btt$ for separate overflow areas on the same cylinder

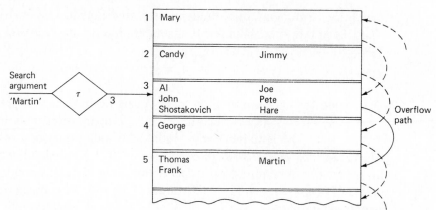

FIG. 19-32   Alternate bucket-overflow accessing

$$2r + btt \quad \text{for linear searching, sequential blocks}$$
$$2btt \quad \text{for linear searching, alternate blocks}$$

and c depends on the complexity of the hashing algorithm and the bucket size.

If the file use is known and stable, advantages may be gained by ordering the records such that the most frequently searched records appear in front of the chains created by colliding record addresses, and the least frequently referenced records are put at the end of the chains.

Fetch for a Record Not in the File   In a fetch for a nonexistent record, we will be forced to search until we find an empty slot. This time is estimated when insertions are evaluated (T_{Iov}), since the same number of slots have to be tested to locate an empty slot. Fetches are limited to the appropriate chain length if a chain is followed. The use of pointer chains also in open addressing is one technique to reduce fetch effort for nonexistent records. Another technique can be used if the overflow chains are kept in an ordered sequence, as indicated in Fig. 19-18. Not only is each record accessed in sequence and checked for a match of fetch argument and key, but the key of the stored record is also transformed to its address, which is matched to the initial fetch address in order to determine whether this record is a member of this chain. The search for a nonexistent record can be terminated when a member record of the chain has a larger key than the fetch argument. To take care of all cases, these records are checked for an end-of-chain flag, which is added to the records and updated when inserting new records into the file. Either method reduces p (not_in_file) to $2p$ or less in the evaluation for T_F above.

Get-Next Record of a Direct File   No concept of serial access exists within the direct file which uses randomizing for its key-to-address translation. If the key for the next record is known, a successor record can be found using the same procedure used to find any record.

$$T_N = T_F$$

If the key for the next record is not known, no practical method exists to retrieve that record. For linear key-to-address translations, which maintain a serial ordering, the successor record can be found by sequential reading, skipping over any unused spaces. The time for getting the next record can be estimated using the procedure for indexed-sequential file if a separate overflow area is used, or from p (not_in_file) if linear searching is used.

Insert into a Direct File   The process of inserting a record into the file has been discussed above in the analysis of the direct-file design. The slot whose address has been computed must be fetched and checked to determine whether the record space contains another record with a different key. For single record per bucket using chaining for overflow,

$$P\,1u = 1 - e^{-n/m}$$

If open addressing is used,

$$P\,1u = \frac{n}{m}$$

The insertion cost can be computed as the sum of the expected cost for the case when the primary slot is empty and the cost for the case where the primary slot is filled and the overflow procedure is invoked.

$$T_I = T_{Ipr} + T_{Iov}$$

When the slot is found empty, the record is rewritten into the empty slot, so that in this case

$$T_{Ipr} = (1 - P\,1u)(s + r + btt + 2r)$$

If it is not empty, one of the overflow procedures discussed has to be followed.

When a **separate overflow area** is used, the simplest procedure is to link the new record as the second member of the chain, as illustrated in Fig. 19-33. Here the new record is placed in the overflow area with the pointer value obtained from the primary record and the primary record is rewritten with the last overflow address.

$$T_{Iov} = P\,1u(s + r + btt + 2r)$$

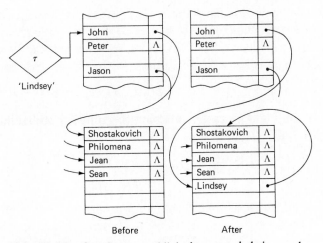

FIG. 19-33   Overflow record linked as second chain member

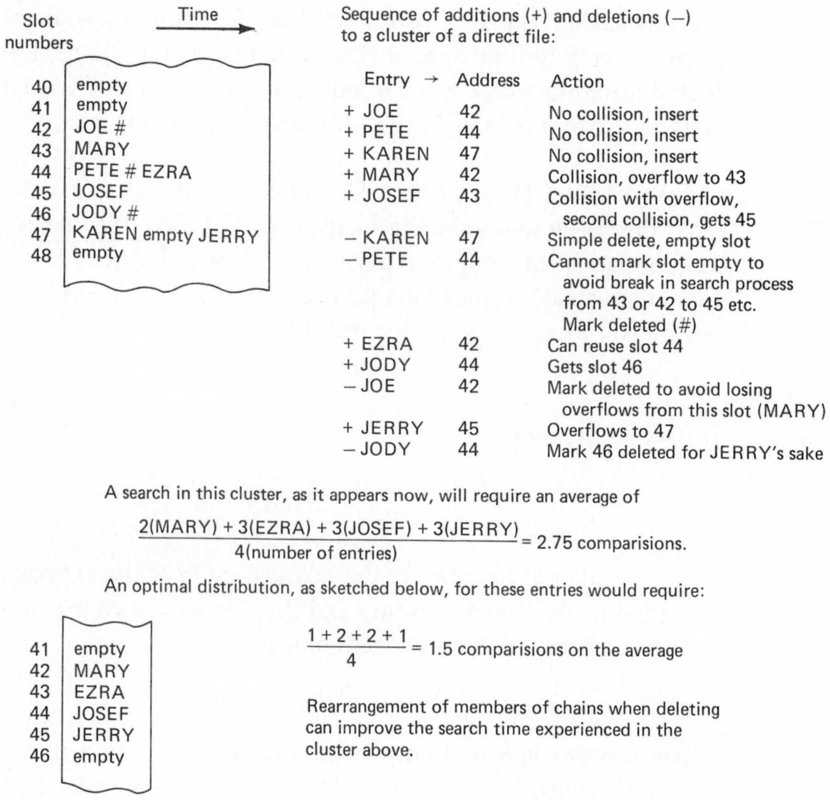

Slot numbers | Time →

40	empty
41	empty
42	JOE #
43	MARY
44	PETE # EZRA
45	JOSEF
46	JODY #
47	KAREN empty JERRY
48	empty

Sequence of additions (+) and deletions (−) to a cluster of a direct file:

Entry →	Address	Action
+ JOE	42	No collision, insert
+ PETE	44	No collision, insert
+ KAREN	47	No collision, insert
+ MARY	42	Collision, overflow to 43
+ JOSEF	43	Collision with overflow, second collision, gets 45
− KAREN	47	Simple delete, empty slot
− PETE	44	Cannot mark slot empty to avoid break in search process from 43 or 42 to 45 etc. Mark deleted (#)
+ EZRA	42	Can reuse slot 44
+ JODY	44	Gets slot 46
− JOE	42	Mark deleted to avoid losing overflows from this slot (MARY)
+ JERRY	45	Overflows to 47
− JODY	44	Mark 46 deleted for JERRY's sake

A search in this cluster, as it appears now, will require an average of

$$\frac{2(\text{MARY}) + 3(\text{EZRA}) + 3(\text{JOSEF}) + 3(\text{JERRY})}{4(\text{number of entries})} = 2.75 \text{ comparisons.}$$

An optimal distribution, as sketched below, for these entries would require:

41	empty
42	MARY
43	EZRA
44	JOSEF
45	JERRY
46	empty

$$\frac{1 + 2 + 2 + 1}{4} = 1.5 \text{ comparisions on the average}$$

Rearrangement of members of chains when deleting can improve the search time experienced in the cluster above.

FIG. 19-34 Operations on a file with open addressing

If the record is to be linked into a specific sequence in the chain, the chain will have to be followed until a larger record key is encountered. This procedure is also required if the chain has to be checked prior to insertion to avoid entering duplicate records with the same key. This time will be equal to the fetch time; then the prior record is rewritten (from an unknown position) and the new record inserted, so that

$$T_{Iov} = P \, 1u(T_F + s + r + btt + s + r + btt)$$

When **open addressing** is used, the entire sequence and the associated cluster (see Fig. 19-34) have to be passed to find a free space. No satisfactory formulation of the problem for linear searching is known to the author. An initial estimate is twice the fetch time, so that in the case of collision

$$T_{Iov} = P \, 1u(2T_F + 2r + s + r + btt)$$

Summing both cases and using the collision probability from open addressing, we find

$$T_I = \frac{2n}{m} T_F + s + 3r + btt$$

Knuth suggests that $T_I \approx (m/(m - n))(s + r + btt)$ when rerandomization is used.

Update Record in a Direct File   The process of updating the record consists of finding the record and rewriting it into the original slot, so that

$$T_U = T_F + 2r$$

When the key changes, a deletion and a new write operation must be performed.

A deletion involves some additional considerations. If any overflows have occurred, these will be found in a chain beginning from the original slot. We have to either move a record from the overflow chain to fill this slot or indicate that this record, while deleted, still has an associated pointer to the overflow records. If we use open addressing, similar considerations hold not only for the chain from which the deletion is made but also for any other chain which crossed this record slot.

Figure 19-34 illustrates what can happen in clusters when we use open addressing with sequential search for slots for overflows.

Some deleted record spaces can be reused as shown above, but the path length for fetches should include all spaces not explicitly marked empty, so that the values of p and $P1u$ are to be based on values larger than the current value of n.

Read Entire Direct File   An exhaustive search of a file using a randomizing key-to-address translation can be done only by searching through the entire space allocated to the file, since the discrete transformations from a sparse set of key values do not allow serial reading. The search is costly, since the working space is larger. Any area used by the overflows will also have to be checked. The overflow area will be dense, except for deletions.

$$T_X = (m + o) \frac{R + W}{t'}$$

Reorganization of a Direct File   Reorganizations are not common in direct files, but when many deletions have occurred in an open-addressing environment, reorganization becomes beneficial. If a high availability is desired, a reorganization can reorganize a single cluster (defined as the space between two empty slots). Possibly a desire to do a frequency-of-access oriented reordering of chained records may cause a reorganization run, which would require

$$T_Y = T_X + T_{Ld}$$

where T_{Ld} is the reloading time discussed below.

Reloading a Direct File   The most obvious way to reload a direct file is to rewrite the records one by one into the new space; then

$$T_{Ld} = nT_F$$

with a continuously changing value of T_F as n/m increases. A first-order estimate can be based on $\frac{1}{2}(n/m)$. This requires much effort, and if open addressing is used, the new file will already show clusters.

A two-pass procedure can be used to reduce the effect of clusters. In the first pass, records are only placed in their primary slots; the remaining records are placed into the still empty slots of the file during a second pass.

A reduction in loading cost can be accomplished by sorting the file to be loaded into the direct-file sequence. This order is obtained by applying the key-to-address transformation to the record keys of the records to be loaded into the file, and attaching the address as the sort key to the records. The load file is sorted and then written into the space for the direct file, skipping slots which do not have a matching address and placing colliding records into successor slots. This writing time is equal to the sequential exhaustive read time, so that

$$T_{Ld} = c + \text{sort}(n) + T_X$$

and the reorganization will require

$$T_Y = c + 2T_X + \text{sort}(n)$$

The advantage of a substantially reduced loading time is that reorganization can become a valid alternative to more complex schemes used to combat clustering and to manage deletions in a dynamic environment. This method can also be used to add a batch of insertions for the file. The batch would have to be quite large. If we use n_I to denote the size of the batch, this insertion method would be profitable only if $n_I > (T_X/T_I)$.

Another reason for a reorganization exists when a file has grown, so that the desired ratio of n/m no longer exists. More space has to be allocated to the primary area for the file, and the randomizing procedure has to be rewritten or adjusted. All data has to be copied using the read-entire technique and rewritten into new slots. The terms T_X and T_{Ld} will be estimated using the old value of m for T_X and the new value of m for T_{Ld}.

19-16   THE MULTIRING FILE

The three previous file-organization methods dealt with the problem of finding individual records fast. This last of the six basic methods is oriented toward efficient processing of subsets of records which contain some common attribute value. The **multiring** approach is used in many database systems; in this section we will consider only the file structure of this design. These subsets are explicitly chained together through the use of pointers which define some order for the members of the subset. One record can be a member of many such subsets. Chains also can be constructed out of header records for such subsets. A header record will contain information which pertains to all its subordinate member records.

The particular type of chain which will be illustrated in this section is the **ring,** a chain where the last member's pointer field is used to point to the header record of the chain. Similar file structures, called **threaded lists** or **multilists** in the literature, can be implemented either with rings or simple chains. The rings considered here can be nested to many levels of depth. This is not necessarily true for threaded lists or multilists. An example of the type of query for which this organization is well suited is

"List all employees in Thule"

Figure 19-35 shows a simple hierarchically linked ring structure.

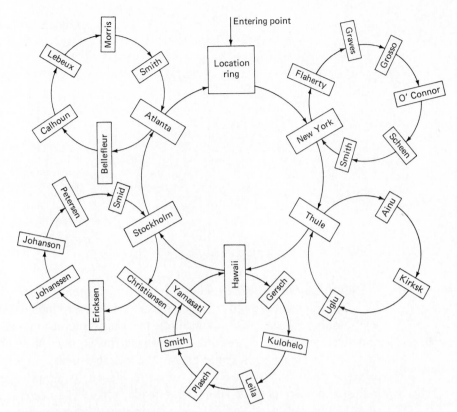

FIG. 19-35   Record linkage in a simple multiple-ring file

A search is made by following a chain for an attribute type until a match is found for that attribute value. Now a new chain is entered to find subordinate attribute values. This process is repeated until the desired record is found. The records in this example could be formatted as shown in Fig. 19-36. Another query of interest might be

"List all welders in our company"

Using the structure shown in Fig. 19-35, this query would require an exhaustive search, traversing the department ring and each personnel subsidiary ring in turn.

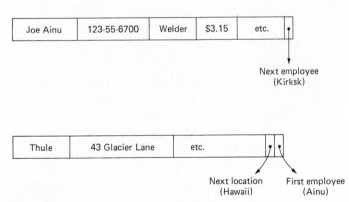

FIG. 19-36   Records in a ring structure

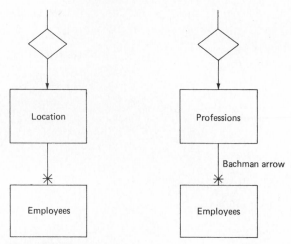

FIG. 19-37 Two employee files

Description of Multiring Files In order to simplify the depiction of these rings, we will use boxes and a specially shaped arrow to indicate rings and their relationship. Figure 19-37 shows both the ring structure of Fig. 19-35 and a ring structure which would allow answering this second query effectively. The shape of the arrow is chosen to denote the fact that many rings will exist at the terminal point but that only one subset is shown. A simple arrow is used to indicate an **entry point,** a ring whose header record is accessible directly. Such rings will be cataloged and will provide an initial point for processing queries.

It is obvious that we should combine the employee files, which can be accomplished by replacing the data field for **profession** with another linkage field, as shown in Fig. 19-38. The actual ring structure with these two relationships has

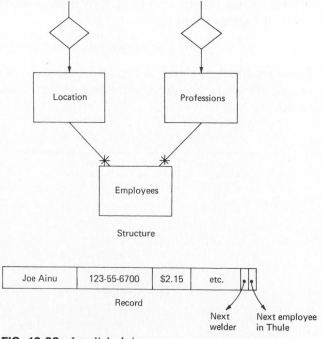

FIG. 19-38 Interlinked rings

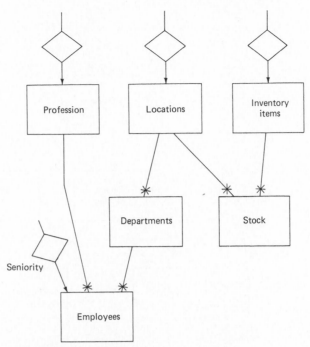

FIG. 19-39 Complex hierarchial structure

already become quite complex, but practical implementations can include many more rings.

If we expand the above example by segregating the employees in the various locations into specific departments, allow access in order of seniority, add a warehouse at each location, and keep stock information available, then the structure diagram would be as shown in Fig. 19-39. If the actual connecting pointers had to be drawn, the diagram would look like a bowl of spaghetti.

Relationships between rings are not necessarily hierarchical. Conceptually linkages may be implemented that relate members of the same ring (Fig. 19-40), that provide multiple pathways between records, or that relate lower rings back to higher-order rings. Two examples of multiple pathways are shown in Fig. 19-41, which may be helpful to readers who understand football.

Not all constructs are allowed or implementable in practice. The ease with which the relational arrows can be drawn hides the complexity of underlying structure very effectively. Loops and other nonhierarchical relationships between records may require a variable number of pointer fields in the records and are hence undesirable. In Fig. 19-40 an implementation may limit the **spouses** relationship to one entry. The **children** to **clinics** relationship may be best implemented using a search argument from **children** to an index for **clinics.**

As the structures become more complex, the optimum method for retrieval of a fact or a subset can require making a choice among alternate access paths. A query such as

> "Find an employee in Thule who can weld"

can be processed beginning at the location or at the profession ring. The appropriate records will be found at the intersection of any department at that location and the **welder** ring.

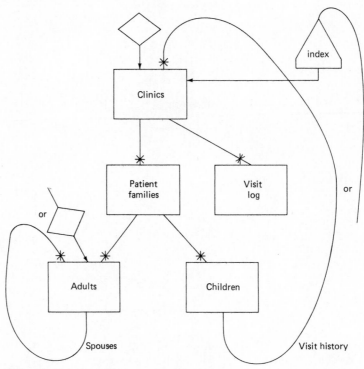

FIG. 19-40 Loops in ring structures

The effectiveness of a process in locating a record depends strongly on a good match of the attribute pairs forming the query argument with the structure of a fact or a subset can require making a choice among alternate access paths. automatically.

If there is no **profession** ring, the path for the query would have to begin at the entry point for **location.** Since the **location** does not contain a **profession** entry, an exhaustive search would be necessary through all **department** rings at this **location.** In an interactive environment, the system might have asked at this point, "Which department do you suggest?" The process of finding the best path for a query to such a database has been termed **navigation** by the principal developer of this file-design concept (Bachman).

Structure and Manipulation of Multiring Files

In the multiring organization the records will have similar structures, but their contents and size will be a function of the rings to which they belong.

Record Formats   In order to enable the records to be linked in the manner shown, many pointers will appear in a typical record. A record can belong to as many rings as it has pointers. A given pointer position in the record format is, in general, assigned to a specific category of rings. In the example above, **profession** may be such a category and **welder** one specific ring of that category. An example for a personnel record in such a file is shown in Fig. 19-42. If an

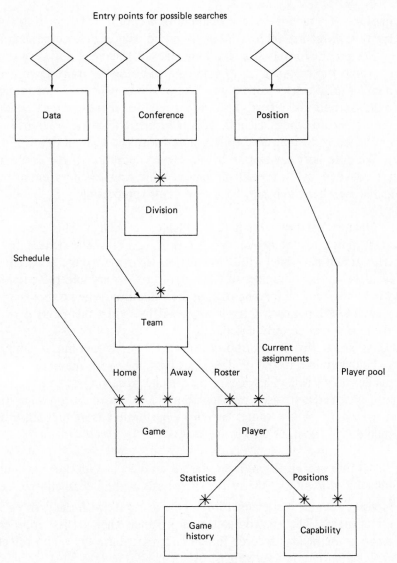

FIG. 19-41   NFL football database from Gonino

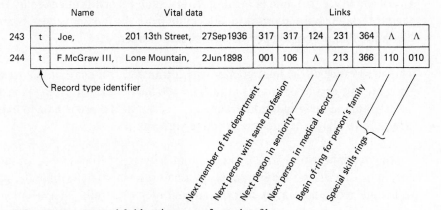

FIG. 19-42   Record field assignments for a ring file

instance of a record is not a member of a certain category ring appropriate to the type of record, there will be an unused pointer field containing a null entry.

The precise format of a record depends on the combination of ring categories of which the record is a member. A multiring file may have a considerable number of distinct record types. The attribute-value pairs could be self-identifying, as were the records used in the pile file; if they are not, each record will need a record-type identifier. This identifier will allow reference to an appropriate record-format description, stored with the general description of the file.

We note here a violation of the earlier definition of a file; the records now are not identical in format of contents, and ring category membership as well as file membership has to be known before processing.

Header Records   Each ring will have a header. This header is either an entry point, a member of another ring, or both. The header for the ring of department personnel will be the list of departments; the header for the ring of welders will be a member of the ring of professions; and the employees records will be the headers for rings listing their families. When a ring is entered during a search, the point of entry is noted so that when this point is reached again, the search can be terminated.

As shown in the examples above, the multiring-file organization avoids redundancy in data by placing data common to all members of a ring in the header of the ring. This means that in the basic ring design, whenever records are to be fetched based on a combination of search arguments, the match of arguments with key values cannot be performed using only information in the record. Two alternatives can be used:

A **parallel search** through all rings identified in the search argument can be made, terminating at the record or records at the intersection of these rings.

A **search** can be made according to the attribute with the greatest partitioning effectiveness. The records collected are then checked for appropriateness by locating the header records for the other attribute types and rejecting records with inappropriate data values.

An example of the latter method for the initial sample query would be

Every employee in Thule is located. Every such record is checked by following the profession chain in order to determine from the header record whether this chain implied a bookkeeper, a salesman, a welder, etc.

The importance of the final pointer which transforms a chain into a ring is clear here, but the cost of obtaining data from the header can be great. Hence it may be desirable to keep redundant descriptive data in the record, or to expand the structure to allow easy access to header records.

Ring Membership   The decisions that determine for which attributes rings should be established are similar to the decisions which determine the attributes to be indexed. The search cost of indexed files rises only logarithmically with increased file size, whereas the cost of following chains increases linearly with chain sizes. The sizes of individual chains can be reduced by appropriate design of the structure of the file. Increasing the number of levels (x) in the chain structure reduces the chain lengths, so that the search time decreases proportionally to the xth root of the record count n. An attribute which does not have structural significance in the file, such as a social security number, would not be useful to use as a ring element in a personnel file, since to find someone in this manner we would expect to require $n/2$ fetches. Finding a specific welder, however, is done efficiently by searching down the profession chain and then down the welder chain. The file designer hopes that both these chains will partition the search space effectively; the optimum is attained when both chains are equal in length, namely, $\sqrt{n}$.

Example 19-15 Given 10,000 employees with 10,000 social security numbers and 50 professions (of equal size, 200 members each).

The first search alternative—by social security number—takes 5,000 fetches.

The second search alternative—by profession—and then within a profession takes $25 + 100 = 125$ expected fetches.

This is much more than the expected number when indexes are used; the retrieval of successor records, however, is more economical in this structure than it is when using indexed files.

If we wish to summarize data for all the welders, we can expect $25 + 200 = 225$ accesses. This number of records probably cannot be obtained more efficiently by any of the preceding methods. In order to gain a complementary benefit in access time, locality of rings has also to be considered in the file design.

Some attributes, such as profession, can be sensibly divided into a number of discrete categories, e.g., welders or bookkeepers. Such a categorization will have a powerful partitioning effect and will match well the natural structure of the data. Attributes that do not represent discrete data, e.g., weight or height, do not provide effective partitioning unless they are artificially categorized. Such artificial categories may be in this case **less than five feet,** 5′0″ to 5′2″, 5′3″ to 5′5″, 5′6″ to 5′8″, and so on. If continuous variables like these are used as secondary categories, so that the memberships of these rings is reasonably small, a simple ordering within the ring may be all that is necessary. Ordering of members of a ring is frequently used.

Ring structures have been implemented in practice with a number of important additional features.

Use of Multiring Files

The concept of header and detail records can be traced to traditional data-processing procedures. Multiring structures are the basis for some of the largest databases currently in use. Management information systems where much of the system operation involves tabulating, summarizing, and exception reporting have been implemented using these multilinked lists. Examples of such operations were shown in the introduction to this section.

Some problems in geographic and architectural space representation also have been approached with a multiring approach. Several current developments in integrated multifile systems depend greatly on the capabilities provided by ring structures. A problem with the multiring structure is that a careful design based on prior knowledge of the data and usage pattern is required before a multiring file can be implemented.

Performance of Multiring Files

The performance of a multiring system depends greatly on the suitability of the attribute assignments to particular rings. In the evaluation below, we will assume that the file structure is optimally matched to the usage requirements.

Record Size in a Multiring File   Record formats in multiring structures tend to be fixed within a record type; but since many types are possible, not many empty fields will exist if the files have been carefully designed. We can hence expect a greater file density than sequential or direct files provide. In each record, there will also be a fixed number of linkage fields, but not many more than required in a particular instance of this record type. For both field counts we may assume that the number is commensurate with the parameter a' which was used to enumerate the number of valid attributes for a record. For a detail design the size should be determined for each record type, since the appropriate value in this structure is strongly dependent on the file design and not only on the record contents, and the values are important in the prediction of file performance. The size of a data field is again averaged at V, a linkage field contains pointer values of size P, and there are a'_{data} data fields and a'_{link} linkage fields in a record. One additional field of size P is used to allow identification of the record type. Then for a record

$$R = a_{\text{data}} V + a'_{\text{link}} P + P$$

If information is not kept redundantly, then an attribute value is represented either by a data value or by a link pointer. If there are furthermore no empty fields,

$$a'_{\text{data}} + a'_{\text{link}} = a'$$

If a record is a member of few rings, the size difference of data values and pointers will not matter, so that

$$R \approx a'V$$

If there is complete duplication of information in attribute fields and linkage fields, but there are still no empty fields, then

$$a'_{\text{data}} = a'_{\text{link}} = a'$$

And the size of the record is

$$R = a'(V + P) + P$$

For an estimate of average record size we can make the conservative assumption that over the entire file the effect of omitted attribute fields due to the linkage is balanced by the effect of empty fields due to the fixed-record structure, so that

$$R \approx a'(V + P)$$

Fetch Record in a Multiring File   The time to fetch a record is a function of the number of chains searched and the length of the chains. We assume now also that the record contains enough data so that when it is found according to one particular accessing sequence, it can be properly identified. The record hence is found by searching through a hierarchy of x levels; the process is similar to the search through the hierarchy of an index. We consider here only one ring membership per record type.

The average length of a ring y depends on the size of the file and how well the file is partitioned into rings, as shown in Fig. 19-43. In this simple hierarchical ring structure the depth of the hierarchy is determined by the decomposition of the level into rings of size y so that

	#(rings)	#(records)
Level x	1	$y_x \approx y$
Level 3	y_x	$y_3 y_x \approx y^2$
Level 2	$y_3 y_x$	$y_2 y_3 y_x \approx y^3$
Level 1	$y_2 y_3 y_x$	$y_1 y_2 y_3 y_x \approx y^4$

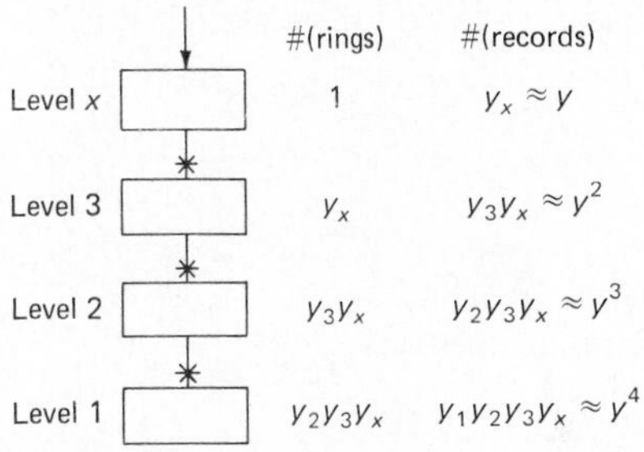

FIG. 19-43 File size at four hierarchial levels

$$x \approx \log^y n$$

The lowest level (1) contains a total of n records in all its rings together, discounting other record types at higher levels or other hierarchies in the file.

If a single record is to be fetched, the number of hierarchical levels should be matched by the number of search arguments a_F in the search key.

If there are fewer search arguments in the key, a ring, i.e., a subset of the records of the file, will be retrieved; if there are more arguments, there is redundancy, and attributes unproductive in terms of an optimum search strategy can be ignored. Otherwise the condition $a_F = x$ holds, and

$$a_F = x = \log_y n \quad \text{or} \quad y = \exp\left(\ln(n)/x\right) = \exp\left(\ln(n)/a_F\right) = n^{1/a_F}$$

In order to traverse one level, we can expect to access $(1 + y)/2$ records. When going from level to level, only $y/2$ new records will be accessed per ring. In order to locate a record at the lowest level, the most likely goal, we will expect to traverse x rings, and if rings on the various levels are of approximately equal size, then ½xy records will be accessed. Assuming random placement of the blocks which contain these records,

$$T_F = \frac{xy}{2}(s + r + btt)$$

Using then the expected number of levels a_F for the hierarchy used by the query and the value for y derived for the optimum hierarchy, we can write

$$T_F = a_F\left[\frac{1}{2}\,e^{\log(n)/a_F}\right](s + r + btt)$$
$$= fna(s + r + btt)$$

where *fna* represents a function based on the values of a_F and n. We see that this relation is critically dependent on the optimum structure of the data, since the file design mimics the relationships inherent in the data. In practice, auxiliary rings or linkages will be employed if the search length for some foreseen search-attribute combinations becomes excessive.

TABLE 19-4   Values for the File-Access Factor fna

a_F	fna		
	n = 10,000	n = 100,000	n = 1,000,000
1	5,000	50,000	500,000
2	100	318	1,000
3	33	72	150
4	20	36	72
5	20	25	32
6	18	24	30

fna = file-access factor
a_F = number of levels of rings in the search hierarchy
n = number of records on the level to be accessed

Table 19-4 lists values for *fna* given some values for n and a_F. Another possibility to reduce the search time is obtained when important rings are placed so that they tend to reside on a single cylinder, reducing the frequency of the seek term s in the equation above. Large databases of this form have been implemented on fixed-head disk hardware where no seeks are required, so that $s = 0$.

Get-Next Record of a Multiring File   The next record, according to any of the linked sequences, can be found simply by following the proper chain

$$T_N = s + r + btt$$

It should be noted that in this file organization, information about serial ordering exists for multiple attributes. The only other file organization that provides this opportunity is the multi-indexed file. If serial access via one particular ring is frequent, the records for one ring can be placed within one cylinder, so that $s = 0$ when accessing members of that ring. Getting a next record tends to be an important operation in data processing using this file structure, so that multiring files will be optimized for this operation rather than for minimum time of fetch operations.

Placing Rings on Disks to Minimize Seeks   Records which are members of only one ring are obviously best placed close together. One ring can, in general, be placed within one cylinder so that seeks are avoided when following this particular **primary** ring. At the higher levels of a ring structure the number of records of a certain record type may be sufficiently small to be kept on one or a few cylinders, and then traversal according to any ring will take no or minimal seeks. In substantial files a given record type at a lower level will require many cylinders, and traversals according to any sequence other than the primary ring will require seeks.

A possible assignment for the data of Fig. 19-39 is sketched in Fig. 19-44. Locating an employee via his department will require only a few seeks to the department ring and to the employee ring for the department; and if there are

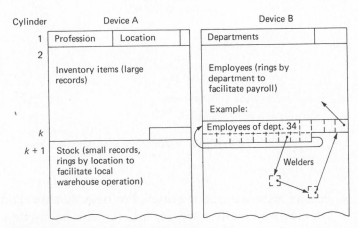

FIG. 19-44   Assignment of rings to storage

many employees in the department, there may be some cylinder breaks in the ring. Finding an employee by profession may require seeks between nearly every employee record. Stock is found with few seeks for a given location; these rings are apt to be long and will require some seeks at cylinder break points. In order to relate stock to the inventory data, in either direction, will take seeks between records, but these rings may be short if an inventory item is kept in few locations.

The evaluation technique used to derive the performance parameters for the ring file balances the optimistic assumption of optimal ring sizes against the pessimistic neglect of benefits obtained by optimized placement of rings. In a dynamically changing database, optimal placement is difficult to maintain and its benefits should be partially discounted. A reorganization may be needed to restore optimal placement.

Insert into a Multiring File   Adding a record to such a file is done by determining a suitable free area, locating all predecessors for the new record, taking the value of the appropriate link from the predecessors, setting it into the new record, and placing the value of the position of the new record into the predecessor link areas.

The total effort is hence equivalent to a'_{link} fetches of such a record plus the actual rewrite times. Some effort can be saved at the bottom levels when the chains are not ordered.

Unordered Attributes   If the records are ordered by attribute value, the chain has to be searched for the correct insertion point. If the chain connects all identical attribute values, such as all welders, only the header record has to

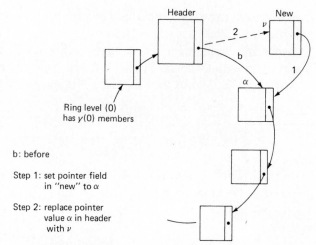

Header   New

Ring level (0)
has $y(0)$ members

b: before

Step 1: set pointer field
in "new" to α

Step 2: replace pointer
value α in header
with ν

FIG. 19-45   Insertion of a record into a ring

be read, modified, and rewritten. For rings that are short and where order does not otherwise matter, new records can also be inserted in the initial position. This will result in an inverse chronological sequence. Such a sequence frequently is also desirable for search purposes, since recent data is easy to find. The process is illustrated in Fig. 19-45. This linking has to be carried out for all a'_{link} rings of which the new record is a member. If we denote the number of unordered or identical attribute links at level 1 as $a''_{unordered}$, then we can save $a''_{unordered}y/2$ accesses.

The sum of the fetches, rewrites, and the placing of the final record is

$$T_I = a'_{link}(T_F + 2r) + s + r + btt + 2r - a''_{unordered}\frac{y}{2}(s + r + btt)$$

The cost of inserting a new record is obviously quite high, especially if the record is a member of many rings.

Update Record in a Multiring File   If only data fields are to be changed, the update requires only finding the record and rewriting it. We can assume that updated records do not change type and keep the same length. Then

$$T_U = T_F + 2r$$

for data-field changes.

Updating of records can also require changes to the linkage. Only linkages whose values have changed need to be altered, since the altered record can be rewritten into the original position. If the changed value is still within the category of the search attribute used to locate the record, then the point where the new record is to be inserted will be in the same ring and will require only $\frac{1}{2}y$ expected fetches. If, for instance, goods of a given type are kept sorted within their ring by weight, a change due to a new design can require an item to shift position within the ring. In this case for search, rewrite of the predecessor record, and rewrite of the new record,

$$T_U = T_F + \frac{1}{2} y(s + r + btt) + 2r + s + r + btt + 2r$$

for a single link-field change within a ring.

If, during the search for the old position of the record, a note is made if the new position is passed, sometimes the fetches required to find the new predecessor record can be eliminated. We cannot expect $2r$ for the rewrite time in this case, since the search for the new position is interposed.

If multiple (a_U) linkages are to be changed or the updates cause ring-membership changes within the same ring category, the new insertion positions have to be located. This could be done by searching from the top, as was necessary in the case of record insertion. An alternative is to use the ring-membership links of the old record.

Searching for the header records of a_U links from the top of the hierarchy again requires a_U fetches of time T_F. It may be faster to go to the header records using the ring, and then search through those header records for the desired place ('Hawaii'). The predecessor in the old ring ('Calhoun') has also to be located and rewritten with a pointer to the previous successor ('Morris'). The expected accesses are again $y/2$. This process is illustrated in Fig. 19-46. The insertion place ('Kulahelo') still has to be found, unless the ring is unordered. The entire process requires for all fields together

$$a_U 4 \frac{y}{2} - a''_{u\,nordered} \frac{y}{2} \text{ accesses}$$

where $a''_{u\,nordered}$ refers to unordered linkages included in the update request. Every update requires also rewrite of the new predecessor and the old prede-

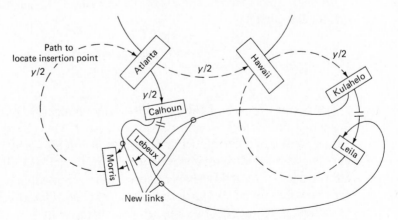

Employee 'Lebeux' is transferred from 'Atlanta' to 'Hawaii'

FIG. 19-46 Finding a new linkage point

cessor. Since the record to be updated is initially located via a fetch or **Get-Next,** one of the access sequences can be an extension of the fetch process. The effect of this is, in general, minor and will not be included below. For updates at less than third level from the top (**level number** $> x - 3$), it is more advantageous to locate the insertion point via fetches from the top.

Both old and new predecessors will have to be located and rewritten for every linkage field to be updated. Then, using the technique described above,

$$T_U = a_U(2y(s + r + btt) + 2r + 2r)$$

$$+ s + r + btt + 2r - a''_{unordered} \frac{y}{2}(s + r + btt)$$

Some reduction of this time can be gained in updating ring memberships where the record remains within the ring. Here again many data-specific considerations have come into play, and these relations will be verified with specific values of chain lengths, locality, and update patterns.

Read Entire Multiring File Exhaustive searches may be carried out by serially following any of a variety of possible linkages. A proper understanding of the file design is required to assure that no records will be read more than once. The cost will be high, since the process will have to follow the linkages given in the records. The alternative, searching sequentially through the space, may not be easy, since the records have a variety of formats, and the description of a record type is necessary to make sense of the fields obtained.

Reading according to the chains requires

$$T_X = n(s + r + btt)$$

but in addition, the header records will be needed more than once. It may be possible to keep a stack of x header records in primary memory.

If the header records cannot be kept available and have to be reread, an additional factor which depends on the length of the average chain has to be included, so that

$$T_X = n\left(1 + \frac{1}{y}\right)(s + r + btt)$$

Reorganization of a Multiring File Reorganization is not required as part of normal operating procedures. This is made obvious by the fact that a database system based on multiring files (IDS), available since about 1966, did not have an associated reorganization program available until 1975. Only when reformatting of record types is required will such records have to be rewritten. This may require only a partial rewrite of the file. This effect is identical to the execution of an update of all records of a chain

$$T_Y(\text{part}) = yT_U$$

A total reorganization is, according to these rules, simply

$$T_Y = nT_U$$

if the rereading of header records can be avoided.

For files where more frequent reorganization is expected, modifications of the basic file structure can provide improved performance in this area.

sec.20

Computer Graphics

William M. Newman and
Robert F. Sproull

20-1 INTRODUCTION

One of the most popular recent inventions for home use is the video game. One such invention, a simulated game of ping-pong, is shown in Fig. 20-1; it is played by two people with a pair of levers and a home television set. When the game is switched on, a small bright spot, representing a ball, is seen bouncing to and fro across the screen. Each player uses his lever to position a "paddle"

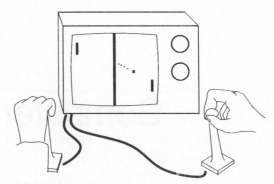

FIG. 20-1 Computer graphics in the home: a video game based on ping-pong

to bounce the ball back to his opponent. A player who hits the ball past his opponent wins a point; the game is won by the first player to reach 15 points.

Video games represent the first major use in the home of **computer graphics,** i.e., the creation and manipulation of pictures with the aid of a computer. Such pictures may be generated on paper or film, using a computer-controlled **plotter;** familiar examples of this form of computer graphics include the titles shown on TV and other forms of computer art (Fig. 20-2). Images like these are examples of noninteractive or **passive** computer graphics; the observer has no control over the image. We can give the observer some control over the image by providing him with an input device, such as the lever of the ping-pong game, so that he can signal his requests to the computer. We then have an example of **interactive** computer graphics.

Interactive computer graphics involves two-way communication between computer and user. The computer, upon receiving signals from the input device, can modify the displayed picture appropriately. To the user it appears that the picture is changing instantaneously in response to his commands. He can give a series of commands, each one generating a graphical response from the computer. In this way he maintains a **conversation,** or **dialogue,** with the computer.

Interactive computer graphics affects our lives in a number of indirect ways;

FIG. 20-2 Computer-generated TV title (courtesy Information International Inc.)

for example, it helps train the pilots of our airplanes. These pilots spend much of their training not in a real aircraft but on the ground at the controls of a **flight simulator.** The flight simulator is a mockup of an aircraft flight deck, containing all the usual controls and surrounded by screens on which are projected computer-generated views of the terrain visible on takeoff and landing. As the trainee pilot maneuvers his "aircraft," these views change so as to maintain an accurate impression of the plane's motion. Flight simulators have many advantages over real aircraft for training purposes, including fuel savings, safety, and the ability to familiarize the trainee with a large number of the world's airports.

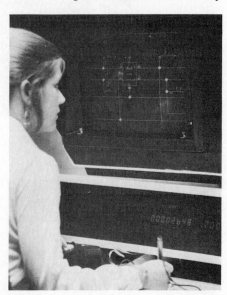

The electronics industry is even more dependent than the airlines on the use of interactive computer graphics. A typical integrated electronic circuit of the kind used in a computer is so complex that it would take an engineer weeks to draw by hand and an equally long time to redraw in the event of a major modification. Using an interactive graphics system, like the one shown in Fig. 20-3, the engineer can draw the circuit in a much shorter time. He can then use the computer to help in checking the design and can make modifications to the design in a matter of minutes. Much

FIG. 20-3 Electronic circuit design using a tablet and graphics display (photo courtesy of Calma Company, a wholly owned subsidiary of the General Electric Company, U.S.A.)

of the trend toward low-cost electronic equipment can be attributed to such advances in integrated-circuit design.

These are examples of industries that have come to depend on interactive computer graphics to carry out tasks that would otherwise be prohibitively expensive to perform. Many other tasks can be made considerably easier or less expensive by the use of interactive graphics. For example, architects can explore alternative solutions to design problems at an interactive graphics terminal; in this way they can test many more solutions than would be possible without the computer. The molecular biologist can display pictures of molecules and gain insight into their structure. Town planners and transportation engineers can use computer-generated maps which display data useful to them in their planning work. Fig. 20-4 shows examples of some of these applications.

The main reason for the effectiveness of interactive computer graphics in these applications is the speed with which the user of the computer can assimilate the displayed information. For example, the engineer designing an integrated circuit can see on the screen features that would never be apparent in an ordinary numerical computer printout. With the ability to interact with the computer, the engineer can quickly correct a design error, and see a revised picture of the circuit. Thus interactive graphics improves the **bandwidth** of communication between the user and the computer in both directions.

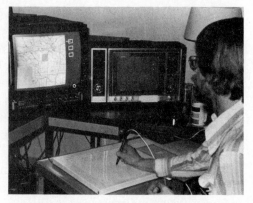

FIG. 20-4 Examples of interactive graphics in map display and architectural layout applications

20-2 THE ORIGINS OF COMPUTER GRAPHICS

Years of research and development have been necessary to achieve all these advances. In 1950 the first computer-driven display, attached to MIT's Whirlwind I computer, was used to generate simple pictures. This display made use of a **cathode-ray tube** (CRT) similar to the one used in television sets. Several years earlier, a CRT had been used by the late F. Williams as an information storage device; this technique was to emerge years later, in the form of the storage CRT incorporated in many low-cost interactive graphic terminals.

During the 1950s, interactive computer graphics made little progress because the computers of that period were so unsuited to interactive use. These computers were "number crunchers" that performed lengthy calculations for physicists and missile designers. Only toward the end of the decade, with the development of machines like MIT's TX-0 and TX-2, did interactive computing become feasible, and interest in computer graphics then began to increase rapidly.

The single event that did most to promote interactive computer graphics as an important new field was the publication in 1962 of a brilliant thesis by Ivan E. Sutherland, who had just received his Ph.D. from MIT. This thesis, entitled *Sketchpad: A Man-Machine Graphical Communication System,* proved to many readers that interactive computer graphics was a viable, useful, and exciting field of research. By the mid-1960s, large computer-graphics research projects were underway at MIT, General Motors, Bell Telephone Laboratories, and Lockheed Aircraft; the Golden Age of computer graphics had begun.

If the 1960s represent the heady years of computer-graphics research, the 1970s have been the decade in which this research began to bear fruit. Interactive graphics displays are now in use in many countries and are widely used for educational purposes, even in elementary schools. The instant appeal of computer graphics to users of all ages has helped it to spread into many applications and will undoubtedly guarantee its continued growth in popularity.

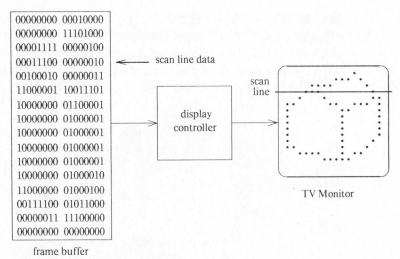

```
00000000 00010000
00000000 11101000
00001111 00000100
00011100 00000010
00100010 00000011
11000001 10011101
10000000 01100001
10000000 01000001
10000000 01000001
10000000 01000001
10000000 01000001
10000000 01000010
11000000 01000100
00111100 01011000
00000011 11100000
00000000 00000000
```

frame buffer

FIG. 20-5 The frame buffer display

20-3 HOW THE INTERACTIVE-GRAPHICS DISPLAY WORKS

The modern graphics display is extremely simple in construction. It consists of three components: a digital memory, or **frame buffer,** in which the displayed image is stored as a matrix of intensity values; a television monitor, i.e., a home TV set without the tuning and receiving electronics; and a simple interface, called the **display controller,** that passes the contents of the frame buffer to the monitor. The image must be passed repeatedly to the monitor, 30 or more times a second, in order to maintain a steady picture on the screen.

Inside the frame buffer the image is stored as a pattern of binary digital numbers, which represent a rectangular array of picture elements, or **pixels.** In the simplest case, where we wish to store only black-and-white images, we can represent black pixels by 1s in the frame buffer, and white pixels by 0s. Thus a 16×16 array of black and white pixels could be represented by the binary values in the 32 8-bit bytes shown in Fig. 20-5.

The display controller simply reads each successive byte of data from the frame buffer and converts its 0s and 1s into the corresponding video signal. This signal is then fed to the TV monitor, producing a black-and-white pattern on the screen, like the wheel shown in Fig. 20-6. The display controller repeats this operation 30 times a second and thus maintains a steady picture on the TV screen.

Suppose we wish to change the displayed picture. All we need do is modify the frame buffer's contents to represent the new pattern of pixels. In this way we can achieve such effects as a rotating wheel or a wheel that grows and shrinks.

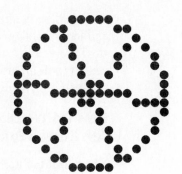

FIG. 20-6 Raster image of a wheel

We can now see how the ping-pong game might be programmed. Each of the sixteen possible positions of the right-hand paddle could be displayed by a different set of bit patterns; some of these are shown in Fig. 20-7. The computer reads the position of the right-hand control lever and selects the appropriate pattern, substituting it for the right-hand column of 16 bytes in the frame

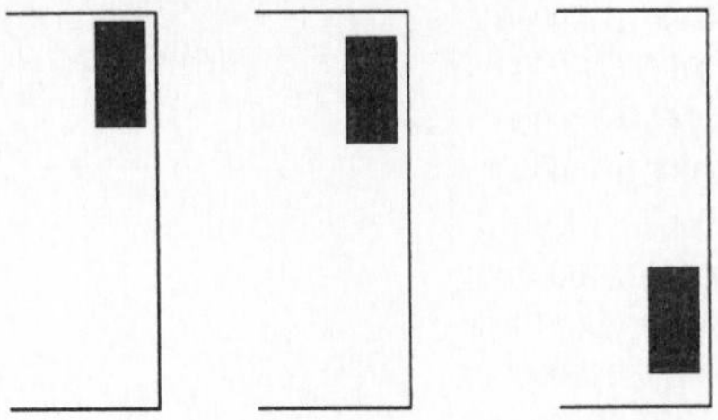

```
00000011      00000000      00000000
00000011      00000011      00000000
00000011      00000011      00000000
00000011      00000011      00000000
00000000      00000011      00000000
00000000      00000000      00000000
00000000      00000000      00000000
00000000      00000000      00000000
00000000      00000000      00000000
00000000      00000000      00000000
00000000      00000000      00000000
00000000      00000000      00000011
00000000      00000000      00000011
00000000      00000000      00000011
00000000      00000000      00000011
00000000      00000000      00000000
```

FIG. 20-7 Frame buffer bit patterns for three of the 16 possible positions of the paddle

buffer. It does the same for the left-hand lever and the left-hand column of the frame buffer. The position of the "ball" is computed, and the appropriate bits are set to 1 in the frame buffer. This entire process is repeated over and over again; meanwhile the display controller continues to pass the contents of the frame buffer to the TV monitor to maintain the moving picture on the screen.

20-4 SOME COMMON QUESTIONS

It should be pointed out, in fairness to those who have spent years of effort and millions of dollars of research money on computer graphics, that there is a great deal more to interactive graphics than the preceding example suggests. Some readers will already have questions about this example. The following are some of the more frequently asked questions about interactive graphics.

How Do We Display Straight Lines? How Are Curves Drawn on the Display?

The wheel picture in Fig. 20-6 illustrates two of the problems in drawing curved and straight lines on a graphic display. First, we must choose which pixels should be black and which white; the choice is not always straightforward. Second, slanting lines and curves in our image will be far from smooth and will instead show unpleasant "staircase" effects.

The first problem is solved by using a procedure, or **algorithm**, that computes which pixels should be black from the equation of the line or curve. Most of these algorithms are so simple that they can easily be implemented in hardware, leading to very fast line and curve generation.

The second problem of staircaselike **quantization** effects in the picture is much more difficult to solve. The most common solution is to use a different sort of display, called a **line-drawing display,** which plots continuous lines and curves rather than separate pixels. With a line-drawing display it is possible to draw lines that appear completely smooth to the unaided eye.

Until recently, line-drawing displays were the only widely used type of graphic display; the cost of digital memories made the frame buffer too expensive to consider. Although this situation is now changing, most computer graphics research has been oriented toward line-drawing displays; the frame buffer and its effective use are relatively unexplored topics.

Why Is Speed So Important in Displaying Pictures?

Again there are two answers. In the first place, any display based on the CRT must be **refreshed** by repeatedly passing to it the image to be displayed. The image must be transmitted to the display point by point (or line segment by line segment, in the case of a vector display). Unless the entire image can be transmitted at least 25 times a second, it will begin to flicker in an unpleasant way. The longer it takes to transmit each element of the picture the fewer elements can be transmitted and the less information can be displayed. Early displays, like the one used by Sutherland to develop the **Sketchpad** system, could display only a few hundred dots before the onset of flicker; nowadays vector displays can show many thousands of lines flicker-free.

A second aspect to the problem of speed concerns the **response** of the computer program to actions by its user. Speed of response depends on the rate at which the computer can generate a fresh picture in response to each action by the user, and on the rate at which this picture can then be transmitted to the display. In many applications, fast response is of paramount importance. For example, if the flight-simulating computer were to respond to movements of the controls only once every few seconds, the displayed view would change sluggishly and in a noticeably jerky fashion. The trainee pilot would not get a realistic impression of flying the aircraft and might even have difficulty in maintaining control. Generally speaking, slow response always makes interactive graphics programs more difficult to operate, and this explains why so much research effort has gone into finding ways of improving the speed of interactive response.

How Are Pictures Made to Grow, Shrink, and Rotate?

Many applications show various parts of the displayed picture changing in size and orientation. Our knowledge of how to apply such changes, or **transforma-**

tions, to pictures is based on standard mathematical techniques: coordinate geometry, trigonometry, and matrix methods. These techniques tell us how to compute the coordinates of a line segment's endpoints after scaling or rotating it. It is therefore relatively easy to apply the appropriate computation and to plot the line segment that results from the transformation. Problems arise only if the computation takes a long time; this can be prevented by using special hardware to perform the transformations.

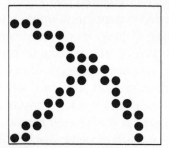

FIG. 20-8   Use of clipping to select part of an enlarged image of a wheel

What Happens to Pictures That Are Too Large to Fit on the Screen?

Display screens are relatively small, and the pictures we wish to display on them are often too big to be shown in their entirety. If we were to enlarge the wheel of Fig. 20-6, for example, it would no longer fit in the frame buffer. In this case, we would probably like to show as much of it as we could (Fig. 20-8). A technique called **clipping** can be used to select just those parts of the picture that lie on the screen and to discard the rest. Clipping can be regarded as a special form of picture transformation, and is indeed often carried out by the same piece of software or hardware that performs other transformations.

How Can the User of the Display Draw on the Screen?

The user's ability to create pictures directly on the display screen is perhaps the most irresistible aspect of interactive computer graphics. A number of different input devices—light pen, tablet, mouse—have been invented to make this kind of interaction more convenient; some of them can be seen in Figs. 20-3 and 20-4. When we draw with these devices, we have the impression of making marks directly on the display screen. In fact the computer is following every movement of the input device and is changing the picture in response to these movements. It is the speed of the computer in changing the picture that creates the impression of drawing directly on the screen.

20-5 NEW DISPLAY DEVICES

The CRT has always been the predominant display device for interactive computer graphics. For many years there was in fact no alternative. Now one or two other devices exist, but they are in many respects inferior to the CRT and have achieved only limited acceptance.

Why should we look for an alternative to the CRT? After all, the CRT is reliable, relatively inexpensive, and capable of displaying rapidly changing pictures. The main problems with the CRT as a computer display device are the very high voltages it requires, its bulkiness, and its weight. The device for which we are all searching could be powered by a 10-volt battery and would be no bulkier or heavier than a briefcase. Display devices with these attributes are just beginning to emerge from research laboratories in the United States and Japan; few of them, however, can compete with the CRT in performance and reliability. None of them solves the CRT's one other severe problem, its limited screen size.

Although we might consider this topic to be a branch of engineering rather than computer science, we cannot afford to ignore it, for it has an enormous impact on interactive computer graphics. We can see very clearly the impact of the CRT, for example, in the many articles that have been published either on ways to exploit the CRT's particular capabilities or on how to cope with its deficiencies. New display devices, as they are introduced to computer graphics, will undoubtedly have a similar impact.

20-6 GENERAL-PURPOSE GRAPHICS SOFTWARE

Many kinds of computer input and output are nowadays programmed in standard ways, using high-level programming languages. For example, languages like Pascal include facilities for file input and output and for handling interactive text terminals. The ability to express such operations within a standard high-level language makes programming much easier and permits the resulting programs to be run on a wide variety of different computers. We would like our graphic application programs to be equally easy to write and equally portable. Unfortunately this is rarely the case.

We can gain ease of programming and portability of programs through the use of a **graphics package,** a set of subroutines that provides high-level access to the graphics input-output hardware. A good graphics package simplifies the programmer's task and makes it possible to write **portable** programs that can be run on different computers and with different displays. This greatly reduces the cost of writing software for graphics applications. Most such packages are **general-purpose,** allowing many different kinds of application programs to be written.

The design of general-purpose graphics packages is a central issue in computer graphics. Since a package of this kind must provide a wide range of functions, its design involves almost every branch of computer graphics. In particular it involves consideration of graphic display devices and their characteristics, and this is where it becomes most difficult. As each new type of display is introduced, it creates new problems in the design of high-level graphics software. The diversity between devices makes it difficult to achieve portability in application programs. Some of the newer devices, including certain kinds of frame-buffer display, have not been in use long enough to permit the development of general-purpose programming techniques for their use. This is one of the problems that will continue to face us.

20-7 THE USER INTERFACE

Every interactive graphics program requires a period of training before the user can expect to operate the program proficiently. Very few are as easy to learn as the ping-pong game described earlier; instead they generally involve anything from hours to weeks of instruction and practice. During this period, the user is learning to understand the functions the program can perform, he is familiarizing himself with the various commands that invoke these functions, and he is learning to recognize the graphic representations used by the program to communicate the results of its computations. These are all aspects of the **user interface** of the program; they are the parts of the program that link the user to the computer and enable him to control it.

A good user interface makes the program not only easy to learn but also easier and more efficient to operate. Conversely, a bad user interface may make things so difficult for the user that the program is unusable. Operating this sort of program is like trying to solve a puzzle of the kind that involves maneuvering several tiny steel balls through a maze: we try to work steadily toward our ultimate goal but keep making mistakes that cause us to lose all the ground we have gained.

When we try to use a program with a faulty user interface, it often seems as if the programmer has tried, as in the case of the puzzle, to create a bad user interface intentionally. In fact this kind of program is merely evidence of how difficult it is to design a good user interface. The programmer designing an interactive graphics program has few guiding principles upon which to base his user-interface design and even fewer ways to analyze his design and predict its performance. User-interface design, more than any other aspect of computer graphics, remains as much an art as a science.

20-8 THE DISPLAY OF SOLID OBJECTS

Look closely at the object shown in Fig. 20-9. It appears to be a champagne glass standing on a checkerboard-patterned surface. In fact it is a computer-generated picture of an object that has never existed, except as a mathematical model stored in the computer's memory. Some extremely ingenious computational methods were employed in converting the computer-stored model into such a realistic displayed image.

The computer techniques we use to generate pictures like Fig. 20-9 fall into three categories:

1. We must model the curved surfaces of the object; this is done by splitting the surfaces into small **patches** and representing each patch by parametric equations in such a way that we can easily modify its shape.
2. We must determine which parts of the object will be invisible, as they will be if they face away from the observer or are obscured by other parts of the object; this is called the **hidden-surface problem,** and is one of the classic problems of computer graphics.
3. We must compute how to **shade** the visible surfaces of the object.

FIG. 20-9 Computer-generated display of a simulated three-dimensional scene (courtesy University of Utah)

The technique used to shade Fig. 20-9, developed at the University of Utah by the late Bui Tuong Phong, requires programming the computer to model how illuminated objects are perceived by the human eye.

Solid-object display is the most analytical branch of computer graphics and over the years has inspired some of the most original research work. The results of this research have been put to a number of uses, perhaps most effectively in the flight-simulation example described earlier. Solid-object display also has many potential uses in aircraft and automobile design, architecture, and planning. The extent to which it can be used in these applications depends on the development of faster and less expensive methods of solid-object display; this remains one of the most challenging research problems in interactive computer graphics.

20-9 POINT-PLOTTING TECHNIQUES

The frame-buffer display described earlier is an example of a **point-plotting** display device. The smallest picture unit accepted by such displays is a single dot, variously termed a **point** or a **pixel**. To construct a useful picture on a point-plotting display we must build the picture out of many hundreds of pixels, each generated by a separate command from the computer. Lines and curves must be drawn with closely spaced pixels; to display a text character, i.e., a letter or a digit, we use a pattern, or **matrix,** of pixels. Figure 20-10 is an enlarged picture of lines and text characters constructed on a point-plotting display.

The very first graphical displays were of the point-plotting variety. They did not use frame buffers but were fed with a stream of point coordinates by the

FIG. 20-10 Lines and text on a point-plotting display, enlarged to show individual pixels

computer. Only a very limited number of points could be displayed in this fashion without flicker.

Point-plotting displays of this kind were made obsolete by the introduction of line-drawing displays in the mid-1960s. The line-drawing display can draw complete segments of straight lines without plotting each individual pixel on the line; it therefore has a much higher capacity than the point-plotting display for line drawings. It also does away with the need to compute the position of each pixel in the picture.

Despite the obsolescence of the original point-plotting displays, the techniques developed for programming them remain relevant today. The main reason is that point-plotting techniques have become essential in programming frame-buffer displays, where once again the intensity of each dot must be separately computed. Point-plotting techniques also serve to introduce us to the **incremental methods** so frequently useful in computer graphics.

20-10 COORDINATE SYSTEMS

Point-plotting techniques are based on the use of a **cartesian coordinate system.** Points are addressed by their x and y coordinates; the value of x increases from left to right and y likewise from bottom to top (Fig. 20-11).

Points are plotted in response to digital signals from the computer. This means that they cannot be positioned with infinite precision; instead we are limited by the precision of the digital values presented to the display. For example, if x and y are passed to the display each as a 10-bit binary number, there can be only 1024 ($= 2^{10}$) distinct x-coordinate values and only 1024 for y. The screen offers us a 1024 $\times$ 1024 array of positions, at any one of which a dot may be displayed.

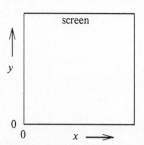

FIG. 20-11 The cartesian screen coordinate system

What determines the precision of a display? In most cases precision is based on the **resolution** of the display screen. This is the number of visibly distinct dots that can be displayed in a given area of the screen. A typical display might have a resolution of 100 dots per inch, indicating that two dots $\frac{1}{100}$ inch apart can just be distinguished from each other. Nothing is gained by increasing coordinate precision much beyond the resolution of the screen because the observer will not be able to tell the difference. If precision is much less than resolution, however, there will be resolvable points on the screen at which it is impossible to display a dot; this will cause visible gaps in lines. Hence when a display is designed, its coordinate precision is made approximately equal to screen resolution.

Given the coordinate precision and the size of the screen, we can arrive at the number of addressable points. A display with 100 dots per inch resolution cannot easily be built with a screen much larger than 12 inches square. Therefore most displays allow no more than 1200 points to be addressed in each direction. The value 1024 is popular, as it makes full use of ten-bit integer coordinates, but displays have been built with as many as 4096×4096 addressable points and with as few as 256×256.

To summarize, most interactive computer displays marketed today use a cartesian coordinate system, with 10 bits of x and y coordinate precision; display screens generally measure about 10 inches (30 centimeters) square. The practice of using integer coordinate values and of placing the origin at the lower left-hand corner of the screen, as shown in Fig. 20-11, is fairly common.

20-11 INCREMENTAL METHODS

The newcomer to a city often finds his way about by an incremental method. If he is at 203 Main Street and is looking for number 735, he gets there by finding the house with a number greater than 203; this might be house number 205. Having found number 205, he proceeds in the same direction past number 207, and so on until the house number reaches 735. The use of house numbers and the arrangement of houses in numerical order make it much easier for him to find his way. If instead he were in Tokyo, where houses are numbered according to their date of construction, the simple incremental method would not work. Incremental methods are frequently used in computer graphics, where again they tend to simplify things. Later in this book we shall see how the introduction of incremental techniques has simplified both scan conversion and the shading of computer-generated pictures of solid objects. It is appropriate to begin our study of incremental methods in this chapter, as these methods are useful in generating lines on point-plotting displays.

Incremental computing techniques are a form of iterative computation, in which each iterative step is simplified by maintaining a small amount of **state,** or memory, about the progress of the computation. The visitor looking for house number 735 needs only three pieces of state information: the direction in which he is going, the number of the house he has just passed, and the number of the house he is looking for. If he reaches a house whose number lies outside the range of these two house numbers, his algorithm tells him to reverse direction.

This algorithm, shown in the following Pascal program, is an example of a simple incremental method.

```
procedure FindHouse(houserequired: integer);
    var housepassed, t, direction: integer;
begin
    direction := 1;
    housepassed := ReadHouseNumber;
    while housepassed <> houserequired do begin
        MoveToNextHouse(direction);
        t := ReadHouseNumber;
        if (t > Max(housepassed, houserequired)) or
        (t < Min(housepassed, houserequired)) then
            direction := - direction;
        housepassed := t
    end
end;
```

Incremental methods come into their own when not only the final result but the intermediate results are of use. When we plot lines incrementally, we start at one end and finish by computing the coordinates of the other end; in between, the incremental technique generates the coordinates of all the dots that lie on the line. Thus one iterative process generates many useful results.

20-12 LINE-DRAWING ALGORITHMS

Straight-line segments are used a great deal in computer-generated pictures. They occur in block diagrams, bar charts and graphs, civil and mechanical engineering drawings, logic schematics, and architectural plans, to name a few examples of commonly displayed pictures. Furthermore, curves can be approximated quite effectively by sequences of short straight-line segments. Since straight lines are so useful, it is worth taking care that they are well drawn.

What are the things a good line-drawing algorithm should do well? To answer this question, we should consider the skills a draftsman must develop in order to draw well. He must learn to make his lines straight, to ensure that they start and finish in exactly the right places, to maintain constant blackness, or **density,** along the length of each line, and to make sure that lines have matching density where appropriate. Given time, he will also learn to draw lines quickly.

Exactly the same criteria apply to computer-generated lines:

Lines should appear straight. Point-plotting techniques are admirably suited to the generation of lines parallel or at 45° to the x and y axes. Other lines cause a problem: a line segment, though it starts and finishes at addressable points, may happen to pass through no other addressable points in between. Figure 20-12 shows such a line. In these cases we must approximate the line by choosing addressable points close to it. If we choose well, the line will appear straight; if not, we shall produce crooked lines, as in Fig. 20-13.

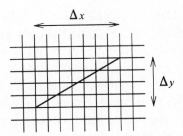

FIG. 20-12 A straight line segment connecting two grid intersections may fail to pass through other grid intersections

FIG. 20-13 Output from a poor line-generating algorithm

Lines should terminate accurately. Unless lines are plotted accurately, they may terminate at the wrong place. The effect is often seen as a small gap between the endpoint of one line and the starting point of the next or as a cumulative error (Fig. 20-14).

Lines should have constant density. With bright lines plotted on a dark background, line density is observed as brightness; when the line is black and the background light, it is seen as blackness. In either case, line density is proportional to the number of dots displayed divided by the length of the line. To maintain constant density, dots should be equally spaced. This can be achieved only in lines parallel or at 45° to the axes. In other cases, we must attempt to achieve as even spacing as possible; bunching of dots will otherwise be visible as particularly bright or dark regions on the line (see the example of Fig. 20-15).

Line density should be independent of line length and angle. This is a difficult requirement to satisfy. As we have just seen, to achieve constant line density we must maintain a constant number of dots per unit length. Before plotting the line we must therefore determine its exact length, which involves computing a square root. Also we must be able to control the rate, in terms of distance traveled, at which dots are plotted. Neither of these is easily done. Normally the best we can do is to compute an approximate **line-length estimate** and to use a line-generation algorithm that keeps line density constant to within the accuracy of this estimate.

Lines should be drawn rapidly. In interactive applications we would like lines to appear rapidly on the screen. This implies using the minimum of computation to draw the line; ideally, this computation should be performed by special-purpose hardware.

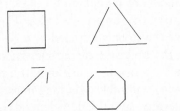

FIG. 20-14 Symbols drawn from lines that fail to connect properly

FIG. 20-15 Uneven line density caused by bunching of dots

Since the line-generation methods described below are all incremental, they share certain features. In particular, each method basically generates two sets of signals; these signals step the x and y coordinates of the point that traces out the line. Thus to draw a vertical line we would issue only y signals, and to draw a line at 45° we would issue x and y signals at an equal rate. For any given line, each of the following methods generates the same total number of x signals and y signals, since these signal totals must sum to the magnitudes of Δx and Δy, the displacements in x and y of the finishing point of the line from its starting point (see Fig. 20-12). The methods differ only in the order in which the signals are issued and in how they are generated.

The Symmetrical DDA

The digital differential analyzer (DDA) generates lines from their differential equations. As we shall see later in this chapter, we can build DDAs to draw curves as well as straight lines provided these curves can be defined by ordinary differential equations. The equation of a straight line is particularly simple:

$$\frac{dy}{dx} = \Delta y/\Delta x \qquad (20\text{-}1)$$

The line-generating DDA is correspondingly straightforward.

The DDA works on the principle that we simultaneously increment x and y by small steps proportional to the first derivatives of x and y. In the case of a straight line the first derivatives are constant and are proportional to Δx and Δy. Thus in the ideal case of an infinite-precision display we could generate a line by incrementing x and y by $\epsilon\Delta x$ and $\epsilon\Delta y$, where ϵ is some small quantity (see Fig. 20-16).

In the real world of limited-precision displays we must generate only addressable points. This can be done by rounding to the nearest integer after each incremental step; after rounding we display a dot at the resultant x and y.

An alternative to rounding is the use of arithmetic overflow: x and y are kept in registers that have two parts, integer and fractional. The incrementing values, which are both less than unity, are repeatedly added to the fractional parts, and whenever the result overflows, the corresponding integer part is incremented. The integer parts of the x and y registers are used in plotting the line. This would normally have the effect of **truncating** rather than rounding, so we initialize the DDA with the value 0.5 in each of the fractional parts to achieve true rounding.

One advantage of this arrangement is that it allows us to detect changes in x and y and hence to avoid plotting the same point twice. The overflow indicator generated by the DDA produce the signals we need to reposition the point that traces out the line. Note that the precision of the incrementing values and of the fractional parts of the registers must be no less than the coordinate precision of the display; otherwise accuracy will be lost on long lines.

The appearance of lines generated by the DDA depends on the value chosen for ϵ. In the case of the **symmetrical DDA** we choose $\epsilon = 2^{-n}$, where

$$2^{n-1} \leq \max(|\Delta x|, |\Delta y|) < 2^n \qquad (20\text{-}2)$$

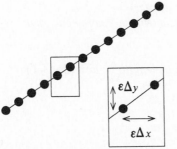

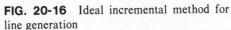

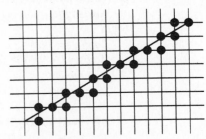

FIG. 20-16 Ideal incremental method for line generation

FIG. 20-17 Line drawn with a symmetrical DDA

In fact ϵ is the reciprocal of the DDA's line-length estimate, in this case 2^n. A line drawn with the symmetrical DDA is illustrated in Fig. 20-17; the organization of a symmetrical DDA is shown in Fig. 20-18.

The symmetrical DDA generates accurate lines, since the displacement of a displayed dot from the true line is never greater than one-half a screen unit.

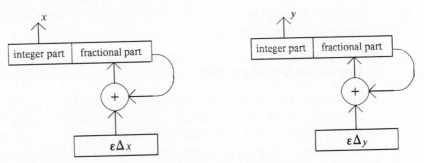

FIG. 20-18 Arrangement of the symmetrical DDA

Logically the symmetrical DDA is simple; the use of a negative power of 2 for ϵ means that the incrementing values can be determined by shifting the Δx and Δy registers rather than by a division. Each step in the line is computed with just two additions.

The Simple DDA

The symmetrical DDA uses a power of 2 as a line-length estimate, since this simplifies the logic. The principle of the DDA tells us, however, that we may use any line-length estimate and any corresponding value of ϵ provided neither $\epsilon \Delta x$ nor $\epsilon \Delta y$ exceeds unit magnitude.

For the **simple DDA** we choose a line-length estimate equal to the larger of the magnitudes of Δx and Δy, so that either $\epsilon \Delta x$ or $\epsilon \Delta y$ is of unit magnitude. This allows us to replace one of the DDA's adders with a simple counter. The simple DDA therefore generates unit steps in the direction of greatest motion; Figure 20-19 shows an example. A Pascal implementation of the simple DDA is as follows:

```
procedure DDA (x1, y1, x2, y2: integer);
    var length, i: integer; x, y, xincrement, yincrement: real;
begin
    length := abs(x2 − x1);
    if abs(y2 − y1) > length then length := abs(y2 − y1);
    xincrement := (x2 − x1)/length;
    yincrement := (y2 − y1)/length;
    x := x1 + 0.5; y := y1 + 0.5;
    for i := 1 to length do
        begin
        Plot(trunc(x), trunc(y));
        x := x + xincrement;
        y := y + yincrement
        end
end;
```

The simple DDA is as accurate as its symmetrical counterpart but generates a different sequence of dots because of its different method of estimating line length. Logically it is simpler, except for the need to perform an initial division to determine the incrementing value. The simple DDA is an ideal basis for a software line generator, but the need for division logic makes it less suited to hardware implementation.

Bresenham's Algorithm

An interesting line-drawing algorithm has been developed by Bresenham. Like the simple DDA, it is designed so that each iteration changes one of the coordinate values by ± 1. The other coordinate may or may not change, depending on the value of an error term maintained by the algorithm. This error term records the distance, measured perpendicular to the axis of greatest movement, between the exact path of the line and the actual dots generated. In the example of Fig. 20-20, where the x axis is the axis of greatest movement, the error term e is shown measured parallel to the y axis. The following description of the algorithm assumes this particular orientation of the line.

At each iteration of the algorithm the slope of the line, $\Delta y/\Delta x$, is added to the error term e. Before this is done, the sign of e is used to determine whether to increment the y coordinate of the current point. A positive e value indicates

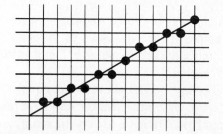

FIG. 20-19 Line drawn with a simple DDA

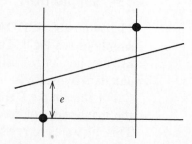

FIG. 20-20 Graphic representation of Bresenham's algorithm

that the exact path of the line lies above the current point; therefore the *y* coordinate is incremented, and 1 is subtracted from *e*. If *e* is negative the *y* coordinate value is left unchanged. Thus the basic algorithm is expressed by the following Pascal program:

```
{ Note: e is real; x, y, deltax, deltay are integers }
e := (deltay/deltax) − 0.5;
for i := 1 to deltax do begin
    Plot(x, y);
    if e > 0 then begin
        y := y + 1;
        e := e − 1
        end;
    x := x + 1;
    e := e + (deltay/deltax)
end;
```

The weakness of this sequence of operations lies in the division required to compute the initial value and increment of *e*. This division can be avoided, however, since the algorithm is unaffected by multiplying *e* by a constant: only the sign of *e* is tested. Thus by multiplying *e* by $2\Delta x$ we produce the following program, requiring neither divisions nor multiplications:

```
{ Note: all variables are integers }
e := 2 * deltay − deltax;
for i := 1 to deltax do begin
    Plot(x, y);
    if e > 0 then begin
        y := y + 1;
        e := e + (2 * deltay − 2 * deltax)
        end
        else e := e + 2 * deltay;
    x := x + 1
end;
```

A full implementation of Bresenham's algorithm involves allowing for other cases besides $0 \leq \Delta y \leq \Delta x$, the case discussed above. At the same time the algorithm can be somewhat simplified by using only integer arithmetic. Like the simple DDA, Bresenham's algorithm avoids generating duplicate points. Because it also avoids multiplications and divisions, it is well suited to implementation in hardware or on simple microprocessors.

20-13 CIRCLE GENERATORS

In certain classes of application, particularly those involving the display of mechanical engineering parts, circles and circular arcs are frequently displayed. A number of incremental methods have been invented to plot circles and arcs. These methods are valuable because most displays, although they have hardware for line generation, have none for circle drawing. Where line-generation hardware exists, incremental circle generators can be used to compute the endpoints of consecutive short line segments; where it does not, circle generators are capable of generating closely spaced dots, suitable for point-plotting displays. We shall discuss one circle-generation method, a variant of the DDA.

The Circle-generating DDA

As we saw earlier, the principle of the DDA can be extended to other curves; one such curve is the circular arc. The differential equation of a circle with center at the origin can be written

$$\frac{dy}{dx} = -x/y \tag{20-3}$$

This suggests that we can implement a circle-plotting DDA by using $-\epsilon x$ and ϵy as incrementing values

$$x_{n+1} = x_n + \epsilon y_n \tag{20-4}$$
$$y_{n+1} = y_n - \epsilon x_n$$

This involves computing the incrementing values afresh at each step, but the computation can be reduced to a pair of shifts and a complement operation if ϵ is chosen to be a negative power of 2; to prevent the spacing of consecutive points from exceeding one screen unit, ϵ should equal 2^{-n}, where

$$2^{n-1} \leq r < 2^n \tag{20-5}$$

r being the radius of the circle.

Unfortunately the method just described plots a spiral, not a circular arc. Each step is made in a direction perpendicular to a radius of the circle; each point is therefore slightly farther from the center than the one before. This problem is easily solved, however, by using x_n+1 rather than x_n to compute y_n+1:

$$x_{n+1} = x_n + \epsilon y_n \tag{20-6}$$
$$y_{n+1} = y_n - \epsilon x_{n+1}$$

This solution is based on the following reasoning: Equations 20-4 can be written in matrix form as

$$[x_{n+1} \, y_{n+1}] = [x_n y_n] \begin{bmatrix} 1 & -\epsilon \\ \epsilon & 1 \end{bmatrix} \tag{20-7}$$

The determinant of the matrix on the right does not equal unity but $1 + \epsilon^2$; this implies that the curve will spiral out. If the determinant can be reduced to unity, the curve will close. We achieve this effect by modifying the matrix as follows:

$$[x_{n+1} \, y_{n+1}] = [x_n y_n] \begin{bmatrix} 1 & -\epsilon \\ \epsilon & 1 - \epsilon^2 \end{bmatrix} \tag{20-8}$$

This is easily reduced to Equations 20-6.

Circles drawn by the DDA need not be centered on the origin, as they must for Equations 20-6 to hold. Instead the displacements in x and y from the circle's center of the point (x_n, y_n) are used in determining (x_n+1, y_n+1). This algorithm is well suited to hardware implementation.

The reader will probably already have discovered that Equations 20-6 generate points on an ellipse, not on a circle. The eccentricity of the resulting curves may be quite noticeable when ϵ is relatively large. Provided ϵ is kept small, this effect is negligible, but the use of very small ϵ values increases the computation considerably.

It is feasible to construct a DDA that draws an exact circle, using the equations

$$x_n+1 = x_n \cos \theta + y_n \sin \theta \qquad (20\text{-}9)$$
$$y_n+1 = y_n \cos \theta - x_n \sin \theta$$

Since θ is generally small, values of $\cos \theta$ and $\sin \theta$ are relatively easy to compute and are then constant for any particular circle radius. This pair of equations can therefore be used to advantage if multiplications can be performed inexpensively. Cohen has extended this approach to the display of general conics.

Several other circle-generating methods have been extended to plot a wider class of curves.

20-14 LINE-DRAWING DISPLAYS

Computer-generated pictures may be divided into two classes, line drawings and continuous-tone images. Examples of each are shown in Fig. 20-21, and others were shown earlier. Not only are these two classes of image very different in appearance, but they require very different techniques for their generation. Line drawings are in most respects easier to create because the algorithms for their generation are simpler, the amount of information required to represent them is less, and they can be displayed on equipment which (at least until very recently) has been more readily available. Continuous-tone images in fact could not be displayed at all until the advent in the late 1960s of the frame-buffer display, and algorithms for generating these images are still being developed. Since the display of line drawings is so much better understood, it forms a more appropriate focus for the first half of this book.

The frame-buffer display is of course capable of displaying lines. Using one of the incremental methods described earlier we can compute which pixels are intersected by a line segment, and can change the contents of the corresponding memory location in the frame buffer. This is a very practical way of displaying line drawings; in fact the line illustrations in this book were all prepared by drawing them on an interactive frame-buffer display. Nevertheless the frame buffer has some shortcomings: it cannot display very smooth lines, since the quantization effects on the screen are almost always noticeable; and it is unsuited to highly interactive image manipulations. To avoid these problems we must use displays that have been designed expressly to draw straight lines.

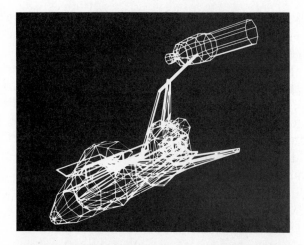

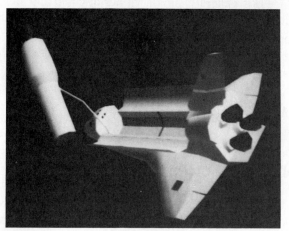

FIG. 20-21 Computer-generated views of the Space Shuttle

20-15 DISPLAY DEVICES AND CONTROLLERS

Two items of display hardware on which we shall focus our discussion are the **display device** and the **display controller.** The purpose of the display device is to convert electrical signals into visible images. The display controller sits between the computer and the display device, receiving information from the computer and converting it into signals acceptable to the device. Tasks performed by the display controller include voltage-level conversion between the computer and the display device, buffering to compensate for differences in speed of operation, and generation of line segments and text characters.

The display controller thus has the overall task of compensating for any idiosyncratic features or limitations that the display device may possess, so as to provide the computer, and its programmer, with a reasonably straightforward interface to the device. This is the original task for which the display controller was invented. Many display controllers are nowadays furnished with additional hardware to perform functions such as scaling and rotation that would otherwise be carried out by software; the purpose of this hardware is generally to improve speed of response.

20-16 DISPLAY DEVICES

In most applications of computer graphics the quality of the displayed image is very important. It is therefore not surprising that a great deal of effort has been directed toward the development of high-quality computer-display devices. When this work began in the 1950s, the CRT was the only available device capable of converting the computer's electrical signals into visible images at high speeds. In those days CRTs were small, dim, and rather expensive. Over the years, however, CRT technology has produced a range of extremely effective computer-display devices. At the same time the CRT's peculiar characteristics have had a significant influence on the development of interactive computer graphics.

Along with the continuing development of the CRT there has been an intensive search for alternatives. This has led to the development of a number of new techniques for converting electrical signals into images. Many of the resulting new devices have been inspired by the needs of the alphanumeric display and television industries; nevertheless most of the new displays are applicable to computer graphics. None of them, however, has been able to displace the CRT as the dominant graphic display device.

20-17 THE CRT

The basic arrangement of the CRT is shown in Fig. 20-22. At the narrow end of a sealed conical glass tube is an **electron gun** that emits a high-velocity, finely focused beam of electrons. The other end, the face of the CRT, is more or less flat and is coated on the inside with **phosphor,** which glows when the electron beam strikes it. The energy of the beam can be controlled so as to vary the intensity of light output and, when necessary, to cut off the light altogether. A **yoke,** or system of electromagnetic coils, is mounted on the outside of the tube at the base of the neck; it deflects the electron beam to different parts of the tube face when currents pass through the coils. The light output of the CRT's phosphor falls off rapidly after the electron beam has passed by, and a steady picture is maintained by tracing it out rapidly and repeatedly; generally this **refresh** process is performed at least 30 times a second.

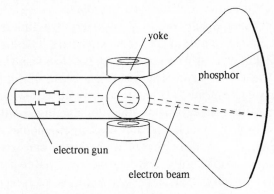

FIG. 20-22 The basic construction of a CRT

The Electron Gun

The electron gun makes use of **electrostatic fields** to focus and accelerate the electron beam. A field is generated when two surfaces are raised to different potentials (voltage levels); electrons within the field tend to travel toward the surface with the more positive potential. The force attracting the electron is directly proportional to the field potential.

The purpose of the electron gun in the CRT is to produce an electron beam with the following properties:

1. It must be accurately focused so that it produces a sharp spot of light where it strikes the phosphor;
2. It must have high velocity, since the brightness of the image depends on the velocity of the electron beam;
3. Means must be provided to control the flow of electrons so that the intensity of the trace of the beam can be controlled.

The electron gun therefore contains a number of separate parts, shown in Fig. 20-23. Electrons are generated by a **cathode** heated by an electric filament.

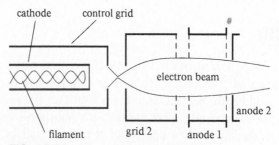

FIG. 20-23   The electron gun of a CRT

Surrounding the cathode is a cylindrical metal **control grid,** with a hole at one end that allows electrons to escape. The control grid is kept at a lower potential than the cathode, creating an electrostatic field that directs the electrons through a point source; this simplifies the subsequent focusing process. By altering the control-grid potential, we can modify the rate of flow of electrons, or **beam current,** and can thus control the brightness of the image; we can even cut off the flow of electrons altogether.

Focusing is achieved by a **focusing structure** containing two or more cylindrical metal plates at different potentials. These set up a toroidal electrostatic field that effectively catches straying electrons and deflects them back toward the axis of the beam. The result is a beam that is extremely finely focused and highly concentrated at the precise moment at which it strikes the phosphor. An **accelerating structure** is generally combined with the focusing structure. It consists of two metal plates mounted perpendicular to the beam axis with holes at their centers through which the beam can pass. The two plates are maintained at a sufficiently high relative potential to accelerate the beam to the necessary velocity; accelerating potentials of several thousand volts are not uncommon.

The resulting electron-gun structure has the advantage that it can be built as a single physical unit and mounted inside the CRT envelope. Other types of gun exist, whose focusing is performed by a coil mounted outside the tube; this is called **electromagnetic focusing** to distinguish it from the more common electrostatic method described in the preceding paragraph. The electromagnetic technique can result in finer focusing, but the electrostatic method is generally preferred in graphic displays because it leads to a cheaper gun construction.

The Deflection System

A set of coils, or **yoke,** mounted at the neck of the tube, forms part of the deflection system responsible for addressing in the CRT. Two pairs of coils are used, one to control horizontal deflection, the other vertical. A primary requirement of the deflection system is that it deflect rapidly, since speed of deflection determines how much information can be displayed without flicker. To achieve fast deflection, we must use large-amplitude currents in the yoke. An important part of the deflection system is therefore the set of **amplifiers** that convert the small voltages received from the display controller into currents of the appropriate magnitude.

The voltages used for deflection are generated by the display controller from digital values provided by the computer. These values normally represent coordinates that are converted into voltages by **digital-to-analog** (D/A) **conversion.** To draw a vector a pair of gradually changing voltages must be generated for the horizontal and vertical-deflection coils. Several methods have been used, including the following:

1. **Integrators.** An integrator is a circuit which, if provided with a constant voltage input, generates a linearly increasing or decreasing voltage as output. Thus if the Δx and Δy values defining a vector are converted into voltages and used as inputs to a pair of integrators, the appropriate deflection signals will be generated.
2. **Digital methods.** A fast digital vector generator, such as a DDA, can be constructed from hardware and used together with a pair of D/A converters. Every time a fresh x or y coordinate is generated, the coordinate value is converted to a deflection voltage, and a dot is displayed.

Phosphors

The phosphors used in a graphic display are normally chosen for their color characteristics and persistence. Ideally the persistence, measured as the time for the brightness to drop to one-tenth of its initial value, should last about 100 milliseconds or less, allowing refresh at 30-hertz rates without noticeable smearing as the image moves. Color should preferably be white, particularly for applications where dark information appears on a light background. The phosphor should also possess a number of other attributes: small grain size for added resolution, high efficiency in terms of electric energy converted to light, and resistance to burning under prolonged excitation.

In attempts to improve performance in one or another of these respects, many different phosphors have been produced, using various compounds of calcium, cadmium, and zinc, together with traces of rare-earth elements. These phosphors are identified by a numbering system, using names like P1, P4, P7, etc. The most popular phosphors for graphic displays are P7, a fairly long-persistence blue phosphor that leaves a green afterglow, and P31, which is green and has a much shorter persistence. Black-and-white television tubes generally use P4, a white phosphor with about the same persistence as P31. Phosphors with much longer persistence than any of these do exist but are rarely used because of smearing problems.

The Beam-Penetration CRT

The normal CRT can generate images of only a single color, due to the limitations of its phosphor. A color CRT device for line-drawing displays has been developed, however; it uses a multilayer phosphor and achieves color control by modulating a normally constant parameter, namely the beam-accelerating potential.

The arrangement of the beam-penetration CRT is similar to that of normal CRTs; the only unusual component is the multilayer phosphor, in which a layer of red phosphor is deposited behind the initial layer of green phosphor. If a fairly low-potential electron beam strikes the tube face, it excites only the red phosphor and therefore produces a red trace. When the accelerating potential is increased, the velocity of the beam striking the phosphor is greater, and as a result the beam penetrates into the green phosphor, increasing the green component of the light output. A limited range of colors, including red, orange, yellow and green, can be generated in this way.

The principal problem with the beam-penetration CRT is the need to change the beam-accelerating potential by significant amounts in order to switch colors. When the accelerating potential changes, the deflection system must react to compensate. The hardware or software must be designed to introduce adequate delays between changes in color, so that there is time for voltages to settle. In order to prevent frequent delays and consequent flicker, it is necessary to display all the red elements of the picture consecutively, then change the accelerating potential and display the yellow elements, and so on through all the different colors.

The Shadow-Mask CRT

The shadow-mask color CRT can display a much wider range of colors than the beam penetration CRT, and is used in the majority of color TV sets and monitors. Its construction is shown in Fig. 20-24. Just behind the phosphor-coated face of the CRT is a metal plate, the **shadow mask,** pierced with small round holes in a triangular pattern. In place of the usual single electron gun, the shadow-mask tube uses three guns, grouped in a triangle or **delta.** These three guns are responsible for the red, green, and blue components of the light output of the CRT.

The deflection system of the CRT operates on all three electron beams simul-

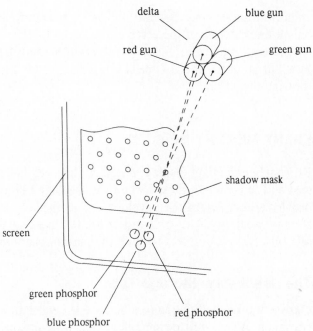

FIG. 20-24 The shadow-mask CRT

taneously, bringing all three to the same point of focus on the shadow mask. Where the three beams encounter holes in the mask, they pass through and strike the phosphor. Since they originate at three different points, however, they strike the phosphor in three slightly different spots. The phosphor of the shadow-mask tube is therefore laid down very carefully in groups of three spots—one red, one green, and one blue—under each hole in the mask, in such a way that each spot is struck only by electrons from the appropriate gun. The effect of the mask is thus to "shadow" the spots of red phosphor from all but the red beam, and likewise for the green and blue phosphor spots. We can therefore control the light output in each of the three component colors by modulating the beam current of the corresponding gun.

Great improvements have been made in the performance of the shadow-mask tube since it was first demonstrated by RCA in 1950. Nevertheless it has remained relatively expensive compared with the monochrome CRT, and still has a relatively poor performance in all respects except color range. The shadow-mask CRT compares particularly unfavorably in resolution and in efficiency of light output. Both these effects are caused by the use of the shadow mask: the grain of the triangular pattern of holes sets a limit on attainable resolution, and the mask tends to block a large proportion of the available beam energy, reducing the total brightness. With the use of very high accelerating potentials it is, however, possible to match the brightness of monochrome CRT images.

A further, unique problem with the shadow-mask tube is that of **convergence.** It is extremely difficult to adjust the three guns and the deflection system so that the electron beams are deflected exactly together, all three converging on the same hole in the shadow mask. Where they fail to converge, the three component colors appear to spread in a manner reminiscent of a poorly-aligned color printing process. Often it is possible to achieve adequate convergence over only a limited area of the screen.

The convergence problem, together with the relatively poor resolution and light output of the shadow-mask CRT, have tended to discourage its use in line-drawing displays.

20-18 INHERENT-MEMORY DEVICES

Refresh line-drawing displays based on the CRT have the disadvantages of high cost and tendency to flicker when the displayed picture is complex. These two problems have led to the development of display devices with inherent image storage capability. The most widely used of these devices is the **direct-view storage tube** (DVST); others include the plasma panel and the laser-scan display.

The Direct-view Storage Tube

Outwardly the DVST behaves like a CRT with an extremely long-persistence phosphor. A line written on the screen will remain visible for up to an hour before it fades from sight. Inwardly, too, the DVST resembles the CRT, since it uses a similar electron gun and a somewhat similar phosphor-coated screen. The beam is designed not to write directly on the phosphor, however, but on a fine-mesh wire grid, coated with dielectric and mounted just behind the screen. A pattern of positive charge is deposited on the grid, and this pattern is transferred to the phosphor by a continuous flood of electrons issuing from a separate **flood gun.** The general arrangement of the DVST is shown in detail in Fig. 20-25.

Just behind the storage mesh is a second grid, the **collector,** whose main purpose is to smooth out the flow of flood electrons. These electrons pass through the collector at a low velocity, and are attracted to the positively charged portions of the storage mesh but repelled by the rest. Electrons not repelled by the storage mesh pass right through it and strike the phosphor. In order to increase

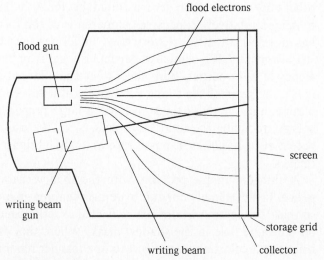

FIG. 20-25   The direct-view storage tube

the energy of these relatively slow-moving electrons and thus create a bright picture, the screen is maintained at a high positive potential by means of a voltage applied to a thin aluminum coating between the tube face and the phosphor.

Until they pass through the mesh, the flood electrons are still moving fairly slowly and therefore hardly affect the charge on the mesh. One of the problems with the DVST is in fact the difficulty in removing the stored charge to erase the picture. The normal erasing method is to apply a positive voltage to the storage mesh for one second or more; this removes all the charge but also generates a rather unpleasant flash over the entire screen surface. This erase problem is perhaps the most severe drawback of the DVST, for it prevents the use of the device for dynamic graphics applications. Other problems are its relatively poor contrast, a result of the comparatively low accelerating potential applied to the flood electrons, and the gradual degradation of the picture quality as background glow accumulates; this glow is caused by the small amounts of charge deposited on the mesh by repelled flood electrons.

In terms of performance, the DVST is somewhat inferior to the refresh CRT. Only a single level of line intensity can be displayed, and only green-phosphor tubes are available. Until recently, the DVST used relatively small-screen tubes; now tubes with 19-inch and 25-inch diagonals are available. The smaller DVST's have the advantage of a flat screen, not present in the larger variety. Some storage-tube displays possess the capability to refresh a limited number of vectors.

The Plasma Panel

The plasma panel is an unorthodox display device. Images can be written onto the display surface point-by-point; each point remains bright after it has been intensified. This makes the plasma panel functionally very similar to the DVST even though its construction is very different.

Construction of the plasma panel is shown in Fig. 20-26. It consists of two sheets of glass with thin, closely spaced gold **electrodes** attached to the inner

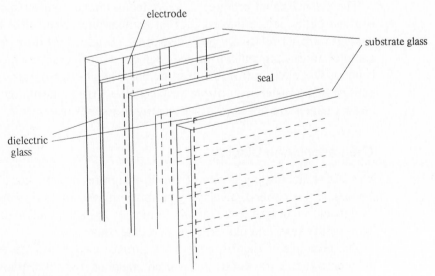

FIG. 20-26   The plasma panel

faces and covered with a dielectric material. The two sheets of glass are spaced a few thousandths of an inch apart, and the intervening space is filled with a neon-based gas and sealed. By applying voltages between the electrodes the gas within the panel is made to behave as if it were divided into tiny cells, each one independent of its neighbors. By an ingenious mechanism, certain cells can be made to glow, and thus a picture is generated. A cell is made to glow by placing a firing voltage across it by means of the electrodes. The gas within the cell begins to discharge, and this develops very rapidly into a glow. The glow can be sustained by maintaining a high-frequency alternating voltage across the cell; the shape of this **sustaining signal** is shown in Fig. 20-27. Furthermore, if the

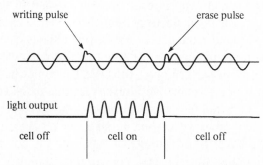

FIG. 20-27 Plasma panel sustaining signal (above) and corresponding cell light output (below)

signal amplitude is chosen correctly, cells that have not been fired will not be affected. In other words, each cell is **bistable:** it has two stable states.

Cells can be switched on by momentarily increasing the sustaining voltage; this can be done selectively by modifying the signal only in the two conductors that intersect at the desired cell. Similarly, if the sustaining signal is lowered, the glow is removed. Thus the plasma panel allows both selective writing and selective erasure, at speeds of about 20 microseconds per cell. This speed can be increased by writing or erasing several cells in parallel.

The plasma panel produces a very steady image, totally free of flicker, and is a less bulky device than a CRT of comparable screen size. Its main disadvantages are its relatively poor resolution, of about 60 dots per inch, and its complex addressing and wiring requirements. Its inherent memory is useful but is not as flexible as a frame-buffer memory. Digital memories are now so inexpensive that a raster-scan display can cost less than a plasma panel. As a result, plasma panels are not used in very many of today's displays.

The Laser-Scan Display

The laser-scan display is one of the few high-resolution, large-screen display devices. It is capable of displaying an image measuring 3 by 4 feet and still has a relatively small spot size of about $\frac{1}{100}$ inch. It has been used in displaying maps, high-quality text, and elaborate circuit diagrams.

The principle of the display is very simple: a laser is deflected by a pair of mirrors so that it traces out the desired image on a sheet of photochromic film.

This material is usually transparent, but the light from the laser leaves a dark trace on it. A light-projection system is used to project onto a large screen the image thus deposited on the film. To produce a fresh image, the display simply winds the roll of film to bring a blank region under the laser.

The mirrors deflecting the laser are extremely small and are controlled by the electrical signals received from the display controller. A complex correction mechanism compensates for the inertia of these mirrors. For interactive purposes, a second laser displays a cursor nondestructively on the screen. The overall arrangement of the display is shown in Fig. 20-28.

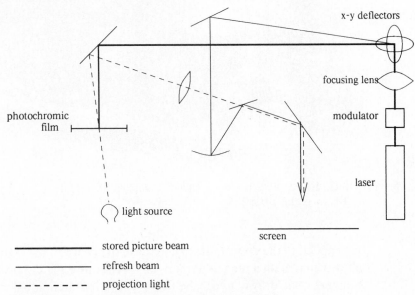

FIG. 20-28   Light beam paths in the laser-scan display

Many other devices besides the plasma panel and the laser-scan display have been proposed as solutions to the problem of generating high-quality images from a computer; none of these has yet been developed into a truly useful display device. The CRT and DVST remain the most popular and successful devices for computer graphics. The remainder of this chapter is devoted to a discussion of display hardware based on these two types of device.

20-19 THE STORAGE-TUBE DISPLAY

A typical storage-tube display, the Tektronix 4006-1, is shown in Fig. 20-29. It incorporates a 7- by 10-inch DVST and a built-in alphanumeric keyboard. The screen coordinate system is divided into 1024 positions horizontally and 760 positions vertically.

The task of generating signals for the DVST from computer-supplied data is carried out by the display controller. The controller receives a series of instructions from the computer, each specifying a single element of the picture. For example, we can display a dot on the screen by supplying the controller with its *x* and *y* coordinates. The controller converts these coordinates into voltages that

FIG. 20-29 The Tektronix 4006-1 Computer Display Terminal (Copyright © 1983 Tektronix, Inc., reproduced with permission.)

are applied to the deflection yoke to move the beam to the right spot; the energy of the beam is then increased momentarily to store the dot on the storage mesh. Complete line drawings can be decomposed into individual dots for display in this fashion, using point-plotting techniques.

To reduce the computational overhead and improve performance, most storage-tube displays are designed instead to plot vectors, i.e., segments of straight lines. The computer supplies the two endpoints of the vector; the display controller positions the electron beam at the first endpoint and moves it in a straight path to the other end. The beam's path is determined by a vector generator which feeds the deflection yoke with voltages that change at a steady rate as the vector is being traced out.

Vector-drawing instructions do not define both endpoints of the vector explicitly, but make use of the **current beam position,** the position reached by the electron beam after plotting the previous point or vector. Every vector starts at the current beam position and finishes at the specified endpoint, which then becomes the current beam position. This provides a convenient means of drawing connected vectors; disjoint vectors must be drawn by preceding each vector-drawing instruction with an instruction that moves the current beam position to the start of the vector.

A storage-tube display that uses 10-bit positive-integer coordinates must supply 20 bits of data with every instruction. At least one additional bit is required as an operation code to distinguish between the various kinds of instructions. To avoid feeding 21 or more bits at a time to the display controller, instructions are broken down into 7-bit instruction bytes. It is then possible to transmit instructions to the display in the same **serial asynchronous** fashion used to transmit alphanumeric data to text terminals. Almost all storage-tube displays will accept serial asynchronous instruction codes; this greatly simplifies the problem of attaching them to a computer.

The use of a 7-bit instruction byte leads to a somewhat complex instruction set for the display. The Tektronix 4006-1, for example, has the instruction set shown in Fig. 20-30. The two commands ENTER GRAPHICS MODE and LEAVE

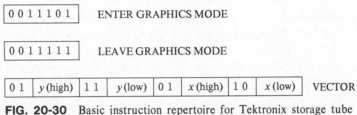

| 0 0 1 1 1 0 1 | ENTER GRAPHICS MODE |

| 0 0 1 1 1 1 1 | LEAVE GRAPHICS MODE |

| 0 1 | y (high) | 1 1 | y (low) | 0 1 | x (high) | 1 0 | x (low) | VECTOR |

FIG. 20-30 Basic instruction repertoire for Tektronix storage tube display. The first VECTOR command following an ENTER GRAPHICS MODE command simply sets the current beam position, without drawing a vector

GRAPHICS MODE permit the display to act both as an alphanumeric text terminal and as a graphic display. When the display is in graphics mode, instruction bytes are interpreted as vector-plotting commands. The LEAVE GRAPHICS MODE command switches the display to a mode in which it interprets instruction bytes as ASCII character codes; each character is displayed on the screen at the current beam position, which is then moved to the right by the width of the displayed character. After plotting characters, the ENTER GRAPHICS MODE command must be given before additional points and vectors can be plotted.

The Tektronix 4006-1 uses a vector instruction format that permits compact representation of pictures containing short vectors. If two successive endpoints have coordinates that differ only in their lower-order five bits it is unnecessary to transmit the higher-order bits. Fig. 20-31 shows the encoding of a storage-tube representation of a simple picture.

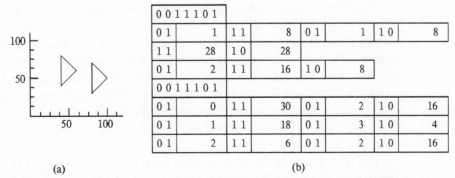

0 0 1 1 1 0 1							
0 1	1	1 1	8	0 1	1	1 0	8
1 1	28	1 0	28				
0 1	2	1 1	16	1 0	8		
0 0 1 1 1 0 1							
0 1	0	1 1	30	0 1	2	1 0	16
0 1	1	1 1	18	0 1	3	1 0	4
0 1	2	1 1	6	0 1	2	1 0	16

(a)   (b)

FIG. 20-31 A simple picture (a) encoded for a storage-tube display, using the instruction set of Fig. 20-30

20-20 THE REFRESH LINE-DRAWING DISPLAY

Before 1968, when the first storage-tube displays were introduced, virtually every graphic display used a refresh CRT. This type of display, although inherently more complicated and expensive than the storage-tube display, is still one of the most popular types of display for interactive work. Its popularity derives mainly from its ability to display dynamically changing pictures. In many applications, such pictures are extremely effective in presenting the results of simulations or in helping the user of an interactive program to operate it.

The refresh line-drawing display, like the storage-tube display, contains a display controller to convert the computer's output signals into deflection voltages for the yoke of the CRT. In some respects this controller is very similar to that of the storage-tube display; it accepts instructions to plot vectors, and it uses the current beam position to define their starting points.

What are the characteristics that make a refresh display controller different? First and foremost, the controller must operate at high speed. The CRT can maintain a steady, flicker-free picture only if it is fed with a fresh description of the picture 30 or so times a second. The picture may contain as many as 5000 vectors, each of which must be passed to the controller during its ⅓₀-second refresh cycle. Thus the controller must be able to process 150,000 (30 × 5000) vector instructions per second. This lies well beyond the comfortable range of serial asynchronous transmission.

In the refresh display controller, speed of refresh is increased in two ways: by using a wider **data path** between the computer's memory and the controller, and by accessing memory more efficiently. The typical computer to which refresh displays are attached has a 16-bit parallel fashion. This can be handled by a program executing in the computer's central processing unit (CPU) that transmits each instruction to the display upon request. To avoid taxing the CPU, however, the display controller will normally use **direct memory access;** it reads display data from memory independently of the CPU, from which it merely "steals" a memory cycle whenever it needs an instruction. The controller contains an **address register,** updated after each instruction has been fetched, and this register tells the controller where to find the next instruction. Instructions are stored in a contiguous sequence of memory locations and are collectively known as the **display file.**

The line-drawing display usually accept instructions for point-plotting as well as for vector-drawing. Typical formats for a set of point-plotting and vector-drawing instructions are shown in Fig. 20-32. Note the use of **relative** endpoint coordinates, i.e., endpoints defined in terms of the current beam position, and the use of one bit to control intensification. Unintensified points may be used to reset the current beam position, and unintensified vectors move the beam position through the distance specified without producing a visible trace. Fig. 20-33 shows the use of this instruction set to describe the picture shown in Fig. 20-31a.

The refresh display needs **flexibility** in addition to high speed in order to take advantage of the CRT's dynamic properties. As we have noted, we can use images that change dynamically, either to display the state of a program during

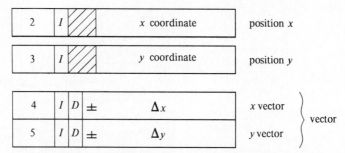

FIG. 20-32 Point-plotting and vector-drawing instructions for a refresh display. I = 0 for unintensified, 1 for intensified; D = 1 to draw vector. In a two-word vector, D = 0 in the first word, 1 in the second. Horizontal or vertical vectors may be drawn with a single instruction, with D = 1

execution or to provide the operator of an interactive program with immediate graphic feedback. These changes are effected by means of corresponding changes to the display file. It is generally somewhat difficult to make rapid changes to a large contiguous block of display instructions, but if the display file can be broken into a number of disjoint sequences, changes can be made more easily. Most display controllers therefore provide an instruction to reset the contents of the address register. This is called a **jump instruction,** since its effect is analogous to a computer's jump or branch instruction.

A display controller that can reset its own address register by means of a jump instruction can of course store in this register the starting address of the display file whenever it reaches the end. This puts the controller in an endless loop, requiring no further attention from the computer; it is even possible to make changes to the display file without stopping the display. We generally use the term **display processor** for any display controller that can function entirely independently of the CPU. Nowadays almost all refresh line-drawing displays have this capability.

It is common to provide a **subroutine-jump capability** in addition to the basic jump instruction. The subroutine-jump instruction sets the display processor's address register to the specified address; a **return-jump instruction** restores the register's previous contents and in this way effects a return from the subroutine. To allow subroutines to call other subroutines we can use a **push-down stack** to store return addresses. This is an array of memory locations with a pointer

2	0		40
3	0		40
4	0	0	20
5	1	1	20
4	0	0	−20
5	1	1	20
5	1	1	−40
2	0		80
3	0		30
4	0	0	20
5	1	1	20
4	0	0	−20
5	1	1	20
5	1	1	−40

FIG. 20-33 A display file representation of Fig. 20-31a using the instruction set of Fig. 20-32

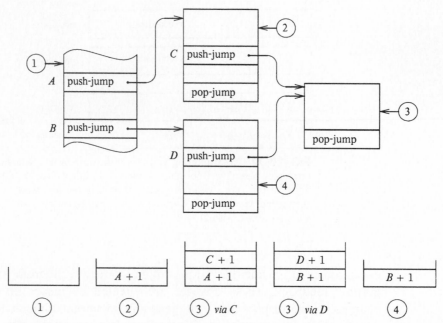

FIG. 20-34 Use of push-jump and pop-jump instructions to call a set of nested display subroutines

addressing the top of the stack, i.e., the most recently used location. When a subroutine-jump instruction is executed, the return address is pushed into the stack, and the stack pointer is raised to point to the next location in which the return address is deposited. A subroutine jump instruction of this kind is often called a **push-jump.** To effect a return, the return address is popped off the stack, the contents of the top location are transferred to the address register, and the stack pointer is lowered. This is akin to "popping" the contents of the top location off the stack, and the return instruction is therefore called a **pop-jump.** Fig. 20-34 shows the state of the stack at various points during the display of a set of nested subroutines.

Display subroutines, like ordinary subroutines, offer a way of eliminating repetitive sequences of instructions; in applications that involve the display of repeated symbols, display subroutines can thus reduce the size of the display file. A pair of positioning instructions must be placed before the subroutine jump to set the position of the symbol; Figure 20-35 shows the use of subroutine-jump instructions to generate the picture of Fig. 20-31a.

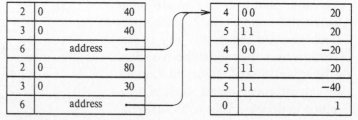

FIG. 20-35 Use of a display subroutine to represent the picture of Fig. 20-31a

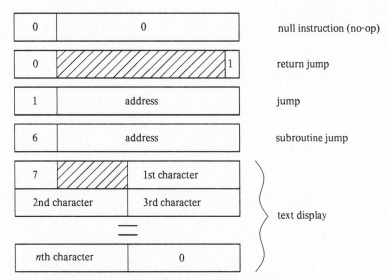

FIG. 20-36 Jump and text-display instruction formats

An obvious use for the subroutine-jump instruction is in displaying text; each character is represented as a subroutine, and strings of characters are included in the display file as sequences of subroutine jumps. This method is wasteful of space since it uses one 16-bit word per displayed character. A more efficient approach involves the provision of a **text-display** instruction and the use of a hardware **character generator,** rather than a set of subroutines, to generate the characters. The text-display instruction allows each displayed character to be encoded in a single 8-bit byte. The character generator receives these bytes from the display processor and generates either sequences of short strokes or matrices of dots, which it reads from a small read-only memory.

The formats of the jump and text display instructions are shown in Fig. 20-36. Most refresh line-drawing displays provide additional instructions to allow control of brightness, display of short vectors or curves, and so on. These instructions are easily accommodated within the instruction repertoire.

sec.21

Artificial Intelligence and Robotics

Harry L. Helms

21-1 INTRODUCTION

Artificial intelligence is generally used to refer to the ability of a computer system to perform tasks, such as reasoning and learning, that human intelligence is capable of. **Robots** may be defined as intelligent machines, or as a computer system with hardware for manipulating and responding to the environment outside the computer system. The body of theory and practice concerning robots has become known as robotics. Both artificial intelligence and robotics have been the subjects of increasing interest in recent years.

21-2 COMPUTERS AND INTELLIGENCE

Despite their popular image, computers actually lack most of the attributes associated with the term "intelligence." Computers can perform tasks quickly and reliably, but such tasks and the rules governing their performance must be precisely defined. If the tasks or their supporting data are outside of the parameters the computer has been programmed to handle, the computer cannot make allowances for such variations.

The problem of designing artificial intelligence systems becomes clearer when we realize "intelligence" consists of two distinct components. One component is factual, comprised of objective, measurable, and quantifiable information about events and objects. The factual component of intelligence can be handled by a computer without great difficulty. However, a second component of intelligence involves associations, pattern recognition, inference, experience, and intuition. This second component of intelligence has proved to be far more difficult to incorporate in a computer system.

Some tasks that involve "intelligence" are quite simple and readily performed on a computer. For example, suppose we have two character strings as follows:

"ABCDEFGHIJK"

"ABCDEFGHIJ"

It would be a simple and rapid operation for the computer system to determine that these two strings are not equivalent. However, for the computer to tell **how** the two strings are not equivalent would be a much more difficult task. A human with a knowledge of the alphabet would realize that one letter was missing. For a computer to do the same, it would have to go through several matching routines (possibly against a reference such as the complete alphabet) before reaching an answer.

Human intelligence is able to fill in gaps in available data through experience, intuition, or even guesses. A computer, on the other hand, must rely on the data given it. Humans are capable of modifying their approach to solving a problem if the correct solution is not found; computer systems must follow the instructions contained in their programs.

The more subjective components of intelligence are present in many situations which may, at first glance, be purely factual. Pattern recognition is one such example. A person and computer can be "taught" to associate the pattern of a person's image (as in a photograph) with a name (such as John Jones). In such a case, purely factual intelligence is involved. A person would still be able to recognize John Jones if he wore different clothes or combed his hair differently. However, a computer would be unable to match the new image of John Jones with the old one.

Another example is how humans may add subjective elements to information that would be interpreted in a strictly factual manner by the computer. For example, the character string

"What do you mean?"

could be interpreted in many different ways by a human. It could be viewed as a simple and direct request for information. It could also be interpreted as a humorous remark, a defensive reaction to an accusation, or even as an accusation. A computer, even one with an entire dictionary in memory, would not be able to give such varying interpretations to the string. Indeed, many problems in artificial intelligence actually are problems involving language and how it is to be interpreted.

A further consideration in artificial intelligence is the "hardware" used by humans and computers. Although the functioning of the brain on the cellular level is not fully understood, it appears that the brain processes information through the almost simultaneous activation of millions of cellular "logic devices." By contrast, a computer passes information through a single processing unit. It may well be that the human brain has a vast, inherent superiority over computer hardware in processing the more subjective components of intelligence. Closing this gap could be the key to developing artificial intelligence systems that begin to approach the abilities of the human brain.

21-3 EXPERT SYSTEMS

Expert systems are an attempt to replicate some human reasoning and decision-making processes in a computer system. Expert systems are made up of three elements: a data base, a rule base, and a rule interpreter.

The **data base** is a term for the working memory where factual information is stored. The **rule base** is sometimes referred to as the knowledge base. It is a file of judgmental rules applicable to a specified set of problems; the rules are obtained from human experts. The **rule interpreter** is also called the general reasoning program. It applies the rules in the rule base to the facts stored in the data base.

The rules in the rule base are written in the following structure:

IF conditions
THEN consequence with a specified probability of being correct

During execution of an expert systems program, rules from the rule base are loaded into the rule interpreter. The rule interpreter then begins to examine the facts in the data base. If it finds a fact or set of facts matching the specified conditions in a rule, it adds the consequence of a rule to the data base. The rule interpreter then resumes examination of the data base.

It is clear that each rule is actually a subroutine. However, it is not called by name or line number; rather, it is executed when certain types of data appear. Such a subroutine is said to be **pattern driven.**

Another approach to expert systems is to specify certain goals to be achieved. The rule interpreter examines the rules for those rules whose consequences match or lead to the desired goals. The rule interpreter scans the data base for those facts which would result in the desired conseqence when used as the conditions for a rule subroutine. If no facts are found to match any of the conditions, and no rule exists to help achieve a specified goal, the interpreter will indicate to the human operator that additional facts or rules are needed.

Expert systems have been successfully applied to a variety of diagnostic problems in fields such as geology and medicine.

21-4 ROBOTICS

Robotics is a term for the body of engineering theory and practice concerning the design and applications of robots. In a very real sense, robotics represents a synthesis of electrical and mechanical engineering.

Many of the problems encountered in development of artificial intelligence also apply to robotics; many new problems also arise. Most of these problems are concerned with a robot's interaction with the environment. For many applications, it is not sufficient for the robot to be able to manipulate objects in the outside world; the robot must have the ability to receive and interpret information about the outside environment and adjust its actions in response to such data. Consider the analogy of a human writing with a pen. It is not enough for the person to be able to manipulate the pen. The person must also be able to judge the amount of pressure to apply to the paper, whether the letters are being correctly formed, and whether the paper is actually making contact with the pen.

As one might surmise from the preceding, the all-purpose robot that has long been a staple of science fiction is still many years away from realization. Robots today tend to be devoted to a specific task or can be programmed to perform desired tasks.

21-5 TASKS IN ROBOTICS

A task in robotics can be described in terms of the individual movements necessary to accomplish a desired action, such as picking up an object or tightening a screw. A task can also be thought of as a cycle, with the individual actions composing the cycle.

Such a definition of a task is ideal for many situations where robots are used today, such as spot welding or picking items from an assembly line. The task to be performed does not have to be varied, and is highly repetitive. It is then easy to specify the various parameters for the actions to be performed, such as how far a robot arm should move, the amount of pressure that an object should be gripped with, and how long a weld should be performed.

The situation gets more more complex as uncertainty enters the task cycle. For example, an item could come down an assembly line out of position and could not be properly welded. Or items may have different strengths and need to be gripped with varying degrees of force. This again illustrates the importance of a robot to be able to detect changes in the environment and respond to them, such as being able to move an object to the proper position for welding. This can be done within the limits of current technology by having a pre-defined range of acceptable parameters in the robot's memory. When it is time to perform a task, the robot can evaluate the parameters of the situation. If the parameters are out of the acceptable range, the task is not performed. The robot could then perform a number of alternative tasks, such as alert a human operator, remove the object from the production line, or perform actions designed to bring the component within the acceptable range of parameters.

Designing a robot physically able to perform a desired task is not a major problem today. However, developing the software is a considerable undertaking even for relatively simple tasks. In fact, development of the necessary software has been the biggest single obstacle to implementing robots in many industrial situations.

21-6 ROBOTS AND PERSONAL COMPUTERS

It was perhaps inevitable that personal computer experimenters and enthusiasts would also turn their attention to robotics. By 1982, several robot devices were available as peripherals for many small personal computers.

A typical unit is the Microbot Alpha, manufactured by Microbot, Inc., of Mountain View, California. It is a robotic arm which moves through five different axes. It also includes a cable operated mechanical gripper capable of handling a load of up to one-half kilogram (or slightly more than one pound). It has an RS-232C serial interface so it can receive operating commands from a microcomputer. There is also a controller on the unit having both RAM and ROM, and a microprocessor controls the operation of the motors on the robot. Like many robots, the motors move in discrete steps rather than in an "analog" fashion.

The integration of microcomputers and robots received a major boost in 1982 when IBM introduced their Model 7535 Manufacturing System. This is a robotic arm which uses the IBM Personal Computer for control and software development. Many observers feel that robotics and microcomputers will become even more closely integrated in the years ahead, since the availability of processing power due to microcomputers solves one of the main problems in developing a robot device.

sec.22

Character Printers

Louis Hohenstein

22-1 INTRODUCTION

Character printers are one of the two devices used to prepare a permanent (or **hard-copy**) record of computer output; the other is the graphic plotter. It is necessary to make a working distinction between printers and plotters as they now exist. Although traditionally printers have printed letters arnd numbers while plotters have plotted lines and curves to form line graphs, drawings, or pictures, actually printers and plotters overlap in function. Most printers can plot graphs in some fashion, using X, *, -, and other type symbols to form lines and coordinates. Even crude pictures are possible with standard characters.

Most plotters, on the other hand, print letters and numbers, since both letters and numbers are merely graphic forms themselves. Devices called **printer-plot-**

Adapted from *Computer Peripherals for Minicomputers, Microprocessors, and Personal Computers*, by Louis Hohenstein. Copyright © 1980. Used by permission of McGraw-Hill, Inc. All rights reserved.

ters by their manufacturers both print and plot with some degree of efficiency. As printer and plotter technology develops, there may be a full merging of the capability of any printing device to plot or print with equal efficiency.

For our present purposes, printers are devices whose purpose is printing letters, numbers, and similar characters in text-readable form, which they do more efficiently than graphic plotting. Plotters are devices whose designed purpose is printing diagrams with continuous lines, which they do more efficiently than printing text characters.

Printers versus Terminals and Teleprinters

A printing terminal consists of a printer with several other peripheral devices grouped together, usually for remote access with a central computer. For example, **teleprinters** are printing terminals with interfaces for communication over telephone lines.

22-2 CLASSIFICATION OF PRINTERS

Printers used in mini- and microcomputers are classified in three broad categories.

IMPACT VERSUS NONIMPACT PRINTERS Impact printers form characters on paper in the traditional way by striking the paper with a print head and squeezing an inked ribbon between the print head and the paper. Nonimpact printers form characters without engaging the print mechanism with the print surface., e.g., by heating sensitized paper or by spraying ink from a jet.

FULLY FORMED VERSUS DOT-MATRIX CHARACTERS Fully formed characters are like those made by a standard typewriter; all parts of the character are embossed in reverse on the type bars of the typewriter. When printed, all type elements appear connected or fully formed. Dot-matrix characters are shaped by a combination of dots that form a group representing a letter or number when viewed together.

CHARACTER AT A TIME VERSUS LINE AT A TIME Character-at-a-time printers (**character printers** or **serial printers**) print each character serially and virtually instantaneously. Line-at-a-time printers (**line printers**) print each line virtually instantaneously. (Some high-technology printers, e.g., those using lasers and xerographic methods, print lines so rapidly that they virtually print a page at a time and are therefore sometimes called **page printers.** They are only rarely used with mini- and microcomputers for special purposes like phototypesetting.)

Figure 22-1 shows the classification of printers within these major categories, along with further classification by printer technology used in subsequent sections of this chapter. Table 22-1 summarizes the characteristics of printers.

TABLE 22-1 Printer Characteristics

Impact classification	Capacity	Printing technology	Approximate speed*	Remarks
Impact	Character at a time	Cylinder font carrier	10 ch/s	Model 33 Teletype
		Ball font carrier	15 ch/s	IBM Selectric typewriter
		Spinning daisy-wheel, thimble font carrier	30–55 ch/s	Highest-speed fully formed character serial printer
		Wire or dot matrix	30–330 ch/s	Highest-speed character impact printer for utility computer use
	Line at a time	Band	To 3000 l/min	Interchangeable character sets
		Chain or train	To 2000 l/min	Interchangeable character sets
		Drum	300–2000 l/min	Subject to slight vertical misregistration at highest speeds
		Print-comb dot matrix	To 600 l/s	
Nonimpact	Character at a time	Thermal dot matrix	30–120 ch/s	Low cost, low noise; requires special paper; no multiple copies
		Electrostatic dot matrix	160–2000 ch/s	Special paper; low print quality
		Ink jet	30–1000 ch/s	No special paper required; no multiple copies
	Line at a time	Electrostatic dot matrix	300–18,000 l/min	Special paper and toner process
		Laser or xerographic	4000–21,000 l/min	High speed, high cost, high maintenance, high-volume printing
		Photooptical	150–1000 l/min	Used for typesetting with minicomputer controllers

*Where ch/s = characters per second; l/min = lines per minute; l/s = lines per second.

22-3 PRINTER CHARACTER SET

Most printers used with mini- and microcomputers use ASCII codes. Printers are specified as using the 48-character set, the 64-character set, the 96-character set, and the 128-character set.

The 48- and 64-character sets include commonly used special symbols, numbers, a space, and the uppercase English alphabet (Fig. 22-2). The 96 ASCII character set includes the lowercase English alphabet and several additional special symbols. Of the 96 characters **space** and **delete** do not print, leaving 94 printable characters.

The entire 128-character ASCII set contains 32 characters normally used for communication and control. These characters usually do not print, and when a printer carries a specification of the 128 ASCII character set, it normally refers to its expanded function as a communication or control terminal. In spe-

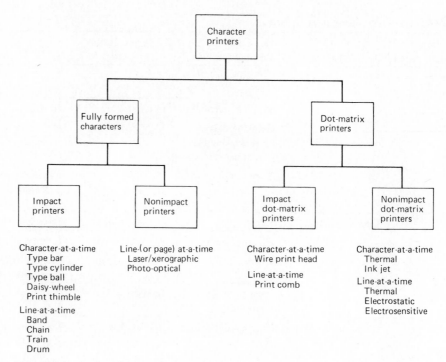

FIG. 22-1 A classification of printers

cial applications, however, the 32 codes are additionally available and can be printed using specially assigned symbols. This method is used when printing symbols for languages other than English, where the English-character ASCII codes do not apply. Any of the 128 forms, whether foreign-language characters or graphic lines and shapes used as graphic building blocks, may be printed. When graphic shapes are used in lieu of text characters, the printer's ability to draw forms, bar graphs, and other nontext graphics is increased.

FIG. 22-2 Teletype printers were adapted early as computer printers. Many of the original model 33 printers are still used. (a) Automatic send-receive (ASR). (b) Keyboard send-receive (KSR). (c) Read only (RO). (Teletype Corp.)

22-4 CHARACTER-AT-A-TIME IMPACT PRINTERS FOR FULLY FORMED CHARACTERS

The classic typewriter is an example of this printer. Characters are fully formed because all character components are embossed on each type bar and the entire character prints at one time. Ordinary type-bar typewriters, however, do not lend themselves to computer use because they lack the computer coding interface for easy communication and are relatively slow. Nevertheless, some ordinary typewriters have been used with computers by mounting solenoids over the keys and interfacing the solenoids with special circuits directly to the computer.

The classic printer used with the mini- and microcomputers in the past was the Teletype model 33 printer, originally designed for printed communication over telephone lines for news transmission (Fig. 22-2). The ready availability and low cost of these printers plus their relatively easy interfacing made them a natural for use with small computers. The model 33 prints at a rate of 10 characters per second, which is slow by today's print speeds of upward from 55 characters per second for similar printers designed for computer use.

The print mechanisms for the model 33 Teletypewriter is a vertical cylinder. Characters are embossed in several rows and columns around the cylinder (Fig. 22-3). The ASCII character code sent to the printer is translated into a motion that rotates the cylinder so that the column containing the desired character faces the paper and raises or lowers the cylinder to present the column containing the desired character directly to the paper. A hammer mechanism propels the cylinder toward the paper, where only the positioned character strikes the ribbon, creating the printed impression of the character on the paper.

Model 33 Teletypewriters are interfaced with small computers by a 20- or 60-milliamp (MA) current loop used to transmit ASCII-coded bits serially. Many home and small-business computers have a 20- or 60-mA input-output port built into the computer or easily available by adapters to convert an RS232C port to model 33 Teletype use. Despite the old design and relative slowness by modern standards, numerous model 33 Teletypes are still in use.

Similar to the model 33 Teletype in print-head concept is the IBM Selectric typewriter, which uses a type head mounted on a sphere (commonly called a **golf ball**) with characters embossed around the surface. To impact the ribbon and then the paper, the transmitted character code ultimately causes the golf ball to rotate around a vertical axis and tilt on a horizontal one until the desired character faces the ribbon. Like the Teletype, the golf ball requires a two-dimensional mechanical motion (Fig. 22-4). Several adapter kits are available to convert the Selectric typewriter for use with mini- and microcomputers.

Both the model 33 Teletype and Selectric typewriter are designed for other purposes and adapted for use as computer printers. Another type of fully formed character printer designed for computer use has characters mounted on the periphery of a spinning print head. Two versions of this printing method, **daisy-wheel** printers (Fig. 22-5) and those using print **thimbles,** operate similarly.

A daisy-wheel print head is mounted on a rotating disk with flexible flower-like petals similar to a daisy. Each petal contains the embossed character in

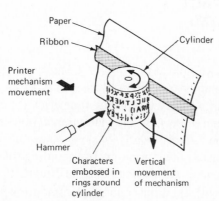

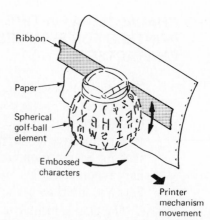

FIG. 22-3 The model 33 Teletype uses a cylinder printer. Character set is embossed around the cylinder, which rotates and shifts up and down to position the character to be printed. The hammer strikes the cylinder to print a character

FIG. 22-4 The golf ball used on the IBM Selectric typewriter is an updated version of a cylinder printer. The sphere rotates to position a character, and the entire sphere strikes the paper

reverse. As the daisy wheel spins, a hammer strikes the desired flexible petal containing the character, in turn impacting the paper with the embossed character through an inked ribbon.

A thimble print head is similar to a daisy wheel except that the flexible petals are turned upward and shaped like a thimble or a basket. Characters are mounted on flexible leaves around the periphery of the basket. As the basket spins and moves horizontally across the paper, a hammer strikes the appropriate character petal as it spins into position.

Because they are designed for computer use, both types of spinning-wheel printers have unique characteristics useful for computer printing. Most important is high-speed printing (about 50 characters per second) with fully formed characters achieving typewriter print quality. These features make spinning-wheel printers useful for word-processing applications.

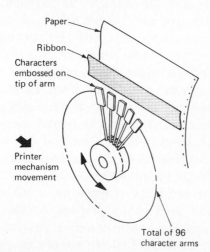

FIG. 22-5 Characters are embossed on the petals of the daisy wheel. The wheel spins to present each character for printing. A hammer strikes the character petal when it is in position

The spinning print head is interchangeable, permitting proportional-spacing type fonts, optical-character-reading fonts, multilingual fonts, and special-application fonts (Fig. 22-6).

Wide-carriage versions permit paper widths up to 16 in, and some models have two print wheels simultaneously printing on the same line (Fig. 22-7). Several models of daisy-wheel printers are illustrated in Fig. 22-8.

Character-at-a-time printing, as we normally think of it, is left-to-right printing to the end of the line, stop,

FIG. 22-6 Daisy wheels are interchangeable to permit printing with different fonts (Qume Corp./ITT)

FIG. 22-7 Dual daisy wheels mounted on one carriage permit double-speed printing (Qume Corp./ITT)

return carriage, and start a second line, again printed left to right. This is unidirectional printing. Spinning-wheel printers are capable of bidirectional printing. The second line of print is stored in a buffer memory within the printer control circuitry and can be printed in either direction, depending on which takes the least printer time. If the next line to be printed is a full line of type and the print head is already in the rightmost print position, the line will be printed right to left, backward from the way we read it. This eliminates the print time otherwise lost by returning the print head across the width of the print line to the leftmost print position. Control circuits in the printer evaluate each printed line and select whichever print direction takes the least time.

Some programmable graphics capability is achieved by fractional horizontal spacing of the print head, along with fractional vertical paper spacing, under program control. Figure 22-9 illustrates a typed curve and the super- and sub-

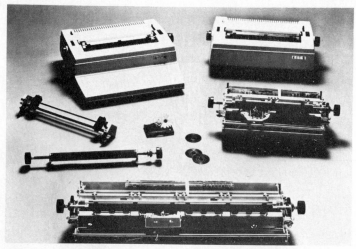

FIG. 22-8 Components and several models of the daisy-wheel impact printer (Qume Corp./ITT)

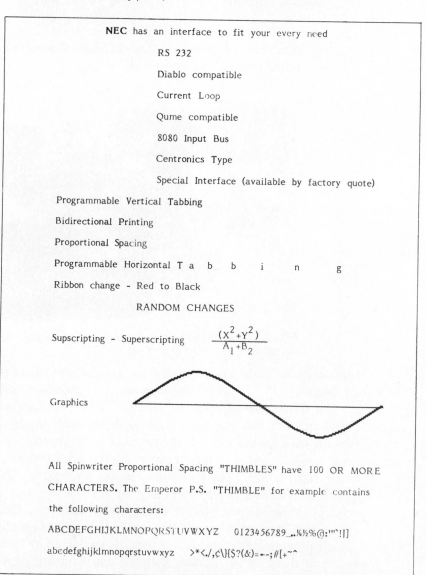

FIG. 22-9 A print sample demonstrating the flexibility of the thimble printer, similar to the daisy-wheel impact printer (NEC Information Systems)

scripting made possible by program-controlled spacing. For example, normal horizontal character spacing is 10 characters per inch (25.4 mm), but under program control horizontal character spacing can be performed in $\frac{1}{120}$-in (0.2-mm) increments.

Correspondingly, paper is spaced vertically (called *line feed*, or *forms feed*) to print six lines per inch normally. Under program control, line-feed spacing is controllable down to $\frac{1}{48}$-in (0.5-mm) increments. With this ability to position the spinning print wheel horizontally in small increments as well as line feed the paper up or down in similar small increments, small-step XY plotting can be achieved as well as normal line printing of text.

22-5 LINE-AT-A-TIME IMPACT PRINTERS FOR FULLY FORMED CHARACTERS

These printers are customarily called **line printers.** Characters or spaces constituting a printable line (typically 132 character positions wide) are printed simultaneously across the entire line. Paper is spaced up and the next line printed. The speeds for line printers range from several hundred to over thousands of lines per minute.

Because of the high print speeds and high equipment costs relative to character-at-a-time printers, line printers are used for high volumes of printed output and less frequently with microcomputers. Examples of use are printing accounts-receivable statements, large payrolls, inventory-stock-status lists, and other volume computer uses for commercial applications.

An embossed type font is positioned across a line for printing by using embossed type either on a carrier, consisting of a chain, train, or band moving horizontally across the paper and print line, or on a drum rotating in front of the paper with characters embossed typically in 132 columns on the drum. As the drum rotates, the columns of characters pass vertically across the paper and the print line. In both methods, hammers (one for each of the 132 print positions) fire when the correct character is positioned, imprinting the character on the paper with an inked ribbon.

Figure 22-10 shows the print band for an impact line printer. Print characters are embossed on the band. The band revolves between two capstans, passing in front of the paper. An inked ribbon is positioned between the moving band and the paper. As print characters on the band move by the 132 horizontal print positions, the 132 corresponding print hammers behind the paper strike the band at the appropriate time, causing the line of characters to print, each desired character printing in the 132-print positions (Fig. 22-11). Timing circuits in the printer controller keep track of when each letter or number is positioned in each print position to control the hammer firing time. A chain printer operates on the same principle (Fig. 22-12). With this technique a chain revolves in front of the ribbon and paper. Each link in the chain is designed to hold a pallet on which type characters are embossed. Hammers are located behind the paper, and each of 132 hammers strikes the moving type pallet when the desired character passes the position in which it is timed to print.

More than one set of characters is embossed on a chain or band; the fewer the characters in the set the more lines per minute are printed. For this reason,

FIG. 22-10 The print band on this band printer is easily changed to permit substitution of character sets (Dataproducts Corp.)

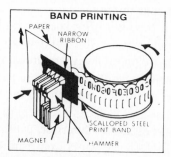

FIG. 22-11 Band printers (also called bell printers) contain characters embossed on the band. A set of hammers, one for each position, strikes the paper. (Mannesmann Tally Corporation).

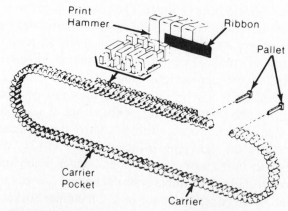

FIG. 22-12 On a chain printer, embossed characters on pallets are rotated on a chain. (Teletype Corp.)

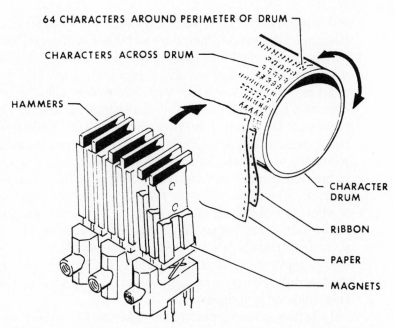

64 CHARACTERS AROUND PERIMETER OF DRUM

CHARACTERS ACROSS DRUM

HAMMERS

CHARACTER DRUM

RIBBON

PAPER

MAGNETS

FIG. 22-13   On a drum printer characters are embossed around the drum, one set of characters for each print position across the paper. A hammer strikes each time a character to be printed on a line is in position. (Data-products Corp.)

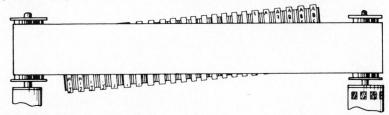

FIG. 22-14   Canting the ribbon across the face of the drum equalizes ribbon wear (Control Data Corp.)

many line printers use only the uppercase 64-character ASCII set. Some printers use even fewer, providing only the 26 alphabet characters, 10 numerals, and a few other symbols. Many printers feature easy removal of the font carrier to make it possible to change character sets and consequently adjust the print efficiency to suit the needs of the immediate printer application.

Figure 22-13 illustrates a drum printer. Each of the 64 or 96 characters used is embossed in 132 columns around the drum corresponding to print positions. The drum rotates in front of the paper and ribbon (Fig. 22-14). Print hammers strike the paper, imprinting the character from the drum through the ribbon and forming the impression on the paper.

22-6 LINE-AT-A-TIME NONIMPACT PRINTERS FOR FULLY FORMED CHARACTERS

These printers are special-purpose devices used for typesetting and extremely high-speed line-printer output. They use photographic, xerographic, and laser technologies to form complete characters without striking the printing surface. Because of their special purpose and high cost, they are used less frequently as peripherals for mini- and microcomputers, but they themselves use mini- and microcomputers as printer control devices.

Laser printers combine laser and xerographic print technologies for extremely high-speed printing; as of 1980, speeds of up to 18,000 to 21,000 lines per minute are possible, corresponding to 300 to 350 lines per second. The laser beam controlled by the computer places print data on an electrically charged rotating drum or belt. Toner particles cling to charged sections and then are transferred to paper to form the printed page. The print toner is finally fused by heat.

Mini- and microcomputers are also used to control **phototypesetters.** In these systems character images of a specified size and font are selected by the computer and optically projected onto a photosensitive paper (or film), where the lines of copy are recorded photographically. The exposed paper or film is developed, and the phototypeset copy is used to make press plates for printing books, magazines, or newspapers.

Projection of the character font is achieved by either a cathode-ray tube with character generators stored in memory or by character masks used for optically projecting selected characters, all controlled by a minicomputer. Figures 22-15 to 22-17 illustrate a minicomputer-controlled cathode-ray tube phototypesetter, which is actually a special-purpose nonimpact line printer.

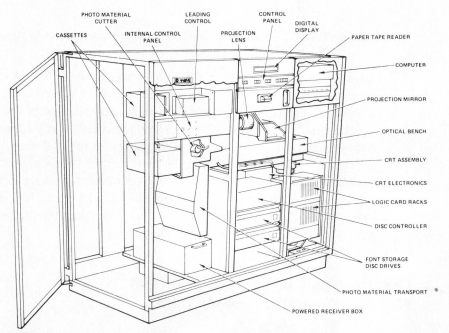

FIG. 22-15 This minicomputer-controlled photooptical line printer is used for typesetting (Harris Corp.)

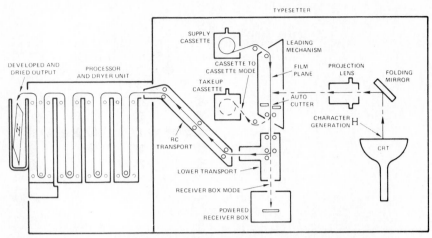

FIG. 22-16 Schematic diagram of a photocopier line printer (Harris Corp.)

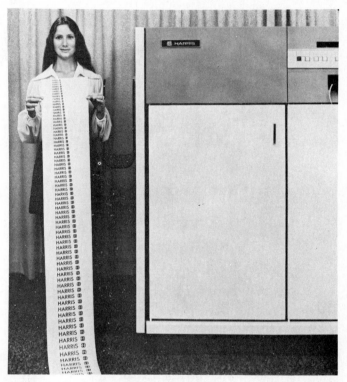

FIG. 22-17 Sample output of photooptical line printer (Harris Corp.)

22-7 DOT-MATRIX PRINTERS

Dot-matrix characters are formed by printing a group of dots to form a letter, number, or other symbol. This method is widely used with mini- and microcomputers.

Dots are formed both by impact and nonimpact print methods, and on both character-at-a-time and line printers. Methods used to print dots are impact,

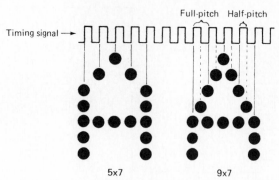

FIG. 22-18 Appearence of the letter A in several dot-matrix sizes (C. Itoh Electronics, Inc.)

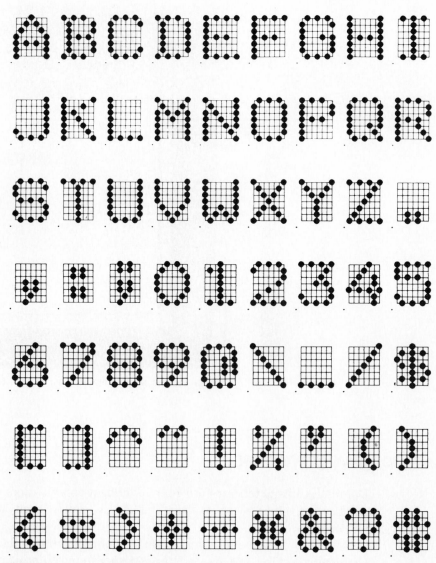

FIG. 22-19 A 63-character set of 7 × 7 dot matrix characters (space omitted). (Gentronics Data Computer Corp.)

thermal, electrosensitive, and ink-jet technologies, each discussed in the following sections.

Figure 22-18 shows the letter A formed by a dot matrix five dots wide and seven dots high (5 × 7) and in a 9 × 7 matrix where the dots are spaced horizontally in nine half-step increments. Other representative matrix configurations are 7 × 7, 8 × 8, 7 × 9, 9 × 9, and 9 × 12. Figure 22-19 shows an entire 63-character set of 7 × 7 characters. Figure 22-20 shows a single normal and expanded character, whereas Fig. 22-21 illustrates normal, compressed (or condensed), and several horizontally expanded character forms, all demonstrating the versatility of dot-matrix characters and printers.

A 5 × 7 dot matrix is frequently used when letters in all capitals are acceptable (it cannot handle regular lowercase letters because there is not room enough for the **descenders,** the part of letters falling below the line). A 7 × 9 matrix prints upper- and lowercase characters and can handle descenders and underlines.

Dot-matrix printers can print any combination of dots with all available print positions in the matrix. The

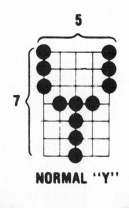

FIG. 22-20 Elongated (expanded) printing of the letter Y (Gentronics Data Computer Corp.)

character printed when one of the 128 ASCII codes is signaled is controlled by a read-only memory (ROM) chip, which in turn controls the pattern of dots. By changing the ROM chip a character set for any language or graphics character set can be used by the printer.

In printers where horizontal and vertical dots overlap, blocks of four or more dots may be printed to form larger block characters and shapes. Figure 22-22 illustrates several foreign-language character sets produced by a dot-matrix printer. Figure 22-23 shows a form printed by a dot-matrix printer simultaneously with the text on the form.

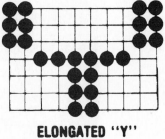

FIG. 22-21 Normal, condensed and expanded uppercase and lowercase dot-matrix print samples (Hewlett-Packard)

USASCII	ABCDEFGHIJKLMNOPQRSTUVW
ARABIC	(Arabic script characters)
CYRILLIC	абцдефгхийклмнопярстужв
KATAKANA	チツテトナニヌネノハヒフヘホマミムメモヤユヨラ
DRAW	(graphics shapes)

FIG. 22-22 Because of the flexibility, dot-matrix printers can print other language characters as well as graphics shapes (Hewlett-Packard)

HEWLETT-PACKARD COMPANY			
DATE: 7/17/78		ORDER #241402176	

SOLD TO:
ABD LIMITED

SHIP TO:
ABD LIMITED
123 E. 32 ST.
NEWTOWN, MONTANA

CUSTOMER ORDER NUMBER	CUSTOMER NO.	H.P. PURCH.NO.	H.P.QUOTE NO.
20329003451	115	CS471	SC30791

REQUIRE DATE	RATING	MFG. DISC.	S.O. DISC	TERMS
9-15-78	-	078	047	NET 30

SHIP VIA INSTRUCTIONS: AIR BEST

SPECIAL INSTRUCTIONS

ITEM	PROD. NUMB.	DESCRIPTION	UNIT PRICE	QTY	TOTAL PRICE
01	2631A	PRINTER	3150	5	15750
02	#240	2640 I/F	105	3	315
03	#210	1000 I/F	650	2	1300

COMMENTS
- - -

SHIP DATE	METHOD	CARRIER	FREIGHT	C.O.D.	BOX NUMB.

FIG. 22-23 A dot-matrix printer printed this form simultaneously with the data on the form (Hewlett-Packard)

22-8 CHARACTER-AT-A-TIME IMPACT DOT-MATRIX PRINTERS

The print head for an impact dot-matrix character printer is usually composed of an array of wires that impact the character through an inked ribbon (Fig. 22-24). For this reason these printers are sometimes also called **wire-matrix printers.** The print head often contains only a single column seven wires high, though it may be two or more columns of wire wide (Fig. 22-25). An entire dot-matrix printer is illustrated in Fig. 22-26. The print head moves horizontally along a rod (Fig. 22-27), usually printing bidirectionally, and multiple print heads may be mounted on the same carriage (Fig. 22-28).

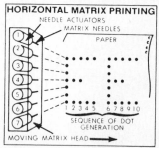

FIG. 22-24 Impact dot-matrix print head. Solenoids actuate matrix needles to print vertical columns of dots (Mannesmann Tally Corp.)

For illustration purposes we will assume that the print head contains a single column of seven wires. The seven wires are thrust from the print head (usually electromagnetically) in whatever combination the print controller calls for to create a character. The wires strike the ribbon and in turn impact the paper, printing one vertical column of a single character. For a 5 × 7 full-step dot-matrix character, the print head spaces one step, prints the second column of dots, and repeats the process until all five columns are printed.

If the printer is designed to print dots in half-steps, the same process is used except that nine horizontal print steps are used to form the character (the five normal steps plus four intervening half-steps), thereby forming a 9 × 7 half-step dot-matrix character.

Virtually all impact dot-matrix printers use one or two vertical columns of wires rather than the full character array, 5 × 7, for example. The mechanical complexity of the print head along with the control circuitry is increased with the multiple wire columns.

FIG. 22-25 Two columns of print wires are visible in this impact dot-matrix print head (Dataproducts Corp.)

Strictly speaking, the dot-matrix character printer does not actually print a character at a time but prints **one column** of a dot-matrix character at a time. However, the print speeds of dot-matrix printers are so high (up to 180 char-

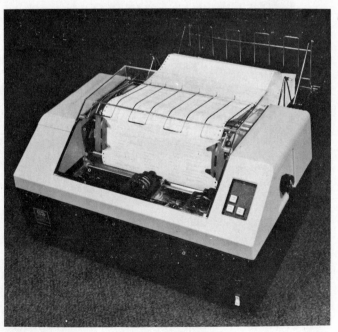

FIG. 22-26 The print head of this dot-matrix printer is in the lower center of the paper (Control Data Corp.)

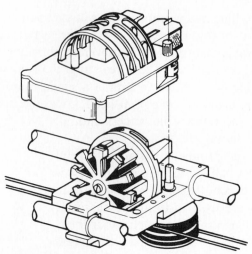

FIG. 22-27 Dot-matrix print head rides across carriage width on two support bars (Control Data Corp.)

FIG. 22-28 Dual dot-matrix print heads mounted on one carriage double printer speed (Control Data Corp.)

acters per second) that they are comparable to many fully formed character-at-a-time printers or even higher.

In addition to the high print speeds, most dot-matrix printers can print in two directions. The major disadvantage is that dot-matrix characters do not have the typewriterlike appearance of fully formed characters and are therefore less useful for word-processing applications. For other computer uses, however, they are highly efficient and mechanically simple. Research efforts now under way may produce practical dot-matrix printers where the dot size is small and the matrix is large enough to produce dot-matrix characters indistinguishable from fully formed characters made by impact printers.

22-9 LINE-AT-A-TIME IMPACT DOT-MATRIX PRINTERS

Impact line dot-matrix printers use a horizontal print comb (Fig. 22-29) stretching across the width of the paper. The single-piece comb consists of 132 fingerlike hammers (corresponding to the teeth on a comb); one raised dot is on

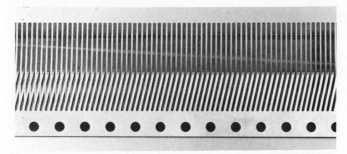

FIG. 22-29 Print comb of dot-matrix line printer (Mannesmann Tally Corp.)

each hammer. Hammers are pulled back by an electromagnet under the control of character generators and released to fly forward, striking the ribbon and paper (Fig. 22-30). Each hammer corresponds to one character print position, and the 132-hammer comb is therefore 132 print spaces wide. The entire comb oscillates horizontally to print any of the overlapping five dots constituting a

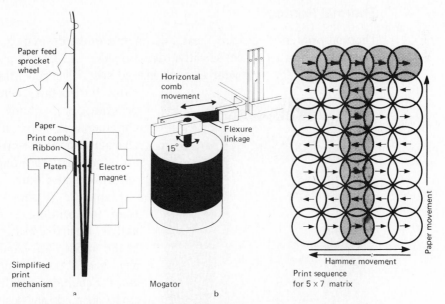

FIG. 22-30 (a) Print-comb fingers are pulled away from paper by an electromagnet at each horizontal character position (b) Raised dots on each finger are moved across each horizontal print position by vibrating linkage to a stepping motor ("mogator") (c) Comb prints dots in sequence (Mannesmann Tally Corp.)

horizontal row of a character matrix. The paper advances vertically one dot position, and the second row of dots (from the character top) print.

The printer therefore prints one row of dots for all 132 characters, and then prints each subsequent row for all 132 characters, and so on, until all seven vertical steps have been completed, printing a 7 × 7 overlapping dot matrix 132 characters wide. The 132 characters are printed substantially a line at a time, but actually only one horizontal row of dots appears across the page at any instant. The effective line-printing speed is 300 lines per minute for one typical printer, and for all practical purposes this is a line-at-a-time printer.

22-10 NONIMPACT DOT-MATRIX PRINTERS

Nonimpact dot-matrix printers cause a mark without directly touching the paper. They are therefore quiet compared with impact printers. They cannot make carbon copies, however, as there is no force to impress the character through multiple carbon copies. Nevertheless, nonimpact printers are useful for printing single copies of computer output, for recording the output of printing calculators and video displays, for logging industrial data, and similar applications.

Four technologies are used for nonimpact dot-matrix printers:

1. Thermal
2. Electrosensitive
3. Electrostatic
4. Ink jet

Thermal Printers

Thermal printers electrically heat a dot matrix in the desired character pattern. The heat activates a heat-sensitive dye embedded in coated paper, causing a black or blue dot to appear at each heated spot. Thermal print heads either move horizontally across the paper, printing each column of dot-matrix characters serially, like any other character-serial dot-matrix printer, or are stationary, printing a horizontal line of dots at a time.

Figure 22-31 shows a serial print head for printing a seven-high dot matrix. Resistive heating elements are in the upper right-hand corner of the print head. Power is applied to the circuit for each dot, resulting in the necessary heat at that position to cause a color change in the paper.

Line-at-a-time thermal printers use fixed print pads containing a row of resistive heating elements screen-

FIG. 22-31   Thermal dot-matrix print head for printing a character at a time (Dataproducts Corp.)

FIG. 22-32   Thermal printer used with a programmable calculator prints a line at a time of 20 characters with stationary heating elements

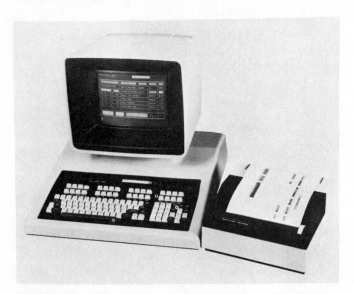

FIG. 22-33   Thermal printer used to record the display of a video monitor

printed on a ceramic substrate. Thermal printers are typically used for calculators, instrumentation printouts, and recording the contents of a video display (Figs. 22-32 and 22-33).

Electrosensitive Printers

Current is passed through the tip of a stylus or a nib in a print head arcing to a specially coated paper sensitive to voltage changes. In many electrosensitive printers the paper coating is aluminum, which vaporizes when voltage is applied to the print head, leaving a black mark. Unlike thermal print paper, which ultimately fades from sunlight or heat, aluminum-coated paper is not affected by

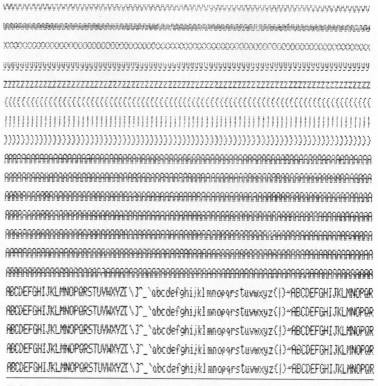

FIG. 22-34 Actual-size print sample produced by an electrosensitive printer often used to record display of video monitor. Paper is coated with aluminum.

heat, light, or water and is therefore a relatively permanent record (Fig. 22-34). Electrosensitive printers are often used to record the display on a video monitor.

Electrostatic Printers

Voltage is applied to an array of needles used to form dot-matrix characters. The energized needles form charged spots on a coated dielectric paper as the

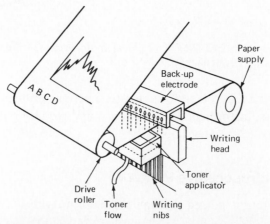

FIG. 22-35 Electrostatic printing. Paper specially coated with dielectric material is charged by an array of needles. Characters in the form of charged spots then attract black toner particles

paper unwinds from a roll and passes the needles. When the paper is passed through a toner, the charged spots attract black toner particles, forming dot-matrix characters (Fig. 22-35).

Ink-Jet Printers

Droplets of ink are sprayed directly on paper to form dot-matrix characters by ink-jet printers. Two major ink-jet printing technologies are in current use.

In the **drop-on-demand** system (Fig. 22-36) droplets of ink under pressure are ejected from nozzles aimed at the paper; each nozzle is opened by an electrical impulse. A vertical array of nozzles one matrix column high ejects droplets of ink, forming one column of the dot matrix. The nozzle is stepped hori-

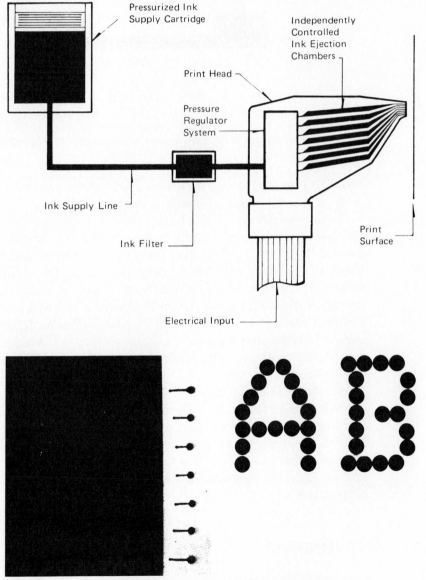

FIG. 22-36 Ink-jet print head sprays droplets of ink to form dot-matrix characters (Silonics)

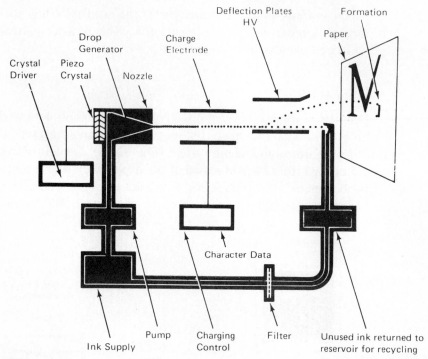

FIG. 22-37 Continuous-stream ink-jet printer forms characters by deflecting a charged ink stream in the same way an electron beam is deflected in a cathode ray tube

zontally to the second matrix column, ink from the selected jets is ejected, and so on, until a dot-matrix character is formed.

Continuous-stream ink-jet printers pump ink continuously through a nozzle. The ink stream passes through a tube where ink droplets are electrically charged (Fig. 22-37). The path of the ink droplets to the paper is electronically aimed by horizontal and vertical deflection plates. The aiming charge on the deflection plates is in turn controlled by an electronic character generator. This method of directing the ink stream is analogous to a video monitor, where an electron stream on its way to the screen is controlled by deflection plates; here, however, **ink droplets** are guided instead of electrons. When a character is not printed, the continuous ink stream is captured and held in a reservoir, from which the ink is recycled.

Strictly speaking, characters formed by the continuous ink stream are not true dot-matrix characters in the sense we have previously used the term. However, they are formed by a composite of dots of extremely small ink droplets. Continuous-stream ink-jet printing approaches the quality of the fully formed character. This ink-jet system is actually a hybrid method of character formation. Unlike other nonimpact printing methods, ink-jet printers require no specially coated paper.

22-11 PAPER HANDLING

Common to all printers is the need to move paper through the printer. There are three methods: friction feed, pin platen feed, and pin tractor feed.

Friction feed is the method used by the ordinary typewriter. Paper is held by friction against the typewriter platen and moves through the printer as the platen turns. Friction feed is used in relatively low-speed printers.

Pin platen feed uses paper with holes perforated in the edges of a continuous form. Pins mounted on the platen engage the holes and move the paper through the printer. Medium-speed printers using continuous forms (in rolls or fan-folded) require a method like this to maintain positive paper alignment in the printer. Because the pins are mounted on the platen and are not horizontally adjustable, only one form width is possible.

Pin tractor feed uses two motor-driven form tractors (Fig. 22-38). Each trac-

FIG. 22-38 Pin-feed form tractors, shown here separated from a printer, permit printing forms of any width (Control Data Corp.)

tor also contains a set of pins, and the horizontal spacing of the tractors is adjustable, permitting use of forms of any width. Motion of the form tractor is often under program control for high-speed skipping. Heavy-duty and high-speed printers usually incorporate tractor feed for handling forms.

Double form tractors are used with split-platen printers. This arrangement permits simultaneous handling of two forms of different widths with separate

FIG. 22-39 Front-feed form insertion is convenient for automatic typing of multipart form sets

vertical spacing requirements as well. Both sets of form tractors are separately controlled and keyed to the vertical spacing requirements of each form used. For example, a split-platen printer permits automatic printing of an owner's name on a stock certificate on the left platen while maintaining a journal of certificates issued on the right platen. Additionally, interactive messages between computer and operator are recorded on the journal on the right platen.

Of course single-sheet forms can be fed manually. As an alternative, automatic single-sheet form-insertion options are available for many printers used for word processing, particularly those preparing letters to look individually typed. These single-sheet forms typically feed from a paper stack at the rear of the printer platen.

Front-form-feeding mechanisms (Fig. 22-39) are used with multipart form sets, like those used for rental-car billing records. This front-form-feeding device enables the printer operator to drop the form in a front plastic chute; subsequent vertical alignment and spacing are performed automatically by the printer and its control mechanisms.

Artificial Intelligence and Robotics

Harry L. Helms

21-1 INTRODUCTION

Artificial intelligence is generally used to refer to the ability of a computer system to perform tasks, such as reasoning and learning, that human intelligence is capable of. **Robots** may be defined as intelligent machines, or as a computer system with hardware for manipulating and responding to the environment outside the computer system. The body of theory and practice concerning robots has become known as robotics. Both artificial intelligence and robotics have been the subjects of increasing interest in recent years.

21-2 COMPUTERS AND INTELLIGENCE

Despite their popular image, computers actually lack most of the attributes associated with the term "intelligence." Computers can perform tasks quickly and reliably, but such tasks and the rules governing their performance must be precisely defined. If the tasks or their supporting data are outside of the parameters the computer has been programmed to handle, the computer cannot make allowances for such variations.

The problem of designing artificial intelligence systems becomes clearer when we realize "intelligence" consists of two distinct components. One component is factual, comprised of objective, measurable, and quantifiable information about events and objects. The factual component of intelligence can be handled by a computer without great difficulty. However, a second component of intelligence involves associations, pattern recognition, inference, experience, and intuition. This second component of intelligence has proved to be far more difficult to incorporate in a computer system.

Some tasks that involve "intelligence" are quite simple and readily performed on a computer. For example, suppose we have two character strings as follows:

"ABCDEFGHIJK"

"ABCDEFGHIJ"

It would be a simple and rapid operation for the computer system to determine that these two strings are not equivalent. However, for the computer to tell **how** the two strings are not equivalent would be a much more difficult task. A human with a knowledge of the alphabet would realize that one letter was missing. For a computer to do the same, it would have to go through several matching routines (possibly against a reference such as the complete alphabet) before reaching an answer.

Human intelligence is able to fill in gaps in available data through experience, intuition, or even guesses. A computer, on the other hand, must rely on the data given it. Humans are capable of modifying their approach to solving a problem if the correct solution is not found; computer systems must follow the instructions contained in their programs.

The more subjective components of intelligence are present in many situations which may, at first glance, be purely factual. Pattern recognition is one such example. A person and computer can be "taught" to associate the pattern of a person's image (as in a photograph) with a name (such as John Jones). In such a case, purely factual intelligence is involved. A person would still be able to recognize John Jones if he wore different clothes or combed his hair differently. However, a computer would be unable to match the new image of John Jones with the old one.

Another example is how humans may add subjective elements to information that would be interpreted in a strictly factual manner by the computer. For example, the character string

"What do you mean?"

could be interpreted in many different ways by a human. It could be viewed as a simple and direct request for information. It could also be interpreted as a humorous remark, a defensive reaction to an accusation, or even as an accusation. A computer, even one with an entire dictionary in memory, would not be able to give such varying interpretations to the string. Indeed, many problems in artificial intelligence actually are problems involving language and how it is to be interpreted.

A further consideration in artificial intelligence is the "hardware" used by humans and computers. Although the functioning of the brain on the cellular level is not fully understood, it appears that the brain processes information through the almost simultaneous activation of millions of cellular "logic devices." By contrast, a computer passes information through a single processing unit. It may well be that the human brain has a vast, inherent superiority over computer hardware in processing the more subjective components of intelligence. Closing this gap could be the key to developing artificial intelligence systems that begin to approach the abilities of the human brain.

21-3 EXPERT SYSTEMS

Expert systems are an attempt to replicate some human reasoning and decision-making processes in a computer system. Expert systems are made up of three elements: a data base, a rule base, and a rule interpreter.

The **data base** is a term for the working memory where factual information is stored. The **rule base** is sometimes referred to as the knowledge base. It is a file of judgmental rules applicable to a specified set of problems; the rules are obtained from human experts. The **rule interpreter** is also called the general reasoning program. It applies the rules in the rule base to the facts stored in the data base.

The rules in the rule base are written in the following structure:

IF conditions
THEN consequence with a specified probability of being correct

During execution of an expert systems program, rules from the rule base are loaded into the rule interpreter. The rule interpreter then begins to examine the facts in the data base. If it finds a fact or set of facts matching the specified conditions in a rule, it adds the consequence of a rule to the data base. The rule interpreter then resumes examination of the data base.

It is clear that each rule is actually a subroutine. However, it is not called by name or line number; rather, it is executed when certain types of data appear. Such a subroutine is said to be **pattern driven.**

Another approach to expert systems is to specify certain goals to be achieved. The rule interpreter examines the rules for those rules whose consequences match or lead to the desired goals. The rule interpreter scans the data base for those facts which would result in the desired conseqence when used as the conditions for a rule subroutine. If no facts are found to match any of the conditions, and no rule exists to help achieve a specified goal, the interpreter will indicate to the human operator that additional facts or rules are needed.

Expert systems have been successfully applied to a variety of diagnostic problems in fields such as geology and medicine.

21-4 ROBOTICS

Robotics is a term for the body of engineering theory and practice concerning the design and applications of robots. In a very real sense, robotics represents a synthesis of electrical and mechanical engineering.

Many of the problems encountered in development of artificial intelligence also apply to robotics; many new problems also arise. Most of these problems are concerned with a robot's interaction with the environment. For many applications, it is not sufficient for the robot to be able to manipulate objects in the outside world; the robot must have the ability to receive and interpret information about the outside environment and adjust its actions in response to such data. Consider the analogy of a human writing with a pen. It is not enough for the person to be able to manipulate the pen. The person must also be able to judge the amount of pressure to apply to the paper, whether the letters are being correctly formed, and whether the paper is actually making contact with the pen.

As one might surmise from the preceding, the all-purpose robot that has long been a staple of science fiction is still many years away from realization. Robots today tend to be devoted to a specific task or can be programmed to perform desired tasks.

21-5 TASKS IN ROBOTICS

A task in robotics can be described in terms of the individual movements necessary to accomplish a desired action, such as picking up an object or tightening a screw. A task can also be thought of as a cycle, with the individual actions composing the cycle.

Such a definition of a task is ideal for many situations where robots are used today, such as spot welding or picking items from an assembly line. The task to be performed does not have to be varied, and is highly repetitive. It is then easy to specify the various parameters for the actions to be performed, such as how far a robot arm should move, the amount of pressure that an object should be gripped with, and how long a weld should be performed.

The situation gets more more complex as uncertainty enters the task cycle. For example, an item could come down an assembly line out of position and could not be properly welded. Or items may have different strengths and need to be gripped with varying degrees of force. This again illustrates the importance of a robot to be able to detect changes in the environment and respond to them, such as being able to move an object to the proper position for welding. This can be done within the limits of current technology by having a pre-defined range of acceptable parameters in the robot's memory. When it is time to perform a task, the robot can evaluate the parameters of the situation. If the parameters are out of the acceptable range, the task is not performed. The robot could then perform a number of alternative tasks, such as alert a human operator, remove the object from the production line, or perform actions designed to bring the component within the acceptable range of parameters.

Designing a robot physically able to perform a desired task is not a major problem today. However, developing the software is a considerable undertaking even for relatively simple tasks. In fact, development of the necessary software has been the biggest single obstacle to implementing robots in many industrial situations.

21-6 ROBOTS AND PERSONAL COMPUTERS

It was perhaps inevitable that personal computer experimenters and enthusiasts would also turn their attention to robotics. By 1982, several robot devices were available as peripherals for many small personal computers.

A typical unit is the Microbot Alpha, manufactured by Microbot, Inc., of Mountain View, California. It is a robotic arm which moves through five different axes. It also includes a cable operated mechanical gripper capable of handling a load of up to one-half kilogram (or slightly more than one pound). It has an RS-232C serial interface so it can receive operating commands from a microcomputer. There is also a controller on the unit having both RAM and ROM, and a microprocessor controls the operation of the motors on the robot. Like many robots, the motors move in discrete steps rather than in an "analog" fashion.

The integration of microcomputers and robots received a major boost in 1982 when IBM introduced their Model 7535 Manufacturing System. This is a robotic arm which uses the IBM Personal Computer for control and software development. Many observers feel that robotics and microcomputers will become even more closely integrated in the years ahead, since the availability of processing power due to microcomputers solves one of the main problems in developing a robot device.

sec.22

Character Printers

Louis Hohenstein

22-1 INTRODUCTION

Character printers are one of the two devices used to prepare a permanent (or **hard-copy**) record of computer output; the other is the graphic plotter. It is necessary to make a working distinction between printers and plotters as they now exist. Although traditionally printers have printed letters arnd numbers while plotters have plotted lines and curves to form line graphs, drawings, or pictures, actually printers and plotters overlap in function. Most printers can plot graphs in some fashion, using X, *, -, and other type symbols to form lines and coordinates. Even crude pictures are possible with standard characters.

Most plotters, on the other hand, print letters and numbers, since both letters and numbers are merely graphic forms themselves. Devices called **printer-plot-**

ters by their manufacturers both print and plot with some degree of efficiency. As printer and plotter technology develops, there may be a full merging of the capability of any printing device to plot or print with equal efficiency.

For our present purposes, printers are devices whose purpose is printing letters, numbers, and similar characters in text-readable form, which they do more efficiently than graphic plotting. Plotters are devices whose designed purpose is printing diagrams with continuous lines, which they do more efficiently than printing text characters.

Printers versus Terminals and Teleprinters

A printing terminal consists of a printer with several other peripheral devices grouped together, usually for remote access with a central computer. For example, **teleprinters** are printing terminals with interfaces for communication over telephone lines.

22-2 CLASSIFICATION OF PRINTERS

Printers used in mini- and microcomputers are classified in three broad categories.

IMPACT VERSUS NONIMPACT PRINTERS   Impact printers form characters on paper in the traditional way by striking the paper with a print head and squeezing an inked ribbon between the print head and the paper. Nonimpact printers form characters without engaging the print mechanism with the print surface., e.g., by heating sensitized paper or by spraying ink from a jet.

FULLY FORMED VERSUS DOT-MATRIX CHARACTERS   Fully formed characters are like those made by a standard typewriter; all parts of the character are embossed in reverse on the type bars of the typewriter. When printed, all type elements appear connected or fully formed. Dot-matrix characters are shaped by a combination of dots that form a group representing a letter or number when viewed together.

CHARACTER AT A TIME VERSUS LINE AT A TIME   Character-at-a-time printers (**character printers** or **serial printers**) print each character serially and virtually instantaneously. Line-at-a-time printers (**line printers**) print each line virtually instantaneously. (Some high-technology printers, e.g., those using lasers and xerographic methods, print lines so rapidly that they virtually print a page at a time and are therefore sometimes called **page printers.** They are only rarely used with mini- and microcomputers for special purposes like phototypesetting.)

Figure 22-1 shows the classification of printers within these major categories, along with further classification by printer technology used in subsequent sections of this chapter. Table 22-1 summarizes the characteristics of printers.

TABLE 22-1 Printer Characteristics

Impact classification	Capacity	Printing technology	Approximate speed*	Remarks
Impact	Character at a time	Cylinder font carrier	10 ch/s	Model 33 Teletype
		Ball font carrier	15 ch/s	IBM Selectric typewriter
		Spinning daisy-wheel, thimble font carrier	30–55 ch/s	Highest-speed fully formed character serial printer
		Wire or dot matrix	30–330 ch/s	Highest-speed character impact printer for utility computer use
	Line at a time	Band	To 3000 1/min	Interchangeable character sets
		Chain or train	To 2000 1/min	Interchangeable character sets
		Drum	300–2000 1/min	Subject to slight vertical misregistration at highest speeds
		Print-comb dot matrix	To 600 1/s	
Nonimpact	Character at a time	Thermal dot matrix	30–120 ch/s	Low cost, low noise; requires special paper; no multiple copies
		Electrostatic dot matrix	160–2000 ch/s	Special paper; low print quality
		Ink jet	30–1000 ch/s	No special paper required; no multiple copies
	Line at a time	Electrostatic dot matrix	300–18,000 1/min	Special paper and toner process
		Laser or xerographic	4000–21,000 1/min	High speed, high cost, high maintenance, high-volume printing
		Photooptical	150–1000 1/min	Used for typesetting with minicomputer controllers

*Where ch/s = characters per second; 1/min = lines per minute; 1/s = lines per second.

22-3 PRINTER CHARACTER SET

Most printers used with mini- and microcomputers use ASCII codes. Printers are specified as using the 48-character set, the 64-character set, the 96-character set, and the 128-character set.

The 48- and 64-character sets include commonly used special symbols, numbers, a space, and the uppercase English alphabet (Fig. 22-2). The 96 ASCII character set includes the lowercase English alphabet and several additional special symbols. Of the 96 characters **space** and **delete** do not print, leaving 94 printable characters.

The entire 128-character ASCII set contains 32 characters normally used for communication and control. These characters usually do not print, and when a printer carries a specification of the 128 ASCII character set, it normally refers to its expanded function as a communication or control terminal. In spe-

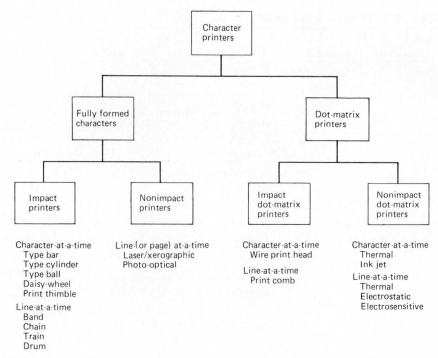

FIG. 22-1 A classification of printers

cial applications, however, the 32 codes are additionally available and can be printed using specially assigned symbols. This method is used when printing symbols for languages other than English, where the English-character ASCII codes do not apply. Any of the 128 forms, whether foreign-language characters or graphic lines and shapes used as graphic building blocks, may be printed. When graphic shapes are used in lieu of text characters, the printer's ability to draw forms, bar graphs, and other nontext graphics is increased.

a   b   c

FIG. 22-2 Teletype printers were adapted early as computer printers. Many of the original model 33 printers are still used. (a) Automatic send-receive (ASR). (b) Keyboard send-receive (KSR). (c) Read only (RO). (Teletype Corp.)

22-4 CHARACTER-AT-A-TIME IMPACT PRINTERS FOR FULLY FORMED CHARACTERS

The classic typewriter is an example of this printer. Characters are fully formed because all character components are embossed on each type bar and the entire character prints at one time. Ordinary type-bar typewriters, however, do not lend themselves to computer use because they lack the computer coding interface for easy communication and are relatively slow. Nevertheless, some ordinary typewriters have been used with computers by mounting solenoids over the keys and interfacing the solenoids with special circuits directly to the computer.

The classic printer used with the mini- and microcomputers in the past was the Teletype model 33 printer, originally designed for printed communication over telephone lines for news transmission (Fig. 22-2). The ready availability and low cost of these printers plus their relatively easy interfacing made them a natural for use with small computers. The model 33 prints at a rate of 10 characters per second, which is slow by today's print speeds of upward from 55 characters per second for similar printers designed for computer use.

The print mechanisms for the model 33 Teletypewriter is a vertical cylinder. Characters are embossed in several rows and columns around the cylinder (Fig. 22-3). The ASCII character code sent to the printer is translated into a motion that rotates the cylinder so that the column containing the desired character faces the paper and raises or lowers the cylinder to present the column containing the desired character directly to the paper. A hammer mechanism propels the cylinder toward the paper, where only the positioned character strikes the ribbon, creating the printed impression of the character on the paper.

Model 33 Teletypewriters are interfaced with small computers by a 20- or 60-milliamp (MA) current loop used to transmit ASCII-coded bits serially. Many home and small-business computers have a 20- or 60-mA input-output port built into the computer or easily available by adapters to convert an RS232C port to model 33 Teletype use. Despite the old design and relative slowness by modern standards, numerous model 33 Teletypes are still in use.

Similar to the model 33 Teletype in print-head concept is the IBM Selectric typewriter, which uses a type head mounted on a sphere (commonly called a **golf ball**) with characters embossed around the surface. To impact the ribbon and then the paper, the transmitted character code ultimately causes the golf ball to rotate around a vertical axis and tilt on a horizontal one until the desired character faces the ribbon. Like the Teletype, the golf ball requires a two-dimensional mechanical motion (Fig. 22-4). Several adapter kits are available to convert the Selectric typewriter for use with mini- and microcomputers.

Both the model 33 Teletype and Selectric typewriter are designed for other purposes and adapted for use as computer printers. Another type of fully formed character printer designed for computer use has characters mounted on the periphery of a spinning print head. Two versions of this printing method, **daisy-wheel** printers (Fig. 22-5) and those using print **thimbles,** operate similarly.

A daisy-wheel print head is mounted on a rotating disk with flexible flower-like petals similar to a daisy. Each petal contains the embossed character in

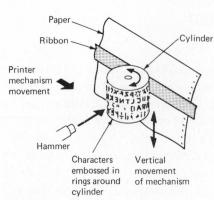

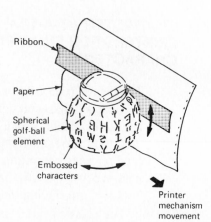

FIG. 22-3 The model 33 Teletype uses a cylinder printer. Character set is embossed around the cylinder, which rotates and shifts up and down to position the character to be printed. The hammer strikes the cylinder to print a character

FIG. 22-4 The golf ball used on the IBM Selectric typewriter is an updated version of a cylinder printer. The sphere rotates to position a character, and the entire sphere strikes the paper

reverse. As the daisy wheel spins, a hammer strikes the desired flexible petal containing the character, in turn impacting the paper with the embossed character through an inked ribbon.

A thimble print head is similar to a daisy wheel except that the flexible petals are turned upward and shaped like a thimble or a basket. Characters are mounted on flexible leaves around the periphery of the basket. As the basket spins and moves horizontally across the paper, a hammer strikes the appropriate character petal as it spins into position.

Because they are designed for computer use, both types of spinning-wheel printers have unique characteristics useful for computer printing. Most important is high-speed printing (about 50 characters per second) with fully formed characters achieving typewriter print quality. These features make spinning-wheel printers useful for word-processing applications.

The spinning print head is interchangeable, permitting proportional-spacing type fonts, optical-character-reading fonts, multilingual fonts, and special-application fonts (Fig. 22-6).

Wide-carriage versions permit paper widths up to 16 in, and some models have two print wheels simultaneously printing on the same line (Fig. 22-7). Several models of daisy-wheel printers are illustrated in Fig. 22-8.

Character-at-a-time printing, as we normally think of it, is left-to-right printing to the end of the line, stop,

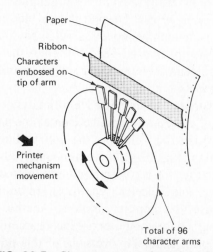

FIG. 22-5 Characters are embossed on the petals of the daisy wheel. The wheel spins to present each character for printing. A hammer strikes the character petal when it is in position

FIG. 22-6   Daisy wheels are interchangeable to permit printing with different fonts (Qume Corp./ITT)

FIG. 22-7   Dual daisy wheels mounted on one carriage permit double-speed printing (Qume Corp./ITT)

return carriage, and start a second line, again printed left to right. This is unidirectional printing. Spinning-wheel printers are capable of bidirectional printing. The second line of print is stored in a buffer memory within the printer control circuitry and can be printed in either direction, depending on which takes the least printer time. If the next line to be printed is a full line of type and the print head is already in the rightmost print position, the line will be printed right to left, backward from the way we read it. This eliminates the print time otherwise lost by returning the print head across the width of the print line to the leftmost print position. Control circuits in the printer evaluate each printed line and select whichever print direction takes the least time.

Some programmable graphics capability is achieved by fractional horizontal spacing of the print head, along with fractional vertical paper spacing, under program control. Figure 22-9 illustrates a typed curve and the super- and sub-

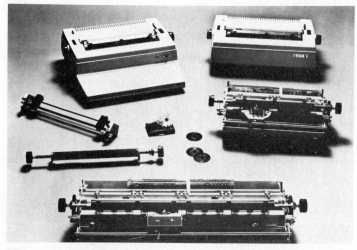

FIG. 22-8 Components and several models of the daisy-wheel impact printer (Qume Corp./ITT)

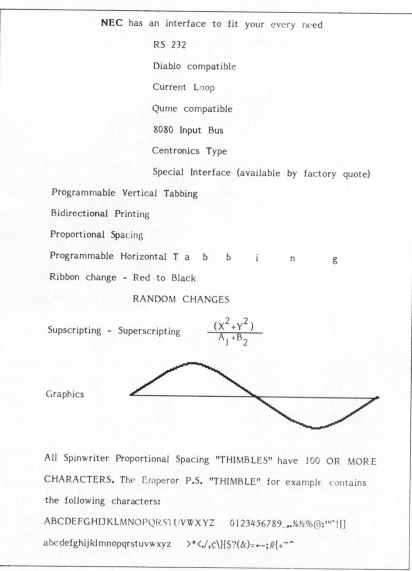

FIG. 22-9 A print sample demonstrating the flexibility of the thimble printer, similar to the daisy-wheel impact printer (NEC Information Systems)

scripting made possible by program-controlled spacing. For example, normal horizontal character spacing is 10 characters per inch (25.4 mm), but under program control horizontal character spacing can be performed in $\frac{1}{120}$-in (0.2-mm) increments.

Correspondingly, paper is spaced vertically (called *line feed*, or *forms feed*) to print six lines per inch normally. Under program control, line-feed spacing is controllable down to $\frac{1}{48}$-in (0.5-mm) increments. With this ability to position the spinning print wheel horizontally in small increments as well as line feed the paper up or down in similar small increments, small-step XY plotting can be achieved as well as normal line printing of text.

22-5 LINE-AT-A-TIME IMPACT PRINTERS FOR FULLY FORMED CHARACTERS

These printers are customarily called **line printers.** Characters or spaces constituting a printable line (typically 132 character positions wide) are printed simultaneously across the entire line. Paper is spaced up and the next line printed. The speeds for line printers range from several hundred to over thousands of lines per minute.

Because of the high print speeds and high equipment costs relative to character-at-a-time printers, line printers are used for high volumes of printed output and less frequently with microcomputers. Examples of use are printing accounts-receivable statements, large payrolls, inventory-stock-status lists, and other volume computer uses for commercial applications.

An embossed type font is positioned across a line for printing by using embossed type either on a carrier, consisting of a chain, train, or band moving horizontally across the paper and print line, or on a drum rotating in front of the paper with characters embossed typically in 132 columns on the drum. As the drum rotates, the columns of characters pass vertically across the paper and the print line. In both methods, hammers (one for each of the 132 print positions) fire when the correct character is positioned, imprinting the character on the paper with an inked ribbon.

Figure 22-10 shows the print band for an impact line printer. Print characters are embossed on the band. The band revolves between two capstans, passing in front of the paper. An inked ribbon is positioned between the moving band and the paper. As print characters on the band move by the 132 horizontal print positions, the 132 corresponding print hammers behind the paper strike the band at the appropriate time, causing the line of characters to print, each desired character printing in the 132-print positions (Fig. 22-11). Timing circuits in the printer controller keep track of when each letter or number is positioned in each print position to control the hammer firing time. A chain printer operates on the same principle (Fig. 22-12). With this technique a chain revolves in front of the ribbon and paper. Each link in the chain is designed to hold a pallet on which type characters are embossed. Hammers are located behind the paper, and each of 132 hammers strikes the moving type pallet when the desired character passes the position in which it is timed to print.

More than one set of characters is embossed on a chain or band; the fewer the characters in the set the more lines per minute are printed. For this reason,

FIG. 22-10 The print band on this band printer is easily changed to permit substitution of character sets (Dataproducts Corp.)

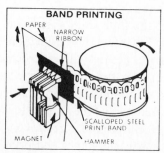

FIG. 22-11 Band printers (also called bell printers) contain characters embossed on the band. A set of hammers, one for each position, strikes the paper. (Mannesmann Tally Corporation).

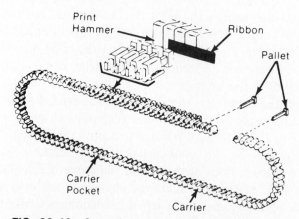

FIG. 22-12 On a chain printer, embossed characters on pallets are rotated on a chain. (Teletype Corp.)

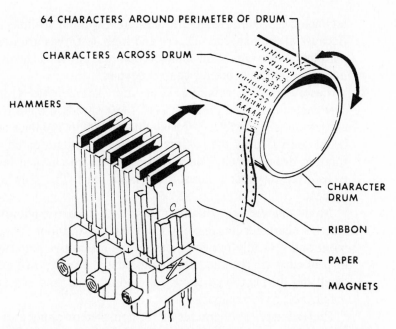

FIG. 22-13 On a drum printer characters are embossed around the drum, one set of characters for each print position across the paper. A hammer strikes each time a character to be printed on a line is in position. (Data-products Corp.)

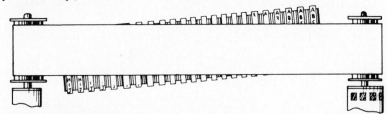

FIG. 22-14 Canting the ribbon across the face of the drum equalizes ribbon wear (Control Data Corp.)

many line printers use only the uppercase 64-character ASCII set. Some printers use even fewer, providing only the 26 alphabet characters, 10 numerals, and a few other symbols. Many printers feature easy removal of the font carrier to make it possible to change character sets and consequently adjust the print efficiency to suit the needs of the immediate printer application.

Figure 22-13 illustrates a drum printer. Each of the 64 or 96 characters used is embossed in 132 columns around the drum corresponding to print positions. The drum rotates in front of the paper and ribbon (Fig. 22-14). Print hammers strike the paper, imprinting the character from the drum through the ribbon and forming the impression on the paper.

22-6 LINE-AT-A-TIME NONIMPACT PRINTERS FOR FULLY FORMED CHARACTERS

These printers are special-purpose devices used for typesetting and extremely high-speed line-printer output. They use photographic, xerographic, and laser technologies to form complete characters without striking the printing surface. Because of their special purpose and high cost, they are used less frequently as peripherals for mini- and microcomputers, but they themselves use mini- and microcomputers as printer control devices.

Laser printers combine laser and xerographic print technologies for extremely high-speed printing; as of 1980, speeds of up to 18,000 to 21,000 lines per minute are possible, corresponding to 300 to 350 lines per second. The laser beam controlled by the computer places print data on an electrically charged rotating drum or belt. Toner particles cling to charged sections and then are transferred to paper to form the printed page. The print toner is finally fused by heat.

Mini- and microcomputers are also used to control **phototypesetters.** In these systems character images of a specified size and font are selected by the computer and optically projected onto a photosensitive paper (or film), where the lines of copy are recorded photographically. The exposed paper or film is developed, and the phototypeset copy is used to make press plates for printing books, magazines, or newspapers.

Projection of the character font is achieved by either a cathode-ray tube with character generators stored in memory or by character masks used for optically projecting selected characters, all controlled by a minicomputer. Figures 22-15 to 22-17 illustrate a minicomputer-controlled cathode-ray tube phototypesetter, which is actually a special-purpose nonimpact line printer.

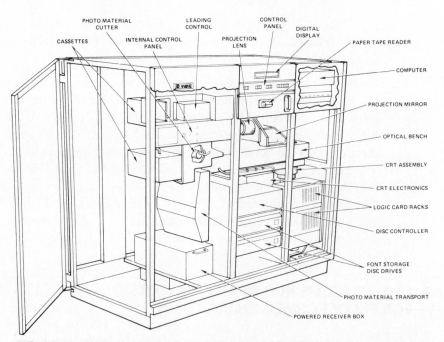

FIG. 22-15 This minicomputer-controlled photooptical line printer is used for typesetting (Harris Corp.)

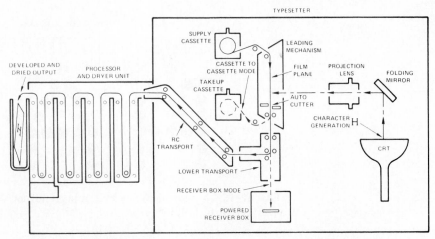

FIG. 22-16 Schematic diagram of a photocopier line printer (Harris Corp.)

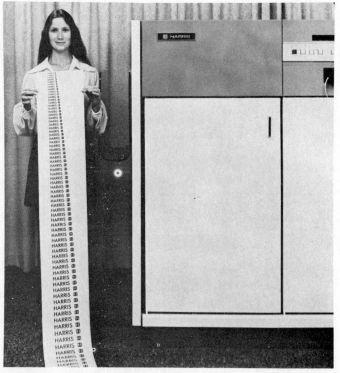

FIG. 22-17 Sample output of photooptical line printer (Harris Corp.)

22-7 DOT-MATRIX PRINTERS

Dot-matrix characters are formed by printing a group of dots to form a letter, number, or other symbol. This method is widely used with mini- and microcomputers.

Dots are formed both by impact and nonimpact print methods, and on both character-at-a-time and line printers. Methods used to print dots are impact,

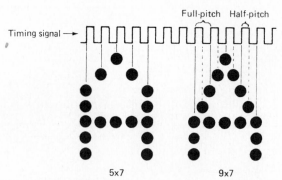

FIG. 22-18 Appearence of the letter A in several dot-matrix sizes (C. Itoh Electronics, Inc.)

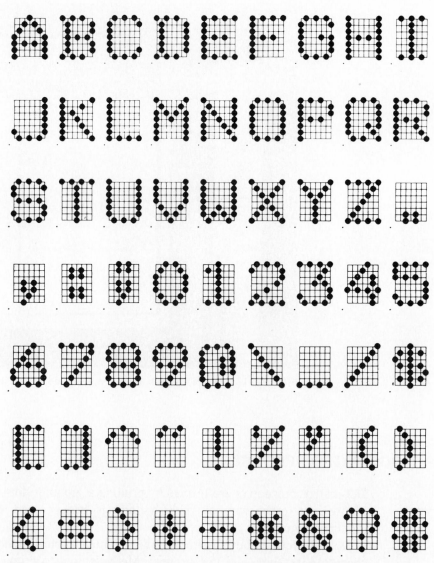

FIG. 22-19 A 63-character set of 7 × 7 dot matrix characters (space omitted). (Gentronics Data Computer Corp.)

thermal, electrosensitive, and ink-jet technologies, each discussed in the following sections.

Figure 22-18 shows the letter A formed by a dot matrix five dots wide and seven dots high (5 × 7) and in a 9 × 7 matrix where the dots are spaced horizontally in nine half-step increments. Other representative matrix configurations are 7 × 7, 8 × 8, 7 × 9, 9 × 9, and 9 × 12. Figure 22-19 shows an entire 63-character set of 7 × 7 characters. Figure 22-20 shows a single normal and expanded character, whereas Fig. 22-21 illustrates normal, compressed (or condensed), and several horizontally expanded character forms, all demonstrating the versatility of dot-matrix characters and printers.

A 5 × 7 dot matrix is frequently used when letters in all capitals are acceptable (it cannot handle regular lowercase letters because there is not room enough for the **descenders,** the part of letters falling below the line). A 7 × 9 matrix prints upper- and lowercase characters and can handle descenders and underlines.

Dot-matrix printers can print any combination of dots with all available print positions in the matrix. The character printed when one of the 128 ASCII codes is signaled is controlled by a read-only memory (ROM) chip, which in turn controls the pattern of dots. By changing the ROM chip a character set for any language or graphics character set can be used by the printer.

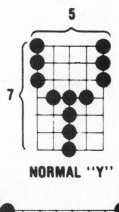

NORMAL "Y"

ELONGATED "Y"

FIG. 22-20 Elongated (expanded) printing of the letter Y (Gentronics Data Computer Corp.)

In printers where horizontal and vertical dots overlap, blocks of four or more dots may be printed to form larger block characters and shapes. Figure 22-22 illustrates several foreign-language character sets produced by a dot-matrix printer. Figure 22-23 shows a form printed by a dot-matrix printer simultaneously with the text on the form.

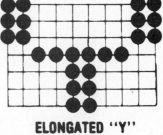

FIG. 22-21 Normal, condensed and expanded uppercase and lowercase dot-matrix print samples (Hewlett-Packard)

```
USASCII    ABCDEFGHIJKLMNOPQRSTUVW
ARABIC     ⁻◊ ₍ᴶᴿ ⁄ ᴶᴿ ⁄ ᴶᴿ ⁄ ᴶᴿ ₘᵤ
CYRILLIC   абцдефгхийк лмнопярстужв
KATAKANA   チツテトナニヌネノハヒフヘホマミムメモヤユヨラ
DRAW       ▟█▌│ ▙▄▟▔▔▔┼╂┘ ┍┚┑╤█
```

FIG. 22-22 Because of the flexibility, dot-matrix printers can print other language characters as well as graphics shapes (Hewlett-Packard)

| DATE: 7/17/78 | HEWLETT-PACKARD COMPANY | | ORDER #241402176 | | | |

SOLD TO:
ABD LIMITED

SHIP TO:
ABD LIMITED
123 E. 32 ST.
NEWTOWN, MONTANA

CUSTOMER ORDER NUMBER	CUSTOMER NO.	H.P. PURCH.NO.	H.P.QUOTE NO.
20329003451	115	CS471	SC30791

REQUIRE DATE	RATING	MFG. DISC.	S.O. DISC	TERMS
9-15-78	–	078	047	NET 30

SHIP VIA INSTRUCTIONS: AIR BEST

SPECIAL INSTRUCTIONS

ITEM	PROD. NUMB.	DESCRIPTION	UNIT PRICE	QTY	TOTAL PRICE
01	2631A	PRINTER	3150	5	15750
02	#240	2640 I/F	105	3	315
03	#210	1000 I/F	650	2	1300

COMMENTS
- - -

SHIP DATE	METHOD	CARRIER	FREIGHT	C.O.D.	BOX NUMB.

FIG. 22-23 A dot-matrix printer printed this form simultaneously with the data on the form (Hewlett-Packard)

22-8 CHARACTER-AT-A-TIME IMPACT DOT-MATRIX PRINTERS

The print head for an impact dot-matrix character printer is usually composed of an array of wires that impact the character through an inked ribbon (Fig.

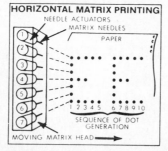

FIG. 22-24 Impact dot-matrix print head. Solenoids actuate matrix needles to print vertical columns of dots (Mannesmann Tally Corp.)

22-24). For this reason these printers are sometimes also called **wire-matrix printers.** The print head often contains only a single column seven wires high, though it may be two or more columns of wire wide (Fig. 22-25). An entire dot-matrix printer is illustrated in Fig. 22-26. The print head moves horizontally along a rod (Fig. 22-27), usually printing bidirectionally, and multiple print heads may be mounted on the same carriage (Fig. 22-28).

For illustration purposes we will assume that the print head contains a single column of seven wires. The seven wires are thrust from the print head (usually electromagnetically) in whatever combination the print controller calls for to create a character. The wires strike the ribbon and in turn impact the paper, printing one vertical column of a single character. For a 5×7 full-step dot-matrix character, the print head spaces one step, prints the second column of dots, and repeats the process until all five columns are printed.

If the printer is designed to print dots in half-steps, the same process is used except that nine horizontal print steps are used to form the character (the five normal steps plus four intervening half-steps), thereby forming a 9×7 half-step dot-matrix character.

Virtually all impact dot-matrix printers use one or two vertical columns of wires rather than the full character array, 5×7, for example. The mechanical complexity of the print head along with the control circuitry is increased with the multiple wire columns.

FIG. 22-25   Two columns of print wires are visible in this impact dot-matrix print head (Dataproducts Corp.)

Strictly speaking, the dot-matrix character printer does not actually print a character at a time but prints **one column** of a dot-matrix character at a time. However, the print speeds of dot-matrix printers are so high (up to 180 char-

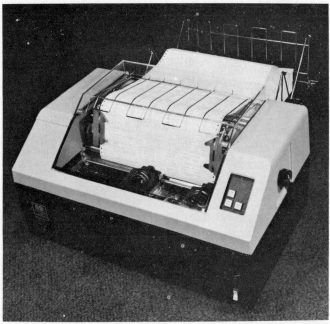

FIG. 22-26   The print head of this dot-matrix printer is in the lower center of the paper (Control Data Corp.)

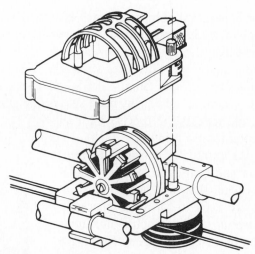

FIG. 22-27 Dot-matrix print head rides across carriage width on two support bars (Control Data Corp.)

FIG. 22-28 Dual dot-matrix print heads mounted on one carriage double printer speed (Control Data Corp.)

acters per second) that they are comparable to many fully formed character-at-a-time printers or even higher.

In addition to the high print speeds, most dot-matrix printers can print in two directions. The major disadvantage is that dot-matrix characters do not have the typewriterlike appearance of fully formed characters and are therefore less useful for word-processing applications. For other computer uses, however, they are highly efficient and mechanically simple. Research efforts now under way may produce practical dot-matrix printers where the dot size is small and the matrix is large enough to produce dot-matrix characters indistinguishable from fully formed characters made by impact printers.

22-9 LINE-AT-A-TIME IMPACT DOT-MATRIX PRINTERS

Impact line dot-matrix printers use a horizontal print comb (Fig. 22-29) stretching across the width of the paper. The single-piece comb consists of 132 fingerlike hammers (corresponding to the teeth on a comb); one raised dot is on

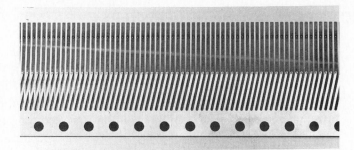

FIG. 22-29   Print comb of dot-matrix line printer (Mannes-mann Tally Corp.)

each hammer. Hammers are pulled back by an electromagnet under the control of character generators and released to fly forward, striking the ribbon and paper (Fig. 22-30). Each hammer corresponds to one character print position, and the 132-hammer comb is therefore 132 print spaces wide. The entire comb oscillates horizontally to print any of the overlapping five dots constituting a

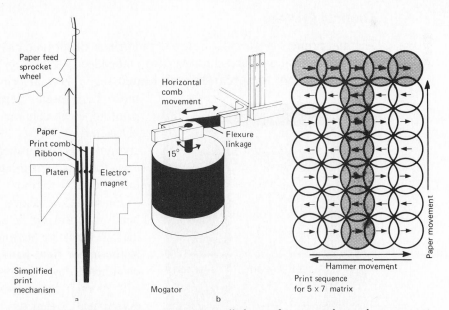

FIG. 22-30   (a) Print-comb fingers are pulled away from paper by an electromagnet at each horizontal character position (b) Raised dots on each finger are moved across each horizontal print position by vibrating linkage to a stepping motor ("mogator") (c) Comb prints dots in sequence (Mannesmann Tally Corp.)

horizontal row of a character matrix. The paper advances vertically one dot position, and the second row of dots (from the character top) print.

The printer therefore prints one row of dots for all 132 characters, and then prints each subsequent row for all 132 characters, and so on, until all seven vertical steps have been completed, printing a 7 × 7 overlapping dot matrix 132 characters wide. The 132 characters are printed substantially a line at a time, but actually only one horizontal row of dots appears across the page at any instant. The effective line-printing speed is 300 lines per minute for one typical printer, and for all practical purposes this is a line-at-a-time printer.

22-10 NONIMPACT DOT-MATRIX PRINTERS

Nonimpact dot-matrix printers cause a mark without directly touching the paper. They are therefore quiet compared with impact printers. They cannot make carbon copies, however, as there is no force to impress the character through multiple carbon copies. Nevertheless, nonimpact printers are useful for printing single copies of computer output, for recording the output of printing calculators and video displays, for logging industrial data, and similar applications.

Four technologies are used for nonimpact dot-matrix printers:

1. Thermal
2. Electrosensitive
3. Electrostatic
4. Ink jet

Thermal Printers

Thermal printers electrically heat a dot matrix in the desired character pattern. The heat activates a heat-sensitive dye embedded in coated paper, causing a black or blue dot to appear at each heated spot. Thermal print heads either move horizontally across the paper, printing each column of dot-matrix characters serially, like any other character-serial dot-matrix printer, or are stationary, printing a horizontal line of dots at a time.

Figure 22-31 shows a serial print head for printing a seven-high dot matrix. Resistive heating elements are in the upper right-hand corner of the print head. Power is applied to the circuit for each dot, resulting in the necessary heat at that position to cause a color change in the paper.

Line-at-a-time thermal printers use fixed print pads containing a row of resistive heating elements screen-

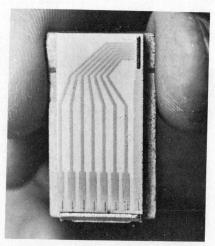

FIG. 22-31 Thermal dot-matrix print head for printing a character at a time (Dataproducts Corp.)

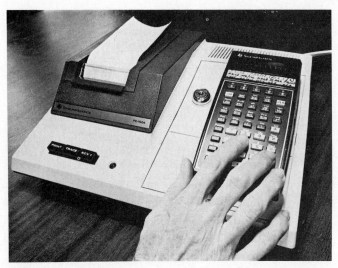

FIG. 22-32 Thermal printer used with a programmable calculator prints a line at a time of 20 characters with stationary heating elements

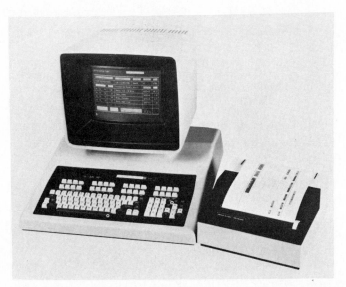

FIG. 22-33 Thermal printer used to record the display of a video monitor

printed on a ceramic substrate. Thermal printers are typically used for calculators, instrumentation printouts, and recording the contents of a video display (Figs. 22-32 and 22-33).

Electrosensitive Printers

Current is passed through the tip of a stylus or a nib in a print head arcing to a specially coated paper sensitive to voltage changes. In many electrosensitive printers the paper coating is aluminum, which vaporizes when voltage is applied to the print head, leaving a black mark. Unlike thermal print paper, which ultimately fades from sunlight or heat, aluminum-coated paper is not affected by

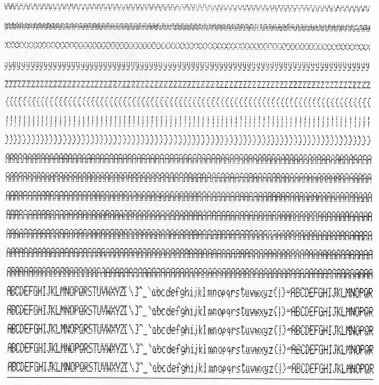

FIG. 22-34 Actual-size print sample produced by an electrosensitive printer often used to record display of video monitor. Paper is coated with aluminum.

heat, light, or water and is therefore a relatively permanent record (Fig. 22-34). Electrosensitive printers are often used to record the display on a video monitor.

Electrostatic Printers

Voltage is applied to an array of needles used to form dot-matrix characters. The energized needles form charged spots on a coated dielectric paper as the

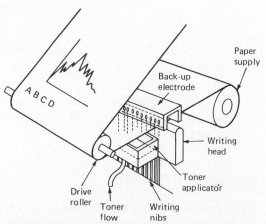

FIG. 22-35 Electrostatic printing. Paper specially coated with dielectric material is charged by an array of needles. Characters in the form of charged spots then attract black toner particles

paper unwinds from a roll and passes the needles. When the paper is passed through a toner, the charged spots attract black toner particles, forming dot-matrix characters (Fig. 22-35).

Ink-Jet Printers

Droplets of ink are sprayed directly on paper to form dot-matrix characters by ink-jet printers. Two major ink-jet printing technologies are in current use.

In the **drop-on-demand** system (Fig. 22-36) droplets of ink under pressure are ejected from nozzles aimed at the paper; each nozzle is opened by an electrical impulse. A vertical array of nozzles one matrix column high ejects droplets of ink, forming one column of the dot matrix. The nozzle is stepped hori-

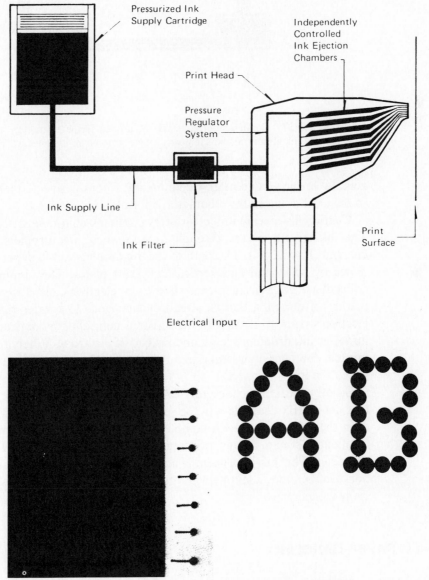

FIG. 22-36   Ink-jet print head sprays droplets of ink to form dot-matrix characters (Silonics)

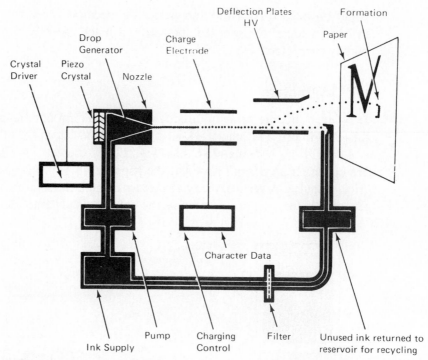

FIG. 22-37 Continuous-stream ink-jet printer forms characters by deflecting a charged ink stream in the same way an electron beam is deflected in a cathode ray tube

zontally to the second matrix column, ink from the selected jets is ejected, and so on, until a dot-matrix character is formed.

Continuous-stream ink-jet printers pump ink continuously through a nozzle. The ink stream passes through a tube where ink droplets are electrically charged (Fig. 22-37). The path of the ink droplets to the paper is electronically aimed by horizontal and vertical deflection plates. The aiming charge on the deflection plates is in turn controlled by an electronic character generator. This method of directing the ink stream is analogous to a video monitor, where an electron stream on its way to the screen is controlled by deflection plates; here, however, **ink droplets** are guided instead of electrons. When a character is not printed, the continuous ink stream is captured and held in a reservoir, from which the ink is recycled.

Strictly speaking, characters formed by the continuous ink stream are not true dot-matrix characters in the sense we have previously used the term. However, they are formed by a composite of dots of extremely small ink droplets. Continuous-stream ink-jet printing approaches the quality of the fully formed character. This ink-jet system is actually a hybrid method of character formation. Unlike other nonimpact printing methods, ink-jet printers require no specially coated paper.

22-11 PAPER HANDLING

Common to all printers is the need to move paper through the printer. There are three methods: friction feed, pin platen feed, and pin tractor feed.

Friction feed is the method used by the ordinary typewriter. Paper is held by friction against the typewriter platen and moves through the printer as the platen turns. Friction feed is used in relatively low-speed printers.

Pin platen feed uses paper with holes perforated in the edges of a continuous form. Pins mounted on the platen engage the holes and move the paper through the printer. Medium-speed printers using continuous forms (in rolls or fan-folded) require a method like this to maintain positive paper alignment in the printer. Because the pins are mounted on the platen and are not horizontally adjustable, only one form width is possible.

Pin tractor feed uses two motor-driven form tractors (Fig. 22-38). Each trac-

FIG. 22-38 Pin-feed form tractors, shown here separated from a printer, permit printing forms of any width (Control Data Corp.)

tor also contains a set of pins, and the horizontal spacing of the tractors is adjustable, permitting use of forms of any width. Motion of the form tractor is often under program control for high-speed skipping. Heavy-duty and high-speed printers usually incorporate tractor feed for handling forms.

Double form tractors are used with split-platen printers. This arrangement permits simultaneous handling of two forms of different widths with separate

FIG. 22-39 Front-feed form insertion is convenient for automatic typing of multipart form sets

vertical spacing requirements as well. Both sets of form tractors are separately controlled and keyed to the vertical spacing requirements of each form used. For example, a split-platen printer permits automatic printing of an owner's name on a stock certificate on the left platen while maintaining a journal of certificates issued on the right platen. Additionally, interactive messages between computer and operator are recorded on the journal on the right platen.

Of course single-sheet forms can be fed manually. As an alternative, automatic single-sheet form-insertion options are available for many printers used for word processing, particularly those preparing letters to look individually typed. These single-sheet forms typically feed from a paper stack at the rear of the printer platen.

Front-form-feeding mechanisms (Fig. 22-39) are used with multipart form sets, like those used for rental-car billing records. This front-form-feeding device enables the printer operator to drop the form in a front plastic chute; subsequent vertical alignment and spacing are performed automatically by the printer and its control mechanisms.

STEP 8. Choose the **large-scale integration (LSI) support chips** once the candidate microprocessor has been selected. Make certain these parts are proven and well-documented by the manufacturer.

STEP 9. Design the central processing unit (CPU), clock, bus drivers, and main address decoding circuits. These are the heart of the system and must have drive capability sufficient to handle the entire system, with margin for growth.

STEP 10. Design the **memory system** using RAM, ROM, PROM, electrically alterable ROM (EAROM), and so on. Choose a microcomputer chip with as much RAM and ROM on board as possible. If high-volume production is anticipated, choose a chip with both PROM available for development and mask programmable ROM available for production.

STEP 11. Design the **I/O circuits** using LSI devices having a good history and adequate documentation. Keep the main microprocessor data and address buses within a few inches of the microprocessor itself. Whenever interfacing with other boards or I/O devices, use secondary data buses and decoded address lines. Many development problems are prevented by keeping all low-level and primary buses on one board within a tightly controlled area.

STEP 12. Design the **control panel** and other **human interfaces.** Make certain as many debugging features are designed into the system as are economically feasible. By making the front panel of the system totally software-operated (both inputs and displays), one can incorporate into hardware and software some highly useful tools that will save hundreds of hours of debugging. These features are invaluable during development of the system and for fault isolation in the field.

STEP 13. Design the **power distribution system.** Most system designers purchase rather than design power supplies. Be sure the current capability of all supply voltages has sufficient margin for growth. Choose established manufacturers who will provide a guarantee and quick turnaround for failed units. Design all printed circuits, cables, and connectors to handle the currents from each supply. Provide adequate numbers of bypass capacitors on each board to keep power supply ripple in the millivolt levels.

STEP 14. Now that more is known of the system, draw a more **detailed flowchart** of the supervisory program. List tradeoffs on locations, sizes, types, and quantities of the various subroutines. Use true modular programming. Keep subroutines as independent as possible. The optimum subroutine is only 20 to 30 statements long, which makes software debugging and corrections easier for the original programmer or for anyone else called upon to isolate problems.

STEP 15. Construct a useful and informative **memory map.** Keep this map in the front of the program listing, where it can be continually edited along with the program.

STEP 16. Write the **supervisory program** and all subroutines. Assemble, debug, reassemble, and prepare the program for test. If possible, simulate the hardware using the MDS system and attempt to run the program.

STEP 17. Load the **assembled program** into RAM, PROM, or a ROM simulator and test on the designed system. Debug, redesign, and rewrite the program as required to get the system operating. This is always the most time-consuming part of system design. Projects usually survive or die in this phase of development.

STEP 18. In the front of the program listing, list all design parameters, temporary registers, scratchpad registers, I/O ports, and so on. Describe each item fully.

References

1. Stout, D. F., and M. Kaufman: Handbook of Microcircuit Design and Application, McGraw-Hill, New York, 1980, pp. 18–20.

2. Nemec, J., and S. Y. Lau: "Bipolar Microprocessors: An Introduction to Architecture and Applications," EDN, September 20, 1977, p. 63.

3. Weiss, C. D.: "Software for MOS/LSI Microprocessors," Electronic Design, vol. 7, April 1, 1974, p. 50.

4. Ungermann, R., and B. Peuto, "Get Powerful Microprocessor Performance by Using the Z80," Electronic Design, vol. 14, July 5, 1977, p. 54.

sec.25

Microcomputers and Programming

Claude A. Wiatrowski
Charles H. House

25-1 INTRODUCTION

The word microcomputer implies a very small computer. Computers in which the central processing unit is fabricated as a single integrated circuit are called microcomputers. The first microcomputers were physically small, had little computation ability, had limited amounts of memory, and had few interfaces to external devices. Their scope of application was also limited. Even these early microcomputers were inexpensive compared with other available computers and were widely used.

Advances in technology have drastically changed the microcomputer since the first crude devices were introduced. Computational power has been increased dramatically. Microcomputers now have large amounts of memory and connect to many external devices. Even with this added capability, microcomputers have become much less expensive than they once were.

In the process of being improved, the microcomputer has become much more difficult to identify. Important identifying characteristics are physical size, cost, and type of application. The term microcomputer is almost always reserved for computers in which the main processing unit is fabricated as a single integrated circuit or, occasionally, a few integrated circuits. Being fabricated as ICs, microcomputers are inexpensive. Even more parts of the computer, such as memory, are being added to this single integrated circuit.

Microcomputers are often dedicated to a single problem or a group of related problems. Formerly, expensive computers had to be shared among several users to justify their cost. The microcomputer's low cost makes it possible to dedicate a computer to a single task or small group of tasks. Thus, we find microcomputers in sewing machines, microwave ovens, and automobiles. More complex tasks, such as control of an industrial plant, have been partitioned into smaller tasks assigned to multiple microcomputers.

Importance of Microcomputers

The scope of the application of microcomputers made possible by their small size and low cost has important implications for the quality of life in the world. Micros help to improve productivity and reduce costs. More importantly, micros often save scarce raw materials and conserve energy that would otherwise be wasted. Microcomputers monitor and control industrial processes to reduce pollution. Microcomputers control automobile timing and fuel injection to maximize gas mileage while minimizing pollutants.

Components of a Microcomputer

The terms microprocessor and microcomputer are often used interchangeably in the literature. Although distinctions can be made, the trend to integrating more of the computer system in a single integrated circuit continually makes it more difficult to differentiate between these terms. The term microprocessor is sometimes used to describe only the processing element, while the term microcomputer describes the entire system of processor, memory, and input-output. For the purpose of this text, the terms microprocessor and microcomputer will be used interchangeably.

A basic microcomputer system is shown in Fig. 25-1. Each block may represent one or more integrated circuits and any additional components needed to make those circuits operational. The microprocessor is the heart of the microcomputer system, controlling the operation of the system.

The memory block contains circuits to remember results of calculations performed by the microprocessors. It also contains the instruction sequence that causes these calculations to be performed. This instruction sequence causes this microcomputer to solve a specific problem. Two kinds of memory are important. The microprocessor can store and retrieve data from Read/Write Memory (RWM). It can also follow instructions contained in RWM. Since RWM for-

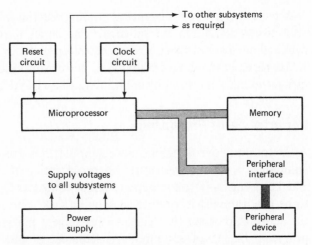

FIG. 25-1 Components of a microcomputer

gets all data and instructions that have been stored in it whenever power is turned off, the instructions would have to be restored somehow each time the microcomputer was turned on. The instructions may be restored from a peripheral storage device, such as a cassette tape unit. Program restoration from magnetic tape is often used in traditional computer applications, such as payroll processing and scientific problem solving.

Including a peripheral mechanical storage device in every microcomputer-controlled sewing machine would be cumbersome and expensive. More seriously, it would be almost impossible to include such a device in some environments, such as an automobile. A mechanical storage unit would not be able to cope with the environment in which an automobile operates and would not be sufficiently reliable. For this reason, the instruction sequence for a microcomputer is usually stored in a Read-Only Memory (ROM). Programmable Read-Only Memories (PROMs) or Electrically Programmable Read-Only Memories (EPROMs) are often used instead of ROMs for reasons of cost or convenience. The terms ROM, PROM, and EPROM will be used interchangeably as they perform the same basic function: the permanent storage of data or instructions.

Strictly speaking, the phrase "Random Access Memory" or RAM applies to all the above memories. Any datum stored in the memory may be immediately accessed by the microprocessor. However, for historical reasons, the term RAM is almost universally used to mean RWM.

External devices to be controlled by the microprocessor are connected to the microcomputer system by an interface. These interfaces are often unique to the system being designed. The interface to a computer printer is different from the interface to a brake cylinder of a truck. Most of the customized hardware or circuitry needed for applying a microcomputer are these interfaces. Fortunately, many interfaces have common functions, and microcomputer manufacturers have integrated this common circuitry into a single circuit, usually called a Programmable Peripheral Interface (PPI). Complete single integrated-circuit interfaces are manufactured for commonly interfaced peripheral devices, such as printers, displays, keyboards, and magnetic disks. Peripheral interfaces will be discussed in a later chapter.

A clock circuit provides master timing for the microcomputer system. The reset circuit initializes the processor and starts it running after the power is switched on. Both of these circuits are often included as integral parts of newer microprocessor integrated circuits. A power supply is required to generate the various voltages required by each integrated circuit in the system.

Importance of Programming

Although the advent of the microcomputer has proliferated the application of computers, it is not obvious that the proliferation of computers is of any benefit. The key benefits from the application of computers lie in the computer's ability to be **programmed** to perform a specific task. The sequence of instructions to the central processor that causes it to solve a particular problem is called the **program**. The art of designing this sequence is called **programming**. Programs are often called **software** in order to distinguish them from the logic circuits, which are **hardware**. Programming is important for several reasons. A microcomputer is applied to solve a problem by designing the program and interfaces needed to solve that problem. All the rest of the microcomputer system remains the same regardless of the application. Since these other components (processor, memory, etc.) are common to all applications, they may be mass-produced, with corresponding economies of scale.

Since the function of a microcomputer system may be changed by altering the program stored in the ROM, such modifications are relatively easily done. Changes in function may be needed to customize a system for a particular application or simply to correct an original design error.

Additional functions may be added by additional programming at little increase in the cost of each system manufactured. Even if additional ROM is required, it may be inexpensive compared to the benefit gained from the functions implemented by the programs it contains.

Designing the program is the major part of designing a microcomputer system. Therefore, programming is the first topic we will discuss.

25-2 PROGRAM PLANNING

Since programs are implementations of algorithms, they may be described by any technique used for algorithms. The most obvious technique is a word description of what the program does. This word description is often the best way to start developing a program. However, word descriptions may get cumbersome when implementing or testing a program; so other techniques are used. We will often use flowcharts to describe a program, although other techniques will and should be used when they are simpler. For example, you might want to use a table of actions required for various conditions. In actual practice, all useful techniques can and should be combined to facilitate development of programs.

The flowcharts we'll use to describe computer programs will be similar to those flowcharts used to describe algorithms. Action boxes and decision diamonds will have the same meaning as before. Figure 25-2 shows an oval that will be used to designate entry and exit points of parts of flowcharts. This notation will greatly simplify our drawings by allowing us to draw flowcharts on multiple sheets of paper. Each sheet may describe a single program, and the ovals show how the programs are interconnected.

Decision diamonds may have more than two exit paths, as shown in Fig. 25-3. Here the temperature is tested to determine whether it is in one of three temperature ranges. Figure 25-4 shows two ways of drawing a multiway branch. The structure of Fig. 25-4a implies that the branch decisions are sequential. Thus, the variable **KEY** is compared with **A** first, **B** second, etc. Figure 25-4b implies simultaneous testing of all branch conditions. It is important that all possible conditions are represented. It is easy to draw simultaneous decision figures that are ambiguous and do not precisely describe the action to be performed for all possible input conditions. Microcomputers can perform both sequential and simultaneous testing. It is best to use the flowchart form for the actual action desired.

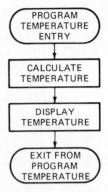

FIG. 25.2 Entry/exit ovals

The variety of possible flowcharts is unlimited. In order to minimize the chance of error, only a few different flowchart forms should be used. We will use one action box followed by another to show sequence of action. Once we start making decisions, we'll have to limit the forms the flowcharts take. Flowchart figures with decisions can be divided into two categories. These are alternate action and repetition. Figure 25-4 shows alternate-action flowcharts. Actions are or are not performed depending on the condition of input variables.

Figure 25-5 shows one common repetition flowchart. All repetition flowcharts are commonly called **loops.** In Fig. 25-5, data are read from a card reader until a datum greater than 999 is encountered. This flowchart is called a **do while** figure because an action is repeated while some condition remains true. **Do**

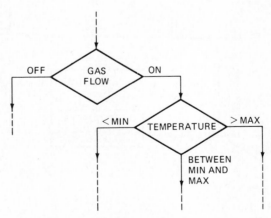

FIG. 25-3 Decision diamonds

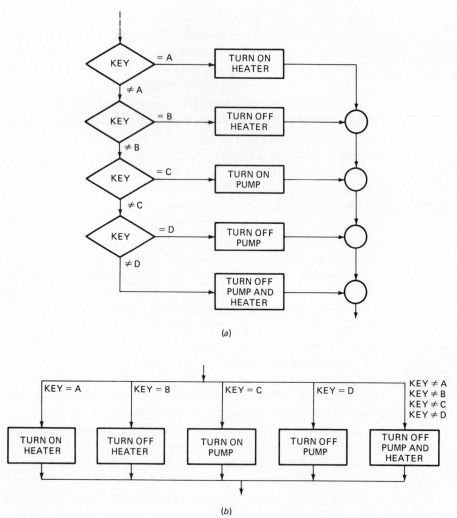

(a)

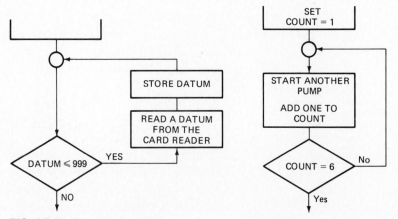

(b)

FIG. 25-4   (a) Sequential multiple decisions (b) Simultaneous multiple decisions

FIG. 25-5   Do while flowchart

FIG. 25.6   Do until flowchart

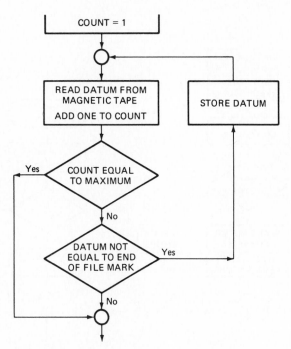

FIG. 25-7 Generalized repetition flowchart

while constructions are often used for indefinite iteration, like this example. The loop of Fig. 25-5 can read one or many data.

A **do until** construction is shown in Fig. 25-6. This flowchart starts exactly six pumps. The action of starting a pump is repeated until some condition is true. In this example the condition is that pump number 6 has been started. **Do until** flowcharts are often used for definite iteration, when the number of actions to be performed is fixed and known in advance. Actually, **do until** and **do while** loops can each be used for definite and indefinite iteration. The loop type that most closely or naturally matches the problem statement should be chosen. There is one important difference between the two loop figures if the loops are entered with the test condition **already true**. The **do while** figure will not perform any action, while the **do until** figure will perform its action once.

Both loop figures can be combined, as shown in Fig. 25-7. Many computer operations involve getting a datum, checking to see if it is the last datum, and processing that datum. This sequence is repeated for all data in a list.

Figure 25-8 shows two flowcharts that represent the same actions. We noticed that two action boxes in Fig. 25-8a were very similar. We've abbreviated the flowchart in Fig. 25-8b by writing the common action only once and referencing it from the main flowchart when needed. The common action could have been much more complex and have involved many action boxes and decision diamonds. You'll notice that we still must specify which motor we want to start each time we reference the MOTORSTRT sequence in Fig. 25-8b. The motor number N is called an **argument.** In the next section, we'll see that these abbreviations are not merely a notational device but may be actually implemented by the microcomputer as **subroutine** programs.

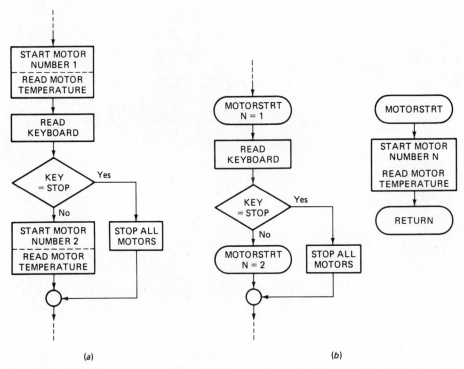

FIG. 25-8 (a) Flowchart with repeated similar actions (b) Abbreviated flowchart

25-3 DATA TYPES

Most instructions performed by the microprocessor cause an operation to be performed on data. Microcomputers use a few standard data types to simplify program development. Of course, the basic unit of data is still the bit, which may have a value of either 0 or 1. Eight bits concatenated are still a **byte.** Bytes are the most-often-used unit of data in microcomputers. Sometimes 8 or more bits concatenated are called a **word.** Sixteen bits is the most common size for a word.

A group of bits may be used to represent many kinds of data. The simple microcomputer we'll use as an example recognizes only a few representations. An unsigned binary integer is shown in Fig. 25-9. As was discussed in a previous section, each bit represents the value of a power of 2. If a bit is a 1, that power of 2 is present in the number being represented. An 8-bit positive binary integer can represent numbers from 0 to 255. The binary point need not be located at the extreme right, but can be anywhere desired, as shown in Fig. 25-10. Although we can no longer represent as large a number, we can now represent some fractional values. The location of the binary point is not automatically stored with the data; the location of the point usually exists only in the mind of the programmer and in the significance he attaches to each of the bits.

As was explained in a previous section, two's-complement notation is most commonly used to represent signed binary numbers. Figure 25-11 shows the weights attached to each binary bit in an 8-bit two's-complement number. The most significant (largest-weight) bit has a negative value. The consequences of this negative weighting are shown in the number line of Fig. 25-12. This number line represents the possible values of an 8-bit two's-complement integer. These values range from -128 to $+127$. Whenever the first bit is a 1, the number will be negative. A 0 first bit indicates a positive number. You should become familiar with the pattern of two's-complement numbers. A microcomputer negates a number in two's-complement form by first changing all bits to their opposites (called complementing or one's complementing) and then adding 1.

Binary representations, as described above, are the most efficient way to store

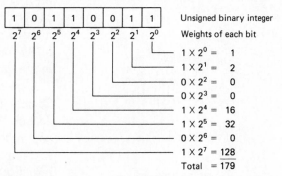

FIG. 25-9 Unsigned binary integer equivalent to decimal 179

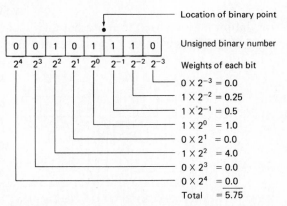

FIG. 25-10 Unsigned binary number equivalent to decimal 5.75

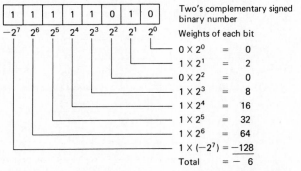

FIG. 25-11 Two's-complement binary equivalent to decimal -6

numbers and compute results. However, binary numbers are not easy to convert from or to decimal numbers to be input by, or displayed to, a human operator. If efficiency of storage and speed of computation are not critical, **binary-coded decimal** (BCD) number representations may be preferable because BCD numbers are easier to convert to a human-compatible format. An 8-bit BCD number is shown in Fig. 25-13. A BCD number is divided into 4-bit groups. The bits within each group are binary-weighted but may take on the values from only 0 to 9. Each group or **BCD digit** has a weight corresponding to a power of 10. Note that an 8-bit BCD number may represent integers from 0 to 99, while an 8-bit binary number may represent values from 0 to 255.

Very often a single bit may be sufficient to represent the required datum. A motor may be either on or off, a door open or closed. In these cases, a single bit will suffice to represent the condition. If the bit is 1, the motor is on. If the bit is 0, the motor is off. Since there are 8 bits in a byte, this most commonly used microprocessor datum may be used to represent eight such on/off conditions, as shown in Fig. 25-14. These bits are naturally called **Boolean** variables.

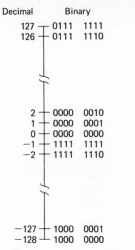

FIG. 25-12 Two's-complement 8-bit numbers

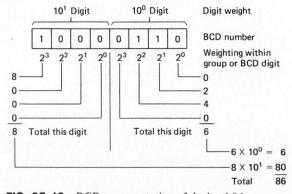

FIG. 25-13 BCD representation of decimal 86

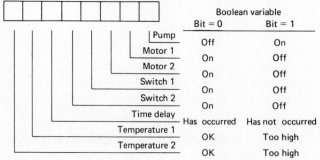

FIG. 25-14 Boolean variables

25-4 DATA STORAGE

Data may be stored and retrieved from registers and memory locations. Physically, the registers are in the microprocessor block of Fig. 25-1, while the memory locations are in the memory block. Each register or memory location will hold a single byte of data. From the programmer's point of view, the primary difference between memory locations and registers is that there are fewer registers than memory locations. Also, operations performed on data in registers are often faster than the same operations on data in memory locations. Registers are usually used as temporary storage for calculations currently in progress, while memory locations are long-term storage for the results of calculations. A microcomputer with eight registers will use 3 bits to specify which register is to be used in a data operation. It is not unusual to find tens of thousands of memory locations available. Sixteen bits will hold a positive binary integer representing values from 0 to 65,535. Each possible integer specifies a memory location, and these 16 bits are called a **memory address.** Each memory location has a unique memory address, which enables the microprocessor to specify that the 8 bits of data stored in that memory location are to be used in a computation.

While they are not strictly used for data storage, data may be stored into, or retrieved from, peripheral interface registers. These registers are used to transfer data in and out of the microprocessor system. Each peripheral interface register has a unique **peripheral address** to allow the microprocessor to specify which peripheral device is to supply or receive data.

25-5 INSTRUCTIONS

The instructions that guide the operation of the microprocessor must be stored in memory locations. Therefore, instructions are groups of bits representing the operation to be performed. Instruction bits are often divided into fields that specify different attributes of the instructions, as shown in Fig. 25-15. The operation code or opcode field specifies the operation to be performed, such as add, subtract, move, complement, etc. Each operation is represented by a unique combination of bits. The register field specifies the register containing the datum to be used in the operation, while the memory address field specifies the memory location containing the datum to be used in the computation.

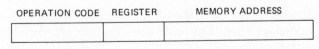

FIG. 25-15 Instruction divided into fields

Instructions are placed in memory in the sequence in which they are to be performed or **executed.** The next instruction to be executed is specified by the contents of a register called the **program counter.** After the execution of an instruction, one is added to the program counter; so it specifies the memory location of the next instruction to be executed. The microprocessor uses the contents of the program counter to retrieve this instruction from its memory location. The instruction is stored temporarily in the microprocessor's **instruction register** while it is being executed.

The representation of some instructions may require more bits than other instructions. For example, some instructions require memory addresses and some do not. Rather than waste bits in some instructions by making all instructions use the largest number of bits required, most microcomputers use variable-length instructions. Some instructions may be 1 byte long, some 2 bytes, and some 3 bytes. Now, to find the next instruction, the microprocessor must add 1, 2, or 3 to the program counter, depending on the length of the last instructions executed.

25-6 8080/8085 MICROCOMPUTER ORGANIZATION

The 8080 and 8085 are very similar 8-bit microcomputers that will be studied in this book. To the programmer these microcomputers consist of:

1. Seven working registers, each containing 8 bits
2. 65,536 memory locations, each containing 8 bits
3. A 16-bit program-counter register
4. A 16-bit stack-pointer register, used to facilitate subroutines and other functions
5. A flag register, containing status flags
6. An input-output interface containing up to 256 input and 256 output bytes

Each register may be referenced by a number or letter as follows:

Name	Number	Letter
Accumulator	7	A
Register	0	B
Register	1	C
Register	2	D
Register	3	E
Register	4	H
Register	5	L

Registers are sometimes used in pairs in order to handle 16-bit operands or addresses. Commonly used pairs may be referenced by a single number or letter as follows:

Name	Number	Letter	Registers referenced
Register pair	0	B	B and C
Register pair	1	D	D and E
Register pair	2	H	H and L
Program status word	3	PSW	A and flags
Stack pointer	3	SP	Stack pointer

Flag Register

The flag register contains five boolean variables, called status or condition flags, as shown below:

Bit number	Letter	Name
7	S	Sign
6	Z	Zero
4	A	Auxiliary carry
2	P	Parity
0	C	Carry

These flags are changed by certain instructions, as will be described later. For convenience, each flag bit has a common interpretation, to which the actions of most instructions adhere.

The Z or zero bit is set (1) if the result of an instruction operation is zero. Otherwise, it is reset (0).

The S or sign bit is set (1) if the result of an instruction operation has a most significant bit which is 1. Otherwise, it is reset.

The P or parity bit is set if the result has even parity; that is, the result has an even number of 1s in it.

The C or carry bit is set if a carry or borrow occurs after an arithmetic operation. The significance of this bit in arithmetic operations will be discussed later. The C bit is also used for other purposes in nonarithmetic operations.

The A or auxiliary carry bit is the carry out of bit 3 into bit 4 from an arithmetic operation. The A bit is used for implementing decimal arithmetic, and its significance will be discussed later.

Addressing Modes

The performance of any computer is very dependent on the convenience with which it can retrieve and store data from memory. The 8085 microcomputer must generate 16-bit memory addresses to specify the memory location in which the desired data is located. The 8085 constructs memory addresses in four ways, called **addressing modes.** These are called direct, register-pair, stack-pointer, and immediate addressing.

Direct Addressing

Direct addressing, shown in Fig. 25-16, is the simplest addressing mode. Each instruction using direct addressing simply contains the complete memory address of the memory location containing the datum to be used. Three bytes are required to hold a direct address instruction. The first byte contains the opcode. The second byte contains the least signif-

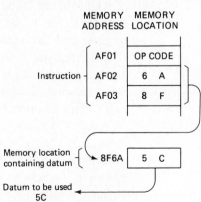

FIG. 25-16 Direct addressing

icant byte of the address, while the third byte contains the most significant byte.

Register-Pair Addressing

A memory address may be specified by the 16-bit contents of a register pair. The contents of this register pair are used as the memory address of the memory location containing the datum to be used, as shown in Fig. 25-17. By holding an address that is used repeatedly in a register pair, each instruction using that address need not contain the extra 2 bytes needed to specify a memory address. Memory size required for instruction storage is reduced. Execution speed is increased because extra address bytes need not be retrieved from memory. A common use of this addressing mode is to manipulate data lists in memory. List manipulation is especially easy because the microprocessor has instructions that will increment or decrement register pairs, so that the address contained in the register pair can be made to point to the next datum in a sequential list.

Usually the **H** register pair is used for register-pair addressing. A few instructions allow the **B** or **D** register pairs to be used for addresses.

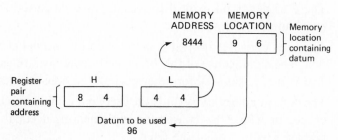

FIG. 25-17 Register pair addressing

Stack-Pointer Addressing

Stack-pointer addressing allows the programmer to automatically add or remove a 16-bit datum from a list. This list is called a **stack** and is contained in RWM. Two stack operations are possible and are called **push** and **pop**. In a stack push, the 16-bit contents of a register pair are transferred to the stack by storing 8 bits at the location specified by 1 less than the contents of the **SP** register and storing an additional 8 bits at 2 less than the contents of the **SP**. The **SP** register is then set to its original value minus 2, in order to prepare it to store another 16 bits of data below the data just stored, as shown in Fig. 25-18. The stack pointer is always left pointing to the last byte pushed onto the stack. This location is called the **top of the stack.**

A stack pop operation retrieves 16 bits from the stack. Eight bits of data located at the location specified by the contents of the **SP** are read first. An additional 8 bits located at the contents of **SP** plus 1 are then retrieved, as shown in Fig. 25-19. Then 2 is added to the original contents of the **SP**, in order to leave it pointing to the next datum on the stack. In this way the **SP** is pre-

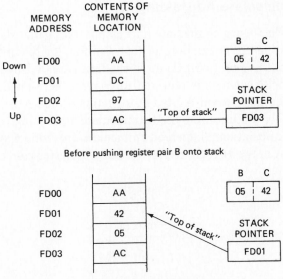

FIG. 25-18   Stack PUSH operation

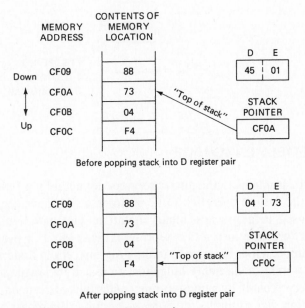

FIG. 25-19   Stack POP operation

pared for an additional pop operation to remove another 16 bits or for a push operation to add 16 bits to the list.

The stack is a variable-length list that expands downward in memory as more data are added to it (pushed) and contracts upward as data are removed (popped). More importantly, the stack is used for implementing subroutines, as will be discussed later.

Immediate Addressing

When using immediate addressing, the actual datum to be used is contained within the instruction, as shown in Fig. 25-20. Immediate instructions exist for both 8- and 16-bit data. In the first case, a 2-byte instruction is required; the additional byte is required to contain the 8-bit datum to be used. If a 16-bit datum is needed, a 3-byte instruction is required; 2 bytes are needed to hold the 16-bit datum to be used. Immediate addressing is used to enter constants into a calculation. Sixteen-bit immediate operands may be memory addresses to be put in the **H** register pair for use as register-pair addresses.

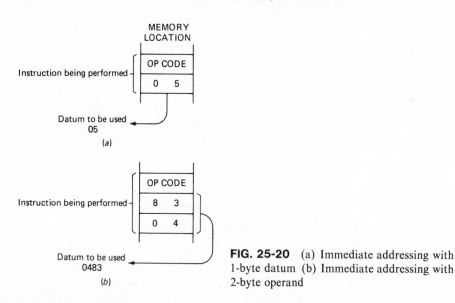

FIG. 25-20 (a) Immediate addressing with 1-byte datum (b) Immediate addressing with 2-byte operand

25-7 ASSEMBLY LANGUAGE

Instructions to the microprocessor are actually groups of 1s and 0s representing the desired operation to be performed. We have seen how hex notation can be used to abbreviate binary notation. Hex notation can obviously be used to abbreviate instruction representations, but hex programs are still difficult to understand. In order to make programs easily understandable, they are usually written in **assembly language.** In assembly language, combinations of bits are represented by names or mnemonics that correspond to the action of the instruction. For example, the 8085 instruction that moves an 8-bit data byte from the **A** register to the **D** register is represented by

$$\textbf{0101 0111} \qquad \text{or} \qquad \textbf{57H}$$

This representation is called machine language because it is the representation actually used by the microprocessor (machine). This instruction has three distinct fields. These fields are the operation, the destination register, and the source register, as shown in Fig. 25-21. Each of these fields is given a mnemonic that makes sense to the programmer. Since the operation field represents the move data instruction, we will call it **MOV.** Similarly, we will call the destination-field contents **D** and the source-field contents **A** for the registers named **D** and **A**, respectively. Written in assembly language, this instruction would be:

MOV   D,A

This is much easier to understand than machine language. Programming is often done in assembly language. After the program has been written in assembly language, it can be converted to machine language manually (called hand assembly) or automatically by a computer program (called an assembler).

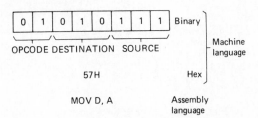

FIG. 25-21 Machine and assembly language

We would also like to refer to memory locations by names representing their memory addresses, rather than cumbersome hexadecimal numbers. The memory location containing the temperature of motor number 1 could be referenced by its address, **TEMP1;** or the first location in a program could be called **START.**

START: MOV   D, A
MOV   B, C

Not all memory locations need be given names. Only those locations which must be referenced by instructions are given names corresponding to their memory addresses. Unnamed locations are assumed to follow named instructions in numerical order in memory. The instruction **MOV B,C** above would be contained in location **3C11H** if **START** represented the address **3C10H.**

If the assembly language program is to be automatically **assembled** (translated to machine langauge) by a computer, it is necessary to indicate to the assembler what memory location the *first* memory address name is to represent or the addresses of memory locations that are not in numerical order. We could specify **START** to be memory location **3C10H** as follows:

ORG   3C10H
START: MOV   D, A
MOV   B, C

The letters **ORG** stand for the word origin. The next memory location after the **ORG** *pseudoinstruction* is given the address specified by the **ORG.** In this case, the next location is called **START** and will represent memory address **3C10H.** The next location after **ORG** need not have an explicit name like

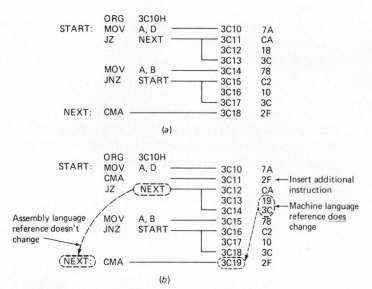

FIG. 25-22 (a) Original program (b) Modified program

START in order to be assigned the memory address specified in the **ORG** pseudoinstruction. Pseudoinstructions do not appear in the machine language program. They are only instructions to the assembler program or hand assembler, telling something about *how* the program should be assembled (e.g., what the first address should be).

In addition to making a program more understandable, symbolic names for memory addresses have other advantages. Very often, correcting a programming error or adding a new function requires that additional instructions be inserted between existing instructions. All instructions following the newly inserted instruction must be moved in memory to make room for these new instructions. The hexadecimal addresses of *all* following instructions will be changed so that all *references* to these following instructions must be changed to correspond to their new hex addresses. The machine language program must be altered. However, since the *names* of these memory locations do not change, the assembly language program will not have to be changed. The assembler will take care of reassigning names to memory addresses, to make room for the new instructions. For example, assume we started with the program shown in Fig. 25-22a. You do not need to know what each instruction means, only that two instructions reference other instructions by the names of their memory locations, **START** and **NEXT.** If we find that we need to add an instruction, as shown in Fig. 25-22b, none of the names by which these instructions are referenced need be changed. However, the assembler *has* assigned new memory addresses to these names to make room for the added instruction. The assembler has also automatically changed all references to changed memory locations to correspond to their new assignments. The assembler eliminates the tremendous burden of keeping track of all references that need to be changed when altering a program.

An assembly language program is divided into fields for convenience as shown on the next page.

Label	Code	Operand	Comment
HERE:	MVI	C, 56H	; LOAD C WITH 56H
THERE:	JMP	NEXT	; JUMP TO NEXT
MAYBE:	XRA	D	; EXCLUSIVE OR A WITH D
	CMA		; COMPLEMENT A

The **label field** contains any symbolic name given to that memory location which will be assigned a memory address. Each name in this field is followed by a colon (:). The code field contains the name of the operation to be performed. The source or destination of data is specified in the **operand field.** This can be a register letter designation, an immediate datum, or a symbolic memory address. If two operands need to be specified, they are both put in the operand field, separated by a comma (,). An additional and very important field is the comment field, separated from the other fields by a semicolon (;). The programmer describes the program in the comment field. The assembler fields we've described are for a particular assembler. Other assembler programs may interpret fields differently, although all assemblers are very similar. Common variations include not using a colon after the label and using different characters to start the comment field.

25-8 DATA MOVEMENT INSTRUCTIONS

We shall study the 8085 instructions grouped by the function that they perform. The first instructions we'll examine are instructions that simply move data. Data may be moved among memory locations and registers. In following sections, each instruction or group of similar instructions will be presented in a standardized format. Each section will begin by listing the instruction's binary representation. The assembly language format will be listed, followed by a list of flag-register bits affected by the instruction.

To simplify our descriptions of instructions, we shall use the following abbreviations:

ADDR.   The mnemonic or name of a memory location

MSPA.   The most significant byte of a memory address

LSPA.   The least significant byte of a memory address

(LABEL:).   An optional address name

DATA.   The name or hex representation of a datum

MSPD.   The most significant byte of a 16-bit datum

LSPD.   The least significant byte of a 16-bit datum

DATA 8.   An 8-bit datum

DST.   The name of a destination for data

DDD.   The bits specifying a data destination

SRC.   The name of a source of data

SSS.   The bits specifying a data source

RP.   The bits specifying a register pair

M.   The memory named as a data source or destination

Comments will be added to the instruction presentations to clarify these abbreviations as necessary.

LDA and STA Instructions

Binary Instruction Format

	LDA	STA
First byte	0 0 1 1 1 0 1 0	0 0 1 1 0 0 1 0
Second byte	LSPA	LSPA
Third byte	MSPA	MSPA

Assembly Language Format

(LABEL:)	**LDA**	**ADDR**
(LABEL:)	**STA**	**ADDR**

Flag Register   Not affected.

As you will see when you study more 8085 instructions, most operations on data require that one operand be located in the **A** register. For this reason, it is important that data can be moved into, or out of, the **A** register in an efficient manner. The load **A** register (**LDA**) and store **A** register (**STA**) instructions allow data to be transferred between **A** register and memory by explicitly specifying the memory address (direct addressing) of the datum. The **LDA** instruction is used to retrieve a datum from memory and put it into a register where the datum may be manipulated by other instructions. The **LDA** instruction does not alter the datum in the memory location. The **STA** instruction is used to store the result of a calculation contained in the **A** register into a memory location. One of the simplest uses of these instructions is the transfer of data from one memory location to another.

START:	LDA	LOG
	STA	CON

The **LDA** instruction copies the data contained in the memory location with address **LOG** into the **A** register. The **STA** instruction copies the data contained in the **A** register into the memory location with the address **CON**. The original contents of **CON** are lost, as are the original contents of the **A** register. The contents of memory location **LOG** are not changed. After this portion of a program is executed, the contents of memory location **LOG** are transferred to memory location **CON**.

LDAX and STAX Instructions

Binary Instruction Format

	LDAX	STAX
First byte	0 0 R P 1 0 1 0	0 0 R P 0 0 1 0

RP = 00 for B register pair and RP = 01 for D register pair.

Assembly Language Format

(LABEL:)	LDAX	B
(LABEL:)	LDAX	D
(LABEL:)	STAX	B
(LABEL:)	STAX	D

Flag Register Not affected.

The load the **A** register indexed (**LDAX**) and store the **A** register indexed (**STAX**) instructions are similar to the **LDA** and **STA** instructions except **LDAX** and **STAX** use register-pair addressing, rather than direct addressing. Either the contents of the **B** or **D** register pair may be used as an address to reference the datum to be accessed. The **LDAX** and **STAX** instructions are often used to retrieve data from a list stored sequentially in memory and to put that data list in a different list.

LDAX	**B**
STAX	**D**

If the register pair **B**, **C** contains **0200** and register pair **D**, **E** contains **0300**, this short program will copy the contents of memory location **0200** into memory location **0300**. Later you'll learn instructions that can increment and decrement register pairs **B** and **D**. These instructions will allow you to change the addresses in **B** and **D** to sequence through a list contained in memory.

MOV Instruction

Binary Instruction Format

	MOV
First byte	0 1 D D D S S S

DDD or SSS may be 000 for B, 001 for C, 010 for D, 011 for E, 100 for H, 101 for L, 111 for A, or 110 for M.

Assembly Language Format

(LABEL:)	MOV	DST, SRC

where **DST** and **SRC** may not both be **M** simultaneously.

Flag Register Not affected.

The move (**MOV**) instruction will move the contents of any data register to any other data register. The **MOV** instruction allows the other registers to be used for storage of intermediate operands in a calculation. Since **MOV** instructions occupy one-third the space in memory and execute 3 times faster than **LDA** and **STA** instructions, it is often better to use registers, rather than memory locations, for temporary storage. No equivalent of the **LDA** and **STA** instructions exists for any other register. The **MOV** instruction, in concert with the **LDA** or **STA** instructions, allows any data register to be loaded from, or stored into, a memory location by direct addressing in two steps.

An important special case of the **MOV** instruction occurs if **110** is specified as either a source or destination register address (**110** cannot be specified as both). You will remember that there is no register designated by the number **110**. However, whenever the microprocessor detects the number **110** in a register field, the processor assumes the operand to be used is contained in a memory location specified by the memory address contained in the **H** register pair. This technique is used by many kinds of instructions to make use of the **H** and **L** registers for register-pair addressing. Instructions using register address **110** to specify data in memory use the symbol **M** to indicate register-pair addressing using the **H** and **L** registers.

MOV   B, M

This instruction moves the datum in the memory location, whose address is in registers **H** and **L**, into the **B** register.

MVI Instruction

Binary Instruction Format

	MVI
First byte	0 0 D D D 1 1 0
Second byte	DATA 8

DDD is 000 for B, 001 for C, 010 for D, 011 for E, 100 for H, 101 for L, 111 for A, or 110 for M.

Assembly Language Format

(LABEL:)   MVI   DST, DATA

Flag Register Not affected.

The move immediate (**MVI**) instruction moves a single byte into a register. The datum is the second byte of the **MVI** instruction. This instruction is often used for entering constants into calculations. Like the **MOV** instruction, the **MVI** instruction allows register-pair addressing using register pair **H**.

MVI   M, 00H

This instruction puts an all-0 byte into the memory location whose address is in the **H** register pair.

LXI Instruction

Binary Instruction Format

	LXI
First byte	0 0 R P 0 0 0 1
Second byte	LSPD
Third byte	MSPD

RP may be 00 for B, 01 for D, 10 for H, or 11 for SP.

Assembly Language Format

(LABEL:)	LXI	B, DATA
(LABEL:)	LXI	D, DATA
(LABEL:)	LXI	H, DATA
(LABEL:)	LXI	SP, DATA

Flag Register Not affected.

The load index register immediate (**LXI**) instruction will place a 16-bit datum into any one of the register pairs: **B**, **D**, **H**, or **SP**. The 16-bit datum is contained in the second and third bytes of the **LXI** instruction. The **LXI** instruction is commonly used to place addresses into register pairs in preparation for either register-pair or stack addressing. The **LXI** instruction can also be used to place a 16-bit constant or two 8-bit constants into registers to be used in calculations.

LXI   B, 1122H

This instruction places the hex constant **11** into register **B** and the hex constant **22** into register **C**.

LXI   H, TEMP1
MOV   M, B

This portion of a program stores the datum in the **B** register into a memory location whose address is **TEMP1.** First, address **TEMP1** is placed in the **H** register pair. Next, the datum in the **B** register is stored into memory location **TEMP1** using register-pair addressing.

LHLD and SHLD Instructions

Binary Instruction Format

	LHLD	SHLD
First byte	0 0 1 0 1 0 1 0	0 0 1 0 0 0 1 0
Second byte	LSPA	LSPA
Third byte	MSPA	MSPA

Assembly Language Format

(LABEL:)	LHLD	ADDR
(LABEL:)	SHLD	ADDR

Flag Register   Not affected.

The load **H** and **L** direct (**LHLD**) and store **H** and **L** direct (**SHLD**) instructions are similar to the **LDA** and **STA** instructions. The **LHLD** and **SHLD** instructions move a 16-bit datum between the **H** register pair and two memory locations. The memory address of the least significant part of the 16-bit datum is contained in the second and third bytes of the **LHLD** and **SHLD** instructions. The most significant part of the 16-bit datum is assumed to be in a memory location whose address is 1 greater than the address of the least significant part. The datum in the first memory location is moved to the **L** register. The datum in the second location is moved to the **H** register. These instructions can be used for temporarily saving a register-pair address in a memory location and restoring it at a later time. The **LHLD** and **SHLD** instructions also are commonly used for moving 16-bit operands. The 8085 has a subset of instructions that use the **H** register pair to simplify 16-bit calculations. Sixteen-bit calculations are common not only for manipulating 16-bit data, but also for manipulating memory addresses.

SHLD	**SAVE**
LHLD	**NEW**

This portion of a program saves the contents of the **H** and **L** registers in two consecutive memory locations, starting at memory address **SAVE**. A new 16-bit datum from two memory locations at address **NEW** is placed in the **H** register pair.

PUSH and POP Instructions

Binary Instruction Format

	PUSH	POP
First byte	1 1 R P 0 1 0 1	1 1 R P 0 0 0 1

RP may be 00 for B, 01 for D, 10 for H, or 11 for PSW.

Assembly Language Format

(LABEL:)	PUSH	B
(LABEL:)	PUSH	D
(LABEL:)	PUSH	H
(LABEL:)	PUSH	PSW
(LABEL:)	POP	B
(LABEL:)	POP	H
(LABEL:)	POP	PSW

Flag Register   Not affected.

The **PUSH** and **POP** instructions add or delete data from the stack, respectively. A 16-bit datum is added to the stack whenever a **PUSH** is executed. A

16-bit datum is removed from the stack whenever a **POP** is executed. The **PUSH** or **POP** instructions specify a register pair as the origin or destination of these 16 bits of data. The stack-pointer register pair **may not** be specified as an operand. The most significant half of the 16-bit operand is pushed onto the stack first (at the highest memory address) and popped off the stack last. Thus, a **PUSH B** operation first places the data in register **B** on the stack and then places the data in register **C** on the stack in the next-lower memory address (remember the stack builds downward in memory). A **POP D** instruction first pops a byte from the stack's lowest address into the **E** register. It then pops the data in the next-higher memory address into the **D** register. The symbol **PSW** stands for program status word. When the **PSW** is specified as the register pair, the **A** and flag registers are the 16-bit datum to be used.

```
PUSH    H
PUSH    PSW
  :
POP     PSW
POP     H
```

This portion of a program first saves the **H**, **L̄**, **A**, and flag registers on the stack. The program is then free to use these registers for any purpose. Later, the program restores the original contents of the flag, **A**, **H**, and **L** registers by retrieving them from the stack. Notice that the data must be popped off the stack in reverse order. The last datum pushed onto the stack is the first datum popped off.

Before you use the stack, you must initialize the **SP** register to the first (highest) address to be used by the stack. An **LXI SP, ADDR** instruction is most often used to initialize the stack-pointer register.

The Flag Register   None of the data movement instructions affect the flags. We will often want to preserve the flags from the last calculation, even while storing the data from that calculation and retrieving new operands for the next calculation.

25-9 BOOLEAN MANIPULATION INSTRUCTIONS

Boolean instructions are most often used to manipulate data bytes in which each bit is an individual boolean variable. Boolean manipulation instructions perform bit-by-bit operations on data. That is, each bit in a byte is only combined with the bit in that same position in another byte. The result of the manipulation is then stored in that same bit position. However, the data manipulation is performed simultaneously on all eight bit locations in a register or memory location.

The flag register is affected by the boolean manipulation instructions. The carry and auxiliary carry bits are always reset by these instructions, while the sign, zero, and parity bits have their usual meaning. That is, the sign bit is set to 1 if the result of the boolean operation has a 1 as its most significant bit. The zero bit is set if the result is 0, and the parity bit is set if the result has even parity.

One operand of a boolean manipulation is always in the **A** register. The other operand can be in any register, or in a memory location through register-pair addressing, or it can be an immediate operand. The result is always stored in the **A** register.

ANA and ANI Instructions

Binary Instruction Format

	ANA	ANI
First byte	1 0 1 0 0 S S S	1 1 1 0 0 1 1 0
Second byte	None	DATA 8

SSS can be 000 for B, 001 for C, 010 for D, 011 for E, 100 for H, 101 for L, 111 for A, or 110 for M.

Assembly Language Format

(LABEL:)	ANA	SRC
(LABEL:)	ANI	DATA

Flag Register

C, AC   Reset to 0.

Z, S, P   Set to 1 if result is zero, negative, or even parity, respectively. Otherwise these bits are reset to 0.

The AND accumulator (**ANA**) instruction computes the boolean AND function of the **A** register and a second operand. The result is stored in the **A** register. In the case of the AND immediate (**ANI**) instruction, the second operand is contained in the second byte of the instruction.

Each bit of the result of the AND operation is set to 1 only if both corresponding bits of the operands are 1. The AND function has two common uses. The AND function can selectively reset 1 or more bits in a byte, while leaving other bits unchanged. Thus, the AND function can be used to reset an individual boolean variable to 0. The byte containing the variable to be set to 0 is ANDed with a **mask** byte. The mask contains 0 bits in those positions corresponding to the boolean variables that are to be reset. All other mask bits are 1. After the AND function is performed, those boolean variables in bit positions corresponding to 0 mask bits will be 0. Boolean variables corresponding to 1 mask bits will be unchanged.

ANI   FEH

This instruction resets bit 0 of the **A** register. All other bits of the **A** register are unchanged.

The second use of the AND function is to select 1 or more bits from a byte so that these bits can be manipulated independently of the other bits in that byte. For example:

> MVI   A,0FH
> ANA   B

This portion of a program selects bits 0 to 3 of the datum in the **B** register and leaves those bits in the corresponding bit positions of the **A** register. Bits 4 to 7 of the **A** register will all be 0, regardless of bits 4 to 7 of the **B** register.

ORA and ORI Instructions

Binary Instruction Format

	ORA	ORI
First byte	1 0 1 1 0 S S S	1 1 1 1 0 1 1 0
Second byte	None	DATA 8

SSS can be 000 for B, 001 for C, 010 for D, 011 for E, 100 for H, 101 for L, 111 for A, or 110 for M.

Assembly Language Format

> (LABEL:)   ORA   SRC
> (LABEL:)   ORI   DATA

Flag Register

C, AC   Reset to 0.

Z, S, P   Set to 1 if result is zero, negative, or even parity, respectively.

The OR function of two boolean variables is 1 if either or both of the variables are 1. In other words, the OR function is 0 only if both of its operands are 0. While the AND function could selectively reset a bit to 0, the OR function can selectively set a bit to one. The byte containing the boolean variable to be set to 1 is ORed with a mask byte. The mask byte contains a 1 in those bit positions corresponding to boolean variables to be set to 1. All other mask bits are 0.

> **ORI   81H**

This instruction sets bits 0 and 7 in the **A** register to 1. All other **A** register bits are unchanged.

XRA and XRI Instructions

Binary Instruction Format

	XRA	XRI
First byte	1 0 1 0 1 S S S	1 1 1 0 1 1 1 0
Second byte	None	DATA 8

SSS can be 000 for B, 001 for C, 010 for D, 011 for E, 100 for H, 101 for L, 111 for A, or 110 for M.

Assembly Language Format

(LABEL:)	XRA	SRC
(LABEL:)	XRI	DATA

Flag Register

C, AC   Reset to 0.

Z, S, P   Set to 1 if result is zero, negative, or even parity, respectively. Otherwise these bits are reset to 0.

The exclusive OR (XOR) function is a 1 only if the bits of its operands differ. The exclusive OR function is 0 if both of its operands are the same. Again, a more appropriate definition can be made for the purposes of programming. An exclusive OR is used to selectively toggle (complement) boolean variables. That is, a bit is made the opposite of what it originally was: a 1 becomes a 0 and a 0 becomes a 1. The byte containing the variable to be complemented is XORed with a mask byte. The mask byte contains a 1 in those bits positions corresponding to boolean variables to be toggled. All other mask bits are 0.

XRI   25H

This instruction complements boolean variables in bits 0, 2, and 5 of the **A** register. All other **A** register bits are unchanged.

CMA Instruction

Binary Instruction Format

	CMA
First byte	0 0 1 0 1 1 1 1

Assembly Language Format

(LABEL:)   CMA

Flag Register   Not affected.

The complement the **A** register (**CMA**) instruction simply toggles or complements all the bits in the accumulator simultaneously. The **CMA** instruction does not affect any flag register bits. This instruction can be used as part of the operation of negating a two's-complement number (complement and add 1) or can be used to invert all the bits in a byte. Common reasons for inverting an entire byte include preparing for one of the boolean operations described previously or preparing data coming from, or going to, a peripheral device that supplies inverted data for electrical reasons.

25-10 ROTATE INSTRUCTIONS

Rotate instructions are used to change the position of bits in a byte, usually to align a boolean variable in one byte with a variable in another byte in preparation for a boolean operation. In addition, a left shift is equivalent to multiplying by 2 and a right shift to dividing by 2 when the byte shifted represents an unsigned binary number.

Rotate instructions **only** affect the carry bit in the flag register.

RLC and RRC Instructions

Binary Instruction Format

	RLC	RRC
First byte	0 0 0 0 0 1 1 1	0 0 0 0 1 1 1 1

Assembly Language Format

| (LABEL:) | RLC |
| (LABEL:) | RRC |

Flag Register

| AC, Z, S, P | Not affected. |
| C | Changed as described in instruction description. |

The rotate left with carry (**RLC**) and rotate right with carry (**RRC**) instructions shift the **A** register's bits to the left or right, respectively. The bit that is shifted out the end of the **A** register is routed back around to the opposite side of the **A** register in order to become the bit shifted in to that side. The bit that is shifted out the end of the **A** register is also stored in the carry bit of the flag register. No bit is ever lost, and the operand can be restored to its original condition if desired. Also, any bit may be stored in the carry bit by an appropriate number of rotate instructions.

The operations of the **RLC** and **RRC** instructions are shown in Fig. 25-23.

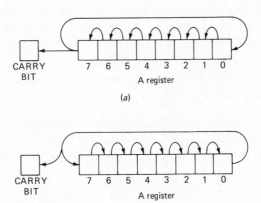

FIG. 25-23 (a) RLC instruction (b) RRC instruction

RAL and RAR Instructions

Binary Instruction Format

	RAL	RAR
First byte	0 0 0 1 0 1 1 1	0 0 0 1 1 1 1 1

Assembly Language Format

(LABEL:)	**RAL**
(LABEL:)	**RAR**

Flag Register

AC, Z, S, P	Not affected.
C	Changed as described in instruction description.

The rotate **A** register left (**RAL**) and rotate **A** register right (**RAR**) instructions are similar to the **RLC** and **RRC** instructions with the exception of the **source** of the bit that is shifted into the **A** register. The operations of the **RAL** and **RAR** instructions are shown in Fig. 25-24.

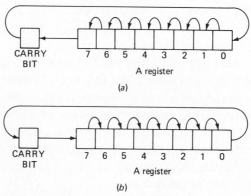

FIG. 25-24 (a) RAL instruction (b) RAR instruction

The bit that is shifted into the **A** register is now the carry bit. The programmer can specify whether a 1 or 0 will be shifted into the vacated bit position by setting or resetting the carry bit before performing a **RAL** or a **RAR**. The bit shifted out during one rotate instruction becomes the bit shifted in during the next instruction. These instructions can be used to implement multiple-byte shifts. To shift a 24-bit operand 1 bit to the left, start with the least significant byte.

```
LDA LSB  ; GET LEAST SIG. BYTE
RAL      ; ASSUME CARRY IS ZERO AT START
STA LSB  ; SAVE RESULT
LDA SSB  ; GET SECOND SIG. BYTE
RAL      ; LAST BIT SHIFTED OUT FOR BIT TO BE SHIFTED IN
STA SSB  ; SAVE RESULT
```

LDA MSB ; GET MOST SIG. BYTE
RAL   ; LAST BIT SHIFTED OUT IS BIT TO BE SHIFTED IN
STA MSB ; SAVE RESULT

A similar sequence can be used to right-shift multiple bytes, starting with the most significant byte.

STC and CMC Instructions

Binary Instruction Format

	STC	CMC
First byte	0 0 1 1 0 1 1 1	0 0 1 1 1 1 1 1

Assembly Language Format

(LABEL:)	**STC**
(LABEL:)	**CMC**

Flag Register

AC, Z, S, P	Not affected.
C	Set to 1 for STC instruction. Complemented for CMC instruction.

The set the carry (**STC**) and complement carry (**CMC**) instructions give the programmer direct control over the carry bit. Control of the carry bit is important for many operations where the initial state of the carry bit is important, such as the **RAL** and **RAR** instructions just described. The set the carry instruction sets the carry bit to a 1. The complement the carry instruction toggles or complements the carry bit to its opposite state. Although there is no clear the carry instruction, there are several ways to clear the carry bit.

STC
CMC

This sequence of two instructions resets the carry bit to 0.

ORA   A
ANA   A

Either of the instructions above will clear the carry and auxiliary carry bits. The contents of the **A** register will be unchanged. However, the **Z**, **P**, and **S** flag-register bits will be changed to reflect the contents of the **A** register.

25-11 BRANCHING INSTRUCTIONS

Branch instructions allow changing the sequential order in which a program is normally executed by explicitly changing the program counter. Each branch instruction occupies 3 bytes in memory. The last 2 bytes hold the new contents of the program counter. This is called the branch address and is the address of the next instruction that will be executed if and when the branch is performed. The processor simply places the branch address in the **PC** register to perform a branch.

JMP Instruction

Binary Instruction Format

	JMP
First byte	1 1 0 0 0 0 1 1
Second byte	LSPA
Third byte	MSPA

Assembly Language Format

(**LABEL:**)　　**JMP**　　**ADDR**

Flag Register　Not affected.

The jump (**JMP**) instruction simply causes the microprocessor to start executing instructions at the address specified by the instruction's branch address. It is used to jump around program segments that are not to be executed at this time. The **JMP** instruction is sometimes called an **unconditional jump** instruction because it always causes a branch whenever it is executed.

JC, JNC, JZ, JNZ, JP, JM, JPE, and JPO Instructions

Binary Instruction Format

	Jxx
First byte	1 1 C C C 0 1 0
Second byte	LSPA
Third byte	MSPA

CCC is 000 for JNZ, 001 for JZ, 010 for JNC, 011 for JC, 100 for JPO, 101 for JPE, 110 for JP, or 111 for JM.

Assembly Language Format

(**LABEL:**)	**JNZ**	**ADDR**
(**LABEL:**)	**JZ**	**ADDR**
(**LABEL:**)	**JNC**	**ADDR**
(**LABEL:**)	**JC**	**ADDR**
(**LABEL:**)	**JPO**	**ADDR**
(**LABEL:**)	**JPE**	**ADDR**
(**LABEL:**)	**JP**	**ADDR**
(**LABEL:**)	**JM**	**ADDR**

Flag Register　Not affected.

This set of eight instructions allows branching only if the condition specified by the instruction is true. If the branch condition is not satisfied, the microprocessor simply executes the next instruction in sequence. The conditions tested are the states of the flag-register bits. Since the flag-register bits are altered by many different instructions, the conditional branch instructions can test the result of many kinds of operations. The eight conditional branch instructions are

JNZ	Jump if result was not zero	(Z bit is 0)
JZ	Jump if result was zero	(Z bit is 1)
JNC	Jump if no carry	(C bit is 0)
JC	Jump if carry	(C bit is 1)
JPO	Jump if parity odd	(P bit is 0)
JPE	Jump if parity even	(P bit is 1)
JP	Jump if result was positive	(S bit is 0)
JM	Jump if result was minus	(S bit is 1)

PCHL Instruction

Binary Instruction Format

	PCHL
First byte	1 1 1 0 1 0 0 1

Assembly Language Format

(**LABEL:**)   **PCHL**

Flag Register   Not affected.

The transfer **H** and **L** to program counter (**PCHL**) instruction simply replaces the contents of the **PC** with the contents of the **H** register pair. The **PCHL** instruction might be called an unconditional jump using register-pair addressing. The branch address is contained in register **H** and **L**. Multiway branches can be implemented by forming an address in the **H** register pair using arithmetic or boolean manipulation and branching to that address with the **PCHL** instruction. One of many techniques for forming such an address is shown below. A table of unconditional jumps is used so that the programs referenced by this multiway jump could be anywhere in memory. The branch address for the **PCHL** is formed by combining the table starting address with the branch number. Since the **JMP** instructions are located every four memory addresses, we multiplied the program branch number by 4. Since the least significant byte of the table address was **00H**, we need only move the quadrupled program number to the **L** register to form the address.

```
          ORG    3C10H
START:    LXI    H, TABL    ; SET UP TABLE STARTING ADDRESS
          LDA    PGMNO      ; GET PROGRAM NUMBER
          RLC
```

```
        RLC                    ; MULTIPLY BY FOUR
        MOV      L, A          ; PUT MODIFIED ADDRESS INTO L
        PCHL                   ; TRANSFER ADDRESS TO PC
        ORG      3D00H
TABL:   JMP      PGMO          ; JUMP TO PROGRAM 0
        0                      ; PLACE HOLDER SO JUMPS OCCUR
                               ;    EVERY 4 BYTES
        JMP      PGM1          ; JUMP TO PROGRAM 1
        0                      ; PLACE HOLDER
        JMP      PGM2          ; JUMP TO PROGRAM 2
        0
        JMP      PGM3
        0
        JMP      PGM4
        0
        JMP      PGM5
        0
        JMP      PGM6
        0
        JMP      PGM7
```

An example might help you understand the operation of this program.

If **PGMNO** contains 5, the two rotates will multiply by 4. Thus, the **L** register will contain 20 decimal or **14H**. The **PCHL** instruction will cause the **JMP PGM5** instruction to be executed next at memory address **3D14H**. Table 25-1 shows how the program number is shifted and how it becomes part of the table address.

TABLE 25-1 Multiway Branch

		0 0 0 0	0 N N N		Contents of PGMNO
	H		L		
0 0 1 1	1 1 0 1	0 0 0 0	0 0 0 0		Original address = TABL
	H		L		
0 0 1 1	1 1 0 1	0 0 0 N	N N 0 0		Modified address for branch

Input and Output Instructions

IN and OUT Instructions

Binary Instruction Format

	IN	OUT
First byte	1 1 0 1 1 0 1	1 1 0 1 0 0 1 1
Second byte	I/O Register No.	I/O Register No.

Assembly Language Format

(LABEL:)	IN	IORN
(LABEL:)	OUT	IORN

Flag Register Not affected.

Data must be input from, and output to, external devices. The **IN** instruction transfers data from a peripheral or I/O register to the **A** register. The **OUT** instruction transfers data from the **A** register to a peripheral or I/O register. The 8085 allows up to 256 input ports or registers and up to 256 ports or registers to be connected to peripherals. The second byte of these instructions contains the address of the I/O port from which the data are to come or to which the data are to go.

Increment and Decrement Instructions

INR and DCR Instructions

Binary Instruction Format

	INR	DCR
First byte	0 0 D D D 1 0 0	0 0 D D D 1 0 1

DDD can be 000 for B, 001 for C, 010 for D, 011 for E, 100 for H, 101 for L, 111 for A, or 110 for M.

Assembly Language

(LABEL:)	INR	DST
(LABEL:)	DCR	DST

Flag Register

C	Not affected.
AC	Set to 1 if there is a carry out of bit 3. Reset to 0 otherwise.
Z, P, S	Set to 1 if the result is zero, even parity, or negative, respectively. Set to 0 otherwise.

The increment register (**INR**) and decrement register (**DCR**) instructions add or subtract 1, respectively, from the quantity contained in any register. In addition, by specifying register **110**, register-pair addressing may be used to increment or decrement the data contained in memory locations. The **INR** and **DCR** instructions affect all the flag-register bits **except the carry bit.**

Besides being used to add or subtract 1 from data, the **INR** and **DCR** instructions are often used to modify binary numbers used as counters in loops. Counters are used to control the number of iterations through a program loop, as has been previously described. For example, multiple passes through a program loop are often used to implement time delays. Each pass through the loop requires a fixed amount of time. Multiple passes through a loop generate longer times.

```
                    ⋮
           MVI      B, 100D
    LOOP:  . . .
                    ⋮
           DCR      B
           JNZ      LOOP
```

This simple program loop repeats 100 times. The **B** register is initialized to 100 (the **D** tells the assembler that 100 is a decimal number). After each execution of the instructions following **LOOP**, the **B** register is decremented. As long as the **B** register is not 0, the **LOOP** instructions will be repeated. After 100 passes through the loop, the **B** register will be decremented to 0 and the instruction after the **JNZ** will be executed.

INX and DCX Instructions

Binary Instruction Format

	INX	DCX
First byte	0 0 R P 0 0 1 1	0 0 R P 1 0 1 1

RP can be 00 for B, 01 for D, 10 for H, or 11 for SP.

Assembly Language Format

(LABEL:)	INX	B
(LABEL:)	INX	D
(LABEL:)	INX	H
(LABEL:)	INX	SP
(LABEL:)	DCX	B
(LABEL:)	DCX	D
(LABEL:)	DCX	H
(LABEL:)	DCX	SP

Flag Register   Not affected.

The increment index (**INX**) and decrement index (**DCX**) instructions add or subtract 1 from a 16-bit quantity contained in any **register pair.** These instructions are used to modify addresses contained in register pairs. Because these instructions are meant to operate on addresses, they do not affect any of the bits in the flag register. Usually, we want to maintain the flags from the last operation on data in the flag register, even while modifying addresses to prepare to retrieve new data. The result of a previous data operation may be needed for the next data operation. For example, the carry bit must be saved when doing multiple-byte shifts. The following program searches through a table in memory looking for a memory location that is all 0. After this program is done, the number of nonzero table entries is contained in the **D** register pair.

```
          LXI     D, 000H     ; SET D, E to 0
          LXI     H, TBL      ; STARTING ADDRESS OF TABLE
LOOP:     MOV     A, M        ; GET BYTE FROM TBL
          ORA     A           ; SET Z BIT IF A IS ZERO
          JZ      DONE        ; DONE IF BYTE IS ALL ZERO
          INX     D           ; D, E COUNTS NONZERO BYTES
          INX     H           ; INCREMENT ADDRESS TO NEXT
                              ;    TABLE LOCATION
          JMP     LOOP        ; GET NEXT BYTE FROM TABLE
DONE:     . . .
```

25-12 A LOGIC CONTROLLER EXAMPLE

A common requirement in an industrial plant is the control of motors and other devices by switches, pressure sensors, etc. The control output is often a simple boolean function of inputs. This control can be accomplished by relay logic, semiconductor gates (a simple ASM), or by a microcomputer with an appropriate program. The functions needed are usually quite simple. For example, a motor should be on only if its switch is on and a heater is also turned on.

It may seem like gross overdesign to use a microcomputer to implement these simple functions, but it is often done for these reasons:

1. The microcomputer is more reliable than relay logic.
2. The microcomputer may be easily reprogrammed to change the functions easily and quickly.
3. Although each function is usually quite simple, hundreds of functions may be required to operate pumps, fans, etc. A single microcomputer may replace hundreds of relays.
4. Additional functions such as time delays or counters are easy to add to the microcomputer system.

Let's program a microcomputer to be a simple logic controller. It will compute four boolean functions of four input variables. The four input variables are called **IA**, **IB**, **IC**, and **ID**. The four output variables are called **OA**, **OB**, **OC**, and **OD**. The relationships between the input and output variables are simple boolean functions.

$$OA = (IA) \cdot (IB) \cdot (IC) \cdot (ID)$$
$$OB = IA + IB + IC + ID$$
$$OC = (IA \cdot IB) + (IC \cdot ID)$$
$$OD = (IA + IB) \cdot (IC \cdot ID)$$

One input and one output register will be sufficient for external signals. The input and output signals will be connected to these ports as follows:

Function	I/O port	Bits							
		7	6	5	4	3	2	1	0
INPUT	02H	0	0	0	0	ID	IC	IB	IA
OUTPUT	F2H	0	0	0	0	OD	OC	OB	OA

The first step in developing the program to implement these functions is the flowchart in Fig. 25-25. We must expand each of the blocks of this diagram into more detailed flowcharts until the flowcharts are sufficiently elementary to allow the program's instruction sequence to be written. Some blocks will be quite simple. The **INPUT DATA** block has been expanded in Fig. 25-26. The flowchart of Fig. 25-26 becomes the portion of the program starting at memory location **DIN**.

```
DIN:    IN      02H         ; READ INPUT PORT
        STA     INPUT       ; SAVE DATA
```

The complete program is listed at the end of this section, and we shall reference memory locations in this listing in our discussion.

The programs to compute functions **OA** and **OB** are flowcharted in Figs. 25-27 and 25-28, respectively. Rotate instructions are used to align the boolean variables for ANDing or ORing. Notice that we have planned ahead and standardized a format for storing the output functions. The output boolean function is always stored in bit 0 of its memory location, and all other bits are reset to 0.

The programs to compute functions **OC** and **OD** are flowcharted in Figs. 25-29 and 25-30, respectively. These functions are slightly more complex and require the temporary storage of intermediate values in other registers. For example, the program of Fig. 25-29 stores the function **IA · IB** temporarily in

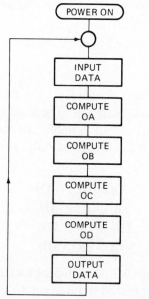

FIG. 25-25 Logic controller flowchart

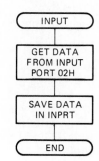

FIG. 25-26 Logic controller input program

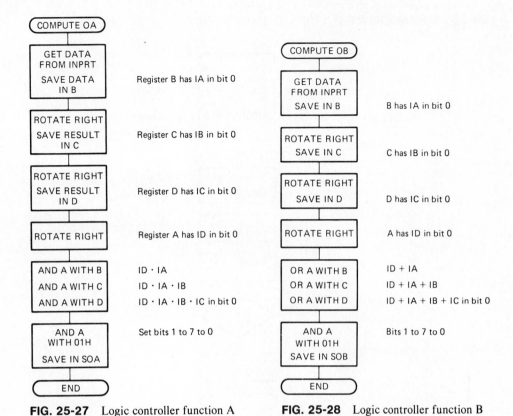

FIG. 25-27 Logic controller function A

FIG. 25-28 Logic controller function B

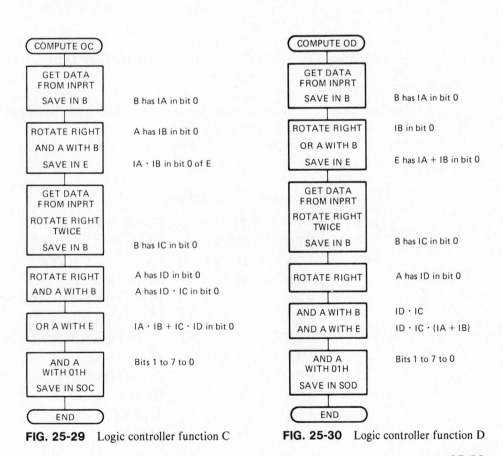

FIG. 25-29 Logic controller function C

FIG. 25-30 Logic controller function D

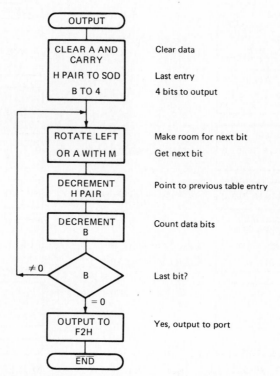

FIG. 25-31   Logic controller output program

the **E** register while computing the function **IC · ID**. The programs that compute functions **OA**, **OB**, **OC**, and **OD** start at memory locations **POA**, **POB**, **POC**, and **POD**, respectively.

The output data program is shown in Fig. 25-31. A loop is arranged to align the four output bits to their correct locations. By placing all the output functions in the same bit position and placing the four memory locations containing these bits together in proper sequence, a simple loop will retrieve each bit from memory and align it to its correct position. The output program starts at memory location **DOUT.**

The complete program is listed next.

DIN:	IN	02H	; READ INPUT PORT
	STA	INPRT	; SAVE DATA
POA:	LDA	INPRT	; GET INPUT DATA
	MOV	B, A	; SAVE IN B
	RRC		; ROTATE RIGHT, ALIGN IB
	MOV	C, A	; SAVE IN C
	RRC		; ROTATE RIGHT, ALIGN IC
	MOV	D, A	; SAVE IN D
	RRC		; ROTATE RIGHT, ALIGN ID
	ANA	B	; ID AND IA
	ANA	C	; AND IB
	ANA	D	; AND IC

```
              ANI      01H       ; RESET BITS 1 TO 7
              STA      SOA       ; SAVE RESULT
       POB:   LDA      INPRT     ; GET INPUT DATA
              MOV      B, A      ; SAVE IN B
              RRC                ; ROTATE RIGHT, ALIGN IB
              MOV      C, A      ; SAVE IN C
              RRC                ; ROTATE RIGHT, ALIGN IC
              MOV      D, A      ; SAVE IN D
              RRC                ; ROTATE RIGHT, ALIGN ID
              ORA      B         ; ID OR IA
              ORA      C         ; OR IB
              ORA      D         ; OR IC
              ANI      01H       ; RESET BITS 1 TO 7
              STA      SOB       ; SAVE RESULT
       POC:   LDA      INPRT     ; GET INPUT DATA
              MOV      B, A      ; SAVE IN B
              RRC                ; ROTATE RIGHT, ALIGN IB
              ANA      B         ; IA AND IB
              MOV      E, A      ; SAVE IN E
              LDA      INPRT     ; GET INPUT DATA
              RRC                ; ROTATE RIGHT
              RRC                ; ROTATE RIGHT, ALIGN IC
              MOV      B, A      ; SAVE IN B
              RRC                ; ROTATE RIGHT, ALIGN ID
              ANA      B         ; IC AND ID
              ORA      E         ; (IC AND ID) OR (IA AND IB)
              ANI      01H       ; SET BITS 1 TO 7 to ZERO
              STA      SOC       ; SAVE RESULT
       POD:   LDA      INPRT     ; GET INPUT DATA
              MOV      B, A      ; SAVE IN B
              RRC                ; ALIGN IB
              ORA      B         ; IA OR IB
              MOV      E, A      ; SAVE IN E
              LDA      INPRT     ; GET INPUT DATA
              RRC
              RRC                ; ALIGN IC
              MOV      B, A      ; SAVE IN B
              RRC                ; ALIGN ID
              ANA      B         ; ID AND IC
              ANA      E         ; ID AND IC AND (IA OR IB)
              ANI      01H       ; SET BITS 1 TO 7 TO ZERO
              STA      SOD       ; SAVE RESULT
       DOUT:  XRA      A         ; CLEAR REG A AND CARRY
```

```
        LXI     H, SOD      ; SET REG TO LAST FUNCTION
        MVI     B, 4H       ; SET ITERATION COUNTER TO 4
LOOP:   RLC                 ; MAKE ROOM FOR NEXT BIT
        ORA     M           ; ENTER NEXT OUTPUT FUNCTION
        DCX     H           ; POINT TO PREVIOUS ENTRY
        DCR     B           ; DECREMENT ITERATION COUNTER
        JNZ     LOOP        ; LOOP UNTIL COUNTER IS 0
        OUT     F2H         ; OUTPUT 4 FUNCTIONS
        JMP     DIN         ; GO BACK AND DO AGAIN
INPRT:  0                   ; STORAGE FOR INPUT DATA
SOA:    0                   ; BIT 0 IS FUNCTION OA
SOB:    0                   ; BIT 0 IS FUNCTION OB
SOC:    0                   ; BIT 0 IS FUNCTION OC
SOD:    0                   ; BIT 0 IS FUNCTION OD
```

25-13 ANOTHER APPROACH TO THE LOGIC CONTROLLER

Although the above program is perfectly satisfactory, it is difficult to change if one or more functions need to be changed. Figure 25-32 shows the flowchart of a program that behaves identically to the previous program but simply **looks up** the functional values in a table, rather than computing them. Since the functions are stored in a table, changes in those functions are easily made by changing entries in that table to correspond to the new function desired. The flowchart for the table-look-up program is shown in Fig. 25-33. The table starting address

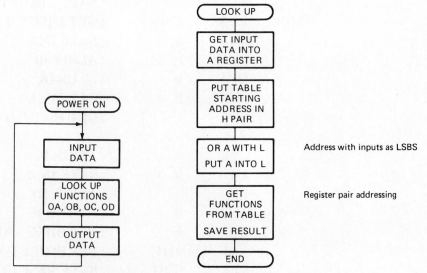

FIG. 25-32 Logic controller with look-up table

FIG. 25-33 Data look-up program

TABLE 25-2 Look-Up Table

Address	Least significant bits of address				Functions				Hex data
	ID	IC	IB	IA	OD	OC	OB	OA	
3D50	0	0	0	0	0	0	0	0	00
3D51	0	0	0	1	0	0	1	0	02
3D52	0	0	1	0	0	0	1	0	02
3D53	0	0	1	1	0	1	1	0	06
3D54	0	1	0	0	0	0	1	0	02
3D55	0	1	0	1	0	0	1	0	02
3D56	0	1	1	0	0	0	1	0	02
3D57	0	1	1	1	0	1	1	0	06
3D58	1	0	0	0	0	0	1	0	02
3D59	1	0	0	1	0	0	1	0	02
3D5A	1	0	1	0	0	0	1	0	02
3D5B	1	0	1	1	0	1	1	0	06
3D5C	1	1	0	0	0	1	1	0	06
3D5D	1	1	0	1	1	1	1	0	0E
3D5E	1	1	1	0	1	1	1	0	0E
3D5F	1	1	1	1	1	1	1	1	0F

is combined with the input port data. The resulting address has 4 least significant bits, which **are** the input variables. Thus, each of 16 possible table addresses corresponds to a combination of these four input variables. Each of these memory locations has 4 bits corresponding to the value of each of the four functions for that combination of input variables. The programmer calculates the proper values of the four functions and constructs Table 25-2. The microcomputer never computes a function but merely looks up a value that has been precomputed by the programmer.

The entire program is listed below. Because the least significant bits of the table address are 0, the 4 input data bits may be just ORed into these four bit positions.

```
           ORG    3C10H
STRT:      IN     02H        ; GET DATA
           LXI    H, TABL    ; TABLE STARTING ADDRESS
           ORA    L          ; INSERT DATA AS LSBS
           MOV    L, A       ; MODIFY ADDRESS IN H, L
           MOV    A, M       ; GET THE TABLE ENTRY
           OUT    F2H        ; OUTPUT THE FUNCTIONS
           JMP    STRT       ; DO IT AGAIN
           ORG    3D50H
TABL:      00H               ; TABLE OF FUNCTION VALUES
           02H
           02H
           06H
           02H
           02H
```

02H
06H
02H
02H
02H
06H
06H
0EH
0EH
0FH

You will notice that not only are the functions much easier to change in this program, but the program is much shorter and simpler. Short and simple programs save design effort and memory, increase the speed of execution, and minimize the chance for programmer error. We seem to have found a much better way of generating functions with a microcomputer. It is generally true that the use of tables for either data look-up or multiway branching will provide the above mentioned benefits. Table-oriented (sometimes called table-driven) programming is highly recommended.

Since there are 4 unused bits in each table entry, we could easily add four more functions to this system. Thus, eight functions of four variables could be represented by the example table. If the input data were shifted left one place before being inserted in the table starting address, as shown in Fig. 25-34, each input combination would specify a 2-byte table entry, in which up to 16 functions could be specified. On the other hand, if we desire to double the number of input variables, 256 bytes would be necessary to specify up to eight functions of eight variables. The size of the table doubles when we double the number of outputs, but the table size doubles for each **single** input variable added. Often, table-driven programming will require large amounts of memory to hold the tables. Remember, though, that the cost of memory is dramatically declining,

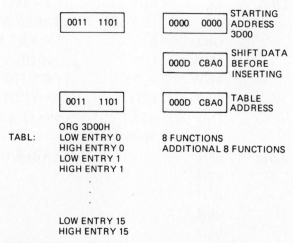

FIG. 25-34 Increasing the size of each table entry

while the cost of designing systems using that memory is increasing. It pays to use memory to save design effort.

Very often the size of a table can be reduced by clever programming. Divide tables into smaller tables when possible. For example, a table of eight functions of eight variables requires 256 bytes. If we examine the functions, we might discover that two outputs are functions of five variables requiring 32 bytes. The other six outputs are functions of five variables requiring 32 bytes. The other six outputs are functions of three variables requiring 8 bytes. By separating the functions into two tables, we require only 40 bytes of memory for the tables.

sec.26

Subroutines, Interrupts, and Arithmetic

Claude A. Wiatrowski
Charles H. House

26-1 SUBROUTINES

Subroutines are subprograms that, although stored in only one place in memory, may be used more than once in the solution algorithm. Commonly used sequences of instructions are implemented as subroutines and occupy much less memory than would otherwise be required. Subroutines also allow commonly used functions to be designed, programmed, and debugged independently of any other program. These subroutines then form a library of common functions that may be inserted into a wide variety of programs.

A subroutine is executed as part of a sequence of programming steps by **calling** the subroutine from the algorithm step that uses the subroutine. The subroutine completes its function and **returns** to the program step after the step that called it, as shown in Fig. 26-1. The subroutine may be called many times from different program steps. A subroutine must remember the place in the program from which it was called so that it can return there. One 16-bit storage location is required to save the address to which the subroutine should return.

Adapted from *Logic Circuits and Microcomputer Systems,* by Claude A. Wiatrowski and Charles H. House. Copyright © 1980. Used by permission of McGraw-Hill, Inc. All rights reserved.

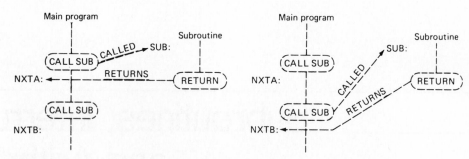

FIG. 26-1 Subroutine calls and returns

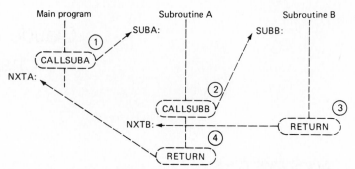

FIG. 26-2 Nested subroutines

Subroutines also call other subroutines, as shown in Fig. 26-2. When the second subroutine is called, a second return address must be saved. When the second subroutine returns to the first, the processor must know which return address to use. Keeping track of return addresses may seem hopeless, with the possibility of the second subroutine calling a third and the third calling a fourth, etc.

We must find a place to store the return address, whether there is one or ten. We also need to retrieve the return addresses in the correct order. The last return address stored should be the first retrieved; the second from the last saved should be the second retrieved; etc. We have already studied a technique for creating a variable-length list that stores and retrieves data in a last-in, first-out fashion. A last-in, first-out list is a stack, and the 8085 uses its stack to store the return addresses for its subroutines.

Figure 26-3 shows the operation of the stack for the subroutines of Fig. 26-2. When subroutine **SUBA** is called, the address **NXTA** of the instruction after the subroutine call is pushed onto the stack. If subroutine **SUBB** is called by subroutine **SUBA,** the second return address **NXTB** is also pushed onto the stack. When the subroutine **SUBB** returns to **SUBA,** the correct return address **NXTB** is popped off the stack. Finally, subroutine **SUBA** returns to the main program by popping the next return address **NXTA** off the stack. Subroutines may call other subroutines as required. The number of subroutines called is limited only by the amount of Read/Write Memory (RWM) available for expansion of the stack.

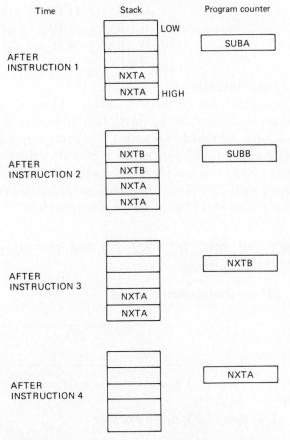

FIG. 26-3 Using the stack for subroutine returns

CALL, CC, CNC, CZ, CNZ, CP, CM, CPE, and CPO Instructions

Binary Instruction Format

	CALL	Cxx
First byte	1 1 0 0 1 1 0 1	1 1 C C C 1 0 0
Second byte	LSPA	LSPA
Third byte	MSPA	MSPA

CCC is 000 for CNZ, 001 for CZ, 010 for CNC, 011 for CC, 100 for CPO, 101 for CPE, 110 for CP, or 111 for CM.

Assembly Language Format

(LABEL:)	CALL	ADDR
(LABEL:)	CNZ	ADDR
(LABEL:)	CZ	ADDR
(LABEL:)	CNC	ADDR
(LABEL:)	CC	ADDR

(LABEL:)	**CPO**	**ADDR**
(LABEL:)	**CPE**	**ADDR**
(LABEL:)	**CP**	**ADDR**
(LABEL:)	**CM**	**ADDR**

Flag Register   Not affected.

Each of these instructions calls a subroutine by storing the contents of the program counter on the stack. This address is the location of the instruction following the **CALL** instruction. The subroutine address in the second and third bytes of the **CALL** instruction is placed in the program counter. Eight conditional subroutine call instructions will call a subroutine only if the specified condition is satisfied. These conditions are identical to those of the conditional jump instructions described in the previous chapter.

RET, RC, RNC, RZ, RNZ, RP, RM, RPE, and RPO Instructions

Binary Instruction Format

	RET	Rxx
First byte	1 1 0 0 1 0 0 1	1 1 C C 0 0 0

CCC is 000 for RNZ, 001 for RZ, 010 for RNC, 011 for RC, 100 for RPO, 101 for RPE, 110 for RP, or 111 for RM.

Assembly Language Format

(LABEL:)	**RET**
(LABEL:)	**RNZ**
(LABEL:)	**RZ**
(LABEL:)	**RNC**
(LABEL:)	**RC**
(LABEL:)	**RPO**
(LABEL:)	**RPE**
(LABEL:)	**RP**
(LABEL:)	**RM**

Flag Register   Not affected.

The return instructions pop a 16-bit subroutine address from the stack to the program counter.

Data for Subroutines

Some subroutines use data stored in the same memory locations each time they are called. Usually at least some of the data will be different at each place the subroutine is called. These variable data are called **arguments** of the subroutine and are said to be passed to the subroutine. Data may be passed to the subroutine in many ways.

If only a small amount of data is to be passed to a subroutine, that data could be stored in registers before the subroutine is called and retrieved from those registers by the subroutine. A single byte is usually passed to the subroutine in the **A** register. Of course, results may be passed back to the main program in the same way. If one or more lists of data or arrays must be passed to the subroutine, the starting addresses of these **arrays** are passed to the subroutine in register pairs in order to allow the subroutine to access the entire list through register-pair addressing.

Another technique, shown in Fig. 26-4, is used when many data need to be passed to a subroutine but these data are scattered throughout memory rather than contained in a sequential list. A list of addresses of each of the data is compiled by the main program and placed somewhere in memory. The starting address of this list of addresses is then passed to the subroutine in a register pair. Two **MOV** instructions using register-pair addressing can transfer the addresses in the table to another register pair where, finally, a **STAX** or **LDAX** instruction can be used to access the data. This is a cumbersome technique but may be the only possible solution

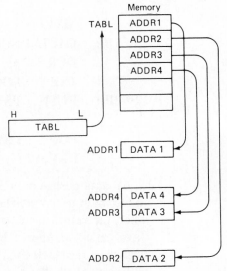

FIG. 26-4 Passing table of addresses to subroutine

Any datum passed via a register could also be pushed onto the stack. The subroutine must pop and save its return address before popping data off the stack. The return address must be pushed back on the stack before returning from the subroutine.

Register Usage

A programmer would specify which registers a subroutine uses. A main program using this subroutine would assume that these registers would not hold the same data after the subroutine returns as they held before the subroutine was called. Unless the subroutine is extremely simple, at least the **A** register usually must be used by the subroutine.

If the programmer desires that the original contents of registers remain inviolate after returning from the subroutine, the subroutine must save these registers before destroying the data in them. The original contents of the registers are restored before returning to the main program. Although these registers may be saved in any fashion, they are most easily saved in pairs on the stack.

Subroutine Example

The following example shows a main program calling a subroutine **SUBR** in two different places. The second **CALL** instruction is imbedded in a loop. The loop may use the **A** register as a counter only because the subroutine saves and restores the **A** register.

```
          .
          .
          .
          CALL    SUBR     ;GO TO SUBROUTINE
          .
          .
          .
          MVI     A, 10D
LOOP:     CALL    SUBR     ;GO TO SUBROUTINE 10 MORE TIMES
          DCR     A
          JNZ     LOOP
SUBR:     PUSH    PSW      ;SAVE A AND FLAGS
          .
          .
          .
          POP     PSW      ;RESTORE A AND FLAGS
          RET              ;RETURN TO MAIN PROGRAM
```

All data pushed onto the stack must be popped off the stack before returning to the main program. The stack pointer will point to the correct return address when the return instruction is executed. This example subroutine could even have called another subroutine. The second return address would then be pushed on the stack after the **PSW** register contents. This second return address will be popped off when the second subroutine returns to the first. The stack pointer will again point to the saved **PSW** register so that it can be popped off the stack.

26-2 INTERRUPTS

An external signal can be used to signal the processor to stop what it is doing and take some other action. This signal is called an **interrupt.** Interrupts are necessary because an external peripheral device may require an immediate action by the microcomputer that cannot wait for the completion of other computations.

The interrupt signal causes the processor to execute a subprogram in much the same way a subroutine is called. The interrupt signal causes the processor to stop after the execution of the instruction in progress. The interrupt system is now disabled; so other interrupts will be disabled. The program counter contains the location of the next instruction to be executed after the interrupt subroutine is finished. This return address is pushed on the stack. The address of the interrupt subroutine is put in the program counter. The processor is now able to execute the interrupt routine to service the peripheral that caused the interrupt. This subroutine will return to the main program by executing an ordinary **RET** instruction to pop the return address from the stack to the program counter.

Each interrupt input on the processor has a fixed memory location that is the address of the subroutine to be executed for that interrupt. These addresses are shown in Table 26-1. Ordinarily, each of these addresses would contain a **JMP** instruction to the interrupt subroutine. The five interrupt inputs are assigned

TABLE 26-1 8085 Interrupts

Priority	Name	Address	Comments
Highest	TRAP	24H	Can't be disabled
	RST7.5	3CH	Internal edge-sensitive flip-flop
	RST6.5	34H	
	RST5.5	2CH	
Lowest	INTR	See below	Only interrupt on 8080
	RST0	00H	All these have same priority but different addresses
	RST1	08H	
	RST2	10H	
	RST3	18H	
	RST4	20H	
	RST5	28H	
	RST6	30H	
	RST7	38H	

priorities, as shown in Table 26-1. The processor services the highest priority interrupt first if more than one interrupt occurs simultaneously. The next-highest-priority interrupt is serviced after the first interrupt serviced has returned to the main program.

Initialization

The 8085 also uses location 0 for initialization. The first instruction executed when power is first applied to the microcomputer is in location 0. This instruction is usually a **JMP** to the start of the main program.

EI and DI Instructions

Binary Instruction Format

	EI	DI
First byte	1 1 1 1 1 0 1 1	1 1 1 1 0 0 1 1

Assembly Language Format

(LABEL:) **EI**

(LABEL:) **DI**

Flag Register Not affected.

When an interrupt is acknowledged by the processor, the interrupt system is automatically disabled for two reasons. First, the cause of the interrupt must be removed (usually by resetting a flip-flop in the peripheral) before enabling the interrupt system. Otherwise, the peripheral would interrupt its own interrupt subroutine. The processor would be completely disabled, caught in a continuous interrupt response. Second, it is usually not desirable to allow one peripheral device to interrupt the service routine of another peripheral. When one device must interrupt another's service routine, special provision must be made to assure proper operation.

The interrupt system must be enabled when leaving the interrupt service routine in order to allow any additional interrupts to be serviced. The **EI** or enable interrupt instruction enables the interrupt system. The enable interrupt instruction is always the last instruction executed before the return (**RET**) instruction. The enable interrupt instruction does not enable the interrupt system until after the execution of the next instruction. By putting the enable interrupt just before the return, we can be sure that the interrupt will not be enabled until after the return address is popped off the stack into the program counter and the microprocessor returned to the main program. At least one main program instruction will be executed before another interrupt is serviced. The return address will always be a correct main-program address.

A **DI** or disable interrupt instruction allows the interrupt to be disabled explicitly by the main program if desired. The main program may be involved in a critical timing loop or computation that cannot be interrupted, or it may simply want to ignore peripherals when it does not need to service them. The main program and interrupt routine may exchange arguments by passing them through memory locations. The main program and interrupt routine may share more than one argument. The interrupt will have to be disabled while the main program is reading or changing related arguments. For example, suppose the interrupt has not been disabled and the main program has changed two of three related arguments. An interrupt occurs. The interrupt routine will use the new value of the first two arguments and the old value of the third!

Finally, the **TRAP** interrupt is not disabled by the **DI** instruction. The **TRAP** interrupt is commonly used for catastrophic events that require immediate service regardless of any other interrupts. For example, a common use of **TRAP** is to signal the processor that the microcomputer's power source has been disconnected. Enough energy remains in the power supply to allow the microcomputer to operate for a few milliseconds. During this time, the microcomputer may disable peripherals and otherwise set the system to a safe state before power is lost.

RIM and SIM Instructions

Binary Instruction Format

	RIM	SIM
First byte	0 0 1 0 0 0 0 0	0 0 1 1 0 0 0 0

Assembly Language Format

(LABEL:)   **RIM**

(LABEL:)   **SIM**

Flag Register   Not affected.

The RIM or **read interrupt mask** instruction transfers the internal processor status bit in Table 26-2 to the **A** register. The SIM or **set interrupt mask** instruction transfers the **A** register to the processor status bits in Table 26-2.

The interrupt mask bits M7.5, M6.5, and M5.5 can be read by RIM and

TABLE 26-2   RIM and SIM Data Formats

Bit	Name	RIM data format
7	SID	Serial input data
6	I7.5	Interrupt 7.5 pending if 1
5	I6.5	Interrupt 6.5 pending if 1
4	I5.5	Interrupt 5.5 pending if 1
3	IE	Interrupts Enabled if 1
2	M7.5	Interrupt 7.5 disabled if 1
1	M6.5	Interrupt 6.5 disabled if 1
0	M5.5	Interrupt 5.5 disabled if 1

Bit	Name	SIM data format
7	SOD	Serial output data
6	SOE	Serial output enable if 1
5	X	
4	R7.5	Reset the 7.5 interrupt flop if 1
3	MSE	Mask set enable if 1
2	M7.5	Mask (disable) interrupt 7.5 if 1
1	M6.5	Mask (disable) interrupt 6.5 if 1
0	M5.5	Mask (disable) interrupt 5.5 if 1

changed by SIM. These mask bits allow their corresponding interrupt inputs to be selectively disabled. Service requests from a particular peripheral might be ignored while some other peripheral is being serviced. The SIM instruction will change the mask bits only if the MSE bit is a 1. Because SIM is used for three diverse functions, it wouldn't be convenient to have it change all three functions each time it was executed.

Bit **IE** of the **RIM** instruction indicates that the interrupt system is enabled or disabled. This **IE** bit is set and reset by the **EI** and **DI** instructions. The **EI** and **DI** instructions enable or disable interrupts **RST7.5, RST6.5, RST5.5,** and **INTR** together. **SIM** can be used to selectively enable or disable **RST7.5, RST6.5,** and **RST5.5**. Of course, **TRAP** can't be disabled.

If the interrupts have been disabled, it is sometimes useful to determine if any require service but **not** to service them via the interrupt. The **I7.5, I6.5,** and **I5.5** bits of the RIM data format indicate the status of their corresponding interrupts. For example, if **I6.5** is a 1, an interrupt is pending on input **RST6.5.**

The **RST7.5** input is edge-sensitive. A positive transition of the logic signal on this input sets an internal flip-flop that remembers the interrupt, even if the **RST7.5** signal disappears. This internal flip-flop is automatically reset by the **RET** instruction after the **RST7.5** interrupt is serviced. The **R7.5** bit of the **SIM** data format will also reset the internal **7.5** flip-flop.

Finally, these two instructions control a 1-bit input port **SID** and a 1-bit output port **SOD** that are built into the processor. The **RIM** instruction reads the input port into the **SID** bit of its data format. The **SIM** instruction changes the output port to the state of its **SOD** bit. The **SOD** bit will be changed only if the **SOE** bit is 1. This allows **SIM** to set the interrupt masks without affecting the **SOD** output port. The bits **SID** and **SOD** are called serial data bits. Neither bit is intrinsically serial in any way. Each bit is simply a 1-bit port. They are called serial ports because they can be, and often are, **programmed** to input and output data serially.

Register Usage with Interrupts

Since an interrupt could occur between any two instructions in a program (except where the interrupt is explicitly disabled), the interrupt routine will almost always have to save the **PSW** and the **A** register on the stack and restore them before returning to the main program. In addition, all other registers will usually have to be saved and restored.

An Interrupt Example

The following example program waits for 10 interrupts to occur on **INTR** at **RST3**.

```
        ORG     0H
        JMP     STRT        ;POWER UP HERE
        ORG     18H
        JMP     INTR        ;INTERRUPT COMES HERE
        ORG     400H
STRT:   MVI     A, 10D      ;INITIALIZE TO COUNT 10
        STA     COUNT
        LXI     SP, TOP     ;INITIALIZE STACK
        EI                  ;TURN ON INTERRUPTS
WAIT:   LDA     COUNT       ;WAIT FOR 10 INTERRUPTS
        ORA     A           ;CHECK COUNT
        JNZ     WAIT
        DI                  ;DISABLE INTERRUPTS IF
        .                   ;NO LONGER NEEDED
        .                   ;REST OF PROGRAM
        .
INTR:   PUSH    PSW         ;SAVE A AND FLAGS
        LDA     COUNT       ;INTERRUPT COUNT
        DCR     A           ;DECREMENT COUNT
        STA     COUNT
        POP     PSW         ;RESTORE A AND FLAGS
        EI                  ;ENABLE INTERRUPTS
        RET                 ;RETURN
```

HLT and NOP Instructions

Binary Instruction Format

	HLT	NOP
First byte	0 1 1 1 0 1 1 0	0 0 0 0 0 0 0 0

Assembly Language Format

```
(LABEL:)    HLT
(LABEL:)    NOP
```

Flag Register Not affected.

The halt instruction might better be called a wait for interrupt instruction. **HLT** simply stops the processor until the next interrupt occurs. Upon returning from the interrupt service routine, the processor executes the instruction following the halt instruction.

The **NOP** or no operation instruction does nothing except increment the program counter. It can be used as a time delay.

26-3 ADDITIONAL PSEUDOINSTRUCTIONS

As was discussed for the **ORG** pseudoinstruction, pseudoinstructions are instructions to the assembler program. The **ORG** pseudoinstruction allows the programmer to tell the assembler where to start assigning memory locations. Pseudoinstructions and their formats will vary from assembler to assembler, but, besides **ORG,** there are two more pseudoinstructions that all assemblers will have.

The first of these pseudoinstructions is **EQU.** These **equate** pseudoinstructions allow the programmer to define new symbols to be used in the program. They have the following format:

NAME   EQU   EXPRESSION

Note that **NAME** has no colon, even though it is in the label field. **NAME** is not the label of an actual memory location. The assembler will substitute the expression listed to the right of **EQU** every time **NAME** appears in the program. For example, in the logic controller example, we could have put the following pseudoinstruction at the beginning of the program:

```
        IRN    EQU    02H      ;INPUT REG. NUMBER
        ORN    EQU    F2H      ;OUTPUT REG. NUMBER
        LBM    EQU    01H      ;LEAST SIG. BIT MASK
        ORG    3CH
        JMP    INTR            ;INTERRUPT VECTOR
        ORG    400H
INIT:   MVI    A, 0
        STA    MODE            ;SET MODE TO NORMAL
        LXI    SP, 3FFH        ;INITIALIZE STACK POINTER
        EI                     ;ENABLE INTERRUPTS
START:  IN     02H             ;READ INPUT
        MOV    B, A            ;SAVE INPUT
        LDA    MODE            ;CHECK MODE
        ORA    A               ;SET FLAGS
        JNZ    MAN             ;NOT ZERO = MANUAL
        LXI    H, TABL         ;TABLE START ADDRESS
                               ;CREATE ADDRESS OF ENTRY
        MOV    L, B
        MOV    A, M            ;GET OUTPUT VALUE
        JMP    OUTPUT
```

```
MAN:      IN     04H       ;GET MANUAL SWITCH DATA
OUTPUT:   OUT    F2H
          JMP    START     ;REPEAT PROCESS
INTR:     PUSH   PSW       ;SAVE A & PSW
          LDA    MODE
```

Then, we could have written the following instruction in the program:

```
IN     IRN    ;READ INPUT DATA
OUT    ORN    ;OUTPUT DATA
ANI    LBM    ;SAVE ONLY LSB
```

This extra cross reference may seem like a useless additional step but is actually a very useful technique. The **EQU** pseudoinstructions are normally written together at the beginning of a program. If the output register number in the previous example needed to be changed to **C3H**, a **single** change in the **EQU** pseudoinstruction would cause the assembler to change the value of **ORN** **everywhere** in the program. Making changes is easier, and the possibility of missing a program line to be changed is eliminated.

By using symbolic names rather than hex constants, the program becomes more easily understood. More importantly, symbolic names allow the programmer to start designing the program even while the microcomputer hardware is being designed and before addresses are known. After the hardware design is finalized, the **EQU** statements can be completed, specifying the memory and peripheral addresses to be used. The use of symbolic names will speed development of the software.

The second pseudoinstruction is **END,** which simply tells the assembler that the physical end of the program has been reached and there are no more instructions to be assembled. It is simply written in the code field:

END   ;END OF THIS PROGRAM

26-4 MANUAL-MODE LOGIC CONTROLLER EXAMPLE

The logic controller example in Section 25 could also include a manual operation mode. In the manual mode, a set of input switches will change the outputs directly, bypassing the algorithms otherwise used to determine the outputs. A pushbutton switch connected to the interrupt will cause the mode to alternate between normal and manual each time it is depressed.

The flowchart for the manual-mode logic controller is shown in Fig. 26-5. The flowchart is similar to the example in the last chapter in normal mode. After data are input, a variable called **MODE** is checked. If the **MODE** is manual, inputs from the manual switches are simply output to the controlled devices.

Each time the pushbutton causes an interrupt, the mode is toggled to its opposite state.

The actual program is listed below. Notice that the main program is almost identical to the last chapter's example except that the **MODE** variable is tested. If the mode is manual, the state of switches connected to port 04H is sent to the output port. The interrupt routine simply toggles all 8 bits in **MODE** each time this routine is executed by pushing the interrupt button.

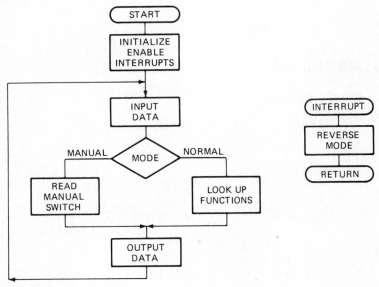

FIG. 26-5 Manual mode logic controller

```
        ORG    0
        JMP    INIT        ;START HERE WHEN POWER
                           ;  APPLIED
        XRI    FFH         ;REVERSE MODE
        STA    MODE
        POP    PSW         ;RESTORE A & PSW
        EI                 ;ENABLE INTERRUPT
        RET                ;RETURN
        ORG    500H
TABL:   00H                ;TABLE OF FUNCTION VALUES
        02H
        02H
        06H
        02H
        02H
        02H
        06H
        02H
        02H
        02H
        06H
        06H
```

```
                    0EH
                    0EH
                    0FH
MODE:               00                        ;0 IS NORMAL MODE, ≠ 0 IS
                                               MANUAL MODE
```

26-5 ARITHMETIC

Binary Addition

The binary addition table is very simple.

$$
\begin{array}{cccc}
0 & 0 & 1 & 1 \\
\underline{+0} & \underline{+1} & \underline{+0} & \underline{+1} \\
00 & 01 & 01 & 10
\end{array}
$$

Multidigit binary numbers are summed least significant digit first, just as in decimal arithmetic. If a carry occurs, it is added to the next most significant bit. Let's add two 8-bit numbers.

```
    0 0 1 1 1 0 0 1     Carry
    0 0 1 0 1 1 0 1     Operand
  + 1 0 1 1 1 0 0 1     Operand
    1 1 1 0 0 1 1 0     Sum
```

In the 8085, as in most computers, the carry out of the most significant bit is stored in the carry bit of the flag register.

When adding unsigned binary numbers, a 1 carry bit out of the most significant bit (the carry stored in the flag register) indicates that the result of the addition was too large to be represented by the number of bits in the register. This is called overflow. The flag-register carry bit may be used to test for arithmetic overflow. Of course, the carry stored in the flag register could be added to the next most significant bit of the result if the result is to be contained in more than one byte.

The same addition table will work correctly for two's-complement numbers. The flag register's carry bit may still be added to the next most significant bit if the result is contained in more than 1 byte. However, the carry bit can no longer be tested for overflow. Adding two numbers of opposite sign will never cause an arithmetic overflow. That is, the register holding the result will always have enough bits to represent the answer properly.

```
              0 1 1 1   1 1 1 1   (127, largest positive number)
              1 1 1 1   1 1 1 1   (−1, smallest negative number)
  Carry = 1   0 1 1 1   1 1 1 0   (126, correct answer)
```

This is the largest positive result from adding opposite-signed operands. Overflow has not occurred.

$$
\begin{array}{ll}
1\,0\,0\,0 \quad 0\,0\,0\,0 & (-128,\ \text{most-negative number}) \\
\underline{0\,0\,0\,0 \quad 0\,0\,0\,0} & (0,\ \text{smallest ``positive'' number}) \\
\text{Carry} = 0 \quad 1\,0\,0\,0 \quad 0\,0\,0\,0 & (-128,\ \text{correct answer})
\end{array}
$$

This is the most negative result from adding opposite-signed operands. Overflow did not occur.

However, when two's-complement numbers of the same sign are added, an arithmetic overflow can occur. An attempt to represent a number greater than $+127$ or less than -128 will cause the result to seem to change sign. Since the sum of two positive numbers should always be positive and the sum of two negative numbers should be negative, a sign change indicates arithmetic overflow. If both operands have the same sign, the result must also have that same sign or arithmetic overflow has occurred.

$$
\begin{array}{ll}
1\,0\,0\,0 \quad 0\,0\,0\,0 & (-128) \\
\underline{1\,1\,1\,1 \quad 1\,1\,1\,1} & (-1) \\
\text{Carry} = 1 \quad 0\,1\,1\,1 \quad 1\,1\,1\,1 & (+127,\ \text{wrong answer})
\end{array}
$$

This addition of negative operands gives a positive result. Arithmetic overflow has occurred.

$$
\begin{array}{ll}
0\,1\,1\,1 \quad 1\,1\,1\,1 & (+127) \\
\underline{0\,0\,0\,0 \quad 0\,0\,0\,1} & (+1) \\
\text{Carry} = 0 \quad 1\,0\,0\,0 \quad 0\,0\,0\,0 & (-128,\ \text{wrong answer})
\end{array}
$$

This addition of positive operands gives a negative result. Arithmetic overflow has occurred.

ADD and ADI Instructions

Binary Instruction Format

	ADD	ADI
First byte	1 0 0 0 0 S S S	1 1 0 0 0 1 1 0
Second byte	NONE	DATA 8

SSS is 000 for B, 001 for C, 010 for D, 011 for E, 100 for H, 101 for L, 111 for A or 110 for M.

Assembly Language Format

(LABEL:)   **ADD**   **SRC**

(LABEL:)   **ADI**   **DATA**

Flag Register   All flag-register bits are affected and have their standard interpretation.

The **ADD** and **ADI** instructions both add an operand to the **A** register and leave the result in the **A** register. The **ADD** instruction will add the contents of any register to the **A** register. The **ADD** instruction will add the contents of any memory location using register-pair addressing to the **A** register. The **ADI** or

add immediate instruction will add an 8-bit immediate operand to the **A** register. All flag-register bits are affected. The carry bit contains the carry out of bit 7, the most significant bit. The auxiliary carry bit contains a copy of the carry out of bit 3 into bit 4. The zero, sign, and parity bits are set according to the result of the addition.

```
STRT:   MVI   A,10D     ;  SET A TO 10
        MVI   E,5D      ;  SET D TO 5
        LXI   H,DATA    ;  H,L POINT TO DATA
        ADD   E         ;  ADD E TO A
        ADI   2         ;  ADD 2 TO A
        ADD   M         ;  ADD CONTENTS OF DATA
        STA   RESLT     ;  STORE RESULT
          .
          .
          .
DATA:   4D              ;  VALUE OF 4
RESLT:  0               ;  CONTAINS RESULTS
```

After this program is executed, memory location **RESLT** will contain 21D.

ADC and ACI Instructions

Binary Instruction Format

	ADC	ACI
First byte	1 0 0 0 1 S S S	1 1 0 0 1 1 1 0
Second byte	NONE	DATA 8

SSS is 000 for B, 001 for C, 010 for D, 011 for E, 100 for H, 101 for L, 111 for A, or 110 for M.

Assembly Language Format

```
(LABEL:)   ADC   SRC
(LABEL:)   ACI   DATA
```

Flag Register   All flag-register bits are affected and have their standard interpretation.

The **ADC** or **add with carry** instruction and the **ACI** or **add with carry immediate** instruction are similar to the **ADD** and **ADI** instructions. The **ADC** and **ACI** instructions add the initial value of the carry bit to the least significant bit of the result. The result of the addition is incremented by 1 if the carry bit is 1. If the carry bit is 1 because of a previous **ADD** instruction, the **ADC** instruction can add the carry out of the MSB of that previous addition into the least significant bit of the current result. The carry can be propagated from 1 byte to another for multiple-byte additions. The operands and result may be 16, 24, 32, or more bits long. An example of a 16-bit addition is shown below.

```
STRT:   LDA   LSG   ;  LEAST SIG. PART OF ONE OPERAND
        MOV   B,A   ;  SAVE IT
        LDA   LSH   ;  LEAST SIG. PART OF OTHER
```

```
                    ;  OPERAND
ADD     B           ;ADD LSP, CARRY OUT IN FLAG REG
STA     LSA         ;SAVE IN LSP OF ANSWER
LDA     MSG         ;GET MSP OF ONE OPERAND
MOV     B,A         ;SAVE IT
LDA     MSH         ;GET MSP OF OTHER OPERAND
ADC     B           ;ADD MSP WITH CARRY OUT OF LSP
STA     MSA         ;SAVE IN MSP OF ANSWER
```

Binary Subtraction   The binary subtract table is also simple.

$$
\begin{array}{rrrr}
1 & 1 & 0 & 0 \\
-0 & -1 & -0 & -1 \\
\hline
1 & 0 & 0 & 1 \\
0 & 0 & 0 & 1
\end{array}
$$
Minuend
Subtrahend
Difference
Borrow

Multiple-bit binary numbers are subtracted like multiple-digit decimal numbers. Start with the least significant bit.

Whenever 1 must be subtracted from 0, a borrow is made from the next most significant bit position. That is, the borrow is subtracted from the minuend.

$$
\begin{array}{l}
0\ 1\ 1\ 0\ 1\ 0\ 0\ 0 \quad \text{Borrow} \\
1\ 1\ 0\ 1\ 0\ 1\ 1\ 0 \quad \text{Minuend} \\
\underline{-\ 0\ 1\ 1\ 0\ 1\ 0\ 1\ 0} \quad \text{Subtrahend} \\
0\ 1\ 1\ 0\ 1\ 1\ 0\ 0 \quad \text{Difference}
\end{array}
$$

In bit position 3, 1 is subtracted from 0. A borrow from bit 4 changes this subtraction to 10 minus 1, which is 1. Thus, bit 3 of the difference is 1. The borrow is subtracted from bit 4 of the minuend and leaves 0 minus 0, which is 0. Thus, bit 4 of the result is 0.

If the register's **most**-significant-bit subtraction needs to borrow from the next most significant bit, the flag-register carry bit will be 1, indicating a borrow occurred that could not be satisfied. Even though the flag register's carry bit is set to the borrow out of the most significant bit of a subtraction, don't assume that a carry is identical to a borrow. For example, a subtract instruction will cause the carry bit (really a borrow) to be set to the opposite state than the carry bit set by the same arithmetic operation performed by the addition of the two's complement of the subtrahend. The following addition performs the previous example subtraction by adding the two's complement of the subtrahend. The carry out of the MSB is opposite the borrow obtained by subtraction.

$$
\begin{array}{l}
\underline{0\ 1\ 1\ 0\ 1\ 0\ 1\ 0} \quad \text{Subtrahend} \\
\underline{1\ 0\ 0\ 1\ 0\ 1\ 0\ 1} \quad \text{One's complement} \\
1\ 0\ 0\ 1\ 0\ 1\ 1\ 0 \quad \text{Two's complement} \\
\underline{+\ 1\ 1\ 0\ 1\ 0\ 1\ 1\ 0} \quad \text{Minuend} \\
0\ 1\ 1\ 0\ 1\ 1\ 0\ 0 \quad \text{Difference} \\
1\ 0\ 0\ 1\ 0\ 1\ 1\ 0 \quad \text{Carry}
\end{array}
$$

When subtracting unsigned binary numbers, a borrow out of the most significant bit indicates the subtrahend was larger than the minuend. The result would have been negative and cannot be represented as an unsigned number. A flag-register carry bit of 1 indicates arithmetic overflow for unsigned subtraction.

When subtracting two's-complement numbers of the **same** sign, arithmetic overflow will never occur.

$$
\begin{array}{ll}
0\,1\,1\,1\,1\,1\,1\,1 & (127, \text{most-positive number}) \\
-\,0\,0\,0\,0\,0\,0\,0\,0 & (0, \text{smallest positive number}) \\
\hline
\text{Borrow} = 0 \quad 0\,1\,1\,1\,1\,1\,1\,1 & (127, \text{correct answer})
\end{array}
$$

This is the most positive result possible from subtracting same-signed operands. No overflow has occurred.

$$
\begin{array}{ll}
1\,0\,0\,0\,0\,0\,0\,0 & (-128, \text{most-negative number}) \\
-\,1\,1\,1\,1\,1\,1\,1\,1 & (-1, \text{smallest negative number}) \\
\hline
\text{Borrow} = 1 \quad 1\,0\,0\,0\,0\,0\,0\,1 & (-127, \text{correct answer})
\end{array}
$$

This is the most-negative result possible from subtracting same-signed operands. No overflow has occurred.

Subtracting two's-complement numbers of opposite sign can cause overflow to occur. When subtracting two's-complement numbers of opposite sign, the result should always have the same sign as the minuend; otherwise arithmetic overflow has occurred.

$$
\begin{array}{ll}
0\,1\,1\,1\,1\,1\,1\,1 & (+127) \\
-\,1\,1\,1\,1\,1\,1\,1\,1 & (-1) \\
\hline
\text{Borrow} = 1 \quad 1\,0\,0\,0\,0\,0\,0\,0 & (-128, \text{wrong answer})
\end{array}
$$

The correct answer is +128. The result appears negative because +128 can't be represented by 8 bits. Overflow has occurred.

$$
\begin{array}{ll}
1\,0\,0\,0\,0\,0\,0\,0 & (-128) \\
-\,0\,0\,0\,0\,0\,0\,0\,1 & (+1) \\
\hline
\text{Borrow} = 0 \quad 0\,1\,1\,1\,1\,1\,1\,1 & (+127, \text{wrong answer})
\end{array}
$$

The correct answer is −129. The answer appears positive because −129 can't be represented by 8 bits. Overflow has occurred.

SUB and SUI Instructions

Binary Instruction Format

	SUB	SUI
First byte	1 0 0 1 0 S S S	1 1 0 1 0 1 1 0
Second byte		DATA 8

SSS can be 000 for B, 001 for C, 010 for D, 011 for E, 100 for H, 101 for L, 111 for A, or 110 for M.

Assembly Language Format

(LABEL:) **SUB** **SRC**
(LABEL:) **SUI** **DATA**

Flag Register All flag-register bits are affected, and all but **C** have their standard interpretation. The **C** bit contains the borrow out of the subtraction.

The subtract or **SUB** and subtract immediate or **SUI** instructions subtract the specified data byte from the **A** register and leave the result in the **A** register. For the **SUB** instruction, the specified data byte can be the contents of any register or the contents of any memory location specified by register-pair addressing. The **SUI** instruction subtracts the 8 bits of immediate data carried with the instruction. The **borrow** out of bit 7 is stored in the flag-register carry bit. However, the auxiliary carry or **AC** bit is set to the **carry** out of bit 3 into bit 4 and **not** the borrow out of bit 3.

SBB and SBI Instructions

Binary Instruction Format

	SBB	SBI
First byte	1 0 0 1 1 S S S	1 1 0 1 1 1 1 0
Second byte		DATA 8

SSS can be 000 for B, 001 for C, 010 for D, 011 for E,
100 for H, 101 for L, 111 for A, or 110 for M.

Assembly Language Format

(LABEL:) **SBB** **SRC**
(LABEL:) **SBI** **DATA**

Flag Register All flag-register bits are affected, and all but **C** have their standard interpretation. The **C** bit contains the borrow out of the subtraction.

The subtract with borrow or **SBB** and the subtract with borrow immediate or **SBI** instructions are similar to the **SUB** and **SUI** instructions. If the flag register's carry bit is 1 before the instruction is executed, that 1 will be subtracted from the result of the subtraction. The flag register's carry bit is set by a borrow out of a previous subtraction. Thus, these instructions can be used for multiple-byte subtraction. The following program subtracts **G** from **H**. Both **G** and **H** are 16-bit binary numbers.

```
STRT:   LDA   LSG   ; LSP OF SUBTRAHEND
        MOV   B,A   ; SAVE IT
        LDA   LSH   ; LSP OF MINUEND
        SUB   B     ; SUBTRACT LSPS, SAVE BORROW
        STA   LSA   ; SAVE LSP OF ANSWER
        LDA   MSG   ; MSP OF SUBTRAHEND
        MOV   B,A   ; SAVE IT
        LDA   MSH   ; MSP OF MINUEND
```

```
SBB    B      ;  SUBTRACT WITH BORROW FROM LSP
STA    MSA    ;  SAVE MSP OF ANSWER
```

DAD Instruction

Binary Instruction Format

	DAD
First byte	0 0 R P 1 0 0 1

RP can be 00 for B, 01 for D, 10 for H, or 11 for SP.

Assembly Language Format

```
(LABEL:)    DAD    B
(LABEL:)    DAD    D
(LABEL:)    DAD    H
(LABEL:)    DAD    SP
```

Flag Register   The C bit is set to the carry out of the most significant bit of the most significant byte of the addition. No other flag-register bits are affected.

Sixteen-bit additions are very commonly performed for both address arithmetic and data calculations. The **DAD** or double add instruction performs 16-bit additions conveniently. The **DAD** instruction adds the contents of any register pair to the 16-bit number in the **H** register pair. The result of the addition remains in the **H** register pair. **Only the carry bit** in the flag register is affected. The C bit is set to the carry out of the most significant bit of the 16-bit addition.

Besides serving as a convenient 16-bit addition instruction, the **DAD** instruction has two other important uses. The instruction **DAD H** adds the **H** register pair to itself. Since **DAD H** doubles the number in **H** and **L**, it is equivalent to the one-place left shift of 16 bits. The **DAD H** instruction is a left shift of the **H** register pair.

The **DAD SP** instruction is the **only** instruction that will allow the program to retrieve the contents of the stack pointer. A program might need to check the contents of the **SP** to determine if the stack still has room to expand. The following sample program will check the **SP** against a limit address stored in memory.

```
STRT:  LDA    LIMIT      ;LSP OF LIMIT ADDRESS
       CMA               ;COMPLEMENT IT
       MOV    L,A        ;SAVE IN LSP OF H PAIR
       LDA    LIMIT+1    ;MSP OF LIMIT ADDRESS
       CMA               ;COMPLEMENT IT
       MOV    H,A        ;SAVE IN MSP OF H PAIR
       INX    H          ;INCREMENT TO FORM 2's
                         ;  COMPLEMENT
       DAD    SP         ;ADD CONTENTS OF STACK
                         ;  POINTER
```

```
JNC     OFLW        ;JUMP IF (SP) IS BELOW LIMIT
                    ;  ADDRESS
NOP                 ;OK TO PUSH ONTO STACK
```

This short program adds the two's complement of the **LIMIT** address to the **SP.** Since the stack expands downward in memory, stack overflow occurs whenever the **SP** is below the **LIMIT.** The result of the calculation **SP-LIMIT** will be positive whenever the **SP** is equal to or above the **LIMIT.** If we were using a subtract instruction, we'd expect a 0 borrow bit. Since we are adding the two's complement, the carry bit will be opposite the borrow. Thus, **C** will be 1 whenever the **SP** is equal to or above the **LIMIT. C** will be 0 when the stack has overflowed the **LIMIT.**

CMP and CPI Instructions

Binary Instruction Format

	CMP	CPI
First byte	1 0 1 1 1 S S S	1 1 1 1 1 1 1 0
Second byte	NONE	DATA 8

SSS can be 000 for B, 001 for C, 010 for D, 011 for E, 100 for H, 101 for L, 111 for A, or 110 for M.

Assembly Language Format

```
(LABEL:)   CMP   SRC
(LABEL:)   CPI   DATA
```

Flag Register   All flag register bits are affected, and all but **C** have their standard interpretation. The **C** bit contains the borrow out of the subtraction.

The **CMP** or compare and **CPI** or compare immediate instructions compare the contents of the specified byte with the accumulator. The datum to be compared can be the contents of any register or of any memory location specified by register-pair addressing. The **CPI** instruction allows the specified byte to be an immediate datum carried with the instruction.

The comparison is performed by subtracting the specified data byte from the contents of the **A** register. All flag-register bits are set as if a **SUB** instruction had been executed. The result of the subtraction is not stored anywhere. The specified data byte and the contents of the **A** register remain unchanged. After performing a compare, the program may conditionally branch on the flag-register bits.

If the zero bit is 1, the two operands were equal; otherwise they were unequal. The sign bit could be used to compare the relative sizes of the two operands **if no arithmetic overflow occurred.** If the sign bit is 1, indicating a negative result, the data byte was larger than the **A** register. If the sign bit is 0, the **A** register is larger than or equal to the data byte. Since we would have to verify that no overflow occurred to believe our comparison and since we may still want to compare the data **even if** overflow occurred, another test must be devised. We can test the state of the carry bit in the flag register to determine relative size.

The carry bit of the flag register will contain the borrow bit out of the most significant bit of the subtraction.

If both operands have the same sign and the **A** register is larger than or equal to the data byte, no borrow will occur and the carry bit will be 0. If the carry bit is set to 1, indicating a borrow, the data byte is greater than the contents of the **A** register. If the signs of the operands are different, the sense of the carry bit will be reversed. We can summarize the compare operation as follows:

Signs of operands	Flag register	Meaning
Any	Z = 1	(A) = Data
Any	Z = 0	(A) ≠ Data
Same	C = 1	(A) < Data
Same	C = 0	(A) ≥ Data
Different	C = 1	(A) ≥ Data
Different	C = 0	(A) < Data

If you are comparing numbers known to be small, it is still easiest to test the sign bit for comparison. Often, numbers to be compared are limited to a range known not to cause overflow.

DAA Instruction

Binary Instruction Format

	DAA
First byte	0 0 1 0 0 1 1 1

Assembly Language Format

(LABEL:) DAA

Flag Register All flag register bits are affected and have their standard interpretation.

The **DAA** or decimal adjust **A** register instruction is used in conjunction with other arithmetic instructions to perform BCD arithmetic. If two valid BCD digits, each having a range of 0 to 9 are added using a binary arithmetic instruction, the result is not necessarily a valid BCD digit. For example:

```
Case 1        0001    (1)
            + 0011    (3)
              0100    (4)    Valid BCD digit

Case 2        0001    (1)
            + 1001    (9)
              1010    (A)    Not a valid BCD digit

Case 3        0111    (7)
            + 1001    (9)
Carry = 1     0000    (0)    Valid BCD digit but incorrect result
```

These three examples represent the only three possible cases. The result could be a valid BCD digit and correct. The result could be a hex digit between A and F. The result could be a valid BCD digit between 0 and 8 but not correct (a carry out of the digit is always generated in this case).

The **DAA** instruction corrects the last two cases to valid BCD numbers representing the correct result. After an **ADD** instruction is executed to add two BCD numbers, a **DAA** instruction is executed to correct the result in two steps.

1. If the least significant digit is greater than 9 (case 2 above) or if the auxiliary carry bit is set (case 3 above), the entire **A** register is incremented by 6. For the case 2 example above, the least significant digit would be 0000 and the most significant digit would be incremented by 1. For the case 3 example above, the least significant digit would be 6. In case 2, when the BCD digit A is corrected to 0, a carry is propagated to the most significant digit to add ten to the entire number. In case 3, the original binary addition propagated a carry to the most significant digit so that, when the digit 0 is corrected to 6, no additional carry need be propagated.

2. Finally, the **DAA** instruction corrects the most significant digit. If the most significant digit is greater than 9 (case 2) or if the normal carry bit is set (case 3), the **most significant** digit is incremented by 6. Any carry out of bit 7 from this operation is stored in the normal carry bit of the flag register. The other flag-register bits are set according to the final result.

After the **DAA** instruction is executed, the contents of the **A** register are valid BCD digits representing the correct sum of the two BCD operands. If the sum should have been greater than 99, the carry bit will be set, which will indicate an overflow or a carry into the next most significant digit. An **ADC** instruction can be used to continue the sum if operands with more than two BCD digits must be summed. The **DAA** instruction will not work after a subtract instruction. Decimal subtraction must be performed by adding the **ten's-complement** representation of the BCD subtrahend. Ten's complement is a representation for negative BCD numbers analogous to two's complement for binary numbers. This example program subtracts the subtrahend by finding its ten's complement and adding it to the minuend.

STRT:	**LXI**	**D,MIN**	;	**ADDRESS OF MINUEND**
	LXI	**H,SBTR**	;	**ADDRESS OF SUBTRAHEND**
	MVI	**C,2**	;	**4 DIGITS OR 2 BYTES**
	STC		;	**NO BORROW**
LOOP:	**MVI**	**99H**	;	**99 BCD**
	ACI	**0**	;	**ADD CARRY**
	SUB	**M**	;	**COMPLEMENT OF SUBTRAHEND**
	XCHG		;	**GET ADDRESS OF MINUEND**
	ADD	**M**	;	**ADD MINUEND**
	DAA		;	**DECIMAL ADJUST RESULT**
	MOV	**M,A**	;	**STORE RESULT**
	XCHG		;	**GET ADDRESS OF SUBTRAHEND**

```
DCR     C          ; CHECK FOR LAST BYTE
JZ      DONE       ; YES, WE ARE DONE
INX     D          ; NO, ADDRESS NEXT BYTE
INX     H          ; NEXT BYTE
JMP     LOOP       ; GET NEXT TWO DECIMAL DIGITS
```

26-6 SOME ADDITIONAL DATA MOVEMENT INSTRUCTIONS

XCHG and XTHL Instructions

Binary Instruction Format

	XCHG	XTHL
First byte	1 1 1 0 1 0 1 1	1 1 1 0 0 0 1 1

Assembly Language Format

```
(LABEL:)   XCHG
(LABEL:)   XTHL
```

Flag Register   Not affected.

The **XCHG** or exchange instruction exchanges the contents of the **D** register pair with those of the **H** register pair. Register-pair addressing must often be used to specify the operand of a logical or arithmetic operation. Only the **H** register pair can be used for register-pair addressing for arithmetic and logical operations. A second address can be placed in the **D** register pair and exchanged with the **H** pair when a different operand is to be addressed. For example, the following program adds a constant to an array, subtracts the corresponding locations of another array from the result, and places the result in the first array.

```
STRT:   LXI     D,AR2      ; ARRAY 2
        LXI     H,AR1      ; ARRAY 1
        MVI     B,SIZE     ; SIZE OF ARRAYS
LOOP:   MVI     A,CONST    ; CONSTANT TO ADD
        ADD     M          ; ADD ARRAY 1
        XCHG               ; EXCHANGE ADDRESSES
        SUB     M          ; SUBTRACT ARRAY 2
        XCHG               ; RESTORE AR1 ADDRESS
        MOV     M,A        ; STORE RESULT IN ARRAY 1
        INX     D          ; NEXT ARRAY 2 LOCATION
        INX     H          ; NEXT ARRAY 1 LOCATION
        DCR     B          ; DECREMENT COUNTER
        JNZ     LOOP       ; CONTINUE IF NOT DONE
```

The **XTHL** or exchange **HL** with top of stack instruction allows the current return address to be changed and the original return address to be saved.

SPHL Instruction

Binary Instruction Format

	SPHL
First byte	1 1 1 1 1 0 0 1

Assembly Language Format

(**LABEL:**)   **SPHL**

Flag Register   Not affected.

The **SPHL** or **HL** to **SP** instruction puts the contents of the **H** register pair into the stack pointer. Like the **LXI SP, DATA** instruction, **SPHL** can be used to initialize the stack pointer. The **LXI** instruction will only initialize the **SP** to a predetermined constant, while the **SPHL** will allow the microcomputer to set the stack pointer to any value calculated in the **H** register pair.

26-7 PROGRAMMED ARITHMETIC OPERATIONS

Multiplication

Some microcomputers, including the 8085, do not have multiply or divide instructions. These arithmetic operations are performed by subroutines written by the programmer. First, we'll consider the multiplication of unsigned binary numbers. Let's examine the multiplication of two decimal numbers:

$$
\begin{array}{r}
483 \\
\times\ 24 \\
\hline
1932 \\
966\ \ \ \\
\hline
11592
\end{array}
\quad
\begin{array}{l}
\text{Multiplicand} \\
\text{Multiplier} \\
\text{Partial product} \\
\text{Partial product} \\
\text{Product}
\end{array}
$$

Start with the rightmost multiplier digit to form the first partial product (by using the decimal multiplication table and propagating carries). The next multiplier digit to the left forms another parital product that is shifted one digit to the left because it represents a number 10 times as large as the first partial product. Continue generating partial products for all multiplier digits. The partial products are summed to obtain the product.

The first thing we need to perform a binary multiplication is the binary multiplication table:

$$
\begin{array}{cccc}
0 & 0 & 1 & 1 \\
\times 0 & \times 1 & \times 0 & \times 1 \\
\hline
0 & 0 & 0 & 1
\end{array}
$$

Let's multiply two 4-bit unsigned binary numbers:

```
      1011    (11)
    ×0101     (5)
      1011
     0000
     1011
    0000
    0110111   (55)
```

Because of the simplicity of the binary multiplication table, a multiplier bit of 1 causes the associated partial to be equal to the multiplicand. If a multiplier bit is 0, the corresponding partial product is 0. In the microcomputer, we will test each multiplier bit and either add or not add the multiplicand. We will not store each partial product, but add the next partial product immediately to form an accumulated partial product.

Let's examine the same multiplication used previously as an example:

0000	1011	Multiplicand
	0101	Multiplier
0000	0000	Accumulated partial product

Since the least significant bit of the multiplier is one, we will add the multiplicand to the partial product. At the same time, we will shift the multiplier right to prepare to check the next bit and the multiplicand left to prepare for the next partial product.

0001	0110	Multiplicand
	0010	Multiplier
0000	1011	Partial product

Since the next multiplier bit is 0, we shall simply shift the multiplicand and multiplier without adding the multiplicand.

0010	1100	Multiplicand
	0001	Multiplier
0000	1011	Partial product

The next multiplier bit is a 1; so we shall add the multiplicand.

0101	1000	Multiplicand
	0000	Multiplier
0011	0111	Partial product

The next and last multiplier bit is 0; so we do not need to add the multiplicand.

1011	0000	Multiplicand
	0000	Multiplier
0011	0111	Product

Although this algorithm could be programmed as shown, it usually is not used for several reasons. First, an 8-bit register is needed for the 4-bit multiplicand,

and, second, an 8-bit addition was required, even though we are using only 4-bit operands. We shift the partial product to the right, rather than shift the multiplicand left.

START	1011		Multiplicand		
	0101		Multiplier		
	0000	0000	Product		
1. **ADD**	1011		2. **SHIFT**	1011	
	0101			0010	
	1011	0000		0101	1000
3. **NO ADD**	1011		4. **SHIFT**	1011	
	0010			0001	
	0101	1000		0010	1100
5. **ADD**	1011		6. **SHIFT**	1011	
	0001			0000	
	1101	1100		0110	1110
7. **NO ADD**	1011		8. **SHIFT**	1011	
	0000			0000	
	0110	1110		0011	0111

Notice that we shift the multiplier right each time we shift the accumulated partial product right. We could have stored the multiplier in the least significant byte of the product. Each time we shifted right we would set up the next multiplier bit to be tested and simultaneously make room for the next product bit.

A multiplication algorithm is flowcharted in Fig. 26-6 for the 8085. The 8085 cannot test the least significant bit of a register without an extra masking step. We will first shift the product/multiplier right, so the least significant bit will be stored in the carry bit of the flag register. The carry bit is easily tested with a conditional jump instruction. A multiplication program may be written from this flowchart.

```
                              ; SINGLE PRECISION MULTIPLY
                              ; MULTIPLIER IN B
                              ; MULTIPLICAND IN C
                              ; RESULT IN A,B (16 BITS)
                              ; BIT COUNTER IN D
MPY:    XRA    A              ; INITIALIZE PARTIAL PRODUCT
        MVI    D,8            ; TEST 8 MULTIPLIER BITS
LOOP:   ORA    A              ; CLEAR CARRY
        RAR                   ; SHIFT PRODUCT RIGHT
        MOV    E,A            ; SAVE PARTIAL PRODUCT
        MOV    A,B            ; GET MULTIPLIER
        RAR                   ; ROTATE
        MOV    B,A            ; RESTORE MULTIPLIER
        MOV    A,E            ; RESTORE PARTIAL PRODUCT
        JNC    NOADD          ; CHECK MULTIPLIER BIT
```

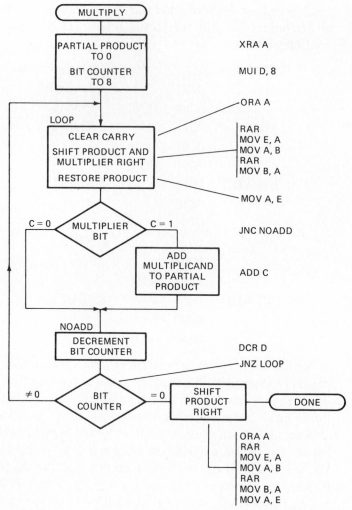

FIG. 26-6   Binary multiplication

	ADD	C	;	MULT. BIT = 1, ADD MULTIPLICAND
NOADD:	DCR	D	;	DECREMENT BIT COUNTER
	JNZ	LOOP	;	NOT DONE. NEXT PARTIAL PRODUCT
	ORA	A	;	CLEAR CARRY
	RAR		;	PRODUCT SHIFTED ONCE MORE
	MOV	E,A		
	MOV	A,B		
	RAR			
	MOV	B,A		
	MOV	A,E		

Division

Binary division is performed similarly to decimal division. Let's examine a decimal division:

$$\begin{array}{r} \underline{021} \quad \text{Quotient} \\ \text{Divisor} \quad 22|478 \quad \text{Dividend} \\ \underline{44} \\ 38 \\ \underline{22} \\ 16 \quad \text{Remainder} \end{array}$$

First, we try to divide the first digit of the dividend by the entire divisor. This division cannot be done, and we enter 0 as the first quotient digit. Next, we try to divide the first two digits of the dividend by the divisor and continue until a division can be performed. We calculate the remainder from that division, bring down the next dividend digit, and attempt to divide again by the divisor. If division cannot be accomplished, we enter 0 in the quotient, bring down the next dividend digit, and try to divide again. If division is possible, we enter the appropriate digit in the quotient and calculate a new remainder.

A binary division will proceed similarly.

$$\begin{array}{r} \underline{0001\ 1011} \quad (27) \\ (6) \quad 0000\ 0110\ |1010\ 0111 \quad (167) \\ \underline{0110} \\ 0100\ 0 \\ \underline{011\ 0} \\ 001\ 011 \\ \underline{0\ 110} \\ 0\ 1011 \\ \underline{0110} \\ 0101 \quad (5) \end{array}$$

As in multiplication, division is simplified in binary. The divisor is either subtracted or not subtracted from the remainder depending on whether the quotient bit is 1 or 0. In fact, the divisor can be subtracted from the dividend to **determine** whether the quotient bit should be 0 or 1. Consider the same division example:

Remainder   Dividend and quotient
   0000 0000   1010 0111
Shift the remainder and dividend left and try to subtract the divisor:

1.   0000 0001   0100 1110
   $-$0000 0110

The result would be negative. Shift left and try again. Enter 0 in the quotient. Since we are shifting the dividend left at each step, we'll use the bits vacated on the right to hold the quotient.

2.   0000 0010   1001 1100
   $-$0000 0110

The result would be negative. Enter 0 in the quotient.

3.   0000 0101   0011 1000
   −0000 0110

The result would be negative. Enter 0 in the quotient.

4.   0000 1010   0111 0000
   −0000 0110
   0000 0100

The subtraction was successful. Enter 1 in the quotient.

5.   0000 1000   1110 0001
   −0000 0110
   0000 0010

The subtraction was successful. Enter 1 in the quotient.

6.   0000 0101   1100 0011
   −0000 0110

The result would be negative. Enter 0 in the quotient.

7.   0000 1011   1000 0110
   −0000 0110
   0000 0101

The subtraction was successful. Enter 1 in the quotient.

8.   0000 1011   0000 1101
   −0000 0110
   0000 0101

The subtraction was successful. Enter 1 in the quotient.

9.   0000 1010   0001 1011

We have run out of dividend bits and have calculated the quotient. In order to enter the last quotient bit, we had to shift the remainder one more place than necessary. We must shift the remainder one to the right to correct it.

Just as in multiplication, where the multiplier and product shared the same register, the dividend and quotient share the same register in division. Every time a new quotient bit is ready, another dividend bit may be shifted into the partial product. Since we are using unsigned binary arithmetic, a negative result is indicated by a borrow bit of 1 (stored in the flag register's carry bit.) Since we need a 1 quotient bit if we have a positive result and a 0 quotient bit if we have a negative result, we can just complement the carry bit and use it as the new quotient bit. The first shift can be accomplished by allowing an extra division step to be performed. Subtracting the divisor from the original 0 remainder will cause a 0 quotient bit and a left shift. This extra division step will be exactly equivalent to the first of the nine shifts in the above example.

This division algorithm is flowcharted in Fig. 26-7. A division program may be written from this flowchart.

```
;  SINGLE PRECISION DIVISION
;  REMAINDER IN B
;  DIVIDEND/QUOTIENT IN C
;  DIVISOR IN D
;  BIT COUNTER IN E
```

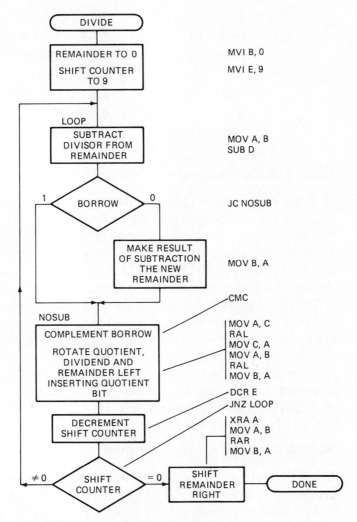

FIG. 26-7 Binary division

DIV:	MVI	E,9	;9 SHIFTS
	MVI	B,0	;ZERO REMAINDER
LOOP:	MOV	A,B	;GET REMAINDER
	SUB	D	;SUBTRACT DIVISOR
	JC	NOSUB	;NEGATIVE RESULT, DON'T SAVE ; RESULT
	MOV	B,A	;POSITIVE RESULT, SAVE NEW ; REMAINDER
NOSUB:	CMC		;FOR NEW QUOTIENT BIT
	MOV	A,C	;GET QUOTIENT/DIVIDEND
	RAL		;ROTATE LEFT
	MOV	C,A	;RESTORE
	MOV	A,B	;GET REMAINDER
	RAL		;INSERT NEW DIVIDEND BIT

```
        MOV   B,A      ;   RESTORE
        DCR   E        ;   BUMP COUNTER
        JNZ   LOOP     ;   DO 9 TIMES
        XRA   A        ;   CLEAR CARRY
        MOV   A,B      ;   GET REMAINDER
        RAR            ;   CORRECT IT
        MOV   B,A      ;   RESTORE
```

Signed Multiplication and Division

One way to perform two's-complement multiplication and division would be to calculate the sign of the result separately and take the absolute value of the operands. Use unsigned multiplication or division and correct the result to the previously calculated sign. When the signs of the operands are different, the sign of the result will be positive. A single subroutine can be used to compute the correct sign for multiplication or division.

The unsigned multiplication algorithm previously described will give a correct result for a negative multiplicand. In this case, only the absolute value of the multiplier need be calculated. The sign of the result is then reversed if the original sign of the multiplier was negative.

Many other techniques exist for performing two's-complement signed multiplication and division but usually offer little or no advantage when programmed for a microcomputer.

Multiplication by Small Constants

It is often necessary to multiply by small constants. For example, a table entry number must be multiplied by 3 for a ROM table that has 3 bytes per entry. In a previous example, we showed how a 3-byte-per-entry table could be padded with do-nothing bytes to make it a 4-byte-per-entry table. We could use two left shifts to multiply by 4 to access the table. If the table had many entries, we would not want to waste a large amount of memory space by inserting do-nothing bytes. On the other hand, it seems that a complete multiplication program is slow and cumbersome if all we need to do is multiply by 3 or 5. Multiplication by a small constant can be performed by only performing the multiplication steps that correspond to each 1 bit in the multiplier. If the multiplier has only a few 1 bits (like the numbers 3 and 5), the multiplication will proceed much faster than a complete multiplication program. The following program uses this technique to access a 3-byte-per-entry jump table.

```
STRT:   LDA   RTNUM    ;NUMBER OF ROUTINE TO EXECUTE
        MOV   B,A      ;SAVE ORIGINAL NUMBER
        ADD   A        ;MULTIPLY BY 2
        ADD   B        ;2*RTNUM + RTNUM = 3*RTNUM
        LXI   H,JTBL   ;STARTING ADDRESS OF JUMP
                       ;  TABLE
        MVI   B,0      ;MSP OF OFFSET
```

```
        MOV   C,A         ;LSP OF OFFSET
        DAD   B           ;ADD STARTING ADDRESS AND
                          ;   OFFSET
        PCHL              ;JUMP TO THIS ADDRESS
JTBL:   JMP   RT0         ;3 BYTE TABLE ENTRY
        JMP   RT1
        JMP   RT2
              .
              .
        JMP   RT84        ;MAXIMUM OF 84 DECIMAL
                          ;ROUTINES
```

If more than 84 entries were needed, the multiplication by 3 would have to accumulate a 16-bit result to accommodate offsets greater than 255.

Moving the Binary Point

The position of the binary point must often be moved when performing arithmetic operations on numbers representing fractional values. The binary points must be aligned in both operands when adding or subtracting. The binary point of the result is in the same position as the point in the operands.

$$
\begin{array}{r}
00101.001 \\
+01010.110 \\
\hline
01111.111
\end{array}
$$

If the binary points are not aligned, one or the other operand must be shifted to align the point. If the operand with the leftmost point is shifted right, the least significant bits will be lost. You can also be certain that the register will be able to represent the shifted operand properly.

$$
\begin{array}{ll}
\text{Original operand} & 101.00101 \\
\text{Shift right} & 00101.001 \\
& +01010.110 \\
\hline
& 01111.111
\end{array}
$$

Shifting an operand to the left to align the binary point will prevent least significant bits from being lost. However, you must be sure that most significant bits are not lost, which would render the result invalid.

When multiplying two binary numbers, the binary point of the result is displaced to the left by the sum of the displacements of the points of the two operands.

$$
\begin{array}{ll}
00101.000 & \text{Point is displaced 3 places to the left} \\
\times000011.00 & \text{Point is displaced 2 places to the left} \\
\hline
00000001111.00000 & \text{Point is displaced 5 places to the left}
\end{array}
$$

When dividing binary numbers, the binary point of the result is displaced to the left by the displacement of the dividend's point minus the displacement of the divisor's point.

Shifting Two's-Complement Numbers

We have previously discussed use of a left shift to multiply by 2 and a right shift to divide by 2 for unsigned binary numbers. Signed binary numbers can also be shifted. A two's-complement number may be multiplied by 2 by shifting it left and filling the least significant bit with a 0. If you are not sure of the initial magnitude of the number, you must check for overflow of the result by looking for a change in sign. The old sign bit is stored in the carry bit after the left shift.

```
DOBL:   ADD    A        ;SHIFT LEFT, INSERT ZERO,
                        ;   SET ALL FLAGS
        JP     POS      ;CHECK NEW SIGN BIT
        JNC    OFLW     ;OLD SIGN WAS 0, NEW SIGN IS 1
        JMP    CONT     ;OLD SIGN WAS 1, NEW SIGN IS 1
POS:    JC     OFLW     ;OLD SIGN WAS 1, NEW SIGN IS 0
CONT:   NOP             ;NO OVERFLOW, CONTINUE
```

A two's-complement number may be halved by shifting it right. Rather than shifting a 0 into the most significant bit, the sign bit must be replicated to preserve the sign and value of the number.

```
HALF:   ORA    A        ;SET SIGN FLAG, CLEAR CARRY
                        ;   FLAG
        JP     ROT      ;POSITIVE NUMBER, CARRY IS 0
        CMC             ;NEGATIVE NUMBER, SET CARRY
                        ;   TO 1
ROT:    RAR             ;HALVE NUMBER, INSERT CORRECT
                        ;   SIGN
```

Floating-Point Numbers

The kinds of numbers we have been using are called fixed-point numbers. To represent a larger fixed-point number than the number of bits allows, we must use additional bits to the left of the binary point. If we must represent very small numbers, we use additional bits to the right of the binary point. Fixed-point numbers can be cumbersome. The programmer must know the range of the numbers expected at all stages of the computation. The original data for the program usually comes from an external device (terminal, temperature sensor, etc.). The range of input data may be very large, and the range of intermediate computational results may be even larger. An excessively large number of bits would be required to represent variables in the computation.

A number representation that does not have the above problems is called floating point. Floating-point binary numbers are analogous to decimal numbers in scientific notation. Each floating-point number is represented by two fixed-point binary numbers, a mantissa and an exponent. The floating-point number represented by these two fixed-point numbers is:

$$(\text{MANTISSA}) \times 2^{(\text{EXPONENT})}$$

In floating-point representation, all numbers have the same precision regardless of their magnitude. Extremely large and small numbers may be represented in a relatively small number of bits. A microcomputer typically uses an 8- to 32-bit mantissa and a 6- to 16-bit exponent. Since the size of the exponent and mantissa are determined by the programmer who writes the floating-point arithmetic subroutine, the mantissa and exponent may be sized to fit the requirements of the problem. However, writing these arithmetic routines is a substantial job; so most programmers try to find standard floating-point arithmetic subroutines that meet their requirements.

Interfacing Concepts

Donald D. Givone
Robert P. Roesser

27-1 INTRODUCTION

A microcomputer system is made up of different types of components, which generally include a microprocessor, memory units, I/O registers, and peripheral devices. The interconnection of these components, which is a primary concern in the design of a microcomputer system, must take into account the nature and timing of the signals that appear at the interfaces between components. For the purpose of achieving compatibility of signals, it is generally necessary to select appropriate components and design supplementary circuits. This is referred to as **interfacing.** In regard to microcomputer systems, interfacing can be separated into two areas of concern. One area involves the connection of the components, such as memory units and input/output registers, to the buses of a microprocessor. Such interfacing is primarily concerned with the timing and control of the buses and the selection of a component so as to effect a data transfer at a given time between the selected component and the microprocessor.

The other area of concern involves interfacing components external to the microcomputer, such as peripheral devices, data channels, and controllers, to a part of the microcomputer. Such interfacing does not directly involve the buses of the microprocessor; so it is comparatively less structured. It is concerned with converting signals associated with the external components, which might be of any nature (including analog), to signals compatible with the buses and vice versa.

27-2 INPUT/OUTPUT PORTS

By convention, the direction of input and output information flow involving a microprocessor is normally regarded relative to the microprocessor itself. Thus, an **input port** refers to any source of data, such as a register, that is connected in a selectable manner to a microprocessor data bus. It supplies a data word to the microprocessor when selected. An **output port** refers to a receptacle of data, such as a register, that is connected in a selectable manner to a microprocessor data bus. It receives a data word from the microprocessor when selected. Most microprocessors use all or part of their address bus to designate which input or output port is selected. Also, input ports and output ports are often distinguished from each other and memory locations by certain control lines.

I/O Ports for the Illustrative Microprocessor

Figure 27-1 shows a network consisting of a typical input port and a typical output port for the illustrative microprocessor. A unique 8-bit device code is assigned to these two ports so that the microprocessor can distinguish them from all other input or output ports. In this case, both ports are assigned the same device code (01100101), which is allowed since the two ports are further distinguished by the separate control lines In and Out. During the execution of an input or output instruction, the device code for the port to be accessed is obtained from the instruction and placed onto the lower half of the Address bus. To detect the presence of the particular device code assigned to the ports of Fig. 27-1, an 8-bit AND gate with the appropriate lines inverted is connected to the lower half of the Address bus. The output line of this AND gate, labeled "Select," is used in the selection of either of the two ports.

The input port includes an 8-bit register that is assumed to contain information supplied by some external device. Eight 3-state drivers couple the output lines of this register to the Data bus. These 3-state drivers are all enabled by the AND of the Select signal and the In control signal from the microprocessor. Thus, the content of the register is placed onto the Data bus when (1) Select is logic-1, indicating that the device code assigned to this input port has been specified, and (2) In is logic-1, indicating that an input instruction is being executed and that it is the proper time in the instruction cycle to input information. Once information is placed onto the Data bus, it is the responsibility of the microprocessor to transfer it to the proper destination within the microprocessor, which is the accumulator.

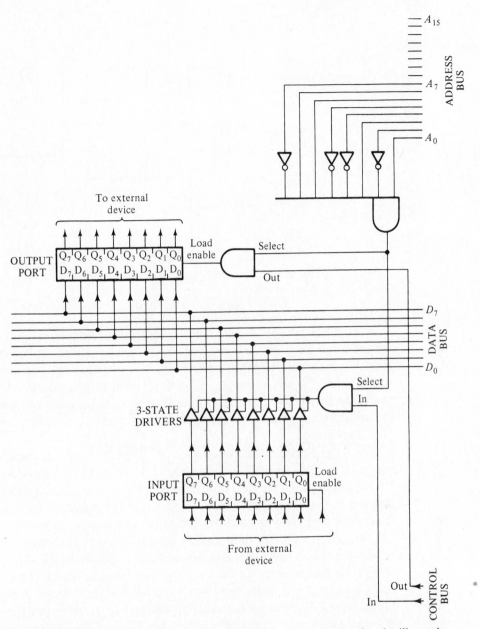

FIG. 27-1 Typical network for an input port and an output port for the illustrative microprocessor

One machine cycle, the third of an input instruction, is used to perform an input data transfer. The timing relationship among the various signals during this machine cycle is shown in Fig. 27-2. Three clock pulses comprise the machine cycle. At the beginning of the first clock pulse T_1 the microprocessor places the appropriate device code onto the lower half of the Address bus. The In control line becomes logic-1 with the trailing edge of T_1 and remains at logic-1 until the leading edge of the third clock pulse T_3. It is assumed that the Data bus, in response to the In signal, will contain valid data from the input port during the time between the leading edges of T_2 and T_3. Finally, this data on the bus is strobed into the microprocessor accumulator at the end of T_2.

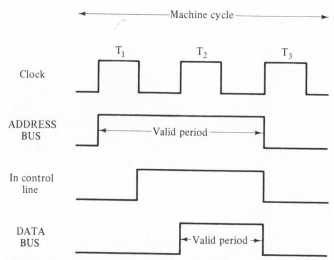

FIG. 27-2 Timing diagram for an input data transfer to the illustrative microprocessor

It should be noticed that two timing constraints are placed upon the circuitry for the input port with this scheme. One time constraint is that the Data bus must become valid within a certain amount of time (i.e., one-half of a clock period) after the In control signal becomes logic-1. This constraint implies that the delay encountered in the 3-state drivers plus the delay encountered in the two-input AND gate connected to the drivers must be no greater than one-half of a clock period.

The second time constraint is that the Data bus must become valid within one clock period after the device code appears on the Address bus. This constraint implies that the sum of the delay encountered in the 8-input AND gate and the connected inverters used to generate the Select signal plus the previously indicated delay must be no greater than one clock period.

Schemes for inputing data used by various microprocessors may differ somewhat from this scheme, but similar time constraints exist for them. These constraints on the external components are usually quite liberal. This is due to the fact that the components comprising an input or output port are usually of a higher speed than that of the microprocessor. For example, medium-scale integrated TTL, which is relatively fast, might be used to implement an input port for a microprocessor that is fabricated with large-scale integrated MOS logic, which is relatively slow.

The output port shown in Fig. 27-1 has an 8-bit register, which is assumed to supply information to an external device. The register consists of D-type clocked latches that are controlled by a common load-enable line. The D input terminals are connected directly to the Data bus. A two-input AND gate that drives the load-enable line combines the Select signal with the Out control signal. Thus, the content of the Data bus, which comes from the accumulator of the microprocessor, is transferred into the output-port register when (1) Select is logic-1, indicating that the device code assigned to this output port has been specified, and (2) Out is logic-1, indicating that an output instruction is being executed and that it is the proper time in the instruction cycle to output information.

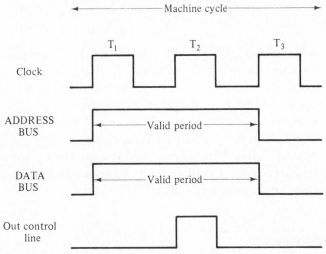

FIG. 27-3   Timing diagram for an output data transfer from the illustrative microprocessor

The third machine cycle for the execution of an output instruction is used to perform the output data transfer. The timing relationship among the various signals during this machine cycle is shown in Fig. 27-3. At the beginning of clock pulse T_1 the lower-half of the Address bus and the Data bus become valid as determined by the microprocessor. That is, both address and data information are placed onto the appropriate buses. The data is then strobed into the output register by a pulse on the Out control line that occurs coincident with the T_2 clock pulse.

Time constraints are placed on the circuitry for an output port that are similar to those for an input port. Again they are normally of little concern due to the relatively fast components that are usually used to implement input and output ports.

I/O Variations

The differences between the I/O scheme just discussed for the illustrative microprocessor and some I/O schemes for commercial microprocessors primarily concern the nature of the control signals that determine the type and timing of data transfers. The In and Out control signals of the illustrative microprocessor serve as strobes that provide for both the necessary timing and control of the I/O transfers. Many schemes for commercial microprocessors, however, require that signals similar to In and Out be derived by logically combining other control signals.

In some cases, a control line from the microprocessor is provided that has the purpose of specifying the direction of the data bus. This control line, referred to as say Data-out, indicates the output direction when at one logic value, say logic-1, and the input direction when at the other logic value. A clock line to the microprocessor or a second control line is then used as a strobe to determine the times of data transfers. Interfacing I/O ports to such microprocessors can be done in a manner similar to that indicated for the illustrative microprocessor by forming signals corresponding to In and Out, as follows:

$$In = (\overline{Data\text{-}out}) \; Strobe$$
$$Out = (Data\text{-}out) \; Strobe$$

where Strobe refers to the control line that determines the transfer time.

Some data-transfer schemes of microprocessors involve sending a control word over the data bus during the beginning of a machine cycle that specifies precisely what type of data transfer is to occur, such as data-in, data-out, memory-read, or memory-write. This control word is then stored in an external register so that it may be used in combination with the clock or other control signals to derive such signals as In, Out, Read, and Write of the illustrative microprocessor. In this way, the corresponding control lines from the microprocessor need not be provided.

27-3 HANDSHAKING

As was indicated in the previous section, input and output ports provide the means for coupling external devices to a microprocessor. An external device can be anything that supplies or accepts digital information, such as a mass storage unit, a data terminal, a data-acquisition instrument, a machine-tool controller, or even another microprocessor. Most external devices operate in a manner that is inherently independent of the timing of the microprocessor. For example, a data terminal having a keyboard and a printer produces a unit of data each time a key is depressed manually and accepts data at a rate dictated by the mechanical limitations of the printer. Some means is needed to coordinate the timing of an external device to the timing of the microprocessor. Otherwise, a data transfer from a given input port might be performed before it contains the desired data or that a data transfer to a given output port might be performed before previous data in that port is used. This coordination of timing is generally known as **handshaking.**

Generally, the operation of an external device involves a specific action based on the mechanism of the device. The end result of this **device action** is either the utilization of one data word at an output port or the provision of one data word to an input port. For example, the device action of a keyboard consists of the depression of a key and the subsequent supply of information to an input port of a microprocessor. Also, the device action of a printer is the activation of the appropriate hammer solenoid for the character that corresponds to the data present at an output port of a microprocessor. It is generally assumed that the data port is engaged by the device during the device action and, therefore, should not be accessed at that time by the microprocessor. Only at times after the completion of the device action is the data port for the device available or ready for either an input or output data transfer, as the case may be, by the microprocessor. There are three overall aspects to the handling of data between a device and a microprocessor:

1. The initiation of the device action
2. The checking for device port availability by the microprocessor
3. The actual transfer of data between the device port and the microprocessor

There are several ways of coordinating data handling based upon the possible combinations of employing the first and second aspects.

Program-Initiated Data Handling

One way of coordinating data handling for some devices is to have the program initiate the action of the device for each data transfer. This is done by a signal sent from the microprocessor to the device at times determined by the program. The device responds to this signal by supplying new data in the case of an input port or using the data in a prescribed manner in the case of an output port. After a sufficient amount of time has elapsed to allow for the device action, the program can access the data port. Very often such access to the port serves as the signal to initiate device action (which, in the case of an input port, is actually for the next access to be made).

A device consisting of a paper-tape reader and punch serves to illustrate program-initiated data handling. Assume that the paper-tape reader is connected to an input port and the punch to an output port. The paper tape consists of a sequence of 8-bit data words. Initially, the input port is filled from the reader with the first data word of an input tape. At various points in a running program, access is made to the input port. In addition to obtaining the data, this access also serves as a signal to operate the reader. The reader responds by reading the next data word from the input tape to replace the previous content of the input port. Likewise, at other points in the running program, access is made to the output port. In addition to loading the output-port register, this access also serves as a signal to operate the punch. It responds by punching the new content of the output port into an output tape.

Figure 27-4 illustrates, in general, how the signals that cause device action can be produced with the illustrative microprocessor. Networks are shown both for input devices and for output devices. Each network involves an unclocked SR flip-flop, which serves as a flag to the external device. Each flag is set by the signal, in either case, that was used in the network of Fig. 27-1 to produce a transfer between the microprocessor and the appropriate port register. Specifically, the output-port flag is set by the AND of the Select signal from the device selection network and the Out control signal from the microprocessor. Likewise, the input-port flag is set by the AND of Select and the In control signal. The output of each flag is sent to the device to cause its action to occur, such as activating the drive motor and punch solenoids of a paper-tape punch. In any case, the result of the device action is the utilization of data from an output port or the provision of data to an input port. After such action takes place, the device places logic-1 onto the reset terminal of the appropriate flag flip-flop. The flag is thus reset at the completion of the action so that the action is not repeated until after the corresponding port is accessed again by the microprocessor.

Device-Initiated Data Handling

A second way of coordinating data handling is to have the device initiate its own action for each data transfer. In this case, after the completion of the device action, information must be provided to the program that the data port con-

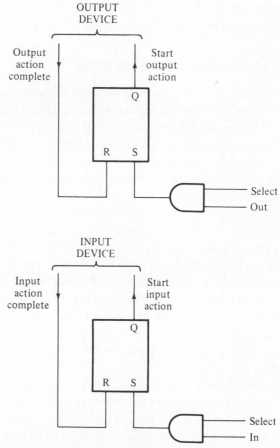

FIG. 27-4 Flags for signaling an external device to perform an input or output action

nected to the device is available for another data transfer. This is done by having the device set a port-ready flat that is repetitively checked by the program during times the program expects to perform a data transfer with the port. Usually an auxiliary input port is used for this purpose that corresponds to the status of one or more devices. The separate bits making up this status port correspond to different conditions that may occur in regard to a group of devices, specifically including a ready condition for each data port.

In a segment of a program in which access to a certain data port is to be made, the ready status of the data port is checked by first inputting the content of the associated status port. The bit that indicates the ready condition for the particular data port is then isolated and tested by the program. If it is determined that the data port is not ready, then this status-checking operation is repeated until the data port is ready.

A magnetic-tape unit is an example that typifies devices that involve device-initiated data handling. Data words are usually grouped on the magnetic tape in blocks, called **records,** with empty spaces in between the records. In operation, the tape is accelerated, within a space between records, to a specified velocity. Thus, during reading or writing, data words in a record are successively encountered and transferred at a fixed rate. The encountering of each data word is the device action.

Generalized Handshaking

A more general scheme for coordinating data handling is to combine the aspects of the first two schemes. In this case, the program initiates the device action and checks the ready status of the data port.

Figure 27-5 illustrates how an interface for this general scheme, including

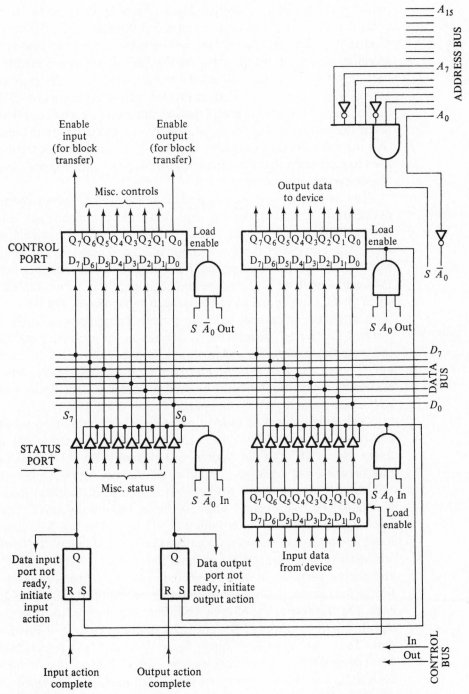

FIG. 27-5 General I/O interface to the illustrative microprocessor including input, output, status, and control ports

both a data input port and a data output port, might be implemented for the illustrative microprocessor. A single input/output device is assumed to be connected to the two data ports. Besides the two data ports there is a status port and a control port.

The status port is an input port that provides the microprocessor with information concerning the set of prevailing device conditions. Two particular conditions are "data input port not ready," corresponding to status bit 7, and "data output port not ready," corresponding to status bit 0. These two status bits each come from the output of an unclocked SR flip-flop. Each flip-flop is set at the time that a data transfer occurs between the microprocessor and the corresponding data port, which indicates that the port is not available for another data transfer. This also informs the device to perform the appropriate device action, which obtains new data in the case of the input port or utilizes the data in the case of the output port. Upon completion of a device action, the device resets the corresponding status bit, which is an indication to the microprocessor that the corresponding data port is ready. The remaining six status bits may be used to represent other device conditions such as "end of tape," "end of block," "input error," etc.

The control port is an output port, which is used to convey commands to the device from the microprocessor. Two particular commands are "enable input," corresponding to control bit 7, and "enable output," corresponding to control bit 0. The purpose of these two commands is to allow an entire block of data words to be inputted or outputted. For example, to read paper or magnetic tape, the enable-input bit is set to 1 at the beginning of a record and then reset to 0 when all data words in a record have been encountered. The device ANDs each of these enable commands with the corresponding port-not-ready status bit as a signal to start or continue the device action for each data transfer. Thus, in the example, tape motion and reading continues from one data word to the next only if both the enable-input and data-input-port-not-ready bits are 1. The remaining six control bits may be used to perform other device functions such as "rewind input tape," "skip a page," "reset error flags," etc.

A selection network is used to partially select the four ports. This network consists of a 7-input AND gate, with some inputs inverted, which is connected to the lower half of of the Address bus excluding bit A_0. The output line S of this network will be logic-1 if either of the two device codes 10110110 or 10110111 is present on the Address bus. The first of these codes corresponds to the status and control ports, whereas the second corresponds to the data ports. Each Port is controlled by a 3-input AND gate. The line S is connected to an input line of each of these AND gates. The complement of the least significant address line $\overline{A_0}$ is connected to an input line of the two AND gates for the status and control ports, while A_0 is connected to an input line of the two AND gates for the data ports. In this way, each port is conditioned upon an assigned device code. The third input line of each AND gate is connected to either the In control signal, if it is for an input port, or the Out control signal, if it is for an output port. Thus, each port is uniquely determined and will respond appropriately when designated by the microprocessor. Also, the output lines of the AND gates controlling the two data ports are connected to the set terminals of the corresponding status flip-flops so that they behave as previously discussed.

TABLE 27-1 Program Segments for Input and Output

Memory location	Machine language instruction	Symbolic form of instruction	Remarks
1000	FD	INP	Input device status word
1001	B6	B6	
1002	61	LRI 1	Load H with mask
1003	80	80	
1004	81	AND 1	Isolate bit 7
1005	7D	JAN	Test bit 7; if equal to 1, then recheck status
1006	10	10	
1007	00	00	
1008	FD	INP	Input data
1009	B7	B7	
2000	FD	INP	Input device status word
2001	B6	B6	
2002	61	LRI 1	Load H with mask
2003	01	01	
2004	81	AND 1	Isolate bit 0
2005	7D	JAN	Test bit 0; if equal to 1, then recheck status
2006	20	20	
2007	00	00	
2008	FE	OUT	Output data
2009	B7	B7	

Table 27-1 shows program segments for input and output that could be used with the network of Fig. 27-5. The input segment is shown starting at memory location 1000_{16}. The first instruction inputs the device status word from the input port $B6_{16}$. The bit in position 7, corresponding to the condition "data input port not ready," is isolated by ANDing the status word with the mask 80_{16}. If bit 7 of the status word is 0, indicating that data is available for input, then the entire accumulator will be zero. If this condition is not met then the next instruction, jump on accumulator not zero, will cause this status checking operation to be repeated. Otherwise, the next instruction will input the data from input port B7, which concludes the input segment.

The output program segment is shown starting at memory location 2000_{16}. It is similar to the input segment except that bit 0 of the device status word is used to indicate "data output port not ready." This status bit is isolated using the mask 01_{16}. Also, of course, the last instruction is an output instruction.

27-4 PROGRAM INTERRUPTS

A powerful facility of most microprocessors is the ability to have a running program interrupted in response to an external event so that a special routine dealing with the event may be executed. This is generally referred to as a **program interrupt.** For example, an interrupting event could be the completion of a data-handling action by an external device for which the microprocessor was waiting. Thus, such interrupt capability provides an alternative to having the microprocessor continually check a status port to determine when a particular I/O port is ready for a data transfer. A considerable advantage is gained by the use of program interrupts because during the waiting time for an I/O port, the microprocessor is free to independently perform other functions, including attending to other I/O ports.

A program interrupt, for most computers, generally resembles a jump to a subroutine. However, it is invoked by an external signal appearing on a specific control line rather than by a program instruction. Such an interrupt signal is referred to as an **interrupt request.** As for a subroutine, an interrupt routine, written to perform a desired task, is placed in memory beginning at the location to which program control is to be transferred. When the microprocessor recognizes an interrupt request while executing a program, it suspends execution of that program and begins execution of the interrupt routine. At the end of an interrupt routine, a return instruction is normally included to cause the microprocessor to resume execution of the suspended program at the point of interruption. Usually, a microprocessor has the capability of disabling interrupts during times in which they are inappropriate. When interrupts are disabled, then any interrupt request will be ignored.

It is common for a microcomputer system to contain more than one device that can request a program interrupt. A need therefore exists in such systems to be able to determine which, if any, device is requesting an interrupt so that the appropriate action can be taken. There are two basic ways in which this determination is made. One way is to have a master interrupt service routine that, when an interrupt request does occur, checks the status of each device to see if it is making the request. This is often referred to as a **polled-interrupt scheme.** The second way is to have a network that provides the microprocessor with information that "points" to a device requesting an interrupt. This is usually referred to as a **vectored-interrupt scheme.**

Polled Interrupts

For the polled-interrupt scheme only a single control line to the microprocessor is necessary for the purpose of requesting an interrupt. This interrupt-request control line is driven by the OR of individual interrupt-request lines for the various devices, so that any device can send an interrupt signal to the microprocessor. Associated with each device is generally a status input port in which one bit position is used to indicate an interrupt request by that device. When an interrupt signal from any device appears on the interrupt-request control line to the microprocessor, a jump will be made to a fixed location upon completing the current instruction provided that interrupts are enabled by the microprocessor. That location is the beginning of a master interrupt service routine, which will successively input the content of each status port in order to test its interrupt-request bit. When a device requesting an interrupt is found, the master routine will then branch to a specific routine that deals with that device.

When two or more devices are simultaneously requesting an interrupt, a conflict arises that must be resolved. The resolution of such conflicts is built into the polled-interrupt scheme. The first interrupting device in the polling order is the one serviced. Of course, after one device is serviced any other pending interrupt requests will cause another program interrupt to occur, which will cause the next device to be serviced, and so on. The order of polling therefore determines a priority for servicing interrupting devices.

The major disadvantage with the polled-interrupt scheme is the amount of time required for the master service routine to poll the separate devices. This polling time is frequently of little concern, since the applications of microprocessors, unlike large-scale computers, often involve a relatively small number of devices. However, there are microprocessor applications in which timing is critical, so that the polling time is of concern. For such applications a vectored-interrupt scheme is a valuable alternative, since then the interrupting device is directly determined.

Vectored Interrupts

For a vectored-interrupt scheme, circuitry external to the microprocessor is provided for the determination of an interrupting device. Of course, this circuitry must be able to resolve conflicts arising when two or more devices simultaneously request an interrupt so that a single device at a time is selected for service.

There are various ways in which an interrupting device can be identified. One way involves a microprocessor with more than one interrupt-request line, each one of which is connected to a separate device. In this case, a signal on any one of the lines causes a program jump to a different location in memory, unless inhibited internally by a higher priority interrupt signal. At each of these locations a specialized service routine begins that treats the particular device. This method is quite common for large-scale computers and is used to a small extent with some microprocessors. However, as can be appreciated, if the number of interrupt-causing devices is not very small, then the necessary number of interrupt-request lines to the microprocessor will be excessive.

Vectored Interrupts Based on Distinguishing Addresses

One scheme for interrupt vectoring, which can be directly or indirectly used with any microprocessor, is to have the beginning address of the service routine corresponding to an interrupting device sent to the microprocessor over the data bus. The address is determined by an external network that selects one of the devices requesting an interrupt according to some priority scheme. Of course, if only one device is requesting an interrupt at the time, it is the one selected.

The illustrative microprocessor was specified with this scheme in mind and will therefore be used to explain it. To handle interrupts, the illustrative microprocessor has two specific control lines, Intr (Interrupt Request) and Inta (Interrupt Acknowledge). The control Intr is an input line to the microprocessor that conveys an external request for an interrupt when it is placed at logic-1. All interrupt requests, however, are conditioned on the internal Interrupt Flag. Only if this flag is set will a request for an interrupt be honored. The control Inta is an output line from the microprocessor that is used to strobe an exter-

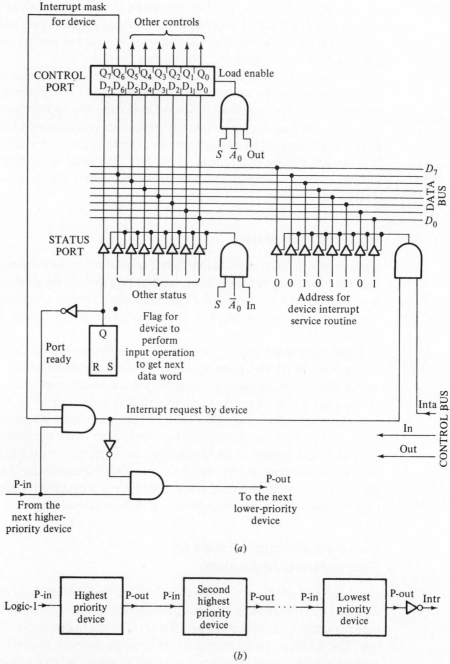

FIG. 27-6 Vectored-interrupt scheme based on device-supplied addresses, which uses a daisy-chain to determine priority (a) Network to provide interrupt address from one device (b) Daisy-chain interconnections

nally supplied jump address onto the Data bus in response to a program interrupt.

Figure 27-6a shows the interrupt circuitry for one device. The device is assumed to include one input port for inputting data (not shown in figure), a second input port for status, and an output port for control. One bit of the status port, the leftmost, is of particular importance in this case. This status bit is used, as it was in Fig. 27-5, to signal the device to begin an input operation. Also, it is available to the microprocessor to indicate when the device is busy with the input operation, and thus the input data port is not ready. The complement of this status bit, Port Ready, is the basis for an interrupt request by the device. Two other conditions must hold, however, before an interrupt is requested by this device.

One of these conditions is that a certain bit, labeled "Interrupt Mask," of the control register is equal to 1. This allows a program to inhibit interrupts by this particular device at times when an interrupt by the device is not appropriate.

The remaining condition for an interrupt request to be made by the device is that the device be given priority by other devices. For this purpose a priority network, in the form of a so-called **daisy-chain,** as shown in Fig. 27-6b, interconnects all devices in an order according to an assigned priority. Each device has an incoming priority line, labeled "P-in," and an outgoing priority line, labeled "P-out." The P-in line to each particular device is defined to be logic-1 when no device having a higher assigned priority is requesting an interrupt. It is connected to the P-out line of the device that has the next higher priority. The particular device in turn computes the value of its P-out line, which is connected to the P-in line of the device that has the next lower priority. Logically, the P-out line of the device is the AND of the P-in line and the negation of an interrupt request by that device. That is, the next device is given priority if its predecessor device is given priority but is not requesting an interrupt. The three signals, Interrupt Mask, Port Ready, and P-in, which correspond to the just mentioned conditions, are ANDed to produce the interrupt-request signal by the device.

When the interrupt-request signal from any of the devices becomes logic-1, the Intr control line to the microprocessor also becomes logic-1. This is accomplished by connecting the Intr control line to the complement of the last P-out line. This last P-out line is logic-0 if any device is requesting an interrupt. When the microprocessor recognizes an interrupt request, it will respond at the proper time with a pulse on the Inta (Interrupt Acknowledge) control line. The Inta line is ANDed with the interrupt-request signal from the device. The output of the AND gate for each device is used to enable a bank of 3-state drivers that couple a specified 8-bit address (which is particular to the device) to the Data bus. In this way, the specified address is brought into the microprocessor to indicate the beginning location of the interrupt service routine. The timing for the transfer of the address into the microprocessor involves one machine cycle and is similar to that for a data transfer from an input port. In this case, however, the Inta control line determines the timing rather than the In control line.

The sequence of events inside the microprocessor for an interrupt is as follows. If the internal Interrupt Flag is logic-0, then any interrupt request is ignored. If this flag is logic-1, then whenever a logic-1 appears on the Interrupt Request line Intr, a program interrupt will be recognized. In this case, however, the execution of the current instruction is first completed. The content of the program counter, which is the address of the next instruction that would otherwise be executed, is then pushed down into the sack. The Interrupt Flag is reset to block any more interrupts until it is set by an instruction. Finally, one machine cycle is used to bring in the 8-bit address from the interrupting device. This 8-bit address forms the lower half of the new content of the program counter, and the upper half is made zero. Consequently, a jump is effected to this address, which is somewhere within the first 256_{10} locations of memory.

The first instruction of an interrupt service routine is often a jump to a location outside of the first 256_{10} locations in order to conserve space there for other interrupt service routines. The routine is especially written to treat the device that caused the interrupt. During the routine the Interrupt Flag of the microprocessor, which was automatically reset (interrupts disabled), might be set (interrupts enabled) by an instruction in order to allow other devices, especially higher-priority devices, to interrupt the routine. Otherwise, the second last instruction of the routine is usually the enable-interrupt instruction, so that the same device or other devices could cause an interrupt in the future. A delay of one instruction is built into the enable-interrupt instruction so that one final instruction of the routine can be executed before any other interrupts are recognized. The last instruction of the routine is always a return instruction, which causes the stack to be popped up into the program counter. This restores the program counter to the address of the location where the program was interrupted.

Priority Encoders for Vectored Interrupts

A second vectored-interrupt scheme, which can be used with any microprocessor, provides the microprocessor with a unique code number representing the interrupting device. In such a scheme, an interrupt causes a jump to a fixed location where a master interrupt service routine begins. This routine then inputs the content of a special port that has been provided to contain the code number for the interrupting device. Based on this code number, a subsequent jump is made to another routine that is particular to the interrupting device. As in other schemes, conflicts which result from more than one device at a time requesting an interrupt are resolved by a priority assignment.

This scheme can be implemented in a manner similar to the previous scheme, in which priority is determined by a daisy-chain network, and in which the code number is supplied by the device requesting an interrupt. However, these two functions can be combined by an alternative manner of implementation, which is often used. In this alternative implementation, a combinational circuit, called a **priority encoder,** produces the code number of the highest priority device requesting an interrupt. The encoder has a number of input lines, each of which corresponds to an interrupt request signal from some device. These input lines are labeled with the code numbers of the devices to which they are connected. In this case, the code numbers are assigned consecutively starting from 0. A sufficient number of output lines from the encoder are provided to represent in binary the number of the highest active (i.e., equal to logic-1) input line.

In particular, consider the design of a priority encoder having eight input lines, labeled $I_0, I_1, \ldots, I_7$. Assume that the priority assignment is the same as the code number assignment with the highest priority corresponding to the highest code number. Since there are eight code numbers there must be three output lines to correspond to the 3-bit binary representation of the selected code number. Label these output bits b_2, b_1, b_0 according to their significance. Using intuitive reasoning to find logic expressions for these 3 output bits, first note that b_2 is to be 1 whenever any input line for a code number greater than or equal to 4 is active. Thus,

$$b_2 = I_7 + I_6 + I_5 + I_4$$

Next, note that b_1 is to be 1 whenever I_6 or I_7 are active, since the binary representation of either 6 or 7 has a 1 in the b_1 position. Also, b_1 is to be 1 whenever I_2 or I_3 are active provided that neither I_4 or I_5 are active, since a 1 appears in the corresponding b_1 position of the binary representation of 2 and 3 but not of 4 and 5. The combination of these two conditions yields the following expression for b_1

$$b_1 = I_7 + I_6 + \bar{I}_5\bar{I}_4 (I_3 + I_2)$$

Finally, note that b_0 is to be 1 if any input line for an odd code number is active, provided no input line for a higher even code number is active. The combination of these conditions for the four odd numbers yields the following expression for b_0

$$b_0 = I_7 + \bar{I}_6I_5 + \bar{I}_6\bar{I}_4I_3 + \bar{I}_6\bar{I}_4\bar{I}_2I_1$$

As a check on these equations, consider the case when the active input lines are I_1, I_2, I_4, and I_5. Substituting 1 for each of these into the three equations the resulting output bits become $b_2 = 1$, $b_1 = 0$, and $b_0 = 1$. These values of b_2, b_1, b_0 form the binary representation of 5, which is the number of the highest active input line in this case.

Figure 27-7 illustrates how this vectored-interrupt scheme using a priority encoder can be used with the illustrative microprocessor. Interrupt-request lines from up to eight devices are connected to the priority encoder, which computes the highest code number of the active lines. The resulting code number, represented by 3 bits, is presented to an input port, so that the microprocessor has access to it.

The interrupt-request lines from the devices are also connected to an OR gate whose output is connected to the Intr line to the microprocessor. Thus, when one or more device interrupt-request line becomes active an interrupt request will be made to the microprocessor. A pulse at the proper time will appear on the Inta control line in response to the recognition of an interrupt request by the microprocessor. This Inta pulse is used to place the fixed address of the master interrupt service routine onto the Data bus, so that it may then be transferred into the microprocessor. Execution of the master interrupt service routine then begins. This routine first inputs the code number of the highest priority device requesting an interrupt. The routine might then use this code number in one of two ways. It could use the code number as a basis to jump to a special routine that treats the corresponding device. Alternatively, it could proceed with a routine that is common to all devices and uses the code number to specify the device code for any accessed ports. This second possibility is especially suitable if the individual devices are similar in the way they are to be handled.

As was mentioned above, this particular vectored-interrupt scheme can be used with any microprocessor. This is true, since only an input port is necessary

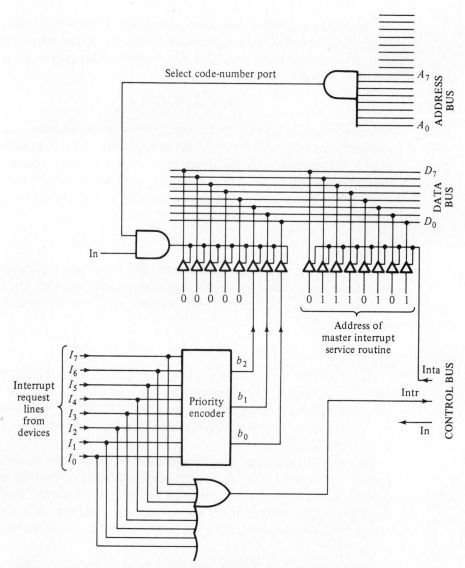

FIG. 27-7 Vectored-interrupt scheme for the illustrative microprocessor using a priority encoder to select the code of one interrupting device

to convey to the microprocessor the information that points to the interrupting device.

Vectored Interrupts Using Device-Originated Instructions

Some microprocessors use a vectored-interrupt scheme that involves an instruction sent to the microprocessor from the interrupting device. When an interrupt request is recognized by such microprocessors, the response is to fetch the next instruction to be executed from the interface network for the interrupting device rather than from memory. The program counter is not automatically saved when an interrupt occurs as it is in other schemes.

Sometimes the single instruction fetched from the interrupting device is sufficient to accomplish the purpose of the interrupt. For example, an event counter might be implemented in software that simply keeps track of the number of times a certain type of interrupt occurs. This could be accomplished by a single instruction that increments a particular register or memory location. In such cases, after the single interrupt instruction is executed, the microprocessor resumes the sequence of instructions it had been executing.

Most of the time, however, a single instruction is not sufficient to service an interrupt. In such cases the instruction fetched from the interrupting device could be a jump to subroutine. The subroutine is then a particular one to treat the interrupting device.

There are various other schemes for carrying out program interrupts, some of which are special to certain microprocessors. Generally, they are variations of schemes that were just discussed.

Programming Considerations for Interrupts

From a programming point of view it is interesting to compare program interrupts with subroutine jumps. They both correspond to the suspension of a given program while a subsidiary routine is executed. Consequently, they both require a linkage between the given program and the subsidiary routine, so that execution can be returned to the given program upon completion of the subsidiary routine. This linkage involves saving the content of the program counter in a place from where it may be retrieved, such as in a pushdown stack or a location in the subsidiary routine.

The fact that program interrupts are invoked by external events while subroutine jumps are caused by program instructions brings about an important difference between the two. The programmer has full control over what points in a program that a subroutine jump can occur. In particular, the programmer has knowledge of what registers and flags are being used by the program at the time a subroutine jump occurs and may save the contents of any of these that are also used by the subroutine. A program interrupt, however, might occur anywhere in a program, thereby hindering the programmer's knowledge of register and flag usage. In this case, all registers and flags used by the interrupt routine must be saved. Some microprocessors, in acknowledgment of this difference, automatically save the contents of all registers and flags into a stack or a special work area whenever an interrupt occurs, but not when a subroutine jump is made. This necessitates two types of return instructions for such microprocessors, one for interrupts that restores the contents of all registers and flags including the program counter, and another for subroutines that only restores the program counter. This automatic saving of registers and flags for interrupts has advantages and disadvantages. It does eliminate the need for extra instructions in an interrupt service routine for the purpose of saving registers. This, however, does not always save time and may actually waste time in cases where no registers and flags need to be saved.

The illustrative microprocessor, for example, does not make such a distinction in the treatment of subroutine jumps and program interrupts. In either case, only the content of the program counter is automatically saved in the stack. Data from the first three scratchpad registers and the content of the carry flag C can be saved and then restored with the use of the instruction pair PUSH and POP. Generally, these three scratchpad registers should be adequate to perform the tasks required of an interrupt routine. In such a case, before any of these three registers or the carry flip-flop is used by the interrupt routine their content is pushed onto the stack. Then, after the interrupt routine has completed its tasks involving these three registers and the carry flip-flop, their original content is restored by popping the stack.

As an example of an interrupt routine for the illustrative microprocessor consider the following simple task. An input/output device supplies 8-bit unsigned integers to the microprocessor. The microprocessor compares each such number with a constant, say $5B_{16}$, and outputs the number only if it is less than the constant. It is assumed that the microprocessor is also performing other computations so that this task will be handled on an interrupt basis. Furthermore, it is assumed that this is the only type of program interrupt that can occur. An interrupt routine for this task is shown in Table 27-2. Whenever a number is available at an input port from the device, a program interrupt occurs causing the interrupt routine to begin. The first instruction is PUSH, which saves the contents of the first three scratchpad registers and the carry flip-flop C. The next instruction inputs the available number from the device (which is assumed to have device code 12_{16}) and places it into the accumulator. Constant 5B is subtracted from the inputted number by first loading 5B into register 1 and then subtracting register 1 from the accumulator. The carry flip-flop C is set if the difference is negative, which indicates that the inputted number is less than the constant 5B. This condition is tested by the jump-on-carry-zero instruction, which causes the next two instructions to be bypassed if C = 0. These next two instructions first add back the constant 5B to the accumulator to restore the inputted number and then output the number to the device (where the same device code 12 is assumed). The POP instruction is then used to restore the

TABLE 27-2 Example of an Interrupt Service Routine

Memory location	Machine language instruction	Symbolic form of instruction	Remarks
0080	77	PUSH	Save Acc, H, L, C in stack
0081	FD	INP	Input number
0082	12	12	
0083	61	LRI 1	Load H with constant 5B
0084	5B	5B	
0085	A1	SUB 1	Subtract 5B from number
0086	7C	JCZ	Test difference, if not negative skip output step
0087	00	00	
0088	8C	8C	
0089	81	ADD 1	Add 5B to restore number
008A	FE	OUT	Output number
008B	12	12	
008C	73	POP	Restore Acc, H, L, C
008D	FB	EIT	Enable future interrupts
008E	F8	RET	Return to interrupted program

values of the first three registers and the carry flip-flop. Before returning to the interrupted program, the Interrupt Flag is set (it had been automatically reset at the beginning of the program interrupt), thus allowing future interrupt requests to be recognized. Finally, the last instruction returns control to the interrupted program.

27-5 MAIN-MEMORY INTERFACING

Main memory is a basic part of a microcomputer that is used to contain program instructions and data. In a few microcomputers, instructions are stored in a separate portion of memory from that of data. In such cases, the basic word size, means of addressing, method of access, and speed may be different for the two portions of memory. Most microcomputers, however, allow arbitrary intermixing of instructions and data within the same portion of memory. The discussion in this section will apply separately to each portion of memory in the former case and to the entire memory in the latter case.

Generally, the main memory of a computer has random access and is made up of a number of words each consisting of a certain number of bits. An address is assigned to each word so that it may be uniquely accessed by the computer. Main memory for a microcomputer is most often implemented with a collection of **memory units** in the form of integrated circuits. The integrated circuits are interconnected in a way that each word is of the appropriate size and has a distinguishing address. Different types of read-only and read/write memory units can be intermixed to serve certain purposes. In particular, some memory locations might be allocated to contain a fixed program or constant data and are therefore implemented with read-only memory units, whereas other locations, allocated to contain variable data, are implemented with read/write memory units. Some or all of the memory units might have a smaller word size than that needed by the microprocessor. In that case, several such units, whose combined word length is equal to that of the microprocessor, are connected so that they are accessed in parallel.

The timing of data transfers between the main memory and a microprocessor is an important concern. Because of the relatively large scale of integration of memory units, they generally operate considerably slower in the transfer of data than do the components for I/O ports. Thus, certain time specifications for a memory unit must be taken into account to ensure that they are met with the timing of the microprocessor.

Prototype Memory Unit

The interfacing of memory units to a microprocessor can be summarized briefly by the two considerations, addressing and timing. In order to proceed with this interfacing, let us assume a prototype for a memory unit that represents most static types of random-access memory. Figure 27-8 indicates the assumed signal lines for the prototype. There are m incoming lines used to address the words in the unit and n bidirectional lines for data corresponding to the bits comprising each word. Thus, the unit consists of 2^m words of n bits each. Finally, there

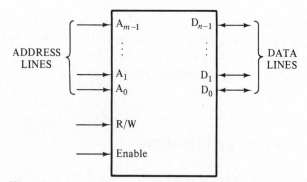

FIG. 27-8 Prototype for a static memory unit

are two incoming control lines, R/W and Enable, which work together to cause a read or write operation to occur. The unit is in a read mode whenever the R/W signal is logic-1; otherwise, it is in a write mode. Neither operation occurs, however, unless the Enable signal is logic-1. When the Enable line is logic-0, the data lines will be in the third state (floating). In the case of read-only memory units, the R/W line is deleted and the unit is always in the read mode. Actual memory integrated circuits might vary from this prototype in ways that include (1) additional enable lines (sometimes called **chip-select** lines) may be provided, which are internally ANDed together; (2) the bidirectional data lines may be replaced by separate input and output data lines; (3) the Enable line might be replaced by two separate control lines to enable the read operation and the write operation; and (4) the data lines may be open-collector or open-emitter rather than 3-state. These variations, however, should not seriously affect the following treatment of interfacing memory units to a microprocessor.

Memory Space of a Microprocessor

In configuring a memory system from memory units for a certain microcomputer it may be useful to think of it as filling a "memory space." The memory space for a particular microprocessor may be viewed as a rectangular area that is divided into rows corresponding to possible address combinations. Each row consists of the number of bits making up a data word for the microprocessor. The illustrative microprocessor, for example, has a memory space that is 2^{16} rows by 8 bits. Memory units of various type and size are placed into the memory space as needed for a specific application. Figure 27-9 indicates how the memory space of the illustrative microprocessor might be allocated.

Once the placement of memory units in the memory space of a microprocessor has been decided, it remains to specify the necessary interconnections. The data lines of every memory unit are each connected to the corresponding line of the microprocessor data bus. The address lines of the microprocessor are used to first select a memory unit or a parallel group of units and then a word location within the selected unit or units. Since the words in a unit usually correspond to consecutive words in the memory space, the address lines of a unit are connected to the lower-order address lines of the microprocessor. The remaining address lines of the microprocessor then are used to select that unit. The selection of a prototype unit is done with the use of the Enable control line.

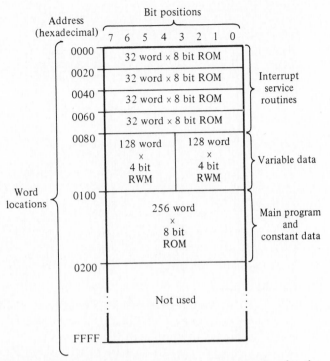

FIG. 27-9 An example of memory space allocation for the illustrative microprocessor

The Enable control line of each memory unit is also used in conjunction with the R/W control line to both effect and time read and write operations. Certain microprocessor control lines are connected in an appropriate manner with the Enable and R/W lines. For a read operation, the R/W line of each memory unit is placed at logic-1, and at the proper time the Enable line of the selected unit or units is placed at logic-1. This causes the content of the addressed word in the selected unit or units to be placed onto the data bus and subsequently transferred into the microprocessor. For a write operation, the R/W line of each memory unit is placed at logic-0, and at the proper time the Enable line of the selected unit or units is placed at logic-1. This causes the content of the data bus as specified by the microprocessor to be transferred into the addressed word location of the selected unit or units.

Example of a Memory System

The manner in which the prototype memory units might be connected to the illustrative microprocessor is shown in Fig. 27-10. The figure assumes the same memory allocation indicated by Fig. 27-9. There are a total of seven memory units of varying size. For each unit, the address lines are connected to the lower lines of the Address bus, and the data lines are connected to the appropriate lines of the Data bus. The Enable line of each memory unit is driven by some combination of Address bus lines ANDed either with the microprocessor control signal Read, in the case of ROM units, or the OR of the microprocessor control signals Read and Write, in the case of RWM units. Thus, a memory

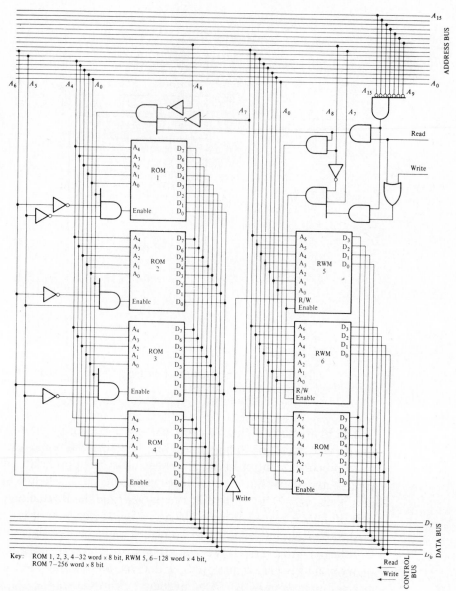

FIG. 27-10 The manner in which prototype memory units might be connected to the illustrative microprocessor in the example of Fig. 27-9

unit is enabled only if selected by the Address bus and when a read or write data transfer is to occur.

The particular conditions that enable each memory unit can be seen more clearly, perhaps, by determining the logic expressions corresponding to each Enable line. Let E_i represent the Enable line of unit i, and A_i represent the Address bus line i. Notice that all Enable lines have the AND of the complements of the highest seven Address bus lines in common. Further conditions for E_1 through E_4 are Read, $\overline{A}_7$, $\overline{A}_8$, and some combination of A_5 and A_6. These first four enable signals are specifically expressed as

$$E_1 = \text{Read }\ \overline{A}_{15}\overline{A}_{14}\overline{A}_{13}\overline{A}_{12}\overline{A}_{11}\overline{A}_{10}\overline{A}_9\overline{A}_8\overline{A}_7\overline{A}_6\overline{A}_5$$

$$E_2 = \text{Read }\ \overline{A}_{15}\overline{A}_{14}\overline{A}_{13}\overline{A}_{12}\overline{A}_{11}\overline{A}_{10}\overline{A}_9\overline{A}_8\overline{A}_7\overline{A}_6 A_5$$

$$E_3 = \text{Read } \overline{A}_{15}\overline{A}_{14}\overline{A}_{13}\overline{A}_{12}\overline{A}_{11}\overline{A}_{10}\overline{A}_9A_8\overline{A}_7A_6\overline{A}_5$$
$$E_4 = \text{Read } \overline{A}_{15}\overline{A}_{14}\overline{A}_{13}\overline{A}_{12}\overline{A}_{11}\overline{A}_{10}\overline{A}_9A_8\overline{A}_7A_6A_5$$

E_5 and E_6 have Read + Write, A_7, and $\overline{A}_8$ as conditions. They are equal to each other and may be expressed as

$$E_5, E_6 = (\text{Read} + \text{Write})\ \overline{A}_{15}\overline{A}_{14}\overline{A}_{13}\overline{A}_{12}\overline{A}_{11}\overline{A}_{10}\overline{A}_9\overline{A}_8A_7$$

Finally, E_7 has Read and A_8 as conditions and is expressed as

$$E_7 = \text{Read } \overline{A}_{15}\overline{A}_{14}\overline{A}_{13}\overline{A}_{12}\overline{A}_{11}\overline{A}_{10}\overline{A}_9A_8$$

It can be noticed that except for E_5 and E_6, which pertain to parallel memory units, the E_i's are mutually exclusive. Also, a simplification might be made to Fig. 27-10 if it is known that there will be no future memory expansion. In that case, the common factor $\overline{A}_{15}\cdots\overline{A}_9$ could be deleted from each E_i. As a result, each word in the memory units will respond to many different addresses in addition to its intended address. This causes no difficulty and might even be exploited in programming.

Timing of Memory Data Transfers

The timing of data transfers to and from the memory is often critical, since memory units are relatively slow in operation, especially when compared to the small-scale integrated components used for I/O ports. Certain delays arising in the sequence of events for the read and write operations of memory units must be taken into account to assure proper operation. The read operation generally involves first sending an address to a memory unit, then placing logic-1 onto its Enable line, and finally using the data when it appears on the data lines. Of prime concern is the delay between the time the address is sent and the time data becomes available. This delay, referred to as the **read-access time,** must be taken into account in the operation of the microprocessor, so that the contents of the data bus are not transferred into the microprocessor before valid data is placed onto the data bus by the memory unit. Also important is the amount of delay between setting the Enable line of a memory unit to logic-1 and the time that the data lines become valid. This delay time, which is usually less than the read-access time, must also be taken into account in the operation of the microprocessor. These read time requirements are illustrated in Fig. 27-11.

A write operation is slightly more complicated as compared to a read oper-

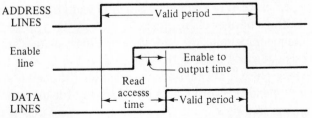

FIG. 27-11 Time requirements for the prototype memory units under a read operation

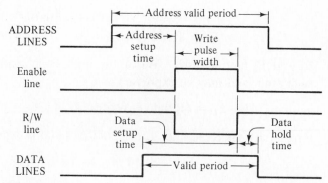

FIG. 27-12 Time requirements for the prototype memory units under a write operation

ation and consequently involves more time considerations. The sequence of events for a write operation generally involves sending an address and data word to a memory unit and holding these while the Enable and R/W lines are momentarily placed at logic-1 and logic-0, respectively. Several periods of time in this sequence are of prime concern and are illustrated by Fig. 27-12. After an address has been specified, a certain amount of time is necessary before the decoding circuit internal to a memory unit can respond. If, while the Enable line is logic-1, the R/W line is brought to logic-0 before the decoding circuit has time to respond to the address, then data may be written into the wrong memory location. This required period of time is often referred to as the **address setup time.** Data presented to a memory unit is written into a word location during the time in which the R/W line is logic-0 and the Enable line is logic-1. This length of time, referred to as the **write-pulse width,** must be sufficient for the memory elements to accept the data being written. The values that are stored in the addressed word location are those that appear on the data lines at the end of this "write pulse" time, provided those values appeared for a sufficient length of time before the end of the write pulse, referred to as the **data setup time,** and a sufficient length of time after the end of the write pulse, referred to as the **data hold time.**

In meeting the above time requirements of the memory units, the additional delays due to the auxiliary gates involved in the interface must be taken into account. Often these additional delays are negligible since the interfacing gates may be relatively high speed owing to their small-scale integration.

Let us now consider how the time requirements of the memory units could be met by the illustrative microprocessor. Consider first the timing diagram shown in Fig. 27-13 for the read operation. A machine cycle consisting of three clock pulses is used to perform this operation. The Data bus is assumed by the microprocessor to contain valid data from memory during the time between the leading edges of clock pulses T_2 and T_3. To provide for the read-access time of the memory units, the address of the location to be read is sent over the Address bus one clock cycle earlier, that is, at the time of the leading edge of the first clock pulse T_1. This address specifies the memory unit (or parallel group of units) and the word location in that unit (or units) to be accessed. A little later, at the trailing edge of T_1, the Read control line of the microprocessor is activated, which causes the selected unit or units to be enabled. The clock-off time

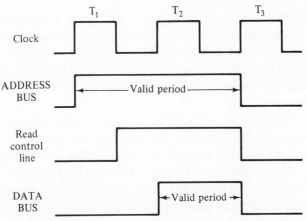

FIG. 27-13 Timing diagram for the read operation of the illustrative microprocessor

between T_1 and T_2 is used to provide for the Enable-to-output delay in the memory units plus delay associated with the gates driving the Enable lines.

The R/W lines of all the memory units are at logic-1 throughout a read operation, since they are driven by the complement of the microprocessor Write line (which is at logic-0). Consequently, the content of the addressed word location in the selected memory units will be placed onto the Data bus, sometime after the units have been enabled. At the end of clock pulse T_2 this data is strobed into a destination register within the microprocessor.

The timing diagram for the write operation of the illustrative microprocessor is shown in Fig. 27-14. For a write operation, data is strobed into a selected memory location during the second clock pulse T_2. To provide for the address and data setup times, both the address and data are placed onto their respective buses beginning with the leading edge of the first clock pulse T_1. The time between the leading edges of T_1 and T_2 is allowed for address setup, while the time between the leading edge of T_1 and the trailing edge of T_2 is allowed for data setup. A pulse occurs on the microprocessor Write control line in coincidence with T_2. This pulse affects the network driving the Enable lines of the memory units so as to enable those units selected by the specified address. The pulse on the Write line also causes the R/W lines of the RWM units to go to

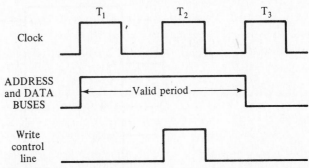

FIG. 27-14 Timing diagram for the write operation of the illustrative microprocessor

logic-0, placing them into the write mode. The time allowed for the write-pulse-width requirement of the memory units is thus approximately the time of duration of a clock pulse, altered by the delay associated with the gates of the enable circuitry. The address and data are held until the leading edge of T_3, allowing the clock-off time between T_2 and T_3 for the data-hold-time requirement of the memory units.

Each of the mentioned time requirements for the memory units must be satisfied. If one or more of the requirements are not met, then the clock repetition rate might be decreased to accommodate the limiting requirement.

It should be mentioned at this point that actual microprocessors vary considerably from one another in their basic time relationships between signals. Some microprocessors have been designed to work with certain types of memory units having a particular time-requirement "profile" that is considerably different from that of other memory unit types. If a different type of memory unit were to be used than that assumed in the design of a microprocessor, then the clock rate might have to be drastically reduced just to meet one time requirement. For example, some microprocessors are designed for memory units that have a data-hold requirement of almost zero. If a memory unit having an appreciable data-hold requirement were to be used with such microprocessors, the clock might have to be reduced to an unreasonable rate. Such situations are sometimes remedied by providing a delayed clock pulse source for either the microprocessor or the memory system.

Dynamic Memory Systems

Dynamic memory units differ in their use from static memory units mainly in their need to be periodically refreshed. Generally, this refreshing is accomplished by performing a read and/or write operation. Let us consider a particular form for a dynamic memory unit that is refreshed by reading it. One control line in addition to those for the static prototype will be assumed for this dynamic-memory prototype, as is indicated in Fig. 27-15. The two control lines Enable and Select operate together to perform a function similar to that of the static-prototype Enable line. The Enable line controls functions that are internal to a memory unit, whereas the Select line controls the data lines by placing them into the third state when Select is at logic-0. These two lines are activated

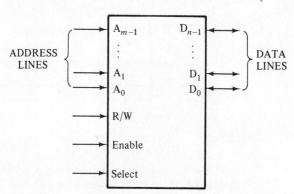

FIG. 27-15 Prototype for a dynamic memory unit

together when a read or write operation is to be performed. However, only the Enable line is used to perform a refresh operation.

Each refresh operation restores the contents of several word locations in a memory unit. Internally, a memory unit has its words placed in an array of columns and rows. The address of a word then consists of two parts, a column address and a row address. The bits in each word can be thought of as lying in a third dimension. All words in a specified row are refreshed during one operation.

A refresh operation consists of specifying a row address and then activating the Enable line while the R/W line is kept at logic-1. The Select line and column address lines are not used during a refresh operation and may be either logic value. Each row of a dynamic memory unit must be refreshed within a certain period of time from the previous refresh. This period of time is generally in the order of a few milliseconds. During this time, as many refresh operations must be performed as there are rows in a memory unit.

Since a refresh operation generally interferes with the use of a memory unit by the microprocessor, some means is necessary to suspend the operation of the microprocessor during the time in which a memory row is to be refreshed. This is done in many ways by the various microprocessors. For some microprocessors a certain control signal is provided that when activated momentarily delays the operation of the microprocessor to allow for a memory refresh. Alternatively, a direct memory access facility of a microprocessor, as discussed in the next section, might be used. Still another way for allowing for memory refresh is to momentarily alter the clock to the microprocessor.

In any case, once the operation of the microprocessor is suspended, the refresh procedure is generally carried out by external circuitry. This external circuitry also determines the time and row address for each memory refresh operation.

Example of a Refresh Scheme

A possible scheme that might be used with the illustrative microprocessor to refresh dynamic memory units is shown in Fig. 27-16. The operation of the microprocessor is suspended during the time a refresh is to occur by the inhibition of the clock line. This will always occur just before a machine cycle begins, at which time it is assumed that the Address bus is placed into the third state by the microprocessor.

In the network of Fig. 27-16, the beginning of a machine cycle is determined with the use of the Sync control line from the microprocessor. A pulse occurs on the Sync control line in coincidence with the third clock pulse of each machine cycle. To determine the time that a refresh operation is to occur, a k-bit up counter is used that is driven by the Sync line. Connected to the output lines of this counter is a k-input AND gate, whose output will be logic-1 when the counter contains all 1s. This condition indicates that it is time for a refresh operation to occur. The next clock pulse is inhibited from reaching the microprocessor and is used for the refresh.

In performing the refresh operation, the content of a 4-bit counter is sent to the row-address lines of the memory unit. Three-state drivers are used for this

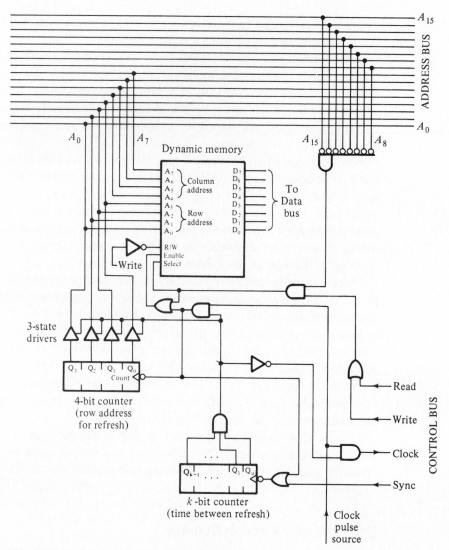

FIG. 27-16 A scheme for refreshing dynamic memory for use with the illustrative microprocessor

purpose. Then, the Enable line is activated by a pulse from the clock source that is coupled through several gates. This refresh pulse is used also to increment the row-address counter for the next refresh operation. In addition, the pulse increments the k-bit counter that determines the refresh time. As a consequence, the k-bit counter becomes all 0s and terminates the refresh operation. The next clock pulse is allowed to pass to the microprocessor as the first pulse of a new machine cycle. The k-bit counter will then be counting Sync pulses to determine the time for the next refresh operation.

It should be noted that methods used for refreshing dynamic memory units vary considerably from one microprocessor to another and even from one application to another for the same microprocessor. Consequently, the method shown here is used to illustrate what might be involved only in the most general sense. An actual design of a memory refreshing circuit requires a careful consideration of the microprocessor to be used as well as the particular memory units and the application for which they are to be used.

27-6 DIRECT MEMORY ACCESS

So far, the discussion has been concerned with data transfers between a microprocessor and external devices or between a microprocessor and main memory. As might be expected, data transfers between external devices and main memory are also of concern. For example, such data transfers could be made to initially load a program into memory from an input device. Also, during the execution of a program, data might be transferred from a device into memory to be manipulated later by the microprocessor, or for that matter, results produced by the microprocessor might be stored in memory to be transferred later to an external device.

When a facility exists in a microcomputer system to transfer data directly between memory and external devices without the immediate intervention of a program, it is referred to as **direct memory access** (DMA). Certainly, by providing sufficient supportive circuitry, a microcomputer system based upon any microprocessor can be made to have direct memory access. In order, though, to keep the number of data pathways to a minimum most microprocessors have a special provision that allows their normal bus system to be used for direct memory access. This is done by releasing the microprocessor's control of the bus system at the time a DMA data transfer is to occur. An external device may then make use of the bus system to perform a data transfer between itself and memory.

Program execution, since it inherently depends upon data transfers to and from memory, usually must be suspended during the time the bus system is released by the microprocessor. Although there are variations among microprocessors, the action of releasing the buses typically occurs whenever a special DMA request control line is activated. The illustrative microprocessor, for example, has the two control lines DMA and DMAA, which are used respectively to request and to acknowledge direct memory access. Whenever logic-1 is placed externally on the DMA control line, the microprocessor will, after completing the current machine cycle, suspend program execution and then release the Address and Data buses by placing each of their lines into the third state (floating). To acknowledge that the Data and Address bus lines are in the third state, the DMAA control line is set to logic-1 by the microprocessor. During this time, the microprocessor retains control of the other outgoing lines of the Control bus. This is necessary so that unintentional events do not arise from undefined control signals, such as writing randomly into memory.

In particular, the control lines Read and Write from the microprocessor are kept at logic-0 during the time DMAA is 1. Normally, these two control lines are connected to the memory system. However, with direct memory access, a modification is necessary in order to allow an external device to determine a memory read or write operation. This modification involves ORing the Read and Write lines from the microprocessor with similar lines from the external device, the result of which is connected to the corresponding lines of the memory system. A particular device may perform a direct-memory-access transfer by first setting DMA to logic-1. It then waits for logic-1 to appear on DMAA. At that time, the device uses the Address bus, Data bus, and its read and write control lines to perform data transfers between itself and memory in a manner similar to that of the microprocessor. When no more such transfers are to be made the device places logic-0 onto the DMA control line, which returns control of the buses back to the microprocessor.

Data transfers using direct memory access can be considered a form of I/O with regard to a microcomputer, which differs from programmed I/O in that it is done under the supervision of external circuitry instead of a program. A savings in program time is gained in the use of direct memory access, since the program is not directly involved in such data transfers. This savings becomes quite important in the case of high-speed data devices, such as disk or tape storage units, which might exceed the capability of a program to keep up with the data flow.

Data Block Transfer Using DMA

Direct-memory-access schemes for high-speed data devices usually involve the transfer of data words in blocks. The microprocessor under program control often initiates the transfer of a block of data and might specify the number of words comprising the block. The transfer of the individual data words is, however, controlled by circuitry that is separate from the microprocessor. For example, a program might involve the inputting of a number of data words from magnetic tape into memory. In this case, the program might include instructions that output to the direct-memory-access control circuitry the number of data words to be transferred and the beginning address of where they are to be located in memory. The program would then set a flag to commence the transfer of data. From that point the program could go on to some other function, while the external control circuitry attended to the data transfer.

Figure 27-17 depicts a network to be used with the illustrative microprocessor for controlling direct-memory-access block transfers from a general input device. In the network, an 8-bit latch is provided to receive input data from the device and place it onto the Data bus at the proper time. Two 8-bit binary up counters are provided to contain each half of the memory address indicating where the input data is to be written. These two counters are connected in cascade to count in unison. The number of data words to be transferred for a block is controlled by an 8-bit binary down counter. The two address counters and the word counter are connected to the microprocessor as output ports.

A program initiates a block transfer by outputting each half of a 16-bit address to the address counters and then outputting an 8-bit number to the word counter. An AND gate with inverted input lines is connected to the word counter as a zero detector. Whenever the word counter contains a nonzero quantity the output of the zero detector will be logic-0, which is a signal to the device to allow the inputting of data. The device responds by sending an input data word each time it obtains one from its source, e.g., magnetic tape. The input data word is strobed by a pulse from the device into the 8-bit latch provided to receive it. This same strobe pulse also sets a flip-flop whose output line is connected to the DMA control line to the microprocessor.

When DMA becomes logic-1, the microprocessor will suspend program execution at the end of the current machine cycle and then release the Address and Data buses. The outgoing control line DMAA becomes logic-1 at this point, causing the start of a 4-pulse sequence that transfers the content of the input-

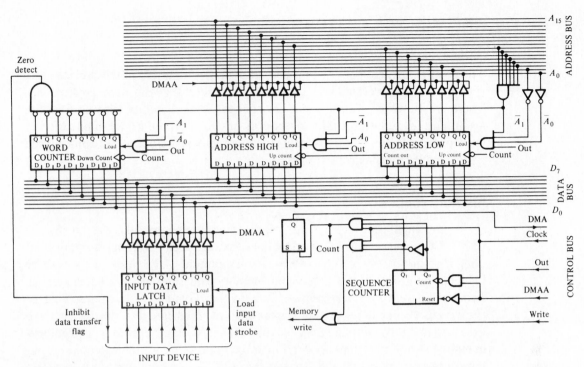

FIG. 27-17 Direct-memory-access controller for an input device connected to the illustrative microprocessor

data latch into memory. The sequence is controlled by a 2-bit counter that is driven by the microprocessor clock conditioned on DMAA.

When DMAA first becomes logic-1 the contents of the two address counters are placed onto the Address bus and the content of the input-data latch is placed onto the Data bus. Each clock pulse increments the 2-bit sequence counter. Nothing else happens for the first two clock pulses, but the third clock pulse causes a write pulse to be sent to memory. This is done by ORing the clock conditioned on the output combination 10 of the sequence counter with the Write control line. The write pulse causes the input data to be stored into the memory location specified by the Address bus.

The clock pulse following the memory write brings the sequence counter to 00 and causes a pulse to be generated on the line labeled "Count." This count pulse causes the 16-bit address counter to be incremented and the word counter to be decremented. It also resets the flip-flop connected to the DMA line. Thus, at this time the counters are ready for the next input data transfer and the microprocessor is allowed to resume program execution. When the word counter eventually reaches zero, the zero-detector output will become logic-1, indicating the end of the block transfer. No further data will be transferred from the device until another block transfer is initiated by the microprocessor.

This type of direct memory access is often referred to as **cycle stealing,** or other similar phrase, since it suspends the execution of a program for about one machine cycle at a time. An alternative type of direct memory access involves stopping program execution while an entire block of data is transferred.

27-7 FURTHER MICROPROCESSOR BUS CONCEPTS

The general arrangement of microprocessor buses assumed in the previous sections basically represents that for most microprocessors and their applications. There are, however, several other bus concepts that should be discussed, which are important to certain microprocessors or are valuable in the application of any microprocessor. These concepts include memory-mapped I/O, multiplexed buses, and memory-bank switching.

Memory-Mapped I/O

To handle input/output transfers many microprocessors, like the illustrative model, have instructions and control lines that are separate from those for handling memory transfers. This allows the assignment of I/O device codes to be independent from the assignment of memory addresses. It is often desirable, however, to treat I/O ports in the same manner as memory locations. That is, the I/O ports for a particular system are given assigned addresses and are accessed as if they were memory locations. This is often referred to as **memory-mapped I/O.** Memory-mapped I/O can be used with any microprocessor, but there are certain microprocessors in which I/O handling must be memory-mapped since separate I/O instructions and control lines are not provided.

An advantage of memory-mapped I/O is that with it all memory-reference instructions in the instruction set of a microprocessor may also reference I/O ports. For some microprocessors the set of memory-reference instructions is very rich, providing various addressing modes and other flexibility. Often, instructions that perform arithmetic or logic with memory operands are included in the set for a microprocessor. With such microprocessors memory-mapped I/O is especially advantageous.

The illustrative microprocessor, as an example, does not have a very rich set of memory-reference instructions, but memory-mapped I/O can still be used to advantage. The two specific I/O instructions only allow a transfer to be made between the accumulator and an I/O port. However, with memory-mapped I/O a transfer can be made between any of the first three scratchpad registers and an I/O port by using the load register, store register, or move instructions. Interfacing I/O ports to the illustrative microprocessor under memory-mapped I/O involves the use of the Read and Write control lines in place of the In and Out lines, respectively.

Multiplexed Buses

The bus system for the illustrative microprocessor, like that for many actual microprocessors, consists of three explicit buses for conveying address, data, and control information. By having a separate bus for each of these three functions, the interfacing of I/O ports and memory units to the microprocessor is accomplished in a simple and straightforward manner. However, some microprocessors combine two of these interfacing functions with the use of one bus. As mentioned in Sec. 27-2, for example, several microprocessors make use of the data bus at certain times to send control information for a data transfer. This is done primarily to keep the pin count of the integrated circuit from exceeding a specified amount (say, 40 pins).

Some microprocessors gain a particular advantage by combining the function of the address bus with that of the data bus. This is done by having a **multiplexed bus,** which will be called the **address-data bus,** that conveys address information at certain times and data at other times. There are several variations to this scheme that primarily concern which address bits are sent over the common address-data bus. If the number of address bits is equal to the number of data bits, which is the case for several microprocessors, then all address bits could be simultaneously sent over the address-data bus. However, if the number of address bits exceeds the number of data bits, as is the case for the illustrative microprocessor and many others, then either additional address lines might be provided or portions of the address could be sent separately over the address-data bus.

In any case, some external means is necessary for recording the address information when it appears on the address-data bus so that it can be used to select the appropriate memory location or I/O port. One way of doing this is with a control line from the microprocessor that is used to strobe the address information into a register at the proper time.

Special memory units having internal address registers are often made available for use with a particular microprocessor having a multiplexed address-data bus. Generally, each such memory unit records from the address-data bus the relevant address information (i.e., the lower-order address bits) needed to designate a memory location within that unit. The high-order bits of an address are then used to select the appropriate memory unit from among all memory units in the system. This step might be done in several ways. The high-order address bits might be obtained either directly from additional address lines of the microprocessor or from a central register in the memory system that recorded these bits from the address-data bus earlier. Alternatively, the selection of the appropriate memory unit might be done with the use of a selection flag within each memory unit. In this case, the selection flag in each memory unit is conditioned to be set when an assigned combination of high-order address bits appear at the proper time on the address-data bus. Once the address of the appropriate memory location is determined, data is then transferred to or from that location over the address-data bus in the usual manner.

As can be seen, a reduction in the number of pins is gained by using a multiplexed address-data bus for a microprocessor. Furthermore, when the special memory units having an address register are used with such a microprocessor, a significant reduction is also gained in the number of wires needed to connect the memory units to the microprocessor. However, the overall operation of such a microprocessor system will tend to be slower due to the need to time share the bus for addresses and data.

Memory-Bank Switching

Typically, the addressable memory space of a microprocessor, as determined by the number of its address bits, is sufficiently large to accommodate the requirements of most microprocessor applications. However, in the event that a particular application has a memory requirement that exceeds the address capability of the microprocessor, the memory space can be extended with the concept of memory-bank switching. To do this, the required memory is divided into memory banks. The selection of a desired memory bank is then determined from the content of a register, called bank designate, that is connected as an output port to the microprocessor.

Let us assume that memory-bank switching is to be done with only that part of the memory containing data and not the part containing the program instructions, since otherwise, switching banks could interfere with the instruction execution sequence. For this purpose, assume that all program instructions are located in the lower half of the normal memory space of the microprocessor. Bank switching, then, will only be done with addresses corresponding to the upper half of the normal memory space. Thus, when the most-significant address bit of the microprocessor is 0 a memory location in the program portion of memory will be designated by just the remaining address bits of the microprocessor. On the other hand, when the most-significant address bit is 1 a memory location in the selected bank will be designated.

With this arrangement a program can determine the memory bank for transferring data by outputting the corresponding number to the bank-designate register. This memory bank will then remain in effect until the program switches to another bank by outputting its corresponding number.

This scheme of switching memory banks can be extended to as large a memory as desired. If the number of bits in an output port is not sufficient to designate all of the required memory banks, then two or more output ports can be used for this purpose.

27-8 ANALOG CONVERSION

Many applications of microcomputers involve physical parameters that take on a continuous range of values. In a mechanical control application, for example, parameters such as speed, position, and force might be monitored or controlled. These parameters are generally represented by some electrical parameter, which will be assumed to be a voltage. Such voltages that directly represent physical parameters are referred to as **analog** quantities. In the case of monitored parameters, the corresponding voltages are generated by appropriate transducers (e.g., tachometers for speed, pressure transducers for force or pressure, and potentiometers for position). Parameters that are controlled are determined from their corresponding voltages by actuators of some sort (e.g., motors for force, speed or position, and heaters for temperature). Now, of course, microcomputers are inherently digital and therefore work with quantities that are digitally represented. In order for microcomputers to handle analog quantities, some means of converting from digital to analog representation and from analog to digital representation is necessary.

Digital-to-Analog Conversion

First, consider the conversion from the digital representation of a quantity into its analog representation. Positive quantities will be assumed at first for sim-

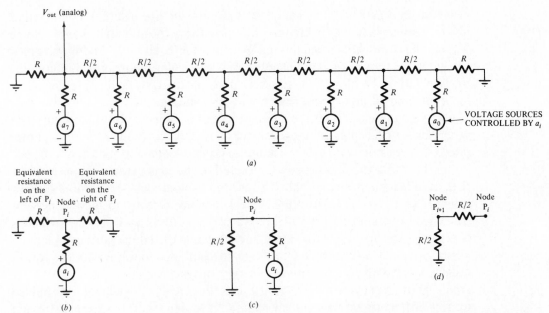

FIG. 27-18 Resistor ladder for digital-to-analog conversion (a) Resistor ladder (b) Equivalent resistances on each side of node P_i (c) Equivalent voltage divider determining effect of the voltage at node P_i upon the voltage at node P_i 1

plicity. The digital representation of a quantity N in binary notation consists of just a string of k bits.

$$a_{k-1}a_{k-2} \cdots a_1 a_0$$

The meaning of these bits is specified by the corresponding polynomial expansion of the quantity N, i.e.,

$$N = a_{k-1}2^{k-1} + a_{k-2}2^{k-2} + \cdots + a_1 2 + a_0$$

This expansion equates N to the result of weighting each bit by an appropriate power of 2 and then adding all such terms together. This operation corresponds to a linear combination of the bits. Such a linear combination is easily performed with a network of resistors. If the voltage equivalent of each bit is available, then the network will effectively yield the analog equivalent of the binary number. One such resistive network, shown in Fig. 27-18a, is in the form of a "ladder" having resistors of just two different values. The number of bits in this case is assumed to be 8. Connected to the resistive network are eight ideal voltage generators each corresponding to one of the bits a_i. Each generator produces either 0 or 1 V depending on the value, 0 or 1, respectively, of the corresponding bit. That is, the voltage of each generator is numerically the same as the value of the corresponding bit a_i. The output voltage V_{out} will be seen to be proportional to the power-of-2-weighted sum of the generator voltages. The resistor ladder therefore performs the desired digital-to-analog conversion of N.

Derivation of Resistor-Ladder Operation

To show that the resistor ladder in Fig. 27-18a performs the indicated weighted summation, the principle of superposition for linear circuits will be used. Each generator acts as a source of an input signal to the linear circuit composed of just the resistors. According to the principle of superposition the output voltage V_{out} can be computed by summing the effect that each individual input signal has upon the output voltage. The effect of a particular input signal is computed by considering the output voltage while that particular signal is present on its input line and all other input lines are at zero voltage.

Consider the effect that the input voltage for a_i has upon the output. The generator for a_i is connected to a resistor of R Ω. Refer to the node at the other side of this resistor as P_i. The resistance to ground looking to the left of the node P_i (not counting the R-Ω resistor connected to the a_i generator) happens to be R Ω, as indicated in Fig. 27-18b. This is seen by combining resistances starting from the left. The R-Ω resistor on the left going directly to ground may be combined in parallel with the R-Ω resistor leading to the a_7 generator (which is effectively grounded since that input line is set at 0 V). The parallel combination yields a value of $R/2$ Ω, which may then be combined in series with the $R/2$-Ω resistor toward the right. This series combination yields a value of R Ω to ground. This process is repeated until node P_i is reached, yielding a combined value of R Ω as stated. In a similar manner, it is seen that the resistance looking to the right between node P_i and ground is R Ω. Thus, the resistor ladder can be represented by the equivalent circuit in Fig. 27-18b.

The voltage at node P_i with respect to ground due to the a_i voltage generator may now be determined using the voltage divider rule for resistances in series. First the resistance looking to the left and to the right of node P_i may be combined in parallel to yield a value of $R/2$ Ω, as indicated by Fig. 27-18c. This resistance and the resistor connecting the a_i generator to node P_i form a voltage divider. This voltage divider produces at the node P_i a fractional amount of the input voltage a_i given by the relation

$$\text{Voltage at } P_i = \frac{R/2}{R + R/2}\, a_i = \tfrac{1}{3} a_i$$

The effect that this voltage of $\tfrac{1}{3}a_i$ V at node P_i has upon the output can be determined by working node by node to the left.

The voltage at the next left node P_{i+1} due to the voltage at node P_i is seen to be one-half of the value. This is determined again by the voltage divider rule. Note that the resistance between the node P_{i+1} and ground, excluding the resistor connecting node P_i to node P_{i+1}, is $R/2$ Ω, as indicated in Fig. 27-18d. This value comes from the parallel combination of the R-Ω resistor from node P_{i+1} to the a_{i+1} generator and the resistance for node P_{i+1} looking to the left, which is also R Ω. This $R/2$-Ω resistance between node P_{i+1} and ground and the $R/2$-Ω resistor connecting node P_i to node P_{i+1} form the voltage divider shown in Fig. 27-18d. This voltage divider produces a voltage at node P_{i+1} equal to one-half that at node P_i. Thus, the voltage at node P_{i+1} due to a_i is given by the relation

$$\text{Voltage at } P_{i+1} = \frac{R/2}{R/2 + R/2} \times \text{voltage at } P_i$$

$$= \frac{1}{2} \frac{a_i}{3}$$

This voltage is further halved for each node that is encountered going to the left. The output voltage due to a_i is the voltage at node P_7, which is now seen to be given by the relation

$$\text{Voltage at } P_7 = \left(\frac{1}{2}\right)^{7-i} \frac{a_i}{3}$$

The total output voltage is next obtained by summing the effects due to all generator voltages, i.e.,

$$
\begin{aligned}
V_{out} &= \sum_{i=0}^{7} \left(\frac{1}{2}\right)^{7-i} \frac{a_i}{3} \\
&= \left(\tfrac{1}{2}\right)^{7} \frac{1}{3} \sum_{i=0}^{7} \left(\tfrac{1}{2}\right)^{-i} a_i \\
&= (\tfrac{1}{2})^{7} \frac{1}{3} \sum_{i=0}^{7} 2^{i} a_i
\end{aligned}
$$

The summation in the expression above is just the polynomial expansion for the quantity N. Thus V_{out} is proportional to N. The constant of proportionality is $(\tfrac{1}{2})^{7}\tfrac{1}{3}$ or generally $(\tfrac{1}{2})^{k-1}\tfrac{1}{3}$.

The conversion of numbers represented by the 2's-complement number system, each of which may be positive or negative, can be accomplished by a slight modification of the scheme for unsigned numbers. The 2's-complement representation for a number may be thought of as a weighted code, similar to unsigned binary representation, with the most-significant bit (the sign bit) having a negative weight. That is, a number N represented in 2's-complement form by the k bits

$$a_{k-1} a_{k-2} \cdots a_1 a_0$$

is given by the polynomial expression

$$N = a_{k-1}(-2^{k-1}) + a_{k-2}2^{k-2} + \cdots + a_1 2^1 + a_0$$

This expression can be implemented in analog by a resistor ladder similar to that of Fig. 27-18, where the polarity of the voltage generator for a_{k-1} is reversed.

Implementation of Voltage Generators

Consider now the implementation of the voltage generators that produce the input signals to the resistor ladder. They are each to be controlled by an a_i bit, so as to produce a voltage equal or proportional to the a_i bit. It is important that the generators be close to ideal so that their output voltage is not affected by the load from the resistor ladder. Also, the voltages must be specified in a precise manner, since they directly affect the accuracy of the output voltage. These requirements can be met by the use of analog switches that connect each input line of the resistor ladder to a precise reference voltage or to ground depending upon the value of the corresponding a_i bit. These analog switches might be just bipolar transistors connected in a "totem pole" arrangement, as

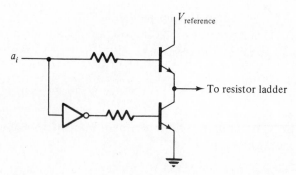

FIG. 27-19 Circuit for voltage generator controlled by
a_i using two transistors

shown in Fig. 27-19. In this case, it is assumed that the voltage level corresponding to logic-1 is somewhat greater than $V_{reference}$. When a_i is at logic-1 the upper transistor will be in saturation, which brings the output to the reference voltage. When a_i is logic-0 the lower transistor is in saturation, which brings the output to ground. The transistors should be chosen to have a negligible voltage drop from collector to emitter when saturated. That is, V_{ce}(sat) should be approximately zero.

For a small number of bits (8 or less), reasonably good results can be obtained with the use of totem-pole output TTL gates and pull-up resistors for the voltage generators, as shown in Fig. 27-20. Normally, the pull-up circuit in a TTL gate, unlike the pull-down circuit, will have a significant voltage drop. The added resistor connected between the output line of the TTL gate and a reference voltage (nominally +5 V) will bring the output reasonably close to the reference voltage, provided that the load from the resistor ladder is kept small. The value of 1 kΩ is chosen for this pull-up resistor, since that is about the minimum value to assure that the pull-down transistor is not overloaded. The input resistors to the ladder should then be set at a much higher value to prevent loading of the 1-kΩ pull-up resistor. A value of 20 KΩ for the input resistors is reasonable.

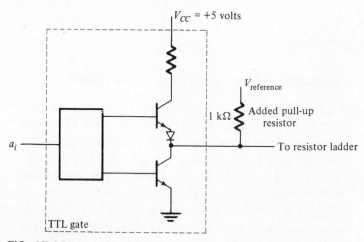

FIG. 27-20 Use of a TTL gate with an added pull-up resistor to a reference voltage as a voltage generator for a resistor ladder

Use of Operational Amplifiers

In place of a resistor ladder, an **operational amplifier** can be used to perform the weighted summation indicated by the polynomial expansion of a binary number. An operational amplifier is a voltage amplifier having a high negative gain $(-A)$, which may be programmed to perform various operations. This programming is done with the interconnection of resistors and other passive components. Figure 27-21 depicts one way an operational amplifier can be programmed to convert a binary number into an analog voltage. The signals labeled V_i are input voltages corresponding to the bit values a_i of the number to be converted. The circuit produces an output voltage V_{out} that is proportional to the quantity represented by the binary number. To verify this, let us analyze the circuit by summing currents into the node labeled "summing junction." The voltage of the summing junction is referred to as V. Each input voltage source V_i is connected to the summing junction through a resistor, which for generalization will be referred to as R_i. Using Ohm's law, the current through each of these resistors into the summing junction can be expressed as $(V_i - V)/R_i$. Also, the output line is connected via the resistor R to the summing junction, contributing a current given by $(V_{out} - V)/R$. The sum of these currents may be equated to 0 as follows:

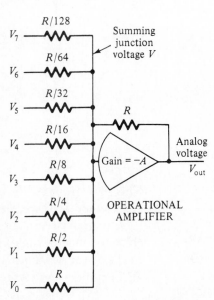

FIG. 27-21 Binary digital-to-analog converter using an operational amplifier

$$\frac{V_0 - V}{R_0} + \frac{V_1 - V}{R_1} + \cdots + \frac{V_7 - V}{R_7} + \frac{V_{out} - V}{R} = 0$$

Now, since V is the input voltage of the operational amplifier the output voltage V_{out} is equal to $-AV$, where A is the gain. This relationship can be rewritten equivalently as $V = -V_{out}/A$. Making this substitution for V and transposing terms involving V_{out}, the previous equation becomes

$$\frac{V_0}{R_0} + \frac{V_1}{R_1} + \cdots + \frac{V_7}{R_7} = \frac{-V_{out}}{A}\left(\frac{1}{R_0} + \frac{1}{R_1} + \cdots + \frac{1}{R_7} + \frac{A}{R} + \frac{1}{R}\right)$$

This equation may be simplified by making an approximation based on the high gain of an operational amplifier. The gain A is normally 50,000 or greater, causing the term A/R on the right side of the equation to be much greater than the other terms to which it is added. The parenthetical quantity on the right side is thus approximated by just the term A/R. The right side of the equation then becomes

$$\frac{-V_{out}}{A}\left(\frac{A}{R}\right) = \frac{-V_{out}}{R}$$

The output voltage V_{out} is therefore given by the expression

$$V_{out} = -R\left(\frac{V_0}{R_0} + \frac{V_1}{R_1} + \cdots + \frac{V_7}{R_7}\right)$$

Now using the values given in Fig. 27-20 for each R_i the expression for V_{out} becomes

$$V_{out} = -R\left(\frac{V_0}{R} + \frac{V_1}{R/2} + \cdots + \frac{V_7}{R/128}\right)$$
$$= -(V_0 + 2V_1 + \cdots + 128V_7)$$
$$= -\sum_{i=0}^{7} V_i 2^i$$

This indicates that the output voltage is equal to the negative of the quantity represented by the input binary number.

A similar circuit can be used to convert numbers represented in 8421 BCD (binary-coded decimal) to analog by adjusting the values of the input resistors to match the weights associated with the bits of a BCD number. A 2-digit 8421 BCD number represented by the sequence of bits

$$N = b_3 b_2 b_1 b_0 a_3 a_2 a_1 a_0$$

has the following polynomial expansion

$$N = (b_3 2^3 + b_2 2^2 + b_1 2^1 + b_0)10^1 + (a_3 2^3 + a_2 2^2 + a_1 2^1 + a_0)$$

The weights for the bits of N are therefore (in the order that the bits appear above) 80, 40, 20, 10, 8, 4, 2, 1. The corresponding input resistor values for a circuit similar to that of Fig. 27-21 are therefore

$$\frac{R}{80} \qquad \frac{R}{40} \qquad \frac{R}{20} \qquad \frac{R}{10} \qquad \frac{R}{8} \qquad \frac{R}{4} \qquad \frac{R}{2} \qquad R$$

Analog-to-Digital Conversion

Several methods for converting an analog quantity into a digital representation will be discussed, all of which use a digital-to-analog (D/A) converter in a "trial and error" manner. Each such method starts with a trial digital number, which is converted with a D/A converter to produce an analog voltage. This analog voltage is then compared to the given analog voltage. Based on the comparison the trial number is either adjusted or left alone. The process is repeated with the new trial number and so on, until an appropriate digital number is found corresponding to the given analog voltage. It is assumed that the input analog quantities are properly scaled so that they fall within the range of the digital-to-analog converter. The methods differ from each other primarily in the way that the trial number is adjusted.

The simplest method of adjusting the trial number is to start with the lowest number in the range (which is zero for positive numbers) and continually incre-

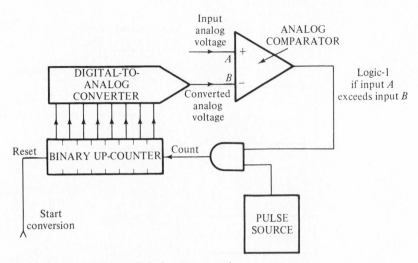

FIG. 27-22   Analog-to-digital converter using an up counter

ment it until the converted voltage first exceeds or equals the given voltage. Figure 27-22 shows how this may be done with an up counter. The bits of the counter are connected to a D/A converter. The analog output voltage of this converter and the given input analog voltage are connected to an analog comparator, which produces a logic-1 on its output line if the given voltage exceeds the D/A voltage. This comparator output line and a pulse source are connected to an AND gate, the output of which is connected to the count line of the counter.

The analog-to-digital (A/D) conversion process is started by resetting the counter to zero. The counter is then incremented with each pulse from the pulse source until the comparator output becomes logic-0. This occurs when the content of the binary counter is sufficient to cause the output of the D/A converter to exceed or equal the given analog voltage. At that time the content of the counter is used as the converted digital number.

A significant improvement to this first method for A/D conversion involves replacing the up counter with an up-down counter. The trial number may then be adjusted by incrementing or decrementing the counter. This allows the counter to track the given analog voltage if it varies in a continuous manner. Figure 27-23 depicts a circuit for this modified method. An analog comparator with two output lines, H and L, is used to compare the given analog voltage with the D/A converter output voltage. The comparator output line H will indicate with a logic-1 when the converted analog voltage exceeds the given analog voltage by at least a certain amount Δ. The other comparator output line L, on the other hand, will indicate with a logic-1 when the converted analog voltage falls short of the given analog voltage by at least the amount Δ. There is thus a "dead zone" of width 2Δ in which neither comparator output line is logic-1. Each of the two comparator output lines, H and L, are used to gate pulses that are applied, respectively, to the down-count and up-count lines of the counter.

The conversion process may start with an arbitrary number in the counter. If the content of the counter is too high compared to the given analog voltage, then the comparator output line H will be at logic-1, causing the counter to decrement with the next pulse. If the content of the counter is too low compared

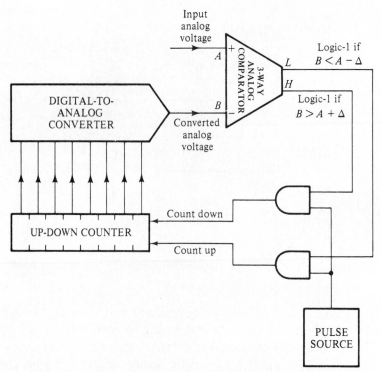

FIG. 27-23 Analog-to-digital converter using an up-down counter

to the given analog voltage, then the line L will be at logic-1, causing the counter to increment with the next pulse. When the content of the counter becomes within $\pm\Delta$ of the given analog voltage, both H and L will be at logic-0, causing the counter to become stationary. If the analog voltage were to subsequently vary, the counter would be incremented or decremented accordingly.

It should be noted that the margin Δ of the comparator should be suitably chosen so that just one number of the counter will fall within the dead zone. The dead-zone width 2Δ should be greater than the amount in which the converted analog voltage varies between successive numbers, which is equal to the analog weight associated with the least-significant bit (W_{LSB}). However, the dead-zone width should not be greater than twice the analog weight of the least-significant bit. That is,

$$W_{LSB} < 2\Delta < 2W_{LSB}$$

The time required for A/D conversion using an up-down counter depends on how far the initial content of the counter is from the value to be determined. The number of pulses can vary from 0 to the range of the counter. In situations where the analog voltage to be converted varies slowly, just a few pulses are needed to complete conversions after the first conversion.

Successive Approximation

In many situations, however, the analog voltage to be converted can vary greatly from one conversion to the next. This is especially true if the A/D converter is shared (multiplexed) among several analog sources in a sequential manner, which is often the case. Furthermore, many applications making use of an A/D converter require that conversions be performed at regular intervals, so that the worst-case time must be assumed regardless of the actual time for conversion. For these latter situations, an alternative method for A/D conversion is available that will complete a conversion in a fixed amount of time that is relatively small. The method, referred to as **successive approximation,** involves adjusting each bit in a successive manner in order to achieve an increasingly-close approximation to the analog voltage to be converted. For converters that work with positive numbers, the method begins with a trial digital number having all bits equal to 0. The most-significant bit is set to 1, and the resulting number is converted to analog and compared with the given input analog voltage. If the comparison indicates that the trial number is too large then the most-significant bit is reset to 0. Otherwise, it is kept at 1. Next, the second most-significant bit is set to 1, and the resulting number is again converted to analog and compared with the input voltage. If this comparison indicates that the trial number is too large, then the second most-significant bit is reset to 0. This process continues with each of the remaining bits, using the values that have been determined for the more-significant bits. When the least-significant bit is tested and adjusted, the A/D conversion is complete.

A circuit that performs A/D conversion by successive approximation is shown in Fig. 27-24. A register consisting of eight negative-edge-triggered SR flip-flops is provided to contain the trial number. As before, the content of this register is presented to a D/A converter. The output voltage from the D/A converter and the input analog voltage to be converted are presented to an analog comparator, the output of which is used to determine whether the bit under trial is to be reset. A 4-bit binary up counter and a 1-out-of-8 decoder are provided to scan the bits of the trial number from left to right. The lower 3 bits of the counter are connected to the input lines of the decoder, to determine which of the eight output lines is to be active (logic-1). A pulse source is connected to the counter and also to the clock lines of the flip-flops comprising the trial-number register. The behavior of the counter and register will therefore be synchronized and state changes of either will occur only at the negative edges of the pulses. The most-significant bit of the counter, which will be 1 for a count of 8, is used to disable the pulse source after eight pulses and thus stop the conversion process. The decoder output lines are each used to select the reset terminal of the corresponding flip-flop in the trial-number register and the set terminal of the next flip-flop. Each reset terminal is also conditioned on the output of the comparator. In this way, when a pulse occurs, the flip-flop corresponding to the active decoder output line will be reset if the trial number is too large, and the next flip-flop will always be set.

The circuit operates as follows. A pulse on the line labeled "start conversion," which is assumed to be synchronized to the pulse source, will initialize the trial number register with 1 for the most-significant bit and 0 for the rest of the bits. This start pulse also resets the 4-bit counter to zero, which enables pulses from the pulse source. The initial trial number is converted to analog and compared with the input voltage. When the negative edge of a pulse from the pulse source occurs, the most-significant bit of the trial number is reset if the trial number is too large. In any event, the second most-significant bit is set. The counter is also incremented to one. This process is repeated for succeeding bits. When the

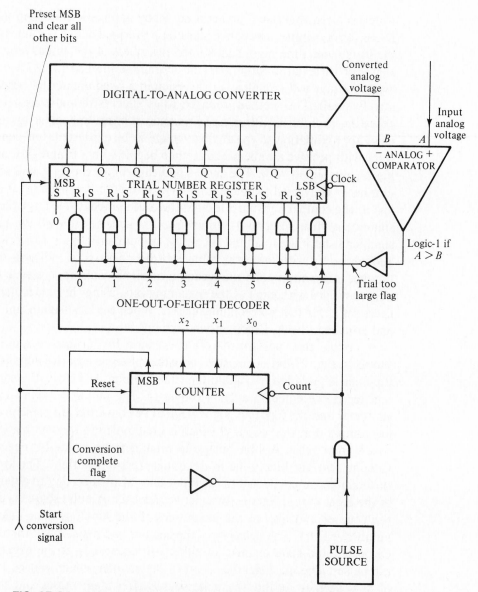

FIG. 27-24 Analog-to-digital converter using successive approximation

counter reaches eight, all bits of the trial-number register will have been tested and adjusted. The process stops at this point, with the converted number in the trial-number register.

Generally, successive approximation requires only k pulses to perform the conversion of an analog voltage to a k-bit number. This is compared to $2^k - 1$ pulses in the worst case for a conversion using the circuit with an up-down counter.

A/D Conversion with a Microprocessor

When analog data is to be converted into digital form for use with a microprocessor, it is possible and often advantageous to have the microprocessor partake in the conversion process. By allowing the microprocessor to perform part of the conversion task, the external circuitry can be simplified. Furthermore, there will be fewer required interconnections between the microprocessor and the external circuitry.

The use of a microprocessor in the conversion process becomes especially advantageous when more than one analog signal is to be converted. In this case, a single D/A converter connected to an output port suffices to convert the trial numbers for all analog signals. A separate comparator for each analog signal is provided to compare that analog signal with the output of the D/A converter. The comparison results for each analog signal are sent to the microprocessor over one line of an input port.

To be more specific, consider a scheme for converting the signals of eight analog channels into digital making use of the illustrative microprocessor. Figure 27-25 shows a circuit to implement this scheme. Included in the circuit are an 8-bit output port and an 8-bit input port, each having the same device code. The output port has an 8-bit register connected to the Data bus to receive trial numbers from the microprocessor. The output lines of this register are connected to a D/A converter, the output line of which is connected to an input line of each of eight analog comparators. The other input line of each comparator is connected to one of the eight analog input channels. Output lines from the comparators are connected to a bank of 3-state drivers that form the input port.

These components provide for sufficient information to and from the microprocessor for a program to be able to perform an analog-to-digital conversion for all eight channels. Generally, the program will begin the conversion for a particular channel by outputting a trial number. This trial number is converted to analog by the D/A converter and then compared with the voltage on each input channel. The results of all eight comparisons are brought in through the input port. The program will then isolate and test the comparison bit corresponding to the particular channel in order to determine a new trial number for this channel. After determining the correct number for the voltage of one channel, the microprocessor will go on to repeat the process for another channel. In this way, all channels are converted in a time-multiplexed manner. It should be noted that no status information concerning the start and completion of the conversion process need be transferred between the microprocessor and the external circuit. This is due to the fact that the conversion is done by the microprocessor, which therefore has control of the starting of the process, as well as knowledge of its completion. If, alternatively, the conversion were done entirely by external components, then such status information would have to be transferred through special I/O ports.

The method used by the program to perform the conversions might be any one of many, including successive approximation, a counting method, or some special method.

There is an interesting programming method that is comparatively fast if the number of bits is rather small (say 4) and the number of channels is large (say 16 or more). The method involves trying every possible number starting from zero and going through the range. As each number is tried, the results from all comparators are noted. If the comparator for any channel has just changed,

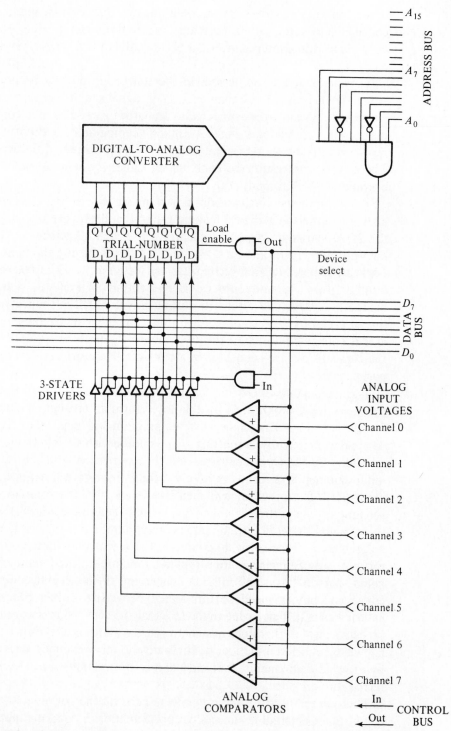

FIG. 27-25 Interface for the illustrative microprocessor to perform A/D conversion for eight analog channels

then the current trial number is used as the value for that channel. After all numbers have been tried, all channels will have been converted. For 4 bits and 16 channels, this method involves just 16 trials to convert all channels, which is an average of one trial per channel.

27-9 SERIAL I/O

In handling I/O data, serial techniques are often used to transfer information between a microcomputer and some I/O device (such as a terminal) or to store information for a microcomputer within a memory unit (such as magnetic cassette tape). Generally, such serial techniques involve a single line that is shared in time to convey a number of bits comprising a data word. The two situations, data transfer and data storage, can be thought of in a similar manner. Each involves an information source and destination. Data is taken from the source and is then either transferred a bit at a time over a line to the destination or stored a bit at a time onto some medium to be later retrieved at the destination. The data path connecting the source to the destination in each case is referred to as a **channel.**

The data is often in a parallel form at the source and/or the destination of a serial channel. In such cases, some means of converting between parallel and serial form is needed. A shift register fills this need quite naturally. To convert parallel data into serial form, first the bits comprising a data word are simultaneously loaded into a shift register. The shift register is then repeatedly shifted in a specified direction, causing each bit of the word to appear sequentially on the output line of the end flip-flop. To convert serial data into parallel form, the line in which the serial data appears is connected to the serial input line at the appropriate end of a shift register. The shift register is then shifted as many times as there are bits in a data word. The bits forming a data word are then available at the output lines of the appropriate flip-flops in the shift register.

There are basically two modes in which information is conveyed over a serial channel, **synchronous** and **asynchronous.** For the synchronous mode, a clock line is provided that is common to the source and destination. Pulses appearing on the clock line serve to separate the individual bits that are conveyed through the channel. Both the source and the destination use the same clock pulses as a time reference for the occurrence of each data bit. As a consequence, the operation of a serial channel in the synchronous mode does not require precision in absolute time. For the asynchronous mode, no clock line common to the source and destination is provided. Instead, the source and the destination each determine the time for each bit by precisely measuring the time from the beginning of a word. For this purpose, the source must mark the beginning of a word in a way recognizable to the destination.

Synchronous Mode

To illustrate the synchronous mode for a serial data channel, consider the network of Fig. 27-26. The network is configured for words of 8 bits, one of which is a parity check bit.

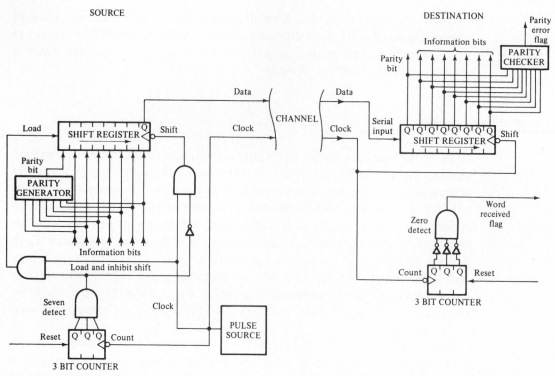

FIG. 27-26 Synchronous serial data channel

At the data source, an 8-bit shift register is provided to convert the parallel input data into serial form. The shift register has input lines controlled by a strobe line, labeled "Load," for the parallel loading of data into the eight flip-flops. Seven bits of input information are presented to the parallel-load input lines of the seven rightmost flip-flops in the shift register. A parity-generator network based on these 7 information bits produces an eighth bit (parity bit) that is presented to the parallel-load input line of the remaining flip-flop. A pulse source is provided to serve as the clock for both the data source and the destination. A 3-bit counter is included at the source to keep track of the number of clock pulses modulo 8. Each time the counter reaches seven a pulse occurs on the Load strobe line of the shift register with the next clock pulse. This causes the source shift register to be loaded with the next data word assumed to be present on its parallel-input lines. When the counter is at a number other than seven, clock pulses are applied to the shift line of the shift register. This causes the 8 bits to appear sequentially on the data line of the channel. The rightmost bit is on the data line immediately after loading, which corresponds to a count of zero. The leftmost bit will appear on the data line after seven clock pulses occur, which corresponds to a count of 7.

An 8-bit shift register is provided at the destination to accept serial data from the channel and convert it into parallel form. Data from the channel is presented to the serial input line on the left end of the shift register. Clock pulses, sent on a second line of the channel from the source, are applied to the shift line of the destination shift register. This causes the shift register to shift in data toward the right. As at the source, a 3-bit counter is provided at the destination to keep track of the clock pulses modulo 8. It is assumed that the 3-bit counters at the source and destination have been reset together at some time and therefore agree in content. Each time the 3-bit counter at the destination reaches zero, a flag labeled "Word Received" is placed at logic-1 signifying that a word has been received and is available at the output lines of the shift register. A network to check parity of a received word is provided that indicates an error if the received word has incorrect parity.

The channel connecting the source and destination could correspond to many types of communication links or storage media. For example, it could consist of two lines connecting a computer I/O port to a peripheral device, a complex communication link utilizing a modulator and a demodulator for a telephone or radio channel, or a pair of tracks of a magnetic-cassette-tape unit. It is important that any time delay occurring in a synchronous channel affects the data and clock lines in the same way, so that their relative time relationship is maintained.

The particular scheme illustrated in Fig. 27-26 is synchronous with respect to the bits comprising a word and also with respect to the words themselves. This is true, since words begin always at a periodic time, specifically the eighth clock pulse. Alternatively, a scheme might be bit synchronous, but word asynchronous. In such a case, a word begins with an externally specified clock pulse.

Asynchronous Mode

With the asynchronous mode of operation, a channel is asynchronous with respect to both bits and words. This means that there is no common clock line connecting the source and destination to delineate bit times and that a word may begin at any time. Source means is necessary to mark the beginning of a word so that the time of appearance of each bit in the word can be determined at the destination. A standard way of doing this is to frame each word with a start bit and a stop bit. During intervals of time in which no word is being transferred the channel is specified to be a certain logic value, say 1. The stop bit, occurring at the end of a word, is assigned this same value 1. The start bit occurring at the beginning of a word is then assigned the opposite value 0. In this way, the front edge of the start bit always corresponds to a transition in values, 1 to 0, and is therefore discernible at the destination. This front edge of the start bit is used at the destination to signify the beginning of a new word and also as a reference to determine the times for all bits in that word.

A network to implement this scheme for an asynchronous serial channel is shown in Fig. 27-27. The network is configured to handle words having 8 information bits. No provision for generating or checking parity is shown in the network to keep it simple. As in the synchronous case, a shift register at the source and at the destination provide respectively for parallel-to-serial and serial-to-parallel conversion. The shift register at the source is 10 bits long to accommodate the start bit, 8 data bits, and the stop bit. The data bits are supplied in parallel to the shift register from a buffer register. The buffer register in turn receives parallel input data that is externally supplied. This external data is loaded in to the buffer register by a pulse externally applied to the line labeled "Load buffer strobe." This may be done during the time that another word is

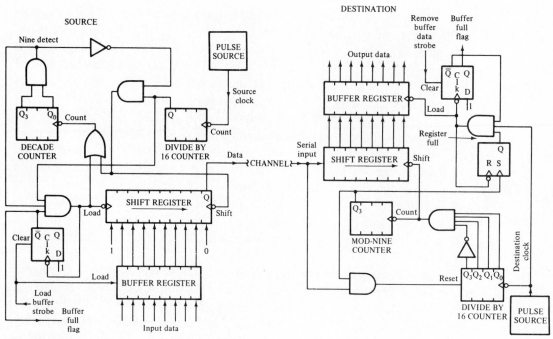

FIG. 27-27 Asynchronous serial data channel

being shifted out of the shift register. In that case, the content of the buffer will be loaded into the shift register as soon as the shift register becomes empty. On the other hand, if the buffer is loaded with data while the shift register is idle, this data will be relayed to the shift register with the next clock pulse. A D flip-flop is used as a flag to signify when the buffer does not contain data ready to be transferred. This flip-flop is cleared when the buffer is loaded and is set (by pulsing its clock line with $D = 1$) when the buffer content is transferred to the shift register.

The pulses used throughout the source network are derived from a pulse source connected to a divide-by-16 counter. It will be seen that this allows the frequencies of the source and destination clocks to be similar.

A decade counter is provided at the source to control the number of shift pulses. Each pulse to the shift register is also applied to the decade counter. A count of 9 (corresponding to the end of a transmitted word) is detected by an AND gate. This nine-detect signal is used to block further pulses from reaching the shift register and the decade counter. The source network at this time is in the idle condition.

While in the idle condition another word can be loaded into the shift register from the buffer. This is done with a pulse that is enabled by the AND of the nine-detect signal and the buffer-full condition. The decade counter is also incremented by this load-shift-register pulse, causing it to go to zero. Consequently, the shift register begins shifting out the new word.

At the destination, an 8-bit shift register is used to accommodate just the 8 data bits. To shift in each bit, a shift pulse is generated at the approximate center of each bit time. These shift pulses are presented to both the shift register and a mod-9 counter. The mod-9 counter starts with a count of 8 before a new word from the channel is encountered. As shift pulses occur for a word, the counter will first go to zero and then count back up to 8, which signifies the end of a new word. This allows 9 bits to be shifted into the register; however, the start bit is lost at the right end.

The shift pulses are generated with the use of a divide-by-16 counter connected to the destination clock. The destination clock is adjusted as close as possible to the pulse rate of the source clock. Connected to the divide-by-16 counter is a seven detector, which produces a shift pulse each time the counter passes through seven. When the mod-9 counter reaches 8, further shift pulses are inhibited by the resetting of the divide-by-16 counter. This is done with the AND of the channel line (which should be logic-1 corresponding to a stop bit) and the most-significant bit of the mod-9 counter. The divide-by-16 counter is kept reset during idle periods of the channel. With the divide-by-16 counter in reset, no shift pulses will be generated.

When the leading edge of a start bit appears on the channel, its 0 value will cause the reset terminal of the divide-by-16 counter to become logic-0. This allows the divide-by-16 counter to begin counting clock pulses. With the seventh clock pulse a shift pulse is generated, which is at the approximate center of the start bit. Every 16 clock pulses later another shift pulse is generated, which will be at the approximate center of a data bit.

It should be noted that if after the start bit begins, but before the first shift pulse, the channel were to return to 1, then the divide-by-16 counter would again be reset. This would signify a false start that is attributed to noise. The network in this case simply continues to wait for a true start bit.

Included at the destination is a buffer register. This buffer register is loaded from the shift register whenever the buffer is empty and the shift register is full. Two flip-flops are used to indicate the full conditions of the two registers. The flip-flop used to indicate the full condition of the shift register is assumed to be of a special type having edge-triggered S and R input terminals. The S terminal is activated by the most-significant bit of the mod-9 counter, which indicates that a new word has been received. The R terminal is activated whenever the content of the shift register is moved to the buffer. A D flip-flop is used to indicate the full condition of the buffer. This flip-flop is cleared by an external strobe whenever the buffer register is read, and is set (by pulsing its clock line with $D = 1$) whenever the buffer is loaded from the shift register.

The buffers at the source and destination are a convenience that allows the channel to operate at full speed while providing time (10 bit times) for external devices to supply and to accept data. This extra time is important when a computer is involved, since a certain amount of program execution time is required before the computer can respond to the status information such as source buffer empty or destination buffer full.

It should be pointed out that the source and destination clocks are not physically the same. They should, however, be adjusted so that their pulse rates are as close as possible. If the two pulse rates differ by some amount, then the destination network will drift away from the center of each bit time as a word progresses. Starting with the front edge of the start bit, the destination circuit must not drift more than one-half of a bit time by the time the 10th bit is received. Otherwise, it will have drifted outside of the time for the tenth bit. This corresponds to a tolerance of 5 percent between the two pulse rates.

There are integrated-circuit modules available that incorporate both a source network and a destination network for synchronous and for asynchronous serial channels. Two such modules thus provide all components for a two-way channel. The source network (referred to as a **transmitter**) of one module is connected to the destination network (referred to as a **receiver**) of the other module and vice versa. In the case where the channel corresponds to a storage medium (such as a magnetic-tape cassette unit), a single module provides both the source and destination networks.

Such modules have various forms and include additional components to make them more flexible. For the asynchronous mode, one available module, referred to as a **universal asynchronous receiver/transmitter** (UART), can be programmed to handle 5, 6, 7, or 8 data bits per word with a possible extra bit for odd or even parity and with 1 or 2 stop bits. The programming is done by wiring certain control lines high or low. The module has additional status lines to indicate various error conditions that might arise, such as wrong parity, framing error (no stop bit when expected), buffer overrun (data supplied too fast to transmitter buffer or removed too slow from receiver buffer). A similar module is available for the synchronous mode, which is referred to as a **universal synchronous receiver/transmitter** (USRT).

Other similar modules are available that are intended to be used with particular microprocessors. They usually have 3-state output lines so that they can conveniently form an I/O port. Programming the options for some of these modules is done by writing a control word from a microprocessor into a special internal register rather than by wiring control lines. This saves a few pins for the module.

The channel connecting the source to the destination often makes use of interface circuits that convert the electrical signals to a certain form. In the case of a two-way asynchronous channel between a terminal and a computer, two standard interface schemes are commonly used. One, which is specified for teletypes or teletype-like terminals, encodes logic-1 as a current of magnitude 20 mA and logic-0 as a zero current. The other scheme, which is part of the EIA RS232C standard, encodes logic-1 as a voltage that is nominally -5 V and logic-0 as a voltage that is nominally $+5$ V.

In the case of asynchronous channels involving long-distance communication, such as telephone lines, or information storage, such as magnetic-tape units, modulators and demodulators of various forms are used. In particular, modules, referred to as **modems,** incorporating a modulator and a demodulator for frequency-shift keying are available for use with telephone channels. Such modems use two frequency bands, one for each direction, so that a two-way channel can be obtained from a single telephone line. One frequency band commonly encodes a logic-1 with a frequency of 1270 Hz and a logic-0 with a frequency of 1070 Hz. The other band commonly uses the frequencies of 2225 Hz for logic-1 and 2025 Hz for logic-0. A modem is needed at each end of a two-way channel. Such modems are also useful to store information asynchronously on audio magnetic tape, since the frequency bands used by the modem fall nicely in the audio range.

27-10 BIT-SLICE MICROPROCESSORS

As has been indicated, a microcomputer is a system of modules that generally includes a microprocessor along with memory and I/O units. The microprocessor might be broken down further into subunits in order to achieve greater flexibility. One such approach involves separating the data-handling portion of a microprocessor from that which generally handles instructions and their sequencing. The data-handling portion, consisting of the arithmetic-logic unit and various data registers, is then formed by cascading several identical data units. Each such data unit, referred to as a **microprocessor slice,** consists of an arithmetic-logic unit and various registers for a certain number of bits.

Many different versions of bit-slice microprocessors are available, each having a particular arrangement of data registers and set of arithmetic-logic functions. No one model can therefore encompass the details involved in each of them. In order to illustrate the general concept, a simplified model will be considered that is representative of the various versions of bit-slice microprocessors. This model, shown in Fig. 27-28, is composed of a 4-bit arithmetic-logic unit (ALU) and a 16-word $\times$ 4-bit scratchpad memory unit. The ALU can perform eight different functions upon two 4-bit operands, A and B, to produce a 4-bit result. Three control lines, K_0, K_1, and K_2, are provided to specify which function is to be performed as shown in Table 27-3. Six lines are provided to the ALU to allow for the cascading of several microprocessor slices. Four of the lines, c_{in}, c_{out}, P, and G, are used to convey carry information for the two arith-

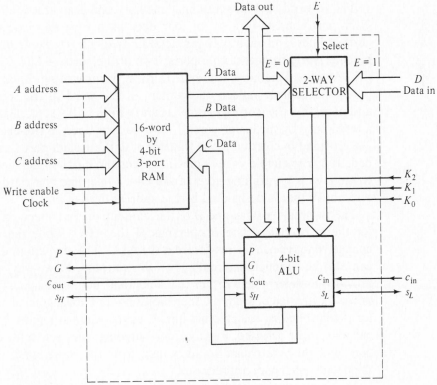

FIG. 27-28 Model for a microprocessor slice

Table 27-3   Functions performed by the ALU in the model bit-slice microprocessor

K_2	K_1	K_0	Function	Effect
0	0	0	Add B to A	Result $= A + B + c_{in}$, $c_{out} =$ final carry
0	0	1	Subtract B from A	Result $= A - B - c_{in}$, $c_{out} =$ final borrow
0	1	0	AND A with B	$r_i = a_i \wedge b_i$
0	1	1	OR A with B	$r_i = a_i \vee b_i$
1	0	0	EXCLUSIVE OR A with B	$r_i = a_i \oplus b_i$
1	0	1	Shift A left	$r_i = a_{i-1}$ $i \neq 0$, $r_0 = s_L$, $s_H = a_3$
1	1	0	Shift A right	$r_i = a_{i+1}$ $i \neq 3$, $r_3 = s_H$, $s_L = a_0$
1	1	1	Pass A	Result $= A$

Note: $A = a_3 a_2 a_1 a_0$, $B = b_3 b_2 b_1 b_0$, and Result $= r_3 r_2 r_1 r_0$.

metic operations, addition and subtraction; whereas the other two lines, s_H and s_L, are used to convey information for the two shift operations. In particular, c_{in} is an incoming line that provides the value of a carry or borrow to the low-order bit and c_{out} is an outgoing line that transmits the value of the carry or borrow produced from the high-order bit. The two lines P and G are outgoing lines that convey additional carry information to allow cascading microprocessor slices with a look-ahead-carry generator. The two lines s_H and s_L are bidirectional. The line s_H provides the value of the bit shifted into the high-order position during a right shift and receives the bit shifted from the high-order position during a left shift. The line s_L provides the value of the bit shifted into the low-order position during a left shift and receives the bit shifted from the low-order position during a right shift.

The 16-word $\times$ 4-bit scratchpad memory unit is assumed to have three ports. Each port consists of a set of four data lines with an associated set of four address lines, and each port can access any of the 16 words of the scratchpad independently from the other ports. Two of the ports, A and B, are for reading the scratchpad memory, while the third, C, is for writing. Each of the two read ports continuously reflects the content of the word in the scratchpad that is addressed by the corresponding address lines. The scratchpad contents are altered only by means of port C. Two control lines, Write-enable and Clock, are provided to coordinate the transfer of data through port C into the scratchpad. If Write-enable is at logic-1, the content of the data lines of port C is written, with the trailing edge of the Clock line, into the word location of the scratchpad that is designated by the address lines of port C.

The two read ports A and B of the scratchpad are connected to provide data for the respective A and B operands of the ALU, while the write port C is connected to receive the results from the ALU. The A-operand data to the ALU can also be supplied externally. For this purpose, a two-way 4-bit selector is provided to determine whether the A-operand data is to come from the A port of the scratchpad or from the four incoming data lines labeled as D. This selector is controlled by the external line E, which when at logic-1 causes the external data to be selected. Finally, four outgoing lines are connected directly to port A of the scratchpad, to allow data from the scratchpad to be brought to the outside of the microprocessor.

In summary, the microprocessor slice performs basic operations upon data obtained from the scratchpad to produce results that are returned to the scratchpad. In addition, external data for an operation can be brought directly in from a set of four lines and data from the scratchpad can be sent out over another set of four lines. The operation to be performed, the source of operand data, and the destination of the results are controlled externally with various control lines to the microprocessor slice. The signals on these control lines are specified by outside circuitry so as to achieve a desired operation of the microprocessor slice. In this way, a microprocessor slice can be adapted for use in a customized microcomputer having a particular behavior. This represents a greater flexibility for bit-slice microprocessors as compared to self-contained microprocessors.

The fact that microprocessor slices can be readily cascaded to achieve a desired data precision represents still more flexibility. Several microprocessor slices in the form of the model may be cascaded by interconnecting their shift and carry lines. In all cases, this involves connecting the shift line s_H of one slice to the shift line s_L of the slice in the next higher position. The carry lines, however, may be interconnected in two different ways. The simplest way is to connect the carryout line c_{out} of one slice to the carry-in line c_{in} of the next higher slice. This results in a rippling of the carry from one slice to the next.

To take full advantage, however, of the look-ahead-carry scheme used in the microprocessor slices, the carry interconnection might make use of a look-ahead-carry generator network. In this case, the look-ahead-carry generator will have the P and G lines from each slice as inputs and will produce as outputs the value for the c_{in} lines to each slice. The c_{out} lines from each slice are not used in this case. Figure 27-29 shows the connections that are made to cascade four microprocessor slices using a look-ahead-carry generator.

To form a complete microprocessor from microprocessor slices, additional components are needed to handle the sequencing and decoding of instructions. Included among these additional components would be a program counter, an instruction register, a timing and control unit, an instruction decoder, perhaps a push-down stack, and other registers to accommodate memory and I/O interfacing. Generally, these components provide for fetching an instruction from main memory according to the program counter and transferring it to the

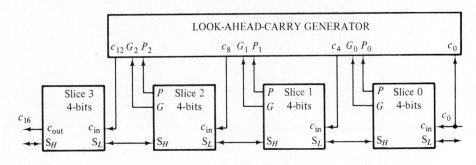

NOTE: The three address buses A, B, and C and the six control lines K_2, K_1, K_0, Clock, Write enable, and E are tied in common.

FIG. 27-29 The cascading of four microprocessor slices using a look-ahead-carry generator

instruction register. The instruction decoder along with the timing and control unit, using the content of the instruction register as input, produce values for the control signals and other input lines to the microprocessor slices in a way to carry out the instruction. The program counter is incremented after each instruction and is appropriately altered in the case of jump instructions.

Implementation of the Illustrative Microprocessor Using Microprocessor Slices

As an example, consider how the illustrative microprocessor might be implemented from the model microprocessor slices. Two slices are cascaded to achieve an 8-bit data width. These two slices contain the ALU and the 16-word scratchpad of the illustrative microprocessor. The remaining necessary components consist of a 16-bit program counter, a 64-word $\times$ 16-bit stack, an 8-bit instruction register, a 16-bit data-address register, an instruction decoder, a carry flip-flop, certain control and timing circuitry, and various bus-driving gates. The interconnection of these components is depicted in Fig. 27-30.

In the figure the block labeled "general logic" directs the flow of data between the various components. Its timing is determined by signals sent to it from the block labeled "timing-and-control logic."

The block labeled "instruction decoder" accepts the content of the instruction register and provides control signals to the general-logic block and to the microprocessor slices. The specific information that the decoder supplies to the micro-

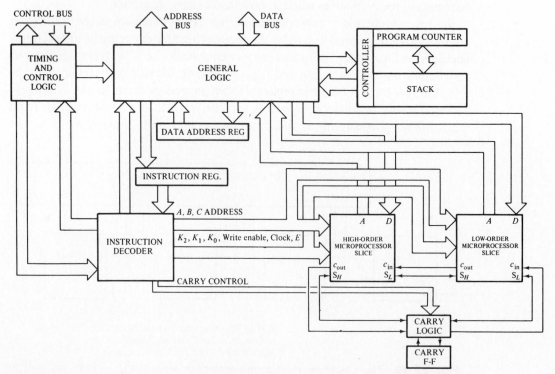

FIG. 27-30 Implementation of the illustrative microprocessor using microprocessor slices

processor slices consists of the *A, B, C* addresses of the scratchpad for operands and results, as well as the 6 control signals K_2, K_1, K_0, Write-enable, Clock, and *E*. The information sent to the general-logic block by the instruction decoder concerns either address modification of the program counter (in the case of jump instructions) or data transfer to or from the microprocessor slices. The time in which specific information is sent by the decoder is influenced by signals from the timing-and-control-logic block.

The timing-and-control-logic block as just indicated determines the timing of all operations performed by other blocks. It also receives signals on the incoming lines of the Control bus and sends signals on the outgoing lines. A major component of this block is a 4-bit sequence counter. This sequence counter is connected to the incoming clock line so that it is incremented with each clock pulse. At the end of each instruction, the sequence counter is reset to zero. The state of the counter is used to determine the clock pulse time of each step in the execution of an instruction. For this purpose the 4 bits of the counter are presented to a 1-out-of-16 decoder, as shown in Fig. 27-31. The output lines of this decoder, labeled S_i, are enabled by the clock line. Thus, for each clock pulse during the execution of an instruction, a pulse will occur on one output line of the decoder, corresponding to the number of clock pulses since the beginning of the instruction cycle. These S_i signals are sent to the blocks labeled "general logic" and "instruction decoder." These two blocks combine the S_i signals with other logic signals to generate pulses on lines that strobe data into the various registers and flags. The timing-and-control block uses the S_i lines also to generate pulses on the outgoing lines of the Control bus.

The general operation of the overall network will now be illustrated by considering the execution of two instructions. The first two clock pulses are common to all instructions, since it is during this time that the operation code of an instruction is fetched from main memory. A pulse on S_0 is used to send an address over the Address bus, commencing with the leading edge. The Read

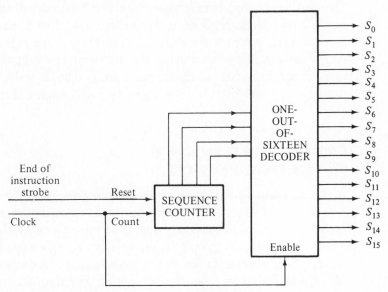

FIG. 27-31 Sequence counter and decoder

control line is then set to logic-1. This causes the first byte of an instruction to be placed onto the Data bus by main memory. This first byte is then strobed into the instruction register with the trailing edge of the S_1 pulse. The instruction decoder then determines the type of instruction and indicates to the general-logic block to bring in additional bytes in the case of a multibyte instruction.

Suppose, for example, that the instruction is add-with-carry. Since this is a single byte instruction no additional bytes will be brought in. This instruction is carried out by the microprocessor slices during the next clock pulse. It involves the addition of the content of some scratchpad register R to the accumulator, which is scratchpad register 0. The results of the addition are stored into the accumulator. To set this up, the instruction decoder places 0000 onto the A and C Address lines to the microprocessor slices, and the specific designator R onto the B Address lines. The control lines $K_2K_1K_0$ are set at 000, corresponding to ADD, and E is set at logic-0, corresponding to select A data. The carry logic is directed to place the value of the carry flip-flop onto the c_{in} line. Finally, the Write-enable control line is set at logic-1 to allow the results to be written into the scratchpad. At this time, the pulse on the S_2 line is passed to the clock line of the microprocessor slices. This causes the computed sum to be written into the accumulator (i.e., scratchpad register 0). At the same time, a pulse is sent to the carry logic that is used to strobe the final carry into the carry flip-flop. The sequence counter is also reset at this time since the execution of the instruction has been completed.

For a second example, consider the unconditional jump instruction, which will not involve the microprocessor slices at all. After the first byte of this instruction is brought into the instruction register, the instruction decoder informs the general-logic block to bring in the two additional bytes. Consequently, the second instruction byte is fetched from main memory and stored into the high-order portion of the data-address register, using pulses on S_2 and S_4 (corresponding to the first two clock pulses of the second machine cycle). The third instruction byte is then fetched and stored into the low-order portion of the data-address register, using pulses on S_6 and S_7 (corresponding to the first two clock pulses of the third machine cycle). The execution of the instruction is completed by transferring the new content of the data-address register to the program counter using the pulse on S_8. This S_8 pulse is also used to reset the sequence counter, since the instruction execution will be completed at this point.

Considerations in the Use of Bit-Slice Microprocessors

It can be generally said that bit-slice microprocessors offer more flexibility as compared to self-contained microprocessors. In particular, the bit slices can be easily cascaded to achieve any degree of data precision. Moreover, the slices can be grouped so as to operate on different components of a vector quantity, allowing the implementation of a microprocessor that deals with vectors instead of individual numbers. Also, the instruction repertoire of a microprocessor using slices can be freely specified by the way the other logic blocks are designed.

Microprocessors constructed from bit slices tend to also have an advantage in speed over self-contained microprocessors, due to the lower scale of integration involved. A disadvantage of bit-slice microprocessors is the need to provide the additional circuitry that is necessary for a complete microprocessor. This causes them to be less convenient to use for most applications. To alleviate this inconvenience, manufacturers generally make modules available that handle the sequencing of instructions. Using such modules in conjunction with microprocessor slices usually requires just the addition of an instruction register, an instruction decoder, and any other registers that are particular to an application. By excluding the instruction register and decoder from the sequencing module the flexibility advantage is retained.

A common approach taken in the design of instruction sequencing modules is to perform the various operations involved in the execution of an instruction as a sequence of microinstructions. These microinstructions reside in a special memory unit and are fetched and executed in a manner similar to that of regular instructions. Fetching the microinstructions in the proper sequence is handled by the instruction sequencing module. A portion of each microinstruction is decoded by additional circuitry to determine the signals to the microprocessor slices. These microinstructions also manage an external program counter and instruction register for handling the regular instructions. The regular instructions (those making up the instruction repertoire) reside in main memory and are fetched into the instruction register according to the program counter. This is done by a routine made up of several microinstructions. The content of the instruction register is then used as an address of a microinstruction subroutine that is especially written to carry out the execution of the regular instruction. Thus, in this case, there exists a computer within a computer, in which the inner computer is programmed with microinstructions to carry out the instructions of the outer computer.

It should be pointed out that **microprogramming** does not refer to the programming of a microcomputer, but rather to the implementation of the instructions in the repertoire of any computer by routines of microinstructions.

27-11 MICROPROCESSOR CLOCKS

Many microprocessors, unlike the illustrative model, require a clock having two or more phases. The phases correspond to separate pulse lines having the same period and a fixed time relationship among each other. Generally, the phases are used within the microprocessor to control different types of data transfers. For instance, two-phase master-slave flip-flops may be used for registers in a microprocessor. In this case, one clock phase is used to strobe information into the master sections of all flip-flops and the other clock phase is used to strobe the content of each master section into the corresponding slave section.

A network that may be used to derive two nonoverlapping phases from a single pulse source is shown in Fig. 27-32. The pulse source is connected to the clock line of a T-type flip-flop, with the T terminal tied to logic-1. The flip-flop therefore changes state after each pulse. The output line of the flip-flop and its complement are each ANDed with the pulse source to produce the two derived

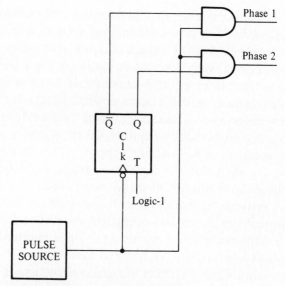

FIG. 27-32 Phase-splitting circuit

phases. When the state Q of the flip-flop is logic-0, a pulse from the source will produce a pulse on the phase-1 line. When Q is logic-1, a pulse from the source will produce a pulse on the phase-2 line. In this way, pulses from the source are alternately applied to the two phases. The "dead time" between phases is equal to the off time of the pulse source, which can be adjusted to meet whatever requirement is specified for a microprocessor. The pulse rate of the two phases is one-half of that of the pulse source. The pulse-duration time for each phase will be equal to that of the pulse source.

A more general time relationship between two phases can be achieved with the network of Fig. 27-33. The network makes use of a Gray-code counter driven by a pulse source. Each phase is derived having an arbitrary pulse duration and position relative to the other phase by combining selected successive

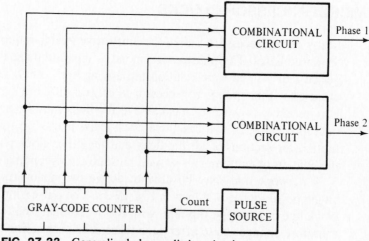

FIG. 27-33 Generalized phase-splitting circuit

counts in the Gray code. Hazard-free combinational circuits are used for this purpose. The Gray code rather than straight binary is used to prevent the occurrence of "glitches" due to multiple bit changes. With a 4-bit counter, as shown in the figure, the pulse rate of the source needs to be 16 times the desired pulse rate of the two phases. This network can be extended to more than two phases by simply including additional combinational circuits to derive the extra phases.

sec.28

Microcomputer Operating Systems

Stanley M. Miastkowski

28-1 INTRODUCTION

An **operating system,** although essentially only a special type of software, is one of the most important components of a computer system. All operating systems, regardless of whether they're designed for a mainframe, minicomputer, or microprocessor-based system, provide an essential logical-to-physical interface between the user and the physical machine.

Besides the man/machine interface, these "traffic police officer" programs provide management of system resources, including the processor, memory, and input/output (I/O).

28-2 OPERATING SYSTEM COMPONENTS

Modern microcomputer operating systems are often designed and implemented in a modular manner in order to provide flexibility and portability. Typical layers include:

Kernel Also called the *nucleus,* this key module is the layer closest to the hardware. It provides basic operating system functions such as scheduling tasks.

Resource Management This layer provides allocation of system resources to other layers. It coordinates read/write to internal memory and microprocessor access.

Physical I/O Often implemented as a set of *device driver* subroutines, this layer coordinates data flow to and from devices such as the console, disk(s), printers, and serial or parallel ports.

Logical I/O This layer allows the operating system to access physical devices without worrying about their physical characteristics. It passes data to and from the physical I/O layer.

File System Maintains a directory of data files of peripheral devices and coordinates data flow between physical and logical I/O.

Human Interface Provides the essential man/machine interface between the user and the system. This outer layer (sometimes referred to as the **shell**) interprets the commands typed into the console by the operator and returns messages and data to the display.

Applications Software Provides the interface between the operating system, languages, utilities, and other applications software.

28-3 SPECIFIC PROBLEMS

Until recently, little thought was given to operating system compatibility or portability, since in mainframe environments operating systems are custom-designed for the capabilities and needs of the system and applications.

With the general acceptance of microprocessor-based systems (i.e., personal computers), the problem of software portability and applications software compatibility has become increasingly important. End users of microprocessor-based systems are understandably concerned that the applications software they purchase from suppliers (who often provide a minimal level of customer support) will run on their systems. The key to the mass-market acceptance of microprocessor-based systems is a **standard interface** between the applications software and the physical machine. As seen below, the microcomputer industry is at least partially on the way to meeting this goal.

28-4 MICROS VS. MAINFRAMES

At their most basic level, operating systems designed for mainframe systems and those designed for microprocessor-based systems differ very little. All provide the needed man/machine interface and management of resources. The primary difference between the large operating system and micro systems is that microprocessor-based systems are called upon to manage a more limited array of resources, including smaller amounts of memory, a comparatively limited amount of I/O, and a slower microprocessor with a much more limited instruction set. In addition, services unique to mainframes such as batch processing and support of a large number of concurrent users are not needed in a small computer environment.

Although this limited resource management results in more compact code, the often-limited directly-addressable memory space of 8-bit microprocessors (seldom more than 64 K) must be dealt with. Full-featured operating systems that take up 100s of kilobytes of memory space cannot possibly be used with small systems. Therefore, despite the limited resource management required on microprocessor-based systems, the code must still be optimized to use as little space as possible.

A further complication in the design of microprocessor-based operating systems is the required high-level of user "friendliness" since the majority of personal computer users are not experienced programmers. These features too require additional code for plain language prompts, help messages, and automatic error trapping and recovery.

Since microcomputer systems based on 16-bit microprocessors have become economically feasible for the typical small system user, the memory space limitation has become a less pressing matter. Cashing in on this memory bonus and the increased computing power of 16-bit microprocessors, manufacturers are developing microcomputer operating systems which rival the complexity and power of systems designed for minicomputer and mainframe use. In fact, as with the hardware, the lines of demarcation between operating systems for the three classes of computers have become increasingly blurred. Microprocessor-based systems have been developed which provide the sophistication and power until recently only available to users of larger systems. These include multi-user and multi-tasking (concurrency) operations, security, sophisticated programmer tools, indexed-sequential access method (ISAM), keyed file typed for more efficient data storage, automatic error-trapping and data recovery, and a high-level of user-friendliness. In addition, more sophisticated operating systems for 8-bit systems have been developed which use paging to address larger blocks of user memory and provide many of the features mentioned above.

28-5 THE PORTABILITY/COMPATIBILITY PROBLEM

In the small computer marketplace, an operating system is commonly referred to as a DOS (for disk operating system), since the standard media for on-line storage are floppy disk drives (both 5¼″ and 8″) and Winchester technology hard disk drives. Although manufacturers of microprocessor-based personal computer systems have come a long way in the past few years, there remains in the market a problem of compatibility and portability. The largest personal computer makers have by and large developed proprietary operating systems designed specifically for their computer systems. Prominent examples are Apple DOS for the Apple II, SOS (sophisticated operating system) for the Apple III, and several versions of TRSDOS for Radio Shack's line of personal computers. Although optimized for the features and capabilities of these particular systems, they lack a standard user interface and command language. Consequently, applications software developed on one system is not transferable to another system without extensive reworking.

Since most applications software require a copy of the operating system on the distribution media, a further problem has developed since some manufacturers (Radio Shack among them) insist on license fees for any applications software that contains their operating system. Some developers have responded to this problem by writing independent operating systems designed specifically to be compatible with the hardware used by proprietary operating systems, yet easy to use and affordable for applications developers. The complexity of the task depends largely on the complexity of the hardware and the accessibility of information about the system.

The TRS-80 "aftermarket" is large because of Radio Shack's former insistence on a stiff license fee for each distribution copy of TRSDOS (TRS-80 Disk Operating System). Examples of closely-compatible operating systems for the TRS-80 include LDOS, NEWDOS, and DOSPLUS.

The situation with Apple Computer, manufacturer of one of the most popular personal computers, is considerably different. Despite Apple's insistence on the details of its operating system (DOS) remaining proprietary, literally thousands of applications software packages are available for the Apple II, with more slowly becoming available for the Apple III. The company has not failed to realize that a large base of applications software virtually guarantees a strong user demand for their hardware. Consequently, they allow applications developers to distribute their operating system with applications without the need of paying a license fee.

28-6 CP/M

There exists a microcomputer operating system which has become a de facto standard. CP/M (Control Program for Microprocessors) was developed in 1975 by Digital Research, Incorporated of Pacific Grove, California. It will run on Z80, 8080, and 8085-based systems, with 16-bit upgrades now available for 8086 microprocessors.

Since CP/M was the first full-featured operating system designed for microprocessor applications, it filled a need and soon developed a devoted following. Because CP/M was the only system for several years, it quickly became the de facto standard. In the interim, it has gone through a number of upgrades and improvements. Despite its widespread acceptance, it has a number of important disadvantages for the developing personal computer market.

Because CP/M has become the major factor in the microprocessor operating system marketplace, we will look at it in a great deal of detail. The following explanation serves as a technical introduction to the specifics of microcomputer operating systems in general since the concepts of CP/M are in many ways similar to all operating systems designed for use with microprocessors.

CP/M Overview

CP/M is a single-user, single-task microcomputer operating system. In a typical microprocessor system, CP/M resides at the top of main memory and is divided into three distinct modules: the BIOS (basic input/output system); BDOS (basic disk operating system); and CCP (console command processor). User memory is referred to as the TPA (transient program area) and resides at the bottom of available memory. Let's take a closer look at each of these.

The BIOS is a hardware-dependent module which interfaces the actual hardware of the microcomputer system to the BDOS. It is unique to the specific hardware environment and includes routines for character I/O and disk control—including setting the address for DMA (direct memory access), locating tracks and sectors, and controlling reading/writing of data. Release versions of CP/M are provided with a "standard" BIOS (actually customized for the Intel MDS-80 microcomputer development system) with detailed instructions for customization to other systems. In most cases, the BIOS is customized by OEMs and other system integrators to work with specific systems.

The BDOS is the key module of the CP/M system. It's responsible for all memory, processor, and I/O management and works through the BIOS.

A boot module is situated at the base of user memory which performs a "warm start" by loading and initializing code sufficient to turn console control over to the CCP.

The CCP provides an interface to the "real world" of the user. When the system is at command level, the CCP awaits instructions from the user through the keyboard. It's responsible for retrieving files from disk as per the user's instructions, executing them, and also writing data to disk.

The user communicates with the CCP by typing in standard commands, usually followed by file names. The CCP then searches the media (usually a floppy or hard disk) for the file. If it is not found, an error message is returned, otherwise the program is loaded into the TPA. The CCP then passes control of the system to the transient program, which begins execution and can use the I/O facilities of the BDOS and BIOS. At the completion of processing, control is passed back to the CCP.

CP/M Disk System Organization

CP/M divides disks into three areas: The first two tracks (0 and 1) are used for the operating system itself. Because they fall outside the "normal" disk area, the operating system cannot be copied to the disk through a normal backup operation. Instead, CP/M provides a special "sysgen" (system generation) command which writes the operating system data to tracks 1 and 0.

The second area of the disk is where the disk directory is maintained. The directory is located on track 2, with its size dynamic—depending on the number of individual files stored on the particular disk.

The remainder of the disk is taken up by the data area, which extends to the end of the disk. (The actual size depends on the type and style of the disk(s) in the system.)

Each file on a disk has a FCB (file control block), which contains the drive number, file name and extension, and length of the file. Space on disks is allocated by blocks with the minimum file size usually being 1 K bytes on a single-density system, and 2 K bytes on a double-density system. Current versions of CP/M allow individual file sizes of up to eight megabytes.

CP/M contains five built-in commands:

TYPE   Display a file

DIR   Directory of files

REN   Rename a file

ERA   Erase a file

SAVE   Save a file

A number of transient utility programs are loaded into the TPA when CP/M is invoked. These include:

SYSGEN   Moves the CP/M system to a disk

PIP   Peripheral interchange program

ED   A line-oriented editor

ASM   Assembler

DUMP   Display a file in Hex format

LOAD   Load a file

STAT   Provides statistics on disk space

MOVCPM   Reconfigure the size of the system

SUBMIT   Chain several commands together

DDT   Dynamic debugging tool

Evaluation of CP/M

Despite it's widespread acceptance and use, CP/M has some serious flaws for today's "typical" personal computer user with limited computer knowledge. First, because it was developed in the early days of microcomputers, it was (and remains) designed to be used by experienced programmers familiar with the intricacies of its command structure. The lack of a "user-friendly" interface is a serious problem in light of the increasing widespread consumer acceptance of personal computers.

Some have called CP/M a "kitchen-sink" operating system, since its design requires the user to learn a complicated series of commands. Perhaps more important is its lack of help commands and error-trapping. It is extremely easy for a new user to accidently erase a whole file or even an entire disk without any way of recovering the information.

The lack of a friendly interface has been circumvented to some extent by custom "front-ends"—comparatively low-priced software which attempts to provide a more understandable and usable interface by providing a layer of software above the CCP which understands less cryptic commands. For example, the command for copying a disk goes from PIP B:=A:*.* to COPY A TO B. User menus are also provided in order to present the user with a number of common choices.

CP/M is (as are most microcomputer operating systems) somewhat of a compromise. Although all operating systems are essentially designed to act as a user/computer interface and provide efficient allocation of system resources, operating systems can further be characterized by systems which are oriented to applications software development, and those designed for optimal resource allocation for already-written software. Because of its history and the early nature of the microcomputer environment, CP/M lies somewhere in the middle. Its complete commands structure and direct access to the system allow applications programmers a powerful tool for software development. Yet, its five built-in commands allow end-users a relatively straightforward (yet, at the same time, often difficult to learn) run-time environment.

CP/M Portability

Because CP/M has been recognized as the de facto operating system standard for microprocessor-based computer systems, it has been accepted and adapted to run on a majority of the personal computer systems available today. However, CP/M is only available to run on 8080 or Z80-based systems. Since the majority of personal computers use either of these, it doesn't create an immediate problem. However, the large base of Apple users (the Apple uses a 6502 microprocessor) were locked out until the development of a plug-in card for the Apple which provides CP/M access. Although it allows Apple users immediate access to hundreds of applications packages written for CP/M, it obviously will not run applications software written for the 6502.

Finally, CP/M is a single-task, single-user system. With the increasing application of 16-bit microprocessors and their increased address space, multi-user operating systems have begun to make a dent in the microcomputer marketplace. A multi-user CP/M called MP/M is available from Digital Research, although at the time this was written, a 16-bit multi-user version was not yet available.

28-7 ADVANCED 8-BIT OPERATING SYSTEMS

Although many operating systems designed for 16-bit microprocessor-based systems have recently been introduced (see below), the large installed base of 8-bit-based systems has resulted in a number of 8-bit operating systems incorporating advanced features. We will use the OASIS system from Phase One Systems, Inc. of Oakland, CA as an example. The operating system, which is now also available in 16-bit versions, is billed by its developers as a "business system" because of its dual orientation toward business applications software developers and end-users in small-to-medium size business environments. The system is designed (for portability) to be implemented on Z80-based microcomputers, yet provides advanced features until recently only available in minicomputer systems. It is also designed to provide a friendly user interface for inexperienced users in a business environment yet provides the advanced features expected by developers of sophisticated applications software.

Organization of OASIS

There are three major sections to OASIS: The system NUCLEUS is comparable to CP/M's BDOS, and provides basic system services. Because OASIS is a multi-user system, it provides much more sophisticated service, including scheduling, memory management, and system resource sharing. The CSI (command string interpreter) is analogous to CP/M's CCP, and provides all I/O, as well as user access to system and user files. Applications programs include over 50 system utilities and languages including BASIC and a macro assembler.

OASIS, like most operating systems, is essentially a file management program. It provides a variety of file types, including direct, sequential, indexed, and ISAM and provides file and record locking to preserve data integrity. System security is provided for through passwords and six privilege levels. This is especially important in a multi-user, multi-tasking environment, and also effectively prevents inexperienced users from inadvertently changing or erasing files.

Transition Systems

With the recent availability of a fully-compatible 16-bit version, OASIS is one of several systems which provide an upgrade path from 8-bit to 16-bit systems. Another example is MS-DOS, a single-user, single task operating system designed for the IBM Personal Computer. Designed primarily for execution rather than program development, MS-DOS has a utility which translates Z80 and 8080 code to 8086 code used by the IBM-PC.

MS-DOS also incorporates a number of features which reflect the state of the art in low-end operating systems and includes the features that users are coming to expect. Requiring only 32 K of RAM (rather than the usual 64 K required by CP/M) MS-DOS can also adapt existing BASIC, COBOL, FORTRAN, and Pascal programs to run on the IBM-PC. MS-DOS also automatically dates each file created, a simple matter which greatly helps developers and users. It also provides sophisticated error recovery and can address up to **one billion bytes** of disk space.

The latest release of MS-DOS reflects the current state of the art in design including the ability to customize user interface, support foreground/background tasks, and handle electronic mail and local networks.

28-8 16-BIT OPERATING SYSTEMS

The proliferation of 16-bit-based systems has focused recent attention on 16-bit operating systems. Unlike 8-bit operating systems, a de facto standard is unlikely to emerge soon for 16-bit systems. The major reason for this is the wide range of expected applications for 16-bit systems ranging from low-end single-user personal computer to sophisticated high-end multi-user, multi-tasking systems for intensive business applications. In addition, real-time operating systems are required for such specialized applications as process control. Real-time capability adds a significant measure of complexity to the designer's task, not to mention the consequent increase in software cost.

The larger amount of RAM directly addressable by 16-bit systems (often up to 512 K) opens up a new world of features. Besides multi-user, multi-tasking, and real-time, users are gaining the availability of sophisticated data security measures, including password access and error trapping.

UNIX

Recently, attention has been drawn to a 16-bit operating system developed at about the same time as CP/M. UNIX was developed by Bell Laboratories specifically for Digital Equipment Corporation's PDP-11 minicomputer line, but has recently become available for systems based on popular 16-bit microprocessors including the 68000 and Z8000. It is even available for Z-80 systems. UNIX provides extremely advanced features—some of which have until recently only been found on large and expensive operating systems designed for mainframes.

UNIX Overview

The UNIX system includes a multi-user operating system, utilities, an assembler for the target microprocessor, and the C language—also developed by Bell Laboratories. Its advanced capabilities include reentrant code, separate memory space for instructions and data, security, timeouts, interprocess monitoring, and multiplexed I/O for high-speed data flow between peripherals.

Despite its powerful features, UNIX suffers from several shortcomings: First, it's much more expensive than most other 16-bit operating systems, although Bell Laboratories provides it free to educational institutions. Secondly, it is a development rather than execution oriented system. Using it requires advanced programming skills, since no user-friendly interface is provided.

One major shortcoming of UNIX is that there is no method of locking files. If more than one user attempts to access the same file at the same time, severe problems can result. In addition, error recovery is primitive. A system crash often destroys much data—even if it's written to disk.

XENIX

Microsoft has endeavored to correct some of UNIX's major deficiencies by developing XENIX under license from Bell Laboratories. XENIX was developed especially to meet the needs of 16-bit microprocessor-based systems, including a reduction in the memory space needed to contain the system, and greatly expanded error-handling facilities. Unlike UNIX, XENIX is primarily a single-user, multitasking system. Its user interface is much more friendly for non-programmers and is consequently oriented toward a business environment.

28-9 CONCLUSIONS

Because of the dynamic nature of the microcomputer marketplace and the many specific needs of users, microcomputer operating systems will continue a rapid evolution for the foreseeable future. The large existing user base of 8-bit-based systems and applications software written specifically to run on operating systems such as CP/M guarantees that existing "standard" operating systems will enjoy a long life. New versions and upgrades will continue to be produced, although the limitations of providing compatibility with past releases prevent major changes to existing systems. Still, new features and more efficient systems will result.

Current technology has already resulted in the release of state-of-the-art operating systems for existing 8-bit systems. We can expect to see the trend continuing because of the above-mentioned user base.

At this writing, the 16-bit operating system market was just beginning to accelerate. The inherent capabilities of 16-bit microcomputer hardware and the varying needs of users will likely result in a number of "standards" designed for specific applications such as software development, business applications, etc. We have only just begun to see the evolution of microcomputer operating systems.

sec.29

Audio Output: Speech and Music

Louis Hohenstein

29-1 INTRODUCTION

Computer output peripherals all have a common function of providing information in a form useful to people. Most of this output is in the form of readable text and visual graphics, but the use of another form, audible output, is growing. Audio output devices are of three major types:

1. Playback of previously recorded speech
2. Music and sound synthesis
3. Speech synthesis

Perhaps the most intriguing of these three audio output devices is the process of speech synthesis. **Speech-recognition equipment** is a separate but related peripheral device.

29-2 AUDIO-RESPONSE UNITS

Peripherals of this category are both called **voice read-out systems** and **automatic announcing systems.** These peripherals store speech as digital signals in nonvolatile solid-state memory and not as analog recorded speech, typical of magnetic-tape recorders. Solid-state audio-response units therefore eliminate the mechanical problems of motor-driven tape drives.

Solid-state audio-response units evolved from the need of the telephone industry for selectively announcing different words, phrases, and numbers, depending on telephone-line status, like the message advising that the number you have dialed has been changed to a new number, which is then stated. The use of audio response units subsequently spread to commercial, industrial, and military applications.

Figure 29-1 illustrates a typical rack-mounted audio-response unit, containing a microprocessor, stored operating program, memory, real-time clock, and RS232C serial interface to a host computer. Vocabulary capacity is 128 s of speech addressable at any ½-s vocabulary position, or up to 256 individually addressable variable-length messages. When additional voice response time (message capacity) is required, additional units are added.

Speech is stored by processing original human speech spoken into a microphone into digital patterns. These digital representations of speech are stored in programmable read-only memory. When the memory location of a digitally stored audio-response word or phrase is addressed, digital signals representing the spoken words are converted back into analog voltages and amplified to output levels for telephone or speaker delivery.

Typically an audio-response unit produces the frequency spectrum sufficient for an understandable voice (50 to 3000 Hz for the audio-response unit illustrated in Fig. 29-1). This closely resembles the sound of the original speaker.

The audio-response unit shown in Fig. 29-1 is capable of responding to a maximum of 64 communication lines. An interesting option is a computer-down operation enabling the audio-response unit to detect when the host computer is not operating. It then answers incoming calls with a message like "System is not available. Please call 829-1988. Good-bye."

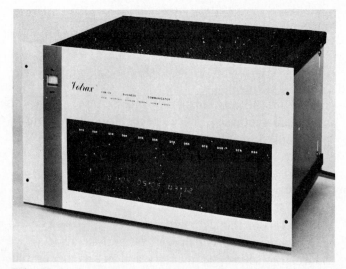

FIG. 29-1 An audio-response unit containing 128 s of speech stored in digital form (Votrax Division of Federal Screw Works)

29-3 MUSIC AND SOUND SYNTHESIZERS

The synthesis of audio tones or other sound differs from audio-response units in that an audio-response unit plays back the same spoken words (or set of sounds) originally provided whereas in a sound synthesizer composite sounds are assembled by the programmer and/or computer from sound elements, usually musical tones. In this way artificial sound is synthesized from its elemental components, not simply played back from a previous recording. Special-purpose sound synthesizers are used (1) by musical groups to add a synthesized rhythm or harmony while a performer provides the melody, (2) by home organs for the same purpose, (3) by artists or composers who wish to create experimental music, (4) in computer games to simulate the sound of rockets, gunfire, ball strikes, or other sound effects, (5) and by the computer hobbyist. Several inexpensive sound synthesizers for personal computers are available.

A simple tone synthesizer usually generates 128 or 256 program-selectable tones through one output channel. One typical 256-tone generator has an amplifier frequency range of 107 to 27,500 Hz, producing sine-wave tones for a programmable tone duration.

More advanced music synthesizers generate multiple tones simultaneously and sample tone waveform tables stored in memory for tone color. Different tone colors are also possible by modifying the digitally stored waveform tables. Numerous assembly programs are available for generating tones. A user can program a musical score including tempo, time, rests, repeats, volume, and tone color over a four- to six-octave range. Sound is typically output through two or four sound channels.

29-4 SPEECH SYNTHESIZERS

Just as music synthesizers differ from audio-response units by building music up from the elements of time-phased tones (rather than playing back a previous recording), computer speech synthesizers construct intelligible speech from **phonemes,** the elements of speech. A typical system uses 63 phoneme commands and 4 stress, or emphasis, commands. With the possible combinations of phoneme commands and stresses, a programmer forms any word desired by assembling the phonemes in a speech program.

Speaking terminals and calculators are currently used to assist visually handicapped persons and in learning aids to assist children with both visual and oral perception of word spelling. As the technology continues to develop, industrial and commercial uses are likely to become more popular.

The components of a speech synthesizer are as follows:

1. An electrical analog of the human vocal track

2. A program to specify desired sound in the vocal-track analog control parameters

3. The control interface of the vocal track

The methods of synthesizing human speech by computer differ slightly from one manufacturer to another. The following method is presented as an example.

Human Vocal Track

The human vocal tract starts with the voice box, in the region of the midthroat (glottis), and is 6.3 to 7.4 in (160 to 190 mm) long, extending up through the oral cavity and lips and nasal cavity and nostrils (Fig. 29-2). As the lungs expel air in a steady stream, the air passes over the voice cords, causing them to vibrate. When the throat closes at the glottis, these vibrations occur effectively in a tube (the vocal tract), with the glottis end closed. At the other end the mouth is open as the primary resonating chamber, and the nasal cavity is selectively opened as a contributing chamber (Fig. 29-3).

Muscles control the entire tube, i.e., the volume of air expelled, the tension on the vocal cords, the shape of the oral cavity, and the position of the tongue. Because words take a finite length of time to say, the time-series configuration of the muscular activities and shapes of the cavities produce elemental sounds, or phonemes, which constitute words.

A representative speech-synthesis system uses 48 consonants and vowel phonemes, 7 special English phoneme sounds, 4 punctuation marks, and 4 stress levels. Phonemes differ from the 26 letters of the alphabet. Ideally, alphabet characters would form groups that could be directly converted into phonemes, but the rules are too complex. The same letters in different words are pronounced differently; even the same words are pronounced differently in different geographic regions.

As a result, the process of human reading and speech (or **program for human speech**) is as follows: to translate a word, written in groups of letters, into speech of the customary pronunciation for a particular person the context of letters in the words recalls a set of specified sounds (phonemes) subconsciously. The phonemes are translated into the muscular control of the lungs and vocal-track components, producing sounds used for human communication, i.e., speech. Virtually the same set of activities takes place in the computer-controlled voice synthesizer.

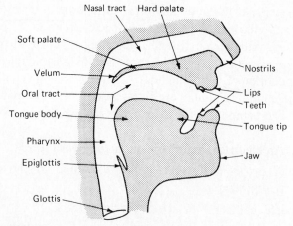

FIG. 29-2 The human vocal tract

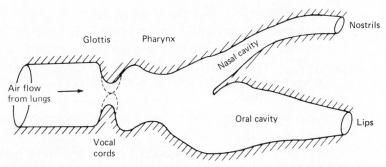

FIG. 29-3   Schematic representation of the vocal tract, illustrating voice source (airflow vibrating vocal cords) and oral and nasal cavities as resonating chambers

Speech-Synthesizer Components

VOWELS   An electronic speech synthesizer is a direct analog of the human vocal tract. The human vocal tract forms a closed-end acoustic resonating tube nominally 6.8 in (173 mm) long. Once air is vibrated in an acoustical resonator of this dimension, standing waves of air pressure form at about 500, 1500, and 2500 Hz. These three resonant frequencies are **formant frequencies** (symbolically F_1, F_2, and F_3) and are actually the center frequencies of resonant **frequency bands** that determine the phonetic quality of a vowel. Frequencies around each of these three center frequencies are controlled in the human vocal tract by muscular control of the throat and mouth. And as the first approximation of an electronic speech synthesizer, these formant frequencies are produced in four amplifiers with digitally controlled bandpass filters (Fig. 29-4). Each amplifier is fed by an amplitude-controlled original voicing frequency that corresponds to the voice box in the throat.

This portion of a frequency synthesizer produces the vowels *a, e, i, o, u,* depending on the frequencies specified by F_1, F_2, and F_3. Each of these bandpass amplifiers is controlled by an 8-bit byte to permit the formant frequency within the band to be adjusted, just as muscles control the shape of the vocal tract.

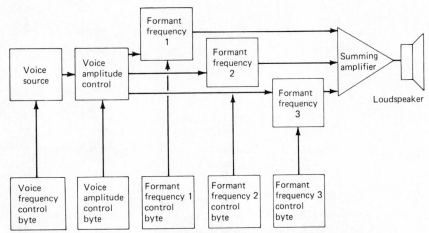

FIG. 29-4   A functional block diagram as an electronic analog of the human vocal tract to produce vowels with three formant frequencies

For example, Fig. 29-5 shows graphically the approximate frequencies for several similar words containing the vowels *a, e, i,* and *o.* These are steady-state vowels; there is no change in the formant frequencies F_1 and F_2 to produce the vowel (F_3 is not shown because it is relatively constant for all the vowels). Therefore to produce the vowels in the words shown with circuit components shown in Fig. 29-4, the 8-bit byte control word for F_1, F_2, and F_3 is placed in a memory location reserved for control of the speech synthesizer and the synthesizer is turned on.

The speech synthesizer reads the F_1, F_2, and F_3 control bytes from the data bus (as well as bytes controlling the voice frequency and amplitude) every 10 or 20 ms, depending on the synthesizer model; this constitutes the **speech frame rate,** i.e., the rate of speech to which the synthesizer is set in order to change speech parameters.

Changing the control parameters for the vowels illustrated in Fig. 29-5 is not required because the vowels illustrated are **steady-state** vowels. However, some words like boy (**bor-ee**) contain more than one vowel. A smooth transition from one vowel to another when the word is spoken is called a **diphthong.** Figure 29-6 shows the frequency starting and ending points of several English words with diphthongs. Since the time to complete the spoken diphthong is between 150 and 250 ms, at a 10-ms frame rate the formant frequencies will change (by changing their control bytes in memory) 15 to 25 times over the duration of the spoken word. To produce a diphthong with a speech synthesizer it is necessary to specify not only vowel formant frequencies but also the timing of these changes over the duration of the vowel transition.

CONSONANTS Three additional functional components are added to the previous vowel circuit components to produce consonants, namely, aspiration noise source, nasal resonator, and fricative resonator.

Aspiration noise produces the beginning noise pulse of air for consonants that start with a burst. These are the **stop consonants** *p, t, k, b, d,* and *g.* For

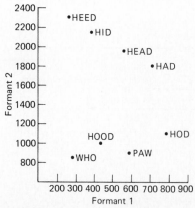

FIG. 29-5 Vowels for words illustrated here are steady-state vowels because formant frequencies F_1, F_2, and F_3 are constant (Copyright © 1979 Byte Publications, Inc. All rights reserved. Produced by permission.)

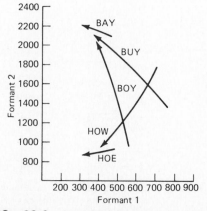

FIG. 29-6 A smooth formant-frequency transition from one vowel to another is a diphthong (Copyright © 1979 Byte Publications, Inc., Peterborough, NH. All rights reserved. Reproduced by permission.)

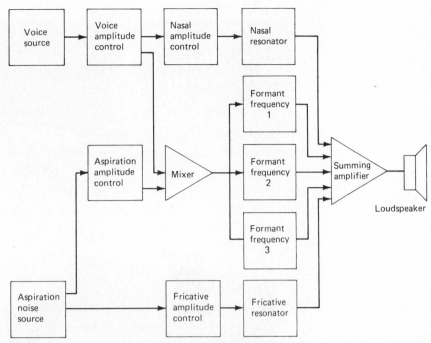

FIG. 29-7 Functional block diagram of a speech synthesizer as an electronic analog of the entire human vocal tract

example, the consonant k starts by quickly opening the rear of the oral cavity and then releasing a burst of air (**ka**) followed by a transition to the vowel a (**kay**).

This beginning aspiration noise (**ka**) is formed in one typical speech synthesizer by the amplified breakdown noise of a zener diode. The amplitude of the aspiration noise is controlled by a byte, which in turn controls eight resistors (a digital-to-analog converter). Aspiration noise of the proper amplitude is combined with the voice frequency (voicing source) in a mixer-amplifer, where it is input to the three formant resonators (Fig. 29-7).

The aspiration noise source is used additionally to produce the **fricative consonants**, sh, zh, s, z, f, v, and th—all characterized by a frequency between 2500 and 8000 Hz. Fricative consonants are produced by adding a frequency- and amplitude-controlled fricative resonator operating within the frequency spectrum of 2500- to 8000-Hz, which is fed sound originally from the aspiration noise source. Depending on which fricative consonant is spoken, the fricative resonator adds the appropriate fricative frequency component.

The **nasal consonants** m, n, and ng are formed with a nasal-formant frequency resonator of about 1400 Hz controlled by bytes regulating resistors for nasal-amplitude control. Electronic components to perform the combination of these functions (previously shown in block form) are mounted on a printed circuit board (Fig. 29-8). (This circuit board is compatible with the bus system of several microcomputers.) The addition of a speaker completes the electronic analog of the human vocal tract.

Figure 29-9 illustrates another speech synthesizer enclosed in a separate cabinet with several alternative parallel and serial interface options. Panel controls of this synthesizer externally regulate speech rate, voicing pitch, and audio level.

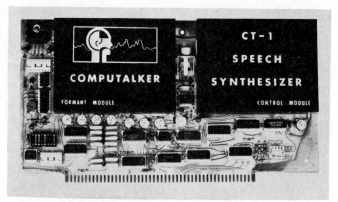

FIG. 29-8 Speech synthesizer mounted on a printed circuit board (Computalker Consultants)

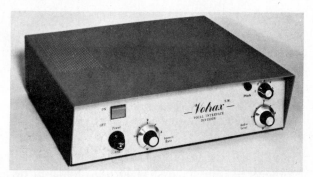

FIG. 29-9 The Votrax model VS-6 electronic voice system speech synthesizer (Votrax Division of Federal Screw Works)

Circuit Control Parameters

Corresponding to the muscular control of the vocal tract, nine different control parameters produce the vowel and consonant sounds of the speech synthesizer. Each is controlled by 8 bits that cut a combination of eight resistors in or out of the electronic circuit. This provides 264 incremental resistor levels and correspondingly controls each parameter, e.g., voice-source amplitude, in 264 steps. Altogether 9 bytes (plus an off-on switch byte) control the functions in the speech synthesizer shown in Fig. 29-9. They are as follows:

Voice-source amplitude	Formant frequency 1
Voice-source frequency	Formant frequency 2
Aspiration-noise amplitude	Formant frequency 3
Nasal-resonator amplitude	Fricative-resonator
Fricative-noise amplitude	frequency

These bytes are stored in random-access memory of the computer at a hexidecimal boundary specified by a four-position DIP switch, as shown in the bottom right section of the circuit board in Fig. 29-8.

These bytes are sequentially placed on the computer data bus and used to specify the utterance produced by the synthesizer in 10 ms speech frames. Changing the parameter control bytes stored in memory each 10 ms controls the parameter string for building vowels, consonants, words, and sentences. For example, the word "hello" lasts about 0.7 s and is composed of 70 sets of the nine control parameters, each constituting a 10-ms utterance.

There are two methods of establishing the string of parameters to generate speech, parameter specification by rule and parameter specification by analysis of the frequency spectrum of spoken words and the energy in each frequency band.

Parameter Specification by Analysis of the Frequency and Power Spectrum of Spoken Words

With this method nearly perfect and natural-sounding speech is possible, but the effort required is substantial. Speech-synthesizer control parameters are developed by analyzing spoken words for their component frequencies and amplitudes as a function of time.

In one method a speech recording is digitized at a sample rate of 10,000 samples per second, and the formant-frequency variations and fundamental voicing frequency are extracted, using mathematical algorithms to separate component frequencies.

As an alternative to separating formant frequencies by mathematical analysis of a single time-series waveform, formant frequencies can be separated first with different bandpass filters and analog-to-digital conversion of each of the formant and fundamental frequencies. Each band is digitized at 10,000 samples per second, and two steps are performed. Average band amplitude is determined once a millisecond; the band frequency data is converted into speech-synthesizer parameters, F_1, F_2, and F_3, and then scaled to the numeric range of one parameter control byte, 0 to 255.

In addition to these computer-performed frequency-analysis steps, manual editing of the formant frequencies is required to fill occasional gaps or remove noise-produced variations. Finally, aspiration and fricative data is inserted.

As an order-of-magnitude estimate, between 10 and 100 h of computer time is required to process a sentence of recorded speech to obtain formant frequencies, depending of course on the computer's computational power and the complexity of the sentence. In addition, manual touch-up of the control parameters is still required to obtain speech perfection.

This method is ideally suited for the development of a series of often repeated sentences where speech perfection is required. Since this computer-plus-manual analysis of speech is independent of language or dialect, it is capable of reproducing both accurately.

Speech-Parameter Specification by Rule

English-language speech synthesis by rule is a method that develops the nine speech-control parameters from letters representing the 63 English phonemes (Table 29-1). Words written with the phoneme letter codes appear rather like

TABLE 29-1 Speech-Synthesis Codes for English Phonemes

Code	Example	Code	Example
	Consonants		
P	pie	SH	shy
T	tie	ZH	vision
K	key	L	lie
B	by	W	we
D	die	R	rye
G	guy	Y	you
M	my	HH	high
N	nigh	CH	chime
NX	hang	JH	jive
F	fie	WH	why
V	vie	EL	battle
TH	thigh	EM	bottom
DH	thy	EN	button
S	sigh	Q	[glottal stop]
Z	zoo		
	Vowels		
IY	heed	ER	herd
IH	hid	AH	Hud
EY	hayed	AY	hide
EH	head	AW	how
AE	had	OY	boy
AA	hod	AX	about
AO	hawed	IX	David
OW	hoed	OH	core
UH	hood	UX	too
UW	who'd		
	Other symbols		
KX	coo (K before back vowel)	DX	pity (T between vowels)
GX	goo (G before back vowel)	YX	diphthong ending
RX	card (R after a vowel)	WX	diphthong ending
LX	kill (L after a vowel)		
	Stress marks		
0	no stress	3	third-level stress
1	maximum stress	4	fourth-level stress
2	second-level stress	5	fifth-level stress
	Punctuation		
space	word boundary	.	falling pitch
,	pause (silence)	?	rising pitch

phonetically spelled words, distantly related to English text. Phoneme coding rules differ with the manufacturer of the speech synthesizer. As an example, phoneme codes for the sentence "I can talk pretty well" with Computalker Consultants phonetic codes comes out "AY2 KAEN TOA1LK PRITIY WEHL," relatively understandable as pronounceable text. Numerals in these words are phoneme stress values. The sentence "PLIY1Z FIH3KS MAY FRIH2KAHTIHVZ" demonstrates unfamiliar words ("Please fix my fricatives"). Another example demonstrates the ability of a computer to describe its mathematical computations verbally: " ... TAY2MZ TEH2EHN TUH DHAX FOH4RTH PAY3WER" is phoneme-encoded speech for " ... Times ten to the fourth power."

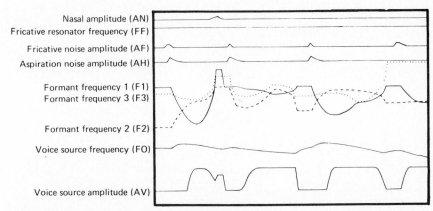

FIG. 29-10 Specification of speech parameters by rule is performed by establishing target levels for the nine controllable parameters for each phoneme code. Target levels specified by different (adjacent) phoneme codes are connected by a smooth parabolic trajectory generated from tables of time constants and boundary values for each phoneme pair (Computalker Associates)

With these phoneme-encoded words and sentences, an assembly program applies a set of rules depending on the phonemes specified and their relationship to each other to generate the nine control bytes used for synthesizer parameter control.

Each phoneme has a set of speech-synthesizer target control parameters with inherent time constants. For adjacent phonemes, the assembly program connects the parameter values for adjacent phonemes with a smooth parabolic trajectory between phoneme boundaries (Fig. 29-10).

As an example of word formation with this system 13 different words are formed by inserting different vowel phonemes between the beginning consonant phoneme HH and the ending stop consonant D:

Phonetic input word	English word
HHIYD	heed
HHIHD	hid
HHEYD	hayed
HHEHD	head
HHAED	had
HHAAD	hod
HHAOD	hawed
HHOWD	hoed
HHUHD	hood
HHUWD	who'd
HHERD	herd
HHAHD	hud
HHAYD	hide

To produce each of these words, rules for each of three phonemes, consonant HH, selected vowel, and consonant D, specify target control parameters connected by parabolic curves used to set the speech-synthesizer parameter control values for the 10-s speech frame rate. The result is assembled parameter values, in turn producing the specified spoken word through the speech synthesizer.

sec. 30

Voice Recognition

Frank Koperda

30-1 HISTORICAL OVERVIEW

Voice recognition, the subject of research for more than 20 years, is a potential application for microprocessors. Initial experimental systems utilized large processors because of the necessary extensive computations. Eventually "minicomputers" were developed; their computing power has increased and new mathematical and programming techniques have evolved. Because today's microprocessor is approaching the computing power of the minicomputer, it is now practical to consider a voice-recognition system based upon a microprocessor.

There is a twofold rationale for a voice-recognition system: (1) It is an easier means for noncomputer professionals to enter data into the computer. (2) In certain applications, such as in semiautomated quality-control inspection procedures, computer users need to use their hands. The cost and generally limited vocabulary of some commercial units have prevented their wide acceptance. One common limitation, for example, is that the system and speaker have to be "trained" to adapt the system to the particular characteristics of the speaker.

Ideally, a truly general voice-recognition system would be capable of recognizing a large vocabulary of words, independent of the speaker.

This section describes an experimental system being developed by the author as a hobby. Although not yet totally implemented, major portions of the system have been completed and are operating. Based upon the results to date, the remainder of the system has been planned and is currently being constructed. The approach to the system design utilizes information about the speech waveform that has been reported in the literature as well as characteristics which can be observed on an oscilloscope or plotter.

30-2 SYSTEM GOALS

The audio waveform created from speech is a complex signal of considerable variation, depending upon the speaker's physical characteristics, emotional state, and learned speaking habits. Fundamentally, speech is created by the vibration of the vocal cords, which gives rise to the sounds, such as the vowels. In addition, different sounds are created by air passing through constrictions formed by the tongue, nose, and lips (for example, the /s/ and /f/ sounds). These basic sounds are modified by the size and shape of cavities in the mouth, nose, and other air passages in the head. Differences in all these physical factors cause variations in the speech waveform from speaker to speaker, and even from day to day in the same person.

To be effective, therefore, a recognition system must be able to deal with these variations; that is, the system should be speaker-independent. In speech waveforms, the variations are manifested as changes in frequency, relative amplitude, and time duration. The system must be designed to normalize these factors, to create parameters independent of absolute time, amplitude, and frequency. This system's approach is to use ratios of quantities that can be measured by the system.

Two additional goals are to make the system insensitive to extraneous sounds and to give it the ability to recognize continuous speech. Insensitivity to extraneous sounds is desired so the system can be used in practical applications where background noise must be tolerated. For example, in a manufacturing location, nearby machinery or other people create sounds. Requiring a noise-free environment is not feasible in such a situation. The ability to recognize continuous speech is also a practical consideration. Certain systems quite accurately recognize discrete words, spoken with distinct interword gaps. Continuous speech, consisting of more than one word spoken in a normal sequence, is much more difficult to recognize because the system must determine when one word ends and the next begins. Since many applications require recognition of sequences of words, a system that restrains the speaker to an artificial way of saying phrases is not satisfactory.

The final goal is to design a system that can be implemented using microprocessors. With this restriction, it is not practical to use some of the approaches that have been investigated in the past because many require processing power in excess of that available with a microprocessor. For example, many research approaches utilize the fast Fourier transform (FFT) to convert the time-domain signal into the frequency domain. It is not practical to implement a real-time FFT on a microprocessor, so the system described here does not convert to the frequency domain. Similarly, because the microprocessor is not as powerful as larger computers, this design utilizes multiple processors to provide concurrency and hence greater apparent processing power. These are examples of the types of tradeoffs necessary when designing a microprocessor-based voice-recognition system.

30-3 SYSTEM OVERVIEW

Six steps in the recognition of speech are common to most voice recognition systems: (1) converting the input analog signal into a digital form by sampling, (2) compressing or selecting the relevant data for subsequent processing, (3) determining the boundaries of the word, (4) detecting patterns within the word, (5) pattern classification, and (6) association of pattern sequences with words in the vocabulary.

With a powerful processor, it is possible to time-share the processor among these six tasks. With microprocessors, however, it is more practical to use several processors in a "pipelined" architecture. The first processor in the pipeline performs one or more of the six tasks and passes the resulting data on to a second processor. The first processor can then continue on the next speech segment while the second performs subsequent steps in the processing. The number of processors required depends upon the complexity of the steps, the speed of the processor, cost considerations, and the desired accuracy.

Figure 30-1 is a block diagram of the pipelined system described in this section. It incorporates three separate microprocessors in addition to the signal-input hardware. The input stage consists of a microphone preamplifier whose characteristics attenuate frequencies above about 8 kHz. The analog-to-digital converter (ADC) changes the input to a digital representation of the analog voice signal. Processor 1, the input microprocessor, receives the data from the ADC and determines when a voice signal, as opposed to noise, is present. It also detects signal peaks (local maxima and minima) and records their amplitude

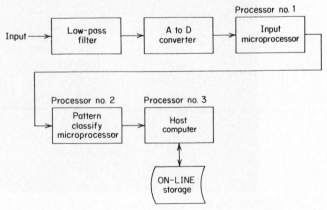

FIG. 30-1 Block diagram of pipeline speech-recognition system

and the time interval between peaks. This significantly reduces the amount of data that must be handled in subsequent processing. The selected data is passed on to Processor 2, which decides when the compressed data constitutes a pattern and then generates parameters based upon the type of pattern. Processor 3, the host computer, uses the sequences of parameters to decide which word has been spoken and to take the programmed action, such as print the word or control an external device. The pipeline configuration essentially follows the six processing steps in the recognition procedure.

An alternate approach, one that reduces computational time at the expense of additional hardware, is to separate the speech into 8 to 15 frequency bands using filters and then sample the filter outputs. The frequency and amplitude information can then be used directly in Fourier series and other frequency-domain computations. In essence, the fine detail of the speech waveform has been transformed from the time domain to the frequency domain. However, the filters are relatively expensive and implementing them digitally requires significant computing power, which is not consistent with the desire to use current microprocessors.

30-4 INPUT-SIGNAL PROCESSING

The speech waveform for the word "ship" shown in Fig. 30-2 illustrates the type of signal that must be processed by the system. The first processing step is to sample the analog waveform and to convert the amplitude of the signal at the sampling instants into a digital word that can be manipulated by the computer. Important considerations in this conversion are the sampling rate and filtering requirements.

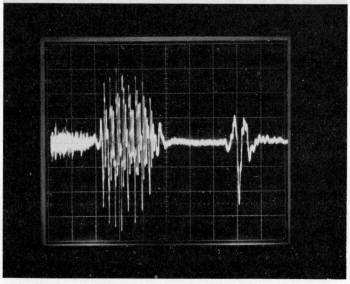

FIG. 30-2 Pattern of the word "ship"

Analog-to-Digital Converters (ADCs)   The basic equipment used to convert an analog signal into its digital equivalent is the ADC, which is essentially a digital voltmeter that can be controlled by the processor. Many different techniques are available to perform the conversion, including successive approximation, voltage-to-frequency conversion, and dual-slope integration. The successive-approximation (S/A) method is fast enough for sampling speech, and low-cost integrated circuit (IC) versions are readily available.

The S/A technique compares the input voltage and a known voltage to generate the successive bits in the binary representation. First the unknown input voltage is compared to a reference voltage equal to half the full-scale range of the ADC. A decision is made as to whether the input voltage is greater than the reference voltage. If it is, the most significant bit is set to binary 1. The next comparison occurs between one-half the reference voltage added to one-fourth the reference voltage. The second bit is set to 1 if the signal voltage is greater than this comparison voltage. By proceeding in this fashion, the total binary representation of the input signal value is generated. This comparison process is inherent in the IC, so the processor merely needs to initiate the conversion and read the data at its completion.

IC ADCs are available with up to 12 bits resolution (1 part in 4096), with 8 bits being quite common and inexpensive. Based upon experimental results obtained with the system, it appears that an 8-bit ADC is adequate for the approach described here.

The speed requirement for the ADC is determined by the sampling rate and the desired time resolution. As discussed in the next section, a minimum sampling rate of 6 kHz is required. However, to provide time resolution, the conversion time should be only a small fraction of the 160-μs period associated with the 6-kHz sample rate. In the implemented system, an ADC having a conversion time of 20 μs is used; this is equivalent to a sampling rate of 50,000 samples per second.

Another way to encode data is pulse-code modulation (PCM). There are several forms of PCM, including delta modulation (DM) and differential pulse-code modulation. These alternative analog conversion techniques are discussed in later sections.

Sampling Rate Requirement   The frequencies in a speech signal range from somewhat less than 100 Hz to in excess of 8 kHz. The Nyquist criterion for sampling states that a periodic signal can be described completely by 2f periodic samples, where f is the highest frequency component of the signal. Thus, accurate representation requires a sampling rate of at least 16,000 samples per second or a sampling interval of about 60 μs. This requires, however, that there be no frequencies greater than 8 kHz; in reality, there are higher frequencies present due to harmonics. To prevent errors caused by inadequate sampling speed ("aliasing errors"), the input signal should be band-limited by using a low-pass filter with a cutoff frequency of about 8 kHz. In the implemented system, the sampling rate of 50,000 samples per second allows a signal bandwidth of 25 kHz which, when coupled with the characteristics of the microphone equalization preamplifier, ensures that the sampled data accurately represents the speech signal.

Noise Suppression The physical environment in which a person speaks is seldom free of background noise. To help suppress these extraneous signals, a unidirectional microphone with a windscreen is recommended. This type of microphone helps ensure that the speech signal will have a significantly higher amplitude than that of the background noise.

Low-frequency (high-pass) filters also can help reduce noise generated by low-frequency mechanical equipment such as electric motors. These filters can be implemented by using analog techniques. However, the microprocessor can provide their digital equivalent. Random sounds with a duration of up to several milliseconds can be efficiently detected and eliminated with a microprocessor.

30-5 DATA COMPRESSION

The amount of data generated by sampling the voice signal at 16,000 samples per second would require a large amount of storage if each sample amplitude were stored. In addition, this quantity of data would overburden the microprocessor in the subsequent processing steps. As a result, it is desirable to find some technique either of reducing the amount of data stored or of storing it more efficiently, without losing the information needed for subsequent recognition.

One technique for reducing the amount of data is to use a different encoding scheme. For a continuous waveform, such as a speech signal, DM can be used. This approach encodes the differential change (the delta) in the signal magnitude between sampling instants. If the differential is less than a preset value, no data is recorded, thus significantly reducing the amount of data for slowly varying signals. In practice, a delta modulator can be implemented with an integrator having a constant input with reversible polarity.

Starting at time t = 0, the output of the integrator is a ramp (the integral of a constant), as shown in the first segment of Fig. 30-3. This output is compared to the input signal at each clock time. When the integrator output exceeds the input signal, the polarity of the integrator input is reversed. The integrator output now decreases, as in the second segment of Fig. 30-3. When the integrator output becomes less than the input signal, the integrator input polarity is again reversed. In this way the integrator's output "tracks" the signal input using a triangular wave that lags slightly behind the differential changes in the input. By recording the times at which the integrator polarity is reversed, a digital representation of the signal is obtained. Either the number of clock pulses in each interval or a 1 or a 0 at each clock pulse can be recorded.

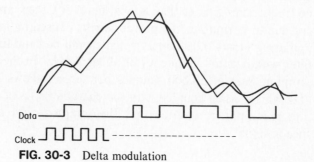

Data ─

Clock ─

FIG. 30-3 Delta modulation

The precision with which the integrator output tracks the actual signal depends upon the clock rate and the magnitude of the integrated voltage. With the proper selection of these parameters, and depending upon the desired precision (quantization resolution), the amount of data can be reduced significantly, as low as 2 kbyte/s for speech signals.

A further improvement (see Fig. 30-4) can be obtained by using several fixed input levels to the integrator. When the input is changing rapidly (i.e., has a high slope or large differential), a large integrator input voltage is used, thus allowing the integrator output to "catch up" to the input signal more rapidly. When the differential is small, a smaller integrator input voltage is used, thus minimizing overshoot of the integrator. To encode the signal, both time of reversal and indication of which integrator input voltage is used must be recorded.

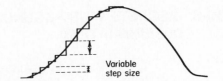

FIG. 30-4 Differential pulse code modulation

In both approaches, determining the actual value of the input requires a numerical integration of the recorded data. The recognition algorithm used in the system described here depends on ratios of actual amplitudes of the input signal. For this reason the DM encoding technique was not used because the requirement for numerical integration would have increased computation, even though the amount of data stored might be less.

Using a similar idea, however, the system employs immediate processing of the data, to select only those data points needed in subsequent processing. As the data from the ADC is received, it is immediately compared to the previous sample to determine if a change in the sign of the slope has occurred. If it has, the amplitude value is stored. In addition, the value of the time interval since the last slope change is recorded. In a sense, the approach is a peak detector in which the input signal is approximated by a triangle wave of variable amplitude and frequency, as shown in Fig. 30-5.

This approach also separates the amplitude and frequency characteristics of the speech signal to the extent that the signal frequency is related to the time intervals between slope reversals. This is called the frequency and amplitude separation (FAS) method of data collection. The reciprocals of the time intervals do represent true frequencies in the sense of the mathematical description of sinusoids. However, they are indicative of the frequency components in the

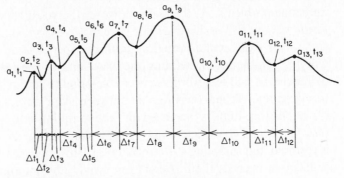

FIG. 30-5 Frequency and amplitude separation

waveform. As an indication of the data compression provided, most small words (like "ship") require about 500 bytes of storage.

The FAS method does require that the time intervals be measured with reasonable precision. Experimentally, it appears that sampling at least every 80 μs (12,500 samples per second) is required. As noted earlier, the implemented system uses a 20-μs interval (50,000 samples per second), providing more than adequate time resolution.

30-6 DISCRETE WORD-BOUNDARY DETERMINATION

The next step in a voice-recognition system is word-boundary determination, the process of determining if a word is present and where it begins and ends. Although this seems to be a trivial process, difficulties arise because of such factors as background noise and electronic interference. There are at least four signal characteristics that can be used to distinguish speech from noise: amplitude, frequency, duration, and sound patterns. Individually, none of these characteristics is sufficient for all cases, but, when used in conjunction with each other, an effective means of word detection is possible.

Because of the multiple characteristics being used, word-boundary determination must be done in several stages within a system. Easily identified word boundaries are determined at the time of input, to allow isolated (discrete) words to be identified. For continuous speech, where one word rapidly follows or is slurred into another, word-boundary determination must be done at a later step of the recognition process.

Variable-Amplitude Threshold A variable-amplitude threshold input section is useful for determining the start and end of valid voice input. This technique is used to lower the threshold amplitude until a signal that exceeds the threshold voltage is received. The pattern-recognition component in the system identifies the data as background noise and increases the threshold amplitude. After a delay that is short compared to the length of a valid speech sound, the threshold amplitude is reduced slightly and the sequence repeats. By using this approach, the system continues to search for a valid speech signal without burdening the system with erroneous noise data.

An interesting phenomenon that occurs in speech can cause end-of-word-detection problems. At the end of a word, the vocal chords have lost their excitation but are still oscillating. The speech waveform begins as erratic decay that sometimes can be interpreted as multiple speech dead times. This decay can cause an ambiguity in defining the exact end of a word. To help more clearly delineate the end of a word, the variable-amplitude threshold can again be used to advantage. When the interval between slope reversals exceeds 10 ms, the threshold amplitude is increased and the sampling rate is reduced to 1,000 samples per second (1-ms intervals). After a short delay, the original threshold level is restored, but sampling still continues at 1-ms intervals. When the input amplitude again exceeds the threshold amplitude, the sampling rate increases to its maximum rate.

There is another phenomenon that can cause false word-end detection. When a word consists of multiple phonemes (the basic acoustic unit of words), there is a finite transition time between phonemes that can be greater than 10 ms. It is very useful to be able to detect these transition times for future processing. After a 10-ms period has elapsed, the pause may be caused by a true end-of-word or by an end-of-phoneme. Further sampling of the input data at the 1-ms time interval and the original amplitude threshold can determine which case exists. If a signal amplitude greater than the threshold is encountered after 10 ms, then an end-of-phoneme signal is saved. If multiple consecutive 10-ms periods exist, during which no signal is detected, then the pause is the end of a word. The 10-ms criterion used was determined experimentally and may vary in the final implementation.

Frequency The frequency of the input signal, as reflected in the time interval between slope reversals, may also be used to distinguish between noise and the presence of voiced input. Many types of background noise (such as that caused by motor-driven machinery) have a low frequency. Although an analog filter could be used to block this noise, a microprocessor can provide a similar function. The microprocessor can check the frequency of an input and determine if it is below 300 Hz. If the FAS method is used for data compression, the microprocessor can reject all input data until the interval between slope changes exceeds about 1.5 ms, or half the period of a 300-Hz sinusoid. Similarly, the endpoint of a word can be determined by the lack of a minimum 300-Hz input. Thus, the microprocessor acts as a fast-attack and fast-decay comparator and low-frequency filter. Even if the background noise is loud, false detection is minimized.

Pattern Another way to distinguish between noise and voice is to examine input patterns. Most noise above 300 Hz is random and of short duration. By examining the pattern and the length of the noise, it is possible to ignore large-amplitude noise. On the basis of experimental results, if an isolated sound lasts less than 100 ms, a word is not in progress and the preceding data can be ignored.

Continuous Speech These techniques have proved effective for rejecting noise and identifying word boundaries in discrete speech or in continuous speech in which words are distinctly separated. Sometimes, however, these techniques may not be effective when speech habits result in connected speech. For example, the southern "you all" is often spoken as the single word "y'all," and therefore must be considered as a distinct word for recognition purposes. Because the specific system being described has not been implemented completely, its ability to recognize continuous speech has not been evaluated. Most likely, additional techniques will be required for word-boundary detection, or certain combinations of words will have to be considered as single words for recognition purposes.

Detection Algorithms The preceding requirements for noise suppression, data compression, and word boundary detection using the FAS approach enable the construction of an algorithm for the initial processing of the speech signal. Figure 30-6 is a flowchart of an algorithm that has been experimentally successful for accurately tracking voice input. On a standard 8-bit microprocessor, the algorithm takes about 100 lines of assembler code.

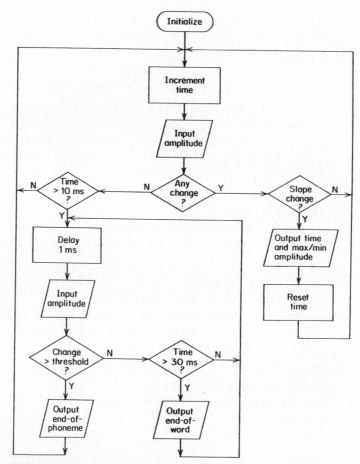

FIG. 30-6 Flowchart of FAS algorithm

The top third of Fig. 30-6 samples for a slope reversal and should be less than 80 μs (preferably faster), so that peak times can be accurately determined. The section on the right side of Fig. 30-6 shows that changing the sampling rate has no effect on the amount of data needed to represent the waveform. Only when the slope of the waveform changes sign are any data saved. Thus, increasing the sampling rates simply provides more precision in determining the time between peaks. When a slope reversal occurs, the maximum or minimum amplitude can be either saved or forwarded to the next microprocessor. The time between slope reversals also is saved, and the scanning continues looking for the next slope change.

The lower-left section of Fig. 30-6 suppresses data output during speech dead times, such as between words or during some consonants. A slow sampling rate and variable-amplitude threshold help eliminate background noise and false end-of-word detection. Because data is not saved until a word actually exists, a considerable amount of data need not be analyzed subsequently. For simple words (e.g., the word "one"), the FAS method reduces the input waveform to only 256 to 512 bytes of data.

As a side benefit, data resulting from the FAS method allows very simple speech-output hardware. A digital-to-analog converter (DAC) may be used in conjunction with the transition time. This data is sent to the DAC to generate triangular wave shapes that approximate the speech waveform. For higher-quality output, the microprocessor can construct a sine-wave segment between two points.

30-7 DEFINITIONS OF LINGUISTIC TERMS

The subsequent sections use certain linguistic terms that may be unfamiliar to most people. Although the definitions are not considered technically rigorous by pure linguists—indeed, there is much disagreement among linguists as to what is the technically correct definition of many of these terms—their purpose here is to provide a common basis for understanding the terms used in the remainder of the section. Definitions of the linguistic components of speech are best clarified by numerous examples. This section also illustrates that voice recognition must concern itself mainly with sounds, not the traditional spellings of words.

Morpheme   A morpheme is the smallest unit of meaning in language. In English, all words are made up of at least one morpheme. Many morphemes are words in their own right, for example, "pin" and "fish." Some morphemes must be combined with others to make what we refer to as words. For example, the morphemes "un," "pin," and "ing" have their own meanings, with "un" being a negative and "ing" indicating an action, but neither can be used independently.

Phoneme   A phoneme is the basic unit of distinctive sound. For example, the word "cat" has three phonemes, with each letter representing a phoneme. This is not always the case because some phonemes require more than one letter, such as the sound represented by "ou" in "house." On the other hand, some letters represent a number of phonemes. For example: "a" can represent the three different phonemes heard in "cat," "father," and "make." Occasionally, a letter does not represent a phoneme at all, as, for example, the silent "e" in "tame." These inconsistencies between spellings and sounds (grapheme-phoneme inconsistencies) are very common in the English language and have led linguists to invent phonetic alphabets, where one symbol represents only one phoneme.

Consonants   Consonants are all the letters of the alphabet except the vowels "a," "e," "i," "o," and "u." Taken singly, most consonants represent a single phoneme. There are exceptions, as, for example, the letter "c," which has no sound exclusive of its own; it sometimes borrows the sound of "k" (cat) and sometimes the sound of "s" (cent). Consonants taken in combination produce even more phonemes.

Vowels   Vowels are the five letters "a," "e," "i," "o," and "u" ("y" also may be used as a vowel). Every English morpheme contains at least one vowel. Vowels present an extreme number of grapheme-phoneme inconsistencies. Even taken singly, vowels represent more than one phoneme, depending on the spelling of the word (graphemic environment). The sounds of "a" in "pan" and "pane" are affected by the silent "e." Vowels are often "overruled" by consonants; for example, the /o/ sound, as in "boat," is significantly affected by the "overruling r" in "more."

Digraph A digraph is a combination of two vowels or two consonants that results in only one phoneme. Examples are the "ch" in "chair" and the "ai" in "sail."

Diphthong A diphthong is a combination of two adjacent vowels in a morpheme, where each vowel is sounded and each produces sounds it does not produce in other graphemic environments. The "oi" in "oil" and "ow" in "out" are diphthongs.

30-8 PATTERN DETECTION WITHIN A WORD

The next processing step in the voice-recognition system begins the analysis phase. There is some uncertainty as to what constitutes the intelligence of speech and what characteristics of a speech waveform allow the brain to recognize words. However, it appears that the intelligence recognized by the brain is related to patterns of frequency and amplitude. Taking this view, speech consists of patterns of several types and transitions between patterns.

It is difficult to describe precisely what constitutes a pattern because of the many waveforms that can occur in speech. A rough definition of a pattern might be multiple occurrences of a particular distinctive waveform.

Observing the waveforms of phonetic sounds on a scope or plotter resulted in identifying three general pattern characteristics. Most unaspirated sounds, such as /s/, appear random in nature, but even randomless can be defined as a distinct characteristic. The vowel sounds are complex periodic oscillations caused by vocal-chord vibrations. Stop consonants are characterized by a short pause followed by a high-amplitude burst of sound. Variations of basic sounds are caused by the mouth, temporary positions of the tongue and lips, and the permanent characteristics of other facial features. Thus, each pattern variation is unique to an individual, and so the patterns must be defined broadly to be useful.

The patterns do not remain constant, even within a phoneme. As one phoneme ends and another begins, there is a transition between patterns that may range from silence to a complex blending of the initial and final pattern. The first processing task, therefore, is to recognize the existence of a relatively stable pattern that, in subsequent analysis, can be classified for use in identifying the spoken word.

The saved input data are the time intervals and amplitudes of maxima and minima. The time intervals are very useful for determining random variation; the amplitude values are used for identifying oscillations. However, neither can be used independently to determine the parameters of a pattern.

Pattern Characteristics The random waveform sounds change slope polarity frequently, and the time between slope reversals is usually less than 160 μs. Potential stop consonants (/b/, /d/, /g/, /p, /t/, /k/) are detected in the data-input section or during the pattern-detection phase of analysis and are identified by a pause followed by a high-amplitude signal. If a 10-ms interval between

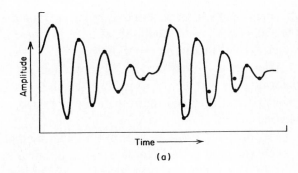

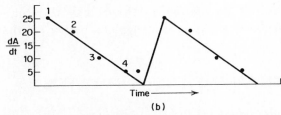

FIG. 30-7 (a) Damped oscillation; (b) absolute value of change in damped oscillation

large amplitude changes occurs, the following pattern is probably a stop consonant.

Amplitude variations associated with periodic oscillations are more difficult to detect. Most types of oscillations observed are damped; that is, the peak amplitudes within a pattern decrease progressively in size, as shown in Fig. 30-7a. The damped type of oscillation can be detected by subtracting successive peak amplitudes, determining the absolute values of the change, and noting that three or more points form a negative slope. The data resulting from performing this algorithm are shown in Fig. 30-7b.

Pattern-Detection Procedure   Determining the precise beginning and ending of a pattern is difficult. Simple words such as "one" contain three to four distinct types of patterns, and each type has 10 to 12 repetitions. Detection of these groups of the same pattern type is a complicated problem because of variations in the same pattern and the leading and trailing transitions between patterns.

In the system being described, the detection of the beginning and ending of a pattern depends upon recognition of the random and decaying oscillation signals previously described. As soon as one or the other is detected, the data is tagged as the beginning of a pattern. When the data no longer satisfies the characteristics of the identified pattern, the data is tagged as the end of the pattern and a search for the next pattern begins.

In more detail, the procedure is as follows. At the identified beginning of a word, the program concurrently examines the data for both randomness, as indicated by slope reversals in less than 160 μs, and decaying oscillations, as indicated by periodic monotonic decreases in the absolute values of the peak amplitudes. If the randomness criterion is satisfied for about 30 slope reversals, the search for damped oscillations is terminated. The random-pattern analysis continues until seven time intervals fail to satisfy the criterion, at which time the end-of-pattern is declared. Similarly, when damped oscillations are found, the end-of-pattern is declared after the appearance of seven slope reversals which do not satisfy the criterion.

After an end-of-pattern is declared, the preceding data are examined to determine the number of slope reversals in the pattern. If there are fewer than about 40, it is assumed that the data represent a transition period and they are ignored in subsequent analysis.

This procedure was derived from experimental results and observations of speech waveforms. Tests to date indicate that it is effective in segmenting the word for subsequent analysis. Due to variations in speakers and utterances of a single speaker, the same word may result in differing members of identified patterns. These multiple patterns must be resolved in the subsequent pattern-classification and word-recognition portions of the system.

30-9 PATTERN PARAMETERS AND ANALYSIS

After segmenting the word into patterns, the next step is to derive a set of measurement parameters that can be used for the further classification and trends of the patterns. If patterns are described too precisely, the chances of finding them again in the same word are small. If patterns are examined too coarsely, the distinction between vowels, for example, is very difficult. To produce speaker-independent recognition, some degree of variation must be accommodated.

A number of parameters can be used to describe a speech waveform. Some parameters require large amounts of mathematical manipulation, implying significant processing time or additional hardware. Cost, performance, and accuracy must be balanced to create a reasonable system configuration.

Types of Patterns In the system being described, two independent searches of a pattern are made to extract the necessary parameters. One search does a detailed analysis of types of oscillations; another search develops the trends of the pattern. In each search, both time and amplitude data are examined. The analysis is based upon changes in time and amplitude between peaks, and the parameters are expressed as ratios, so as to make the resultant parameters independent of the absolute time and amplitude.

Eighteen parameters currently are calculated in this system; sixteen are grouped into four categories. The remaining two parameters are single values: one is a number and the other is an average taken over the total pattern. The eighteen parameters can be summarized thus:

1. Damped oscillations—amplitude analysis (four ratios)
2. Damped oscillations—time-interval analysis (four ratios)
3. Peaks—amplitude analysis (four ratios)
4. Peaks—time-interval analysis (four ratios)
5. Number of repetitions
6. Average time interval

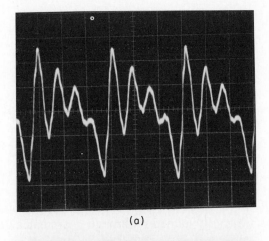

(a)

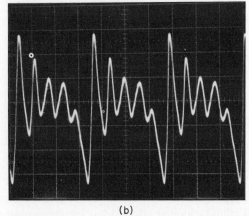

(b)

FIG. 30-8 Patterns of (a) the vowel /a/, and
(b) the vowel /o/

Damped Oscillations—Amplitude Analysis As described earlier, a damped-
oscillation pattern is identified by comparing the absolute value of the amplitudes of successive peaks and noting that three or more of them are monotoni-
cally decreasing. Within a pattern of this type, there typically are a number of
repetitions of the damped behavior. Within each repetition, the number of oscillations (peaks) appears related to the particular vowel. The existence of the
repetitions and of the varying number of peaks in a repetition is illustrated in
Fig. 30-8 for two vowel sounds.

The pattern data based upon these observations is examined to identify the
repetitions. The total number of repetitions is determined and saved. Similarly,
the number of positive peaks in each repetition is saved. The time intervals
between the first five positive peaks also are saved for use in the later time-
interval analysis. The saved data are indicated graphically for two repetitions
in Fig. 30-9. For convenience, only the positive peaks are used in this analysis.
The concept could be used with both positive peaks (maxima) and negative
peaks (minima), but this has been found unnecessary in this experimental
system.

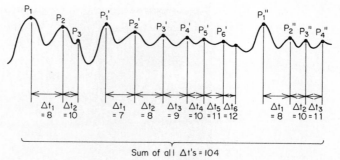

Sum of all Δt's = 104

FIG. 30-9 Example of damped oscillation analysis

If we let R be the total number of repetitions (reps) in the pattern, four ratios arbitrarily named r_1 through r_4 are calculated:

$$r_1 = \frac{R}{\text{no. of } P_2\text{'s in R reps}}$$

$$r_2 = \frac{R}{\text{no. of } P_3\text{'s in R reps}}$$

$$r_3 = \frac{R}{\text{no. of } P_4\text{'s in R reps}}$$

$$r_4 = \frac{\text{total no. of peaks (P) in R reps}}{R}$$

Because it is conceivable that the denominator of some of these ratios might be zero, the program must test its value to avoid an attempt to divide by zero.

All calculations are done by using integer arithmetic, which is usually faster than floating-point arithmetic. This is why the ratios are designed to provide numbers greater than 1. The ratio r_4 provides the average number of peaks in a damped oscillation; this number is a clue as to the type of vowel or pattern. If there are more than 16 damped-oscillation segments (R > 16), the pattern is a candidate for classification as a vowel.

Damped Oscillations—Time-Interval Analysis Referring again to Fig. 30-9, a similar set of ratios, arbitrarily designated r_5 through r_8, are calculated. They represent the average time intervals associated with each of the first four peaks and with the entire pattern.

The ratios are calculated as:

$$r_5 = \frac{\text{sum of } \Delta t_1\text{'s in R reps}}{\text{no. of } P_2\text{'s in R reps}}$$

$$r_6 = \frac{\text{sum of } \Delta t_2\text{'s in R reps}}{\text{no. of } P_3\text{'s in R reps}}$$

$$r_7 = \frac{\text{sum of } \Delta t_3\text{'s in R reps}}{\text{no. of } P_4\text{'s in R reps}}$$

$$r_8 = \frac{\text{sum of all } \Delta t\text{'s in R reps}}{R}$$

Again, the program should test the denominator for zero before attempting division. Also note that r_8 is the average time duration of the damped oscillations.

As a specific example of the calculation of r_1 through r_8, consider the waveform in Fig. 30-9, which shows three repetitions of a damped-oscillation pattern so that R = 3. The number of P_1's, P_2's, P_3's, and P_4's, are 3, 3, 3, and 2, respectively. The time intervals are as shown in the figure. Using this data, the ratios are:

$$3/3,\ 3/3,\ 3/1,\ 13/3,\ 23/3,\ 28/2,\ 20/2,\ 104/3$$

Peaks—Amplitude Analysis   This analysis provides four additional ratios that describe characteristics relating to the peaks in the waveform. Both positive and negative peaks (maxima and minima) are used, and the ratios represent relative occurrences of certain characteristics compared to the total number of peaks P in all repetitions R. The ratios arbitrarily are designated as r_9 through r_{12}. In the calculation of r_9, "equality" means that the peak amplitudes are equal to within 6 of the 8 data bits; that is, the subsequent peaks vary less than 4 parts out of 2^8, or 256.

The ratios are defined as:

$$r_9 = \frac{P}{\text{no. of sequential peaks almost zero in total pattern}}$$

$$r_{10} = \frac{P}{\text{no. of sequential peaks equal in total pattern and} > \text{zero}}$$

$$r_{11} = \frac{P}{\text{no. of sequential peak amplitudes monotonic (positive or negative) in total pattern}}$$

$$r_{12} = \frac{P}{\text{no. of sequential peaks in total pattern for which differentials alternate}}$$

The last parameter requires further explanation. The denominator is determined by considering three peaks at a time. If $P_1 > P_2 < P_3$, then one differential $(P_1 - P_2)$ is positive, and differential $(P_2 - P_3)$ is negative. This is what is meant by alternating differentials. It is extended to $P_4, P_5, \ldots$, until the condition is no longer true.

Peaks—Time-Interval Analysis   This analysis is analogous to that used for the amplitude data. Because the numbers of peaks and time intervals in the pattern differ by only 1, P is used in calculating the ratios. With the same interpretations of equality and alternating differentials, the ratios r_{13} through r_{16} are defined as:

$$r_{13} = \frac{P}{\text{no. of sequential } \Delta t\text{'s} < 280\ \mu s \text{ in total pattern}}$$

$$r_{14} = \frac{P}{\text{no. of sequential } \Delta t\text{'s} = \text{ or } > 280\ \mu s \text{ in total pattern}}$$

$$r_{15} = \frac{P}{\text{no. } \Delta t\text{'s monotonic (positive or negative) in total pattern}}$$

$$r_{16} = \frac{P}{\text{no. of sequential } \Delta t\text{'s in total pattern for which differentials alternate}}$$

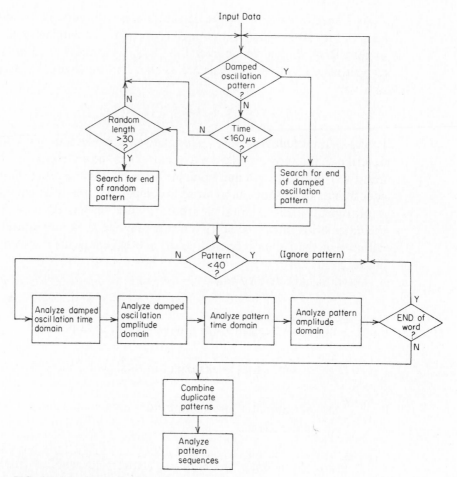

FIG. 30-10 Block diagram of pattern classification

Parameter-Calculation Procedure The remaining two parameters are the number of repetitions in the pattern (earlier defined as R) and the average time interval in the entire pattern. This is defined as:

$$r_{17} = \frac{\text{sum of all } \Delta t\text{'s in total pattern}}{P}$$

The total procedure is summarized in Fig. 30-10. The word-boundary and data-compression (selection) procedures were described earlier and are shown in more detail in Fig. 30-6. This procedure executes very quickly on a microprocessor. It is implemented in about 300 lines of assembler code and requires about 600 bytes of storage.

Pattern Analysis Specific computer routines that examine the parameters described have not yet been completed. As a result, experimental evidence that the 18 parameters are sufficient for voice recognition has not yet been obtained. Development of the pattern-analysis and word-recognition algorithms may result in modifications, additions, or deletions to the set of parameters. However, the work to date suggests that this set may be sufficient. On the basis of manual computation and visual observation of the ratio parameters for many different words, several observations can be made that will be the basis for developing the analysis routines.

There are multiple parameters generated for a pattern, and a decision as to the nature of a particular pattern cannot be made until all patterns are considered. The pattern must be examined as a total entity because of the number of identifying characteristics within that pattern.

The hard consonant (such as /t/ in "two") has as its main characteristic r_{13}, r_{14} (small ratio). Words like "one" and "four" have similar parameters (r_9 through r_{16}) across a pattern and similar oscillation types in the amplitude domain (r_1 through r_4) but vary in the time domain of the oscillations (r_5 through r_8). Unaspirated sounds have a large number of random changes and small average time within a pattern (r_{13}, r_{17}).

These observations can be illustrated by using the actual ratios generated by the system for the word "ship." A facsimile of the output is shown in Table 30-1. Pattern 1 shows a large number of peaks which change slope (r_{12}). The time associated with this change is short (r_{17}), and the short time interval is the predominant occurrence (r_{13}). The large number of damped oscillations (R and r_{15}) is consistent with the idea of randomness because all pattern types can exist in a random pattern. Pattern 1, then, is at the least an unaspirated sound (that is, /s/, /t/, /f/); to help distinguish these ratios (r_5 through r_8) indicate a probable /s/ sound. Patterns 2 to 3 represent the middle of the word. Pattern 3 is terminated by a stop-consonant flag derived by the input processor. Pattern 4 then identifies the /p/ as the stop consonant.

It appears that the unique identification of vowels will be very important in the success of this, or any, speech-recognition system. There are many similar words that differ in only the vowel sound, as, for example, "hit," "hat," and "hot." As shown in Table 30-2, half the phonemes are vowel-like sounds (i.e., vowels, semivowels, and diphthongs). Although characterized by the multiple repetitions of decaying oscillations, unique identification appears to depend upon the ability to identify the frequency content of the sound.

Some techniques for voice recognition depend heavily upon a frequency-domain analysis of the sound. Directly (by use of a filter bank) or indirectly (by the FFT, for example), the relative energy in certain frequency bands has been measured. Vowel-like sounds typically show three or more distinct frequency ranges, called "formants," in which significant energy is concentrated. Table 30-3 shows the frequencies on which these bands of energy are centered for the vowel sounds. The values are averages taken over different speakers uttering a variety of words.

TABLE 30-1 Parameters for "Ship"

| | Damped oscillations | | | | | | | | | Peaks | | | | | | | |
| | Amplitude | | | | | Time interval | | | | Amplitude | | | | Time interval | | | |
	r_1	r_2	r_3	r_4	R	r_5	r_6	r_7	r_8	r_9	r_{10}	r_{11}	r_{12}	r_{13}	r_{14}	r_{15}	r_{16}	r_{17}
Pattern 1	1	1	1	3	109	4	5	6	38	15	2	8	2	2	8	3	16	23
2	1	1	2	3	5	21	32	44	80	42	42	2	2	13	40	2	2	37
3	1	1	1	2	12	8	27	34	128	0	0	1	2	50	50	2	2	39
4	1*	1	1	4	3	7	32	16	64	0	12	2	3	...	10	2	2	48

*Represents an inter-phoneme-gap flag.

TABLE 30-2 Orthographic Representations of Phonemes in American English and Representative Words

Vowels		Semivowels		Diphthongs	
IY	beet	W	wag	eI	bay
I	bit	L	lamb	oU	boat
E	bet	R	rod	aI	buy
AD	bat	Y	yes	aU	how
UH	but			oI	boy
A	hot			jU	few
OW	bough	(These sounds are particu-			
U	foot	larly dependent upon their			
OO	boot	location in the word and			
ER	bird	surrounding vowels.)			

Consonants					
Nasals		Stops		Whisper	
M	miss	B	big	H	hand
N	knot	D	dig		
NG	sing	G	give		
		P	pin		
		T	tin		
		K	cat		

Fricatives		Affricates	
V	van	DZH	gem
TH	then	TSH	chin
Z	zip		
ZH	rouge		
F	fan		
THE	thin		
S	sod		
SH	shove		

TABLE 30-3 Table of Formant Frequencies for Vowels

Typewritten symbol for vowel	Typical word	F1	F2	F3
IY	beet	270	2290	3010
I	bit	390	1990	2550
E	bet	530	1840	2480
AE	bat	660	1720	2410
UH	but	520	1190	2390
A	hot	730	1090	2440
OW	bought	570	840	2410
U	foot	440	1020	2240
OO	boot	300	860	2240
ER	bird	490	1350	1690

In this system, the burden of converting to the frequency domain was not considered reasonable, so all analyses are being done in the time domain. However, some frequency information is inherent in the time-interval data that has been saved by the system. The exact relationships have not been derived, but it is expected that the average values of the various time intervals can be related consistently to the formant frequencies. For example, the average length of the repetitions in the first cycle of a damped-oscillation waveform appears to be related to the third formant frequency, and r_8 is related to the first formant frequency.

Phoneme Sequences   The concepts discussed serve to associate the individual patterns with phonemes. The procedures do not result in a unique relationship between any given pattern and a single phoneme. The patterns resulting from transitions between phonemes and limitations in the analysis techniques limit the ability to totally and accurately identify phonemes.

However, it is expected that the procedures will narrow the possible phonemes for a given pattern to a manageable number. To a greater or lesser degree, the procedures will permit the construction of possible phoneme sequences that approximate the actual phoneme sequence in the word. Using the phoneme sequences in conjunction with the calculated ratios, a search technique of the dictionary of words, their phoneme sequences, and probable variations of these sequences can be constructed to lead to the actual word recognition.

As a more specific example, the word "six" (phonetically, /siks/) is rather easily separated into a sequence of four types of phonemes: a random sound, a vowel sound, a stop consonant indicated by a pause, and a final random sound. The identification procedures discussed for the vowel sounds can provide more detail about the vowel sound. Similarly, random sounds will be analyzed to separate some of the fricatives, such as distinguishing /s/ from /z/.

An intelligent pattern-analysis algorithm is very necessary for identifying phoneme sequences. Some patterns are meaningless because they merely indicate a transition, and some patterns are only repeats of previous patterns. An exact match of the parameters for each phoneme is not possible because of the variations of each voice. What is possible is a trend analysis of the patterns. The key parameters of each pattern parameter are used, and a best-fit approach is used for comparison.

30-10 WORD-IDENTIFICATION TECHNIQUES

The final step in the word-recognition sequence is the association of phoneme sequences to words. This will be done by establishing a dictionary that relates actual words to phoneme sequences and other identifying parameters. Finding the exact word involves searching the dictionary for a reasonable match.

The more powerful 16- and 32-bit microprocessors perform this task more efficiently than do the 8-bit microprocessors. Their powerful instruction sets, larger addressing space, additional addressing modes, and word size can be used to reduce computation time and main storage requirements.

The search technique, the amount of storage, and the desired sophistication of "understanding" will influence the amount of storage required for the dictionary. Simple digit-recognition systems might require as little as several hundred bytes of storage. Very complex phrase- or sentence-understanding systems require multimegabyte dictionaries with syntactical parsing that breaks down a sentence into nouns, verbs, and other components of a sentence.

A number of well-known searching techniques are available. In some cases, combinations of the techniques are used in a sequential procedure. The following paragraphs introduce three of the search techniques likely to be useful in this system: binary, indexed, and hashing.

Binary Search   The binary search technique can be very efficient for a reasonable number of entries, such as might be encountered in digit recognition. The lookup table can reside in memory; a search divides the table in half and decides which half the observed phoneme sequence is in. That half is cut in half, and a similar decision is again made. This process continues until the word is found. A table of 1024 entries can be searched with only 10 decisions by using this method.

Indexed Search   An indexed search is used for larger vocabularies. A table of parameters is maintained that gives an address of a group of words with similar properties. For example, an index table composed of phonemes can be used for start-of-word sounds. If the first pattern of a word contains an /s/ sound, the /s/ entry has associated with it a starting address for a table in memory. The table contains all words with a starting /s/ sound, their likely phoneme sequences, and other key parameters. This table of phoneme-constructed words can have the English spelling as part of its entry. This spelling entry could be used to directly print the word or to initiate some other computer response.

Hashing Parameters   Hashing algorithms take all the key parameters from the phoneme sequence and generate an address based upon some algorithm. Some key parameters that can be used are the number of unique patterns, the placement of vowels within a word, and beginning sounds. Hashing algorithms are very efficient for converting the large number of parameters (40 to 50 bytes) in a word to a 16- to 24-bit address.

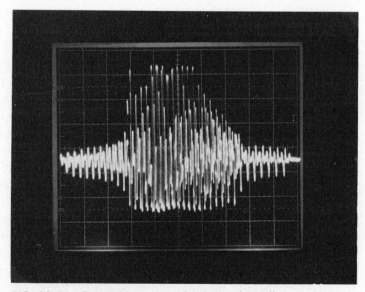

FIG. 30-11   Recognition pattern for the word "one"

30-11 HARDWARE IMPLEMENTATION

There are many possible hardware configurations for performing voice recognition. The configuration that was implemented is shown in Fig. 30-1. Now that some of the problems and possible techniques associated with recognition have been mentioned, a more descriptive functional hardware implementation is possible. Using this system, the parameters associated with a word can be determined in about 1.5 s, and several words may be in the process of being analyzed because of the pipeline architecture.

The first processor is the input and includes an ADC that has 128 bytes of random access memory (RAM) and 512 bytes of read-only memory (ROM). The sampling rate of the ADC is 50,000 samples per second. Implemented in the code are the variable-amplitude threshold, word-boundary determination, and the data-compression algorithms. About 500 to 1000 parameters per second are transferred to the next processor for subsequent processing.

Processor 2 has 8 kbyte of RAM and 8 kbyte of ROM. It performs the pattern-detection algorithm and calculates the 18 ratios. The data from Processor 1 is received and buffered while the previous word is being analyzed. This processor sends 100 to 200 parameters per second to the subsequent processor.

Processor 3, the system processor, has a standard complement of input-output (I/O) devices, such as keyboard/CRT and disk (diskette). This processor has 64 kbyte of RAM and will perform the dictionary lookup using a combination of indexed and hashing search techniques. It will also perform the response to the verbal request.

30-12 STATUS

As indicated earlier, not all of this system has been constructed. Processors 1 and 2 have been implemented, and the software up through the calculation of the ratio parameters is operational. The basic operating system kernel is currently being written.

Because the system implementation is incomplete, it is not now possible to verify the accuracy of its voice-recognition capabilities. It is certainly likely that, when completed, the system will not be completely successful initially. Further experimentation, which could involve modifications to the procedures described in this chapter, may be necessary. It is even conceivable that the system cannot reach its initial goals because of limitations in currently available microcomputer processing power or fundamental errors in the experiments, research, or heuristic reasoning upon which the system is based.

Nevertheless, this experimental system represents an investigation that is possible only because of the emergence of the microprocessor. The problem of voice recognition has been a topic of research for more than 20 years and a low-cost, speaker-independent, large-vocabulary system has yet to become commercially practical. Someday professionals will find a microprocessor-based system which meets the elusive goals and which could be of significant value in hundreds of practical applications. In the meantime, voice recognition continues as a fascinating and challenging problem for researchers in this field.

Acknowledgments

I would like to express appreciation to my wife Bonita for her linguistics support and to Dr. Thomas J. Harrison for his efforts in the preparation of this section.

References

1. Dinneen, Francis P.: An Introduction to General Linguistics, Holt, New York, 1967.

2. Dixon, N. Rex, and Thomas B. Martin: Automatic Speech and Speaker Recognition, IEEE Press, New York, 1979.

3. Rabiner, L. R., and R. W. Schafer: Digital Processing of Speech Signals, Prentice-Hall, Englewood Cliffs, N.J., 1978.

4. Harrison, Thomas J.: Handbook of Industrial Control Computers, Wiley-Interscience, New York, 1972.

5. Heilman, Arthur W.: Principles and Practices of Teaching Reading, Merrill, Columbus, Ohio, 1972.

6. Peterson, G. E., and H. L. Barney: "Control Methods Used in a Study of the Vowels," J. Acoust. Soc. Am., Vol. 24, No. 2, March 1952, pp. 175–184.

Glossary

Abend An error resulting in the abnormal termination of a program.

Accumulator A temporary, holding register for arithmetic and logic operation used in conjunction with an arithmetic and logic unit (ALU).

Acoustic Coupler A device which converts computer output to audio tones for transmission by telephone or radio.

Ada A Pascal-based language developed under the auspices of the U.S. Department of Defense. Like Pascal, it is highly structured and offers the potential for high portability.

ADC Abbreviation for analog to digital converter.

Adder A circuit whose output is the sum of two or more inputs.

Address The identification of a particular point in a computer memory or data source.

Algorithm The processes or steps used to solve a problem.

ALU Abbreviation for arithmetic and logic unit.

Analog In computer science and electronics, a signal or data which varies in a continuous fashion, such as voltage, temperature, etc.

Analog to digital converter A circuit to convert analog data to digital form.

ANSI Abbreviation for American National Standards Institute.

Applications program A program written to accomplish a specific task or purpose on a computer.

Architecture The internal structure and organization of a microprocessor or other integrated circuit device.

Arithmetic and logic unit The part of the central processing unit (CPU) which performs arithmetic calculations and logical operations. The result is stored in the accumulator.

Array A set of data or other items in a structured pattern.

ASCII Abbreviation for American Standard Code for Information Interchange, a system for representing alphanumeric data using seven-bit data "words."

Assembler   A program used to translate an assembly language program into the machine language used by a processor.

Assembly language   A language consisting of mnemonic symbols which can be converted to the machine language of a processor by the assembler.

BASIC   Abbreviation for Beginners All-purpose Symbolic Instruction Code.

Baud   A unit of measurement used with the transmission of data, usually in terms of bits per second.

BCD   Abbreviation for binary-coded decimal, a code in which decimal digits are expressed as 4-bit binary "words."

Benchmark   A program which can be executed on several different computers to compare their speed and performance.

Binary   A term to describe a circuit or situation which can assume one of two possible states.

Bit   Contraction of "binary digit," the smallest unit of data in a computer (usually 0 or 1).

Bootstrap   A program which instructs the processor to load its operating system into memory and get ready to execute the applications program.

Branch   An instruction which causes program execution to jump to a new point in the program sequence rather than execute the next instruction in the program.

Breakpoint   A point in the program where execution stops and various conditions may be examined.

Buffer   A circuit used to isolate or match two or more different items of hardware.

Bus   A wiring network used to carry data between the various components of a computer system.

Byte   An 8-bit "word."

CAD   Abbreviation for computer-aided design.

CAM   Abbreviation for computer-aided manufacturing.

Central Processing Unit   The part of a processor that executes instructions and controls the operation of the ALU, accumulator, and various registers.

Chip   Term used to describe any integrated circuit device.

Clock   A circuit which provides synchronizing signals for the various components of a computer system.

CMOS   Abbreviation for complementary metal-oxide semi-conductor. CMOS devices are coming into wide use with portable or battery-powered microcomputer systems due to their low power consumption and wide range of acceptable supply voltages.

Compiler   A program which translates a high-level language into the machine code used by a computer.

Console   A unit of hardware where the control keys are located.

CPU   Abbreviation for central processing unit.

Cross assembler An assembler which will accept source code for one processor type and compile it using a system based upon a different type of processor.

CRT Abbreviation for cathode-ray tube, often used in the video display unit of a computer system.

Data base A large file of information used with a computer system.

Data buffer A register or small memory device used to temporarily hold data when the CPU and peripheral devices are operating at different speeds.

Data pointer A register used to hold the memory location of data to be processed.

Debugging The process of detecting and correcting errors in a computer program.

Diagnostic A program or message used to isolate and diagnose faults in a program or computer system.

Digital Signal or data in the form of discrete steps rather than one in a continuous stream.

DIP Abbreviation for dual in-line package, the most common form of packaging for integrated circuits.

Direct memory access A technique where a peripheral can directly access a computer system's memory without going through the CPU.

Disk A magnetically coated disk used in a computer system to store data in binary form.

Diskette A name applied to smaller disks, particularly the 5¼ and 8 inch sizes.

Dynamic A type of memory that stores data as a charge on a capacitor. Such a memory needs to be "refreshed" from time to time to maintain the data since capacitors slowly lose their charge.

EAROM Abbreviation for Electronically Alterable Read Only Memory, a device in which data may be changed electronically but will be retained if power is interrupted.

EBCDIC Abbreviation of Extended Binary Coded Decimal Interchange Code, a code consisting of 8-bit characters used in computer systems and associated communications equipment.

ECL Abbreviation for emitter coupled logic, a semiconductor technology resulting in very fast chips. ECL microprocessors are found in high speed computers.

Editor A text editing program which allows text to be entered into a data file and manipulated as desired.

EEPROM Abbreviation for Electrically Erasable Programmable Read Only Memory, a read only memory that can be erased with an electronic signal.

EIA Interface An interface for terminals and modems conforming to signal standards established by the Electronic Industries Association (EIA).

Emulator A combination of hardware and software that allows the instruction set of one microprocessor to be executed on a computer system using a different microprocessor.

EPROM Abbreviation for Erasable Programmable Read Only Memory, a read only memory that can be erased using ultraviolet light or an electrical signal.

Execute To perform an action specified by a program or computer operator.

File A collection of data stored in memory.

Firmware A set of programs stored permanently in read only memory (ROM).

Flag A data bit used to indicate the state of a device or the result of an operation.

Floppy disk A magnetically coated plastic disk used for mass storage with microcomputer systems. The usual size is 5¼″.

Flowchart A diagram showing the sequence of operations a computer program performs to solve a problem or accomplish a task.

Hardware The physical, tangible components of a computer system.

Hard disk A rigid, magnetic disk used for mass storage.

High level language A computer programming language using English words for instructions.

Instruction An expression or code defining what the CPU is to do and the data it will use in performing the action.

Instruction set The set of instructions a processor is able to execute.

Interpreter A program which translates instructions written in a high level to machine code as the program is executed.

Interrupt Interruption of the normal sequence of program execution due to a software instruction or an external signal.

Jump Essentially another term for a branch.

Kilobyte 1024 bytes, sometimes abbreviated K.

Library A set of programs for common functions and operations.

Linker A program used to link together blocks of assembly language code to form an executable program.

Loader A program which calls up machine code from mass storage and loads it into memory for execution.

LSI Abbreviation for large scale integration, a technique which places thousands of logic circuits on a single chip.

Machine language Data groups which are interpreted as instructions to be executed by the processor.

Macro A sequence of instructions treated as a single instruction by the assembler; this saves programming time.

Macro-assembler An assembler which handles macro instructions.

Mass storage The storage and retrieval of large amounts of data in various peripheral devices.

Memory The section of a computer system where data is stored.

Microcomputer   An entire computer system integrated on a single chip or a computer system made up of single chips.

Microprocessor   The central processing unit of a micro-computer.

Mini floppy   Another term for a 5¼″ floppy disk.

Modem   Abbreviation for modulator-demodulator, a device which converts computer output to audio tones for transmission and reverses the process on the receiving end.

Monitor   A program which provides basic utility routines for a computer system.

Nibble   A 4-bit "word."

Non-volatile memory   A type of memory which still retains data stored in it even if power to the memory is interrupted.

Object program   The program produced by a compiler or interpreter from a high-level program.

Op code   The binary, octal, or hexadecimal code representing a microprocessor instruction.

Operating system   A set of programs controlling the operations of a computer system, such as assemblers or input and output facilities.

Parallel   A method of data handling in which all the bits composing a word are transmitted simultaneously.

Parameter   A variable which may be assigned a different value each time a subroutine is used and transmits the value to other variables in the program.

Parity   An extra bit added to a data element for error checking.

Peripheral   A device connected to the CPU, such as keyboard, video monitor, disk drives, printer, etc.

Pointer   A register containing the memory address of data or instructions.

Polling   The process of periodically checking peripherals to determine their operating status.

Port   A connecting point between a computer and various input/output peripherals.

Portability   A term used to describe software which can be used on other computer systems than the one the software was originally written for.

Processor   A generic term for that part of computer hardware performing arithmetic and logical operations.

Program   A sequence of instructions to be followed by the computer to carry out desired operations.

PROM   Abbreviation for Programmable Read Only Memory, a read only memory device which can be programmed in the field.

RAM   Abbreviation for Random Access Memory, a memory device in which data can be entered into or read from as desired.

Read   The process of taking data from a memory device.

Register A single word memory location used to temporarily hold data during program execution.

RPG Abbreviation for Report Program Generator, a programming language for the establishment, maintaining, and report generation for business-related data.

ROM Abbreviation for Read Only Memory, a memory device from which data can be read but the data cannot be altered or added to.

Serial A method of data handling in which the bits composing a word are transmitted one after the other.

Software The programs and documentation for a computer system.

Stack A series of registers or memory used to hold addresses or data.

Statement An instruction line in a high-level language.

String A sequence of alphanumeric data.

Subroutine A section of frequently used operations in a program which are treated as small separate programs.

Terminal A console from which programs can be entered, run, and output data received.

Text editor A program which allows alphanumeric data to be entered into memory and manipulated to produce a file.

Trace A debugging method in which the program is executed one instruction at a time and the register contents can be examined after each step.

UART Abbreviation for Universal Asynchronous Receiver Transmission, a device used to control serial data transmission.

User friendly A term used to describe hardware or software which does not require extensive computer knowledge or experience to successfully use.

USRT Abbreviation for Universal Synchronous Receiver Transmitter, a device which accepts parallel data from a processor and converts it to serial form on transmission. On receive, it converts serial data to parallel.

Utility A program which performs a specific duty such as program checking, text preparation, user accounting, etc.

Word A group of data treated as a single entity, usually consisting of 4, 8, 16, or 32 bits.

Index